Human Resource Management

A case study approach

MICHAEL MULLER-CAMEN, RICHARD CROUCHER
AND SUSAN LEIGH (Eds)

The CIPD would like to thank the following members of the CIPD Publishing editorial board for their help and advice:

Pauline Dibben, Sheffield University
Edwina Hollings, Staffordshire University Business School
Caroline Hook, Huddersfield University Business School
Vincenza Priola, Keele University
John Sinclair, Napier University Business School

The Chartered Institute of Personnel and Development is the leading publisher of books and reports for personnel and training professionals, students, and all those concerned with the effective management and development of people at work. For details of all our titles, please contact the publishing department:

Tel: 020 8612 6200

Email: publish@cipd.co.uk

The catalogue of all CIPD titles can be viewed on the CIPD website: www.cipd.co.uk/bookstore

Human Resource Management
A case study approach

Michael Muller-Camen, Richard Croucher
and Susan Leigh (Eds)

Chartered Institute of Personnel and Development

Published by the Chartered Institute of Personnel and Development
151, The Broadway, London, SW19 1JQ

First published 2008

Designed by Mercer Design, London

Typeset by Columns Design Ltd, Reading, Berkshire RG4 7DH

Printed in Spain by Graphycems

British Library Cataloguing in Publication Data

A catalogue of this publication is available from the British Library

ISBN 978 1 84398 165 7

Chartered Institute of Personnel and Development, CIPD House,
151, The Broadway, London, SW19 1JQ
Tel: 020 8612 6200
E-mail: cipd@cipd.co.uk
Website: www.cipd.co.uk
Incorporated by Royal Charter.
Registered Charity No. 1079797

Contents

HRM AND EMPLOYEE REPRESENTATION

CONTEMPORARY AND CRITICAL ISSUES

CONCLUSION

List of Figures and Tables

Contributors

CHRIS BREWSTER

Chris Brewster is Professor of International Human Resource Management at the University of Reading in the UK. Previously he held the same title at Henley Management College and before that at London South Bank and Cranfield Universities. He has conducted extensive research in the field of international and comparative HRM; and published twenty-five books and over a hundred articles. In 2002 Chris Brewster was awarded the Georges Petitpas Memorial Award by the practitioner body, the World Federation of Personnel Management Associations, in recognition of his outstanding contribution to international human resource management.

MICHAEL BROOKES

Dr Michael Brookes is a Senior Lecturer in Economics at Middlesex University Business School. He became an academic relatively late in life, having for many years taught Economics and Business Studies in a number of secondary schools. His research interests include labour market discrimination, industrial relations and comparative HRM and he has already published a number of articles in each of these areas.

TRICIA CHASE

Patricia Chase is a graduate member of the CIPD and former programme leader for MA HRM at Middlesex University with experience of working in the Public Sector. Her special interests cover issues relating to violence in the workplace, diversity and performance.

TRACEY COCKERTON

Dr Tracey Cockerton is Associate Director in the School of Health and Social Sciences at Middlesex University and a Chartered Occupational Psychologist and Coaching Psychologist. She teaches selection and assessment methods and theories of personality and individual differences. Her research interests include: psychometric evaluations of various tools for assessing individual differences, coping and psychological well-being at work; emotional intelligence and personality; learning styles; attitudes to mental illnesses.

PETER CRITTEN

Dr Peter Critten is a Principal Lecturer at Middlesex University Business School and coordinates and teaches on the subjects aligned to Human Resource Development. Prior to joining Middlesex University he had 25 years' experience of introducing and evaluating training and development systems, mainly in service industries. His experience was written up in *Investing in People: Towards Corporate Capability* (1993). His current professional and research interests involve work-based-learning and the Doctorate in Professional Practice programme at Middlesex.

RICHARD CROUCHER

Richard Croucher is Professor of Comparative Employment Relations and Associate Dean: Research at Middlesex University Business School. He earned his PhD from the University of Warwick and was previously Senior Research Fellow at

Cranfield University. His research interests are in regulation of the employment relationship in different national, sectoral and workplace regimes and his work has been published in journals such as the *European Journal of Industrial Relations, Industrial Relations, International Journal of Human Resource Management, International Journal of Labour Law* and *Work, Employment and Society.* He has held research grants from the Economic and Social Research Council, the Leverhulme Trust, the Anglo-German Society for the Study of Industrial Society, the Department of Trade and Industry, the Low Pay Commission and the British Academy. Richard is a Fellow of the Royal Society of Arts.

PAUL ELLIS

Paul Ellis has worked for the Ministry of Defence since 1990 in 18 different countries. As Assistant Director at the Defence Leadership and Management Centre, part of the Defence Academy of the UK, he leads on the use of coaching with strategic leaders in the Armed Forces and Ministry of Defence. His main interests are the application of coaching, leadership, and organisational development.

IAN FAVELL

Ian Favell is a Visiting Professor at Middlesex University Business School, where he has designed and delivered undergraduate and postgraduate programmes for many years. He is a Chartered Fellow of CIPD, Chief Verifier Professional Assessment for CIPD, a member of the CIPD Membership & Education Committee, and a CIPD Quality Panel Chair. His main interests are professional management development, personal, organisational and work-based learning, and the accreditation of professional experience.

MATT FLYNN

Dr Matt Flynn is a Senior Lecturer at Middlesex University Business School. His main area of expertise is age management. He has carried out research for the UK government (Department for Work and Pensions, Department for Trade and Industry and the South East of England Development Agency) on age discrimination and retirement; and participated in an EU-funded project on age and knowledge management in the automotive industry (ESF); older workers as a vulnerable occupational group (EQUAL); and the relationship between gender, qualification and work in later life (HE-ESF).

PHILIP FRAME

Dr Philip Frame is Principal Lecturer in Organisational Development and Director of Work Based Learning Programmes at Middlesex University Business School. He is both a Middlesex and a National Teaching Fellow. Philip's first degree in Social Anthropology was followed by eight years with the Race Relations Board. He subsequently obtained an MSc in Organisational Development and a PhD in Management Studies. He is a Fellow of both the RSA and the Higher Education Academy, and is co-chair of SEDA's publishing committee. He has provided staff development workshops and published on student induction, work-based learning, managing diversity and business ethics.

SEBASTIAN FUCHS

Sebastian Fuchs is a Lecturer in Human Resource Management at Middlesex University Business School. Sebastian holds a BA (Hons) in HRM and Marketing from Middlesex University, and an MSc in HRM from the London School of Economics and Political Science. Currently, he reads for a PhD at King's College London, where he looks into the concept of Organisational Identification from a comparative perspective. Prior to his academic career, he worked for the Daimler AG in his native Germany, and gathered international working and teaching experience in Brazil, Peru and China.

MARY HARTOG

Dr Mary Hartog is a Principal Lecturer at Middlesex University Business School and Head of the Department of Human Resource Management. She has been awarded a National Teaching Fellowship for teaching excellence. Her research interests include the use of self-study for professional development; Critical reflective practice; Ethics and Professional Development; and Productive Diversity in teaching and learning. Mary has taught at Middlesex on both undergraduate and postgraduate Business & Management programmes since 1990. Mary also undertakes consultancy and research assignments through the university. Prior to joining Middlesex University, Mary worked as an HRD practitioner in local government, an employment law consultant for a publishing company, and before that, she had a career in community development and social work.

PAUL HIGGINS

Dr Paul Higgins is Senior Lecturer in Human Resource Management. He has worked on research projects funded by the European Social Fund and the Higher Education Academy and has published research papers in such journals as *Work Employment and Society*, *Public Money and Management* and *Local Government Studies*. His main research interests are employee relations, public sector reform and work-based learning.

CAROLINE HORNER

Dr Caroline Horner is an experienced coach and Director of an international coaching consultancy, i-coach academy. Prior to becoming a coach, she had over 12 years international experience in the technology, telecommunications and financial services sectors. In addition to her 1:1 coaching practice, Caroline facilitates post-graduate courses in coaching for both academic and corporate programmes, and is the Director of the Africa Centre for Individualised Learning and Coaching at the University of Stellenbosch Business School. Her research interests focus on the development of a professional coaching practice.

TERENCE JACKSON

Terence Jackson is Professor of Cross Cultural Management at Middlesex University. Before becoming an academic he was manager and internal training and development consultant in NatWest Bank. He has published widely in the area of Cross-cultural management and International HRM, is editor of the *International Journal of Cross Cultural Management* and has more recently directed projects on people management in Africa.

PHIL JAMES

Philip James is Professor of Employment Relations at Oxford Brookes University and a Visiting Professor at Middlesex University Business School. He has researched and published widely in the fields of both human resource management and occupational health and safety. In the second of these areas, he has acted as a Specialist Adviser to the Work and Pensions Select Committee and is Deputy Editor of the journal *Policy and Practice in Health and Safety*.

ANNA KYPRIANOU

Anna Kyprianou is the Dean of Middlesex University Business School. She has worked with the strategic development of organisations and their management teams for more than fifteen years. Her areas of specialism are organisational behaviour, managing people and learning and development with a particular emphasis on managing and developing people in the virtual organisation. She has extensive research experience in survey design and data analysis at organisational, national and international levels.

SUSAN LEIGH

Susan Leigh is a Senior Lecturer in the department of HRM. She joined Middlesex University in 1997 as a Research Fellow and then progressed on to being a lecturer. For a number of years she was the programme leader for the Postgraduate Diploma in HRM. She is Chair of the North London Branch of the CIPD and is on their academic quality panel. She is also on the membership upgrading panel of the CIPD. Her research interests are the psychological contract and managing absence and retention.

DAVID LEWIS

David Lewis is Professor of Employment Law and member of the Centre for Legal Research at Middlesex University. David has considerable experience as a consultant and is an ACAS arbitrator. He is also a member of the editorial board of the *Industrial Law Journal* and an elected member of the executive committee of the Industrial Law Society.

SUZAN LEWIS

Sue Lewis is Professor of Organisational Psychology at Middlesex University. Her research focuses on work-personal life issues and workplace practice, culture and change in different organisational and social policy contexts. She has published numerous books and papers on these topics and is a founding editor of the international journal Community, Work and Family. She has advised governments and worked with employers and policy makers on work-life issues in Europe, the USA and Japan.

ANDREW MAYO

Andrew Mayo is Professor of Human Capital Management at Middlessex University Business School with particular research interests in people-related measures. He is also a Fellow of the Centre for Management Development at London Business School, and designs and directs executive programmes for companies. He spent 28 years in international industry, and is the author of five books including *The Human Value of the Enterprise – Valuing People as Assets* (2001) and *Creating a Learning and Development Strategy* (2004). He is Chartered Fellow of the CIPD and is President of the HR Society.

CLIVE MORTON

Dr Clive Morton OBE is Professor of Corporate Governance at Middlesex University Business School. He is a corporate development director with an impressive record of achieving successful change in revitalising an unusually broad range of major organisations in private, public and not-for-profit sectors, offering specialist knowledge of HR at the cutting edge, and consults to organisations on change management. He is the author of four books including *Becoming World Class*, (published in 1994), *Leading HR* (published in 2001) and *By the Skin of Our Teeth* (published in 2003). He is a former Vice President of CIPD and a Chartered Companion of CIPD.

MICHAEL MULLER-CAMEN

Michael Muller-Camen is Professor of International Human Resource Management at Middlesex University Business School and has formerly worked at the International University in Germany, DeMontfort University in Leicester and the University of Innsbruck. His main research interests are the comparative study of human resource management, age diversity and sustainable human resource management. He has held research grants from the Anglo-German Foundation, the European Union (Marie Curie) and the ESRC and has published widely in academic journals such as *British Journal of Industrial Relations, Human Relations, Human Resource Management Journal, International Journal of Human Resource Management*, and *Organisation Studies*.

ALEXANDROS PSYCHOGIOS

Dr Alexandros G. Psychogios holds an MSc in Public Policy & Public Finance from the University of Athens, an MA in Public Services Management from the University of York and a PhD in Industrial & Business Studies from the University of Warwick. Currently, he is a Lecturer on Management, Organizational Behaviour and Human Resources and an Academic Research Coordinator at the Department of Business Administration & Economics of City College in Thessaloniki, Greece (Affiliated Institution of the University of Sheffield). He has published several articles in academic journals concerning contemporary issues of management.

IAN ROPER

Dr Ian Roper is Principal Lecturer and Director of HRM Programmes at Middlesex University Business School where he teaches employee relations and contemporary issues in HRM. His main research interests are concerned with (1) the government regulation of the employment relationship, and (2) the employment implications of public service reform, particularly in relation to UK local government. He has published widely in academic journals and has co-edited two books: *Modernising Work in Public Services* (2007) and *Contesting Public Sector Reforms: Critical Debates, International Perspectives* (2004).

MALCOLM SARGEANT

Malcolm Sargeant is Professor of Labour Law. He specialises in the implementation of EU labour law and has written widely on such subjects as transfers of undertakings and age discrimination in employment. He is author and co-author of a number of books including being co-author of *Essentials of Employment Law* and joint consulting editor for *Employment Law for People Managers*. Prior to his career as an academic he was HRM Manager of a large financial services company and helped run a specialist recruitment consultancy for a number of years.

LESLIE T. SZAMOSI

Leslie Szamosi is a Senior Lecturer and Academic Director of the EMBA at City College in Thessaloniki, Greece (Affiliated Institution of the University of Sheffield) and has published extensively in the areas of change management and human resource management practices. He has consulted extensively in both North America and South-Eastern Europe and his main research interests are in the areas of change management and international management practices.

MARTIN UPCHURCH

Martin Upchurch is Professor of International Employment Relations at Middlesex University Business School. His research interests cover trade unions, industrial relations and the political economy of work in the UK, Germany and transformation economies. He is editor of *The State and Globalization* (Mansell 1999), co-author of *New Unions, New Workplaces* (Routledge 2003), *Partnership and the High Performance Workplace* (Palgrave 2005), *The Reality of Workplace Partnership* (Palgrave 2008 forthcoming) and *The Crisis of Social Democratic Trade Unionism in Western Europe* (Ashgate 2008 forthcoming). He has held research grants from the Leverhulme Trust and British Academy and was Principal Investigator for an ESRC-funded major project on the Future of Work. He is currently undertaking research into workplace transformation, the international financial institutions and social dialogue in the former Yugoslavia funded by the British Academy.

DOIREAN WILSON

Doirean Wilson is a Senior Lecturer, HR Professional Practitioner, and member of the HRM Department at Middlesex University Business School. Her research is in the area of culture, diversity, gender disparity, leadership and management. She is also studying for a Doctorate in Professional Studies at Middlesex. She has been author and co-author for several academic papers and is lead compiler for a consultancy book based on a third-year undergraduate consultancy module for which she is module leader. Doirean, who is a former business consultant, journalist and television presenter, is also a Fellow of the CIPD.

GEOFFREY WOOD

Geoffrey Wood is Professor in HRM in the School of Management at the University of Sheffield. Previously he was Professor and Director of Research at Middlesex University Business School. He has authored/co-authored/edited seven books, and over one hundred articles in peer-reviewed journals (including journals such as *Work, Employment and Society, Organization Studies, International Journal of Human Resource Management, British Journal of Industrial Relations* and *Human Resource Management* (US). His current research interests centre on the systematic testing and development of contemporary institutional theory in the light of large-scale survey evidence. This has encompassed assessments of variations in industrial in different institutional settings, the relative fortunes of organized labour in emerging markets, and developments and extensions of regulationist theories.

Book Map

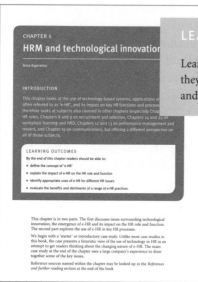

LEARNING OUTCOMES

Learning outcomes enable students to focus what they should have learned by the end of the chapter and evaluate their progress.

CASE STUDIES

At least two case studies per chapter, taken from a wide range of sources, help students make links between theory and real-life, practical examples.

Starter case studies establish the significance of the topic under discussion and stimulate thinking around it.

Main case studies incorporate a wider range of issues and illustrate complex issues facing HR professionals.

Each case study is accompanied by a set of questions or tasks encourage students to analyse the example in groups or individually.

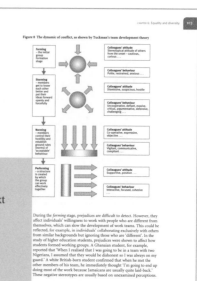

FIGURES AND TABLES

Visual learning aids scattered throughout the text illustrate key concepts, including tables relating British practice to that in other major European countries.

REFLECTIVE ACTIVITIES

A series of reflective activities in the form of questions and exercises encourage students to consider and apply what they have learnt.

KEY ISSUES

Key learning points summarise the main issues addressed in each chapter and distil a central set of messages to students and tutors - a useful revision tool.

EXPLORE FURTHER

Explore further boxes at the end of each chapter direct students to relevant and contemporary sources for further study, including web resources.

REFERENCES AND FURTHER READING

A comprehensive list of references at the end of the book pulls together the main works cited in each chapter and encourages students to build on their knowledge.

COMPANION WEBSITE

Comprehensive and interactive websites for students and tutors include features such as multiple choice questions for each chapter, allowing students to test their knowledge, and weblinks to help develop understanding. Go to **http://www.cipd.co.uk/letures/student/tsmfs/**

CHAPTER 1
Introduction

Richard Croucher, Susan Leigh *and* Michael Muller-Camen

This textbook is aimed to fulfil a need the contributors have experienced in their own daily practice as teachers of HRM at undergraduate level. We believe that it meets a need for a specific type of textbook, built around case studies, which is both practical and yet theoretically informed. It is anchored in the British national context while also seeking to place British practice within the wider global situation. Above all, this book aims to be accessible and yet challenging.

The textbook provides a comprehensive and practical text for use in the classroom and for background reading, aimed mainly at undergraduates with some preliminary knowledge and understanding of HR. Its overarching aim is to provide a clear exposition of practical issues that confront the HR practitioner, without over-simplifying or ignoring wider debates. It is therefore suitable for undergraduates at or around second-year level or for students embarking on their professional studies who have only a limited amount of knowledge of HR. We have attempted to recognise the busy and even pressured reality that many teachers and students find themselves in by providing a text that is comprehensive, systematically structured, accessible in language, and which is conceptually clear and easy to use. The chapters which describe subjects in an introductory way are grouped together in the book's earlier sections. Those requiring more background knowledge, which introduce more theoretical issues, or are more critical in approach, are in the last section. The text is also useful for a wider group of students than second-year undergraduates because of the inclusion of case studies in each chapter.

The case study approach is central to the text. Each chapter contains two case studies, to encourage students to think about issues in a concrete way that connects with contemporary realities. The case studies are derived from real-life situations, allowing teachers and students to use them in a range of different contexts and in their own way, bringing their own insights to the situations described. It is recognised that students will have a variety of cultural backgrounds; they may well not be native speakers of English and may have only minimal practical experience. There are also many opportunities to apply the knowledge that has been acquired in the 'Exercise' features that have been positioned at important points in each chapter. References have been kept to a minimum, to promote clarity of exposition and presentation. Furthermore we have tried to prioritise clarity of exposition and ease of use. For these reasons, some topics are touched on in more than one chapter, but these cases are always cross-referenced and the most in-depth treatment is to be found simply by looking for the chapter with the appropriate title. The emphasis has also been on establishing the practical significance of all the topics covered from the outset, and to provide multiple opportunities for relating general and theoretical concepts to practical situations. The text may appear dauntingly large, but it has been designed to allow a 'mix and match' approach by teachers and students, so that particular chapters may be selected as they appear relevant. We hope that these features will help teachers to use the book as the basis of a wide-ranging discussion on HRM's central issues.

Each chapter follows a similar pattern, with the following common features:

- an initial set of clearly articulated intended learning outcomes
- an introductory or 'starter' case study at the beginning of each chapter designed to establish the significance of the topic under discussion and to stimulate thinking around it
- a main case study at the end of each chapter intended to incorporate a wider range of issues and designed to illustrate the dilemmas and complexity often faced by the HR professional
- reflective activities, interspersed throughout, designed to help students make links between theory and practice
- illustrative tables systematically showing how British practice relates to that in other major European countries, in order to illustrate national variations in HR practices; we have generally sought where possible to include illustrative material from a range of countries
- a list of key learning points at the end of each chapter, designed to sum up major 'take-away' points and to allow busy students and teachers to distil a central set of messages.

The illustrative material provided in each chapter adds a distinctive dimension by taking an important practice and showing its incidence in a selection of European countries. They are taken from Cranet data (which one of the editors and a chapter author played a part in collecting) and the British Workplace Employment Relations Survey (WERS). Cranet is a network of academics spread across some 40 countries that has conducted surveys of HR practices in those countries since 1989. It asks the most senior HR practitioner in each surveyed organisation a wide range of questions about HR practices. WERS, by contrast, is a more detailed survey of employment relations practices conducted since 1980 that asks questions of both managers and employee representatives. Both surveys completed their most recent iterations in 2004. Further details of the surveys are available in Brewster and Hegewisch (1993), Tregaskis, Mahoney and Atterbury (2004) [both for Cranet] and Kersley, Alpin, Forth, Dix, Bryson and Bewley (2005) [for WERS].

At the very end of the book is a list of references and works for further reading, intended to show the main works in each area and to build on the insights offered herein.

The chapters are grouped in sections to allow teachers and students to select them for study both by subject and approach. In terms of their subject matter, the first section deals with both societal and corporate contexts and facilitates discussion of how these impact on the work of HR professionals. The second group of chapters provides a bridge with the third, by discussing issues linked with resourcing, which we think of as being positioned at the interface between external contexts and the workplace practices that occupy HR professionals. The third section deals with these latter issues, and is concerned with the important topics of employee development and performance management through reward and appraisal systems. The fourth section is about areas that potentially bring practitioners into contact with employee representatives, such as communication, employment relations and health and safety. Our fifth section contains more discursive and theoretical discussion, dealing as it does with subjects that we think of as of great contemporary significance (such as CSR) or at the borders between HR and other subjects such as organisational behaviour (including work organisation). A further characteristic of many of the chapters in these intermediate sections is that authors such as Terence Jackson on cross-cultural management and Peter Critten on HRD have taken novel and stimulatingly alternative perspectives on their subjects. The sixth and final section contains only a shortish chapter that looks at possible future developments in the HRM context.

The text's underlying philosophy is that of the 'collaborative' rather than the 'calculative' view of HR, which emphasises employees' as participants in a project based on commitment and participation (Gooderham, Nordhaug and Ringdal, 1999). To this extent, it takes a European rather than a US or 'calculative' view. It is therefore in the 'human relations' tradition discussed by several chapter authors. Although a further theme is the necessity to relate all HR issues to the business needs, we also recognise that businesses should be meeting the needs of all stakeholders, including employees. While there is still room to debate the precise contribution HR makes to the 'bottom line', there is in our view little room for debate on whether employees should be treated as more than simply a 'resource'. The text also recognises the continued relevance of the industrial relations tradition, largely because of that tradition's awareness of the possibility of conflicting interests in the employment relationship. Finally, there is a general concern in the text with issues of diversity, ethics and sustainability.

The book is the product of a group of teachers, most of them based at or associated with Middlesex University Business School, with long practical experience of HR issues and with considerable collective experience of teaching HRM at undergraduate and postgraduate level. The editors would like to thank many people for their help in what has been a considerable undertaking. We would especially like to thank Dr Michael Brookes, who compiled the tables in each chapter and Dr Pauline Dibben who led the project initially. The CIPD's staff have been supportive and unfailingly helpful. We also thank our six anonymous external readers for taking the time to read through and comment on the text, and Heike Schröder and Sebastian Fuchs for help with editing. Finally, we thank our students, for without them the experience that the book draws on would not exist – nor would the future of HRM look as positive as it does. Thank you also to Kate McClunes for her contributions to the website.

SECTION 1

HRM in Context

CHAPTER 2

The context of HRM

Paul Higgins *and* Philip Frame

INTRODUCTION

This chapter concerns the context of HRM within an organisation's environmental setting. It involves a critical examination of the key environmental factors that influence and shape organisations and the practice of HRM within them.

LEARNING OUTCOMES

By the end of this chapter readers should be able to:

- identify the key characteristics of organisations
- describe and analyse the key environmental factors that influence the HRM process within different types of organisations
- critically discuss ways in which organisations can monitor these environmental influences with particular reference to labour markets
- identify sources of information that can help HR managers to gain a detailed understanding of what is happening in employment markets affecting their organisation.

After the starter case study we identify the key characteristics of organisations by reference to their common features, ownership type, orientation and size. This part concludes with a discussion of the role of the HR process within organisations (there is more information on this subject in Chapter 20), and also provides the chance to test the reader's understanding of some of the key characteristics of organisations.

In the second part of the chapter, attention turns to the organisational environment and in particular how it can be described and analysed. We explore two models: the systems and the PEST model, using examples taken from a variety of different organisational settings, and pay particular attention to the HRM process. During this part the chance is afforded readers to apply these models to organisations known to themselves. We conclude with a summary of the environment in its entirety.

The third part of the chapter then builds upon the frameworks provided by the systems and PEST models by outlining and critically examining the ways in which organisations can monitor both potential and actual changes that they have identified in their environment. This is considered from the perspective of the monitoring of labour markets and the impact they have on the HR function within different types of organisations. Again, during this part, readers are asked to apply their knowledge to the various issues raised.

The chapter concludes with the main case study.

Reference sources named within the chapter may be looked up in the *References and further reading* section at the end of the book.

STARTER CASE STUDY

John, the HR manager has just arrived, and joins the team for its weekly meeting, a standing item for which is the latest instructions from headquarters. The team comprises John himself, his assistant Julie and their three administrators: Gary, Keith and Michelle. Headquarters is in London, but their outpost is located in the north-east of England. There is a general feeling that headquarters is ill-informed about outlying branches and that often its directives are totally irrelevant to local conditions. As a result, the team actively tries to avoid as many of these directives as it can without putting its members' future or that of the branch in danger.

Today's directive concerns the environment. There is a new requirement that branch employees actively monitor the local external environment. Something has happened at another branch which evidently came as a complete surprise and initially posed a significant threat to the branch's continued operations there. Headquarters does not want any more such surprises! The organisation intends to include this requirement in each and everyone's job description, but before it does so, it intends to try out a pilot scheme.

Members of the team are a little uncertain of what 'the environment' means. Is it about green issues and carbon footprints? There is general agreement that they are doing their bit on the recycling front, with ink cartridge and paper re-use. Most of the branch's products are produced locally, so the carbon issue is of no great significance, it is felt. So what is left and how can they find out? And then 'monitoring' – what does that mean, and how are they to go about it? Someone suggests that it is similar to what the sensible person might do when thinking about buying something new and major, such as a car – you'd ask your friends and neighbours and look at relevant consumer magazines. In other words, you would try to get as much information as possible before making a decision on what to do. But no, monitoring is not just focused on the customer, it is suggested, although the methods might be the same. And everyone who works at the branch is felt to be doing something similar, but on a private basis, not as an employee. Think of the impact if this personal activity is used for the organisational good.

The resources just aren't there, it is strongly asserted. And 'We have enough to do already' without additional tasks, the outcomes from which may well be difficult to quantify, which will make it difficult to sell to the staff because it seems unrelated to the outcomes-oriented focus of everyone's annual performance review. 'We are a small organisation here, unlike the bureaucracy in London.' Yet it is suggested that there may well be some advantages to becoming more aware of what is going on locally ... over and above reducing the likelihood of surprises.

Questions for discussion

1 What do you think is meant by the term 'environment'?

2 How do you find out about or 'monitor' the outside world? Think of as many sources of information as you can and make a note of them.

3 What might the benefits of supplying local knowledge to headquarters be?

1 CHARACTERISTICS OF ORGANISATIONS

Organisations have been a key feature of human society for many years. They come in many different types, shapes and sizes, have various organisational and ownership structures, and exist in order to achieve goals and objectives (Mullins, 2007). Despite this, there are thought to be three major elements common to all organisations. These are ownership type, orientation and size.

OWNERSHIP TYPE

The broad strategic direction that managers take on behalf of the organisation depends in many respects on the type of organisational ownership. Ownership could be public, charitable/independent or private. The type of ownership is important to strategic direction because it helps to determine the purpose and financing of the organisation (Needle, 2004).

Firstly, the public sector is a broad area covering central government departments, local government departments, universities, schools, hospitals and public sector corporations. Organisations of this type are funded mostly by taxation and exist to serve society as a whole. Considered in terms of the UK government and society as a whole, the most important body is the state, which is normally thought of as: the executive, Parliament, the civil service, the judiciary, the armed forces and the police. Its purpose is to establish a legal framework, to develop economic policies, to provide basic services and infrastructure, and to protect the vulnerable and the environment.

Secondly, organisations from within the charities/independent sector, meanwhile, are non-governmental, non-profit-making in orientation, their funding coming from donations, government grants, user charges, subscriptions and merchandising. Charities tend to focus on particular areas of need. They therefore specialise in these chosen beneficiaries rather than seeking to serve society as a whole. Some organisations from this sector also take responsibility for services contracted or tendered out by such government organisations as health and local authorities (Hodge and Greve, 2005; Dibben, James, Roper and Wood, 2007).

Thirdly, private organisations are owned and financed by individuals, partners or shareholders, and they are principally accountable to these owners, their duty to society being regarded as very much a secondary responsibility, although this is currently changing (see Chapter 25). Their main aim is commercial in nature – to make a profit. In the UK context, three main types of private organisations can be identified: these are sole traders, partnerships and limited companies. Of these, limited companies comprise both public limited companies (plc) and private companies (ltd). The main difference between these two is that a plc has shares that are available for the general public to buy and the company is quoted on the stock market whereas the ltd does not and is not. Shares in private companies tend to be owned by the founders, family interest and/or current management. In both cases, the owners' liability is restricted to the amount that they have invested in the company, usually in the form of shares. Meanwhile, a sole trader is the most common form of ownership in the UK and is found in most small business start-ups. A key feature here is that of unlimited personal liability, which means that any debts are the responsibility of the owner. Finally, a partnership is essentially a collaboration for the shared interests of partners, and is found most commonly in such professions as law, accountancy and medicine. Ownership is shared on the basis that each partner puts capital into the firm, which is then taken out according to that share given when the partner leaves or retires. In common with sole traders, partnerships also have unlimited personal liability.

ORGANISATIONAL ORIENTATION

In addition to ownership, organisations can be distinguished on the basis of whether they are production- or service-oriented. Products relate to physical, material goods that can be seen and touched and which remain with the customer. Services, meanwhile, are called 'intangible' in the sense of being consumed at the point of delivery. Services cannot be stored, therefore, and estimations of their quality are influenced by users' subjective perceptions and expectations. A user's estimation of service quality also involves reference to service output and delivery, such as the consumption of a meal at a restaurant.

The orientation of an organisation can also be gauged by reference to its activities, which fall into the three key sectors of the national economy. These are the primary sector, the secondary sector and the tertiary sector. The primary sector refers to agriculture, fishing and the extraction of natural resources, such as oil and minerals. The secondary sector refers to manufacturing industry: the production of industrial products and the processing of commodities such as food. The tertiary sector, finally, refers to service industries, including distribution, hotels and restaurants, transport and communications, finance and business services, public administration, education and health.

ORGANISATIONAL SIZE

Organisations vary according to size. At the lower end of the scale are micro-businesses. These are organisations with fewer than 10 employees. In the middle range are those of small to medium size, with fewer than 250 employees. At the high end are those organisations with thousands of employees. These include such large public sector organisations as the NHS and local government and multinational organisations. Some famous brand companies exist in name only, their operating functions passed on to subcontractors (Kaletsky, 2006). At the same time, core and committed HR departments are more likely to be found in larger organisations where the problems of co-ordination and control of large and very varied groups of employees become important (Kersley *et al*, 2006).

Larger organisations are more likely to have someone like an employment relations or industrial relations manager who spends more than half his or her time on employment relations issues – as Table 1 shows. Readers may find more about employment relations in Chapter 17.

Table 1 The existence of an employee relations specialist within different types of organisation

Organisational characteristic	Employee relations specialist at the workplace or higher (%)
10–99 employees	17
100–999 employees	74
1,000–9,999 employees	91
10,000 or more employees	91
Stand-alone organisation	18
Part of a larger organisation	77
Private	53
Public	82

Source: Kersley *et al* (2006; p.41)

REFLECTIVE ACTIVITY

Look at Table 1.

What reasons can you give to explain the different percentage figures for employee relations specialists in stand-alone organisations and those in a part of larger organisations?

Likewise, why is it that a greater proportion of public sector organisations have employment relations specialists at the workplace level or higher, do you think?

2 DESCRIBING AND ANALYSING THE HRM CONTEXT

Having examined the key characteristics of organisations, we can now move on to consider the environmental factors that shape and influence their actual behaviour. Every organisation is influenced by factors in the environment which it is unable to fully control. These factors can be grouped and conceptualised in various ways so as to construct environmental models. HR managers can use these models to describe and analyse their organisational environment with a view to ensuring that the functions that they are responsible for are shaped accordingly, or that they take action to influence the environment in which they operate.

In this section we focus on two environmental models: the systems model and the PEST model. We then conclude by considering the environment as a whole.

THE SYSTEMS MODEL

HR managers can use the systems model to consider the environment in terms of inputs and outputs – the organisation's response to these two external elements is derived from its internal transformation process. The organisational transformation process is what adds value to the inputs so that as reformed outputs they can becomes sales to customers, or services to clients, and is therefore extremely important (Haslam, Neale and Johal, 2000).

Thus, taking for example the hypothetical car manufacturing organisation shown in Figure 1, we can see how it utilises such inputs as human resources, materials, finance, technology and information from the environment which it then transforms through its operational processes – such as manufacturing and servicing – to deliver these resources once more to the environment as goods and services.

Figure 1 A systems model of car manufacturing and servicing

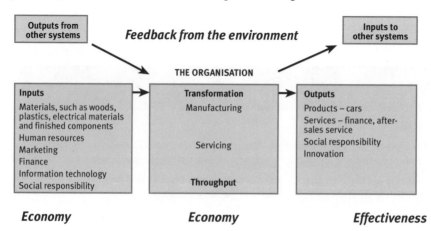

Source: adapted from Needle (2004, pp.38–9)

It is important to note in this model that although for many years it has been the function of car manufacturers to produce cars, the general oversupply and low margins associated with making cars has led many to focus on more profitable areas, such as finance for purchase. Many cars are no longer purchased in cash but are bought with financing deals such as loans or hire purchase. Thus the outputs of car producers, in addition to cars, are the financial packages they offer (Haslam *et al*, 1994). Of course the other feature that car producers spend vast amounts of money on – in addition to research and development – is marketing and advertising, as indicated in Figure 1.

In larger organisations it tends to be the task of HR managers to facilitate the process of efficient value adding, or transformation, by making sure that they hire the correct human resources and then retain them (see Chapters 7 and 8). In addition to this, human resource managers have also to provide training and development courses to ensure that employees can do their job (see Chapter 14); they must ensure that staff are provided with sufficient compensation and rest that they feel motivated to work hard, and ensure too that they are given appraisals and promotion opportunities for further development (see Chapters 12 and 13).

REFLECTIVE ACTIVITY

Apply the systems model to a service provider known to you.

What would the inputs, throughput and outputs be for your chosen organisation?

How does it add value to its inputs?

THE PEST MODEL

Another way to describe the external environment is by using the PEST model. The PEST model provides a particularly good tool to examine the general HRM context because it captures four important elements that shape and influence broad HR decisions. These elements are the Political, Economic, Social/Cultural and Technological aspects (see Figure 2), and each is considered in turn below.

Figure 2 The PEST model

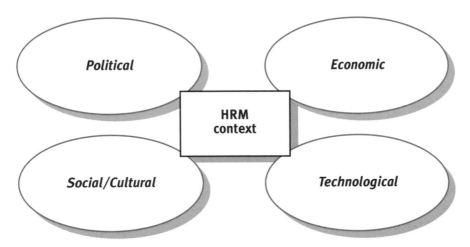

Political

The political environment is generally very important to HR managers, not least because included within it is the state and government. These have the power to make law and, therefore, to regulate the employment relationship between capital and labour, which trained HR managers are required to mediate (see Chapter 5). For example, the introduction of the National Minimum Wage by the Labour Government in 1999 determines minimum pay levels for UK workers, which HR managers must follow (Croucher and White, 2007). In addition, the law also shapes the bargaining power of employees and employers by detailing strike procedures, statutory recognition procedures and the minimum levels of employee information and consultation required in different types of organisations (see Chapter 19). Government laws and polices also shape the HRM context in less direct ways. Thus, for example, a policy of privatisation could provide a threat or an opportunity to an organisation depending on whether it faced the threat of losing contracts or had the opportunity to gain new markets (Domberger and Jensen, 1997).

In addition to national and local political factors there is also a wide range of international political factors. These too help to shape the general HRM context. Depending on the type of organisation, its ownership, size and activities, international political factors could involve the actions of the United Nations, such as an army or food agency; the activities of the World Trade Organisation (WTO), which might directly influence the operations of multinational corporations by opening up new markets and removing tariffs and other barriers to trade; and the activities of the European Union (EU), through such legal Directives as the Working Time Directive and the Part-Time Workers Directive. Finally, organisations might also be influenced by the activities of political pressure and interest groups that operate on the local, regional, national and international levels, and which may support or object to the organisation's intentions or behaviour.

Economic

Closely aligned to the activities of the state and general political pressures are economic influences which, in the HR context, include not only wage levels but also inflation (and housing costs), interest rates, currency and exchange rates, unemployment levels, social costs such as pensions, National Insurance contributions, direct and indirect taxation, and GDP growth. These economic factors influence the HR context in different ways and according to differing organisational contexts.

For example, the rate of inflation can be a trigger for increased wage demands so that workers can at least maintain their standard of living. Conversely, a high level of unemployment might help to ease inflationary pressures because unemployed people accept poorer terms and conditions of employment in return for scarce work. Meanwhile, currency and exchange rate movements influence the competitiveness of domestic goods and services traded in the international market, and these have a knock-on effect in terms of jobs and prosperity (Rugman and Collinson, 2006). Thus, for example, a strong currency would make a country's exports more expensive to overseas importers – with perhaps negative consequences for the security of jobs – whereas the country's imports would become cheaper. Finally, gross domestic product (GDP) growth and distribution might offer HR managers an insight into the strength of the economy and their confidence of it in the future. Under good conditions managers might try to expand through recruiting more workers, for example.

Social/cultural

The third part of the PEST model is social or social/cultural. This factor relates mainly to shifts in values and lifestyle, and in the HR context could involve a consideration of employees' attitudes to work and leisure, a consideration of wider demographic changes and potential pension costs, and general cultural values towards age, gender, sexuality and mobility, which may have an impact on recruiting strategies (see Chapters 6 and 8). The public's opinion towards Third-World debt, pollution, ethical trading and national competitiveness also helps to shape the general environment which HR managers are a part of.

Technological

Technological factors relate to the application of available knowledge and skills to create and use materials, processes and products. Technological change is very relevant to the HRM context. It can lead both to the displacement of labour by machines and to the creation of new jobs that require the skills to work with new technologies and jobs in companies making and supplying technological equipment. Indeed, in terms of job creation the emphasis has, in recent years, been put on the importance of employees' having transferable skills and of maintaining 'employability' as the opportunity for a 'job for life' disappears and as technological advances demand a skilled and trained labour force.

At the same time, technological advances have raised issues about the impact of e-/mobile communication between managers and the workforce and the surveillance of employees via sophisticated logging-on procedures for Internet use at work. It has also led to concerns about its impact on stress factors and tiredness, particularly amongst employees who are always on demand and contactable via email and mobile phone technology.

Teleworking, whereby employees use ICT to perform work at some distance from the organisation, can also add to the issues that HR managers should be aware of, and can bring advantages and disadvantages to the employee. For example, although teleworking can offer advantages to both employees (flexibility, reduced travelling costs) and employers (reduced costs), it does bring changes to the relationship between workers and the organisation that have to be carefully managed. These include potentially reduced promotion prospects caused by a lack of being visibly present, reduced chances for peer and professional development, reduced job security, confusion over the boundaries between home and work that influence social relationships, and greater feelings of social isolation that can lead to low motivation.

REFLECTIVE ACTIVITY

So far we have considered the PEST model from the perspective of the HRM environment.

Now apply the four factors of the PEST model to an organisation known to you.

For each of the four factors consider the respective influences.

PRIORITISING EXTERNAL INFLUENCES

When identifying key environmental factors, they must additionally be prioritised in terms of their importance and potential impact. In doing this, it is important to recognise that the nature of these influences changes both on a daily basis and, more seriously, as shocks to the system arise, often unexpectedly. There are four dimensions of analysis that can be employed to get a general feel of the organisation's overall environment: these are shown in Figure 3.

Figure 3 Dimensions of environmental analysis

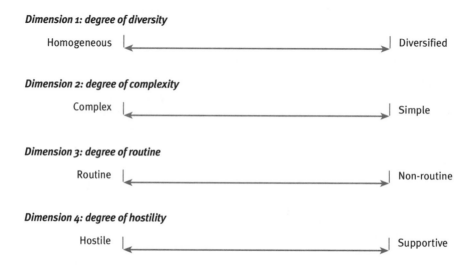

Dimension 1: degree of diversity

Homogeneous ⟷ Diversified

Dimension 2: degree of complexity

Complex ⟷ Simple

Dimension 3: degree of routine

Routine ⟷ Non-routine

Dimension 4: degree of hostility

Hostile ⟷ Supportive

The first dimension, the degree of diversity, draws attention to the degree of diversity in the organisation's market. For example, a firm who supplies a single product to a single customer would have a homogeneous market. Conversely, a multi-product conglomerate serving a diverse group of clients would have a diversified market. Homogenous markets tend to be simpler to monitor than diversified markets.

The second dimension measures the degree of complexity. This dimension focuses on a) the number of significant environmental factors, and b) the degree of similarity or diversity between them. The greater and more diverse the number of significant environmental factors, the more complex is the environment.

The third dimension is concerned with the degree of routine. It concerns environmental change and the extent to which elements in the organisation's environment stay the same over time. In other words, is the organisation's environment static or dynamic? In making judgements about the degree of routine, much will depend on the degree of predictability or uncertainty in the organisation's environment and the rate of change within it.

The fourth dimension measures the degree of hostility and especially how far the environment supports or undermines the organisation's activities. A supportive or hostile environment could emerge as a result not only of favourable and unfavourable government policy but also as a result of the activities of a pressure group which might be supportive or hostile to an organisation's activities and behaviour.

REFLECTIVE ACTIVITY

Drawing upon the same organisation you applied the PEST model to earlier, consider its overall environment by reference to the four dimensions of analysis.

3 MONITORING ENVIRONMENTAL INFLUENCES

So far we have identified two useful ways to describe and analyse the general HRM context – the systems and the PEST models. We have also noted how managers can consider the overall complexity of the environment by referring to four further dimensions of analysis. Attention can now be turned to how organisations monitor changes in their identified environmental influences. For it is one thing to know what the most significant environment factors faced by organisations are, but it is quite another to know how to monitor and to respond to them.

In considering how organisations monitor changes in their environment, we remain focused on the HRM context and, in particular, examine the impact of labour markets on planning and strategic choice in HRM (see Chapters 3 and 7). The reason for this focus is that the labour market influences the supply and demand of one of the most important organisational resources – the human resource. This section therefore continues by first providing a brief and simplified overview of the labour market and then by investigating the implications of changes in it for HR managers. It ends by identifying the sources of information that can help HR managers to obtain a detailed understanding of changes in the labour market so that they can orientate their organisational strategy accordingly.

THE EMPLOYMENT MARKET

The simplest way to conceptualise the labour market is to see it as an economic exchange between two equal parties comprising the employer and the employee. The former buys or demands labour and the latter provides or supplies labour.

The demand for labour – the number of jobs offered by employers – is the total number of employees in employment plus the number of unfilled jobs. The extent of demand for labour depends on the amount of goods and services produced by the employer in a specific market. When the demand for the organisation's goods and services increases, the organisation's demand for labour rises, and when the demand for goods and services falls, the organisation's demand for labour also falls.

The supply of labour, in contrast, is the total number of people of working age (between school-leaving and state retirement ages) who are in employment and the number of hours that they are able and willing to work. In real terms, the amount of labour available to firms at any one time is influenced by the number of people of working age who are in employment or are *seeking* employment, and these people as a whole are classified as being *economically active*. Not everyone of 'working' age is therefore in employment at any one time because there are always some people who are not in work or seeking work. This part of the workforce is described as *economically inactive* and it typically includes those with caring responsibilities for children or other dependants, those who have retired from work, and people who are incapacitated through ill health or disability.

In addition to describing the potential size of the workforce in terms of economically active and inactive people, the actual workforce can be considered in terms of employment and unemployment. The employed segment of the workforce contains those in paid work, including those working full-time or part-time, temporarily or permanently, and as employees, workers or on a self-employed basis. In contrast, the term 'unemployed' is used to describe those people who are currently not in work but would like to be. Unemployed people can generally be classified in three different ways. Firstly, they might be classified as structurally unemployed – those who are unemployed as a result of the loss of whole industries such as (in Western Europe) mining and ship-building. Secondly, they might be classified as frictionally unemployed – those who are temporarily out of work because they are between jobs. Thirdly, the unemployed might be classified as being seasonally unemployed, which affects those who have no work during non-active seasons such as winter or summer.

Nationally, the unemployment rate in the United Kingdom stands at between 4 and 5% (2005–2007), or at about 1·5 million people. Although this figure might appear to be fairly high, it is less than half the amount of unemployment that was registered in 1993, when the number of people out of work was around the 3 million mark. It is also less than half of the equivalent rate in Germany and France. However, much of the explanation behind the relatively low levels of unemployment in recent years is a result of tightening definitions of unemployment and the increasing use of non-standard employment, including self-employment, part-time work, temporary agency work, temporary or fixed-term contracts, and home-working (Grimshaw, Marchington, Rubery and Willmott, 2005). In 1993, for example, 40% of the UK workforce was employed on either a part-time, self-employed or temporary basis. Another significant development in the supply of labour has been the growing feminisation of the labour force. Women's share of total employment increased from about one third (33%) in the late 1950s to 42% in 1980 to nearly half (50%) in 1998. Although this has contributed to greater levels of employment and lower levels of unemployment, the work undertaken by women remains largely distinct from that undertaken by men: the majority of women workers are engaged not only in clerical, serving and cleaning work but also often on a part-time or temporary basis.

REFLECTIVE ACTIVITY

What is the difference between being economically active and economically inactive and being employed or unemployed – and how does this affect the work of HR professionals?

SOME IMPLICATIONS OF CHANGING EMPLOYMENT MARKETS FOR HR MANAGERS

At an organisational level the composition of the labour supply in terms of skills and other attributes greatly affects the sourcing of different types of employees and the wages and salaries they are able to get. In industries where employers have recruitment difficulties and skill shortages, such as those dependent on new technologies, it is very important for the HR managers concerned to target their recruiting efforts accordingly. Another strategy that HR managers can use to deal with skill shortages is to focus on candidates' potential rather than current ability. In this way, candidates with the potential to perform to the desired standards can be recruited and then trained until they are sufficiently qualified. HR managers can also analyse the employment market from the perspective of its current workforce so as to gain a fuller understanding of such problems as low employee retention, particularly if current employees are being 'poached' or lured away by other employers.

The age structure of the population is also an important determinant of labour supply as firms draw labour from the portion of the total population that is of working age. The overall trend in the UK, Japan and Germany is of an ageing population, with increasing numbers of people aged over 65 and decreasing numbers of children under 16. For HR managers the implications of changes in the age structure of the population are many. For example, there could be more competition amongst employers for young workers. Likewise, as the average age of the working population increases, HR managers will be asked to develop employment strategies which succeed in attracting and retaining older workers (McNair and Flynn, 2005). They will also have to develop sophisticated means to manage sickness absence.

In addition to the age and skills of people, what other issues should HR managers be aware of when considering the potential impact of employment markets on HRM?

What can they do to plan for the issues identified?

RESPONDING TO CHANGES IN EMPLOYMENT MARKETS

At an organisational level, HR managers are required to ensure that their demand for suitably qualified staff is matched with what is available to them in terms of supply. In seeking to attract and retain suitably qualified staff, this balancing process involves a variety of HRM activities including recruitment, induction, appraisal, promotion, training, reward, retirement and redundancy. Such human resource planning can be seen to lie at the heart of the HRM function's recognising the importance of people to organisational strategy and performance.

Conventionally, human resource planning involves forecasting the supply and demand of labour so that the necessary actions can be implemented to rectify situations of labour shortage or surplus. The most common approach to this is managerial judgement whereby managers estimate the human resources necessary for the achievement of corporate goals. Estimates are likely to be based on a combination of past experience, local knowledge and instinct.

HR planners will also collect data from local, national and international labour markets, depending on the nature of jobs and the skills required, helping them to make these judgements. Data can be collected by formal or informal means, including national and local surveys, and information provided by applicants on application forms and CVs. Analysis may also relate to the ways in which human resources are currently managed – for example, to the extent that the current workforce structure, job design and reward system enhance or restrict productivity and performance levels.

In addition to specific labour market data, HR managers tend also to find out about general changes in environmental conditions by reading newspapers, industry publications and business periodicals. Of these, the latter tend to capture news items and developments within a fairly focused but still broad area of interest such as economics, law and HRM. Industry publications, meanwhile, are journals specific to particular industries such as nursing, accountancy and engineering.

Benchmarking also has a central role in understanding organisational performance within a particular labour market because by definition it involves managers' learning and adopting best (or at least better) HR practices by comparing their own practices with those of other more successful organisations. In undertaking HR benchmarking, HR managers must first identify which practice they wish to benchmark. This could be, for example, HR training, recruitment or reward systems, or the collecting of productivity and performance data. Managers must then identify suitable benchmark partners who not only use recognised best practices but who are also prepared to participate in the benchmarking exercise. Chosen benchmark comparators may include internal departments or external competitors and non-competitors in the same industry, national organisations or international organisations. Following analysis of benchmarking data, managers should thirdly identify the performance gaps between the way things are currently undertaken within their own organisation and the desired or best practice of others. Action plans should then be created so as to enable their organisation to close the gap between the current and desired performance.

REFLECTIVE ACTIVITY

List industry publications and business periodicals that HR managers might regularly read to keep them informed of changes in the HR environment.

How would you, as an HR manager, seek to monitor changes in the type and supply of labour sourced from university graduates?

KEY ISSUES IN THE CONTEXT OF HRM

We now pull together ten key points about the context of HRM raised in this chapter:

- Organisations come in many different types, shapes and sizes, have various organisational and ownership structures, and exist in order to achieve goals and objectives.

- Organisations can also be distinguished on the basis of whether they are production- or service-oriented and by reference to their core activities, which fall into one or more of the three key sectors of the national economy: primary, secondary and tertiary.

- HR managers can use environmental models such as the systems model and the PEST model to describe and analyse their organisational environment.

- The systems model can be used to consider the environment in terms of inputs and outputs, with the organisation's response to these two elements centring on its internal transformation process. HR managers are particularly involved in ensuring the effective operation of the organisation's value-adding processes.

- The PEST model provides a particularly good tool to examine the general HRM context by capturing four salient elements that shape and influence broad HR decisions: these are political, economic, social and technological.

- In addition to identifying key environmental factors HR managers can also prioritise them in terms of their importance and potential impact. This can be achieved by reference to four dimensions of analysis to garner the overall environmental complexity.

- One of the key influences on HR managers is the employment market. Perhaps the simplest way to conceptualise the employment market is to view it as an economic exchange between the employer who purchases or demands labour and the employee who provides or supplies labour.

- The composition of the labour supply in terms of skills and other attributes impacts greatly on the sourcing of different types of employees and the wages and salaries they are able to command.

- Human resource managers can collect data about employment markets from numerous sources including surveys, application forms and CVs.

- Benchmarking can be used as a tool for evaluating the organisation's HRM strategy and HRM practices in the light of information about other organisations' practices.

Perhaps there are other key points that you would like to note for yourself.

The main case study in this chapter now follows. It gives an example of the importance that organisations should place on the monitoring of the external environment.

MAIN CASE STUDY

Look at the description of the case set out below. Then decide on the recommendations that you would make as an HR manager for dealing with the issues raised. Try to think beyond the level of a 'quick fix' or simple solutions by developing a longer-term strategy as well as responding to the immediate issue.

Atif is sitting in the staff lounge of the white goods company where he works, reading the local paper. It's his mid-morning break and he's on his own – which is a pity, he thinks, because there is something really interesting on page 4 which he'd like to tell his colleagues about, not least because items of interest are few and far between in the *Coketown Times*.

Back once more in the HR section of the open-plan office, Atif starts talking to his four colleagues: two administrators like himself, Garry and Alice, the HR assistant Shilpa, and their manager Darren. They all find the news he's spotted equally interesting and decide to book a meeting-room to discuss the issue properly without attracting the glares of their open-plan colleagues.

The story is about the Council's decision to agree to a change of use, from office accommodation to retail, for a town centre property following some lengthy and not-so-subtle lobbying on the part of a rival white goods firm. And it has come as a bit of a surprise to Atif and his colleagues. But is it a threat? Or is it perhaps even an opportunity?

Alice says that her next-door neighbour knows a councillor and they have been complaining about the time taken in meetings to listen to different stakeholders' arguments, whatever development was proposed for the town centre.

'It won't affect us. We've been here for years, and our reputation's good,' says Darren cheerfully.

'They sell discounted stuff, though – cheaper than us,' counter Gary and Shilpa.

Darren replies, 'But people buy from people at the end of the day, and we've got some real selling experts.'

'Well, they might drive us under unless we do something,' suggests a rather gloomy Atif.

'So what is this something we need to do?' is what Alice wants to know.

They agree to raise the matter with the director responsible for HR issues and to make recommendations for action, both for the immediate future and the longer term.

Questions for discussion

1 What is the potential impact of this development on Atif and his colleagues, both as HR specialists and as employees?

2 Recalling the work you did on sources of information for the starter case study of this chapter, what sources are Atif and his colleagues using, and what others could they use?

3 Why has the development described come as a surprise?

4 What range of responses to this development should be recommended to the director?

5 What long-term strategy would you recommend?

EXPLORE FURTHER

BROOKS, I., WEATHERSTON, J. and WILKINSON, G. (2004) *The International Business Environment.* Harlow, Prentice Hall/Financial Times
This is a very useful book which provides a broad coverage of the external environment confronted by both large and small organisations in an international context. It is particularly strong on PEST analysis and considers competitive, ecological and legal issues too.

MORRISON, J. (2006) *The International Business Environment: Global and local marketplaces in a changing world.* Basingstoke, Palgrave Macmillan
This slightly more up-to-date textbook again charts the key dimensions of the international business environment, highlighting transitional and developing economies as well as advanced economies.

MULLINS, L. (2007) *Management and Organisational Behaviour.* Harlow, Prentice Hall/Financial Times
This book provides a thorough overview of organisational behaviour and management, large chunks of it devoted to organisations, the management of human resources and the organisational environment.

NEEDLE, D. (2004) *Business in Context.* London, Thomson Learning
This excellent textbook provides a detailed and rounded examination of the business environment, drawing upon many useful examples and case studies.

CHAPTER 3

People and human resources strategies

Andrew Mayo

INTRODUCTION

'Strategy' is a much overused word, but essentially it is about making choices. Typically, these are choices about which direction the organisation should take in order to meet a goal. Strategies then also have to be implemented through practical plans, sometimes called 'tactics'. When we talk about 'HR strategy' it can have two meanings. The first meaning is a strategy for 'people management', which should follow clearly from the organisational or business strategy, because – as mentioned at the beginning of Chapter 2 – this is what makes HRM different from personnel management. The second meaning corresponds to a strategy for the HR function itself – how it will be structured, what it will or will not outsource, what skills and software support it needs. Readers may have encountered phrases like 'being linked with' (eg Boxall and Purcell, 2003; p6), 'being aligned to' (Holbeche, 2001), and 'being driven by' the business strategy. The last one of these is the closest to how it should be. Ulrich and Brockbank (2005; p.150) phrase HR's primary deliverable as 'organisational capability' – the capability to meet the business strategy.

In formulating any strategy we have to decide what we will do and why, what we will *not* do (the difficult bit) and why, and how we will implement it. All of these involve *choices* – and that is what strategies are about.

LEARNING OUTCOMES

By the end of this chapter readers should be able to:

- explain the basics of strategy formulation in general
- identify the factors that have to be considered in order to create or revise a strategy for people management
- explain the steps to be undertaken to develop such a strategy
- list and explain the factors to be considered in building a strategy for the HR function itself.

The chapter is divided into two parts. Part 1 is about how we create a strategy for people in an organisation. This leads to determining what HR activities – both ongoing and specific initiatives – are the *right* things to do. Part 2 is about a strategy for the HR function itself – for example, how it will be organised, what professional tools it will use – in order to deliver the people strategy.

Reference sources named within the chapter may be looked up in the *References and further reading* section at the end of the book.

STARTER CASE STUDY

ABC Software is located in south London. The founder, now chairman, created a unique software product 10 years ago that does geographic profiling based on postcode. Customers buy the product once, but they need to buy annual updates to maintain its usefulness. This is a very profitable business model. After considerable success in the UK, the company has since expanded into some European countries, Australia and the USA. Today, about 15% of revenues come from international operations and the five-year plan is to move this to 50%.

The company has about 350 people. Of the 310 in UK, about 90 are in sales and marketing, 150 in product development and support, 30 in customer service, and the rest in senior management and support functions. In addition to London, there are offices in Birmingham and Manchester, which have about 25 people between them. Headcount growth over the next five years is expected to be about 60 net, and to involve some jobs in the UK being eliminated and more being created abroad.

The chairman recruited a CEO early on and let him get on and run the company. However, he has liked to interview every new recruit to make sure they 'fitted' the culture he wanted to build. He did this until the company reached about 250 staff. The average age of the staff is just over 30, and a strong culture has been created which might be described as 'work hard, play hard'. Unlike many software companies, everyone comes to work in suits, even developers, and employees generally join in the many social events organised by the company.

Your task

You have just joined as the first HR director reporting to the director of support services. There are two HR people, looking after administration and recruitment but with little time for anything else. The CEO has asked you to prepare a people strategy for the company as soon as you have settled in.

What questions do you need to ask, and of whom?

1 BUILDING A PEOPLE STRATEGY

UNDERSTANDING WHAT WE MEAN BY 'STRATEGY'

There are many words connected with planning that can cause confusion. We have goals, objectives, values, visions, missions, plans, strategies, targets and policies – how do all these fit together coherently?

- *A mission* describes what the purpose of the organisation is and what it is there to do.

- *A vision* is an end point of where we want to get to in the long term – maybe what we will be known for or a position we will attain.

- *Goals* are specific targets on the way to the vision, usually over a time period of two to five years.

- *Targets* are the measures that apply to the goals.

- *Strategies* are the routes we have chosen to achieve the goals.

- *Values* are the ways in which we want to behave in achieving our goals. This may (and should) include beliefs and principles about how we will do business – how we will treat our employees, our customers, our suppliers and/or the public.

- *Policies* are about how we will do certain things, consistent with our values.

- *Plans* are detailed actions for implementation in the foreseeable period ahead.

All of these can apply to an organisation as a whole, or to a part of it. Usually one organisation shares the same values and policies. Visions and missions may be written for parts of an organisation as subsets of 'umbrella' statements.

 REFLECTIVE ACTIVITY

Jot down on a piece of paper all the options you have to travel from your home to your place of study. One will be your preferred option. We might call this your 'travel strategy'.

What factors did you weigh up and balance to make your choice?

In the case of the exercise above you probably made your choice based strongly on the *resources* available. There is an important lesson here – that chosen strategies have to be implementable. The secret with strategies does not lie with analysis but with the ability to turn strategy into practical plans and then to do what we have decided.

Organisations have to decide their main business strategies, and then departments put together their own, which support the main strategy. In the commercial world the strategy will be about how to achieve goals of revenue, profit and market share. The public sector is more about implementing policy – either political policy or to meet the needs of the section of the public it serves. This is another important lesson – that all the supporting strategies must be *driven* by where the organisation itself wants to go. We do not write a people strategy based purely on our own beliefs and what we know is good practice in HR.

This assumes that organisations do have a strategy. Whether it is written down or not, choices have been made. Often the strategy is not written down but emerges in an opportunistic way. Frequently, organisations have formally articulated neither their beliefs nor their principles. We will come back to that later, but clearly it makes life more difficult if there is nothing openly agreed and written. Table 2 shows some data about the existence of strategic plans in UK workplaces.

Table 2 The existence of strategic business plans in British organisations

	Percentage of organisations with no strategic plan
All workplaces	30
Organisation size 10–99 employees 10,000 or more employees	53 7
Manufacturing Hotels and restaurants Financial services Public sector	46 50 7 6

Source: Kersley *et al* (2006)

This data has changed very little since 1998 and suggests that smaller organisations in particular often have no formal strategic plans.

SOME BASIC TOOLS FOR CREATING A STRATEGY

Thousands of books have been written on strategic planning and this is not the place to go into them in detail. Figure 4 captures the steps needed very well (Davies, 1993).

We must start with understanding where we are and where we want to get to. There are then a series of steps to go through. The first set is about formulating

Figure 4 A model of the strategic planning process

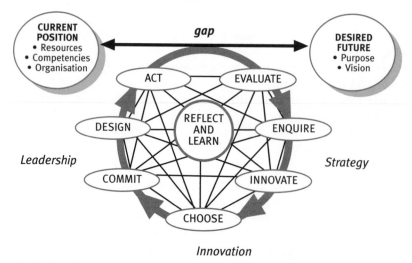

Source: Davies (1993)

the strategic options – evaluating the situation, researching and analysing, being creative and breaking out of the past – all to generate the choices. The second set of steps is about making the choices happen.

There are two well-known tools to use in the first phase. One looks predominantly at the external environment and is the PEST framework (see Chapter 2). The second useful tool is called SWOT analysis. It is a simple evaluation of our Strengths, Weaknesses, Opportunities and Threats in relation to what we want to achieve. It is more directed to looking internally at our capability, although opportunities and threats will look externally as well. Normally, it is drawn up on a page as four quadrants, with relevant items placed in each. What we want to be able to do is to see how we can harness the positives and mitigate the negatives.

Why would we want to write a strategy?

It is important to think through the *purpose* of writing a strategy and the *audiences* for it. The obvious answer is 'to decide systematically what we are going to do'. But there are other goals to be achieved too. A strategy may be demanded by an internal process or by external 'masters' (such as parent companies or governments). If we do not see benefits for ourselves in doing it, we will be tempted to do the minimum. It can be an important communication vehicle. We can use it to explain to others what we are doing and why, not least the HR people themselves. Furthermore, a strategy can be a means of seeking endorsement and resources. If it is logically argued from the business strategy and designed to support it, it can be powerful. Finally, it can provide visibility and credibility for colleagues and for external partners.

The style and tone of any document (or part of it) would be conditioned by its audiences. Note that a lot of people strategies or HR strategies look as if they have come straight from a textbook, using vague generalisations of 'good things' to do with people. They could refer to any organisation. A people strategy should be designed for *your* people in *your* organisation and be distinctive and specific. The methodology that follows will help readers do that. We also have to be realistic about what we can achieve – we have culture and traditions, and particular types of employees, and these things do not change easily or quickly: they take time.

A MODEL FOR DECIDING OUR PEOPLE STRATEGY

In practice we never start from nothing. You might tell me that you do not have a people strategy – meaning that it is not written down. But in fact you are doing some things and not doing others. So when we talk about 'creating' a people strategy it is more likely to be 'revising' – taking a new look at where we are, where we are going and how to get there.

Figure 5 illustrates the key drivers of our strategy. This is modelled on Schuler (1992; p.20), who then leads the analysis into a '5P' set of HR activities – HR philosophy, policies, programmes, practices and processes.

As we have said, the business strategy itself is key. We then have to think about the external factors – using PEST – from the point of view of HR and people. These are usually significant: there is always changing legislation about employment and

Figure 5 The drivers of an HR strategy

external factors affecting the labour market. Thirdly, there are internal issues. Every organisation has problems – things that do not run as well as they might. We may have morale, turnover or absentee problems: processes like performance management that are not working well, lack of skills to do a good job, conflicts in the organisation, and so on. Finally (and it *is* finally), the last influence is HR professional practice. Developments in HR practices must be watched to see if they would benefit *our* organisation. All these are encased in our values, beliefs and principles. If these are diverse and not commonly held, we will lack coherence in the implementation of any strategy. When we examine any one driver we have one simple question to ask. What are the implications of values, principles and beliefs on people in the organisation, specifically in six areas of HRM? These are:

- organisation and culture

- rewards and recognition

- communications and employee relations

- resourcing

- general HR policies, and

- learning and development.

Let us take three examples. Suppose that one of the values of the organisation is 'teamworking'. Tables 3, 4 and 5 show some possible implications of this for our strategy in people management. You might have thought that none of these examples had much to do with HR, except perhaps the first. Wrong! Every manager's objective and every problem has people implications. Even plain financial forecasts have them.

Table 3 HR implications of business strategy: example 1

SUPPORTING: the value of teamworking	
Organisation and culture	• organisation structure team-based • building a culture of teams helping one another • 'the team is as important as the individual'
Rewards and recognition	• team bonus schemes • team awards • reduced emphasis on individual performance
Communications and employee relations	(not affected)
Resourcing	• a promotion factor would be team orientation
General HR policies	(not affected)
Learning and development	• effective teamworking, inter-team facilitation, being a team leader • multi-skilling

Table 4 HR implications of business strategy: example 2

SUPPORTING: EMEA division's target to grow market share in Africa	
Organisation and culture	• new team needed, based in Nigeria
Rewards and recognition	• review incentive scheme • local packages, salary and benefits
Communications and employee relations	(not affected)
Resourcing	• recruit local salespeople • appoint experienced international manager
General HR policies	• review foreign service policy • create local policies as needed
Learning and development	• sales training • African culture training

Did you notice that each table of Tables 3 to 5 supports a different *level* of issue? (See Mayo, 2004; pp13–14.) They have quite different time-scales. Each one fits on the continuum below in a different place:

Today's problem	*Current targets*	*The way we want to be*
Reacting	**Proacting**	**Continuing**
(Table 3)	(Table 4)	(Table 5)

The 'continuing' strategy fits with our mission, vision, values, beliefs and long-term business goals. It incorporates the key principles of people management, with processes and programmes that we operate each year. It is not of course continuing for ever. We would revise it every time there was a significant change

Table 5 HR implications of business strategy: example 3

SUPPORTING: reducing problem of customer complaints in large store	
Organisation and culture	• test general culture towards customers • check analysis of complaints to see if caused by organisational process inefficiencies such as shortages • conflicts between store needs and head office targets? • jobs suitably designed?
Rewards and recognition	• check rewards not a source of employee dissatisfaction • consider awards based on customer feedback
Communications and employee relations	• ensure all staff are aware of volume and reasons for complaints • institute regular 'service quality' groups
Resourcing	• enough staff? • shift patterns?
General HR policies	• review why people leave • check whether any policies (such as flexible working) are a source of discontent
Learning and development	• customer focus training needed? • personal skills training needed?

in the nature of the organisation itself, and from time to time we would test it for still being relevant. (In practice, whenever the CEO of an organisation changes, or the HR director, it is natural for them to review and often change the strategy in order to make their mark.)

The 'proacting' strategy is a set of initiatives to support the business units or departments in what they are seeking to achieve. It will include resourcing needs, and then specific initiatives, projects and learning programmes to support them.

The 'reacting' strategy is not really a strategy at all. Nevertheless, we still have to make choices. Every organisation has problems that are people-related – HR has to decide which are the priority ones to address and feed them into its plans. Since all strategies must lead to implementation plans, we cannot ignore this often very important category.

 EXERCISE

Imagine you are the HR director in a significant garden centre business. This year the company has decided to go online and offer its products for customers to order and have delivered to their doorstep.

Draw up a table similar to Tables 3 to 5, and think through the implications for people of this decision.

What questions should be asked in each category?

THE 'CONTINUING' PEOPLE STRATEGY

When we try and put this together, or review where we are, what factors will guide us? We need to follow the general outline of Figure 5 but start with the business and move clockwise. There is a great temptation by ambitious and idealistic people in HR to want the 'perfect' people management strategy according to every good practice that has been read about. Particularly in the public sector one can find HR strategies so far from reality as to have lost all credibility. You just cannot move some deeply entrenched cultures very fast. It actually is counterproductive to publish aspirations and then for employees to see no signs of them in reality.

What are the factors to be considered in putting together this part of the strategy? They are the following, and each will be explained in more detail:

● the vision and values of the organisation

● the beliefs and principles we have regarding people management and development

● the long-term business goals and strategies

● the core competencies of the organisation that we want to maintain

● the general external factors that affect our kind of organisation.

Vision and values

If we assume that the organisation does want these to become a reality (and one sometimes wonders whether some organisations do), then HR must ask how it will help that to happen. The values must be supported in many ways, such as through recruiting people who share them (see Chapter 8); training people to live them in their jobs (see Chapter 24); arranging peer or manager feedback to employees (see Chapter 12); rewarding the right behaviours *and* sanctioning undesired behaviours; promoting and rewarding people who demonstrate the values (see Chapters 12 and 13); designing processes that exhibit the values; and reinforcing them in communications (see Chapter 19). All too often this does not happen. HR can have an enormous influence in this area, and this is not a one-off programme at the time of launching of the values. It is an ongoing part of the people management strategy.

REFLECTIVE ACTIVITY

You are the HR director and one of the values of your organisation is 'taking responsibility'.

How would HR support such a value?

Beliefs and values in people management

Beliefs and values are a very important subject. HR people are generally in HR because they care about people being respected, valued and treated well. Not all line managers share their perspectives, and they have pressures on them to deliver results. This causes conflicts. On the one hand idealistic HR people have to move more towards reality, and on the other managers may have to be educated to understand that well-treated people produce better results. A *shared* philosophy of the principles of people management is therefore important. And there *are* choices. Figure 6 shows some of these choices. Whichever one is chosen will significantly impact the work HR has to do and its priorities. It will affect the *kind* of training we do, the *kind* of pay systems, the *kind* of organisation, and the *kind* of policies we create.

Figure 6 Options in people management beliefs

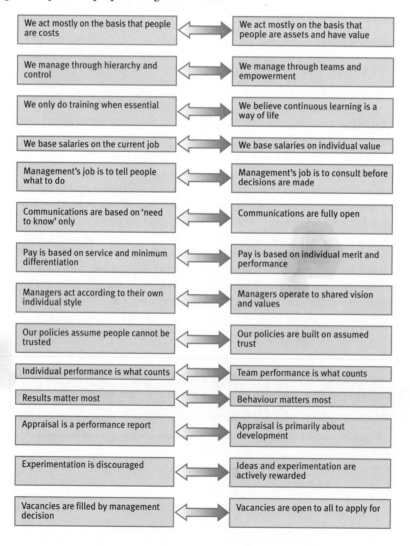

We act mostly on the basis that people are costs	We act mostly on the basis that people are assets and have value
We manage through hierarchy and control	We manage through teams and empowerment
We only do training when essential	We believe continuous learning is a way of life
We base salaries on the current job	We base salaries on individual value
Management's job is to tell people what to do	Management's job is to consult before decisions are made
Communications are based on 'need to know' only	Communications are fully open
Pay is based on service and minimum differentiation	Pay is based on individual merit and performance
Managers act according to their own individual style	Managers operate to shared vision and values
Our policies assume people cannot be trusted	Our policies are built on assumed trust
Individual performance is what counts	Team performance is what counts
Results matter most	Behaviour matters most
Appraisal is a performance report	Appraisal is primarily about development
Experimentation is discouraged	Ideas and experimentation are actively rewarded
Vacancies are filled by management decision	Vacancies are open to all to apply for

Organisation A sees people only as resources and a cost. Organisation B sees people as valuable assets.

List some of the implications for the six categories of people management that we looked at earlier for both A and B, and contrast them.

What is important is that HR does not itself decide what the beliefs should be. There is a great temptation to do so, and there is no reason why HR should not try to *exert influence* towards what it believes is the best philosophy. But the senior management team must decide –because they must 'own' and believe personally in what is decided. It is a good idea for the senior team just to write down a series of statements. The American pharmaceutical company Johnson & Johnson have a whole set of statements for all their stakeholders and call it their 'Credo' – here is the section for employees:

We are responsible to our employees, the men and women who work with us throughout the world. Everyone must be considered an individual. We must respect their dignity and recognise their merit.

They must have a sense of security in their jobs. Compensation must be fair and adequate, and working conditions clean, orderly and safe.

We must be mindful of ways to help our employees fulfil their family responsibilities.

Employees must feel free to make suggestions and complaints.

There must be equal opportunity for employment, development and advancement for those qualified. We must provide competent management, and our actions must be just and ethical.

Extract from Johnson & Johnson's 'Credo'

The long-term business goals and strategies

Long-term business goals and strategies are the third set of factors to consider. It may be that the organisation just plans to do more of the same (as today), hopefully better and more efficiently as years go by. But if it has ambitions – to acquire other companies, to create new subsidiaries, to expand internationally, and so on – we need to have 'the right people in the right place at the right time with the right skills' to meet the challenges. Some of these business goals might also require quite new HR policies and pay systems, for example.

Maintaining core competencies in the organisation

There are two different kinds of 'core competencies'. The first refers to the expertise that we need to have to be in our kind of business. If we are running an airline, for example, we have constant needs for pilots, yield optimisation experts and schedulers (to name a few). So we are constantly recruiting and training such people because it is our life. Another type of core competence is that which gives us a competitive advantage – we are better at them. Easyjet and Ryanair have all the experts other airlines do, but they are better at aircraft utilisation and it gives them a clear advantage. Our people strategy must be one that maintains all these core competencies.

External factors

Every organisation has its own external factors to take into account in the medium term – trends in the market or in regulation, for example, that must be considered in shaping our strategy. The PEST analysis (see Chapter 2) will help us identify these factors. For every factor we have identified under the five headings above, we are going to ask the same question as we asked earlier – what are the implications for the six areas of HRM? The implications may be of different kinds:

- they may shape our HR policies (the beliefs about people management may almost be policies in themselves, depending on how they are worded)
- they will shape sub-strategies for rewards, resourcing, organisation design and development and communications/employee relations
- they may lead to a long-term resourcing plan
- they may define a desired culture to aim for
- they may lead to people processes that we do not have
- they may lead to ongoing programmes of learning.

Bringing the 'continuing strategy' together

If we have done the above systematically, we will have a large number of tables such as Tables 3, 4 and 5 that need to be integrated into one. One way to do that is to have one sheet for each of the six HRM areas as shown in Table 6. Strategies often have just a series of intentions, such as the first (top) box in Table 6. But it is the other three boxes that will make it all work. Running the processes and developing short-term action plans which progress the strategy forwards will make a significant contribution to the question right at the beginning of the chapter-deciding 'what we should do and why'.

REFLECTIVE ACTIVITY

Go back to the garden centre we introduced in one of the previous exercises – the garden centre which serves both visiting and online customers. Imagine it has 250 employees, half of whom are part-time and/or seasonal, and 10 managers.

Go through the five areas to consider for putting together the 'continuing' strategy, with particular reference to the area of learning and development.

Draw up a table like Table 6 for learning and development.

Table 6 Example of an integrated sub-strategy for 'organisation and culture'

1	Policy statements

- We want an organisation that is agile and adaptable; therefore we will aim for a minimum number of layers between the front line and senior management.
- Wherever possible we will organise by process teams to maximise efficiency of flow and minimise hierarchy.
- We want to build a culture that truly reflects our values, and all stakeholders will experience them.
- It is essential for our business that new knowledge is rapidly shared. We will organise to minimise boundaries and generate a culture that is willingly and skilfully knowledge-sharing.

2	Processes

- We will have a steering committee on organisation design which will advise and approve all proposed changes in line with the policy statements.
- We will at least annually test our culture through perception surveys against the desired cultural template.
- We will set up a series of knowledge-sharing processes, such as communities of practice, project reviews, expert seminars and virtual discussion groups.

3	Supportive learning programmes

- We will have a section of new employee induction that emphasises the cultural behaviours expected.
- We will have regular programmes to learn effective knowledge-sharing techniques.

4	Resource requirements to implement this ongoing strategy

- The organisation steering committee will consist of part-time representatives from each main area of the business.
- An 'organisation development' team of two people within HR will be needed to facilitate this ongoing strategy.

THE 'PROACTING' AND 'REACTING' STRATEGIES

Some would say these are not really strategies but just plans and initiatives for the current year. Let us not worry about the words – we still need to make choices and priorities for what we will do in addition to running the 'continuing' strategy – supporting operational managers in their objectives and tackling problem areas.

Supporting operational managers (proactively)

It is normal in organisations for all managers to have current objectives and targets to go with them. HR typically might talk to each manager about a headcount plan and a training plan for the department concerned, but this approach starts off with many assumptions. A better way is to sit down with each manager when he or she has his/her objectives and go through a process of getting answers to questions like the following:

For each objective:

- What is the objective, and does it have a measurable endpoint?
- What factors are working for its achievement and what are working against it?

- Who (individuals or groups) are involved in these factors?

- What are the implications (if any) for each set of people in the six areas of HRM?

After doing this for all the objectives one by one:

- Which of all the actions and initiatives that we have noted would have the biggest impact on your goal achievement?

Note here that we are not talking about people generically, but specifically by group – or even by individual. What kind of actions might result? Examples are a recruitment task, a new bonus plan, special learning programmes, a new skill test, or some form of coaching.

Supporting operational managers (reactively)

Above, we sat down with managers to look forward and ask how we could support them in achieving their goals. At the same time we might ask another question: 'Are there any existing *problems* that you need help with?' If the organisation has a good metrics system (see Chapter 16), we might already have some data that would tell us about problems – signals coming from opinion surveys, labour turnover and attrition statistics, health and safety audits, and so on. But there may be problems less obvious to HR but still with people solutions. Problems with quality, productivity, project over-runs, compliance, budgets – all of these may benefit from professional HR attention. So we apply the five questions above in the same way – except that we substitute 'problem' for 'objective' and 'solution' for 'achievement'.

Integrating and prioritising

You can imagine that we might well end up with a long list of issues and potential initiatives as we go round all the managers. We will inevitably be limited to resources available and have to make choices. There will be items that we have no choice over and we just have to make a plan to get on with them – essential training or recruitment, for instance. But how do we decide about the rest? Figure 7 is a well-known method of helping to make prioritising easier. Look at the long list of all the things that could and should be done, and allocate them to one of the boxes in the figure. The two dimensions are the *impact* on the organisation's achievement and the *difficulty* of implementation. 'Quick wins' are always a temptation, especially for building credibility, and some are good – but it is the top two boxes that demand the most attention. Remember, it is fine to do the analysis and make statements of what we will do – the reality is in the detailed planning that implements it all. *Strategy should be 10% analysis and 90% implementation,* not the other way round. So all this has to be turned into practical, phased and resourced plans to make it happen.

We finally have to make sure that all the various initiatives do not conflict and that they support each other. This is called 'horizontal integration'. For example, we do not want to find that we have set cultural aspirations but are pursuing policies and processes in the reward sub-strategy that work against them.

Figure 7 Prioritisation of demands

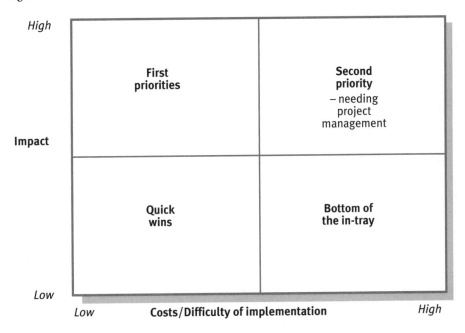

Lynda Gratton (2000) wrote a book called *Living Strategy*, which was about what she called 'the *path* of the journey'. It is about the environment in which our strategy will (or will not) be realised, and how to bridge philosophy or ideals to action. It is beyond the scope of this chapter to discuss the book in detail, but it is recommended for further reading.

Part 1 of this chapter has been about an organisation's people strategy – what policies, processes, programmes and projects we need for good people management and how HR and line managers can work in partnership to achieve this. These are all in addition to everyday administration which, as explained at the beginning of Chapter 2, is a fundamental part of HR work. Now it is time to look at the strategy for the HR function itself.

2 A STRATEGY FOR THE HR FUNCTION

The HR function, like other support functions (such as IT and Finance), exists to do the following:

- to carry out necessary administrative activities – in this case to do with people
- to ensure compliance and integrity with relevant legislation and company policies
- to represent the company externally on people issues as required
- to manage, usually jointly with line management, people management processes

- to apply professional knowledge to support the organisation and its managers in their goals

- to provide data and information that enables management to manage effectively.

The last three of these activities clearly interface with the people strategy discussed in Part 1. The function needs a strategy that will deliver all of these efficiently and effectively.

That means making choices about organisation of the function and the resources needed; the capabilities of people in the function; ongoing process evaluation and review; 'tools' to support the processes; people-related measures and standards of performance; involvement and dialogue with business managers; and external benchmarking and networking. Each of these is now examined in turn.

ORGANISATION AND RESOURCES

How the HR department should be structured is an important strategy choice. One key influence is the demands of the people strategy, but another is also the approach we want to take to resourcing. Historically, an HR department would have seen three main roles – administration, the professional generalist and the professional specialist. The *generalist* would look after a section of people – usually linked to a business or division – and the role often included some administration and specialist activity. The *specialist* would be dedicated to one area of HR.

Today, things are not so different in practice, but new words are in use and technology has had a big impact. Administration and quite a lot of what the generalist used to do is encompassed in the term 'transactional HR'. It includes all the routine tasks involved in employing people. Some of this can be made 'self-service' using intranet facilities; it is usually centralised today, and also is frequently outsourced.

'Shared services', as the centralised option is often called, may go beyond just administration and include legal advice, grievance support, training programmes and a lot of day-to-day activities that an HR generalist used to do. The new generation of generalists is more likely to be called 'advisers' or 'business partners', and their role is more to support business priorities and take initiatives that will help their dedicated area of the organisation. It is more of an 'organisational effectiveness' role than traditional HR, and is sometimes referred to (somewhat pretentiously) as 'transformational HR' or 'strategic HRM'. Line managers need some time to adjust to the fact that they now have to go to more than one HR person for their needs. Meanwhile the 'specialist' roles (experts in our six areas of HRM) still continue and may be supplemented by consultants as needed.

A CASE STUDY OF A SHARED SERVICE MODEL

A large London-centred law firm used the Peoplesoft HR system to provide a technical base for moving to a new HR operating model. The model comprised three parts. An HR solutions group was established to deal centrally with the vast majority of HR enquiries concerning people. All routine transactions were centralised and standardised to give a consistent and responsive HR service across the firm. They used a 'contact management tool' to capture and progress all enquiries. This enabled the senior HR managers to provide a more strategic HR service through developing and implementing specific strategies for the practice areas. In addition, a new centre of expertise was established, consisting of specialists in areas such as resourcing, benefits and rewards whose aim was to ensure that HR policies and processes for the firm were of best HR professional practice. This change saved the firm £1 million in reduced staff costs in the HR function.

CAPABILITIES

The changes to HR departments outlined above have been driven not only by the continual desire for cost reduction and by technological opportunities, but very much by the inspiration given to the HR profession by Professor Dave Ulrich of the University of Michigan. He maintained that the delivery of the strategy depends on the capability of HR people. Ulrich (1997; p.253) illustrated the requirements under four headings. At the heart we have 'personal credibility'. HR people have lots of ideas, and indeed an often idealistic view of what managers and organisations should be like. But if they want to be listened to, they must have some fundamentals in place. These include:

- efficiency, responsiveness and reliability – they do what they say they will do, and do it well

- realism, recognising the pressures that managers have from day to day

- using language that is free from jargon

- demonstrating that they really care about what the business and its managers are trying to achieve.

Then we have 'business mastery'. 'Mastery' is a strong word and perhaps too strong, because if you have chosen HR as your profession and not worked operationally in the business, you cannot expect to master all the intricacies of a business. But it does mean that at least the 'business partner' professionals:

- understand the basics of the financial model of the business and the effect on costs of initiatives we propose

- are able to do credible 'return on investment' calculations

- know what people *do* in the organisation – what the different roles entail

- can discuss the business objectives and ask intelligent questions.

Thus 'human resource mastery' refers to professional knowledge of HR, or at least having access to it.

'Change and process mastery' is essential if we want to play the role of change catalyst and facilitator, and in order to ensure that our own processes are effective. It means we understand:

- process design and re-engineering
- measuring process effectiveness
- models of effective change
- helping people through change.

Our strategy will include a 'functional development strategy' – our priorities and goals for the development of our HR people in order to ensure that the value of our own human capital is maximised.

REFLECTIVE ACTIVITY

Go back again to the garden centre of the previous exercises – the garden centre which serves both visiting and online customers.

What kind of resource in HR do you think it could afford to have?

What do you think would be the top ten capabilities that the HR director should have to be effective?

PROCESS EVALUATION

Table 7 features a list of processes that HR would typically design and 'own', even though line management is jointly responsible for implementing most of them. We do not have to have every people process in the HR textbook, but we need those that will support our 'continuing' strategy. Other chapters in this book cover many of these processes in detail. There may be processes that we need but do not have, or we may have some that need revision. Criteria we might use to test whether a process is 'fit for purpose' include:

- Its purpose is clear.
- It makes the business more effective in some way – it adds value to one or more stakeholder.
- The cost and time of running the process is justified by the value it brings (as seen by line managers).
- The process is consistent with our values.
- The process has been recently examined for possible simplification.

Table 7 List of HR processes

Resourcing	Remuneration	Learning and development
Job profiling	Job grading	Personal development planning
Recruitment	Salary banding	Training needs analysis
Selection	Salary increases	Training design
Induction/Orientation	Variable pay/bonus systems	Training evaluation
Vacancy management	Market benchmarking	Knowledge management
Promotion	Recognition schemes	Further education
Succession planning	Performance management	Training authorisation
		Use of coaching and mentoring
Organisation and culture	**Communications/ER**	**HR policies**
Organisation design	Communication processes	Discipline
Organisation restructuring	Employee consultation	Grievance
Culture analysis	Suggestion schemes	Absence management
Workforce planning	Use of intranet	Poor performance
Opinion and engagement surveys	Upwards communication	Sickness
		Time off and leave
		Use of company equipment

Our strategy will include the 'map' of needed processes, and – resources permitting – our plans will include making sure they are all fit for purpose.

TOOLS WHICH SUPPORT PROCESSES

Perhaps the most important tool to support HR processes is technology. We need a human resources information system (HRIS) that will provide us with data and reports and that keeps track of our people. We need to decide how distributed it will be – what information managers and employees will have access to. We may use specialised software for particular processes also – such as performance management or talent management. The intranet provides us with many opportunities for communication (see Chapter 19), such as having policies and forms online. A whole part of our strategy will be how technology is deployed, and this is covered in Chapter 4.

Then there are professional tools which may or may not be automated. These are instruments that are purchased, or specially designed internally, to help a process work more effectively. HR is constantly bombarded by suppliers who offer tools and methodologies, and its choices have significant effects on resources. Table 8 gives some examples of the tools that may be used.

How would we evaluate the choices over tools to be used? Criteria we might use to test whether a tool is 'fit for purpose' include:

- It makes a process more effective.
- It is consistent with our values.
- It *works* – it fulfils its promise.
- The cost of purchase, development and implementation is justified by the value it produces.

Table 8 Some of the tools used in HR

Resourcing	*Remuneration*	*Learning and development*
Assessment centres	Job evaluation systems	E-learning programmes
Personality tests	Salary planning software	Development centres
Ability tests	Salary surveys	Competency frameworks
Web-based recruitment		Role specifications
Structured panels		Learning resource centres
Graphology (mainly in France)		Talent management software
Biodata questionnaires		Training management software
Application forms		360-degree assessments
Organisation and culture	*Communications/ER*	*HR policies*
Organisation design software	Web-based tools	Intranet and web-based tools
Culture surveys	Virtual discussion groups	
Questionnaires	Conferencing tools	
Workforce planning models	Satellite broadcasting	
	Pulse surveys	

- It is easily understandable by non-HR people.
- It preferably can be used in several processes.
- It is appropriate for our culture.

PEOPLE-RELATED MEASURES AND STANDARDS OF PERFORMANCE

Part of our HR strategy will be to measure and monitor our own effectiveness. This is covered in Chapter 16.

INVOLVEMENT AND DIALOGUE WITH BUSINESS MANAGERS

The business-oriented HR function cannot operate in isolation. We have already described the need for our people strategy to be driven by the business strategies and objectives. But our HR strategy must include regular contact with the operations.

A lot of angst appears in the HR media about 'having a seat at the top table' and 'being a member of the board'. A lot depends on the role of a board and the requirements of its members. The most senior HR person is more likely to be on a board sub-committee, such as the remuneration committee, than on the board itself, particularly for a holding or large parent company. The 'top table' should be interpreted as the 'executive committee', and it is clearly desirable for HR to be represented there. It is more the personal qualities and credibility of the individual that will bring this about than the 'right by job title'.

Nevertheless, there are many other opportunities to be involved in. HR can set up 'steering committees' of operational executives to advise it on some issues, such as management development and internal communications. Individuals can represent the function in project committees and task forces and be regular attenders at business reviews so that they pick up people-related issues. They may have to take the initiative for this to happen.

EXTERNAL BENCHMARKING AND NETWORKING

Finally, the HR strategy will include a part which is keeping up to date. The HR world offers many opportunities – perhaps too many – and a systematic choice of which to be involved in is important. The function may want to go in for the many awards and league tables that are on offer (such as the various annual 'great place to work' surveys), which can help build the employee brand. 'Benchmarking clubs' in the organisation's own commercial sector provide useful knowledge of good practices and comparative data. We may also want to participate in research projects, particularly in areas which relate to the initiatives we have decided to take in our main HR and people strategies.

KEY ISSUES IN PEOPLE AND HR STRATEGIES

We now pull together ten key points about HR strategies raised in this chapter:

- 'Strategy' means choosing routes to get to a goal. It merges into objectives and plans. It is important to remember that it also involves choices of what *not* to do.

- HR has to prepare two different strategies. One is the 'people strategy' and the other is a strategy for the HR function itself.

- The people strategy is one of the strategies that supports the business in maintaining its competitive advantage and achieving its goals. There are well-established processes for defining strategies and tools, such as PEST and SWOT.

- The key drivers that help us to define our people strategy are: the business strategy itself, our guiding principles and beliefs on people management, external factors we must take into account, and internal factors such as organisational problems.

- In deciding what should be in a people strategy, we can divide it into three parts. The first part is 'continuing' – the core policies and processes we want in place to achieve our ongoing goals in people management. The second is 'proacting' – specific initiatives that will support current business goals. Finally, we have things we should do as 'reacting' to problems and issues that need solving.

- The people strategy can be divided into six sub-strategies – organisation and culture, learning and development, rewards and recognition, communications and employee relations, general HR policies, and resourcing.

- We integrate the demands of these sub-strategies into policies, processes, learning requirements and resources, ensure that they are 'horizontally integrated', and then prioritise them. This leads us to practical implementation planning.

- The HR functional strategy is about choices it must make for itself. It includes how to organise, how to use resources, and how to debelop the capabilities of the in-house resources.

- Then we have to decide which processes and tools we need to deliver the people strategy, what technology will support us, how we will measure our performance, how we intend to keep close to the business and how we will keep track of the outside world.

- Finally, HR should do none of this in isolation. People management is a shared partnership between HR and managers, and all HR policies and programmes should be mutually agreed.

Perhaps there are other key points that you would like to note for yourself.

The main case study in this chapter now follows. It gives an example of the HR strategy of a British local government authority.

THE HR STRATEGY OF HERTFORDSHIRE COUNTY COUNCIL

Make an initial reading of the case study to gain an overview of the situation, and then read the questions that you will need to address. Now read the case study again, making notes of issues and facts that will help you in your analysis and responses to the questions. Remember to 'read between the lines' as well as picking out the obvious points, and also to consider what is not said as well as what is presented here.

This is an extract from the people strategy of Hertfordshire County Council (2001).

Introduction

The people strategy is the County Council's statement of how it will achieve its objectives through its people. The County Council has in place the infrastructure needed to achieve its promises to its communities. The 'Herts Connect' programme, the creation of new children's schools and family services and a new integrated adult care service are just a few examples of transformations in the way the County provides its services. However, infrastructure alone is not enough. To achieve successful change we need to engage, value and enthuse the unique contribution of all employees. At Hertfordshire we recognise that our success as an organisation is totally dependent upon the commitment and dedication of the very talented people who work here. This people strategy sets out how we will continue to value and develop our people in order to maintain our success in the future and mark ourselves out as the best-performing local authority in the country.

Bill Ogley, Chief Executive,
Hertfordshire County Council

Linking strategy to objectives: 20–20 vision

The County Council's promises to the people of Hertfordshire create the strategic objectives that will drive the County through the early years of the twenty-first century. These objectives also shape the people requirements for the organisation. Any people strategy must be closely aligned to organisational objectives in order to ensure that the right people are achieving the right things at the right time. Our starting point in developing this people strategy has therefore been an analysis of the people objectives contained within the following:

The promises: Four key promises have been made to the communities of Hertfordshire about how the County Council will improve their lives. These promises provide a framework for the planning and development of all services across the organisation. They will play an important role in determining the skills, competencies and behaviours needed from employees now and in the future so that we can:

- make Hertfordshire a better place to live and work

- improve education and promote prosperity

- help people to help themselves

- get better in all that we do, and involve and serve the public.

Herts Connect is a major county-wide initiative that is fundamentally changing the way we operate. So far it has resulted in:

- the introduction of an all-service call centre, a new interface with customers via the website (Herts Direct)

- a rationalisation of the way we use our property and transport and a focus of service delivery on the needs of our customers, a major structural change in the development of the new children's schools and family services and adult care services to focus service delivery on the needs of our customers.

These initiatives will all require employees to work more flexibly, in different ways, across professional boundaries and using new competencies.

Best value: Although a government initiative, the principles of best value are closely aligned to the principles of Herts Connect. Every service of the County Council will be fundamentally reviewed within the next five years. These reviews, along with advances in technology, will change the way that the County Council operates and the way that people work.

What you told us . . .

In developing this strategy it was important that we listened to people across the organisation. We wanted to understand what the key people requirements for the business success were and to develop a common agreement on what the people strategy is aiming to achieve. This is what you told us:

- There are significant recruitment and retention difficulties that have arisen as a result of national skills shortages. These shortages are now impacting on the ability to deliver quality services.

- We need to do more to diversify our workforce.

- We need to become a more flexible employer.

- We need to develop more effective methods of rewarding contribution.

- We need to do more to enable our employees to embrace new communications technologies.

- We need to do more as an employer to actively demonstrate how we value our people.

- We need to develop new leadership capabilities.

- Departmental and professional silos need to be challenged so that people can work more effectively together.

Delivering the people strategy

The people strategy will form an organisation-wide framework for the delivery of people management objectives over the next three to five years. All departments of the County Council will be responsible for developing their own tailored strategy for delivering the five key people objectives identified in this document.

Strategic people objectives

The five strategic people objectives set out in this document are the building-blocks of our people strategy. They will ensure that the work of the personnel function across the County Council is always closely aligned to organisational objectives. Our performance in achieving our strategic objectives will be closely monitored and measured. The value added by the personnel function will be identified through tangible performance measures.

The building-blocks of success

To be an employer of choice, we will aim to be an organisation that people aspire to work for by:

- creating flexible employment, development and reward packages that employees highly value

- creating a challenging and exciting working environment

- being a good employer and looking after our people.

To be a developer of people, we will develop the organisation through its people by:

- developing strong leaders

- promoting and assisting career development through coaching, mentoring, shadowing and secondment schemes

- developing a culture of learning through practice

- developing structured professional qualification strategies and personal development opportunities based on our development charter and organisational objectives

- ensuring that employees take responsibility for their own continuous development and lifelong learning.

We will enable all the elements of this strategy to be delivered by embracing new information and communication technologies. People practices in the organisation will become more effective and more efficient by our:

- making access to personnel services much easier for all our customers and partners

- communicating with people within and outside the organisation more effectively through a variety of communication and technology portals

- providing effective and timely management information on people-related issues.

We will continuously influence the success of organisational change by:

- involving and empowering employees to contribute to innovation and change within their services

- developing a performance culture

- recognising the importance of engaging employees in organisational change at the earliest opportunity to ensure effective culture change

- developing more effective partnerships with our trade unions and employees

- developing flexible employment packages that reflect the new paradigm of work.

We will value and embrace the creativity and uniqueness of all employees by:

- harnessing the diversity of our employees to improve service delivery

- enhancing Hertfordshire's reputation inside and outside the organisation by our actions, not just our words

- ensuring the fair and consistent treatment of all our employees

- monitoring personnel practice and workforce profiles and taking positive action to redress any imbalances found.

Note: These are followed by quite extensive lists of actions to be taken, with targets, performance indicators and accountabilities under each of the five building-blocks.

Questions for discussion

Consider and come to conclusions on the following questions, and be prepared to discuss your answers.

1 How does the above case study relate to the principles outlined in the chapter?

2 What do you think is particularly good about it?

3 If you were a consultant to the Council, would you suggest any areas the Council might consider adding or changing?

EXPLORE FURTHER

ARMSTRONG, M. and BARON, A. (2002) *Strategic HRM*. London, CIPD
This draws on previously unpublished research to provide authentic voices from real-life managers discussing how they set about developing and implementing HR strategies. The research includes interviews with HR directors and chief executives from a variety of organisations, demystifying the concept and practice of 'strategic HRM', and placing it firmly within the context of the wider organisational strategy and business goals.

BOXALL, P. and PURCELL, J. (2007) *Strategy and Human Resource Management*. Basingstoke, Palgrave Macmillan
A thorough review of the literature and the evolution of strategic HRM thinking. The authors also develop a conceptual framework to provide an exploration of the the field.

GRATTON, L. (2000) *Living Strategy*. London, Prentice Hall/Financial Times
Based on Gratton's experience leading a consortium of companies over the years in exploring added-value HR, this book shows how to design strategies that have meaning and purpose for people without whose commitment they remain drawings on the wallchart. It shows how to create a people vision, how to analyse gaps from where we are and where we want to be, and how to turn strategy into implementation.

MAYO, A. J. (2004b) *Creating a Learning and Development Strategy*. London, CIPD
Although focused specifically on learning and development, the methodologies in the book are very similar to this chapter. The ideas are developed more thoroughly and is written as a practical guide for HR professionals.

CHAPTER 4

HRM and technological innovation

Anna Kyprianou

INTRODUCTION

This chapter looks at the use of technology-based systems, applications and tools, often referred to as 'e-HR', and its impact on key HR functions and processes. It therefore looks at subjects also covered in other chapters (especially Chapter 20 on HR roles, Chapters 8 and 9 on recruitment and selection, Chapters 14 and 24 on workplace learning and HRD, Chapters 12 and 13 on performance management and reward, and Chapter 19 on communication), but offering a different perspective on all of those subjects.

LEARNING OUTCOMES

By the end of this chapter readers should be able to:

● define the concept of 'e-HR'

● explain the impact of e-HR on the HR role and function

● identify appropriate uses of e-HR for different HR issues

● evaluate the benefits and detriments of a range of e-HR practices.

This chapter is in two parts. The first discusses issues surrounding technological innovation, the emergence of e-HR and its impact on the HR role and function. The second part explores the use of e-HR in key HR processes.

We begin with a 'starter' or introductory case study. Unlike most case studies in this book, the case presents a futuristic view of the use of technology in HR in an attempt to get readers thinking about the changing nature of e-HR. The main case study at the end of the chapter uses a large company's experience to draw together some of the key issues.

Reference sources named within the chapter may be looked up in the *References and further reading* section at the end of the book.

STARTER CASE STUDY

It is 3am GMT and Julie George, talent strategist for the multinational technology organisation Global Industries, wakes up in a cold sweat having forgotten to deal with some urgent applications for the post of Global HR Director. She sits up in bed and immediately goes to her inbox on her videophone and downloads the applications. The five digital CVs she downloads are mapped onto her core competencies and corporate fit model for an initial pre-screen and the results reveal that three of the applicants have matches between 95% and 98%. Julie sends each of the three an email inviting them to a preliminary first interview, which will be conducted virtually, using video-conferencing. She also ensures that an automatic, yet personalised, 'rejection' letter is sent to the other two applicants who only scored a 70% and 75% fit respectively. Julie then goes back to sleep, feeling relieved.

The following morning, Julie logs on to the corporate employee portal to check how many people have chosen their flexible benefits for the year 2021–22. It appears that gym membership is proving more popular than ever before and outstrips private healthcare. Julie thinks it is not surprising that staff are more interested in the way they look in that their average age is 25.

Julie has a four-year-old son and Global Industries' flexible working policy means that she works from home most days and as long as she completes her tasks by 3pm GMT, she can spend the rest of the time with her son. The last job on her electronic list is to train herself in voice recognition software. So she goes to her password-protected personal development folder on the employee portal and downloads the appropriate training module . . .

Questions for discussion

1 What would it be like to work for Global Industries? List the benefits and detriments for both Julie George and Global Industries.

2 What impact would such a heavy reliance on technology have on the HR function?

Source: adapted from S. Weekes and S. Beagrie (2002) *E-People*, Capstone Publishing

Some would argue that it is no longer possible for HR without technology to realise its strategic potential (see Chapter 20) and provide the necessary wide range of services and products that an organisation needs (Fein, 2001).

Just as HR's role is changing, technology has continued to evolve. If HR's role has come to be to deliver employee support and management based on the needs of the organisation, then technology's role has helped that. Technology can provide an effective and efficient way for organisations to capture, edit, store, retrieve and share the essential information about people. But the key to ensuring a streamlined information-sharing service is by integrating them into a robust HR network. It is important to note that there is no one technological solution or innovation that meets the needs of all organisations.

1 TECHNOLOGICAL INNOVATION IN HR: TOWARDS A DEFINITION

What is e-HR? Ulrich (2002; p.91) says:

E-HR means a lot of things ... I see it as a matrix with two columns: transaction – doing the administrative things faster and better; enabling employees to be self-sufficient and self-reliant; building employee portals, etc;

and transformation – becoming more strategic and building sustainable competitive advantage. My sense is that most of the e-HR work is in the transactional column, doing the administrative parts of HR systems.

At an advanced level, e-HR represents a fully integrated, organisation-wide electronic network of HR-related data, information, services, databases, tools, applications and transactions that are generally accessible at any time by end-user groups. Because e-HR does mean a lot of things, we now give a quick overview of the terms, often used interchangeably, relating to technology and HR.

A human resource information system (HRIS) is a system that helps an organisation 'acquire, store, manipulate, analyse, retrieve, and distribute information about an organisation's human resources' (Tannenbaum, 1990; p.28).

E-HR in its simplest sense refers to the use of technology within the HR function. E-HR in its broadest sense is 'the planning, implementation and application of information technology for both networking and supporting at least two individual or collective actors in their shared performing of HR activities' (Strohmeier, 2007; p.19).

Other terms, often used interchangeably, are:

● *virtual HR* (Lepak and Snell, 1998) – virtual HR refers to technology-mediated networks of different internal and external stakeholders that provide an organisation with the HR services needed, so obviating any requirement for a conventional HR department

● *web-based HR* (Ruel *et al*, 2004) – The use of Internet technologies

● *business-to-employee* (B2E) (Huang, Jin and Yang, 2004) – this focuses on internal stakeholders such as line managers, HR professionals and employees. In contrast e-HR has a greater reach in that it includes other, external, stakeholders such as applicants and consultants.

In this chapter, 'e-HR' is used in both its simplest and its broadest senses.

EVALUATING TECHNOLOGICAL INNOVATION IN HRM

Historically, HR was one of the first departments in organisations to automate its processes. This has sometimes led to a legacy of unconnected applications, systems and attitudes that has not helped the development of coherent technological HR strategies. Table 9 provides a brief historical outline of the relationship between technological innovations and HR.

Today's technology frees HR from its administrative history. The technology can range from simple spreadsheets to all-embracing integrated HRIS to web-enabled applications and systems covering all HR functions, processes and strategies.

As can be seen from Table 10, technology can extend HR services directly to managers and employees through self-service systems. Furthermore, technology can both facilitate the management of HR more efficiently and enable the adoption of practices across the whole organisation.

Table 9 Technological innovations and HR: a 40-year chronology

1960s	First payroll processing systems appear
1970s	Emergence of HR information systems with functional features such as compensation, benefits and pensions
1980s	HR begins to develop its own systems as desktop computers offer local solutions relatively cost-effectively
1980s	Cost-effective software facilitates the spread of HR information systems to an increasing number of organisations
1989	Creation of the World Wide Web enables the effective navigation of the Internet
1995	Online job boards are introduced
1996	ICL launches Café VIK, an employee portal designed to share knowledge
1998	The term 'e-business' is coined; major HR technology vendors move increasingly to the Internet; terms such as 'e-HR' and 'web-enabled HR' appear
1999	Outsourcing comes into its own; BP sign one of the biggest HR outsourcing deals
2000	Increasing number of business-to-employee (B2E) services emerge
2001	All major corporations embark on some form of e-HR

The use of technology in HR

Organisations are approaching the introduction and development of e-HR from several perspectives, often combining several elements. These elements include:

- HR transaction processing systems for employees

- knowledge servers for instructions and queries

- self-service tools

- information system tools for managers

- integrating systems to link different existing systems.

How far are these used? A CIPD survey in 2005 found that 77% of organisations used some sort of technology for HR-related activities. The 2003 Cranet survey found high levels of use, 82% of UK organisations having some form of HRIS. This survey also suggests that in terms of e-HRM use UK organisations are not necessarily ahead of those in other European countries. On the one hand, Table 11 shows that in 2003 only 18% of UK organisations surveyed reported no use of technology in HR compared to just under 30% in Slovakia. Interestingly, Germany, Greece and Slovakia reported greater integration of HR systems into wider management systems than Sweden and the UK – this may be explained by the time at which these countries began using HR-related technology (the earlier, the more likely that legacy systems are more important).

Table 12 shows the level of HR web development for those organisations that reported e-HR facilities. The UK and Greece mainly use e-HR for one-way communication with minimal employee access to personal information. Employee access to update personal data appears to be even less common. Complex HR transactions were indeed a rarity in 2003 across Europe.

The general application of technology in HR has spread. However, it remains on an administrative level, as Table 13 shows. Administrative tasks such as personnel records and payroll were clearly supported by technology across the countries surveyed, whereas advanced, complex strategic or decision-support applications had yet to be fully realised (Ball, 2001; Teo *et al*, 2001).

Table 10 The application of technology in support of HR

Recruitment	Learning and development	Core HR	Policies and procedures	Performance management
The enablers				
• corporate job boards • external job sites • applicant tracking and management systems • online candidate screening, testing, skills matching and ranking • task-specific skills matching	• e-learning • blended learning and community learning • knowledge management and best practice sharing systems	• self-service tools for employee transactions • online flexible benefits system • payroll systems • employee portals	• employee portal/corporate intranet for storing information • email for disseminating information • online induction	• internal incentive and reward systems • external incentive and reward sites • online flexible benefits systems • email for collaborative discussion on staff appraisal • online benchmarking against core competencies • online 360-degree feedback
Individual aim				
Reduce the cost and time to hire; more responsive recruiting; extend reach of candidate pool	Develop staff more effectively and cultivate, maintain and retain company knowledge	Reduce administration so HR can be strategic; empowered employees	Reduce administration for HR to become more strategic; improve corporate communications and empower employees	Tailored recognition and rewarding; more effective and collaborative performance assessment
Overall aim				
To create a strategic HR function and an empowered, motivated workforce, performing at optimum efficiency				

Source: adapted from Weekes and Beagrie (2002)

Table 11 'What type of HR Information System do you have?'

	UK	Sweden	Germany	Greece	Slovakia
No computerised HR information system	18%	13%	16%	12%	29%
Primarily independent HR system	57%	68%	52%	52%	39%
Integrated into wider management system	25%	19%	31%	36%	32%

Source: Cranet (2003)

Table 12 'If you have e-HR facilities, what is the level of HR web deployment?'

	UK	Sweden	Germany	Greece	Slovakia
One-way communication	65%	41%	48%	75%	50%
One-way, but allowing employee access to some personal information	15%	31%	35%	13%	27%
Two-way: employee is able to update simple personal information	11%	16%	8%	6%	8%
Two-way: employee is able to perform complex transactions	2%	9%	2%	5%	1%
Other more complex transactions	0%	2%	0%	0%	1%
Don't know	7%	1%	7%	1%	13%

Source: Cranet (2003)

Table 13 'In which of the following areas is the HR Information System used?'

	UK	Sweden	Germany	Greece	Slovakia
Individual personnel records	98%	46%	33%	97%	95%
Payroll	74%	96%	93%	95%	94%
Benefits	66%	72%	80%	80%	48%
Time registration and attendance	48%	20%	90%	86%	82%
Recruitment and selection	66%	19%	39%	60%	35%
Training and development	68%	38%	55%	69%	44%
Performance management	36%	12%	29%	52%	28%
Career planning/Succession planning	15%	12%	24%	30%	17%
Work scheduling	11%	54%	28%	64%	40%
Health and safety	21%	18%	24%	29%	29%

Source: Cranet (2003)

REFLECTIVE ACTIVITY

Look at Tables 11, 12 and 13 carefully and explore the similarities and differences of the data between the countries.

Can you provide reasons for the similarities and differences identified?

KEY DRIVERS AND BENEFITS OF TECHNOLOGY IN HR

The adoption of e-HR stems largely from the wish to improve the efficiency and effectiveness of HR-related activities. The three key drivers for the increasing importance of e-HR in the twenty-first century are (Snell, Stueber and Lepak, 2002; Kettley and O'Reilly, 2003):

- the need for *operational efficiency* – The increasing cost of administering HR throughout the 1990s has led HR to seriously consider ways of reducing costs and enhancing the speed and accuracy of data

- the *relational impact* – The increasing expectations and reported low levels of satisfaction of employees with HR has necessitated a change in the relationship between HR, managers and employees

- the *transformational impact* – It has been perceived necessary to change the HR role from primarily administrative to one of a strategic business partner.

Two technological applications have contributed to the timely delivery of accurate and detailed information: corporate intranets, and employee and manager self-service. Starting with the intranet – a 2005 CIPD survey found that 71% of organisations had an intranet providing HR information including policies, practices and HR forms. HR intranets have become one-stop shops for HR-related queries and routine transactions (through employee and manager self-service applications). Nevertheless, the complexity and content of HR intranets can vary. At the simplest, an HR intranet gives access to comprehensive HR policy content and associated guidelines and constitutes a means for employee communication. At a more sophisticated level, self-service applications allow HR transactions to be streamlined and devolved to line managers and employees. Intranets provide a *single repository for HR information*. They offer an alternative channel of communication with employees and line managers by carrying organisation-wide news stories and highlighting policy changes. Discussion groups allow employees to share knowledge, while colleagues with particular expertise can be found by using staff profiles in an online employee directory.

As for employee and manager self-service – one of the fastest-growing trends in the delivery of HR information is employee self-service. Again there are international differences: 80% of US organisations delivered some information to employees through self-service in 2000 whereas only 22% of UK organisations had such a system (CIPD, 2005). These applications help employees to access and maintain HR information about themselves. In organisations such as Nationwide and ICL, employees are able to select their own benefits package. Similarly, managers' self-service provides a variety of HR tools and information for managers thereby improving managerial effectiveness. Increasingly, employees can carry out some basic HR transactions using interactive self-service applications. By handing over primary responsibility to staff for maintaining their own personal details a major administrative burden can be removed from HR and the accuracy of records is often improved.

There are a number of drivers of e-HR, but how successful is it in fulfilling expectations?

Table 14 offers a comparative assessment by HR managers and gives an impression of relative success.

Table 14 Success in meeting objectives for the introduction of HRIS

Criteria	North America (%)	Rest of the world (%)
Improving data accuracy	92	82
HR staff acceptance	91	100
Employee acceptance	84	88
Manager acceptance	84	82
Employee services improvement	80	88
Meeting administrative cost savings goal	77	59
Enabling HR to be more strategic	76	81
Aligning workforce with organisational objectives	70	47
Accountability	70	63
Enabling organisation to recruit key talent	68	41
Enabling employees and managers to make better decisions	67	59
Revenue growth	42	59

Source: Cedar Crestone, 2006. Workforce Technology and Service Delivery Survey, 9th Edition

The evidence to support the claim that these benefits have indeed been fully realised is patchy – HR managers may give an optimistic picture. On the one hand some surveys have reported reductions of up to 60% in transaction costs, the length of time taken to deal with queries, reductions in enquiries directly to HR, and less HR administration. Other reports suggest, however, that e-enabled HR has not delivered its potential (Ruel *et al*, 2004).

REFLECTIVE ACTIVITY

In the light of the benefits of e-HR in freeing HR of burdensome administration and the evidence of the uptake of e-HR, consider the reasons why some argue that HR has yet to realise its full transformational potential.

Below are some practical considerations and challenges that may help us to understand why that potential may not be reached.

Practical considerations and challenges

Some organisations have used 'off-the-shelf' packages (packages that can be used in more than one organisation), whereas others have decided to tackle all elements through the development of a custom-made, coherent integrated e-HR system. Both types of system can have their problems, but the choice of technological solutions has shifted dramatically from the generic to the specific and customised. Whether to use off-the-shelf or customised e-HR solutions can only be decided by looking at the requirements of HR and the organisation and at what they want to achieve. For HR a key criterion is to consider which solution best streamlines administration and transaction processing tasks.

Dissatisfaction can come from a number of causes.

First, e-HR is still predominantly used by white-collar employees. This group of staff generally has personal access to a computer and is usually familiar with the technology. There is some risk, therefore, that although these staff are increasingly empowered, their blue-collar colleagues may be less so. In response, organisations are beginning to find alternative ways for making HR applications available to their manual workers. Among the options already being implemented are shared-access kiosks or PCs situated in communal areas.

Second, employees, line managers and HR itself must be convinced that such HR delivery is of real benefit to them and the organisation. Senior management are more likely to accept the benefits by projected cost savings. Employees can be persuaded of the benefits of self-service. However, line managers must be reassured that processes will be simplified and that the whole exercise is not just a case of work being transferred from HR to them. HR staff themselves may be the hardest to convince because technology often leads to a significant change in the role and structure of HR.

Third, staff and line managers have to be persuaded to use and keep using the technology and its associated applications once it is up and running. Above all, the system must be attractive, easy to use and well maintained. Making sure that it delivers practical benefits as well as cost reductions by removing unnecessary bureaucracy from routine transactions is vital.

The biggest challenge that HR faces with the many complexities and uncertainties around e-HR is to effectively adjust and learn to manage the world of technology at both transactional and transformational levels. As will be seen in Part 2 of this chapter, many functions and processes of HR have embraced technological solutions, at least at a transactional level. E-HR provides HR with the opportunity to take on the challenge of *transformation*.

REFLECTIVE ACTIVITY

Imagine you are advising the HR director of an organisation on the practical considerations he/she will face in introducing e-HR.

What recommendations would you make to overcome the potential difficulties and help the director rise to the challenge?

2   E-ENABLED HR FUNCTIONS AND PROCESSES

There is clear evidence of the widespread use of a number of e-enabled functions and processes. What follows is a fuller discussion on a range of HR functions in which technology has had a large impact. We begin by looking at technology used in recruitment.

E-RECRUITMENT

Technology has dramatically changed recruitment practices. Some estimates are that 100% of large organisations currently use the Internet for recruitment purposes, with 82% using intranet systems to advertise posts internally (Cedar, 2002). E-recruitment practices include the use of recruitment pages on existing corporate websites, kiosks, specialist recruitment websites (job portals, online job boards), state-of-the-art online games, websites devoted to helping users make new friends, and podcasts offering career advice to attract job applicants. Interactive tools for processing applications (online applications, email auto-responding), and using online screening techniques such as online interviews or personality assessment further enhance e-recruitment.

Corporate websites are becoming more important in attracting candidates because they enable potential applicants to find out more than simply about the vacancies. They can also provide applicants with visuals on what offices, break areas and amenities look like. Add this to employee blogs and applicants can now get a better sense of what it is like to work for an organisation.

To make the most of corporate website recruiting it is important that it should include: a link to the careers section from the homepage, information on benefits and culture, separate graduate recruitment section, job search by job category, location, and keyword, urgent jobs highlighted, complete job descriptions, one click to apply, pre-assessment tools for each job, choice of cut-and-paste form or CV builder, attachment of formatted CV, application automatically connected to a job position, anonymous application, email to friend, job agent, profiling, re-use of candidate information for multiple applications and online user feedback (**www.recruitsoft.com**).

The popularity of websites such as Facebook, Bebo and Myspace, whose original intentions were to work as social sites, has been used by organisations with a desire to establish work-related interactions such as recruitment. Such taking over of social Internet spaces is further illustrated by the Yell Group which has undertaken a recruitment campaign in the virtual world of Second Life. Yell put up company posters and created three-dimensional characters wearing Yell T-shirts in the virtual world where they can be asked for more information on current vacancies. Some recruiters use mobile technology to notify candidates of potential job opportunities: a number of mobile access websites being have been developed enabling applicants to search, view and apply for positions directly from a mobile phone.

These practices have the potential benefit of reaching large numbers of qualified applicants globally (Gueutal and Stone, 2005; Stone *et al*, 2003). They can bring down recruitment costs, decrease cycle time, streamline administrative processes and enable organisations to more effectively evaluate their recruitment strategy – but e-recruitment is still seen by most employers as an add-on tool. E-recruitment has not replaced traditional methods of recruitment. Some have argued that there may be a number of detriments. For example, replacing traditional recruiters with computerised systems may make the recruitment process much more impersonal and inflexible and therefore have a negative impact on applicants' attraction and retention rates. Likewise, the use of online recruitment may have a negative impact on minority groups who may not have access to the Internet or possess the skills needed to use it. Applicants may think that online systems are more likely to invade personal privacy than other recruitment processes and may therefore be less willing to use e-recruiting systems than traditional systems to apply for jobs.

There is evidence that applicants still prefer traditional recruitment sources (especially newspaper advertisements and employee referrals) to e-recruiting, and surveys consistently indicate that the Internet is not the number one source of jobs for most candidates (Galanaki, 2002; Zusman and Landis, 2002). E-recruiting is more likely to be used by young, highly educated white job candidates than those who are older, less well-educated or members of ethnic minority groups (Galanaki, 2002; McManus and Ferguson, 2003). E-recruiting systems are more likely to produce candidates who appear to change their jobs frequently (McManus and Ferguson, 2003). Whereas e-recruiting systems may attract more applicants, those applicants are not always of higher quality than the applicants attracted by traditional recruiting systems (Chapman and Webster, 2003).

In one sense e-recruitment works too well, bringing a large response from applicants, many of them unqualified. An effective selection process that sorts these applications quickly without screening out good applicants is therefore essential (Capelli, 2005).

E-SELECTION

E-selection uses filtering tools to filter out unqualified applicants through online pre-employment testing and to apply selection and assessment tools, often tailored to each job, to match applicants to the job requirements. Such systems and tools may use a variety of specific strategies (eg interviews, ability tests, personality measures) to find out which applicants have appropriate levels of knowledge, skills and attitudes.

Organisations use online testing for a number of purposes. Some use it to assess the knowledge skills and attitudes of applicants in a cost-effective manner. For example, Home Depot placed kiosks in stores to test applicants and reported saving $135 per applicant in administrative costs. They also found an 11% reduction in turnover among candidates who were tested in kiosks (Gueutal and Falbe, 2005).

Other organisations use e-selection systems to do online interviews or simulations designed to find out the critical thinking or decision-making skills of applicants. One such interviewing tool is activ8's 'a8i Recruitment', a product that promises to offer 'the potential to remove the traditional face-to-face interview completely' with the help of artificial intelligence. Others provide applicants with the opportunity to complete online self-assessments of personality to assess the degree of fit between the applicant's traits and the organisation's culture.

Despite the increasing use of e-selection tools and systems, there is still little research on their effectiveness (Kehoe *et al*, 2005). The OPP survey of British HR professionals found that two thirds of respondents had reservations about using online personality tests at the recruitment stage. The main concerns were over lack of control – whether the candidates had understood the instructions properly, and not knowing who had completed the form (OPP 2001).

 REFLECTIVE ACTIVITY

How can organisations overcome some of the concerns over e-selection tools that have been raised by the OPP survey?

E-LEARNING, TRAINING AND DEVELOPMENT

Of all HR processes, learning, training and development is the most technologically enabled. It has been argued that 'web-based training is replacing traditional training as the most effective educational tool' (Greengard, 1999; p.95). The use of such technology for learning includes shop-floor as well as white-collar workers.

Although computer-based training (CBT) continues to have a presence in organisations, the shift to web-based learning, training and development is inevitable. As Cohen (2001; p.137) states:

> *Unlike traditional, off-line classes, web-based training can typically be accessed on demand, so users have much more flexibility when scheduling sessions. And because of the interactive nature of the Net, classes are often far more engaging and lively. Beyond boosting the efficiency of training, the web can also make it affordable.*

Many organisations keep their own libraries of reference materials and some have their own virtual university. There are a number of examples of this. American Airlines has its own university where it provides learning and development for a wide range of staff across a variety of methods including computer- and Internet-based programmes. Biolink, a group of scientific companies in the south of England, has joined with academic partners to provide a virtual university for their members, where they can access a variety of resources connected to management development. The UK financial services company Egg has also launched a virtual university where its staff can have access to learning and development from around the world using the Internet.

What are the key drivers for these changes? We look at the question from three perspectives: the organisational, work team and individual perspectives.

Starting with the *organisational perspective*, there are two main advantages: cost and effective targeting. Firstly, learning materials can be purchased or designed in electronic format, bringing cost savings. Learning and training materials can be deposited on the organisation's intranet and employees can access them from their desks or from home as and when required. The organisation can also target particular learning specifically to the individual who needs it rather than designing events using a 'one-size-fits-all' approach for everyone. Learning materials can also be made available to remote staff, as is particularly relevant for large, global or virtual organisations. Secondly, effective targeting is an advantage, because organisations spend a great deal of money on learning, training and development without always knowing what the real return on investment is. One could go as far as to say that there is often no direct link established between learning, training and development and performance improvement. Technology provides the tools to create a skills database, track competencies and skills, identify gaps in employee knowledge and then create the necessary courses using appropriate learning technologies to address specific needs.

Adding the *work team perspective* to the organisational perspective, there are a number of advantages to the virtual classroom. People do not actually need to leave their place of work – they can 'attend' the event via their computer. They can also interact with others on the same programme through the use of:

- *online briefings* – Each person receives the same information at the same time from the person who is facilitating the event although he/she does not have to act on it at the same time. They can wait until their work pattern allows a convenient opportunity for them to focus on their learning. They can also make any response in their own time

- *discussion rooms* – These allow people to exchange ideas. They can be particularly useful for finding innovative approaches or for sharing experience. The 'rooms' are usually facilitated by a trainer, although informal networks can also be an effective vehicle for exchanging ideas. Discussion rooms can take several formats including real-time, where people are online at the same time, and noticeboards, where messages can be posted and responded to one at a time as people log on to the programme

- *conferencing* – 'Meetings' can be set up in which people in remote places can both talk and see each other simulating to some extent the networking and sharing of ideas often associated with a conventional training event where people turn up in person.

Finally, there are many benefits to the use of e-learning, training and development from the *individual perspective*. As Greengard (1999; p.95) states:

> *An employee can log on and peruse a course syllabus, click to specific lessons to get an idea of what the course entails, and then sign up electronically. At that point, the student can receive lessons and coursework online, take tests and advance to the next level. Best of all, it's possible to study at home, at work or while sitting in a hotel room in Dubuque.*

There are further advantages for individuals: tutor support and helplines from which learners can seek advice from their tutors on a one-to-one basis; access to other learners – learning networks can be established, providing an effective way of sharing knowledge and experiences; working at their own pace as and when appropriate and convenient; and easy access to information at any time.

Despite the advantages of e-learning outlined above, the value of traditional methods should not be overlooked. Learning works better when participants can physically meet and talk to each other. Social interaction and feedback are important. Maintaining participant motivation is problematic in programmes where there is little or no face-to-face contact. Computer and web-based training can be a lonely experience. Imaginative use of newsgroups, dedicated chatrooms and webcams can help reduce isolation. E-learning, training and development is an additional set of tools which when combined with traditional methods can provide powerful learning and development solutions.

 REFLECTIVE ACTIVITY

Develop an action plan by which a 'blended' approach can be used to greater effect in relation to learning, training and development.

E-PERFORMANCE MANAGEMENT SYSTEMS

The main purpose of any performance management process is to manage and control employee behaviour, ensuring its alignment with organisational goals (see Chapter 12). E- systems enable managers to measure performance, write performance reviews and provide employees with feedback (Cardy and Miller, 2005; Stone *et al*, 2003). For instance, computerised performance monitoring (CPM) systems facilitate the measurement of performance by storing such information as number of items produced, time spent on tasks, and error and wastage rates. Some estimates indicate that CPM systems are used to monitor the work of over 40 million workers. One of the many reasons for organisations' using such systems is that they allow for greater spans of control and eliminate the need for managers to spend time observing the behaviour of employees and assessing their performance (Cardy and Miller, 2003).

E-performance management systems also help with writing appraisals and providing employees with feedback. One benefit is that employees can be appraised more frequently. The e-system simplifies the process of completing appraisal forms through the use of predefined sentences and paragraphs. Intranet systems are used for 360-degree feedback. Such systems send emails to evaluators and ask them to complete online evaluations of employees. The data are subsequently merged and feedback is provided for the appraisee. These systems also can be used to track and compare individual, team and organisational performance with respect to such areas as attendance, lateness, grievances and turnover (Stone *et al*, 2003). Such data can be used to identify specific performance problems, highlight exceptional performance, and more importantly provide managers with feedback on these in order for informed decisions to be made.

But many e-performance systems can only be used for low-level jobs with clearly definable objective performance standards. They often measure the quantity rather than the quality of products and services produced. Nor do they have any real capacity to assess organisational 'citizenship' and co-operation. Little research has focused on their overall effectiveness (Cardy and Miller, 2003).

E-COMPENSATION SYSTEMS

E-compensation systems are used for developing and implementing pay systems, providing benefits and evaluating the effectiveness of compensation packages. They facilitate the process in a variety of ways. First, they allow HR to collect job analysis data through online questionnaires. The systems automatically collect job analysis data from 'experts', summarise the data, and generate standardised job descriptions. In addition, they convert the job analysis data to job evaluation point scores. Furthermore, they integrate the job evaluation point scores with online labour market data. Then they use the data to create pay grades and establish pay levels in organisations.

E-compensation systems are also used to communicate data about benefits options to employees, and give them the opportunity to select benefit plans online (Gueutal and Falbe, 2005). Employees are not always aware of the types of benefits offered by organisations (Cascio, 2006), often because information is hidden in large employee handbooks. E-systems also facilitate the use of 'cafeteria' or flexible benefit packages. The typical use is through employee self-service systems that give employees the opportunity to alter their benefit packages as their needs change. Such systems may meet employees' needs to a greater degree than traditional benefits systems.

E-compensation systems also allow managers to model the impact of incentive systems and ensure the fairness of salary allocation decisions. These systems can be linked to e-performance management systems, increasing the likelihood that pay rises are based on performance. They can be used to make sure that rewards have internal and external equity. Research reveals that individuals have higher satisfaction and retention levels when pay systems are perceived as fair (Bergmann and Scarpello, 2002).

REFLECTIVE ACTIVITY

Consider how traditional HR practices compare with e-HR practices.

What are the benefits and drawbacks of each?

Consider how organisations need to rethink their HR functions, and what skills and competencies HR professionals would need to have in order to add real value using e-HR.

KEY ISSUES IN HRM AND TECHNOLOGICAL INNOVATION

Properly designed e-HR systems can increase organisational efficiency by increasing an organisation's ability to gather, access and disseminate information. Thus, e-HR can help the HR function to become more strategic, although there are still HR functions which are lagging behind due to poor data systems or poor web applications. The true value of technology is only realised when it is perceived as a tool.

We now pull together ten key points about HRM and technology raised in this chapter:

- E-HR strategies are a combination of the transactional and transformational. The first deals with traditional HR functions such as payroll and benefits. The second is more concerned with developing employees and building competitive advantage. It is the automation of the former that facilitates the latter.

- Operational efficiency, relational and transformational impact are key drivers for the growth of e-HR.

- Consideration of organisational culture, processes and understanding the business are essential in developing e-HR.

- There is no one technological innovation or solution that meets the needs of all organisations.

- Technology is not the major driver of change for HR – rather, it is the desire to integrate its multifunctional nature that technology enables.

- An intranet can be a powerful platform for an organisation to deliver effective e-HR.

- Self-service and employee portals are critical to any online HR strategy.

- Technology offers new opportunities for delivery of HR services such as recruitment, learning, performance management and reward and compensation.

- Individuals can access learning and development materials in a convenient manner.

- Blended HR systems that combine e-HR with traditional systems have a greater chance of success.

The main case study in this chapter now follows. It is based on the experience of ICL and the development of their employee portal, Café VIK.

ICL, the IT solutions organisation owned by the Japanese Fijitsu Group, has brought all of its web-enabled processes into what they refer to as e-ICL. An integrated web-enabled e-HR system is a key aspect of ICL's vision to put into practice the values and vision of the organisation.

ICL was one of the first organisations to create an organisation-wide intranet in 1996. The intranet is seen as much more than just an HR tool – it is seen as a business tool. The knowledge-sharing initiative was branded as Café VIK ('valuing ICL knowledge'). Café VIK is a set of portals which enable employees to access a range of information and services. By its first anniversary in November 1997, Café VIK was already being used by about 50% of ICL's 19,000 employees. As awareness of the service spread, the number continued to grow. Key staff state that 'It's helping HR to play a leading role in developing strategy and managing people. After that, the next phase will be to use it as a management tool.'

In 1998, a number of cross-function groups were set up to explore how the company could get more staff involved with the intranet. During 2000, ICL re-launched the intranet to allow greater personalisation of content (introduction of My Café VIK tool) and to encourage employees to share their knowledge through online communities. The second-generation model was housed on a single server which brought to an end the duplication of materials associated with the original version. The search facilities were improved and the new HR intranet became far more interactive. The self-service application has reduced the administrative activity of the HR function and has encouraged employees to take greater responsibility for keeping their data up to date by entering it directly onto the HR database.

Employees can view their current employment terms and benefits online, update personal details directly on the HR database via the Café VIK interface, and can order equipment that they need for their jobs, such as IT kit and mobile phones via an online authorisation process. Café VIK also incorporates a flexible benefits system which allows employees to make choices on their benefits package and view its value at any time. The range of benefits can be tailored to suit individual lifestyles or circumstances, and they can be exchanged and traded online. Employees can trade up to three days' holiday for their cash value. The benefits are elected annually and staff are given a four- to five-week window to decide on them. Staff with 30 days' holiday who find that they can not use it all tend to trade down. Employees can choose from a range of discounted benefits such as travel insurance and health club membership, and company-provided schemes such as life assurance and dental cover – pet insurance is also on the menu. ICL uses its buying power to get good rates to pass on to employees.

The learning gateway provides a single portal to all available learning and development opportunities. Learning programmes are supplied by the e-learning provider KnowledgePool. The portal features a database of information of over 5,000 learning options including online, CD-ROM and classroom-based courses, books and videos. A community homepage has links to a range of additional material such as management development information and online libraries. A system of online professional and knowledge communities has established Café VIK as the centre for knowledge management throughout the organisation.

By 2002, 35% of ICL's employees were mobile workers, and its growing number of remote workers can access the intranet to ensure that they can operate effectively from home or wherever via the Extended Connected Office which gives them access to mobile phone networks and fixed lines, email facilities, the Internet and the Café VIK intranet. These are available on laptops, PCs, PDAs or WAP phones. New joiners to the organisation can access a short walk-through on general information about ICL, its values, employment policies and key information about being an ICL employee.

ICL is continually improving the transactional scope of Café VIK for its employees. It is, however, clear that some staff do not make the time to browse through the HR intranet and to take advantage of its knowledge-sharing capabilities. In fact, some staff have not registered on My Café VIK and are therefore missing out on the advantages it offers and reducing the operational scope of the intranet.

Questions for consideration and discussion

1 Using your knowledge of this chapter and the case, what are the benefits of such an e-HR system to ICL, its managers and individual employees?

2 Why do you think that some employees fail to use Café VIK?

3 And what recommendations can you make that will help ICL boost the user rate of applications such as employee self-service?

EXPLORE FURTHER

CIPD (2005) *Technology and People Management: The opportunity and the challenge*. London, CIPD

CIPD (2006) *HR and Technology: Beyond delivery*, Change Agenda. London, CIPD

CIPD (2006) *The Changing HR Function: The key questions*, Change Agenda. London, CIPD
This selection of CIPD material concerning technology in HRM provides a professional overview of the development and issues of the topic. Written in a very accessible style, they are useful for students and practitioners alike.

CIPD (2007) *HR and Technology: Impact and advantages*. London, CIPD
This latest report from the CIPD examines the use of technology in nine public, private and not-for-profit sector organisations, focusing on its impact on the delivery and support of HR activity and processes, employee communications and engagement, and the changing role and skills of HR and other managers.

ASHTON, C. (2001) *E-HR: Transforming the HR function*. London, Business Intelligence
This is an in-depth report on how organisations are making the shift to e-HR. It features a survey of 91 organisations and case studies including Cisco, IBM, Oracle, BP, BT and Nokia (see **www.businessintelligence.co.uk**).

GUEUTAL, H. G. and STONE, D. L. (2005) *The Brave New World of e-HR: Human resource management in the digital age*. San Francisco, Jossey-Bass
This textbook offers an overview of the major technological trends in e-HR and shows how to use technology to enhance organisational effectiveness.

CHAPTER 5

Labour law

David Lewis *and* Malcolm Sargeant

INTRODUCTION

This chapter is about the legal and policy contexts of HR management, or, put another way, how the labour market is regulated and what the objectives of such regulation are. In this way, it goes beyond the previous chapter and also lays an important basis for most of the following chapters. 'Regulation' is the way that the state sets rules for how people are treated at work, through laws and the other tools such as funding that it can use to manage the national economy. It is important for HR professionals to understand these state policies and laws because they are expected to advise other managers on how they apply. If you work in HR, one of your major responsibilities will be ensuring that your organisation complies with current employment law. This chapter talks about the law as it is currently, but there are always changes and updates. You should therefore be prepared to make use of the Internet links at the end of this chapter to keep yourself up to date.

LEARNING OUTCOMES

By the end of this chapter readers should be able to:

- explain the different elements that make up the national policy on employment regulation
- explain the role of the public and the private sector in the labour market
- give an account of employment law relating to equalising employment opportunities.

This chapter is structured in three parts. The first part deals with the policy context, and employment services in particular. The second part examines discrimination at the workplace. The third part considers the legal status of workers in the labour market.

The chapter concludes with the main case study.

Reference sources named within the chapter may be looked up in the *References and further reading* section at the end of the book.

STARTER CASE STUDY

Patricia Dacas was a cleaner who had a 'temporary worker agreement' with an employment agency, Brook Street Bureau. This agreement stated that its terms 'shall not give rise to a contract of employment between Brook Street and the temporary worker, or the temporary worker and the client'.

Brook Street had a contract with Wandsworth Borough Council to provide agency staff. This set out the agency's responsibilities and provided that the Council would pay Brook Street on the receipt of invoices. These invoices were calculated from timesheets completed by the agency staff supplied to the Council.

For a number of years Ms Dacas worked exclusively at a hostel run by the Council. The Council had day-to-day control over her work and supplied her with cleaning materials, equipment and an overall. She worked fixed hours for five days a week. The agency fixed her pay rate and paid her wages out of the sums received from the Council. Brook Street also deducted PAYE and National Insurance contributions and issued payslips. Ms Dacas arranged her holidays and notified any sickness absence to the agency.

As a result of a dispute between Ms Dacas and a visitor to the hostel, the Council requested that she be withdrawn from the contract. In the light of this incident and a previous one when she was thought to have been rude, Brook Street notified her that it would no longer be finding work for her. Ms Dacas claimed unfair dismissal on the basis that she was an employee either of the agency or the Council.

Questions for consideration and discussion

1 Would an employment tribunal be entitled to conclude that Ms Dacas was employed by neither the agency nor the Council?

2 Should an employment tribunal be free to look at the reality of the relationship between Ms Dacas and Brook Street and disregard the label that the parties put on their contract?

3 Alternatively, would a tribunal be entitled to decide that even though there was no written contract between Ms Dacas and the Council, a contract of employment could be implied between them?

4 What requirements would have to be met for a contract of employment to be implied?

When you have considered how you might answer these questions, it is recommended that you read the Court of Appeal's judgment in *Dacas v Brook Street Bureau*. The case citation is [2004] IRLR 358.

1 THE POLICY CONTEXT

The United Kingdom Government has a national plan for employment. This is part of a wider European employment strategy for employment organised by the European Union. Some of the UK targets are therefore influenced by European policies. An example of this was set out in 'the Lisbon strategy' in 2000. This established a ten-year plan to make Europe 'the most dynamic and competitive knowledge-based economy in the world, capable of sustainable economic growth with more and better jobs and greater social cohesion, and respect for the environment'. The Lisbon strategy called for governments to – amongst other matters – develop policies with the intention of increasing the total employment rate to 67% by 2005 and 70% by 2010; increasing the female employment rate to 57% by 2005 and 60% by 2010; and increasing the employment rate of older workers to 50% by 2010. It was a policy of combining economic growth with a concern to advance social cohesion (see *Facing the Challenge: The Lisbon strategy for growth and employment,* Report from the High-Level Group chaired by Wim Kok, November 2004).

In order to help achieve this and its own policies, the UK Government has set a number of objectives, which include developing:

● active labour market policies, including help for those without work

● policies that make work pay – such as incentives to work, paid through the tax and benefits system

● policies that reduce barriers to work, such as those concerned with education, skills development and training.

One way of implementing these objectives is by a programme of promoting training and lifelong learning – this is about increasing the skills and the qualification levels of the working age population (less than 15% of the population now have no qualification).

THE ROLE OF THE PUBLIC AND PRIVATE SECTORS

Since the 1980s, the UK Government has given many of the functions relating to labour market regulation and other public service areas to executive agencies and similar bodies. These bodies are usually financed by a parent department of the civil service and are responsible for carrying out many aspects of the public sector's contribution to the regulation of the labour market. The Government's review of executive agencies describes their role thus (in *Creation, Review and Dissolution of Executive Agencies, April 2004*: Cabinet Office, 2004):

> *Executive agencies were created to enable executive functions within government to be carried out by a well-defined business unit with a clear focus on delivering specified outputs within a framework of accountability to Ministers.*

By the mid-1990s the agency model had become the principal organisational type for public service delivery. And by 1997, when most of the 'creation' phase was over, some three-quarters of all civil servants were working for executive agencies. The present Government has continued to develop this policy. Examples of such bodies in the employment sector are Jobcentre Plus and the Learning and Skills Council. There is an agencies and public bodies website which provides more information on such agencies. It can be found at **www.civilservice.gov.uk/improving_services/agencies_and_public_bodies/index.asp**.

The United Kingdom also has a history of the private sector playing an increasingly important role throughout the twentieth century in the employment field. This has been predominantly in the supply of temporary workers and candidates to fill permanent vacancies with client organisations.

REFLECTIVE ACTIVITY

Do you have any knowledge or experience of government employment agencies?

What effects might this sort of agency have on an HR professional's work?

PRIVATE EMPLOYMENT SERVICES

There is a long-established and active private sector concerned with the placement of people in permanent employment and with the provision of temporary workers. Today, some 500,000 workers use its services each week. The industry has been regulated since 1973, when the Employment Agencies Act 1973 came into force. This contained a system for licensing and regular inspections by the Department of Employment. The implementation of this Act was changed by the Conduct of Employment Agencies and Employment Businesses Regulations 2003 (SI 2003/3319), which came into effect in April 2004 (see **www.opsi.gov.uk**).

The 1973 Act and the 2004 Regulations distinguish between employment businesses and employment agencies. Employment businesses are those that are concerned with the supply of temporary staff, whereas employment agencies are those that are concerned with the supply of work-seekers to fill permanent vacancies with client organisations (see sections 13(1) to 13(3) Employment Agencies Act 1973). Many organisations are both employment businesses and employment agencies.

The main provisions of the Act and the Regulations are:

- Neither an employment agency nor employment business may charge fees to work-seekers for finding them work or seeking to find them work. Neither an agency nor an employment business may make help to a work-seeker conditional upon using other services which require a fee. There is a restriction on the terms that can be included in contracts between employment businesses and hirers which have the effect of preventing temporary workers from taking up permanent jobs unless a fee is paid to the employment business first.

- An employment business may not introduce a work-seeker to a hirer to perform the normal tasks carried out by a worker who is taking part in an industrial dispute or other industrial action, unless it is an unofficial strike or industrial action – ie one that does not take place within the rules governing such actions contained in the Trade Union and Labour Relations (Consolidation) Act 1992.

- Employment businesses are not able to withhold pay owed to a temporary worker just because the worker has not obtained a signed worksheet from the hirer.

- When an agency or business first offers to provide a work-seeker with services, the agency or business must supply the work-seeker with details of its terms of business and fees (if any). The agency or business will obtain the agreement of the work-seeker on fees, if any, and the type of work the agency or business will try to find for the work-seeker.

- Employment businesses must agree whether the work-seeker is, or will be, employed under a contract of service or a contract for services. The work-seeker will also be given an undertaking that the business will pay him or her for the work that he or she does, regardless of whether the business is paid by the hirer. Other terms of business will include the rate of remuneration paid to the work-seeker and the minimum rate of remuneration to be paid to the employment business, details of any entitlements to holidays and to payment in respect of holidays.

- Similar requirements are imposed upon employment agencies to explain to work-seekers what services will be provided and details of any fees to be paid to the agency for work-finding services, although fees may only be charged to work-seekers wanting work in such areas as sport, music, dance and theatre.

- Agencies and businesses are required to keep documentation showing the work-seeker's agreement to the terms of business and any changes to them. Neither an agency nor a hirer may introduce or supply a work-seeker unless the agency or business has sufficient information about the hirer, the dates on which the work-seeker is required and the duration of the work, the position to be filled and the experience, training and qualifications necessary to work in this position, including the rate of remuneration to be paid to the work-seeker. There are similar conditions concerning the finding out of information about a work-seeker before that person can be introduced to a hirer. Agencies and employment businesses must obtain references on job-seekers wishing to work with vulnerable persons.

- Every advertisement must carry the full name of the agency or business and state the nature of the work, its location and the minimum qualifications necessary when advertising rates of pay.

- Employment agencies must not introduce an employer to a young person under the age of 18 years if that person is attending school or has just left school, unless that person has received vocational guidance from their local careers service.

- There are strict rules on record-keeping.

Generally, the Act and the Regulations regulate the relationship between the hirer and the agency or business and the relationship between the job-seeker and the agency or business. They set down the requirements for communicating information between all the parties involved and the terms of the agreements between each of the parties.

Anyone who contravenes the prohibition on charging fees to work-seekers, fails to comply with Regulations to secure the proper conduct of the agency or business, falsifies records or fails, without reasonable excuse, to comply with a prohibition order, will be guilty of an offence and subject to a fine not exceeding £5,000. There is a further fine of up to £1,000 for obstructing any officer from carrying out enforcement functions. An employment tribunal may make an order prohibiting a person (or company) from conducting or being concerned with an employment agency or business for up to 10 years on the grounds that the person is unsuitable because of misconduct or any other sufficient reason.

In addition, terms of contracts with hirers or work-seekers which are invalid in terms of the Act or Regulations will be unenforceable. Any contravention of the Act or Regulations which causes damage, including death or injury, will be actionable in civil law.

REFLECTIVE ACTIVITY

Do you have any experience of private employment agencies?

How important are they and the rules regulating them to the work of an HR professional?

PUBLIC EMPLOYMENT SERVICES

Jobcentre Plus is an executive agency of the Department for Work and Pensions and provides the public sector part of the UK employment service (see **www.jobcentreplus.gov.uk**). The purposes of the Agency are outlined in its annual report. In summary, these are to:

- increase the effective labour supply by helping as many unemployed and economically inactive people of working age as possible to move into jobs or self-employment

- provide employers with high-quality demand-led services to help fill vacancies

- help people of working age in the most disadvantaged groups and areas to move closer to the labour market

- work towards parity of outcomes for minority ethnic customers

- ensure that people receiving working age benefits fulfil their responsibilities and are offered appropriate high-quality help and support

- pay people of working age the correct amount of benefit to which they are entitled.

Initiatives include Internet jobpoint terminals on its website, making it the most heavily used Government website; providing details of local job vacancies on digital television; building up direct payment of benefits (to individual bank accounts) so that these amounted to 2,648,182 such payments in April 2004.

2 DISADVANTAGED PEOPLE IN THE LABOUR MARKET

Other ways of improving the supply of labour include increasing the employment rate of those who are disadvantaged in the market.

WOMEN

The Commission for Equality and Human Rights provides the following information (**www.equalityhumanrights.com**): 44% of women and 10% of men work part-time. The average hourly earnings for women working full-time are 18% lower than for men; for women working part-time, earnings are 40% lower than for men working full-time. Women are the majority in administrative and secretarial and personal service jobs, whereas men hold the most skilled trades.

The Government tries to encourage women's participation in the labour market through various work–life balance initiatives, including improved childcare help, financial incentives and flexible working. Outlined below are some of the key provisions relating to flexible and part-time working and equal pay.

Flexible working

The Flexible Working (Procedural Requirements) Regulations 2002 (SI 2002/3207) and the Flexible Working (Eligibility, Complaints and Remedies) Regulations 2002 (SI 2002/3236) set out the rules for encouraging individuals to apply to their employer for more flexible work arrangements, and to have that request treated seriously. Employees have the right to:

- apply to work flexibly

- have their application considered in accordance with the procedures set out in the regulations

- be turned down only where there is a clear business reason for doing so

- be accompanied when having the meeting with the employer to discuss the application

- have a written explanation as to why it was turned down

- appeal and to complain to an employment tribunal if the Regulations have not been followed.

Employers have the right to reject an application when the work arrangements sought cannot be reconciled with the needs of the business.

Part-time work

The treatment of part-time workers is a discrimination issue, because the great majority of part-time workers are female (see *R v Secretary of State, ex parte Equal Opportunities Commission* [1994] IRLR 176 HL). In the United Kingdom, women represent 33% of all those working full-time and 81% of all those working part-time.

Evidence given by the Equal Opportunities Commission to the Education and Employment Committee of the House of Commons contained examples of how part-time workers were disadvantaged. Over 75% of female part-timers, for example, earn less than the average hourly wage. About 54% of male part-timers and 42% of female part-timers work for employers who do not have a pension scheme, compared with 25% of full-time employees. Part-time work is still mostly confined to the low-paid in a relatively narrow range of occupations. There appear to be limited opportunities for part-time employees to be promoted.

The Part-time Workers (Prevention of Less Favourable Treatment) Regulations which came into force on 1 July 2000 (SI 2000/1551) are an attempt to improve the situation of part-time workers. Regulation 2(1) of the Regulations identifies a full-time worker as someone who is paid wholly or partly by reference to the time worked, and, having regard to the custom and practice of the employer in relation to its other workers, is identifiable as a full-time worker. Regulation 2(2) has the same definition for part-time workers as this, except that they must be identifiable as part-time workers. To be an appropriate comparator, a full-timer must be:

- employed by the same employer under the same type of contract

- engaged in the same or broadly similar work having regard, where relevant, to whether he/she has similar levels of qualifications, skills and experience

- based at the same establishment or, if there is no full-time comparator at the same establishment, at a different establishment.

What happens if there is no full-time person who can meet the criteria? Where a workforce is made up entirely of part-time employees in a particular category, the Regulations will be of no assistance in enabling them to claim discrimination on the basis of being a part-time worker. (In *Wippel v Peek & Cloppenburg Gmbh* [2005] IRLR 211 the European Court of Justice suggested that a part-time casual worker might be covered by the Framework Agreement. However, Ms Wippel could not find a full-time comparator who worked on a casual basis.) One example might be a contract cleaning operation. All the employees concerned with cleaning might be part-time and all the supervisory, management and administration employees might be full-time. The result is that there is no full-time comparator.

Equal pay

The Equal Pay Act (EPA) 1970 came into effect in 1975. Although the legislation has undoubtedly had an impact on the relative pay of men and women, a significant gap still remains. In 2003 female employees who worked full-time earned 82% of the average gross hourly earnings of male full-time employees. This is an improvement, however, on the situation when the EPA was passed. In 1971, women earned only 63% of the average hourly earnings of full-time male employees (see Commission for Equality and Human Rights, *Women and Men in Britain – At The Millennium* (2000)).

Section 1(1) EPA 1970 implies an equality clause into all contracts of employment. According to section 1(2) EPA 1970, such a clause applies to all the terms of a contract under which a woman is employed, and not just pay. The clause has effect where a woman is employed on:

- like work with a man in the same employment

- work rated as equivalent with that of a man in the same employment

- work which, not being work in (1) or (2), is, in terms of the demands made upon her, of equal value to that of a man in the same employment.

In these situations any term of the woman's contract that is less favourable to the woman than the comparable man should be modified so as to be not less favourable. Similarly, if the woman's contract does not contain a term conferring a benefit on her that is contained in the comparable man's contract, the woman's contract will be deemed to include the term.

ETHNIC MINORITIES AND RACIAL DISCRIMINATION

Generally, people from ethnic minorities have lower levels of economic activity and higher levels of unemployment than white people. Ethnic minority households are more likely to suffer lower income levels. Pakistani and Bangladeshi homes have an average household income that is more than 50% below the national average income.

Protection from discrimination

The United Kingdom has the following legislative measures against race and sex discrimination:

- The Sex Discrimination Act (SDA) 1975 provides protection from discrimination on the grounds of gender, gender re-assignment, civil partnership and being married. Further protection for women is provided by the Equal Pay Act 1970 (see above).

- The Race Relations Act (RRA) 1976 provides protection from discrimination on racial grounds. Section 3(1) defines racial grounds as meaning 'colour, race, nationality or ethnic or national origins'. The Race Relations (Amendment) Act 2000 came into effect in April 2001. It amended the 1976 Act and, amongst other matters, it placed a statutory duty on a wide range of public authorities to promote racial equality and to prevent racial discrimination. Protection is provided against direct and indirect discrimination as well as against victimisation and harassment.

Both the SDA 1975 and the RRA 1976 provide for a situation where being of a particular sex or of a particular racial group is a genuine occupational qualification. There are certain situations where it is permissible to use sex or racial origin as a criterion in the selection of an applicant or in providing access to promotion and training. Section 7(2) SDA lists the situations in which being a man may be a genuine occupational qualification. These exceptions apply where only some of the duties of a job fall within the categories, as well as when all the duties do so. They apply where:

- 'The essential nature of the job would be materially different if carried out by a woman.'

- There are decency reasons for a job to be held by a man – such as a job involving physical contact with men where they might reasonably object to the job being carried out by a woman or where the men are likely to be in a state of undress or using sanitary facilities.

● The job concerns working in, or living in, a private home and the job has to be held by a man because of the degree of physical or social contact and the knowledge of the intimate details of a person's life.

● The nature or location of the establishment make it impracticable for the job-holder to live anywhere but on the premises supplied by the employer and there are no separate sleeping or sanitary provisions for men and women, nor is it reasonable to expect the employer to provide them.

● The nature of the establishment, or the part in which work is done, requires the job-holder to be a man.

● The job-holder provides individuals with personal services promoting their welfare or education, or similar services, and this can best be done by a man.

● The job has to be done by a man because it is likely to involve the performance of some of the work in a country where a woman would not be able to effectively perform the duties.

● The job is one of two held by a married couple.

Section 7A SDA 1975 provides similar rules to be applied in situations relating to gender reassignment, and section 7B provides that there is a further genuine occupational qualification concerning those who are planning a gender reassignment or are undergoing the process of gender reassignment. This exception includes jobs that are concerned with, firstly, being called upon to conduct intimate searches; secondly, with living or working in a private home; thirdly, where the location or establishment requires the person to live on the premises and there are not separate facilities for preserving decency and privacy; and, finally, where the job-holder is providing personal services for vulnerable individuals, promoting their welfare or similar, and where the employer decides that the services cannot be provided by someone undergoing gender reassignment.

Under the RRA 1976 there are fewer situations in which a genuine occupational qualification applies. These are where:

● authenticity in drama or other entertainment requires a person of a particular racial group

● the production of visual imagery in art or photography requires a person from a particular racial group for reasons of authenticity

● the job involves working in a place where food and drink is served to the public and membership of a racial group is required for authenticity

● the job-holder provides persons of that racial group with personal services promoting their welfare, and where those services can be most effectively performed by a person of that racial group.

DISCRIMINATION ON THE GROUNDS OF RELIGION, BELIEF OR SEXUAL ORIENTATION

The Employment Equality (Religion or Belief) Regulations 2003 and the Employment Equality (Sexual Orientation) Regulations 2003 were introduced to comply with the Framework Directive on Equal Treatment at Work (Directive 2000/78/EC).

'Religion' means any religion and 'belief' means any religions or philosophical belief. This is not a helpful definition because it provides no meaning to the terms 'religion' or 'belief'. It has been deliberately left to the courts, relying on Article 9 of the European Convention on Human Rights, to decide whether any particular religion or belief meets this definition. The Government guidance on these Regulations states that this definition is a broad one and will clearly include those religions that are widely recognised, such as Christianity, Islam, Hinduism and Judaism. Equally, it will apply to groups within religions, such as Roman Catholics and Protestants.

'Sexual orientation' is defined as a sexual orientation towards persons of the same sex, thus covering both gay men and gay women; opposite sex, which provides for heterosexual relationships; and same sex and opposite sex, which covers bisexual men and women.

Protection is also provided against direct and indirect discrimination, victimisation and harassment.

In the employment context, there is an exception for a genuine occupational requirement. This must be:

- a *requirement* of the job, which means that it must be essential for a person to be able to carry out the job

- a *determining* requirement – something that is crucial to the job

- an *occupational* requirement, meaning a close connection with the job in question

- a *genuine* occupational requirement and not one created just to avoid the regulations.

PEOPLE WITH DISABILITIES

The Disability Discrimination Act (DDA) 1995 was the first measure to outlaw discrimination against disabled people in the United Kingdom and included an obligation upon the employer to make adjustments (the approach prior to the DDA 1995 had been to establish quotas of disabled people in an employer's workforce – see Disabled Persons (Employment) Act 1944; this approach failed). The Act gives disabled people rights in employment and other areas. It is enforced by the Commission for Equality and Human Rights.

The need for action is illustrated by the fact that there are over 6.8 million disabled persons of working age in Great Britain (**www.equalityhumanrights.com**). They account for nearly one fifth of the working age population but only for one eighth of all those in employment. When employed, disabled people are more likely than the non-disabled to be working part-time or as self-employed. Disabled people are over six times as likely as non-disabled people to be out of work and claiming benefit. However, employment rates vary with the type of disability. Some types, such as those concerned with diabetes, skin conditions and hearing problems, are associated with relatively high employment rates. Other types, such as those associated with mental illness and learning disabilities, have much lower employment rates.

The DDA 1995 makes a number of forms of discrimination unlawful (see also Chapters 4 and 5 of the Code of Practice, which give a very good description of these types of discrimination with many examples, some of which are used here). These are direct discrimination, disability-related discrimination, victimisation and failure to comply with a duty to make reasonable adjustments. Each of these is now discussed in turn.

Direct discrimination

Direct discrimination results from treatment of a disabled person that:

- is on the grounds of the person's disability

- is treatment which is less favourable than that given to, or would have been given to, a person not having that particular disability, when

  - the relevant circumstances, including the abilities, of the person being used as the comparator are the same as, or not materially different from, those of the disabled person.

Thus the discriminatory treatment must be on the grounds of the person's disability. There is no requirement for there to have been a deliberate and conscious decision to discriminate. Indeed, much discrimination may be the result of prejudices about which the discriminator is unaware. The comparator must be someone who does not have the same disability and may be someone who is not disabled. It is important, however, that the comparator's relevant circumstances, including his or her abilities, are the same as, or not materially different from, those of the disabled person. It is not necessary to identify an actual person to use as a comparator. Where someone with similar relevant circumstances is not available, a hypothetical comparator can be used.

An example of direct discrimination given in the DRC Code of Practice is where a person who becomes disabled takes six months' sick leave because of his or her disability and is dismissed by the employer. A non-disabled fellow-employee also takes six months' sick leave, because of a broken leg, and is not dismissed. The non-disabled employee is an appropriate comparator because the relevant circumstances are the same – ie having six months' sick leave. Direct discrimination has occurred because of the less favourable treatment of the disabled person.

In relation to direct discrimination there is no justification defence for the employer. Treatment that amounts to direct discrimination cannot be justified, as it can in some other circumstances (see below).

Disability-related discrimination

Section 3A(1) DDA 1995 states that an employer discriminates against a disabled person when:

- it is for a reason related to his or her disability

- the treatment is less favourable than the treatment given, or would have been given, to others to whom the reason does not or would not apply, and

- the employer cannot show that the treatment in question can be justified.

The phrase 'disability-related discrimination' is not used in the Act, but is used in the CEHR Code of Practice to describe discrimination that falls under section 3A(1) DDA 1995 but that does not amount to direct discrimination. It therefore has a wider scope – and a good example of this is given in the CEHR Code of Practice:

> A disabled woman is refused an administrative job because she cannot type. She cannot type because she has arthritis. A non-disabled person who was unable to type would also have been turned down. The disability-related reason for the less favourable treatment is the woman's inability to type, and the correct comparator is a person to whom the reason does not apply – that is, someone who can type. Such a person would not have been refused the job. In respect of that comparison, the disabled woman has been treated less favourably for a disability-related reason and this will be unlawful unless it can be justified.

Importantly, this discrimination is not direct discrimination, because, in that case, the correct comparator would have been someone who did not have arthritis and who had similar disabilities – ie someone who could not type. This comparator would not have obtained the job either, so there would not have been less favourable treatment.

There are strict limitations to any justification defence. There may be situations when the employer will still not be able to justify the treatment, even if there are material and substantial justifications for the less favourable treatment. This may occur if the employer has failed in the duty to make reasonable adjustments (see below). The employer will, in such circumstances, have to show that the material and substantial circumstances would have applied even if the adjustments had been made.

Victimisation

An employer discriminates against an employee or another person if the employer treats that employee or other person less favourably than it treats or would treat other employees in the same circumstances because the employee or other person:

- brought proceedings against the employer or any other person under the DDA 1995, or

- gave evidence or information in connection with such proceedings brought by any other person, or

- otherwise does anything under the DDA 1995 in relation to the employer or any other person, or

- alleged that the employer or other person has contravened the DDA 1995.

Treating the employee or other person less favourably because the employer believes or suspects that the employee or other person has done or intends to do any of these actions is also unlawful. Unlike the other forms of discrimination outlawed by the DDA 1995, this form can be claimed by non-disabled people as well as disabled people. The treatment, however, will not amount to less favourable treatment if any allegation of the employee or other person was false and not made in good faith. There is also protection for ex-employees in a situation where there has been a relevant relationship between an employer and a disabled person that has come to an end. A relevant relationship is where there has been an employment relationship during which there was an act of discrimination or harassment. In such a situation it is unlawful for the ex-employer to discriminate against or harass the disabled person concerned.

Duty to make reasonable adjustments

The employer also discriminates against a disabled person if the employer fails to comply with a duty to make reasonable adjustments in relation to the disabled person. Thus, where the disabled person is placed at a substantial disadvantage compared to persons who are not disabled because of a provision, criterion or practice applied by or on behalf of an employer, or any physical feature of premises occupied by an employer ('physical feature' includes any feature arising from the design or construction of a building, approaches to it, access or exits, fixtures, fittings, furnishings, furniture, equipment or material in the building; section 18D DDA 1995).

It is the duty of the employer to take reasonable steps, in all the circumstances of the case, to prevent the provision, criterion, practice or feature from having that effect. This obligation applies in respect of applicants for employment as well as in respect of existing employees. There is, however, no obligation placed upon the employer if the employer does not know, or could not have reasonably been expected to know, that the applicant or employee had a disability. Provision, criteria or practice includes any arrangements. The arrangements referred to include, firstly, the arrangements for determining who should be offered employment, and, secondly, any term, condition or arrangements on which employment, promotion, transfer, training or any other benefit is offered. The arrangements referred to are strictly job-related. Employers are required to make adjustments to the way that the job is structured and organised so as to accommodate those who cannot fit into the existing arrangements. This appears to exclude providing assistance with personal arrangements and care so as to enable an individual to attend work (see *Kenny v Hampshire Constabulary* [1999] IRLR 76). Examples of steps which may have to be taken are making adjustments to premises, allocating some of the disabled person's duties to another person, or transferring the disabled person to an existing vacancy.

An example of the scope of the duty to make reasonable adjustments arose in *Archibald v Fife Council* [2004] IRLR 651 HL. This concerned an employee of Fife

Council who was employed as a roadsweeper. As a result of a complication during surgery she became virtually unable to walk and could no longer carry out the duties of a roadsweeper. She could do sedentary work and the Council sent her on a number of computer and administration courses. Over the next few months she applied for over 100 jobs within the Council, but she always failed in a competitive interview situation. Eventually she was dismissed because the redeployment procedure was exhausted. The issue for the Court was the limits of the duty to make reasonable adjustments. It was agreed that the DDA 1995 required some positive discrimination in favour of disabled people, but did this include finding them another job if their disability stopped them from performing their current one? The Court held that the DDA 1995, to the extent that the provisions of the Act required it, permitted and sometimes obliged employers to treat a disabled person more favourably than others. This may even require transferring them to a higher-level position without the need for a competitive interview. (This was one of the problems for the employer – most positions were at a higher level than that of a roadsweeper and the local authority assumed that it had an obligation to make all promotion interviews competitive.)

REFLECTIVE ACTIVITY

Do you have any experience of discrimination at work?

How important do you think this aspect of an HR professional's job is?

Harassment

It is unlawful for an employer to harass a disabled employee or a disabled job applicant. A person subjects a disabled person to harassment if he or she engages in unwanted conduct which has the purpose or effect of violating the disabled person's dignity, or creating an intimidating, hostile, degrading, humiliating or offensive environment for him or her.

Conduct will be seen as harassment only if, having regard to all the circumstances, especially the perception of the disabled person, it can reasonably be considered as having the effect of harassment. Thus, although there is a reasonableness test, it is not necessarily an objective test because the view of the disabled person affected by the conduct is important.

Section 53A of the Disability Discrimination Act provides for the Disability Rights Commission to give practical guidance on how to avoid discrimination in relation to the DDA 1995 and to promote equality of opportunity. The current Code of Practice was issued by the Disability Rights Commission and took effect in October 2004. Failure to observe the provisions of the Code does not in itself make a person liable to proceedings, but any provision of the Code that appears to be relevant to a question arising in any proceedings will be taken into account.

OLDER WORKERS

There is ample evidence that age discrimination takes place in the EU. One EU-wide indicative survey (Marsh and Sahin-Dikmen, 'Discrimination in Europe', *Eurobarometer*, May 2003) of people's perceptions of discrimination in relation to racial or ethnic origin, religion or beliefs, disability, age and sexual orientation found that the most often-cited ground for discrimination was age (5%) followed by racial or ethnic origin (3%), religion or belief, physical disability, learning difficulties or mental illness (2% each). In the same survey people were asked which of the following would have the most difficulty in finding a job, training or promotion: a person from another ethnic origin, a person with minority beliefs, a physically disabled person, a person with learning difficulties, a person aged under 25, a person aged over 50, or a homosexual. Some 87% of respondents thought those with learning difficulties would be the most disadvantaged, and some 77% thought that the physically disabled would be the next most disadvantaged. In third place was the over-50-year-old. Some 71% thought that such a person would have less chance. There was a significant variation between countries, though, ranging from 17% in Greece to 83% in Finland. The fourth choice, for information, was the person from another ethnic origin.

The Employment Equality (Age) Regulations 2006 (SI 2006/1031) provide protection against direct and indirect discrimination, harassment and victimisation. The definition of direct and indirect discrimination is the same as in the other equality enactments. However, unlike other forms of discrimination (except in relation to genuine occupational qualification), it is permissible to directly discriminate on the grounds of age in some circumstances. There is a requirement to show that the less favourable treatment is a 'proportionate means of achieving a legitimate aim'.

One major issue is whether making people retire is a form of age discrimination. The 2006 Regulations introduced a default retirement age but the Government proposes to review this after five years. Until then employers will be able to enforce retirement at the age of 65 years, and at other ages if this can be objectively justified. Retirement below the age of 65 years will have to be objectively justified. Section 98 of the Employment Rights Act 1996 is amended to add another fair reason for dismissal, which will be 'retirement of the employee'. There is, however, no requirement to go through any statutory dismissal procedure. This is replaced by a statutory retirement procedure as outlined in new sections 98ZA to 98ZF of the Employment Rights Act.

For retirement to be taken as the only reason for dismissal, it must take place on the 'intended date of retirement'. There is still the opportunity for the employee to claim that the real reason for dismissal was some other reason and that the retirement would not have taken place but for this other reason, or that the dismissal amounts to unlawful discrimination under the Regulations. This will not be easy and there will be a heavy burden of proof on the employee. The operative retirement date is the 65th birthday unless there is an alternative date which is the normal retirement age, in which case it is that date. There is then a procedure in which the employer and employee must participate. Failure on the employer's part may render the dismissal unfair.

REFLECTIVE ACTIVITY

What will be the advantages and disadvantages of equalising employment opportunities for older workers?

What impact do you think the new laws will have on younger people?

3 THE LEGAL STATUS OF THE WORKER IN THE LABOUR MARKET

EMPLOYEES AND WORKERS

The legal status of the worker in the labour market is an important issue because some of the protection afforded by legislation affects only those who are employees and not, for example, the self-employed. Many organisations now 'outsource' a good deal of their work, sometimes to the self-employed (see Chapter 10).

One of the features of employment law in the United Kingdom is the distinction between employees and workers. The latter tends to have a wider meaning. The Employment Rights Act 1996 defines an employee as 'an individual who has entered into or works under (or, where the employment has ceased, worked under) a contract of employment'. The definition of a worker is broader – ie an individual who has entered into, or works under, a contract of employment or any other contract 'whereby the individual undertakes to do or perform personally any work or services for another party to the contract whose status is not by virtue of the contract that of a client or customer of any profession or business undertaking carried on by the individual'. Thus there are some individuals who are not under a contract of employment but are under a contract to perform personally any work or services for an employer. Often the latter are treated as self-employed, although they may be as dependent on one employer as those who are employees.

In *Byrne Brothers (Formwork) Ltd v Baird* [2002] IRLR 96 the Employment Appeal Tribunal (EAT) held that Parliament had intended to create an intermediate class of protected worker – one who is not an employee but also could not be regarded as carrying on a business. In this case the EAT concluded that self-employed sub-contract workers in the construction industry fitted into this category. The court stated:

> *There can be no general rule, and we should not be understood as propounding one; cases cannot be decided by applying labels. But typically labour-only sub-contractors will, though nominally free to move from contractor to contractor, in practice work for long periods for a single employer as an integrated part of his workforce.*

By way of contrast, in *Inland Revenue v Post Office Ltd* [2003] IRLR 199, the EAT decided that sub-postmistresses and sub-postmasters were not workers for the purposes of the National Minimum Wage Act 1998 because they had a choice whether or not to do the work themselves.

THE SELF-EMPLOYED

The numbers of self-employed workers has grown significantly in the last 20 years and, in 2004, amounted to approximately 3.5 million people, compared to almost 25 million employees. Over two thirds of the self-employed have no employees themselves and are dependent upon using their own skills and labour. For some workers, self-employment is an illusion. They will be dependent upon one employer for their supply of work and income, but may be lacking in certain employment rights because of their self-employed status.

There is then a real difficulty in distinguishing between those who are genuine employees and those who are self-employed, especially if they have the same dependence on one employer as do employees. To some extent this is recognised by the Government when certain employment protection measures are applied to workers and others to employees only. The Working Time Regulations 1998, for example, refer, in regulation 4(1), to a 'worker's working time', whereas the Maternity and Parental Leave etc Regulations 1999 apply only to employees.

There are a number of reasons why it is important to establish whether an individual is an employee or self-employed:

- Some employment protection measures are reserved for employees, although there are measures which refer to the wider definition of 'worker' including the Working Time Regulations 1998, the Sex Discrimination Act 1975 and the Race Relations Act 1976.

- Self-employed persons are taxed on a Schedule D basis, rather than the Schedule E basis for employed earnings. This allows the self-employed person to set off business expenses against income for tax purposes.

- Employers are vicariously liable for the actions of their employees, rather than for independent contractors.

- The employer also owes a higher standard of care to employees. This was demonstrated in *Lane v Shire Roofing* [1995] IRLR 493, where the claimant was held to be an employee rather than a self-employed contractor. As a result of this, damages in excess of £100,000 were awarded after a work-related accident which would not have been awarded if the claimant had been carrying out work as an independent contractor.

KEY ISSUES IN LABOUR MARKET REGULATION

We now pull together ten key points raised in this chapter:

- It can be seen that both the public and the private sectors are regulated as regards their relationships with employees. However, much of the regulation by the Government is of the private sector and is concerned with the protection of employees and equalising the balance of power in the relationship between employer and worker.

- It is important to note particularly the context in which labour market regulation takes place, such as the requirements of the national plan and the Lisbon strategy.

- Both public and private employment agencies are regulated, and details can be found in the relevant sections.

- Since 1970 there has been increasing protection for employees who have been disadvantaged in the past.

- Women and ethnic minorities were the first groups to be protected in the 1970s and disabled people have been protected since 1995. Age discrimination was outlawed in 2006.

- The anti-discrimination laws are frequently updated to take account of new situations. For example, sex discrimination now covers sexual orientation and gender reassignment. Regulations now protect against discrimination on the grounds of religion or belief.

- All HR activities are affected by anti-discrimination practices including recruitment, selection, promotion and access to training.

- Employees are protected from exploitation by numerous acts including the Working Time Directives, the Employment Act 2002 and its updates.

- In recent years, there have been a number of measures introduced to reduce illegal working such as the Asylum and Immigration Acts and the updates controlling workers from the new EU states.

- HR professionals must understand the importance of the type of employment status enjoyed by individual workers in order to respond appropriately.

Perhaps there are other key points that you would like to note for yourself.

The main case study in this chapter now follows. It gives an example of the possible legal implications of discrimination in the workplace.

MAIN CASE STUDY

Make an initial reading of the case study to gain an overview of the situation, and then read the questions that you will need to address. Now read the case study again, making notes of issues and facts that will help you in your analysis and responses to the questions. Remember to 'read between the lines' as well as picking out the obvious points, and also to consider what is not said as well as what is presented here.

This case study is based on a Court of Appeal decision in 2004. Lakhbir Rihal is an Indian-born Sikh who has been a UK resident for many years. He worked for the London Borough of Ealing as a surveyor in the housing department and then as a senior surveyor in the central technical team. The head of this team and the capital programmes subdivision was Ms Herman. In May 1996, Mr Relf, the acting head of the planned maintenance subdivision, retired. He was not replaced and Mr Rihal, who was as well qualified as Mr Relf, was not given that position. Instead, a white employee junior to Mr Rihal was promoted and shared Mr Relf's responsibilities with Mr Rihal.

In September 1996 Ms Herman retired and was replaced as head of the central technical team by a white man, Mr Foxall. The position of head of the capital programmes subdivision was filled on an acting-up basis by a Mr Gaffikan, who was white and had fewer qualifications and less experience than Mr Rihal.

In 1998 new posts were created as a result of a reorganisation. These were filled by a process of 'assimilation' whereby an existing employee whose post matched sufficiently closely to a new position was entitled to the new post, unless more than one person qualified on this basis, in which case there were competitive interviews. Mr Rihal unsuccessfully applied for a new managerial position as housing investment manager and for the two posts below that as investment planning and standards manager and programme delivery manager. In February 1999 he applied again for the post of investment planning and standards manager but this was given to Mr Gaffikan on the grounds that he had interviewed better. Mr Rihal then brought a grievance under the Council's procedure but this was not dealt with for over 14 months. Subsequently, he complained to an employment tribunal that he had been discriminated against on racial grounds.

Questions for consideration and discussion

1   In deciding whether there are racial grounds for less favourable treatment, is an employment tribunal entitled to look at evidence about the conduct of the alleged discriminator both before and after the act about which a complaint has been made?

2   Where there are allegations of direct or indirect discrimination by an employer over a substantial period of time, should the tribunal look at the individual incidents in isolation from one another?

3   If an employer has an arrangement which is racially discriminatory, does it make any difference that the manager in charge changes?

4   How relevant is it that there was 'a "force" in existence throughout that prevented Mr Foxall and others from picturing a turban-wearing Sikh with a pronounced accent in the managerial roles, which a person of the applicant's qualifications and experience could easily have achieved?'

5   Where a selection process focuses on experience, should any handicap which the employer has inflicted on a candidate by earlier discriminatory behaviour be taken into account?

6   Is a tribunal entitled to take into consideration the fact that a 'glass ceiling' operated in a particular department, which made it very difficult for those who were not white to obtain senior management positions?

7   Where direct or indirect discrimination is alleged, how relevant is the manner in which the complainant's grievance is dealt with?

8   If Mr Rihal had chosen to resign as a result of his treatment by the employer, could he have complained of unfair constructive dismissal?

[Note that a contructive dismissal occurs where an employee terminates the contract with or without notice in circumstances such that he or she is entitled to terminate it without notice by reason of the employer's conduct. Employees are entitled to treat themselves as constructively dismissed only if the employer is guilty of conduct which is a significant breach going to the root of the contract or which shows that the employer no longer intends to be bound by one or more of its essential terms.]

When you have considered your answers to these questions, you may wish to read the Court of Appeal judgment. The case citation is *Rihal v London Borough of Ealing* [2004] IRLR 642.

EXPLORE FURTHER

Advisory, Conciliation and Arbitration Service	**www.acas.org.uk**
Age Positive	**www.agepositive.gov.uk**
Basic Skills Agency	**www.basic-skills.co.uk**
Business Link	**www.businesslink.gov.uk**
Cabinet Office	**www.cabinetoffice.gov.uk**
Central Arbitration Committee	**www.cac.gov.uk**
Certification Officer	**www.certoff.org**
Commission for Equality and Human Rights	**www.equalityhumanrights.com**
Corporate social responsibility	**www.csracademy.org.uk**
Department for Business Enterprise and Regulations	**www.berr.gov.uk**
Department for Education and Skills	**www.dfes.gov.uk**
Department for Work and Pensions	**www.dwp.gov.uk**
Home Office	**www.homeoffive.gov.uk**
Information Commissioner	**www.informationcommissioner.gov.uk**
Job Centre Plus	**www.jobcentreplus.gov.uk**
Learning and Skills Council	**www.lsc.gov.uk**
Lifelong Learning	**www.lifelonglearning.co.uk**
Low Pay Commission	**http://www.lowpay.gov.uk/**
National Institute of Continuing Adult Education	**www.niace.org.uk**
Recruitment and Employment Confederation	**www.rec.uk.com**
Sector Skills Development Agency	**www.ssda.org.uk**
Small Business Council	**www.smallbusinesscouncil.org**
Small Business Service	**www.sbs.gov.uk**
Stationery Office	**www.opsi.gov.uk**
Statistics	**www.statistics.gov.uk**
Trades Union Congress	**www.tuc.oug.uk**

CHAPTER 6

Equality and diversity

Doirean Wilson, Matt Flynn *and* Philip Frame

INTRODUCTION

This chapter examines the management of equality and diversity in the workplace as a way of ensuring that organisations both operate within the law and make best use of workers' diverse skills and talents. As the previous chapter has shown, laws in Britain and many other countries now protect workers from discrimination on the basis of race, gender, disability, ethnicity, religion, sexual orientation and age. All employers are therefore obliged to make sure that their staff are not subject to workplace discrimination in how they are managed, how their pay, rewards and benefits are determined, or how decisions on training and development, promotion and dismissal are made.

Employers are also responsible under discrimination law for protecting their employees from bullying and harassment from colleagues and managers. See Chapter 5 in this book for an overview of discrimination laws in the UK.

Compliance with discrimination law is not the only reason why workplace equality and diversity are important. Discrimination has a demoralising effect on employees and can lead to poor work output and a waste of their skills and talents. However, employers who take steps to stop discrimination in the workplace could benefit by using fully the wide range of skills, talents, experience and cultural resources of their workers. In other words, equality and diversity are important to any well-run organisation.

In using the terms 'equality' and 'diversity', we note that they are often regarded as identical, but they are not in fact completely interchangeable. For example, 'equality' means not treating somebody less favourably on the basis, of for instance, his or her gender or age. Here, the focus is on the individual. 'Diversity', on the other hand, refers to approaches which employers can take to make sure that people from different backgrounds, and with different perspectives, are suitably represented, and valued in the workplace. Equality and diversity are closely associated since promoting equality is likely to lead to a diverse workforce; and an employer who promotes diversity is more likely to treat employees equally than one who does not. The first part of this chapter is about age equality, and the second examines cultural diversity.

LEARNING OUTCOMES

At the end of this chapter readers should be able to:

- describe ways in which discrimination can occur in the workplace
- discuss the negative impact that discrimination can have on workplace morale and performance
- adopt a positive approach to working with those of difference
- identify the organisational benefits of having strategies for equality and diversity
- list ways of embedding equality and diversity in all aspects of management
- describe ways in which to harness positive working relationships
- pinpoint ways in which to resolve workplace conflict.

This chapter is divided into two parts. Part 1 discusses the importance to employers of having a strategy for managing equality and diversity in the workplace. This is illustrated in the context of developing an age-positive workplace. In 2006, age discrimination in the workplace was made unlawful in Britain. Although most employers have equal opportunities policies, few have developed strategies for appropriately translating the policies into HR management. This chapter is not meant to give an overview of the new law – see chapter 5 for a detailed discussion of UK law and the Employment Equality (Age) Regulations 2006 – but to examine how an organisation's approach to equality and diversity can impact on how people are managed.

In Part 2 of this chapter we look at how equality and diversity policies can be used to improve team performance. This is demonstrated using the concept of 'cultural positivity' as a twenty-first-century tool for promoting, understanding and addressing conflict among those people who are different from each other, especially those working in teams.

This chapter also draws readers' attention to various diversity-related issues from a theoretical perspective, in order to broaden their knowledge and to encourage their support for a positive approach towards dealing with negative stereotypes. Although the issues raised in this chapter are illustrated by examples of age and cultural equality and diversity, the lessons learned can be used more widely, to tackle other forms of discrimination.

STARTER CASE STUDY

Consolidated Motors is a small manufacturer which supplies car parts to major automotive companies. Factory workers are divided into teams of five, and each team puts together a specific part. One of the teams is responsible for assembling wing mirrors. It is made up of four workers who are in their twenties and John who is 58. John has been with the company since it opened in the 1970s. He gets on well with his colleagues, and they often go out for a beer together at the end of the working day. John is considered the wise man of the team. When things go wrong with the machine, John is usually asked to sort things out. He appreciates that his experience is respected and enjoys the friendships he has at work. However, the job is very hard, and he has told his foreman that he might want to retire on a reduced pension when he reaches 60.

Earlier this year, one of the car companies began complaining about the quality control of the wing mirrors. Some were scratched and had to be returned. The quality control manager investigated and found that workers were not using the machines properly. He ordered the four younger workers to go through retraining. He also advised the HR manager to cancel their annual productivity bonus. John, on the other hand, was treated more leniently. The manager didn't want to embarrass John by making him relearn how to use a machine which he had operated for years, and didn't feel there was much point in training him, since he was going to retire the next year. Besides, there is a cost associated with training, and it did not make sense to waste money on someone who would be leaving soon anyway. He also let John keep his bonus as a 'retirement gift'.

Questions for discussion

1 How would John's colleagues feel about this situation?

2 Might John feel singled out by being treated differently from the others?

3 What might happen to the work team if one of them is singled out for better treatment?

4 Can John remain productive if he doesn't go through the same training as the others?

5 Is the quality control manager guilty of age discrimination?

Throughout, the reader is encouraged to reflect on his or her previous experiences of equality and diversity in work and learning.

The chapter concludes with the main case study.

Reference sources named within the chapter may be looked up in the *References and further reading* section at the end of the book.

1 EQUALITY: THE EXAMPLE OF AGE

The starter case study above shows that discrimination can often be unintentional, as demonstrated by the quality control manager, who probably had good intentions. However, the manager is clearly discriminating on the basis of age in that some workers are being treated less favourably because they are being denied a bonus in comparison to another employee because of their age. (Remember that age discrimination can affect young as well as older employees.) Under the new age discrimination laws, this is unlawful.

Consider the situation from John's perspective. His manager assumes that he will retire early, and decides not to provide training which is essential for him to remain productive. Perhaps he will later decide not to take early retirement; but without training it will be difficult for him to continue in his job. Even if he does keep his plans to retire early, he may still have a few more years of service which will be marked by worsening performance in comparison with his colleagues. Those colleagues may also resent the fact that he received a bonus when they did not – despite similar performances. He may therefore be pushed out of work with a sense that he is no longer a contributing team member.

The scenario described is often called allowing staff to 'coast into retirement', and is common to many organisations. It can appear to be the easy way to remedy performance problems of older workers, since uncomfortable discussions can be avoided, but is one of the factors that can lead to premature exit from the labour market.

THE POLITICAL CONTEXT

Governments across Europe have become increasingly concerned about age discrimination because of the effect it has on older people's employment. Both the EU and the UK have set targets for increasing older people's participation in work. The UK government wants 80% of the working age population (including 1 million additional older workers) to be economically active (European Commission, 2005). To achieve this goal, it has changed state pension rules, as well as tax regulations on occupational pensions, to restrict early retirement and make later retirement more attractive to workers (DWP, 2005).

All EU member states have strategies for increasing the number of older workers, although some are taking a different approach. Sweden, like Norway, has a state pension age of 65, but older workers have the right to continue in work for a further two years (OECD, 2003). Belgium, Germany and Italy are all countries with very low real retirement ages which are now focusing on state pensions and redundancy laws to restrict opportunities for early retirement (OECD, 2005). Finland has seen the sharpest growth in the number of older workers, which reflects employers' and unions' application of 'Workability' tools to help people remain economically active longer. The Workability model, developed by the Finnish Institute for Occupational Health (Ilmarinen, 1999), is used to identify factors early which might lead to premature exit from the labour market. Workers who are at risk of early exit through incapacity, for example, are given support such as changes to work design to help them stay in work. Across most of the EU, negotiations between employers' groups and unions have been shaping the scope and application of age discrimination regulations. In the UK, employers will be uncertain about how the new regulations will apply to them until the courts interpret the law – particularly on the justifications for discrimination (discussed below).

The age discrimination regulations are part of the Government's efforts to meet its 1 million older workers target. Much of the law is what the Government itself termed 'light touch' (DTI, 2005) employment regulation. Retiring employees now have the right, for example, to request an extension to their working lives and the right to request flexible working should they have eldercare responsibilities. Although neither right-of-request gives older workers any new employment rights, they do force employers to respond to employees' requests by considering (however superficially) the possibilities for facilitating the extension of working life.

Too often, employers' management of performance and development is built on expectations that older workers want to, or could at least be persuaded to, retire early. Measures which could be taken to help older employees, such as training or small changes to work design, are not considered cost-effective, as judged against when retirement could be assumed to take place. Yet a worker in his late fifties is likely to have as long a future with his employer as one in his twenties. Whereas the former may eventually leave through retirement, the latter is more likely to change workplaces.

A number of studies have found that most older workers would like to work beyond what they consider to be their normal retirement age, but they need support from their employers to do so (Owen and Flynn, 2004; Loretto, Vickerstaff and White, 2005; Loretto, Vickerstaff and White, 2006). One found that half of those who are retired now would have preferred to stay in their jobs but to work more flexible hours (McNair and Flynn, 2004). In the UK at the time the age discrimination regulations were coming into effect there was a dramatic increase in the real retirement age, which is now 64.2 for men (just below the state pension age) and 61.8 for women (just above). Changes to employers' behaviours as a response to the law can therefore have a direct impact on older workers' employment.

In the UK, part of the reason for the fact that ageism is to be found everywhere is that the age discrimination laws are so new, and employers have only recently been confronted with the need to define what unacceptable behaviour is. Half a century ago, employers who dismissed female employees when they married were not uncommon – the Civil Service itself was one! Now, after more than 30 years of sex discrimination law, almost everyone would consider the practice unfair and absurd. Age discrimination has, until very recently, gone unchallenged by the law, and practices which are long on discrimination but short on merit have been allowed to continue.

Many employers took steps to eliminate age discrimination before the regulations forced them to do so. In the UK, skills shortages and an expanding economy have persuaded employers to look for new ways to recruit and retain older workers (McNair and Flynn, 2005). According to the Cranet survey, 14% of British employers say that they have an action programme to encourage older workers to remain economically active longer. This is twice the proportion of employers who responded from Germany, where the economy is going through a period of high unemployment. Employers in London and the south-east of England are particularly likely to have policies for keeping older workers employed longer.

Leading efforts to encourage older people to stay in work are 'age champions' which include Barclays, British Telecom, Coca-Cola, Tesco and Nationwide. However, large employers are not the only ones who are benefiting from an increase in older workers' participation. In fact, many of the most innovative ways of addressing workplace ageism derive from small firms, which come from a range of sectors. The most common feature of age champions is a recognition that they need to recruit and retain skilled workers, and age discrimination is inconsistent with these objectives. In other words, age discrimination does not make business sense.

Perhaps one of the highest-profile age champions is B&Q. Rapid expansion in the early 1990s forced the company to look to recruit beyond the pool of their typical job applicants and to challenge the assumptions made about older workers' ability to work in DIY stores. They soon found that, with machines and technology, there are few tasks which are too physically demanding for a 60-year-old employee. The retailer has also found that its older employees have lower rates of absenteeism and turnover than their younger colleagues. Many of their older employers have experience working in a trade, and use their skills and knowledge to help customers. Today, 21% of B&Q front-line employees are over 50.

 REFLECTIVE ACTIVITY

Think of an industry you are familiar with.

When do people normally expect to retire? Are employees expected to retire early? What does the employer do, if anything, to help or encourage people to stay on at work longer?

What are the costs to an employer, and the workforce, of operating ageist policies? What are the benefits of age equality?

A STRATEGY TO ELIMINATE DISCRIMINATION

The starting point for employers has often been establishing or amending an equal opportunities policy prohibiting discrimination in the workplace. However, simply drafting a statement into the staff handbook or annual report to say that the company does not discriminate does little to change workplace culture. With ageism, there is a real gap between what HR managers *say* corporate policy is, and what line managers *think* to be the case.

Equal opportunities policies require employers to review HR policies and practices in order to remove discrimination from the workplace and to make policy a working reality. The new age discrimination regulations have brought calls for employers to build 'integrated age strategies' (Walker, 1999) – that is, to have age policies which are pushed firmly into all aspects of HR policies and practices. They also require employers to raise awareness of age management within their workplaces, particularly amongst managers. In this way the barriers which older workers face in staying economically active are more likely to be removed.

Although age equality policies are common in the UK workplace, age strategies are more rare. According to WERS 2004 data, 73% of workplaces have equal opportunity policies (see Table 15). However, only a minority regularly review activities to eliminate ageism (see Table 16). Around 16% of employers regularly review their recruitment and selection procedures – and yet only one in 18 reviews pay rates to eliminate age biases in its pay system. Employers are almost as slow to review policies in order to eliminate other forms of discrimination. For example, only one in five reviews recruitment and selection procedures to identify discrimination on the basis of gender, ethnicity or disability.

Table 15 The incidence of equal opportunity policies in UK workplaces

	Equal opportunity policy (%)
All workplaces	73
Organisation size	
10–99 employees	46
10,000 or more employees	97
Industry	
Manufacturing	52
Hotels and restaurants	50
Financial services	96
Public sector	98

Source: Kersley *et al* (2006; p.238)

Table 16 The incidence of regular organisational reviews, by workforce characteristics

	Percentage of workplaces		
	Review recruitment and selection procedures	Review promotion procedures	Review relative pay rates
Gender	19	11	7
Ethnic background	20	11	5
Disability	19	10	4
Age	16	9	6

Source: Kersley *et al* (2006; p.248)

EMBEDDING EQUALITY INTO HR PRACTICES

Having integrated age equality strategies and practices to carry them out requires employers to consider the effect discrimination has on all aspects of management. Unlike other discrimination law, the age discrimination regulations allow some forms of direct discrimination which are determined by the courts to be objectively justifiable. For example, a restaurant manager may decide not to train any staff under 18 in bartending because it is unlawful for minors to serve alcohol. Although the manager's decision is based directly on age, there is a legitimate business reason for it.

The Government has set two criteria which employment tribunals will use in assessing whether an age discriminatory practice is objectively justifiable. Firstly, it needs to reflect a legitimate business objective; and secondly, it has to be proportionate – that is, the costs to the employee must be compared to the benefits to the employer.

The courts will decide exactly what practices are unlawful, but these criteria are a good starting point to think about age discrimination and HR practices. Think back to the starter case study. There, the manager decided not to send John on a training course because he expected that the company would not benefit enough to recoup the costs. Was this a legitimate business objective? In some circumstances, employers might have a valid reason for using an employee's proximity to retirement (or even the likelihood of his leaving for another job) in deciding whether to send him on a long or expensive training programme. The EU Directive from which the regulations come specifically gives the example of training costs as objectively justifiable. But is it proportionate? If you think of the cost of the training, and the benefits which John (not to mention the employer itself) would have gained through increased productivity and improved job prospects, the decision does not seem to be justifiable.

It is now worth thinking about some of the ways in which age discrimination can affect HR practices. We start with *appraisals and performance management*. We showed above how managers can allow problems with performance not to be looked at, hoping that poor performers will retire early (and often persuading them to do so). In contrast, older workers who have unmet skills needs are often reluctant to ask for additional training for fear of signalling to their employers that they have gone beyond their productive years and should therefore be encouraged to retire.

Age bias in *pay and benefits* is also common, although pay systems that are directly related to age are rare. Usually, such pay systems offer a lower rate to those at the younger end of the age scale. ('Development rates' for the UK National Minimum Wage remain lawful, for example.) Indirect age discrimination is more likely, such as pay scales which reflect length of service. Performance-related pay and individually negotiated remuneration packages can also reflect age bias if they are based on discriminatory ideas – for example, the idea that young people are generally undependable.

Turning to *working hours and job design*, research suggests that older workers would stay longer if their work could be designed to meet their individual circumstances, such as reducing their working hours or reducing the stress associated with their work. In addition, many older workers have caring responsibilities for elderly relatives or grandchildren. Older carers often have fewer opportunities to work flexibly, and the stress associated with balancing home and work responsibilities often accelerates their desire to retire. In 2007, the statutory right to request flexible working was extended to employees with eldercare responsibilities.

Age-related selection criteria for *redundancies* can work in both directions. Common compulsory redundancy procedures – such as 'last in, first out' – disadvantage younger workers (as well as workers from ethnic minorities) who tend to have shorter service. Voluntary redundancy schemes often provide financial incentives to older workers to retire early. In contrast, age equal redundancy systems focus on the skills and competencies which are needed for retention by the organisation, regardless of age.

Older workers are more likely to face age discrimination when applying for jobs, and unemployed people over 50 are among the least likely to find employment. We need to ask ourselves why, if ever, age should be a factor in *recruitment* decisions, and note the recent moves of many leading employers to remove requests for age-related information from application forms. Even when this is removed, selectors may still make negative assumptions about applicants' age, abilities and expectations. In order to deal with this problem many employers now use recruitment tools which are based on competencies rather than biographies in order to limit information (for example, whether someone sat a particular sort of examination that is no longer used) which could be used to guess age.

Employers have a duty to protect employees from *harassment and bullying* which is based on any form of discrimination, including age. Structures should be put in place to make sure that such claims are recognised as legitimate, and addressed effectively, fairly, and in a timely manner.

Perhaps the most difficult issue which the age discrimination regulations address is that of *retirement*. Employers can lawfully set a compulsory retirement age which is 65 or over without needing to justify it. However, an employee who remains in work beyond 65 is protected against *unfair dismissal*. It has been widely suggested that the default retirement age, as well as the statutory framework for handling retirement, are age discriminatory and do not fully implement the EU Directive from which the regulations derive. The European courts are currently considering this issue. Nevertheless, good age management practices should include clear and understandable criteria for handling requests to stay in work beyond retirement age.

The above list of issues highlights just some of the issues which employers and HR specialists must consider when developing strategies for promoting equality, including those related to age, in the workplace. What should be clear is that equality issues affect management at all levels of an organisation. Discriminatory practices could exist in all corporate HR policies (for example, pay scales with long-service-related higher pay), or could continue in the prejudices of individual managers. It is important, therefore, that employees – particularly those involved in HR decisions – are trained in equal opportunities, are aware of the organisation's policy, and appreciate how this should be reflected in HR decisions.

Many employers are using the introduction of age equality strategies to review other anti-discrimination policies to ensure their continued effectiveness and harmonisation. This is also a way to address multiple discrimination. It is easy to think of older workers as a uniform group, but this is not so. Those who experienced discrimination (for example, on the basis of gender or disability) at a younger age are more likely to be disadvantaged in later working life than those who did not. In summary, it is important not to consider age discrimination as separate from other equality issues.

REFLECTIVE ACTIVITY

As a manager, or potential manager, are there any assumptions you would make about employees or job-seekers based on their ages or, indeed, their other characteristics?

If there are, can you justify these assumptions?

2 DIVERSITY IN WORK TEAMS

In the first half of this chapter we noted the importance of having strategies for embedding equality and diversity in the management of employees. We will now show how equality and diversity strategies can be embedded into HRM practices, thereby enhancing the performance of managers and those people they manage.

One of the most important responsibilities of a manager is to foster the development of effective teams in which employees can work together to meet shared objectives. Daniels and MacDonald (2005; p.30) acknowledge that 'Teamwork also allows the strengths and weaknesses of individuals to be matched so that overall the team is stronger than the individuals who are within it.' This is something that tends to be fairly common among teams of students.

REFLECTIVE ACTIVITY

Were you ever part of a team where it was obvious that other individual members possessed particular team strengths or weaknesses?

Did these strengths or weaknesses have an impact on the team's performance – and if they did, how?

How could weaker members of a team be developed to improve their team performance, do you think?

As members of groups who have traditionally been under-represented in the workforce enter the labour market, work teams have become much more diverse than they were a decade ago. It should come as no surprise, therefore, to learn that 'No one is untouched by the impact of diversity' (Parvis, 2007; p.1). In a recent publicity article, WWP Training Limited (2007; p.1) acknowledged that 'The blending of skills from different cultures has become a major engine of human and corporate development.' Hence the potential benefits that can be gained from incorporating suitable diversity policies and procedures in an organisation.

For example, 'The Latino Employee Network at Frito-Lay, the snack division of PepsiCo, did just that, during the development of Doritos guacamole-flavoured tortilla chips. Members of the network provided feedback on the taste and packaging to help ensure that the product would be regarded as authentic in the Latino community.' This helped to make the product 'one of the most successful new launches in the company's history, generating more than $100 million in sales in its first year' (Rodriquez, 2006; p.1), which was indeed a positive outcome. It is also speculated that 'Diverse teams actually perform better than non-diverse teams because they have a greater range of knowledge and cognitive skills to draw on' (Daniels and MacDonald, 2005; p.31). However, it could be argued that this would depend on whether individuals in the team were working well together.

Diversity in the workplace can also present challenges which managers need to meet in order to maximise the performance of their work teams. Everyone holds stereotypes or assumptions about people who are different from themselves (whether, for example, they are different in terms of age, gender, ethnicity, race, sexual orientation or ability/disability). Usually these prejudices are not spoken, because social traditions and the law prohibit people from sharing their prejudices. False assumptions persist because they are usually not voiced and therefore remain unchallenged. But if we were to 'imagine a world without diversity, it would be hard to tell one person from another, because we would all look alike and have the same conversations since everyone would think alike. We couldn't have team sports because they require varied skills, and only one political party would exist' because there would be 'no need to vote on anything, since we would all see things the same way' (WWP Training Limited, 2007; p.2). When exploring this ideology, we would have to be mindful of the possible implications on societal development.

CULTURAL POSITIVITY

In the starter case study, we saw how a manager's action undermined a positive work team – the workmates who were of different ages got on well with each other until one was treated differently. Now we will discuss how managers can foster good relationships within a diverse team. We will do this by using a concept known as 'cultural positivity'. It is a method which facilitates collaborative working in an internationalised higher-education environment. Here, we will show how it can be applied in a workplace context as a means to break down cultural barriers.

'Cultural positivity' encourages an attitude shift from negativity or pessimism to one which builds a more positive and optimistic outlook. An additional aim is to acknowledge and celebrate cultural differences in order to build pride in self and ethnicity, while addressing potential conflicts that can occur when working with cultural diversity in practice. In America there are several similar culturally positive initiatives such as the Martin Luther King Junior Award and the NH Martin Luther King Coalition that is aimed at honouring 'young people who make diversity, civil rights and tolerance a part of their lives' (Powell, 2006; p.1).

The idea of cultural positivity came from observations made of the ongoing hostilities and conflict that could occur among students working with those who were from different backgrounds. Conflict can occur in any group with more than one team member, but is more likely to happen in teams that are large and diverse, particularly if there is a negative attitude to those from diverse backgrounds. Daniels and MacDonald (2005; p.30) noted that 'Diversity can lead to a reduced group cohesion and greater levels of conflict within the group.' In turn, this can have a negative impact on team relationships and morale, and thus, the standard of work produced.

REFLECTIVE ACTIVITY

Think back to a time when you worked or studied with people from backgrounds that were different from your own.

What was your initial impression of them?

Were your perceptions based on personal experiences or from what you had read, heard or been told?

Were these impressions based on reality?

Did your perceptions influence your approach towards those of difference – and if so, how?

Do you now tend to adopt a different approach when interacting with those from backgrounds that are the same or similar to your own – and if so, why?

How cultural conflict can manifest itself

Conflict in work teams can continue if managers are unaware of the impact that it is having on the members' ability to work together, or if they just don't care. Cultural differences, and the unresolved conflicts that result, are sometimes put down to 'clashes of personality'. But this may not always be the case and managers must be aware of the range of sources from which conflict may emerge.

A good way to analyse conflict is to use Bruce Tuckman's 1965 team development theory (Daniels and MacDonald, 2005; p.32; Tuckman and Jensen, 1977; pp419–27) by which he shows how conflict can emerge, peak, and, with proper management, be resolved (see Figure 8).

Figure 8 The dynamic of conflict, as shown by Tuckman's team development theory

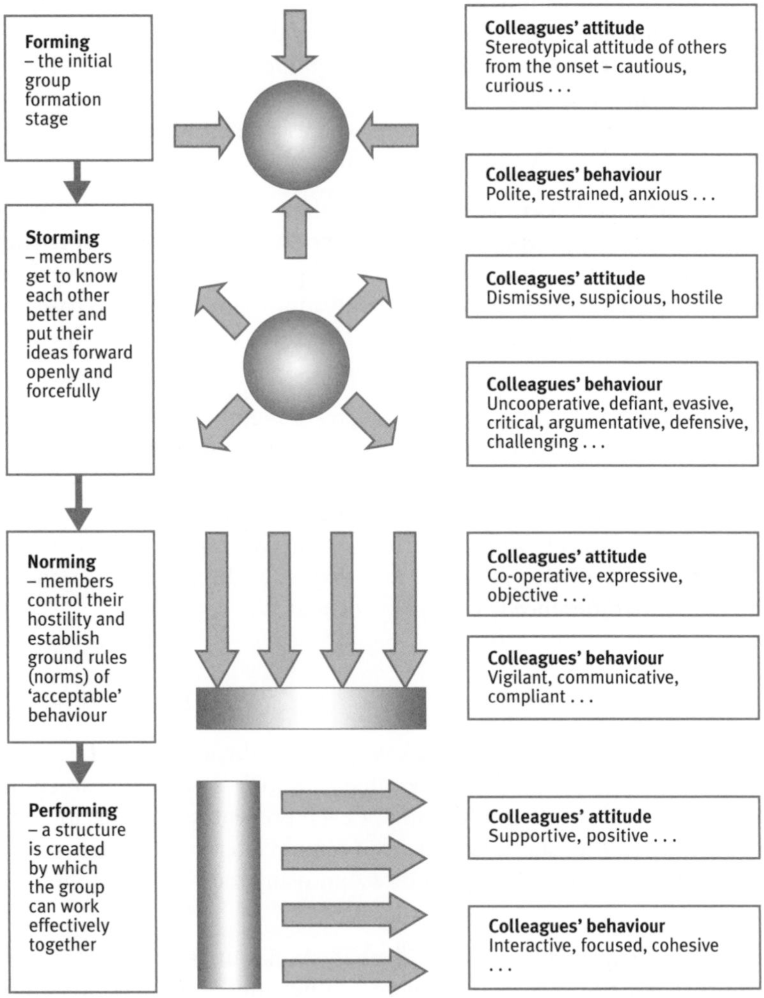

Forming – the initial group formation stage	**Colleagues' attitude** Stereotypical attitude of others from the onset – cautious, curious ...
	Colleagues' behaviour Polite, restrained, anxious ...
Storming – members get to know each other better and put their ideas forward openly and forcefully	**Colleagues' attitude** Dismissive, suspicious, hostile
	Colleagues' behaviour Uncooperative, defiant, evasive, critical, argumentative, defensive, challenging ...
Norming – members control their hostility and establish ground rules (norms) of 'acceptable' behaviour	**Colleagues' attitude** Co-operative, expressive, objective ...
	Colleagues' behaviour Vigilant, communicative, compliant ...
Performing – a structure is created by which the group can work effectively together	**Colleagues' attitude** Supportive, positive ...
	Colleagues' behaviour Interactive, focused, cohesive ...

During the *forming* stage, prejudices are difficult to detect. However, they affect individuals' willingness to work with people who are different from themselves, which can slow the development of work teams. This could be reflected, for example, in individuals' collaborating exclusively with others from similar backgrounds but ignoring those who are 'different'. In the study of higher education students, prejudices were shown to affect how students formed working groups. A Ghanaian student, for example, reported that 'When I realised that I was going to be in a team with two Nigerians, I assumed that they would be dishonest so I was always on my guard.' A white British-born student confirmed that when he met the other members of his team, he immediately thought 'I'm going to end up doing most of the work because Jamaicans are usually quite laid-back.' These negative stereotypes are usually based on unexamined perceptions.

They can frequently result in conflict among team members, which occurs at the *storming* stage of team formation. As a result, work outcomes and the ability to complete tasks within agreed deadlines can be badly delayed. This leads to increased work pressure on the team which in turn increases hostilities. The study also showed that those members of the team who were being negatively stereotyped were aware that this was the case, and as a result were less cooperative and more defensive and mistrustful.

At the *norming* stage, team members realise that the ongoing conflict is counterproductive, and so attempt to resolve their hostilities by discussing and agreeing on ground rules. Although hostilities and grievances can still be evident at this stage, they are less disruptive as the group adopts a more reality-based approach than one based on presuppositions. This results in a more cooperative working attitude.

As the team progresses to the *performing* stage, team members become more interdependent and supportive of each other, as a result of their experience of having to manage with difference and in a productive way. They are also mindful of completing the task within the specified deadline. It was also noted that as team members grapple with and critique their assumptions and beliefs, they also become aware of what is similar and shared, enabling the emergence of a complementarity of difference (Frame, Hartog and Wilson, 2005).

RESOLVING CULTURAL CONFLICT — AN EXERCISE

Of course, team development does not always progress through all of Tuckman's stages. Left unchecked, cultural difference can lead to teams becoming stuck in the storming phase, with conflict inhibiting or even preventing the development of effective working relationships. Conflict can remain latent, with team members keeping quiet about their prejudices but using them to shape their views of colleagues.

Effective cultural management, and thus diversity management, starts at an early stage and is proactive, rather than reacting to conflict after it emerges. Managers must encourage good team relationships, particularly when cultural conflicts have the potential to act as barriers to effective working.

One exercise that has been used to achieve this in an academic context can be applied to a workplace setting. It is based on the approach of 'cultural positivity' detailed above. Participants are asked to form work teams which are based on mixed gender, ethnicity, age and location. The above criteria helped to ensure that there was a mix of members in each team, while also preventing them from being dominated by certain groups of individuals. The steps outlined in Figure 9 below can encourage a better awareness of difference, in addition to creating more trusting and harmonious working relationships, by helping to expose and address potential sources of team conflict. Each team was required to follow the three steps identified below and then present to the whole group.

When the model was first used, the audience watching each team presentation would gasp in surprise whenever members revealed things about themselves that

Figure 9 The three steps that encourage better awareness of difference

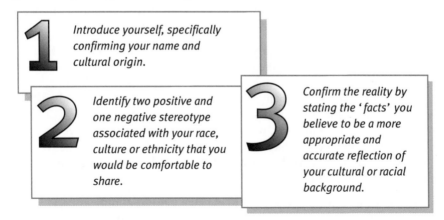

1 Introduce yourself, specifically confirming your name and cultural origin.

2 Identify two positive and one negative stereotype associated with your race, culture or ethnicity that you would be comfortable to share.

3 Confirm the reality by stating the 'facts' you believe to be a more appropriate and accurate reflection of your cultural or racial background.

did not match the stereotypical perception of them, which was, as is often the case, based on physical appearance. This was evident when a blue-eyed Caucasian-looking white female member of one team introduced herself as being a 'Jamaican whose parents and grandparents were also born and raised in Jamaica'. The audience was very surprised by this, especially in the light of the student's strong Jamaican accent. The reaction from the audience was the same when a female member of another team, who looked Asian, revealed that she was of 'mixed race with an Irish mother and an Afro-Caribbean father'.

This exercise challenged and undermined the pre-existing perceptions of participants based on physical appearance; the gasps were the oral representation of this. Since its introduction there has been a drop in the number of reported conflict among team members by as much as 50%. The exercise showed that there are clear benefits for the development of teams in addressing cultural issues in an open, direct and constructive manner:

- People generally welcome the opportunity to present themselves and their culture from a perspective of which they can feel proud.

- Although participants notice aspects of culture, these issues were less prominent between people of the same background.

- Participants discovered their similarities as well as their differences.

- Exercises like this can motivate participants to address negative stereotypes in a non-confrontational and positive way which can significantly undermine the stereotypes' power.

- Diversity exercises can make participants view those of difference from a less negative and guarded viewpoint, in addition to making them curious to learn more about the upbringing and background of the others.

- The same is true of the often unrealistic expectations associated with positive stereotypes.

- Diversity exercises can trigger a shift in the students' perception of others from one that was primarily influenced by culturally driven stereotypes to one that focuses on the individual and their 'here and now' behaviour.

Finally, and perhaps most importantly, the exercise demonstrated the significant role that managers have in taking the initiative and addressing cultural issues at an early stage of collaborative working. If ignored, stereotypes can have a negative effect on team development and effective working which can lead to subsequent management difficulties. When individuals can discuss their differences, and indeed similarities, in a supportive environment, positive cultural identities can emerge which support, rather than hinder, constructive team formation. Productive work teams are then more likely to emerge, which will have a positive impact on the organisation.

Of course, the same ideas can be applied to managing teams of different age, gender or disability. By taking action to enable people to present themselves in a positive way, managers can help to break down stereotypes of team colleagues and their abilities.

REFLECTIVE ACTIVITY

Have you ever been in a team or work situation in which you felt you were being disadvantaged because of your age, ethnicity, gender, background, disability or ability?

If you have, how did it affect you?

KEY CULTURAL POSITIVITY ISSUES

Finally, we turn to the four key 'cultural positivity' issues that must be considered before taking organisational action. When considering how to take action against discrimination in your work team, you should think about:

- your approach
- the timing
- the benefits of participation
- obtaining feedback.

Approach

This relates to the need to choose a suitable approach that is relevant and appropriate for encouraging involvement from participants. The approach chosen should focus primarily on the positive aspects of diversity, and on similarities as well as differences.

Timing

The timing for introducing 'culturally positive' diversity activities is important and should preferably begin at the *forming* stage of the team development relationship. Should this not be possible, a team process intervention at a later stage is advisable, along the lines noted above in Figure 9.

Participation

It is important to communicate the benefits of 'culturally positive' diversity activities from the outset, in order to secure involvement and commitment from participants.

Feedback

This relates to the need to obtain feedback from participants on the relevance and benefits of the diversity activities, and how these can be improved, as well as learning whether the activities resulted in an improvement in interpersonal relations.

Let's think about the difficulties that can arise with regard to the four key issues mentioned above. They include those outlined below.

Approach

A biased 'culturally positive' approach – that is, one that is partial rather than inclusive, in that it does not reflect the diverse backgrounds of all team members – can be counterproductive. Similarly, an inflexibility which results in an unwillingness to recognise the negative effects of positive stereotypes will undermine the effectiveness of this process. For example a manager who assumes that older workers don't need training is denying them opportunities to learn and remain productive.

Timing

An attempt to introduce positive diversity activities when conflict has become the norm within the team is likely to be viewed with suspicion or be met with some hostility. It is better to take a positive approach to diversity from the start rather than trying to make repairs when things go wrong.

Participation

If participants have already had negative experiences of working in teams with those from diverse backgrounds, it can make it more difficult to get their participation in 'culturally positive' activities – unless, of course, the benefits of such activities are made clear.

Feedback

If no action is taken following feedback obtained from participants regarding 'culturally positive' activities, it can lead to the suspicion that there is a lack of commitment on the organisation's part. This in turn can lead to an unwillingness to participate in future activities.

KEY ISSUES IN EQUALITY AND DIVERSITY MANAGEMENT

We now pull together ten key points about sustainable HRM raised in this chapter:

- Workplaces are becoming more diverse as people from different backgrounds enter the labour market. This can be good for business since diversity brings new ideas.

- Taking a positive approach to equality and diversity can benefit you and your organisation by encouraging employees to make best use of their talents and fostering positive working relationships.

- Ageism is the latest form of discrimination to be made unlawful, and most employers will find it a challenge to eliminate it from the workplace. Ageist attitudes are often hidden as 'common sense' and it is difficult to make people realise that they are discriminatory.

- Tackling ageism early can give an employer a competitive edge, since it can make use of an unused source of skilled and experienced labour.

- Discrimination, even if done with good intentions, is unlawful and can do more harm than good to a person whom you are trying to help. It can also have unintended consequences in the workplace.

- Simply having an equal opportunity policy is not enough to stop discrimination. You must make sure that all HR policies and practices treat people equally, and that employees understand that discrimination is not tolerated.

- Stereotypes can hurt team formation, as colleagues hold false assumptions about their colleagues.

- Stereotypes can be broken down by discussing them within a team, but dialogue must take place in a positive and constructive environment.

- It is better to take a positive approach to equality and diversity at an early stage rather than after things go wrong.

- Governments across Europe are taking steps to eliminate discrimination because it harms people and is bad for the economy.

Perhaps there are other key points that you would like to note for yourself.

The main case study in this chapter now follows. It is based on a team conflict situation.

MAIN CASE STUDY

Read through the case study and decide on the recommendations that you would make as an HR manager for dealing effectively with the issues raised.

A medium-sized niche retailer decided to start using the Internet to sell its products to a wider group of customers. The head of the marketing department was asked to put together a team to develop an online marketing strategy for the company. The project team needed a mix of skills, such as a range of information technology skills, design, manufacturing, commercial law, and, of course, marketing.

Because of the range of skills needed, a large team was formed, and conflicts between team members soon became apparent. The IT technicians, who were mostly the younger members of the group, wanted to use the firm's intranet system for collaborating, while other team members complained that they lacked the training and equipment to participate in this way. Older employees from the legal department said that they had had experience advising on earlier campaigns which could benefit this project, but their views had been ignored. People with childcare responsibilities had times when they could not work on the project, and others felt that they were not contributing their fair share. The team was also culturally diverse, and some team members were overheard making inappropriate remarks about colleagues. In addition, it became clear that some team members were working on the project out of hours, excluding others in their collaboration. Because the working relationships within the group broke down, the project team was unable to meet its objectives. The head of marketing had hoped to present a comprehensive online marketing strategy to the board of directors, but it was not achieved.

Questions for discussion

1. How could the conflict have been reduced? If you were managing this team, what would you have done to resolve these tensions?

2. At what stage would you intervene in order to reduce or avoid conflict? How might you raise awareness within the team of the challenges of working with a diverse group of colleagues? Is there a stage at which intervention is too late to avoid a breakdown of communications?

3. The 'cultural positivity' model which was described in Figure 9 was explained using a culturally diverse group of management students. In this case study, differences in the team can be seen in respect to gender, age, class and culture. How could the model be used in order to reduce conflicts based on these dimensions?

4. What are the costs of conflicts such as this? How might the team's performance be affected by the differences outlined above?

5. Are there benefits to team diversity? In this case, can the differences of background be used to the advantage of the team? How might the team be organised to encourage the participants to think about the positive aspects of diversity?

EXPLORE FURTHER

DANIELS, K. and MACDONALD, L. (2005) *Equality, Dversity and Discrimination*. London, CIPD

This book is relevant for various equality-and-diversity-type HR and business degree modules. Designed for those students taking such modules it includes case studies and useful real-life examples.

FLYNN, M. and MCNAIR, S. (2007) *Managing Age: A guide to good employment practice*. London, CIPD/Trades Union Congress

This guide explores in more detail the issues around age, work and retirement. It is focused on a practitioner audience and aims to support the development of good approaches to age management.

HARVEY, C. P. and ALLARD, M. J. (2005) *Understanding and Managing Diversity*, 3rd edition. London, Pearson/Prentice Hall

This book provides a combination of varied readings, real-life case studies and various thought-provoking exercises. Its treatment of the topic of workplace diversity helps to prepare students today for working in an environment where it is necessary to understand all the issues that relate to diversity.

TAYLOR, P. (2006) *Employment Initiatives for an Ageing Workforce in the EU-15*. Luxemburg, Office for Official Publications of the European Communities

This guide provides interesting examples of good practice that have emerged throughout Europe.

SECTION 2
Employee Resourcing

CHAPTER 7

HR planning

Andrew Mayo

INTRODUCTION

'The right people in the right place with the right skills at the right time' is a fundamental goal of HRM. This chapter explores the balance between external and internal resourcing – both the strategic considerations and practical planning techniques. It also looks at the dynamics of internal movement and promotion, career patterns, types of potential and managing continuity for the organisation. The next chapter deals with the processes of recruiting – this one is about what leads up to that.

LEARNING OUTCOMES

By the end of this chapter readers should be able to:

- explain and apply the basic principles of workforce planning

- explain the different kinds of potential for growth that employees have and how these can be utilised in longer-term planning

- define the different steps needed in putting together a system of succession planning, and explain what is needed for it to operate successfully

- explain how individual career planning can be helped and encouraged, and how this interacts with succession planning.

Resourcing in today's organisations is much more complex than the recruitment and selection of permanently contracted employees. There are many ways by which a person may contribute to an organisation, and we see very different mixes from sector to sector. Especially desirable resources are described by Boxall and Purcell (2007; p.75) as 'valuable and scarce, inimitable (hard to copy), non-substitutable and appropriate (meaning that they are directly relevant to the purpose of the organisation)'.

The first part of this two-part chapter can be seen as 'macro' in that it analyses the organisational-level requirements for human resources in terms of numbers and skills. This will give us ways to ensure that each group of employees is correctly resourced at a given time, to meet the business plan. The future is always uncertain, but without a plan we are left merely reacting to events. The second part is more at the 'micro' level – seeing how individuals fit into the plan, and also what plans they should have for themselves.

The chapter concludes with the main case study.

Reference sources named within the chapter may be looked up in the *References and further reading* section at the end of the book.

STARTER CASE STUDY

The holding company of a series of retail brands left the operational side firmly in the hands of the local management of each subsidiary. However, the staff functions, such as Finance and HR, were strongly co-ordinated from the centre. The company made two or three acquisitions per year, and in addition its revenues grew organically at about 6% per year.

The Finance Director became increasingly concerned, despite having good compensation packages, that the company was constantly losing professional finance people. There were about 120 such positions across the Group and about 20 left each year. He often had to resort to interim appointments, because recruitment was a long process.

Questions for discussion

You are a consultant called in to help him solve this problem. What kind of questions would you ask?

1 THE RESOURCING STRATEGY

Organisations always have a choice of whether to plan for the future or whether to be agile, responsive and opportunistic based on the needs of the moment. There are risks in both approaches. The former can result in masses of analysis and lengthy papers which soon become out of date and in practice may not be used. If we do no planning, we risk being short of our most essential resource, people, and incurring expensive ad hoc recruitment or temporary staffing that eats into our budgets. The strategically minded HR professional will, however, want to look ahead and be prepared – both to meet the demands of the business plan and for emergencies should they arise.

There is also overwhelming evidence that companies that plan for *continuity* achieve more sustainable results and growth. Collins and Porras (1994), in a book called *Built to Last,* researched organisations that had been consistently successful for between 50 and 100 years to see what common characteristics there might be. They found that one was a focus on internal promotion. In a total of 1,700 years of corporate history of these great companies, only four occasions were found of hiring an external CEO. This is a long way from today's normal practice, where the average life of a CEO in public companies is less than three years. Planning for succession means planning development experiences for people over time. McCall, Lombardo and Morrison (1998; p.5) argue for the importance of systematically managing experiences as the fundamental source of executive learning. They assert (from their research) that 'companies viewed as better managed do more of this than less well-managed companies.'

Questions on which an organisation has to make crucial strategic decisions include:

- At different levels, in filling vacancies, what would be the ideal ratio of internal promotion to external recruitment?

It may be that strategically you need to attract in as much experience as you can from outside, or you feel you really do need a shake-up by bringing in new blood. But once things have stabilised, the desired ratio will generally be in the 80% internal promotion range.

- What should be the ratio of 'fixed' resource (employees with contracts) to 'variable' resource (sub-contract, temporary, interim people)?

This of course depends on the nature of the organisation – whether it is seasonal in its business or subject to other peaks and troughs. 'Interim' people are contracted for a short time to fill a job – typically for three to nine months – to cover (for example) a maternity leave or a lengthy recruitment period for a full-time person.

- Which positions are critical in terms of continuity?

These are the ones we want to plan succession for – we look at this in more detail later.

- How will our diversity policy influence resourcing?

Many organisations today positively seek to reflect the community in which they operate and/or their customers through their employment profile. This leads to setting targets at particular job levels.

WHAT CAN WE KNOW ABOUT THE FUTURE?

There are things we know and things we do not know – things that will happen and things that may never happen – but for which we want to be prepared. Figure 10 shows the factors that must be taken into account in resource planning.

Let us briefly look more closely at the factors involved.

- *The vision and strategy,* the goals of the organisation – Where is the organisation heading? Is it on a strong growth path? Expanding into new

Figure 10 Factors that affect a resourcing plan

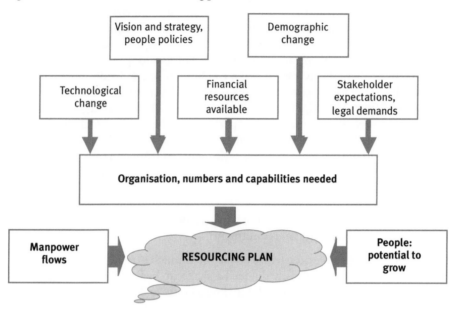

Source: based on Mayo (2004; p.115)

areas? Restructuring the organisation design (such as reducing levels)? Or planning to outsource functions in the future? What will all this mean for numbers and capabilities of people over, say, six monthly chunks ahead?

● *The people policies* – This is where the answers to the strategic questions outlined above come in. What are the policies on resourcing? If there are long-term diversity goals, what effect will this have on recruitment?

● *Demographic change* – Within our normal labour pools are there going to be enough skilled people available in the future?

● *Technological change* – Future technology changes the requirements for people, bringing in new capabilities and making redundant older ones. Planning enables us to reskill employees and reduces actual people redundancies, which both cause pain to people and cost a lot of money. Technology also affects productivity – we may need fewer people to get the same amount of work done.

● *The financial resources available* – Too often this is allowed to define the 'headcount' of an organisation on its own, taking a short-term view. Nevertheless, sometimes budgets are cut in both private and public sectors, and there are limits to what can be afforded. Activities have to be reduced or eliminated.

● *Stakeholder expectations and legal demands* – The law constantly changes and affects resourcing. Examples are the 48-hour week restriction, provision of holidays for long-term temporary staff, and extensions to maternity allowances. Customers are ever more demanding and may look for new services (such as internet purchases), and politicians both central and local make continually changing demands on public servants.

All the above are factors to take into account as an organisation looks ahead. Some will be more precise than others in their implications. But, job family by job family, we should be able to make estimates of how the numbers will change over time – and whether those families will need new capabilities to continue their role. Now, instead of looking to the future we want to look at history and the data we have at present about our employees.

- *Manpower flows* – Our organisation should be divided into job families, and for each we need to be able to answer a lot of questions (see below) to help us understand what is likely to happen to that family in the future. This analysis is essential to compare with the requirements of future resource needs,

- *People and potential* – Finally, at the individual employee level, assuming we are committed to internal development, we need to know the *potential* of people to grow and do different jobs in the future.

WORKFORCE PLANNING

'Workforce planning' is sometimes used wrongly to mean 'HR planning in general', but is actually the modern name given to what used to be called 'manpower planning'. Bennison and Casson (1984; p.8), who wrote still the best guide to this subject, said that 'A stand-alone manpower planning system must be replaced by manpower management.' In other words, any system is but a means towards more effective resource management. If we can do it effectively, it helps us to do the following:

- make a recruitment plan and be ahead of the game, so that vacancies are minimised

- specifically define the number of young entrants, such as graduates and trainees, that we need

- plan for continuity of key expertise and positions

- plan for individual career development to ensure that we have the managerial responsibility and technical/professional leadership to meet the needs

- plan for core competence training to be available as needed.

To do this we need to have a very good understanding of the internal demographics of the organisation – by function, division, location and staff category. For the latter it is useful to use the concept of *job families* – defined as groups of employees who share common characteristics in terms of entry requirements to the job, and a similar job market.

REFLECTIVE ACTIVITY

Think of a university as an organisation.

List as many job families as you can think of that work there.

What do we need to know about job families?

To help us with forward planning, we would like to know – from analysis of the factors that affect a resourcing plan (see Figure 10) – the expected number of people needed in this job family quarter by quarter, plus any critical capability changes. Benison and Casson (1984) talk of 'push' and 'pull' flows – the former being when people move into a job family and the latter when they move out. We therefore need to know:

- the distribution of length of service

- losses for, say, the last two years and the reasons for loss

- where people transfer to and from within the organisation

- the number of people expecting to retire

- the distribution of potential

- the map of key competency distribution.

Stephen Connock (1991) also recommends studying where employees live in relation to the location of the organisation as an additional factor in understanding employee movements.

This data, together with our forward look, enables us to get a picture of what is happening, and what we can predict will happen *within* a job family – but as we link job families together, we can also achieve a number of outcomes, such as:

- forecasting future flows out of, into, and within the organisation

- consequent decisions about young entrant recruitment and actions to reduce attrition in some areas

- planning accelerated development for some individuals

- strengthening of areas that are weak in potential and succession

- taking action on retention of key and potential staff

- creating new career paths

- planning significant capability shifts (and preparing for them).

Modelling a job family itself

Figure 11 illustrates the flows into and out of a job family group.

Figure 11 Flows in and out of a job family

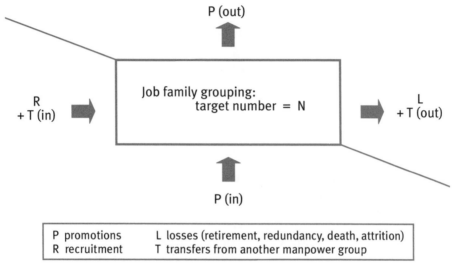

P promotions   L losses (retirement, redundancy, death, attrition)
R recruitment   T transfers from another manpower group

*Note: 'Attrition' is a word often used for people leaving the organisation.
It may be voluntary or involuntary. 'Labour turnover' is a term used for
the percentage of attrition compared with the total workforce.*

First, we decide our planning period – it might typically be six or twelve months
ahead. The target number at the end of the period is N. We then feed in our
predictions, based on history plus future expectations, of:

- **L**: losses out of the organisation (for which we are planning)
- **T** (out): lateral transfers out of this group to other groups
- **T** (in): lateral transfers into this group from another
- **P** (out): promotions to the group above
- **P** (in): promotions from the group below.

Finally, we can calculate the expected recruitment requirement (R) over the
period ahead. If R turns out to be a negative figure, we will need to either
increase the transfers out (if possible) or will need to manage some redundancies.
Note that time takes care of many workforce changes, many organisations
(especially in the public sector) just cut off recruitment, increase transfers and
wait for the N to stabilise over time.

REFLECTIVE ACTIVITY

Suppose we have a call centre with 140 operators currently. The expansion of the company means that at the end of the six-month period for which we are planning we need 160. There are no promotions into the group, and typically two are promoted to supervisor per year. An average of 10 per year transfer to other tasks in the organisation, and four per year transfer in from other groups. Losses average 20% per year.

What will be the recruitment requirement over the next six months?

You will see, in this case, that the recruitment requirement is quite high and will in practice be continuous. *Supposing the overall number was reducing to 130 – what difference would this make?*

In endeavouring to find answers for the exercise above, historical data is where we start, but we must be careful not to calculate ahead using this as our sole base. Other interventions may affect the future figures. Perhaps the group of supervisors will show signs of stabilising and there will be fewer promotion possibilities than before. Perhaps we do not have enough people with potential to fill the three vacancies if they occurred. Maybe we are taking positive steps to reduce the level of attrition losses, and expect them to be lower than the 20% average. So the numbers we use will always be a judgement of all the facts available to us.

Figure 11 has four arrows in two directions which interact with other parts of the organisation. So we go on to integrate all the job families together, as shown diagrammatically in Figure 12. This is a simplification, especially at the

Figure 12 Integrating the manpower flows horizontally and vertically

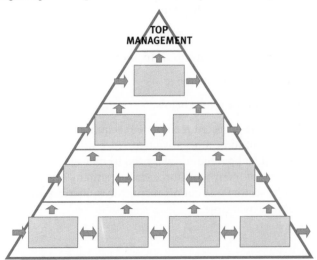

horizontal level, because the transfer arrows from one box may go in to more than one other. However, a model can be built up using Excel or special software that represents a particular organisation.

Using staffing ratios

One common technique in determining numbers needed is to use some guiding ratios. For example, in the exercise above, how many employees will we have per supervisor? The more we have, the lower our costs, but the more difficult it is for a supervisor to provide individual attention and feedback – a classic cost-versus-quality dilemma in staff planning. How many support staff do we need per salesperson? Answers to questions like this vary enormously with the business sector and how complex a sale is. How many employees per HR professional? With such ratios we always start with the bottom of the organisation, or the 'front line' and work inwards. So far we have concentrated only on the numbers. However, workforce planning is not just about the right number of people at the right time – but also about people with the right skills.

Capability planning

For each job family we need to identify the critical core skills essential for the job to be done. There may be others we wish to develop in people, but our business planning focus is on the core. To do this we must have a 'scale of expertise' – and this would typically be a description of four or five levels. Here is one such scale:

- A: Aware: knows what it means
- B: Basic: can talk about it
- C: Competent: can put it into practice
- D: Distinguished: people come and ask how
- E: Expert: teaches others.

One of several pictures we can build up about a job family is shown in the example in Figure 13. Note that this distinguishes between an 'entry level' – the minimum needed to get the job – and a 'fully competent level' – the level we would expect after training and experience. Under each person we have an estimate of his or her current level.

This profile describes our current situation: we can draw up a second one for how we would like it to be at the end of our planning period. Note that it takes time to grow capabilities and we may therefore use a longer planning period here. The comparison of the desired future and where we are now clearly informs our training requirements, but may also dictate the recruitment of specific expertise if we are short of it. No team can operate with every person at the 'entry level', for example. Also, our forward look may dictate *new* capabilities needed – required by technology change, for example.

The requirement for young entrants

For many jobs, the age of people we recruit is not important, and the law does not allow us to discriminate on this basis. Nevertheless, young people with

Figure 13 Core skill profile of assistants in a retail store

KNOWLEDGE OR SKILL	Entry level	Fully competent level	Person 1	Person 2	Person 3	Person 4
Product knowledge and demonstrations	A	C	D	B	C	C
Operation of discount/promotion schemes	A	C	C	C	C	B
Operation of guarantee and service	A	C	C	C	C	C
Sourcing of items	A	D	C	D	C	B
IT systems	B	C	C	D	C	C
Team cooperation	C	C	B	D	C	C
Personal customer delight skills	B	D	C	D	B	C

varying qualifications enter the job market all the time and we need a strategy for their recruitment. Some organisations will say that because young people rarely stay with them more than two or three years, it does not make sense to go to all the expense of recruitment and training just to lose them. It is better, therefore, they would say, to bring in people already trained. Others will say quite the opposite – that it is vital to get the best talent available from Day 1, immerse them in the culture, train them thoroughly and do the best to keep them. Deloittes, for example, is one of the large professional firms putting immense effort into recruiting the best possible graduates.

The range of qualified young entrants is large and we may need to consider several groups. These may include school-leavers with no qualifications other than GCSEs or A-levels, school-leavers with vocational qualifications, ordinary graduates, high-quality graduates, specialised Masters, MBAs, and PhDs. Each of these groups needs different recruitment approaches. Many organisations build up special relationships with academic institutions to ensure good access to the best students in order to regenerate their 'talent bank'. Where graduates have a choice, surveys repeatedly show that training schemes feature strongly in their priorities.

OPTIONS FOR RESOURCES

We naturally think of the people in organisations as employees, and indeed, all the models we have discussed above relate to such. However, in today's world reality is more complex, especially in the highly flexible UK environment. What we call 'employees' are those who have an employment contract with the organisation that makes them a part of the organisation and brings them under the umbrella of all the appropriate benefits, policies and disciplines. They may be 'full-time' or 'part-time' – the latter typically describing a stated number of hours per week. Some jobs may be shared by two part-time people. Because of this mix, the term 'full-time equivalents' or FTEs is often used as the basis of workforce planning. It is not the same as 'headcount' – which is the number of people actually on the payroll. The decision for part-time may be dictated by the workload or is often by employee request in line with their work–life balance.

For many reasons we may supplement the employees with additional people, sometimes called the 'contingent workforce' (see Chapter 10). Among these are temporary and interim contracts, typically used for filling absences, coping with temporary overload or leading a special change project; and sub-contract staff – people with specialised knowledge or skills used on projects. These both typically have a fixed-term contract, which may be renewed. They work within the organisation and after a time develop certain legal rights. In addition, there may be sets of consultants, doing research and analysis, providing advice, suggesting change, working to fixed deliverables rather than for a fixed time. The requirement for consultants is dictated primarily by the capability and capacity of the existing staff. In addition, they may be used to specifically tap into the external world, or for 'political' reasons – using outsiders to bring into the open uncomfortable truths.

REFLECTIVE ACTIVITY

Should we minimise or maximise the core resource – our employees?

List the advantages of dedicated employees on the one hand, and contingent workers on the other.

What kind of organisation would have a higher-than-average ratio of contingent workers?

2 PLANNING FOR THE INDIVIDUAL

THE POTENTIAL OF PEOPLE TO GROW

Figure 10 showed that an essential input to a resourcing plan is the knowledge we have about people's potential to grow and their ability to do something different in the future. Each job family needs a profile of the potential that exists within it. 'Potential' is often seen in very limited way as referring to those who have the ability to become future senior managers. Actually, this is very unlikely to exceed more than 1% of the workforce – and surely, we cannot say that 99% have *no* potential. Figure 14 illustrates three dimensions of potential. 'Height' is about the traditional high-flyers – people rising up through the management ranks. 'Depth' is about creating world-class expertise in core competences, the potential to

Figure 14 The three dimensions of 'potential'

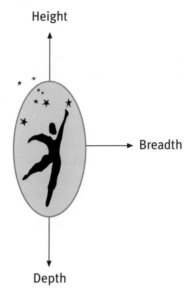

Source: Mayo (1994; p.118)

deepen knowledge and eventually provide technical leadership. 'Breadth' recognises the value that comes from individuals who can turn their hands to several different kinds of job – 'lateral' potential.

To achieve the profile of a group, we must have a system of classification – a shorthand. However, there are many dangers in 'labelling' people. After all, any classification is only a judgement at a point in time – and people change. A good term to use, therefore, is 'current perception of potential'. This also makes it much easier to have an open dialogue with individuals about it.

In choosing classifications, options for describing 'height' available include an assessment of the *speed* of rising responsibility (eg two levels within four years); an assessment of *levels* beyond the current one (eg able to rise two levels); and an estimate of the person's *ceiling* (eg 'will make Grade 15'). We will want a broader classification if we take the extended view of talent. The classification used by a young software company is as follows:

M1 = Able to progress to a senior management position within three years

M2 = Able to progress to take management responsibility

TP = Able to progress to a leadership role (not necessarily managing people) in his/her technological or professional expertise

L = Able to progress laterally and learn new skills outside of his/her current job

O = Likely to stay in present job at present level, and develop with the job

E = Ability not suited to the current position and level.

Should we classify certain groups only in the workforce, or everybody? Talent may lurk in unexpected quarters. Besides, it will be very useful to know the distribution of talent for the population as a whole – and where strong and weak pockets currently exist.

REFLECTIVE ACTIVITY

What do you think would be the key characteristics you would look for in deciding whether a person had the potential of 'height', 'depth' or 'breadth'?

POTENTIAL ASSESSMENT

How can we find out what a person's classification should be? We must not be confused by great performance in the current job. It is good news, of course, but is not a certain indicator of an ability to do a bigger job in the future. The problem is that we are trying to judge whether someone would succeed in a job he/she is not yet doing.

Figure 15 summarises some of the methods that can be used. One dimension is that of the number of assessors – the more we have, the better judgement we are likely to make. An 'assessment centre' is a series of simulated exercises reflecting the target job level, with trained multi-assessors and a systematic evaluation of required capabilities. As is often the case in professional HR, there is a trade-off between cost and quality. The second dimension is that of the observation period. Some methods take into account what we have observed over time.

Figure 15 Options for assessing potential

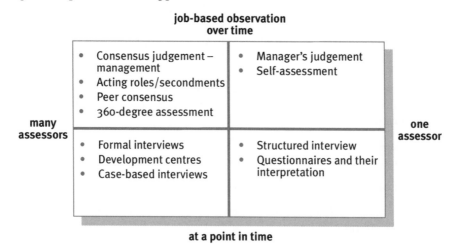

Others, like the psychologist interview and the assessment centre, take an in-depth look at a point in time. For a first evaluation, we would rely on a manager's judgement. We would deploy the more sophisticated approaches with those who are thought to have the highest potential (height or depth).

'TALENT MANAGEMENT'

'Talent management' is a term frequently heard. What does it mean? It refers to the processes of:

- recruitment: seeking the best people in the marketplace
- motivation: enabling them to give of their best
- retention: doing one's best to keep them in the organisation
- development: growing their capability
- career progression: meeting their career ambitions.

As applied to people judged to be 'talented' – ie capable of providing superior added value to the organisation and its stakeholders – the definition of 'talent' is key here. How broad will we make it? Will it include people who do a superb everyday job but who are not going to get promoted? Sadler (1993) talks of the 'talent-intensive organisation', and lists four main categories of talent: specialist expertise, the ability to lead, business-getting talent, and hybrid talent (a combination of the others).

There is a good argument for saying that if we apply these processes to *all* employees, we will avoid being discriminatory and open to accusations of favouritism – and still we will be looking after our 'talent'. Further, we will expand the pool of talent available beyond the narrow way it is often conceived of in organisations.

SUCCESSION, OR CONTINUITY, PLANNING

Organisations can survive without planning for the future, but they will almost certainly incur costs that they could avoid. Particularly at senior levels, the cost of recruitment is very high. Unfortunately, it is rarely highlighted as a separate cost in the accounts but is swallowed up in various cost lines – salaries, consultants, advertising expenses, and so on. We will never avoid it completely, and sometimes we have good reasons to deliberately bring in new blood. But what we might call *continuity* is highly valuable. It means that vacant posts are not sitting waiting to be filled, and that knowledge and experience is passed on from one person to another in a systematic way. It is a good idea to set some targets, appropriate for the particular business, such as:

- the percentage of vacancies to be filled by inside promotion (this may depend on the level in the organisation – so we may have several targets), or
- the number of key posts with identified successors.

There are additional benefits from the planning process. It provides the basis for a 'health audit' in terms of the potential that does or does not exist in the organisation, and also for individual discussions with people about their careers. It helps too in achieving diversity targets as we systematically audit and plan the development of people. This kind of planning is often called *succession planning*. The outcomes of the process are:

- a plan for filling unexpected vacancies
- a longer-term plan for providing continuity of posts and development of people
- an audit of continuity strength
- proactive career moves
- regular lists of people for whom action is required.

Selecting the jobs that need planning

It would be a bureaucratic overkill to plan succession for every job in an organisation. Some jobs are more critical than others in terms of the need for continuity. A 'critical position' is one where:

- success depends on an intimate knowledge of the organisation and its people, and/or
- a time gap in continuity of the position would have serious business effects (leadership and direction, customer relationships, key investment decisions, programme momentum), and/or
- the skill/experience is very hard to find.

Such positions could be individual jobs or generic jobs. Figure 16 shows an example of identifying the jobs for which long-term planning is needed. There are at least two 'planning horizons'. The first is 'now' – what we do in the event

Figure 16 Mapping critical positions in an organisation

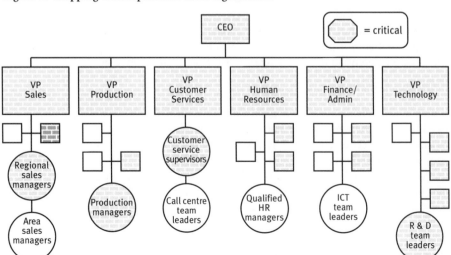

of an unexpected vacancy. The second is some time in the future – two years ahead, for example, or maybe both two years and five years. Note that today's organisation chart is unlikely to be the same in five years' time, but our future scanning – which we talked about at the beginning of the chapter – may help identify new positions that are anticipated and that require planning. It is the names that we are able to put in the longer-term slots that lead to proactive career and development planning.

The information that is needed

For each position we have identified, we need to know the following information:

- *the key requirements for the job: essential levels of knowledge, skills and experience*

  If we are recruiting from outside we will want the best and most experienced person we can find. Internally, however, all jobs are part of the process of development and are learning opportunities in themselves. So the level we look for does not need to be so high. Despite the temptation to pick someone who is already very capable, all jobs should be used as part of the process of continuing development. Each job therefore has a 'minimum entry' level and a 'maturity level' – the knowledge, skills and experience of someone who has mastered the job.

- *information about the person(s) in the job today*

  We will probably have a lot of information about all employees, but what we need specifically here is data related to the current job-holder's likelihood of moving on. There may be a planned retirement date, although this is by no means as cut-and-dried as it used to be. A judgement of the 'risk of leaving' is helpful – the higher we judge the risk, the more concerned we would be about succession. A particularly useful piece of data is 'earliest date for a move'. This will be based on the ideal time to be in a job – the higher or more complex the job is, the longer that will be. The date is then calculated based on the date of starting the job – and it signals action. We will not necessarily move someone on at that date, but it tells us he or she is ready for a move – and may indeed be getting impatient for one. We will also need to know the current perception of the person's potential: in what direction will his/her next move be?

- *information about the possible successors*

  For each possible successor, we need the above information as well. We also need to know their profiles of knowledge, skills and experience to match against the job requirements. The very choice of considering them as a successor is based on our judgement of their ability to reach the entry level of the job. They may be ready now – or will be ready after some specific development actions. This is what leads to the individual career and development plans.

A process to make it all work

It is no use doing all this planning if nobody takes any notice of it when a vacancy occurs. It cannot be a backroom task done in isolation by HR people, and must involve line managers. The most successful organisations are those in which the CEO chairs review and decision meetings, and requires a high standard of data and of commitment by all concerned.

An approach developed by ICL, now Fujitsu Systems, and subsequently widely adopted is one that integrates succession discussions with operational business reviews (see Mayo, 1994; p.267). Generally termed the 'organisational and management review' (OMR) or similar, it synchronises a formal review of issues such as succession, key people development, strategic training issues, and potential strength with the cycle of business reviews. Typically, this might take place every four to six months, being 'cascaded' upwards through business units and subsidiary companies, eventually reaching the CEO. Each level in the cascade generates information that feeds into the next level.

This approach puts the ownership with line management, links business performance with people capability, recognises the dynamism of organisational and people development, and provides continually updated succession information. Actions to close gaps or deal with problems can be taken regularly. Items that might be on the agenda of the meeting include:

- the current structure and people; the changes anticipated

- the distribution of potential

- who should be considered for a move in the next period

- who is at risk

- succession problems and gaps

- series of planned moves

- review of process and data – are they satisfactory?

HR has a number of key roles to play. It will be the designers and owners of the process, responsible for making it successful. It should try to ensure consistent standards of judgements and classification. HR is a broker and boundary-spanner – enabling successors to be considered from, and career moves to take place, across the whole organisation. Its personnel may also be counsellors and advisers to managers.

Several specialised software systems have been created, aimed at succession planning and talent management. Particularly useful for large, complex and changing organisations, they enable immediate identification of successors. However, whatever system is used, its strength is always dependent on the quality, reliability and recency of the data in the system.

PERSONAL CAREER PLANNING

So far we have looked at everything from the point of view of the organisation. But every individual also evaluates his or her own progress and ambition. Most people are not actually very ambitious in the sense of wanting to have a senior role. But they still care about their career – having a sense of moving forward in life.

Just as many organisations are opportunistic in respect of vacancies when they do not have good plans, so most individuals think most about their careers when a change is imminent. Is it better to have a plan, even though the future is uncertain, or not to bother? That is a personal decision, of course. But an organisation that believes in strategic resourcing would encourage employees to plan. The organisation should help individuals to look at options by making information available. The organisation should make information available about the nature of jobs and their requirements – the minimum entry levels referred to above. The organisation can be drawn diagrammatically in the form of a 'map of learning opportunities' showing which jobs provide particular areas of knowledge and experience. There are some career moves that are easier to make than others – so we can identify some typical career paths and acceptable 'bridges' across boundaries and functions. There will be more bridges at the lower levels of the organisation than further up, because specialised knowledge is less of a requirement. So each person should be able to see the options from his or her current job for where he or she could move next. This vision of possibilities is likely to be conditioned by the department the person is in – ie what he or she is familiar with. This additional information will broaden horizons.

The other kind of help is to enable people to understand themselves and their ambitions, using motivational and interest tests, perhaps career guidance events or skilled career counselling. To help them plan ahead, they should always be encouraged to look beyond the next step alone – five to seven years ahead with a clear aiming-point would be reasonable for most. Choosing the aiming-point (there could be two or three alternatives) is the critical and often the most difficult part. Once it is chosen, we can look at the routes to get there – some training perhaps, but mostly the focus should be on 'building-blocks of experience'. These will provide most of the knowledge, skills, contacts and, of course, experience itself that is needed to bridge the identified 'career gap'. Such experience derives not only in the form of job changes but may be achieved by secondments, job enlargement, assignments, projects, committee involvement, and so on.

Secondments are one of the most valuable forms of development, and essential in 'flatter' organisations. Relatively low-risk to all parties, they provide an opportunity for new learning through real-life experiences. This has been the traditional route for international assignments, and many organisations have deployed secondees on a broader basis – to project teams, to new departments, or from line to staff posts and vice versa. Herts County Council, in an effort to mitigate a reduction in traditional career opportunities, introduced a 24-page booklet entitled *Guidelines for Effective Secondments, Job Swaps and Job Shadowing*.

Career paths

In many national and corporate cultures, development is 'silo-driven' right up to high levels. This creates a problem because when people become senior, they lack an understanding of what other functions and operations do. However, there are several general models of career development, and one has to be chosen (or evolve). Models include (Mayo, 1994):

- *the Narrow T* – In this model people remain specialists until the highest level, managing groups of their own specialism but not working outside it. It is not until the top of the 'tree' that they take broader collegiate responsibilities

- *the Wide T* – This is a model more common in the UK, where beyond, say, the first ten years of specialism and junior management, people broaden across functional boundaries and become a 'management resource' thereafter

- *the I* – Here, young entrants are given a general knowledge of the organisation and its business for perhaps up to three years. They then specialise in a chosen area, and remain in that area until reaching senior management, when they become more general again

- *the Y* – Found in highly technical organisations, career opportunities and matching rewards exist to a more or less equally high level for both specialists and generalists.

Career development is an important policy decision that has to be matched with rewards, and that clearly influences people's ability to manage their own careers. It is a classic problem of naturally hierarchical organisations that good specialists become poor managers because there is no alternative route for progress. It is a double loss. An organisation that believes in the value of varied experience has to facilitate movements across boundaries. One large international pharmaceutical company had a policy of 'two functions plus two countries plus two business units' for future general managers. Its succession planning process enabled the right movements to take place to achieve this goal over time.

 REFLECTIVE ACTIVITY

Many organisations believe it is unwise to discuss with individuals what is on the succession plan, in that it might create expectations that are never fulfilled. Others argue that openness is the only route.

List the points of argument for both sides.

On balance, which do you think is the stronger side?

Bringing personal and organisational goals together

The plans that are made must come together and match. This can only happen through open dialogue, sharing ambitions on the one hand and the collective view of potential on the other. At the end of the day we need an agreed development plan that both sides work together to put into practice. Who should conduct this dialogue? Many would say it is the job of a person's manager (and it is often expected at appraisal time) – but it could be a careers professional either within or outside the organisation. Nobody should leave an organisation because of uncertainty of the opportunities available or of how his or her potential is viewed. Sadly, such departures are all too often the case – the right dialogue has not taken place.

Vacancy management – how does succession management live alongside open job advertising?

There is an apparent dilemma between open access to jobs (via an intranet) and planned development, where the two might seem to be in conflict. This need not be so. Some organisations make it clear that above a certain level jobs will not be advertised. Others would say 'You are on the succession chart, but this is not a guarantee – it means you will be considered alongside any other suitable candidates who apply.' Some, especially in the public sector, advertise externally anyway – however, this is hard to justify if internal successors are available, and it only demotivates existing staff.

Whatever is done has to have credibility, and not appear be a showcase behind which selection is fixed. The more 'shared' the information about aspirations and perceived potential, the easier it is to have coherence between the planned and the open.

KEY ISSUES IN RESOURCING

We now pull together ten key points about resourcing raised in this chapter:

- Organisational success is totally dependent on people – on having the right people with the right skills in the right place at the right time.

- Organisations have a choice of planning for their future or being reactive and opportunistic. Successful organisations invest in planning and make clear and consistent strategic decisions over resources.

- Workforce planning starts with scanning the future, looking both at where the business wants to go and at the environment in which it expects to operate.

- The organisation can be divided up into discrete job families to find out relevant data about the members of each family and the flows in and out of it.

- Selecting a planning period, and feeding in the knowledge available, we can predict the resourcing requirements – both in numbers and in capabilities.

- There are options for resourcing – decisions to be taken about the ratios of core and peripheral staff.

- A classification for potential is a vital tool – potential has several dimensions and is not just about ascending the management ranks. A range of methods are available for assessing this.

- Succession planning, sometimes called 'continuity planning', is a key process for critical jobs in an organisation, using two categories – 'availability in the event of an emergency' and 'longer-term successors' – for whom we will have a development plan.

- To facilitate succession planning we need career paths, and we can provide significant help for individuals in their own career planning – not least of which is talking to them about it.

- Finally, we need to ensure that our policy on vacancy notification and management is consistent with all other processes.

Perhaps there are other key points that you would like to note for yourself.

The main case study in this chapter now follows. It gives an example of career planning in one particular organisation.

Make an initial reading of the case study to gain an overview of the situation, and then read the questions that you will need to address. Now read the case study again, making notes of issues and facts that will help you in your analysis and responses to the questions. Remember to 'read between the lines' as well as picking out the obvious points, and also to consider what is not said as well as what is presented here.

The Limassol Manufacturing Company is based in Cyprus and produces technical equipment for the wine industry. It employs 4,000 people. The structure of this organisation is indicated by the organisational chart (see Figure 17). In addition you have got an overview of the talent pool (see Table 17).

Table 17 Talent pool: Limassol Manufacturing Company

Department and group	Level below VP	Total number	Potential A ready for move now	Potential A not yet ready for move	Potential B ready for move now	Potential B not yet ready for move	Potential C and/or D
Manufacturing							
Production managers	1	7	0	0	1	1	5
Senior staff roles	1	4	0	0	0	0	4
Supervisors	2	20	1	0	2	1	16
Purchasing							
Senior purchasing officers	1	4	0	0	1	0	3
Junior purchasing officers	2	6	0	0	0	0	6
Sales and marketing							
Regional sales managers	1	4	1	0	1	0	2
Area sales managers	2	12	0	0	1	1	10
Marketing managers	1	3	1	0	0	1	1
Marketing officers	2		1	0	1	0	3
Finance and IT							
Finance/IT managers	1	6	0	0	1	0	5
Accountants etc	2	19	2	2	2	1	3
IT team leaders	2	6	0	0	1	0	5
Human resources							
Senior HR managers	1	3	0	0	0	0	3
HR officers	2	7	0	0	0	0	7
Comms and government							
Communications officers	1	3	0	0	0	1	2
Technology							
Technology managers	1	4	0	0	1	0	3
Team leaders	2	8	1	0	0	1	6

Figure 17 Organisation chart: Limassol Manufacturing Company

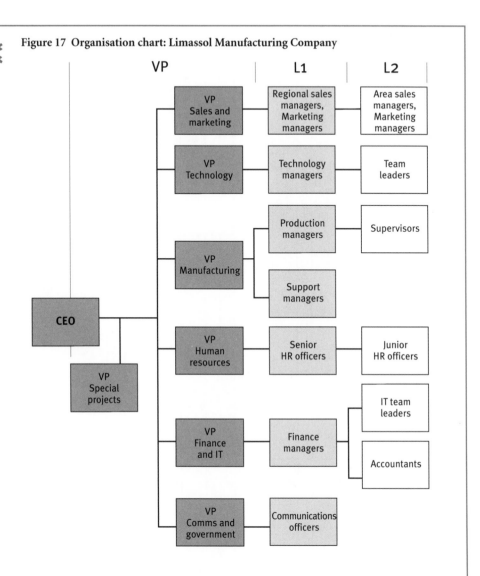

Your task

You are the Organisation and Manpower Planning Committee reviewing the attached succession plan (see Table 18). Consider the following issues:

1 What actions would you take if the VP for Finances and IT resigned?

2 How would you prepare Mr N for the position of VP Technology?

3 How would you prepare Mr O for VP Purchasing?

4 What would you do about succession to VP Communications and Government?

5 What do you conclude from examining the 'talent pool'? What actions would you place on the HR Director?

Table 18 Succession plan (January 2007): Limassol Manufacturing Company

Job title	Current holder, date app'ted, age	Exp'd date of move	risk	P'tial	Pfmance	Planned next job and date	Emergency successors	Longer term-successors and date ready	Development required
Chief Executive	Dr A 9/01, 62	6/09	L			retire	Mr D	Mr D: 3/09 / Mr I: 2013	
VP Manufacturing	Mr B 1/97, 54	now	L	D	**	early retire 2009	Mr C	Mr C / Mr O: 2010	
VP Purchasing	Mr C 5/02, 46	now	M	C	****	VP Mfg 2009	Mr O	Ms L: 2009 / Mr I: 2009	
VP Finance and IT	Mr D 3/02, 48	now	H	B	***	CEO 2009	None		customer involvement
VP Sales and marketing	Mr E 1/00, 51	now	M	B	***		Mr J	Mr K: 2009	
VP Human resources	Ms F 8/04, 43	Q4 07	M	D	***		None	Ms M: 2008 / Ms Q: 2011	
VP Comms and government	Ms G 3/05 45	09	M	C	**		None	None	
VP Technology	Dr H 1/97, 61	now	L	D	**	retire 2010	None	Mr N	
VP Special projects	Mr I 6/05, 38	07	H	B	****	VP Finance 3/09	None needed		
Level 1 below VP: Potential A and B									
Regional sales manager	Mr J 3/01, 42	now	H	A	****	VP Sales and marketing	from pool	from pool	involvement with gov'ment sales
Regional sales manager	Mr K 2/99, 48	now	L	B	***	marketing role, 2008	from pool	from pool	needs marketing experience
Management accounting manager	Ms L 4/04. 41	now	M	B	***	IT manager, 2007	from pool	from pool	wider experience of finance/IT
Factory HR manager	Ms M 6/05, 36	08	H	B	***	Managemt developmt mgr, 1/08	None	None	involvement in HR strategy
Product marketing manager	Mr N 4/03, 45	now	M	A	****		from pool	from pool	
Production manager	Mr O 4/02, 47	now	L	B	***		from pool	from pool	more people mgt exper'nce staff role in Manufac'ing
Production manager	Mr P 5/04, 39	Q3 07	M	B	***	Senior staff, Mfg	from pool	from pool	appropriate courses
R&D manager, Tech dept	Mr R 4/99, 47	now	L	B	***	?	from pool	from pool	
Press relations officer	Ms Q 3/06, 27	6/07	M	B	****	Job in HR, 2008	Recruit	Recruit	HR generalist position

Notes   Risk: **H** high   **M** medium   **L** low
Potential (P'tial):   **A** high potential; fast mover   **B** some potential; move one level   **C** lateral move   **D** in the right job

EXPLORE FURTHER

BENNISON, M. and CASSON, J. (1984) *The Manpower Planning Handbook*. Maidenhead, McGraw-Hill

This is the classic textbook on workforce planning. It covers most of the areas we have examined, including a variety of other planning models. It also deals with creating strategies and has a chapter on managing careers. The chapter on analysing wastage is a classic.

McBEATH, G. (1992) *The Handbook of Human Resource Planning*. London, CIPD

This highly practical book examines the implications for organisations of rapid business change and of constant changes in manpower. It presents a systematic approach for analysing the flows and current skills of existing employees and for formulating strategies to acquire and develop skills for tomorrow from new and from existing staff.

MAYO, A. (1994) *Managing Careers – Strategies for Organisations*. London, IPM

This was the first book in Europe to look at career management from the organisation's perspective. It starts with looking at future needs and the influence of culture on the way careers work. It examines all the systems and data needed, and includes chapters on individual counselling and managing personal growth. Chapter 6 particularly discusses the data needed for the purposes of this chapter.

CHAPTER 8

Recruitment

Ian Favell

INTRODUCTION

Recruitment and selection is a core area of HRM (French, 2007), and is crucial to the successful functioning of an organisation (Pilbream and Corbridge, 2006). It is a critical mechanism to make sure that the organisation has the right skills, expertise and qualifications to deliver the key organisational objectives. This chapter looks at some of the important issues that should be considered in an effective recruitment process. It should be read in conjunction with Chapter 7 on HR Planning and Chapter 9 on Selection, because these go hand in hand – one being 'pre-' and the other being 'post-' the recruitment process.

LEARNING OUTCOMES

By the end of this chapter readers should be able to:

- list some of the factors that should be considered before starting a recruitment process

- identify a range of methods for reaching potential candidates

- explain aspects and approaches to advertising that can be critical to an effective recruitment process

- give an overview of the timing and topics that should be part of an effective induction programme.

The chapter is in three parts. Part 1 is an overview of the whole recruitment process, and the key steps involved. Part 2 then picks up some important but often glossed-over issues that should be considered in trying to attract the best applicants for a job. Finally, Part 3 considers effective induction, to make sure that the organisation keeps the good people who have been recruited.

The chapter concludes with the main case study.

Reference sources named within the chapter may be looked up in the *References and further reading* section at the end of the book.

STARTER CASE STUDY

Billy Brown's Butchers is a chain of seven butcher's shops preparing and providing fresh meat and cooked meat products for several small and medium-sized market towns in Hampshire. Each shop has a senior butcher, a junior butcher and a sales assistant. Three of the shops also have as part of the premises a small teashop that serves (for example) hot pies, sausage rolls and pasties. Following the recent retirement of the senior butcher in Fareham, the junior butcher at Lambton (who the owner had been watching with approval for some months now) was invited to move to Fareham to take over as the senior butcher as a replacement. This left a vacancy in Fareham for a junior butcher. One of the young women teashop assistants expressed interest in being trained up to take this vacancy, and the junior butcher at Liphook also asked to change branches to progress to this larger branch and build on his experience. However, the owner – always bullish in his approach – decided that the chain needed some new blood, and saw this as an opportunity to recruit externally, effectively cutting out the two existing members of staff who were interested.

The owner placed a small advertisement in the local paper for two weeks, and was pleased to find that a number of people applied. However, when looking through the applications, the owner was not pleased to find that most were inexperienced, and that some very unsuitable people had applied (including some who were obviously not English and were therefore unlikely to understand the needs of a typical English family's meat requirements). Several of the applications also appeared to be from young women, who obviously had not considered the nature of the business and the strength required. He did, however, have one application from an ex-serviceman, who appeared to have worked in a kitchen on a battleship. He was appointed immediately, and started the following week.

Questions for consideration and discussion

1   What could have caused the number of poor applications? What could the owner have done to widen the range of applications?

2   How do you think the staff might have reacted to the appointment to the senior butcher posts from within the ranks? What are the issues about how this appointment was made?

3   How do you think the staff might have reacted to the external advertisement, when internal staff had expressed interest?

4   What was unlawful about the approach taken by the owner?

5   How far might such poor practice be present in your own organisation (or one you know well)?

6   How should the situation have been handled, for maximum effectiveness?

1 THE RECRUITMENT PROCESS

WHY IS EFFECTIVE RECRUITMENT IMPORTANT?

Organisations are only able to provide goods and services because of the efforts of the people employed by them. Without good people, working effectively together, the organisation is much less likely to be able to provide what is needed by its customers. Having the right person in the right job at the right time is therefore critical to success (Bilsberry, 1996).

Another point that many organisations do not yet realise is the importance of the link between effective recruitment and other processes within the organisation. If the recruitment process is weak, it is possible that a person recruited will not perform particularly well. This is likely to give rise to performance management issues, which in turn may lead to significant training and development to enable him or her to work effectively and efficiently. If the individual had been recruited effectively, this chain reaction would have been avoided, or at least minimised, saving time, effort and costs.

If the recruitment process is not effective, then as well as probably causing these issues, the individual concerned is likely to quickly become demotivated and may well leave, giving rise to a need to start the recruitment process all over again (Taylor, 2005b). Effective recruitment is therefore key to business success.

Who should be involved in the recruitment process?

Recruitment is usually undertaken for one of two reasons: either to fill a vacancy (Taylor, 2005b) or – as with many graduate schemes – to enable promising individuals to enter the organisation on a fixed-length work-based development programme leading to later permanency.

With a graduate programme, those involved are usually the HR department and specialist training managers or project managers, who recruit into the scheme and then as part of the ongoing programme arrange secondments in various parts of the organisation for those recruited. For a vacancy, however, much depends on the size of the organisation. In larger organisations, the HR department often has the most important role, the section manager taking part mainly in specifying the job to be done and attending the interviews. In a smaller organisation there may not actually be an HR department, so section managers are more likely to take full responsibility themselves, perhaps guided by a manager who has a specialist responsibility for people issues.

To ensure effectiveness in recruitment, it is important to identify the key parts of the recruitment process (see the box below). Although there is no exactly 'correct' approach, the following is drawn from a wide range of authors (for example, ACAS; Roberts, 1997; Taylor, 2005b) and is absolutely typical of what many organisations might use.

The effective recruitment process

- identification of basic need
- job analysis
- make the case and gain approval to recruit
- job description
- person specification
- decision regarding selection methods
- decisions regarding advertising and application methods
- design and place advertisements
- receive applications
- shortlist
- interviews and tests
- selection decision
- acceptance/rejection letters
- references
- contractual issues
- induction

REFLECTIVE ACTIVITY

Think about the approach taken by an organisation you know well.

To what extent does it include the elements listed in the box above? Are all the elements present? What might be the effect of having some missing, or perhaps in a different order? Are there any additional steps taken? In what ways do these add value and assist in making the process effective?

Identification of recruitment need

Before beginning any recruitment activity, the first step is to make sure that there is a need (Taylor, 2005b, particularly stresses this). There may well have been a previous post-holder, but that in itself does not necessarily mean that the person has to be replaced. Perhaps the components of the job are not required any more, or not in the same form, or maybe the work could be divided and spread between other jobs. Another option is to outsource the job perhaps overseas or to use agency staff to do the work as and when there is a need. It is important therefore to establish exactly what the work requirement is, and whether that is sufficient to give rise to a recruitment situation. Normally, once decided, this will need authorisation because organisations are rightly concerned to control recruitment

Job analysis, making the case and gaining approval

Having decided that there is indeed a need, the job or details of the activity should be analysed and examined to find out exactly what sort of requirement there is, so that a case can be made for finance or permissions and authority to undertake recruitment. Organisations of course vary in their approach. Some managers are given their budgets, and they are able to recruit as and when they see fit to meet the demands of their sections. This might be especially true in larger organisations where, for example, each region may be able to work autonomously. However, increasingly, organisations are trying to minimise the number of employees since people costs are some of the highest outgoings for an organisation (CIPD research, highlighted in Taylor, 2005b). As a result, it is becoming normal for permission to be requested to recruit, usually after a formal proposal, fully costed, is put forward to justify why recruitment is necessary. This is even the case in many organisations where a vacancy has occurred naturally – the replacement has to be justified and permission given before recruitment can begin. This permission is granted usually by senior managers, although in many organisations the decision may be devolved to HR and personnel departments, who manage the activity on a day-to-day basis (see Chapter 20 on HR roles).

Job analysis is a series of techniques used to explore exactly what the job entails. A job is unlikely to have remained static and it is advisable to take the time to find out what the current job requirements are before starting a recruitment process. There are a number of ways of gaining this information (Pearn Kandola, 1993; Armstrong, 1999; Taylor, 2005b), including watching someone doing the role, and talking to or interviewing current job-holders and their managers and, if possible, the person or people who have left. It may be better to utilise the services of a specialist consultant to analyse the jobs – and they will probably use a questionnaire-based approach. Once a job analysis has been completed and the recruiter has up-to-date knowledge of the job and the skills, experience and qualifications of the person required to do it, the job description and person specification can be drawn up.

Job description

Most authors agree that a detailed description of the job is then essential – to clearly spell out what it is the post-holder will have to achieve (for example, Taylor, 2005b; Lucas, Lupton and Mathieson, 2006). Note that a good job description is not a list of tasks (this is the historical approach, and is potentially quite constraining) but clear statements of targets, outputs or outcomes that the post-holder will be required to achieve.

Clearly, there are some jobs – especially operational jobs – where some of the activities are so essential that they do form part of the job description, and it is quite common to have specific tasks listed in the job description. However, it is not best practice to do this, because as soon as aspects of the job change (for example, with the introduction of a new machine, or a change of process), all of the job descriptions in that area may have to be revised (and this might also give rise to potential union argument and pay issues). With a job description that is worded in outcome-achievement format, the actual detailed tasks are left open, allowing changes to be made without making the job descriptions useless. It is important, though, that readers are aware that many job descriptions do not follow this good practice approach but continue to list the tasks to be undertaken, and many staff expect this to be the case, especially at more high-skills levels. The job description will lead to the person specification.

Person specification

Whereas the job description details the job to be done, the person specification details the characteristics of an ideal person who has the capability to do the job. This document therefore uses the job description to identify the skills, knowledge, experience, attributes and characteristics of the type of person that is needed to fulfil the job requirements (Lucas *et al*, 2006; Taylor, 2005b). It should contain clear, measurable statements of these attributes, because these will be the benchmark to decide whether a candidate is or is not suitable. Within the selection process the person specification is what determines whether an individual is capable of doing the job or not, and so the person specification is the key document at the point of selection.

There are three main approaches used for person specifications:

- focusing on the needs of the job, and the personal characteristics required for someone to do the job (and he or she is then expected to learn about the organisation and team, and develop to fit in with them)

- focusing on the organisation and team, and the person's abilities to fit in (and he or she is then expected to learn about and develop into the job itself)

- a competency approach, in which skills, attributes and behaviours required for both the job and the team are listed, and the applicant measured against them.

What is key for a person specification is that it should be used equally across all applicants in providing a basis for measuring the characteristics of each individual to determine the extent to which he or she fits that description.

Decision regarding selection methods

Now the selection method has to be decided. This is critical – there are many different ways of selecting candidates from among those who have applied. Chapter 9 of this book should help with more information on this topic.

Advertising and application decisions

There is no point in having an excellent selection system if no one applies. The first step towards getting applicants is to raise awareness of the vacancy and what is required in the job. Although there are a number of different ways of finding people to apply, all start with some form of awareness-raising, usually by advertising. (Where this is not the case, it is usually because agencies are used – but even these advertise.) There are a number of important issues with advertising, which are discussed more fully in Part 2 of this chapter.

Before even thinking about raising awareness and attracting applications it is essential that you should be clear on what applicants need to do to apply. This should, of course, be spelled out clearly in any advertisement. Often the application method is chosen to be part of the selection process. As Table 19 shows, different application methods might be used to check different issues.

Table 19 Application methods and their use

Application method	May be used to check (eg)
Completing an application form	• Ability to complete forms • Ability to summarise key points • Handwriting skills • Ability to understand key requirements
Writing a letter of application	• Handwriting skills, if relevant to the job • Ability to understand key requirements • Capability of constructing a structured document
Sending in a CV	• Capability of compiling a structured document • Ability to summarise key points
Telephoning for information and initial detail-giving	• Tone and quality of spoken voice • Use of the English language • Level of formality or customer service used • Image projected
Online questionnaire	• Experience, qualifications, factual understanding • Ability to use web-based applications

The next steps in the recruitment process are usually considered part of the selection process, and are examined in the following chapter.

2 SEEKING APPLICANTS

One of the key issues of recruitment is where to start to look for potential candidates. As the world becomes smaller, travel and mobility now being more the norm than the exception, the potential source of candidates is huge. In practice, though, many of these people are not actually easily available, and unless you are seeking a specialist or someone with a specific combination of skills that is unusual, it is more likely that you will first look locally or nationally.

So where should you look for candidates? It does of course depend very much on a number of important issues relating to the reason you are recruiting, and the job role you are intending to fill. There are five main areas to consider: the person needed, the job role you want him/her to undertake, your department and organisation, the wider context of your subject discipline and marketplace, and the details of the constraints on the recruitment process itself. For each of these areas there are a number of questions to think over before making any decisions about how and where to seek applicants. We now examine them in more detail.

About the person

The person specification should help to answer questions about the person you are looking for. Key questions should include:

- What experience, skills, qualities and other attributes are you looking for? This might affect whether you seek internally or externally, and how widely you need to look. The more specialised or focused your requirements, the more likely it is that you will need to look far afield or use multiple or national advertising methods to reach those who are likely to meet your needs.

- Which qualifications and other achievements would be ideal, or essential (like a Heavy Goods Vehicle driving licence, for example)? Answers to this question might point you towards specialist journals or particular national newspapers or professional bodies. At senior levels, some achievements or qualifications might need a specific search perhaps through a recruitment agency or head-hunters.

- How available should the person recruited be? This of course depends upon how quickly you must have him/her in the job – urgently, in a month or two, or later? This is likely to affect the extent to which you have time to advertise widely, since some journals need a significant time to prepare their publication. It may also affect the style and content of the advertisement.

About the job

Most authorities (for example, Bilsberry, 1996; Taylor, 2005b; Roberts, 1997) clearly state that the job description should provide information about the job. Key questions might include:

- Are you looking for someone who will be permanent, temporary, casual or on a specified contract? Apart from pointing towards different media for an advertisement, for all except permanent positions this might suggest a more local than a national approach.

- Is the main work long-term, short-term or perhaps only project-based? Again, this should cause you to consider local versus national methods of raising awareness of the vacancy.

- Part-time, full-time or variable?

- Day work, evening work, night work or shift work?

The following two questions should help you to define particular requirements and consider the extent to which advantage can be taken of how closely those who live within easy reach of the place of work. Local advertising might appear appropriate, but those from afar might be prepared to move to join your organisation. You will have to consider the implications for any moving costs and how these might be met by the organisation. Clearly, for more senior positions this may be necessary, but for relatively straightforward jobs this might be less important. Again, this should help you with the decision over whether advertising should be local or wider.

What about the physical and geographical location of the workplace, and its accessibility? Will the position be office-based, home-based or mobile? This should inform the extent to which your search for applicants is local or wider.

Are there any issues of resources or facilities needed by the job that might affect who you are seeking (use of a car or van, or own set of kitchen knives, or own guitar and amplifier, for example)? These are important issues for the job, but really only affect the search for applicants in terms of the practicality of their travelling to the place of work or removing to your location from far away.

About the organisation

Lucas *et al* (2006) note that the organisational context should be considered (see Chapter 2). The following questions are important in relation to an organisation that is seeking to fill a position:

- Is the organisation multinational, national, regional or local? This might affect people's perceptions of possible career paths, as well as geographical mobility potential. Decisions about advertising method and design may well be affected by your answers here.

- What is the profile of the organisation (for example, high-profile, well-known or small and relatively unknown)? A brand name can often influence people's wish to apply. Decisions about advertising method and design may well be affected by your answers here too.

- Multiple products or services or of specific focus? The issue of breadth versus depth of work potential can influence applicants. Specialists often seek out specialist firms, for example, whereas a generalist or person with uncertain career plans might favour a more diverse organisation. This should help you to think through whether a specialist journal or professional body will be needed for your advertisement, as well as the actual content of the advert.

- What is the structure and culture of the organisation? Much has been written about structure and culture (for example, Handy, 1993; Johnson and Scholes, 1999; Blundell and Murdock, 1997), and for most people the extent to which they perceive that they might 'fit' usually determines the extent to which they apply seriously (if at all). The design and content, as well as the medium chosen, should be delineated with care, because they will subconsciously convey some of the underlying philosophies of the organisation, and therefore its apparent attractiveness to individuals.

- How far is career progression available, expected and welcomed within the organisation? These days, knowing how they will progress (usually measured in financial and in status terms) is often important to people's willingness to explore job opportunities. Any advertisement may have to reflect such opportunities, for maximum effectiveness.

About the profession or business sector

The profession or business sector has also to be considered:

- Which sector are you in – for example: art, science or support? Clearly, this is a key point for placing advertisements to match the desired audience.

- What is the main job focus – for example, manufacturing, service, distribution or research? Similarly, the placing of any advertisements should be influenced by this point.

- Is the business environment highly regulated, restricted or very organic and freeform? Personal style and approach to work differs significantly, and this point ties in with the questions about organisational structure and culture. Some people cannot settle to work in a highly controlled or regulated environment, whereas others might struggle if the organisation and work is too organic and freeform. Care should be taken in the placing of an advertisement to reflect this aspect of the job content, and the wording itself must reflect any special focal points or requirements, to avoid many applications from those who are not of a suitable disposition.

The recruitment process itself

In order to plan an effective recruitment process it is necessary to ask a number of questions, many of which are listed below. The information obtained from the job analysis is helpful in finding out the answers to the questions, which is why it is advisable to plan recruitment with an up-to-date job analysis available.

- Is the position for internal applicants, external applicants or both? Ideally, of course, you should aim for the widest possible search for candidates by looking inside and outside the organisation. However, time-scales, experience or succession planning might cause you to decide to look internally first, and only look externally if a suitable internal candidate cannot be found. Alternatively, if your aim is to bring fresh blood or new ideas and experience into the organisation, external candidates should presumably be sought.

- What is the timeframe available – how soon must the person be in the post? Does that allow for enough time for the various steps necessary to achieve this result? Timing is one of the most important issues, and will most likely affect what you are able to do to raise awareness of the position and attract candidates. Wherever possible, you should allow enough time to be able to attract the best candidates, and so if you can, you should decide the recruitment methods first, and then work out the timing needed afterwards. In most situations, however, this is not possible, and you are likely to be under significant time pressures, and probably have to compromise your recruitment approaches to fit operational requirements.

- What is your resource availability – for example, how much can you spend? How easy is it to place advertisements? What steps internally do you need to undertake? Being clear about the time (as above), finance, people and physical resources required and available may also affect the approach you are able to take.

- What is the people situation – who must be involved in the process, and what limits are there on those people's availability? How will you establish the best combination of people to involve, and how will you get their participation and commitment to the process?

- What is the experience of the staff involved – are there any training issues or additional people that must be involved in the design or preparation of the process? Any such issues might also take up time and additional resources.

Before thinking about where to look for possible applicants, questions like these should be considered. The answers should help you to decide where to put your efforts in seeking out those you would like to apply.

FINDING YOUR APPLICANTS

So where can you find potential applicants? Having thought through the details of the situation, context and requirements, there are a number of options. The key issues here are whether you are going to focus on internal or external candidates, and also how far you wish to handle things yourself or work through others to help you. The WERS data on recruitment channels by workplace characteristics (see Table 20) identifies three distinct approaches to finding applicants. The data clearly shows that although workplaces do use informal methods and formal methods that use professional help, most organisations use the formal processes that they themselves devise and implement without professional assistance.

Table 20 Recruitment channels, by workplace characteristics

	Formal channel – professional help (job centres, careers services and private employment agencies)	Formal channel – no professional help (newspapers, specialist press, notices, replying to speculative applications, and Internet)	Informal channel (direct approaches to potential recruits, recommendation or enquiry by existing employees and word of mouth)
All workplaces with vacancies in core group of employees in previous year	69	88	64
Organisation size 10–99 employees 10,000 or more employees	68 71	80 95	70 60
Industry Manufacturing Hotels and restaurants Financial services Public sector	76 69 66 51	78 83 93 98	72 77 64 32

Source: Kersley *et al* (2006; p.73)

Let's look in detail at the different ways in which applicants might be found. Newell and Shackleton (2000) suggest that most private sector organisations attempt to fill vacancies internally before looking outside. Internal candidate search might, for example, be from within a single department, other departments, other geographical sites or partner sites and organisations. Internal methods of letting people know about the vacancy include word of mouth, organisational intranet or emails to all employees, staff newsletters, newspapers and bulletins, and noticeboards (paper or electronic).

An internal promotion or appointment can cause bad feeling among colleagues who were not selected, so managers in the area concerned will have to handle the transition carefully. Also, staying internal to the organisation does not bring in any new ideas from outside, even if it is perhaps cheaper and quicker to appoint from within. As the Cranet data suggests, internal promotion is more common in some countries than in others. Whereas in the UK and Sweden only about a third of organisations fill management positions internally, most do in Greece and Slovakia (see Table 21).

Table 21 'How are management positions most commonly filled?'

	UK	Sweden	Germany	Greece	Slovakia
Internally	37%	37%	44%	56%	56%

Source: Cranet (2003)

EXTERNAL — WORKING THROUGH OTHERS

There are many methods for letting people know about a vacancy by working through others (Taylor, 2005b). These include:

- word of mouth and personal contact
- previous applicants on file (usually held and accessed through those overseeing HR in the organisation)
- using job centres, careers services and youth and adult training schemes and placement programmes
- recruitment and employment agencies
- head-hunters (those who actively seek out suitable people in other organisations, to see if they can be encouraged to leave).

Of these, one of the most widely used is that of the recruitment agency, who can advertise on behalf of employers, and who also may well have a large file already of people looking for such an opening. However, an agency needs careful briefing, especially when using an agency that you do not really know, or that does not already know you and your organisation well. A clear briefing has to be backed up by an effective job description and person specification. If at all possible you should talk to the person who will be working on your case, and then ask to see the final brief that he/she builds in order to check that it really does meet your requirements.

Keep a close eye on the activities of the agency, because some may well not screen (or filter out) people very well, and send you people to interview on the off-chance that you will take them, rather than screening them properly first. This may happen particularly if your contract with the agency stipulates payment on finding someone, rather than for its services in general. Remember that just because you use an agency does not take away your responsibility for the effectiveness of the recruitment. It simply means that someone else is doing the detailed basic work for you. You should therefore be clear in dealing with the agency about what is and is not acceptable, and make sure you give it clear information about the criteria that you expect it to use in screening people. You might also ask it to give you details of those that it turns away (with its reasons for doing so) as well as those that it passes to you for the selection process, so that you can check that it is truly carrying out your wishes fully.

EXTERNAL – DEALING WITH IT YOURSELF

This largely involves some form of advertising, to let people know of the opportunity. The question here is where to choose to advertise – for example:

- a card in a shop window
- an advert in local paper
- an advert on local radio/TV
- a national advert in the press or a magazine or journal
- the Internet (passive information-giving – or interactive, perhaps even pre-checking suitability).

Additional issues that you will need to address include:

- exactly which professional journals, magazines, national and local papers you use, and your reasons for choosing those
- the format of the advertisement itself, involving:
  - the style of wording you use
  - the graphic layout and design of the advertisement
  - the actual detail and content of the message.

Below is a checklist you might use when you are putting an advertisement together:

About the job:

- title, rate of pay, location
- who reports to or is responsible for whom.

About the application:

- who to contact, how to apply, the deadline for doing so
- the address to send application to
- the telephone number for further enquiries
- when and where interviews will be held (if decided in advance).

About the person needed:

- the key must-have points from your person specification
- any special requirements.

About the writing style:

- Keep it brief and factual.
- Keep it professional.
- Keep it legal (see Chapters 5 and 6).

Time spent on getting the advertisement right will save you time later on, because the resultant applications should be exactly the kind you were looking for, rather than including a large number that are no real use to you because the advertisement did not explain your requirements properly.

REFLECTIVE ACTIVITY

In light of the ideas in this chapter so far, consider which of the various methods of recruitment would be most suitable for a job you know well – such as course tutor in a college or cashier at a supermarket. Be able to explain exactly why you think these are suitable, and why you have rejected the other methods.

If you decide to advertise, what issues are particularly important for you to remember?

Compare your decisions with what actually happens in the organisation. What changes or improvements would you make to ensure greater effectiveness?

EQUALITY OF OPPORTUNITY

Recruitment and selection are areas in which there are many pitfalls in terms of equality of opportunity, and if you are involved with recruitment in any way, you should always check the latest legal position before proceeding. (Chapter 5 deals with legal issues in general, and is a good starting point for this.)

You must certainly think about whether the method you choose might disadvantage certain types of people who might wish to apply for the job. For example, if you always advertise in a particular newspaper, only the people who read that newspaper will get to hear about the job. People who read a different newspaper (who might be – for example – of a different religion, ethnicity or social standing) will not have the chance to apply because they will not know about the vacancy. Word of mouth can have equal opportunities issues too, because it relies on people recommending friends and acquaintances. In this instance the pool of applicants is artificially limited, and certainly not necessarily inclusive or representative across religions, gender, age, race or disabilities.

REFLECTIVE ACTIVITY

What are the main equal opportunities issues that you should be aware of when seeking applicants? Where might such issues arise within the recruitment process?

In an organisation you know well, how much attention is paid to these sorts of issues?

What might you have to do to ensure compliance with the law, and to ensure that you receive the best applications?

3   INDUCTION

Induction (or 'orientation', as it is known as in many countries) is the name usually given to the process by which a new employee (or someone in a new position) is integrated into the organisation, the team and the work role. It is the method by which these people can effectively learn issues of organisational purpose, policies and procedures, and (for example) ways of working. The process should help them to become aware of the organisational culture, the skills, knowledge and behaviours required for the job, and to fully understand their responsibilities.

Although the induction process is often not considered to be part of the recruitment and selection process, it is actually key to success. After all, if you spend significant amounts of time and money on getting the right people into the organisation, it is clearly sensible to look after them once they arrive, so that they can not only feel at home quickly but they can become productive immediately. Indeed, a number of studies have shown a direct relationship between the effectiveness of the induction process and retention – the length of time a new employee stays with the organisation (Taylor, 2005b; Fowler, 1996; Reid, Barrington and Brown, 2004). Where induction has been well thought through and undertaken, there is a much higher likelihood that the new member of staff will settle quickly. Where the induction process is weak or absent, new staff often do not settle and may quickly move on. An effective induction is an essential part of the formation of a positive psychological contract, and a positive psychological contract reduces absence and turnover and maximises performance (see Chapter 11).

The induction programme is usually regarded as part of the new employee's development programme – which of course it is – but it is also the link between the recruitment process and the performance management process (see Chapter 12). The effectiveness of this link can easily set the tone for the new staff and show them the value that you place on their services and the way they will be managed in the future. It is for this reason that induction is key to effectiveness of the recruitment process, because a weak induction can undermine and completely devalue all the good work put into obtaining the services of those individuals in the first place. Where an effective induction programme is not present, there can be poor integration into the organisation, team and job role, leading to low morale for the individual and the team, and less effective performance. In turn, this may also lead to disillusionment, and eventually resignation of the new team member, which of course might then demotivate the team, and require the whole recruitment process to be gone through again, at significant cost.

Taylor (2005b) has suggested that a 'standard' process may not be as effective as a tailor-made process from the viewpoint of retaining those recently recruited. Again, perhaps you should consider how you might feel if you were 'processed' for your induction in a mechanical standard manner rather than in a more personalised and job role-related way.

Who needs an induction programme? Anyone who takes on a new role should have some form of induction. This includes new full-time, part-time and temporary staff, trainees (for example, on a graduate training scheme), and those appointed internally to a different role or those returning after a long absence (for example, after maternity/paternity leave or after recovery from long-term sickness). The principle can also be extended to those who are on secondment or attachment, or perhaps at the start of a medium- to large-sized project assignment. The variety of situations in which induction is useful is quite wide, and this further reinforces the need for induction programmes to be tailor-made rather than standard or 'off the shelf'.

An effective induction programme ensures that a number of issues are well covered. These should include the physical facilities of the workplace and details of the job role and how it fits within the larger organisational and team purpose and objectives. They should include health and safety information – this is a legal requirement: see Chapter 18 – and clear coverage of the terms and conditions of service that apply. In larger organisations an employee handbook is distributed which can be used to set out contractual and non-contractual information. The employee is often asked to sign to say that he or she has received this information, and it can be used in the future as a source of information provided it is kept up to date when there are changes.

There are other issues that can be covered in the induction, such as information about the organisation, perhaps its history, services and products, and mission, values and culture. Although they may not be essential elements of an induction, they are nonetheless very desirable to ensure full integration. Most writers on the subject of induction recommend that some form of mentor or 'buddy' is appointed in the early days, so that the new person has a specific point of contact for support and enquiries, and someone who can help to introduce him/her to others in the organisation as essential contacts, colleagues and potential friends.

The way in which the programme is constructed is critical to its success. Traditionally, organisations used to set aside a few days at the start of the employment contract for this activity, and then gave people large amounts of information, booklets, documents, visits to various areas, and introductions to everyone in the department (and anyone who happened to pass by). Overload was often the result, and even the most motivated and focused individual soon found that he/she was confused.

Some parts of this approach are of course essential within the first few days, but for real effectiveness the process is best spread over a much longer time, with a planned approach. In this way the required information can emerge gradually and in a structured manner for the newcomer in a way that enables him or her fully to understand each aspect. There should be a review meeting planned after the employee has been in post for some time at which the employee can ask for any further information or training if needed. This can form part of an annual appraisal meeting. It is not only helpful to the new employee, it also helps managers to evaluate the effectiveness of the induction and to make any changes for the benefit of future new starters.

Marchington and Wilkinson (2005) suggest that line managers should hold the responsibility for the effectiveness of the induction process for their staff. After all, they are the ones who need the staff, and the new member is one of their team, performing a role that contributes to their section's operational performance objectives and targets. However, in many organisations the induction programme is viewed as 'an HR issue', and therefore either left to HR to sort out or formally delegated to the HR department. This may be effective, but often is not, because induction can so easily be assumed to be only about meeting legal requirements, and about the rules and regulations, totally ignoring the integration issues discussed above. A good compromise is to have the induction programme designed by both line managers and HR in cooperation with each other, and then perhaps for the HR department to oversee its delivery (calling upon the line manager and team colleagues for input where needed).

So exactly what should be included? The actual content will vary according to the type of organisation, the person being inducted, his or her contractual terms and conditions, job role and prior experience of work, and the organisational context itself. There have been many books and articles written about effective induction, including lists of the specifics that should be included in the wider programme, which might cover, say, the first three months of service in the job. A good starting point to read further on this topic are the factsheets and checklists provided by ACAS, the CIPD and the CMI .

REFLECTIVE ACTIVITY

What are the effects of the induction process in an organisation?

How can any negative effects be minimised? What are the reasons that induction programmes can be less successful?

What legal requirements are there that should be included?

KEY ISSUES IN RECRUITMENT AND INDUCTION

We now pull together ten key points about recruitment and induction raised in this chapter:

- Effective recruitment is essential to ensure that the right people are brought forward for consideration for every job.

- The first step is to ensure that a job analysis is undertaken, leading to a clearly specified job description.

- The job description should be used as the basis for determining and clearly specifying the personal attributes and characteristics of the ideal individual for the job, written in a person specification.

- Finding the right applicants is an important step, and there are many ways of ensuring that people get to hear about a vacancy.

- Before advertising, a decision should be made on exactly how a potential candidate should apply.

- The content of an advertisement should reflect not only the core duties of the job, taken from the job description, but also details from the person specification of the key characteristics required.

- Agencies can be used to bring forward suitable applicants, but the process should be managed effectively from within the organisation to ensure that the agency does provide appropriate shortlisted applicants.

- Staff involved with the recruitment process should be fully trained to ensure that they take action that is effective and meets legislative requirements.

- Effective induction is essential to retain and make productive all those who join the organisation or commence new job roles.

- Only by effectiveness throughout the recruitment and induction processes is it possible to get and keep the best talent available for your organisation, upon which to build a sound and growing business.

Perhaps there are other key points that you would like to note for yourself.

The main case study in this chapter now follows. It gives an example of recruitment and induction issues faced by many organisations.

MAIN CASE STUDY

Make an initial reading of the case study to gain an overview of the situation, and then read the questions that you will need to address. Now read the case study again, making notes of issues and facts that will help you in your analysis and responses to the questions. Remember to 'read between the lines' as well as picking out the obvious points, and also to consider what is not said as well as what is presented here.

A large broadcasting organisation, operating on a 24-hours-a-day, seven-days-a-week basis, regularly recruits new operational engineers to operate specialist sound, lighting, vision and computer equipment. In this organisation recruitment occurs typically every two years to ensure that a good number of staff are properly trained and are available to apply when actual full-time operational post vacancies occur. It takes about two years' training for staff to become sufficiently proficient to take on regular

duties, and historically there is low turnover, so that a phased entry has worked well. Within the organisation, career opportunities to progress and diversify are readily available, and this form of succession planning has always previously been appropriate to ensure continuity of staff in the main operational areas, while at the same time providing seasoned practitioners to rise to more senior and specialist jobs.

Because the organisation has undertaken this recruitment exercise regularly over the last 20 years, a normal process has become established. When the due date arrives (determined by the date of the last recruitment round, usually the first week in July) the departmental manager confirms the wish to proceed, and HR looks out the job description and issues a standard advertisement, which is placed in the media section of the Tuesday edition of the Daily Blurb national newspaper for two consecutive weeks.

Are you what we need to join
our next generation of Operational Engineers?

Major broadcasting organisation is seeking bright, lively, committed and enthusiastic people to join the pool of trainees that will eventually provide the backbone of our services. You will have a proven interest in engineering or operations in your current role or hobbies, an 'A'-level in physics, maths and English, and normal colour vision.

You will be working initially at our training centre in Kent, followed by a series of three- to six-month attachments and secondments at various locations throughout the UK. This will involve weekend, bank holiday, and shift working. A permanent operational unit position may be applied for at any time after the first year, and subject to satisfactory progress, is guaranteed at the end of Year 2.

Expenses are paid, and salary will initially be £18,000 pa, rising to £21,000 on successful completion of the training programme. Large city weighting is paid additionally for postings to the major conurbations.

For further information and an application form, please ring

Fiona Jarvis on 0208-123 45678

We are an equal opportunities employer, and welcome applications from all sections of society.

The advertisement contains details of the job prospects and salary (see above), and how to apply. HR collects the application forms that are sent in by candidates, which are then sorted into alphabetical order and sent on to the departmental manager for selection.

Four years ago, 54 people applied but most were found at selection to be unsuitable. Seven were appointed where 10 positions had been available. Two years ago, 23 people applied and not one was found to be suitable, so a second recruitment round was held six months later. Then, only a handful of applicants came anywhere near the required standard. Clearly, something was not going well. The departmental manager complained to the HR department, demanding that something be done to improve matters before the next round of recruitment commenced.

Once in the organisation, the new staff attended a two-day induction programme alongside other staff recruited around the same period from a range of departments. Staff records show that about 15% of those recruited did not stay in the organisation, although there was a higher level of retention in the technical departments (about 10% leaving within a year).

Your task

Consider the following questions, making notes of the key points of your responses. If you are studying in a group, discuss your responses, and come to an agreed set of answers. Then draft a short report to the department manager and HR manager, explaining and justifying your suggestions.

1 What are the factors that have contributed to the lack of success?

2 What changes should the HR department make to its recruitment processes?

3 What changes should the departmental manager make to the recruitment approaches and processes in the department?

4 What are the implications to be considered before making the changes you suggest?

5 To what extent does this organisation comply with legislation on equal opportunities?

6 What should the organisation do to increase the retention of those recruited?

EXPLORE FURTHER

CIPD (2005) *On-Line Recruitment*, Factsheet. London, CIPD
CIPD (2006) *Recruitment*, Factsheet. London, CIPD
CIPD (2006) *Induction*, Factsheet. London, CIPD
The three factsheets are aimed at the practitioner with an overview of the main issues involved in recruitment. Very accessible, and a great help to anyone who already works in HR or who wants to say something productive during a first interview on recruitment.

ROBERTS, G. (2005) *Recruitment and Selection*, 2nd edition. London, CIPD
This text provides a very comprehensive overview of the main issues involved in recruitment and selection, written in a clear and succinct style.

TAYLOR, S. (2005b) *People Resourcing*, 3rd edition. London, CIPD
A wider look at resourcing issues, with clear guidance on recruitment processes for both the practitioner and the academic.

CHAPTER 9

Selection

Tracey Cockerton

INTRODUCTION

This chapter considers the selection process as a means of predicting performance in the workplace. Identifying the right person for a position is essential for individual and organisational success. Planning, developing, implementing and evaluating a selection process can be time-consuming and costly, but the long-term benefits outweigh the costs of hiring an unsuitable candidate unable to perform well in the position. Both the organisation and the individual may suffer and the individual may need extra support.

LEARNING OUTCOMES

By the end of this chapter readers should be able to:

- describe the selection process and state how the organisational context can influence selection outcomes and in turn impact on organisational performance and development

- give an overview of the different methods of assessment for selection and the factors determining choice

- explain how selection can be a predictive process using the concepts of reliability and validity (particularly criterion-related validity)

- identify appropriate ways of evaluating selection strategies

- explain how to use psychometric tools within the required legal framework with sensitivity to issues of diversity.

The chapter is structured in two parts. The first part discusses the wider issues around choice and use of selection methods, and the second part focuses on the more technical issues of reliability, validity and evaluating selection procedures.

The introductory case study is drawn from a real-life situation and is designed to examine some of the common problems with selection procedures. There follows an investigation of the meaning of selection and the importance of considering selection within the organisational context. Next, we look at the range of selection and assessment methods available, with particular reference to those methods UK companies most often use. The following section describes the factors that determine the choice of selection procedures and the advantages and difficulties associated with each.

Part 2 defines the concepts of reliability and validity and discusses the technical issues surrounding the different types of validity and reliability, explaining also how selection can be a predictive process adopting a criterion-related validity approach. This leads on to a section on how to evaluate selection strategies that also examines some of the current issues in relation to the required legal framework with sensitivity to issues of diversity.

STARTER CASE STUDY

An HR administrator has convinced her boss that personality assessment would add value and objective information to the selection process for senior manager appointments, particularly in relation to identifying leadership qualities. She has obtained a copy of a well-known personality questionnaire from her postgraduate programme. Although she has never been trained in psychometric testing, she is permitted by her boss to administer it to candidates for a high-level and very responsible management position as part of the selection process. A job description documenting the responsibilities and outcomes of the position has been produced, but not based on a job analysis. A person specification or competency profile has not been finalised.

Senior manager candidates are interviewed at different times during the week by different interviewers, asking different questions. Unfortunately, organising a schedule for the administration of the personality questionnaire during a busy week proves difficult, and as a result, the candidates all undertake completion of the questionnaire on an individual basis, some before interview, some after interview, and not everyone is informed of the purpose of this part of the selection process. In addition to this, some candidates write their answers on the questionnaire booklet instead of the answer sheet. The HR administrator has only one copy of the booklet and some of the candidates' answers cannot be removed. However, she had photocopied the questionnaire booklet in advance and uses these photocopies with the remaining candidates. Her only problem is getting these back in time from her flatmates who asked to borrow them.

In due course it turns out that the personality questionnaire is an outdated version of the instrument. Moreover, due to time constraints the candidates receive no feedback on their responses, and the profile information produced by the HR administrator includes only brief summary information relating to each candidate's score. Also, the personality questionnaire is not one that is work-related. As the week of interviewing ends, there is little time to produce feedback summary reports, although all the information relating to each candidate, by name, is on computer and can be made available to the selection panel to help their decisions. However, the members of the panel are not trained in psychometric testing, nor do they have any understanding of that particular personality questionnaire or how it relates to the vacant management position.

Questions for discussion

1 How many examples of unprofessional practice can you find in this case study? List them.

2 What elements of the process would you keep – and what would you change, and how?

Notes:

There are many lessons to be learned from this case study and improvements can be made at every point in the process as described. Personality questionnaire assessments may provide additional and objective information for a selection process. However, the information will be most useful when there is evidence of a predictive relationship between particular personality characteristics and job performance (Furnham and Heaven, 1999). Inconsistent, ad hoc administration of personality questionnaires by an untrained individual can even then reduce the value of such personality information.

The chapter concludes with the main case study, which draws together most of the issues covered in the form of a real-life example of selection practice – albeit a very bad one!

Reference sources named within the chapter may be looked up in the *References and further reading* section at the end of the book.

1 SELECTION METHODS AND ORGANISATIONAL CONTEXT

Selection procedures are used to enable an employer to appoint the most 'appropriate' person for employment to a vacant post. Selection procedures are means of assessing individual candidates who have applied for a post against a set of agreed criteria which are deemed relevant. From an organisational perspective, selection procedures must be as fair, reliable, valid, objective, ethical, cost-effective and efficient as possible, while differentiating as accurately as possible between candidates to determine the right choice – ie someone who can perform most successfully in the post. However, the process of selecting the right person for the job adopting the person–job-fit model – which refers to the match between the abilities of the person and demands of the job (Edwards, 1991) – may not be as appropriate or as simple as it appears. Alternatively, the person–organisational-fit model (Kristof, 1996) acknowledges the wider two-way compatibility-matching process which may occur between a person and an organisation during selection and recognises the significance the organisational context may have on the selection process.

The culture of an organisation includes the organisation's philosophy, which can both explicitly and implicitly determine the approaches to recruitment and selection, selection decisions, and measures of successful performance at work. Organisational culture is also likely to be reflected in the organisation's identity, and this in turn will influence who applies for a vacant post. Selection does not occur in a vacuum. It takes place within an organisational context and the culture of the organisation may influence who applies, as well as the outcome. The assessments occurring during a selection process are not all one-way. Individuals also carefully select the organisation they apply to and evaluate the potential employer at each stage of the process.

Beyond the organisational context, there is the legal framework to consider. Selection processes have to be conducted appropriately to ensure that there is no unlawful discrimination on the grounds of sex, race, disability, age, sexual orientation, or religion or belief (see Chapter 5). In Britain and more widely in Western Europe, equality of opportunity is an integral part of the recruitment and selection process. Employers and HR practitioners have to regularly monitor the outcomes of each selection process stage for potential discrimination and address accordingly. Furthermore, as organisations adopt global resourcing strategies the recruitment, selection and assessment process becomes an ever-increasing challenge (see Sparrow, 2006).

SELECTION METHODS CURRENTLY USED IN EUROPE

A wide range of selection methods are currently available but differ considerably in frequency of application and according to the type and level of vacant position. The range includes application forms and CVs, biographical data, interviews, references, psychological testing, job or work samples, in-tray exercises, group assessment, presentations and assessment centres.

Table 22   Most popular selection methods used for managerial staff

	UK	Sweden	Germany	Greece	Slovakia
Interview panel	77%	59%	57%	21%	48%
One-to-one interviews	51%	72%	60%	87%	35%
Application forms	66%	34%	14%	39%	16%
Psychometric test	47%	66%	6%	17%	15%
Assessment centre	26%	12%	23%	18%	10%
Graphology	1%	3%	2%	7%	1%
References	79%	85%	45%	41%	24%

Source: Cranet (2003)

As is evident in Table 22, the most commonly used selection methods for management positions in the UK and many other countries are application forms, interviews and references. These are followed by psychometric testing and assessment centres for management positions. Despite the range of selection methods available, many organisations, large, medium-sized and small, employ the most long-standing approaches, such as interviews. Why is this? It may be because they are part of their custom and practice, and because without evaluating the effectiveness of a selection process it is difficult to know whether it is worth changing.

FACTORS THAT AFFECT THE CHOICE OF SELECTION METHOD(S)

Choosing the right selection method(s) depends on a number of factors:
- the available budget
- the time-scale for appointment
- the accuracy required
- the type, specialism and level of post to be filled
- previous custom and practice
- selection criteria for the post to be filled
- the acceptability and appropriateness of the methods
- the abilities of the staff involved in the selection process
- administrative ease.

Selection tools can assess a variety of individual characteristics such as knowledge, skills, abilities and attributes relevant to the vacant post. Perhaps one of the most significant steps in the design of a selection procedure is to ensure that the most applicable skills, abilities, knowledge and attributes are identified and accurately assessed according to the requirements of the vacant position. This raises the important question of a 'one-size-fits-all' approach versus individually tailored selection processes. To answer this, HR managers must focus on their organisation's strategic aims and thereby ensure that selection processes are part of an overall coherent and integrated approach reflecting the organisation's values and designed to meet the organisation's vision. On a practical level, HR managers may carry out a series of interviews or data-collection sessions with stakeholders, line managers and co-workers to find the capabilities required for successful performance, once they understand and agree on exactly what 'successful job performance' is and how it may relate to wider organisational values and behaviours. This is the key to ensuring that the selection process is a way of predicting performance in the workplace.

It is now quite common for external experts – 'head-hunters' – to be employed as professional recruiters (see Chapter 8). Head-hunters search out potential applicants and invite them to apply for vacant positions which they may not have considered or even been aware of. Applicants are then systematically screened and through a process of elimination reduced to a select few candidates presented to the recruiting organisation for further assessment. For the rejected applicants who were not considering the vacant post before they were encouraged to apply for it, the process can be demoralising. However, for organisations and for HR managers in particular, this service can guarantee, if managed properly (as discussed in Chapter 8), that they select candidates from a diverse and competitive pool of applicants, and is often essential when recruiting to specialist senior positions and/or key leadership roles.

2 SELECTION METHODS

We now examine the selection methods most commonly used, highlighting the pros and cons of each.

APPLICATION FORMS AND CVS

Application forms are produced by organisations to allow applicants to present essential information in a standardised format. They also provide an insight into the organisation – and the image they present to candidates may influence the response level and content provided by the applicant. Potentially successful applicants may be lost at this stage because they do not complete the application form; it may appear too long, too complicated, to require irrelevant information, or not to fit with the applicant's image of his/her ideal employer.

Application forms are rarely used as the only method of selecting candidates, but are useful for screening and identifying a short-list of suitable candidates to go forward for a further selection process. A well-designed application form, available online and used in conjunction with relevant short-listing criteria helps in reducing costs of the overall selection process. However, if the application form is unclear and/or the short-listing criteria are not relevant to the job, those rejected at this stage may include a number of potentially successful applicants.

Not all organisations rely on application forms. Some – particularly US, Australian and German organisations – request a CV or résumé from the applicant in addition to or instead of a completed application form. A CV is a summary document designed and produced by the applicant. CVs include information similar to that requested in application forms, but the content, presentation, order and wording are at the discretion of the applicant. The applicant may even include a photograph of himself/herself. A well-designed and presented CV can make an excellent impression although it is not necessarily an appropriate indication of job performance, particularly if the candidate received professional assistance in compiling the CV.

BIOGRAPHICAL DATA

Biographical data or 'biodata' uses a biographical inventory or questionnaire to collect factual information about a candidate's life history to build a profile of employees in a particular role. Candidates' responses are scored and matched against successful employees in a particular occupational role. Biographical data questionnaires may be presented in multiple-choice format and include both 'hard' items, which are easy to verify, and 'soft' items, which are easy to fake. Typical items cover educational background, previous work experience, educational background, hobbies and interests, aspirations and attitudes. Impression management scales may be included to deal with faking. There is no underlying theory determining the inclusion of questions. However, the empirical basis of biodata questionnaires has been the focus of considerable research, and they have generally been found to be a good predictor of job performance (Robertson and Smith, 2001). Biographical data may be used in the selection process in numerous occupations and questionnaires are more commonly used in the USA than the UK.

REFLECTIVE ACTIVITY

Which selection tool – application form, CV, or biographical data questionnaire – do you think is best at differentiating applicants and predicting performance at work in respect of each of the following occupations?

        construction worker
        librarian
        store manager
        company director
        call centre operator

Both application forms and biographical data are more discriminatory between applicants than CVs because they are standardised – they ask the same questions of everyone. However, whereas application form information is compared to job requirements and identified competencies (eg teamworking), possibly identified from job analysis, biographical data is collected and matched against biographical characteristics identified from statistical analysis of the profiles of successful employees. But statistical relationships between different biographical characteristics (eg living abroad before the age of 12) and job performance (eg as airline cabin crew member) may not reflect a causal relationship.

INTERVIEWS

Interviews may be carried out as one-to-one selection processes or involve a panel of interviewers. The interview itself may be unstructured and free-flowing or structured according to an ordered set of questions; these may relate to a criterion-based or competency-based interview format which includes questions focused on obtaining evidence against particular criteria or competencies. Interviews are the most used, most abused and also most well-researched selection procedure. So not only do we know why interviews are used so often, and how differently interviews can be designed and carried out, we also have some idea about how to enhance them to improve job performance predictions.

Interviews are relatively inexpensive compared to other methods, such as assessment centres or psychometric testing, although they are often wrongly assumed to require little training and preparation. Interviews by their nature are an exchange of views and therefore allow interviewers to become acquainted with the interviewees and assess a number of knowledge, skills, abilities and training requirements as part of one assessment process. Overall, interviews appear to be – and can be – cost-effective and efficient. Unfortunately, there is also a high price to pay if interviews are not well designed and conducted appropriately.

Interviews can be designed to assess relevant knowledge, skills, experience, abilities, training needs, aspirations and person–organisation fit, but quite often this approach is too broad and the quality of the experience and information obtained can be further undermined by a limited and relatively short time period allowed for the interview. Even well-designed interviews can be problematic since the skills of the interviewer are of great importance in determining interview outcomes. Interviewers may display their own nervousness, dominate the interview process, allow the interviewee to provide lengthy, irrelevant answers, be influenced by the physical appearance or communication skills of the interviewee, fail to remember important answers and be distracted by irrelevant information. Decisions can be reached too quickly or on the basis of irrelevant information, and undue weight may be placed on negative information provided by the candidate.

Unlike most other selection methods, interviews are interactive and allow an exchange of communications between two or more people. This means they are not only heavily influenced by the verbal and non-verbal communication skills of those taking part – the interviewees and the interviewers – but also by their thoughts, feelings and judgements. Social psychologists such as Anderson and Shackleton (1993) have focused on identifying factors that shape interview decision-making and understanding individuals' implicit personality theories, cognitive biases and judgement errors. Potential sources of error that can influence interviewer evaluations of candidates have been the focus of considerable research and are summarised in the list below (Taylor, 2005).

Expectancy effect

An excellent application form or reference can lead interviewers to expect and judge a candidate's interview performance as excellent and confirm the initial expectations.

First impressions

The first few minutes of an interview can have long-lasting effects and determine the final outcome – in either a negative or a positive way.

Stereotyping

This can occur when interviewees are evaluated against the interviewer's personal understanding of categories of interviewees – eg females, ethnic groups, a good applicant.

Halo and horns effect

This is a tendency to generalise one aspect of an interviewee's good (halo effect) or bad (horns effect) performance to all performance or perceived abilities.

Contrast effect

It can be difficult not to compare each interviewee with the previous one, contrasting them on certain aspects which may not be relevant to the selection process.

Leniency and harshness effect

This is a general tendency to judge people's performance favourably (leniency effect) or unfavourably (harshness effect).

Negative information bias

This occurs when an initial unfavourable piece of information is weighted more significantly than any following positive information. Bolster and Springbett (1961) suggested that it can take eight pieces of positive information to outweigh the damaging effect of one piece of negative information

'Similar to me' effect

This refers to a favourable bias towards interviewees who are judged by the interviewer to be similar to himself/herself.

REFLECTIVE ACTIVITY

The role of the assessor in the selection process is to objectively evaluate candidates' performance.

Consider each of the biases listed above and decide how each of them might be avoided in an interview situation.

ASSESSING INTERVIEW PERFORMANCE AND PREDICTING JOB PERFORMANCE

Robertson and Smith (2001) summarise some of the research on the job interview which has been extensively investigated. Briefly, interviews are more likely to accurately predict job performance when the interview format is structured, standardised and incorporates situational interviewing. This is where candidates are asked the same situation-specific questions relating to how they would do the job and are examined on their hypothetical performance. Answers are scored by specialists and interpreted according to a pre-defined set of criteria. Alternatively, behaviour description interviewing may be adopted, which focuses on the candidate's actual behaviour. However, although it has been said that past behaviour is the best predictor of future behaviour (Janz, 1989), the review by Robertson and Smith (2001) found that situational interviews tend to be slightly better at predicting successful job performance than behaviour description interviews (see Taylor and Small, 2002, for other recent research in this field).

Assessing individuals' performance in any context is difficult and requires precise definition of the main criteria behaviours as a starting point (see the above section on factors that affect the choice of selection method). One approach in appraisal contexts and selection processes includes the use of behavioural anchored rating scales (BARS) to improve objectivity in assessments by limiting biases and assumptions. However, using BARS will not ensure that the process of evaluation is objective. Assessors require understanding, training and practice in the use of BARS or any other behaviour rating system.

BEHAVIOURAL ANCHORED RATING SCALES (BARS)

BARS are hierarchical descriptions of behaviours which assessors use to evaluate candidates' responses to interview questions or behaviours demonstrated in job sample tests or assessment centre exercises. Developing BARS can be a lengthy process but uses the information collected from repertory grid and critical incident techniques and visionary interviews used for getting objective information about superior job performance. These techniques gather a lot of information and examples of ideal, good and poor performance which can be grouped into dimensions (eg communication or leadership or problem-solving) and specify the behaviours associated or expected of superior performers. These behaviours can be ranked and presented in a BARS format so that each point on the rating scale is tied to a behaviour description to make the rating as meaningful as possible. (See Cook, 2004, for further details on how to create a BARS and example.)

Training assessors to observe and then record what they have seen may seem like unnecessary skills to focus on, but observations and records of candidates' behaviours are often distorted by the biases and assumptions that can affect the selection process. To avoid such biases candidates' behaviours should be observed, recorded and then classified (or categorised) and finally evaluated. In many assessment situations candidates are observed and evaluated without behaviours being accurately recorded and classified.

REFLECTIVE ACTIVITY

How would you improve a one-to-one unstructured interview?

REFERENCES

As is evident in Table 22 above, references are widely used throughout Europe and particularly in the UK. References require applicants to provide details of the names, occupation and addresses of at least two individuals who can be contacted to provide a written or verbal statement about the applicant. Reference requests generally seek information in relation to the applicant's employment history and experience and to verify objective information such as the applicant's qualifications, rate of absenteeism, reliability, standard of work and achievements. Standardised reference forms are becoming more common to ensure consistency in information gathered about applicants.

References may be obtained as part of the assessment and selection process or at the end of the selection process and once a provisional offer has been made to the applicant. This means that the value and importance of references in determining the outcome of a selection process may vary considerably. The CIPD recruitment, retention and turnover survey (2006) found that 50% of organisations rate pre-interview employment references as one of the methods they use to select applicants.

Referees may be chosen by applicants to provide a positive assessment, although references from relatives and friends are rarely accepted. Usual practice requires that applicants' current and former employers are named as main referees. The information given in references must be carefully considered and as accurate as possible and not present a misleading impression of the applicant, overly favourable or otherwise. Under the Data Protection Act 1998 it can be possible for applicants to obtain copies of their references.

In terms of the usefulness of references, the findings from the Recruitment Confidence Index (RCI) produced by Cranfield School of Management (2006) reveal that 86% of HR managers who take up written references do not find them useful predictors of future success.

REFLECTIVE ACTIVITY

What value do you think references add to the selection process?

How would you try to ensure that references assist in predicting candidates' job performance?

PSYCHOLOGICAL TESTING

Psychological tests or instruments are sophisticated tools – usually developed by psychologists – for measuring individuals' characteristics such as personality, abilities, intelligence, interests and aptitudes (ie abilities to acquire further knowledge and skills). They are designed to measure psychological characteristics in a systematic way, according to standardised measurement dimensions, and for this reason are also known as psychometric tests. (Psychometrics is the theory and practice of psychological test construction.) Psychological testing is adopted for a variety of purposes, employment selection being a common use.

It is important to note that psychological tests invariably take considerable time and expertise to develop and refine to reach a high standard of acceptability, reliability and validity. HR practitioners must be familiar with the concepts of reliability and validity and understand the different types of reliability coefficients and validity coefficients and what they mean. Most psychological instruments are available through publishers who provide training for each particular test or questionnaire before they can be purchased. Manuals are also available, and these are necessary for in-depth information and future reference to ensure that they are used appropriately to provide standard and consistent assessment. Psychological tools are protected by copyright laws, which mean that they must not be reproduced without prior permission of the publisher.

Guidelines for using psychological tests in the selection process

Individuals who use psychological tests for assessment are expected to follow the British Psychological Society's Code of Good Practice for Psychological Testing. This means they should hold the relevant Certificate(s) of Competence in Psychological Testing, continue to develop their competence, and work within their competence.

Procedures for administration, scoring and interpretation should be followed in accordance with the appropriate test manual. The administration of psychological tests should be the same for everyone. This includes the same questionnaire booklets, answer sheets, time constraints, sequence in the selection process, environmental conditions, scoring of responses and interpretation. Unqualified individuals should not have access to the materials, and all information relating to the materials and individuals' responses and scores should be kept securely. Confidentiality must be respected.

All potential test-takers must be informed of the purpose of psychological testing and how their results will be used. They should also be provided with feedback. If all this guidance to ensure that psychological tests are used appropriately is followed, they can promote fairness and equality of opportunity. This is because they are designed to be as objective as possible. On the other hand, inappropriate use of tests or inadequate testing processes can lead to bias and unfair discrimination against some candidates.

In general, psychological tests can be divided into two main categories: personality questionnaires, and ability and aptitude tests.

Personality questionnaires

Personality questionnaires are not tests because there are no right or wrong answers. The use of personality questionnaires in the selection process has been the subject of some debate based on two main issues. Firstly, can personality be measured? And secondly, how important is personality in job performance? There are no simple answers to these questions but the case for personality assessment in selection continues to be argued (see Robertson, 1994). The underlying assumption in the adoption of personality questionnaires is that an individual's personality is relatively stable and can be accurately assessed using questionnaires to identify key characteristics which are thought to be of significant importance in determining successful job performance.

The type of personality characteristics assessed by questionnaires include interpersonal style, thinking style, management style, emotional responsiveness, sociability, independence, empathy, conscientiousness, self-discipline, decision-making, impulsivity, and so on. Each personality measure is based on a particular theory of personality – for example, the NEO-PI personality measure is based on the 'Big Five' theory of personality. The big five personality dimensions are **N**euroticism, **E**xtraversion, **O**penness, Agreeableness and Conscientiousness, and NEO-PI stands for the first three dimensions of personality theory measured by the **P**ersonality **I**nventory. However, occupationally related measures of personality reflect theory and research findings on the role of personality (behaviours, preferences and attitudes) in work performance and assist in assessing the suitability of an individual for a particular role. There are a wide range of occupational personality questionnaires.

Ability and aptitude tests

Ability and aptitude tests may measure general or specific abilities or aptitudes. In general, these psychometric tests are carefully designed to assess clearly defined concepts and skills. For example, specific ability tests look at individual abilities such as critical reasoning ability, numerical critical reasoning and spatial ability. Specific aptitude tests are designed to assess skills that are required for particular job activities or training, such as computer programming. Ability and aptitude tests are often developed to cover a range of ability levels and form part of a battery of several tests. They may be very general in application and applied in a selection process for a wide variety of different jobs, or be relevant to a specific skill set.

General ability tests, however, assess what is often referred to by psychologists as 'general intelligence'. Like the concept of personality, general intelligence has been the subject of considerable debate. General ability tests provide an overall measure of mental ability for a wide range of activities across a wide variety of situations, and this may not provide enough information on how well an individual will perform in relation to specific job requirements. Examples of ability tests commonly used in the selection process include the Watson Glaser Critical Thinking Appraisal test, the Employee Aptitude Survey, which is a set of employment tests designed to meet the practical requirements of a personnel office, and the Advance Assessment Series for Managerial and Graduate Tests VRT1 and NRT1 for verbal reasoning and numerical reasoning. The ABLE (Aptitude for Business Learning Exercises) Series is designed to measure aptitude for learning new competencies and to reduce the potential for discrimination against minority groups. As the WERS data indicates (see Table 23), the use of personality questionnaires for selection purposes is not as common as performance tests, and overall the popularity of these psychological tools has not increased a great deal since 1998.

Table 23 Selection tests, 1998 and 2004

	(1998)		(2004)	
	Personality questionnaires used routinely for some occupations (%)	Performance tests used routinely for some occupations (%)	Personality questionnaires used routinely for some occupations (%)	Performance tests used routinely for some occupations (%)
All workplaces	18	44	19	46
Organisation size				
10–99 employees	12	41	7	38
10,000 or more employees	22	48	29	58
Industry				
Manufacturing	12	44	17	37
Hotels and restaurants	15	23	20	33
Financial services	53	69	25	61
Public sector	16	56	18	63

Source: Kersley *et al* (2006; p.77)

JOB OR WORK SAMPLES

Standardised job or work samples may be the most appropriate, reliable and valid approach to selecting the best candidate for the job according to predetermined structured performance criteria, as reviewed by Robertson and Smith (2001) and Schmidt and Hunter (1998). However, practical constraints may prevent the inclusion of work samples in the selection process and may disadvantage those candidates lacking specific job-related knowledge or experience. It is also critical to carry out a job analysis to identify the content of the job that is to be sampled for selection purposes.

In-tray exercises

In-tray exercises are often used to assess individuals on some of the core administrative functions of a job and may be regarded as a sub-set of work samples. In-tray exercises may require candidates to produce a report based on an analysis of a variety of information or prioritising and co-ordinating various actions in response to a number of competing demands and requirements. Such tasks are intended to assess candidates' analytical skills, problem-solving ability, resourcefulness and initiative, etc. In-tray exercises can be assessed quite objectively with a clearly structured scoring system and are often included in assessment centres.

GROUP ASSESSMENTS

Where working with others is a fundamental aspect of a job, group discussions provide an opportunity to assess individuals' interpersonal and communication skills and the ability to work with or lead others in a social work-related situation. An analysis of the content and relevance of the discussion may also provide an evaluation of individuals' reasoning skills. Group discussions can be organised to focus on different aspects of individuals' verbal and non-verbal behaviour and communication skills, and – like in-tray exercises – group assessments are often included in assessment centres.

A common group assessment involves candidates' completing a task as a group exercise. This approach allows assessors to evaluate a wide range of abilities including problem-solving, initiative, creativity, teamwork, flexibility, and so on. Structured criteria for assessment are needed to ensure consistency and relevance in evaluating individuals' contributions in group discussion sessions or group assignments.

PRESENTATIONS

Managerial and leadership roles generally require a high standard of communication skills in all situations including presentations to large, possibly very diverse, groups of employees. Selection processes for this type of position therefore often involve a presentation on a specific topic which is formally assessed. Various aspects of the presentation can be evaluated, including the structure, content, style of delivery, persuasiveness, relevance, accuracy, and so on.

ASSESSMENT CENTRES

An assessment centre is not a place but an approach to selection that includes a number of exercises and assessment methods which simulate the main requirements of the job. A typical combination of assessment methods which compromise an assessment centre might include psychometric tests such as personality and aptitude tests, a criterion-based structured interview, an in-tray exercise, a group exercise, a group discussion and a presentation. Each assessment method will be carefully designed to evaluate particular competencies required for the job. Each part of the selection process is observed and evaluated by trained assessors to be as consistent and objective as possible in scoring candidates' behaviours. Assessment centres are an expensive selection process but increasing in popularity. Some 48% of organisations surveyed by the CIPD in 2006 then utilised assessment centres, compared to 34% in 2005. However, research studies (see Robertson and Smith, 2001) question whether cheaper methods could produce the same selection outcomes with the same, or better, chances of predicting the candidates' job success.

THE ACCURACY OF SOME METHODS OF SELECTION

The accuracy of different selection methods varies considerably. This means that some selection methods are better than others in identifying the candidate who will perform most successfully in the job. In general, various research studies suggest that assessment centres, work sample tests, ability tests and structured interviews tend to be more accurate than unstructured interviews and references.

REFLECTIVE ACTIVITY

Why are some selection methods better than others in identifying candidates who will perform more (or less) successfully in the job?

How would you know if a selection method was successful?

Different selection methods vary in how closely they match and measure the key abilities and skills required for the particular job. In other words, they vary in content validity (matching the tasks and duties of the job) and criterion-related validity (measuring performance on the tasks and duties). A statistical procedure such as correlation can help us evaluate the effectiveness of our selection processes or methods. The next section covers these key points in more detail.

3 SELECTION AS PREDICTION AND MEASURE OF SUCCESSFUL SELECTION

There are two concepts that are central to understanding what is meant by successful selection. These are validity and reliability. Valid means sound, authentic and genuine. A valid selection method accepts good applicants and rejects poor ones. Reliability, on the other hand, means consistent, unchanging and stable. A reliable selection method achieves the same outcome given the same circumstances and the same individuals.

VALIDITY

Validity is a most important concept. There are several types of validity. This means that a selection method may be or appear to be sound, genuine and authentic in different ways.

- *Face validity* refers to whether a selection method *appears* relevant, appropriate and acceptable to the selection participants. This is important. Yet face validity may result in false validity, because a selection method may appear appropriate when it is not. How is face validity assessed? By asking participants if they think the selection method is plausible.

- *Content validity* is present when the questions or items in a test *are* relevant, appropriate and measure what they are designed to measure. Content validity relies on job analysis to ensure that the content of the selection method is relevant and allows required skills, knowledge, experience, etc, to be demonstrated. How is content validity assessed? Experts in the particular area – eg individuals who perform in the role, managers or supervisors – are asked to assess the content in relation to breadth and depth of information covered by the selection method. It is a logical assessment, not a statistical one.

- *Construct validity* is concerned with concepts and overarching theories. Different ability tests, personality questionnaires, aptitude tests, intelligence tests, etc, are based on particular theories and are designed to measure concepts defined within such theories. For example, there are different theories of personality, which in turn means that each different personality questionnaire is built on a different theory of personality and attempts to measure the different constructs of each theory that predict how people behave. These predictions are reflected in the questions or items that make up the questionnaire. Construct validity is about analysing the meaning of the questions, items and the responses in relation to defined concepts or constructs to ensure consistency with the overarching theory. How is construct validity assessed? Statistical procedures such as correlation, t-tests and factor analysis are often employed to explore and offer evidence of construct validity.

- *Criterion-related validity* studies are at the heart of selection as prediction of successful job performance. Criterion-related validity studies compare performance assessed by the selection method (eg an ability test) to a relevant external measure of job success or 'performance criterion'. Criterion-related validity is high when the selection method identifies individuals who are or will be successful on the job as defined by the particular measure of job success chosen as the performance criterion – eg number of sales, supervisor rating, etc. Criterion-related validity can be assessed as *concurrent validity* or as *predictive validity*.

- *Concurrent validity* assessments are often carried out with current employees. The purpose is to identify highly successful and less successful performers according to a measure of job performance (eg manager ratings), which correspond well with a particular test or task (eg ability test) that can be used for selection purposes. Comparing individuals' test performance with another assessment – eg a job sample task – can also assess concurrent validity. Concurrent validation provides an assessment of individuals' current level of performance and is quicker and easier to conduct than predictive validity studies.

- *Predictive validity* is assessed by comparing or correlating results of assessments taken before individuals are employed and once they are in post. The aim is to predict future successful job performance at the point of selection. The main problem with assessing for predictive validity is identifying a relevant and meaningful job performance measure, and it may not be possible to use the same measure at the point of selection for various practical reasons.

RELIABILITY

Reliability refers to consistency, stability and equivalence. Selection processes must include reliable methods or tools to ensure that the assessments of individuals are consistent from one assessor to another, stable over time and can be repeated, so the same outcome decisions are obtained every time. Selection methods lack reliability if the same interview performance, for example, is rated high by one interviewer and low by another, and completely differently three weeks later. If there is a lack of consistency in the process, selection decisions will be unreliable.

The concept of reliability is mostly used in connection with statistical assessments of psychological tests. In most test manuals, information on the reliability of the test is reported as the correlation obtained between one set of test scores and another. However, the same approaches can be adopted for assessing any selection method, including structured interviews, job samples, in-tray exercises, etc, so long as there is a means of obtaining objective scoring for candidates' performance included in the process.

The most effective way to improve reliability of selection methods is to standardise the process – the interview, assessment exercise, job sample, etc – as far as possible. In effect this means ensuring that all candidates are treated in the same way – eg asked the same questions in the same way, under the same assessment conditions, with the same time constraints and with responses to questions observed, recorded, classified and evaluated according to a predefined rating system.

REFLECTIVE ACTIVITY

Which do you think is more important – validity or reliability?

Why?

EVALUATING SELECTION STRATEGIES

A selection strategy involves a process of selection using different methods – often application forms, references and interviews are included as a minimum – with the aim of identifying the candidate(s) who will perform most successfully in the post. But how do we know this aim is achieved and our selection strategy has been successful? We need to evaluate the selection methods adopting a predictive-criterion validity study design. This involves correlating the objective, reliable and valid scores obtained at the point of selection (eg test results or interview BARS results) with the valid and reliable job performance criteria collected once the employees are well established in their jobs (after between one and three years). This is often not done, even though the costs of using poor selection processes are high.

KEY ISSUES IN SELECTION

We now pull together ten key points about selection raised in this chapter:

- Selecting appropriate employees is a key activity in any organisation since failure is costly and can threaten organisational performance, development and even survival.

- Success depends on using appropriate and effective selection methods.

- It is important to remember that the selection process is two-way: applicants are also engaged in a selection and evaluation process of organisations and may reject offers from organisations if there is a lack of 'fit'.

- Selection processes reflect the organisation's culture and values.

- Different European countries adopt a different mix of commonly used selection methods which reflects different cultures and values.

- Various factors can determine the selection methods adopted because a 'one-size-fits-all' approach is not appropriate.

- Legal issues must be considered in the design of any selection process to avoid unlawful discrimination.

- The different psychological processes at play in interview situations must be controlled as far as possible.

- There are many psychometric tools available – however, the value of such tools may be lost if they are not chosen carefully nor used appropriately.

- Evaluation of the selection process itself, however simple, is a vital exercise to undertake.

Perhaps there are other key points that you would like to note for yourself.

The main case study in this chapter now follows. It illustrates some examples of good practice and highlights the importance of a well-designed, coherent approach to selection. In addition, it demonstrates the benefits of evaluating the selection methods and overall selection strategies, however simply.

MAIN CASE STUDY

This case study is based on a selection process developed by a large private sector employer based in the UK. Custom and practice relied on a structured interview method for assessment and selection of candidates to manager-level positions, most of whom were recruited locally or promoted from within the company. However, as the company expanded, struggled to keep step with technological advancements, strove to beat off international competition, and at the same time began to attract more highly qualified and more overseas applicants with additional experience and skills, it became apparent that the selection process was not sufficiently discriminatory. Inconsistent hiring decisions were made in different part of the company and there was no focus on future needs. In sum, the selection process was no longer adequate. Consultants were commissioned to review, design, train and implement a revised selection process.

The consultants began by taking account of the company's new strategic plan and involved discussions with senior executives, who were required to answer two key questions to drive the focus of the redesigned selection process: What sort of people does the company want? How does the company describe people who are really good? Job analyses were then employed to identify the main tasks and responsibilities of particular roles, how good performance might be measured, and how these roles might change in the future, and therefore what these people would be required to do in the future. The main criteria – skills, abilities, knowledge, etc – could then be described in meaningful terms for all senior executives and line managers to provide feedback on. Involving all key stakeholders in the organisation in the redesign of the selection process was an important contributory factor in its success implementation and in ensuring that individuals would be selected who 'fitted' with the organisation.

An online application form was designed that was carefully assessed against the company's recruitment needs and the requirements of the vacant positions. Successful applicants were then invited to a two-day selection process which included a group task, a job sample, a psychological test and a structured interview which has since become competency-based as candidates are now asked for specific examples of experience and how they have resolved difficult situations. Current interviewers are trained in on-going interviewing skills workshops on competency-based interviewing to improve objective and justifiable selection decisions against a tailored rating system. Performance on each of the selection methods is rated according to the agreed dimensions, such as working with others, communication and influence, technical orientation, problem-solving and drive to reach an overall selection decision. The same dimensions are used in the six-monthly appraisal system to track individual performance and can be used to evaluate the components of the selection process.

Your task

Not all organisations can afford consultants to construct the selection and evaluation process described above. If you were asked to create a selection process to recruit your new boss, what method(s) would you adopt, what steps would you take to establish the process, and how would you reassure yourself that you had chosen the right person?

EXPLORE FURTHER

BPS (2002) *Code of Good Practice for Psychological Testing*. Available from: **www.psychtesting.org.uk**
This provides clear guidance for the appropriate use of psychological tests for testers and test-takers.

Cook, M. (2004) *Personnel Selection. Adding value through people*, 4th edition. Chichester, John Wiley & Sons
A research-focused textbook written from the perspective that there is a clear link between selection and productivity.

Searle, R. H. (2003) *Recruitment and Selection: A critical text*. Milton Keynes, Palgrave/Open University Press
A research-focused textbook which aims to critically evaluate various practices in recruitment and selection.

Sparrow, P. (2006) *International Recruitment, Selection and Assessment*. London, CIPD
A research-informed report covering recruitment, selection and assessment issues facing HR professionals working in an international context.

CHAPTER 10

Flexibility and work–life balance

Suzan Lewis *and* Ian Roper

INTRODUCTION

This chapter is about matching the personal needs of employees outside of work with the operational and commercial needs of employers in the workplace.

LEARNING OUTCOMES

By the end of this chapter readers should be able to:

- explain what employers may mean when they refer to 'flexibility'

- explain the growing significance of 'work–life balance' as a key source of employees' need for flexibility

- identify where the apparently competing needs of employers and employees may be put together effectively

- recognise and challenge aspects of workplace culture that undermine flexible working arrangements

- understand that achieving mutual flexibility involves processes and not just policies.

The chapter is structured in four parts. The first part discusses the development of the term 'flexibility' in the field of HRM, comparing employer-oriented needs with those of workers. (The term 'employee' is not used here, specifically because one form of flexibility is the use of non-employment-based contracts.) The second part examines what employees want from flexibility; the third part focuses on work–life balance; and the final part looks at how these various issues can be integrated into HR best practice.

The starter case study highlights some uses of flexibility in a real-life organisational situation. The text then explains in more detail some of the different forms of flexibility that employers have sought to utilise, and examines one or two problems with some of these approaches. This is followed by a discussion of some more recent uses of the term 'flexibility', which appear to be more employee-led and strongly associated with the concept of work–life balance. The third part of the chapter then goes on to discuss the development

STARTER CASE STUDY

LonBoro is a London metropolitan borough council with a large and ethnically diverse workforce. In the period being described here, the Council had gone through a number of years of political turmoil resulting in some negative publicity. The political leadership was seeking radical restructuring of the organisation, moving away from a traditional bureaucratic model of management to one where much greater devolution was assigned to the services themselves. This strategy had a number of stages. First, services were turned into cost centres for which budget targets were delegated to service heads and managed accordingly. Service managers were therefore 'empowered' to make more decisions about staff issues than had been the case before. Combined with this there was a large reduction in the size of the workforce, together with a series of decisions to tender out, completely, a number of services to private contactors. Overall, this package of changes could be called a strategy based on *numerical flexibility* (which we explain later).

In the next stage of reform, LonBoro embarked upon an ambitious quality management project to enhance the reputation of its services. Service managers were encouraged to make innovations in working practices to realise this aim – a strategy that could be described as focusing on the *functional flexibility* of its staff (which we again explain later).

A further stage involved the decision to outsource all of what remained of in-house provided services, effectively transferring all the front-line staff over to private contractors bidding to run the services, leaving only

'strategic' commissioning units in the Council, In the end, however, much of this final stage was actually abandoned when LonBoro's political leadership changed in subsequent local elections.

The effects of these various changes were mixed. The early round of severe job cuts and outsourcing – through numerical flexibility – led to a steep downturn in staff morale. Later, however, the introduction of the quality policy – partly associated with functional flexibility – led to improved staff morale, albeit, in the light of the previous round of job cuts, described somewhat lugubriously by one manager who said that 'morale among the survivors' was good. This generally improved picture was further boosted by the enhanced reputation that LonBoro was receiving for the quality of its services – which further boosted morale. However, this virtuous circle was again broken by the further announcement of more outsourcing. Among other issues of concern, staff surveys were now reporting a perception of how this was all badly affecting LonBoro's previous commitment to equality issues and it was also leading to direct confrontation with the union. Figure 18 shows the effects of these changes on morale, as described by a senior manager.

Questions for discussion

Basing your response on what has been described in this case study, what would you say were the likely advantages and disadvantages of *numerical flexibility* and *functional flexibility*?

Figure 18 Staff morale at LonBoro

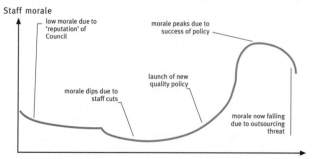

Staff morale

low morale due to 'reputation' of Council

morale peaks due to success of policy

launch of new quality policy

morale dips due to staff cuts

morale now falling due to outsourcing threat

of flexible working arrangements within a work–life balance framework, using case study examples to illustrate the reason for their development, their advantages and limitations. In this section we explore an approach to flexibility that is both employer- and employee-led. The chapter then concludes with the main case study, which describes the introduction of work–life balance policies and practices into an organisation.

Reference sources named within the chapter may be looked up in the *References and further reading* section at the end of the book.

FLEXIBILITY FROM THE EMPLOYER'S PERSPECTIVE

WHAT IS FLEXIBILITY?

First we should explain some of the flexibility terms used and see how certain types of flexibility may be used in conjunction with others. One of the issues arising from the case study above is the definition of 'flexibility' being used. Quite clearly, there appear to be very different consequences involved in using *numerical flexibility* than in pursuing *functional flexibility*. Another issue is the question of who is intended to benefit from any particular type of flexibility. The word itself implies a call to be 'reasonable', and it is very hard see how anyone could object to being asked to be flexible. As Tailby (2003; p.490) has succinctly put it, when flexibility is

> applied to the world of work and employment, however, this obviously raises the issue of whose interests are at stake. Practices deemed to be rigid by management, for example, may be the source of stability and security for employees. Consequently, job protection rights and the employer's freedom to hire and fire may be a source of conflict between the parties.

For this reason we need to be precise about *who* is being expected to be flexible and *in what way*. Blyton (1996) provides a useful starting point for us here. He has consolidated many of the definitions of flexibility into four basic types: numerical, functional, temporal and financial flexibility. Each of these is now explained.

Numerical flexibility (as the name implies) is concerned with management's ability to make rapid adjustments to the number – and also the composition – of its workforce. We could think of how this has been traditionally used in seasonal industries like tourism: running a holiday camp at the seaside requires the recruitment of large numbers of staff during the peak season in the summer, but only a very basic skeleton staff during the winter. Being numerically flexible allows such an organisation to make these rapid adjustments to seasonal market conditions. Crucially, though, this type of flexibility works in *this* industry partly because it meets the expectations of the workers in it.

REFLECTIVE ACTIVITY

Referring back to the LonBoro case described in the Starter case study, in what circumstances and in what ways might the use of numerical flexibility be more problematic than is the situation at a seaside holiday camp?

Fuctional flexibility refers (again as the name implies) to the functions that employees carry out when employed. It implies a multi-skilled, multi-tasking worker keen to carry out a range of duties. It is functional flexibility that has been identified by numerous commentators to have been at the heart of Japanese industrial success from the 1970s onwards and is credited as being equally crucial to Japanese transplants such as Nissan and Toyota that came to Britain in the 1980s and 1990s (Oliver and Wilkinson, 1992). From an employee perspective, functional flexibility would seem to be a much better option than that of numerical flexibility – offering the possibility of getting skills that would be transferable to other employers. However, critics have pointed to a bleaker side to functional flexibility, often referred to as 'work intensification' – whereby it is not so much responsibility and increased autonomy that are being improved, but rather 'horizontal job loading' by which more tasks are added into the working day. (See Chapter 11 on the importance of autonomy.)

A third type of flexibility is *temporal flexibility*. Yet again as the name suggests, this is to do with adjustments to time – the working day or the working year. Examples include the use of flexitime, annualised hours, or the use of termtime working. It also extends to some more long-standing practices such as the use of part-time work and even 'overtime' – although many of the innovations in temporal flexibility are designed to reduce the need for employers to resort to paying an overtime premium to cope with high peaks in demand.

REFLECTIVE ACTIVITY

One example of temporal flexibility that has been used by large retail organisations such as Sainsbury's is that of 'temporary vacation contracts', designed so that students can work part-time and increase their hours when they are between terms.

How do a) students, and b) retail employers benefit from this arrangement?

The final form of flexibility defined by Blyton (1996) is that of *financial flexibility*. Financial flexibility describes practices relating to variations to standard methods of payment. A 'standard' method of payment could be assumed to mean payment based on a flat rate for the job, based on hours worked. Flexibility, on this theme, might include performance-related pay – based upon some idea of management being able to adjust pay rates individually according to some method of assessing each individual's contribution (see Chapter 13). It may also involve the inclusion, within the pay package itself, of bonus schemes and employee share ownership schemes. Flexibility within the 'reward system' may also include a range of non-pay aspects such as variations in fringe benefits. More recently, innovations in 'flexible benefits' packages have involved organisations allowing employees to trade off various aspects of their benefits package to optimise to their own personal circumstances – trading in their company car allowance in favour of more generous holiday entitlement, for example.

COMBINING TYPES OF FLEXIBILITY: THE IMPACT OF (DE)REGULATION AND THE FLEXIBLE FIRM

We have so far examined and categorised different types of flexibility separately. In practice, however, firms are likely to use versions of these approaches to flexibility in combination. In 1984, John Atkinson proposed a model for an integrated approach to flexibility in the model known as 'the flexible firm'. This now well-known model compared the traditional firm – employing sufficient numbers of permanent full-time employees to enable the firm to carry out all activities at any given time – with an emerging flexible firm in which the long-term commitment of the firm to such large numbers of people was seen as impossible. In the flexible firm the workforce is divided into two elements. The first element is a 'core' workforce of functionally flexible employees on secure permanent employment contracts, typically being highly trained, qualified and on high salaries. Outside this core, however, is the second element, a 'periphery workforce' – based on the principles described under numerical flexibility. This group would conduct a whole range of activities not perceived to be of strategic importance to the core activity of the business. In the Atkinson model, this periphery is further divided into different peripheral sub-groups comprising different types of employment with varying degrees of job security.

Although there are some important criticisms that can be made of the flexible firm model, it is helpful in describing what most large UK organisations, private and public now look like, compared to how they may have looked, say, 30 years ago. However, this situation did not take place purely through the persuasive strength of the model alone. Making labour markets this flexible required changes to the external environment. During the 1980s, Britain experienced a step-change in the way that government treated employment regulation – one that was significantly different from past approaches and one that was significantly at odds with the way such matters were dealt with in continental Europe. The Conservative governments of this period were committed to making the labour market more flexible, as the following quote from their election manifesto indicates (Conservative Party Manifesto, 1983):

We shall go on reducing the barriers which discourage employers from recruiting more staff, even when they want to. And we shall help to make the job market more flexible and efficient so that more people can work part-time if they wish, and find work more easily.

Table 24 shows some examples of regulatory and deregulatory changes made during the 1980s and early 1990s, and how they impacted upon employers' use of flexibility.

Table 24 Changes to regulation and the impact on flexibility

Regulatory change(s)	Impact on flexibility
Restriction of trade union powers	Reduces collective employee resistance to introducing functional flexibility
Abolition of Wage Councils	Allows lower rates of pay for new job categories created by numerical flexibility
Reduction in unfair dismissal protection for employees	The reduced risk for employers incentivises a growth in the use of fixed-term temporary employment
Opt-out of EU Social Chapter	The reduced cost, through reduced rights for part-time and temporary employees, allows growth in non-standard employment
Forcing of public services to tender out series of activities to private contractors	Transference of the logic of the flexible firm into the public sector

In fact, if we look at figures from the WERS data, the evidence is mixed. For example, although the outsourcing of various peripheral functions is common, there are differences between functions. For example, whereas 59% of organisations outsource building maintenance, still only 12% outsource catering services (Kersley, Alpin, Forth, Dix, Oxenbridge, Bryson and Bewley, 2006); and it is public sector organisations that are more likely to make use of fixed-term contract workers (61% of workplaces) rather than what we might assume to be the more ruthless cost-conscious private sector equivalents, where only 23% used these types of contracts (*ibid*; p.80).

2 FLEXIBILITY FROM THE EMPLOYEE'S PERSPECTIVE

The case for flexibility that has been made so far has all been based on the perceived benefits to employers. From this logic it is assumed that if the business benefits from reduced costs and enhanced efficiencies gained from such flexibilities, then the employees go on to benefit too, through the enhanced job security and job prospects that they receive from this. However, it could be argued on the other hand that if *all* organisations can gain maximum flexibility from their workforces, no *single* workforce will be able to gain this added job security, because any one organisation will only be as efficient as all the other organisations. It was for this reason that in the early part of the twentieth century employers were constrained by government regulation in their ability to compete on the terms and conditions of their employees; to prevent, as Winston Churchill is reputed to have stated at the time, 'the good employer being undercut by the bad employer, and the bad employer being undercut by the worse employer'. The most recent example of this trait is probably the increasing concern being felt by those – in manufacturing and in services – unable to compete on cost terms with emerging economies such as China and India. For employees this is the 'race to the bottom' scenario: that in being so 'flexible' to the needs of employers, employees are now having their jobs outsourced, not to local sub-contractors with whom they might expect to obtain employment in the future but to remote locations thousands of miles away. The argument here is that such one-sided flexibility makes it increasingly difficult for employees to achieve personal financial stability to plan a normal family life outside of the workplace.

This brings us to the other side of flexibility – that of the increased employee demand for work–life balance. But before this, we should return to some more recent changes – and continuities – to the themes mentioned in the previous section.

It was noted that 'flexibility' was not just something that occurred as a result of 'best practice': it was positively encouraged by the government by various means. When the Conservatives left office in 1997, to be replaced by Labour, a shift occurred in relation to the attitude to regulation. It was not, however, a radical shift. The new government entered into office with a stated desire to improve basic employment rights and bring them more into line with European norms, but not in a way that undermined employers' basic desire for flexibility. The approach has therefore been to 'opt in' to the European Social Chapter, thereby bringing in regulations affecting equal rights, parental rights, working time issues and employee consultation rights. Some critics from employers' lobby groups have complained about the 'regulatory burden' involved in complying with such regulations, while other lobby groups representing employee rights issues have complained that the regulations that have been introduced have been significantly watered down when applied in Britain.

The effect of this has been mixed. Most observers agree that Britain still has the most flexible labour markets in Europe even though there are high costs to geographical mobility because of home ownership. It has the least employment protection and the longest working hours, for example. However, since the equalisation of rights for non-standard workers, the overall pattern of job growth in Britain has been in permanent full-time and part-time employment, with a decline in temporary employment. Table 25 shows the growth in temporary employment in the early 1990s compared with its decline in the late 1990s and 2000s.

Table 25 UK employment growth, 1992–2002

Employees	1992–1997		1997–2002	
Full-time	+234,000	+1.4%	+1,165,000	+6.9%
Part-time	+641,000	+12.5%	+409,000	+7.1%
Permanent	+410,000	+2.0%	+1,787,000	+8.5%
Temporary	+465,000	+35.9%	−213,000	−12.1%

Source: TUC (derived from Labour Force Survey data)

So to some extent, the agenda of merely providing flexibility for employers at employees' expense has been kept under control. However, the area of 'employee-led' flexibility that has grown most in recent years is probably that related to what has been termed 'family-friendly policies' or 'work–life balance'. The case can be made that raising children makes a significant contribution to the economy as a whole (even if we think, very crudely, of the future generations that will have to be in work in order to pay for our own pensions in future years), and that this burden has fallen too much on women in the past, in terms of the loss in direct earnings and career development. Government figures estimate that the average difference in lifetime earnings between an unskilled man and an unskilled woman with no children is £197,000. This may in itself be unfair. However, if both are parents of two children, this gap increases to £482,000. Even for graduates, the lifetime pay gap between a father and mother is £161,000 (DTI, 2000). If women are not able to contribute to the labour market in line with their qualifications and experience, there are also implications for the national economy (DTI, 2001).

There has consequently been a change in government policies to address some of these issues. At the most basic level, maternity rights have been steadily improved since 1997, providing more paid maternity leave. This agenda has also, however, attempted to affect wider cultural assumptions about childcare responsibilities, providing extended rights to extended parental leave, the right to take time off work to deal with 'family emergencies', the introduction of paid paternity leave – introducing, for the first time, the rights of fathers in the workplace equation. Most recently, the government's 'family-friendly' agenda has introduced the right for parents of children up to the age of six to request flexible working, with a duty on employers to consider it (see Croucher and Kelliher, 2005, for more details). Figure 19 shows evidence from WERS 2004 that some of these initiatives seem to have had some effect on British workplaces – at least at the level of policies.

3 AN INTEGRATED APPROACH TO FLEXIBILITY

Having considered what flexibility might mean from an employer's and from an employee's perspective, we now go on to examine how these two different agendas can potentially be integrated.

WHAT IS WORK–LIFE BALANCE?

Work–life balance has been defined (Employers for work–life balance, **www.employersforwork-lifebalance.org.uk**) as being

> *about people having a measure of control over when, where and how they work. It is achieved when an individual's right to a fulfilled life inside and outside paid work is accepted and respected as the norm, to the mutual benefit of the individual, business and society.*

However, the term 'work–life balance' is problematic. It has been criticised for a number of reasons (Fleetwood, forthcoming; Lewis *et al*, forthcoming). In particular it is argued that the concept (Lewis and Cooper, 2005):

Figure 19 Percentage of workplaces with flexible working arrangements, 2004

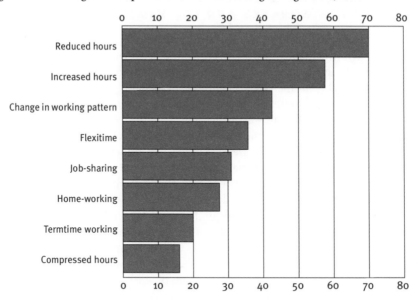

Source: Kersley, Alpin, Forth, Dix, Oxenbridge, Bryson and Bewley (2006)

- implies that work and life are separate spheres, rather than that work is a part of life
- is often interpreted as viewing lack of 'balance' as an individual rather than a workplace issue
- assumes 'balance' is always good and imbalance bad
- neglects workers' changing needs for different forms of 'balance' at different points in their lives
- as an approach tends to focus on policy rather than practice and culture change, which are necessary for policies to be effective.

Despite the ongoing discussion about the term, work–life balance has for many reasons – as explained below – become increasingly significant for organisations.

 REFLECTIVE ACTIVITY

Consider your own circumstances and those of others in your group.

How much would your own home commitments affect the patterns of work you feel able to do? What differences emerge within your group?

What kind of work would not be suitable for some people's home commitments, and what might organisations be able to do to make it more suitable?

WHY HAS 'WORK–LIFE BALANCE' BECOME INCREASINGLY SIGNIFICANT FOR WORKERS AND FOR HRM?

At first, demands for flexibility to 'balance' or integrate employment and personal life – especially family demands – came largely from women with children (see Chapter 6). Historically, the norm of full-time, continuous and inflexible working hours was made possible for men by women's role in the family. But as more women entered and stayed in the labour market, and employers recognised the need for women's labour and skills, this was challenged. From the 1980s employers began to respond with what were then termed 'family-friendly policies'. For example, Midland Bank – now part of HSBC – was one of the early leaders in this respect. Banks traditionally rely on a largely female workforce. When it was recognised in the 1980s that there was a high turnover of women after maternity leave because of childcare-related problems, policies were developed to help to meet business objectives as well as enhancing equal opportunities (see Chapter 11 on staff turnover). These included a range of flexible working arrangements such as job-sharing, family-related leaves and career breaks as well as the opening of workplace nurseries, all aiming to improve recruitment and retention of women. Outcomes included enhanced retention rates and flexible forms of work that enabled, for example, the development of 24-hour banking (Lewis, Watts and Camp, 1996).

A move from a focus on 'family-friendly' to 'work–life balance' policies occurred from the mid-1990s associated with a number of trends:

- Family-friendly policies usually focused on women. But as families and social norms shift, men – especially younger men – also want or need to be more involved in families or just to have a life outside work.

- With the trends towards long working hours and an intensification of work, more people feel the need for some 'balance' between their paid work and the rest of their lives.

- The government developed a work–life balance campaign, partly in response to EU pressure (as noted above).

- Britain still has fewer employment regulations and statutory supports (such as state-funded childcare) than many other European countries for reconciling employment and family life. This leaves considerable room for employers to develop a competitive edge by developing work–life balance policies.

FLEXIBLE WORK ARRANGEMENTS

Development of flexible working arrangements is key to work–life balance strategies. Most of the flexible working arrangements developed under the work–life balance umbrella are a form of temporal flexibility. Some forms of flexible working arrangements, such as part-time work and some flexitime or shift systems, have a long history and were introduced as productivity or efficiency measures, although it is increasingly recognised that these strategies have implications for work–life 'balance'. Others are newer and are depicted as tools for reducing work–family conflict or enhancing work–life balance, but it is increasingly recognised that they are also beneficial to employers (Lewis, 2003). It makes a difference whether these initiatives are seen primarily as productivity or work–life balance measures.

For example, a company in Japan developed a career break scheme for carers and also a flexitime scheme. The carers' scheme was open to men and women but only women used it. The flexitime was presented as a productivity measure and both men and women used it. In fact, there were business advantages to both.

REFLECTIVE ACTIVITY

Write down your considered answers to the following questions.

1 *What difficulties do you see with the implementation of flexible working arrangements within a work–life balance framework rather than as a productivity measure?*

2 *Where might resistance come from, and why?*

3 *What other barriers might there be to the effective implementation of such arrangements?*

These issues are examined in detail later in this chapter.

Table 26 shows the percentage of full-time and part-time employees who use formal flexible working arrangements. There are of course many others, particularly in smaller businesses or in professional and managerial roles, who have opportunities for informal flexibility of working times and place.

Table 26 Percentage of employees with flexible working patterns, by sex, 2004

	Males	Females	All employees
Full-time employees			
Flexible working hours	9.2	14.6	11.3
Annualised working hours	5.0	4.8	4.9
Four-and-a-half-day week	1.5	0.7	1.2
Term-time working	1.2	5.5	2.8
Nine-day fortnight	0.3	0.3	0.3
Any flexible working pattern	*17.4*	*26.2*	*20.7*
Part-time employees			
Flexible working hours	5.3	8.1	7.6
Annualised working hours	3.1	4.3	4.0
Term-time working	4.2	11.2	9.9
Job-sharing	1.0	2.7	2.4
Any flexible working pattern	*15.0*	*27.0*	*24.7*

Note: Some of the percentages in this table are based on totals which exclude people who did not state whether or not they had a flexible working arrangement; respondents could give more than one answer.

Source: Labour Force Survey, Office for National Statistics

There are of course variations across countries, as illustrated by the Cranet-E data (see Table 27).

Table 27 'Does your organisation use the following working arrangements?'

	UK	Sweden	Germany	Greece	Slovakia
Weekend work	65%	65%	77%	68%	60%
Shiftwork	61%	74%	74%	85%	67%
Overtime	92%	99%	56%	89%	87%
Annual hours contract	26%	46%	30%	10%	66%
Part-time work	97%	99%	98%	48%	12%
Job-sharing	55%	34%	41%	7%	60%
Flexitime	48%	94%	90%	43%	60%
Temporary/casual	86%	94%	65%	51%	54%
Fixed-term contracts	75%	97%	97%	79%	7%
Home-based work	32%	34%	13%	7%	16%
Teleworking	20%	44%	43%	9%	45%
Compressed working week	29%	20%	26%	2%	0%

Source: Cranet-E (2003)

4 THE ROLE OF HR PROFESSIONALS IN WORK–LIFE BALANCE

The role of HR professionals in work–life balance is not limited to the development of policies. It includes assessing the needs of workers and the business and finding the best way of meeting both agendas. This is important for convincing senior and line management of the need for flexible working arrangements. HR professionals also have an important role to play in monitoring the effectiveness of work–life balance policies, including implementation and take-up rates, and for developing strategies for overcoming resistance to change amongst managers and others, and barriers to success.

REFLECTIVE ACTIVITY

How would you convince management that work–life balance policies are important for organisational effectiveness?

Below are listed some of the business benefits that have been proved to follow from policies that are well implemented:

- compliance with regulations, and using this to positive advantage – for example, treating the parents' right to request flexible working as a challenge and opportunity to innovate rather than as a threat
- better recruitment and retention
- becoming an employer of choice by keeping up with and possibly even exceeding the flexible options offered by other employers in the same sector, especially where there are skills shortages
- reduction in stress associated with conflicting demands at work and beyond
- reduced absenteeism (flexible working arrangements, for example, enable workers to make up time lost through family or other issues)
- raised morale – workers are more engaged if they feel that their needs are recognised and if they have more autonomy and control over their time
- good public relations
- attracting ethical investors who are increasingly asking about equal opportunities and related policies
- achieving mutual flexibility (give and take between workers and their manager), which makes for additional forms of flexibility, as noted below.

For example, in a small printing business (see Lewis and Cooper, 2005) workers were encouraged to learn multiple skills so that colleagues could cover for each other on a reciprocal basis if they took time off for any reason. Workers collaborated in finding flexible solutions that they saw as fair and which also sustained production.

 REFLECTIVE ACTIVITY

Can you think of further scenarios in which the sort of flexibility associated with work–life balance enhances other forms of flexibility, or vice versa?

BARRIERS AND RESISTANCE TO THE EFFECTIVE IMPLEMENTATION OF FLEXIBLE WORKING ARRANGEMENTS

Evidence indicates that work–life policies can be successful up to a point, but much depends on how they are implemented and managed (Lewis and Cooper, 2005). They can, for example, improve recruitment but they do not necessarily maximise the use of women's (or in some cases, men's) skills. This is because flexible working policies are necessary – but not sufficient – to make the changes needed to enable all workers to develop their full potential at work and at home. Flexible working arrangements without culture change have limited impact. This is illustrated by the case of 'Proffco', a large multinational professional services firm.

Proffco has developed an impressive raft of work–life policies. They include not only family-related initiatives such as time off to care for dependants (recognising that staff have elder care and other care commitments and not just childcare-related issues) but also initiatives relating to other work–personal life commitments and aspirations. For example, a nine-day fortnight is used by some members of staff to participate in sport or other activities. The policies have increased the rate of return from maternity leave and improved scores on a staff satisfaction questionnaire. However, long working hours and inflexible work remains the norm, and those members of staff – mostly women – who do take up flexible working practices are often thought to be less committed than other employees. Consequently, most men and many women say they do not make use of flexible working arrangements because they know it would be career-limiting. Assumptions about ideal workers are deeply embedded in the culture. A woman who worked full-time, but flexibly, explained:

I am the first at work every day. Also, I usually work through lunch. The fact that I leave work on time quite often (even though I might have a caseful of work at peak periods) means that I get comments like 'I know that it's difficult for you to put in the hours, with the children.'

Those who do work flexibly believe that they are equally effective with – and in many cases, more effective than – their colleagues. Most of their managers agree with this. Yet despite the impressive policies and the success of flexible working arrangements in some departments, the organisational culture is very slow to change. People who are considered for promotion – often referred to as 'strong players' or those who 'are 'willing to go the extra mile' – are not those who use flexible working arrangements. Selection for promotion is thus made from a limited pool. Hence, the effectiveness of policies in helping all staff to work most effectively and to enhance career development is undermined. Turnover has been reduced but is still high because many employees leave to go to smaller, more flexible firms or to become self-employed.

Questions for discussion

HR professionals in many organisations will recognise the problems faced at Proffco.

Do you have any ideas about how to challenge workplace cultures in which ideal workers are still assumed to be those who do not need flexibility of working arrangements?

One possible approach is explored in the next section of text.

EMPLOYER- AND EMPLOYEE-LED: MUTUAL FLEXIBILITY

The previous sections showed how flexible working arrangements that focus on employee demands or needs are implemented for business reasons. This can be a win/win solution for employers and workers, but the effectiveness of these policies is limited if they are implemented without culture change. For example, the opportunities for reduced hours or flexible work have limited success if only full-time non-flexible workers are valued.

A further approach to flexibility is based on a dual agenda. That is, changes are implemented to meet the needs of both employer and employees, with both given equal weight. Initiatives based on the needs only of employers or only of employees are less effective (Rapoport, Bailyn, Fletcher and Pruitt, 2002). This approach stresses the importance of going beyond policy development to start a process which first challenges assumptions that sustain ineffective practices and then draws on collaboration to develop more appropriate and effective norms and practices. This is illustrated in the case of a Customer Administration Centre described below.

(See Rapoport *et al*, 2002, and Lewis and Cooper, 2005, for more details of this approach.)

CASE STUDY

At the Customer Administration Centre, where the workforce comprised largely women, many with family commitments, there were high levels of unexpected absence, resulting in problems of lack of cover. There was also high staff turnover. Management was attempting to shift the structure towards more empowered self-managed teams so that staff could manage their own absences ensuring cover at all times, but it was not working smoothly. Collaborative interviews with members of the team, including managers, revealed that employees were not trusted to manage their own time flexibly and sustain productivity. A culture of control by management was undermining the goal of empowerment. Although there was a range of flexible work policies available, managers were reluctant to allow employees to use them because they feared that it would 'open the floodgates' and undermine productivity. Consequently, employees had to make their own arrangements to try to juggle work and family commitments. Often these arrangements broke down, so they would have to call in sick or use holiday time, creating absence problems.

Bringing these assumptions, which were embedded in the culture and not just individual manager perspectives, to the surface enabled managers to reflect on their reluctance to give up control because of short-term productivity concerns. They came to understand why they were experiencing so much difficulty moving towards empowered teams. In response to this, the managers and employees worked together to design an experiment in which flexible working policies were made available to all, regardless of family situation or management discretion. There was, of course, some resistance and it was important to engage with this, again exploring the assumptions underpinning the culture of control. The experiment was implemented and ultimately there was a move away from individual accommodation to meet the needs of specific employees, towards a situation where flexibility became ingrained in the culture. The outcome was that teams came up with collective approaches to flexibility to meet productivity and personal needs. This resulted in a 30% decrease in absenteeism. In addition, customer responsiveness increased as times of coverage were extended. Employee satisfaction also improved. It became possible to move to more self-managed teams which gradually took on more responsibility and participated in decisions about work schedules.

The principles of this approach, illustrated in the case above, include:

- starting by looking at a key business need (in this case the need to reduce absenteeism and turnover by empowering self-managed teams)

- working together to develop mutual understandings of working practices, underlying assumptions and their impact on the dual agenda (employees' work–life needs and workplace effectiveness)

- keeping the dual agenda in focus at all times – dropping either perspective prevents positive outcomes
- working together to come up with innovative solutions
- experimenting with new ways of working
- engaging with resistance throughout.

The next stage is to evaluate interventions and communicate outcomes in order to diffuse learning within the organisation.

REFLECTIVE ACTIVITY

Think of a specific workplace situation where flexible working arrangements are not working, and consider how you might apply the dual agenda approach.

What difficulties might you face?

What strategies could you, as an HR professional, develop to overcome them?

KEY ISSUES IN FLEXIBILITY AND WORK–LIFE BALANCE

We now pull together ten key points about flexibility raised in this chapter:

- Flexibility became a popular concept in HRM from the 1980s.
- It is important to see that different types of flexibility result in different outcomes for employers and employees. It is important to understand *who* is being flexible and *in what way.*
- The initial emphasis in the popularity of flexibility was concerned with advantages for employers, rather than for employees.
- The types of flexibility being used by employers are related to government regulations. In the 1980s the emphasis was on numerical flexibility; from 1997 there has been a greater emphasis on work–life balance.

- Work–life balance policies are not just employee-led. They are usually introduced for business reasons.
- Solutions that meet the dual needs of employers and employees can be very effective.
- Work–life balance policies are just a first step. Good implementation and manager support are essential.
- Flexible working arrangements without culture change have limited impact.
- It is important to question assumptions that undermine mutual flexibility.
- Mutual flexibility is best developed through collaboration rather than top-down.

Perhaps there are other key points that you would like to note for yourself.

The main case study in this chapter now follows. It gives an example of how it is possible to advance from work–life policies to culture change. It also highlights some of the pitfalls and barriers to success.

Look at the description of the case set out below. Then decide on the recommendations that you would make as an HR manager for dealing with the issues raised. Try to think beyond the level of a 'quick fix' or simple solutions and to be wary of assumptions that undermine opportunities for mutual flexibility.

The company, which we are calling Peak, is a large insurance company that has undergone mergers, takeovers and restructuring in recent years. There is now a drive for flexibility: numerical (mostly through the use of agency workers but also some staff on temporary contracts), functional (via multi-skilling), and temporal (via flexible working policies) as well as culture change (primarily through management training and development).

Downsizing and reorganisation have brought increasing job insecurity and intensification of work for those who survived redundancies. The most recent merger/takeover was followed by a strategic drive to develop a distinctive culture for the new merged company, including a decision to develop policy, practice and culture change to increase flexibility of working hours. The goal was to move to a more people-focused culture, based on trust, mutual flexibility, autonomy and self-management at all levels, non-hierarchical, non-status-based relationships and collaboration and mutual responsibility between managers and employees. Traditional ways of working were challenged and there was wide talk of the value of two-way flexibility. In the new culture, ideal employees would be regarded as those who were flexible, adaptable and self-motivated.

A number of flexible working arrangements thus came into existence at Peak involving some major shifts in policy following the merger. In particular, there were changes to the existing flexitime system, which involved a shift from formal clocking-in to an informal trust-based flexitime system. This was viewed by management as consistent with the drive for culture change towards greater flexibility and autonomy. It was also justified in terms of financial savings, in that workers had previously been able to clock in 10 minutes early each day and build up days off, which was regarded as no longer beneficial to the

organisation. An on-site crèche at the main premises was also replaced with childcare vouchers throughout the company.

There was an implicit dual agenda of pursuing business needs by meeting staff flexibility needs. However, policy change solutions were not always reached collaboratively. Rather, decisions were often made at management level and communicated in a top-down way. Because of this, some workers did not understand the reasons for the new policies and resented them. For example, the change in flexitime system and loss of the crèche created major problems for some employees, making it more difficult for them to manage their work and private lives, and this was then associated with higher levels of absenteeism and turnover.

Similarly, some line managers had not accepted the rationales for the new policies even though managers underwent training and development to spread the new management values and style. Consequently, management support for mutual flexibility was patchy. Employees with 'new-style' supportive managers were very satisfied with the enhanced level of trust, autonomy and flexibility. However, the new values and discourses of empowerment raised expectations of support, so employees who worked under 'old-style' non-supportive managers were particularly resentful. Nor was the lack of change restricted to line managers. Some HR managers were very slow to take on and live by the new values.

The drive for a shift in culture, and the changes in structures and practices that this was intended to bring about, incorporated a deliberate questioning of deeply held assumptions that ideal workers were those who worked full-time and inflexibly. Although the effectiveness of flexible working arrangements was increasingly apparent, one assumption remained stubbornly intact. This was the belief that managers and supervisors must work full-time and long hours (although flexible working hours made it impossible for single managers to cover all the working hours of their subordinates). Many managers returning from maternity leave requested reduced working hours or other flexible working arrangements, and this was granted – but they were moved to non-managerial posts. Consequently, many managers and supervisors left the company after maternity leave. The failure to question assumptions about the nature of jobs involving people management, and the lack of trust implied in these assumptions, despite the high-profile drive for a trust-based culture shift, prevented Peak management from treating these requests as opportunities for learning and innovating.

So the current position is that on the positive side there is an understanding of the need to go beyond policy to changes in culture, structures and practice, and this is used strategically at Peak as a way of pursuing business aims in a rapidly changing and competitive environment. There is a concerted effort to train and develop managers as agents of change and to work towards putting espoused values into practice. These strategies have achieved some success, both in terms of workplace effectiveness and of satisfying the personal needs of some employees, but with some gaps and limitations. There has been some listening to employees' needs, but this falls far short of a collaborative approach. Above all, however, there has been limited questioning of assumptions about ideal workers, especially at more senior levels. At this point in time the longer-term impacts of the changing practices have not been monitored in terms of the dual agenda.

Your task

Imagine you are an HR professional working in Peak. Prepare a short report based on the information you have been given above, making recommendations to your colleagues about how the situation can be improved.

EXPLORE FURTHER

DTI (2001) *Work–life Balance: The business case*. London, Department of Trade and Industry
This report sets out the business case for introducing work–life balance initiatives in organisations.

LEWIS, S. and COOPER, C. (2005) *Work–life Integration: Case studies of organisational change*. London, John Wiley & Sons
A book of case studies using a work–life integration approach to bring about organisational change and flexibility. This provides a range of practical examples and has learning points at the end of each chapter.

RAPOPORT, R., BAILYN, L., FLETCHER, J. and PRUITT, B. (2002) *Beyond Work–family Balance: Advancing gender equity and workplace performance*. London, Jossey-Bass/John Wiley
A very detailed but readable account of an action research model of organisational change using a work–life balance lens.

STREDWICK, J. and ELLIS, S. (2005) *Flexible Working Practices*. London, CIPD
Using case studies from leading organisations and many practical tools, the authors show how to develop and implement effective and flexible working policies.

WOOD, G., HARCOURT, M. and ROPER, I. (2006) 'The limits of numerical flexibility. Continuity and change'. In G. Wood and P. James (eds) *Institutions, Production and Working Life*. Oxford, Oxford University Press
This chapter provides a comparative look at the use of numerical flexibility across Europe, highlighting its incompatibility with other forms of flexibility.

Managing Employee Performance and Development

CHAPTER 11

The psychological contract, absence and turnover

Susan Leigh

INTRODUCTION

This chapter discusses the psychological contract between employees and their employer, with special emphasis on its use to maximise employee contribution – a subject relevant to HR management anywhere in the world. The chapter also looks at one of the most important results of problems with the psychological contract: absence. There are two perspectives on workplace absence – temporary absence (authorised or unauthorised), and permanent absence in the form of people leaving their jobs, the measure or rate of which is called turnover. Turnover is usually perceived as negative, for reasons that are examined later in the chapter. People being away from their jobs temporarily or permanently can have a negative effect on productivity, so both types of absence are discussed here.

LEARNING OUTCOMES

By the end of this chapter readers should be able to:

- describe the psychological contract, understand why it is important, and suggest HR practices to improve its state
- identify the causes of absence and explain how it can be managed effectively
- understand the importance of managing turnover and discuss some strategies for keeping good performers in the organisation.

The chapter is structured in three parts. The first part introduces the psychological contract and explains why it is key to managing employee performance. The second part introduces absence management and discusses various way of managing it effectively. The third part covers labour turnover and examines how organisations can increase the likelihood that key employees will be happy to stay with the organisation.

STARTER CASE STUDY

Whitegoods plc has long been an established retail company selling kitchen appliances such as fridges, freezers and cookers from a chain of showrooms spread all over the UK. Over many years they built up a good reputation based on their competitive prices and knowledgeable sales staff. Customers liked to visit their local showroom to discuss their requirements with the staff there. Once they had placed their orders they knew they could rely on Whitegoods to deliver and even install their new appliance, if that was needed. In order to give this level of service, Whitegoods built up a team of talented managers and staff many of whom had been with the company for years. The company encouraged promotion from within – many of the managers started off as junior sales staff and worked their way up.

Pay and benefits were not much better than at other retailers but the staff discount was particularly valuable. Staff could get a discount of 30% on anything they bought, and the discount was also available to family members and friends. Another benefit much appreciated by the staff was time off to attend classes and tuition fees for those who wanted to improve their product knowledge.

After many years of successful trading, Whitegoods are currently finding that their sales are dropping despite the high level of customer service provided. Last year's trading figures revealed that Whitegoods plc was in serious financial trouble. As a result, the chief executive decided it was time to take early retirement and several senior managers also decided that it was time to either retire or go elsewhere. A new chief executive was found quite quickly – her name was Jennifer Smith and she had previously been in charge of the kitchen appliances division of one of the country's most successful retail chains. The reward package she demanded was very generous, but the board of Whitegoods decided that the right CEO could turn the company round and prevent branch closures.

Jennifer Smith quickly made changes. Firstly, she had the layout of the stores changed and new work practices introduced to increase efficiency. However, she did not consult the

staff about these changes. Secondly, she cut the staff discount from 30% to 15% – and it was no longer available to their friends and family. No explanation was given for this. Thirdly, she introduced a profit-sharing scheme for senior managers which meant that they could earn substantial bonuses if the company's trading improved.

The staff working in the shops were furious at the changes, especially since they had not been consulted. Many felt that they should also have been consulted about the layout of the stores in which they worked, because they believed that they had a much better understanding of customers' requirements than anyone coming from outside the company. The new working practices included a requirement for staff to clock in and out at the beginning and end of their shifts. Up till now staff had been trusted by their managers to come in on time and to work a full shift. In addition, the staff had less flexibility about which shifts they worked. Previously, staff had been able to work flexibly by making their own arrangements with their colleagues to cover shifts. Now the store managers had to insist that staff worked the shifts they were contracted to do – and staff who did not work their contracted shifts were disciplined. Staff were particularly upset about the halving of their staff discount, and that senior managers were going to be entitled to large bonuses and profit-sharing while shopfloor staff were not was another source of disappointment. Many shopfloor staff wrote angry letters of complaint which they sent to head office. However, their letters were not acknowledged by head office and no one received an answer.

Questions for discussion

1 What has happened to the psychological contract as far as the staff are concerned in this case study?

2 What effect is the situation likely to have on employee engagement?

3 What advice would you give Jennifer Smith and the senior managers to help them manage the psychological contracts of their employees more effectively?

The chapter concludes with the main case study.

Reference sources named within the chapter may be looked up in the *References and further reading* section at the end of the book.

1   THE PSYCHOLOGICAL CONTRACT: THE KEY TO MAXIMISING EMPLOYEE PERFORMANCE

THE PSYCHOLOGICAL CONTRACT AND THE WRITTEN EMPLOYMENT CONTRACT

British employees receive a written Statement of Terms often (wrongly) called a 'contract' although the full contract, legally speaking, actually contains implied terms as well. The written statement normally includes the job title, the pay, the place of work, whether the job is permanent or temporary, full-time or part-time, and the number of hours to be worked. Other information can be included in the main terms and particulars such as holiday entitlements and sick pay arrangements or these can be presented in a different format such as an employee handbook. Some other contractual arrangements can be seen on noticeboards in large organisations. Regardless of the way the information is presented, it is in writing. This written statement of terms could be as simple as a letter confirming the job offer or it could be a series of documents (see Chapter 5). Nevertheless, can these written documents, or the legally implied terms (in English law, terms can be 'implied' by practice without ever being written), give the employee information on the expected behaviours and the culture of the organisation he or she has joined? They cannot: this is where experience of working in the organisation comes in, and the result is the psychological contract.

The psychological contract is developed between the employee and the organisation over an extended period of time. It starts with the experiences the candidate has when applying for the job, develops during the recruitment and selection process, and continues to be formed during the induction and settling-in period. The psychological contract is constantly being revised and adjusted throughout the period of employment. If this process of revision and adjustment is well managed, we can say that there is a positive, or good, psychological contract. If it is not well managed, we can say that there is a poor psychological contract. This is known as the 'state' of the psychological contract and, as is explained later in this chapter, the state of the psychological contract has implications for motivation, performance, attendance and retention.

What exactly *is* the psychological contract? First of all, it is subjective. This means that each employee and employer has his or her own view of what is expected. The psychological contract is a unique combination of beliefs held by an individual and his or her employer about what they expect of each other. This is in contrast to the written, legal contract, the Statement of Terms, which is likely to be the same for groups of employees doing the same job. The psychological contract consists of expectations and obligations as opposed to the tangible content of the written Statement of Terms.

The psychological contract is based on the idea of mutuality and exchange, which means that a good psychological contract depends on an agreement being made and understood as to what is expected and the idea that there is 'give and take'. With the written Statement of Terms there may not be agreement on both sides because the employee has to accept the terms and conditions offered by the employer in order to get the job. Although it is implied that the employee will work hard for the employer and be honest and protect the employer's interests in exchange for pay and benefits, this exchange is rarely set out in detail in the written Statement of Terms.

The psychological contract can be fulfilled or unfulfilled. If the expectations of the parties are met to their mutual satisfaction, it can be said that their psychological contract has been fulfilled. In reality, it is rare for all expectations to be fulfilled – but so long as most are, then a satisfactory balance is achieved. It is also important to understand that the psychological contract can be violated or broken. This happens when one party makes a significant change without first getting the agreement of the other party.

THE EMPLOYEE'S AND THE EMPLOYER'S PERSPECTIVES ON THE PSYCHOLOGICAL CONTRACT

There are two perspectives to the psychological contract – the employee's and the employer's or manager's. These two perspectives are different, and ensuring that the two perspectives are not *too* different is one outcome of a well-managed psychological contract.

Guest and Conway's (1997) research carried out for the CIPD found that the psychological contract from the *employee's* perspective consists of six parts:

1 *Fairness, equity and consistency* – Employees who see their managers treating members of their teams differently, by, for example, being lenient when one person is late but reacting harshly to another team member when he/she is equally late, are likely to have a less positive psychological contract.

2 *Security of employment* – Although most people realise that one can no longer expect a job for life, a certain amount of job security is expected. In cases where job security is in doubt, employees will have a poorer psychological contract compared to employees who feel that their jobs are not threatened.

3 *Scope to demonstrate competence* – A good psychological contract is more likely when employees are given the skills, knowledge and tools to do their job properly. A computer that is constantly giving problems but not replaced can have a very negative effect on the psychological contract.

4 *Career expectations and the opportunity to develop skills* – Although there are a few employees who do not wish to develop themselves and improve their career or job prospects, the majority are more likely to have a positive psychological contract if they see that there are opportunities for advancement.

5 *Involvement and influence* – Having some involvement with decision-making that affects your job and some influence over the way you carry out your work has a strong influence over the state of the psychological contract as well as improving retention and motivation generally. Jobs should be designed to maximise the control the employee has over his/her work.

6 *Trust in the organisation to keep its promises* – When people start a job they have certain expectations and these expectations are often seen as promises.

One way in which we can understand the *employer's* perspective on the psychological contract is to think about it as being the same as the implied terms as defined by employment law. These implied terms for workers are effort, compliance, commitment and loyalty. In other words, all workers who are being rewarded in some way for their contribution are expected to put as much effort as possible into their jobs, they are expected to obey orders and do what is expected of them in their job role, they are expected to show a level of commitment to their organisation and fellow workers, and, in addition, they are expected to protect their organisation's interests by showing loyalty.

REFLECTIVE ACTIVITY

Having read the first section of this chapter, you will by now probably have realised that we all have psychological contracts not only with the organisation we work for (or will work for) but also with everyone else with whom we have a relationship. In pairs or as individuals, think about the psychological contract you have with the place where you are currently studying.

First think about your university or college. What do they expect of you? How do you know that they have those expectations? Have those expectations changed at all during your relationship?

Now, as a student, ask the same questions of the university/college. What do you, as a student, expect of them? How did these expectations come about? Have these expectations changed during your relationship?

If you are responding in pairs, one of you can be 'the student' and the other can be 'the university/college'.

An example of one expectation a student might have of his or her university or college is that there will be somewhere to park the car. How was this expectation formed? Well, when I came to an open day on a Saturday there was a large car park which appeared to have plenty of room for students' cars, so I expected that to be the case during termtime. Has this expectation changed? Yes – when term started I realised that parking was only available for staff and postgraduate students.

REFLECTIVE ACTIVITY

Now think of some more expectations on both sides.

When you have thought of a minimum of six expectations on each side, write a paragraph about how this exercise made you feel.

If you are working or have had a job in the past, write another paragraph about your thoughts about the psychological contract you have/had with your employer.

WHO IS INVOLVED IN CREATING AND MAINTAINING THE PSYCHOLOGICAL CONTRACT?

As we have seen above, there are many different people and practices involved in creating the psychological contract, although it is usually the employee's line manager or supervisor who plays the major role in maintaining the contract once it is formed. It is usual for the manager to be seen as the organisation's representative even though, as we have seen, he or she is not the only person involved in this process. Co-workers also play an important part in the making of the psychological contract because new employees see how their co-workers behave and model their behaviour according to what they see. So if co-workers regularly come back late from lunch, it will be perceived as an acceptable part of the organisation's culture.

Top management also plays a major role in formulating the psychological contract because they set an example to middle managers who are generally the main architects of employees' psychological contracts. If an organisation wishes to change its culture, it must be done from the top down. Top managers must adopt the new behaviours first and cascade them downwards.

HR professionals also play a key role in creating the psychological contract because they are often the first contact a future employee has with the organisation and are usually involved with the employee's induction. Recruiters are the first point of contact with the organisation and the impression they make forms the basis of the psychological contract. Recruiters should present unfavourable as well as favourable aspects of the job so that expectations are realistic. During the selection process it is common for promises to be implied or made in order to encourage a good candidate to take up a job offer. For example, an interviewer may promise that an employee will be given training – but when he/she takes the job he/she finds that the department where he/she works is under-staffed and cover cannot be found to enable him/her to participate in the promised training.

Once the employee has settled in, HR's role is to help managers to manage the psychological contract effectively.

THE IMPACT OF HR PRACTICES ON THE PSYCHOLOGICAL CONTRACT

Most HR practices suggested in this book can influence the psychological contract positively. For example, a good induction, a fair and objective performance management system, the provision of training and development as well as good employee communication can have a significant impact on the state of the psychological contract (see Chapters 8, 12, 14 and 19). This is shown by Guest and Conway's (1997) research. Employees were asked about the HR practices in their organisations and the application of these practices was correlated with the state of those employees' psychological contract. These HR practices are listed in the box below, with the practice mentioned most frequently at the top and the practice mentioned least frequently at the bottom.

HR practices and the psychological contract

- providing opportunities for training and development

- *keeping employees informed about business issues and performance*

- providing employees with formal appraisal reviews

- ensuring that the job provides opportunities to learn new things

- *whenever possible trying to fill vacancies from within the organisation*

- *trying to make jobs as varied and interesting as possible*

- having a policy of single status

- *having a policy of avoiding compulsory redundancies and lay-offs*

- providing a bonus or merit payment if employees perform well

- having some form of workplace involvement

Note: Points in *italics* represent the strongest links to a positive psychological contract

Source: Guest and Conway (1997)

All the HR practices (or the absence of them) listed in the box above had an effect on the state of the psychological contract, but those printed in *italics* correlate most strongly. Organisations should therefore make sure that keeping employees informed, avoiding compulsory redundancies, filling vacancies from within and making jobs as interesting and varied as possible are given top priority.

Although HR policies and practices are only one input to a positive psychological contract, they have been found by researchers to have an important influence on organisational performance by motivating people and getting the best out of them. Guest and Conway (1997) make this clear in their research. They believe that *a positive psychological contract is worth taking seriously because it is strongly linked to higher commitment to the organisation, higher employee satisfaction and better employment relations. Again, this reinforces the benefits of pursuing a set of progressive HRM practices.*

More about the psychological contract is available on the CIPD website. Visit especially: **http://www.cipd.co.uk/subjects/empreltns/psycntrct/psycontr.htm? IsSrchRes=1**

2 MANAGING ABSENCE

One outcome of a poorly managed psychological contract can be persistent unauthorised absence. What is meant by absence? The broadest definition is that it is any time when an employee is not doing the job he or she is employed to do. A good deal of absence is by previous arrangement (annual leave, educational leave, medical appointments and trade union activities). These prearranged absences have to be monitored and recorded and should not cause major problems. It is the other two types of absence that cause problems – sickness and unauthorised absence – and we now consider these in detail.

Sickness absence is usually divided into three types. *Uncertificated* absence is when the organisation allows the employee to return to work without filling in any paperwork giving reasons for the absence. It is *self-certificated* when the organisation allows the employee to report the reasons for the absence without a doctor's certificate to back them up. In the UK, self-certificated absence is often permitted for the first few days but after a certain number of days – typically four to seven – a doctor's certificate is required. This is then *certificated* absence.

Sick pay is at the discretion of the organisation and there is a wide range of different provision made. Some companies pay absent employees their full wages or salary from the first day of sickness whereas others pay nothing for the first few days or even weeks of sickness. The length of time for which companies go on paying their sick employees also varies greatly. For example, some employees may be entitled to only a couple of weeks of sick pay whereas many public sector employees could be entitled to six or even 12 months of sick pay (although normally the second six are half-pay). Regardless of any company sick pay entitlement, after four days an employee may be entitled to Statutory Sick Pay which his or her employer may be required to pay for the first 28 days of sickness.

Many organisations distinguish between short-term and long-term sickness because they have to be considered differently. Longer spells of sickness are sometimes easier for managers to deal with because they may be possible to plan for, and cover can be arranged when, for example, someone has to go into hospital for an operation. However, most long-term sickness is unplanned.

THE EXTENT AND COSTS OF ABSENCE

Survey evidence for the UK suggests that the average figure for absence is just below 4%, equivalent to about 8.5 working days per employee based on a working year of 228 days. There are variations between different sectors and different sizes of organisations. Absence in the public sector is generally higher than in the private, and it is much lower in organisations with fewer than 100 employees than in large organisations employing more than 2,000. Most absence is short-term – approximately 60% is for five days or less, with a further 20% for six days to four weeks. The remaining 20% of absences last for more than six weeks.

Absence costs can be calculated from both the employer's and the employee's perspectives. From the employer's point of view there are direct and indirect costs. *Direct* costs include the sick pay and fringe benefits paid, the overtime payments to others doing the sick person's job, and the costs of having to employ extra staff to ensure that absences do not cause disruption. These costs are relatively easy to measure – but *indirect* costs must also be taken into account. These include disruptions or even shutdown due to frequent or prolonged absences, reduced productivity or lower productivity when staff are absent, and perhaps even loss of customers where there has been a good relationship between customers and an absent member of staff. There are also the indirect costs of extra management time needed to organise cover and supervise replacements, and the time needed to do return-to-work interviews, the extra administration cost to organise cover and deal with sick pay and sickness reporting, and possibly also the extra recruitment costs if an employee can no longer do the job because of sickness.

REFLECTIVE ACTIVITY

Think about a job that you have done or that you know well.

Estimate the cost to your employing organisation if you were to be absent for one month. Take both the direct costs and the indirect costs into consideration.

There are also costs to other employees though these cannot usually be calculated in monetary terms. However, they can have a very negative impact on motivation. These costs occur when staff have to cover for an absent employee and/or deal with the problems that arise because of that absence. There is likely to be resentment at having to do other people's work, poor performance due to the tiredness it causes or due to inexperienced staff having to do the absent person's work. If the absence continues for an extended period, there may be a decrease in morale generally. An outcome could be poor attendance due to stress and heavy workload and even increased turnover as a result of having to cover for an absent colleague too frequently.

REASONS FOR ABSENTEEISM

Certain types of work are more likely to cause illness due to the nature of the tasks involved. Any form of manual work, especially where there are heavy items to be moved or lifted, is likely to cause injury. Excessive use of a keyboard can cause repetitive strain problems. Miners and people who worked with asbestos frequently contracted illnesses because of their work before the links were established between coal dust and asbestos dust and their illnesses. Even people who have to fly long distances as part of their jobs can suffer from short-term medical problems due to jet lag or more serious problems due to deep vein thrombosis (see Chapter 18). A very British problem that leads to a lot of absence is poor job design. Jobs that are designed to give employees control over how they work and as much autonomy as possible will prevent boredom and make it less likely that an employee will be absent. Work–life balance can also be important. Very limited provision for family-friendly working is a major cause of absence in people who have caring responsibilities. Family responsibilities can cause significant absence when there are elderly relatives and young children to care for. Employers can respond with time off for family emergencies and other family-friendly policies, flexible working hours, baby and granny crèches, and so on.

Many of the above reasons for absence are linked to stress. Poor working conditions, shiftwork, work overload, poor relationships at work or lack of consultation in decision-making are among the most important causes of stress.

When employers are asked to list common reason for sickness absence in their organisations, the most usual cause of absence is minor illness – for example, coughs, colds and headaches. However, there is one very important factor that affects whether or not people stay away from work when suffering from minor ailments: the organisational culture. The attitude of the organisation to staying away from work with minor illnesses is extremely significant. New starters soon work out the organisation's attitude to calling in sick with minor complaints. They see managers and colleagues either coming in to work with a bad cold or even flu – or alternatively calling in sick with relatively small illnesses. In addition, the organisation's policies, practices and procedures relating to sickness absence may encourage or discourage an individual. If he/she believes that his/her manager or supervisor has a less than sympathetic attitude to absence due to minor illnesses, the unwell person is more likely to decide to attend.

The British Disability Discrimination Act (1995, and updates) is relevant in managing long-term sickness absence because an employer cannot just dismiss an employee because he or she is unable to work. If the sickness has resulted in a disability under the Act, the law requires employers to make reasonable adjustments to the job content or the workplace to make sure that the disabled person is not placed at any disadvantage in the workplace. This includes people applying for a job and employees who become disabled while in employment. In addition, information held about employees' disabilities is sensitive personal data and must be handled carefully to avoid contravening both the Disability Discrimination Act and the Data Protection Act. Finally, any issues concerning absence and pregnancy must be handled equally carefully to avoid contravening the Sex Discrimination Act.

In summary, the way in which managers handle absences amongst their staff can make a huge difference to the amount of unauthorised and non-genuine sickness absence. It has been found that if managers adopt the following guidelines these types of absence can be minimised.

DO:

- Make employees aware that they have been missed and insist on return-to-work interviews.

- Be sympathetic on the telephone to encourage employees to call in as soon as they know they will be absent.

- Go through the procedure with new employees at induction to ensure that they know exactly what to do if they cannot attend.

- Compile a computerised database and use the information to keep managers informed.

- Consider stress management training and minimise stress factors as far as possible. Consider allowing employees to access employee assistance programmes.

- Be flexible by allowing employees to take leave where appropriate.

- Be firm where necessary and use disciplinary processes in cases of unacceptable absence.

- Consider paying attendance bonuses or making other awards for a perfect attendance record.

- Consider using a potential employee's previous absence record as a selection criterion.

- Improve job design and the working environment.

- Examine the family-friendliness of work arrangements.

DON'T:

- Set a level of acceptable absence measured as a number of days so that employees treat up to that number of days as extra holidays.

- Allow individuals to leave messages with anyone except their line manager.

- Jump to conclusions about reasons for absence.

- Be inconsistent when granting leave – it is important to treat all employees equally when they ask for time off.

- Make taking leave so difficult that calling in sick is the easy answer.

- Let staff use up all their holiday in the first half of the holiday year so that they have no leave left for unplanned eventualities.

For more information about managing absence, visit the CIPD website, and especially: **http://www.cipd.co.uk/subjects/hrpract/absence/absncman.htm ?IsSrchRes=1.**

A poorly managed psychological contract can also result in high employee turnover. Employee turnover is the number of people leaving an organisation over a given period of time. Most organisations want to minimise employee turnover where the people who are leaving are good performers and have benefited from in-company training. To keep track of the number of people involved, most organisations measure their turnover rates on a month-by-month or year-by-year basis. The measurement commonly used is the crude turnover or wastage rate, which is based on a simple formula:

$$\text{Labour turnover rate} = \frac{\text{Total number of leavers over a given period}}{\text{Average number of employees in that period}} \times 100$$

THE EXTENT AND COSTS OF LABOUR TURNOVER

The CIPD recruitment, retention and turnover survey 2006 reported that the overall annual employee turnover rate for the UK is 18.3%. It varies considerably between industries. The highest levels (22.9%) are found in private organisations rather than the public sector where the average turnover rate averages 13.3%. In the private sector the highest annual levels of turnover are found in call centres, retailing, hotels and restaurants, where turnover often exceeds 50%. Turnover levels also vary between regions. The highest rates of turnover occur where unemployment is lowest. However, there is little evidence of any long-term trends towards higher staff turnover. Over the 10 years from 1996 to 2006 the average turnover rate was 18.4%. One third of UK employees have been in their jobs for more than 10 years, and 10% for over 20. As a proportion of total turnover the number of people leaving organisations as a result of redundancy is small. In the private sector about 8% of the turnover is due to redundancy, and in the other sectors (public, not-for-profit and manufacturing) it is about 5%.

When people leave an organisation and have to be replaced, substantial costs are incurred. These consist of *direct recruitment* costs, such as recruitment administration and selection costs. There are also *development* costs, such as those of training the replacement member of staff. The extra effort required from existing staff to cover while a new member of staff is recruited can result in pressure that makes them consider leaving too. Alternatively, existing employees may not go as far as resigning from their jobs but there is likely to be a reduction in their motivation and productivity as a result of increased turnover in their team.

Whether or not the levels of turnover are problematic depends on the type of labour market the organisation operates within and the types of jobs that are affected. In retailing, for example, it is relatively easy to find and train new employees to replace those who have left, so it is possible to keep good-quality levels of service despite having a high turnover rate. By contrast, where jobs involve skills that are relatively scarce, where recruitment is costly or where it takes a while to fill a vacancy, high turnover is likely to present problems for management and employees. This creates severe problems when staff are lost to direct competitors or where customers have built up relationships with particular employees. In 2005, 73% of the respondents in the CIPD's annual recruitment and retention survey reported retention difficulties, and the survey showed that managerial and professional staff are the most difficult to retain, especially in the public sector.

A limited amount of turnover is positive for organisations. It can enable a poor performer to be replaced by a more efficient employee or create an opportunity for career development and promotion when someone in a senior position leaves. A new employee can bring fresh ideas into the organisation. Also, payroll costs can be reduced if the new employee is paid less than the person he or she replaces. In situations were business is poor, a delay in replacing someone who has left can be an effective way of reducing payroll costs.

UNDERSTANDING THE EMPLOYEE TURNOVER STATISTICS

Crude turnover figures as described in the previous section are used by all the major turnover surveys. They represent all leavers, including those who leave involuntarily due to dismissal, redundancy or retirement. They also do not distinguish between functional (or beneficial) turnover and turnover that is dysfunctional and harmful to the organisation.

So in order to make sense of the turnover figures in an organisation it is important to do a more detailed analysis. This means looking at the turnover figures in the context of that particular organisation. For example, the average annual turnover figure for a supermarket chain might be 40% – but that is not much help if you are trying to find out what is going on in a particular store or with a particular group of employees. One store may have a turnover of 20% and another of 60%. This would make you want to investigate what was going on in the store with the low turnover, because it is obviously doing something right. This might help us understand any problems there are with the management in the store with 60% turnover. A similar logic applies to work teams. Crude turnover figures therefore have to be broken down by location, department and team.

It would also be useful to break down the crude figure to find out more about the types of people who were leaving. For example, turnover figures could be broken down by age, sex, ethnic origin, grade or job title and job tenure. If the people who are leaving have been in their jobs for less than a year, it may indicate a problem with poor recruitment decisions or perhaps with induction. In some cases it might be appropriate to look at the appraisal records or performance rating of the people who are leaving. If it is discovered that the good performers are leaving whereas the poor performers are staying, it would merit urgent investigation.

INVESTIGATING THE CAUSES OF TURNOVER

Well-managed organisations want to know why people are leaving their jobs, particularly if the people who are leaving are people who they would prefer to retain. However, most organisations make no attempt to find out the reasons for dissatisfaction until the employee has given in notice or has actually left. This is too late – there is no chance of getting a valuable employee to change his or her mind at that stage.

Usually, companies use exit interviews to discover why an employee is leaving, although exit surveys or word-of-mouth sources of information are used in some cases. These methods can be unreliable because the employee leaving is usually reluctant to tell the employer the real reason why he or she is leaving in case it jeopardises the chances of getting a good reference to take to his/her new employer. Exit surveys, or 'separation questionnaires' as they are sometimes called, can be equally unreliable unless the people filling them in feel confident that their answers are completely anonymous. This is difficult to achieve unless the organisation has a large number of people leaving all at the same time.

So what is the best way of finding out why people are leaving? It is continuously to monitor employee satisfaction throughout the entire employment relationship. In other words, to stop the problem in the first place. This can be done in two ways: by regular staff attitude surveys and, for particular groups of employees who you really want to keep, by conducting focus groups.

Staff satisfaction surveys have to be carried out regularly so that trends in staff satisfaction can be monitored. It is very important that management are seen to be responding to feedback from staff satisfaction surveys so that staff can see the benefit in giving their honest opinions on workplace issues. Benchmarking your organisation's turnover rates against that of similar organisations is a good idea. If similar organisations have similar turnover issues, there is less to be concerned about – but if your organisation has turnover rates that are considerably higher than average, it may be possible to look at the retention strategies of a successful organisation to see if anything can be learned from them.

REFLECTIVE ACTIVITY

Ask as many people as possible who have worked for an organisation and left the job voluntarily to tell you their reasons for leaving.

Make a list of the reasons and see which of the above categories they fall into.

(You will need to exclude reasons such as 'I moved away from the area,' or 'I left because I'd finished my studies,' in order to make this exercise more meaningful.)

RETENTION STRATEGIES

What can be done to encourage good employees to stay? Below, we examine four areas in which an organisation might invest to improve its retention record.

Improving corporate culture and management style

People are more likely to leave their jobs because of dissatisfaction with their manager than for any other reason. Organisations that wish to improve retention should therefore concentrate on improving their managers' people management skills. They should help managers to develop a management style that encourages staff participation, develops teamworking, promotes individual autonomy and provides regular communication. Managers must develop a leadership style that supports rather than commands, and give employees autonomy through empowerment. Managers need to be aware of the importance of explicitly recognising good employee performance and saying 'Well done.'

Investing in training and development

Many employees leave because of a lack of opportunity to develop their skills, knowledge or competencies. Strategies to improve retention could therefore include introducing a mentoring scheme, encouraging multi-skilling, improving career development opportunities and investing in succession planning. Many organisations also encourage their employees to make use of general development opportunities because these can develop transferable skills that can be used at work (see Chapter 14 and Chapter 24).

Improving work–life balance

As older employees move into retirement, often with elderly parents of their own to take care of, a degree of flexibility is needed (see Chapter 6). In addition, many more women and single parents are now working and a number of government initiatives are aiming at increasing the proportion of working mothers. All these groups need to have flexibility in their working hours, and this has been supported by legislation. Recent legislation gives parents of children aged under six the right to ask to work flexibly, and there have been extensions to maternity and paternity leave. Another possibility is to offer assistance with childcare to help a parent to work. It is not just people with eldercare and childcare responsibilities who may want to work flexibly. Some organisations offer career breaks after an employee has been working for a number of years, and this allows the employee to take time off while keeping his or her job open. A menu of different types of benefits can meet more employees' needs and can cater for all age groups and life stages. Older people might opt for an increased pension whereas younger people may prefer more time to travel. Parents of school-age children may prefer time off in the school holidays, and so on.

Improving pay and benefits

Dissatisfaction with pay and benefits is a major reason for employee turnover. Some organisations target rewards at key individuals and groups. However, this can cause resentment and demotivation of other employees and often has no lasting influence on retention. A simple pay increase is a useful strategy – it can put off someone's intention to leave ... but only for a short time if the real reason for dissatisfaction goes beyond pay issues. Other possibilities are to pay retention bonuses to stop people from leaving from hard-to-fill jobs or to develop share ownership plans or other rewards which benefit employees over the long term. To maximise retention it is important to ensure that market rates of pay are matched or bettered, although high pay alone is not always the answer to keeping key employees.

More information about managing retention is available on the CIPD website, and especially from **http://www.cipd.co.uk/subjects/hrpract/turnover/ empturnretent.htm?IsSrchRes=1.**

KEY ISSUES TO DO WITH THE PSYCHOLOGICAL CONTRACT, ABSENCE AND TURNOVER

We now pull together ten key points relating to the psychological contract, absence and turnover raised in this chapter:

- The psychological contract is shaped by employment practices and employment experiences.

- The psychological contract influences employee attitudes and behaviour and, if well managed, can improve employee performance.

- There are considerable variations in the state of the psychological contract within different sectors.

- The most common causes of short-term absence are minor illnesses such as coughs, colds, headaches and back pain. Stress is a major reason for longer-term absence.

- Absence can be minimised by good management control and the use of return-to-work interviews.

- Employees are less likely to be absent if they have a positive psychological contract.

- The organisational culture has a major influence on employees' attitudes to attendance.

- The causes of turnover should always be investigated, preferably by using such techniques as performance appraisals, focus groups and staff satisfaction surveys.

- Retention can be improved through a number of different initiatives including offering opportunities for employee development, improving pay and benefits, improving work–life balance and by making the job content and work environment as interesting and comfortable as possible.

- Most people leave a job because the relationship between them and their supervisor or manager becomes poor. Considerable effort should therefore be put into training managers to manage their staff well if they want them to stay.

Perhaps there are other key points that you would like to note for yourself.

The main case study in this chapter now follows.

MAIN CASE STUDY

Look at the description of the case set out below. Then decide on the recommendations that you would make as an HR manager for dealing with the issues raised. Try to think beyond the level of a 'quick fix' or simple solutions.

Getwell Hospital is situated in a small town on the south coast of England. Many of the people who live in the town retired to the seaside, so the majority of the hospital's patients are aged over 60. The hospital is housed in a crumbling Victorian building which is difficult to keep clean and has big wards, unlike most modern hospitals. But as is usual with hospitals nowadays, accommodation is not provided for nurses or other staff, and the only places available to rent in the town tend to be bed-and-breakfast places which fill up with tourists in the summer. Because the hospital is in the centre of the town there are very few parking spaces for staff or visitors. The pay-and-display car parks in the town centre are a viable alternative for visitors but are expensive for staff to use if they need to stay for a full shift. There are no social amenities for the staff, and even if there were, many of the staff have to travel long distances and need to set off for home as soon as they finished their shift. Because the population of the hospital's catchment area consists mainly of retired people, there are no clubs and few shops of interest to younger people in the town.

The hospital's HR department has noticed that there are increasing problems in filling a number of key positions – in particular, finding enough qualified and experienced nurses to work on the crowded geriatric wards. There is also a shortage of other professionally trained staff, such as physiotherapists, pharmacists and radiotherapists. In fact, the only areas in which there are no shortages of staff are the hospital shop and refreshment counters, and these are normally staffed by volunteers anyway.

The problem does not lie in attracting the qualified staff the hospital needs. Because the NHS is currently making cutbacks to save money, there are fewer jobs about, so there is no shortage of good applicants for every job that is advertised. The problem is with getting them to stay. For example, the university in

the nearest larger town runs a course leading to a nursing qualification, and many nurses complete the practical part of their qualification at Getwell Hospital. On completing their qualification many of the nurses join the permanent staff – but most do not stay for very long. Once they have gained sufficient experience to allow them to apply for jobs in London or to work abroad, they resign from their jobs at Getwell Hospital and do not stay long enough for the hospital to benefit from the experience they have gained while working there. The same thing happens with other staff: they seem to be using Getwell Hospital as a stepping-stone to jobs elsewhere and only stay long enough to get the experience they need to move on.

The hospital decided to engage the services of a consultant, who designed a staff satisfaction survey. All members of staff, including the nurses, filled in the questionnaire, hoping that the managers would respond to their complaints. For example, days that had been set aside for training the new nurses often had to be postponed due to staff shortages and there seemed to be problems in some wards, with some nurses not getting on very well with the ward managers. When people went off sick, which happened rather frequently, the managers did not seem to be very interested in finding out why. Working on the wards was often very stressful due to staff shortages resulting from the high turnover and the demanding nature of the work. Elderly and infirm people need a lot of care and often become confused and disorientated when hospitalised. However, nothing changed as a result of the survey, and the turnover rate has since remained higher than that of other hospitals nearby.

The hospital has been experiencing many problems as a result of this high level of turnover. To keep the wards running at all, the management recruited a number of nurses from abroad. Although they were highly qualified and skilled, the nurses mostly spoke

English with an accent that the elderly people – many of whom had impaired hearing – had difficulty understanding. Another way of keeping the wards fully staffed has been to employ agency nurses, especially on the less popular shifts. Some of these nurses work only one or two shifts at the hospital and so never know much about the hospital's routines and certainly do not know any of the patients' names. In other cases, the 'agency' shifts are filled by the hospital's regular staff working double shifts to earn extra money. This makes it more likely that mistakes are made due to tiredness, and is not a satisfactory long-term solution.

Your task

What advice would you give the hospital's management team to improve retention generally, but particularly the retention of qualified and skilled nurses?

EXPLORE FURTHER

Evans, A. and Walters, M. (2002) *From Absence to Attendance*, 2nd edition. London, CIPD
A useful book which covers all aspects of managing absence.

Guest, D. and Conway, N. (1997) *Employee Motivation and the Psychological Contract*, IPD Report. London, IPD

Guest, D. and Conway, N. (2000) *The Psychological Contract in the Public Sector*. London, CIPD
Two of a series of reports published by the IPD/CIPD looking at different aspects of managing the psychological contract.

Taylor, S. (2005a) *The Employee Retention Handbook*. London, CIPD
This book gives an insight into the best ways of retaining employees and helps readers understand the reasons why people leave their jobs.

CHAPTER 12

Performance management and appraisal

Patricia Chase *and* Sebastian Fuchs

INTRODUCTION

This chapter examines performance and how organisations assess and evaluate whether the performance levels of their employees are acceptable by utilising performance management systems and employee appraisals. It looks at how a performance management system can support an organisation's overall performance through maintaining or improving the performance of its employees. It offers key drivers that should be considered both when designing and when re-evaluating them.

LEARNING OUTCOMES

By the end of this chapter readers should be able to:

- describe the differences between a performance management system and a performance appraisal

- explain how customised performance appraisals can be used as a strategic tool in improving individual performance as part of a performance management system

- identify good practices and the different ways of assessing performance

- evaluate the effectiveness of systems already in place.

The chapter is divided into three main parts. Part 1 discusses performance, motivation and performance management systems in relation to the organisation. Part 2 looks at performance assessment in general and shows how it reinforces the strategic aspect of performance management. Part 3 considers performance management in relation to the balanced scorecard, coaching and 360-degree appraisal.

The chapter concludes with the main case study.

Reference sources named within the chapter may be looked up in the *References and further reading* section at the end of the book.

Metalik Creations [a fictional company] provides interior designers with metallic sculptures made from scrap metals and more recently has started a direct sales mail-order operation for anyone interested in owning one. The rapid rise in popularity of these sculptures due to the new service has led to a need to increase production to meet demand without losing creativity, innovation or quality.

Because production of the sculptures is team-based, the managing director has decided to involve two teams in increasing the production levels. He calls in the team leaders of Team A and Team B and informs them both that due to higher demand for the sculptures they are required to increase their levels of production over the next year to meet this increase without compromising on the build quality. Both team leaders are told they can interpret and communicate the new objectives set by the managing director to their teams.

Team A are told by their team leader that they are required to produce more sculptures to meet the increase in demand. As a result of this, the team agrees on the following measurements to assess their performance:

- how quickly the materials for producing the sculptures can be obtained

- who obtains the most scrap metal (for which an award would be given)

- how many sculptures the team produced.

Team B are told by their team leader that they are required to produce more sculptures of the same quality as those already being produced to meet the increase in demand. The team leader makes it clear that the innovative nature, creative qualities and overall quality of the sculptures must be maintained despite having to produce more sculptures. The agreed performance measurements are as follows:

- the amounts of good-quality scrap metal found by the team and used in the sculptures

- the number of good-quality sculptures produced.

To help Team B in identifying their performance levels a bulletin board was set up to monitor their progress. The measurements agreed focused on the quality of the scrap metal obtained, the quantity effectively used against the wastage from each batch of work, and the successful identification of high-quality sources of materials. Team B also had an opportunity to assess their level of performance through regular feedback sessions during the year, and an incentive scheme was introduced based on the production levels of good-quality sculptures and the profits made.

Questions for discussion

Consider what the possible consequences might be from the way the organisation's goals and objectives are communicated downwards to the teams.

At the end of the year, what do you think the outcomes were specifically as a result of the way the team leaders communicated the objectives set by the managing director?

Answer first for Team A, and then for Team B.

1 PERFORMANCE, MOTIVATION AND PERFORMANCE MANAGEMENT SYSTEMS

To put the following discussion in context, sit for a moment and consider what it was like when you first started senior school, college, university or a job. There are features common to all of these that apply here, especially when starting in a new place where you do not know what is really expected of you. People who are new to any scene are often left feeling very isolated until they know what they need to do, how they should do it, what is expected of them and how their success is measured to show that they have reached the standards required.

Let us consider a simple example at this stage. A programme of study usually includes a syllabus and descriptors, which provide an outline of the quality of work for each grade of assessment. This determines a level of understanding of what might be expected of you. Different courseworks and examinations are set to test your ability to perform; the grades you receive are feedback on your performance.

When you see your teacher or tutor for feedback, that is the time when your performance is reviewed and, depending on your grades, for discussion on what you have done well and where you might improve. At the end of the session you may go away with an action plan to help you continue to perform well or improve your performance for the future. So, taking these analogies forward, let us look at what is meant by 'performance'.

The role of performance is a complex one. It is a mixture of inputs based on an individual's knowledge, skills and actions combined with the available organisational resources and/or support. The outcome can be a service or a product, or a combination of both. The quality of the outcome will be reflected in the expertise of the individual and the supporting resources. For example, the quality of call centre front-line operators' responses to customers on particular products and services will reflect their levels of knowledge, training and supervisory support. Equally, the quality of teaching and the level of resources available can impact on the overall performance of students.

In the case of the call centre front-line operators, the performance is directly linked to what their job descriptions are likely to entail: providing answers to questions and issues customers might have on a range of products and services. There are, however, many areas in organisational settings where employees' behaviour can have a positive impact on individual and organisational performance, even though it is not related directly to their jobs. For instance, convincing your friend that he or she should use the products and services offered by the company you work for is likely to have a positive – albeit small – effect on sales and ultimately on the performance of the organisation. This type of behaviour refers to contextual (as opposed to task) performance and relates to the idea that employees engage in 'citizenship behaviour' as one element of performance (Organ, Podsakoff and MacKenzie, 2006). Regardless of whether organisations want to improve task or contextual performance, we must look at what makes people engage in performance-related behaviours. Understanding employees' motivation to work is one important way of getting to grips with this.

WORK MOTIVATION

Part of generating higher levels of performance is recognising the uniqueness of each individual and what motivates him or her. To some extent the motivational process is within the individual's control.

REFLECTIVE ACTIVITY

Think of the times you have had coursework to do and left it to the last moment because there were more interesting things to do.

What finally motivated you to do the work?

Individuals need to know that what is being offered to them not only has purpose and direction but will be beneficial and provide a fair outcome for their efforts. This may explain why motivators vary in their degree of effectiveness over time. In 1943, Maslow suggested that a 'hierarchy of needs' exists. According to his theory, once the basic physiological need has been satisfied to some degree, the individual's concerns move in turn towards safety, belongingness, self-esteem and self-actualisation (Arnold *et al*, 1995). His theory is very popular with managers because it seems plausible that, for instance, once you feel safe, you can start getting concerned with other things such as finding a suitable partner. Moreover, it would be a convenient way of managing people just to exhibit higher levels of motivation by passing people through these stages. However, the theory was developed during a time of significant uncertainty in many countries, and more basic things such as food and shelter were on people's minds. There is not much conclusive evidence to suggest that people actually function in a way where they climb from one stage to the next, nor do we know whether people can switch between these different stages in short time-spans.

McClelland (1971) identified three related important needs – namely, 'power', 'affiliation' and 'achievement'. Identifying these helps us to understand the impact of power relations – for example, management's behaviour, the necessity of valuing individuals, and how achievement can be encouraged to enhance performance through training.

Equity is also important – the need to be treated equally and fairly. Individuals make comparisons between the levels of recognition and rewards they receive with others giving the same level of effort. Should there be any differences, they may decide to increase their efforts further to maintain a balance or, alternatively, if they see this as not worthwhile, their effort may be reduced (Adams, 1965). Thus, to some extent justice, transparency and the distribution of rewards and other organisational resources determines the extent to which people are motivated to perform.

The way performance is assessed can affect the level of motivation: the goals and targets individuals are expected to achieve must be clearly set out and challenging. So goal-setting is another motivational theory in that it clarifies, specifies and prioritises what is expected of individuals at work. The attainment of such goals closes the feedback loop and provides important feedback. This, it is argued, encourages people to focus their actions on achieving these goals (Locke, 1968; Latham and Locke, 1990). If you think about setting yourself targets and goals in your academic or personal life, ideally 'SMART' ones (specific, measurable, attainable, realistic and time-bound), you are more likely to get results. For instance, creating the goal of completing your undergraduate studies within three years – so that you can finally start earning some money afterwards – is likely to get you through your degree smoothly. The same principle applies to organisations. Clear targets have been found to lead to an increase in goal attainment, and this, if designed in correspondence with the organisational strategy (see Chapter 3), is likely to increase organisational performance.

Expectancy theory is based on work by Vroom (1964). He suggests that 'valence', 'instrumentality' and 'expectancy' impact on how successfully individuals take up realistic and challenging goals. The successful outcome of goal-setting to some degree may depend on how individuals perceive the extent to which they have the ability to achieve these goals (expectancy), whether their performance is rewarded (instrumentality), and whether or not they value the reward being offered (valence). In other words, individuals expect certain outcomes (referred to as performance) to result from their efforts, and those efforts are made more strenuously when these outcomes are of personal importance to them.

REFLECTIVE ACTIVITY

Think of a time when you were faced with a challenge to produce a project or some coursework by a specified deadline.

What motivated you to do it – and how did it motivate you?

Try to consider some of the theories outlined above.

Once you have completed this exercise, look back at the starter case study and consider how you might relate your experiences to it.

To encourage higher rates of performance, organisations can use different performance measurement criteria within either a more overarching performance management system (PMS) or an appraisal system. These criteria can vary from results-oriented outcomes to competency-based assessments, or they may be combined. Although performance is managed in a variety of ways, it is still often used by managers in terms of 'objective-setting and appraisal', and where it focuses on individual performance it tends to be linked to talent management, succession planning, development or career management (CIPD, 2005).

Recognising that a performance management system strategically manages the inputs and outputs of individuals or teams by aligning the performance criteria with the business objectives is the first step to realising how important it is. For this, it is crucial:

- to understand the business of the organisation

- to have the ability to interpret the more abstract goals and objectives at board level into more practical operational goals and objectives at employee level to meet them – that is, to place in context the expected levels of performance required of employees, and to communicate them to them

- to practically align individual or team objectives with those of the organisation, including a review process to ensure that they are on track to meet the expected outputs

- to monitor the outputs to ensure that they achieve the required levels of service or quality and quantities of products.

The system's process creates a platform to develop better human resource plans, assess promotion potential and training needs and develop consistency in standards and performance. It is an on-going process requiring some flexibility so that adjustments can be made to maximise levels of performance.

REFLECTIVE ACTIVITY

Think of an experience you have had with customer services when purchasing a product or a service.

What was your overall impression of the service you received? Did the way in which you were dealt with provide any insight into the capabilities and motivation of those who served you?

THE PERFORMANCE MANAGEMENT SYSTEM CYCLE

Figure 20 shows corporate goals and objectives being communicated downwards to the divisional or departmental level, where they are interpreted in combination with the job description, person specification and work situation to provide operational-level performance criteria. Once agreement is reached between line managers and individuals on their performance criteria, action plans are drawn up to help them in their performance. Their performance is monitored and feedback provided on a regular basis, which at the end of the agreed reporting period results in a review feedback report. Feedback provides the opportunity to assess actual against expected performance and to identify any performance gaps or development needs. It can be used to deal with inefficiencies and poor performance by providing more focused performance criteria and frequent monitoring.

In conjunction with the cycle, the vertical integration of the performance management system with other processes (eg training, development, reward, etc) provides the focus for interpreting organisational goals as operational ones, so identifying for teams and individuals the levels of performance needed to ensure sustainable operations, including an opportunity for two-way feedback between management and individuals/teams.

Figure 20 The performance management system cycle

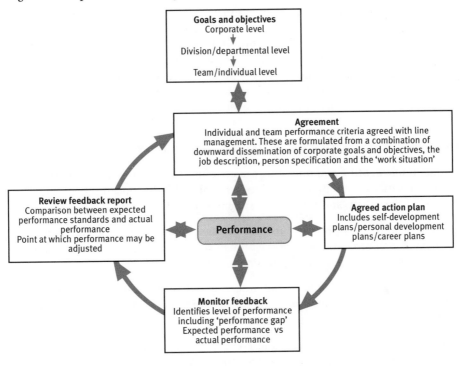

Although its horizontal integration provides a platform on which the organisation can either improve its performance or adjust it when necessary, the PMS recognises that any changes within the organisation can affect the process and that there should therefore be a degree of flexibility to accommodate such changes. A combination of both vertical and horizontal integration of the PMS ensures that the process incorporates elements in its design that allow it to support other processes and procedures within the organisation.

Effective use of technology is important in supporting these processes because essentially it allows for faster sharing of information on the local, national and global level, making it a powerful tool provided it is controlled and not in control. To design and produce a fully functional HR system requires input from all relevant stakeholders to ensure that it supports both the HR function and an effective PMS. It requires trained operators, on-going support and the recording and storage of relevant data, which are ideally linked to other systems within the organisation (eg the data controller).

In practical terms, the most difficult aspect of a PMS is managing people effectively to gain their commitment to perform. There are a number of major variables that can affect the process – for example, the type of organisation (eg retail, health sector, etc), the styles of leadership and management (transformational, autocratic, etc), the make-up of the workforce (eg full-time, part-time, professional, etc), motivation levels and the products or services being offered.

A key aim is thus to provide a clear recognition of levels of performance, and ways of dealing with inconsistencies in performance that will ensure improved outputs and commitment. Part of this process is to develop managers to the point at which they are able to think more strategically and add value by looking at ways to improve the overall performance (see Chapter 3). To assist them further, there is a need to identify levels of performance by providing clear performance indicators. These should provide for an equitable assessment of rewards, future development needs, succession planning and training.

CREATING A PERFORMANCE MANAGEMENT SYSTEM

Creating, implementing and operating a successful PMS requires a number of interventions that are essential to the process, which should concentrate on the 'purpose' of the system and not on the 'system' itself. These are:

- a clear alignment between the business strategy, the information technology strategy, the reward strategy and the human resource strategy, and integration with other systems operating in the organisation

- senior managers driving the overall process and disseminating the mission, vision, corporate goals and objectives downwards so that they are interpreted as operational performance indicators

- moving away from a 'command-and-control' ethos that coerces performance from the individual to one that creates commitment, empowerment and loyalty

- managers coming to a mutual agreement on the methods by which individuals will reach their set targets, on regular reviews to monitor their progress and on the ability to adjust the targets to match any changes

- providing an opportunity to bring about change – for example, creating a shift in culture or workforce attitudes by targeting them through the performance indicators

- a clearly structured review or appraisal process to ensure clearer channels of communication at all levels and provide a better understanding of the part each employee plays in the organisation. Translating organisational objectives and goals into individual ones allows for a better understanding not only of the relationship of reward to performance but the necessity of improving individuals' skills and knowledge. Where a more development-focused culture is encouraged, it provides a level of security in respect of multi-skilling employees, improving areas requiring further development and building on their strengths

- ensuring that line managers take early 'ownership' (CIPD, 2005) via training and provision of on-going advice and support, which reinforces and updates them

- providing informative feedback, action planning regarding work and career development, empowerment and recognition of good performance to create higher levels of job satisfaction and retention

- inculcating a context of Keep It Simple (KIS): if designed correctly it can assist in focusing on SMARTer working practices (CIPD, 2006)

- finally, monitoring and evaluating the system's progress and building into it the ability to adapt to changes caused by legislation, globalisation, social trends, political and economic change and technological developments created by internal and external factors that can impact on the design and delivery of the organisation.

REFLECTIVE ACTIVITY

Why is it important to consult with all interested parties when developing a performance management system?

List the parties who should be involved in the process, and provide justifications for your selection of parties.

There are key advantages in having a clearly structured PMS which incorporates an appraisal (as discussed in detail later on in this chapter). It provides for an equitable evaluation of wages, eligibility for rewards/promotion and feedback. It identifies for employees their level of performance, gives recognition of good practices and assists in clarifying and directing their work. It defines 'performance' and channels development to achieve this end, which helps in improving the quality or standards of the outputs and maximises task performance in relation to products or services. It can support management development and succession planning through identifying staff's management and leadership potential through their performance appraisals. This is especially important in developing future leaders, who can be groomed for top positions (high-fliers).

It supports human resource planning (see Chapter 7) in that it identifies the right people with the relevant skills and experience to do specific jobs. It also highlights skills and training gaps and assists in targeting training and development that will help in improving productivity and supporting the organisation's business. It can identify and resolve issues related to job structure through restructuring the way the work is done (this relates to the work profile described in the final section of this chapter, on appraisal).

Feedback and performance reviews provide a platform for drawing up action, personal development and career plans for developing individuals which can provide a positive impact on their perception of being valued members of the organisation. Clear recognition of individual and team contributions also aids this perception, which can be motivating and often lead to higher retention rates. Improving employee skills, knowledge and retention rates can have a positive impact on the reputation of an organisation, and, ultimately, on its performance.

However, a PMS also has some potential drawbacks:

- It can be a time-consuming and costly process.

- There may be problems where it is linked directly to pay and rewards, especially if it is an off-the-shelf package and not designed specifically for the organisation. The design of the rating scales can cause issues in respect of pay decisions and identifying good and poor performers, especially where it encourages a central tendency – managers taking the average of the rating scale due to reluctance to identify the true state of an individual performance – which may create difficulties. Pay expectations among employees may be unrealistically raised, creating discontent.

- Lack of support or clarity regarding performance expectations can result in lower retention rates because it may be seen as being unfair or inequitable in operation – especially if the assessments are too subjective and based on favouritism.

2 PERFORMANCE ASSESSMENTS

The way in which performance is assessed in organisations can provide a chance to identify individual and team potential and any skills and knowledge gaps, whether it is in terms of performance development reviews or staff appraisals. The performance indicators used may vary across the organisation as the targets of managers differ in relation to the staff they supervise. The assessment may involve the use of rating scales, objective setting, BARS or competencies, and where practicable, combinations of them.

In the light of the UK Government's initiatives regarding 'dignity at work' (ECU, 2007), the designing of the performance criteria (or indicators) should be clearly linked to diversity, equal opportunities policies and disability issues, and should moreover reinforce zero tolerance to conceivable negative behaviours. This should essentially reduce discriminatory behaviours against any one group in relation to, for example, race, age, sexual orientation or disability (see Chapter 6). Organisations have a great variety of performance indicators to choose from. The main ones are examined below.

Rating scales assess an individual's performance against a set of agreed descriptors that indicate the standard of work produced and whether he or she has fulfilled his/her main duties (from the job description) to a satisfactory level. The performance indicators can reflect certain employee characteristics that are needed to successfully perform the work; each may be rated on a scale ranging from 'unacceptable' to 'outstanding'. The scale may be linked to a numerical rating ranging from one to five, which can be used to provide an overall rating. This form of rating can cause problems with employees where the descriptors and rating provides a more subjective assessment, especially if it is linked to pay rewards and promotion prospects.

Orange recently experienced problems with using a numbered five-point rating scale where staff were having difficulties in accepting that a rating of 'three' meant they had 'met their objective and were doing a good job'. To solve the problem and make the ratings more transparent, the five-point scale was retained but in the form of descriptors ranging from 1 = 'unacceptable', 2 = 'getting there', 3 = 'great stuff' (used to reflect 'effective performance'), 4 = 'excellent' and 5 = 'exceptional', which is referred to as the 'Orange thing' (Johnson, 2006).

Objective-setting in management by objectives programmes monitors the feasibility or achievability of the objectives or targets set, and whether they have been successfully reached. Employee objectives should be aligned with organisational objectives. Because the objectives are focused on achievement of the work goals set, there is an opportunity for self-assessment and feedback during the reporting period. This is often used together with rating scales to provide a clearer overview of performance. The process does require management to recognise that situations can arise that are outside the control of the individual, which may affect achieving the set objectives and lead to suitable adjustments having to be made to the performance requirements.

Behaviourally anchored rating incorporates a number of rating scales that are customised to evaluate the expected performance levels that reflect the particular job in question. In deriving these ratings, managers first identify the key areas essential to successfully performing the job; descriptors are then drawn up that reflect varying levels of performance within each of the key areas. Once this process has been completed, the 'typical or expected' level of performance for each individual across the scale is drawn up by their appraiser (individual rating scale). This more focused approach is useful in identifying potential and development needs.

Competencies are a form of assessment that looks at the level of competence individuals display in respect of each of the competencies (standards to which individuals are expected to perform) they are being assessed on. Competencies may be measured in respect of a number of capabilities which can focus either on behaviours or functional/technical know-how, or a combination of these, within an agreed framework.

A good example of the competencies approach is the *transformational government initiative* The initiative has produced the *transformational government framework*, which provides a set of core competencies in order to improve performance, increase skills and expertise in the public services; it is seen as part of the way forward (Cabinet Office, 2007).

As part of this initiative, there is now a Chief Information Officer Council which is involved in developing the 'government gateway', which will provide services for sharing information across the public sector and with the public. To ensure that, for instance, IT professionals have the relevant specialist and technical skills and knowledge, a *core skills framework for IT professionals* has been developed consisting of five core competency groups, namely:

- architecture, information and innovation

- business change management

- solutions delivery and implementation

- service delivery

- procurement and management support

plus two competency groups for senior managers:

- delivery management

- enterprise strategy and architecture.

This enables IT professionals to identify their profiles and development needs, and it can be used as a part of the performance management or recruitment processes for IT specialists (CIO, 2007).

The British National Health Service is another example where a 'knowledge and skills framework' has been introduced to standardise performance criteria and encourage a learning and development environment as part of the broader agenda for change programmes. The framework's design incorporates regulatory-required competencies and identifies six *core dimensions* considered essential to the performance of all health staff covered by the framework; these are: 'communication', 'personal and people development', 'health, safety and security', 'service improvement', 'quality' and 'equality and diversity'. Support materials are provided for managers and staff online to assist them in using the framework and the development review process. Successful implementation of such frameworks arguably will depend on whether managers and employees alike understand and accept them.

THE PERFORMANCE APPRAISAL

The performance appraisal is an opportunity for employees to discuss their performance with their line manager. It provides a platform for clarifying the quality of performance through feedback on both an informal and a formal basis throughout the year. To ensure meaningful and effective feedback the performance targets must have been set as the employee commenced work. Some organisations use personal development reviews rather than appraisals – although there are similarities between the two, the personal development review tends to be more development-oriented.

The appraisal analyses employees' past performance over a set period of time and considers their future potential. The 2004 WERS survey suggests that even for non-managerial employees, regular appraisals are common (see Table 28). However, larger organisations are more likely to do them than smaller organisations, and there are also differences between industries, appraisals being more common (for example) in financial services.

Performance appraisals are part of a formal process which provides an opportunity to assess the individual's suitability for promotion, further training and/or development and appropriate levels of reward. It monitors:

- the quality of performance in relation to achievements and failures over the reporting period

- the work profile content, load and volume

- the agreement and setting of future objectives.

Table 28 Percentage extent of performance appraisals, by workplace characteristics

	Regular appraisals for 60% or more non-managerial employees
All workplaces	64
Organisation size	
10–99 employees	49
10,000 or more employees	82
Industry	
Manufacturing	41
Hotels and restaurants	48
Financial services	96
Public sector	77

Source: Kersley *et al* (2006; p.83)

Whether it is a stand-alone process or part of the performance management system, it provides performance indicators that reflect organisational goals and objectives, including at least two of the following three elements.

Performance review

This looks back on performance during a given period and whether or not performance objectives, goals or targets are being achieved or have been reached. The aim is to improve current performance. It should focus on the strengths of the individual/team to create a positive work ethos that encourages higher levels of commitment, proactivity and levels of achievement. Areas that need improvement should be approached with a positive attitude that allows the individual or team the opportunity to work with the appraiser on ways to improve. Current performance can be used to set the objectives for the coming year, especially where progress is on-going. This is an opportunity to be proactive and to set objectives that will reflect future needs as opposed to just the organisation's present needs. We can see clear links here with how organisations make use of goal-setting theoretical foundations in order to increase individual performance in the future.

Potential review

This part of the appraisal focuses on development needs and could be related to areas needing improvement which require a mutually agreed action plan that encourages and supports such improvement. It can also be used as part of the career plan whereby the future potential of the individual is identified and areas for development or 'opportunities for progression' are defined within the action plan. Where the performance management system focuses on development, this particular element is often dealt with in a separate session. The reasoning behind the separation is that although the appraiser may be focused on developing the employee, the employee's own focus may be more on whether or not his/her level of performance meets requirements and he/she receives the due reward.

Employees are less likely to admit to difficulties regarding their performance when there is a chance that any such admission on their part may affect their reward.

Reward review

There is evidence to suggest that the inclusion of the reward element in the appraisal can be demotivating. A leading police service has moved away from assessing reward and development within the same review because it has been identified as having a negative impact on performance. There are, however, national variations. The Cranet-E survey suggests that in the UK as well as in Continental Europe appraisals are most often used for development and training purposes (see Table 29). The link to reward is strongest in Sweden and Germany.

Table 29 'Is the performance appraisal system used to inform the following?'

	UK	Sweden	Germany	Greece	Slovakia
HR planning	64%	51%	46%	71%	44%
Analysis of training/development needs	98%	79%	87%	86%	51%
Career	86%	66%	87%	82%	35%
Pay determination	55%	87%	74%	80%	62%
Organisation of work	53%	43%	42%	65%	45%

Source: Cranet-E (2003)

The review session is also an opportunity for an exchange between the line manager (appraiser) and the employee (appraisee). The reviews should be undertaken on a regular basis and at least once a year. It is a way of making sure that performances are on target and of having the tools to deal with poor performance. The reviews can be both informal and formal. Having informal reviews on a regular basis allows for a closer monitoring of performances and gives an earlier opportunity for addressing any issues. The completed appraisal form is usually signed both by the appraiser and appraisee and countersigned by the appraiser's line manager to make sure that reporting is transparent.

A crucial factor in driving the appraisal system, which must be noted here, is the buy-in of line managers (appraisers) to the process. They not only need to take ownership of the process, which may be encouraged through making it one of their performance targets, they also need on-going training, advice and support to sustain it.

The appraisal also should be seen as being transparent and equitable, providing reporting consistency and regular feedback on performance. It should be simple, straightforward and easy to understand with objectives that are 'SMART' – ie specific, measurable, attainable, realistic and time-bound (Armstrong and Baron, 2005).

Issues can occur in relation to a poor buy-in to the system creating a lack of commitment. Poor training or the complete lack of it can encourage a mistrust of performance ratings, which may also not be clearly set out to provide a realistic reflection of performance. The system if seen negatively may be sabotaged through lack of active support.

The appraisal process requires a number of conditions to ensure that it is carried out effectively:

- There must be preparation prior to the formal review meeting on the part of both the reviewer (appraiser) and the reviewee (appraisee).

- Where appraisees are required to fill out a self-assessment form, the form should be given to the reviewer before the apparaisal meeting because it will allow the reviewer a useful insight into the reviewee's perspective of his/her performance.

- The reviewer should be familiar with the reviewee's performance record, and should therefore be comfortable with setting aside time in a quiet and private area to discuss it in confidence.

- The reviewer may start by discussing positive aspects of the reviewee's performance before going on to areas that may require further development.

- The reviewees should be encouraged to put forward their views and should be encouraged to do most of the talking while the reviewer listens carefully to the responses. This two-way communication should result in the preparation of a development or action plan which encourages and motivates the reviewee to meet agreed targets over the coming year.

- Reviews can take place both formally and informally: there are times where during the process issues may be highlighted that need further monitoring, especially where there may be grievance, disciplinary or counselling implications.

3 CURRENT ISSUES IN PERFORMANCE MANAGEMENT

THE BALANCED SCORECARD

The 'balanced scorecard', developed by Kaplan and Norton (1996), provides the organisation with a framework for communicating the company's vision and strategy by expressing them in the form of strategic objectives, measures and goals (Olve *et al*, 2001).

It facilitates the integration between different functional areas and translates the business mission, vision and goals to provide measurable short-term performance goals that relate to the long-term organisational ones. It translates strategic processes into operational ones and encourages continuous improvement and accountability mainly in respect of the team rather than the individual (Armstrong and Baron, 2005). It uses feedback as part of the learning and as a process for adapting strategies to improve organisational performance. This allows the company to deal with changes in the marketplace.

The overall business's performance is assessed through four different perspectives:

● *learning and growth* – which encourages 'self-improvement' both at the corporate and operational level

● *financial* – which looks at the importance of providing accurate and up-to-date financial data in support of the organisation's overall performance

● *customer* – which identifies the importance of retaining customers and making sure they are satisfied with the quality of services and products

● *internal/business process* – which focuses on the effectiveness of the business in its provision of goods and services.

The focus of the balanced scorecard relates to the alignment of the performance management system with other aspects of the business and how long-term goals are translated into short-term performances (Armstrong and Baron, 2005). Its design varies according to the focus of the mission, vision and objectives of the organisation. For instance, an airline's focus will differ from that of a public sector organisation.

Used correctly, it is an important instrument for expressing a vision and strategy in more concrete terms (Olve *et al*, 2001). The Highways Agency has developed a scorecard which contains five perspectives that mirror its objectives. These are *customer service, teamwork, improvement, diversity* and *best value*. It also includes *integrity* (Highways Agency, 2007). This has led to clearly defined performance indicators that have set the types of behaviours it requires to deliver a more effective service. Part of the process has been the introduction of the 'valuing employees reward'. The Highways Agency provides a good example of ways to move performance forward.

REFLECTIVE ACTIVITY

Access the Highways Agency website, **http://www.highways.gov.uk/ default.aspx** and look at the development plans and performance indicators there.

What is so interesting about them?

Another interesting example is Orange. Orange now links objectives to the balanced scorecard, translating them downwards to provide individual objectives that clarify the role of employees in the organisation. This is achieved through the 'strategy' and 'business excellence' teams working with HR to set the scorecard and translate strategy into operational targets along four dimensions:

shareholders, customers, partners, and people/the workforce (Johnson, 2006). This too is an on-going process.

360-DEGREE FEEDBACK

This may be referred to as '360-degree appraisal or multi-rater feedback' (DBA, 2002), and is a process that seeks to create more effective feedback on performance from a number of sources linked to the individual concerned (eg peers, supervisors, colleagues, project teams, internal and external customers) through raising his/her awareness of how his/her behaviour and performance is perceived by others. It measures competencies through the use of a questionnaire specifically designed to provide feedback relevant to the organisation and the individual. It requires trained raters, facilitators and managers so that the feedback can be effectively produced and interpreted.

A well-designed 360-degree feedback format can thus be used to measure the relevant knowledge, skills, abilities and/or competencies that are required to meet the organisation's needs. It can provide a unique opportunity for individuals to make an objective comparison of their self-assessment with the assessments of their peers, managers and customers or other interested parties involved in the process. Moreover, it provides assessed feedback from a number of sources that when combined present a clearer picture of an individual's overall performance.

It is particularly useful in the development of managers and senior managers because it gives an insight into how they are seen by others. It is a time-consuming process that needs a skilled interpretation of the results of the assessments obtained, but on the other hand it does provide a more accurate picture of an individual's performance. The person elected to provide the feedback for the individual concerned has an opportunity to discuss any development needs from a more informed perspective.

The Cranet-E data implies that 360-degree feedback is not yet widespread in European organisations. Table 30 suggests that appraisals are mainly based on the input of the supervisor and employee. In contrast, the review of subordinates, peers and customers count less.

Table 30 'Who is formally expected to input/provide data for the performance appraisal process?'

	UK	Sweden	Germany	Greece	Slovakia
Immediate supervisor	100%	100%	100%	100%	59%
Supervisor's superior	80%	69%	70%	89%	28%
Employee himself/herself	99%	89%	68%	74%	66%
Subordinates	22%	36%	19%	17%	18%
Peers	26%	26%	6%	17%	23%
Customers	15%	20%	9%	21%	25%

Source: Cranet-E (2003)

COACHING

Coaching appears to be increasing in popularity and managers are being encouraged to use it to assist in improving employees' performance. Coaching in the right hands can be a powerful tool in directing individuals and improving their performance. It sits comfortably with self-awareness and encourages coachees to look forward and be proactive in their own development. There are different types of coaching, which focus on different levels of the organisation. There are, for example, executive coaches and development ones. How successful the coaching is depends on a number of variables, including the coach's experience, the type of coaching, the type of intervention used and ultimately the coachee. It can – if used effectively – focus, improve and motivate an individual to move forward.

FURTHER CONSIDERATIONS ON PERFORMANCE MANAGEMENT

After examining a solid range of frequently used tools to measure performance in organisations, let us consider some of the major problems we still find in relation to performance. Perhaps you are doing a part-time job besides your studies and have already come across such tools. If so, what were the problems you encountered? In some jobs, such as in sales, task performance can be measured relatively easily: sales per day/shift/week/month/quarter/year. Other jobs, such as HR or marketing-oriented ones, for instance, are much harder to quantify. How can we set 'SMART' objectives for developing an effective human resource development system for these kinds of jobs?

Another problem is that some employees might visibly exert more effort than others, but it does not always increase actual measured performance. For instance, your teacher may try very hard to help students in their learning, but the final marks (as moderated by external examiners) may turn out to be very similar to those of students of another teacher who has been far less energetic in teaching. It is likely that anybody who puts in a special effort would prefer to be rewarded on the basis of that effort, whereas management generally deems output the more important criterion. This is likely to create ill-feeling, which in turn is likely to result in demotivation and disillusionment, and in reducing or withholding contextual performance.

There is also ample evidence that rater biases do exist and are difficult to minimise. People who are liked by the rater are often more favourably assessed – regardless of the final outcome – than those who have a weaker relationship with the rater. Moreover, appraisers may be reluctant to express severe criticism during a performance appraisal because it creates an unpleasant atmosphere and, after all, people generally have to go on working with each other. It has got to be awkward to spend the rest of the day (or week or month) in the same office with someone you have just told is not good enough at his or her job.

REFLECTIVE ACTIVITY

Think about the problems we have just outlined with regard to performance management in organisations.

To what extent might the methods we described in earlier sections of this chapter overcome such problems?

KEY ISSUES IN PERFORMANCE MANAGEMENT AND APPRAISAL

We now pull together ten key points about performance management and appraisals raised in this chapter:

- A clearly structured performance management system can improve organisational performance by providing simple and straightforward appraisals that monitor performance.
- The system must be aligned to the strategic plans. The performance goals must be clearly identified and set in relation to individuals, teams, processes, etc, and cascaded downwards.
- The system has to provide for the learning and development needs of individuals and teams. This includes coaching and mentoring, skills audit and succession planning.
- The appraisal should represent an opportunity to encourage the development of action, personal development and career plans.
- All parties with an interest in the process should be identified, because their commitment is an ingredient essential to the success of the process. This may include managers, individual or trade union representatives, customers and shareholders.

- The assessment design for individual or team performance should reflect the nature of the work concerned – the ratings must be objective to encourage confidence in the system.
- Line managers should be supported in developing the expertise to operate the system and encourage their staff to perform to higher levels.
- Performance management systems should be ethical and provide a platform for cultural and job profile changes, should promote the values of the organisation, and should be integrated into the HR process. There should be in-built monitoring and evaluating processes which allow improvements to be made to the systems through re-structuring and adaptations.
- Piloting or testing them on designated areas of the organisation to evaluate their effectiveness would provide an opportunity to modify or adjust them to ensure that they can be effectively implemented.
- There are some crucial problems which even well-designed performance management systems may not overcome.

Perhaps there are other key points you would like to note for yourself.

The main case study in this chapter now follows. It provides an example of how performance-related interventions can be used to engineer a change from a quantity- to a quality-oriented culture.

The production history of the Halewood plant, Merseyside, offers an insight into how one of the worst-performing car plants in the Ford portfolio was transformed into the exemplar of the Japanese-style Ford production system and six-sigma quality system, producing high-quality motor vehicles. Halewood's production of the Ford Escort (1968–2000) was plagued by poor industrial relations and poor build quality. During this time the British car industry was in flux to the extent that in 1989 Ford purchased Jaguar. During 1999 their Jaguar plant at Castle Bromwich, Birmingham, became operational and doubled their production of the S-type. In 1998, as part of increasing Jaguar's model productions it was decided to produce the new X-type at Halewood. This nearly did not happen in the light of the opposition that Ford experienced from the workforce.

Jaguar took over operation during this turbulent time and began the process of changing to Jaguar working practices. The Gateway Agreement, as part of the changes in working, was signed up to by the unions. Unfortunately, strikes ensued when management attempted to implement the Agreement. Because of these poor industrial relations, Ford threatened to pull out – but this was resolved when 90% of the workforce signed up to the Halewood charter and the rest took voluntary redundancy or early retirement. The changes in working practices relating to the move to producing Jaguars were supported by government grants for re-training the workforce.

The senior management team at Halewood sought to obtain buy-in by the workforce to the new more flexible working arrangements. It was important to move from being volume-driven to being quality-driven – which meant changing mindsets. The plant was shut down in 2000 for nine weeks for modification in readiness for production of the new module. This provided an opportunity for a series of interventions to be put into operation to support the new more flexible working practices and the reopening of the plant.

The creation of centres of excellence was part of the move to sustain quality. These centres delivered specific elements of the business, which focused on cultural change and improved quality. This, combined with the new processes and a more open management style, provided a platform whereby managers and the workforce alike were able to hold open discussions on the changes. Provisions were made for shopfloor workers to draft their job descriptions and for the creation of teams of six to eight workers whose team leaders were able to monitor quality control.

Assessment centres were used to identify new managers who would not only be committed to running the centres of excellence but be comfortable with the changes and with operating the new production processes. The successful operation of the new centres of excellence created a positive impact, which encouraged others to buy in to this more enthusiastic approach to work.

One intervention that really encapsulated the new approach was empowering the workers to stop the production line to deal with any quality issues. This freedom to act independently to some extent recognised the value of each worker in the production process and helped the drive for better-quality products.

All the training programmes set up during the closure of the plant were designed to support the change process. Senior managers and volunteers from the workforce underwent training to become facilitators so that they could deliver the new programme to the rest of the workforce. Production workers undertook college courses focused on IT, numeracy and literacy skills training to support their role in record-keeping. Community projects were set up to encourage the integration of the new production teams – this was initially viewed with caution by those concerned, but as the projects progressed, attitudes changed, and the experience appeared to have a positive impact.

Some operators and all supervisors and group leaders were seconded to the new S-type Jaguar plant to obtain an overview of the new production process and a level of expertise that they could take back to Halewood. Training on trial car-building runs enabled them to train other operators on their return by becoming product coaches.

The combination of interventions resulted in teams being formed that had a clearer idea of what performance levels and product quality were expected of them in the new teams and working conditions. Senior management recognised that to sustain performance the process needed on-going monitoring. Production started in 2001, and an audit of the new working practices has since provided a template that others might put into practice.

Source: Pickard (2002)

Questions for discussion

1 Why did this combination of interventions succeed in changing the performance record of the workforce from one of the worst to the best?

2 Analyse each intervention noting the individual aspects of each one that demonstrate good practice. Can they be used for similar changes elsewhere?

3 What else might you do to sustain high-quality performance?

Note: It is your response to Question 2 – asking yourself why individual aspects worked and whether different combinations of them might be used elsewhere to produce similar outcomes – from which you should be able to develop your ideas as recommendations in response to Question 3.

EXPLORE FURTHER

ARMSTRONG, M. and BARON, A. (2005) *Managing Performance – Performance management in action*. London, CIPD
These are useful in providing a base from which people management policies, procedures and process can be developed to contribute to the overall performance of the business.

CABINET OFFICE (2007) *Transformational Government Enabled by Technology*, Annual Report. Online version available at:
http://www.cio.gov.uk/documents/annual_report2006/ trans_gov2006.pdf [accessed July 2007]
The Cabinet Office provides reports on a number of HR-related areas including the framework.

CIO (2007) *IT Skills Framework and the Focus of the Council*. Online version available at: **www.cio.gov.uk/about_the_council/index.asp** [accessed July 2007]

CIPD (2005) *Performance Appraisal*. London, CIPD

CIPD (2005) *Performance Management*, CIPD Survey Report. London, CIPD
The report looks at the performance management arrangements in different organisations and analyses the effectiveness of the activities that feature in them.

CIPD (2007) Performance management factsheet. Online version available at:
http://www. cipd.co.uk [accessed March 2007]WALTERS, M. (2005) *People and Performance: Designing the HR process for maximum performance delivery*. London, CIPD

HIGHWAYS AGENCY (2007) *Business Plan*. Online version available at:
www.highways.gov.uk/ aboutus/1283.aspx; general access:
http://www.highways.gov.uk/default.aspx [accessed July 2007]
These sites provide not only information on performance indicators and the balanced scorecard but also an insight into the activities of the agencies.

CHAPTER 13

Reward systems

Geoff Wood, Leslie T. Szamosi *and* Alexandros Psychogios

INTRODUCTION

This chapter aims to provide an introduction to and an overview of reward systems in the modern organisation. It takes a comprehensive look at recent developments in the deployment and administration of reward systems and examines the practical implications for organisations.

LEARNING OUTCOMES

By the end of this chapter readers should be able to:

- discuss the links between overall organisational strategies and reward systems in practice
- introduce and describe the limitations and uses of job evaluation in the modern organisation
- introduce and critically discuss the individual performance-oriented pay ('new pay') approach to reward systems
- appreciate the role of team pay and the contexts in which it may be the most appropriate
- provide an overview of key ethical questions in the deployment and use of reward systems.

The chapter is structured in two parts. The first part discusses the context of reward and the second part deals with different types of reward systems.

The chapter concludes with the main case study.

Reference sources named within the chapter may be looked up in the *References and further reading* section at the end of the book.

Central to the employment contract are questions related to reward (Snell, 1992). All jobs – even voluntary ones – are performed in the anticipation of some reward, whether as wages or in personal satisfaction. Quite simply, organisations have to take the process of reward seriously in order to attract and retain talented staff (Brewster, 1995). In looking at reward within an organisation, we tend to look at reward systems (Snell, 1992). These are the

In 1960, Northstar was one of five steel producers located in Oldstown, which, in all employed some 26% of the town's mill-age-eligible adult population. Today, it is the sole surviving steel producer, employing some 2% of the eligible adult male population. Traditionally, Northstar supplied the shipping industry but today it owes its survival to a gradual shift to smaller batch production, providing specialist products in niches of the market not covered by major Far Eastern steel producers.

As a result of this shift, Northstar has been forced to redefine the manner in which it manages its human resources. Most recently, senior management has begun to explore the possibility of adopting an employee involvement programme (EIP). It is hoped that such a programme will encourage commitment, facilitate further multi-skilling and ultimately enhance the quality of the products produced. Theoretically, the success of an EIP is predicated on both parties' adopting co-operative norms of power-sharing to a lesser or greater extent.

Work at Northstar has for many years been characterised by employee defiance of many of the rules imposed by the company (and in many cases, by the union as well). Workers 'know their jobs', and have committed their lives to making the world's best steel. However, they have also found time to redefine the work area to meet their own needs and norms. A workplace survey revealed that workers tended to see supervisors as incompetent, 'lacking family values' and big drinkers, and senior management seemed to be held in even lower esteem. Moreover, workers 'make their own tea breaks', engaging in recreational activity on company time – a practice that supervisors turn a blind eye to, within certain parameters. Finally, Northstar has always been dogged by high levels of petty theft of company property.

Questions for discussion

What changes to or reforms of the reward system might help solve some of the problems faced by management in this organisation?

overall structures and processes that are in place to ensure that each individual is adequately rewarded for his or her output or general contribution to the organisation. There must be some consistency in this process.

1 REWARD SYSTEMS

The employment contract is about an exchange relationship by which a specified amount of labour power is traded for various rewards – a tenet of all motivation theories. The *traditional approach* to motivation emphasises economic rewards linked to productivity (ie scientific management). The *human relations approach* emphasises non-monetary rewards as the prime motivating factor (eg the Hawthorne studies) while the *human resource approach* suggests that workers are motivated by many individualised reward systems (eg Theory X and Theory Y).

For almost all employees, the most important reward is monetary compensation. Wages are an *extrinsic* reward ('hygiene factors', according to Herzberg's two-factor motivation theory) – in other words, it is given for a certain amount of work, and does not directly constitute a part of the actual working experience. The other major extrinsic reward is job security. Most employees prefer secure employment in view of their personal and family commitments, or, at the very least enough notice period to make alternative arrangements should their employment end. On the one hand it could be argued that only incompetent staff will set a premium on job security – the best staff will have good externally marketable skills, and will rapidly be able to find another job. Organisations might thus become more flexible by concentrating extrinsic rewards towards pay only, and be able to rapidly cut or increase workforce sizes (and overall pay obligations) in the light of changing circumstances. On the other hand there is considerable evidence to suggest that job-seekers in a strong bargaining position will naturally demand some job security, if nothing else to reduce the costs incurred during employment transitions. It is perhaps telling that most executive board members in the UK ensure that they will receive generous payouts in the event of having to leave the organisation.

Intrinsic rewards are those that form part and parcel of the working day ('motivating factors', according to Herzberg's two-factor motivation theory). They could include issues such as recognition from peers and superiors, personal fulfilment from the nature of the tasks performed, celebrations on attaining work goals, and/or the sense of belonging to a community. Although a large proportion of the literature on reward systems concentrates on extrinsic rewards, the importance of intrinsic rewards should not be underestimated.

The reward that a worker takes from his or her efforts indicates whether his/her behaviour was appropriate and sufficiently compensated. Organisations must seek to determine the right balance of rewards to keep workers motivated. For example, in terms of the content theories of motivation (eg Maslow's hierarchy of needs, ERG Theory) needs must be satisfied and the appropriate reward linked to fulfilment of those particular needs. On the other hand, through Reinforcement Theory, rewards (and punishments) are used to immediately link behaviours and consequences.

 REFLECTIVE ACTIVITY

Think of an organisation you know.

How important are/were intrinsic rewards in motivating employees?

It is difficult to accurately measure the exact worth of a particular amount of labour time, and, for that reason, there is inevitably some room for a conflict of interest between employer and employee. The employer naturally has an interest in closely tying perceived output – and the general value of the employee to the enterprise – to payment. Although employees are in employment precisely because they wish to be rewarded – above all, in the form of pay – they have an interest in a reward system that is predictable (in view of personal financial commitments), is fair, and does not impose undue amounts of stress.

So the manner in which organisations administer and distribute rewards reflects a desire to mould the behaviour of their staff. This would include the monitoring of their performance and/or the controlling of their output. In other words, companies administer reward systems in a manner that directs staff towards the realisation of organisational objectives. However, organisations may choose – or choose not – to empower staff with considerable room for manoeuvre in the way in which outputs may be attained. They may act unilaterally, or they may allow staff some input in the process of goal-setting, in the manner in which performance is measured, and in the nature and extent of the actual rewards given.

On the one hand, most organisations naturally seek to optimise their output (in terms of goods manufactured or services offered). This would including giving greater rewards to the most productive, skilled and/or capable employees (Koch and McGrath, 1996). On the other hand, too much emphasis on closely controlling the work of employees and/or the distribution of rewards in a manner that is perceived to be unfair or overly punitive will result in the migration of the most competent staff members to organisations where the quality of working life is better, leaving behind a discontent group of less capable and mobile staff who have to put up with the system in the absence of alternative options. The operation of reward systems may thus have effects opposite to those intended. Again, the close monitoring of employee performance may encourage dishonesty, with employees lying or systematically breaking rules to attain preset outcomes.

There is very much more to reward than output and moulding the behaviour of staff. Reward systems also aim to control costs, to be fair and to increase staff morale (Lado and Wilson, 1994). In addition, many countries prohibit pay discrimination on the grounds of gender and race – the operation of a reward system has legal implications. Organisations have to monitor pay rates to ensure that legislation is not being breached, even if inadvertently. Quite simply, reward is one of the key, fundamental policy-making areas of HRM.

REFLECTIVE ACTIVITY

What is more important in designing a reward system – controlling costs or promoting fairness?

STRATEGY, HR AND REWARD

Since the early 1980s, a growing emphasis has been placed on the strategic dimension of people management (see Chapters 3 and 20 for a more in-depth discussion of the issues that are only summarised below). Historically, personnel administration was just that – the administration of pay and reward systems and other elements of the personnel function in a predetermined manner according to formal rules and procedures. The increasingly turbulent global environment has forced firms to take *strategic* issues in the management of human resources more seriously.

There is a very simple reason for this. The resource-based view of the firm suggests that many of a firm's attributes cannot be readily bought or sold on the external labour market, and yet may be the source of sustained competitive advantage. For example, staff may have skills, attributes or knowledge specific to the organisation that may not have a commensurate value on the external job market, or even be known to competitors. So what a firm does with its people may be the key to greater organisational competitiveness: the manner in which they are rewarded may provide the basis of success, even if external conditions are bleak. Any inclusive HR strategy therefore has rewards as one of its core components. Ideally, reward systems should be linked directly to overall organisational strategies, and concern not just issues of motivation and control but also provide incentives for higher productivity.

In the early years of the Industrial Revolution, pay was generally set on the basis of output. In practice, pay-setting in early industrial organisations was often arbitrary. The rise of trade unions in Britain saw a shift towards pay rates for the job – in other words, all those doing a similar job were paid according to the same pay-scale. With the decline of unions in Britain, pay by results or performance has returned to popularity. Interestingly, many organisations have also tended to decentralise the operation of rewards systems away from a central HR department and towards greater involvement by line management. There is something of a contradiction here in that although there is a greater emphasis on the need for reward systems to be strategic – and hence, flexible – considerable attention in the literature has been focused on promoting 'best practices': customer-focused pay, variable pay linked to individual performance, and pay as the primary reward for good performance. Indeed, critics have charged that most HR systems are a collection of issues rarely integrated or designed from a 'total systems' perspective – that in the real world, pay systems are rarely integrated into overall HR, let alone internal organisational strategies (Drucker and White, 1997). After all, reward systems are often inconsistent even internally, reducing their general effectiveness.

Moreover, many companies create or maintain reward systems that are not linked with the overall organisational strategic aim (Kerr, 1975). When rewards are aligned with strategic goals, employees can coordinate and emphasise their efforts and their daily labours. The challenge is therefore to guarantee that the reward systems are enhancing strategic intent instead of being a drag on it. For this reason it would be appropriate to involve in the design process of the reward systems not only HR specialists but also those people that are fully aware of the strategic goals of the organisation (Meyer, 1994).

REFLECTIVE ACTIVITY

It is often argued that reward systems should be adjusted in line with changing organisational strategic objectives – yet in the real world, this is not often the case.

Why is that, do you think?

2 TYPES OF REWARD SYSTEMS

There are three basic approaches to reward systems. The first, and simplest, is to pay all individuals in the same job grade the same rate, or on a similar pay-scale (allowing gradual progression on the grounds of seniority). Secondly, individuals may be ranked in their own right, some individuals being judged superior, some average and some inferior; pay rates are adjusted accordingly. Thirdly, team pay is a variation of performance-related pay, allocated on the basis of teams of employees, rather than individuals.

TRADITIONAL APPROACHES TO PAY

As noted above, up until the 1980s most British organisations tended to make use of formal bureaucratic pay systems. Typically, staff were placed on predetermined pay-scales. The latter had often been pre-negotiated with a trade union, representing the outcome of a *collective agreement* that in turn represented the outcome of *collective bargaining* between the union and management. Today, only about a third of employees are covered by collective bargaining in the UK. The coverage is particularly low in private services, but relatively high in the public sector (see Table 31).

Table 31 Aggregate collective bargaining coverage, 1998 and 2004

	Percentage of employees	
	1998	2004
All workplaces	38	35
Industry		
Manufacturing	43	35
Hotels and restaurants	12	4
Financial services	49	35
Public sector	66	75

Source: Kersley *et al* (2006; p.187)

In the traditional approach, the pay scale is contingent on the job, and the individual's position on the pay-scale on seniority. The advantages of such systems include internal consistency, legitimacy (in the case of collective agreements), and administrative ease. Central to such a process is job evaluation – in other words, the ability to tell what a particular job really is about and worth, rather than the performance of the individual carrying it out.

Job evaluation

Job evaluation is the analysis of a particular set of roles typically performed in carrying out a job. Because it is specific to the job, it should be a process less prone to personal prejudice or discrimination than the assessment of a particular individual. There are two basic types of job evaluation. The first, 'non-analytical' ranking system assigns rank to a job as a whole, vis-à-vis others: in other words, what the job as a whole entails in relation to others. The second, 'analytical' approach breaks up a job into individual factors and elements, and looks at each in turn, which, in theory at least, should enable greater objectivity. Non-analytical systems leave more room for job stereotyping, which may reflect embedded gender, age or ethnic stereotypes, but does recognise that jobs represent more than simply packages of tasks, and may be harder to manage in the case of jobs that entail a wide range of duties.

Job evaluation simply is the process of deciding the relative contribution of a particular job to the organisation as a whole, and its worth both *internally* (that is in terms of the organisation) and *externally* (in terms of comparable jobs in other organisations). In other words, it is about finding out the relative worth of a job to assign pay to it. As such, it is distinct from *job analysis.*

Job analysis is essentially *the compilation of information on what a particular job really is about* – in other words, the duties attached to a particular job, and the context thereof. No job evaluation is possible without some form of job analysis in advance: one has to gather information about a job in order to evaluate it or decide on its relative worth. Job analysis is used not only for subsequent job evaluation but also to compile *job descriptions* (what a job entails), *job performance standards* (what is expected in a particular job) and *job specification* (what is required to do a particular job – eg skills, knowledge, physical and psychological attributes, etc).

Job evaluation is a somewhat subjective process, although it is also a formal and procedural one. Table 32 highlights some of the principal forms of job evaluation system. Job evaluation is about finding out the relative value of a job and assigning pay rates to it – not an individual, who may, at a particular time, carry out the job. On entering a particular job, individuals will be assured of a particular pay rate – either a simple fixed wage (eg the national minimum wage) – or a place on the pay-scale attached to the relevant job grade. The individual will then gradually progress on the scale (eg on the basis of seniority).

Table 32 Job evaluation systems compared

Type of system	System	Description
Non-analytical	Ranking	Places jobs in an order, from the least to the most important for the organisation
Non-analytical	Job grading/ Job classification	A number of possible job grades are identified, each attached to a particular pay-scale. These grades may be defined on skill, knowledge and responsibilities. Individual jobs are then slotted into these predetermined grades
Analytical	Quantitative methods	*Factor comparison schemes* identify a number of factors (scales), such as skill, responsibility, effort, etc. Each job is ranked on each factor, and pay is set accordingly per factor, ultimately leading to an overall pay package. A variation of this is the *point comparison system*, in which instead of assigning components of pay to each factor, points are assigned (eg 10 out of 100 for skill). Overall points assigned to a particular job are then added up, and this is used as a basis for differentiating pay

Critics have charged that such approaches are inflexible, and do not allow enough room to award individual excellence (or punish poor performance): 'old pay fits old bureaucratic organisations', whereas more modern flexible organisations require more modern pay systems. In other words, traditional pay rewards individuals according to their place in the organisation and their accomplishments, but is not congruent with 'knowledge- or quality-oriented organisations' (Allen and Killmann, 1999).

REFLECTIVE ACTIVITY

What do you think are the positive and negative aspects of job evaluation schemes?

(If you have had experience of a job evaluation scheme, draw on it for your answer.)

INDIVIDUAL PERFORMANCE-ORIENTED PAY

Often referred to as 'the New pay', a term coined by Edward Lawler, individual performance-oriented pay systems are depicted by their proponents as a more up-to-date strategic approach to pay and reward. It is argued that pay systems should be integrated and mutually supportive with other areas of HRM, and organisational strategies at large (Lewis, 1998). New pay is about flexibility, and a more direct linking of individual performance to reward (Heery, 1996; Dickinson, 2006). As such, it reflects the declining influence of unions and collective bargaining. New pay approaches argue that fixed base pay rates only reward a job, not the nature or quality of an individual's input; it is argued that, in an increasingly competitive world, it is necessary to tailor pay to what individuals *really* contribute to an organisation (ie both tangibles and intangibles). Person-based systems aim explicitly to promote the attainment of certain pre-decided organisational outcomes. 'New pay' systems focusing on the individual are a form of individual performance-related pay (PRP) – in other words, a system where an individual's pay is at least partly dependent on his or her performance appraisal or ranking (Kerrin and Oliver, 2002). Current research has shown, however, that traditional reward systems are still strong throughout Europe (Willems, Janvier and Henderickx, 2006).

Individual performance-related pay assumes that rewards can be adjusted to changes in organisational circumstances, enabling firms to become 'fast and nimble'. The literature on 'New pay' makes little reference to collective bargaining, and assumes that determining reward is ultimately the prerogative of management. New pay also argues that individual rewards should reflect both the state of the external market and the net worth of the individual staff member. As with any other benefits, pay rates should be flexible and readily adjustable to changes in circumstances, and encourage entrepreneurial behaviour among staff (Carraher, Hart and Carraher, 2003). However, in reality, the rate at which New pay systems have been adopted remains uneven, reflecting both an abiding reluctance by senior management to abandon tried and trusted measures and the continued popularity of job-evaluation-based reward systems. In part, the latter would reflect the effects of equal pay for equal work legislation (for example, legislation that outlaws differential pay on the basis of gender or ethnicity), which would encourage firms to become more, rather than less, consistent in the manner in which they pay their staff.

The adoption of an individual PRP system does not mean that the entire salary package should be based solely on performance. However, the base pay (that is, the set amount that is related to the job, rather than individual performance) should be kept at the bare minimum necessary to attract and retain key staff. Thereafter, performance-related payments would top up salaries, ensuring that the 'best' workers are the 'best rewarded'. This would also assist in motivating employees (eg Equity Theory).

It has been argued that the PRP model is most appropriate to more 'flexible' employment contracts, by which incumbents have lower degrees of job security, but with more room for redeployment, and, perhaps advancement (see Chapter 10). It represents a move away from the formal regulation of the employment contract, and, as such, may be most appropriate in cases where the ability of individuals to depart from preset norms is particularly valuable (ie thinking outside the box).

Proponents have argued that the new pay is particularly appropriate to firms operating in the high technology sector. Rapid change in such environments poses the risk that reward systems will fall behind changing organisational needs (eg Twomey and Quazi, 1994). New pay assumes that wages should be variable; in practice, pay packages are often designed in such a manner that some indirect costs can be shifted on to the individual in the event of sub-optimal performance. This also turns fixed costs into variable costs thereby allowing easier budgeting and forecasting expenses. Such reward systems may be supplemented and improved by objective bonus plans and the availability of firm-specific training to increase the value of the employment relationship, making it more worthwhile for talented staff to stay with the organisation (Ichniowski and Shaw, 2003).

Critics have charged that this model is overly simplistic, and that it merely assumes there is a direct link between compensation strategy and individual performance, whereas classic theories of motivation (eg Vroom's Expectancy Theory) would point to more complex relationships between the two. In today's work environment these links may be becoming even more complex as workers also seek to balance work and family concerns against straight compensation. Individual PRP thus takes little account of the social context in which work takes place, which we are seeing as becoming even more critical in today's environment. Individuals may restrict their output in order to maintain good relations with their peers, or work together to ensure that targets are mutually attainable.

Again, New pay is based on the assumption that managers and employees have essentially the same interests – interests that can be readily reconciled. Through high-quality work, individuals contribute to the broader well-being of the organisation, and are also well rewarded through flexible pay systems (Scott and Dean, 1992; Dickinson, 2006). It has accordingly been referred to as *neo-unitarist* – that is, that managers and employees should have *united* interests.

Reward systems are investments to attract talented individuals and ensure that they perform well over time. Yet if rewards are seen as inequitable, individuals are more likely to leave, qualified individuals are also less likely to join, or staff may stay and produce at a lower level. In reality, there have been many cases where employees have opposed the introduction of new pay systems, and/or voted by their feet by choosing to move away from organisations where the administration of reward is seen as unduly coercive.

The introduction of New pay may be used as a device for undermining unions – employees are rewarded according to the perceived value they add, rather than through a collectively negotiated contract.

There are also other practical concerns. The evaluation of any staff member is necessarily a subjective process, based on managerial perceptions of customer satisfaction and/or the perceived quality of goods or services that are produced. This level of vagueness leaves management with a great deal of discretion, which may perpetuate existing inequalities in the organisation – for example, those on race or gender lines. Indeed, the introduction of individual PRP systems may raise equity and fairness concerns, contribute to employee anxiety, result in unduly negative evaluations of specific categories of employee, and inevitable injustices may contribute to perceptions of organisational inefficiency (Pearce, Branyiczki and Bakacsi, 1994). Because the New pay is individually (or at best, team-) focused, workers may lack an effective collective voice to challenge managerial judgements.

On the one hand, there is substantial evidence to suggest that large numbers of organisations have moved towards more flexible benefits systems – or redesigned existing systems – particularly in certain job categories. On the other hand, this may reflect the influence of external factors. The latter could include factors as disparate as changes in tax policy and declining union power – and hence, collective bargaining and centrally agreed pay-scales.

 REFLECTIVE ACTIVITY

What would you say are the benefits and disadvantages of individual PRP in practice in organisations – in particular, in service and manufacturing industries?

TEAM-BASED PAY

Performance-based pay may be administered not only on the basis of individual effort and achievement but also, alternatively, on the performance of autonomous work teams (Cacciope, 1999). When firms cannot measure accurately the contribution of individual workers, group-based incentive pay may be particularly appropriate. This includes rewarding employees according to physical output or firm-wide profit-sharing (Ichniowski and Shaw, 2003). However, it can create the problem of 'free-riding', less productive workers relying on the efforts of others (Kerrin and Oliver, 2002). This has often led to a focus on small groups or teams of workers; work teams may boost group identity (Brown, 1996).

It may be difficult to decide on suitable measures of team performance in organisational settings other than manufacturing or frontline services. Even in the case of the latter, performance measures may have perverse effects. For example, the speed with which customers may be dealt with may result in difficult or time-consuming requests being deferred or ignored, with the bulk of attention being directed towards dealing with customers who can be speedily processed (even in cases where the potential revenue that may flow from the latter is less). There is also the problem of excessive competition between teams, which can undermine organisational solidarity and lead to employees being reluctant to share information with each other. Finally, team-based incentive systems are not always compatible with the use of individual bonuses or other forms of performance recognition – and in fact, if exercised, can cause catastrophic team dysfunction. This has meant that, in practice, organisations may choose to go for gestures or symbolic rewards for exceptional team performance, rather than completely redesigning reward systems on team lines (Cacciope, 1999).

Teams may be rewarded not only through the payment of bonuses but also through resetting base pay rates, through the future allocation of resources (including supporting infrastructure) and the allocation of work. The allocation of rewards may be uniform across the entire team, or be customised to take account of particular effort (or lack thereof). This is a complex process, and packages that work in one context may not work in another. Any package should be flexible, and capable of coping with structural and technological changes. Again, the process must be integrated into the process of building teams and reallocating individuals between teams. Finally, it seems that team-based pay can be also linked with overall organisational strategy. Because team-based rewards can be adjusted in line with the firm's strategic goals, team members' attention can be directed to follow specific strategic patterns (Meyer, 1994). This will enhance the fulfilment of strategic challenges that organisations face.

SHARE OWNERSHIP AND PROFIT-SHARING

Employees may also be rewarded through share ownership schemes or by profit-sharing. Table 33 compares and contrasts firm-level practices in a range of different national contexts, based on the findings of the Cranet-E survey (full details are supplied elsewhere in this volume). As can be seen, employee share schemes (in other words, schemes that assist workers in buying shares) and stock options (opportunities for employees to buy shares at favourable rates) are less common in Sweden and Germany – countries where there is a strong tradition of collaboration between firms and unions – than in the United Kingdom and, indeed, Greece – where there are traditions of more adversarial industrial relations (Table 33).

In other words, it is suggested that firms appear more likely to offer such schemes when unions are weaker. This would reflect the fact that such schemes closely tie workers to overall organisational performance as reflected by short-term share prices, the pursuit of which may undermine long-term job security and, indeed, collective bargaining between unions and employers as a means of pay-setting. This variation is also reflected at the level of managerial staff. Again,

Table 33 Profit-sharing, employee share ownership and stock options in different national contexts

Do you offer the following managerial staff?	UK	Sweden	Germany	Greece	Slovakia
Employee share schemes	25%	10%	15%	25%	15%
Profit-sharing	20%	21%	65%	16%	43%
Stock options	21%	11%	12%	30%	9%
Do you offer the following for manual staff?					
Employee share schemes	15%	5%	8%	8%	7%
Profit-sharing	11%	13%	23%	6%	13%
Stock options	2%	2%	2%	11%	1%

Source: Cranet-E (2003)

giving managers a strong interest in immediate share prices is likely to incentivise certain forms of behaviour: an immediate fascination with the bottom line and with factors likely to impact on the share price.

In contrast, profit-sharing was very much more common in Germany – where, in other words, workers were given a proportion of overall profits. Typically, this would be linked to collective bargaining and reinforce the collective identity of the workforce and effectively that of the union. This collective basis is also likely to make for greater long-termism – because the interests of all workers at all stages of their careers have to be considered – rather than where each worker seeks to maximise his or her own interests and/or the immediate concerns of the firm.

ETHICS AND REWARD SYSTEMS

The operation of reward systems raises a number of ethical and related concerns. Firstly, there are questions of *equity*. Reward systems have to take account not only of external equity (that is, prevailing rates for a particular job) but also of internal equity (fairness vis-à-vis others in the organisation) and individual equity (whether an individual is being fairly rewarded for his or her efforts). Balancing these three equity concerns may prove to be extremely difficult in practice. The issue of internal equity has become an increasingly important one. In Britain, the pay gap between senior managers and other employees has substantially widened since the 1970s. This is grounds for particular concern in that winning organisations in sustainable areas of economic activity, where competitiveness is particularly dependent on quality – such as high-value-added manufacturing (in which Britain performs particularly poorly) – have, in most contexts, had relatively narrow gaps between senior managers and rank-and-file. Greater quality, trust and employee commitment are more likely when pay differentials are muted (Baron and Cooke, 1992). There is little doubt that high pay inequality within an organisation greatly undermines notions of 'partnership' or 'mutual commitment' (Jansen and Glinow, 1985).

Again, although organisations are quick to penalise individual employees for poor performance, often senior managers are rewarded for poor performance with ever greater pay increases, and, at the worst, 'golden goodbyes' – substantial payments to encourage them to move on. Critics have charged that the New pay has allowed managers to transfer increasing amounts of risk to employees, who are blamed and punished for organisational failures. Senior managers optimise their own rewards while delegating many responsibilities.

 REFLECTIVE ACTIVITY

Do you think it is possible for organisations ever to reconcile internal, external and individual equity concerns?

Secondly, there are questions of employee well-being. As noted earlier, the appraisal of performance depends, in the end, on the subjective judgement of managers. This may result in the perpetuation of existing organisational inequalities, on race and gender lines. It may also open up individual workers to bullying or harassment (at both ends of the spectrum – working too hard or not working enough) (Scott and Dean, 1992). Managers may use the additional power opened up by an appraisal in an inappropriate manner, even if their behaviour is illegal in terms of formal organisational rules. Again, most employees desire some stability and predictability in their earnings (in order to meet financial commitments such as bond payments, rent, loan repayments, etc); variable New-pay-inspired systems may challenge their ability to meet everyday financial commitments in a consistent way.

 KEY ISSUES IN REWARD

We now pull together some key points about reward raised in this chapter:

- In the UK context, there has been a trend for the last 30 years towards more individually based reward systems, with pay being more closely linked to perceived performance.
- This trend has allowed organisations to better reward exceptional achievement and penalise failure.
- To critics, this has resulted in increasing internal inequality within organisations, and may undermine relationships with long-standing employees.
- Growing numbers of organisations are seeing reward as of *strategic* importance rather than simply a formal *administrative* function centring on the administration of predetermined pay rates.

Perhaps there are other key points that you would like to note for yourself.

The main case study in this chapter now follows. It gives an example of how the increasingly important issue of communicating with people who work for the organisation, but are not directly employed by it, can affect a company in practice.

MAIN CASE STUDY

Look at the description of the real-life case set out below. Then decide on the recommendations that you would make as an HR manager for dealing with the issues raised. Try to think beyond the level of a 'quick fix' or simple solutions.

The firm, making textiles and trimming, was established in 1964. The factory originated in a small building with one crochet loom machine, and a group of local people who were subsequently trained by the family on how to create hand-made trimming. In the last ten years the company has been growing at an average rate of 20% per year, and has become a major global player in the trimming business. The company exports 80% of its products to 71 countries worldwide. The major market is the US market, followed closely by the European market. The company is viewed today as one of the top three companies in the world within its field and provides employment for approximately 1,000 people. The success of the company has, according to management, been due to its being innovative, flexible and aggressive with regard to the export market. More specifically, by concentrating on specialised niche markets the firm has managed to survive the flooding of global markets by cheap textiles manufactured in the Far East. The firm received an Exporter of the Year award in 1994. Management are proud of the fact that many employees have been with the firm for many years and that the enterprise has one of the lowest staff turnover rates in the textile industry.

The organisation decided many years ago to focus and to become a leading force in the international arena. In the mid-1980s the organisation manufactured basic trimming that required a simple level of manufacturing. It made use of only 30 types of combinations of raw materials and colours. Today, this figure has expanded to over 350 types of yarns/colours. From a range of combinations of products in the region of 20,000 at the beginning of the 1990s, the organisation now deals with over 130,000 combinations of products. This ability to meet specialised niche demand, through the production of individualised batches, has, in part, insulated the firm from head-on competition with high-volume low-cost Far Eastern producers.

In the late 1980s and at the beginning of the 1990s, customers abroad bought large quantities of relatively few items. However, increased competition forced the firm to concentrate on niche markets. In the latter areas, it seems that a very real market break-up has occurred, many customers now demanding small quantities of very complicated items in thousands of combinations and variety of colours, whereas 15 years ago a much more limited range would have sufficed. In addition, the established lead time for delivery on handmade articles was 13 weeks in the late 1980s. By the onset of the 1990s customers expected a lead time of no longer than four weeks, probably on account of a desire for reduced inventory stocks. This diversification necessitated more flexible methods of production, hinging around a multi-skilled workforce. After making a survey of the international literature on multi-skilling, a formal training plan was formulated. Thereafter, extensive (and lengthy) consultation took place with departmental heads, shop stewards, and finally the employees themselves.

At the time of the case study, production was divided into four main divisions: i) crochet knitting, which produced mainly *crochet-knitted* decorative trimmings (for example, fringes), ii) the handmade division, where activities revolved around the assembly of decorative trimmings by hand (for example, tiebacks and tassels), iii) *twisting and component manufacturing*, and iv) *narrow weaving*, which manufactured woven material, such as ribbons and narrow-width decorative trimming.

Within the crochet knitting division, the set-up time on the machine for each article could take between a minimum of four hours and maximum of 12 hours (for a qualified mechanic). To produce 100 metres of knitted material could take within the region of one hour. As the market conditions changed and short runs had to be put through the machines, management decided to recast the division of labour on the shop floor. Prior to the implementation of the development initiative, the ratio of operators to mechanics was 10:1. Within this area, human resource development plans aimed to train all the operators to become mechanics – a process that is still on-going. This has not reduced employment, but it has enabled the organisation to produce shorter runs and to have many more changes of products in order to fulfil market requirements. An accurate list was undertaken of all employees' educational qualifications, and psychometric tests were then undertaken to evaluate their mechanical abilities, whereby they proceeded to choose the best potential operator. This operator was then assigned to a qualified mechanic as a trainee. Meanwhile, the most capable mechanics were then chosen to acquire additional skills in the engineering workshop.

The handmade division comprised two sections. The tassel fringe section consisted of workers manually tying tassels to the end of braids. The loose tassel section mainly assembled tiebacks and key tassels by hand. Even though the two operations of covering and tying yarn to different components seemed to be similar activities, they were, in fact, not compatible. During periods when there was a shortage of orders in one department, management attempted to transfer workers from one department to the other. This proved to be unsuccessful in the sense that, according to management, workers were unable to reach a reasonable level of productivity within a short time-frame. Thereafter, management decided to train new multi-skilled operators, capable of performing both tasks, from scratch. According to the departmental manager:

People who were used to performing certain hand movements for long periods found it difficult to change this habit.

However, a few existing employees proved capable of operating in both sections and, unlike their 'repetitive peers' enjoyed relatively high levels of job security.

Within the twisting and component manufacturing section, management saw multi-skilling as particularly desirable, in that it would enable any worker to operate all the machines should a peer be absent. Each operator has since been trained, or is currently undergoing training, to be able to operate all the machines. In both the cord-making and mould-covering sections, a single worker may have to operate between two to six machines at any one time.

The organisation therefore decided to train operators from cord-making and mould-covering to be able to function in each others' department. The entire department underwent assessment and evaluation to ascertain their ability and skill level. Those who were discerned to be 'more capable' were asked to undergo intensive training in order to be able to operate the other section's machines. Management motivated employees by stating that, due to being multi-skilled, their position within the organisation would be much more secure than that of their single-skilled co-workers.

Staffing levels in the narrow weaving division were extremely tight, each worker 'being trained to the maximum of his ability'.

Source: G. Wood and R. Sela (2000) 'Making human resource development work', *Human Resource Development International*, Vol. 3, No. 4, 451–64. Fuller information on the case can be found in the original article

Questions for consideration and discussion

1 What type of reward system would be most appropriate for this organisation and how would it differ (or not) between the four departments?

2 Assume there is a trade union in this organisation. How would this affect the choice of reward system?

3 How could a reward system best be integrated into teamwork in an organisation of this type?

EXPLORE FURTHER

ARMSTRONG, M. (2002) *Employee Reward*. London, CIPD
This CIPD textbook provides a comprehensive coverage of employee reward systems from an applied practitioner perspective.

CACCIOPE, R. (1999) 'Using team-individual reward and recognition strategies to drive organizational success', *Leadership and Organization Development Journal*, Vol. 20, No. 6, 322–31
This article provides a look at the role of team-based reward systems from a practitioner perspective.

HEERY, E. (1996) 'Risk, reward and the New pay', *Personnel Review*, Vol. 25, No. 6, 54–65
This article locates reward systems within a broader ethical framework.

ICHNIOWSKI, C. and SHAW, K. (2003) 'Beyond incentive pay', *Journal of Economic Perspectives*, Vol. 17, No. 1, 155–80
This theoretically rigorous account looks at the limitations of incentive-based reward systems and alternatives thereto.

KERRIN, M. and OLIVER, N. (2002) 'Collective and individual improvement activities: the role of reward systems', *Personnel Review*, Vol. 31, No. 3, 320–37
This article links theoretical questions to the practical implementation of reward systems.

CHAPTER 14

Training and development

Ian Favell

INTRODUCTION

This chapter is about learning in the workplace.

> ### LEARNING OUTCOMES
>
> By the end of this chapter readers should be able to:
>
> - explain the range of different methods available for workplace learning
> - describe some key issues of on-the-job and off-the-job methods of training and development
> - identify the benefits and disadvantages of a range of different workplace learning methods.

The chapter is closely related to Chapter 24 on HRD, and is structured in three parts. The first part deals with formal training and development. The second part then turns to informal learning initiatives in organisations. The third part examines formal schemes based around a mixture of formal and informal learning methods, blended to suit the context of the individual and the subject. The final case study then shows a number of ideas in operation within an organisational context, with mixed success and effectiveness.

Reference sources named within the chapter may be looked up in the *References and further reading* section at the end of the book.

Most organisations recognise the importance of learning and development for their staff, and usually have some form of training and development scheme. Many schemes are based around the organisation's performance management scheme (appraisal), in which development needs and aspirations are discussed and a development plan agreed for each individual each year (see Chapter 12 on performance management and appraisal). The plans will range in approach according to individual needs and the issues involved, and may call upon any appropriate training and development methods.

STARTER CASE STUDY

John leaves school with almost no qualifications. He has decided that he would like to work as an electrician. He applies to a number of local firms for a job. However, he is not even invited to interview by any of them. After several frustrating months he decides to talk to a local training provider about how he should train himself for his chosen career, in order that he might get on the first rung of the ladder. The provider, by chance, is one that offers qualifications that involve an Individual Learning Plan, associated with an apprenticeship. This involves some classroom attendance, for learning of theory and practical skills, and some work-placement for on-the-job practice and experience. John is overjoyed to find that for his workplace practical experience he is placed in one of the organisations that he had previously applied to, and that some of the assessment is competency-based in the workplace as well as at the training provider. At his Induction event, John is surprised to find an observer from an inspection agency.

At the training provider a learning resource centre is available, which provides a wide range of facilities, freely available, including e-learning packages, books, journals, videos,

practice tests, and other materials – everything that he needs to progress. As well as the written tests, his apprenticeship contains a vocationally based technical certificate, which confirms his competence in the basics of the job. Having successfully completed his training programme, John then accepts a paid secondment with the firm that he has been working with during his programme, to further his career, in the hope that if he is successful it will eventually take him on, on a full-time basis.

Questions for discussion

1 What are the key points about workplace learning that can be drawn from this case study?

2 What are the components of the final qualification that John will achieve?

3 Why do you think that the firm would not take John on initially?

4 How will the resource centre be helpful to John?

5 What problems might John experience if the resource centre was not available or so well equipped?

Learning and development in the workplace falls into one of two categories – formal schemes, and informal, more self-managed approaches, each on the job or off the job. Both are important, and the approach taken within organisations ideally should include both components (Blundell and Murdock, 1997; Lucas, Lupton and Mathieson, 2006; Marchington and Wilkinson, 2005). Nevertheless, both to be comprehensive and to aid comprehensibility in this chapter we separate them, examining formal schemes in Part 1 and informal ones in Part 2.

1 FORMAL SCHEMES

Any learning and development scheme that forms part of the formal processes within an organisation could be considered a formal scheme, especially if there is a prescribed approach or reporting mechanism in use. Formal schemes are most commonly found in the form of training courses, coaching and mentoring schemes, as well as job rotation and shadowing. Job rotation is widely used in some countries, such as Germany and Japan, where it is used for all staff and not just for graduate recruits. Each of these methods is examined in turn below.

TRAINING COURSES

Although (for example) a college course and qualifications may well help organisations and individuals, these are often not considered to be 'workplace learning' unless the programme of learning has been specially designed to support organisational needs or goals, and is sponsored by and/or run in conjunction with the organisation itself. There are of course exceptions to this, where individuals must get or maintain a qualification or licence in order to be operational, and staff are scheduled to attend external provision of training and examination. Examples of this include, in the financial sector, the qualifications that allow an individual to give mortgage or other financial advice, and in the building industry the qualification to allow an engineer to install and repair gas appliances.

Outside the formal college and qualification context, training courses in workplace learning are usually designed and delivered with specific focus on and in the specific context of the organisation and job roles. They are generally designed to last a couple of hours, half or a full day, or several days. They are most likely to be led by a trainer or tutor, who is a subject expert, with the main purpose of passing on knowledge or skills. There are two main types of framework for these training courses – they are meeting-based or activity-based.

A meeting-based course involves some presentation from the trainer or expert, and then discussions around the subject and how it relates to practical issues in the workplace. The activity-based approach is more likely to start with a practical work-related or simulation activity that is then analysed and discussed as a practical example of some aspect of work, often then generalised to make wider workplace learning points. Each approach can be trainer- or participant-focused, and it is frequently beneficial on longer courses to use a mixture of the two approaches. The decision over which is used is often made by thinking about how far those doing the training are experienced in learning, the subject matter under consideration, and whether the training centres on knowledge, skills or behaviours. However, the organisational structure and culture can often have a significant effect on the approach chosen, because it affects participant and trainer expectations and norms (Marchington and Wilkinson, 2005). A highly autocratic and hierarchical organisation is more likely to favour and therefore use a meeting approach (since it lends itself to a 'lecture' style of training) than a 'flatter', more collegiate organisation (which is more likely to favour an experiential, facilitative approach).

Many authors (for example, Lucas *et al*, 2006) explore the relative merits of formal education and training. Benefits of formal training courses include the fact that the content can be designed in advance, and checked as being appropriate before delivery. It can make sure that a consistent message is delivered in a structured manner to a large number of individuals over a long period of time. Costs and length are usually known in advance and therefore the approach may be useful in those situations where many staff are involved, or consistency is very important. Planning of the programme of courses is also relatively straightforward, because demand and requirements are largely known, or possible to anticipate.

Disadvantages of training courses include the fact that they can so easily be ineffective, the people attending only because they are required to, and the content and approach to delivery being somewhat fixed and potentially inappropriate to individuals' needs. The focus can also be more on attendance than on learning. Training courses can additionally be costly for the benefits gained.

 REFLECTIVE ACTIVITY

Think about an organisation you know well, and the type of formal training that takes place.

How effective is this approach?

How might it be improved?

COACHING SCHEMES

Both formal and informal coaching schemes can be very effective for workplace learning (see Chapter 15 on coaching). In a formal scheme, expert staff are formally allocated or scheduled for a period to 'buddy' one or more members of staff, to oversee their activity and help them to become more effective at specific tasks or job activities. The coach does this mainly on regular occasions (often scheduled) when the staff being coached have opportunities to discuss problems and issues, to explore areas of uncertainty or inconsistent or poor performance, or to demonstrate an activity under the guidance of the coach. The coach then offers his or her expertise to suggest ways in which the performance can be improved or changed to be more effective.

In an informal scheme, coaching relationships are encouraged but not necessarily formalised or scheduled, and staff mutually support each other on an 'as required or requested' basis. They undertake coaching activities as above, but only for the issue under consideration that gave rise to the request. Most managers in organisations have this informal role built into their job descriptions, to oversee and guide their staff to effectiveness, although managers themselves do not necessarily undertake the coaching activity personally on every occasion.

Coaching schemes have the benefit that they are seen by staff to be highly relevant to their job, with the focus on what is required to assist them to become effective or maintain effectiveness. They are often cost- and time-effective, and can be used at all levels and at any time, as well as being scheduled for regular performance monitoring, updates or enhancements. However, the coaching approach does depend on the personal skills of the coach, especially in his or her ability to build a positive relationship with the staff he/she is supporting, and assumes that those who are coaching also have the expert knowledge and skills in the first place. Without these, of course, poor practice can so easily be reinforced and spread in the organisation.

MENTORING SCHEMES

Like coaching schemes, mentoring schemes can also be formal or informal, and involve one-to-one relationships between the mentor and the member of staff being supported (sometimes called the 'mentee' or the 'protégé[e]'). The key difference between mentoring and coaching is mainly in the focus of the relationship (Lewis, 2000). Coaching largely focuses on the work tasks to be completed, and is clearly job-role-related. Mentoring tends much more to have as its focus the individual and his or her personal development and growth needs which may relate to wider issues than just the current work role. It is common, for example, for lower-level managers to get career advice by this route. Whereas coaching is often undertaken by a colleague or line manager, mentoring is usually done by a senior manager or a manager in a different department or field altogether, to enable wider perspectives to be brought into consideration. As with coaching, the effectiveness of mentoring schemes is affected by the personal skills and expertise of the mentor, and also his or her organisational influence in being able to access wider perspectives, information and contacts (Lewis, 2000).

JOB ROTATION AND JOB SHADOWING

Job rotation and job shadowing are two simple techniques that are often used formally within a section or department to give variety in the work that an individual might do, while offering an opportunity to develop a wider understanding of the department and of other job functions. Job shadowing might take the form of sitting alongside another individual to 'shadow' them by watching what they do, how and when (Mumford, 1996). Much can be learned about the other job from the individual undertaking it, although one obvious potential disadvantage is that the technique assumes that the person being watched is fully effective in the job that he or she is displaying to the visiting shadow.

Job rotation takes a similar form to the technique of secondments and attachments discussed below, except that it occurs usually internally within a section or department, and several people change job roles on a planned and sometimes regular basis.

REFLECTIVE ACTIVITY

Think about an organisation you know well.

To what extent is job rotation or job shadowing undertaken?

In what ways does job rotation/shadowing support individual development?

How might mentoring help further?

2   INFORMAL SCHEMES

Although formal schemes are still used significantly within organisations, training and development schemes are increasingly focusing upon more informal methods of workplace learning. These might include working through a series of workbooks, or electronic (eg online, CD-ROM, DVD) packages or private reading. Such self-managed schemes are occasionally provided as part of a formal development programme but are much more likely to be found as informal individual learning. The packages usually give key information on a topic and include a way of checking understanding, or in some cases formally testing knowledge or responses.

There are several benefits to such individual learning packages. One is location, because individual learning packages can be worked through in a variety of different locations, such as a normal workstation or desk, in a specially provided area or resource centre, while travelling or at home. Another is context flexibility. Individual learning packages can be used in a range of different ways, such as individually to suit specific time-scales, requirements and learning style; in small groups, with review points set along the way; in a classroom setting, with a tutor providing monitoring and support. Also, they can be provided and updated relatively quickly and delivered to large numbers of people at the same time. With informal learning and development in the workplace there are usually many more options. These can also include coaching, mentoring, self-selected and self-directed reading (which can include the packages described above), and action learning from reflection on workplace activities or projects (Lucas *et al*, 2006).

E-LEARNING PACKAGES

With the arrival of the Internet and in-house intranets, increasing use is now being made of e-learning packages (Sloman, 2007; Marchington and Wilkinson, 2005). These have a significant advantage in that they can be worked through at the individual's workstation at his or her own speed, with opportunities to go back over the work to review, refresh and summarise if wanted. Furthermore, with some packages it is possible to score or mark the work done in a way that can contribute to a final score and even to a formal qualification.

However, e-learning has several important disadvantages (Sloman and Rolph, 2003). For example, the learner has to be self-motivated. A less committed or very busy individual might not start or complete the package, or may enter into it half-heartedly. Also the work is largely unsupervised, and so tutors and trainers are less likely to be available to answer questions, clarify issues or develop themes further. This often means that learners can become 'stuck' at a given point, and give up because of the lack of easily available help. A further issue is that technology is fine when it works, but from time to time creates problems that can disturb the learning or even put a participant off completely – and of course the individual undertaking the development cannot carry on if the package, or the equipment, is for some reason unavailable.

Blended learning

The expression 'blended learning' describes a mixture of formal and informal learning, using a range of different learning media and methods such as described in this chapter. It is thought by learning professionals and participants alike to offer an effective approach, because it enables the selection of the method most appropriate to each individual aspect that has to be learned, and of a delivery method that most suits the organisation, the department, the team and the individuals concerned. The main disadvantage is that it is much more difficult to plan (needing attention to each individual and each topic) and more difficult to monitor progress across the many methods in use. It can also be more expensive, because a wider range of options might be used than would be the case if a more specific approach were to be used.

Links to appraisal

One area that is used particularly for workplace learning and development is that of a performance management (appraisal) system. Many systems exist, and some are more successful than others (see Chapter 12). However, an organisation that truly wishes to embed effective workplace learning and development into its culture and operations will need an effective appraisal system that has a forward-looking positive focus and developmental approach to performance measurement and support (Pedlar, Boydell and Burgoyne, 1991).

REFLECTIVE ACTIVITY

Think about your own organisation or one you know well.

In the organisation, is the focus more on formal or on informal leaning and development? Why is this, do you think?

What facilities are there in the organisation to support informal learning and development?

TRAINING IN CONTEXT

The WERS data (see Table 34) shows that there are some clear differences in the way in which different organisations and sectors use formal or informal learning methods. For example, the data indicate that across all organisations surveyed, only 47% of them use formal off-the-job training for the majority of their core workforce, and of those organisations that do, the larger organisations are more likely to use this approach than the smaller organisations. The WERS data also shows some clear differences in approach across the industries too, with a very marked difference in responses. Manufacturing and catering industries are shown to use relatively little off-the-job training compared to public sector and financial institutions, which are reported to use it significantly.

Table 34 Off-the-job training in British organisations

	Percentage of organisations with off-the-job training for 60% or more experienced core employees
All workplaces	47
Organisation size	
10–99 employees	35
10,000 or more employees	59
Industry	
Manufacturing	28
Hotels and restaurants	27
Financial services	77
Public sector	72

Source: Kersley *et al* (2006; p.83)

Much is therefore dependent on a number of issues, and when thinking through the range of workplace learning methods in order to make a selection, matters such as the availability of resources, the size and type of business, the internal training capability and the structure and culture of the organisation should be considered. Each of these is examined in turn below.

Firstly, how much an organisation has of significant resources to put into workplace learning will clearly affect the organisational provision. Key issues in this area are particularly the time and money to fund what might be needed, although the location and space for physical resources are also important. Examples of this include whether a learning centre can be provided, whether time off can be given to key employees to further their learning, and whether the cost and time for the design and delivery of formal workshops and courses is within acceptable parameters.

Secondly, as the WERS data has indicated, the size of the organisation can be important because a small organisation may be less likely to be able to find a high level of resource than a larger organisation. Also, a smaller organisation may not have the space (or potential use) of other supporting facilities, nor the ability to release staff for training sessions.

Thirdly, the type of business is worth considering. Some businesses operate in a highly regulated context (for example, legal services, financial services, gas and petrochemical operations). To meet the needs of the regulators and legislative requirements, formal training courses (often followed by examinations) are a requirement, and much of the learning and development initiative in these organisations is likely to have this as a focus. This might go some way to explain the bias in the WERS data for those sorts of organisations towards the use of off-the-job training. However, other businesses operate in arenas that are less regulated, if at all (for example, fashion and design, publications, performing arts). Here there might be some formal courses, but much of the learning and development may well be informal and even fully self-driven in approach (and, for that matter, not necessarily fully business-focused). Again, the infrequent use of off-the-job training in the catering and manufacturing areas reported in the WERS data may well be because of the highly skills-based nature of the work, and the fact that there may be a need for some learning to be done in a practical sense on-the-job where first-hand and live experience can be used as the basis for performance improvement.

Fourthly, whether the workplace learning is formally based or informally based, on-the-job or off-the-job, one key issue to be considered is how far the organisation has experienced and qualified training and learning facilitators on the staff or easily available. Without skilled trainers and learning facilitators, formal on- or off-the-job training programmes are less likely to be considered or possible. However, they could be outsourced or bought in if resources are available.

Fifthly, the way in which the business is organised can also play a part in how learning and development takes place. For example if the organisation is structured as a tall hierarchy (ie with many different levels of staff, the real power strongly concentrated at the higher levels, as described by, for example, Handy, 1993), then particular types of training or subject areas may only be open to those at particular levels or positions in the organisation. This might be associated with different needs at different levels, or a sense that a certain level of seniority is required before certain areas of training are appropriate (even though this judgement is often incorrect). However, in a flatter structure an organisation might be more willing to enable every individual to undertake development at any point that he/she, or the organisation, feels it to be useful.

Finally, the general style and culture of the organisation also often greatly influences the approach to learning and development (Lucas *et al*, 2006). Some organisations may well have a supportive coaching and developmental approach to the whole of their activities. In this case, there may well be a formal framework in which informal learning takes place all the time, both on-the-job and off-the-job components being brought together into a programme of learning that supports both individual and organisational goals. At the other extreme might be an organisation that is rather formal, traditional, and with the business bottom line as the whole driver of all activities. In this case there is a much higher likelihood that learning and development will only be focused on activities to meet specific business needs, and will probably only take the form of formal 'courses', and these may not be optional or available to all because selection for attendance is only based upon demonstrable business needs. In some organisations, legally appointed union learning representatives may operate, seeking to encourage employees who might have reservations about 'going back to school' (see Chapter 17 on employment relations). They may also play a role in helping to change both employees and managements towards being more open to different types of learning.

3   LEARNING WHILE WORKING

Although most aspects of workplace learning can be described as formal or informal, there are many schemes that combine these two approaches within an overall formal (and sometimes externally funded) programme. Such programmes can be for those not yet in employment, as a way of starting their career, or for those already employed who need to expand or change their role. This section looks at some of the most well-known and widely used of such programmes. It starts with induction, since this usually combines both the formal and informal, and is a process that almost all new staff come across.

INDUCTION

One key learning occasion for every employee is the induction process. Without a successful induction, not only will the new member of staff not come up to speed so quickly, it is more likely that he or she will not be so effective and may not settle well into the new job. Indeed, there is plenty of evidence that organisations that suffer from high turnover of staff do so because they do not put sufficient effort into their recruitment and selection *and induction* processes.

Ideally, induction is a process that is on-going, rather than (as many organisations seem to think) a single event (Marchington and Wilkinson, 2005). If all of the details are contained in a single event, the new member of staff is likely to become 'overloaded', and be unable to remember or take on board much of what is covered. In an ideal situation, the induction programme is spread over a number of weeks or perhaps months, and blends naturally into the organisation's learning and development programme.

APPRENTICESHIPS

The importance of this type of learning varies over different countries. In many British industries workplace learning is inbuilt, since to become fully qualified and experienced a period of apprenticeship is required (eg gas-fitters, plumbers and hairdressers). An individual is taken on by the company as an apprentice, with a specific focus on a learning and development programme that may lead to some form of qualification as well as practical experience. Many of the qualifications in the craft skills areas actually assess performance in the job as part of the qualification process. Training is given on the job by those who are actively employed in that field (undertaking real work), on the job in simulated or laboratory/workshop situations (so that skills can be practised), and in more theoretical classroom sessions. In other countries, apprenticeship and formal training is given more importance. In Germany, people are trained systematically for professions, and apprenticeship is very common even for jobs that are not usually regarded as needing one in Britain (sales, for instance).

Many apprenticeships in Britain are government-funded through, for example, Learning and Skills Councils (governed by the National LSC), and the learning and training undertaken is therefore closely monitored by government agencies as well as internally within the organisation by assessors and verifiers. These 'inspectors' will visit training centres and organisations from time to time with checklists to make sure that the training programme that has been sold to the individual and funded with government money is actually meeting the criteria that the government has set for the use of such funds.

VOCATIONAL AND COMPETENCY-BASED SCHEMES

Increasingly, British organisations are basing their performance management schemes upon competencies. Competencies define and describe the capacity actually to do something, such as change a lorry tyre. Competencies determine the key job activities, behaviours and knowledge that are required to undertake the job fully. They use descriptors to illustrate and exemplify how a performer in a specified role might show effectiveness (Favell, 2005). This inevitably leads to competencies being used for recruitment and selection for the various jobs, and to a focus upon developing the skills defined by the competencies as a main focus for learning and development activities. In some organisations and occupational areas (for example, the medical profession, airline flight crew instruction, and financial services) occupational competence is a requirement to get the licences that are legally required for operations in that arena. The whole area of apprenticeships (see above) also is focused around learning and development towards vocational and occupational competence.

In Britain, most occupational areas have National Standards, which detail the competencies needed for effectiveness in that arena. They are put together by standard-setting bodies (currently known as Sector Skills Councils – but from time to time names and organisations change).These bodies hold the responsibility for determining the National Standards in that occupational arena, and for confirming with, for example, the Qualifications and Curriculum Authority (QCA) their suitability for granting of awards, such as an NVQ (a National Vocational Qualification) in that subject.

PLACEMENTS, SECONDMENTS AND ATTACHMENTS

Many organisations, especially the larger ones, use placements, secondments and attachments as a key method of development for their staff. Although we have used three expressions here, they are all really one mechanism – that by which an individual is temporarily placed in (seconded or attached to) a department or team that does not do his or her usual work, sometimes in a very different discipline. The main idea is to enable the individual concerned to attain an insight into this particular new discipline and working arrangement, and into the wider issues and perspectives that this will bring to his or her experience. Secondments are often for three, six, nine or 12 months, according to how long the individual can be spared from his or her permanent job, and for how long the experience has to continue in order to achieve the optimum development aimed at.

Clearly, there are a range of important implications for this type of development activity. The work in the placed/seconded employees' own job role has to be covered in their absence, and this has to be accounted for as part of the development plan. What often happens is that someone else comes to the department on attachment/secondment, or perhaps an agency temp fills in.

Another consideration is how quickly the individual will be fully up to speed in the job he or she is now temporarily doing, and how any gaps will be covered during his/her development. Gaps are often covered by a permanent member of staff in that department doing work of a higher level than usual, as a way of developing them also, as well by giving them some responsibilities for things that they are fully capable of but normally do not have the opportunity to do. Monitoring the work during the attachment, to make sure that the incoming individual is progressing, and that the work is being done to a good standard, is also something that must be considered, to ensure that the secondment is effective. This is also likely to involve the question of how the individual on the attachment/secondment is to be trained in those areas where it is needed. Finally, any costs that might be involved, including the possible cost of temporary accommodation for the individual concerned, should also be taken into account during the planning stages. Good examples of this type of workplace learning and development are apprenticeships (see above) in which an apprentice might be assigned to different sections during a programme, and a graduate programme (see below) in which those on the programme might be rotated through a number of departments.

GRADUATE PROGRAMMES

Many larger organisations have graduate programmes so that each year they can take promising people into the organisation and train them in the ways of the business in readiness for a permanent position either at the end of the programme or as vacancies arise (Mumford, 1996). A programme usually involves a series of study days, both business- and management-focused, and placements in various sections of the organisation in real positions with real work to do, but under close guidance or a coach or mentor. Those on the programme are rotated through a range of areas to ensure that a broad experience is obtained of the business, but also to try to see if any area or type of work particularly suits the individual's skills and interests. Often a resource centre is available for further individual study, or open learning programmes carried out perhaps to obtain an appropriate qualification. Graduate programmes typically last one or two years, by which time the individual is thought suitable for permanent employment (or decides that the business is not for him or her and moves on).

RESOURCE AND LEARNING CENTRES

Organisations that are serious about the development of their staff often provide appropriate resources in support. In larger organisations this may take the form of a resource centre – a physical location that might resemble a small library – where these resources can be used or borrowed. A fully equipped resource centre might have available such things as books, magazines and journals, videos and DVDs, details of courses and programmes of study (both in-house and external), computers with Internet access for research or investigation, access to in-house intranet resources and information, and e-learning packages. The resources provided usually have a work focus but often also include other high-interest topics (for example, foreign-language-learning packages). In the largest of organisations there may even be a resident tutor or resource manager present to provide coaching and learning support, although with the arrival of e-learning this is becoming rarer in Britain.

FUNDING AND INSPECTION

One key aspect of workplace learning and development is that often it may be funded, part-funded or supported in some way by government funding bodies (for example, the Learning and Skills Councils). Also, where vocationally based qualifications are offered, awarding bodies have an interest in what takes place. Many work-based schemes are therefore subject to external inspection from time to time to ensure that the learning and development being provided is complete and to the standard required to meet the qualification of funding contract, and this is common in all European countries. In Britain, these Inspections or External Verification Visits are undertaken by government or awarding body inspection teams, generally working to the remit of QCA/SQA or QIA (the government bodies responsible for overseeing qualifications and quality of provision). Such an Inspection samples a range of things – for example, the work of all tutors, assessors and the learning environment, together with the administrative infrastructure of the organisation in respect of its training and development activity – to ensure that quality standards are being met, and therefore that government funds are being used appropriately.

REFLECTIVE ACTIVITY

Think about an organisation you know well.

Which training and development methods are used most frequently in the organisation? Why is it that they are used most frequently?

What issues promote or inhibit the selection of the methods in use?

Which other methods offer some advantages?

KEY ISSUES IN WORKPLACE LEARNING

We now pull together ten key points about workplace learning raised in this chapter:

- Within organisations, training, learning and development opportunities can take many forms and be very wide in approach and content.

- There are no real rules or boundaries to limit what is offered and how it takes place, so long as the organisation feels it is effective in achieving what is required, and the activity meets any legal requirements.

- The key must always be what it is that should be learned, and exactly how this can be best done bearing in mind the context, the nature of the work, the people involved, and the cost in both time and money.

- Getting the best fit between the form of training, the organisation and the individual is often a challenge, and each organisation should check the effectiveness of initiatives to ensure that the workforce is as skilled and knowledgeable as possible at all times in a way that disturbs the workflow the mimimum amount for maximum organisational achievement.

- Weak induction programmes can often prompt new staff to leave prematurely. An effective induction is a programme of study that is on-going and deals with key issues over a period of time, that slowly merges and leads naturally into the organisation's mainstream development programme.

- The exact nature of workplace learning and development might be affected by funding and associated inspection regimes that are specific requirements of a programme that is funded.

- Workplace learning and development is often linked to a robust and well-operating appraisal or performance management scheme. This enables each development activity to be planned and monitored as a natural part of everyday performance.

- The extent to which learners have access to resources in the form of materials and personal learning support often determines the effectiveness of the learning.

- Workplace learning can be associated with a wide range of qualifications, or be simply for the benefit of the organisation, the team and the individual.

- Learning benefits people and organisations. However, it may be more difficult to access in a smaller organisation or department.

Perhaps there are other key points that you would like to note for yourself.

MAIN CASE STUDY

Make an initial reading of the case study to gain an overview of the situation, and then read the questions that you will need to address. Now read the case study again, making notes of issues and facts that will help you in your analysis and responses to the questions. Remember to 'read between the lines' as well as picking out the obvious points, and also to consider what is not said as well as what is presented here.

The senior managers of a large financial institution recognise the importance of training and development for their staff. They have a clear policy that not only should staff be trained and developed to meet the licensing and legislative requirements that apply to their area of business, but that staff should also be encouraged and enabled to engage in other appropriate development activities. The middle managers, who largely look after staff performance and development, all welcome this policy. They have made it clear to all of their staff that development opportunities are available and . can be applied for at any time. Many individual managers have therefore put together a list of courses that they think might be of interest to their staff, and make these available to staff so that individual members of staff can pick-and-mix the courses that they feel they would like to attend. There is no restriction on the number of courses that are allowed for each staff member, and it is up to each middle manager whether to allow attendance. Common practice is that staff just mention to the manager what they would like to do, and then a secretary books the place. The staff member then receives the letter from the training provider inviting him or her to the event, which he or she then attends when the due date arrives.

The staff appraisal system is good in that the process described in organisational paperwork is good practice, but in reality it does not happen, because managers do not have time and have not been properly trained. When an appraisal interview does take place, it is usually short, and development needs tend to be addressed at the appraisal interview with the question 'What do you want to do this year?', and then arrangements made after listing the responses. Costs have never been a barrier because money is said to be freely available for developmental purposes.

When staff are to attend a course, they are supposed to let their line manager know about their impending absence, but this does not always happen. Neither does the manager hold any pre- or post-attendance discussions, nor does the organisation have any mechanism for evaluating the effectiveness of any course (or, for that matter, any mechanism for checking that the member of staff actually attended). Some courses are held in-house for those areas of specialism where there is plenty of expertise, but these do not seem to be very effective. One employee recently missed half a day of a two-day course – and no one even noticed.

Some courses are particularly important to the organisation, especially those that re-license staff to enable them to operate in their specific financial area. However, staff are responsible for their own updates and re-licensing – the organisation does not keep records of when events are due or attended for any except the most essential staff. Rumour has it that many update courses are boring and inessential, so that it is not actually clear whether staff are or are not attending, and therefore may or may not be fully up to date.

Following a merger with a similar but slightly smaller concern, new staff are now to be incorporated into the wider organisation. In the smaller firm, training and development was of a very focused nature and a very high standard, as it had to be to keep the small firm competitive. The larger firm is now faced with some pressing issues. The recently arrived staff appear to be expecting detailed development discussions prior to training course attendance, and a debrief of what was learned following the course. They are also complaining about the appraisal system that appears to be blocking what they call proper discussion about their future, and the development needs that they have in order to position themselves to be ready when promotion opportunities arise. They have noted that training appears only to be courses, and are questioning this approach.

In the meantime, shareholders have begun to ask questions about the size of the training budget when compared to the size of the dividend budget that was recently set. Managers in the wider organisation, feeling suddenly under the spotlight, are now said to be unhappy with what they see as challenges to their way of doing things by both these newcomers and the shareholders. A further complication is that new legislation requires all of the professionals in one of the major fields of operation to be retrained and tested to ensure that they are advising customers in an appropriate way.

As a result of these growing challenges, the new bigger organisation has appointed a Head of Learning and Development to

oversee the whole area of staff development, with the remit to obtain an overview of the key issues that have to be tackled, and to implement the most effective and cost-effective development scheme possible.

Your task

Imagine you are the new Head of Learning and Development.

1 Make a list of the issues that you should consider tackling.

2 Put that list in priority order, so that urgent business needs can be addressed first.

3 Consider how you might address the issues on your list.

4 Who else should be involved? Why them?

5 How will you know that the development activities are successful?

EXPLORE FURTHER

CIPD (2006) *Latest Trends in Learning, Training and Development*. London, CIPD
Excellent summary of the latest trends in workplace learning.

HARRISON, R. (2005) *Learning and Development*, 4th edition. London, CIPD
Textbook that provides a more extensive introduction to the concepts of workplace learning.

CHAPTER 15

Understanding coaching

Caroline Horner *and* Paul Ellis

INTRODUCTION

This chapter aims to help readers become more knowledgeable about coaching and its application within organisations.

LEARNING OUTCOMES

By the end of this chapter readers should be able to:

- explain what coaching is and is not
- describe the role of HR in putting in place coaching for an organisation
- consider some of the challenges faced.

This chapter is structured in two parts. Part 1 begins with the starter case study which, like the other case studies in this book, is based on a real-life situation. We then go on to look at the definition of coaching, and how coaching is distinctive. We also outline what coaching is used for and provide examples of when to use and when not to use it. Part 2 examines the three principal approaches to delivering coaching in the workplace. Throughout Part 2 the reader is asked to consider how to use the various coaching interventions, what the issues and challenges of each approach are, and the role of the HR professional in applying coaching within organisations.

The chapter concludes with the main case study.

Reference sources named within the chapter may be looked up in the *References and further reading* section at the end of the book.

STARTER CASE STUDY

Despite a run of good years, a large international financial services organisation was subject to a hostile takeover bid. The organisation successfully prevented the bid but discovered through the process that its leadership profile was perceived to be old-fashioned by being too rigid and instructional. An assessment of senior leaders across the organisation confirmed this. The CEO understood that the people issues had to be resolved if business results were going to be sustained in the future. A preliminary study showed that leadership development activities were being undertaken on an ad hoc basis and were evidently having limited impact. Coaches were being hired without reference to any organisational aims, in an unregulated coaching market that had no professional barriers to entry and no agreed measures for quality control. At the same time, the company wanted to fast-track the careers of minorities in the business and actively follow a strategy of diversity and inclusiveness.

Recognising the need to invest in its employees to resolve the problems it faced, the organisation decided to invest in the development of a leadership centre, including the development and implementation of a comprehensive coaching and mentoring framework to meet the needs of all its business units. Coaching was thought to be the most suitable method to ensure that new behaviours and learning from leadership development programmes were effectively carried through back in the workplace.

The company introduced a series of coaching interventions. Managers were encouraged to use and rewarded for using a coaching approach to help staff discover solutions for themselves, through posing powerful questions and providing 'in-the-moment' feedback. A peer-coaching network was started in addition to the existing mentoring scheme to assist new entrants to the organisation to pick up key skills and

organisational processes. Team coaching was offered to large project teams, and external group process facilitators were employed to support teams to leverage the diversity of their teams to improve the quality and effectiveness of project work. Internal coaches were used to support individuals participating in leadership development programmes to effectively translate their learning into their day-to-day work as well as to provide a safe environment to explore their own leadership style and behaviours and to work at improving these behaviours. A group of external coaches was brought together through a rigorous assessment process to support senior leaders in a variety of challenges ranging from individual development areas to transition (taking on a significantly bigger role or project, moving to another country, managing a change programme for the organisation), and for a few executives to provide a safe supportive space in which to reflect and develop innovative thinking during an intense period of transition.

Coaching was the process that pulled multiple initiatives together across the organisation to shift old-style leadership behaviours and embed new skills and behaviours. There were many other elements – for example, the reward system and other organisation development initiatives – that supported the culture change. However, coaching was a key part of the mix, and today the organisation is beginning to be seen as a modern, innovative organisation that is a market leader and an attractive employer.

Questions for discussion

1 Why do organisations use coaching more frequently for the purposes described in the case study?

2 With reference to the case study, what are the main challenges of introducing coaching in an organisation?

1 UNDERSTANDING THE FUNDAMENTALS OF COACHING

DRIVING FORCES BEHIND COACHING

An increasing number of organisations are recognising the value of using coaching to support individuals to achieve sustained improvements in personal and organisational performance. In the CIPD learning and development survey 2006, eight out of ten respondents reported that they used coaching in their organisations (CIPD, 2007).

The increase has been driven by a number of organisational and societal trends, such as the globalisation of business and a fiercely competitive marketplace which experiences rapid and constant change (de Geus and Senge, 1997). Organisations have reacted by creating flatter, leaner structures that can respond more quickly to developments. However, these structures – along with increasing reliance on technology for business functions – mean that managers find it hard to know those who report directly to them, and therefore there are fewer opportunities to build a relationship between employees. Also, managers are often promoted into senior positions without the opportunity to develop their leadership skills over a series of roles. At the same time there is a growing recognition of the costs associated with executives who fail (Greco, 2001). Organisations now recognise the benefits of coaching to help key employees in developing appropriate leadership skills and behaviours.

Coaching is no longer seen as a remedial intervention triggered only when there is a problem. Leaders are expected to be challenged with tasks that they have never undertaken before or that may be entirely new to the organisation. Many coaching assignments are now initiated entirely to help the client's overall development as a leader.

WHAT EXACTLY DO WE MEAN BY COACHING?

Coaching draws on a variety of fields including psychology, leadership, organisational development, counselling and therapy; it is a vast topic. However, despite the fact that coaching is increasingly popular, there remains some confusion over what exactly coaching is and how it differs from other helping interventions such as mentoring and counselling (Kampa-Kokesch and Anderson, 2001; Kilburg, 1996).

The Chartered Institute of Personnel and Development (Jarvis, 2004; p.19) defines coaching as:

Developing a person's skills and knowledge so that their job performance improves, hopefully leading to the achievement of organisational objectives. It targets high performance and improvement at work, although it may also have an impact on an individual's private life. It usually lasts for a short period and focuses on specific skills and goals.

Although there is no common definition, most coaching professionals agree on the following characteristics of coaching:

- It is frequently a one-to-one intervention in which the recipient of the coaching is referred to as the client (or coachee).

- The main purpose of coaching is individual learning and the expectation is that through this learning the current and future performance of the individual (and therefore team and organisational performance) will be improved; coaching is not about addressing the past.

- The client sets the agenda for the coaching and the role of the coach is to help the client in working through the issue, not to give advice or direct what the client should or should not do. That is, coaching is a non-directive intervention by which clients are helped to develop awareness and take responsibility for their own development.

- The client is seen as resourceful and is not engaging in coaching to be 'fixed' but rather supported to resolve his or her own issues.

- The coaching relationship is one of partnership in which coach and client are equals.

- The focus of coaching is to empower the client to manage his or her own learning and not to build dependency on the coach.

- It is a skilled activity which draws on skills such as active listening, effective questioning and feedback.

- Coaching is frequently time-limited and usually agreed for a specific length of time.

- The individual who receives coaching is psychologically healthy; he/she requires no clinical intervention.

 REFLECTIVE ACTIVITY

Is there anything missing from this list of bullet points that you might have expected to see?

In the light of the CIPD definition above, how is coaching different from mentoring and counselling?

Clarity of understanding is important if the HR professional is to make sure that the individual and organisation use the right type of intervention, and it is useful to establish how coaching differs from the other helping disciplines.

The term 'mentoring' is often used interchangeably with 'coaching'. However, traditionally, mentoring is a relationship with someone who is older, more senior and experienced than the mentee. A mentor is also someone who transfers knowledge and gives advice often to those who are new to a role or the organisation. The mentoring relationship can extend over a long period, even years, and usually focuses on the professional and career development of the mentee. Organisations often have a formal mentoring programme whereby individuals who meet certain criteria – such as new entrants, employees with high potential and minority groups – are offered a mentor to help their development; such an arrangement is usually managed by HR departments (Clutterbuck, 2001; Garvey, 2004).

The difference between coaching and *counselling* is also not always clear. For the purposes of the HR professional, the key distinction to be drawn is that coaching is always for people who are psychologically well, but counselling may be used for both psychologically well and unwell people.

WHAT IS COACHING USED FOR?

One way to categorise the main ways in which coaching can be used in organisations is described by the following typology from Witherspoon and White (2004), who distinguished between coaching for skills, coaching for performance, coaching for development, and coaching for the executive agenda.

Coaching for skills is about helping the client to get knowledge and skills which are relevant to the individual's current role or work. The need for this coaching is often unambiguous, the goals being specific and clear. Such coaching is frequently delivered by peers, technical specialists or by the individual's line manager. This form of coaching is not usually outsourced to external coaches because of the need to apply a specific skill within a specific organisational context: it often includes more content because it recognises the stage of development of the client/coachee. Coaches may be more directional with those early in their development of the skill-sharing ideas, offering suggestions and where necessary providing advice. For some this level of coaching seems more like mentoring or one-to-one instruction.

Coaching for performance usually focuses on helping an individual to improve his or her performance in a current role. This coaching is normally the responsibility of the individual's line manager who works with the individual on a day-to-day basis and is ideally placed to give 'in-the-moment' feedback and ask questions that will help the individual to consider alternatives for delivering immediate results.

Coaching for development is focused on the future direction and development of an individual as he or she prepares for a new role or new responsibilities. The responsibility for development of direct reports is often that of the individuals' line manager. However, therein lies a conflict of interest because in times of pressure the line manager may focus on performance and results, and the time available to support individuals with development is limited. The focus is on 'stretch' learning goals and possibly behavioural change. Depending on the results that are targeted and the organisational culture, this coaching can be delivered by internal or external coaches. HR professionals must consider their role in the 'management' of the learning goals in this environment and the balance between controlling the coaching process to ensure consistency and quality against trusting individuals to manage their own development, and so empower them through coaching.

Coaching for the executive agenda is offered to support senior-level individuals usually with a wide variety of concerns. Leadership, especially at senior executive levels, can be an isolated role and coaching often offers a safe and confidential place in which individuals can be supported to explore new ideas, take time to reflect and be encouraged. This level of coaching is almost exclusively delivered by external coaches who are recognised to have the credibility required by the client population and also who maintain a level of confidentiality that should relieve concerns about privacy. HR professionals are often involved in the selection and assessment of coaches to work at this level. HR will also often provide a matching process to ensure an appropriate fit between coach and executive. After an effective relationship is established, the role of HR lessens and the process is frequently self-managed by the client. These interventions are often longer-term – ie lasting a year or more – and sessions may be ad hoc, set up in relation to specific client needs.

REFLECTIVE ACTIVITY

What would you use coaching for in an organisation?

What learning interventions might you use instead of coaching?

WHEN WOULD YOU USE COACHING?

Coaching is one of a range of interventions that organisations can use to meet identified learning and development needs. Deciding whether coaching is an appropriate intervention is a key responsibility of the HR professional. The benefits of a formal coaching intervention from an internal or external coach must be considered alongside other possibilities such as training courses, stretch assignments, mentoring or on-the-job training. It will also be important for the HR professional to work alongside the line manager of the individual in question so as not to displace the responsibility for day-to-day performance from the line manager. Should line managers be struggling with coaching people who report directly to them, HR professionals may have to consider training line managers to help them develop their own coaching skills, as opposed to removing the responsibility for managers to effectively coach their team members by getting help from outside.

Coaching for development is frequently offered together with other learning interventions such as training courses or leadership development programmes (see Chapter 14). This sort of coaching is often initiated with some assessments (such as 360-degree feedback or psychometrics) to raise awareness in individuals of their development areas and to draft an individual learning plan. The coaching then works alongside the learning plan, encouraging individuals to use the programme and opportunities in their work environment to experiment with new behaviours. Coaching can also be offered as a stand-alone intervention to support particular development needs – for example, individuals who are undertaking large projects and organisation change initiatives, and recently recruited or promoted individuals who may benefit from coaching to fast-track them in their new role. This ad hoc coaching is frequently organised through HR professionals, and thus it is important for the HR professional to understand the variety of purposes for coaching and have access to coaches who are specialised in delivering particular outcomes.

When NOT to use a coach

Coaching is not a panacea and there are situations which need a different intervention. Before engaging a coach, it is the responsibility of an HR professional to determine on behalf of individuals whether coaching is the appropriate intervention (Lee and Valerio, 2005). Common examples of where coaching may not be appropriate include:

- The individual is told to have a coach when he/she does not want coaching.

- Coaching is offered to an individual who has already been identified as no longer required in the organisation.

- The issue is more systemic in nature and outside the individual's control – this is where an organisational development intervention is required.

- The coachee has significant personal and emotional problems for which a different intervention may be more appropriate – for example, substance abuse, bereavement, marital breakdown, conflict resolution, etc.

- Specific advice or knowledge is required – a consultant may be more appropriate.

2 COACHING INTERVENTIONS AND THE ROLE OF HR

In recent CIPD research, Clutterbuck and Megginson (2005; p.19) describe a coaching culture as one in which

> coaching is the predominant style of managing and working together and where commitment to improving the organisation is embedded in a parallel commitment to improve the people.

Some 93% of respondents of the CIPD learning and development survey 2006 who then used coaching considered a coaching culture to be 'very important' or 'important' to the success of their organisation, and 72% identified improving individual and business performance as the core objective for developing a coaching culture.

There are a variety of activities that can be used to develop such a culture, and in this section we aim to explore three main approaches: the use of external coaches, the use of internal coaching, and the development of coaching skills in line managers. A core part of an HR professional's role is to decide the range of activities required for the specific organisation to meet its unique challenges. In the CIPD learning and development survey 2006, 47% said they were using training to develop coaching skills in line managers, whereas 18% said they were providing coaching through a network of internal and external coaches, and 35% said they were combining both of these approaches. These methods are examined in turn below.

EXTERNAL COACHING

An external coach is a professional who specialises in coaching and is separate from the purchasing organisation. External coaches frequently come to coaching after a career in business, psychology or counselling. Many have formal qualifications in coaching and related areas. External coaches may be dedicated full-time to coaching or have a portfolio career where they also offer services such as facilitation and consulting. External coaches are frequently reserved for senior-level leaders and executives because they are expensive. External coaches have a wide range of purposes for their coaching, and it is important for HR professionals to understand the specific niche of each external coach working in their organisation to effectively match an appropriate coach for the client's 'presenting issue' (a 'presenting issue' is what the client at first thinks the issue is). External coaches can be used for stand-alone interventions or to support leadership development and other programmatic interventions. HR professionals must consider what type of coaching they need and then find coaches who are informed by an appropriate philosophy and use an appropriate approach, and who can demonstrate their experience in delivering that type of intervention.

What are the advantages of using an external coach?

For senior-level clients, external coaches are often perceived as more 'credible' than internal coaches. This is because they are external to the organisation rather than because they necessarily have more coaching skills and experience than internal people. It may also be that external coaches offer clients a degree of confidentiality which a coach within the organisation may not be demonstrably able to offer.

The purpose of coaching for an individual at this level of the organisation often requires a shift in behaviours and perspectives to ensure a step-change in his or her own performance and in that of the organisation – so using external coaches can be helpful because they offer clients a fresh way of looking at existing issues which coaches and other colleagues within the organisational system may not see.

The challenge of using external coaching services

For the HR professional there are a number of challenges in using external coaching services. In particular, who is the client when the organisation pays for the coaching? It is common practice for coaches to treat what is discussed with the coachee as confidential, a model taken from the therapy professions. Yet this poses a conflict for a commercial organisation whose responsibility is to its shareholders. How does HR demonstrate value from procuring coaching? How should a coach employed by the company respond when a member of staff wants to be coached on leaving the company? And what of the coaches' ethical duty when they become privy to internal information which might, for example, be useful for insider trading (Peltier, 2001)?

To avoid potential problems and set up an ethical framework for coaching to take place that respects the needs of all parties involved, the initial agreement which outlines the contractual responsibilities and expectations is critical for ensuring a clear understanding for all those involved. The nature of coaching means that it is difficult to foresee every eventuality, in which case openness between the coach and client, and direct discussions about potential problem issues as they arise, are a useful guideline (Peltier, 2001; Lee and Valerio, 2005).

REFLECTIVE ACTIVITY

Should organisations dictate what employees focus on in coaching?

Selecting external coaches

Choosing an external coach who is fit for the purpose is an important task for the HR professional. A coach often works over a long period of time with key individuals in an organisation. In these relationships clients may talk about extremely sensitive and important issues for them and the organisation, and coaches are thus potentially in a very powerful position in which they can influence the behaviours, attitudes and decisions of the client and ultimately the organisation. Yet the coaching industry is currently unregulated. There are no barriers to entry for new coaches into the marketplace – anyone can become a coach. The early years of the twenty-first century saw a massive growth in the number of people offering coaching services, many with only a simple understanding of a coaching process, and often without any psychologically informed knowledge (Berglas, 2002; Freas, 2004). Who you choose as a coach is therefore very important: selecting a coach who is not appropriately skilled could harm your employees.

To develop the expertise to be able to choose the right coach, HR professionals must understand coaching and the organisational imperatives for using it. This can involve training in coaching techniques, networking with the coaching industry, attending conferences – and receiving coaching. Before you begin selecting coaches, establish what it is you are trying to achieve for your corporate clients, because that will often have a direct influence on the type of coach that you want. When you begin the selection, there can be a temptation to evaluate coaching companies, but best practice is to look at each individual coach. Critical areas to consider in assessing coaches' suitability include: the experience of the coaches, the level of seniority and the particular organisations, their coaching style, their supervisory arrangements, whether they practise continued professional development, and whether references are available.

Some organisations use a formal selection process to make sure they have coaches that are the correct 'fit' for their organisation and meet the standards they have set for coaches at that level (Horner and Dolny, 2006). The selection process also provides information to support the effective matching of coach to coachee. Such selection processes are time-consuming and costly and are usually undertaken only by larger organisations. However, given the variety of coaching styles (de Haan, 2005), approaches and backgrounds, an effective selection process ensures that you have access to a diverse group of coaches who meet the organisation's criteria for coaching at the level for which they are being recruited, and who share the philosophy of coaching and learning within your organisation. Where demand is sufficiently high, some organisations are now establishing a specific HR function as 'head of coaching' (Stern, 2007).

Supervision

Supervision is where a coach has regular structured opportunities to reflect with a more experienced coach or group of coaches to help him or her understand how he/she is working with his/her clients. The purpose of supervision is first to protect the clients, in that it provides the coach with a better understanding of the impact of his/her work and enhances the coach's self-awareness. These opportunities also help coaches to continuously develop their skills and provide coaches with support. Supervision can be an important quality-assurance activity for organisations as well as a useful source of learning for the organisation. In the light of its importance, the absence of regular supervision for internal or external coaches is a concern; participation in supervision is therefore often considered a prerequisite for employment of the coach. Recent research by the CIPD found that despite a dramatic growth in the use of coaching in organisations in recent years, very few firms are using supervision to support their coaches and to get the best value from their coaching services. Less than half (44%) of coaches say they are receiving regular supervision, and less than a quarter (23%) of organisations who use coaching are providing coaching supervision. Nevertheless, the picture has improved significantly in recent years, some 58% of those coaches who receive supervision having begun the process in the last two years (Hawkins and Schwenk, 2006).

REFLECTIVE ACTIVITY

How would you organise a selection process for external coaches?

How might you get insights from external coaches about the organisation without impinging on the confidentiality agreements they have with their individual clients?

INTERNAL COACHING

Given the cost of external coaching and the demand for this intervention, organisations are starting to develop internal coaches. Internal coaching is the same as external coaching with the obvious difference that the internal coach is a fellow-employee of the organisation. One definition (Frisch, 2001; p.242) is:

Internal coaching is a one-on-one developmental intervention supported by the organisation and provided by a colleague of those coached, who is trusted to shape and deliver a programme yielding individual professional growth.

Internal coaches tend to be outside the line management chain to differentiate from manager coaching on the job and avoid potential conflicts of interest.

There are many benefits in using internal coaches. An internal coaching service is likely to be more cost-effective than paying external coach fees. Being more affordable means that the coaching can be made more accessible across the organisation. Internal coaches know the organisational context, the culture and power relationships. They are more easily contactable and also have opportunities to observe the coachee and bring those observations into the coaching intervention (de Haan, 2005).

There are, however, some challenges in using internal coaching effectively. The main concern is about confidentiality and potential conflict of interests that arise in internal coaching, because the internal coach does not enjoy the same separation from the organisation as the external coach. Clear contracting between internal coaches and the client can address those concerns. Internal coaching requires organisational support to arrange training at a suitable level; to manage contracting and coaching relationships; to arrange supervision; to maintain continued professional development for the internal coaches; and to negotiate with management to allow the internal coaches to be used. The development of an internal coaching pool is therefore a significant investment. However, as well as the direct benefits of internal coaches, such a programme also provides evidence of the commitment to working towards a 'learning organisation' (Senge, 1990). Organisations that embrace internal coaching help model behaviours that individual managers have to adopt to enable cultural change.

 REFLECTIVE ACTIVITY

What are the strengths and the limitations of using internal coaches?

What are the challenges for HR in managing a team of internal coaches?

COACHING SKILLS FOR LEADERS AND MANAGERS

The changing face of organisations has seen an increase in the need for a coaching culture in organisations by which managers and leaders adopt a different style of leadership. This is frequently because rapid change makes it difficult for managers to keep abreast of technical detail and they are thus all too frequently managing staff whose work they know too little about and so are unable to advise on technical aspects of the role. The use of coaching techniques is more useful in supporting leaders to deliver through others, rather than the old-style instructional 'Do as the boss says' approach. Although organisations have been slow to develop capacity among their leaders, this is changing as demand for leaders to deliver results through others and actively develop staff increases (Clutterbuck and Megginson, 2005). Training courses to build coaching skills in leaders are focused on supporting leaders to change from a leadership style which is directive (solving staff's problems for them) to a non-directive (helping staff to solve their own problems) approach. To reinforce this change, core coaching skills and techniques – for example, active listening, building rapport, open questions and effective feedback – are taught.

Whereas a coaching style may require a greater investment of time and effort on the part of the manager, the staff feel empowered because the manager does not seek to direct them but, by coaching, encourages them to solve their own issues. In the longer term staff become more productive, because a coaching approach encourages personal responsibility and promotes staff learning. This approach is also perceived as more attractive for a modern workforce because it recognises the independence and individuality of the employee.

The role for HR is to ensure that the managers have the appropriate skills to use coaching techniques in their daily work. HR should additionally be responsible for evaluating and choosing the training course and measuring any impact in such areas as organisational culture. It is also important to ensure that managers do not overstep the boundaries of their capabilities and start coaching at a level beyond their training. Explaining the purpose, approach and limits of the coaching skills provided is a useful way for the wider workforce to understand what it is their managers are trying to do, and why.

REFLECTIVE ACTIVITY

What is required to ensure the successful implementation of a programme to teach and/or improve coaching skills for managers?

How might you ensure that managers develop their coaching skills and actively use them with the people who report directly to them?

THE CENTRAL ROLE OF HR IN COACHING

Coaching's widespread popularity is a relatively recent phenomenon, and there is still considerable misunderstanding about what coaching is and how best to use it to be most effective. The lack of established standards, professional bodies and qualifications frameworks means that using coaching effectively is usually the responsibility of the HR department.

The role of the HR professional is critical to ensuring that coaching is used appropriately and that all the stakeholders involved understand, and are able to fulfil, their roles. HR professionals must understand the different types of coaching and know when it is the right intervention in preference to other learning and development options. They must understand how to select appropriately qualified coaches and then match them to both the organisational culture and the needs of the individuals. Finally, HR professionals are often responsible for setting up coaching contracts, ensuring that there are some means of quality control, and developing a way of evaluating the effectiveness of the coaching activities.

KEY ISSUES: COACHING

We now pull together ten key points about coaching raised in this chapter:

- Coaching draws on a variety of fields including, psychology, leadership, organisational development, counselling and therapy.

- There is no single definition of coaching, but most professionals would agree that its core purpose is individual learning that will contribute to the current and future performance of the individual – and therefore team and organisational performance. Coaching is not about addressing the past.

- Coaching is a skilled activity which relies on skills such as active listening, effective questioning and feedback. It is usually non-directional: the coach helps clients to find their answers to their issues, thus empowering the clients to be self-directed in their approach to performance and development.

- Coaching is normally time-limited.

- Organisational and societal trends have seen organisations increasingly use coaching techniques as a style of leadership and management to support

their staff development, and to achieve better performance and enhanced self-direction.

- Although one-to-one coaching is mostly used by senior management because of the costs involved in its provision, it can be successfully used at all levels in an organisation.

- The three ways of implementing coaching are: external coaching, internal coaching, and the use of coaching skills by managers as part of day-to-day work conversations.

- Coaching can be used to address a number of issues, such as skills, performance, development, or for the client's own agenda.

- The role of HR is vital to ensuring that coaching is used appropriately and that all stakeholders involved understand and are able to fulfil their roles.

- HR professionals must understand the different types of coaching and know when it is the right intervention in preference to other learning and development options.

Perhaps there are other key points that you would like to note for yourself.

The main case study in this chapter now follows.

Make an initial reading of the case study to gain an overview of the situation, and then read the questions that you will need to address. Now read the case study again, making notes of issues and facts that will help you in your analysis and responses to the questions. Remember to 'read between the lines' as well as picking out the obvious points, and also to consider what is not said as well as what is presented here.

The Great Energy Business (GEB) is a large energy generation and supply company with a diverse and international workforce. Its leaders need a wide array of skills, and coaching is regarded as key in helping its leaders to deliver the highest levels of performance. Over the last few years the GEB has created a team of internal coaches to work with leaders across the business. It now has 50 trained coaches available. The GEB has used external executive coaches for a number of years with its board-level and directorate-level leaders, with some success. External coaching is a popular learning intervention, but seen across the business as a privilege for the executive community.

Having initially grown rapidly, the business has experienced below-market growth for a number of years. New companies have entered the market, competition for trained personnel is fierce, and new environmental regulation means that the industry is becoming a more challenging market to operate in. The arrival of a new CEO has led to a capability review of the organisation's management at all levels. This review has established that the old-fashioned directive style of leadership is unpopular with the workforce and leaders are perceived as unhelpful and unsupportive of employees. The cost implications of offering external coaches to all of the management team are far too high, so the head of HR has decided to create a pool of internal coaches to support a new leadership programme aimed at changing the leadership style and culture in GEB.

Coaching is viewed as essential because it offers a personal intervention which can be tailored to the requirements of the leader. The long-term nature of the coaching relationship, stretching over several months, also makes it an attractive method of learning because it is seen as having a greater chance of embedding new leadership styles and behaviours. Because coaching focuses on future performance, it is perceived as sending out a positive message that the business is not going to dwell on the past but seek to move forward.

The challenge for the head of HR is to find people capable of performing as internal coaches. People with a sound understanding of the business, experience in the dynamics of change and a well-developed understanding of people are needed. Initially, the HR department, using its knowledge of the workforce, approached people who had a known interest in and passion for improving the organisation; this was then followed with a recruitment campaign which advertised the benefits for personal development in becoming a coach and asked for volunteers to become internal coaches

Selection of appropriate candidates was regarded as a crucial part of the programme. The HR department ran a selection and assessment process to screen out those people who did not demonstrate the potential to coach. The GEB used an external consultancy to help the department develop its own set of competencies to describe the behaviours of a trainee coach and meet the organisational requirements. Applicants had to have the support of their line managers because their role of internal coach was to be in addition to their normal duties. Applicants were asked to provide a presentation on what they understood about coaching and how they thought it could be applied within the organisation. This was followed by a criteria-based interview. Those who passed the assessment were offered a place on a training course.

Initially, a new programme started every eight weeks in order to quickly grow the pool of coaches; today, it runs once a year to maintain the pool. The course aims to equip GEB's internal coaches with the knowledge, skills and experience to coach effectively across the business, particularly, but not exclusively, in support of the leadership programme. The programme consists of taught elements, observed practice sessions and assessed fieldwork. Coach trainees also have an opportunity to undergo a series of coaching sessions with an external coach so that they can appreciate coaching from the client's perspective. The course lasts for six months, with the emphasis on skills development. At the end of the programme all trainees are formally assessed on a presentation on their understanding of coaching and how they have applied it, a demonstration of their coaching practice, and supporting evidence of the fieldwork undertaken.

Once in the internal coaching pool they are allocated clients on the leadership development programme. However, after they have completed six months of this coaching, they may be approached by anyone in GEB who wants coaching. This open market has created challenges for some coaches who are popular within GEB and has resulted in the HR department's having to negotiate with line managers to ensure that core work commitments are not compromised when certain internal coaches are doing several days of coaching a week.

Even as the internal coach programme was being launched, the HR department started to think about continuous professional development and supervision for the internal coaches. This was regarded as essential for the credibility of the programme. Continuous professional development ensured that coaches maintained their skill set and learned new techniques. The coaches were required to participate in continuous professional development as part of the right to practise, and quarterly workshops with outside speakers were offered. Supervision was vital in ensuring that the coaches could have a safe place to discuss their clients and learn about their coaching. In the first year as a coach, one-to-one supervision was mandatory for all coaches. There after, coaches went into a peer group of coaches supported by an external supervisor who ensured the independence of the discussions.

Despite a high initial cost in setting up the selection and training programmes, a cost-benefit analysis showed that by Year 2 of the programme it was offering better value for money than relying on external coaches. The use of internal coaches enabled coaching to be available at more management levels in the organisation. The long-term nature of the coaching – over several months in comparison to the traditional week-long training course – saw the learning become embedded because the coaching clients were supported in their changes through the coaching relationship. Those trained as internal coaches started to model coaching behaviour in their daily work, helping to implement a cultural change in the organisation.

Case study learning points

The GEB's internal coaching pool has now been operating for a number of years. Key learning points for HR were:

- Individuals receiving coaching must be committed to continuous learning.

- The board-level executives and some directorate-level leaders preferred to use external coaching because it was perceived to be more confidential.

- There must be clarity about how the coaching fits into the culture of the organisation. GEB HR now runs briefings on coaching, what it is, and how it works, for staff who are interested in receiving coaching.

- The internal coach volunteers must be prepared to put in considerable time and energy.

- A clear process has to be established for how internal coaches are selected, trained and then supported. HR must support and work with line managers to ensure that they are content for their staff to become internal coaches.

- Those who become internal coaches have found it to be a profound learning experience with considerable personal benefits for themselves, and a rewarding activity in supporting leaders and the organisation to develop.

Questions for discussion

1   Who in the business would be best placed to play the role of internal coach?

2   How might they be selected, developed and rewarded?

3   What support would be offered to them once they were in the internal coach pool?

4   How would the organisation establish a return on investment from the coaching skills programmes and the development of internal coaches?

5   What options are there to develop leaders' individual coaching skills?

6   How would you gather information from the coaches to benefit organisational learning without compromising the confidentiality of their clients?

7   How would the organisation measure the impact of coaching on its leadership development?

EXPLORE FURTHER

CIPD (2007) *Coaching at Work*, Magazine and online resource. London, Chartered Institute of Personnel and Development. Available online at:
http://www.cipd.co.uk/coachingatwork/ presales.htm
A bi-monthly publication which offers articles on current trends, developments and techniques in the coaching industry.

CLUTTERBUCK, D. and MEGGINSON, D. (2005) *Making Coaching Work: Creating a coaching culture*. London, CIPD
This work looks at the importance of creating an organisational culture that will effectively support the introduction of coaching.

JARVIS, J. (2004) *Coaching and Buying Coaching Services. A guide*. London, CIPD.
Available online at: **http://www.cipd.co.uk/guides**
A useful and succinct guide to the issues involved in procuring coaching services.

LEE, R. J. and VALERIO, A. M. (2005) *Executive Coaching: A guide for the HR professional*. San Francisco, Pfeiffer
One of the few published works on executive coaching written specifically for the HR professional.

WITHERSPOON, R. and WHITE, R. P. (2004) *Four Essential Ways That Coaching Can Help Executives*. Greensboro N.C., Center for Creative Leadership
A clear and concise guide to how coaching can be used within an organisation.

CHAPTER 16

People-related measures and high-performance HRM

Andrew Mayo

INTRODUCTION

HR departments want to be seen as 'business partners'. This means that they work with operating managers to help them with their objectives, but also that they are businesslike themselves. It is a general truth in business that 'Numbers speak louder than words.' This chapter provides a framework for distinguishing between the requirements for metrics for HR as a function, and separately for 'people in the organisation', and examines practical ways of meeting them. It also identifies the parameters for delivering high performance from the HR function.

LEARNING OUTCOMES

By the end of this chapter readers should be able to:

- explain the distinction between human capital management and HRM

- understand the types of measures appropriate to people

- define and link measures on human capital

- build an HR functional scorecard.

This chapter is in two parts – firstly, measures for managers to use; and secondly, measures for the effectiveness of the HR function's performance.

The chapter concludes with the main case study.

Reference sources named within the chapter may be looked up in the *References and further reading* section at the end of the book.

STARTER CASE STUDY

Extract from Shell Annual Report, 2005

Resourcing for the future
In 2005 we recruited more than 700 graduates and almost 2,000 experienced people from over 70 different nationalities, underlining our focus on recruiting from a wider range of countries and regions, especially Asia-Pacific and the Middle East. Our successful large-scale recruitment drive for experienced exploration and production professionals in 2005 means that Shell is well positioned to deliver on the increased level of investment in our upstream business. The recent appointment of chief scientists also demonstrates our continued commitment to technical excellence, and confirms the strength of Shell's career and development opportunities for technical staff. We place strong emphasis on local careers and employee development with 49 nationalities represented amongst our senior leaders.

Strengthening leadership and deepening professionalism
Shell's ability to capitalise on growth opportunities in emerging markets relies on the skills and professionalism of our employees. We continue to invest in training and development through a balance of on- and off-the-job learning. The establishment of Project and Commercial Academies will provide new opportunities for staff to develop expertise in these areas. Just as important is the ability to manage change effectively, and in 2005 we increased both resources and capability in support of business critical change initiatives. In addition, we are committed to the development of leadership capability through the integrated cross-business Shell Leadership Development programmes. These are delivered through strong partnerships with major international academic institutions, and in 2005 more than 7,000 people with leadership potential participated in these programmes.

Communication and involvement
The success of our business depends on the full commitment of all employees. We encourage the involvement of employees in the planning and direction of their work, and provide them with safe and confidential channels to report concerns. Employees in all countries where we operate have access to staff forums, grievance procedures or other support systems. A global Ethics and Compliance Helpline was introduced during December 2005, offering an independent, confidential and anonymous facility for reporting non-compliance and resolving dilemmas and concerns. The Shell People Survey is conducted every two years, and asks employees for their opinions on a number of topics relating to how they feel about working at Shell. The last survey in 2004 had a 78% response rate and showed an overall satisfaction rate of 64%. The next survey will take place in 2006. We seek to establish and maintain high-quality, direct and open dialogue with employees. Our staff are represented by collective labour agreements, unions and staff councils in many countries in which the group has operations.

Diversity and inclusiveness
Shell has had a long-standing commitment to the integration of diversity and inclusiveness into every aspect of our operations and culture. We set explicit expectations for all employees and leaders, underpinned by clear plans and targets. There are three global objectives: improving the representation of women in senior leadership positions to a minimum of 20% in the long term; improving the representation of local people in senior positions in their own countries; and improving the positive perceptions of inclusiveness in the workplace. At the end of 2005, women in senior leadership positions had increased to 9.9%, compared with 9.6% in 2004. In 36% of countries, local nationals fill more than half of senior leadership positions. The Shell People Survey (2004) reported that 64% of employees perceived workplace inclusiveness favourably. These results represent good progress, but further improvement is needed to meet our aspirations.

Questions for discussion

If you were an investor or potential investor in Shell, what would you conclude was good and bad about the organisation's people and about people management? What else would you like to know?

1 HUMAN CAPITAL MEASURES

WHAT DO WE MEAN BY 'HUMAN CAPITAL'?

It is important to start by understanding the difference between 'human resources' and 'human capital'. Both terms refer to the people in the organisation. People are of course costly resources – in most organisations today, the major cost that they have. But people are also the creators of value.

Why do organisations exist? Only for one purpose, and that is to create value – or benefits – for their stakeholders. A stakeholder is a person or group that has an interest in the organisation's being successful. Most organisations have at least three sets of stakeholders – their owners, their customers and their employees. In a commercial organisation the owners, or shareholders, want the organisation to be financially successful so that they receive a good return on their investment. But they can only do that if they have satisfied customers, and employees who are committed to their work and want to do a good job. In the public sector, the owners are policy-makers – usually the government – and the customers are the public.

Every organisation has two types of assets that it uses to create the value for its stakeholders. One type of assets is 'tangible' – these include money, buildings, equipment, machines and stocks of materials. They are regularly valued by accountants and from time to time a 'stocktake' is made of what the organisation has, what it owes to others and what it is owed itself – and this is carefully documented on what is called a 'balance sheet'. The second category comprises 'intangible' assets. These are not generally measured by accountants, but include things which a buyer would have to pay for (in addition to the tangibles) when buying the organisation. Intangible assets were first described by Swedish thinkers, and a comprehensive summary of them can be found in Edvinsson and Malone (1997). They may include a customer base, brand names, reputation, valuable contracts, systems, processes, knowledge and methodologies . . . and the people – their skills, experience, relationships and creativity. In fact, without people, nothing happens. That is why it is popular to say that 'People are our most important assets' – although in fact it is the *qualities* of people that are the actual assets. Just as money is often called 'financial capital', this aspect of people is called 'human capital'.

'Human capital management' is therefore to do with thinking about people as assets and not just costs. It is about the value they have as individuals and teams, and the value they create for others. 'Human resource management', we could say, is about administering the resource called people, and about processes, tools and programmes which maximise people's value and contribution.

REFLECTIVE ACTIVITY

Think of two different kinds of organisation that you are familiar with – maybe ones you have worked for, or ones you interact with as a customer.

Make a list of the kinds of tangible and intangible assets they have. For each organisation, rank approximately the importance of each type of asset.

If you were able to buy the organisation, what would you want to make sure you did not lose after the purchase?

WHY MEASURES ARE IMPORTANT

It is often said that 'What gets measured gets managed.' Managers all over the world are trained to work with numbers, and human capital management is therefore often associated quite rightly with people-related measures. However, Albert Einstein is quoted as saying 'What counts can often not be counted, and what is counted often does not count.' In other words, in looking for measures that relate to people we will not necessarily be looking through an accountant's lens, seeing everything as financial numbers – we have to be smarter than that and use a range of different kinds of measures.

We use a variety of different kinds of measures, such as:

- proportions, percentages and ratios
- indices, which weight and combine several measures
- ranking in order
- time-based trends
- perceptions of how people feel or see things
- levels of expertise
- costs and cost-based ratios
- the absence of negative events (like accidents and occupationally caused ill-health).

For a comprehensive survey of measurement options, see Becker, Huselid and Ulrich (2001).

Remember that all measures depend on the reliability of the measuring process. Perceptions of how people feel are particularly vulnerable to misinterpretation, unless the questions are phrased with careful and neutral objectivity. Whenever scales are used – such as estimating expertise – we have to be sure that the people who use them will all use them in exactly the same way, which will depend on how closely the scales are defined.

How do we know whether to be pleased with a particular measure or not? When is a measure 'a good result' and when is it 'a bad result'? Sometimes it is obvious, but often just a raw figure does not mean very much. There are three means of evaluation to help us answer the question:

- *By seeing if it is increasing or decreasing* compared to a previous figure. Whichever way it is going, we want to understand why. Some measures vary over short periods (for example, attrition rates may be quite different month on month) and we must look at trends such as three-month moving averages.

- *By comparison with similar measures* from other organisations – *benchmarking*. In fact, organisations like to make comparisons to see whether their figures are better or worse than those of competitors or sister organisations. Often third parties produce league tables, especially in the public sector.

- *By comparison against a target* we have set.

The different audiences for measures

The starter case study above was from the published Annual Report of Shell. It actually has much more information than most of this sort of report often does about people. The 'audience' for an annual report includes investors, journalists, academics, regulatory bodies and other external observers. It also includes competitors. What we choose to tell the world is governed by compliance with regulations, plus what we feel will give confidence in us as a good company in which to invest.

In 2003, the UK Government commissioned a report into what might be put about people in annual reports – it is known as the Kingsmill Report and is available online at **www.accountingforpeople.gov.uk**. It made a number of suggestions for data about people to be included in a section of an annual report called the Operating and Financial Review. As an input to this the CIPD produced a report of its own called *Human Capital: The external reporting framework* (Scarbrough, 2003). So far, nothing has been mandated for companies in law, although the best companies include a section on people which is most likely to be a narrative.

What is published externally must be separated from the need for management *within* an organisation to have good human capital management. We will inevitably use some of the same numbers, but in an annual report they are consolidated for the company as a whole. Just as we have to break down financial budgets into units and departments, so we must do the same for people measures for them to be useful. We may also want to focus on some detail that we might not want to make public.

There are four categories of measures we can have for our human capital (in Part 2 of this chapter we look at measures relevant to the work of the HR function itself), which are now considered in turn below. They are: statistics about the workforce and movements in it; the value of the people; the motivation of the people; and the productivity of the people.

STATISTICS ABOUT THE WORKFORCE

Consider the following exercise before reading any further.

REFLECTIVE ACTIVITY

A supermarket company has 32 stores and a total of 4,500 people.

What kind of breakdown of this population might we be interested in at any given point in time?

What kind of information would be useful over a specific period of time, such as three months?

For the first question we might look at the total company, or by area or individual store. We should then divide our data first into *job families* – this would include groups such as senior management, middle management, store management, store staff, professional support staff, buyers, and distribution operators. We could then be interested in the following distributions for each job family: length of service, time in job, age, disability, gender, ethnic origin, full-time/part-time, qualifications, vacancies, etc.

For the second question, we might be interested in the following:

- labour turnover, sometimes called attrition – this is the loss of people over a certain period (see Chapter 11)

- movements of people *in* to a job family or store over the period

- other transfers or promotions – all of these three measures might be consolidated into a 'headcount change report'

- the use of temporary or subcontract staff – again by job family or store

- absenteeism and sickness (see Chapter 11)

- accidents and ill-health (see Chapter 18).

REFLECTIVE ACTIVITY

Your monthly human capital (statistics) report has been produced. If you notice the following, what would you conclude, and what action would you consider taking?

Two stores show an unusually high loss of people occurring between three and six months of service.

Five stores have much worse absenteeism rates than the average.

In the job family of store managers, only 14% are women, and only 3% are from ethnic minorities.

There are three stores in which the age distribution shows 50% of the staff are aged over 50.

The ratio of HQ staff to store staff is 18% across the country – in a recent study of retail companies the average for the sector was given as 14%.

Note that we have here introduced the concept of *ratios* of one job family to another, or of one as a percentage of the whole workforce. These can be more revealing than simple statistics.

THE VALUE OF PEOPLE

We know the costs of people. But what do we know about their value? Is it the same? Clearly, it is not. We can have five different members of a team, all paid the same. But their manager knows they are all individuals, with different experience, knowledge, skills and attitudes. He or she would miss them in different ways if they left the team. There might indeed be an individual whose leaving would delight the manager because it meant that there was an opportunity for a *better* replacement. One of the problems for most organisations is that they are unable to balance the costs of people with any quantitative assessment of their value. 'Price is what you pay; value is what you get,' says one enlightened CEO. Whereas a team leader knows the unique and relative value of his or her people – and can describe it qualitatively – as we go above and beyond his or her level of management, that value is lost in a fog and those individuals just become 'headcount' and costs. As a result, poor decisions are often made and the value walks out of the door before we have finished counting the cost savings.

The great thing about people is they have the capacity to *increase* their value with time. They get new experience and new skills; they may be promoted and take higher responsibility. Provided we give the chance to people, most of them will grow with us – and we will reward them accordingly. If we are an organisation, it is in our interest to do this. Some academics have attempted to build formulae for the financial valuation of people (see, for example, Flamholz, 1999). We need not concern ourselves with these because they are not in any general use. We have to find a way of quantifying the *characteristics* of value that people bring to us. We can use a common framework but it is important that we do not assume that the same detailed components of value will fit all employees. What makes a call centre operator valuable to us is different from what makes an electrician or an HR business partner valuable to us.

Here we have two questions to ask. Firstly, what are the distinctive characteristics of these employees which epitomise their special value in the department of which they are part? There are some characteristics that we always value in any employee – positive attitudes, willingness, being a team player, reliability. But for each task there are additional abilities which distinguish one from another in the ability to achieve levels of performance. The kind of things we would look for might be (Mayo, 2001; pp80–1):

- *personal attitudes* – eg positive approach, flexibility, team member, takes initiative
  These are often to be found in competency frameworks. We are referring here to those which are more personality-oriented – ie are generally not developed through training. Most teams value people with these kinds of attitudes regardless of their work mission.

- *values alignment with the organisation* – its values, ethos, and mission
  People who comfortably align themselves to our values have particular worth. They become 'part of us' and are likely to be loyal to us.

- *job-relevant capability/expertise* – knowledge, skills, specialised experiences and people contacts
  Note: the widespread use of 'universal competency frameworks' – by which every employee at a certain level is expected to shine at a large number of behavioural competencies – makes no sense. It is more than behaviours: it is professional and technical expertise uniquely critical to the role in question that we want to identify.

- *productivity/contribution* – people vary in their ability to actually achieve things
  Some people are better at getting results than others – even with the same base level of knowledge and skill. It is to do with the way they prioritise time and effort. We always value more those who 'get things done'.

REFLECTIVE ACTIVITY

Think of a job that you know well.

What would be the characteristics of a really valuable person in such a job?

The second question to ask is: What additional characteristics does an individual have which indicate the promise of future value, beyond the current task? People may have previous experiences not used in the current job, or may just have the potential to grow and undertake a more demanding role in the future – higher or broader responsibilities. Another factor here may be 'mobility' – the willingness to take up positions in other locations or countries.

Compiling a 'human capital index'

Having identified the factors affecting high performance, we should then do the following. We need to weight the factors for relative importance; decide how to rate the factors as observed – both in terms of a scale and a process to apply it; design a display format for them; and summarise the data in an overall index of value. We may call this overall index by any suitable name. Elsewhere (Mayo, 2001; pp78–84) it is called the ' Individual Asset Multiplier', but we could use other terms such as 'Individual Value Index', 'Human Capital Index', or whatever suits the culture of the organisation best.

Table 35 shows a way to display the value of people in a team. It uses a rating scale of 0 to 2, where 1.0 represents 'a person who demonstrates the level of value we would expect for what we are paying'. This helps us do a number of useful things in human capital management. We can compare the value of different teams, and focus training on the characteristics that matter and recruitment on where we have gaps. The objective is to constantly increase the total index we have.

Table 35 Displaying the value in a group

Employee	Personal attitudes (20%)	Capability factor (20%)	Contribution factor (30%)	Values factor (15%)	Potential factor (15%)	Human capital index (100%)
A	1.7	1.6	1.8	1.6	1.9	*1.725*
B	0.7	1.0	0.8	0.8	0.7	*0.805*
C	1.4	1.1	0.8	1.6	0.9	*1.115*
D	1.6	1.7	1.5	1.0	1.5	*1.485*
E	1.0	0.8	0.9	1.1	1.0	*0.945*
Average per employee	*1.28*	*1.24*	*1.19*	*1.22*	*1.20*	*1.215*

THE MOTIVATION OF PEOPLE

We can have great people in our team or organisation, but creating the maximum value for stakeholders is not guaranteed just because of that. Extraordinary and well-qualified people can produce very little. The good news is that quite ordinary people can produce extraordinary results. What makes the difference? Their motivation – how the organisation (through its HR and other policies) and their manager inspires them, meets their personal needs, provides them with challenge and achievement, and so on.

We must define some terms here. *Satisfied* employees do not necessarily produce great results, but at least it is better than *dissatisfied* employees, so we have to know how employees are feeling about their work and the environment in which they perform it. The aspiration we have today is to have *engaged* employees – not just satisfied with the organisation but *committed* and keen to do the best job they can. Figure 21 names two types of motivation – 'intrinsic' and 'extrinsic'. The first is people's natural enthusiasm for what they do. It can be strengthened or sapped by 'extrinsic' factors – what the organisation or the manager does or does not do. What we want is for all the influences to be strong so that the end result is 'engaged employees'. And we want to know what is happening – to measure it, monitor it and manage it.

Figure 21 Motivation and engagement

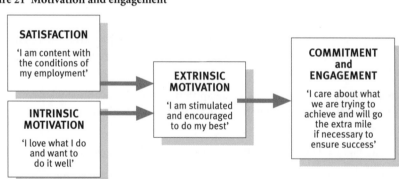

There are numerous surveys carried out by consultants on the levels of engagement of employees. Most of them find that between 10% and 20% of employees are 'highly engaged', between 10% and 15% are 'disengaged', and the remainder are 'somewhat engaged' (eg Corporate Leadership Council, 2004). Because engagement has direct and strong links to performance, the challenge for managements is to improve the first category. There are two things we want to measure. Firstly, 'Are people engaged or not?' And secondly, 'What are the factors that make them engaged?'

REFLECTIVE ACTIVITY

From your own experience, make a list of the kind of things in a work situation that a) make you frustrated and discontented, and b) make you enthusiastic and keen to do a great job.

How do we know people are engaged?

There are five ways to know whether people are engaged:

1 Ask the people. At this stage we are not interested in what makes people engaged or not, but just whether they *are* or not. Below are some statements to evoke responses which test that. As with all surveys the responses need a scale – typically a Likert-type scale ranging from 'Absolutely true for me' to 'Absolutely not true for me'.

  ● I would recommend my company to a friend as a good place to work.

  ● I am proud to tell others I work for the company.

  ● I really care about the future of my company.

  ● I am willing to put in a great deal of effort beyond what is normally expected to help my company succeed.

  ● I am personally motivated to help my company be successful.

2 Have an independent company ask the people. Surveys like The Great Place to Work conducted by consultants on behalf of the *Sunday Times* are very comprehensive in finding how employees feel.

  ● Voluntary resignation rates – although we should be a bit careful here and analyse the reasons, people who love their job do not leave it. So if the rates are above the historical or industry norms, they may be an indicator.

4 Excessive absenteeism rates – the same applies. If the rate is above what we might reasonably expect, it may be an indicator that people do not want to come to work.

5 Ask the managers. They know who goes the extra mile and who does not.

It is wise to use a combination of these and not any one measure alone.

How do we find out about the factors that make people engage or not?

As noted earlier, the answer to this question is different for different groups of people. We can take a compromise based on research of what *generally* makes a difference to people, or we can ask the group concerned and then draw up a survey based on what they said. Research into occupational psychology tells us fairly consistently about the things that motivate people in general. Factors include the nature of the work they do, whether they can feel a sense of achievement and whether they get recognition and opportunities for advancement. The most commonly used survey on engagement today is devised and copyrighted by Gallup (see **http://www.gallupconsulting.com/content/?ci=52**). It is known as the Q12™ (see the box below). It comprises 12 questions, and if the answer to a majority of them is 'yes', there is a strong chance that the employee is engaged. How do these relate to your answers to the previous apply your knowledge exercise?

The Gallup Q12™ Engagement Survey

1 Do I know what is expected of me at work?

2 Do I have the materials and equipment I need to do my work right?

3 At work, do I have the opportunity to do what I do best every day?

4 In the last seven days have I received recognition or praise for good work?

5 Does my supervisor, or someone at work, seem to care about me as a person?

6 Is there someone at work who encourages my development?

7 At work, do my opinions count?

8 Does the mission/purpose of my company make me feel my work is important?

9 Are my co-workers committed to doing quality work?

10 Do I have a best friend at work?

11 In the last six months have I talked to someone about my progress?

12 At work, have I had opportunities to learn and grow?

Now check on how these questions relate to your answers to the previous exercise.

REFLECTIVE ACTIVITY

Our chain of supermarkets has decided to go beyond statistics about the workforce and do some engagement surveys of each store every four months. They are using a slightly modified version of the Q12 with a five-point scale. The two upper parts of the scale are 'Always true for me' and 'Usually true for me'. One third of stores show 40% or more employees in the top two categories. One sixth show only 10% or less; the others are in between. Two stores have made dramatic increases in their percentage since the last survey four months ago. The worst responses, more or less everywhere, were those to question numbers 7 and 11. Number 8s had improved significantly since last time, but number 12s had become worse.

If you were the HR director, what messages would these figures tell you?

Good organisations have always done employee opinion surveys. Usually, these are annual or even less frequent and cover many areas. Today they may be supplemented by local, short, frequent 'pulse surveys'. In the survey we need two to three questions which check whether people *are* engaged, plus a set covering the key influences such as in Q12.

Note: With all surveys of how people feel it is good to ask 'How important is this item for you?' in addition to asking for their scores on an item.

THE PRODUCTIVITY OF PEOPLE

People bring their value to organisations in order to create value for others. We need to know how successful they are – ie what they are creating. Each group of people should be linked to one or more stakeholders. Sales people add value to customers (through helping them get the right product and providing them with good service) and to the shareholders (by bringing in revenues). We would measure the value they add in terms of customer satisfaction and loyalty, *and* in sales revenues.

Productivity is defined as output over input – it is a ratio. The input is the denominator in the ratio, and we want it to relate to people. We can use:

● numbers of people (such as revenue per salesperson)

● time spent (such as customer satisfaction compared with time spent by salespersons in checking it)

● people cost (such as revenues in relation to total sales compensation cost).

A detailed study of ratios such as this can be found in Fitz-Enz (2000).

Remember, the output measure is a measure of value added. It is not mere activities. Take for example a public sector organisation. Our interest is not in the number of cases handled per person per week. It is the number of cases *resolved*. That is the value added.

REFLECTIVE ACTIVITY

For our chain of supermarkets, what measures of productivity might you have for one store?

What measures might you use for the purchasing and distribution departments?

PUTTING IT ALL TOGETHER

We now have four kinds of measures to form our human capital report. We do not want them to stand alone or just be bundled into a basket. We are interested in how they link together and their correlations, especially with performance (productivity). What is it about our people and what is it about their working environment that makes a difference to productivity? Some companies, especially in banking and retail, have been able to demonstrate a clear quantitative correlation between engagement and a business parameter. The 'human capital monitor' (Mayo, 2001; p.12ff) is one example of how the various measures can be shown together (see Figure 22). This kind of report is something we would compare with a previous one, to see in what areas we are making progress or otherwise.

Figure 22 A human capital (or 'people') monitor

The People Monitor – Group XX				
People as assets		**Commitment and engagement**		**Contribution to added value**
GREAT PEOPLE The value of the people we have, using our chosen index	×	IN A GREAT PLACE TO WORK Input measures The factors that lead to engagement of this group	=	GREAT RESULTS The measures of *value* for stakeholders or of productivity
Maximising the value Measures of human capital management processes – both inputs and success indicators		**Success indicators** The measures of commitment and engagement		

Source: Mayo (2001)

Then, just as in looking at our money we create a balance sheet, we can create one for people. It is a summary at a point in time of where we are. Of course, the people balance sheet is not written in money. It is a summary of what is positive and what is getting better on one side, and what is negative or getting worse on the other (see Table 36).

Table 36 Example of a 'people balance sheet'

THE HUMAN CAPITAL BALANCE SHEET	
ASSETS	**LIABILITIES**
Factors on the Monitor that are at or ABOVE target	Factors on the Monitor that are BELOW target
OUR PEOPLE	OUR PEOPLE
. . . . .	. . . . .
. . . . .	. . . . .
MOTIVATION/ENGAGEMENT	MOTIVATION/ENGAGEMENT
. . . . .	. . . . .
. . . . .	. . . . .
VALUE ADDED	VALUE ADDED
. . . . .	. . . . .

Of course, organisations will find their own ways to present the data and information. It is not just the information that is important but the process and the action that follows it. HR in its 'business partner' role should play a key part in this process.

Final note: Whatever measures and presentation we use, it should feed into any organisational performance management systems such as the 'balanced scorecard' (Kaplan and Norton, 1996). Such a system focuses on the *most* important measures for supporting company strategy. They will not be enough in themselves to manage human capital – we need the detail we have discussed.

2 HIGH-PERFORMING HR MANAGEMENT

We noted on page 291 that there is considerable confusion under the heading of 'HR metrics' between measures of human capital and measures of the HR department's effectiveness. Often a mix of measures is presented in one freestanding report – a 'basket' of measures. These have little meaning if they are not connected together.

An HR department is a group of people in its own right, of course, and so the human capital measures apply to them – we are interested in their value, their motivation and the value they add. But professionally, we would want to go further into the activities and effect of what the department does. What should we want to know? Any support function has two roles. One is administrative – looking after the regulatory requirements and ensuring that people are properly paid, and so on. The other role is often described as 'strategic'. This is not a good word because nobody spends much time in a year thinking about strategy. A better term is 'value-adding'. The administrative side of HR is not really value-adding to any stakeholder – it is ensuring compliance with the law and with company policies, and providing good housekeeping. It has to be done well, and we come back to that later. However, HR – assuming it is more than just administrative personnel management – also has the capacity to add value to several stakeholders. It designs and owns a number of important people management processes, and it is there to support managers in achieving their own objectives.

THE VALUE THAT HR ADDS

So what should we want to know and measure? First, we want to understand and measure the value HR adds. Then there are two categories of effectiveness measures of *how* the value is delivered:

- *operating effectiveness* – This is how efficient we are; how well our processes achieve their purpose, how good a service we deliver, and what our productivity levels are.

- *project effectiveness* – This is whether we get a good return on what we spend on special initiatives and programmes.

Before we examine these in more depth, we must briefly consider the value added to stakeholders.

REFLECTIVE ACTIVITY

List the stakeholders for whom HR can add value.

What kind of value (or benefits) can/does HR add?

To check with your answer for the first part of the exercise above, there are three main stakeholders for HR. They are the owners (via senior management), managers and employees. Often there is a parent company to consider if the company is a division or subsidiary. HR may also provide benefits for suppliers, trade unions, communities, other functions such as IT and Finance, government departments and industry bodies. Can we measure the value HR adds? We start from the idea that everything can be measured if we try hard enough.

Financial value added is measured in money saved, or the return on money invested. We have to be careful we do not save money at the expense of benefits for other stakeholders. However, senior management is always pleased if we can save. Sometimes we have to spend to save – that is why we have to know how to do 'return on investment' calculations. Financial value added to employees is different – they want their salary, benefits and bonuses to be fair (so the measure is a perception), and we can also benchmark against market salaries and see which quartile of the salary ranges we are in.

Most of the other value-added items are measured by surveys of perceptions of one kind or another – of service provided, or of the value of a policy. Sometimes it is useful to measure 'negatives' or the extent to which things did *not* happen. Examples of this would be low rates of accidents or grievances. Having chosen how to measure what we are there to do, we move to measuring how well we do it, starting with operating effectiveness.

Table 37 The contribution of an HR function to stakeholder added value

HR stakeholders and areas of added value	Examples of practical contribution from HR and L&D initiatives
Senior management (and via them owners, shareholders, parent companies)	
● financial	● People management or people development projects with a good return on investment ● Cost-saving initiatives
● reputational	● Employment brand ● Handling of legal issues
● strategic	● Creating HR strategies and policies that support business strategy ● Achieving employee alignment with company goals ● Describing and achieving a cultural vision supporting the business goals
● continuity	● Talent and succession management ● Retention strategies
● organisational effectiveness	● Organisational design ● Communication strategies ● People-related processes designed to make the organisation more effective
Operational management	
● strategic	● Creating people initiatives which support operational goals
● tactical	● Providing problem-based consultancy ● Advising on legal and policy issues
● employee engagement	● Recognition programmes ● Information on engagement ● Performance management
Employees	
● financial	● Salary, bonus and benefit structures
● motivational	● HR policies and programmes ● Good communications ● Recognition programmes
● developmental	● Knowledge and skills enhancement ● New experiences ● Career planning and progression
● health and safety	● Absence of accidents ● Employee health support

 REFLECTIVE ACTIVITY

Look at Table 37.

In the light of what you have learned so far, what kind of measures would you use for each of the items in the right-hand column? Add another column to the right, and write in it the measures you suggest for each of those items.

OPERATING EFFECTIVENESS

We could deliver great added value, at least non-financially, but it could cost a fortune to do so. Every support function like HR must know whether it is good value for money. That is why we have to have some good 'internal' measures which we can monitor and manage. The four areas we now examine are: the quality of service provided for the cost; what our productivity is, and what value for money we give; how well HR processes work; and how time is utilised.

REFLECTIVE ACTIVITY

Jot down quickly all the things you look for in good service from a professional organisation.

Service

Many organisations today have 'service-level agreements' which describe how they will perform for their customers. They cover things like accuracy, timeliness, responsiveness, quality of advice, attitude of the people delivering the service, and ease of dealing. Which of these might require a survey? One might be done every quarter to see how customers of the HR service are experiencing it. Other things can be measured internally. For example, we can regularly track the time it takes to fill vacancies, or the number of mistakes in paying people, or how long it takes to process a benefit application.

Productivity and value for money

Earlier we examined the productivity of people (in a section of that heading). We are now looking for output measures of human effort. From Table 37 we could potentially have a lot of outputs. We could be selective or we could combine some into an index. If an HR person is dedicated to one type of added value (like training people, for example), we can just take his/her outputs (learning achieved index) and divide by his/her costs. Often HR professionals do many things – some service delivery, some projects, some other value-added contributions. So the only way we can fully comprehend our productivity is to have some division of people's time between various areas. Let us suppose that one thing we are trying hard to do is to improve the company's employment brand – its attractiveness to new employees. We would measure this in three ways – external league tables such as The Best Companies to Work For, the acceptance rate of offers made, and the number of employees leaving through dissatisfaction with the company (because they will tell other people). The productivity ratio is the increase in employment brand (as measured consistently) divided by the time spent on it. (If we have employed consultants, we must use the cost of time.) Of course Rome, and an employment brand, is not built in a day – so we might get quite low (or even negative) productivity levels in the short term.

'Value for money' is a very similar concept. One often-used ratio is the overall HR costs per employee in the organisation. This is not a good ratio, even though it is quick and easy to work out, because it depends what HR produces. So we have to combine it with service levels and value-added areas and ask 'Does this feel like value for money?' It is a judgement – but we can use benchmarking figures from other organisations to help us make that judgement.

How well HR processes work

HR owns, designs and either runs or helps run many processes that are to do with people management – many of which are discussed elsewhere in this book in detail. They include such areas as performance management, recruitment, development centres, promotion and absence management. They do not always run according to plan, often because managers do not play their full part (or we have made them too complicated). We need to be very clear about the *purpose* and *aims* of a process to be able to assess how well it is working. For example, there are actually several possible purposes of an appraisal system and people are often confused as to which they are.

Measures that can be used include:

- the 'penetration' of the process – What percentage of the people who are supposed to use it are actually doing so? For example, how many appraisals get done each year?

- the success of the process – To what extent are the intended outcomes achieved? In training it is one thing to measure the percentage of people who have training plans, but how many of them *complete* them?

- the time and/or cost taken for completion of a round of the process – Is it worth the goals achieved? For example, development centres are fun things for everybody involved, but very expensive. Is the time and cost justified by the achievement?

Someone should own every process – and they should be responsible for setting up and monitoring its success.

REFLECTIVE ACTIVITY

Take the process of recruitment – one (like many) that is designed by HR but shared in implementation with line managers.

What measures would you choose to monitor if the process was working well?

How well time is utilised

The truth is that very few people are productive (in terms of adding value) every minute of the day. We are not talking about rest breaks or the occasional chat, but about work itself. We all spend time doing internal and non-productive things (many of which really have to be done). We attend meetings, write reports, pass on communications, travel to meetings, have waiting time, read superfluous emails, comply with regulations, solve problems that should not have happened – and so on. All this is *non-value-added* work. It stops us spending our time directly contributing to one of the areas of value added we have identified. So from time to time we must take a rain check for a month or so and just ask people to jot down what their time is being spent on. The results are often quite disturbing. (For more on this, see Mayo, 2001, pp.221–5.)

PROJECT EFFECTIVENESS

Support functions like HR initiate projects and programmes for various reasons. Sometimes it is because senior management thinks it would be a good idea, or it may be that other organisations are doing it and HR thinks it would be beneficial to its own organisation. It could be that there is a problem to be solved – there are too many accidents, or too many people are getting stressed, or there is a quality problem in customer service. Remember that most operational difficulties have a people problem behind them.

It is important to register that it is no use going ahead and then later deciding we should find out whether there was a return on what we did, and try to evaluate its effectiveness. That is not what we do with financial capital investments. We first decide *whether* it will bring a return – we evaluate its anticipated effectiveness. All projects have some wishful thinking and optimism behind them, and this is why so many are an embarrassment and quietly forgotten afterwards. A problem in HR and training is that so many initiatives look naturally like good things to do. The question is whether they will make any difference.

It is not easy in HR because many of the projects have a lot more than purely financial benefits. But by now we are experts at understanding 'non-financial added value' and how we measure it. The simple formula for return on investment (ROI) is as follows (see Phillips, Stone and Phillips, 2001, Chapter 8, for a full explanation):

$$\% \text{ ROI} = \frac{\text{Financial benefits} - \text{Project costs}}{\text{Project cost}} \times 100 + \text{Non-financial benefits}$$

We may have to make an estimate of the financial benefits and sometimes can do that for the effects of a non-financial benefit. We might estimate that a 5% 'increase in engagement' affects productivity by 2%, which is worth £*x*. Or we can see what it looks like for just the financial benefits on their own. Does this itself show an acceptable rate of return? If so, the non-financial benefits are a bonus. Otherwise, we have to make a judgement – does this look like value for money? So there are two possible processes here: either preparing a case to justify an initiative or evaluating whether the initiative met its anticipated returns.

In making the case, we have four steps to go through:

1 Define the measurable objectives of the initiative.

2 Calculate the estimated costs of the project.

3 Estimate the returns (both financial and non-financial) to be expected from the initiative.

4 Balance the two and conclude that the initiative is or is not a worthwhile use of resources.

If we want to subsequently evaluate how right we were, we have to add some more steps (Mayo, 2004, p.187).

5 Make a data collection and evaluation plan.

6 Collect data before the initiative if before/after comparisons are to be made.

7 Collect data during the initiative as needed.

8 Collect data after implementation.

9 Calculate all costs involved at each stage.

10 Isolate the effects of the programme.

11 Calculate the financial impact of the data.

12 Compare with the costs.

13 Present together with the non-financial benefits.

14 Judge whether the actual ROI was satisfactory.

This is a lot of work – which is why it is often not done. You have to be good at understanding costs, and be realistic about the costs of implementation. Note Step 14, which is difficult – other factors may have influenced the benefits, especially if a long time period was involved. So we have to estimate how much of the benefits were actually *due to the programme*.

PUTTING IT ALL TOGETHER

As before, we have to make choices about exactly how many measures we choose to monitor. We do not have time to measure everything, so choose those that are preferably not difficult to do and that will have the biggest impact. Figure 23 shows a model format which would embrace all we have examined.

CASE STUDY

150 high-potential middle managers from 40 different operating companies of a multinational telecommunications company were sent, in groups of 25, on a three-day management conference. The management conference consisted of group discussions to work out how the company values could be practically implemented and how change was taking place within the organisation to achieve the strategic business objectives, together with exercises to identify and share best practice. The direct cost per three-day programme (including travel and accommodation) was £60,000. After the management conference, it was noticed that the turnover for this highly mobile group dropped from 12% to 8% (50% were replaced from outside – generally it was reckoned that the replacement of a middle manager from outside cost about nine months' salary). Also, motivation levels of two thirds of the group perceptibly increased. This was supported by anecdotal and written evidence from appraisals (managers often reported gaining 'significant motivation' from the programme) and was also measured as an increase in productivity of the teams being led. 50% of the managers were from sales teams whose annual revenues before the programme averaged £500,000 per team. The average cost centre had total costs of £200,000 per year. The productivity changes were an average of 10% per employee for the sales teams, and for the cost centres a decrease in 5% costs per employee. The average managerial salary (including benefits and bonuses) was £100,000. The average sales margin on revenues was 12%.

Your task

Using the information in the short case study above, calculate the value of the financial benefits, calculate the return on investment, and list other non-financial benefits that were probably achieved.

Figure 23 A model for an HR scorecard

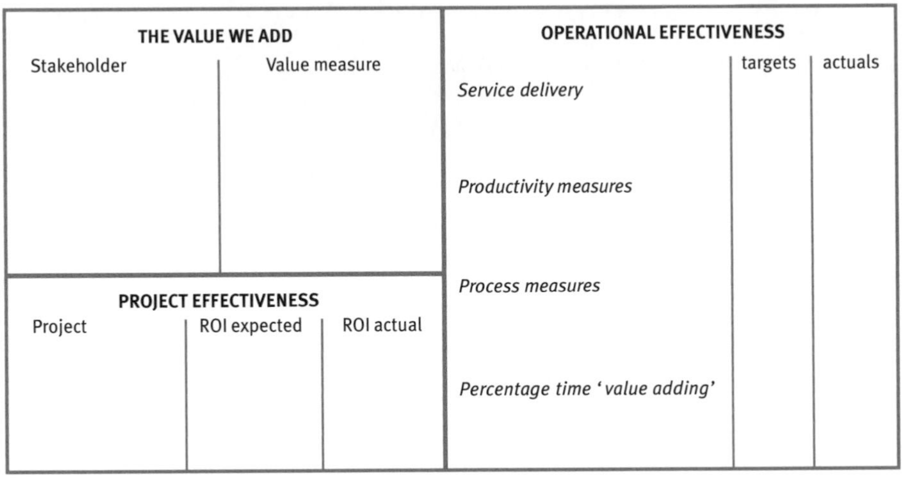

THE VALUE WE ADD		OPERATIONAL EFFECTIVENESS		
Stakeholder	Value measure		targets	actuals
		Service delivery		
		Productivity measures		
PROJECT EFFECTIVENESS		*Process measures*		
Project	ROI expected	ROI actual		
		Percentage time 'value adding'		

KEY ISSUES: PEOPLE-RELATED MEASURES AND HIGH-PERFORMANCE HRM

We now pull together ten key points about the main issues raised in this chapter:

- There are two main areas of people-related measures – those to do with the human capital of the organisation and those to do with the HR function.

- 'Human capital' is linked in to the whole HRM concept, as distinct from personnel management. It is about seeing people as value-creating assets and managing them accordingly. It implies measurement as in any other part of a business, and is as valid for public sector organisations as well as private.

- There are four areas to consider in human capital measurement: workforce statistics, the value of people, the motivation of people, and finally their productivity.

- Statistics is about who we have and where – by job family and by department.

- We need to value people quantitatively in order to have a balance with the focus on costs – but we cannot do this in financial terms. We have to evaluate the characteristics of people that make them valuable.

- Satisfaction is not the same as engagement – we need to measure the latter using custom-made surveys.

- Productivity is the added value to stakeholders divided by some measure of the human input.

- When we look at the effectiveness of the HR function, we need to know the value it adds to its own stakeholders and quantify it.

- Then we look at 'operating effectiveness' – service delivery, process efficiency, productivity and value for money, and time utilisation – and finally 'project effectiveness' – return on investment for projects.

- For both sets of measures we need an integrated presentation of the measures – for human capital a 'monitor', for HR a 'scorecard'.

Perhaps there are other key points that you would like to note for yourself.

The main case study in this chapter now follows.

MAIN CASE STUDY

Make an initial reading of the case study to gain an overview of the situation, and then read the questions that you will need to address. Now read the case study again, making notes of issues and facts that will help you in your analysis and responses to the questions. Remember to 'read between the lines' as well as picking out the obvious points, and also to consider what is not said as well as what is presented here.

This case study concerns a university. The Summa cum Laude University has some 25,000 students and 3,750 staff, split approximately 50:50 between academic and support staff. It has six schools, mostly on one distributed city campus, but also with an outlying campus 40 miles away which serves part of two of the faculties. The schools differ in size but their functions are all similar – namely, to provide teaching for students and to undertake and publish research. Each school has a head and a group of senior department leaders, although strong hierarchical management is not a feature of academia and decisions are more taken by consensus. Each school has support staff – secretaries, administrators and technicians. These are managed by a facilities manager, and typically total 100–130 or so staff per school. The university centre houses corporate functions such as HR, finance, IT and estates (which looks after all the buildings).

In the faculty support department, measures of performance are not formalised. However, for administrators success is all about meeting deadlines in the faculty timetable – accuracy and efficiency. For the technicians it is the right materials in the right place at the right time, adherence to health and safety requirements, and housekeeping, stock-keeping and managing equipment maintenance.

It is a general problem in universities that support staff feel they are regarded as second-class citizens compared to the academics, and this makes a particular challenge for the manager. Technicians particularly often feel undervalued and strikes have not been unknown.

HR comprises some 25 people, located together in one building. Under the HR director (who sits on the university senior executive team) are two deputy directors who share responsibility for particular projects and initiatives. Each school has an HR adviser dedicated to them, plus an assistant. A service centre deals with all administration and recruitment. In addition, there are six

people working under a learning and development manager. They do a few basic training courses themselves but most staff training is outsourced and they manage the suppliers. As a department HR has enjoyed good stability of the key staff over the last five years although the absenteeism rate is about the public sector average.

HR keeps good data on attrition and absenteeism, although the breakdown of the reasons for each is very general. A comprehensive employee opinion survey is run every three years which covers many aspects of working for the university and is broken down by department in each school. HR is responsible for an appraisal system for all staff. Each year about 80% of appraisals are actually done. The appraisal links into a training planning system. There is no succession planning. HR is also responsible for internal communications and trade union negotiations.

Your task

You are a consultant who has been asked by the HR director to do two things. Firstly, she would like first a scorecard for the HR function to enable her to monitor the right indicators that will tell her the department is being effective.

What would you have in the scorecard and what measures would have to be built? Be specific and not general – you may have to be somewhat creative to think of what would be useful in this context.

Secondly, she would like a human capital monitor for the group of technicians.

Think about what makes such people valuable in the organisation, what is likely to motivate them, and how the result of their efforts can be measured in value added. How would you summarise clearly such a monitor for the manager?

In preparing the monitor and the scorecard, can you foresee any practical difficulties? Likewise in implementation?

EXPLORE FURTHER

BECKER, B. E., HUSELID, M. A. and ULRICH, D. (2001) *The HR Scorecard: Linking people, strategy, and performance*. Boston, MA, Harvard Business School Press
A book designed for HR business partners, from the most famous HR thinktank in the world. It discusses HR's strategic role and has an excellent chapter on measurement in general. It tells readers how to create and implement the HR scorecard and how to do cost-benefit calculations.

EDVINSSON, L. and MALONE, M. S. (1997) *Intellectual Capital*. London, Piatkus
From the founder of the intellectual capital movement while in Skandia Assurance, this gives the logic of intangible assets, why people are so important, and how people-related measures can be made and used.

FITZ-ENZ, J. A. C. (2000) *The ROI of Human Capital: Measuring the economic value of employee performance*. New York, Amacom
The father of HR metrics and founder of the Saratoga Institute provides lots of numerate ideas for measurement. This book shows how to gauge productivity and people costs at the levels of the organisation, a function and HRM. Essential reading for somebody going into the subject in more depth.

MAYO, A. J. (2001) *The Human Value of the Enterprise – Valuing people as assets, measuring, managing, monitoring*. London, Nicholas Brealey
This book provides an overview of human capital management and the measures associated with it. It argues why they are important and introduces the concept of 'the human capital monitor' for linking people, engagement and performance. It goes into detail in the possible measures for each area, and in so doing draws out the implications for 'value-based HRM'. It examines the impact on mergers and acquisitions of human capital management, and finally the issue of public reporting.

HRM and Employee Representation

CHAPTER 17

Employment relations

Paul Higgins *and* Richard Croucher

INTRODUCTION

This chapter is about employment relations – ie the *collective* relations between managers and employees and the influence that various actors have on the terms and conditions of employment, discipline and grievance.

LEARNING OUTCOMES

By the end of this chapter readers should be able to:

- identify the most important actors in employment relations

- recognise the importance of collective bargaining to the management of the employment relationship

- consider the impact of recent national and European legislation on unionised and non-unionised workplaces

- describe the appropriate grievance and discipline procedures for different employee issues.

The chapter is structured in three parts.

After the starter case study, designed to outline some of the issues that emerge in the employment relations field, the first part of the chapter endeavours to identify the characteristics and motivations of the key actors in employment relations. Attention then focuses upon trade union recognition and in particular the reasons why some organisations might choose to be pro- or anti-trade union. The section concludes by examining the prevalence of the two main forms of collective representation by workplace characteristics.

In the chapter's second section, we consider in more detail the interplay between the key employment relations actors by reference to two of the most important pieces of employment relations legislation in recent years. The first of these is the statutory recognition procedure introduced by the New Labour government in 1999. This is followed by an examination of 'partnership' between management and unions. The second piece of legislation is that which requires companies

This case study is based around a debate undertaken by four employees – Angela, Ashok, Charlene and Jim – regarding the virtues of joining and not joining a trade union. The debate subtly illuminates the complicated relationship between collectively organised employees, individual employees, union firms, non-union firms and government.

Charlene begins proceedings.

Charlene: I wouldn't join a trade union – they're troublemakers. Look at how trade unions caused havoc during the miners' strike in the 1980s and nearly brought the country to its knees. If it hadn't had been for the Conservatives, the country would never have changed. Look at all of the opportunities now! Much better jobs.

Jim: I agree – and besides, since Margaret Thatcher, trade unions haven't got much power anyway, so what's the point in joining them? In artificially raising wages they increased inflation, raised prices, made Britain uncompetitive and overburdened the taxpayer. I'm glad they've been disciplined.

Ashok: But can't you see it from the opposite perspective? Without trade unions wages would fall and employment conditions would worsen.

Charlene: No, not any more. Many organisations try to prevent union growth by offering better wages than agreed rates and also highly reward good individual performance – so if you work hard, you get paid more. That's fair. Look at some lazy people who fail to contribute to group work but get 'carried' by others and still get the same pay. It's a similar sort of thing. I'm an achiever. I don't want to be held back by others.

Angela: Actually, many professionals and well-paid people are members of trade unions as well – even professional footballers – so trade unions don't necessarily hold you back. On average, trade union members tend to be better paid than the average worker anyway. Ashok's right – you must also consider the situation of workers on lower pay without a trade union. They often have poor terms and conditions of employment, without protection. You only need to consider the work experience amongst retail staff, waiters and waitresses, bar staff, carers, call centre operatives … The list goes on.

Jim: Well, there's the minimum wage for them.

Angela: But that doesn't bring security nor necessarily mean good conditions of employment. You have to consider what each hour of work actually demands.

Ashok: I agree with Angela. People need a say at work, a countervailing power to management and capital. And anyway, in some organisations it might even be beneficial for both sides – employers and employees – to talk and improve matters for everyone. Employees are often closer to the user and can present management with good ideas that can help to achieve its goals. And if you treat staff well and pay them fairly, they will give back, too.

Jim: Yeah, but the conditions aren't there now. You can't treat waiters and waitresses or call centre staff too well because if you do, they'll lose their jobs. It's part of the global environment now. People will swear at you whatever. And there are plenty of people around the world who will accept inferior conditions, so if you don't put up, you shut up or leave.

Angela: And the employer loses someone with some ideas of their own, who's a bit more than just a 'yes' person and who can probably be used to help improve the ways things are done at work.

Questions for discussion

1 What can be learned from this debate?

2 Whose perspective do you most agree with, and why?

3 What would be your reasons for joining or for not joining a trade union?

with more than 50 employees to inform and consult with their staff on matters important to the employment relationship. The implications of both statutes for union and non-union organisations are carefully considered.

In the third section of the chapter we move on to consider the twin issues of discipline and grievance. These are vitally important issues for all HR professionals because they can be brought up in employment tribunals and courts of law. Taking each of these issues in turn we provide a definition of the terms, consider some trends in respect of their prevalence, and then go on to examine their statutory procedures.

The chapter concludes with the main case study.

Reference sources named within the chapter may be looked up in the *References and further reading* section at the end of the book.

1 KEY ACTORS IN EMPLOYMENT RELATIONS

WHO ARE THE KEY ACTORS?

The starter case study centred on the impact of trade unions, which are regarded as a key actor in employment relations. Trade unions are important to the study of employment relations because they represent an exclusively collective orientation to the employment relationship which might further entail representation and collective bargaining. Their existence and function within employment relations can therefore be contrasted with the more widespread individual forms of employee representation or even those conducted through unrecognised systems of collective representation.

Trade unions and individual employees are not, however, the only actors in employment relations, the complexity of which also includes the actions of the direct employer and its relationship with external employer associations and subcontractors and, of course, legislative authorities both domestic and, in the case of the United Kingdom, European. In this first section we consider the general characteristics and motivation of these various actors before focusing upon the issue of the importance of collective bargaining to the management of the employment relationship.

The key actors in employment relations can be identified as:

- the Government
- employers and management
- individually and collectively represented employees.

Government

The Government exerts a major influence on employment relations by enacting legislation, devising and executing economic policy and acting as an employer, directly or indirectly within the public sector. The Government is also involved to maintain order, to improve competitiveness, to redistribute wealth and to ensure social justice and fairness, to attract investment and to improve well-being. The Government can also pass direct employment relations legislation such as the Race Relations Act 1976 and the Sex Discrimination Act 1975 (see Chapter 5). It can also influence employment relations issues in indirect ways – for example, by its management of the economy, by passing other laws, by shaping the public mood through its politics and ideology, and by embarking upon the policies of nationalisation and privatisation. Over time, various governments in the United Kingdom have also created a number of independent employment relations agencies. These include employment tribunals, the Advisory Conciliation and Arbitration Service (ACAS), the Central Arbitration Committee (CAC) and the Certification Officer.

Although the Government is a key and overriding employment relations actor, there are no agreed limits to its actions because it intervenes for a number of reasons and in a number of ways. The Government has intervened strongly in employment relations since the 1960s, particularly, as suggested by the opening case study, during the Thatcher period (Wedderburn, 1991; Smith and Morton, 1993; Harvey, 2003). In more recent years, since the election of New Labour in 1997, some of the Government's most important legislative developments with respect to employment relations have included the establishment of the National Minimum Wage Regulations and the implementation of various European Union Directives such as the Working Time Directive and the Part-Time Workers Directive (Crouch, 2001; Smith and Morton, 2006).

Despite these broader regulatory shifts, however, Labour's approach to employment relations has not led to a radical departure from the approach adopted by the Conservatives. The reason for this is that New Labour shares its predecessor's enthusiasm for encouraging a flexible labour market, many of the more notable reforms, which might serve to regulate this, originating from the European Union rather than being purely domestic measures. This suggests that New Labour is not so much *responding* to the 'globalisation' threat but rather *creating* its very conditions. The following quote from former Prime Minister Tony Blair (1998) provides a good example of this:

> There will be no going back. The days of strikes without ballots, mass picketing, closed shops and secondary picketing are over. Even after the changes we propose, Britain will have the most lightly regulated labour market of any leading economy in the world.

Employers and management

Employers and management can relate either to those people responsible *in* organisations for carrying out the strategic and decision-making responsibilities or to those from *outside* the organisation who may have a direct or indirect influence on organisational goals. The second are subcontractors for the organisation, employers' associations and consultants.

In the first instance, we are referring to those organisational-based managers and employers responsible for the effective operation of the organisation. Precisely how these managers influence the employment relationship depends upon whether they, and particularly those specialists known as personnel officers or human resource managers, adopt a 'hard' or 'soft' approach to employment relations issues (Guest, 1987; Storey, 1992). The 'hard' approach takes its description from the perspective that the human resource is simply a factor of production together with land and capital and is largely treated as an expense to be cut rather than as potential for turning production into wealth. In contrast, the 'soft' model treats employees as valued assets, as a source of competitive advantage to be nurtured, trained and improved.

Our second instance includes subcontractors. At the extreme are organisations whose managers conduct employment relations through the medium of various forms of subcontracting. This involves employing the labour force indirectly or externally through an agent or subcontractor who deals with recruiting the workforce, monitoring production and paying workers (Grimshaw, Marchington, Rubery and Willmott, 2005). Subcontracting has the advantage to the host firm that labour issues are passed over to another organisation, and because of this it is easier to lay workers off as necessary. It has the disadvantage, however, that organisations using subcontracted labour have less direct control over the effort and compliance of workers.

Meanwhile, in more generally seeking to influence the employment relations landscape, employers and managers from different organisations sometimes organise together to collectively represent themselves through a employers' or management association. These associations are formed from representatives of firms within a particular industry and provide various services for member firms. They vary in size and influence from the very small with no full-time staff to large and highly influential organisations such as the Engineering Employers Federation, the Road Haulage Association and Retail Motor Industry Federation. These, along with consultants and lawyers, frequently advise companies about employment relations issues.

Individually and collectively represented employees

The final key actor in employment relations we can consider is employees. Employees are responsible for carrying out the day-to-day activities that lead to the achievement of organisational goals and might be employed on a full-time, part-time, temporary or casual basis. They might work for a single or for multiple employers and generally have other commitments outside of their paid work such as caring for dependants, specific ways of spending leisure time, consumption and studying. In terms of their paid work, employees may decide to represent themselves to their employer on either an individual or a collective basis. A number of the ways in which employees might individually represent themselves are examined in the chapter on communication (Chapter 19). For the purposes of this section, however, we are more concerned with employees who represent themselves collectively.

There are two main ways in which employees might decide to collectively represent themselves. The first is with the assistance of an independent trade union. The second is without trade union representation by setting up a body such as a joint consultative committee (JCC). These are usually organised within a single organisation and tend to involve consultation rather than negotiation.

Taking the latter first, there are numerous reasons why some organisations might not have trade union representation. For example, in smaller self-employed or family-run organisations no formally employed labour might be used and therefore there are no formal employment relations processes. Meanwhile, in smaller-scale organisations with few employees, staff often engage in interpersonal and face-to-face interaction without formal processes. However, at the same time, such organisations might instead be very autocratic in style such that The Boss compels employees to accept his/her commands. In contrast, for larger, medium-sized firms employing between 100 and 500 people a range of soft and hard human resource management styles are likely to be in evidence. However, unlike small businesses, most will operate with formal procedures and will have varying degrees of hierarchically organised control systems.

Finally, although there are only a few large non-union firms they do still, nonetheless, have a high profile in human resource textbooks. In the current climate, it is questionable what benefits such organisations that seek to avoid unions can achieve, particularly if they embark upon 'union substitution' strategies (Fiorito and Maranto, 1987; Guest and Conway, 1999). These are strategies that seek to gain the commitment of employees to corporate goals by, for example, paying above the union-negotiated pay (see below), and other employment conditions. In other words, in trying to keep unions out, non-union firms must in theory satisfy their workers in ways that independent trade unions would seek to do anyway. In turn, this means that such companies must have an interest in the outcome of collective bargaining (see below) although they are not direct parties to it.

For all of these reasons many non-union organisations are described as utilising 'best practice' HRM strategies which involve ensuring good pay and benefits, good complaints procedures, good job security and good communication. At the same time, a number of non-union firms might also display the characteristics of the 'ugly' face of non-unionism, with poor terms and conditions of employment and negligible or one-dimensional consultation strategies. This is particularly likely to be the case in low-skilled subcontracted work.

Meanwhile, the power of a trade union to actively influence the management of the employment relationship depends greatly upon whether it is 'recognised' by its members' employers for the purposes of collective bargaining. Unless otherwise compelled (see below), there are various arguments that an employer might put for and against choosing to recognise a trade union. In the first instance, an employer might choose to work with a union because it regards the union as an essential part of the communication process, particularly, as suggested above, in larger workplaces where it might be too time-consuming to talk to each employee separately. Similarly, such union-friendly organisations might think that by reaching agreement with union representatives, in contrast to imposing decisions, they will make superior decisions. On the other hand, employers are often concerned that trade unions make decision-making and communication in companies slow, cumbersome and inflexible. There is a view that unions tend to resist change and take a long time to get things done. The result is a reduction in the ability of managers to respond quickly and flexibly to market pressures and opportunities. In the light of these concerns, it might seem appropriate that they consider to what extent collective consent can be achieved by other means.

Either way, the step of 'being recognised' marks a very significant movement away from unilateral decision-making by management and involves the joint determination between management and trade union representatives of two sets of rules: substantive and procedural. Substantive rules establish terms and conditions of employment, such as pay, working hours, overtime arrangements, fringe benefits and holidays. Also included are training and promotion prospects. Procedural issues focus upon the issue of *how* the substantive issues are decided and relate to the rules and regulations determining decision-making at industrial, organisational and workplace levels.

In practice, the substantive outcomes of collective bargaining are not confined to union members. Unionised organisations apply collectively bargained terms and conditions of employment to their non-union employees as well as to their unionised ones. Equally significant to these collective rights, recognition imposes a duty on the employer to inform and consult about training, redundancy, pensions and health and safety.

Although there are various arguments that can be put for and against an employer's choosing to recognise a trade union, in the last 30 or so years the United Kingdom has moved from a position in which a large majority of people worked in establishments which recognised trade unions to one in which the large majority do not. The latest workplace employment relations survey, conducted in 2004 (Kersley, Alpin, Forth, Dix, Oxenbridge, Bryson and Bewley, 2006), details the percentage of workplaces that recognise a trade union and/or entertain a workplace-level JCC. The data is reproduced in Table 38.

Table 38 Percentage extent of trade union recognition and joint consultative committee coverage

	Trade union recognition	Workplace-level JCC
All workplaces	30	14
Organisation sector		
Private	16	11
Public	90	28
Industry		
Manufacturing	13	21
Wholesale retail	10	11
Hotels and restaurants	0	4
Financial services	72	5
Public administration	100	42
Education	81	30
Health and social work	41	13

Source: Kersley *et al* (2006)

REFLECTIVE ACTIVITY

Why do the substantive outcomes of collective bargaining apply to both union and non-union employees?

Why are the trade union figures for public sector organisations in Table 38 much higher than for private sector organisations?

Why are the trade union recognition figures for retail and restaurants so low?

The scale of difference between union recognition and JCC representation is low in some industries but high in others – how has this come about?

Note that we have here introduced the concept of *ratios* of one job family to another, or of one as a percentage of the whole workforce. These can be more revealing than simple statistics.

2 THE IMPACT OF NATIONAL AND EU LEGISLATION ON UNIONISED AND NON-UNIONISED WORKPLACES

So far we have considered the three most important actors in employment relations. It was explained that the Government, via requirements of the European Union, determines the overall legal framework and creates specific employment relations organisations such as ACAS. Then, from within these broad parameters managers, employers, employees and their representatives seek to influence organisational goals and outcomes.

Against this backdrop we now move on to consider in more detail the employment relationship between the key actors with respect to some of the most recent and important employment relations legislation. The first piece of legislation to be considered is the Employment Relations Act 1999, which introduced a statutory recognition procedure and paved the way for the development of social partnerships between employers and unions. The second is the Information and Consultation of Employee Regulations 2004, which compel qualifying employers to inform and consult with their workforce on a range of matters.

STATUTORY RECOGNITION PROCEDURE

Employers' attitudes to trade union organisation do not operate in a vacuum and depend on, among other things, a willingness for trade union participation and on government policy. In the first instance, as was suggested above, employees might feel safe in their jobs, with good terms and conditions of employment and thus not regard trade union membership and representation as necessary. Likewise, employers might work hard at both securing and maintaining employee consent and commitment through other means. Alternatively, sufficient numbers of employees might have a grievance at work (see below) and seek trade union representation to express this on more equal terms with their employer.

In the second instance, by passing legislation, the Government can have a tremendously important impact on employment relations. In recent years, government policy under the guise of New Labour has shifted with respect to collective representation via the passing of the Employment Relations Act 1999 (Waddington, 2003). This piece of legislation has provided trade unions with a legal right to trade union recognition provided the following conditions are met:

- the organisation has more than 20 employees

- the organisation has a minimum 10% 'threshold' union membership.

If these requirements are met, the following steps have to be taken for the union formally to secure recognition:

- Step 1: The union must formally approach the Central Arbitration Committee (CAC).

- Step 2: The employer must define the 'bargaining unit'.

- Step 3: The employer must allow the union access to canvass votes/members.

- Step 4: The vote must be taken, with due concern for confidentiality.

- Step 5: The union must receive a minimum of 50% of the vote, and at least 40% of those eligible to vote must have voted.

In fact, as Step 5 implies, if the trade union already has over 50% membership in the employer's organisation, recognition is largely automatic.

Since the passing of the Employment Relations Act 1999, cases of union recognition have increased, although much of this increase has occurred through voluntary recognition deals rather as a result of the statutory process. The reason for this is that by signing a voluntary deal, employers have much more influence over the content of the agreement and avoid a potentially damaging confrontation with their workforce. Lewis, Thornhill and Saunders (2003; p.159) adapt TUC data to show this trend in Table 39.

Table 39 The incidence of union recognitions by voluntary agreement 1996–2001

Period	Number of months	Number of voluntary agreements
Jan–Dec 1996	12	110
Jan 1997–Feb 1998	14	81
Mar 1998–Oct 1999	20	109
Nov 1999–Oct 2000	12	159
Nov 2000–Oct 2001	12	450

Source: Lewis *et al* (2003; p.159)

REFLECTIVE ACTIVITY

From Table 39 calculate the average number of recognition agreements per month.

What has been the trend over time, and what factors might account for this?

'Partnerships'

Given the difficulties that can be faced by some organisations over determining the terms and conditions of employment, a 'partnership approach' to the employment relationship has been adopted by some employers who have been faced with a claim for union recognition or who have decided to reassess and change their approach and relationship with employees and their representative bodies.

Many commentators view the adoption of a partnership approach to employment relations as being more reflective of a co-operative, joint problem-solving atmosphere where employers, employees and trade unions work together to achieve common goals such as fairness, competitiveness and job security (Ackers and Payne, 1998; Haynes and Allen, 2000). A variety of research suggests that partnerships might yield benefits for both parties. For the employer the beneficial outcomes might include higher employee commitment, a greater willingness to contribute, less absence, less labour turnover, less industrial conflict and superior performance. For the employees the benefits might include opportunities to exercise greater autonomy and direct participation, a more positive psychological contract, and an opportunity to share in the financial gains through employee share ownership. Likewise, other research has highlighted that there may also be gains for employee representatives, such as greater influence over employment issues and better representative organisational structures.

However, both the Confederation of British Industry (CBI) (Taylor, 1997) and the Chartered Institute of Personnel and Development (1998) have expressed concern that the onus of partnership is on employer–employment relations rather than employer–trade union relations. The basis for this argument is that employees' best interests are met when they can have some input into decisions which affect their day-to-day work activities, so long as these activities are restricted to work issues rather than wider organisational matters. It is suggested that 'communication programmes' geared to improve employee commitment to company goals and values might supplement such an approach.

Alternatively, there are trade union-sponsored approaches to partnership which embrace a central role for trade union representation, to help secure an independent employee voice in the workplace. This second approach centres on various forms of employee participation and involvement in everyday workplace activities. Indeed, a good way of distinguishing between the forms of communication that might prevail under the various forms of partnership is to utilise the terms 'employee involvement' and 'employee participation'.

Both methods assume that employees have a say at work, although the nature of such 'voice' differs tremendously. Put simply, employee involvement can be seen as enhancing the support and commitment of the organisation, and employee participation as providing employees with the opportunity to influence and take part in organisational decision-making. The key differences between the two are detailed in Table 40.

Table 40 Employee involvement and employee participation

Employee involvement	Employee participation
Inspired and controlled by management	Aims to harness collective employee inputs through market regulation
Oriented towards encouraging individual employee inputs through market regulation	Collective representation
Directed to responsibilities of individual employees	Management and organisational hierarchy's chain of command broken
Employees are often passive recipients of information and decisions already made	Active involvement of employee representatives
Decisions tend to be task-based	Decision-making at higher organisational levels
Assumes common interests between employer and employees	Plurality of interests recognised and machinery for their resolution provided
Aims to concentrate strategic influence among management	Aims to distribute strategic influence beyond management

REFLECTIVE ACTIVITY

Do you think it is possible for employers and employees to work together as a genuine partnership, or is there some underlying conflict of interest?

Which do you think requires better communication – involvement or participation? Why?

INFORMATION AND CONSULTATION

As a member state of the European Union, the UK is now subject to the terms of the Information and Consultation of Employee Regulations (ICE Regulations) 2004 (Hall, 2006), which began to take effect in 2005. The ICE Regulations are based on a framework agreed between the CBI and the Trades Union Congress. Under the standard provisions of these Regulations, qualifying employers must inform and consult with their workforce on measures that are expected to entail substantial changes in work organisation or contractual relations such as pay, redundancies and job transfers. Also included are training and development, equal opportunities, health, safety and environment and pension and welfare issues. Moreover, qualifying employers must inform and consult on recent and probable developments of the undertaking's activities and economic situation, such as profit and loss, sales performance, productivity, market developments and strategic plans. The implementation of the Regulations was staggered, beginning first by covering undertakings with more than 150 employees. From April 2008 the Regulations apply to undertakings with 50 or more employees.

The Regulations are intended to facilitate voluntary, rather than standard, agreements to emerge so that the characteristics of particular organisations can be accommodated, thus avoiding the laying down of detailed 'one-size-fits-all' rules that apply to everyone. Employers that have 'pre-existing' information and consultation agreements that cover all employees only have to consider making changes if they receive a request supported by 40% of employees to negotiate new arrangements. In such pre-existing and negotiated agreements it is possible for information and consultation arrangements to be either direct (between managers and employees) or indirect (through employee representatives) or a combination of the two.

In contrast, organisations that do not have formally approved information and consultation agreements may be vulnerable to having the Regulations' standard provisions for informing and consulting employees imposed on them if just 10% of employers make a request for new arrangements. Employers in this position will be required to negotiate new arrangements, but if agreement cannot be reached, the standard provisions apply. In particular, the Regulations' standard provisions allow for the election of employee representatives and the establishment of indirect methods of informing and consulting with the workforce.

The implications of the ICE Regulations for union and non-union organisations

The information and consultation regulations could potentially change the interface between employers and their employees substantially, whether trade unions are recognised or not. Because few organisations have 100% union membership or collective bargaining arrangements covering all employees, it is likely that strongly unionised occupational groups will be found alongside other groups with weak or non-existent union organisation. Many managers will have to decide whether to develop integrated or parallel systems of employee representation. Some commentators suggest that there is likely to be growth in the number of hybrid systems, and that the new legislation may test the degree of commitment that managers have for trade union-based collective bargaining. At the same time, the Regulations also give unions an opportunity to have structured contact with the non-unionised sections of the workforce, allowing the former to demonstrate to the latter the logic and benefits of union membership. Table 41, drawing upon WERS 2004, shows the types of issues, and their perceived importance, dealt with by union and non-union representatives over a 12-month period.

Table 41 Issues dealt with by employee representatives

Type of issue	Union representative		Non-union representative	
	Spent time on issue in past 12 months	Most important issue in past 12 months	Spent time on issue in past 12 months	Most important issue in past 12 months
Terms and conditions	79	38	65	31
Selection, development and staffing	69	18	77	31
Welfare issues	68	11	60	15
Individual disputes	73	16	44	6
Other issues	10	17	12	16

Source: Kersley *et al* (2006)

REFLECTIVE ACTIVITY

What differences in the significance of issues to union representatives and to non-union representatives can you spot in the figures as listed in Table 41?

To what extent do you think the figures in Table 41 support the argument that one feature of the ICE Regulations is that they allow union representatives to demonstrate to non-union employees the logic and benefits of union membership?

The impact of the ICE Regulations will be greater in organisations with no union recognition. The reason for this is that the preference among non-union employers is not to create any formal indirect structure of employee representation. Amongst such organisations, the Regulations mean that employers will find it more difficult to conduct their relationship with the workforce on a strictly 'need to know' basis. Instead, they will have to continuously inform and consult with employees on a broad range of issues and in a structured manner. Information and consultation agreements must not only be in writing and cover all employees of the undertaking, they must also set out how the employer is to give information to the employees or their representatives and to seek their views on such information. Employees will also be able to seek information from their employers rather than having to be content to receive whatever information management feels is in the best interest of the employees to receive.

In considering these requirements, it should finally be reiterated, however, that the practice of information and consultation is not the same as collective bargaining. Whereas the former is linked to the exchange of information and ideas, collective bargaining is the process by which employers and recognised trade unions jointly reach and negotiate decisions regarding the employment relationship such as pay and terms and conditions of employment. Moreover, although under the ICE Regulations employees will be given the opportunity to express their views and opinions about specific issues, the employer is not compelled to act upon them. The employer simply has to consider those opinions, provide feedback, and where necessary explain why actions have not been taken.

Having said that, organisations should ensure that they are compliant with the ICE Regulations or they could face a maximum penalty of £75,000. Organisations should also be aware that employees can challenge existing arrangements – and they may find that they are compelled to negotiate new arrangements.

3   DISCIPLINE AND GRIEVANCE

Thus far, we have considered the main actors in employment relations and, in particular, how national and European legislation has shaped the employment relations landscape in recent years and its impact on union and non-union forms of representation. Attention now turns to the twin issues of discipline and grievance, which form part of a two-way process that concerns complaints by managers and workers against one another. From 1 October 2004, the Employment Act 2002 made it a legal requirement for all organisations to follow minimum disciplinary, dismissal and grievance procedures in certain circumstances. These statutory procedures amount to a minimum standard that must be followed by all employers and employees, although many employers have more detailed and elaborate procedures than these minima. This section considers the implications of this Act for grievance and discipline procedures, and in addition presents a wider context because in issues of this sort HR managers need to know enough to speak with some authority.

GRIEVANCE

A grievance usually arises because an aggrieved individual regards some management decision (or act of indecision) or behaviour on the part of another employee (normally a manager) as unfair and unjust in its application to him or her. Grievances can be extremely serious, such as a sexual assault or a severe safety hazard. They may be less serious in totality but of serious concern to the employee, such as a new shift rota, a failure to consider for promotion, a critical appraisal report, a lack of opportunity for overtime or too much pressure of work. The types of grievance respondents mentioned to the 1998 and 2004 Workplace and Employment Relations Survey are provided in Table 42.

Most minor grievance and disciplinary matters can be dealt with in the day-to-day informal contact between employees and management, and in some respects this is perhaps the best way of dealing with them. There is something to be said for keeping things informal – the cost of formal hearings and the way that they 'raise the stakes' on the issue are two significant points here. However, there is also something to be said for formal procedures because these procedures enable everyone concerned to know exactly where they stand. For more serious cases, the Employment Act 2002 therefore sets out two statutory grievance procedures: standard and modified.

Table 42 Most common grievances raised in WERS 1998 and 2004

Grievance	Workplaces % 1998	Workplaces % 2004
Pay and conditions	25	18
Poor relations with supervisors, line managers	16	16
Work practices, pace of work	14	12
Working time, annual leave or time off work	13	10
Physical working conditions, health and safety	12	10
Promotion, career development	14	8
Bullying at work	3	7
Job grading or classification	13	6
Use of disciplinary sanctions, including dismissal	–	5
Performance appraisal	7	4
Sexual harassment	3	2
Selection for redundancies	–	2
Relations with other employees	–	2
Sex or race discrimination	3	1
Racial harassment	1	1
No grievances raised formally in past 12 months	44	53

Source: Kersley *et al* (2006)

The *standard procedure* has the following three steps:

● Step 1: the employee informs the employer of the grievance in writing

● Step 2: they meet to discuss the grievance

● Step 3: an appeal, if requested, is held.

The *modified procedure* is intended to apply where a dismissal has already occurred and comprises two steps:

● Step 1: the employee must set out the grievance and the basis of it in writing and send the statement or a copy to the employer

● Step 2: the employer must set out its response in writing and send the statement or a copy to the employee.

All grievance procedures, then, aim to ensure that the employee's case is heard quickly, that the employee concerned has a fair hearing with an opportunity for full discussion to take place, and that a response from management follows without too long a gap. The procedure should make clear to whom the grievance is to be addressed, who should accompany employees if they require somebody to help them in the process, and specific time limits for the meeting to be held and the decision given, plus the stages of any appeal. This really does mean at all times that people 'know where they stand'.

The right to appeal is important, and it must be noted here that the legal principle of natural justice requires that the person who hears the appeal should not be the person who previously heard the case at an earlier stage in the procedure. If this is not the case, the appeal may well not be regarded as valid at an employment tribunal and the employer is likely to lose this aspect of any case.

Failure to address grievances can be a serious matter and cause problems with motivation or demotivation – failure to address issues often leaves employees with 'residual anger' which can escalate into general unrest and disputes in the workplace. Thus, employees must know to whom they can turn in the event of a grievance and the support, such as counselling or sources of advice, that is available to them. Likewise, all line and senior managers must be familiar with their organisation's grievance procedure. HR managers need to impress this on line managers, and training can often be a useful way of doing this. Meanwhile, individuals should be encouraged to discuss ordinary, day-to-day issues informally with their line manager. This helps concerns to be heard and responded to as soon as possible.

The key risk for HR practitioners is not following the organisation's own procedures. It is this that most commonly causes employers to lose cases at employment tribunals. Perhaps more importantly, however, it can bring the procedures themselves into disrepute since employees are likely to notice breaches of procedure. Having procedures brought into disrepute is not likely to be positive for the HR department.

DISCIPLINE

One major consequence of employing people is that there must be a series of rules which regulates their behaviour. In many cases, disciplinary procedures are used to ensure compliance with these rules and a controlled and effective employee performance. This can, however, be one of the most difficult issues with which a manager has to deal because it brings to close attention matters relating to an individual's performance/capability and conduct.

In the first instance, all employers are likely to encounter some difficulties with the performance and capability of some of their employees (although such difficulties might derive from insufficient training and support). It is therefore good practice that such issues are addressed informally by managers via discussions which clarify what good performance 'looks like' and include goal-setting, support and timely positive feedback. Only when these options have been exhausted and where there is no alternative should managers enter a more formal disciplinary procedure.

In the second instance, employee conduct – or rather more accurately, *mis*conduct – could range from continued lateness or a failure to follow a reasonable management instruction through to theft, fighting and the committing of a more serious criminal offence. The most serious offences may constitute gross misconduct in the meaning of the disciplinary procedure, in which case the employee has clearly indicated that he or she has gone beyond the bounds of the contract and the employer has the right to instantly dismiss the employee. 'Gross misconduct' is a problematic term, however, in that there are often no solid safeguards that ensure that the allegation is actually proven. To draw an analogy: if someone is accused of a serious offence that may be punished with a serious penalty, the accusation is not tested according to *lower* standards of proof in a court of law. So for managers it is important to ensure that allegations are subjected to reasonably full investigation before dismissal. 'Gross misconduct' allegations are for this reason occasionally misused by managers seeking to impose strong penalties with little use of time-consuming procedures. HR managers must therefore monitor such situations closely, because their misuse can lead to demotivation on the part of those employees not disciplined who feel that a colleague has been treated unfairly and fear that the same could happen to them.

With misdemeanours, which are lesser offences, there is no right of dismissal for a first offence so warnings are the appropriate penalty. The practical distinction between gross misconduct and misdemeanours is, however, a delicate one and the boxes below provide a list of actions that would normally fall into either of the categories.

Examples of misdemeanours	**Examples of gross misconduct**
• Time-keeping not up to the required standard	• Fighting
• Attendance not up to the required standard	• Working under the influence of drink or drugs
• Performance not up to the required standard	• Giving confidential information to competitors
• Inappropriate attitude towards management, fellow employees, customers or suppliers	• Theft
	• Fraud
	• Sexual harassment
	• Deliberately damaging the organisation's property

As part of their employment, employees need to know what actions or lack of actions can lead to a formal disciplinary process being initiated, and ultimately, if serious enough, dismissal. Disciplinary practices, ranging from oral warnings to the termination of the employment relationship, aim to make employees' behaviour predictable and for those employers and managers with an autocratic style there is a framework of legal rights regulating the disciplinary process. Thus, disciplinary procedures are necessary:

● so that employees know what is expected of them in terms of standards of performance or conduct (and the likely consequences of continued failure to meet these standards)

● to identify obstacles to individuals' achieving the required standards (for example, training needs, lack of clarity of job requirements, lack of timely support) and to identify appropriate action to be taken

- as an opportunity to agree suitable goals and time-scales for improvement in an individual's performance or conduct

- as a point of reference for an employment tribunal should an employee make a complaint about the way he or she was dismissed

- to provide employees with clear guidance on what is acceptable in the workplace in terms of both behaviour and performance.

One of the main problems HR managers often encounter with these procedures is that different line managers see things differently, and as a result employees are not dealt with equitably across the organisation. That is, one employee receives a severe penalty in one case but another employee elsewhere receives a lesser penalty for what is essentially an identical case. A way of dealing with this is to maintain good, detailed records of cases and their outcomes.

Overall, a fair and effective disciplinary procedure is one that concentrates on improving or changing behaviour, rather than one that relies on the principle of punishment. It usually operates by a system of warnings – and an organisation's policy should outline exactly what warnings will be given and when. The following, in order of severity, are the most commonly used warnings:

- a formal oral warning (of which a record is kept)

- a first written warning

- a final written warning.

Any warning should specify a review period during which the individual receives appropriate support and during which his or her performance can be monitored. Similarly, a decision must also be made in relation to the length of time warnings will remain in place. This is sometimes called a 'slate clean' clause. The reason for this is that if it is too short a time, the employer runs the risk of achieving only short-term changes in behaviour. Yet if it is a long time, a sanction that remains on an employee's record for an excessive period of time relative to the original breach of discipline can act as a demotivating influence. Typical time-scales for the continued 'validity' of the three types of warning are:

- a formal oral warning: six months

- a first written warning: one year

- a final written warning: two years.

Where misconduct has been very serious, it may be appropriate for the warning to continue in force indefinitely.

More generally, employers have to be sure that any decision to dismiss an employee will be seen as 'reasonable' by an employment tribunal. Managers must be able to show that they have acted reasonably having regard to all the circumstances. As noted above, the employer must have followed the statutory and any other procedures in the organisation's procedural system prior to any dismissal and also have been fair. Other reasons employees might be dismissed include:

- they are employed under a fixed-term contract and that contract comes to an end without being renewed

- they are made redundant

- they lack the capability and qualifications to do the job – this covers the area of poor performance or the lack or loss of a necessary qualification

- they are in breach of statutory provision – such as the lack of a work permit or security clearance in parts of the public sector

- some other substantial reason – this covers areas such as making a false statement on their application form.

An individual is entitled to be accompanied by a work colleague or trade union official at formal disciplinary and grievance interviews, and for that purpose to select a companion of his or her choice. It is important to note that the right to be accompanied applies to every individual, not just union members, and it is of no consequence whether the organisation recognises unions or not.

REFLECTIVE ACTIVITY

List several employee actions/events each of what you think constitutes a) a misdemeanour and b) gross misconduct.

What disciplinary measures do you think are justified for the examples of grievance, misdemeanour and gross misconduct you have listed?

KEY ISSUES: EMPLOYMENT RELATIONS

We now pull together key points about the main issues raised in this chapter:

- Collective relations with employees remain important in many parts of the economy and large companies.

- Collective organisation of employees can bring benefits for companies as well as the employees.

- Trade unions are one important form of employee organisation, but not the only one. Employers also have to follow the law in consulting with employees by other methods.

- Relations with employee bodies can be partnership-based and need not be confrontational.

- HR managers have to be aware of the possibility of trade union recognition claims and how they operate.

- Following grievance and disciplinary procedures is vital for HR professionals, because the alternative is employment tribunals and court cases.

Perhaps there are other key points that you would like to note for yourself.

MAIN CASE STUDY

Look at the description of the case set out below. Then decide on the recommendations that you would make as an HR manager for dealing with the issues raised. Try to think beyond the level of a 'quick fix' or simple solutions by developing a longer-term strategy as well as responding to the immediate issue.

A large City financial services firm employs large numbers of very well-paid financial services staff in its plush offices in Canary Wharf in London. It has outsourced its office cleaning to a firm of contract cleaners. Most of the cleaning staff work when the offices are empty (or nearly empty, since some of the financial staff work very late and sometimes into the night). The contract cleaning staff come from many countries of the world. In fact, very few of the dozens of cleaners are British and almost all of them are women.

Recently, a Union sent a young organiser to work at the contract cleaners, and this young woman has interested many of the contract cleaning staff in joining the union. There are many grievances among the cleaners. Some allege that they are not being paid the National Minimum Wage because they are often asked to do more hours than they are actually paid for. If they refuse to do them, they can lose their jobs. Some of the cleaners also make allegations of sexual harassment. These allegations have been taken up by the union organiser with the contract cleaning company, but the company's representatives have said that they want nothing to do with the union and will not recognise it.

The large City firm was picketed by the Union one morning. The demonstrators handed out leaflets explaining the situation to City workers coming to work in the morning, and have attracted a good deal of press publicity. The firm is now embarrassed by the bad publicity, which has had even more impact than it otherwise might have done because the company has recently lost a high-profile case of its own involving a young woman stockbroker who won considerable damages because of the sexual harassment she suffered at the hands of male stockbrokers. The company is now in a dilemma. Although it has outsourced the cleaning work, it sees only problems coming from this direction in the future. Whatever the contract cleaners think, they find themselves in the position of having to try to get it to deal with the allegations made by the union.

Questions for discussion

1 What lessons do you think this case study holds for HR professionals in the financial services company?

2 What actions should the company take?

EXPLORE FURTHER

ACAS provides a wealth of up-to-date information concerning best practice employment relations. Its website is: **http://www.acas.org.uk**

The Involvement and Participation Association (IPA) is a centre of excellence for organisations developing world-class strategies for employee involvement and partnership. Its online searchable database provides free and instant access to over 150 examples of workplace partnership, over 100 examples of employee consultation arrangements, and over 550 other entries dedicated to employee involvement and participation in the workplace. Its website is:
http://www.ipa-involve.com/

KERSLEY, B., ALPIN, C., FORTH, J., DIX, G., OXENBRIDGE, S., BRYSON, A., and BEWLEY, H., (2006) *Inside the Workplace: Findings from the 2004 Workplace Employment Relations Survey.* London, Taylor & Francis
The Work Employment Relations Survey (2004) provides a wealth of information concerning the state of employee relations in Britain.

The Information and Consultation of Employee Regulations 2004 (2004)
SI 2004/3426. London, Stationery Office. Available online at:
http://www.opsi.gov.uk/si/si2004/ 20043426.htm
Provides full details of the Information and Consultation of Employee Regulations 2004.

CHAPTER 18

Health and safety at work

Phil James

INTRODUCTION

This chapter is about the importance of managing health and safety at work effectively, and how such management can be achieved. It is a subject all HR professionals should understand because it strongly affects employee welfare and an organisation's costs, and cannot therefore simply be left to specialists.

LEARNING OUTCOMES

By the end of this chapter readers should be able to:

- explain why an organisation should see the issue of health and safety at work as a central part of its people management activities

- identify the main causes of workplace injuries and ill-health

- put an effective health and safety management system in place, and

- build into such a system legally required arrangements for workforce involvement in the identification and resolution of workplace health and safety issues.

The starter case study is followed by three sections which explore, in turn, the extent of work-related injuries and ill-health and the costs that organisations incur as a result of such harm, some of the main factors that cause such harm, how employers can adopt a systematic approach to the management of workplace health and safety, and the arrangements that organisations must put in place with regard to workforce consultation and more general involvement in health and safety matters. The chapter concludes with the main case study which focuses attention on the management of stress – one of the most important sources of work-related ill-health.

Reference sources named within the chapter may be looked up in the *References and further reading* section at the end of the book.

STARTER CASE STUDY

An experienced mechanical fitter was asked by her employer to remove the motor from an extractor fan located five minutes' walk from her department – a task which involved unscrewing the nuts on two rows of bolts. During this work the fitter, who had worked for this firm for 10 years, discovered that one of the nuts could not be unscrewed. She therefore decided to remove the nut by wedging a chisel between it and the bolt in order to create tension between them so that one could be turned without the other. However, when she tried to do this, by inserting the chisel and striking it with a hammer, a piece of metal flew into her right eye; she was not wearing protective goggles.

The employee knew that the risk of such an injury existed when hammering metal on metal, a task that she undertook on an almost daily basis. She also knew that although goggles had not been supplied to her as an individual, they were available on a communal basis in the department where she was based.

Questions for discussion

1 To what extent was the employee involved in this incident responsible for its happening?

2 Did the accident occur partly because of weaknesses in how health and safety was managed in the workplace?

3 What actions could management take to prevent a similar event from occurring in the future?

1   THE IMPORTANCE OF HEALTH AND SAFETY AT WORK

The scale of injuries and ill-health arising from work activities around the world is large. In 2005 there were 199 deaths in South African mines, but in China's mines the rate of deaths per tonne of coal mined is four times as high as in South Africa. Around 300 British workers die each year as a result of accidents, according to official statistics, and this figure does not include those deaths arising from road transport accidents that take place during employment (HSE, 2006). Survey data also suggests that around 1 million workers annually suffer an accident at work, and that there are currently over 2 million people in Britain who consider themselves to be suffering from a health condition caused or made worse by their work. By far the most common of these health conditions are not 'traditional' occupational diseases but musculo-skeletal disorders (MSDs) and stress, depression and anxiety.

It is clear, therefore, that health and safety problems can arise not only among manual workers and those working in 'heavy' industries, such as construction, mining and manufacturing, but also in non-manual occupations, and in private and public sector service organisations. In fact, those employed in the health and social work, public administration, and education sectors are among those that are most likely to report that their health has been damaged as a result of work.

Health and safety is therefore an issue of relevance to all organisations. It is also one that has potentially significant cost implications for employers. According to the British Health and Safety Executive over 20 million working days are lost each year through absences arising from occupational injuries and ill-health, and a further 300 million days' work activities are in some way limited by work-related health conditions. More generally, it has been found that accidents can incur considerable costs for organisations, including the management time spent on their investigation and payments on sick pay, the replacement or repair of damaged equipment and the employment of temporary staff to cover for those absent as a result of their injuries. It has been found that in one hospital these costs amounted to the equivalent of 5% of its total operating expenditure, and that in the case of a transport company they represented 37% of its annual profits.

These costs exist alongside potential legal liabilities. Two main sources of such liability exist: that arising from personal injury litigation brought by those harmed by their work activities, and that arising from non-compliance with legal health and safety duties (James and Walters, 2005).

Personal injury litigation involves common law actions for compensation, or what are legally called 'damages'. British law, like US law, is different from that in many other countries. There is 'common law' – ie law made by judges that has built up through decisions in the past – and statute law enacted by Parliament.

Legal actions under common law may be taken on the grounds that an employer has been negligent – that is, it has failed to comply with its common-law duty to take reasonable steps to protect employees from reasonably foreseeable risks. They may also take the form of actions for breach of statutory duty and involve claims for compensation based on the fact that an employer did not comply with a relevant duty and that this failure contributed directly to the harm suffered by an employee. Any compensation awarded as a result of either of these two types of action is usually paid by insurance companies because employers are legally required to purchase employers' liability insurance to cover it. Insurance premiums may rise if claims are made by employers.

Not carrying out their statutory health and safety duties can lead to employers' being served with Improvement Notices which require them, within a specified period of time, to make changes, or Prohibition Notices which stop them from carrying out activities involving a risk of serious personal injury or ill-health. They can also result in their being prosecuted before magistrates or, on indictment, in the Crown Court.

The statutory duties on which failure can bring these penalties and actions are extensive. The central ones take the form of general duties under the Health and Safety at Work (HSW) Act 1974. These require employers to ensure, so far as reasonably practicable, the health, safety and welfare of employees and similarly to protect all those who may be affected by the conduct of their undertaking, including non-employees and members of the public (Gunningham and Johnstone, 2000; James and Walters, 2005). Employers are also prohibited from charging employees for anything provided in order to protect them in pursuance of statutory requirements – a prohibition that, for example, applies to any protective equipment and clothing so provided.

These general duties are supplemented by an extensive range of duties contained in a large number of supporting regulations made under the 1974 Act, such as the Control of Substances Hazardous to Health Regulations 2002, the Health and Safety (Display Screen Equipment) Regulations 1992, the Control of Noise at Work Regulations 2005, the Workplace (Health, Safety and Welfare) Regulations 1992, the Personal Protective Equipment Regulations 1992, the Provision and Use of Work Equipment Regulations 1998, the Manual Handling

Operations Regulations 1992 and the Management of Health and Safety at Work Regulations 1999. The last of these sets of Regulations are of particular importance. Among other things, they require employers to:

- carry out, record and revise risk assessments in respect of both employees and non-employees

- appoint competent persons – that is, those possessing suitable skills, qualifications and competences – to provide management with health and safety assistance

- establish procedures for handling situations involving 'serious and imminent danger'

- provide various types of information for employees, fixed-term employees, non-employees and temporary workers

- supply various types of information to visiting employers and other employers sharing the same workplace and employment businesses, and

- give adequate training to employees.

These same Regulations also impose a number of specific duties on employers in relation to the protection of young workers and new or expectant mothers.

THE CAUSES OF WORKPLACE INJURIES AND ILL-HEALTH

A huge range of factors can lead to workers' suffering harm as a result of their work. An insight into some of the more important of them can be obtained by looking at those that are commonly associated with the occurrence of workplace accidents, work-related stress and MSDs.

Accidents

The most common sources of accidents are, on the face of it, fairly straightforward, including slips and trips, falls from a height or on the same level, being struck by a falling or moving object, and handling, lifting or carrying. The causes of them are, on the other hand, not necessarily straightforward since they can include a number of contributing elements. As a result, a distinction can often be drawn between the immediate event that 'triggers' or gives rise to an accident and more distant, but nevertheless important, causal factors (Turner and Pidgeon, 1997).

A clear illustration of this last point is the Clapham Junction railway disaster, which happened in 1988 and resulted in the death of 35 people and the injury of nearly 500 others (Hutter, 2001). The immediate cause was the failure of a worker, carrying out rewiring in a signal box, to remove a redundant wire from the fuse to a signal and cut back the other end of it so it could not come into contact with the electrical relay serving the fusebox concerned. The outcome of this was that when the wire was dislodged during later work it came into contact with the relay, and the signal, rather than staying at red while another train was on the stretch of track it regulated, therefore turned to green, causing another train to enter the same stretch and crash into the one already on it.

On detailed investigation, it was found that this failure by the worker had occurred against the background of a number of weaknesses in the structure and operation of the surrounding system of health and safety management. These weaknesses included:

- the fact that the worker had been allowed to work in the same way for some time without anybody telling him that it was incorrect
- a lack of clarity as to who in the supervisory and management structure was responsible for checking that his work had been done properly
- a failure to give him adequate training in correct working methods
- the time-scale for carrying out the overhaul of re-signalling in the area – an overhaul of which the worker's work formed part – that required high levels of overtime working (he himself had, in the three months prior to the accident, had just one day off work).

In short, what the Clapham disaster shows is that the causes of accidents can be multi-dimensional and that care must be taken to avoid too readily jumping to the conclusion that the event which immediately gives rise to them – say, a worker error – is the only, or even primary, cause of it. (This is a point that the earlier starter case study hopefully highlighted in the context of a rather more routine incident.)

Research done into the reasons underlying worker deviations from laid-down safety rules and procedures reinforces this point by showing that the factors causing such deviations can include (Turner and Pidgeon, 1997):

- time pressures
- an incompatibility between laid-down procedures and required work activities
- a desire by workers to carry out work tasks in a way which avoids or relieves boredom
- operational pressures stemming from production and broader financial considerations, including those associated with piecework payment systems intended to encourage workers to produce more and which cause supervisors to ignore, and even encourage, unsafe work practices.

Many factors can therefore contribute to the occurrence of an accident. Failures on the part of workers can clearly play an important role. So too, though, can broader management ones such as inadequate training and supervision, the use of poorly maintained and installed equipment, the imposing of excessive workloads, and the poor design of work tasks and processes – to name just a few.

Stress

Stress can give rise to behavioural responses that have negative implications for both the individuals affected and their employing organisations (Stansfeld *et al*, 1999). These responses can include increased alcohol consumption and smoking, drug use, poor eating habits, irritability and aggression, an inability to concentrate (resulting in 'presenteeism'), absence from work, and domestic conflict. (See also Chapter 11 on absenteeism.)

Some of these responses can have adverse health consequences for workers as a result of the physiological changes they cause (Cox *et al*, 2000). Amongst these outcomes are bronchitis, coronary heart disease, mental illness, thyroid disorders, obesity, peptic ulcers and certain forms of rheumatoid arthritis, skin diseases and diabetes.

Today, stress is most commonly conceptualised from a psychological perspective and as an outcome of some form of imbalance between the work environment and the physical and psychological characteristics of workers (Cox *et al*, 2000). Several aspects of the working environment have been identified as potentially contributing to this imbalance (Anderson-Connolly *et al*, 2002; Taylor *et al*, 2003). Some of the more important of these are:

- lack of control over work tasks
- negative work relationships, including bullying behaviour on the part of managers and other work colleagues
- inadequate information and support from colleagues and managers
- lack of role clarity and the perception of role conflict
- poor work–life balance
- excessive work demands arising, for example, from overly long working hours and too high workloads
- unchallenging work tasks
- poor management of change, often through failing to adequately consult staff and provide them with information on the changes taking place (see Chapter 19).

Also, the above factors can combine together in a negative way to increase the likelihood that stress occurs. A number of research studies have found stress to be particularly associated with a combination of high work demand and low task control.

It must be recognised, as pointed out earlier, that the precise impact that such factors have is influenced by the characteristics of those exposed to them – notably the nature of their personality and the emotional, coping, resources they are able to draw on. For example, some studies suggest that people who have a strong commitment to work and a high level of involvement in their job, a strong sense of urgency and a high degree of competitiveness are more vulnerable to work-related stress.

The role that these individual factors play draws attention to the fact that the management of work-related stress can include not only preventive strategies of the type discussed later but also 'secondary' ones aimed at increasing the ability of individual workers to cope better with their work situation through counselling and other support services, including training in the identification of stress symptoms and the management of stress. Such support is provided in some organisations via what are often called employee assistance programmes (EAPs) that provide not only access to stress counselling but also such forms of support as financial planning advice and 'marriage' guidance.

Musculo-skeletal disorders

Musculo-skeletal disorders (MSDs) are conditions that affect muscles, joints, tendons and other parts of the musculo-skeletal system. They therefore include low back pain, joint injuries and repetitive strain injuries of various types. MSDs can occur as a result of any activity that involves some movement of the body, including typing, lifting and repetitive manual activities, and so may arise among those working in a wide range of occupations and sectors. The likelihood of their occurring, however, is influenced not only by the nature of the work tasks done but also by the physical and psychological characteristics of workers and aspects of the work environment within which tasks are carried out (Buckle and Devereux, 1999). They can therefore be the outcome of the interaction that occurs between these three sets of factors, rather than just the nature of the work undertaken.

Certain types of work tasks have, nevertheless, been found to be particularly associated with the onset of MSDs. Those tasks include repeating the same sequence of movements many times (as may happen in production-line situations and in the case of high-speed data entry work), lifting or moving heavy loads, twisting or stooping when lifting or moving such loads, working with hands at or above shoulder height, exerting considerable force (as when pushing or pulling heavy items), repeated gripping and releasing between finger and palm, and, more generally, working at a fast pace. As a result, some of the forms of work that are particularly likely to give rise to MSDs are manufacturing assembly activities, packing or sorting components or products, driving, machine operations and keyboard work.

The strength and fitness of workers can act to increase or reduce the potentially harmful effects of some of these work tasks. The same is true of the degree of stress they are under, because muscular tension increases the likelihood that the effects will cause damage. It therefore follows from this last point that the type of psychosocial factors already identified as contributing to workers' suffering stress – such as high job demands, low task control and time pressures – can also play a role in the occurrence of MSDs. Other contributing factors include working in overly hot or cold temperatures, the former acting to increase the degree of physical effort that has to be expended on a task and the latter, in common with stress, reducing muscular flexibility; carrying out tasks in confined or otherwise unsuitable physical environments; and working too long and without adequate breaks.

REFLECTIVE ACTIVITY

Think of a job you have either done yourself or have observed.

In the light of the above sections of text, list the potential sources of risk to worker health and safety involved in it.

(The text suggested that such sources might be related to the personal characteristics of workers, the nature of the work tasks and processes they are engaged on, and aspects of the broader organisational environment within which they are employed.)

2 THE MANAGEMENT OF HEALTH AND SAFETY

The above review of some of the main causes of accidents, stress and MSDs has highlighted that their prevention can require employees to undertake a wide range of different types of preventive activities. In the case of accidents, for example, it points to the fact that these activities can include:

● the safe installation of plant and equipment, as well as their adequate maintenance

● the provision of preventive 'hardware', including machine guards and ventilation systems

● the appropriate design of work tasks and processes

● the clear communication of safety rules and procedures

● the adequate supervision of worker compliance with these rules and procedures

● the provision of training for workers and line managers on work-related risks and the actions necessary to control them.

In addition, and more generally, the review has highlighted the fact that accidents, stress and MSDs can be reduced by creating work environments, tasks and processes that are more compatible with the physical and psychological characteristics and capabilities of workers by, for example, making sure that:

● working hours are not excessive

● work pressures are not overly demanding

● manual handling tasks do not require the physical lifting or moving of too heavy loads.

It is now widely accepted that such preventive activities are likely to be most effectively undertaken as part of a systematic approach to the management of workplace risks containing the following central elements (Dawson *et al*, 1998; Health and Safety Executive, 1997):

● comprehensive assessment of workplace risks and the related identification of those that must be better controlled

● identification of the methods through which this control can be obtained, with priority given to removing risks and use being made of alternative solutions, such as the provision of protective equipment or the laying down of new rules and procedures

● the development of mechanisms such as training, giving relevant information and the laying down of required rules and procedures, to enable the effective implementation of these solutions

● the adoption of adequate arrangements to monitor and review the effectiveness of the control measures put in place.

Consequently, it is argued that what is needed is a dynamic – rather than a static, once-for-all – approach to health and safety management in which the adequacy of existing control measures undergoes a continuous process of monitoring and, where needed, subsequent adjustment. Such monitoring can be done in two ways: firstly, through the use of various 'output' measures which show how far the existing health and safety system has been successful in preventing (or not preventing) worker ill-health and injury; secondly, through the use of 'process' methods aimed at assessing the adequacy and operation of the health and safety arrangements in place. These are now examined in turn.

In relation to output measures, a number of different indices can be used to measure the scale of work-related harm caused by work activities. These include employee sickness absence records, occupational health records (including first-aid treatments and the results of health assessments), self-report data provided by workers, and accident statistics.

Commonly, these last statistics are used to calculate accident rates that (a) provide a way of tracking trends in accident performance that are not due to variations in hours worked or numbers employed, and (b) enable an understanding of variations in the severity of the injuries caused. Three of the most commonly used of these are accident frequency rates, accident incident rates and accident severity rates. These are calculated on the following bases:

Accident frequency rate

$$= \frac{\text{Total number of accidents}}{\text{Total number of person hours worked}} \times 1{,}000{,}000$$

ie accidents per 1,000,000 hours worked

Accident incident rate

$$= \frac{\text{Total number of accidents}}{\text{Total number of persons employed}} \times 1{,}000$$

ie accidents per 1,000 employees

Accident severity rate

$$= \frac{\text{Total number of days lost}}{\text{Total number of person-hours worked}} \times 1{,}000$$

ie the average number of days lost per 1,000 hours worked.

Accident statistics therefore not only provide a potentially valuable source of information on overall and comparative standards of safety performance but also can be used to spot areas of activity where remedial action is needed. At the same time, a potentially important limitation of them is that, by definition, they only relate to 'undesirable' events that have actually resulted in injury. They exclude from consideration other such events that, perhaps by chance, did not cause harm, and in doing so can potentially give a misleading picture of health and safety performance. It is for this reason that they can usefully be supplemented by the use of process measures that try to proactively assess the degree to which workplace risks are being managed.

Several different techniques can be used to more proactively assess the adequacy and operation of the existing health and safety management system. These include:

● workforce 'safety climate' surveys that give information on the adequacy of current policies, practices and attitudes

- the use of 'hardware' like noise meters to measure worker exposures to particular occupational health hazards, such as noise and fumes

- health surveillance aimed at monitoring whether workers' health is being affected by such exposures

- investigations into the causes of accidents and dangerous occurrences

- inspections and audits which systematically assess whether organisationally required and/or legally acceptable arrangements are in place and are adequately implemented and, more generally, identify areas where improvements must be made.

SYSTEMATIC MANAGEMENT AND STRESS

Work-related stress can be managed following the same systematic approach as that described above. Indeed, the use of such an approach is now encouraged by the Health and Safety Executive (HSE) through its Stress Management Standards. These Standards form part of a five-step risk assessment process which encompasses the identification of hazards, the making of a decision on 'who might be harmed and how', the evaluation of risk and the taking of relevant action, the recording of the assessment findings, and monitoring and review.

An Indicator Tool that can be used to more precisely gauge the extent and nature of the stress problems in an organisation is provided by the HSE, along with guidance on how to use employee focus groups to help find solutions to any problems that are discovered. The Indicator Tool is a self-completion questionnaire that can be given to all employees. Responses from the completed questionnaire can then be analysed through an accompanying Analysis Tool to compute average scores in relation to the Standards the HSE has specified in respect of the following six features of work tasks and environment: demands, control, support, relationships, role, and change (these tools, as well as more general information on the HSE's Stress Management Standards, are available at **http:// www.hse.gov.uk/stress/standards/sitemap.htm**). In this way, the HSE not only enables organisations to obtain an insight into their current situation regarding workforce stress and how far it is satisfactory, but also gives them a way of identifying where remedial action is most needed.

The challenges to systematic management

The value of adopting a systematic approach to health and safety management is clearly affected by the competence with which it is done and hence by the knowledge and skills of those involved in carrying out its central components (Dawson *et al*, 1998) – an issue that can be a source of difficulty in smaller organisations (Walters, 2001). The degree of commitment to health and safety amongst managers, and particularly senior ones, is important to how well these processes are undertaken.

Even if appropriate health and safety precautions are developed, it does not follow that they will be implemented effectively, particularly if no action is taken to define clearly the health and safety responsibilities of line managers and establish systems to hold them accountable for their performance in fulfilling them (Callagher, 2002). Unless there is such accountability, there is a clear danger that compliance with health and safety rules and procedures may suffer in the face of conflicting work pressures and a view that such compliance is of relatively little importance. For example, line managers may encourage workers to ignore safety rules in order to maintain production levels, workers can be tempted to cut corners as a way of protecting or enhancing their earnings, and workers may feel free to get round laid-down working methods in order to avoid the restrictions they impose on them.

In recent years and in recognition of the way in which such factors can adversely affect health and safety performance, increasing attention has been paid to taking actions to improve health and safety cultures or climates through the provision of training (Turner and Pidgeon, 1999). It must, however, be recognised that cultural change is difficult, particularly within a context of poor management support and commitment. Indeed, centrally driven culture change programmes may, by downplaying countervailing workforce views and values, actually generate conflict rather than consensus and therefore ultimately be counterproductive. Consequently, although programmes aimed at creating more positive attitudes to workplace health and safety may bring beneficial results, it is only likely where considerable care is taken with regard to their design and implementation.

REFLECTIVE ACTIVITY

Go online and find a substantial newspaper article that reports a major work-related accident.

In the light of the above sections of text on the management of health and safety, list the managerial factors that may have contributed to the accident's occurrence.

Note that we have here introduced the concept of *ratios* of one job family to another, or of one as a percentage of the whole workforce. These can be more revealing than simple statistics.

(The text suggested that such factors might include inadequacies in existing management systems and weaknesses in their implementation. Do these two categories of factors seem sufficient, in your view, to explain why the accident you have researched took place?)

3 WORKFORCE INVOLVEMENT

It has long been accepted that the involvement of workers in health and safety can make a positive contribution to the establishment of good health and safety standards (Walters and Nichols, 2007). In particular, such involvement is seen to:

- enable the detailed knowledge workers have of work tasks and processes, as well as the broader working environment, to be used to identify risks and what has to be done to control them

- engender worker ownership and support for laid-down preventive arrangements

- provide a platform for workers to voice their health and safety concerns and challenge current management actions.

The importance of workforce involvement to effective health and safety management is underlined by the fact that all employers in Britain are legally required to consult their workforces over health and safety matters. The relevant legal requirements are laid down in two sets of regulations: the Safety Representatives and Safety Committees (SRSC) Regulations 1977 and the Health and Safety (Consultation with Employees) Regulations 1996 (Walters and Nichols, 2007).

Under the SRSC Regulations, an independent trade union is entitled to appoint safety representatives from amongst the employees of an employer by whom it is recognised (see Chapter 17 on employment relations). Once appointed in accordance with the Regulations representatives have to be consulted by employers over a range of matters and are accorded a number of functions which entitle them to:

- investigate potential hazards and dangerous occurrences, and causes of accidents

- investigate complaints relating to an employee's health, safety or welfare at work

- make representations to employers on these and on general matters affecting the health, safety and welfare of employees

- carry out workplace inspections

- represent employees in consultation with health and safety inspectors

- receive information from such inspectors

- attend safety committee meetings.

In addition, safety representatives are entitled to the paid time off that is necessary for them to carry out their functions and to undergo such training as is reasonable in the circumstances. Employers are also obliged to make available information within their knowledge that is similarly necessary and to establish a safety committee, if requested to do so by two or more safety representatives.

The 1996 Regulations impose a duty of consultation on employers in relation to employees not covered by safety representatives appointed under the 1977 ones. This duty is the same as that which applies in the case of union safety representatives. However, employers may choose whether they consult employees directly or via elected representatives, known as representatives of employee safety (RES).

If this representative route is chosen, employers must provide the RES with adequate information for them to fully and effectively participate in consultations and to carry out their functions of making representations and consulting with inspectors. Representatives are also entitled to training, time off, and such other facilities and assistance as they may reasonably require to carry out their functions. However, in contrast to union-appointed safety representatives, they have no rights to carry out workplace inspections, to inspect statutory health and safety documents or to investigate employee complaints and accidents and dangerous occurrences that have to be legally reported. Nor are they able to require the establishment of a safety committee.

Table 43 below provides data, drawn from the Workplace Employment Relations Survey 2004, which shows how far employers do, in practice, consult over health and safety matters and the types of arrangements through which this consultation happens (Kersley *et al*, 2006). This data suggests that virtually all employers do so consult, that consultation is most commonly undertaken via direct, rather than representative, arrangements, and that arrangements of the latter type are more common where one or more unions are recognised.

Table 43 Health and safety consultation arrangements, 2004

Type of arrangements	All workplaces (%)	At least one recognised union (%)
Single or multi-issue joint consultative committees	20	41
Free-standing worker representatives	22	22
Direct methods	57	37
No arrangements	1	0

Base: All workplaces with 10 or more employees
Source: adapted from Kersley *et al* (2006; p.77)

Meanwhile, existing research evidence shows that the effectiveness of consultative arrangements is very much influenced by both the structures and broader organisational environment within which they operate (Walters *et al*, 2005). Research findings on the factors that affect the operation of health and safety committees illustrate this point clearly. For example, they suggest that committees are usually more effective where:

- there is a high level of commitment from employers, particularly through the appointment of at least one senior corporate officer who is able to exercise real authority and implement change in the workplace

- members have the information and knowledge to contribute effectively

- management–worker relationships are good

- worker representation operates through trade union channels.

In addition, committee effectiveness has been found to be influenced by such structural factors as the quality of communications between them and the workforce, the regularity of meetings and attendance at them, and the size of their membership.

REFLECTIVE ACTIVITY

The text in this section has suggested that workforce involvement can play an important role in supporting the effective identification and control of potential risks to worker health and safety.

Now re-read the earlier text section on the causes of work-related injuries and ill-health.

How far do you think that this earlier text provides support for these benefits of workforce involvement?

KEY ISSUES: HEALTH AND SAFETY AT WORK

We now pull together ten key points on health and safety at work as raised in this chapter:

- The scale of work-related injuries and ill-health is large and brings considerable costs on employing organisations, as well as on the economy as a whole.

- MSDs and stress-related conditions are the most common forms of occupational ill-health.

- The causes of accidents are often multi-dimensional and frequently include organisational failures beyond the immediate events that triggered them.

- Although the causes of MSDs and stress-related conditions are varied, their occurrence is often intimately connected to the way in which work activities are designed and managed.

- A failure to adequately manage health and safety can lead to prosecutions and the imposition of Improvement and Prohibition Notices, and also to the award of compensation to those harmed.

- It is widely accepted that a systematic and well implemented approach to the management of workplace health and safety is necessary if it is to be managed effectively.

- Such an approach needs to encompass the assessment of workplace risks and the related identification of those that need to be better controlled.

- Such an approach needs to encompass the determination of the methods through which this control can be obtained, and the development of mechanisms to enable the effective implementation of these solutions.

- Such an approach needs to encompass the adoption of adequate arrangements to monitor and review the effectiveness of the control measures so put in place.

- Worker consultation and representation can make an important contribution to the carrying out of these various processes.

Perhaps there are other key points that you would like to note for yourself.

The main case study in this chapter now follows. It gives an example of the effects of change both on the employees of an organisation and on the organisation itself in terms of productivity and cost-effectiveness caused primarily by health and safety factors.

MAIN CASE STUDY

Look at the description of the case set out below. Then decide on the recommendations that you would make as an HR manager for dealing with the issues raised.

In recent years competition facing this publishing company has been increasing and has impacted negatively on sales and profits. Against this background, senior management have been actively seeking to cut costs and increase efficiency. In the case of the editorial department, a key action taken to increase efficiency has been the purchase of an 'off-the-shelf' and more up-to-date computer system to store and transfer news stories. Meanwhile, in the production department the way in which its various activities are carried out has been changed. This change has entailed a move away from the previously existing system whereby individual staff were mainly responsible for carrying out all of them in relation to particular products to one where they specialise in just one of the department's central tasks – namely, subediting, typesetting or proofreading – a change that has further involved staff working, in a much less intensive way, with a much larger number of editors.

These changes were introduced without any real consultation with staff. They were also introduced in a way which sought to minimise the costs associated with making them. In particular, no adjustments were made to the office furniture of journalists to take account of the larger nature of the new desktop screens that they were now required to use and the implications that this had for the positioning of keyboards and work surface space. Nor was any action taken to develop and circulate detailed operational procedures relating to how production staff were to interface with each other, as well as with magazine editors, while carrying out their new 'sequential' system of working.

In the year that has passed since the changes significant rises in sickness absence and labour turnover have occurred. Much of these increases have, in turn, been found to be attributable to marked increases in the number of staff from both departments reporting stress-related problems and, in the case of the editorial department, an increase

also in musculo-skeletal disorders affecting the lower back, arms, wrists, neck and shoulders. Furthermore, there are signs that the number reporting these conditions is increasing as a consequence of the higher workloads that the staff are bearing because of the increased level of sickness absence.

More generally, there are clear signs that staff morale and job satisfaction has been declining. Amongst journalists, an important factor underlying this decline has been the frustration caused by the new computer system's lack of suitability for use in respect of lengthy features, as opposed to short news items. As regards production staff, the chief factors at work would seem to be the way in which their work has become more repetitive and more vulnerable to disruption because of breakdowns in the flow of work in the new sequential method of working, and a perceived reduction in 'work quality' as a result of being far less able to identify with particular products and build up close working relationships with individual editors.

The upshot of all of this is that the changes made have neither led to the desired reductions in operational costs nor served to increase efficiency. Indeed, costs have actually risen because of the need to recruit and train more new staff as a result of the higher level of turnover, and to pay for more overtime working and to employ temporary staff to cover those on sick leave. These increased costs, moreover, exist alongside a growing concern amongst management that sooner or later they are likely to face legal actions from staff for the damage to health that they have suffered.

Your task

As an HR professional working in this company, prepare a report detailing a) what it should do to address the problems identified above, and b) how it should change its approach to the management of change in order to avoid similar problems occurring in the future.

EXPLORE FURTHER

Dawson, S., Clinton, M., Bamford, M. and Willman, P. (1998) *Safety at Work: The limits of self-regulation*. Cambridge, Cambridge University Press
This book contains detailed case studies which shed light on health and safety management in a number of organisations and pinpoint the factors that influence it.

James, P. and Walters, D. (2005) *Regulating Health and Safety at Work: An agenda for change?* London, Institute of Employment Rights
This report provides an overview and critical analysis of the legal framework for health and safety.

Stansfeld, S., Head, J. and Marmot, M. (1999) *Work-Related Factors and Ill-Health: The Whitehall II study*. Research Report 266. Sudbury: HSE Books. Available online at: **http://www.hse.gov.uk/ research/crr_pdf/2000/crr00266.pdf**
This research report provides a good insight into how aspects of the psychosocial work environment can impact on worker health.

Walters, D., Nichols, T., Connor, J., Tasiran, A. and Cam, S. (2005) *The Role and Effectiveness of Safety Representatives in Influencing Workplace Health and Safety*. Research Report 363. Sudbury: HSE Books. Available online at: **http://www.hse.gov.uk/ research/rrhtm/rr363.htm**
This is a detailed study of the operation and impact of arrangements for worker representation in respect of health and safety, and the factors that influence their operation.

CHAPTER 19

Employee communication

Richard Croucher

INTRODUCTION

This chapter is about the HR aspects of communication from management to employees and vice versa.

LEARNING OUTCOMES

By the end of this chapter readers should be able to:

- explain the importance of HR's role in communication to employees in their workplace

- explain the growing significance of communication in British organisations in recent years

- describe the appropriate means of communication for different HR issues

- identify optimal communication methods to and from employees, and explain their potential advantages and difficulties.

The chapter is structured in two parts.

After the starter case study we define what exactly we mean by communication and discuss why it is important. Next, we look at the role of HR professionals in communication. Then we present some information on how British companies are making increasing use of communication to employees. We follow this with a section about who is communicating about what and with whom. In a third section of Part 1 we deal with an important new development in HR – that of communicating electronically with employees.

Part 2 discusses the potential advantages and difficulties involved in different forms of communication from employees: suggestion schemes, employee surveys and employee forums. This brings us to our main case study, which is about HR's role in trying to communicate with people doing work for the organisation but who are not directly employed by it.

STARTER CASE STUDY

The case study organisation is a financial services company in the City of London employing several thousand people. The best-paid employees are the salesmen directly involved in selling financial products to consumers, but these only constitute about 30% of the workforce. Most employees are 'back office' staff processing the business initiated by the salesmen; a majority of them are women, almost all of them less well paid than the mostly male salesmen. The company does not find it especially easy to recruit or retain staff in the 'back office' because although they are not especially highly skilled, there are reasonable opportunities for them to move on to work in other central London companies.

On 6 April 2003, working parents in the UK with young or disabled children gained the legal right to request flexible working arrangements; their employers acquired a statutory duty to give these requests serious consideration. The company HR director advised the board's employment subcommittee before the legislation became effective that although the legislation was intended for the parents of young children, this might prove rather divisive and demotivating for non-parents and that therefore consideration should be given to extending the right to all employees. However, this was rejected – operational managers were afraid that this would lead to a flood of requests and the company simply announced in the company newsletter for employees that it would follow the law.

In the event, after April 2003 many parents of young children – concentrated in the 'back office' – requested the right to work flexibly from their operational managers. The applications were dealt with by operational managers in consultation with HR. Several difficulties arose. Operational managers noticed, however, that employees thought that they had a right to work flexibly rather than (in fact, in law) a right to *request* to work flexibly. Secondly, a number of salesmen complained to their managers that they, too, wanted the right to work flexibly because at least parts of their work could be done at home. Thirdly, older people in the 'back office' put the same argument as that put by the salesmen.

The result in the spring and summer of 2003 was increased turnover throughout the central London operation, as employees felt that they were not getting their legal rights or saw that other companies had in fact extended the right to all employees.

Question for discussion

What can be learned from this real-life case study?

Readers should note that there are several important aspects of communication that we do not deal with in this chapter because they are tackled in depth in other chapters. So, for example, we do not deal with communications with prospective employees, nor do we deal with important types of communication with employees such as appraisals (see instead Chapter 12). A third very relevant subject dealt with elsewhere is that of communication to and from employee representatives (see Chapter 17). Nor do we deal with the important but different subject of communication *between* employees – an aspect that is closely related to organisational culture.

Reference sources named within the chapter may be looked up in the *References and further reading* section at the end of the book.

1 COMMUNICATION TO EMPLOYEES

WHAT EXACTLY DO WE MEAN BY 'COMMUNICATION'?

Everyone has their own 'common-sense' definition of 'communication'. But for the purposes of this chapter we must define it more precisely. We therefore define communication as a two-way process: it is communication by management *to* employees, and communication *from* employees to management.

In this chapter, we focus on the first aspect, communication *to* employees (sometimes known as 'downward' communication) in Part 1, and on communication *from* employees (sometimes known as 'upward' communication) in Part 2. Having said that, the distinction between the two is for convenience only because in the end most communication is really two-way. So, for example, briefings to employees about issues often provide opportunities for questions and feedback (Marchington, Wilkinson, Ackers and Dundon, 2001).

Managers have to communicate with employees all the time at work. It is impossible to imagine them doing their jobs without talking to the employees that they work with. Plentiful communication with employees has been shown to be linked to good company performance (Pfeffer, 1998). There are therefore both relatively informal as well as more formal communications to be considered under our general heading of 'communication'. Smaller companies often rely on informal methods and have few, if any, formal methods of communicating with employees, which they may perceive as 'bureaucratic'. In some cases, they prefer to encourage social events such as going to the pub for promoting mutual communication (Marchington, Wilkinson, Ackers and Dundon, 2001). In this chapter, although we do touch on informal channels, we deal mainly with the more formal methods. This does not mean that informal communications are unimportant (which is clearly not the case).

There are two reasons for our focus:

- First, formalised communications practices are linked to a positive 'psychological contract' between organisations and employees (see Chapter 11). This may be why they are also linked to high performance.

- Second, most organisations have a degree of formalisation in their practices, because not everyone wants to go to the pub with their manager.

In addition, we examine HR's role in advising and training other managers in communication – something that is relevant even where there are no formal communications practices.

More formal communication can take different forms, deal with different subjects, and be done by different groups of people and aimed at different groups within the workforce. These differences are an important theme of this chapter.

'Downward' communication (ie from management to employees) spans a number of different practices including:

- workforce briefings for all or part of the workforce on key issues

- quality circles, regular meetings with all or part of the workforce

- appraisal interviews

- newsletters, electronic circulars and DVDs

- electronic communication.

As noted above, some of these 'downward' methods may also involve some 'upward' communication (Marchington, Wilkinson, Ackers and Dundon, 2001). For example, appraisal interviews, workforce briefings or electronic communication may all also involve employees voicing their views.

'Upward' forms of communication (ie from employees to management) also include a number of different practices, such as:

- employee attitude surveys

- suggestion schemes

- employee forums

- project teams.

KEY ISSUES IN COMMUNICATION

There are a number of key issues in communication with employees. We summarise these under six main headings:

- *Subject*: What is communicated is perhaps the most important issue of all. Some information is regarded as sensitive. This is closely related to the issue of 'depth' (see below).

- *Quality*: This can also be subdivided into two aspects:

    - how good the information is, and especially how coherent

    - how credible it is. Bear in mind that some issues are both matters of debate and opinion and also vitally important to employees – information about employees' pensions, for example.

    If you recall the starter case study, you might already have thought that part of the problem was that the company did not really explain either the law or its own policy clearly or convincingly enough to employees.

- *Depth*: How many people in the organisation have access to the information? Many organisations now distribute information quite widely among employees. On the other hand, a lot of information is often distributed on a 'confidential' or 'need to know' basis in British organisations, and they have sometimes been criticised for being too restrictive with much information.

- *Timing*: Information may be released too early or too late for different stakeholders. A good example here is redundancy information. Stock market rules prevent listed companies from making internal announcements on this before the stock market is told, because it is 'price-sensitive' information. On the other hand, employees are themselves sensitive when they read about their own redundancy in the newspapers.

- *Receptiveness*: Employees should feel that they are being listened to. Action on their views may or may not be considered a good idea, but employees need feedback on them.

- *Regularity*: Employees learn to trust the communication if it is regular and tells them the good and the not-so-good news. Regular communication means it is less likely that rumours which are quite incorrect circulate in workplaces.

Let us examine some aspects of these key issues a bit more closely at this point. What problems can we foresee? Below, we raise a few issues under these six headings.

Subject

Organisations can send messages to employees only on subjects which they choose to communicate with them. For example, certain information such as commercially important material may not be passed on to certain employees because the organisations do not trust them with it.

Quality

The information may not be consistent with other information employees have. (For example, they may have read sensational articles in newspapers about employment law.)

Employees may simply not believe the information. (For example, on important matters they might only believe the most senior managers.)

There may be too much information so that employees have problems in digesting it.

The issues being communicated about may not in fact have been made clear to employees. Very often, managers think they have explained something whereas in reality employees are still quite unclear about the issues.

Depth

The information may not be fit for its purpose – for example, it may be too detailed and confusing for those it is aimed at. It may, say, have been initially designed as a management circular, re-worked slightly and then circulated to part-time workers.

Timing

Information may be released when leaked information has already reached employees as rumour, and it may then be treated with contempt.

Receptiveness

Employees may voice their ideas but feel that they are not listened to, creating a negative effect amongst them and actually demotivating them.

Regularity

A balance must be struck between giving people information so regularly that they are swamped with it, and too infrequently so that uncertainty arises.

REFLECTIVE ACTIVITY

What issues can you imagine arising in the subject, quality, depth, timing and regularity of information given by management to employees, or in receptiveness to their ideas?

THE ROLE OF HR PROFESSIONALS IN COMMUNICATION

In one sense, communicating with employees is the business of all managers. As we have already said, all managers have to communicate with employees all the time, and much of the communication is informal. In fact, HR professionals frequently see it as their job to communicate with employees (Croucher *et al*, 2006). But the important issue here is that it is the line manager's job, with help and support from HR (see Chapter 20). This help has to be with important, basic issues, and not just with complex ones.

REFLECTIVE ACTIVITY

So what is HR professionals' *particular* role in communicating with employees? Some important roles for HR professionals in communication are listed below. Read through the list and see if you can add to it.

- At the strategic level, the HR director, advised by other HR colleagues, will seek to influence corporate communications policies by advising on such matters as how and when major policy decisions (eg on family-friendly working practices, training policy, redundancies, etc) affecting employees are communicated.

- At the more day-to-day level, HR professionals will act as advisers to individual operational managers on how to communicate to employees on issues such as their pension or legal rights, or alternatively communicate directly with individual employees on such subjects. These matters are of vital importance to employees, for whom areas like pensions and benefits packages are central issues. Getting communication right in these areas is therefore also at the centre of HR professionals' jobs.

- HR professionals sometimes have to advise both senior and operational managers on employees' feelings on different subjects. It is usually HR professionals who are called on to run or at least to source and oversee employee attitude surveys, for example. To some extent, they may also try to act as employee advocates in order to maintain employee commitment and motivation. However, this role is in many ways difficult for HR professionals also trying to be business partners with senior management – they cannot substitute for elected employee representatives, who have less conflicting roles.

For the exercise above you may have added a number of different roles for HR professionals in communication. For example, one important additional role not listed in the exercise is in sourcing inputs from outside experts and/or themselves directly providing briefings for groups of other managers and groups of employees on a range of issues. Additionally, HR professionals are likely to play an important role in building other managers' presentational and communications skills, since operational managers are often appointed mainly for other skills that they have, such as technical capacities. They may not have thought very much about the nature of their exchanges with other employees and may sometimes need help in developing their interpersonal skills more generally. Some may never have asked themselves the important question 'Do my subordinates have reservations about talking to me?' Further, because HR professionals have people issues at the forefront of their minds, they may advise on where and when sensitive meetings such as appraisals or disciplinary meetings might best be held.

Overall, the role is a very significant one for HR professionals at all levels.

COMMUNICATION AS A KEY PART OF HIGH-INVOLVEMENT MANAGEMENT

Few people would deny that employees are at the centre of any organisation's capacities to operate effectively. Equally, it is one of the themes of this book that HRM should play a strategic role in organisations. There is therefore an important role for policies and practices that seek to involve employees in the organisation in a strategic way.

Intensive communication to employees is an important part of 'high-involvement management' (HIM), which seeks to win competitive advantage for the organisation by involving employees intensively in the organisation. Indeed, intensive communication is the cornerstone of HIM. HIM may include some or all of the following:

- first, increased information ('flow') down the organisation
- second, increased information ('flow') up the organisation
- third, changes in job design
- fourth, financial involvement or participation
- fifth, changes in leadership or management style towards a more participative approach.

For readers who want to know more, HIM is a major topic in Pfeffer (1998).

Intensive communication is important for several key reasons. These include:

- Communication by management to employees on certain key issues (organisational strategy and financial issues) has been shown to be linked to superior organisational performance (see Pfeffer, 1998).
- Communication can increase employee commitment to the organisation. Many employees prefer well-structured situations ('I like to know where I am' is often heard in organisations) to uncertainty. Cutting down on uncertainty helps people feel secure and to perform better.

- Inadequate or poor communication to employees can have a demotivating effect on them. Sending mixed messages (in which one statement apparently contradicts another) to employees is a common problem in organisations and means that employees are unclear as to what it is that the organisation wants of them, and what its priorities are.

- Some large companies may insist on it from small suppliers, anxious to ensure that the suppliers meet demanding quality standards.

- Employers may feel that these practices make it easier for them to make themselves an 'employer of choice'. Employees may feel more committed to the company and less inclined to leave it. In respect of certain highly skilled categories of employee, the costs of their leaving are especially high and employers try to minimise the possibility.

 REFLECTIVE ACTIVITY

List any other reasons you can think of for the importance of good communication.

THE INCREASE IN COMMUNICATION IN BRITAIN IN RECENT YEARS

Communication in British organisations has not historically been especially intensive in comparison with organisational communication in some other countries such as Germany (Hall and Soskice, 2001). The increased use of practices to facilitate communication between management and employees in the private sector was, according to a study carried out by Forth and Millward (2002) for the CIPD, one of the more striking developments in employment relations in the 1990s. Table 44 illustrates this by reproducing some of the study's figures. It shows the increased use of different types of communication to employees; two-way communication methods are included, as well as just 'downward' methods. The table highlights a number of quite dramatic developments in the 1990s, in particular a considerable increase in the incidence of workforce meetings. These were meetings where senior management met employees either all together or section by section. It also shows a great increase in the proportion of organisations that were using briefing groups, defined as regular meetings taking place at least once a month between junior managers or supervisors and all the workers for whom they were responsible. The same was true of problem-solving groups – ie regular work-group or team meetings taking place at least once a month to discuss aspects of performance (such as quality circles). These went from zero in the mid-1980s to a situation where almost half of the organisations surveyed reported using them. Even traditional methods of communication with employees, such as the company newsletter, were used more in 1998 than in 1984.

Table 44 The incidence of direct communication methods, 1984–1998

	1984	1990	1998
Two-way communication or consultation:			
Workforce meetings	34	41	48
Briefing groups	36	48	65
Problem-solving groups	–	35	49
Suggestion scheme	25	28	33
Downward communication:			
Management chain	62	60	6
Newsletters	34	41	50

Percentage of organisations employing 25 or more people
Source: Forth and Millward (2002; Table 2, p.4)

Table 45 shows the same developments, broken down by sector. It indicates that the public sector showed the greatest propensity to communicate with employees during the 1990s, although private sector organisations did move in a similar direction. This was true both of the percentage of organisations using any one of five communications practices, and of the number of these practices used. More recent data from organisations shows that the trend has continued since 1998.

Table 45 Use and breadth of direct communication by ownership sector, 1990–1998

	Private sector		Public sector	
	1990	1998	1990	1998
Use: Percentage of organisations using any one of five direct communication methods	74	84	92	94
Breadth: mean number of arrangements where they are used	2.4	2.7	2.6	3.2

Percentage of organisations employing 25 or more people
Source: Forth and Millward (2002; Table 3, p.7)

WHO IS COMMUNICATED TO ABOUT WHAT?

If, as suggested above, the purpose of communication is to increase the understanding and commitment of all who do work for organisations to overall goals, it follows that information about the organisation's strategy should be communicated to all these people. Yet if we look at the data on communication, we see that this is often not the case.

Cranet data shows that there is a hierarchy of information distribution in European organisations. In terms of formal briefings about business strategy and financial performance, managers are top of the information tree, followed by technical and professional workers (see Tables 46 and 47). These receive the best

Table 46 Briefing on business strategy for different employee categories

	UK	Sweden	Germany	Greece	Slovakia
Management	93%	97%	91%	94%	82%
Professional/technical	75%	79%	49%	46%	48%
Clerical	60%	77%	37%	23%	42%
Manual	46%	58%	23%	12%	23%

Source: Cranet-E (2003)

Table 47 Briefing on financial performance for different employee categories

	UK	Sweden	Germany	Greece	Slovakia
Management	93%	98%	93%	95%	80%
Professional/technical	78%	86%	78%	57%	40%
Clerical	64%	86%	70%	42%	48%
Manual	51%	70%	50%	21%	20%

Source: Cranet-E (2003)

information on business strategy, financial performance and work organisation. Next come clerical staff – and manual workers come last.

It is also important to remember here that other people who do work for organisations such as agency and subcontractors are not included in the survey, and almost certainly have even less information than those directly employed.

In many organisations, electronic communication plays an increasingly important role, and we turn now to this subject.

ELECTRONIC COMMUNICATION

What do we mean by 'electronic communication' here? We mean providing employees with information by electronic means. It is not, in other words, the electronic information systems used within HR departments. Its main feature is that the information is directed at employees. Electronic communication typically provides employees with information in the following areas: individual personal records/payroll/benefits/time-keeping and attendance/recruitment and selection/training and development/performance management/career planning/succession planning/work scheduling/health and safety. It is a part of 'e-HRM' (*Personnel Today*, 2005).

Electronic communication systems in HRM can typically take any of a number of different forms. The different forms depend on how interactive they are – in other words, how much employees can affect what information they can obtain from the system and how much they can affect that information themselves by changing it. Take for example 'downward' communication, which is probably the most common form. In this, employees can access some personal information (eg work schedules, current benefits they are entitled to). A more developed form allows two-way communication. In this form, an employee is able to update simple personal information such as address or bank details.

A third, even more developed form allows two-way communication in a more complex way. In this, the employee is able to perform intricate transactions and select items (such as the composition of benefits) which can be calculated by the system, approved or declined, and confirmed to the employee. So, for example, where 'cafeteria' benefits (ie benefits that award employees points, and allow them to use their points total by choosing whether they prefer to have childcare or health club membership, etc) are provided, the employee can personalise his or her mix of benefits and have it approved online. A few companies' systems allow even more complex transactions.

Why do organisations introduce electronic methods of communicating?

There are several key reasons why organisations do this:

- to reduce the administrative load on HR staff by cutting down on routine inquiries (Ulrich, 2002)

- to make sure that mistake-free, consistent information is given to all employees who ask the same question

- to become more focused on their internal (other managers, employees) and external (outsourced activities, employment agencies, customers) clients

- to cut costs.

These reasons are, of course, real benefits, and some companies have certainly succeeded in realising the first three even if the fourth has proved more difficult to achieve. There are several additional reasons for introducing or extending electronic methods. To take just one: there is an increasing demand from employees for career management information, some of which can be quite complex. But a further reason is especially important: it frees HR staff from more routine tasks and allows them to develop a more genuinely *strategic* role. HR staff can become more focused on the vital issues such as recruitment, staff development and retention or motivation rather than have always to be dealing with relatively routine inquiries.

The reasons for organisations' introducing these methods could be slightly contradictory; improving HR services for managers and other employees is not necessarily compatible with cutting costs. As in many areas, it is important for all organisations to be clear about the priorities they have when seeking to meet multiple aims: what is the order of importance of the different aims? It is often the case that cost savings do not materialise, or at least do not materialise in the medium term. In some cases, costs are effectively shifted within the organisation, so that fewer people are employed in HR and more of operational managers' time is taken up with answering employees' HR enquiries. The argument that savings would occur appears in some cases to have been put simply because it could help 'sell' the idea to senior managers.

What problems can arise with electronic methods of communication?

These methods may in some ways seem like an obvious and 'natural' development: people in society in general are using electronic methods, so why should employing organisations be any different? But this simple and optimistic view does not recognise that in society in general there are many people with little or no access to computers. In some companies, these people form a majority of the workforce. This means that the 'digital divide' between those with access to electronic information and those with little or none will be reproduced inside employing organisations. This in turn could mean that only part of the organisation's employees feel involved and committed to it. It is a considerable problem in some large manufacturing companies, where manual workers have little or no time or opportunity to use electronic information.

Secondly, many organisations that use these methods do not have a clearly defined strategy on which its introduction can be based. In other words, if organisations do not have clear strategies (including one for electronic communication), this is likely to become more obvious to employees when they are introduced. This is simply because the information will become more transparent to employees and they will see that the organisation is not sending them very clear messages through it.

Thirdly, electronic systems can overburden even the IT-literate employees, many of whom may only make use of a small proportion of the information available.

Fourthly, it can take employees years to catch up with the information that is available to them through electronic sources. In some companies, periods of over three years have been reported. This is not just because people take time to adapt to new things; it is also because line managers often have to pick up responsibilities that were previously those of HR, and have to accept this and learn to deal with it in practice. The problem is likely to be even more acute where people not directly employed by the organisation but who nevertheless need to know its policies and procedures (for example, contractors who need to know health and safety policies and procedures) are concerned (see Chapter 18).

 REFLECTIVE ACTIVITY

List ways in which you think the problems outlined above could be handled.

In answer to the exercise above, we have just three points to make. Firstly, our view is that all of the problem areas show that both the HR strategy and the reasons for introducing electronic communication, and the relationship between the two, need to be thought through thoroughly if electronic communication is to realise its promise. So, for example, if the strategic aim is to increase employee satisfaction rather than to reduce costs, it may be that only small to moderate amounts of key information are put on the website, backed up by a good telephone enquiry service. Secondly, in relation to the important 'digital divide' issue, it may be that it will have to be recognised in certain organisations that more HR communication will have to be done through conventional methods than they would ideally like. Finally, there is the issue of the uses of and attitudes to email. Many people see email and electronic communication more widely as overloading them. The ease with which emails can be sent probably encourages a huge amount of communication much of which used to be done on the telephone or in person. So the electronic information becomes too heavy, and much of it is ignored or regarded as low-grade information. In other words, increased volume may also have brought at least a perception of information overload of low-grade information much of which can be ignored.

In view of these points, it might be thought worrying that a small minority of organisations reported to the Cranet survey in 2003 that they *only* used electronic methods to communicate to employees. However, in most cases the same survey showed that the great majority of organisations were increasing communication through *every* available channel.

2 COMMUNICATION FROM EMPLOYEES

WHY EMPLOYEE VOICE?

Communication from employees to the organisations they work for (as opposed to day-to-day communication with their operational managers), sometimes called 'employee voice', is often not a conspicuously evident aspect of life in British organisations.

However, effective voice mechanisms can, as suggested at the beginning of this chapter, be a major source of competitive advantage for companies (Pfeffer, 1998) and can help improve service delivery in the public sector (Blumberg, 1976). Employees clearly know a lot about how work is done, and are often in customer-facing roles. They are therefore in a position to help improve efficiency. Sometimes, operational managers can feel that it is they who have to improve efficiency because it is central to their jobs and they may therefore resist 'employee voice'. But the HR professional has to recognise and overcome this resistance; it can be difficult.

In addition to the efficiency argument just made, employees can have valid and useful ideas about the organisation's strategic direction. However, many managers suggest the opposite and argue that employees' ideas are mainly in the operational area. We would suggest that this is in part because many employees have little opportunity to voice ideas about the organisation's overall direction. Good ideas are not necessarily the sole preserve of senior management. Opportunities for employees to voice their ideas on the subject are usually rare, however, and perhaps they should be encouraged.

Finally, for some this sort of communication is also about responding to employees' feeling that the organisation they spend much of their waking time working for should allow at least an element of democracy for employees.

One reason for giving all who do work for the organisation an opportunity to give their views on the organisation's strategic direction is that it tends to make employees feel positive about the organisation, and to increase levels of commitment and trust within it.

FORMS OF EMPLOYEE VOICE

Employee voice can take many different forms. Five of the most common forms, and the potential advantages and possible difficulties associated with them, are examined in some detail below. They are:

- 'open door' policies
- suggestion schemes
- employee attitude surveys
- employee forums
- work team, project team and general meetings.

'Open door' policies

Many companies operate 'open door' policies, whereby senior managers invite employees to voice individual concerns to them whenever they feel the need. Formal policies of this sort are particularly common in larger companies but many smaller companies suggest that the practice is common with them too even though it is not enshrined as a formal policy. 'Open door' policies are often advocated by senior managers as an 'ideal' way of dealing with employee concerns – and indeed they may be for them and for some employees – but there are at least three important difficulties to be considered.

First, individual employees often lack confidence in front of senior managers and may feel that if their views are considered 'off-message', they may suffer for them, so they therefore keep them to themselves. This is especially true of temporary staff. Organisations, including small companies, are hierarchies and those lower down the hierarchy are likely to have reservations about what they say to those higher up the hierarchy. Many managers in small companies have limited understanding of this and imagine that everyone speaks to them quite openly.

Second, many organisations have working patterns such as shiftworking that make 'open door' policies difficult to operate in practice.

Third, they can also be an excuse *not* to communicate. 'My door is always open to you' may be further interpreted as '... but don't come to me when I am busy or unless you have something really worthwhile to say' – which will put people off from trying the open door.

Suggestion schemes

Suggestion schemes are a long-standing method of seeking employee views on how savings may be made, or how improvements could be made in work organisation or service delivery. Typically, in formalised systems employees send their suggestions in to a central point, where they are evaluated for their usefulness. Employees are then sometimes rewarded for their suggestions. Organisations which claim to espouse continuous learning are likely to encourage people to suggest improvements rather than using a formal suggestion scheme. Japanese organisations may have more formal schemes but are less likely to pay for suggestions – on the basis that good ideas are part of what they expect/hope for from employees. That view has extended to some other manufacturing organisations.

In some companies, and especially in small ones, such practices may not exist as formal systems but are nevertheless there so that employees who make a good suggestion are given a reward of some type.

Suggestion schemes have obvious advantages for organisations seeking to improve efficiency. They are obviously very limited in that they only deal with ways of improving efficiency in a narrow sense. One potential disadvantage of them is that they can become a source of ill-feeling if a suggestion leads to employees' losing jobs.

Employee attitude surveys

Employee attitude surveys, like suggestion schemes, also have a long history and are becoming increasingly important in many organisations. They can have the advantage of getting a wide range of employee opinions on a range of subjects. There is now much more use of e-surveys as a means of collecting and analysing responses very quickly. These are commonly used where employees have access to email – but shopfloor employees can still join in through email kiosks on assembly lines. In other words, they can allow those people with less confidence to have a voice, and to have one across a wide range of issues.

They also have their problems. It is important to recognise that holding a survey raises employee expectations that something will be done. Also, although they are often used in organisations, they are also frequently only done once, or done irregularly. This means that employee satisfaction cannot be measured over time and particular problems identified. A less common but more serious problem can arise if they are in fact 'one-way' communication because management does not itself feed back the results to employees, or tell them what actions they propose to take on matters of concern. They can be demotivating if this is not done.

Employee forums

Many companies operate employee forums where small groups of employees meet with managers to discuss issues of mutual interest. Their scope can vary, from forums which deal only with production issues and are in reality close in nature to quality circles, to forums where no subject is ruled out of order. A number of these forums sometimes exist in each workplace, and these relate to an overall workplace forum. In some instances there are national employee forums. Employee forums may include union representatives in their participants (see Chapter 17). Readers can find more about communication with employees through unions and works councils in Brewster *et al* (2007) and Croucher *et al* (2006).

The strength of these methods can be that they allow employees a collective voice so that support can be offered to an individual voicing a general concern that some individuals might feel reticent about raising on their own. The disadvantages can be that some managers may think employees' concerns 'trivial'. Also, if managers do not themselves have the skills required to structure issues in a meaningful way, or to encourage people to speak and make them feel they are being listened to, this can disappoint employees and lead to a degree of cynicism.

Work team, project team and general meetings

This category includes many different types of meeting. Some work and project teams may be asked for their opinions on issues wider than just simple work problems as defined by management. Work teams are in some ways possibly the most important and successful form of employee communications, because this is where employees may be able to have the greatest impact on their daily working lives through chatting with their direct manager and making small suggestions for progress. They depend for their success on the skills of the line managers in drawing out employee suggestions.

General meetings may be held on a regular basis, and indeed in some workplaces are held as often as monthly. These methods have the advantages of collective systems already mentioned, and once again depend for their success to a great extent on the skills of the managers who run them. How well the facilitators can chair a meeting, how clearly they structure issues for discussion, how well they listen and how much feedback on previous discussions they provide are all significant issues.

KEY ISSUES: COMMUNICATION

We now pull together ten key points about communication raised in this chapter:

- Communication to employees is important because giving information to employees on issues such as business strategy and financial performance is linked to superior organisational performance.

- The subject, quality, depth and timing of information 'cascaded' down within organisations are important issues: information must be fit for purpose.

- In British organisations there has been a steady increase in the information flow to employees in recent years, but there is still a good deal of room for improvement in British organisations' information-giving to employees.

- Many managers in small companies rely mainly on informal communication, which they may or may not be skilled at. Managers may not have all the skills required for effective communication. Employees need to feel that they are being listened to even though their concerns may appear 'irrelevant' or 'trivial' to the manager concerned.

- Many who do outsourced or contracted work for organisations are given relatively little information compared to others who may be directly employed, even in 'lower' positions.

- HR has a key role to play in improving communication, including by providing training and coaching for other managers and workers which can improve their informal and formal communication.

- Electronic communication is playing an increasingly significant role in information-giving to employees. It can enable HR to increase its strategic role in organisations.

- Electronic communication faces the same problem as other forms of communication and indeed runs the risk of exacerbating existing inequalities between different types of worker in terms of the amount and quality of information they receive.

- Communication from employees is frequently done within strict limits imposed by management, and it is therefore important to recognise this and to provide opportunities for more wide-ranging expression of employees' views.

- Employee attitude surveys are often only done once, and how management acts on them is frequently not reported back to employees. This can lead to a negative effect on motivation.

Perhaps there are other key points that you would like to note for yourself.

The main case study now follows. It gives an example of how the increasingly important issue of communicating with people who do work for the organisation but are not directly employed by it can affect a company in practice.

MAIN CASE STUDY

Look at the description of the case set out below. Then decide on the recommendations that you would make as an HR manager for dealing with the issues raised. Try to think beyond the level of a 'quick fix' or simple solutions by developing a longer-term strategy as well as responding to the immediate issue.

The company (which we shall call Company A) is a major US-based data-handling company with a number of sites scattered throughout the UK, employing several thousand people. Its core business is processing data received from its customer organisations. The data arrives at the company in either paper or electronic form, and may (for example) be respondents' completed questionnaires to market surveys. It is then processed by entering it into data files in different forms, providing analyses and reports. In some cases, reports are then printed and bound for the customer companies. There are therefore three main types of employee: data entry clerks, data processing employees, and printers. Much of the data is confidential, some of it is highly confidential, and security of both the raw and processed data is an issue of commercial sensitivity for client companies, government departments and the National Health Service. Work is often carried out to demanding deadlines.

The company has two types of staff, making up about 15% of the workforce, who it does not directly employ. One type is agency staff, employed mainly for only short periods (up to six months) to carry out relatively routine tasks such as data entry. These staff are managed by Company A's managers. Agency staff are mainly employed because the company wants to retain some flexibility for dealing with peaks and troughs in demand, for which the agency staff offer a cheap, responsive and 'no commitment' service. The second type is staff employed by two external companies (Companies B and C), chosen for their technical expertise in their areas – for example, providing computer trouble-shooting services for core staff and other technical support services. Company B's staff are managed by Company B managers working on Company A's premises; Company C's staff are managed by Company C managers on a remote basis (ie they are not on Company A's premises unless they

feel they have to be for some specific reason). The company employs these staff for reasons that are mainly to do with the high quality of their work, their reliability and relatively low costs.

However, a range of difficulties and concerns associated with both agency and contracted-out staff has become increasingly evident.

First, the contractors' staff have sometimes been the cause of complaints recently not because of the general quality of their work (which is high) but rather because they sometimes appear not to understand what is vitally important work and what is of less importance. So they are reluctant to drop a trouble-shooting task of relatively low importance to go to deal with a problem that is holding up a job that is vital for the company. Recently, when a Company X manager approached them as a matter of urgency, two Company B employees asked him to 'hang on for a bit'. When he asked them to drop what they were doing, they told him to approach their Company B manager if he had a problem and wanted help straight away – they said they only had four hands between them. The Company B manager was himself not available at that time, and the delay required Company A employees to have to work late, causing annoyance to the women employees involved and costing the company overtime payments to them.

Second, although relations between agency and contract staff on the one hand and Company A staff on the other are generally good, there have been some problems between established Company A staff and both agency and Company B and C staff. So, for example, some non-core staff do not seem to know about Company A's health and safety policies. One Company C employee recently left a computer cable trailing across a gangway, allegedly causing a Company A employee to trip and bruise his arm. The

Company C employee refused to fill in an accident report form, saying it was not his fault and Company A's forms were nothing to do with him.

Third, fears have arisen among managers where highly confidential work has been involved, that non-core staff do not seem fully to appreciate the sensitivity of the data and how important this is to certain customers. Company B employees have, for example, recently taken highly confidential electronic records belonging to a government department out of Company A's building to work on them at home.

Your task

Imagine you are an HR professional or professionals working in Company A. Prepare a short report based on the facts you have been given above, making recommendations to your colleagues on how the situation can be improved.

EXPLORE FURTHER

FORTH, J. and MILLWARD, N. (2002) *The Growth of Direct Communication*. London, CIPD
This is a short British study of the communications reality in organisations, conducted for the CIPD and written in an accessible style.

HARLEY, B., HYMAN, J. and THOMPSON, P. (eds) (2005) *Participation and Democracy at Work*. Basingstoke, Palgrave Macmillan
This collection of essays discusses questions of 'industrial democracy' in an interesting and accessible way.

KERSLEY, B., ALPIN, C., FORTH, J., DIX, G., OXENBRIDGE, S., BRYSON, A., and BEWLEY, H., (2006) *Inside the Workplace: First findings from the 2004 Workplace Employment Relations Survey*. London, Taylor & Francis
This is the summary version of the most comprehensive survey of communications practices in Britain's private and public organisations. It is probably the best brief summary of what actually goes on in the country's organisations.

MARCHINGTON, M., WILKINSON, A., ACKERS, P. and DUNDON, T. (2001) *Management Choice and Employee Voice*. London, CIPD
This is a CIPD-commissioned report on British managers' use of different channels for employee voice (ie communication with employees through employee representatives).

PFEFFER, J. (1998) *The Human Equation: Building profits by putting people first*. Boston, MA: Harvard Business School Press
This is an important text, giving a US view of the subject in a clear way.

Contemporary and Critical Issues

CHAPTER 20

Changing roles in HRM

Chris Brewster

INTRODUCTION

This chapter looks at the changing nature of roles in HRM, exploring the various actors and their effects on the way that HRM is done within organisations. Different people play a part in HRM, and this chapter is about those different actors and their roles. HRM differs from traditional personnel management in that HRM tries in addition to personnel administration to take a more strategic role in the way people are managed. This is one of the main reasons why it involves more people in organisations than personnel management did: if HRM is 'strategic', it potentially at least involves more people, since 'strategy' describes the organisation's overall direction.

LEARNING OUTCOMES

By the end of this chapter readers should be able to:

- identify the most important actors in the area of HRM (HR specialists, line managers, employees, trade unions, outsourcers and consultants)

- recognise the impact of each of those actors and the changes effected by changes in their roles

- describe the effects of the changing roles on the way that HRM is done.

The chapter is linked to the strategic HRM debates (Chapter 3), the role of trade unions (Chapter 17) and international and comparative approaches to the study of HRM (Chapters 22 and 23). It considers only the parties immediately involved in organisational-level HRM. There are important changes going on amongst the parties external to HRM too, and these are covered in this chapter.

The chapter is structured in relation to the immediate parties to HRM – ie those most obviously and closely involved in it. After the starter case study we identify the most important actors in HRM and their key characteristics. We examine the role of the HRM department and those working in it. Attention is paid to the current debates about the strategic nature of HRM and the impact of e-HRM. We then address some of the other actors in HRM.

In the second part of the chapter we explore the important role of line managers in HRM.

STARTER CASE STUDY

Justine Doit, the relatively new CEO of Middlesex Educational and Support Services (MESS), recently attended a free seminar offered by one of the big consultancies at which she heard that modern organisations are moving towards a more strategic model of HRM in which small but powerful HRM departments work more or less directly for the CEO, as she understood it, and getting out of the low-value-added transactional work involved in the record-keeping and systems-operating role that old-fashioned personnel departments used to adopt.

MESS has until now been a fairly traditional education and training establishment, focused on the end product and with little real concern for management processes. The HRM department has undertaken a mixed role of supporting employees when they have problems, supporting line managers with problem employees, 'policing' the rules to make sure that systems operate as fairly as possible, and negotiating with the trade union.

Justine has organised an informal 'after-work meeting' with the consultants, Adam Cash and his new and apparently bright assistant, May Good: they have arranged that the meeting takes place in an upmarket restaurant recently featured in the Sunday papers.

Justine: I was very impressed with your presentation. I have to say that MESS is a long way from the sort of picture you present.

Adam: Well, that's not unusual. We have worked with a lot of organisations like yours, developing an added-value results-oriented approach to HRM.

Justine: Hmmm – but you know, it's not going to be easy. There are a lot of people with interests involved here. For a start, I wonder

why our own HRM department hasn't been bringing these ideas to me. I'm not sure they would have the right competencies to manage the kind of HRM you were discussing.

May: Are you sure they haven't? We often find that the HRM people do put forward these ideas, but somehow they are not heard by the rest of the management team.

Adam: Well, whatever. The fact is that you have taken these ideas on board and, to be blunt, as the CEO you cannot ignore them. Like everyone responsible for results you have to be working on these kinds of issues.

Justine: Yes, but it's not just the HRM specialists. To be honest, I think they might even welcome some of this stuff. But what about my line managers? They expect the HRM department to be there to help them with the difficult and embarrassing people problems. And there will certainly be a reaction, too, from the trade union and from the employees.

May: Yes, somehow the employees always get left out of these debates.

Adam: Well, let's organise another meeting with some of your people and see how they react in practice. Another glass of this excellent Chilean Sauvignon?

Questions for discussion

1 What might be the reaction of the HRM department in MESS to the next meeting?

2 What is it that line managers expect from their HRM department?

3 Why might the trade union be opposed to a new strategically oriented HRM department?

In the third part we discuss the role of other important parties in HRM.

The chapter concludes with the main case study.

Reference sources named within the chapter may be looked up in the *References and further reading* section at the end of the book.

THE PARTIES TO HRM

At the start of this chapter we want to introduce the most important actors in HRM and their role (see Figure 24). Two parties are always and obviously involved in HRM, as indicated by the phrase itself: the human resources (the people working in the organisation) and the managers. In most larger organisations there are one or more HRM specialists, so we can split the management group into HRM specialists and the rest of the management group – usually called, in this context, 'line managers'. The HRM specialists may outsource some of their activities (such as, most commonly, payroll or training) to other people outside the organisation, and they may be advised by or work with HRM consultants. For their part, the employees may include trade union members and may call on the external union officers for help in their part of HRM (see Chapter 17). These 'internal' roles are the subject of this chapter.

Figure 24 The parties to HRM

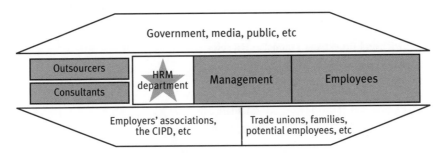

Around these roles, of course, no organisation is context-free (Brewster, 2007). What the government does in terms of the economy and of labour legislation has a big influence and some authors include the government as a party to HRM. Also influential is media coverage of the organisation and what the public thinks about it. If the organisation belongs to an employers' association, that will have an effect and so will the CIPD. The families of the employees and the potential employees and the general labour market also have an effect. But our focus in this chapter is on the people immediately concerned with HRM within the organisation.

1 THE ROLE OF THE HR DEPARTMENT

There have been many debates about the role of HRM departments and the specialists working in them. What is generally agreed is that there are several models of HRM determined largely by the relationship between two of the key factors that distinguish HRM from the older notion of 'personnel management': the link between HRM and corporate strategy, and the link between the HRM department and the line managers. HRM is assumed to include a closer link to corporate strategy and a focus on getting all line managers to act as people managers, with the HRM department establishing the appropriate environment and providing support for the line managers.

There is in some people's view a wish to see everyone in the department operating at the strategic level, but clearly that is not possible or desirable. The US guru Dave Ulrich and his colleague Wayne Brockbank (Ulrich and Brockbank, 2005) identify five main roles that have to be carried out within the HRM department (see Figure 25):

- the *employee advocate* focuses on the needs of today's employees, ensuring that people are paid appropriately, that their concerns are listened to and acted upon and, where relevant, dealing with the trade unions and the consultative arrangements
- the *human capital developer* focuses on ensuring that employees, are continually developing the skills and capabilities they will need to be successful in the future

Figure 25 Ulrich and Brockbank's model of HR roles

Source: Ulrich and Brockbank (2005)

- the *functional expert* deals with the administrative practices that are central to what the HR department offers the organisation (recruitment, selection, payroll, etc)

- the *strategic partner* has multiple dimensions: business expert, change agent, strategic HR planner, knowledge manager and internal consultant

- the *HR leader* pulls this all together, collaborating with other functions, setting and enhancing the standards for strategic thinking, and ensuring good corporate governance.

As Ulrich himself says, HR departments have to be good at all these things. In many cases, particularly in smaller organisations and in the less developed world, the department with responsibility for these areas is still most accurately entitled 'personnel administration'. That is what it does. The experts argue that this misses the roles that Ulrich's other categories represent: HRM departments should be more strategic in order to create value within organisations (Wright and McMahon, 1992). Further, many would go on to say that most of these administrative tasks can now be done more effectively through the use of information technology or through outsourcing (and we examine this shortly).

THE STRATEGIC INVOLVEMENT OF THE HRM DEPARTMENT

In many organisations the HR people do not have the credibility to play a strategic role. HR is not always represented at the top decision-making level of organisations (Brewster, Larsen and Mayrhofer, 1997). In some countries, HRM issues are taken into account anyway. Thus in Germany the law requires that many larger organisations have an employee representative on their supervisory board – even if the head of the HR function is not represented, HRM issues are discussed. In other countries, most senior HRM specialists are represented at the top level. In Britain about half the organisations with more than 200 people have an HRM representative on the main board or equivalent. In general, these figures seem to change very little over the years. It is clearly more likely that an organisation with an HRM specialist on the board will have a more strategic approach to HRM.

Other data from the Cranet research indicates that where there is no specialist presence at this level, the responsibility for HRM rests most frequently with the managing director or an administration manager. This could mean either that the topic is taken seriously, the top person seeing it as a crucial part of his or her responsibilities, or it could mean that it is not taken seriously at all, being swept into an 'and everything else' category. In either case it is not clear that the specialist input to decisions from the HRM angle is always going to be available when key strategic decisions are made.

The extent of strategic involvement of the HRM specialists varies by size and sector of organisations but also, significantly, by country (Brewster *et al*, 1997). The strategic implications of a management decision in Germany or the Netherlands are subject to the involvement of powerful works council representatives or the worker representatives on the supervisory board of the company. In these companies the knowledge that their decisions are subject to close examination – and can be reversed or varied – at that level means that managers tend to operate with HRM issues in mind (Wächter and Muller-Camen, 2002). Ideas that strategies are the preserve of senior managers (or even just managers) may be questioned too: in some countries employees have a much more significant input than in Britain. It is not a surprise, therefore, to find that the Cranet research shows that in some countries HRM is involved in the development of corporate strategy in more organisations than there are who have HR directors on the board. In Britain there is a close relationship between the two.

REFLECTIVE ACTIVITY

How might having an HR director on the main board help an organisation to develop competitive corporate strategies?

THE CHANGING NATURE OF THE HRM FUNCTION

The role of the HRM department is perhaps always ambiguous and dynamic. Like other functional specialists, HR professionals are constantly challenged to meet three competing aims: to make themselves more cost-effective through reducing the costs of services and headcount (the *operational* driver), to improve their services to meet the increasing demands of line managers and employees (the *relational* driver), and to address the strategic objectives of organisations (the *transformational* driver). The difficulty is that these drivers do not necessarily all point in the same direction. Indeed, often they cannot all be done at the same time.

As the CIPD has noted, in order to meet these challenges HRM departments are turning to changes in supply chain management and organisational restructuring policies including:

- greater use of electronic HRM

- downsizing the function

- allocating more responsibility to line managers

- outsourcing transactional or routine activities.

In each case, it is worth pointing out, the rhetoric may have moved ahead of the reality but there are clearly some kinds of development going on here. We examine these issues in turn.

ELECTRONIC HRM AND DOWNSIZING

In theory, at least, the extension of existing information and communications technology (ICT) systems, and the implementation of new ones, could transform the internal operations of the HRM department. This process, known as 'the e-enablement of HRM (e-HRM)', is qualitatively different from earlier applications of ICT to the information function of HR itself (known as HRIS). E-HRM refers to the application of ICT to HRM so that the process is changed from a face-to-face or paper relationship to an increasingly 'virtual' one. The concept is that line managers or employees can get from their computer all the information and advice they might otherwise get from the HRM specialists (Florkowski and Olivas-Lujan, 2006). In addition, the HRM department can do much more with the information that it has: checking the costs and effects of training more fully, linking pay and benefits costs more closely to output, and so on (Gueutal and Stone, 2005). According to those who take a very positive view of it, e-HRM has the potential to fundamentally transform the nature of the HRM function just as e-business has already done in sectors such as financial services and retailing.

Currently, the application of ICT to HRM accounts for a substantial element of the total technology-spend in organisations (as much as 10% of all ICT investment in British organisations, according to estimates). In 2006 one of the two main sellers of e-HRM systems, SAP, claimed that 9,500 companies worldwide used its applications to manage over 54 million employees, while the other main provider, Oracle, claimed that 76 of the US top 100 companies had adopted its software. Nevertheless, despite these claims, at present the use of e-HR technologies is uneven, varying between countries, sectors, sizes of organisations and showing marked differences even between organisations in the same country, sector and size. The effects are also unclear.

Little is known about the long-term cost-effectiveness of generic e-HR systems, whether they promote off-shoring and job losses in the UK (or whether this is offset by the creation of high-value jobs), or their overall contribution to organisational productivity and effectiveness. For every success story there is a horror story somewhere else. And, despite the claims of those who endorse them, it is not clear how generic systems will enable companies to obtain a competitive advantage if they all end up operating similar business processes to their competitors. We do know that the implementation of these systems has brought problems, in part because practitioners lack a sound body of theory and evidence on which to proceed. HRM specialists say that lack of guidance is one of the most important problems making the adoption of e-HR systems difficult. There are only a few studies, including some by the CIPD, that have systematically looked at the nature of e-HR technologies in use, the rationale for their adoption, problems influencing their implementation and their broader organisational effects. At this point in our knowledge, the consequences of e-HRM for HRM specialists, line managers and other employees are not well understood (Martin, 2005).

One particular area which is unclear is e-HRM's effect on the size of the HRM department. In theory, more e-HRM should lead to fewer people in the HRM function. In practice the relationship between organisational size, sector, national context and the size of the HR department within organisations is complex. Across Europe, the average ratio is about one and a half people in the HRM department for every 100 people employed, but this varies a lot (Brewster *et al*, 2006). Summarised, the proportion of staff engaged in the HR function tends to be smaller where the organisation is larger. It is lower in specific areas of the service sector, retailing and distribution – probably reflecting the importance of relatively low-value-added HR policies in this area – but HR departments are relatively large in the state sector, probably reflecting political pressures against excessive outsourcing. The impact of e-HRM so far seems to be very small.

REFLECTIVE ACTIVITY

Answer the following questions, and in each case relate your answer afterwards to the situation in your own organisation or an organisation you know well.

How might e-HRM assist in creating a cost-effective HRM department?

What changes would e-HRM mean to the capabilities required by the HRM department?

How would an organisation determine whether it had too many or too few people in the HRM department?

2 LINE MANAGEMENT RESPONSIBILITY FOR HRM

A crucial issue in HRM – one that is said to make it quite different from 'personnel administration' – is the responsibility placed on line managers for the management of their people. The balance of responsibilities for the management of people between the specialists in the HR department and the line managers who have day-to-day responsibilities for organising the work and the progress of their subordinates is unclear, contested and changing.

The British expert David Guest argued many years ago that because HRM is central to the well-being of an organisation and to its ability to perform effectively, the subject has to be central to the responsibilities of every single manager in an organisation. In a famous statement, Guest, 1997 argued that 'If HRM is to be taken seriously, personnel managers must give it away.' Others, however, have claimed that only a knowledgeable, experienced and influential HR department focused on nothing but HRM can provide the organisation with the expertise needed in this competitively crucial area of management. These commentators point to failures of line managers to manage their people effectively and argue that if the subject is not driven by a specialist department, the reality is that it gets ignored (at least until there is a crisis).

It seems that the trends in giving HRM responsibilities to line managers have been almost tidal, ebbing and flowing like the sea as the HR specialists move between opposition to the line, through the roles of power-holder, administrative centre, advocate for co-determination and change agent (Larsen and Brewster, 2003). Currently, there is a strong push to increase the degree of line management responsibility. The Cranet-E data shows that organisations across Europe have increased line management responsibilities. For each aspect of HRM and in each country, there are always significantly more organisations increasing line management responsibility than reducing it (Mayrhofer and Brewster, 2005). The evidence also shows that recruitment and selection, health and safety and the expansion and reduction of the workforce are more likely to have been given to the line managers, whereas industrial relations and training are more likely to stay with the HR function.

The reasons for these increases include the fact that line managers cannot avoid taking at least some responsibility for their subordinates. Perhaps the ability to give work to people, to make people enthusiastic about their work and to develop their potential are the marks of a good manager. Allocating time, money and energy to the management and development of subordinate staff is not only an investment in improved effectiveness and future success but a necessary precondition for that success. This is not a role that the HRM department can play. The HRM function is seen as playing the role of co-ordinator and catalyst for the activities of the line managers, working with line managers to deal with people-related business issues.

The emphasis on the line management role in HRM has come about for four closely linked reasons:

- There has been a trend towards managing organisations through the development of cost centre- or profit centre-based approaches. In such systems it does not make any sense to exclude from the managers' responsibilities the major operating cost of their centre: the cost of the people they employ.

- It is line managers, not the HRM specialists, who are in frequent, often constant, contact with employees, allocating tasks, making people enthusiastic about their jobs and monitoring performance.

- There is a growing emphasis on providing a responsive service for customers: line managers have to be able to respond quickly without having to get permission for changes to working hours or practices from the HRM department.

- There has been a widespread movement towards reducing the numbers in 'overhead' departments, such as HRM. In such circumstances the role of line management in HRM can be seen as an alternative to outsourcing the function – the 'internalising' shift. More responsibility taken by line managers should mean fewer people in the HRM department.

However, in many countries and in particular in the UK, the allocation of HRM responsibilities to the line has not got very far (Larsen and Brewster, 2003). There are six reasons why the assignment of HR responsibilities to the line has not gone further. These are that:

- Line managers are often not enthusiastic about taking on responsibility for HRM for the people in their area. They feel they have enough to do without that.

- Line managers under pressure often give HR responsibilities a low priority – they are often ignorant about legal requirements, trade union agreements and agreed practices or training.

- There is little evidence that organisations are providing any formal training to help their line managers handle the HR tasks that are being allocated to them.

- They are not particularly interested in HR issues and are unable to keep up to date with the latest HR thinking.

- Line managers are focused on their department and may not see the bigger picture (for example, when management development requires that one of their best people should move to another department, or when pay increases from their department could have a knock-on effect for others).

- Perhaps most significantly, the devolvement of HRM responsibilities to the line will not achieve the objectives hoped for if it is done in a policy vacuum, as it often is, just as a way of bringing costs down.

The balance of these different pressures means that the responsibility that line managers and HRM departments take over the next few years will continue to be discussed and will continue to change. Of course, allocating more responsibility for managing their people to line managers means, potentially, big changes in what line managers do and how they are judged – and equally big changes to the activities of the HRM departmental specialists.

The theoretical dividing line sometimes drawn between policy and practice is not so obvious on the ground. It is one thing to be asked to decide whether to recruit people for the immediately required work or for long-term careers with the overall organisation, or whether to recognise a union; it is another to place advertisements and to conduct negotiations. In practice, however, this distinction may be less clear and we should not make easy assumptions that the way forward would be to split the roles so that specialist HR directors set policies and line managers implement them. In practice, many of these less attractive tasks still have to be done, and there will in many cases be advantages in having them brought together under one specialist. Alternatively, with the spread of intelligent information and communications systems, much of this work will be available to the line manager without the intervention of an HR specialist.

In theory, HR specialists have to be closely involved with their line management colleagues if they want to perform their role successfully. As partners, the theory is, they share totally in the creation of policy and also in its implementation. They expect – and are expected – to contribute their specific expertise, knowledge and skill to the discussion. They will not be expected to agree with everything the line manager proposes, or expected to accept something when their professional expertise tells them that it is wrong to do so. To this extent they will not be such comfortable colleagues as the much-discussed 'internal consultants'. There is evidence that HR specialists can, indeed, be influential 'strategic change-makers'. On the other hand, it is clear that line managers as such are not a coherent group. Some senior executives may want their HR departments to take a strategic role, but many line managers just want their HR department to deal with the bureaucratic and sometimes difficult issues necessarily involved in managing people. They want a responsive operational partner, not a strategic one. Can partnering mean you ignore what your partner wants in order to do what you think is best for them?

REFLECTIVE ACTIVITY

Look back over

- the reasons for the growth of the allocation of HR responsibilities to line managers

- the reasons why that allocation has expanded no further.

How would you judge the importance of the two sets of explanations?

3 THE ROLE OF OTHER PARTIES IN HRM

It is worth taking a quick excursion now to mention the role of the people that work in an organisation as a factor in HRM. HRM is, after all, just another phrase for managing the people that the organisation uses. These may not, of course, be employees. Other people can contribute to an organisation – as self-employed contractors, as consultants (see below) and as agency workers. The majority are usually employees. But what is their role in HRM? People are the one resource that an organisation employs that is not a passive asset. All the other assets need people to give them value, but people are a value in themselves. The kind of people that an organisation can draw upon is very important: success depends not just on HRM policies or the capabilities of line managers – although they may make a critical difference – but also on the people the organisation has, the labour market they are drawn from, the educational characteristics they bring with them, their characters, their training, their attitudes and their values.

The people in every organisation are different. And that is one of the key things for the success of an organisation.

REFLECTIVE ACTIVITY

What kind of people does your organisation – or an organisation that you know well – employ?

What effect does that have on their HRM?

THE ROLE OF TRADE UNIONISTS

Trade unions include union members within organisations, activists (members who continue to be employed in an organisation but devote a lot of time and energy to the work of their union) and full-time trade union officials who do not work for anyone other than the union. For many organisations, therefore, the unions are not external players in their HR approach but internal actors. For others they are a mix of both. For HRM specialists the question of the role that the unions play is one to be managed in the same way that other aspects of the employer–employee relationship are managed: do we want to avoid the unions (is that a realistic option)? Do we want to fight them? Do we want to work with them? The employees' views, history, tradition and the behaviour of line managers are all important parts of this mix. Although it is not necessarily true that 'managers get the trade unions (and the industrial relations) that they deserve', it is certainly true that they get the trade unions (and the industrial relations) that history and the actions of managers up to and including the present group of managers deserve.

There are enormous numbers of examples from across the world of the effect of different approaches to trade unionism, to consultation and communication with and from managers and employees. Some organisations have developed individualistic relationships, so that the only real channel of communication is between management – particularly the immediate line manager – and employees. Some organisations have developed hard, antagonistic relationships with trade unions as the representatives of their employees, where there is so little trust that almost any action that the management takes is perceived as an attack on the employees or their unions. Some organisations have developed powerful partnership arrangements between themselves and their unions, so that the union sees its role as being to support but to challenge the management in order to make sure that the decisions that are taken actually deliver the best outcomes for the organisation so that the organisation remains successful and can deliver high pay levels and employment security. Like all simple pictures, these options emphasise certain characteristics and downplay others – but the truth of the picture is apparent.

Of course, the picture is complicated: some countries do not allow trade unions at all, some have government-controlled trade unions, and some allow the market to decide. The role that the trade union adopts in its relationship with the employers and their management representatives varies with country, sector, size of organisation and history. But whatever decisions are taken, the role that the trade unions adopt makes them more or less of an important player in the HRM scene.

REFLECTIVE ACTIVITY

Read through a fortnight's editions of a broadsheet newspaper and the current edition of *People Management*. See if you can find an article about an organisation in which a trade union is mentioned.

What role does the trade union have in that case?

THE PRESSURE TO OUTSOURCE

Outsourcing certain HRM activities – paying another organisation to carry them out for you – is part of the new rhetoric of HRM (CIPD, 2005; Paauwe, 1995). We should say that it is not actually new. Many management training institutions have existed for well over half a century, for example, and would not have been able to do that unless more than 50 years ago organisations had been outsourcing some of their training and development activities. Banks have long-established and profitable businesses in managing payroll for other organisations. What has happened is that there are now many new providers in the market and they are creating a demand for outsourcing and trying to talk up the changes that have gone on in order to improve their businesses. Many organisations remain resistant to the idea – and there is a clear country effect in that the 'outsourcers' are finding it very difficult to make any money in certain countries. The arguments for outsourcing include:

- HR departments should be freed from the boring low-value-added transactional work, so that they can focus on the strategic roles.

- Specialist organisations that do a lot of this work (management training centres, for example) can provide certain services better than the organisation itself.

- Economies of scale mean that the outsourcers may be able to provide the service more cheaply than the organisation can.

The opposition to outsourcing is built on arguments that:

- It does not make sense to put parts of the control of the organisation's most valuable resource (its people) in the hands of someone outside the organisation.

- The way that organisations manage their people gives them a competitive edge over other organisations that find it increasingly difficult to provide distinctive products, equipment or services, and outsourcers provide standard packages for all their (perhaps competitive) clients.

- E-HRM means that the advantages of using outsourcers may be less than the cost of developing an electronic in-house system to manage aspects of HRM – and those systems will be fully integrated with the rest of the organisation's HR policies and practices.

- In practice, it is often not cheaper to use outsourcers.

REFLECTIVE ACTIVITY

Have a discussion with others on the subject of outsourcing. No doubt there will be some arguments for and some arguments against the concept.

Which do you find the more convincing?

THE ROLE OF CONSULTANTS

There are now many large consultancy companies and a wide range of small independent consultants offering HRM services. Both offer two different kinds of service: they provide people who will do some activities in the place of, or sometimes alongside, people employed in the organisation; and they do activities aimed more at changing the policies of the organisation. Thus, consultancies offering redundancy services, expatriation services or headhunting tend to be doing activities that could be done by people within the organisation; consultancies that undertake culture change or organisational redesign projects are aiming to create or embed new policies. As elsewhere, the line between these two kinds of offerings is not clear, especially because many of the consultants and the people who employ them prefer to use the language of strategic change even when the task is just one of providing bodies to carry out an activity.

Why would organisations want to use consultants? There are a number of linked and overlapping reasons (we take here the example of a redundancy services consultant, but the same reasons could be applied to any other consultancy service):

- The consultants may have an expertise currently not available in the present HRM department: a redundancy services consultancy, for example, may be more up to date with the way the law has developed through the tribunals than the HRM department of an organisation that has never dealt with redundancies before. They may be more experienced and skilled at advising people in outplacement interviews of the alternative employment, financial and emotional implications.

- There may be good public relations reasons for using a consultant – 'We are taking the implications of this difficult situation for everybody very seriously: we have called in and will pay for experts to advise and assist us and to help you.'

- The consultants are temporary: they will soon be gone – any bad feeling that remains will, it is hoped, not attach to the permanent staff left behind, including those in the HRM department.

- Perhaps looking at the issue rather cynically, by employing consultants, managers can spread the blame – 'It wasn't my fault. We hired the most famous and expensive consultants and they advised us to do this . . .'

For whichever of these reasons, the use of consultants is now common and many consultancies make a lot of money from offering HRM services. For individuals, a few years in consultancy is either, at the start of a career, a good way to get experience of working in a wide range of different circumstances; in the middle of a career, a good way to make a comfortable income; or, at the end of a career, a good way to keep doing interesting things without the pressure and responsibility of working for a particular organisation.

REFLECTIVE ACTIVITY

At the top of a sheet of paper write 'As an HRM practitioner I would be in favour of using consultants because . . . ' and list as many reasons as you can think of.

Then list an opposing argument against each of those reasons.

When might using consultants be especially helpful? In what circumstances might it be particularly problematic?

KEY ISSUES: CHANGING ROLES IN HRM

We now pull together ten key points about changing roles in HRM raised in this chapter:

- The roles of all the actors in HRM are changing greatly.

- The strategic involvement of senior HR specialists may be changing and new roles for these specialists as function leaders and contributors to strategic thinking in the business are being identified. The relationship between HR specialist and line manager is very important.

- The strategic partner and HR leader roles are complex and equivocal.

- Increasing pressure is being put on line managers to do a better job of people management. In many cases, good HR policies are of little value without effective line management implementation.

- The impact of outsourcing, e-HRM and consultancy operations are all being felt.

- The implications of e-HRM, outsourcing and the role of consultants remain to be resolved and in practice vary on a case-by-case basis.

- There are a number of implications in the changing roles of those involved in HRM for how we think about the subject, and significant implications in practice for the role of the HR function.

- The different roles that the specialists in HR departments can play are a useful way to look at some of the implications of the allocation of HR responsibilities. All the roles are important and all must be handled effectively and with credibility.

- The assumptions that people within an HRM department make about their role may not be shared by the other parties involved: they have to be continually tested.

- The 'interplay' between the many actors involved (corporate, national and plant-level HR specialists, line managers, trade unionists, consultants, outsourcers, etc) is complex and varies with context.

Perhaps there are other key points that you would like to note for yourself.

The main case study in this chapter now follows. It gives an example of what can happen when an organisation decides to restructure its HR function and operations.

MAIN CASE STUDY

Look at the description of the case set out below. Then decide on the recommendations that you would make as an HR manager for dealing with the issues raised.

Megaco is a service company based in Britain but with substantial overseas investments. It has been through a radical and massive downsizing process stretching across several years in order to cut costs. The company began with some 200,000 employees, mostly in Britain, but now only employs around half of that number. In the process it has lost many very experienced and well-trained people with a lot of understanding about their complex industry. Now that the process is nearing completion, there is very real pressure on the HRM department to downsize too, and to cut costs. The company's HR function has long been very traditionally structured and organised. Sub-departments within the HR department (recruitment, payroll, employee relations, training and other sub-departments) all reported up to the top of an organisational pyramid that ended with the Head Office HR department and ultimately the HR director.

Decisions were taken at board level drastically to reduce the size of the department. Many HR functions were devolved to mid-level managers for the first time. This enabled senior management to reduce the HR department and to focus the remaining HR professionals on 'lines of business' (ie different key products and services) rather than the HR functions (recruitment, training, etc) to get HR professionals reporting to the heads of these lines of business, not to Head Office HR and also to co-ordinate HR through 'centres of excellence'. These 'centres of excellence' are loose electronically connected groups of experts in each HR area who can respond creatively to difficult problems and come up with new ideas. All relatively straightforward transactional work such as payroll, providing information on rates of pay, pensions and so on was to be outsourced to consultants. To facilitate all of this, the company bought expensive electronic information systems. Large numbers of HR people left as a result, disliking the changes. In fact, very few redundancies had to be made in the HR function because many left anyway.

There are now a number of problems as a result of this restructuring of the HR function. Many of the middle-level line managers are not happy with what has happened. They now have to deal with HR issues themselves, something they have not been trained for, and they feel they have to learn by costly and stressful trial and error. Meanwhile, the HRM department has the wrong skill set for the new roles it is being asked to perform. Many people in the company make cynical jokes about the 'centres of excellence'. In addition, it is widely rumoured in the company that consultants are working quite hard to get into positions where they can win large new contracts for advising middle-level managers.

Your task

Can you think of any wider consequences for the business of the decisions that were made to restructure the HR department?

If you were the HR director, how would you have responded to the board's demands to cut the costs of HR?

EXPLORE FURTHER

FARNDALE, E. and BREWSTER, C. (2005) 'In search of legitimacy: national professional associations and the professionalism of HR practitioners', *Human Resource Management Journal*, Vol. 15, No. 3, 33–48
This article presents the results of a worldwide survey of professional associations for personnel specialists, arguing that the function shows signs of professionalism but is not yet a profession.

GUEST, D. E. (1997) 'Human resource management and performance: a review and a research agenda', *International Journal of Human Resource Management*, Vol. 8, 263–76
A seminal, critical, study by one of the UK's leading thinkers about HRM on the link between HRM and firm performance.

MARTIN, G. (2005) *Technology and People Management: Transforming the function of HR and the HR function*. London, CIPD
A useful summary of the literature on developments in the technology available to, and increasingly used by, HRM departments and the implications that technology will have for the role of the function.

CHAPTER 21

The organisation of work

Martin Upchurch

INTRODUCTION

This chapter examines new ways of organising work in the modern workplace. The last 30 years have seen large changes in the organisation of work in workplaces all over the world. In the British workplace, change has been a direct product of new employer strategies to compete in an increasingly internationalised product market. The new wave of work organisation has included the development of both hard and soft techniques of HRM, has adapted to the Japanese production model, and has more latterly taken on the 'high performance' concept. The Government, in adapting to these developments, has also sought to encourage employers to work in partnership with their employees and trade unions in an effort to raise productivity in jointly agreed initiatives. This consensus-based approach is presented as an alternative to the confrontation between unions and employers in British industry. There is little disagreement amongst academics and practitioners that these changes have happened, although there remains considerable division as to the scale and scope of change, and probably more importantly, as to the effects the changes have had on the quality of working life and the intensity of work itself. All of this is important context for the HR professional.

LEARNING OUTCOMES

By the end of this chapter readers should be able to:

- appreciate the reason for change within a globalised economy

- describe government and employer strategies and reasons for reorganising work

- review the evidence of changing work organisation

- discuss the major points of debates and controversies associated with the organisation of work

- understand what all this means for the HR professional.

The chapter is in four parts. First, we consider the reasons for change, as they are located in a globalising economy. Then we review the importance of Japanese production methods and the concept of HRM for work organisation. Finally, we look at the high-performance work approach. Throughout we consider the debates and controversies around this new world of work.

The chapter concludes with the main case study.

Reference sources named within the chapter may be looked up in the *References and further reading* section at the end of the book.

STARTER CASE STUDY

Goos and Manning (2003) have produced evidence to suggest that a polarisation of job skills is taking place in Britain (reflecting the experience of the USA) between low-paid low-skilled jobs and high-skill knowledge-intensive jobs. Both sets of jobs are said to be growing faster in total than 'middling' types of jobs such as clerical, administrative and lower managerial jobs. Most of the low-skill jobs, however, are in service work in areas such as catering and tourism and in personal services in the caring sector, whereas in manufacturing there appears to be a decline in low-skill jobs in the USA and Europe as routinised jobs become automated. The pattern of job growth produced by these trends is reflected in a 'U-bend' profile.

The scenario described above has been questioned by other academic commentators. The starter case study is intended firstly to help understanding of the debate, and secondly to relate the recorded evidence to the situation in organisations.

Dorling and Thomas (2004), using 2001 Census data, record a relatively faster increase in 'associate professional' jobs (eg nurses, social workers, fire service operatives and police) than in any other jobs, and a second-fastest growth of 'elementary occupations' (such as those employed in shelf-stacking in retail and cleaning in the service sector). These trends would support a 'polarisation thesis', with a drift at the ends of the skills spectrum to low-skill poor-quality jobs at one end and to high-skill high-value-added jobs at the other, together with a stabilisation of middle managerial and administrative occupations.

However, using evidence from the Government's Annual Surveys of Hours and Earnings, the Director of Research at the Department of Trade and Industry Grant Fitzner (2006) shows that 'since 1998, the share of low-paid UK jobs has shrunk and the proportion of high-paid jobs has increased. The proportion of jobs paying around median earnings has remained relatively unchanged, contrary to the thesis of a "disappearing

middle".' There seems also to have been a reversal in the managerial 'de-layering' process. A survey of 2,000 UK managers in 2002 showed that on average 22% of managers said that the proportion of managerial and professional staff had risen in the previous three years, against 8% who thought there had been a decline and 69% who reported little change.

Question for discussion

1 How can this seemingly contradictory evidence be explained?

2 Is it because there has been an increase in 'manager' jobs after two decades of managerial de-layering?

3 Does low-paid work by migrant labour (much of it illegal) register in the statistics? In your organisation or in one you know well, what trends can you observe which may confirm or refute the 'U-bend' profile?

4 What might these changes mean for the HR professional?

1 THE GLOBALISATION OF PRODUCTION AND SERVICES

The 1970s saw the end of the long period of post-war economic growth and stability. Rising oil prices added to inflationary tendencies and put extra strains on those advanced industrial nations, such as Japan, that were more dependent on imported oil than competitors. The economic downturn came with a crisis of profitability amongst corporations in the Western economies, leading them by the end of the 1970s to search for new production locations (to cut costs) and new markets (for sales of products).

The new era of globalisation started by this process was accompanied by changes in international political economy. Typically, it involved moves within supra-national institutions such as the International Monetary Fund, the World Bank, and later the World Trade Organisation (WTO), to pressurise the under-developed countries to lower tariff barriers and allow the free movement of capital, goods and services. This was thought necessary by the countries of the richer world to allow their enterprises access to the new markets in the form of foreign direct investment (FDI), the establishment of new production facilities, or the control and ownership of services.

The eventual reaction by countries of the developing South to this pressure from the industrialised North brought in the decline of their 'import substitution model' of national self-sufficient development and the creation of a new international division of labour. This division of labour was based on comparative advantage and free (but not necessarily fair) trade whereby the countries of the South produced goods and service for the world market linked either to commodity production or to cheap labour costs. The process of searching for ever-cheaper production locations has led many commentators to warn against a 'race to the bottom', which might negatively affect labour standards and conditions in both South and North. Table 48 shows the enormous gap which exists in wage costs for workers in manufacturing – workers in Sri Lanka, for example, earning just over half a US dollar an hour, whereas workers in Norway earn on average almost 35 dollars per hour. Even in the European Union, manufacturing wages vary from just over 7 dollars per hour (Portugal) to just over 34 dollars per hour (in what used to be West Germany).

In many ways globalisation is a double-edged sword. On the one hand the drive towards market liberalisation and downward regulation of labour and financial markets has created real fears about job insecurity, income inequality and declining democratic participation at work. On the other hand demands for some re-regulation to bring market forces under control have arisen in opposition. In terms of fears, the need to improve competitiveness in the world product market has clearly led employers to flexibilise their employment contracts and try to reduce employment. This fear (real or perceived) is increased by the upturn in takeovers, mergers and alliances as capital restructures and consolidates on an international dimension.

Second, the expansion of corporate activity across national boundaries has weakened government ability to regulate corporate activity without fear of offending the very corporations whose investment decisions are seen by pro-

Table 48 Hourly compensation costs (in US dollars) for production workers in manufacturing, 2004

United States	22.87
Brazil	3.03
Canada	21.42
Mexico	2.50
Australia	23.09
Hong Kong (1,2)	5.51
Israel	12.18
Japan	21.90
Korea	11.52
New Zealand	12.89
Singapore	7.45
Sri Lanka	0.51
Taiwan	5.97
Austria	28.29
Belgium	29.98
Czech Republic	5.43
Denmark	33.75
Finland	30.67
France	23.89
Germany, former West	34.05
Germany, all	32.53
Hungary	5.72
Ireland, Republic of	21.94
Italy	20.48
Luxembourg	26.57
Netherlands	30.76
Norway	34.64
Portugal	7.02
Spain	17.10
Sweden	28.41
Switzerland	30.26
United Kingdom	24.71

(1) Hong Kong Special Administrative Region of China.
(2) Average of selected manufacturing industries.
Source: US Bureau of Labor Statistics, February 2006

market regimes to be important to national well-being and economic health. Corporate taxation, for example, has fallen by an average 3.5% in all advanced industrial countries since the mid-1990s, and tax rates on US MNCs in developing countries have dropped from an average 54% in 1986 to 28% in 1996. The UK economy is relatively highly exposed to the world market when compared to other advanced industrial nations. The UK has disproportionately high rates of both outward and inward investment, spread across both manufacturing and service industries, making the UK economy extremely dependent on decisions taken by non-UK owners abroad. Also, the UK has also experienced a higher rate of mergers, takeovers and strategic alliances than competitors. This is due in part to Britain's high exposure to the world economy and the consequent need for restructuring, and in part because of the Anglo-Saxon corporate governance regime with its emphasis on short-termism, shareholder value and propensity to hostile takeover.

Globalisation is also affecting provision of public services as regulatory regimes are liberalised to allow entry into national markets of foreign-owned service providers. The EU Services Directive will reinforce this trend by opening up public service markets within the EU, while the World Trade Organisation General Agreement on Trade in Services (GATS) has the same intention. What is highlighted by this evidence is the extreme volatility of investment and corporate ownership within the UK, which in turn makes both employee relations regimes and the labour market uncertain and unstable. This means that is hard for HR professionals to minimise redundancies and to avoid the negative effects described in Chapter 19.

Government strategy has responded to the high risks of a globalised economy by promoting both the high-performance workplace (see below) and partnership in the workplace between employers and employees. The aim is to improve UK productivity by building a consensus in the workplace on the need to modernise work practices through flexibility and skill training. Partnership is promoted as a method for such practice, by engaging employees through participation and establishing trust and job security (see Chapter 19).

The effects of these global processes on the organisation of work in the trading sector of advanced economies such as Britain are considerable.

Firstly, the pressures from stronger international competition have meant that *enterprises have reassessed their labour and production costs.* Low-skill labour-intensive industries in richer countries are less likely to survive, and employers will be tempted to shift production facilities or outsource production abroad to take advantage of lower labour costs. In the UK, for example, jobs needing degree-level qualifications have grown much faster than non-degree jobs in the last 15 years, while jobs needing low-level or no qualifications have declined sharply. According to WERS 2004, employers are also much more likely to provide off-the-job training than in the past, 64% of employers doing so in 2004 compared to 42% in 1998. Other enterprises may also re-examine their production operations and, if necessary, re-focus on core production while abandoning, subcontracting or outsourcing peripheral or lower-skill functions.

The textile and clothing industries show interesting examples of these processes. Cheaper labour costs in Morocco have led Courtaulds to move much of its textile production to that country, while the retailer Marks & Spencers has also moved where it gets a lot of its clothing brand away from the UK to Morocco. However, in some developed countries clothing production has been kept, due to government protectionist tariffs and cheap immigrant labour in the case of the Los Angeles area, or by marketing and cultural/networking links to the fashion industry in the case of the north Italian Emiglia-Romana industrial district. Considerable media attention has also been directed at companies' moving call centre operations abroad in cheaper labour locations such as India. However, surveys estimate that in 2004 only about 6% of call centre jobs have been offshored in this way.

Secondly, the nature of work itself is likely to change as *employers seek to restructure working methods*, either by using more creative and knowledge-based applications to production (eg robotics and computer-aided design), by intensifying levels of labour exploitation to cut down 'waste' time at work, by redesigning production processes with new technology, or by the introduction of more flexible working arrangements to allow multi-tasking and multi-skilling (see Chapter 10). The proportion of UK workers using information technology as part of their job, for example, is estimated to have risen from just over half in 1992 to almost three quarters in 2001.

Many commentators suggest that the two trends combined have led to a *polarisation* of job skills between those better jobs – MacJobs – which require an upgraded knowledge-based skill set, and those lower-graded routine-based-skill jobs in personal services, fast food and shops – McJobs (eg Goos and Manning, 2003). Other forms of flexibility – such as numerical, contract and temporal flexibility – may be used to create a tighter fit between organisational requirements and staffing. WERS 2004 records that some core employees have been trained to be functionally flexible in two thirds of UK workplaces with 10 or more employees. However, despite predictions in the 1980s and 1990s of the end of the 'job for life', the evidence shows that permanent full-time work is still the norm for the British worker, with 94% of employed men and 92% of employed women in permanent-contract jobs at the turn of the century. 96% of workers also have one job, rather than a 'portfolio' of different jobs, although portfolio working may exist within organisations as employees take on a range of tasks for a single employer.

One additional product of increased working with information technology has been a rise in working remotely from home as well as an increase in working via a laptop 'on the move'. According to the Government's *Labour Force Survey*, the proportion of people working mostly at or from home has risen to one in 10 (about 2.8 million people) in 2002 from one in 25 in 1981. IT has also encouraged the phenomenon of 'hot-desking' and open-plan offices. Hot-desking is now used by one in four employers, and most employers now use open-plan offices, often creating the appearance of office 'factories'.

Thirdly, because of the increased likelihood that new global companies will be able to enter product markets, *manufacturers and service providers have to be more responsive to consumer demands* if they are to retain and increase their market share. This will require production processes to be more functionally flexible. This need for *flexible specialisation* brings a 'new industrial divide' between the old mass production techniques and more flexible techniques based on cellular or alternative methods of production. More importantly, Japanese management and production techniques became increasingly seen as the way forward for production. British employers have tried to upgrade workers' skills as part of this process, particularly through work-based training.

Fourthly, there has been *an integration of tasks within the organisation*, achieved most importantly through teamworking. Teams are used to co-ordinate tasks between people in contrast to hierarchically based divisions of labour observed under Taylorist systems. WERS 2004 shows that 88% of public sector workplaces and 66% of private sector workplaces now operate with some core employees in formally designated teams. Teamworking might also involve some form of quasi self-governance (or autonomy) through which problem-solving can take place. A mixture of skills within teams can also remove the need for specialist individual operations such as quality checking and work allocation. The 2004 WERS survey showed that 21% of workplaces with more than 10 employees at that time had problem-solving groups amongst their core employees, up from 16% in 1998. The introduction of cellular teamworking in high-technology industries such as aerospace has also created opportunities for employers to outsource less profitable or lower-value-added production processes. Finally, as the classic Human Relations school of thought showed, teams have a distinct social role which may be used to integrate employees into the values and culture of the organisation, to reduce feelings of 'them' and 'us', and to facilitate the development of social capital through networking (see Chapter 24). Coaching and mentoring of employees is increasingly used as a way of instilling organisational culture and values (see Chapter 15).

Fifthly, many of the above changes *have social implications*. Although unemployment has fallen in the UK over the last decade, the proportion of inactive men in the labour market has stayed consistently high, reflecting a shift away from older traditional industries (in which men dominated) to newer information- and service-based industries with more women and younger employees. More workers are also coming from abroad, especially since the expansion of the EU into central and eastern Europe. Immigrant workers also show a polarised skill base – some are recruited to skilled jobs within industry and the public services, while others work in the informal economy. The net effect is to make the UK workplace and work regimes in general much more diverse.

REFLECTIVE ACTIVITY

What effect has globalisation had on an industry and/or organisation in which you work or which you know well?

What evidence is there of the industry's/organisation's outsourcing or shifting production to developing countries?

Has there been an upskilling of knowledge-based work in the industry/organisation?

What are the limits to working at home? Why might the office still live on as the core place of work?

2 JAPANESE METHODS

The 'Japanese production model' of the 1970s and 1980s was characterised by high-quality goods produced at low costs. Japan set new standards in production. Lower cost was a result not so much of cheaper basic wage costs but of lower *unit* wage costs which came from more efficient production methods based on teamworking, just-in-time production and business process engineering. High quality, according to the model, came from self-checking, quality circles and an ethos of continuous improvement (*kaizen*). Such was the power of the model that it led to a US-Government-commissioned enquiry by the Massachusetts Institute of Technology (MIT) to look at the nature, significance and possible use of the model in American manufacturing. The results of the study, written into book form as *The Machine that Changed the World* (Womack, Jones and Roos, 1990), praised the Japanese 'lean' production process and suggested that only a Toyotan 'best way' could solve the problems of US manufacturing competitiveness. Womack *et al* claimed that lean production meant working 'smarter, not harder', suggesting that the recommended new production methods should be a paradigm break with the alienating Taylorist methods of the past. Furthermore, they suggested (Womack *et al*, 1990; p.101) that the everyday experience of work would be better as a result:

> *While the mass production plant is often filled with mind-numbing stress, as workers struggle to assemble unmanufacturable products and have no way to improve their working environment, lean production offers a creative tension in which workers have many ways to address challenges. This creative tension involved in solving complex problems is precisely what has separated manual factory work from professional 'think' work in the age of mass production.*

As Japanese production methods began to be adopted in Western industrialised countries in the 1980s and 1990s, many studies tried to measure their impact. Oliver and Wilkinson (1992) produced an important work, *The Japanisation of British Industry*, in which they explained the prescriptions of the Japanese model designed to stop waste in production. They outlined Total Quality Management (TQM), continuous improvement (*kaizen*), just-in-time production (JIT), teamworking, job rotation and multi-skilling as key parts of the system and suggested that, in the UK context, such new methods might damage industrial relations. New techniques of HRM would be necessary to overcome labour resistance, including careful employee selection techniques, direct communications between the employer and employee, performance-related pay and longer-term job security. These practices thus combined both production methods and management techniques, and work was reorganised against the potential interests of collective labour but in favour of more satisfying work for the individual. By the end of the century, the impact of such work practices in UK workplaces was considerable. In 2000 quality circles covered three in ten workers – half as many again compared with 10 years earlier. The majority of UK workers now work in groups, an increase of 10% from the early 1990s.

REFLECTIVE ACTIVITY

Could the full range of Japanese practices be transferred to British factories and offices despite the great differences in cultural and institutional background?

Do Japanese production methods in fact mark a break with Taylorist mass production methods, or are they simply a revised and refined version of Taylorism?

Are workers liberated through self-checking of quality and through teamworking – or are they actually just working harder with extra surveillance?

Note that we have here introduced the concept of *ratios* of one job family to another, or of one as a percentage of the whole workforce. These can be more revealing than simple statistics.

In discussing the questions of the exercise above, many studies point to the enhanced effect on performance generated by worker peer pressure through teamworking, or highlight the autonomy of workers achieved under computer-aided teamworking. Labour-oriented perspectives are more critical. Garrahan and Stewart (1992), in their study of the Nissan transplant in Sunderland, focused on the ideological nature of control over workers in the factory, leading to intensified worker exploitation. Danford (1999), in his study of Japanese factories in South Wales, draws similar conclusions, and suggests that Japanese production methods intensify work through semi-Taylorist methods with limited opportunities for worker creativity and self-expression. A study for the Department for Education and Skills (DfES) by Felstead, Gallie and Green

CASE STUDY

'I must admit, a lot of the earlier ideas we were looking at were based on the idea that everybody would be encouraged to spend time off production on *kaizen* activity. But I'm afraid that's not reality, is it? Life isn't like that. We still want involvement from the shop floor, but our 100% priority – and I stress 100% – must be making parts. Therefore the direction we're moving in now is that team leaders, the unit managers, will be the problem-solvers and they will just involve team members in more of a consultative manner through effective communications with the employees.'

Personnel manager in car components factory, from Danford (1999) *Japanese Management Techniques and British Workers* (p.153)

Questions for discussion

1 What might explain the constraints on managerial ability to introduce full worker autonomy?

2 Should effective teamworking bring about the abolition of the role of team leader?

3 How might good performance for teamworking be rewarded?

(2002) reported that although responsibility might have increased, the amount of 'task discretion' in UK workplaces had decreased significantly for both professionals and skilled workers throughout the 1990s. Discretion and control for managers, however, seems to have increased, often with the use of remote surveillance techniques aided by information technology.

3 HUMAN RESOURCE MANAGEMENT AND THE ORGANISATION OF WORK

We now focus on how techniques of HRM may have reshaped the organisation of work in advanced economies such as Britain's. An important aspect of HRM has been the focus on individual value added, and its quantification by systems of performance measurement and appraisal (see Chapter 12). The measurement of performance is notoriously difficult. This is due to the sometimes contradictory pressures between the need for quantity and the need for quality; the inexact science of performance measurement itself (especially in public services); the likelihood of the creation of anomalies between jobs, grades and occupations; and the effects of bonuses on performance systems. In addition, no definite link has been confirmed between individual effort and the incentives (such as pay).

Despite these difficulties a move towards individual performance measurement has been a central feature of British workplace practice since the 1980s. According to WERS 2004 formal performance appraisal was conducted in 78% of British workplaces. The systems needed to conduct such performance review have been a major influence on the organisation of work.

- *New systems of financial control and accountability within organisations have been constructed*, including the creation of cost centres, budget centres and strategic business units and the marketisation of services between these units. Such units are made accountable not only for budgets but also for their value added or profitability. Because of this, the process of outsourcing activities which produce less value within the 'value chain' is encouraged, and the likelihood of organisational restructuring to maximise value added is increased. Techniques of HRM are subordinated to the process of financial accountability, leading to the development of 'hard' HRM and human asset accounting, as well as individual and group target-setting.

- Within the public sector, the development of '*new public management*' has tried to copy many of the features of divisional financial accountability seen in the private sector. However, the measurement of individual value added is much harder in the public sector than in the private sector due to the lack of profit imperative. A substitute for this has been the introduction by the Government of principles of marketisation through private finance initiatives, public–private partnerships and internal trading of services. This has had a parallel effect on organisational restructuring and the creation of organisational targets in sectors such as the NHS and education.

- In many organisations performance measurement has moved beyond quantitative assessment towards *softer competency objectives* such as the ability to work in teams, leadership, etc. A good deal of competency assessment reflects TQM processes whereby attitudinal structuring is undertaken by HRM-led initiatives to promote ideas of customer consciousness. Teamworking has been especially encouraged, both to reflect 'Japanese' best practice and to encourage commitment through employee task participation.

- Other occupationally specific competencies include concepts of emotional and even aesthetic labour. Both *emotional and aesthetic labour* measurement is justified by organisational needs to satisfy customer demand. As well as the employee 'selling' manual effort to the employer (manual labour) and intellectual effort (intellectual labour) the need might also be to 'sell' positive aspects of personality (emotional labour) or how one looks (aesthetic labour).

REFLECTIVE ACTIVITY

What are the main purposes of creating flatter spans of control in organisations by de-layering managerial jobs?

Why might methods of performance-related pay be more contested in public sector employment?

How can teams be used to create a greater customer or consumer consciousness?

JOB REDESIGN AND BUSINESS PROCESS ENGINEERING

In looking at the above developments some commentators suggest that HRM techniques represent a return to motivational theory popularised by theorists of the Human Relations school such as Maslow, Herzberg and McGregor. This is in reaction to the alienation of workers associated with Taylorist and Fordist principles of scientific management and automated mass-assembly production. For these reasons renewed efforts to revisit *job design* (eg job rotation, job enrichment, job enlargement) through teamworking processes do not just fulfil the needs of lean production but also employees' needs for and desires for intrinsic and extrinsic motivation. Allied with these developments are debates about contract status and content, as job boundaries and job descriptions are deliberately blurred or even absent and the 'new psychological contract' is open-ended, with greater expectation of self-initiative and lower expectation of paternalistic and heavily regulated employment relationships.

Alongside new contractual expectations are efforts to reorganise hierarchical structure within organisations through business process engineering. Such new organisational design allows more horizontal communication between employees and networking to complete specified tasks and projects. Traditional structural boundaries are by-passed or abolished in order to generate employee creativity and initiative. The resulting organisational form can be described as the 'virtual corporation'. The blurring of contract boundary is potentially negative for employee interests, as organisational control may adversely affect controls over health and safety, and working hours, whereby the 'norm' expectation of the eight-hour working day disappears and a long hours culture of 'presenteeism' is substituted. Business process re-engineering has also often resulted in substantial de-layering of managerial and other jobs, as organisational redesign happens. Because of this, the process has often been criticised for forgetting the 'human dimension' of working life.

This has been recognised by Michael Hammer, the computing academic and business consultant who first coined the phrase 'business process re-engineering', when interviewed for an article in the *Wall Street Journal* in 1996.

> *Dr Hammer points out a flaw: He and the other leaders of the $4.7 billion re-engineering industry forgot about people. 'I wasn't smart enough about that,' he says. 'I was reflecting my engineering background and was insufficient appreciative of the human dimension. I've learned that's critical.'*

REFLECTIVE ACTIVITY

How might the 'virtual corporation' differ in organisational design from a traditional hierarchically organised enterprise?

What extra skills might be required of employees in a task-based networking organisation?

What would be the consequences for HR professionals working in 'virtual corporations' or in task-based networking organisations?

The difficulties of organisational redesign experienced in the 1990s, combined with the structural limitations to continued productivity improvement through lean production techniques, have led commentators to refer to a 'crisis of HRM'. Sparrow and Marchington (1998) talk about a *contribution dilemma* of HRM which questions the technical validity of many HRM techniques, argues for a need to define the link between HRM and organisational performance, and refers to the growing sophistication of the role of HRM within organisational strategy. Out of such reflection new approaches have emerged centred on the notion of the 'high-performance work system', which is examined below.

4 HIGH-PERFORMANCE WORK SYSTEMS

In the early 1990s, there was increasing concern on the part of employers and US political leaders that productivity growth in America was possibly suffering from the aftershocks of a decade of de-layering of jobs within corporations. One potential byproduct of increasing job precariousness was a decline in workplace trust seen as necessary in business process engineering to develop a spirit of creativity and innovation. Applebaum, Bailey, Berg and Kallenberg (2000) argued that a shift in management–employee relations was now needed if organisations were to overcome lack of trust and create the conditions for increased productivity. Their book *Manufacturing Advantage: Why high-performance work systems pay off* makes an argument for the high-performance work system (HPWS) that placed job security, management–worker trust, worker participation and upskilling as central features:

- direct worker participation in decisions over operational functions – sharing power with management rather than individual worker empowerment

- agreement to increase worker skills

- creation of incentives for worker participation

- facilitation of co-ordination and communication between employees.

It is argued that the above high-skill model must be based on management's willingness to devolve power within the organisation, if necessary in consultation/negotiation with trade unions (see Chapter 17). Such an approach leads, it is suggested, to a win/win situation based on mutual gains for both employers and employees. Earlier experiments at the 'high-performance' approach were introduced at the Volvo car factory in Kalmar, Sweden, in the form of *semi-autonomous teams* (although it should be noted that the factory has since been closed).

CASE STUDY

Volvo defined five levels of group-working at its Kalmar plant. Level 1 is simply working as a group. Level 5 (the highest level) allows for the increased possibility that the group can make its own decisions. Payments to each group are linked both to training and to the consequent level of attainment.

Level 1 – working as a group

Level 2 – job enlargement

Level 3 – increases in responsibility for planning

Level 4 – job rotation

Level 5 – increased possibility of making own decisions.

Questions for discussion

1 Why might it be argued that such job re-design will increase worker productivity?

2 How might such changes in the organisation of work affect managerial authority and control?

The central proposition of HPWS is that previous efforts to drive workers to work harder by lean production, peer pressure, surveillance and control are inferior to systems which allow more worker discretion and greater autonomy. The ideas of HPWS have since been taken up by the UK Government in its publications on the subject (DTI, 2002; 2004) as well as the CIPD (2004). The Engineering Employers' Federation (EEF) also promotes the concept and in its pamphlet *Catching Up with Uncle Sam: The final report on US/UK manufacturing productivity* (2001) a link is made between more responsible and discretionary working methods and improved productivity. A joint CIPD/EEF Report (2003) argues that in introducing HPWS:

> *Job design is very influential. Where people have some influence over how they do their job, and where they find their job interesting and challenging, they are much more likely to have job satisfaction, be motivated and be more committed to the organisation.*

The CIPD (2004) report produced by David Guest lists 18 high-performance work practices associated with HPWS, which may be introduced as bundles of practices and which have implications both for the organisation of work and for HR practice. Examples are shown in the box below.

Flexible job descriptions
Open-ended job description with lack of precise roles and expected tasks. Implication of continual skill upgrading

Work improvement teams
Task-based semi-permanent multi-skilled teams enacted to boost quality and design more efficient and less wasteful working method

Problem-solving groups
Ad hoc (often voluntary) multi-skilled groups drawn from different work departments with the aim of suggesting methods of overcoming design problems and improving quality; similar to quality circles

Single status
System of awarding equal benefits to all occupational groups in the workplace – such as pension entitlement, holiday entitlement, sick leave entitlement, car-parking spaces, etc, but excluding pay and remuneration

Harmonisation
Process of moving to single status or near single status

Job redesign
Job rotation to allow employees to utilise a greater range of skills on a greater range of tasks, thus reducing alienation
Job enrichment to allow employees to expand their skills and responsibilities

Continuous learning
Promotion of learning and development within organisation through formal and informal means and through permanent and semi-permanent organisational structures

In particular flexible job descriptions, multi-skilling, work improvement teams, problem-solving groups, single status and harmonisation are all considered important factors within an environment of continuous learning. However, central to the HPWS approach is the important role of employee discretion in improving organisational performance. Purcell *et al* (2003), in their case study research on behalf of the CIPD, emphasise this link, and suggest that for organisational performance to improve employees must not only do their job but act 'beyond contract' to do more. Their willingness to do so is in turn a function of improvements in job satisfaction and the consequent supposed link between job satisfaction, organisational commitment and individual performance. It follows that for such discretionary behaviour to really work well, organisations must relax supervisory and hierarchical control.

 REFLECTIVE ACTIVITY

List examples of high-performance working in organisations you are familiar with.

What barriers might there be in organisations to the introduction of HPWS?

How might such barriers be overcome?

The concept and operational effects of HPWS have been criticised. Although Appelbaum *et al*'s (2000) US-based study appeared to show positive outcomes of HPWS for employees in terms of trust and job satisfaction, some other studies have been less enthusiastic. Both White, Hill, McGovern, Mills and Smeaton (2004a) and Danford, Richardson, Stewart, Tailby and Upchurch (2005) in surveys conducted for the Economic and Social Research Council's Future of Work Programme found that HPWS can negatively affect employees' work–life balance and intensify work. Discretion is often limited to management grades, and does not reach down to lower-grade occupations. Danford *et al* (2005; p.8) further argue that many of the constraining and controlling aspects of lean production 'have been cannibalised most successfully in the current ideology of the high-performance workplace'.

The difficulties of introducing effective HPWS are recognised by practitioners. Porter and Ketels' (2003) report into UK competitiveness suggested that UK companies are less likely to adopt modern management techniques than their competitors. The role of line managers in implementing the process is crucial, and it is here that some resistance to relaxing control may take place. Findings from WERS 2004 seem to confirm the pessimism, as the proportion of workplaces using a combination of high-involvement practices has shown only a 'marginal increase' since the 1998 survey. Most importantly, there appeared to be a continued lack of trust between employers and employees. Trust appeared in only 'a minority' of workplaces. Because of this the Government has been keen to link up HPWS with 'partnership'-based practices, emphasising the micro-institutional benefits of employee–employer consensus and joint problem-solving. The Government has since established a Partnership Fund to encourage joint problem-solving initiatives between employees, their unions and employers. Both the TUC and the CBI have also embraced the concept of partnership at work, seeing it as both a route to higher productivity and of mutual benefit to employers and the workforce. However, important differences exist between the US, UK and the 'European Social Model' institutional environments. The European 'social partnership' model offers greater institutional support for employee voice and representation than that of the USA. Partnership in Britain appears a hybrid case lying between the US mutual gains model and the EU social model.

KEY ISSUES IN WORK ORGANISATION

We now pull together ten key points about the organisation of work raised in this chapter:

- Increased internationalisation of the world economy has intensified product market competition and has been a major driver of outsourcing and industrial restructuring. In an attempt to remain competitive and increase productivity, employers have turned to new production methods and business process engineering and sought to focus on core activities which maximise value added for the organisation. Value chains have expanded across national boundaries and a new international division of labour has emerged.

- As for the workplace itself, evidence points to an intensification of work as wasteful production is gradually eliminated and time porosity in the working day is squeezed by self-disciplinary processes induced by teamworking, surveillance and monitoring of performance, and multi-skilling and tasking of the workforce.

- An associated effect appears to have been a polarisation of skills within the workforce as lower-skilled jobs are automated and routinised and 'knowledge'-based jobs are credited with more discretion and autonomy.

- A rejoinder to this process has been the new paradigm of high-performance working and partnership, with an emphasis on organisational trust and employee consultation constructed to channel workers' creativity into the production regime.

- Within the non-trading public sector many of the processes associated with manufacturing and service provision have

been replicated. Encouraged by marketisation and privatisation, a new disaggregation of function has emerged within organisations which has encouraged cost-consciousness and relaxed hierarchical controls in favour of a networking-based organisational culture.

- Much of the discussion of high performance has been framed within concerns over a 'crisis of HRM' by which doubts have arisen over the usefulness of HRM techniques in enhancing organisational performance.

- Workplace-based evidence also suggests that increased discretion appears to have been focused on managers, while staff remain subject to continuing and new forms of control.

- As we move from the present to the future it is clear that no simple picture of work and the workplace will emerge.

- Employers in advanced industrial nations such as Britain will have enormous pressure placed on them to move up the value chain in order to compete in the world economy. Such a move will not only define the type of jobs that are available in the labour market, but will also define the ideal 'type' of worker that is required to fill the job.

- More innovative production will require a more innovative workforce, and this may continue to challenge both employers and workers alike.

Perhaps there are other key points that you would like to note for yourself.

The main case study in this chapter now follows. It reflects the context of the finance sector in the UK over the last decade – a sector that might be said to have undergone more than its fair share of restructuring during that period.

MAIN CASE STUDY

Make an initial reading of the case study to gain an overview of the situation, and then read the questions that you will need to address. Now read the case study again, making notes of issues and facts that will help you in your analysis and responses to the questions. Remember to 'read between the lines' as well as picking out the obvious points, and also to consider what is not said as well as what is presented here.

The finance sector in the UK now represents about 19% per cent of all UK employment. In the past, divisions between the three sub-sectors (banking, insurance and building societies) in the UK were fairly well established but since the 1980s boundaries within the sector have become blurred as they have undergone the 'financial services revolution'. The sector has been especially affected by mergers, acquisitions and takeovers alongside de-regulation and then re-regulation of financial markets and de-mutualisation within the sector. This process has been a response to increased competition, as organisations seek to develop economies of scale and secure an increased market share.

The restructuring of the industry has also adversely affected job security as cost efficiency and capital concentration has taken its toll. New forms of delivery based on call centre operation followed the telephone-based creation of *Direct Line* in the 1980s and this has been followed in turn by Internet and digital television access as well as new entrants into the product market. New technology has also allowed much of the administration and case work to be computerised, and as a consequence many jobs are now routinised and closely monitored for output. The introduction of cash machines, for example, has eliminated the need for so many front desk staff in retail banks, but increased the need for 'white-collar factories' of staff processing the transactions. Those that do work in the high street banks are now also expected to be able to sell the bank's products over the counter. All new insurance claims or applications are usually scanned in the post room and then sent electronically to a claims or new business handler via the computer network. Once one claim is completed, the next one simply pops up on the screen. At the other end of the spectrum, insurance advisers, for

example, are expected to have knowledge of a range of products that could be made available to a customer or client. Because of this, their own knowledge of a company's products (and its competitors' products) is likely to add value to the employing organisation.

In terms of staff representation the sector exhibits the complete range of relationships from non-union (or indeed anti-union), through recognition of dependent staff association, independent staff associations, to independent trade union. The independent unions representing the sector (predominantly Amicus through its old MSF section, and UNIFI) have traditionally recorded low levels of militancy. This has been explained in the past with particular reference to banking, as a reflection of the conservative organisational culture of the industry. More recently, commentators have noted a change in bank workers' attitudes towards a more collective and pro-union orientation driven by work intensification and regimentation, which may be a precursor of similar developments in the rest of the finance sector. Employer strategy in response includes the development of partnership arrangements – 14 signed in the sector between 1997 and 2000.

Alongside capital concentration have been major changes to the organisation of work as employers have sought to become more cost-efficient in an increasingly competitive product market. Both de/re-regulation and de-mutualisation are reasons for the emergence of a new management 'model' whereby the old model based on paternalism, conservatism and bureaucracy has given way to a new model of sales and performance orientation and technocracy. However, evidence from the banking sector and from insurance suggests that this new model has not always been successfully translated into creation and consolidation of softer HRM techniques based on employee involvement and participation. This is partly because of a continuation of the old management culture and partly because of the background of staff reductions and low trust of management motives fed by job insecurity. De-layering of management jobs has been accompanied with the break-up of the whole business into separately accountable business divisions. Restructuring of work has been driven by the perceived need to cut operating costs, leading to work intensification through computerisation and increased case-loading. New forms of pay are prevalent in the sector, based on individual performance and sometimes linked with job evaluation to accommodate shifting skills in relation to new technology. Competency-based pay is also common, emphasising the ability to work in teams, and sales and customer consciousness. Some organisations within the sector also have market-based pay systems, with pay rates set to the ability to recruit and retain staff within a localised labour market. As with much UK industry, teamworking has been introduced throughout the sector and operational targets have been introduced for these teams based on sales performance, completed case work, or other quantifiable measures.

Case study adapted from: Upchurch, M., Richardson, M., Tailby, S., Danford, A. and Stewart, P. (2006) 'Employee representation and partnership in the non-union sector: a paradox of intention?', *Human Resource Management Journal*, Vol. 16, No. 4, 393–410

Qustions for discussion

1 In the light of this background to recent developments in the finance sector, what do you consider to be priority areas for the management of human resources in the sector?

2 What problems might an HR practitioner envisage with the introduction of widespread teamworking?

3 In what ways might jobs in such organisations be subject to enlargement or rotation?

EXPLORE FURTHER

APPELBAUM, E., BAILEY, T., BERG, P. and KALLENBERG, A. L. (2000) *Manufacturing Advantage: Why high-performance work systems pay off*. Ithaca, Cornell University Press
This is an excellent description of a high-performance workplace in the USA.

DANFORD, A. (1999) *Japanese Management Techniques and British Workers*. London, Mansell
This provides a critique of Japanisation in the UK.

GOOS, M. and MANNING, A. (2003) 'McJobs and MacJobs: the growing polarisation of jobs in the UK'. In R. Dickens, P. Gregg and J. Wadsworth (eds) *The Labour Market Under New Labour: The state of working Britain*. New York, Palgrave Macmillan
This study illustrates the polarisation of work-based skills in the UK economy.

WHITE, M., HILL, S., McGOVERN, P., MILLS, C. and SMEATON, D. (2004a) *Managing to Change?* Basingstoke, Palgrave
A useful survey of UK workplaces from the ESRC's Future of Work programme.

WOMACK, J. P., JONES, D. T. and ROOS, D. (1990) *The Machine That Changed the World: The triumph of lean production*. New York, Rawson Macmillan
This is a seminal account of lean production conducted at the request of the US Government.

CHAPTER 22

International HRM

Michael Muller-Camen *and* Chris Brewster

INTRODUCTION

This chapter is about the HRM issues faced by companies operating internationally.

LEARNING OUTCOMES

By the end of this chapter readers should be able to:

- describe factors that encourage international firms to standardise or globalise HR practices

- discuss the extent to which HR practices can be globally standardised

- list the different approaches to transfers of employees

- evaluate the ways multinational firms can select, prepare, compensate and reintegrate expatriates.

This chapter is in two parts. The first part deals with the 'global versus local' dilemma and discusses whether and how multinational companies (MNCs) can standardise HR policies and practices across their subsidiaries. We analyse the contradictory pressures towards global integration and local responsiveness faced by multinationals and describe some examples of their impact on HRM. The second part deals with HR issues to do with the transfer of employees abroad. We explore some of the ways that the process has been analysed and then work round the 'expatriate cycle' of selecting them, preparing them, managing them and bringing them back.

The chapter concludes with the main case study.

Reference sources named within the chapter may be looked up in the *References and further reading* section at the end of the book.

IT Company is a large multinational corporation that has more than 100 years of history, a global workforce of more than 100,000 employees and is headquartered in the USA. Up until the early 1990s, the corporation was structured around geographical areas, each of which was afforded relatively powerful independence. So, for example, the UK headquarters in London had high decision-making autonomy in relation to the US headquarters in New York and the European headquarters in Paris. One outcome of this so-called area structure was that hardly any global HR policies existed, so that HR practices in areas such as pay, training and flexitime differed widely between countries. Nevertheless, a strong corporate culture ensured that some core values applied throughout the organisation. For example, since its foundation IT Company has been known for its strong anti-union stance. Combined with an emphasis on sophisticated and innovative HR policies, the parent company has been able to defeat several recognition campaigns by trade unions. The same has happened in the UK, where local management prided itself on defeating a strong union recognition campaign in the 1970s. However, in other countries IT Company does recognise trade unions. For example, the German subsidiary has a powerful body of elected employee representatives (as encouraged by German law), some of whom are trade union members, who have a strong say in any decisions affecting the workforce. Up to the early 1990s the company also participated in industry-wide bargaining which determined pay and conditions for the large majority of its workforce.

In the early 1990s, IT Company – which had enjoyed a near monopoly status in its markets until then – encountered economic problems due to higher global and domestic competition. A new CEO made far-reaching changes to the business strategy and the organisational structure. In particular, the decision-making authority of local managers was reduced and responsibility transferred to regional headquarters such as Paris and to the US headquarters. Furthermore, the company was structured around business units, each responsible for a certain range of products such as printers or IT solutions. Business units were encouraged to standardise management functions such as finance, marketing and human resources as far as possible on a worldwide basis.

Question for discussion

You are in charge of HR for the global business unit printer of IT Company which has production and distribution organisations in almost 100 countries.

1 Which HR practices would you standardise on a global basis?

2 Where would you allow different approaches?

3 How would you ensure that global policies are implemented by the subsidiaries?

4 Why would you choose these options?

1 STRATEGY, STRUCTURE AND STANDARDISATION OF HR POLICIES

THE 'GLOBAL VERSUS LOCAL' DILEMMA

The issues facing IT Company in the starter case study are to some extent experienced by all organisations that operate in more than one country. On the one hand there are pressures for global integration and standardisation. Among these are global competitors and products that can be sold throughout the world, meaning that customers can compare prices across national borders, rapid technological change (which must be transferred across borders as quickly as possible), and the need to achieve economies of scale (which means doing things in a similar way in every location). On the other hand there are pressures for local responsiveness and differentiation due to differences in consumer preferences, distribution channels, workforce cultures and national institutions, such as legislation, labour markets and taxation. This tension is often called the 'global versus local' dilemma (Evans, Pucik and Barsoux, 2002). Unfortunately, the consultants' advice to 'think global and act local' sounds good but is in practice rather meaningless. Furthermore, where an organisation stands on this issue depends on factors such as the competitive situation which the business faces, how integrated its business is (whether goods, for example, are manufactured from parts supplied from different countries), how easily its business can be moved to different countries, how globalised its branding is, etc. It may well be that an organisation such as IT Company might reach different answers for different parts of its operation.

REFLECTIVE ACTIVITY

In which industries are pressures for global integration very strong, and in which is local responsiveness very important? How can international firms deal with such differences?

Among the industries that face high pressures for global integration and in which it is important to achieve high economies of scale you may, in your answer to the above exercise, have included sectors where manufacturing is integrated across borders and moving the process is very expensive: engines, construction equipment, semi-conductors and industrial chemicals, for example. Although there is, due to the demands cited earlier, a general trend towards global standardisation, there are still some industries where local responsiveness is a key requirement for business. You may have thought about industries such as food, healthcare and household appliances.

Clearly, the type of global environment a multinational organisation is facing should have an impact on its business strategy. Bartlett and Ghoshal (1989) developed a typology of three strategies that are appropriate for a particular combination of local and global pressures an organisation faces. We now briefly introduce three of these:

- the multi-domestic strategy
- the global strategy
- the transnational strategy.

The *multi-domestic strategy* is recommended for firms in industries that are under high pressure for local responsiveness, but that only face low pressure for global integration. Firms in such industries have to customise product offering and marketing to local conditions. This means that they have to have a complete set of value-creation activities in all major markets. Although there are some businesses for which such a strategy makes sense – similar to IT Company portrayed in the starter case study – growing global competition, and perhaps fashion, has made a multi-domestic strategy less popular and many international firms have attempted to adopt a global strategy.

A *global strategy* aims to standardise product offering and marketing strategy across different markets. Value-creation activities such as production and R&D are in a few favourable locations to achieve economies of scale.

The *transnational strategy* corresponds to the central argument of Bartlett and Ghoshal – that irrespective of industry, businesses have to be globally integrated and locally responsive at the same time, and to move from a headquarters-subsidiary approach to a truly 'stateless' approach, in which the location of headquarters is incidental. We might question how many companies are truly transnational (Dickmann and Muller-Camen, 2006). Can you think of a major multinational company where you are not sure which country dominates its policies?

One means to make sure that the strategy chosen is implemented is to adopt an appropriate structure. Similar to IT Company up to the early 1990s, firms that follow a multi-domestic strategy often have a global area division structure. This means they are organised geographically on the basis of countries or regions that report directly to the main headquarters. In contrast, businesses with a global strategy are usually organised in product divisions that have worldwide responsibility for a certain product. For firms with transnational strategies, Bartlett and Ghoshal foresee a matrix structure within which each manager has two reporting lines – for example, one to the product division to ensure that global integration is as high as possible, and one to the area to ensure that local responsiveness is achieved.

REFLECTIVE ACTIVITY

You are the HR manager of an MNC's foreign subsidiary.

How much autonomy in decision-making would you like to have? What arguments would you put forward to localise decision-making? How might headquarters justify attempts to centralise decision-making?

Irrespective of the structure that a business has or intends to introduce, a crucial issue is the allocation of responsibility between headquarters and subsidiaries. We now examine this issue in the context of centralisation and decentralisation of HR policies and practices.

CENTRALISATION AND DECENTRALISATION OF HR POLICIES

You may have argued, in your response to the exercise above, that high autonomy of the subsidiary in strategic HR decisions would reduce the burden on headquarters and increase motivation at lower levels. It should also lead to better decisions locally by the people directly involved and, last but not least, increase accountability. In contrast, amongst other arguments you may have suggested that the corporate HR function will argue that centralised decision-making will make global co-ordination easier. It will ensure consistency between global strategies and local decisions. If headquarters take decisions and just inform local managers, duplication of efforts will be avoided. However, instead of such very broad answers you may have concluded that it depends on the specific HR practice whether this is best decided for the organisation as a whole or locally.

At the extremes the arguments are clear: pay levels for locally recruited and employed staff are determined locally; management development systems for those selected as future organisational leaders should be worldwide. Relevant pay rates within the local community will be unknown to specialists at the headquarters of the organisation. They can only make such decisions by drawing on and then second-guessing the local specialists – a waste of resources. Paying people the same salaries wherever they work makes little sense in a world where living standards vary considerably between countries. Reward issues other than levels of pay may be subject to worldwide policies – for example, that the top quartile always includes a performance-related salary element.

On the other hand, the organisation must retain the right to promote and encourage its best and brightest, beyond the local unit if necessary, wherever they are found. An organisational objective, common to many MNCs, of drawing on the best talent available irrespective of country of origin, requires that the management development systems have some cross-border coherence. Identifying the best people in each country will be of maximum benefit if there is some way of comparing these individuals across countries. Here, too, reality is not as simple as this statement implies. For example, one very successful international bank, Citicorp, has a uniform system throughout the world. This, the company argues, facilitates identification of the best wherever they are in the world – and its results would seem to suggest that they are good at it. Another equally successful international bank, and a direct competitor, the Hong Kong and Shanghai Banking Corporation, has different systems in different regions and countries, and compares leading individuals after they have been identified by these different systems. This company argues that the different cultural environments in which it operates mean that imposing a worldwide system would cause it to overlook people who may not be brought forward by a uniform, and therefore probably culturally biased, system (see Chapter 23). And this company too has good people coming through at the senior levels.

Between these extremes there is considerable uncertainty and significant problems arise (Harris, Brewster and Sparrow, 2004). Should there be a local performance assessment system, so that performance can be related to the local pay scales and take account of local cultures? Or should the performance assessment system be international, so that it can identify likely future leaders wherever they are found in the organisation? And should the organisation communicate with its employees individually or through trade union or representative structures (see Chapter 17)?

A few examples highlight these problems. Taking performance appraisal first, we have enough knowledge of the effects of culture (see Chapter 23) to know that there is no easy answer to this question. The US-style performance appraisal process assumes that employees will work jointly with their boss to set targets, to assess their own performance, to comment on the extent to which their boss has helped them with achieving their targets – or made things more difficult for them. It also assumes that they will do much of this through a face-to-face interview. It is not likely that such performance appraisal systems will work in the same way in many Eastern societies, where open responses to seniors are discouraged, where challenging the boss's expectations of what is possible would be seen as insubordination, where admitting faults amounts to a loss of face, and where, for example, the idea of criticising the boss's work in front of that boss would be seen as a sort of organisational suicide.

The organisation will try to ensure the objectives which appraisals are seen as meeting: encouraging improved performance, assessing career options and identifying training needs. But how to do this? The more the organisation attempts to enforce a worldwide system, the more likely it is that managers will bend the system to their local requirements (Ferner *et al*, 2004). Often this will involve exaggerated or incomplete reports or even reporting back on interviews that never in fact took place. So what appears to be exactly comparable data may be very misleading. The more the organisation is responsive to these cultural issues, the less likely it is to have information that it can use to assess people across national boundaries.

The question of communication channels (see Chapter 19) is complicated by national institutions. In Europe, for example, employers are required to recognise trade unions for collective bargaining in different circumstances in different countries – when certain thresholds (usually the existence of a certain number of union members among employees) are reached, when employees request it, or, exceptionally, when unions win ballots. In many European countries employers are required to establish and pay for employee representation committees that may have extensive powers, including, for example, the right to review appointments or to be consulted prior to major investment decisions. Of course, national laws and institutions are in part a reflection of and a support to national cultural values.

MNCs therefore have a series of decisions to make. Will they deal with trade unions? Will they refuse to? Will they check the legislation carefully and do the minimum necessary to comply with the legislation? Or will they embrace the law and the purposes behind it on the grounds that such behaviour will show them as good citizens and that other MNCs in that country have been successful while adopting the local employment systems in full? Or will they allow individual countries (and, by extension, individual country management teams) to make their own decisions (Almond *et al*, 2005)? At the extreme, will they – as Walmart, a famously anti-union US company, is reputed to have done – simply refuse to open operations where they would have to recognise a union? (Note, however, the pull of profits. When Walmart was told it could not open in China without recognising the union, the potential profits were too big to be overridden by policy, and in 2006 Walmart signed an agreement with the Chinese trade unions – possibly because they are not internationally recognised as independent trade unions.)

Overall, every international organisation will always have a continual tension between the costs of and the advantages to be gained by standardisation, and the costs of and the advantages to be gained from being locally responsive. This applies to all aspects of an MNC's operations but is particularly relevant for HRM, where local sensitivities are most pronounced. Recently, standardisation has become not only more popular but also more possible. The development of significantly improved telecommunications, the Internet and intranets have allowed organisations to develop shared services and centres of excellence which are often virtual – drawing together the best experts they have from across the globe and generalising the messages across their various operations in all countries (Tregaskis, Glover and Ferner, 2006). Employees logging in with a question about their training provision might (sometimes unrealised by them) be getting their answers from the company's top development expert half a world away. Obviously, for these systems to work well an increased degree of standardisation is required.

CONTROL MECHANISMS

Research has shown that there is a potential conflict of interest between the wish of headquarters to control affiliates and the subsidiaries' managers' desire for autonomy. Foreign managers in particular can use various strategies to obstruct the implementation of global policies. For example, they can argue that local trade unions prevent them from introducing a global pay policy (Ferner *et al*, 2004). This raises the question of how an MNC can make sure that all its units are committed to common goals.

REFLECTIVE ACTIVITY

You are employed in the HR department of a UK MNC, and you have to ensure that foreign units implement HR practices.

How are you going to do that?

There are four possible methods of control. One means of control is to *measure and benchmark results and outputs*. For example, your HR strategy might be to have a fair representation of females in management positions. In order to achieve this you may set and measure the goal of increasing the ratio of female managers by 2 percentage points until this strategic aim is achieved. A second type of control is rules and regulations. This is *bureaucratic control* (Ferner, 2000). For example, you could produce manuals that specify in detail how certain HR processes such as resourcing should be organised. A third type of control is social or cultural control. For example, Bartlett and Ghoshal (1989) suggest that senior managers in MNCs should have a matrix in their mind so that for every decision they take they have in mind the needs of global standardisation and local responsiveness. In this way, without being explicitly told, managers strive to implement organisational goals. Such control mechanisms may work well in organisations that have a strong organisational culture and that make great use of training and development to socialise managers into the behaviours and values expected of them. For the remainder of this chapter we concentrate on another means of control which is arguably the most important one in any organisation. This is our fourth method, *control through personnel.*

2 INTERNATIONAL STAFFING AND EXPATRIATION

INTERNATIONAL STAFFING

Staffing is a crucial issue for all organisations and it is certainly important for MNCs (Harzing, 2001). One option is for the international organisation to transfer its people between different countries: such transferees are usually referred to as 'expatriates'. Research suggests that there are important strategic issues that can be addressed by long-term international assignments. Most importantly, expatriates are supposed to improve the performance of the subsidiary they are assigned to. They can do this by solving technical problems, developing local talent, opening new international markets and by developing, sharing and transferring best practices. They can also help to improve the communication between headquarters and subsidiary and assure that global policies are implemented by a particular subsidiary. They can do this by fostering the parent corporate culture in the subsidiary, by developing networking processes and by controlling financial results. Where expatriates are sent from the headquarters operation to the subsidiaries, this operates as a powerful – perhaps the most powerful – form of control.

Some 40 years ago, Perlmutter (1969) identified four main approaches used by MNCs. First, there is the *ethnocentric* staffing approach. In firms that rely on this approach, foreign subsidiaries are managed by employees sent from the parent company, who are usually parent-country nationals (PCNs). This approach is perhaps the most common, even if in theory it should only be used in firms with a global strategy that aim to centralise decision-making and are interested to implement global policies and practices. Second, there is the *polycentric* approach. MNCs that favour a polycentric approach normally rely on managers recruited locally, who are usually host-country nationals (HCNs). This can normally be found in firms that pursue a multi-domestic strategy and where each subsidiary has relatively high decision-making autonomy. For example, the senior management of a UK firm in Germany consists mainly of German nationals. Third, there is the *geocentric* approach, by which firms emphasise passport diversity and employ PCNs, HCNs and third-country nationals (TCNs) in their subsidiaries, as well as managers from the subsidiaries in their headquarters. This is normally favoured by MNCs that aim to pursue a transnational strategy. It could, for example, mean that the board of a Swedish electronics firm in the UK consists of managers with British, Canadian, German and Swedish passports. The fourth and final approach is the *regiocentric* staffing policy. Similar to the geocentric approach, it favours passport diversity, but TCNs only move within a region such as Europe or Asia.

REFLECTIVE ACTIVITY

What are the advantages and disadvantages of the ethnocentric staffing approach outlined above?

Among the advantages of an ethnocentric staffing approach you may have noted, in your response to the exercise above, that parent-company employees or PCNs are familiar with the products, technology and culture of the MNC. Some of this knowledge is tacit (ie knowledge that people have but cannot fully explain or transfer to others – see Chapter 14 on HRD) and cannot be transferred except by people. Employees from the parent company can therefore play a vital role in implementing corporate-wide quality standards, business strategies or styles of management. They can facilitate communication between headquarters and subsidiaries and are an important means of control for headquarters. Finally, they may also compensate for the inadequacy of local managerial skills.

However, an ethnocentric strategy also has severe disadvantages. If most senior management positions are filled with PCNs, as is the case in many Japanese MNCs, local staff lack opportunities for promotion, which may lower morale. At least initially, PCNs may be unfamiliar with the local culture, which could lead to costly mistakes in dealings with co-workers, customers and governments. Most importantly, if holding a passport of the country where a MNC has its worldwide headquarters is a criterion for promotion, that may not only be considered discrimination but the firm may also be wasting a large share of its pool of talent (see Chapter 6 on diversity).

A similar advantages and disadvantages analysis could be applied to each of Perlmutter's approaches. Clearly, what is going to be the best approach will vary between, and perhaps even within, MNCs.

THE EXPATRIATE ASSIGNMENT CYCLE

Although research demonstrates that expatriation can bring significant benefits to business, it also shows that this will only be achieved if expatriates are managed properly. There is therefore a need to manage the expatriate cycle properly. Its key elements – which are discussed in more detail in the next section – can be seen in Figure 26.

Figure 26 The expatriate assignment cycle

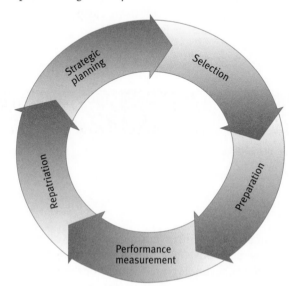

Source: Harris *et al* (2004; p.148)

Expatriate selection

Many MNCs have no formal system for selecting employees whom they send on an international assignment. Expatriates are often chosen in an informal way and at short notice. The employees selected have usually demonstrated high technical competence and good managerial skills. Because there is often an underlying assumption that managerial skills are universal, it is assumed that the candidate will be similarly successful in a foreign context. However, research has shown that technical ability is not enough and that interpersonal and cross-cultural skills are also important for expatriates.

Mendenhall and Oddou (1985) identified four key attributes of successful expatriates. *Self-orientation* suggests that expatriates should have high self-esteem, self-confidence and psychological well-being. At the same time, they should also exhibit a high degree of *others-orientation* in order to be able to develop relationships with host-country nationals. In this respect, knowledge of the local language is also important. A third desired attribute is *perceptual ability* – the capacity to understand why host-country nationals behave the way they do. Finally, and particularly if there is a high degree of cultural distance between home country and country of assignment, *cultural toughness* is required. This can help the expatriate to deal with factors such as loneliness, crime and language difficulties.

So far we have only talked about the expatriate. However, particularly if they are senior managers, they may well have a partner, and also perhaps children, who may or may not follow them on the assignment. Some organisations therefore also consider the cross-cultural adaptability of the spouse when selecting an employee for a foreign assignment.

Preparation

Employees who are going abroad can be prepared, at least to some extent, for the cross-cultural interactions they are likely to encounter. Some organisations therefore offer pre-departure training or other preparation with the objective of reducing misunderstanding, inappropriate behaviours and culture shock when expatriates (and families) arrive in their new location.

Preparation can consist of the following elements:

- Environmental briefings can give documentary information about the host country's political system, economics and history, management processes, markets, etc.

- Cultural awareness training aims to help expatriates to understand cultural differences between their own culture and the host country's culture. For this purpose, cultural assimilators are a useful tool. These use programmed learning approaches to provide the trainee with intercultural encounters. For example, South Americans would learn that punctuality for meetings is essential in Germany. Germans would learn that being seen as a rounded person, and not just being business-focused, is vital for doing business in South America. In order to communicate effectively with host-country nationals it is also recommended that expatriates learn the language of the new culture.

- There is also a need for training in the laws, institutions and common practices of the host country.

- If time permits, a prospective expatriate should visit the country of assignment. Such a preliminary visit can also be a final test of the suitability of an employee for a particular assignment.

- Perhaps the cheapest and most effective form of preparation is to get the transferee to meet with people who are from, or who have worked in, the country that will be their new home.

Some firms also involve the spouse and children of an expatriate in the preparation. In addition they provide not only training but also practical assistance for the relocation, which could include the organisation of housing.

REFLECTIVE ACTIVITY

In the light of the challenges of managing performance (see Chapter 12), what do you think are the major issues facing international firms that want to assess the performance of employees working abroad?

Assessing performance

International organisations are concerned with the performance of their subsidiary operations and the key expatriates in them. Accurately measuring the performance of an employee who may be thousands of miles away and who is operating in a different context from most of the other employees in the system is not easy. Most large MNCs operate some form of formal performance measurement system. Some corporations have standardised this worldwide to facilitate the exchange of people. However, even in such cases it may be difficult to judge the performance of an expatriate due to unintentional bias. If the expatriate is assessed by a home-country manager, this person may lack knowledge of the local situation and thus might not be able to appreciate issues that may have adversely affected performance. In such circumstances, the appraiser may rely on the information from the expatriate himself/herself or on hard data such as market share and profitability that are likely to reflect factors outside the control of the expatriate. In either case the understanding is likely to be partial. In contrast, host-nation managers may not understand that expatriates transfer home-country standards and expectations to the subsidiary. In addition they may have performance standards that differ from those of the parent firm. One solution is to have multiple people (raters) in the home and host country who assess the expatriate.

Compensation

Rewarding, or compensating expatriates is more complicated than the always problematic issue of pay and rewards in one country (Perkins, 2006). This is largely for two reasons. Firstly, there are large differences in salaries, cost of living, taxes and benefits between countries. On top of this there are the difficulties created by differences in tax regimes, currency movements, etc. Secondly, as noted, most MNCs try to link at least some element of pay to performance – and that is going to be difficult.

MNCs usually try to make sure not only that their expatriates maintain their standard of living when going abroad, but that they also compensate for any additional costs incurred, or for the level of perceived hardship involved. The most common method to ensure this is the balance sheet approach. Its first element is the base salary. This is the same as in the home country, but adjusted for differences in cost of living and the currency exchange rate. A UK manager (TCN) working for a US MNC in Germany will therefore have a base salary that is tied to the salary structure of the British subsidiary. Benefits such as pension plans and stock options are equalised as well. Besides the base salary and benefits, expatriates usually receive various allowances for relocation, housing, private education of children or the hardships incurred. Finally, the MNC has to equalise any differential tax effects that are caused by the relocation. All these costs make an expatriate much more expensive than if a host-country national is employed. An additional factor, of course, is that many employees who accept a foreign assignment do it not only because they hope to gain additional experience and to boost their careers but also because they are aware of the generous allowances and incentives so that even if they take their families with them they expect to be much better off than at home. For any HRM specialist, juggling costs, labour market requirements and expectations is fundamental to all reward packages (see Chapter 13). In the case of expatriates the pressures are high.

Repatriation

The final element in the expatriate assignment cycle is repatriation, which is the process of returning home from the foreign assignment. Research shows that many expatriates leave their organisation shortly after their return. This is a significant loss to the organisation. As we have seen, the costs of each expatriate are considerable and the learning that they have achieved will be substantial. Researchers find that expatriates are almost always very positive about the experience and its effects on their knowledge and their careers – but between a quarter and a third of them do not continue their careers in the organisation that has paid for that experience. From the organisation's viewpoint, not only does this mean a loss of a valuable resource, it means (because people tend to stay in the same industry or occupation) that these people tend to get picked up by their competitors. It also reduces the organisation's ability to internationalise thinking in the company. For these reasons, this wastage is currently occupying the time of many international HR specialists.

A number of factors account for this high level of turnover. Organisations may, either because of poor HR planning or through practical changes that have occurred in the meantime, not have an adequate re-entry position that makes use of the international experience of the repatriate. Combined, often, with a loss of status and pay, initial expectations that an international assignment would lead to rapid career progression are often disappointed. In addition, the expatriate and the family, if unprepared, may find that readjusting to 'home' is not as smooth or as comfortable as they had expected. In short, a lot of problems come together to make these, now more knowledgeable and hence more marketable, employees consider their employment position. This may be unsatisfactory for the repatriate, but certainly means that critical knowledge is lost to the organisation.

To avoid this level of wastage, international HR specialists in MNCs have begun to set up repatriation programmes. One element can be a repatriation agreement which, before the start of the assignment, stipulates the type of job that will be given to the expatriate upon returning. Of course, in the current rapidly changing situation, few companies feel confident enough to give such guarantees. More promisingly, it seems that ongoing communication and contacts with the home organisation during the assignment is linked to retention. For this purpose it is increasingly common, at least amongst the larger MNCs, to assign coaches or mentors to the soon-returning expatriate (see Chapter 15). The role of the mentor is to ensure that career and performance are on track and that discussions about a suitable re-entry position start in good time

 REFLECTIVE ACTIVITY

In the light of the costs and difficulties of sending employees abroad on a long-term assignment, what alternatives can you suggest?

As you may have considered in response to the exercise above, long-term expatriates are only one of a number of different types of international assignment (Harris *et al*, 2004). Expatriates can be on short-term assignments of less than one year. Then there are international commuters who travel on a regular weekly or fortnightly basis between their home country and an operation of the MNC in another country. Frequent flyers, who undertake regular international business trips, are a third assignment type. Among the problems associated with these assignments are work–life balance issues, travel fatigue and the difficulty of dealing with foreign cultures to which one is only exposed for short intervals. There is also the increasing growth of 'virtual assignments' in which people use modern communication technologies to work in international teams although they may rarely, or in some cases never, meet face to face. All these different types of assignment have become more widespread recently – but then, so has the typical, standard, expatriate assignment. International working is just becoming more common.

KEY ISSUES: INTERNATIONAL HRM

We now pull together ten key points about international HRM raised in this chapter:

- IHRM covers all the same topics as HRM generally, but is inevitably more complex.

- International organisations are always dealing with the twin pressures of standardisation across the organisation and responsiveness to the local environment.

- There is increasing pressure for organisations to standardise, and modern technology is making it possible to move further in that direction.

- Different approaches to IHRM are likely to be relevant for different kinds of organisations and for different organisational structures and philosophies.

- MNCs would benefit from close alignment of their IHRM with their corporate strategy. Often it is not aligned at all.

- Controlling local operations is a key to success for MNCs. Transfer of individuals from one country to another is a powerful mechanism for such control.

- International transfers also bring benefits in internationalising the thinking of MNCs.

- But international assignees are an expensive option: they are, post for post, the most expensive people that MNCs employ.

- Many employees assigned to other countries leave their organisation just before or after they are due to return home, with a consequent loss of the organisation's investment.

- Better management of the expatriate cycle will benefit the expatriates and the organisation they work for.

Perhaps there are other key points that you would like to note for yourself.

The main case study in this chapter now follows. It gives an example of the professional and work–life balance issues faced by expatriates.

MAIN CASE STUDY

Look at the description of the case set out below. Then decide on the recommendations that you would make as an HR manager for dealing with the issues raised. Try to think beyond the level of a 'quick fix' or simple solutions.

Sonja has a senior position in an investment bank in London, which recently opened a branch in Moscow. Shortly after starting the foreign operation, the manager selected to head the subsidiary was poached by another bank. Sonja was asked to step in at short notice, although she had had no previous international exposure. The main reasons for choosing her were her excellent track record and experience in setting up and managing a new department in the home office. It was suggested to her that after the successful completion of the assignment in Russia she would be a major factor in any future promotion decisions. Given the urgency of the situation, Sonja was given three days to decide whether she would accept the offer. Intensive discussions with her partner, who is a freelance IT consultant, and their 10-year-old child followed. Although both were sceptical about the move, eventually Sonja was able to persuade them to move with her to Moscow.

Sonja and her family were housed in a gated compound in an expensive suburb of Moscow, where many of Russia's new millionaires have their homes. A driver took her to work and collected her each day. During the first month in Moscow, which was in August, Sonja and her family enjoyed working and living in a different world, made friends with other expatriates who lived near by and her husband and daughter spent a lot of time in exploring the city. Within a few weeks, Sonja's daughter was established in the local 'international school' and her partner began to pick up some work from their new friends. However, shortly after this initial honeymoon, problems started to develop.

Sonja became increasingly aware that Russia is a hard place to do business. Much of the country seems to operate without the attention to standards, ethics, the following of regulations and the honouring of contracts that she was used to in London. She was often told that she was expected to socialise (which seemed to mean get drunk) with key clients and that she 'had to adjust to the Russian way' when it seemed to her that she was being asked to go beyond good business practice.

It was difficult to establish good relationships in the office. Because she did not speak Russian she had asked the staff, all of who had been selected partly because they could, to speak English in the office. Nevertheless, a lot of the work was conducted in Russian, and she did not feel that she was fully in control of what was being done. The staff often worked late, as she did herself, but whereas some of them then went out for a drink or a meal, she was driven back to her family.

After the first few projects for other expatriates, her partner found it difficult to get much work because he could not speak Russian. He did not spend much time with the other expatriates' non-working partners, mostly women (although Sonja was beginning to worry that he was spending too much time with one of them). He spent a lot of time at home working on his computer.

The winter had set in. The centre of Moscow, where the office was, became particularly dirty and unpleasant. Going out in the evenings or weekends became a major expedition.

Sonja and her partner had begun to fall out increasingly frequently. The only one who seemed to be adapting well was their daughter.

The combined effect of all of these problems was irritation and hostility. On a business trip to London, Sonja asked for a meeting with the international HR specialists. The Bank's senior managers, who had recently visited Moscow, suspected that she might be about to ask to return home. They made it clear to the HR department that this assignment was already costing them more than they wanted to see spent and they didn't want to see their investment wasted.

Your task

Imagine you are one of the international HR professionals working for this multinational firm. Prepare a short report based on the facts you have been given above, making recommendations to your colleagues. Analyse what went wrong and how the situation can be improved.

EXPLORE FURTHER

BARTLETT, C. A. and GHOSHAL, S. (1989) *Managing Across Borders: The transnational solution*. Boston, MA: Harvard Business School Press
An excellent analysis of the global environment faced by multinational enterprises and how this is influencing strategic choices.

HARRIS, H., BREWSTER, C. and SPARROW, P. (2004) *International Human Resource Management*. London, CIPD
A very useful analysis of the many important issues involved in IHRM.

PERKINS, S. J. (2006) *International Reward and Recognition*, Research Report. London, CIPD
Clear and concise presentation of new qualitative and quantitative research results in this contentious area by one of the specialists in the field.

PERLMUTTER, H. V. (1969) 'The tortuous evolution of the multinational corporation', *Columbia Journal of World Business*, Vol. 4, 9–18
A classic of the IHRM literature – still a much-used starting point, even if later critics have pointed to a lack of supporting evidence and the rather simplistic unitary assumptions of organisational structures.

SPARROW, P. R. (2006) *International Recruitment, Selection and Assessment*, Research Report. London, CIPD
Thorough and up-to-date analysis of this critical topic drawing on new research and previously published data.

CHAPTER 23

Instead of HRM: a cross-cultural perspective

Terence Jackson

INTRODUCTION

HRM is mainly a concept developed in the Anglo-Saxon world and applied to other cultural contexts, often unsuccessfully. To think of people as a 'resource' may be at odds with many non-Western cultures, and this is where problems might arise. This chapter critically examines the transfer of HRM to other cultures. It explores alternative cultural models, and looks at the future of HRM in a multicultural world.

This chapter therefore aims to develop an understanding of the cultural boundedness of the concept of human beings as a resource; to explore the nature of HRM in a global world; to discuss the problems encountered by international companies when transferring HRM practices abroad; and to look at alternative ways of thinking about the value of people in organisations, and the implications for people management. It does this mainly within the context of so-called 'developing' countries.

LEARNING OUTCOMES

By the end of this chapter readers should be able to:

- explain the cultural origins of human resources management
- describe different concepts of the value of people in organisations across cultures
- analyse the problems of transferring Western HRM practices across cultures
- identify alternative approaches to managing people in different countries
- develop a critical attitude towards HRM principles in a cross-cultural context.

The chapter has five parts. The first part deals with the origins of HRM as an American concept. The second part looks at how we might break out of this culturally bound concept of managing people. The third part looks at how we might compare approaches to managing people across cultures. The fourth considers the transfer of HRM approaches to other countries. Finally, the fifth part considers how we might develop international approaches to managing people by considering stakeholders and their different values and concepts of people.

The chapter concludes with the main case study.

Reference sources named within the chapter may be looked up in the *References and further reading* section at the end of the book.

STARTER CASE STUDY

Johnny Mbeki was late for work again. He had already had a couple of warnings from the HR manager, not simply for being late but because he was slow at his job. He had a lame leg. He'd had it since birth. On the whole he coped with it, but sometimes it affected his work. On this occasion, he was called into the HR manager's office.

'I'm afraid that this has gone a bit too far. I've tried to make allowances, but you are affecting overall production. If I have to speak to you again, I will have to let you go.'

The next morning the HR manager received a delegation from the workforce – colleagues of Johnny. They asked that he be given special treatment. They explained that Johnny had an extended family that depended on him. His were the only wages coming in. They lived in a township far from the factory. It takes him a long time to get to work, depending on public transport that is not always reliable. Sometimes when a family member is sick, he has to stay behind, and this can make him late for work.

They asked the HR manager to give Johnny another chance. They, as members of his work team, promised to cover for him, to make up for his slowness and his sometimes coming in late. Overall production in the work group would not be affected. The HR manager agreed.

Questions for discussion

1 Do you agree with the HR manager's decisions?

2 Johnny has been given due warning, and is not very productive. It doesn't matter that his work mates stick up for him – he should be sacked on the next occasion. Do you agree?

3 This incident takes place in South Africa. Does this make any difference to the decision? Should Western standards of HRM apply in this instance?

1 THE ORIGINS OF HRM: AN AMERICAN CONSTRUCTION?

The term 'human resource management' (which arose originally in the United States, and is now almost universally accepted), and the concept behind it, is laden with value. Values are part of the fabric of culture and are specific to countries or communities. That human beings are a resource to further the executive ends of an organisation is a concept that is against the values of many non-Western cultures. Perhaps in its most extreme or instrumental conceptualisation – ie one that really does look at people as a way of meeting organisational aims – this may also be against the values of many 'Western' cultures. Certainly, the ideas behind what constitutes the principles, policies and practices of managing people in organisations differ even among and within Western European countries, and certainly between US and most Western European countries.

From its origins in the individualistic achievement-oriented management culture of the United States, the term 'human resource management' has spread in a globalised world. Particularly in writing about the management of people, it is very difficult not to use this term. Sometimes little thought is given to the implications of its underlying concept, or of its manifestations in the policies and practices that multinational corporations use across different countries.

This is not to denigrate the contributions to global managing that HRM in many of its principles – such as the competences approach (Boyatzis, 1982) – can often make. The point here is to place HRM in its cultural context, and to examine its appropriateness in other cultural contexts. Before doing this we must first situate the concept of HRM in its original cultural setting.

The importance of the contribution of the HRM function to the bottom line and to shareholder value is a key issue in US and other Western-based human resource management (Becker, Huselid, Pickus and Spratt, 1997). The cultural perception that human beings are a resource to be used in the pursuit of shareholder value may be challenged by a view that people have a value in their own right. For example, a developmental approach that sees people as an integral part of the organisation, and as the subject for organisational objectives, seems to be implicit within Japanese people management policies and practices (Allinson, 1993).

This may be reflected in practices that seek to integrate employees as key stakeholders in the organisation and to gain commitment to the corporate endeavour. Human resource practices among corporations in Japan such as employment security, extensive job rotation, continuous on-the-job training, evaluation of the total person, seniority-/ability-based wage structure and promotions, welfare facilities and even the cooperation with 'enterprise unions' or trade unions limited to the company, are used to build a *moral* involvement of staff as part of a corporate community (Ishido, 1986).

This contrasts with 'Western' practices that may only try to gain a *calculative* involvement of staff based on an exchange where the organisation is seen by the employee as a means to an end, and where employees will work spontaneously and cooperatively if that is seen as benefiting them directly, but will leave the organisation if a better opportunity occurs outside.

This is reflected in HRM practices that take a 'competencies' approach. Job descriptions are defined by specific duties, and by the competencies needed to perform those duties well. This reflects operational requirements, which in turn reflects the strategic objectives of the corporation. The best person is recruited to the specific position, and is seen as a resource to achieve the executive ends of the organisation. Hence, HRM practices have competency- and objectives-based appraisal systems that determine pay and promotion.

REFLECTIVE ACTIVITY

Think about the differences in the way you are valued, as a person, in different situations and by different groups of people – in your family, in your community, within a social group, at university, in the workplace.

Are there major differences between the way you (or people you know) are valued in work and non-work situations? In your culture, are you valued within your local community like a family member? If so, does this contrast with the way people are valued in work situations? Is it possible to value people in the work situation the same as in the family or community situation? Should work be completely separate from the community?

2 HARD AND SOFT APPROACHES TO HRM: BREAKING OUT OF THE PARADIGM?

STAKEHOLDER APPROACHES AND 'SOFT' HRM

There has increasingly been an emphasis in Western HRM literature on the stakeholder approach to managing organisations (perhaps driven by the interest in Japanese approaches). A hard *instrumental* approach had already been challenged in a limited way within the context and conceptual framework of Western human resource management (Legge, 1989). This caused a distinction to be drawn in the strategic human resource management literature between the 'hard' perspective reflecting utilitarian instrumentalism, which sees people in the organisation as just a resource to achieving the ends of the organisation, and the 'soft' developmental approach, which sees people more as valued assets capable of development, worthy of trust, and providing inputs through participation and informed choice (Storey, 1992; Tyson and Fell, 1986).

Yet the concept of human resource management is itself a product of a particular Anglo-US culture, as we noted above. It is likely that the 'hard' and 'soft' approaches taken within Western organisations are both a reflection of an inherent cultural concept that perceives human beings in organisations as a means to an end. They are simply two poles representing high to low *instrumentalism.*

If managers and human resource professionals are unable to break out of this concept or paradigm, it is likely that when they, or managers educated in the Western tradition, try to implement 'Western' human resource practices in cultures which have a different concept of people, and a different regard for people in organisations, incompatibilities will be shown through employees' lack of motivation and alienation leading to low productivity and labour conflicts (see Chapter 17 on employment relations).

For example, the current author has carried out many interviews in many different organisations in sub-Saharan African countries. Many times he has been told by employees, and managers, that when going into work in the morning they are stepping out of their own culture and going into a foreign culture. And when they go home in the evening, they step back into their own culture (Jackson, 2004).

WESTERN AND INDIGENOUS APPROACHES: TRANSITIONAL AND DEVELOPING ECONOMIES

The importance of cultural values to organisational life is well established in the literature. The most well-known theory in this area is that of Hofstede (1980; 2003). From a survey of managers and staff of IBM in more than 50 countries, he identified four cultural values that varied among the cultural groups. These are:

- *Power distance* – This is the extent to which inequalities among people are seen as normal. This dimension stretches from equal relations being perceived as normal to wide inequalities being viewed as normal.

- *Uncertainty avoidance* – This refers to a preference for structured situations versus unstructured situations. This dimension runs from being comfortable with flexibility and ambiguity to a need for extreme rigidity and situations with a high degree of certainty.

- *Individualism/collectivism* – This looks at whether individuals are used to acting as individuals or as part of cohesive groups, which may be based on the family (which is more the case with Chinese societies or the corporation as may be the case in Japan).

- *Masculinity/femininity* – Hofstede distinguishes 'hard values' such as assertiveness and competition, and the 'soft' or 'feminine' values of personal relations, quality of life and caring about others, where in a masculine society gender role differentiation is emphasised.

Yet Hofstede's original study published in 1980 included very few developing countries. What his theory did rather well was to provide a critique of Western (particularly American) management applied in other countries, and it has opened up a great debate in this area.

More recently there is growing interest in the relationship between indigenous and foreign (mainly Western) cultures in the practice and development of management and organisation in the transitional economies of the former Soviet bloc, in China, and to a lesser extent in the so-called 'developing' countries of South Asia, Africa and Latin America. These issues have also been explored in the newly industrialised countries of East Asia, as well as in the 'hybrid' East-West cultures of the economies of Hong Kong and Singapore. This literature on the whole challenges the assumptions upon which human resource management is based in the Western world, and its applicability to managing people in countries of which the economies have more recently been launched into the global marketplace (Jackson, 2002a).

REFLECTIVE ACTIVITY

Have another look at the starter case study. To what extent do you think the HR manager is stuck within the Western paradigm of human resource management? He has conceded the point to Johnny's work colleagues – but does he understand the real differences between the Western/Anglo-Saxon approaches he has been trained in, and the rather different community-based values the African employees have been brought up with? Think about this for a while . . . and then read on.

3 THE INSTRUMENTAL AND THE HUMANISTIC LOCUS OF HUMAN VALUES: OPPOSITES OR COMPLEMENTARY?

The differences in perspectives towards the value of people in organisations, and the validity of human resource management, particularly in non-Western countries, is best understood in terms of the concept of *the locus of human value*.

We can define the locus of human value as the way, culturally, people place a value on other people. Two main orientations or *loci* have been discussed in the literature (Jackson, 2002b):

- *Humanism* is a regard for people as an end in themselves, and having a value for themselves and of themselves within an organisational context. So the locus of value or worth of persons in a work organisation is towards those persons in themselves rather than towards organisational objectives as appropriate ends. In other words, the question might be asked, what can the organisation do for its people? The organisation can be used in a developmental way to develop talents in a holistic way.

- *Instrumentalism* is defined as a regard for people as a means to an end, where the locus of value or worth is towards the ends (objectives) of the organisation. In other words, the question might be asked, what can this person do for the organisation? The person is seen as a resource (albeit a valuable one), like any other resource: money, plant, machinery, etc. He or she is recruited because of his/her specific set of competences that can help meet the objectives of the organisation.

INDIVIDUALISTIC AND COLLECTIVISTIC CULTURAL VALUES

This way of conceptualising the perceived value of human beings has its roots in the distinction between *individualistic* and *collectivistic* cultures (Hofstede, 1980 and 2003; discussed above). There seems to be a simple split between the individualistic Western cultures in which individuals are brought up in nuclear families and where individualism and individual achievement is often emphasised, and collectivistic non-Western cultures in which people are more likely to be part of an extended family and group involvement is emphasised. The lifetime protection of people which collectivism affords (either in corporations as in traditional Japanese companies, or within extended family groups such as in communities as different as those in China, India and the African continent) would seem to indicate a valuing of people in their own right, and as part of a collective. The expectation of people in individualistic cultures of having to look after themselves would indicate a more instrumental view of people in organisations.

But the connection between humanism and collectivism, and instrumentalism and individualism is not as straightforward as it might at first appear. Firstly, collectivism is target-specific and obligatory in nature. Japanese men may be more psychologically involved with their organisations, and Chinese more involved with their families, but at the expense of those outside the collective (Hui, 1990). Hence, those outside the in-group may be regarded instrumentally (as a means to an end). This is often shown in the large numbers of casual workers on short-term contracts employed by Japanese corporations. These workers can be 'let go' at short notice in times of economic downturn, and thus protect the jobs of the 'salarymen': those within the corporate in-group who have a lifetime commitment for employment.

Secondly, the work of cross-cultural researcher Shalom Schwartz (1999) in the 1990s contrasts 'conservatism' and 'egalitarian commitment'. 'Conservatism' correlates negatively with Hofstede's individualism, and 'egalitarian commitment' correlates positively with it. So, while the socio-centric values linked to 'conservatism' are those that would be expected to be associated with collectivism, 'egalitarian commitment' expresses going beyond selfish interest (loyalty, social justice, responsibility and equality), but places a voluntary rather than an obligatory aspect on this towards the in-group. In other words, it could be possible that individualism might give rise to humanistic values.

Instrumentalism and humanism may not relate, therefore, in a *direct* way to the level of individualism and collectivism in a society, because there may be different cultural influences in different societies that lead to a lessening of a humanistic locus of human value within the organisation and/or a softening of an instrumental locus of human value. We can look at some examples of this from around the world.

EXAMPLES OF HUMANISM-INSTRUMENTALISM IN DIFFERENT COUNTRIES

Australia has an individualistic 'Western' culture, yet has also been seen as having a 'humanistic' orientation that leads to a concern for the well-being of the workforce and for quality of work life. More accurately (in Schwartz's research), this may reflect a moderately high level of egalitarian commitment, and in terms of the popular management literature, the 'mateship' of Australian society (Westwood and Posner, 1997).

More recent research has suggested that Americans are not as individualistic as Hofstede's original 1980 study has suggested. The GLOBE (House *et al*, 2004) study undertaken in the late 1990s and early 2000s is worth noting in this respect. This view is reflected in the USA's moderately high scores on Schwartz's 'egalitarian commitment' scale.

Yet Australian and US values towards people in organisations may still be different. With Australia having a higher historical level of protectionism of both business and of the workers in the labour market, American work culture may be expected to show a higher level of individual achievement orientation than that of Australia. However, both countries have similar moderately high scores on Hofstede's 'masculinity' values dimension, which in part measures the level of competitiveness and results focus, and Australia has more recently gone through a time of economic liberalisation and increase in competitiveness and less worker-friendly labour markets (Tixier, 2000).

Both Australian and American organisations have been shown to have a command-and-control orientation with a top-down management approach (Wheeler and McClendon, 1998). Again, this may be a factor that promotes the view that employees may be used instrumentally towards the objectives of the organisation's executive. Yet there are other reasons, apart from the recent conceptualisation of 'egalitarian commitment' within the cross-cultural values literature, why the harder forms of instrumentalism are being 'softened' in the Anglo-Saxon countries and probably also in Western Europe, but also why the 'harder' versions may be being adopted uncritically in the rather short-term orientation of transitional countries in the former Soviet bloc, and in the newly industrialised countries of East Asia.

There are influences on HRM policies and practices in Anglo-Saxon countries that appear to have given rise to a 'softer' instrumentalism. These include the maturation of Western HRM systems, the influence of Human Relations theory, and influences from Japanese management.

CULTURAL 'CROSSVERGENCE': DEVELOPING HYBRID MANAGEMENT

This brings us to the issue of 'crossvergence' of cultural influences, where different cultures come together to form specific 'hybrid' management approaches. Hong Kong is a good example of this. One study of crossvergence in Hong Kong found Hong Kong managers closer in their values to those from America than managers from the nearby Guangzhou Province in mainland China (Priem, Love and Shaffer, 2000). Another study of Hong Kong notes the different treatment of employees of in-group members and out-group members in Chinese family firms (Hui, 1990). Hong Kong society is culturally complex. It has been at the interface of Eastern and Western society for many years. The evidence in the literature in terms of its level of individualism-collectivism and the way it is changing is contradictory (Ho and Chiu, 1994). So because of both cultural crossvergence and differential treatment of employees within a 'hybrid' collectivist management, both instrumentalism and humanism will be modified by the influence of the other.

THE INFLUENCE OF WESTERN INSTRUMENTALISM ON TRANSITIONAL AND NEWLY INDUSTRIALISED COUNTRIES

The influence of instrumentalism on transitional and newly industrialised countries should also be mentioned. Studies of Russia have noted a tendency of corporations to adopt uncritically imported HRM solutions, which underestimate the complexities of the 'free market' economy in the context of the Russian situation (May, Bormann Young and Ledgerwood, 1998). Also noted is the lack of commitment by employees to the organisation, a lack of managerial responsibility, disregard for health and safety issues, and strained labour-management relations. This would seem indicative of a high level of instrumentalism.

This may also be the case in Eastern and Central European post-Soviet countries. Yet countries such as the Czech Republic and Poland are historically different from Russia, with traditions of pre-Soviet industrialisation and entrepreneurship, and relative efficiency under the Soviet system (Koubrek and Brewster, 1995). They may be far closer to Western Europe than Russia in their cultural orientation, yet suffer from a lack of maturity of their HRM systems.

Russia may also have a stronger tradition of collectivisation, and perhaps even 'Asiatic' humanistic orientations than Poland and the Czech Republic. Russian cultural values appear much higher on conservatism and lower on egalitarian commitment than Poland (Smith, Dugan and Trompenaars, 1996).

The newly industrialised countries in East Asia are also likely to come under influences of the older industrialised countries to adopt short-term measures that have been successful elsewhere in order to effectively compete in the global economy. They may be influenced by both Japanese models of industrialisation and US models (Chen, 1995).

In one study, Korean organisations have been shown to be different from those of Japan in terms of the level of solidarity shown by employees towards their co-workers (Bae and Chung, 1997). Although Korean employees expect a higher level of commitment from their companies towards them, and from them to the company, the corporation shows a lower level of solidarity to workers than both their Japanese and American counterparts. Korean people management appears to be less consultative than Japanese firms, and have a lower loyalty downwards. Yet loyalty is expected upwards. This represents a more authoritarian system than that of Japan. Hard instrumentalism may therefore be a feature in the newly industrialised countries of East Asia as well as of transitional countries. However, there will also be humanistic influences on such countries.

DIFFERENCES BETWEEN COLLECTIVISTIC AND INDIVIDUALISTIC COUNTRIES

If organisations are seen as meeting collective social needs such as providing full employment as in the case of the former Soviet bloc, or serving the needs of people as part of a collective in-group as in the case of Japan and Korea, this may reflect in the level to which people see their organisation fulfilling the needs of its people. A view of contractual obligations only within individualistic societies may work against this type of view. In a society with such collectivistic socio-cultural values, individuals may be valued as part of the wider collective.

This may be different from the values implicit within 'egalitarian commitment' and the 'human relations school' in Western society where a consideration of the 'valuing' of people may still be oriented towards a particular end that is separate from the individual. In a collectivist society, the 'end' may not be separate from the individual. It may also be the case that the relationship between the collectivism and a humanistic locus in organisations may be more simple than the relationship between individualism and instrumentalism. In other words, humanistic approaches may be appropriate in both collectivistic and individualistic culture, but instrumental approaches will be against the humanistic values of collectivistic cultures. Attempting to transplant Western HRM practices directly to collectivist societies will therefore be problematic. Yet collectivistic societies can be quite different in the type of people management systems adopted.

'CAPTURING' THE WIDER SOCIETAL COLLECTIVISM IN THE CORPORATION

The difference noted in the literature between the lower loyalty of the Korean corporation and the higher loyalty of the Japanese corporation has already been noted (Bae and Chung, 1997). This may affect the degree of concern of managers for employees with a value in themselves (humanism). Unlike in other collectivist cultures, such as India and African countries, Japanese corporations have been successful in using a wider societal collectivism for the corporation by 'utilising social and spiritual forces for the organisation's benefit, and in accepting the responsibilities to their employees' in the words of the classic study on Japanese management by Pascale and Athos (1981). Although people management practices arising from this (eg lifetime employment, payment by seniority) have come under increasing pressure, there still seems to be a people and relationship focus that is important in obtaining employees' moral commitment to the organisation.

This relationship focus is also found in Chinese business organisations where familial relations are important both internally and in *guanxi* relations in business dealings (Chen, 1994). Although there are differences in the ways corporations capture this societal collectivism in people identifying with the corporation and the corporation identifying with its people, the mindset or locus of human value is still likely to be humanistic in a collectivist society. Where corporations cannot or do not use and work with this, alienation between people's 'home' culture and the alien culture they step into when they go to work in the morning is likely.

 REFLECTIVE ACTIVITY

This section has mainly been about the different, often hybrid, approaches to valuing and managing people in various emerging economies. Most of your training and education so far in HRM has no doubt been from a Western perspective. However, how much of this would you be able to apply in countries that are quite different from Anglo-Saxon ones?

For example, at this stage you could review theories you have learned about motivating staff. How does practice vary in Japan and Korea?

How could the HR manager in our starter case study better motivate staff? (We will return to this issue later in our main case study at the end of this chapter.)

4 LOOKING AT HRM IN A CROSS-CULTURAL PERSPECTIVE: DOES IT WORK OVERSEAS?

THE RELATION BETWEEN HOME AND WORK: DIFFERENT SOLUTIONS

The contradictions between life outside and inside the world of work organisations have been investigated in various ways since the Industrial Revolution in the West, from the concept of 'alienation' in the Marxist tradition onwards.

Organisations in different cultural settings may have different responses to this contradiction. These include:

- the calculative/contractual responses of US HRM systems which recognise and work within the instrumental relationship between employer and employee (trying to humanise this through quality of work-life initiatives and employee involvement while firmly focusing on the bottom line)

- the moral, spiritual and obligatory responses (such as creating an internal labour market – ie ways of helping people to rise inside the organisation) of traditional Japanese organisations which capture the collectivistic and humanistic orientations within the wider society (humanistic approaches).

There seems little doubt that between these different approaches, which have been represented here as *humanism* and *instrumentalism*, policies and practices are being shared across cultures through the processes and activities of firms who are internationalising through different types of strategies and expatriates' activities and functions in host countries.

This may not be through convergence (the coming together of value systems) but by *crossvergence* (developing of hybrid value systems as a result of cultural interactions), as we outlined above. Hence raw 'Taylorism' (the instrumental, stop-watch approach of the American Frederick W. Taylor publicised in the early twentieth century), concerned with finding the most efficient methods and procedures for co-ordination and controlling work and workers, may not be a feature of the mature HRM systems in, for example, the United States as a result of the influences discussed above, but may be seen in the policy manifestations of organisations in Russia and other post-Soviet countries, identified in the post-Soviet system as a move towards greater efficiency, higher workforce discipline, less paternalism and more instrumentalism and a decline in human contact – as well as short-termism and deterioration in employee–manager relations.

THE HEGEMONY OF WESTERN PRACTICES

In HRM practice this means borrowing from the West. In Russia one study (Lawrence, 1994) suggests that HRM systems are built more explicitly around business objectives, with formal systems of staffing, career planning, management development, skills training and appraisal systems with 'management by objectives' (MBO).

This tendency may also be the case in Korea (Chen, 1995), with workers putting a strong emphasis on extrinsic (such as pay) rather than intrinsic factors of motivation (such as inherent satisfaction drawn from the job), and some organisations having MBO systems and focusing more on wages and conditions, and performance being seen as an important factor (see Chapter 13 on reward). Yet there appears in addition to be retention of seniority systems. Western-style appraisal systems also seem to be used, but include other considerations apart from performance, and an emphasis on harmony militating against negative judgements and reflecting tolerance and appreciation of people's best efforts.

THE COMPETENCES APPROACH IN WESTERN HRM

The manifestations of an instrumental locus of value are best explained by the competences approach to human resource management. A competence has been defined as 'the ability to demonstrate a system or sequence of behaviour as a function related to attaining a performance goal' (Boyatzis, 1982). The required competences are therefore determined by operational objectives, which are related to strategic objectives, and link the various human resource functions such as selection, training and reward, in seeking organisational objectives. It is also supported by a systems concept of organisation, where people (as resources) are organised in the best way, and having the best skills, to ensure efficient throughput through the system (see Chapter 2 on the systems approach). For example, job descriptions would identify appropriate persons for particular positions within the system, ensuring the required competences.

This may be one of the more important implications and manifestations of an instrumental locus of control, which may remain although certain features of a 'softer' instrumentalism such as quality of work–life initiatives may resemble features of a 'harder' humanism. This may be an appropriate response of HRM policies in getting higher levels of mutual contractual involvement of employees in cultures that show an instrumental locus of human value.

A DEVELOPMENT APPROACH IN HUMANISTIC CULTURES

In cultures that have a humanistic locus of human value, the development of a moral commitment may be more appropriate. So Japanese firms may show a higher commitment to people and community welfare by keeping (in-group) employees in work through economic downturns, which in turn encourages stability, commitment and a sense of belonging.

This element of social welfare and responsibility was also shown in the Soviet countries, as well as obtaining the commitment of workers through ideological means. However, it is likely that the two systems are different on the level of commitment to developing people, although the same opportunities may have presented themselves through longer-term planning and a lack of pressure from a concern for shareholder value in the case of Japan and the Soviet economy.

Rather than based on a competences approach which links individuals to the operational and strategic objectives of the organisation, a developmental approach based on job flexibility and rotation (rather than fitting a person to a job), and promotion based on experience through seniority seems to show a more holistic approach to the person. So the organisation, and experience within it, tries to develop the person as a committed part of the human organisation.

The concept of locus of human value (Jackson, 2002b) may therefore be helpful in understanding an inherent contradiction between the world outside work organisations and life inside. The different attempts at reconciling these two worlds, and the possible effects of crossvergence through global cultural interaction, may bring the two loci into conflict or contradiction. Yet they may come together to form a hybrid people management system.

Through crossvergence, management systems may be borrowed and adapted, rather than the cultural orientations of those being managed substantially changing. Hence, it is the managers from emerging and transitional economies who are trained and influenced by Western traditions, rather than the workers who staff the enterprises.

Similarly, the literature on international and comparative HRM practices in different countries reflects those policies and practices being introduced, rather than telling us very much about how employees react to such policies, and how successful they might be in the long term. The wholesale adoption of Western HRM principles, albeit with necessary adaptations, in Russia, for example, may ultimately be ineffective as inappropriate ways to manage people within a culture that may reflect a humanistic locus of human value.

This view is currently being reflected in the growing management literature in at least two parts of the world: South Africa (eg Mbigi, 1997) and India (eg Rao, 1996):

- In practice this is reflected in the *Ubuntu* movement in South Africa (this comes from a phrase that means 'people are only people through other people'), where enlightened corporations are trying to integrate indigenous African approaches within their people management systems.

- In India an Indian approach to human resource development is providing a synthesis of Western and Indian approaches, but the spiritual/holistic/developmental aspects of humanness are emphasised.

It may also be the case that the so-called K-type management of Korea may reflect an effective synthesis of indigenous Korean with Japanese and American approaches (Chen, 1995).

In developing effective international and cross-cultural systems, managers should learn to think outside the parochial box of HRM. Blindly introducing Western HRM practices that reflect an *instrumental* view of people may be ineffective, if not an affront to the humanity of people outside Western traditions. Yet managing globally goes further than simply adapting effectively practices from one culture to another. Managers should ask themselves what could be learned from the *humanism* of South Asia and from Africa in managing global enterprises successfully. What can be learned from the attempts of reconciling instrumental and humanistic approaches in the countries where this is becoming more successful?

REFLECTIVE ACTIVITY

Revisit the starter case study. Write a recommendation to the HR manager on how the situation can be managed. How can consideration be given to the more communally minded humanistic values of the African staff?

5 MANAGING PEOPLE INTERNATIONALLY: STAKEHOLDERS, HUMAN VALUE AND INTERNATIONAL STRATEGY

In summary, from the above discussion, it is possible to draw three interdependent conceptual threads – stakeholder consideration, the locus of human value, and multicultural/strategising oppositions – that must be considered in managing people internationally. Firstly, an understanding and consideration of stakeholders is important in any enterprise. Within the context of corporate life, two categories of stakeholder may be identified: corporate and community. In many societies, these two sets of stakeholders may be quite distinct. For example, a high regard for shareholder value in societies emphasising a free market economy may see the local community within which it operates as only a source of labour (see Chapter 25). Where there is a high governmental or institutional involvement in the finances and control of enterprises, government and local communities may be high-profile stakeholders in the enterprise.

Secondly, one of the major jobs of the management of people within the enterprise is to reconcile the distinctions between these two sets of stakeholder groups, and the lives of people in the community, and their lives in the enterprise. Across cultures, there are different ways in which this is approached. A major cultural influence in how this is approached is the way in which people are seen in organisations (the locus of human value). An *instrumental* cultural perspective may therefore bring a contractual relationship with the employee who provides his or her time in exchange for wages. A *humanistic* cultural perspective may bring an obligatory relationship of commitment amongst members of the corporation.

Thirdly, as a result of the often competing local and global forces in international management, which on the one hand leads to local cultural adaptation and adoption, and on the other leads to universalisation of management principles through international strategies, there are different combinations of solutions to this issue – some highly adaptive and successful, and some not so successful. So hybrid solutions adopted in Korea may be regarded as successfully reconciling corporate and community life, whereas solutions in many sub-Saharan African countries have not adapted well to the situation.

KEY ISSUES: COMPARATIVE HRM

We now pull together ten key points showing the main lessons that can be learned from the above discussion for HRM professionals working across cultures:

- Seeing people in organisations as just a means to an end may be an affront to human dignity in many non-Western countries including Japan, Korean and Russia and other transition countries in Central Europe and Asia, and emerging countries in Africa, Latin America and South Asia.

- Inappropriate HR policies and practices in countries with humanistic cultures may lead to alienation, poor motivation and labour conflict.

- Staff may see themselves as stepping out of their own culture into an alien one when they go to work in the morning where approaches to managing people in the organisation are different from the way people are valued in their own communities.

- HR practices based on the competences approach may be interpreted in humanistic cultures as fitting a person to the requirements of the job and the organisational objectives, rather than developing a person around a number of jobs and developing him or her holistically. This may be contrary to practices reported in Japanese organisations, and may lead to a lack of identification with the organisation and a lack of commitment.

- Thought should therefore be given to introducing a more developmental/holistic approach in other collectivistic societies such as in sub-Saharan Africa.

- Payment by results and performance-related reward may also be inappropriate in humanistic cultures, and may be seen as reflecting an instrumental perception of people.

- In these circumstances it may be better to reward people on the basis of their commitment to the group and the organisation, and their development as a valued group member.

- Instrumental approaches may be appropriate in instrumentally oriented cultures, but humanism also has value as a concept and approach toward people.

- Developing moral commitment and involvement, aiming corporate resources towards the advancement of its people, focusing on the whole person rather than as a resource with a set of competences may also bring positive results in instrumental cultures.

- A 'soft' instrumental approach does not equal a humanistic approach. To break out of the parochial box needs an understanding of the cultural differences between an instrumental and a humanistic locus of human value. This represents the difference between aiming people as a resource towards executive goals of the organisation, and aiming the resources of the organisation towards achieving the development of human capacity of people with a value in their own right.

Perhaps there are other key points that you would like to note for yourself.

The main case study in this chapter now follows. Returning to South Africa, the case study presents different sets of value systems for a Western manager and African staff: readers are asked to consider how these might be reconciled.

MAIN CASE STUDY

Cashbuild, a supplier of building material mainly to the home market, was set up in 1978 by Albert Koopman (see Koopman, 1991). Despite initial problems, he was able to quickly turn these around and it became a successful business. It has since been sold by Koopman as a highly profitable going concern. It is quoted on the Johannesburg Stock Exchange, operates in a number of southern African countries, and is today a household name in South Africa. At the beginning it struggled with very high turnover of staff and low motivation. Koopman, a white Afrikaans-speaking businessman brought up within Western management traditions, had to do some hard thinking about the value systems of his predominantly Zulu workforce. He had to address these differences and gain the commitment of the African workforce if he was to turn the company around.

He conceptualised the differences between what he sees as his own 'individual' value system and that of his 'communal' workforce. Some of the distinctions that he drew are as follows.

INDIVIDUAL	**COMMUNAL**
• I control my life: I therefore say that I missed the bus	• Outside forces control me – therefore I say the bus left without me
• I want to show you who is in charge by gripping your hand hard when I greet you – I am your opponent	• I want to show my connectedness to you by greeting you with a soft hand and hold it longer – I am your friend
• I am self-reliant	• I am cooperative and emotional
• I like job descriptions, status and rank because I know who has to be in which place; I like to alienate people	• I prefer operating in a team working towards a common goal and not divided from my human being – I like solidarity amongst people
• I pay bonuses to motivate you to work harder because this works for me; I like to compete against my fellow man through higher earnings	• As part of a group, I dare not separate myself from my group by earning more through hard work; you will therefore be throwing good money after bad because I don't want to be separated through money
• I will only support my brother for a short while in case of his financial embarrassment, then he must find a job	• The more I earn, the more I tend to care for my brothers and sisters for as long as necessary
• I normally have a small family so that we can have a better quality of life and hopefully avoid financial destitution	• I have an extended family to help me during times of destitution
• The more I have, the more I am	• I am, therefore the more I am prepared to give and share
• My concern is for production	• My concern is for people
• I am driven by merit and reward for individual effort	• I am driven by group reward for group effort
• I am individually competitive – everyone is my opponent	• I am cooperative – we're all in this together and should assist one another

Your task

Look at these differences in values, and recommend how they can be reconciled. In particular, how can people management systems and practices be developed to gain commitment and motivate people?

Now look below at what Koopman did, and what he recommends.

What Koopman did

Koopman describes how in Cashbuild, shared values were built mainly by getting people together in order to develop an understanding of values and principles upon which they might wish to work. He goes on to make recommendations on how motivational systems may be developed, drawing on his experience in Cashbuild, in order to take account of the more communal orientation of managers and staff. Basing reward on a belief that people do not work purely for money, and that the need for dignity, pride, belonging and freedom should be fulfilled first, they addressed those needs first at Cashbuild before any additional rewards for money were introduced. Maintenance factors were also addressed as they were raised, such as funeral policies, housing loans and educational assistance – although these were only addressed once additional productivity and wealth, as well as 'human freedom' had been created.

What Koopman recommends

His recommendations from his experience were:

- Avoid rewarding staff for something they do not have control over. This involves avoiding long-term goals (over 12 months) and things beyond the workplace. This addresses the orientation towards an external locus of control.

- Only share profit if profitability is raised. If not, this is tantamount to paternalism. Loyalty is difficult to buy in this way if staff see through this.

- Giving staff share ownership is not meaningful when, for example, food prices are a main concern in Africa. Their ability to sell their shares defeats the objective.

- Avoid rewarding communally oriented staff on an individual basis that will separate them into classes by money and grading systems, and avoid the principle of capitalist meritocracy, because it does not apply in Africa.

- Develop communal reward schemes for communal effort, for example, by group or section.

- Reward only those things that people feel they can control and measure themselves.

- Reward for upward movement of productivity indices.

- If share schemes are created, do so via a collective, with people gaining a meaningful proportion of shares that can directly influence their voting rights on issues within the organisation.

Your task

These recommendations represent at least one organisation's attempt to introduce motivational measures that address the issue of rewarding more communally minded staff. How can this now be applied to resolving the situation in the starter case study? How can motivational people management practices be introduced?

EXPLORE FURTHER

JACKSON, T. (2002a) *International HRM: A cross-cultural approach*. London, Sage
This book is a fairly comprehensive overview of different approaches to people management in a wide range of countries.

JACKSON, T. (2002b) 'The management of people across cultures: valuing people differently', *Human Resource Management*, Vol. 41, No. 4, 455–75
This article discusses the concept of the locus of human value and provides some empirical data for country differences.

JACKSON, T. (2004) *Management and Change in Africa: A cross-cultural perspective*. London, Routledge
This book provides a comprehensive study of people management in sub-Saharan Africa, and discusses many of the issues raised in the current chapter.

KOOPMAN, A. (1991) *Transcultural Management*. Oxford, Basil Blackwell
This book provides additional information on the main case study of this chapter.

PASCALE, R. T. and ATHOS, A. G. (1981) *The Art of Japanese Management*. New York, Simon & Schuster
This is a classic study of Japanese management which had tremendous influence on management in the United States and the UK.

CHAPTER 24

Creating corporate capability: a new agenda

Peter Critten

INTRODUCTION

The aim of this chapter is to help readers understand how the role of human resource development (HRD) is changing from being a deliverer of training solutions to being a facilitator of learning. In the newer role, it better builds 'intellectual capital' as part of the wider HR strategy.

LEARNING OUTCOMES

By the end of this chapter readers should be able to:

- describe the defining characteristics of an HRD strategy designed to build corporate intellectual capital

- recognise the difference between such an HRD strategy and a more traditional 'training-oriented' approach

- appreciate how such a strategy is part of a corporate-wide approach to knowledge management

- recognise what role HR professionals can play in contributing to such an HRD strategy.

This chapter offers another view of workplace learning, also outlined in Chapter 14. It makes a case for a new approach to HRD in the context of a developing knowledge economy, in which 'strategies have to be dynamic, changeable and, to an extent, opportunistic' (Garvey and Williamson, 2002). It argues that HRD has never been able to decide whether its focus should be on individual needs (personal development as well as skills and knowledge improvement) or the organisation's business and strategic needs. But to understand this tension – still a factor in most companies' approach to HRD – it is necessary to understand how thinking about HRD has changed over the last 50 years.

The chapter is in four sections which chart the key developments in HRD in Britain from the 1960s until now. Part 1 gives an insight into the legislation of the 1960s that was pivotal in shaping attitudes to what was called 'systematic training', which was overseen by Government-appointed Industry Training Boards. Part 2 moves on to the 1980s. Then, again, a Government initiative – Investors in People – focused attention onto seeing training and development as an investment in rather than as a cost to the business. The third part describes the principles behind the idea of the 'learning organisation', which was introduced in the early 1990s and is still an espoused vision for many organisations today. The final section, Part 4, moves the agenda on from the mid-1990s to now and, we suggest, the future. This is the agenda of 'knowledge management'.

As well as being a 'historical' journey, it might be seen also as 'developmental' in that all of the approaches to HRD we highlight are still with us.

The chapter concludes with the main case study.

Reference sources named within the chapter may be looked up in the *References and further reading* section at the end of the book.

STARTER CASE STUDY

An expanding chain of DIY shops called DIY Solutions was started in the early 1980s by John Miles, an engineer by profession who took early retirement to indulge his passion, DIY. He opened a shop in a leafy London suburb with a particular mission in mind.

Now, in the early 1990s, he is genuinely retiring and about to hand over the business as a successful going concern to an employee, Matt Dyson, who is to take on a new role as MD. On his last day at work, John Miles is being interviewed by a reporter from a local paper.

Interviewer: Can you tell us, John, what made you start up this business in the first place?

John Miles: Well, I'd spent about 30 years working as an engineer in various construction companies and got to a point when I'd had enough working for other people so I decided to retire early and invest in a shop which allowed me to indulge my secret passion, DIY.

Interviewer: Wasn't that the time when the big chains like Homebase and B&Q were also recognising the DIY boom and beginning to capitalise on it? How did you expect to compete with them?

John Miles: That's the point – I wasn't going to compete but could provide something

none of the big stores could provide – friendly practical advice which was available to local householders, on their doorstep, as it were.

Interviewer: Well, you certainly read the market well at the time, because over the last 10 years you've grown from one shop to 10. And one of the benefits that I know all your customers talk about (including me) is the expertise of your staff. Did you start by recruiting staff who already had such expertise, or did you train them yourself?

John Miles: A bit of both, actually. When I started my first shop I was lucky to still be in contact with former colleagues, engineers, who were practical people, like me, and who had all been trained and developed themselves in ways which which I'm sorry to say have passed away. When I was a young engineer, I had an apprenticeship with a firm that made sure I learned my craft but also allowed me time to attend the local college where I took my City and Guilds qualifications so I understood the theory as well as the practice. I was lucky that one or two of my colleagues also decided to take retirement a year after me and they joined me in a partnership which meant the business could expand – plus I knew I had people in charge who knew what they were talking about.

But as we expanded we had to take on new staff who hadn't the same background as ours and needed developing. Here I was also lucky, and was able to draw on experience working with engineering companies. In the 1970s the Government introduced what were called Industry Training Boards (ITBs) to monitor the training given by different industries and provide financial incentives for effective – what they called 'systematic' – training. At first we did not like interference from our own ITB, the Engineering Industry Training Board (EITB), but after a while we realised they could teach us a lot about how to get the best out of our people by systematic development. Beforehand we'd wasted a lot of money sending staff on courses that added nothing to the business. But the concept of 'systematic' training meant we were able to draw up individual plans for each employee based on what knowledge/skill they needed to acquire to be effective at a particular task.

Despite Maggie Thatcher's destruction of the ITBs in the late 1980s – I liked her support for individual enterprise, but she didn't understand how the ITBs were beginning to help business add value to itself – I've remembered the lessons learned and now have a full-time 'training officer' who was made redundant from the EITB whose job it is to develop training plans for all our new (and old) employees.

Interviewer: That's quite unusual, isn't it, to have a training officer in such a small company?

John Miles: Maybe it is, but you've remarked yourself on how customers value our expertise, and that's all down to training. But we don't stop with initial training – which Derek, my training officer does himself in each of the shops. All our staff are encouraged to keep up to date with the latest developments in our field by attending courses and subscribing to trade journals. And this applies to my managers as well.

Interviewer: So in conclusion, John, what's the legacy you would say you're handing over to your successor?

John Miles: Matt comes from the same background as me. He was one of my former colleagues I told you I took on in a partnership in the early years. I know he will make sure our staff are as up to date on latest developments to match any training that the big chains can provide. But we have the advantage in having staff who are dedicated to giving quality advice which they believe in.

Interviewer: Thanks very much, John. Enjoy a 'proper' retirement now, and I look forward to interviewing Matt after another 10 years have passed.

Questions for discussion

1 How would you compare the way staff were helped to perform their jobs by the training officer, Derek, in the DIY Solutions of the 1980s and early 1990s with your understanding of how staff are 'trained' and 'developed' in organisations today?

2 In fact, what exactly is your understanding of the terms 'development' and 'training', and do you see any difference between their meanings?

Note: At the end of this chapter, in the main case study, we return to the business 15 years later. That case study features a report by an outside consultancy into how effective Matt Dyson has been in growing and developing the workforce of DIY Solutions. Your task after reading the report will be to recommend just how you would put the consultancy's recommendations into action based on what you have learned about HRD in the chapter.

1   THE LEGACY OF THE LEGISLATION OF THE 1960s AND 1970s

In 1986 the Institute of Personnel Management published *Training Interventions* by John Kenney and Margaret Reid, which replaced a former publication, *Manpower Training and Development* first published in 1972. In 2004, the seventh edition of 'Training Interventions' was published by the CIPD under a new title *Human Resource Development: Beyond training interventions* (Reid, Barrington and Brown 2004). The change in titles over the last 30-plus years reflects the transition from 'Training' to 'Learning' to 'HRD', which is the subject of this chapter.

Our story begins in the 1960s when the Government was concerned about the need to improve skills level of those in work – not such a different story from today. It was also concerned that bigger companies were taking, or 'poaching' experienced staff from other companies and not undertaking training themselves. These were the main reasons for the passing of the Industry Training Act in 1964 whereby each of the major industries had to establish its own Industry Training Board to set and monitor training standards for their industry sector. In our case study, John Miles remembered the influence of the Engineering Industries Training Board.

The Industry Training Act gave each Training Board the right to collect a payment called a levy (based on a percentage of a company's payroll) of companies of a certain size in their industry. With this money they were then able to reward companies that did train according to specified standards – what became known as 'systematic training'. In the way that each industry specified its own standards, it was in fact similar to the German training system that still largely works in this way today. The British ITB system followed the cycle of four stages shown in Figure 27.

Figure 27 The systematic training cycle

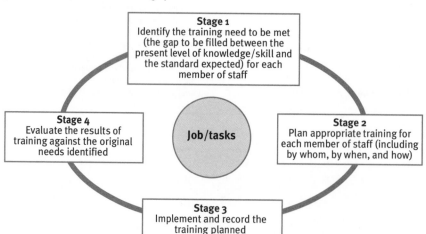

REFLECTIVE ACTIVITY

How does the four-stage cycle shown in Figure 27 compare with how you described your understanding of how staff are 'trained' and 'developed' to perform effectively above?

(If you read the interview with John Miles again – in the starter case study – you will see that this is probably the way the training officer Derek trained new staff. He would have most likely followed the 'systematic training cycle' as practised by his own Industry Training Board of the time, the Engineering Industry Training Board.)

CHANGING VIEWS OF TRAINING

Reid *et al* (2004; p.2) remind us of a definition of training that was first proposed in the Manpower Services Commission's *Glossary of Training Terms* in 1981:

> *Training is a planned process to modify attitude, knowledge or skill behaviour through learning experience to achieve effective performance in an activity or range of activities. Its purpose, in the work situation, is to develop the abilities of the individual and to satisfy the current and future needs of the organisation.*

Ten years before that a slightly different definition had been proposed by the then Department of Employment in its *Glossary of Training Terms* of 1971:

> *Training is the systematic development of the attitude/knowledge/skill behaviour pattern required by an individual to perform adequately a given task or job.*

REFLECTIVE ACTIVITY

Look at the 1971 and 1981 definitions of training as cited and list what you think are significant differences between them.

In these two definitions we may consider that there are three significant differences of emphasis:

- The 1971 definition talks about 'systematic development' whereas in the 1981 definition it becomes a 'planned process'.

- The most important addition in the 1981 definition is a focus on 'learning experience'; learning plays no part in the 1971 definition.

- The 1981 definition talks about the purpose of training (albeit in the work situation) as being not just for the benefit of the organisation but for that of the individual as well – whereas the context of training in the 1971 definition is firmly within the organisation in a given task or job.

As we go on to argue in this chapter, these are important distinctions which reflected changing views in society. But for those practising training in the 1960s and 1970s, like the starter case study DIY Solutions' training officer Derek, these principles would underpin their practice for all time. So although the starter case study interview was conducted in the early 1990s, Derek's approach to development of staff was *still* based on a 'systematic approach to training' as reflected in the 1971 definition: 'Training is the systematic development of the attitude/knowledge/skill behaviour pattern required by an individual to perform adequately a given task or job.'

In fact, this attitude towards training 'the workers' to enable companies to achieve their business objectives has its roots in the early twentieth century with the American Frederick W. Taylor's concept of 'scientific management'. Harrison (2002; p.18) points out that:

> If we locate the true origins of organisational HRD here, we can more easily understand those tensions in purpose and values that still bedevil the learning and development process in many organisations today. They arise from trying to combine a business imperative with a genuine concern for the well-being and development of the individual.

To be fair to Derek, his plans went beyond training as such, as John Miles remarked to the interviewer in the starter case study:

> But we don't stop with initial training – which Derek, my training officer does himself in each of the shops. All our staff are encouraged to keep up to date with the latest developments in our field by attending courses and subscribing to trade journals. And this applies to my managers as well.

This reflects more the principles of the 1981 definition with a move towards the importance of learning experience and, just as importantly, the professional needs of the individual as well as goals of the organisation. Today we would call this 'continuous professional development' (CPD).

In Figure 27, note that Stage 4 of the systematic training cycle focuses on 'evaluation'. During the 1960s and 1970s 'evaluation' of training meant little more than how the 'trainees' on a training course/programme rated the 'training experience' on what became known as a 'happy sheet' given out at the end. But towards the end of the 1960s, Kirkpatrick introduced a model which helped trainers collect evidence of 'value' not just according to a favourable or unfavourable comment about the training experience, but at higher levels. What had they learned from the training? And at a higher level still, how had their behaviour changed? And then the final level which really opened up a debate which continues until today: what evidence is there that the training has led to real, concrete, tangible results like reduction of costs, increase in profits? (More information about models of evaluation that followed soon after is to be found in Reid *et al*, 2004; pp200–1.)

The move to thinking about training in a more strategic way that had implications not just for the individual and his or her job but for the enterprise as a whole leads us into Part 2 of the chapter and a description of a more strategic approach to development put forward at the end of the 1980s that set the agenda for the 1990s.

2 THE INVESTING IN PEOPLE ERA: ADDING VALUE TO THE ORGANISATION

Towards the end of the 1980s the training initiatives of the 1960s and 1970s were perceived not to have created the skilled workforce that had been hoped for, and in 1988 the Government White Paper *Employment for the Nineties* set out a strategy for the next ten years. This meant the end of the ITBs and the creation of a National Training Task Force which spent a year talking to business about what were the 'people' factors that made one company more effective than another. They identified key criteria which successful companies used, to show that investment in people made a difference to an organisation's performance. These criteria became the basis for a National Award of 'Investor in People' (IiP) to those companies that met them. Over the years, the criteria have been reviewed, as has the institution administering the scheme. The current criteria are divided into three categories (see the box below). These are the criteria companies have to show they can meet if they are to be given the national 'kite-mark' proudly displayed in the reception area of many organisations today. Originally run by the Department of Education and Employment, the scheme is now run by a private company: Investors in People UK (see the website for further information: **www.investorsinpeople.co.uk**).

Investors in People criteria
Developing strategies to improve the performance of the organisation

An investor in People develops effective strategies to improve the performance of the organisation through its people.

1 **A strategy for improving the performance of the organisation is clearly defined and understood.**

2 **Learning and development is planned to achieve the organisation's objectives.**

3 **Strategies for managing people are designed to promote quality of opportunity in the development of the organisation's people.**

4 **The capabilities managers need to lead, manage and develop people effectively are clearly defined and understood.**

Taking action to improve the performance of the organisation

An Investor in People takes effective action to improve the performance of the organisation through its people.

5 **Managers are effective in leading, managing and developing people.**

6 **People's contribution to the organisation is recognised and valued.**

7 **People are encouraged to take ownership and responsibility by being involved in decision-making.**

8 **People learn and develop effectively.**

Evaluating the impact on the performance of the organisation

An Investor in People can demonstrate the impact of its investment in people on the performance of the organisation.

9 **Investment in people improves the performance of the organisation.**

10 **Improvements are continually made to the way people are managed and developed.**

Source: **www.investorsinpeople.co.uk**

Look at the Investors in People criteria listed in the box above and note down the ways in which they differ from the definitions of training and development that shaped HR development strategies over the previous 30 years.

One difference is that in the IiP criteria the word 'training' does not appear anywhere. In the same way as 'training courses' were understood to be methods by which companies met the demands of ITBs in the 1970s and 1980s, many organisations claimed to meet the criteria of IiP by showing evidence of the number of training courses they were running – which is still true of many organisations trying to meet the criteria today. And that is why a note published by the Department of Employment in 1990 clearly (if slightly plaintively) stated:

> *Investors in People is not just one more training programme scheme or initiative. Nor is it simply about persuading companies to spend more on training. It's about helping companies to realise the value of their most potent investment – their own people.*

There are other definitions of HRD in the latter half of this chapter – but the above is as good as any.

The focus is on how 'learning and development' can help improve the **business** as a whole and not on training. This is also the focus of HRD. But how do you show the link between HRD and performance? This has been at the centre of 'evaluation' for decades and was what the ITBs were trying to achieve. The ten criteria for the Investors in People Award come closest to measuring some of the 'activities' organisations might undertake to make the link possible.

Look once more at the ten Investors in People criteria listed in the box above and note down the kind of evidence that you might look for in a company that is seeking IiP accreditation.

If you look at the Investors in People website and go to the Investors in People Standard, you will find evidence of the following kind listed against the criteria:

- People are clear about the business strategy and are involved in the decision-making process.

- People's ideas for improvement are welcomed and rewarded.

- People can describe how their learning and development has contributed to improvement in themselves, their teams and the organisation overall.

Clearly, this is good HRM practice and reflects principles of communication and performance management which appear in other chapters in this book (see Chapters 19 and 12 on communication and performance management). But is this enough to show that the business has really changed? What if a business is to be defined not by the product it sells or profit it makes but by its capacity to learn? A former CEO of IBM is said to have remarked that the business of his company was learning – the design and selling of computers was a by-product of that learning. This brings us to the third stage in our journey, which explores the practical value of what has been called 'the learning organisation'.

Again, in the UK at least, this concept was championed by a state-sponsored organisation. In 1986 the Director of the Manpower Services Commission said that 'If we are to survive – individually or as companies, or as a country – we must create a tradition of "learning companies"'. Thus was begun the Learning Company Project the results of which we examine in the next part of the chapter.

REFLECTIVE ACTIVITY

List ways in which you think an organisation might be said to *learn*. What evidence would you be looking for to prove it?

3 THE COMING OF THE 'LEARNING ORGANISATION'

If your response to the above exercise was to question the question – to say that it is difficult to imagine how an organisation could be said to learn – you are in good company. Although it is reasonable to think of individuals and even teams of individuals learning, somehow it is difficult to see how an organisation can be said to be learning. Yet if we can talk about an organisation 'changing', what is learning if it is not about changing? The Learning Company Project led to the publication in 1991 of *The Learning Company* in which Mike Pedlar, John Burgoyne and Tom Boydell explained their strategy for what steps could practically be taken to create a 'learning organisation', which they defined (Reid *et al*, 2004; p.274) as:

> an organisation which facilitates the learning of all its members and continuously transforms itself.

They provided guidelines under five key headings:

Strategic

- a learning approach to strategy – company policy and strategy continuously being revised as a result of feedback from all members of the organisation

- participative policy-making – everyone encouraged to participate in decision-making and facilities made available for this to happen.

Looking in

- information – the empowerment of everyone through the use of ICT to share information

- formative accounting and control – the opening up of bureaucratic control procedures to review and change by all who use them

- internal exchange – the encouragement of cross-departmental exchange and projects which bring together a variety of business functions and expertise

- reward flexibility – the encouragement of creative ways of rewarding innovating thinking and learning.

Structures

- enabling structures – the breaking down of top-down control structures in favour of a more flexible network wherein information and knowledge can be more easily shared.

Looking out

- boundary workers as external scanners – the encouragement of all staff to be the 'ears and eyes' of the organisation in their interaction with the external world and ensuring that the organisation 'learns' from their feedback

- inter-company learning – the encouragement of all staff to interact with other companies and again ensure that the organisation learns from their feedback.

Learning opportunities

- a learning climate – the creation of an internal culture which supports learning and the exchange of information and knowledge resulting from that learning

- self-development for all – the encouragement of everyone to take ownership of their own learning and development.

Like the 10 criteria for Investors in People, the above 11 principles would be a good basis for any HRD strategy. They would certainly help to bring about the goal expressed in the first half of the definition proposed by Pedlar, Burgoyne and Boydell (1991) – ie 'the facilitation of learning of all its members' – but would they necessarily lead to the second requirement, continuous transformation of the organisation? This is the difference between good HR *transactions* – which the 11 criteria put forward – and a change in what Peter Senge calls our 'mental models' which shape the way we see the world and can thereby lead to a *transformation* of the world (see Reid *et al*, 2004, pp273–4 for another view of learning organisations, which Peter Senge introduced in the early 1990s and which is based around 'systems thinking').

To be fair, Pedlar and his colleagues (1991) recognised that

We can't take you to visit a learning company or bring in a blueprint of what worked elsewhere – it's not like that. The magic of the Learning Company has to be realised from within. The key word is 'transformation' – a radical change in the form and character of what is already there.

The paradox is that since the publication of these guidelines there have been very many other publications with titles like 'Twenty Steps to Becoming a Learning Organisation', suggesting, in contradiction to Pedlar *et al*'s advice, that there is a blueprint to be had.

REFLECTIVE ACTIVITY

You have an opportunity to create from scratch an organisation that meets all 11 criteria listed by Pedlar, Burgoyne and Boydell as those of the learning organisation. What will it look like? Describe how it is structured and give suggestions for its culture, vision and values.

Hint: Start with a structure very different from the familiar top-down hierarchical one regarded as standard. Think of the organisation as a network.

If I were a visitor to the organisation you have been asked to describe in the exercise above, what might I see happening around me? Examples of what I might see, listed under each of the headings cited, could include:

Strategic

- Organisation policies reflect the value of all members, not just those of top management.
- Organisation regularly conducts surveys to take account of both customers' and staff's views.

Looking in

- Accountants and finance people act as consultants and advisers as well as score-keepers and 'bean counters'.
- Organisation recognises the value of teamwork by appropriate rewards.

Structures

- Organisation encourages and supports the creation of informal networks that cut across organisation silos.
- Roles and career paths are flexibly structured so that cross-department working is encouraged.

Looking out

- Staff are encouraged to engage in and learn from activities/projects outside work.

- Regular meetings are held with customers, suppliers and community members to agree on common areas of interest which impact on company policy.

Learning opportunities

- Every member of staff has a self-development plan which is regularly updated, and a budget allocated to them to be spent on personal as well as professional and vocational development.

- Everyone is encouraged to develop coaching and mentoring skills to help and develop colleagues and staff.

If I saw these kinds of activities taking place, it would show that the organisation certainly valued learning, which would meet the requirements of the first half of Pedlar *et al*'s definition of a learning organisation – namely, that it can be seen 'to facilitate the learning of all its members' – but would this be enough to meet the second criterion so that it 'continuously transforms itself'? The capacity of an organisation to change is also at the heart of Peter Senge's definition of a learning organisation, which he sees as one that is 'continually expanding its capacity to create its future'.

In the 1990s the car company Rover were enthusiastic supporters of the concept of the 'learning organisation' and supported staff's learning in many ways – but this was clearly *not* a 'sustainable' development for them because they failed to use that learning to create their own future. The next and final part of the chapter looks at what was the missing link and what any HRD strategy needs if it is to help its organisation survive into the future – ie the translation of learning into corporate knowledge.

REFLECTIVE ACTIVITY

Write down your own definition of 'knowledge'.

What form or forms do you think it might have in an organisation?

4 THE AGE OF THE KNOWLEDGE COMPANY AND THE KNOWLEDGE ECONOMY

The term 'knowledge society' is much in use today but it was first used over 50 years ago by the Daddy of all management gurus, Peter Drucker (see Reid *et al* 2004; p.267). He first suggested that an organisation's health in the future would depend more on its 'intellectual assets' rather than the traditionally valued assets like machinery, land, property and money. This must have sounded very strange to his colleagues 50 years ago, but today the Internet has meant that 'intellectual capital' is seen as a key competitive advantage. As the CEO of Hewlett-Packard said: 'If HP knew what HP knew, it would be unbeatable.' Helping an organisation become aware of what it knows and how it can know more is the central role of HRD.

Philosophers have argued about what knowledge is for thousands of years and in the definitions you have come up with in response to the exercise above you have no doubt added to the debate. We are not about to join in here, but it *is* important to distinguish between 'information' and 'knowledge', which are often used interchangeably, and 'data'. As the word's etymology suggests, 'data' means 'what are given' – ie symbols, some form of record which requires interpretation and only then has meaning or significance. Information is data which has been given a meaning or conveys a message. This word's etymology implies 'what has been given shape'. It is the receiver of the message who gives it shape, meaning. But to do that he/she needs 'knowledge', some form of personal framework within which new information is processed and evaluated (Stewart, 1997; Davenport and Prusak, 1998).

It is generally accepted that what has become known as 'knowledge management' dates from 1995 with the publication of Nonaka and Takeuchi's *Knowledge Creating Company* (see Reid *et al*, 2004; p.275). This brought to public attention the notion of 'tacit' knowledge which was first expressed by a social philosopher, Michael Polanyi, nearly 40 years earlier. Polanyi (1966) said that *all* knowledge (including so-called objective facts of science) involves a personal and subjective component – tacit knowledge. But for this knowledge to be realised and shared it has to be made explicit. Nonaka and Takeuchi suggest that companies can make such knowledge explicit by a process of socialisation, externalisation, combination and internalisation.

Personal knowledge, or what became known as *human capital*, is just one part of what has been described as 'intellectual capital'. The term 'intellectual capital' emerged out of the belief of the then CEO of Sweden's company Skandia in the 1980s that a knowledge-intensive service company's competitive strength in the future would rely less on traditional accounting assets (eg property, equipment, etc) than on less concrete, intangible factors like individual talent, skills and competencies. By the early 1990s it had created an Intellectual Capital function under the direction of Leif Edvinsson, who defined intellectual capital as having two parts: human capital (similar to personal knowledge) and structural capital. In our starter/main case study, human capital would be the knowledge each employee has. But this knowledge would also include what Polanyi calls 'tacit knowledge' as well as the 'explicit knowledge' that might be outcome of a training course, for example. As we will see, it is this kind of knowledge that most organisations are unaware their organisation possesses but which may be vital to them (see Mayo, 2001).

A few years later, as a result of a collaboration between Hubert Saint-Onge of the Canadian Imperial Bank of Commerce and Leif Edvinsson of Skandia, a third component – *customer capital* – was identified as being necessary to define the capital that emerges from synergistic relationships with customers. We give examples of this when we return to our case study at the end of the chapter.

The task of knowledge management is helping individuals and organisations to make explicit what they know (this is often called 'codifying') and to share it in such a form that others can not only use but add to. In our view this provides a bridge to bring individual and organisational learning together. We suggest that a knowledge management strategy provides a much stronger HRD strategy by providing a process whereby individual and collective learning can be codified and shared in such a way as to add value to an organisation's intellectual capital. So the HRD strategy for the future might be more closely linked with valuing people as assets (see Chapter 4).

However, although 'knowledge management' might be thought a step forward in the link between individual and organisational learning, there is an underlying assumption that knowledge somehow exists 'out there' as a 'thing' to be captured. The mainstream view is of knowledge being located in people's heads. Some years ago some organisations appointed so-called 'knowledge officers' whose job it was to 'extract' knowledge essential to the organisation's survival and 'codify' it in some way – ideally in some form of database – but that was never going to work.

 REFLECTIVE ACTIVITY

From what you have learned above about the distinctions between data, information and knowledge, think about and/or discuss with colleagues what it is that can be 'captured' in the ways suggested.

Depending on what Senge calls your 'mental model' you might – as your answer to the exercise above – have said that knowledge, information or even data can be captured. If you believe that knowledge can be stored in people's heads, it is likely that you think it can be stored in a computer. But there is another view of knowledge, which is that it is a *social* phenomenon and comes out of our relationships with each other. In such a context 'knowledge' is not an 'it' but a *process*. This leads to the fourth part of 'intellectual capital', the idea of *social capital*, which is the knowledge that comes out of our sharing ideas and knowledge with each other. It is a process that in turn generates *new* knowledge. We suggest that this process is the missing link whereby individual learning becomes group learning, which becomes organisational learning.

It is also the process which is at the heart of the next generation of the WorldWide Web, which goes beyond individual access to information, which may or not become knowledge, but which can become knowledge when shared with others. The best example of this is the notion of 'wikis' and 'wikipedia' through which anyone can contribute to shared knowledge. So knowledge becomes a shared property which can not only be accessed but *changed* and so lead to the kind of transformation that should be the goal of a learning organisation. It should also be the goal of an HRD strategy. But for that to happen we need to 'see' organisations in new ways. This kind of sharing will not happen where organisations operate in top-down control-oriented hierarchies where 'information' (**not** knowledge) is filtered down on a 'need to know' basis. In our starter case study, John Miles and his training officer operated in such a world. This was fine when it was a small operation – but we shall soon see (in the main case study) what happens when it grows and has to meet changing demands both from the inside (diversity of staff) and outside (changing customer expectations).

At this stage the organisation has to be run on more 'organic' principles, and the way staff are developed has to take into account the need for them to continually update themselves. But taking a lesson from above, the organisation must recognise that in developing themselves the staff have knowledge to share which can change the way the organisation operates. In this way every member of staff can help to 'co-create' corporate capability.

Often staff can build what have been called 'communities of practice' in which professional staff meet informally to discuss ways in which they can improve their professional practice (Wenger, 1998). In contrast to 'training', which is often imposed, communities of practice are entered into voluntarily by staff looking to develop themselves through reflection on their practice. The trick for HRD is to encourage such communities, provide them with the support mechanisms they need, and above all, provide the means whereby lessons learned can be spread throughout the organisation. (For more about communities of practice, see Harrison and Kessels, 2004, and Wenger, 1998.)

Finally, here is the definition given to HRD by Harrison and Kessels (2004; pp4–5) who describe it as 'an organisational process' which:

> comprises the skilful planning and facilitation of a variety of formal and informal learning and knowledge processes and experiences, primarily but not exclusively in the workplace, in order that organisational progress and individual potential can be enhanced through the competence, adaptability, commitment and knowledge-creating activity of all who work for the organisation.

KEY ISSUES IN HRD

We now pull together ten key points raised in this chapter:

- An organisation's current approach to HRD may have its roots in the past where the priority was to 'train' staff to meet company objectives by observing 'systematic training' principles.

- HRD has to balance nurturing and 'developing' individuals' skill and knowledge on the one hand and 'training' staff to meet the company's objectives on the other.

- An important contribution to the development of current HRD good practice was emphasis in the 1980s on individuals' 'learning experience'.

- The notion of an organisation also having the capability to learn created a new context in which individuals' learning could have a 'transforming' impact on the organisation itself.

- The structure of the organisation can help or disable learning, thus affecting an HRD strategy's effectiveness.

- For learning to be spread and shared, organisations must be structured like organic networks rather than in the more typical hierarchy.

- For an organisation to be able to 'value' its learning it has to be translated into knowledge which can be shared and codified in such a way as to contribute to an organisation's 'intellectual capital'.

- Knowledge is created and shared through social exchange.

- A key role of an HRD practitioner is to encourage the creation of 'communities of practice' within which knowledge is shared and good practice codified to contribute to an organisation's 'structural capital'.

- In this way an HRD strategy for the future will be to develop an organisation's 'corporate capability' by encouraging the 'co-creation' of new knowledge.

Perhaps there are other key points that you would like to note for yourself.

The main case study in this chapter now follows. It continues the story narrated in the starter case study, although the action now takes place 15 years later. It comprises a report from an HRD consultancy group that the Chief Executive Matt Dyson has brought in to examine the company's development needs and to recommend an appropriate HRD strategy. The recommendations give examples of principles that reflect the themes addressed in the final part of this chapter.

MAIN CASE STUDY

Look at the structure of the organisation as it is currently (as shown in Figure 28), reflecting a growth over the 15 years from 10 outlets to 20, and then read the consultant's report.

Figure 28 DIY Solutions organisation chart

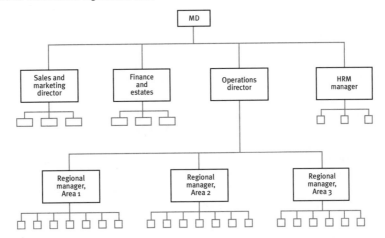

Report to the MD of DIY Solutions

Thank you for the opportunity of spending time with a range of employees in your organisation over the last two months. We have begun to form a better picture of your business, how your current employees fit into this picture, and how they and future employees ought to be developed.

In no order of importance, we list below three observations on your business, how it has changed and how your staff feature. At the end of each observation we have raised one or more questions we would like to discuss further with you.

Observation 1

Growth in number of employees from 20 ten years ago to 150 now. Growth primarily in shop staff as you continue to open up new premises. Units are organised within three geographical areas each under a regional manager who reports directly to you.

- Does the organisation structure best serve your needs, and does it serve the relational and development needs of your staff?

Observation 2

Change in the age, experience of staff recruited to your shops. Over the last ten years recruitment has primarily been in the hands of the three area managers who have the same background as John Miles and yourself – ie engineering. But over the last ten years you have not been able to recruit experienced engineers (which was your former recruitment strategy). According to your regional managers, you seem to be going for previous experience in retail rather than recruiting staff with engineering or indeed DIY expertise. In some outlets there is tension between those with broader retail experience – who also tend to be younger – and the older staff with engineering/DIY experience.

- Can you use the new mix of skills and talent to your advantage?

Observation 3

The directional flow of information is 'top-down'. There have been recent occasions when information needed in the shops has taken some time to percolate down via the regional managers. For example, your sales team recently attended a sales exhibition where they made an important link with an outside company who had developed a new type of patio heater which was fraction of the price of those currently on the market. A number of your shops have been approached recently by local customers stocking up on equipment for the barbecue season. Had this information been available earlier, you could have capitalised on this new market earlier.

- This new information faced two hurdles before it was communicated to the people who needed it. First the sales team had to report to the board and then the board reported to the shops through the regional managers. Can you create a structure where such information can be communicated more directly to people who need it?

The three issues raised above are at heart of a new approach to both development and communication we would like to debate with you. It reflects a move away from individuals being trained up to a standard which often becomes out of date very quickly. In a rapidly changing market all your staff need to update and share their knowledge continuously. We suggest that you think about how you develop your staff in terms of sharing 'knowledge' rather than training individuals against individual standards of competence.

We suggest that you discuss with us how to:

- re-frame your organisational structure to make knowledge-sharing easier
- make the most of your employees' existing knowledge both as individuals and as work-groups.

Your task

Building on the consultant's recommendations, what would you suggest the company does when you meet with them to discuss how they could improve?

EXPLORE FURTHER

DAVENPORT, T. H. and PRUSAK, L. (1998) *Working Knowledge: How organisations manage what they know.* Boston, MA, Harvard Business School Press
This book is a good introduction to the concept of 'knowledge management'.

GARVEY, B. and WILLIAMSON, B. (2002) *Beyond Knowledge Management – Dialogue, creativity and the corporate curriculum.* London, FT/Prentice Hall
This book takes a pragmatic approach to HRD emerging out of learning in the workplace. It provides useful case studies to illustrate principles introduced.

HARRISON, R. and KESSELS, J. (2004) *Human Resource Development in a Knowledge Economy – An organisational view.* London, Palgrave Macmillan
This book makes a case for HRD to be seen as a separate discipline in its own right and for the HRD practitioner to be the catalyst for the creation of new knowledge.

REID, M. A., BARRINGTON, H. and BROWN, M. (2004) *Human Resource Development – Beyond training interventions,* 7th edition. London, CIPD
This book is a good introduction to how HRD has developed from being seen as 'training', and is a good source of reference for a variety of HRD practices.

WENGER, E. (1998) *Communities of Practice: Learning, meaning and identity.* Cambridge, Cambridge University Press
This book introduces the concept of 'communities of practice' and how they can be enabled to grow in an organisation.

CHAPTER 25

Corporate social responsibility and sustainable HRM

Mary Hartog, Clive Morton *and* Michael Muller-Camen

INTRODUCTION

In this chapter we examine the growing importance of corporate social responsibility and the implications that concepts such as sustainability have on HRM and the HR function.

LEARNING OUTCOMES

By the end of this chapter readers should be able to:

- understand the business rationale for corporate social responsibility (CSR)

- describe links between CSR and HRM

- evaluate the role HR departments have in developing CSR

- examine ethical issues that can arise when operating globally.

This chapter is structured in five parts. The first part introduces sustainability issues facing organisations. The second examines links between CSR and HRM. We then in the third part consider the role HR departments can play in developing CSR by implementing the process and in the fourth part by making it sustainable. The final, fifth part of the chapter examines ethical issues that are faced by companies that operate internationally.

The chapter concludes with the main case study.

Reference sources named within the chapter may be looked up in the *References and further reading* section at the end of the book.

A UK water company had been in the public sector until privatisation, and thereafter the goals of profit and shareholder value loomed large in the mind of top management. Although in the public sector the dominant theme had been 'service', many employees had joined the organisation to pursue professional goals and standards. After privatisation, top management had changed their focus rapidly towards commercial requirements, but further down the organisation the public sector values and culture remained rooted in 'how we do things around here'. There was a desire for change at the top but a feeling of insecurity below, leading to inflexibility and rigidity.

An ambitious change programme was launched, designed to introduce flexibility, working across boundaries and a commercial outlook. 'Transformation Journey' teams were formed composed of 'diagonal-slice multi-disciplined' groups to unite levels in the hierarchy and departments. They were encouraged to choose their own projects and given the freedom to do so. Management were disappointed when 90% of the Journey teams chose community-based projects such as redecorating a hostel for the homeless or producing a children's garden at a hospice when the expectation had been that they would choose ways of reducing costs, improving efficiency and increasing profit. However, having given groups the choice, there was no going back and the project continued.

Some four years later top management wished to diversify the business and brought in consultants to advise on the feasibility of selling other products to the existing (monopoly) customer base. The consultants duly reported to the board that they had been pleasantly surprised by their surveys. 'Your customers trust you and this gives a good base for further business initiatives.' The executives congratulated themselves, assuming the credit for efficient and effective management of water resources and disposal of sewage. 'No, no!' the consultants quickly responded. 'Your customers expect that as part of paying their water bills – the source of the trust is the work your employees do in the community!'

The company went ahead with the new venture. What was an unexpected by-product of a successful change programme became a new business. The view of the outside, for those participating in the Transformation Journey teams, encouraged flexibility and teamwork. A win/win/win all round!

Questions for discussion

1 What lessons can management learn about the relationship between society and business from this example?

2 What would you say to shareholders of the company to convince them that 'community work' can contribute to the bottom line?

1 CORPORATE SOCIAL RESPONSIBILITY AND SUSTAINABLE ORGANISATIONS

Over recent years the concept of corporate social responsibility (CSR) that first emerged in the 1950s and 1960s in the USA has become widely accepted by multinational corporations and governments. This is because of the recognition of sustainability as a management concept, the increasing importance of non-government organisations, the growth of socially responsible investment, consumer pressure and recent corporate scandals. It is expected that CSR has, and will have, a strong impact on corporate reporting practices, investment strategies, the management of supply chains and public relations (Matten and Moon, 2007).

But what is CSR? For the purpose of this chapter we have chosen the following definition, which acknowledges that firms serve a broad range of stakeholders and which highlights the importance of striking a balance between economic performance, meeting the stakeholders' expectations and responsibility towards society (Hopkins, 2006; p.214):

> *CSR is concerned with treating the stakeholders of the firm ethically or in a socially responsible manner. Stakeholders exist both within a firm and outside. The aim of social responsibility is to create higher and higher standards of living, while preserving the profitability of the corporation, for its stakeholders both within and outside the corporation.*

THE LINK BETWEEN CSR, SUSTAINABILITY AND HRM

The PWC Global Survey 2003 of 1,000 CEOs entitled *Leadership Responsibility and Growth in Uncertain Times* defines 'sustainability' in the following terms:

> *We prefer the single word 'sustainability' – borrowed from the world of sustainable development and in this context to mean adding economic, environmental and social value through a company's core business function. Another way of saying it is 'Doing business with your grandchildren's interests at heart.'*

The link between sustainability, CSR and HRM is aptly demonstrated in the following quote (Etzioni, 2001):

> *The challenge in any multicultural society is to gain a shared framework in order to flourish.*

Etzioni argues that

> *the most profound problems that plague modern societies will be fully addressed only when those whose basic needs have been met shift their priorities up Maslow's scale of human needs. That is, only after they accord a higher priority to gaining and giving affection, cultivating culture, becoming involved in community service and seeking spiritual fulfilment.*

Etzioni was aiming this at individuals in society. This chapter will argue that the same applies to organisations that make up the institutions in our society and as was demonstrated in *Beyond World Class* (Morton, 1998), which suggested that the individual, the organisation and the community needed each other for growth. The thesis was that 'No organisation or company is an island and can hope to maintain or go beyond being world-class unless it operates in partnership with the world outside the factory gates.'

WHAT IS THE BUSINESS RATIONALE FOR CSR?

CSR is closely linked to the sustainability of organisations. Research has shown that three conditions must be in place for organisations to demonstrate sustainability. Firstly, organisations need world-class practices to ensure efficiency, effectiveness and competitiveness. Secondly, the organisation must be 'extrovert' and continually scan the horizon taking in data on trends, customer needs, community views and supplier interaction. Thirdly, agility is important. Based on the first two conditions the organisation is in a position to change or modify direction to ensure sustainability. The premise is that it is 'in the business interest' to pursue CSR policies within this model (Morton, 2003).

Alternative models take as their premise that businesses have to be forced by law or 'licence to operate' to act on behalf of 'stakeholders' or society as a whole. They are guided by external pressures such as industry and market standards, the media, industry reputation, pressure groups and public opinion. Other models point to the perceived need of businesses to advertise their CSR credentials to gain reputation. This may be a product of the first premise, 'the business case', which suggests 'I don't mind doing the right thing if it pays!'

The growth of CSR cannot be separated from the 'stakeholder philosophy'. Only a generation ago businesses saw themselves as solely responsible to shareholders. Indeed, even today, some business leaders would agree with this, protesting that others outside the business have no influence on the conduct of business. In contrast, the stakeholder philosophy assumes that an organisation has not only shareholders but a number of key relationships with groups such as employers, customers and the community (see Figure 29).

Figure 29 What are our key relationships?

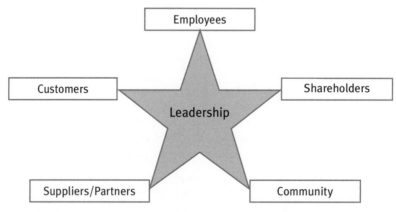

Source: Tomorrow's Company

Acknowledging the existence of various stakeholders is a question of opportunities rather than threats. For example, globalisation can give the opportunity for ideas to be translated with ease around the world that are industry-specific and can translate via chains into other unrelated sectors locally. Environmental sensitivities can with positive approaches lead to new business (for example, BodyShop) or at least prevent losses (such as the consumer reaction against Shell over Brent Spar). Consumer groups can help rather than hinder, and knowledge-based companies have 70 to 80% of their assets (intellectual capital) 'owned' in the brains of their employees. Taken together, on the one hand there are more demanding employees, customers and communities who expect their individual needs and values to be respected, but on the other hand this gives an opportunity for greater dialogue and contribution that can aid the objectives of the enterprise.

The approach is not without its critics (see, for example, Stoney and Winstanley, 2001). The term 'stakeholder' is open to misinterpretation in that the only people who *own* the business are shareholders and therefore are the only 'stakeholders' to be able, by policy, to grow the business or cease trading. The main criticism of the stakeholder approach is the supposed possibility of confusion and possible removal of concentration on the 'bottom line'. One answer might be that the results can be seen over the long term from stakeholder or 'inclusive' companies such as Marks & Spencer and Boots – the bottom line is the winner over the long term rather than just the short-term horizon.

TOMORROW'S COMPANY

In 1995, the Royal Society of Arts and Manufactures developed the concept of 'Tomorrow's Company'. Such a company would compete at world-class levels through the adoption of an inclusive approach. In terms of vision 'Tomorrow's Company' places a positive value on each of its relationships. Firstly, it works in partnership with stakeholders and maintains a healthy reputation – in other words, a strong licence to operate. Secondly, it has an inclusive approach to business leadership. This means accepting the need for change and rating long-term 'trust' relationships higher than short-term low-trust relationships as a source of competitive advantage, thus reinterpreting directors' duties – that is, to stakeholders not just shareholders – and producing annual reports that mean something to all stakeholders, not just obeying company law. Thirdly, an inclusive approach to people is recommended, which is discussed in more depth below. Fourthly, an inclusive approach to investment needs is required, which avoids an exclusive concern with immediate returns and puts a higher emphasis on fundamentals and future prospects. Finally, there has to be an inclusive approach to society. For example, business leaders can help create a climate for success, by developing community partnerships, by working with the government, by improving business representation and networking structures, and by clearing the way for the growth of small businesses. Overall, these elements will create value as indicated by Figure 30.

REFLECTIVE ACTIVITY

In respect of an organisation or a business with which you are familiar, think through the rationale behind CSR and dealing with stakeholders.

Is it the moral case – ie should we be treating those external to the firm in this sort of way?

Is it the 'licence to operate' – ie if we do not maintain a good reputation, we go out of business?

Is it the 'business case' where good relationships built by CSR bring additional business and good publicity?

Or is it a mixture of all three?

Figure 30 What does success look like?

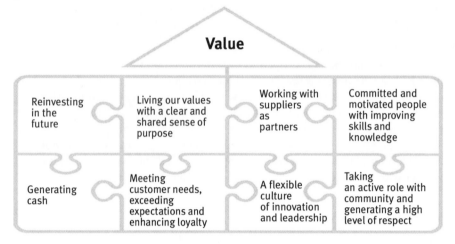

Source: Tomorrow's Company

2 CSR AND EMPLOYEES

After examining how it can be positive for an organisation to engage in CSR, we now want to look at the implications for HRM. According to 'Tomorrow's Company' the following people issues are preconditions for success. 'Tomorrow's Company':

- anticipates and responds to changes in employment patterns and in individuals' expectations

- supports individuals in developing their capabilities

- motivates people to make the best possible contribution

- adapts its organisational structure to enable people's contributions to be used fully

- participates in exploring the future of work.

What can this mean in practice? Because there is so far hardly any literature about the link between CSR and HRM, we now turn to the results of a study of HR issues in CSR reported by Muller-Camen *et al* (2008). Over recent years most global firms have started to publish CSR reports annually although their names reflect different ways of saying that – for instance, we have a Global Citizenship Report (eg Microsoft), a Corporate Responsibility Report (eg GlaxoSmithKline), a Human Resources and Social Report (eg Deutsche Post), a Social Environment Report (eg British Telecom), a Sustainability Report (eg Johnson & Johnson) and similar titles. The study, based on an analysis of 59 reports of the world's 100 largest corporations, found that five HR practices are commonly reported and, at least for these companies, are compatible with CSR. We now discuss each item separately according to how often they are disclosed in the reports (see Table 49). In our analysis, we differentiate between companies

Table 49 Social disclosure on selected items in CSR reports by Fortune 100 companies

	Liberal market economies+	%	Cooperative market economies+	%	All	%
Number of reports analysed	26		33		59	
Diversity and inclusion policy	26	100	25	76	51	86
Health and safety reporting	22	85	30	91	52	83
Extensive training	21	81	28	85	49	82
Direct communication	19	73	23	70	42	71
Indirect communication	12	46	26	79	38	64
Employment stability	3	12	14	42	17	29

Notes: + Figures represent the number of companies in each category. Liberal market economies includes CSR reports of companies from the USA, the UK, Australia and Canada. Cooperative market economies includes corporations headquartered in the Netherlands, Belgium, Germany, Switzerland, France, Japan and Italy.
Source: Muller-Camen *et al* (2006)

from 'liberal market' economies and those from 'cooperative market' economies (Hall and Soskice, 2001). The former consists of organisations from Anglo-Saxon countries and the later of companies from continental Europe and Japan.

DIVERSITY AND INCLUSION POLICY

The large majority of companies analysed disclose information on diversity and inclusion (see Table 49). For example, in its Global Citizenship Report 2004, Hewlett-Packard gives statistics on the ethnic and gender balance of its US workforce, states its diversity policy, and gives an overview of the programmes to promote diversity and the awards it has received. One reason for the popularity of diversity is the high importance attached to diversity management and equal opportunity in Anglo-Saxon countries. This is not only because of legal pressure but also because there is a business case for diversity management (see Chapter 6). In contrast, diversity management is still not fully accepted in continental Europe and Japan. This is also shown by our data, in that only 76% of companies from these regions – and thus significantly less compared to Anglo-Saxon firms – have a diversity management and inclusion policy. Some of those not disclosing information about diversity, however, give data on gender equality and disability (Muller-Camen *et al*, 2008).

HEALTH AND SAFETY REPORTING

Health and safety together with diversity and inclusion are the most frequently disclosed social indicator according to the CSR reports analysed (see Table 49). Most of the firms that do not disclose information on this item are banks and insurance companies where it is less of an issue. In contrast to industry, differences between business systems are minor. A good example for health and safety reporting is BP's Sustainability Report 2003, which describes safety policies, provides data on safety performance and reports on the improvement of standards. In contrast to diversity, international differences are not obvious (Muller-Camen *et al*, 2008).

TRAINING

Most CSR reports provide data on training initiatives and data on expenditure and number of employees covered. International differences are not obvious. Nevertheless, in the absence of standardised reporting practices it is difficult to estimate the extent to which they are committed to extensive training and to compare and contrast this data between firms (Muller-Camen *et al*, 2008).

DIRECT COMMUNICATION

Employees will contribute to enhancing organisational performance if the company shares with them information on issues such as financial performance, strategy and operational measures (see Chapter 19 on communication). Only very few CSR reports disclose information on this aspect. Nevertheless, what they do is provide insights into methods of employee communication. For example, BP's Sustainability Report 2003 shows results from an attitude survey and introduces BP's intranet-based worldwide complaints tool OpenTalk. Whereas there is no major difference between business systems in the disclosure of direct communication efforts, a difference exists with indirect communication (Muller-Camen *et al*, 2008).

INDIRECT COMMUNICATION

International CSR standards suggest that businesses should respect the the right to join unions and the right to collective bargaining (see Chapter 17 on employment relations). It is therefore not surprising that 64% of the reports disclose information on how the respective corporations deal with trade unions and employee representatives. However, whereas such information was found in 79% of the CSR reports from continental European and Japanese firms, only 46% of Anglo-Saxon firms, and thus significantly less, disclose information on this item. This applies in particular to those US MNCs that are non-union firms in the United States. They either do not touch this issue or state that although they respect the law, they prefer direct communication (Muller-Camen *et al*, 2008). An example of this is IBM, which expresses such a view in its Corporate Responsibility Report 2002 (p.36):

> *Throughout the company's history, IBM has respected the rights of employees to organise, and has made managers at all levels aware of those rights. It is our long-standing belief, however, that the interests of IBM and its employees are best served when managers and employees deal directly with each other. However, IBM complies with legal requirements worldwide regarding employee and third-party involvement.*

IBM's report does not show any examples of dialogue with trade unions. This is in strong contrast to many continental European and Japanese MNCs who describe negotiations with employee representatives (eg the European Works Council) and offer a much more positive view of social partnership with works councils and unions (Muller-Camen *et al*, 2008). An example is the following statement from the Belgian/Dutch finance firm Fortis (Fortis Sustainability Report 2004, p.34):

> *At Fortis we attach great importance to smooth and effective consultations with works councils and unions. We ensure that employee representatives receive the time and resources necessary (meeting-rooms, electronic communication, etc) to fulfil their role properly. Their role is twofold: joining in deliberations and talks on strategy, growth of profitability and employment opportunities at the different Fortis entities and at Fortis as a whole and, additionally, protecting the interests of employees collectively and individually. They also make sure that employees who find themselves in conflict with their superior possess a published and documented procedure for lodging an appeal. Senior management all the way up to the CEO and COO exercise their personal efforts to provide relevant company information first-hand to the local works councils and the European Works Council of Fortis.*

STABLE EMPLOYMENT

Stable employment is not generally perceived as part of CSR by multinational companies, as demonstrated by the relatively low reporting. The rationale for employment stability is that otherwise a high-trust relationship will not develop and workers will not fully cooperate in becoming more efficient and productive, if their jobs are at risk. The Japanese car producer Toyota is one of the few firms that state explicitly in their CSR reports that they offer stable employment (Toyota Environmental and Social Report 2004, p.72):

> *Stable employment that avoids simple layoffs and terminations is a key pillar in the relationship of mutual trust between labour and management. In addition, the Toyota management system is based largely on bringing out to the greatest extent employee abilities, reasoning skills and creativity. Consequently, the simple disposal of human resources, a major management asset, not only damages the relationship of trust but also hinders the spontaneous display of ability by employees. Accordingly, Toyota always takes a medium- to long-term management perspective and has made the realisation and continuation of stable employment through all possible employment policies the fundamental basis of its management philosophy.*

Although other CSR reports are not as explicit as Toyota, a high percentage of European/Japanese corporations (42%) report on how they have tried to downsize and restructure in a socially responsible manner. For example, the Dutch ABN Amro Bank explicitly discusses in its Sustainability Report 2004 (p.59) the dilemma a major workforce reduction in 2004 caused and the communication, consultation, training, outplacement advice and internal redeployment activities that were taken in order to minimise the impact on the workforce. In contrast, Anglo-Saxon firms usually do not report on the handling of restructuring in their CSR reports and/or seem to offer much less assistance than continental European firms. This difference also affects operations of the same firms. For example, the Dutch insurance company AEGON disclosed in its Corporate Responsibility Report 2003 that staff reductions in the Netherlands will be achieved via natural attrition whereas in the USA and UK reorganisation will involve compulsory redundancies (Muller-Camen *et al*, 2008).

3 HOW CAN CSR BE IMPLEMENTED?

The Centre for Tomorrow's Company has shown that those companies that are inclusive in their relationships inside and with their communities are consistently more profitable and more able to make strategic choices for the future. We know that individuals need organisations in which to develop and that communities need both companies and people to contribute for mutual benefit. Organisations benefit from being active in the community and HR needs to champion such policies. Looked at deeply, HR can see that its own strategies can benefit from linking with and supporting CSR policies.

The challenge for HR today is to define their role in ways that will give the best contribution to the sustainability of the organisation that employs them. We have seen that HR practices must contribute to organisational sustainability and environmental sustainability. This implies that there should be a shared responsibility between employer and employee concerning their contribution to sustainability – hence a linking together on vision, values, ethos and ethics, purpose (of the enterprise, its worth and products). We know that HRM practices that involve and engage employees improve productivity and individual well-being. Similarly HR practices that encourage protection of the environment have multiple benefits – eg a 'cycle to work' scheme where the employee benefits from an interest-free loan, and via salary sacrifice, reduces tax liability, and the employer gains through less car parking and fitter employees.

If the initial premise for a sustainable organisation is accepted, HRM policies should be focused on engaging employees towards those mutually beneficial goals. Creating and maintaining the 'extrovert' organisation requires employers to be continually scanning the horizon for opportunities and relationships for the organisation, feeding back perceptions and measures on how the organisation is succeeding in markets and sectors, with suppliers and customers and in wider CSR terms within the communities that it operates. If employees can be encouraged to be proactive in their commitments, a sustainable virtuous cycle can exist. This is shown in Figure 31.

The greatest HRM policy and practice contribution towards success in this area is encouraging change in a supportive atmosphere of trust. The values of the sustainable organisation should include 'openness, transparency, honesty and integrity'. In this, the approach taken here links closely with the evolved approach of corporate governance and should come naturally to the organisation that pursues the approach outlined in this chapter. The trust that is the necessary ingredient for change is a product of how an organisation treats others – whether employees, suppliers, customers or communities. Again, this is the 'oil' for a sustainable virtuous cycle which should be reflected in the HR policies and practice.

Figure 31 Products of the three-legged stool: mission accomplished – sustainability

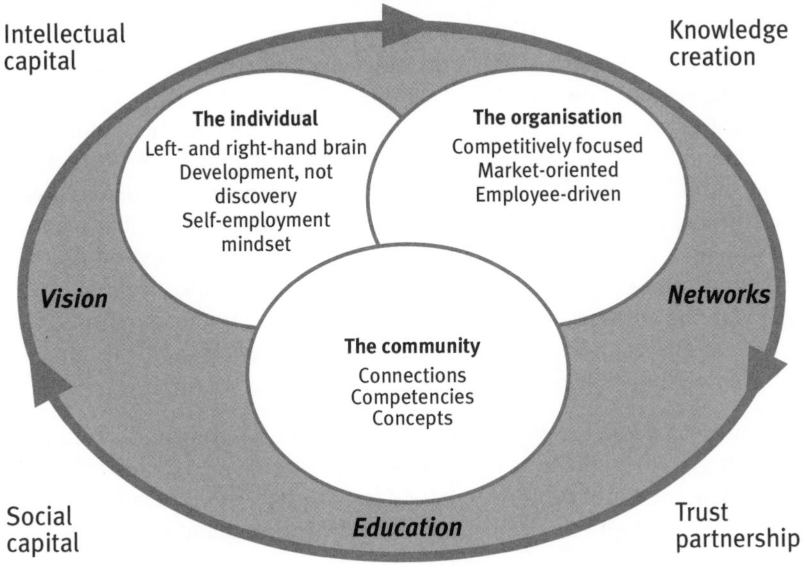

Intellectual
capital

Knowledge
creation

The individual
Left- and right-hand brain
Development, not
discovery
Self-employment
mindset

The organisation
Competitively focused
Market-oriented
Employee-driven

Vision

Networks

The community
Connections
Competencies
Concepts

Social
capital

Education

Trust
partnership

Source: Morton (1998; p.276)

REFLECTIVE ACTIVITY

Is the idea of sustainable human resource management just the latest fad or does it have any enduring substance to it? Indeed, is it just another idea or does it have something practical to offer? (Some might even say it is a contradiction in terms.)

Brainstorm your ideas and share them with a friend. Then make a note of your key thoughts before reading on.

At the end of this chapter come back to them and see if you have changed your point of view.

4 SUSTAINABLE HRM AND THE HR FUNCTION

Cynics might say that corporate social responsibility has little or nothing to do with human resource management – after all, most HR practitioners have enough to do tackling the day-to-day jobs of recruitment, absence management, disciplinary matters and training and development without having to worry about saving the planet as well. In any case, most CSR departments are separate from HR and have a role more in common with the marketing department and the task of brand management. Indeed, some would go so far as to say that saving the planet is not the job of business, let alone the HR department. However, the Stern Report (2006) might change a few minds. It forecast that climate change has the potential to shrink the economy by 20%. In response, the Chartered Institute of Personnel and Development's chief economist John Philpott argued that although HR practitioners may not see the connection or regard measures such as training in energy efficiency as 'hassle', in the long term this type of intervention now could be a significant investment in the economy. Additionally, Stern made clear that responsibility for the management of climate change lay with industry rather than government, although it recommended that government should provide legislative direction through measures such as green taxes. Nonetheless, many people are suspicious of organisations that engage in CSR, believing their motives to be merely self-serving. In some cases, no doubt, this may have elements of truth – but we suggest that if we can educate managers to see the links between CSR and HR practice at both a global and local level, we might just help them make the shift in thinking about sustainable HRM viable enough to change our understanding of it in practice.

In this section we are going to explore what sustainable HRM means for human resource practice. We discuss how it can make real difference to employee engagement, happiness and productivity, and in addition we show how it can support personal development, leadership and teamworking and diversity. To do this we use the case of HSBC.

HSBC is a global bank which decided five years ago to take a global approach to CSR – one that would serve to join up its global workforce. To do this it took up the concept of business partnership with three charitable organisations working with global environmental projects: Botanical Gardens Conservation International, The World Wildlife Fund and Earthwatch. HSBC donated in the region of £25 million to help fund the work of these new business partners. Partnership was also developed in a practical way with over 2,000 HSBC employees sponsored to take part in two-week educational field trips to work on environmental projects in places like Amazonia and Belarus, with scientists and conservationists. Significantly, the learning experience did not stop there. Taking the learning back home has become an important feature of this project, and although not initially planned for, it serves to demonstrate the potential benefits of this type of global CSR for people and organisation development generally. And it is this potential we would argue that HR has to pay attention to and actively support.

Based on the experience that HSBC participants had working on a global environmental project, it was thought that this would motivate them to set up local projects when they returned home. And indeed, approximately 50% of participants were sufficiently motivated to do something either in their local community or in their workplace that improved or contributed to environmental sustainability on their return. But more significantly, the project brought surprises in respect of personal and organisational development. For example, an employee who was known to be particularly shy, returned self-confident and able to share her learning with her colleagues. Other examples included employees gaining a better understanding of other cultures, having met people of different nationalities in the global CSR project teams, while others reported that they were more able to work with people who had strong personalities, and able to recognise and work more effectively with people who had different learning styles. These outcomes were commonly reported, and although one might expect participants to return full of enthusiasm for environmental concerns and a greater appreciation of CSR, what had not been expected was the extent to which it would engage teams.

An evaluation was undertaken by the Cambridge Programme for Industry to look at the programme's impact on both individual development and organisation development. This discovered that for many participants the experience had been deep and transformative. One explanation is that the experience of taking part in the project had been a meaningful activity for many employees, linking with their personal passions for the environment. People met others and had important new experiences. This type of learning process is believed to help loosen our mental models – in other words, our perspectives of how we see the world. In this case it helped employees see the link between the global environmental issues and our day-to-day lives and work practices.

By linking into the personal values of employees through the CSR project and creating awareness of the links between global issues and local practice, the company had created an opportunity to align personal values with espoused corporate values, and in the process improved the psychological contract between employees and the employer (see Chapter 19). It also created a feel-good factor, raising employee satisfaction and pride in the organisation, all of which have a positive impact on employee retention and productivity.

The CPI survey showed that 74% of participants reported increased development of skills and competencies in team work and leadership following their experience in the CSR project. Another 84% reported building and maintaining relationships. They further noted that line managers had not been prepared for the potential impact this project had for team engagement and thus they could not always take the opportunity to embed the learning that this CSR project generated.

CSR projects like that of HSBC's have the potential to impact on organisation development and learning – but this potential will only be fully realised if work is done to make sure that the transfer of learning from the project to the workplace is made easier by creating and maintaining a culture of learning and support. This will entail training those in line management with skills in coaching and facilitation if the benefits of such interventions are to help the development of the organisation. This is a job for the human resource development practitioner. It is this appreciation of human capital theory in practice that will help a company capitalise on learning opportunities that this type of CSR intervention can create, effectively facilitating the process of individual and organisational learning and change. In so doing, it will help create many changes in attitudes, and further understanding in the culture of the organisation towards what CSR can achieve and what sustainable HRM means in practice. Finally, as well as the benefits this type of CSR activity can bring in terms of brand management, with added value created through employee engagement, it will be positive for the reputation of the company itself as an employer of choice. For HR practitioners getting on the inside of the CSR agenda and using it to facilitate sustainable HR can add value and improve HR's contribution to the organisation as a strategic business player (Redington, 2005).

We can understand this in the following way. We are all connected to one another and live interdependent lives, pooling resources from the same planetary source. To understand sustainability in this fashion connects the planet to all our lives in communities and workplaces in a way that goes further than what we traditionally think of as the role of business and management.

So what does all this mean for the relationship between HRM, CSR and their respective tasks and functions? Firstly, we would suggest that these functions ought to be strategically integrated into the business. Although CSR is perceived mainly to have an external or extrovert function and HR is seen to serve an internal function, we suggest that these traditional divisions are in part to blame for a lack of integration and joined-up thinking. Better communication between HR teams and CSR implementers could make sure that HR issues figure prominently within CSR planning, reporting and target-setting, and in turn HR could better support and complement the efforts of CSR departments in terms of recruitment, people management and individual and organisational learning. Also, companies could include communication between management and staff, staff associations, works councils and unions within the scope of CSR stakeholder dialogue, with the aim of fostering environmental sustainability. Selection criteria for HR staff and general managers might include consideration of environmental knowledge and skills and/or commitment to developing corporate socially responsible work practices. Compensation and reward policies should aim to encourage eco-initiatives by employees, particularly initiatives that would have relevance and add value to the workplace and local communities in which the business operates. Job descriptions could include responsibilities for environmental goals and training and development provided to increase ecological awareness and foster eco-centric values appropriate to and in support of the vision and mission of the company (Ramus and Steger, 2000). The HRD practitioner has a particular job to support the creation of an ethical learning culture – one that is itself sustainable and contributes beyond the bottom line. Taken together, CSR could encourage companies to develop more long-term HR strategies that create win/wins for employees and employers alike.

5 MNCS, CSR AND ETHICS

So far we have argued that any organisation should at least to some extent fulfil the expectations of its stakeholders and behave in a socially responsible way. However, there may be different standards of acceptable or desirable behaviour in different countries (Jackson, 2000). Over the last decades, MNCs have been in the headlines for and been accused of not fulfilling ethical requirements. For example, well-known firms such as British Aerospace and the German electronic group Siemens have been involved in corruption scandals. In particular, they were accused of paying bribes to government officials to get large contracts. Another problem, which has become particularly obvious in the textile and footwear industries, is sweat-shops and child labour. Companies such as Levi-Strauss and Nike have been accused of exploiting workers in Third World countries by working with suppliers that violate labour standards. This particularly applies to plants that use child or forced labour, have an unsafe working environment, do not allow workers to unionise, require extensive working weeks and pay wages that do not meet employees' basic needs (Kolk and van Tulder, 2004). A final issue is discrimination. For example, in many countries gender discrimination is still common and often not challenged by the subsidiaries of multinational firms.

There are basically three approaches that MNCs can take to deal with these issues. The first one is ethical relativism. Basically, this means adapting corporate practices to the ethical standards of the host country. However, these vary widely. For example, the Corruption Perception Index of Transparency International shows that although in some countries such as Finland and Denmark there is almost no corruption amongst public officials and politicians, corruption is rampant in Nigeria and Bangladesh. The second option of dealing with moral obligations is ethical ethnocentrism. Firms that follow such an approach will apply ethical standards common in the home country to their operations abroad. In some cases this can lead to subsidiaries of multinational companies following higher standards and being more socially responsible than local companies. The downside is, however, the imposition of HR practices that do not fit host-country requirements. For example, a US MNC may forbid the recruitment of relatives of current employees, which could be normal practice in other countries. The third approach is ethical universalism. This assumes that there are worldwide standards that can be applied universally. A manifestation of this approach is the international code of conduct from organisations such as the OECD, the UN and the International Labour Organisation (ILO). For example, the ILO suggests that MNCs should follow HR practices such as stable employment, equal opportunities, recognition of the right to form and belong to a union, and training and consultation with employee representatives (Dowling, Welch and Schuler, 1999).

Today, most large MNCs try to impose global standards based on one or more of the internationally accepted codes of conduct. They draw up their own code of conduct and often introduce a monitoring system. In addition, employees are trained how to deal with ethical dilemmas.

KEY ISSUES: CSR AND HRM

We now pull together ten key points about CSR and HRM raised in this chapter:

- CSR takes a stakeholder approach that recognises the overlapping interests of stakeholders – ie the business, the community, employers and employees – and pays equal regard to them, and it takes both an external and an internal focus on its affairs.

- CSR is in the interest of the business to pursue. CSR can support the business brand and reputation and help the business become an employer of choice.

- Organisations need to prepare fully to use the potential impact that involvement in CSR can achieve for the business.

- Tomorrow's Company tells us that successful companies adopt partnership, stakeholding, inclusivity and trust, and commitment to the long term.

- HR practices such as diversity, health and safety, training, direct and indirect communication and stable employment are compatible with CSR.

- Values of sustainable organisations include openness, transparency, honesty and integrity.

- If HR practitioners see the link between global issues and local concerns of running the business, it will make a significant investment in the economy.

- Sustainable HRM requires joined-up thinking – the concept that CSR looks outward and HR looks inward is no longer helpful.

- Sustainable HRM supports responsive long-term policies and practices that promise to create win/wins for all.

- Major ethical issues facing international firms are bribery, gender discrimination and child labour.

Perhaps there are other key points that you would like to note for yourself.

The main case study in this chapter now follows. It gives an example of an HR/CSR issue faced by many organisations that has strong ethical implications for developing the business in a global economy.

Look at the description of the case set out below. Then decide on the recommendations that you would make as an HR manager for dealing with the issues raised. Try to think beyond the level of a 'quick fix' or simple solutions and to draw on the lessons learned from this chapter.

The Wellness at Work Foundation is an established private sector health company that has provided services for business organisations in the United Kingdom for the past 25 years. Although it does not provide private medical insurance, it supplies a range of services that support companies in achieving their occupational health and well-being policies, such as employee counselling and assistance programmes, and return-to-work services for staff who have suffered serious illness. In recent years it has opened more than ten small hospitals providing minor surgical procedures and optical and dental services for employees and companies who have private health insurance. More recently, it has opened corporate gymnasiums in five companies in the South-East, and has devised corporate training programmes and published advice on topics such as stress management, keeping fit, and managing absence and retention through well-being for HR practitioners and line managers. In 2003 it decide to expand the business by setting up a partnership company in an emerging market in one of the international emerging economies.

A small hospital has been established in Tiger City in the free-trade zone, which allows international business to set up with local partners who hold a minimum of a 51% share in the business. This has proved to be an attractive proposition for local entrepreneurs who can stand to make considerable profits from partnering with international companies – businesses that are well established without having the expertise of running the business..

When the company was set up in Tiger City, a senior executive was sent by the UK business partner to work alongside an appointed executive for the local entrepreneur. In addition, several key staff with a range of experience including marketing and sales, hospital management and administration, and nursing and ancillary services were also sent out from the UK on fixed-term two-year

contracts to establish the business. It was anticipated that these employees would return to the UK after that time to resume their posts. The aim was that once the business was established, it would employ local staff and international staff employed on local contracts.

Whereas multinationals traditionally offered high salaries, rewards and status for expatriate workers, this is no longer guaranteed. There is growing competition for jobs and an increasing desire fuelled by national legislation to employ locals wherever possible. However, it is still a period of transition in which some locals hold senior positions based on who they are and who they know, rather than on merit, and the gap between rich and poor is so great that many locals who would want to work lack the education and skills required to do the job. The cost of living is also rising, with a property boom to match business growth. This has led to a steep rise in rental accommodation in the past year.

In the four years in which the business has been operating, it has successfully established a number of its products in Tiger City and is beginning to establish a healthy client base. It has yet to break even in terms of the investment that has gone into establishing the business in this international market, but with predicted growth it is on target to do so by 2012. With the exception of the senior executive, all the original UK employees have now returned to the UK. None, however, has remained with the company; all have chosen to move on.

A common point of feedback in exit interviews has been that 'The profit-before-service position demanded by the local entrepreneur created tension and concerns of a professional nature.' In this environment individuals felt unable to voice their concerns and felt they had to keep their heads down and try to get on with their jobs. This, they claimed, created stress because they felt at times that professional integrity and quality of service was being compromised, and indeed, they expressed the view that the reputation of the company itself might also have been damaged. Deeply affected by the experience, these employees reported a need for 'a fresh start somewhere else' on their return to the UK.

With high turnover of both UK staff before or on return to the UK and a 25% turnover in new hires since 2005 of international staff that have joined this venture, the UK partner decided to conduct a confidential employee opinion survey similar to its UK Quality of Working Life survey to elicit feedback from employees. Additionally, it sent a quality inspection team to Tiger City to undertake a quality audit of practices and procedures. The inspection quality team has yet to report back its findings and recommendations, but in the meantime the HR department has analysed the results of the employee survey. Some of the key findings are:

- 60% of staff describe feeling stressed at work and confirm the feeling that there is a tension between service and profit that is causing anxiety.

- A number of staff report being made to feel uncomfortable by a memo sent out by the local entrepreneur's representative prior to the visit of the quality audit team which stated: 'You can say what you like – please feel free to express your opinions: you will not be fired.'

- International staff (many of whom had been recruited from the UK by way of Internet recruitment and telephone interview) reported that their expectations with regard to pay, resettlement allowance, help with accommodation, employment visas, holiday entitlement and hours of work were not as good as presented in the recruitment process. For example, the resettlement allowance was not sufficient to cover the recent rise in rents in the local area, which is booming, and even where the company had provided accommodation in property that it owned, the allowance did not cover replacement of worn or soiled furniture and broken equipment.

Holiday entitlement was calculated on a seven-day week as opposed to a five-day week as in the UK. The consequent 45 days' holiday per annum, with only one day for Christmas and no bank holiday allowance, left staff feeling that what initially looked generous was misleading, leaving insufficient time to visit home and have proper breaks. Several members of staff reported that they had been called in to the manager's office by a representative of the local entrepreneur to 'talk through their concerns'. The manner in which the interview was conducted was reported as intimidating and not at all reassuring, and the management style of the local partner's representative was described as brusque. Indeed, one new hire said she felt powerless to discuss her expectations freely because they were dismissed from the first with comments such as 'We know how you are feeling – you have ex-pat syndrome.' Unable to go home for fear of conspicuously failing, a number of new hires reported adopting the strategy of making the best of it until such time as they could find a better offer – but because visas were issued by employers, this was easier said than done.

- Working hours were described as problematic by over 50% of employees. The local contract specifies a 47-hour week. In light of the long hours culture in the UK, compared to the rest of Europe, at first international employees from the UK were not concerned about this – but as the expectations became clearer about the work schedules and expectations, this changed. In Tiger City the normal operating hours for business are 8:30 am to 5:30 pm, but the business was also open in the evenings and at weekends. It was in addition the local custom that most employees worked a shift during the weekend. Thus, six-day working patterns were frequently the case. With staff numbers limited while the business was growing, staff were expected to service the rising demands of the business, and several said that although in theory they could take time off in lieu, the clause

'Additional hours may be required to accommodate the needs of the business at the employer's discretion' was invoked all too often.

- 40% of staff reported that their journey to work caused them stress. Because of the very high rents in Tiger City, many staff could not afford to live in the centre of town or within easy commuting distance of the business. Indeed, many of them lived several kilometres away in a satellite city so that the journey-to-work time was regularly in the region of two hours by car, which meant leaving before 6 am if they were to be at work by 8:30am. The return journey met with similar delays. Because this was the only means of transport since the city's infrastructure was still under construction and the transport system had yet to be established, staff found the journey stressful and said this impacted on their performance once they reached the workplace.

- Over 40% of staff reported that they felt professionally challenged by their work. Because the business was growing, staff numbers were still relatively low compared to those in the UK, and staff were frequently asked to take on duties and responsibilities that stretched their professional competence and experience. Without adequate training and experienced and senior colleagues to call on for advice, this led to increased anxiety and stress.

- 60% of staff reported that they had no induction and were just left to get on with it when they arrived.

- Over 50% of staff reported that they did not know about or understand the business strategy, and that there was little or no indirect or direct communication.

- 30% of staff said that they often felt embarrassed that the company was promoting some services that it couldn't yet deliver and that it fell to them to put customer expectations right about what services actually were currently available.

- 30% of staff revealed that they found noise pollution a problem, saying that they could not get away from the constant noise of construction either at home or at work in daylight hours.

Your task

You are the HR manager who has been asked to advise on this case. Prepare a short report based on the facts you have been given above, making recommendations to your colleagues on how the ethical dilemma presented can be solved. Bear in mind the recommendations of Tomorrow's Company and the findings of Muller-Camen *et al* (2008) in making your case. The goal is to achieve recommendations for sustainable HRM while achieving good bottom-line results.

EXPLORE FURTHER

HOPKINS, M. (2006) *CSR and International Development – Are corporations the solution?* London, Earthscan
One of the best introductions into CSR with a special emphasis on developing countries.

MORTON, C. (2003) *By the Skin of our Teeth*. London, Middlesex University Press
This book argues that businesses that pay only lip service to the idea that their people are a key source of sustainability survive only 'by the skin of our teeth'. It shows how to create sustainable organisations through people.

MULLER-CAMEN, M., HARTOG, M., HENRIQUES, A., HOPKINS, M. and PARSA, S. (2008) 'Corporate social responsibility and human resource management', *Human Resource Management Journal*, under review
One of the first studies that empirically examines the relationship between HRM and CSR.

REDINGTON, I. (2005) *Making CSR Happen: The contribution of people management.* London, CIPD
This CIPD report is one of the first analyses of the link between CSR and HRM and how the HR function can become actively involved in CSR.

SECTION 6

Conclusion

CHAPTER 26

Potential future developments in HRM

Richard Croucher *and* Andrew Mayo

This textbook has covered the great variety of activities that engage the HR practitioner, and some of the inevitable tensions and dilemmas inherent in satisfying a range of different stakeholders. We now briefly point to some of the main complexities in the role, and to some of the continuing issues that come from the HR professional's position.

As the HR function has steadily shifted from being only concerned with employees and employment to a greater involvement in the overall business direction, so the tensions and dilemmas have become greater. Today's HR practitioner has to be able to advise managers on a wide range of different HR issues and to develop lawful policies that are felt fair by employees. They have to ensure that these policies are followed by line managers in order to ensure that organisational performance is maximised and that relevant legislation is adhered to. In addition, an HR practitioner is expected to understand and contribute to other aspects of the business outside of the traditional sphere of HR. In some cases additional tensions have been caused by a sense of inferiority in the perceived lack of recognition of the value that HR can potentially deliver.

One important issue is the enduring effort to establish the importance of people management issues – often described as 'soft' matters – with other managers. This is shown in the current concern with 'strategic' HRM, but has been around for many years. Everyone has heard the assertion that 'People are our greatest asset', but this may appear glib and can often draw a cynical response. Understandably, managers primarily concerned with providing a product or service at as low a cost as possible and often to demanding deadlines are not always receptive to declarations that training, supporting and motivating people are organisational priorities. How HR professionals show their understanding of other business issues is also relevant here. Although there are positive signs that in many cases they have been showing a greater awareness of wider business matters recently, having to deal with the daily weight of relatively non-strategic (but essential) personnel administration tasks as well as maintaining a strategic and business-oriented perspective is always a challenge.

Nevertheless, products and services are ultimately provided by people, and although 'labour' is undoubtedly a 'factor of production' like raw materials or data, it is not a factor of production like any other. A second enduring theme is therefore the changing role of HR professionals in relation to employees. In the past, what we call HR today was called 'welfare'. HR professionals are also very mobile today and spend little time building up relationships at all levels in an organisation. Ulrich (1997) suggested one of the four key roles is that of 'employee champion', but HR seems more obsessed with 'strategic partnership' with other managers today. Nevertheless, few things can be more important than engagement, productivity and 'well-being'. The key bottom-line calculations that derive from absenteeism and attrition (labour turnover) are largely related to motivation. It is one of the responsibilities of HR professionals to ensure that the creation and maintenance of a positive psychological contract is taken seriously by line managers and supervisors because it is one of the key factors producing the desired outcomes. There are both possibilities and tensions between this and another trend, in the form of the move away from 'consistency = fairness' to 'flexibility = fairness'. This is matched by personalised flexible benefit packages – a sea-change from the rigidity of HR's historic approach. A further challenge is that of managing those who do work for the organisation but are not employed by it. HR managers increasingly have to manage across organisational boundaries, trying to ensure that organisational goals are met by those who are not the organisation's employees.

HR always feels it is in a maelstrom of crisis. In fact the evidence is that there is a strong and remunerative market for highly professional and experienced players in HR, plus a growing recognition that intangible assets drive value in modern organisations. The contribution that HR can make is increasingly relevant, but it must embrace more consultancy skills and business knowledge. Ulrich described four areas of HR capability – business mastery, change and process mastery, professional knowledge, and personal credibility. The editors hope at least that this text has contributed to providing the third of these. The first two have to be learned too, and the last is all about the ability to create high-trust relationships. In the end it is this that counts most of all.

References and further reading

ACKERS, P. and PAYNE, J. (1998) 'British trade unions and social partnership: rhetoric, reality and strategy', *International Journal of Human Resource Management*, Vol. 9, No. 3, 529–50

ADAMS, J. S. (1965) 'Inequity in social exchange'. In L. Berkowitz (ed.) *Advances in Experimental Social Psychology*, Vol. 2, pp267–99

ALLEN, R. and KILLMANN, R. (1999) 'The role of the reward system for a total quality management-based strategy', *Journal of Organizational Change and Management*, Vol. 14, No. 2, 110–31

ALLINSON, R. (1993) *Global Disasters: Inquiries into management ethics*. New York, Prentice Hall.

ALMOND, P., EDWARDS, T., COLLING, T., FERNER, A., GUNNIGLE, P., MULLER-CAMEN, M., QUINTANILLA, J. and WÄCHTER, H. (2005) 'Unraveling home and host country effects: an investigation of the HR policies of an American multinational in four European countries', *Industrial Relations*, Vol. 44, No. 2, 276–306

ANDERSON, N. and SHACKLETON, V. (1993) *Successful Selection Interviewing*. Oxford, Blackwell

ANDERSON-CONNOLLY, R., GRUNBERG, L., GREENBERG, E. and MOORE, S. (2002) 'Is lean mean? Workplace transformation and employee well-being', *Work, Employment and Society*, Vol. 16, No. 3, 389–413

ANSOFF, H. I. (1986) *Corporate Strategy*. New York, McGraw-Hill

APPELBAUM, E., BAILEY, T., BERG, P. and KALLENBERG, A. L. (2000) *Manufacturing Advantage: Why high-performance work systems pay off*. Ithaca, Cornell University Press

ARMSTRONG, M. (2002) *Employee Reward*. London, CIPD

ARMSTRONG, M. and BARON, A. (2005) *Managing Performance – Performance Management In Action*. London, CIPD

ARMSTRONG, M. and BARON, A. (2002) *Strategic HRM*. London, CIPD

ARNOLD, J., COOPER, C. L., ROBERTSON, I. T. (1995) *Work Psychology – Understanding human behaviour in the workplace*, 2nd edition. London, Pitman

ASHTON , C. (2001) *E-HR: Transforming the HR function.* London, Business Intelligence

ATKINSON, J. (1984) 'Manpower strategies for flexible organisations', *Personnel Management*, August, 28–31

BAE, K. and CHUNG, C. (1997) 'Cultural values and work attitudes of Korean industrial workers in comparison with those of the United States and Japan', *Work and Occupations*, Vol. 24, No. 1, 80–96

BALL, K. S. (2001) 'The use of human resource information systems: a survey', *Personnel Review*, Vol. 30, No. 6, 677–93

BARON, J. and COOKE, K. (1992) 'Process and outcome: perspectives on the distribution of rewards within organizations', *Administrative Science Quarterly*, Vol. 37, No. 2, 191–7

BARTLETT, C. A. and GHOSHAL, S. (1989) *Managing Across Borders: The transnational solution.* Boston, MA: Harvard Business School Press

BECKER, B. E., HUSELID, M. A. and ULRICH, D. (2001) *The HR Scorecard: Linking people, strategy, and performance.* Boston, MA, Harvard Business School Press

BECKER, B. E., HUSELID, M. A., PICKUS, P. S. and SPRATT, M. F. (1997) 'HR as a source of shareholder value: research and recommendation', *Human Resource Management*, Vol. 36, No. 1, 39–47

BENNISON, M. and CASSON, J. (1984) *The Manpower Planning Handbook.* Maidenhead, McGraw-Hill

BERGLAS, S. (2002) 'The very real dangers of executive coaching', *Harvard Business Review*, June, 86–92

BERGMANN, T. J. and SCARPELLO, V. G. (2002) *Compensation Decision-making.* Cincinnati, OH: South Western Publishing

BILSBERRY, J. (1996) *The Effective Manager: Perspectives and illustrations.* London, Sage

BLUMBERG, P. (1976) *The Sociology of Participation.* New York, Schocken

BLUNDELL, B. and MURDOCK, A. (1997) *Managing in the Public Sector.* London, Butterworth-Heinemann

BLYTON, P. (1996) 'Workplace flexibility'. In B. Towers (ed.) *The Handbook of Human Resource Management.* Oxford, Blackwell

BOLSTER, B. I. and SPRINGBETT, B. M. (1961) 'The reaction of interviewers to favourable and unfavourable information', *Journal of Applied Psychology*, Vol. 45, 97–103

BOXALL, P. and PURCELL, J. (2003) *Strategy and Human Resource Management.* Basingstoke, Palgrave Macmillan

BOYATZIS, R. E. (1982) *The Competent Manager.* New York, John Wiley & Sons

BPS (2002) *Code of Good Practice for Psychological Testing.* Available from: **www.psychtesting.org.uk**

BREWSTER, C. (2007) 'Comparative HRM: European views and perspectives', *International Journal of Human Resource Management*, Vol. 18, No. 5, 769–87

BREWSTER, C. (1995) 'Towards a European model of human resource management', *Journal of International Business Studies*, Vol. 26, No. 1, 1–21

BREWSTER, C. and HEGEWISCH, A. (1993) 'Methodology of the PriceWaterhouse Cranfield project on European human resource management', *P+Journal of the European Foundation for the Improvement of Living and Working Conditions*

BREWSTER, C., LARSEN, H. H. and MAYRHOFER, W. (1997) 'Integration and assignment: a paradox in human resource management', *Journal of International Management*, Vol. 3, No. 1, 1–23

BREWSTER, C., WOOD, G., BROOKES, M. and VAN OMMEREN, J. (2006) 'What determines the size of the HR function? A cross-national analysis', *Human Resource Management*, Vol. 45, No. 1, 3–21

BREWSTER, C., WOOD, G., CROUCHER, R. and BROOKES, M. (2007) 'Are works councils and joint consultative committees a threat to trade unions? A comparative analysis', *Economic and Industrial Democracy*, Vol. 28, No. 1, 49–77

BROOKS, I., WEATHERSTON, J. and WILKINSON, G. (2004) *The International Business Environment*. Harlow, Prentice Hall/Financial Times

BROWN, D. (1996) 'Team rewards: lessons from the coal face', *Team Performance Management*, Vol. 2, No. 2, 12

BUCKLE, P. and DEVEREUX, J. (1999) *Research on Work-Related Neck and Upper Limb Musculo-Skeletal Disorders*. Luxembourg, Office for Official Publications of the European Union

CABINET OFFICE (2007) *Transformational Government Enabled by Technology*, Annual Report. Online version available at: **www.cio.gov.uk/documents/ annual_report2006/trans_gov2006.pdf** [accessed July 2007]

CACCIOPE, R. (1999) 'Using team-individual reward and recognition strategies to drive organizational success', *Leadership and Organization Development Journal*, Vol. 20, No. 6, 322–31

CALLAGHER, C. (2002) 'Occupational safety and health management systems in Australia: barriers to success', *Policy and Practice in Health and Safety*, Vol. 1, No. 2, 67–81

CAPELLI, P. (2005) 'Making the most of online recruiting', *Harvard Business Review*, Vol. 79, 139–46

CARDY, R. L. and MILLER, J. S. (2003) 'Technology implications for HRM'. In D. Stone (ed.) *Advances in Human Performance and Cognitive Engineering Research*. Greenwich, CT: JAI Press

CARDY, R. L. and MILLER, J. S. (2005) 'E-HR and performance management: a consideration of positive potential and the dark side'. In H. G. Gueutal and D. L. Stone (eds) *The Brave New World of e-HR: Human resource management in the digital age*. San Francisco, Jossey-Bass

CARRAHER, S. M., HART, D. E. and CARRAHER, C. E. (2003) 'Attitudes towards benefits among entrepreneurial employees', *Personnel Review*, Vol. 32, No. 6, 683–93

CASCIO, W. F. (2006) *Managing Human Resources: Productivity, quality of work life, profits.* New York, McGraw-Hill

CEDAR (2002) *Human Resources self-services/postal survey.* Available from: **www.cedar/com**

CHAPMAN, D. S. and WEBSTER, J. (2003) 'The use of technologies in the recruiting, screening and selection process for job candidates', *International Journal of Selection and Assessment*, Vol. 11, No. 2/3, 113–20

CHEN, M. (1995) *Asian Management Systems.* New York, Routledge

CIO (2007) *IT Skills Framework and the Focus of the Council.* Online version available at: **http://www.cio.gov.uk/about_the_council/index.asp** [accessed July 2007]

CIPD (2007) Performance management factsheet. Online version available at: **http://www.cipd.co.uk** [accessed March 2007]

CIPD (2007) *HR and Technology: Impact and advantages.* London, CIPD

CIPD (2007) *Coaching at Work*, Magazine and online resource. London, Chartered Institute of Personnel and Development. Available online at: **http://www.cipd.co.uk/coachingatwork/ presales.htm**

CIPD (2006) *HR and Technology: Beyond delivery*, Change Agenda. London, CIPD

CIPD (2006) *The Changing HR Function: The key questions*, Change Agenda. London, CIPD

CIPD (2006) *Recruitment*, Factsheet. London, CIPD

CIPD (2006) *Induction*, Factsheet. London, CIPD

CIPD (2006) *Latest Trends in Learning, Training and Development.* London, CIPD

CIPD (2006) *Recruitment, Retention and Turnover survey.* Available from: **http://www.cipd.co.uk/surveys**

CIPD (2006) *Public Policy Perspectives: People, productivity and performance.* Online version available at: **http://www.cipd.co.uk/subjects/maneco/ecolabmrkt/_smrtwrk.htm** [accessed March 2007]

CIPD (2005) *Technology and People Management: The opportunity and the challenge.* London, CIPD

CIPD (2005) *On-Line Recruitment*, Factsheet. London, CIPD

CIPD (2005) *Performance Management*, CIPD Survey Report. London, CIPD

CIPD (2005) *Performance Appraisal.* London, CIPD

CIPD (2005) *HR Outsourcing: The key decisions.* London, CIPD

CLUTTERBUCK, D. (2001) *Everyone Needs a Mentor*. London, Chartered Institute of Personnel and Development

CLUTTERBUCK, D. and MEGGINSON, D. (2005) *Making Coaching Work: Creating a coaching culture*. London, CIPD

COHEN, A. (2001) 'Corporate e-ducation', *PC Magazine*, 2 January, 137

COLLINS, J. and PORRAS, G. (1994) *Built to Last*. New York, Harper Business

CONNOCK, S. (1991) *HR Vision*. London, IPM

COOK, M. (2004) *Personnel Selection. Adding value through people*, 4th edition. Chichester, John Wiley & Sons

CORPORATE LEADERSHIP COUNCIL (2004) *Driving Performance and Retention Through Employee Engagement*. London, CLC

COX, T., GRIFFITHS, A. and RIAL-GONZALEZ, E. (2000) *Research on Work-Related Stress*. Luxembourg, Office for Official Publications of the European Union

CRANFIELD SCHOOL OF MANAGEMENT (2006) *Selection Methods Letting Employers Down*. Available from: **http://www.manufacturingtalk.com/news/can/can166.html**

CROUCH, C. (2001) 'A third way in industrial relations?' In S. White (ed.) *New Labour: The progressive future?* Basingstoke, Palgrave

CROUCHER, R. and KELLIHER, C. (2005) 'The right to request flexible working in Britain: the law and organisational realities', *International Journal of Comparative Labour Law and Industrial Relations*, Vol. 21/3, 503–20

CROUCHER, R. and SINGE, I. (2005) 'Consultation in a British utilities company: reinforcing the hierarchy?', *Journal of Industrial Relations*, Vol. 47, No. 4, 471–5

CROUCHER, R. and WHITE, G. (2007) 'Enforcing a national minimum wage: the British case', *Policy Studies*, Vol. 28, No. 2, 145–61

CROUCHER, R., GOODERHAM, P. and PARRY, E. (2006) 'The influences on direct communication in British and Danish firms: country, "strategic HRM" or unionization?', *European Journal of Industrial Relations*, Vol. 12, No. 3, 267–86

DANFORD, A. (1999) *Japanese Management Techniques and British Workers*. London, Mansell

DANFORD, A., RICHARDSON, M., STEWART, P., TAILBY, S. and UPCHURCH, M. (2005) *Partnership and the High-Performance Workplace: Work and employment relations in the aerospace industry*. Basingstoke, Palgrave Macmillan

DANIELS, K. and MacDONALD, L. (2005) *Equality, Dversity and Discrimination*. London, CIPD

DAVENPORT, T. H. and PRUSAK, L. (1998) *Working Knowledge: How organisations manage what they know*. Boston, MA, Harvard Business School Press

DAVIES, R. (1993) 'Making strategy happen: common patterns of strategic success and failure', *European Management Journal*, Vol. 11, No. 2, 210–13

DAWSON, S., CLINTON, M., BAMFORD, M. and WILLMAN, P. (1998) *Safety at Work: The limits of self-regulation.* Cambridge, Cambridge University Press

DBA (2002) *360-Degree Feedback,* Training Handbook Bulletin by Diane Bailey Associates. London, GEE Publishing

DE GEUS, A. and SENGE, P. M. (1997) *The Living Company.* Boston, MA, Harvard Business School Press

DE HAAN, E. and BURGER, Y. (2005) *Coaching With Colleagues.* Basingstoke, Palgrave Macmillan

DIBBEN, P., JAMES, P., ROPER, I. and WOOD, G. (2007) *'Modernising' Work and Employment in Public Services: Redefining roles and relationships in Britain's changing workplace.* London, Palgrave

DICKINSON, J. (2006) 'Employees' preferences for the bases of pay differentials', *Employee Relations,* Vol. 28, No. 2, 164–83

DICKMANN, M. and MULLER-CAMEN, M. (2006) 'A typology of international human resource management strategies and processes', *International Journal of Human Resource Management,* Vol. 17, No. 4, 580–601

DOMBERGER, S. and JENSEN, P. (1997) 'Contracting out by the public sector: theory, evidence, prospects', *Oxford Review of Economic Policy,* Vol. 13, No. 4, 67–78

DORLING, D. and THOMAS, B. (2004) *People and Places: A 2001 census atlas of the UK.* Bristol, Polity Press

DOWLING, P. J., WELCH, D. E. and SCHULER, R. S. (1999) *International Human Resource Management,* 3rd edition. Cincinnati, OH, South-Western College Publishing

DRUKER, J. and WHITE, G. (1997) 'Constructing a new reward strategy', *Employee Relations,* Vol. 19, No. 2, 128–46

DTI (2005) *Equality and Diversity, Coming of Age: Consultation on the Employment Equality Regulations 2006.* London, Department of Trade

DTI (2001) *Work–Life Balance: The business case.* London, Department of Trade and Industry

DWP (2005) *Opportunity Age.* London, The Stationery Office

ECU (2007) *Dignity at Work: Final project report.* The Equality Challenging Unit. Online version available at: **https://www.ecu.ac.uk** [accessed April 2007]

EDVINSSON, L. and MALONE, M. S. (1997) *Intellectual Capital.* London, Piatkus

EDWARDS, J. R. (1991) 'Person–job fit: a conceptual integration, literature review, and methodological critique'. In C. L. Cooper and I. T. Robertson (eds) *International Review of Industrial and Organisational Psychology,* Vol. 5, 283–357. New York, Wiley

EEF/CIPD (2003) *Maximising Employee Potential and Business Performance: The role of high performance working.* London, EEF/CIPD

ETZIONI, A. (2001) *Sustaining the Community of Communities.* Demos Collection, Vol. 16

EUROPEAN COMMISSION (2005) *Lisbon Action Plan incorporating EU Lisbon programme and recommendations for actions to member states for inclusion in their national Lisbon programmes*

EVANS, A. and WALTERS, M. (2002) *From Absence to Attendance,* 2nd edition. London, CIPD

EVANS, P., PUCIK, V. and BARSOUX, J.-L. (2002) *The Global Challenge.* New York, McGraw-Hill

FARNDALE, E. and BREWSTER, C. (2005) 'In search of legitimacy: national professional associations and the professionalism of HR practitioners', *Human Resource Management Journal,* Vol. 15, No. 3, 33–48

FAVELL, I. (2005) *The Competency Toolkit.* London, Fenman

FELSTEAD, A., GALLIE, G. and GREEN, F. (2002) *Work Skills in Britain 1986–2001.* London, DfES

FERNER, A. (2000) 'The underpinnings of "bureaucratic" control systems: HRM in European multinationals', *Journal of Management Studies,* Vol. 37, No. 4, 521–40

FIORITO, J. and MARANTO, C. (1987) 'The contemporary decline of union strength', *Contemporary Policy Issues,* Vol. 5, No. 4, 12–27

FITZ-ENZ, J. (2002) *How to Measure Human Resources Management.* New York, McGraw-Hill

FITZ-ENZ, J. A. C. (2000) *The ROI of Human Capital: Measuring the economic value of employee performance.* New York, Amacom

FLAMHOLZ, E. G. (1999) *Human Resource Accounting: Advances in concepts, methods and applications,* 3rd edition. Norwell, Kluwer

FLEETWOOD, S. (forthcoming)

FLORKOWSKI, G. W. and OLIVAS-LUJAN, M. R. (2006) 'The diffusion of human resource information technology innovations in US and non-US firms', *Personnel Review,* Vol. 35, No. 6, 684–710

FLYNN, M. and MCNAIR, S. (2007) *Managing Age: A guide to good employment practice.* London, CIPD/Trades Union Congress

FORTH, J. and MILLWARD, N. (2002) *The Growth of Direct Communication.* London, CIPD

FOWLER, A. (1996) *Employee Induction: A good start.* London, CIPD

FRAME, P., HARTOG, M. and WILSON, D. (2005) 'Productive diversity: capitalising on human resources. How can we harness our knowledge of diversity?', *International Journal of Knowledge Culture and Change Management,* Vol. 4

FREAS, A. and SHERMAN, S. (2004) 'The Wild West of executive coaching', *Harvard Business Review,* November

FRENCH, R. (2007) *Cross-Cultural Management in Work Organisations*. London, CIPD

FRISCH, M. H. (2001) 'The emerging role of the internal coach', *Consulting Psychology Journal*, Vol. 53, No. 4, 240–50

FURNHAM, A. and HEAVEN, P. (1999) *Personality and Social Behaviour*. London, Arnold

GALANAKI, E. (2002) 'The decision to recruit online: a descriptive study', *Career Development International*, Vol. 7, 243–51

GARRAHAN, P. and STEWART, P. (1992) *The Nissan Enigma: Flexibility at work in a local economy*. London, Mansell

GARVEY, B. (2004) 'The mentoring/counselling/coaching debate', *Development and Learning in Organizations*, Vol. 18, No. 2, 608

GARVEY, B. and WILLIAMSON, B. (2002) *Beyond Knowledge Management – Dialogue, creativity and the corporate curriculum*. London, FT/Prentice Hall

GOODERHAM, P.N., NORDHAUG, O. and RINGDAL, K. (1999) 'Institutional and rational determinants of organisational practices: human resource practices in European firms', *Administrative Science Quarterly*, Vol. 44, 507–31

GOOS, M. and MANNING, A. (2003) 'McJobs and MacJobs: the growing polarisation of jobs in the UK'. In R. Dickens, P. Gregg and J. Wadsworth (eds) *The Labour Market Under New Labour: The state of working Britain*. New York, Palgrave Macmillan

GRATTON, L. (2000) *Living Strategy*. London, Prentice Hall/Financial Times

GREENGARD, S. (1999) 'Web-based training yields maximum returns', *Workforce*, Vol. 78, No. 2, 95

GRIMSHAW, D., MARCHINGTON, M., RUBERY, J. and WILLMOTT, H. (2005) 'Introduction: fragmenting work across organisational boundaries'. In M. Marchington, D. Grimshaw, J. Rubery and H. Willmott (eds) *Fragmenting Work, Blurring Organisational Boundaries and Disordering Hierarchies*. Oxford, Oxford University Press

GUEST, D. E. (1997) 'Human resource management and performance: a review and a research agenda', *International Journal of Human Resource Management*, Vol. 8, 263–76

GUEST, D. (1987) 'Human resource management and industrial relations', *Journal of Management Studies*, Vol. 24, No. 5, 503–21

GUEST, D. and CONWAY, N. (2000) *The Psychological Contract in the Public Sector*. London, CIPD

GUEST, D. and CONWAY, N. (1999) 'Peering into the black hole: the downside of the new employment relations in the UK', *British Journal of Industrial Relations*, Vol. 37, No. 3, 367–89

GUEST, D. and CONWAY, N. (1997) *Employee Motivation and the Psychological Contract*, IPD Report. London, IPD

GUEUTAL, H. G. and FALBE, C. M. (2005) 'E-HR: trends in delivery methods'. In H. G. Gueutal and D. L. Stone (eds) *The Brave New World of e-HR: Human resource management in the digital age.* San Francisco, Jossey-Bass

GUEUTAL, H. G. and STONE, D. L. (2005) *The Brave New World of e-HR: Human resource management in the digital age.* San Francisco, Jossey-Bass

GUNNINGHAM, N. and JOHNSTONE, R. (2000) *Regulating Workplace Safety: Systems and sanctions.* Oxford, Oxford University Press

HALL, M. (2006) 'A cool response to the ICE regulations? Employer and trade union approaches to the new legal framework for information and consultation', *Industrial Relations Journal,* Vol. 37, No. 5, 456–72

HALL, P. A. and SOSKICE, D. (eds) (2001) *Varieties of Capitalism: The institutional foundations of comparative advantage.* Oxford, Oxford University Press

HANDY, C. (1993) *Understanding Organisations.* London, Penguin

HARLEY, B., HYMAN, J. and THOMPSON, P. (eds) (2005) *Participation and Democracy at Work.* Basingstoke, Palgrave Macmillan

HARRIS, H., BREWSTER, C. and SPARROW, P. (2004) *International Human Resource Management.* London, CIPD

HARRISON, R. (2005) *Learning and Development,* 4th edition. London, CIPD

HARRISON, R. and KESSELS, J. (2004) *Human Resource Development in a Knowledge Economy – An organisational view.* London, Palgrave Macmillan

HARVEY, C. P. and ALLARD, M. J. (2005) *Understanding and Managing Diversity,* 3rd edition. London, Pearson/Prentice Hall

HARVEY, D. (2003) *The New Imperialism.* Oxford, Oxford University Press

HARZING, A. W. (2001) 'Who's in charge? An empirical study of excecutive staffing practices in foreign subsidiaries', *Human Resource Management,* Vol. 40, No. 2, 139–58

HASLAM, C., NEALE, A. and JOHAL, S. (2000) *Economics in a Business Context.* Cornwall, Thompson Learning

HASLAM, C., WILLIAMS, K., JOHAL, S. and WILLIAMS, J. (1994) *Cars: Analysis, history, cases.* Oxford, Berghahn Books

HAWKINS, P. and SCHWENK, G. (2006) *Coaching Supervision: Maximising the potential of coaching. A guide.* London, CIPD

HAYNES, P. and ALLEN, M. (2000) 'Partnership as union strategy: a preliminary evaluation', *Employee Relations,* Vol. 23, No. 2, 164–87

HEALTH AND SAFETY EXECUTIVE (2006) *Health and Safety Statistics 2005/06.* Sudbury, HSE Books

HEALTH AND SAFETY EXECUTIVE (1997) *Successful Health and Safety Management.* Sudbury, HSE Books

HEERY, E. (1996) 'Risk, reward and the New pay', *Personnel Review,* Vol. 25, No. 6, 54–65

HIGHWAYS AGENCY (2007) *Business Plan.* Online version available at: **http://www.highways.gov.uk/aboutus/1283.aspx**; general access: **http://www.highways.gov.uk/default.aspx** [accessed July 2007]

HO, D. Y-F. AND CHIU, C-Y. (1994) 'Component ideas of individualism, collectivism and social organization: an application in the study of Chinese culture'. In U. Kim, H. Triandis, C. Kagitcibasi, S.-C. Choi and G. Yoon, *Individualism and Collectivism: Theory, method and application.* Thousand Oaks, Sage

HODGE, G. and GREVE, C. (2005) *The Challenge of Public–Private Partnerships: Learning from international experience.* Cheltenham, Edward Elgar Publishing

HOFSTEDE, G. (2003) *Culture's Consequences*, 2nd edition. Thousand Oaks, Sage

HOFSTEDE, G. (1980) *Culture's Consequences.* Thousand Oaks, Sage

HOLBECHE, L. (2001) *Aligning Human Resources and Business Strategy.* London, Butterworth-Heinemann

HOPKINS, M. (2006) *CSR and International Development – Are corporations the solution?* London, Earthscan

HORNER, C. and DOLNY, H. (2006) 'Choosing the right coaches for your company', Paper presented at i-Coach Academy and Standard Bank, Knowledge Resources Conference, Johannesburg, South Africa

HOUSE, R., HANGES, P. J., JAVIDAN, M. and DORFMAN, P. W. (eds) (2004) *Leadership, Culture and Organizations: The GLOBE study of 62 societies.* Thousand Oaks, Sage

HUANG, J. H., JIN, B. H. and YANG, C. (2004) 'Satisfaction with B2E benefit systems and organisational citizenship behaviour: an examination of gender differences', *International Journal of Manpower*, Vol. 25, No. 2, 195–210

HUI, C. H. (1990) 'Work attitudes, leadership styles and managerial behaviour in different cultures'. In R. W. Brislin (ed.) *Applied Cross-Cultural Psychology.* Newbury Park, Sage

HUTTER, B. (2001) *Regulation and Risk: Occupational health and safety on the railways.* Oxford, Oxford University Press

ICHNIOWSKI, C. and SHAW, K. (2003) 'Beyond incentive pay', *Journal of Economic Perspectives*, Vol. 17, No. 1, 155–80

ILMARINEN, J. (1999) *Ageing Workers in the European Union: Status and promotion of workability, employability and employment.* Helsinki, Finnish Institute of Occupational Health

IPD (1998) *The Future of Employment Relations*, a Position Paper. London, IPD

ISHIDO, H. (1986) 'Transferability of Japanese human resource management abroad', *Human Resource Management*, Vol. 25, No. 1, 103–20

JACKSON, T. (2004) *Management and Change in Africa: A cross-cultural perspective.* London, Routledge

JACKSON, T. (2002a) *International HRM: A cross-cultural approach.* London, Sage

JACKSON, T. (2002b) 'The management of people across cultures: valuing people differently', *Human Resource Management,* Vol. 41, No. 4, 455–75

JACKSON, T. (2000) 'Management ethics and corporate policy: a cross-cultural comparison', *Journal of Management Studies,* Vol. 37, No. 3, 349–69

JAMES, P. and WALTERS, D. (2005) *Regulating Health and Safety at Work: An agenda for change?* London, Institute of Employment Rights

JANSEN, E. and VON GLINOW, M. (1985) 'Ethical ambivalence and organizational reward systems', *Academy of Management Review,* Vol. 10, No. 4, 814–22

JANZ, J. T. (1989) 'The patterned behavior description interview: the best prophet of the future is the past'. In R. W. Eder and G. R. Ferris (eds) *The Employment Interview: Theory, research, and practice.* Newbury Park, CA: Sage

JARVIS, J. (2004) *Coaching and Buying Coaching Services. A guide.* London, CIPD. Available online at: **http://www.cipd.co.uk/guides**

JOHNSON, A. (2006) 'Orange blossoms', *People Management,* Vol. 12, No. 21, 57–60

JOHNSON, G. and SCHOLES, K. (1999) *Exploring Corporate Strategy.* London, Prentice-Hall

KALETSKY, A. (2006) 'Why the sun is rising over Britain, not Japan', *The Times,* 10 November

KAMPA-KOKESCH, S. and ANDERSON, M. Z. (2001) 'Executive coaching: a comprehensive review of the literature', *Consulting Psychology Journal,* Vol. 53, No. 4, 205–28

KAPLAN, R S and NORTON, D. P. (1996) *The Balanced Scorecard.* Boston, MA: Harvard Business School Press

KEHOE, J. K., DICKTER, D. N., RUSSELL, D. P. and SACCO, J. M. (2005) 'E-selection'. In H. G. Gueutal and D. L. Stone (eds) *The Brave New World of e-HR: Human resource management in the digital age.* San Francisco, Jossey-Bass

KERR, S. (1975) 'On the folly of rewarding A, while hoping for B', *Academy of Management Journal,* Vol. 18, No. 4, 769–83

KERRIN, M. and OLIVER, N. (2002) 'Collective and individual improvement activities: the role of reward systems', *Personnel Review,* Vol. 31, No. 3, 320–37

KERSLEY, B., ALPIN, C., FORTH, J., DIX, G., BRYSON, A. and BEWLEY, H. (2005) *Inside the Workplace: First findings from the 2004 Employment Relations Survey.* London, Routledge

KERSLEY, B., ALPIN, C., FORTH, J., DIX, G., OXENBRIDGE, S., BRYSON, A. and BEWLEY, H. (2006) *Inside the Workplace: Findings from the 2004 Workplace Employment Relations Survey.* London, Taylor & Francis

KILBURG, R. R. (1996) 'Towards a conceptual understanding and definition of executive coaching', *Consulting Psychology Journal,* Vol. 48, No. 2, 134–44

KOCH, M. and MCGRATH, R. (1996) 'Improving labor productivity: human resource policies do matter', *Strategic Management Journal*, Vol. 17, 335–54

KOLK, A. and VAN TULDER, R. (2004) 'Ethics in international business: multinational approaches to child labor', *Journal of World Business*, Vol. 39, 49–60

KOOPMAN, A. (1991) *Transcultural Management*. Oxford, Basil Blackwell

KOUBREK, J. and BREWSTER, C. (1995) 'Human resource management in turbulent times: HRM in the Czech Republic', *International Journal of Human Resource Management*, Vol. 6, 223–47

KRISTOF, A. L. (1996) 'Person–organization fit: an integrative review of its conceptualizations, measurement, and implications', *Personnel Psychology*, Vol. 49, No. 1, 1–49

LADO, A. and WILSON, M. (1994) 'Human resource systems and sustained competitive advantage', *Academy of Management Review*, Vol. 19, No. 4, 699–727

LARSEN, H. H. and BREWSTER, C. (2003) 'Line management responsibility for HRM: what's happening in Europe?', *Employee Relations*, Vol. 25, No. 3, 228–44

LAWRENCE, P. (1994) 'German management: at the interface between Eastern and Western Europe'. In R. Calori and P. de Woot (eds) *A European Management Model: Beyond diversity*. London, Prentice Hall

LEE, R. J. and VALERIO, A. M. (2005) *Executive Coaching: A guide for the HR professional*. San Francisco, Pfeiffer

LEGGE, K. (1989) 'Human resource management: a critical analysis'. In J. Storey (ed.) *New Perspectives on Human Resource Management*. London, Routledge

LEPAK, D. P. and SNELL, S. A. (1998) 'Virtual HR: strategic HRM in the 21st century', *Human Resource Management Review*, Vol. 8, No. 3, 215–34

LEWIS, G. (2000) *Mentoring Manager*. London, Prentice Hall

LEWIS, P. (1998) 'Exploring Lawler's New pay theory through the case of Finbanks' reward strategy for managers', *Personnel Review*, Vol. 29, No. 1, 10–32

LEWIS, P., THORNHILL, A. and SAUNDERS, M. (2003) *Employee Relations: Understanding the employment relationship*. London, FT/Prentice-Hall

LEWIS, S. (2003) 'Flexible working arrangements: implementation, outcomes and management'. In C. L. Cooper and I. Robertson (eds) *International Review of Industrial and Organisational Psychology*. London, John Wiley & Sons

LEWIS, S. and COOPER, C. (2005) *Work-life Integration: Case studies of organisational change*. London, John Wiley & Sons

LEWIS, S., WATTS, A. and CAMP, C. (1996) 'The Midland Bank experience'. In S. Lewis and J. Lewis (eds) *The Work Family Challenge: Rethinking employment*. London, Sage

LEWIS, S. *et al* (forthcoming)

LOCKE, E. A. and LATHAM, G. P. (1990) *A Theory of Goal-Setting and Task Performance*. Cited in J. Arnold, C. L. Cooper and I. T. Robertson (1995) *Work Psychology – Understanding human behaviour in the workplace*, 2nd edition. London, Pitman

LORETTO, W., VICKERSTAFF, S. and WHITE, P. (2006) 'What do older workers want?', *Social Policy and Society*, Vol. 5, No. 4, 479–83

LORETTO, W., VICKERSTAFF, S. and WHITE, P. (2005) *Older Workers and Options for Flexible Work*. Manchester, Equal Opportunities Commission

LUCAS, R., LUPTON, B. and MATHIESON, H. (2006) *Human Resource Management in an International Context*. London, CIPD

LUNDY, O. and COWLING, A. (1996) *Strategic Human Resource Management*. London, Routledge

MCCALL, M., LOMBARDO, M. and MORRISON, A. (1998) *The Lessons of Experience*. Lanham, Lexington Books

MCCLELLAND, D. C. (1971) *Motivational Trends in Society*. Cited in M. Steers and L. W. Porter (1987) *Motivation and Work Behaviour*, 4th edition. New York, McGraw-Hill

MCMANUS, M. A. and FERGUSON, M. W. (2003) 'Biodata, personality and demographic differences of recruits from three sources', *International Journal of Selection and Assessment*, Vol. 11, No. 2/3, 175–83

MCNAIR, S. and FLYNN, M. (2005) 'The age dimension of employer practices: employer case studies'. Department of Trade and Industry, Vol. 42

MCNAIR, S., FLYNN, M., OWEN, L., HUMPHREYS, C. and WOODFIELD, S. (2004) *Changing Work in Later Life: A study of job transitions*. Guildford, University of Surrey

MARCHINGTON, M. and WILKINSON, A. (2005) *Human Resource Management at Work*. London, CIPD

MARCHINGTON, M., WILKINSON, A., ACKERS, P. and DUNDON, T. (2001) *Management Choice and Employee Voice*. London, CIPD

MARTIN, G. (2005) *Technology and People Management: Transforming the function of HR and the HR function*. London, CIPD

MATTEN, D. and MOON, J. (2007) '"Implicit" and "explicit" CSR: a conceptual framework for a comparative understanding of corporate social responsibility', *Academy of Management Review*. Forthcoming

MAY, R., BORMANN YOUNG, C. and LEDGERWOOD, D. (1998) 'Lessons from Russian human resource management experience', *European Management Journal*, Vol. 16, No. 4, 447–59

MAYO, A. J. (2006) *What's the Future for Human Capital? Measuring and reporting – the fundamental requirement for data*. London, CIPD

MAYO, A. J. (2004a) *Understanding HR Return On Investment*. One Stop Guide Series. London, *Personnel Today* Management Resources

MAYO, A. J. (2004b) *Creating a Learning and Development Strategy.* London, CIPD

MAYO, A. J. (2001) *The Human Value of the Enterprise: Valuing people as assets – monitoring, measuring and managing.* London, Nicholas Brealey

MAYO, A.J. (1994) *Managing Careers – Strategies for Organisations.* London, IPM

MAYRHOFER, W. and BREWSTER, C. (2005) 'European human resource management: researching developments over time', *Management Review,* Vol. 16, No. 1, 36–62

MBIGI, L. (1997) *Ubuntu: The African dream in management.* Cape Town, Knowledge Resources

MENDENHALL, M. and ODDOU, G. (1985) 'The dimensions of expatriate acculturation: a review', *Academy of Management Review,* Vol. 10, 39–47

MEYER, C. (1994) 'How the right measures help teams excel', *Harvard Business Review,* Vol. 72, No. 3, 95–103

MORRISON, J. (2006) *The International Business Environment: Global and local marketplaces in a changing world.* Basingstoke, Palgrave Macmillan

MORTON, C. (2003) *By the Skin of our Teeth.* London, Middlesex University Press

MULLER-CAMEN, M., HARTOG, M., HENRIQUES, A., HOPKINS, M. and PARSA, S. (2008) 'Corporate social responsibility and human resource management', *Human Resource Management Journal,* under review

MULLINS, L. (2007) *Management and Organisational Behaviour.* Harlow, Prentice Hall/Financial Times

MUMFORD, A. (1996) 'Special needs, different solutions'. In J. Bilsberry (ed.) *The Effective Manager: Perspectives and Illustrations.* London, Sage

NEEDLE, D. (2004) *Business in Context.* London, Thomson Learning

NEWELL, S. and SHACKLETON, V. (2000) 'Recruitment and selection'. In S. Bach and K. Sisson (eds) *Personnel Management: A comprehensive guide to theory and practice.* London, Blackwell

NONAKA, I. and TAKEUCHI, H. (1995) *The Knowledge Creating Company.* Oxford, Oxford University Press

OECD (2003) *Ageing and Employment Policies (Vieillissement et politiques de l'emploi).* Stockholm, OECD

OLIVER, N. and WILKINSON, B. (1992) *The Japanisation of British Industry.* Oxford, Blackwell

OLVE, N., ROY, J. and WETTER, M. (2001) *Performance Drivers: A practical guide to using the balanced scorecard.* London, John Wiley & Sons

ORGAN, D. W., PODSAKOFF, P. M. and MACKENZIE, S. B. (2006) *Organizational Citizenship Behavior: Its nature, antecedents, and consequences.* Thousand Oaks, Sage

OWEN, L. and FLYNN, M. (2004) 'Changing work: mid to late life transitions in employment', *Ageing International,* Vol. 29, No. 4, 333–50

PAAUWE, J. (1995) 'Personnel management without personnel managers: varying degrees of outsourcing the personnel function'. In P. Flood, M. Gannon and J. Paauwe (eds) *Managing Without Traditional Methods*. Wokingham, Addison-Wesley

PARVIS, L. (2007). *Understanding cultural diversity in today's complex world*. Available from: **www.lulu.com/browse/search.php?fkeywrds= diversityparagraph1**

PASCALE, R. T. and ATHOS, A. G. (1981) *The Art of Japanese Management*. New York, Simon & Schuster

PEARCE, J., BRANYICZKI, I. and BAKACSI, J. (1994) 'Person-based Reward Systems', *Journal of Organizational Behavior*, Vol. 15, 261–82

PEARN, M. and KANDOLA, R. (1993) *Job Analysis*. London, IPM

PEDLAR, M., BURGOYNE, J. and BOYDELL, T. (1991) *The Learning Company*. London, McGraw-Hill

PELTIER, B. (2001) *The Psychology of Executive Coaching: Theory and application*. Hove, Brunner-Routledge

PERKINS, S. J. (2006) *International Reward and Recognition*, Research Report. London, CIPD

PERLMUTTER, H. V. (1969) 'The tortuous evolution of the multinational corporation', *Columbia Journal of World Business*, Vol. 4, 9–18

PERSONNEL TODAY (2005) *UK Makes Use of e-HRM*. 12 April

PFEFFER, J. (1998) *The Human Equation: Building profits by putting people first*. Boston, MA: Harvard Business School Press

PHILLIPS, J. J. and PHILLIPS, P. P. (2005) *Proving the Value of HR*. Alexandria, SHRM

PHILLIPS, J. J. and PHILLIPS, P. P. (2002) *Measuring Intellectual Capital*. Alexandria, VA, ASTD

PHILLIPS, J. J., STONE, R. D. and PHILLIPS, P. P. (2001) *The Human Resources Scorecard*. Boston, MA, Butterworth-Heinemann

PILBEAM, S. and CORBRIDGE, M. (2006) *People Resourcing: HRM in practice*. London, Prentice-Hall/FT

POLANYI, M. (1966) *The Tacit Dimension*. New York, Doubleday

PORTER, M. and KETELS, C. H. M. (2003) *UK Competitiveness: Moving to the next stage*. DTI Economics Paper No. 3. London, DTI

PRIEM, R. L., LOVE, L. G. and SHAFFER, M. (2000) 'Industrialization and values evolution: the case of Hong Kong and Guangzhou, China', *Asia-Pacific Journal of Management*, Vol. 17, No. 3, 473–92

RAMUS, C. A. and STEGER, U. (2000) 'The roles of supervisory support behaviours and environmental policy in employee "eco-initiatives" at leading-edge European companies', *Academy of Management Journal*, Vol. 43, No. 4, 605–26

RAO, T. V. (1996) *Human Resource Development: Experiences, intervention, strategies.* New Delhi, Sage

RAPOPORT, R., BAILYN, L., FLETCHER, J. and PRUITT, B. (2002) *Beyond Work–family Balance: Advancing gender equity and workplace performance.* London, Jossey-Bass/John Wiley

REDINGTON, I. (2005) *Making CSR Happen: The contribution of people management.* London, CIPD

REID, M. A., BARRINGTON, H. and BROWN, M. (2004) *Human Resource Development – Beyond training interventions,* 7th edition. London, CIPD

ROBERTS, G. (2005) *Recruitment and Selection,* 2nd edition. London, CIPD

ROBERTSON, I. T. (1994) 'Personality and personnel selection'. In C. L. Cooper and D. M. Rousseau (eds) *Trends in Organisational Behaviour.* London, John Wiley & Sons

ROBERTSON, I. T. and SMITH, M. (2001) 'Personnel selection', *Journal of Occupational and Organizational Psychology,* Vol. 74, No. 4, 441–72

RODRIQUEZ, R. (2006) 'Diversity finds its place', *HR Magazine,* Vol. 51, No. 8

RUEL, H. J. M., BONDAOUK, T. and LOOISE, J. C. (2004) 'E-HRM: innovation or irritation? An expansive empirical study in five large companies on web-based HRM', *Management Review,* Vol. 15, No. 3, 364–81

RUGMAN, A. and COLLINSON, S. (2006) *International Business.* Harlow, Prentice Hall/Financial Times

SADLER, P. (1993) *Managing Talent.* London, Economist Books

SCARBROUGH, H. (2003) *Human Capital: The external reporting framework,* Change Agenda. London, CIPD

SCHMIDT, F. L. and HUNTER, J. E. (1998) 'The validity and utility of selection methods in personnel psychology and theoretical implications of 85 years of research findings', *Psychological Bulletin,* Vol. 124, 262–74

SCHULER, R. S. (1992) *Linking the People with the Strategic Needs of the Business.* American Management Association

SCHWARTZ, S. H. (1999) 'A theory of cultural values and some implications for work', *Applied Psychology: An International Review,* Vol. 48, No. 1, 23–47

SCOTT, S. and DEAN, J. (1992) 'Integrated manufacturing and human resource management: a human capital approach', *Academy of Management Journal,* Vol. 35, No. 3, 467–504

SEARLE, R. H. (2003) *Recruitment and Selection: A critical text.* Milton Keynes, Palgrave/Open University Press

SENGE, P. M. (1990) *The Fifth Discipline: The art and practice of the learning organization.* London, Random House

SENGE, P., ROSS, R., SMITH, B., ROBERTS, C. and KLEINER, A. (1994) *The Fifth Discipline Fieldbook: Strategies and tools for building a learning organisation.* London, Nicholas Brealey

SLOMAN, M. (2007) *The Changing World of the Trainer*. Oxford, Butterworth-Heinemann

SLOMAN, M. and ROLPH, J. (2003) *E-learning*, Change Agenda. London, CIPD

SMITH, P. and MORTON, G. (2006) 'Nine years of New Labour: neoliberalism and workers rights', *British Journal of Industrial Relations*, Vol. 44, No. 3, 401–20

SMITH, P. and MORTON, G. (1993) 'Union exclusion and the decollectivisation of industrial relations in contemporary Britain', *British Journal of Industrial Relations*, Vol. 31, No. 1, 97–114

SMITH, P. B., DUGAN, S. and TROMPENAARS, F. (1996) 'National culture and values of organizational employees: a dimensional analysis across 43 nations', *Journal of Cross-Cultural Psychology*, Vol. 27, No. 2, 231–64

SNELL, S. (1992) 'Control theory in strategic human resource management', *Academy of Management Journal*, Vol. 35, No. 2, 292–327

SNELL, S. A., STUEBER, D. and LEPAK, D. P. (2002) 'Virtual HR departments: getting out of the middle'. In R. L. Henneman and D. B. Greenberger (eds) *HRM in Virtual Organisations*. New York, NY: Information Management Publishing

SPARROW, P. R. (2006) *International Recruitment, Selection and Assessment*, Research Report. London, CIPD

SPARROW, P. AND MARCHINGTON, M. (1998) 'Is HRM in crisis?' In P. Sparrow and M. Marchington (eds) *Human Resource Management: The new agenda*. London, FT/Pitman

STANSFELD, S., HEAD, J. and MARMOT, M. (1999) *Work-Related Factors and Ill-Health: The Whitehall II study*. Research Report 266. Sudbury: HSE Books. Available online at: **http://www.hse.gov.uk/research/crr_pdf/2000/crr00266.pdf**

STERN, S. (2007) 'The rise of the listening guru', *Financial Times*, 19 July, 14

STEWART, T. A. (1997) *Intellectual Capital – The new wealth of organizations*. London, Nicholas Brealey

STONE, D. L., STONE-ROMERO, E. F. and LUKASZEWSKI, K. (2003) 'The functional and dysfunctional consequences of human resource information technology for organisations and their employees'. In D. Stone (ed.) *Advances in Human Performance and Cognitive Engineering Research*. Greenwich, CT: JAI Press

STONEY, C. and WINSTANLEY, D. (2001) 'Stakeholding: confusion or Utopia? Mapping the contextual terrain', *Journal of Management Studies*, Vol. 38, No. 5, 603–26

STOREY, J. (1992) *Developments in the Management of Human Resources*. Oxford, Blackwell

STREDWICK, J. and ELLIS, S. (2005) *Flexible Working Practices*. London, CIPD

STROHMEIER, S. (2007) 'Research in e-HRM: review and implications', *Human Resource Management Review*, Vol. 17, No. 1, 19–37

TAILBY, S. (2003) 'Flexibility'. In G. Hollinshead, P. Nicholls and S. Tailby (eds) *Employee Relations*, 2nd edition. Harlow, Pearson

TANNENBAUM, S. I. (1990) 'Human resource information systems: user group implications', *Journal of Systems Management*, Vol. 41, 27–32

TAYLOR, P. (2006) *Employment Initiatives for an Ageing Workforce in the EU-15.* Luxembourg, Office for Official Publications of the European Communities

TAYLOR, P. J. and SMALL, B. (2002) 'Asking applicants what they *would* do versus what they *did* do: a meta-analytic comparison of situational and past behaviour employment interview questions', *Journal of Occupational and Organizational Psychology*, Vol. 75, No. 3, 277–94

TAYLOR, P., BALDRY, C., BAIN, P. and ELLIS, V. (2003) 'A unique working environment: health, sickness and absence management in UK call centres', *Work, Employment and Society*, Vol. 17, No. 3, 435–58

TAYLOR, R. (1997) 'CBI chief signals support for partnership with unions', *Financial Times*, 11 September

TAYLOR, S. (2005a) *The Employee Retention Handbook.* London, CIPD

TAYLOR, S. (2005b) *People Resourcing*, 3rd edition. London, CIPD

TEO, T. S. H., SOON, L. G. and FEDRIC, S. A. (2001) 'Adoption and impact of human resource information systems', *Research and Practice in Human Resource Management*, Vol. 9, No. 1, 101–17

TIXIER, M. (2000) 'Communication and management styles in Australia: understanding the changing nature of its corporate affairs', *Cross-Cultural Management: An International Journal*, Vol. 7, No. 1, 12–22

TREGASKIS, O., GLOVER, L. and FERNER, A. (2006) *International HR Networks in MNCs*, Research Report. London, CIPD

TREGASKIS, O., MAHONEY, C. and ATTERBURY, S. (2004) 'International survey methodology experiences from the Cranet Network'. In C. Brewster, W. Mayrhofer and M. Morley (eds) *Human Resource Management in Europe: Evidence of convergence?* London, Butterworth-Heinemann

TUCKMAN, B. and JENSEN, N. (1977) 'Stages of small group development revisited', *Group and Organisational Studies*, Vol. 2, 419–27

TURNER, B. and PIDGEON, N. (1997). *Man-Made Disasters.* London, Wykeham

TWOMEY, D. and QUAZI, H. (1994) 'Triangular typology approach to studying performance management systems in hi-tech firms', *Journal of Organizational Behaviour*, Vol. 15, No. 6, 561–73

TYSON, S. and FELL, A. (1986) *Evaluating the Personnel Function.* London, Hutchinson

ULRICH, D. (1997) *Human Resource Champions.* Boston, MA: Harvard Business Press

ULRICH, D. and BROCKBANK, B. (2005) *The HR Value Proposition.* Boston, MA: Harvard Business

ULRICH, D. and BROCKBANK, W. (2005) 'Role call', *People Management*, Vol. 16, June, 24–8

ULRICH, S. (2002) 'From e-business to e-HR', *International Human Resource Information Management Journal*, Vol. 5, 90–7

VROOM, V. H. (1964) *Work and Motivation.* Cited in J. Arnold, C. L. Cooper and I. T. Robertson (1995) *Work Psychology – Understanding human behaviour in the workplace*, 2nd edition. London, Pitman

WÄCHTER, H. and MULLER-CAMEN, M. (2002) 'Co-determination and strategic integration in German firms', *Human Resource Management Journal*, Vol. 12, No. 3, 76–87

WADDINGTON, J. (2003) 'Annual review article: heightening tension in relations between trade unions and the labour government in 2002', *British Journal of Industrial Relations*, Vol. 41, No. 2, 335–58

WALKER, A. (1999) 'Ageing in Europe – challenges and consequences', *Zeitschrift für Gerontologie und Geriatrie*, Vol. 32, No. 6, 390–7

WALTERS, D. (2001) *Health and Safety in Small Enterprises.* Oxford, PIE Peter Lang

WALTERS, D. and NICHOLS, T. (2007) *Worker Representation and Workplace Health and Safety.* Basingstoke, Palgrave Macmillan

WALTERS, D., NICHOLS, T., CONNOR, J., TASIRAN, A. and CAM, S. (2005) *The Role and Effectiveness of Safety Representatives in Influencing Workplace Health and Safety.* Research Report 363. Sudbury: HSE Books. Available online at: **http://www.hse.gov.uk/_research/rrhtm/rr363.htm**

WALTERS, M. (2005) *People and Performance: Designing the HR process for maximum performance delivery.* London, CIPD

WEDDERBURN, L. (1991) 'Freedom of association and philosophies of labour law', *Employment Rights in Britain and Europe: Selected papers in labour law.* London, Lawrence & Wishart

WEEKES, S. and BEAGRIE, S. (2002) *E-People.* Knoxville, TN: Capstone Publishing

WENGER, E. (1998) *Communities of Practice: Learning, meaning and identity.* Cambridge, Cambridge University Press

WESTWOOD, R. J. and POSNER, B. Z. (1997) 'Managerial values across cultures: Australia, Hong Kong, and the United States', *Asia-Pacific Journal of Management*, Vol. 14, 31–66

WHEELER, H. N. and MCCLENDON, J. A. (1998) 'Employment relations in the United States'. In G. J. Bamber and R. D. Lansbury, *International and Comparative Employment Relations.* London, Sage

WHITE, M., HILL, S., MCGOVERN, P., MILLS, C. and SMEATON, D. (2004a) *Managing to Change?* Basingstoke, Palgrave

WHITE, M., HILL, S., MCGOVERN, P., MILLS, C. and SMEATON, D. (2004b) '"High performance" management practices, working hours and work–life balance', *British Journal of Industrial Relations*, Vol. 41, No. 2, 175–95

WILLEMS, I., JANVIER, R. and HENDERICKX, E. (2006) 'New pay in European civil services: is the psychological contract changing?', *International Journal of Public Sector Management*, Vol. 19, No. 6, 609–21

WITHERSPOON, R. and WHITE, R. P. (2004) *Four Essential Ways That Coaching Can Help Executives.* Greensboro, NC, Center for Creative Leadership

WOMACK, J. P., JONES, D. T. and ROOS, D. (1990) *The Machine That Changed the World: The triumph of lean production.* New York, Rawson Macmillan

WOOD, G. and SELA, R. (2000) 'Making human resource development work', *Human Resource Development International*, Vol. 3, No. 4, 451–64

WOOD, G., HARCOURT, M. and ROPER, I. (2006) 'The limits of numerical flexibility. Continuity and change'. In G. Wood and P. James (eds) *Institutions, Production and Working Life.* Oxford, Oxford University Press

WRIGHT, P. and McMAHON, A. (1992) 'Theoretical perspectives for strategic human resource management', *Journal of Management*, Vol. 18, No. 2, 295–320

WWP DEVELOPING PEOPLE (2007) *Managing diversity.* Available from: **www.wwp.co.uk/ diversity _ cultural _ equality _workplace.htm?gclid=COP8V**

ZUSMAN, P. R. and LANDIS, R. S. (2002) 'Applicant preferences for web-based vs traditional job postings', *Computers in Human Behaviour*, Vol. 18, No. 3, 285–96

Index

Organizational Behavior

Global Edition

Organizational Behavior

EDITION

15

Global Edition

Stephen P. Robbins
—San Diego State University

Timothy A. Judge
—University of Notre Dame

PEARSON

Boston Columbus Indianapolis New York San Francisco Upper Saddle River
Amsterdam Cape Town Dubai London Madrid Milan Munich Paris Montréal Toronto
Delhi Mexico City São Paulo Sydney Hong Kong Seoul Singapore Taipei Tokyo

Editorial Director: Sally Yagan
Director of Editorial Services: Ashley Santora
Acquisitions Editor: Brian Mickelson
Senior International
  Acquisitions Editor: Laura Dent
International Print and Media
  Editor: Leandra Paoli
Editorial Project Manager: Sarah Holle
Editorial Assistant: Ashlee Bradbury
VP Director of Marketing: Patrice Lumumba Jones
Senior Marketing Manager: Nikki Ayana Jones
International Marketing Manager: Dean Erasmus
Senior Managing Editor: Judy Leale
Production Project Manager: Becca Groves
Senior Operations Supervisor: Arnold Vila

Operations Specialist: Cathleen Petersen
Senior Art Director: Janet Slowik
Art Director: Kenny Beck
Text Designer: Wanda Espana
OB Poll Graphics: Electra Graphics
Cover Designer: Jodi Notowitz
Cover Art: © Freudenthal Verhagen/Getty
Sr. Media Project Manager, Editorial:
  Denise Vaughn
Media Project Manager, Production:
  Lisa Rinaldi
Full-Service Project Management:
  Christian Holdener, S4Carlisle Publishing
  Services

Pearson Education Limited
Edinburgh Gate
Harlow
Essex CM20 2JE
England

and Associated Companies throughout the world

Visit us on the World Wide Web at:
www.pearson.com/uk

© Pearson Education Limited 2013

ISBN 13: 978-0-273-76529-5
ISBN 10: 0-273-76529-9

British Library Cataloguing-in-Publication Data
A catalogue record for this book is available from the British Library

10 9 8 7 6 5 4 3
16 15 14 13 12

Typeset in 10.5/12 ITC New Baskerville Std by S4Carlisle Publishing Services
Printed and bound by Courier/Kendallville in The United States of America

The publisher's policy is to use paper manufactured from sustainable forests.

Brief Contents

4   The Organization System

Contents

2   The Individual

4 *Emotions and Moods* 131

5 *Personality and Values* 165

6 *Perception and Individual Decision Making* 199

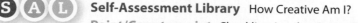

7 *Motivation Concepts* 235

8 *Motivation: From Concepts to Applications* 273

3   The Group

12 *Leadership* 401

4 The Organization System

16 *Organizational Culture* 545

About the Authors

Stephen P. Robbins

Education

Ph.D. University of Arizona

Professional Experience

Academic Positions: Professor, San Diego State University, Southern Illinois University at Edwardsville, University of Baltimore, Concordia University in Montreal, and University of Nebraska at Omaha.

Research: Research interests have focused on conflict, power, and politics in organizations, behavioral decision making, and the development of effective interpersonal skills.

Books Published: World's best-selling author of textbooks in both management and organizational behavior. His books have sold more than 5 million copies and have been translated into 20 languages; editions have been adapted for Canada, Australia, South Africa, and India, such as these:

- *Essentials of Organizational Behavior*, 11th ed. (Pearson Education, 2012)
- *Management*, 11th ed. with Mary Coulter (Pearson Education, 2012)
- *Fundamentals of Human Resource Management*, 10th ed., with David DeCenzo (Wiley, 2010)
- *Prentice Hall's Self-Assessment Library 3.4* (Pearson Education, 2010)
- *Fundamentals of Management*, 8th ed., with David DeCenzo and Mary Coulter (Pearson Education, 2013)
- *Supervision Today!* 7th ed., with David DeCenzo and Robert Wolter (Pearson Education, 2013)
- *Training in Interpersonal Skills: TIPS for Managing People at Work*, 6th ed., with Phillip Hunsaker (Pearson Education, 2012)
- *Managing Today!* 2nd ed. (Pearson Education, 2000)
- *Organization Theory*, 3rd ed. (Pearson Education, 1990)
- *The Truth About Managing People*, 2nd ed. (Pearson Education, 2008)
- *Decide and Conquer: Make Winning Decisions and Take Control of Your Life* (Pearson Education, 2004).

Other Interests

In his "other life," Dr. Robbins actively participates in masters' track competition. Since turning 50 in 1993, he has won 18 national championships and 12 world titles. He is the current world record holder at 100 meters (12.37 seconds) and 200 meters (25.20 seconds) for men 65 and over.

Timothy A. Judge

Education

Ph.D., University of Illinois at Urbana-Champaign

Professional Experience

Academic Positions: Franklin D. Schurz Chair, Department of Management, Mendoza College of Business, University of Notre Dame; Matherly-McKethan Eminent Scholar in Management, Warrington College of Business Administration, University of Florida; Stanley M. Howe Professor in Leadership, Henry B. Tippie College of Business, University of Iowa; Associate Professor (with tenure), Department of Human Resource Studies, School of Industrial and Labor Relations, Cornell University; Lecturer, Charles University, Czech Republic, and Comenius University, Slovakia; Instructor, Industrial/Organizational Psychology, Department of Psychology, University of Illinois at Urbana-Champaign.

Research: Dr. Judge's primary research interests are in (1) personality, moods, and emotions; (2) job attitudes; (3) leadership and influence behaviors; and (4) careers (person–organization fit, career success). Dr. Judge has published more than 140 articles on these and other major topics in journals such as *Journal of Organizational Behavior, Personnel Psychology, Academy of Management Journal, Journal of Applied Psychology, European Journal of Personality*, and *European Journal of Work and Organizational Psychology*.

Fellowship: Dr. Judge is a fellow of the American Psychological Association, the Academy of Management, the Society for Industrial and Organizational Psychology, and the American Psychological Society.

Awards: In 1995, Dr. Judge received the Ernest J. McCormick Award for Distinguished Early Career Contributions from the Society for Industrial and Organizational Psychology. In 2001, he received the Larry L. Cummings Award for mid-career contributions from the Organizational Behavior Division of the Academy of Management. In 2007, he received the Professional Practice Award from the Institute of Industrial and Labor Relations, University of Illinois.

Books Published: H. G. Heneman III, T. A. Judge, and J. D. Kammeyer-Mueller, *Staffing Organizations*, 7th ed. (Madison, WI: Mendota House/Irwin, 2011)

Other Interests

Although he cannot keep up (literally!) with Dr. Robbin's accomplishments on the track, Dr. Judge enjoys golf, cooking and baking, literature (he's a particular fan of Thomas Hardy and is a member of the Thomas Hardy Society), and keeping up with his three children, who range in age from 23 to 9.

Preface

Welcome to the fifteenth edition of *Organizational Behavior!* Long considered the standard for all organizational behavior textbooks, this edition continues its tradition of making current, relevant research come alive for students. While maintaining its hallmark features—clear writing style, cutting-edge content, and engaging pedagogy—the fourteenth edition has been updated to reflect the most recent research within the field of organizational behavior. This is one of the most comprehensive and thorough revisions of *Organizational Behavior* we've undertaken, and while we've preserved the core material, we're confident that this edition reflects the most important research and topical issues facing organizations, managers, and employees.

Key Changes to the Fifteenth Edition

- The **most substantial updating ever.** The following sections of each chapter are new to the fifteenth edition:
  - *Opening Vignette*
  - *Myth or Science?*
  - *Ethical Choice*
  - *Point/Counterpoint*
  - *Case Incident*

- In addition, the following material is substantially revised and updated:
  - *Opening Vignette*
  - *Case Incident* (those not entirely new are revised and updated)
  - *OB Poll* (more than half are new to this edition)
  - *Ethical Dilemma* (more than half are new to this edition)
  - *Photos/captions* (more than half are new to this edition)

- New feature: **glOBalization!,** which features organizational behavior in an international context.

- Improved integration of **global implications:** With the explosion of international research, global OB research is now woven into each chapter, rather than in a stand-alone section at the end of the chapter.

- Revision to **Summary and Implications for Managers** section, with more focus on practical ways to apply the material on the job.

- NEW videos—up-to-date videos showing management topics in action, access to the complete management video library, as well as instructional materials for integrating clips from popular movies into your class, are at **www.pearsonglobaleditions.com/mymanagementlab**.

Chapter-by-Chapter Changes

Chapter 1: What Is Organizational Behavior?

- New feature: **glOBalization!**
- New *Myth or Science?* ("Most Acts of Workplace Bullying Are Men Attacking Women")

- New *OB Model,* with better integration with pedagogy (structure) of book
- New *Point–Counterpoint* (Lost in Translation?)
- New *An Ethical Choice* (Can You Learn from Failure?)
- New *Case Incident* (Lessons for 'Undercover' Bosses)
- New *Case Incident* (Era of the Disposable Worker?)

Chapter 2: Diversity in Organizations

- Entirely new *Opening Vignette* (Diversity in Singapore)
- New feature: **glOBalization!**
- New *Myth or Science?* ("Dual-Career Couples Divorce Less")
- Enhanced coverage of stereotyping and discrimination research
- Revised content regarding age discrimination and implications of an aging workforce
- Updates to discussion of disability in the workplace
- Expanded coverage of sexual orientation discrimination
- New material and integration of diversity with international/cultural diversity
- New *Point–Counterpoint* (Men Have More Mathematical Ability Than Women)
- New *An Ethical Choice* (Religious Tattoos)
- Updated *Case Incident* (The Flynn Effect)
- New *Case Incident* (Diversity at Work: Nestlé Malaysia)

Chapter 3: Attitudes and Job Satisfaction

- Entirely new *Opening Vignette* (Tannourine Hospital: The Ultimate Challenge!)
- New feature: **glOBalization!**
- New *Myth or Science?* ("Favorable Job Attitudes Make Organizations More Profitable")
- Review of recent studies on within-person variation in job attitudes
- New developments in organizational commitment
- Updated material on organizational citizenship behaviors
- New perspectives on attitudes and organizational performance
- New ethical dilemma
- New *Point–Counterpoint* (Employer–Employee Loyalty Is an Outdated Concept)
- New *An Ethical Choice* (Do Employers Owe Workers More Satisfying Jobs?)
- New *Case Incident* (Crafting a Better Job)
- Updated *Case Incident* (Long Hours, Hundreds of E-Mails, and No Sleep: Does This Sound Like a Satisfying Job?)

Chapter 4: Emotions and Moods

- New feature: **glOBalization!**
- New *Myth or Science?* ("We Are Better Judges of When Others Are Happy Than When They Are Sad")
- Revised introduction to the topic
- Review of research on moods and employee attachment
- New section on "moral emotions"
- Discussion of emotion regulation strategies and their consequences
- New research on gender and emotions
- Updated content on emotional displays at work
- New section on *Emotional Intelligence,* with substantially more coverage and a new exhibit
- New *Point–Counterpoint* (Sometimes Blowing Your Top Is a Good Thing)
- New *An Ethical Choice* (Schadenfreude)

- New *Case Incident* (Is It Okay to Cry at Work?)
- Updated *Case Incident* (Can You Read Emotions from Faces?)

Chapter 5: Personality and Values

- Entirely new *Opening Vignette* (Changing of the Guard in Japan: Is it the Economy, or the Values?)
- New feature: **glOBalization!**
- New *Myth or Science?* ("Personality Predicts the Performance of Entrepreneurs")
- Introduces concepts related to dispositional self- and other-orientation
- New material regarding vocational choices
- New discussion of values and reactions to violations of employee values
- Major revision regarding Hofstede's model of culture and its consequences
- Updated information on personality and expatriate success
- New *Point–Counterpoint* (Millennials Are More Narcissistic)
- New *An Ethical Choice* (Should You Try to Change Someone's Personality?)

Chapter 6: Perception and Individual Decision Making

- Entirely new *Opening Vignette* (Do Machines Make Better Decisions?)
- New feature: **glOBalization!**
- New *Myth or Science?* ("Creative Decision Making Is a Right-Brain Activity")
- Review of recent work on self-serving biases
- New information on stereotyping processes
- Discussion of latest trends in decision errors research
- Updated discussion of culture and perceptions
- New section on *Financial Decision Making* and how it informs to understand recent and current crises
- New Experiential Exercise
- New *Point–Counterpoint* (Checklists Lead to Better Decisions)
- New *An Ethical Choice* (Whose Ethical Standards to Follow?)
- New *Case Incident* (Career Promotion at Emox: Rationalizing under Uncertainty')

Chapter 7: Motivation Concepts

- Entirely new *Opening Vignette* (The Motivations of the 99ers)
- New feature: **glOBalization!**
- New *Myth or Science?* ("The Support of Others Improves Our Chances of Accomplishing Our Goals")
- New material on psychological need theories
- Increased discussion of employee engagement
- Updates to the discussion on goal-setting theory
- New perspectives on equity and organizational justice
- New *Point–Counterpoint* (Fear Is a Powerful Motivator)
- New *An Ethical Choice* (Motivated to Behave Unethically)
- Updated *Case Incident* (Bullying Bosses)

Chapter 8: Motivation: From Concepts to Applications

- Entirely new *Opening Vignette* (Motivation Minus the Moolah)
- New feature: **glOBalization!**
- New *Myth or Science?* ("CEO Pay Can't Be Measured")
- Updated discussion of job characteristics
- New coverage of flextime, telecommuting, and related work practices
- Revised discussion of employee empowerment and its effects

- Discussion of innovations in gainsharing practices
- New *Point–Counterpoint* ("If Money Doesn't Make You Happy, You Aren't Spending It Right")
- New *Case Incident* (Bonuses Can Backfire)
- Updated *Case Incident* (Multitasking: A Good Use of Your Time?)

Chapter 9: Foundations of Group Behavior

- Entirely new *Opening Vignette* (To the Clickers Go the Spoils)
- New feature: **glOBalization!**
- New *Myth or Science?* ("Asians Have Less Ingroup Bias Than Americans")
- New material on dysfunctional behavior in teams
- Discussion of minority influence on group decision making
- Introduces material on team mental models
- Updated information on group decision errors and groupthink
- New information on international variations in group behavior
- New *Point–Counterpoint* (Affinity Groups Fuel Business Success)
- New *An Ethical Choice* (Should You Use Group Peer Pressure?)
- New *Case Incident* (Third Circle Asset Management)
- Updated *Case Incident* (Herd Behavior and the Housing Bubble [and Collapse])

Chapter 10: Understanding Work Teams

- Entirely new *Opening Vignette* (Killing bin Laden)
- New feature: **glOBalization!**
- New *Myth or Science?* ("Teams Work Best Under Angry Leaders")
- Updated discussion of strategies to improve team performance
- Review of research on team decision-making strategies
- New perspectives on creativity in teams
- New material on team proactivity
- Presents new literature on work teams in international contexts
- New *Point–Counterpoint* (We Can Learn Much about Work Teams from Studying Sports Teams)
- New *An Ethical Choice* (Using Global Virtual Teams as an Environmental Choice)
- New *Case Incident* (Why Don't Teams Work Like They're Supposed To?)
- Updated *Case Incident* (Multicultural Multinational Teams at IBM)

Chapter 11: Communication

- Entirely new *Opening Vignette* (Goldman Rules)
- New feature: **glOBalization!**
- New *Myth or Science?* ("We Know What Makes Good Liars Good")
- New section on *Social Networking*
- New section on *Persuasive Communication* strategies
- Discussion of how to frame messages for maximum impact
- Discussion of the effects of authority, expertise, and liking on communication effectiveness
- Updated discussion of body language in communication
- Introduces new ideas about the effects of electronic communications
- New *Point–Counterpoint* (Social Networking Is Good Business)
- New *An Ethical Choice* (The Ethics of Gossip at Work)
- New *Case Incident* (Using Social Media to Your Advantage)

Chapter 12: Leadership

- New feature: **glOBalization!**
- New *Myth or Science?* ("Power Helps Leaders Perform Better")
- Expanded discussion of leader effects on employee attitudes
- New perspectives on culture and leadership
- New material regarding emotional intelligence and leadership
- Increased consideration of contemporary theories of leadership
- Consideration of "servant leadership"
- Discussion of how leaders can increase employee creativity
- New *Point–Counterpoint* (Heroes Are Made, Not Born)
- New *An Ethical Choice* (Do Leaders Have a Responsibility to Protect Followers?)
- New *Case Incident* (Healthy Employees are Happy Employees)

Chapter 13: Power and Politics

- Entirely new *Opening Vignette* (Appearances Can Be Deceiving)
- New feature: **glOBalization!**
- New *Myth or Science?* ("Corporate Political Activity Pays")
- Coverage of latest research on influence tactics
- Revised discussion of sexual harassment
- Updated discussion of political behavior in organizations
- Revision to international issues in power and politics
- New *Point–Counterpoint* (Power Corrupts People)
- New *An Ethical Choice* (Should All Sexual Behavior Be Prohibited at Work?)
- New *Case Incident* (Delegate Power, or Keep it Close?)
- Updated *Case Incident* (The Persuasion Imperative)

Chapter 14: Conflict and Negotiation

- Entirely new *Opening Vignette* (No Conflict at the Post Office. . . Is That Good?)
- New feature: **glOBalization!**
- New *Myth or Science?* ("Communicating Well Is More Important in Cross-Cultural Negotiations")
- Updated material on gender and negotiation styles
- New material on individual differences in negotiation styles
- Discussion of emotions in negotiation
- New information on suspicion and deception in negotiation
- Updates to discussion on conflict and conflict management processes
- New *Point–Counterpoint* (Player–Owner Disputes Are Unnecessary)
- New *An Ethical Choice* (Using Empathy to Negotiate More Ethically)
- New *Case Incident* (Choosing Your Battles)
- Updated *Case Incident* (Mediation: Master Solution to Employment Disputes?)

Chapter 15: Foundations of Organization Structure

- Entirely new *Opening Vignette* (Dismantling a Bureaucracy)
- New feature: **glOBalization!**
- New *Myth or Science?* ("Employees Resent Outsourcing")
- Latest research on boundaryless organizations and their functioning
- Discussion of technology's influence on organizational structure
- Updated review of the relationship between organizational structure and attitudes
- New *An Ethical Choice* (Downsizing with a Conscience)

- New *Case Incident* (Creative Deviance: Bucking the Hierarchy?)
- Updated *Case Incident* (Siemens' Simple Structure—Not)

Chapter 16: Organizational Culture

- Entirely new *Opening Vignette* (Ursula M. Burns and the Culture of Xerox)
- New feature: **glOBalization!**
- New *Myth or Science?* ("Employees Treat Customers the Same Way the Organization Treats Them")
- New review of basic issues in organizational culture and subcultures
- Enhanced discussion of ethical culture
- Review of culture and organizational performance
- Revised discussion of organizational socialization practices and outcomes
- New *Point–Counterpoint* (Organizations Should Strive to Create a Positive Organizational Culture)
- New *An Ethical Choice* (Designing a Culture of Ethical Voice)
- New *Case Incident* (Are Employees Happier Working in their Own National Cultures?)
- Updated *Case Incident* (Mergers Don't Always Lead to Culture Clashes)

Chapter 17: Human Resource Policies and Practices

- Entirely new *Opening Vignette* (Human Resources at KiMantra)
- New feature: **glOBalization!**
- New *Myth or Science?* ("Work Is Making Us Fat")
- Discussion of the implications of the Great Recession
- New material on legal issues
- Updated discussion of the effects of high performance work practice on employee attitudes and behavior
- Expanded discussion of the effects of staffing decisions on employee turnover
- New section on *Job Performance and Workplace Civility*
- New material related to performance appraisals and rater goals
- New *Point–Counterpoint* (Social Media Is a Great Source of New Hires)
- New *An Ethical Choice* (Recruiting the Unemployed)
- New *Case Incident* (Who Are You?)

Chapter 18: Organizational Change and Stress Management

- Entirely new *Opening Vignette* (Sweet Changes at Cadbury?)
- New feature: **glOBalization!**
- New *Myth or Science?* ("Men Experience More Job Stress Than Women")
- Updated review of research on individual readiness for organizational change
- Discussion of maladaptive behavioral response to stress at work
- Updated discussion of coping strategies
- Implications of the stress-health relationship
- New *Point–Counterpoint* (Responsible Managers Relieve Stress on Their Employees)
- New *An Ethical Choice* (Responsibly Managing Your Own Stress)
- New *Case Incident* (Starbucks Returns to Its Roots)

Teaching and Learning Support

MyManagementLab (www.pearsonglobaleditions.com/mymanagementlab) is an easy-to-use online tool that personalizes course content and provides robust assessment and reporting to measure student and class performance. All the resources you need for course success are in one place—flexible and easily adapted for your course experience.

Instructor's Resource Center

At www.pearsonglobaleditions.com/robbins, instructors can access a variety of print, digital, and presentation resources available with this text in download-able format. Registration is simple and gives you immediate access to new titles and new editions. As a registered faculty member, you can download resource files and receive immediate access and instructions for installing course management content on your campus server.

If you need assistance, our dedicated technical support team is ready to help with the media supplements that accompany this text. Visit 247pearsoned .custhelp.com for answers to frequently asked questions and toll-free user support phone numbers.

The following supplements are available to adopting instructors (for detailed descriptions, please visit www.pearsonglobaleditions.com/robbins):

- Instructor's Manual—updated and revised to provide ideas and resources in the classroom.
- Test Item File—Revised and updated to include questions that require students to apply the knowledge that they've read about in the text through Learning Objectives and Learning Outcomes. Questions are also tagged to reflect the AACSB Learning Standards.
- TestGen Test Generating Software—Test management software that contains all material from the Test Item File. This software is completely user-friendly and allows instructors to view, edit, and add test questions with just a few mouse clicks.
- PowerPoint Presentation—A ready-to-use PowerPoint slideshow designed for classroom presentation. Use it as is, or edit content to fit your individual classroom needs.
- Image Library—includes all the charts, tables, and graphs that are found in the text.

Videos on DVD

Adopters can access the 48 videos on the 2013 Organizational Behavior Video Library DVD. These videos have been produced to depict real-world OB issues and give students a taste of the multi-faceted nature of OB in real companies.

Self-Assessment Library (S.A.L.)

A hallmark of the Robbins series, S.A.L. is a unique learning tool that allows you to assess your knowledge, beliefs, feelings, and actions in regard to a wide range of personal skills, abilities, and interests. Self-assessments have been integrated into each chapter, including a self-assessment at the beginning of each chapter. S.A.L. helps students better understand their interpersonal and behavioral skills as they relate to the theoretical concepts presented in each chapter.

Highlights

- **69 research-based self-assessments**—All 69 instruments of our collection are from sources such as *Journal of Social Behavior and Personality, Harvard Business Review, Organizational Behavior: Experiences and Cases, Journal of Experimental Education, Journal of Applied Measurement,* and more.
- **Work–life and career focused**—All self-assessments are focused to help individuals better manage their work lives or careers. Organized in four parts, these instruments offer you one source from which to learn more about yourself.
- **Online**—The Self-Assessment Library is available in online.
- **Save feature**—Students can take the self-assessments an unlimited number of times, and they can save and print their scores for class discussion.
- **Scoring key**—The key to the self-assessments has been edited by Steve Robbins to allow students to quickly make sense of the results of their score.
- **Instructor's manual**—An *Instructor's Manual* guides instructors in interpreting self-assessments and helps facilitate better classroom discussion.

Acknowledgments

Getting this book into your hands was a team effort. It took faculty reviewers and a talented group of designers and production specialists, editorial personnel, and marketing and sales staff.

More than one hundred instructors reviewed parts or all of *Organizational Behavior*, Fifteenth Edition. Their comments, compliments, and suggestions have significantly improved the final product. The authors wish to thank John D. Kammeyer-Mueller of the University of Florida for help with several key aspects of this revision. The authors would also like to extend their sincerest thanks to the following instructors:

Lee Boam, University of Utah

Andres Johnson, Santa Clara University

Edward Lisoski, Northeastern University

Douglas Mahony, Lehigh University

Douglas McCabe, Georgetown University

Bradley Norris, Baylor University

Jonelle Roth, Michigan State University

Philip Roth, Clemson University

Dale Rude, University of Houston

Holly Schroth, University of California at Berkeley

Jody Tolan, University of Southern California

Debra Schneck, Indiana University

Marilyn Wesner, George Washington University

Over the last editions this text has grown stronger with the contribution and feedback of the following instructors:

David Abramis, California State University

Chris Adalikwu, Concordia College

Basil Adams, Notre Dame de Namur University

Janet Adams, Kennesaw State University

Cheryl Adkins, Longwood College

Vicky Aitken, St. Louis Community College

David Albritton, Northern Arizona University

Bradley Alge, Purdue University

Lois Antonen, CSUS

Lucy Arendt, University of Wisconsin, Green Bay

Anke Arnaud, University of Central Florida

Mihran Aroian, University of Texas, Austin

Gary Ballinger, Purdue University

Deborah Balser, University of Missouri at St. Louis

Christopher Barlow, DePaul University

Joy Benson, University of Wisconsin at Green Bay

Lehman Benson III, University of Arizona

Jacqui Bergman, Appalachian State University

Anne Berthelot, University of Texas at El Paso

David Bess, Shidler College of Business at the University of Hawaii

Bruce Bikle, California State University, Sacramento

Richard Blackburn, University of North Carolina–Chapel Hill

Weldon Blake, Bethune-Cookman College

Carl Blencke, University of Central Florida

Michael Bochenek, Elmhurst College

Alicia Boisnier, State University of New York

William H. Bommer, Cleveland State University

Bryan Bonner, University of Utah

Jessica Bradley, Clemson University

Dr. Jerry Bream, Empire State College/Niagara Frontier Center

Jim Breaugh, University of Missouri

Peggy Brewer, Eastern Kentucky University

Deborah Brown, North Carolina State University

Reginald Bruce, University of Louisville

Jeff Bruns, Bacone College

Pamela Buckle, Adelphi University

Patricia Buhler, Goldey-Beacom College

Allen Bures, Radford University

Edith Busija, University of Richmond

Holly Buttner, University of North Carolina at Greensboro

Michael Cafferky, Southern Adventist University

Scott Campbell, Francis Marion University

Elena Capella, University of San Francisco

Don Capener, Monmouth University

Dan Caprar, University of Iowa

David Carmichael, Oklahoma City University

Carol Carnevale, SUNY Empire State College

Donald W. Caudill, Bluefield College

Suzanne Chan, Tulane University

Anthony Chelte, Midwestern State University

Bongsoon Cho, State University of New York—Buffalo

Savannah Clay, Central Piedmont Community College

David Connelly, Western Illinois State University

Jeffrey Conte, San Diego State University

Jane Crabtree, Benedictine University

Suzanne Crampton, Grand Valley State University

Douglas Crawford, Wilson College

Michael Cruz, San Jose State University

Robert Cyr, Northwestern University

Evelyn Dadzie, Clark Atlanta University

Joseph Daly, Appalachian State University

Denise Daniels, Seattle Pacific University

Marie Dasborough, Oklahoma State University

Nancy Da Silva, San Jose State University

Christine Day, Eastern Michigan University

Emmeline de Pillis, University of Hawaii, Hilo

Kathy Lund Dean, Idaho State University

Roger Dean, Washington & Lee University

Robert DelCampo, University of New Mexico

Kristen Detienne, Brigham Young University

Doug Dierking, University of Texas at Austin

Cynthia Doil, Southern Illinois University

Jennifer Dose, Messiah College

Ceasar Douglas, Florida State University

David Duby, Liberty University

Ken Dunegan, Cleveland State University

Michael Dutch, Greensboro College

Kathleen Edwards, University of Texas at Austin

Berrin Erdogan, Portland State University

Ellen Fagenson Eland, George Mason University

Lenny Favara, Central Christian College

Claudia Ferrante, U.S. Air Force Academy

Andy Fitorre, Nyack College

Kathleen Fleming, Averett University

Erin Fluegge, University of Florida

Edward Fox, Wilkes University

Alison Fragale, University of North Carolina at Chapel Hill

Lucy Franks, Bellevue University

Dean Frear, Wilkes University

Jann Freed, Central College

Crissie Frye, Eastern Michigan University

Diane Galbraith, Slippery Rock University

Carolyn Gardner, Radford University

Janice Gates, Western Illinois University

Ellen Kaye Gehrke, Alliant International University

James Gelatt, University of Maryland University College

Joe Gerard, University of Wisconsin at Milwaukee

Matthew Giblin, Southern Illinois University

Donald Gibson, Fairfield University

Cindi Gilliland, The University of Arizona

Mary Giovannini, Truman State University

David Glew, University of North Carolina at Wilmington

Leonard Glick, Northeastern University

Reginald Goodfellow, California State University

Jeffrey Goldstein, Adelphi University

Jodi Goodman, University of Connecticut

Claude Graeff, Illinois State University

Richard Grover, University of Southern Maine

W. Lee Grubb III, East Carolina University

John Guarino, Averett University

Rebecca Guidice, University of Nevada at Las Vegas

Andra Gumbus, Sacred Heart University

Linda Hackleman, Concordia University Austin

Deniz Hackner, Tidewater Community College

Michael Hadani, Long Island University

Jonathon Halbesleben, University of Missouri-Columbia

Dan Hallock, University of North Alabama

Tracey Rockett Hanft, University of Texas at Dallas

Edward Hampton, University of Central Florida

Vernard Harrington, Radford University

Nell Hartley, Robert Morris University

Barbara Hassell, Indiana University, Kelley School of Business

Erin Hayes, George Washington University

Tom Head, Roosevelt University

Douglas Heeter, Ferris State University

David Henderson, University of Illinois at Chicago

Scott Henley, Oklahoma City University

Ted Herbert, Rollins College

Susan Herman, University of Alaska Fairbanks

James Hess, Ivy Tech Community College

Ronald Hester, Marymount University

Patricia Hewlin, Georgetown University

Chad Higgins, University of Washington

Kim Hinrichs, Minnesota State University Mankato

Kathie Holland, University of Central Florida

Elaine Hollensbe, University of Cincinnati

Kristin Holmberg-Wright, University of Wisconsin at Parkside

Brooks Holtom, Georgetown University

Lisa Houts, California State University Fullerton

Abigail Hubbard, University of Houston

Paul Hudec, Milwaukee School of Engineering

Stephen Humphrey, Florida State University

Charlice Hurst, University of Florida

Warren Imada, Leeward Community College

Gazi Islam, Tulane University

Alan Jackson, Peru State College

Christine Jackson, Purdue University

Marsha Jackson, Bowie State University

Kathryn Jacobson, Arizona State University

Paul Jacques, Western Carolina University

David Jalajas, Long Island University

Elizabeth Jamison, Radford University

Stephen Jenner, California State University, Dominguez Hills

John Jermier, University of South Florida

Jack Johnson, Consumnes River College

Michael Johnson, University of Washington

David Jones, South University

Ray Jones, University of Pittsburgh

Anthony Jost, University of Delaware

Louis Jourdan, Clayton College

Rusty Juban, Southeastern Illinois University

Carole L. Jurkiewicz, Louisiana State University

John Kammeyer-Mueller, University of Florida

Edward Kass, Saint Joseph's University

Marsha Katz, Governors State College

James Katzenstein, California State University

John Keiser, SUNY College at Brockport

Mark Kendrick, Methodist University

Mary Kern, Baruch College

Robert Key, University of Phoenix

Sigrid Khorram, University of Texas at El Paso

Hal Kingsley, Erie Community College

Jeffrey Kobles, California State University San Marcos

Jack Kondrasuk, University of Portland

Leslie A. Korb, University of Nebraska at Kearney

Glen Kreiner, University of Cincinnati

James Kroeger, Cleveland State University

Frederick Lane, Baruch College

Rebecca Lau, Virginia Polytechnic Institute and State University

David Leuser, Plymouth State College

Julia Levashina, Indiana State University Kokomo

Benyamin Lichtenstein, University of Massachusetts at Boston

Robert Liden, University of Illinois at Chicago

Don Lifton, Ithaca College

Ginamarie Ligon, Villanova University

Beth Livingston, University of Florida

Barbara Low, Dominican University

Doyle Lucas, Anderson University

Alexandra Luong, University of Minnesota

Rick Maclin, Missouri Baptist University

Peter Madsen, Brigham Young University

Lou Marino, University of Alabama

Catherine Marsh, Northpark University

J. David Martin, Midwestern State University

Timothy A. Matherly, Florida State University

John Mattoon, State University of New York

Paul Maxwell, Saint Thomas University

Brenda McAleer, University of Maine at Augusta

Christina McCale, Regis College

Don McCormick, California State University Northridge

James McElroy, Iowa State University

Bonnie McNeely, Murray State University

Melony Mead, University of Phoenix

Steven Meisel, La Salle University

Nancy Meyer-Emerick, Cleveland State University

Catherine Michael, St. Edwards University

Sandy Miles, Murray State University

Janice Miller, University of Wisconsin at Milwaukee

Leann Mischel, Susquehanna University

Atul Mitra, University of Northern Iowa

Linda Morable, Richland College

Paula Morrow, Iowa State University

Mark Mortensen, Massachusetts Institute of Technology

Lori Muse, Western Michigan University

Padmakumar Nair, University of Texas at Dallas

Judy Nixon, University of Tennessee at Chattanooga

Jeffrey Nystrom, University of Colorado at Denver

Alison O'Brien, George Mason University

Heather Odle-Dusseau, Clemson University

Miguel Olivas-Lujan, Lujan Clarion University

Kelly Ottman, University of Wisconsin at Milwaukee

Cynthia Ozeki, California State University, Dominguez Hills

Peg Padgett, Butler University

Jennifer Palthe, Western Michigan University

Dennis Passovoy, University of Texas at Austin

Karen Paul, Florida International University

Laura Finnerty Paul, Skidmore College

Anette Pendergrass, Arkansas State University at Mountain Home

Bryan Pesta, Cleveland State University

Jeff Peterson, University of Washington

Nanette Philibert, Missouri Southern State University

Larry Phillips, Indiana University South Bend

William Pinchuk, Rutgers University at Camden

Eric Popkoff, Brooklyn College

Paul Preston, University of Montevallo

Scott Quatro, Grand Canyon University

Aarti Ramaswami, Indiana University Bloomington

Jere Ramsey, Cal Poly at San Luis Obispo

Amy Randel, San Diego State University

Anne Reilly, Loyola University Chicago

Clint Relyea, Arkansas State University

Herbert Ricardo, Indian River Community College

David Ritchey, University of Texas at Dallas

Chris Roberts, University of Massachusetts Amherst

Sherry Robinson, Pennsylvania State University Hazleton

Christopher Ann Robinson-Easley, Governors State University

Joe Rode, Miami University

Bob Roller, LeTourneau University

Andrea Roofe, Florida International University

Craig Russell, University of Oklahoma at Norman

Manjula Salimath, University of North Texas

Mary Saunders, Georgia Gwinnett College

Andy Schaffer, North Georgia College and State University

Elizabeth Scott, Elizabeth City University

Mark Seabright, Western Oregon University

Joseph Seltzer, LaSalle University

John Shaw, Mississippi State University

John Sherlock, Western Carolina University

Daniel Sherman, University of Alabama, Huntsville

Heather Shields, Texas Tech University

Ted Shore, California State University at Long Beach

Stuart Sidle, University of New Haven

Bret Simmons, University of Nevada Reno

Randy Sleeth, Virginia Commonwealth University

William Smith, Emporia State University

Kenneth Solano, Northeastern University

Shane Spiller, Morehead State University

Lynda St. Clair, Bryant University

John B. Stark, California State University, Bakersfield

Merwyn Strate, Purdue University

Joo-Seng Tan, Cornell University

Karen Thompson, Sonoma State University

Linda Tibbetts, Antioch University McGregor

Ed Tomlinson, John Carroll University

Bob Trodella, Webster University

Tom Tudor, University of Arkansas at Little Rock

William D. Tudor, Ohio State University

Daniel Turban, University of Missouri

Albert Turner, Webster University

Jim Turner, Morehead State University

Leslie Tworoger, Nova Southeastern University

M. A. Viets, University of Vermont

Roger Volkema, American University

William Walker, University of Houston

Ian Walsh, Boston College

Charles F. Warren, Salem State College

Christa Washington, Saint Augustine's College

Jim Westerman, Appalachian State University

William J. White, Northwestern University

David Whitlock, Southwest Baptist University

Dan Wiljanen, Grand Valley State University

Dean Williamson, Brewton-Parker College

Hilda Williamson, Hampton University

Alice Wilson, Cedar Crest College

Barry Wisdom, Southeast Missouri State University

Craig Wishart, Fayetteville State University

Laura Wolfe, Louisiana State University

Melody Wollan, Eastern Illinois University

Evan Wood, Taylor University Fort Wayne

Chun-Sheng Yu, University of Houston-Victoria

Jun Zhao, Governors State University

Lori Ziegler, University of Texas at Dallas

Mary Ellen Zuckerman, State University of New York at Geneseo

Gail Zwart, Riverside Community College

We owe a debt of gratitude to all those at Pearson Education who have supported this text over the past 30 years and who have worked so hard on the development of this latest edition. On the development and editorial side, we want to thank Elisa Adams, Development Editor; Steve Deitmer, Director of Development; Ashley Santora, Director of Editorial Services; Brian Mickelson, Acquisitions Editor; and Sally Yagan, Editorial Director. On the design and production side, Judy Leale, Senior Managing Editor, did an outstanding job, as did Becca Groves, Production Project Manager, and Nancy Moudry, Photo Development Editor. Last but not least, we would like to thank Nikki Ayana Jones, Senior Marketing Manager; Patrice Lumumba Jones, Vice President Director of Marketing; and their sales staff, who have been selling this book over its many editions. Thank you for the attention you've given to this book.

Pearson gratefully acknowledges and thanks the following people for their work on the Global Edition:

Global Contributors

Caroline Akhras, Notre Dame University

Charbel Aoun, Lebanese American University

Chan Kheng Ping, Patrick, Nanyang Technological University

Hadia FakhrElDin, British University in Egypt

Elham Hasham, Notre Dame University

Daisy Kee Mui Hung, Universiti Sains Malaysia

Linzi Kemp, American University of Sharjah

Achim Leeser, FRABA AG

Chantal Olckers, University of Pretoria

Matthias Spitzmuller, National University of Singapore

Betina Szkudlarek, The University of Sydney Business School

Marcus O. Weber, Hochschule Niederrhein

Anna Po Yung Tsui, Chinese University of Hong Kong

Dahlia Zawawi, Universiti Putra Malaysia

Global Reviewers

Rania A. Azmi, University of Portsmouth

Michèle Boonzaier, Stellenbosch University

Gonca Günay, Izmir University of Economics

Ralph Kattenbach, University of Hamburg

Anthony C. Lok, The Hong Kong Polytechnic University

Organizational Behavior

Global Edition

LEARNING OBJECTIVES

After studying this chapter, you should be able to:

1 Demonstrate the importance of interpersonal skills in the workplace.

2 Describe the manager's functions, roles, and skills.

3 Define *organizational behavior (OB)*.

4 Show the value to OB of systematic study.

5 Identify the major behavioral science disciplines that contribute to OB.

6 Demonstrate why few absolutes apply to OB.

7 Identify the challenges and opportunities managers have in applying OB concepts.

8 Compare the three levels of analysis in this book's OB model.

MyManagementLab

Access a host of interactive learning aids to help strengthen your understanding of the chapter concepts at **www.pearsonglobaleditions .com/mymanagementlab**

A DAY IN THE LIFE OF HUSSAM

Hussam is the general and marketing manager of a small subsidiary of the German company Electro in Dubai that was founded two years ago. Hussam is the first Arab manager in the company, an achievement that he attributes to the fact that he graduated from Germany's best engineering university and is proficient in English, Arabic, and German.

Today, Hussam arrives at the office early to review his schedule for the day.

9.00: Meeting with all employees to communicate the revised business goals for 2010. Hussam has scheduled 30 minutes to revise his presentation: this subsidiary has 45 employees from 15 different cultures, and misunderstandings occur frequently. The company is experiencing financial difficulties, and Hussam needs to be an inspirational leader.

10.30: Meeting with the IT and sales managers. These two managers have been in constant conflict for the past two months. Hussam has already met with them individually. Today, he will try to get them to resolve their differences. The conflict is related to the implementation of a new IT system for the sales department.

11.30: Call the two best advertising agencies in the country. Hussam has to decide which agency to work with for next season's campaign. One agency has a better reputation, but Hussam is developing a friendship with the manager of the other one. Hussam has to make sure he makes the right choice for the company.

2.30: Meeting with Petra, his personal assistant. Hussam has noticed that her performance has declined recently and that on some occasions she did not treat irritated clients properly. Hussam wants to understand what is happening with her, to clarify her job objectives, and to remotivate her. He wants every employee to respect the key organizational values: "Clients are kings" and "Excellence in everything we do."

4.00: Call Holger, the international human resources manager in Berlin, to discuss the "German expat problem." Of the German expatriates sent to Dubai, 20 percent returned to Germany before the end of their assignment. Moreover, the expatriates that stayed in Dubai never performed up to their supervisors' expectations. Hussam needed some advice from Holger. Hussam also has to call three important clients today.

What Is Organizational Behavior?

The stellar universe is not so difficult of comprehension as the real actions of other people. —Marcel Proust

Photo: Electronic diary. Source: © Dmitrij Yakovlev/Fotolia.com

Those who work in and with organizations are often not the purely rational actors we assume, but neither is most behavior wholly unpredictable. In fact, there is a lot to learn about how people act in organizations, why they act as they do, and what we can do to predict and manage their behavior. This is where organizational behavior comes into play. And, as we'll learn, it is much more than common sense and intuition.

You've probably made many observations about people's behavior in your life. In a way, you are already proficient at seeing some of the major themes in organizational behavior. At the same time, you probably have not had the tools to make these observations systematically. This is where organizational behavior comes into play. And, as we'll learn, it is much more than common sense, intuition, and soothsaying.

To see how far common sense gets you, try the following from the Self-Assessment Library.

SELF-ASSESSMENT LIBRARY

How Much Do I Know About Organizational Behavior?

In the Self-Assessment Library (available on CD and online), take assessment IV.G.1 (How Much Do I Know About OB?) and answer the following questions:

1. How did you score? Are you surprised by your score?
2. How much of effective management do you think is common sense? Did your score on the test change your answer to this question?

The Importance of Interpersonal Skills

1 Demonstrate the importance of interpersonal skills in the workplace.

Until the late 1980s, business school curricula emphasized the technical aspects of management, focusing on economics, accounting, finance, and quantitative techniques. Course work in human behavior and people skills received relatively less attention. Over the past three decades, however, business faculty have come to realize the role that understanding human behavior plays in determining a manager's effectiveness, and required courses on people skills have been added to many curricula. As the director of leadership at MIT's Sloan School of Management put it, "M.B.A. students may get by on their technical and quantitative skills the first couple of years out of school. But soon, leadership and communication skills come to the fore in distinguishing the managers whose careers really take off."[1]

Developing managers' interpersonal skills also helps organizations attract and keep high-performing employees. Regardless of labor market conditions, outstanding employees are always in short supply.[2] Companies known as good places to work—such as Starbucks, Adobe Systems, Cisco, Whole Foods, Google, American Express, Amgen, Pfizer, and Marriott—have a big advantage. A recent survey of hundreds of workplaces, and more than 200,000 respondents, showed the social relationships among co-workers and supervisors were strongly related to overall job satisfaction. Positive social relationships also were associated with lower stress at work and lower intentions to quit.[3] So having managers with good interpersonal skills is likely to make the workplace more pleasant, which in turn makes it easier to hire and keep qualified people. Creating a pleasant workplace also appears to make good economic sense. Companies with reputations

Succeeding in management today requires good interpersonal skills. Communication and leadership skills distinguish managers such as John Chambers, who rise to the top of their profession. Chambers is CEO of Cisco Systems, the world's largest maker of networking equipment. He is respected as a visionary leader and innovator who has the ability to drive an entrepreneurial culture. As an effective communicator, Chambers is described as warm-hearted and straight talking. In this photo Chambers speaks during a launch ceremony of a green technology partnership Cisco formed with a university in China.

Source: China Photos/Getty Images, Inc.

as good places to work (such as *Forbes'* "100 Best Companies to Work For in America") have been found to generate superior financial performance.[4]

We have come to understand that in today's competitive and demanding workplace, managers can't succeed on their technical skills alone. They also have to have good people skills. This book has been written to help both managers and potential managers develop those people skills.

What Managers Do

2 Describe the manager's functions, roles, and skills.

MyManagementLab
For an interactive application of this topic, check out this chapter's simulation activity at **www.pearsonglobaleditions.com/mymanagementlab**.

Let's begin by briefly defining the terms *manager* and *organization*—the place where managers work. Then let's look at the manager's job; specifically, what do managers do?

Managers get things done through other people. They make decisions, allocate resources, and direct the activities of others to attain goals. Managers do their work in an **organization**, which is a consciously coordinated social unit, composed of two or more people, that functions on a relatively continuous basis to achieve a common goal or set of goals. By this definition, manufacturing and service firms are organizations, and so are schools, hospitals, churches, military units, retail stores, police departments, and local, state, and federal government agencies. The people who oversee the activities of

manager *An individual who achieves goals through other people.*

organization *A consciously coordinated social unit, composed of two or more people, that functions on a relatively continuous basis to achieve a common goal or set of goals.*

others and who are responsible for attaining goals in these organizations are managers (sometimes called *administrators,* especially in not-for-profit organizations).

Management Functions

In the early part of the twentieth century, French industrialist Henri Fayol wrote that all managers perform five management functions: planning, organizing, commanding, coordinating, and controlling.[5] Today, we have condensed these to four: planning, organizing, leading, and controlling.

Because organizations exist to achieve goals, someone has to define those goals and the means for achieving them; management is that someone. The **planning** function encompasses defining an organization's goals, establishing an overall strategy for achieving those goals, and developing a comprehensive set of plans to integrate and coordinate activities. Evidence indicates this function increases the most as managers move from lower-level to mid-level management.[6]

Managers are also responsible for designing an organization's structure. We call this function **organizing**. It includes determining what tasks are to be done, who is to do them, how the tasks are to be grouped, who reports to whom, and where decisions are to be made.

Every organization contains people, and it is management's job to direct and coordinate those people. This is the **leading** function. When managers motivate employees, direct their activities, select the most effective communication channels, or resolve conflicts among members, they're engaging in leading.

To ensure things are going as they should, management must monitor the organization's performance and compare it with previously set goals. If there are any significant deviations, it is management's job to get the organization back on track. This monitoring, comparing, and potential correcting is the **controlling** function.

So, using the functional approach, the answer to the question "What do managers do?" is that they plan, organize, lead, and control.

Management Roles

In the late 1960s, Henry Mintzberg, then a graduate student at MIT, undertook a careful study of five executives to determine what they did on their jobs. On the basis of his observations, Mintzberg concluded that managers perform ten different, highly interrelated roles—or sets of behaviors.[7] As shown in Exhibit 1-1, these ten roles are primarily (1) interpersonal, (2) informational, or (3) decisional.

Interpersonal Roles   All managers are required to perform duties that are ceremonial and symbolic in nature. For instance, when the president of a college hands out diplomas at commencement or a factory supervisor gives a group of high school students a tour of the plant, he or she is acting in a *figurehead* role. All managers also have a *leadership* role. This role includes hiring, training, motivating, and disciplining employees. The third role within the interpersonal grouping is the *liaison* role, or contacting others who provide the manager with information. The sales manager who obtains information from the quality-control manager in his or her own company has an internal liaison relationship. When that sales manager has contacts with other sales executives through a marketing trade association, he or she has an outside liaison relationship.

Exhibit 1-1	Minztberg's Managerial Roles

Role	Description
Interpersonal	
Figurehead	Symbolic head; required to perform a number of routine duties of a legal or social nature
Leader	Responsible for the motivation and direction of employees
Liaison	Maintains a network of outside contacts who provide favors and information
Informational	
Monitor	Receives a wide variety of information; serves as nerve center of internal and external information of the organization
Disseminator	Transmits information received from outsiders or from other employees to members of the organization
Spokesperson	Transmits information to outsiders on organization's plans, policies, actions, and results; serves as expert on organization's industry
Decisional	
Entrepreneur	Searches organization and its environment for opportunities and initiates projects to bring about change
Disturbance handler	Responsible for corrective action when organization faces important, unexpected disturbances
Resource allocator	Makes or approves significant organizational decisions
Negotiator	Responsible for representing the organization at major negotiations

Source: Adapted from *The Nature of Managerial Work* by H. Mintzberg. Copyright © 1973 by H. Mintzberg. MINTZBERG, HENRY, THE NATURE OF MANAGERIAL WORK, 1st Edition, © 1980, pp. 92–93. Reprinted with permission of Pearson Education, Inc., Upper Saddle River, NJ.

Informational Roles   All managers, to some degree, collect information from outside organizations and institutions, typically by scanning the news media (including the Internet) and talking with other people to learn of changes in the public's tastes, what competitors may be planning, and the like. Mintzberg called this the *monitor* role. Managers also act as a conduit to transmit information to organizational members. This is the *disseminator* role. In addition, managers perform a *spokesperson* role when they represent the organization to outsiders.

Decisional Roles   Mintzberg identified four roles that require making choices. In the *entrepreneur* role, managers initiate and oversee new projects that will improve their organization's performance. As *disturbance handlers,* managers take corrective action in response to unforeseen problems. As *resource allocators,*

planning   *A process that includes defining goals, establishing strategy, and developing plans to coordinate activities.*

organizing   *Determining what tasks are to be done, who is to do them, how the tasks are to be grouped, who reports to whom, and where decisions are to be made.*

leading   *A function that includes motivating employees, directing others, selecting the most effective communication channels, and resolving conflicts.*

controlling   *Monitoring activities to ensure they are being accomplished as planned and correcting any significant deviations.*

managers are responsible for allocating human, physical, and monetary resources. Finally, managers perform a *negotiator* role, in which they discuss issues and bargain with other units to gain advantages for their own unit.

Management Skills

Still another way of considering what managers do is to look at the skills or competencies they need to achieve their goals. Researchers have identified a number of skills that differentiate effective from ineffective managers.[8]

Technical Skills   **Technical skills** encompass the ability to apply specialized knowledge or expertise. When you think of the skills of professionals such as civil engineers or oral surgeons, you typically focus on the technical skills they have learned through extensive formal education. Of course, professionals don't have a monopoly on technical skills, and not all technical skills have to be learned in schools or other formal training programs. All jobs require some specialized expertise, and many people develop their technical skills on the job.

Human Skills   The ability to understand, communicate with, motivate, and support other people, both individually and in groups, defines **human skills**. Many people are technically proficient but poor listeners, unable to understand the needs of others, or weak at managing conflicts. Because managers get things done through other people, they must have good human skills.

Conceptual Skills   Managers must have the mental ability to analyze and diagnose complex situations. These tasks require **conceptual skills**. Decision making, for instance, requires managers to identify problems, develop alternative solutions to correct those problems, evaluate those alternative solutions, and select the best one. After they have selected a course of action, managers must be able to organize a plan of action and then execute it. The ability to integrate new ideas with existing processes and innovate on the job are also crucial conceptual skills for today's managers.

Effective versus Successful Managerial Activities

Fred Luthans and his associates looked at what managers do from a somewhat different perspective.[9] They asked, "Do managers who move up the quickest in an organization do the same activities and with the same emphasis as managers who do the best job?" You might think the answer is yes, but that's not always the case.

Luthans and his associates studied more than 450 managers. All engaged in four managerial activities:

1. **Traditional management.**   Decision making, planning, and controlling.
2. **Communication.**   Exchanging routine information and processing paperwork.
3. **Human resource management.**   Motivating, disciplining, managing conflict, staffing, and training.
4. **Networking.**   Socializing, politicking, and interacting with outsiders.

The "average" manager spent 32 percent of his or her time in traditional management activities, 29 percent communicating, 20 percent in human resource management activities, and 19 percent networking. However, the time and effort different *individual* managers spent on those activities varied a great deal. As shown in Exhibit 1-2, among managers who were *successful* (defined in terms of speed of promotion within their organization), networking made

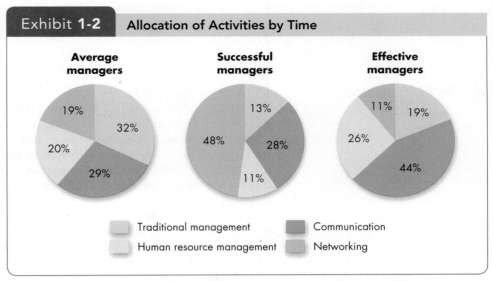

Exhibit **1-2**	Allocation of Activities by Time

Average managers

19%
32%
20%
29%

Successful managers

13%
28%
48%
11%

Effective managers

11%
19%
26%
44%

Traditional management   Communication
Human resource management   Networking

Source: Based on F. Luthans, R. M. Hodgetts, and S. A. Rosenkrantz, *Real Managers* (Cambridge, MA: Ballinger, 1988).

the largest relative contribution to success, and human resource management activities made the least relative contribution. Among *effective* managers (defined in terms of quantity and quality of their performance and the satisfaction and commitment of employees), communication made the largest relative contribution and networking the least. More recent studies in Australia, Israel, Italy, Japan, and the United States confirm the link between networking and social relationships and success within an organization.[10] And the connection between communication and effective managers is also clear. A study of 410 U.S. managers indicates those who seek information from colleagues and employees—even if it's negative—and who explain their decisions are the most effective.[11]

This research offers important insights. Successful managers give almost the opposite emphases to traditional management, communication, human resource management, and networking as do effective managers. This finding challenges the historical assumption that promotions are based on performance, and it illustrates the importance of networking and political skills in getting ahead in organizations.

A Review of the Manager's Job

One common thread runs through the functions, roles, skills, activities, and approaches to management: Each recognizes the paramount importance of managing people, whether it is called "the leading function," "interpersonal roles," "human skills," or "human resource management, communication, and networking activities." It's clear managers must develop their people skills to be effective and successful.

technical skills   *The ability to apply specialized knowledge or expertise.*

human skills   *The ability to work with, understand, and motivate other people, both individually and in groups.*

conceptual skills   *The mental ability to analyze and diagnose complex situations.*

Enter Organizational Behavior

3 Define *organizational behavior (OB)*.

We've made the case for the importance of people skills. But neither this book nor the discipline on which it is based is called "people skills." The term that is widely used to describe the discipline is *organizational behavior*.

Organizational behavior (often abbreviated OB) is a field of study that investigates the impact that individuals, groups, and structure have on behavior within organizations, for the purpose of applying such knowledge toward improving an organization's effectiveness. That's a mouthful, so let's break it down.

Organizational behavior is a field of study, meaning that it is a distinct area of expertise with a common body of knowledge. What does it study? It studies three determinants of behavior in organizations: individuals, groups, and structure. In addition, OB applies the knowledge gained about individuals, groups, and the effect of structure on behavior in order to make organizations work more effectively.

To sum up our definition, OB is the study of what people do in an organization and how their behavior affects the organization's performance. And because OB is concerned specifically with employment-related situations, you should not be surprised that it emphasizes behavior as related to concerns such as jobs, work, absenteeism, employment turnover, productivity, human performance, and management.

Although debate exists about the relative importance of each, OB includes the core topics of motivation, leader behavior and power, interpersonal communication, group structure and processes, learning, attitude development and perception, change processes, conflict, work design, and work stress.[12]

Online shoe retailer Zappos.com understands how organizational behavior affects an organization's performance. Zappos maintains good employee relationships by providing generous benefits, extensive customer service training, and a positive, fun-loving work environment. Employees are empowered to make decisions that increase customer satisfaction and are encouraged to create fun and a little weirdness." At Zappos, employee loyalty, job satisfaction, and productivity are high, contributing to the company's growth. In this photo, employees view a line of shoes in one of the company's quirky offices.

Source: Isaac Brekken/The New York Times/Redux Pictures

Complementing Intuition with Systematic Study

4 Show the value to OB of systematic study.

Each of us is a student of behavior. Whether you've explicitly thought about it before, you've been "reading" people almost all your life, watching their actions and trying to interpret what you see or predict what people might do under different conditions. Unfortunately, the casual or common sense approach to reading others can often lead to erroneous predictions. However, you can improve your predictive ability by supplementing intuition with a more systematic approach.

The systematic approach in this book will uncover important facts and relationships and provide a base from which to make more accurate predictions of behavior. Underlying this systematic approach is the belief that behavior is not random. Rather, we can identify fundamental consistencies underlying the behavior of all individuals and modify them to reflect individual differences.

These fundamental consistencies are very important. Why? Because they allow predictability. Behavior is generally predictable, and the *systematic study* of behavior is a means to making reasonably accurate predictions. When we use the term **systematic study**, we mean looking at relationships, attempting to attribute causes and effects, and basing our conclusions on scientific evidence—that is, on data gathered under controlled conditions and measured and interpreted in a reasonably rigorous manner. (See Appendix A for a basic review of research methods used in studies of organizational behavior.)

Evidence-based management (EBM) complements systematic study by basing managerial decisions on the best available scientific evidence. For example, we want doctors to make decisions about patient care based on the latest available evidence, and EBM argues that managers should do the same, becoming more scientific in how they think about management problems. A manager might pose a managerial question, search for the best available evidence, and apply the relevant information to the question or case at hand. You might think it difficult to argue against this (what manager would say decisions shouldn't be based on evidence?), but the vast majority of management decisions are still made "on the fly," with little or systematic study of available evidence.[13]

Systematic study and EBM add to **intuition**, or those "gut feelings" about what makes others (and ourselves) "tick." Of course, the things you have come to believe in an unsystematic way are not necessarily incorrect. Jack Welch (former CEO of GE) noted, "The trick, of course, is to know when to go with your gut." But if we make *all* decisions with intuition or gut instinct, we're likely working with incomplete information—like making an investment decision with only half the data.

Relying on intuition is made worse because we tend to overestimate the accuracy of what we think we know. In a recent survey, 86 percent of managers thought their organization was treating their employees well, but only 55 percent of the employees thought so. Surveys of human resource managers have also

---

organizational behavior (OB) *A field of study that investigates the impact that individuals, groups, and structure have on behavior within organizations, for the purpose of applying such knowledge toward improving an organization's effectiveness.*

systematic study *Looking at relationships, attempting to attribute causes and effects, and drawing conclusions based on scientific evidence.*

evidence-based management (EBM) *The basing of managerial decisions on the best available scientific evidence.*

intuition *A gut feeling not necessarily supported by research.*

"Most Acts of Workplace Bullying Are Men Attacking Women"

This statement is true in the broad sense that most research indicates men are more likely to engage in workplace bullying, and women are more likely to be targets of bullying behavior.

However, the full picture of gender and workplace bullying is more complicated than that.

First, the gender differences are narrowing. A recent study of workplace bullying by the Workplace Bullying Institute (WBI) suggested that 60 percent of workplace bullies are men and 40 percent are women. That is still a significant gender difference. But it is not as large as was once the case. Some of the narrowing in the gender of bullies is due to the ascension of women up their organizations' ladders. Evidence indicates that the vast majority of incidents of workplace bullying are "top-down": the supervisor is intimidating the subordinate. As more women are becoming supervisors, this is changing, to some degree, the gender balance of workplace bullies.

A second complication is that when women bully others at work, other women are overwhelmingly their targets. The same WBI study of workplace bullying revealed that 58 percent of victims of bullying are women. However, almost all of this gender difference in victims is due to *who women bullies target;* in 80 percent of the cases, it was other women. Male bullies are actually more likely to target their own sex, though to a less dramatic degree than female bullies do.

Finally, it does appear that women are more adversely affected by bullying. A recent study of 183 victims of bullying found that the prevalence of trauma was higher for women (49 percent) than men (35 percent). The complexity of these relationships shows us that gaining a true understanding of organizational behavior phenomena often means understanding that the causes and consequences of work behavior are complex.

Back to bullying, experts suggest some ways to cope with workplace bullies regardless of your sex.

1. **Talk to your bully.** "Perhaps your boss is one of those people who aren't aware of how they come across," says Stanford's Robert Sutton, author of several books on bullying in the workplace.
2. **Get help.** Keep a diary of the behavior. Be specific and focus more on actions than feelings. At some point, it might be necessary to involve others, such as human resources.
3. **Ignore it.** This is often easier said than done, but sometimes the only thing you can do is to try to ignore the bully. "Try not to let it touch your soul," says Sutton.
4. **Polish your résumé.** Bullies sometimes go away, and sometimes they listen. But if they aren't going to change and aren't going away, you may want to plan your exit strategy. Take your time and don't panic. But not every workplace is filled with bullies, and you'll likely be happier if you're in one of those.

Source: L. Petrecca, "Bullying in Workplace Is Common, Hard to Fix," *USA Today* (December 28, 2010), pp. 1B–2B; R. I. Sutton, *Good Boss, Bad Boss: How to Be the Best...and Learn from the Worst* (New York: Business Plus, 2010); A. Rodríguez-Muñoz, B. Moreno-Jiménez, A. Vergel, and E. G. Hernández, "Post-Traumatic Symptoms Among Victims of Workplace Bullying: Exploring Gender Differences and Shattered Assumptions," *Journal of Applied Social Psychology* 40, no. 10 (2010), pp. 2616–2635.

shown many managers hold "common sense" opinions regarding effective management that have been flatly refuted by empirical evidence.

We find a similar problem in chasing the business and popular media for management wisdom. The business press tends to be dominated by fads. As a writer for *The New Yorker* put it, "Every few years, new companies succeed, and they are scrutinized for the underlying truths they might reveal. But often there is no underlying truth; the companies just happened to be in the right place at the right time."[14] Although we try to avoid it, we might also fall into this trap. It's not that the business press stories are all wrong; it's that without a systematic approach, it's hard to separate the wheat from the chaff.

We're not advising that you throw your intuition, or all the business press, out the window. Nor are we arguing that research is always right.

Researchers make mistakes, too. What we are advising is to use evidence as much as possible to inform your intuition and experience. That is the promise of OB.

Disciplines That Contribute to the OB Field

5 Identify the major behavioral science disciplines that contribute to OB.

Organizational behavior is an applied behavioral science built on contributions from a number of behavioral disciplines, mainly psychology and social psychology, sociology, and anthropology. Psychology's contributions have been mainly at the individual or micro level of analysis, while the other disciplines have contributed to our understanding of macro concepts such as group processes and organization. Exhibit 1-3 is an overview of the major contributions to the study of organizational behavior.

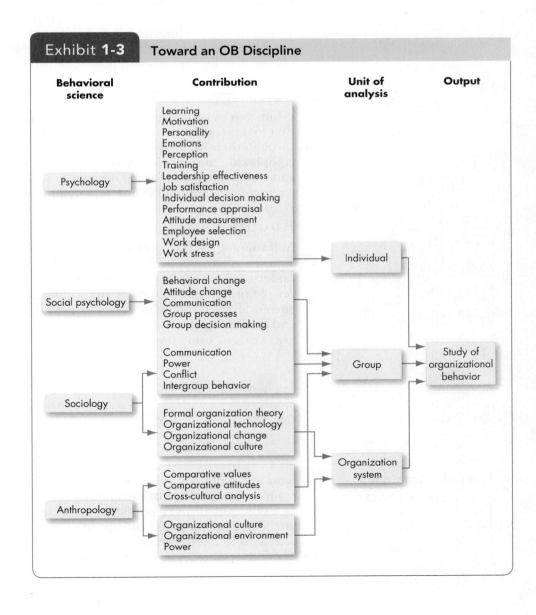

Exhibit 1-3   Toward an OB Discipline

Psychology

Psychology seeks to measure, explain, and sometimes change the behavior of humans and other animals. Those who have contributed and continue to add to the knowledge of OB are learning theorists, personality theorists, counseling psychologists, and, most important, industrial and organizational psychologists.

Early industrial/organizational psychologists studied the problems of fatigue, boredom, and other working conditions that could impede efficient work performance. More recently, their contributions have expanded to include learning, perception, personality, emotions, training, leadership effectiveness, needs and motivational forces, job satisfaction, decision-making processes, performance appraisals, attitude measurement, employee-selection techniques, work design, and job stress.

Social Psychology

Social psychology, generally considered a branch of psychology, blends concepts from both psychology and sociology to focus on peoples' influence on one another. One major study area is *change*—how to implement it and how to reduce barriers to its acceptance. Social psychologists also contribute to measuring, understanding, and changing attitudes; identifying communication patterns; and building trust. Finally, they have made important contributions to our study of group behavior, power, and conflict.

Sociology

While psychology focuses on the individual, **sociology** studies people in relation to their social environment or culture. Sociologists have contributed to OB through their study of group behavior in organizations, particularly formal and complex organizations. Perhaps most important, sociologists have studied organizational culture, formal organization theory and structure, organizational technology, communications, power, and conflict.

Anthropology

Anthropology is the study of societies to learn about human beings and their activities. Anthropologists' work on cultures and environments has helped us understand differences in fundamental values, attitudes, and behavior between people in different countries and within different organizations. Much of our current understanding of organizational culture, organizational environments, and differences among national cultures is a result of the work of anthropologists or those using their methods.

There Are Few Absolutes in OB

6   Demonstrate why few absolutes apply to OB.

Laws in the physical sciences—chemistry, astronomy, physics—are consistent and apply in a wide range of situations. They allow scientists to generalize about the pull of gravity or to be confident about sending astronauts into space to repair satellites. But as a noted behavioral researcher observed, "God gave all the easy problems to the physicists." Human beings are complex, and few, if any, simple and universal principles explain organizational behavior. Because we are not alike, our ability to make simple, accurate, and sweeping generalizations is limited.

Two people often act very differently in the same situation, and the same person's behavior changes in different situations. Not everyone is motivated by money, and people may behave differently at a religious service than they do at a party.

That doesn't mean, of course, that we can't offer reasonably accurate explanations of human behavior or make valid predictions. It does mean that OB concepts must reflect situational, or contingency, conditions. We can say x leads to y, but only under conditions specified in z—the **contingency variables**. The science of OB was developed by applying general concepts to a particular situation, person, or group. For example, OB scholars would avoid stating that everyone likes complex and challenging work (the general concept). Why? Because not everyone wants a challenging job. Some people prefer routine over varied, or simple over complex. A job attractive to one person may not be to another; its appeal is contingent on the person who holds it.

As you proceed through this book, you'll encounter a wealth of research-based theories about how people behave in organizations. But don't expect to find a lot of straightforward cause-and-effect relationships. There aren't many! organizational behavior theories mirror the subject matter with which they deal, and people are complex and complicated.

Challenges and Opportunities for OB

7 Identify the challenges and opportunities managers have in applying OB concepts.

Understanding organizational behavior has never been more important for managers. Take a quick look at the dramatic changes in organizations. The typical employee is getting older; more women and people of color are in the workplace; corporate downsizing and the heavy use of temporary workers are severing the bonds of loyalty that tied many employees to their employers; global competition requires employees to become more flexible and cope with rapid change. The global recession has brought to the forefront the challenges of working with and managing people during uncertain times.

In short, today's challenges bring opportunities for managers to use OB concepts. In this section, we review some of the most critical issues confronting managers for which OB offers solutions—or at least meaningful insights toward solutions.

Responding to Economic Pressures

When the U.S. economy plunged into a deep and prolonged recession in 2008, virtually all other large economies around the world followed suit. Layoffs and job losses were widespread, and those who survived the ax were often asked to accept pay cuts.

During difficult economic times, effective management is often at a premium. Anybody can run a company when business is booming, because the difference

psychology *The science that seeks to measure, explain, and sometimes change the behavior of humans and other animals.*

social psychology *An area of psychology that blends concepts from psychology and sociology and that focuses on the influence of people on one another.*

sociology *The study of people in relation to their social environment or culture.*

anthropology *The study of societies to learn about human beings and their activities.*

contingency variables *Situational factors: variables that moderate the relationship between two or more variables.*

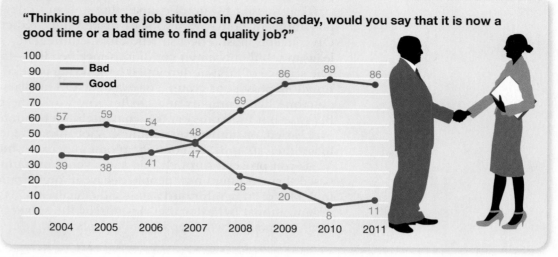

OB Poll   Working in Good Times—and Bad

"Thinking about the job situation in America today, would you say that it is now a good time or a bad time to find a quality job?"

— Bad
— Good

Year	Bad	Good
2004	57	39
2005	59	38
2006	54	41
2007	48	47
2008	69	26
2009	86	20
2010	89	8
2011	86	11

Source: Gallup tracking polls of random samples of roughly 1,000 adults, aged 18 and older, living in the continental U.S., selected using random-digit telephone sampling. See F. Newport, "Americans' Views of Job Market Improve; Still Mostly Negative" (April 18, 2011), www.gallup.com.

between good and bad management reflects the difference between making a lot of money and making a lot more money. When times are bad, though, managers are on the front lines with employees who must be fired, who are asked to make do with less, and who worry about their futures. The difference between good and bad management can be the difference between profit and loss or, ultimately, between survival and failure.

Consider Enterprise Rent-A-Car. The company prided itself on never having laid off a U.S. employee in its 51-year history. Even in the 2001–2002 recession after the 9/11 terrorist attacks, Enterprise kept hiring. In 2008–2009, however, Enterprise was forced to lay off more than a thousand employees. "These types of declines are unprecedented," said Patrick Farrell, Enterprise's vice president of corporate responsibility. Gentex Corp, a Michigan-based auto parts supplier, had never had a layoff in its 34-year history—until 2008–2009. "We didn't even have a layoff policy," said Gentex's vice president of human resources.[15]

Managing employees well when times are tough is just as hard as when times are good—if not more so. But the OB approaches sometimes differ. In good times, understanding how to reward, satisfy, and retain employees is at a premium. In bad times, issues like stress, decision making, and coping come to the fore.

Responding to Globalization

Organizations are no longer constrained by national borders. Burger King is owned by a British firm, and McDonald's sells hamburgers in Moscow. ExxonMobil, a so-called U.S. company, receives almost 75 percent of its revenues from sales outside the United States. New employees at Finland-based phone maker Nokia are increasingly being recruited from India, China, and other developing countries—non-Finns now outnumber Finns at Nokia's renowned research center in Helsinki. And all major automobile makers now manufacture cars outside their borders; Honda builds cars in Ohio, Ford in Brazil, Volkswagen in Mexico, and both Mercedes and BMW in South Africa.

The world has become a global village. In the process, the manager's job has changed.

Increased Foreign Assignments If you're a manager, you are increasingly likely to find yourself in a foreign assignment—transferred to your employer's operating division or subsidiary in another country. Once there, you'll have to manage a workforce very different in needs, aspirations, and attitudes from those you are used to back home.

Working with People from Different Cultures Even in your own country, you'll find yourself working with bosses, peers, and other employees born and raised in different cultures. What motivates you may not motivate them. Or your communication style may be straightforward and open, which others may find uncomfortable and threatening. To work effectively with people from different cultures, you need to understand how their culture, geography, and religion have shaped them and how to adapt your management style to their differences.

Managers at global companies such as McDonald's, Disney, and Coca-Cola have come to realize that economic values are not universally transferable. Management practices need to be modified to reflect the values of the different countries in which an organization operates.

Overseeing Movement of Jobs to Countries with Low-Cost Labor It's increasingly difficult for managers in advanced nations, where minimum wages are typically $6 or more an hour, to compete against firms that rely on workers from China and other developing nations where labor is available for 30 cents an hour. It's not by chance that many in the United States wear clothes made in China, work on computers whose microchips came from Taiwan, and watch movies filmed in Canada. In a global economy, jobs tend to flow where lower costs give businesses a comparative advantage, though labor groups, politicians, and local community leaders see the exporting of jobs as undermining the job market at home. Managers face the difficult task of balancing the interests of their organization with their responsibilities to the communities in which they operate.

In the global economy, jobs tend to shift from developed nations to countries where lower labor costs give firms a comparative advantage. In this photo, an employee wearing a sign on his head reading "Capital Interests" joins co-workers at a Nokia factory in Germany to protest the company's decision of terminating mobile phone production at the plant, resulting in the loss of 2,300 jobs. Nokia announced plans to shift production from Germany to Romania, where labor costs are lower.

Source: Henning Kaiser/Getty Images

Managing Workforce Diversity

One of the most important challenges for organizations is adapting to people who are different. We describe this challenge as *workforce diversity.* Whereas globalization focuses on differences among people *from* different countries, workforce diversity addresses differences among people *within* given countries.

Workforce diversity acknowledges a workforce of women and men; many racial and ethnic groups; individuals with a variety of physical or psychological abilities; and people who differ in age and sexual orientation. Managing this diversity is a global concern. Most European countries have experienced dramatic growth in immigration from the Middle East, Argentina and Venezuela host a significant number of migrants from other South American countries, and nations from India to Iraq to Indonesia find great cultural diversity within their borders.

The most significant change in the U.S. labor force during the last half of the twentieth century was the rapid increase in the number of female workers. In 1950, for instance, only 29.6 percent of the workforce was female. By 2008, it was 46.5 percent. The first half of the twenty-first century will be notable for changes in racial and ethnic composition and an aging baby boom generation. By 2050, Hispanics will grow from today's 11 percent of the workforce to 24 percent, blacks will increase from 12 to 14 percent, and Asians from 5 to 11 percent. Meanwhile, in the near term the labor force will be aging. The 55-and-older age group, currently 13 percent of the labor force, will increase to 20 percent by 2014.

Though we have more to say about workforce diversity in the next chapter, suffice it to say here that it presents great opportunities and poses challenging questions for managers and employees in all countries. How can we leverage differences within groups for competitive advantage? Should we treat all employees alike? Should we recognize individual and cultural differences? How can we foster cultural awareness in employees without lapsing into political correctness? What are the legal requirements in each country? Does diversity even matter?

Improving Customer Service

American Express recently turned Joan Weinbel's worst nightmare into a non-event. It was 10:00 P.M. Joan was home in New Jersey, packing for a weeklong trip, when she suddenly realized she had left her AmEx Gold card at a restaurant in New York City earlier in the evening. The restaurant was 30 miles away. She had a flight to catch at 7:30 the next morning, and she wanted her card for the trip. She called American Express. The phone was quickly answered by a courteous and helpful AmEx customer service representative who told Ms. Weinbel not to worry. He asked her a few questions and told her, "Help is on the way." To say Joan was flabbergasted when her doorbell rang at 11:45 P.M. is an understatement—it was less than 2 hours after her call. At the door was a courier with a new card. How the company was able to produce the card and get it to her so quickly still puzzles Joan, but she said the experience made her a customer for life.

Today, the majority of employees in developed countries work in service jobs, including 80 percent in the United States. In Australia, 73 percent work in service industries. In the United Kingdom, Germany, and Japan, the percentages are 69, 68, and 65, respectively. Service jobs include technical support representatives, fast-food counter workers, sales clerks, waiters and waitresses, nurses, automobile repair technicians, consultants, credit representatives, financial planners, and flight attendants. The common characteristic of these jobs is substantial interaction with an organization's customers. And because an organization can't exist without customers—whether it is American

The Ritz Carlton Hotel Company is recognized worldwide as the gold standard of the hospitality industry. Its motto—"We are ladies and gentlemen serving ladies and gentlemen"—is exemplified by the employee shown here serving a guest on the summer terrace of the Ritz-Carlton Moscow. The Ritz-Carlton's customer-responsive culture, which is articulated in the company's motto, credo, and service values, is designed to build strong relationships that create guests for life.

Source: ITAR - TASS / Anton Tushin / Newscom

Express, L. L. Bean, a law firm, a museum, a school, or a government agency—management needs to ensure employees do what it takes to please customers.[16] At Patagonia—a retail outfitter for climbers, mountain bikers, skiers and boarders, and other outdoor fanatics—customer service is the store manager's most important general responsibility: "Instill in your employees the meaning and importance of customer service as outlined in the retail philosophy, 'Our store is a place where the word "no" does not exist'; empower staff to 'use their best judgment' in all customer service matters."[17] OB can help managers at Patagonia achieve this goal and, more generally, can contribute to improving an organization's performance by showing managers how employee attitudes and behavior are associated with customer satisfaction.

Many an organization has failed because its employees failed to please customers. Management needs to create a customer-responsive culture. OB can provide considerable guidance in helping managers create such cultures—in which employees are friendly and courteous, accessible, knowledgeable, prompt in responding to customer needs, and willing to do what's necessary to please the customer.[18]

Improving People Skills

As you proceed through the chapters of this book, we'll present relevant concepts and theories that can help you explain and predict the behavior of people at work. In addition, you'll gain insights into specific people skills that you

workforce diversity *The concept that organizations are becoming more heterogeneous in terms of gender, age, race, ethnicity, sexual orientation, and inclusion of other diverse groups.*

can use on the job. For instance, you'll learn ways to design motivating jobs, techniques for improving your listening skills, and how to create more effective teams.

Stimulating Innovation and Change

Whatever happened to Montgomery Ward, Woolworth, Smith Corona, TWA, Bethlehem Steel, and WorldCom? All these giants went bust. Why have other giants, such as General Motors, Sears, Boeing, and Lucent Technologies, implemented huge cost-cutting programs and eliminated thousands of jobs? The answer is to avoid going broke.

Today's successful organizations must foster innovation and master the art of change, or they'll become candidates for extinction. Victory will go to the organizations that maintain their flexibility, continually improve their quality, and beat their competition to the marketplace with a constant stream of innovative products and services. Domino's single-handedly brought on the demise of small pizza parlors whose managers thought they could continue doing what they had been doing for years. Amazon.com is putting a lot of independent bookstores out of business as it proves you can successfully sell books (and most anything else) from a Web site. After years of lackluster performance, Boeing realized it needed to change its business model. The result was its 787 Dreamliner and a return to being the world's largest airplane manufacturer.

An organization's employees can be the impetus for innovation and change, or they can be a major stumbling block. The challenge for managers is to stimulate their employees' creativity and tolerance for change. The field of OB provides a wealth of ideas and techniques to aid in realizing these goals.

Coping with "Temporariness"

Globalization, expanded capacity, and advances in technology have required organizations to be fast and flexible if they are to survive. The result is that most managers and employees today work in a climate best characterized as "temporary."

Workers must continually update their knowledge and skills to perform new job requirements. Production employees at companies such as Caterpillar, Ford, and Alcoa now need to operate computerized production equipment. That was not part of their job descriptions 20 years ago. In the past, employees were assigned to a specific work group, gaining a considerable amount of security working with the same people day in and day out. That predictability has been replaced by temporary work groups, with members from different departments, and the increased use of employee rotation to fill constantly changing work assignments. Finally, organizations themselves are in a state of flux. They continually reorganize their various divisions, sell off poorly performing businesses, downsize operations, subcontract noncritical services and operations to other organizations, and replace permanent employees with temporary workers.

Today's managers and employees must learn to cope with temporariness, flexibility, spontaneity, and unpredictability. The study of OB can help you better understand a work world of continual change, overcome resistance to change, and create an organizational culture that thrives on change.

Working in Networked Organizations

Networked organizations allow people to communicate and work together even though they may be thousands of miles apart. Independent contractors can telecommute via computer to workplaces around the globe and change employers as the demand for their services changes. Software programmers, graphic designers, systems analysts, technical writers, photo researchers, book

Dr. Orit Wimpfheimer performs her job by linking to others through networks. Shown here at her home office near Jerusalem, Israel, she is a radiologist who analyzes test results from hospitals in the United States over the Internet. Networked organizations that use e-mail, the Internet, and video-conferencing allow Dr. Orit Wimpfheimer and other telecommuters to communicate and work together even though they are thousands of miles apart. The manager's job in a networked organization requires different techniques from those used when workers are physically present in a single location.

Source: AP Photo/Emilio Morenatti

and media editors, and medical transcribers are just a few examples of people who can work from home or other nonoffice locations.

The manager's job is different in a networked organization. Motivating and leading people and making collaborative decisions online requires different techniques than when individuals are physically present in a single location. As more employees do their jobs by linking to others through networks, managers must develop new skills. OB can provide valuable insights to help with honing those skills.

Helping Employees Balance Work–Life Conflicts

The typical employee in the 1960s or 1970s showed up at a specified workplace Monday through Friday and worked for clearly defined 8- or 9-hour chunks of time. That's no longer true for a large segment of today's workforce. Employees are increasingly complaining that the line between work and nonwork time has become blurred, creating personal conflicts and stress.[19] At the same time, today's workplace presents opportunities for workers to create and structure their own roles.

How do work–life conflicts come about? First, the creation of global organizations means the world never sleeps. At any time on any day, thousands of General Electric employees are working somewhere. The need to consult with colleagues or customers eight or ten time zones away means many employees of global firms are "on call" 24 hours a day. Second, communication technology allows many technical and professional employees to do their work at home, in their cars, or on the beach in Tahiti—but it also means many feel like they never really get away from the office. Third, organizations are asking employees to put in longer hours. Over a recent 10-year period, the average U.S. workweek increased from 43 to 47 hours; and the number of people working 50 or more hours a week jumped from 24 to 37 percent. Finally, the rise of the dual-career couple makes it difficult for married employees to find time to fulfill commitments to home, spouse, children, parents, and friends. Millions of single-parent households and employees with dependent parents have even more significant challenges in balancing work and family responsibilities.

Employees increasingly recognize that work infringes on their personal lives, and they're not happy about it. Recent studies suggest employees want jobs that give them flexibility in their work schedules so they can better manage work–life conflicts.[20] In fact, balancing work and life demands now surpasses job security as an employee priority.[21] The next generation of employees is likely to show similar concerns.[22] Most college and university students say attaining a balance between personal life and work is a primary career goal; they want "a life" as well as a job. Organizations that don't help their people achieve work–life balance will find it increasingly difficult to attract and retain the most capable and motivated employees.

As you'll see in later chapters, the field of OB offers a number of suggestions to guide managers in designing workplaces and jobs that can help employees deal with work–life conflicts.

Creating a Positive Work Environment

Although competitive pressures on most organizations are stronger than ever, some organizations are trying to realize a competitive advantage by fostering a positive work environment. Jeff Immelt and Jim McNerney, both disciples of Jack Welch, have tried to maintain high-performance expectations (a characteristic of GE's culture) while fostering a positive work environment in their organizations (GE and Boeing). "In this time of turmoil and cynicism about business, you need to be passionate, positive leaders," Mr. Immelt recently told his top managers.

A real growth area in OB research is **positive organizational scholarship** (also called *positive organizational behavior*), which studies how organizations develop human strengths, foster vitality and resilience, and unlock potential. Researchers in this area say too much of OB research and management practice has been targeted toward identifying what's wrong with organizations and their employees. In response, they try to study what's *good* about them.[23] Some key independent variables in positive OB research are engagement, hope, optimism, and resilience in the face of strain.

Positive organizational scholars have studied a concept called "reflected best-self"—asking employees to think about when they were at their "personal best" in order to understand how to exploit their strengths. The idea is that we all have things at which we are unusually good, yet too often we focus on addressing our limitations and too rarely think about how to exploit our strengths.[24]

Although positive organizational scholarship does not deny the value of the negative (such as critical feedback), it does challenge researchers to look at OB through a new lens and pushes organizations to exploit employees' strengths rather than dwell on their limitations.

Improving Ethical Behavior

In an organizational world characterized by cutbacks, expectations of increasing productivity, and tough competition, it's not surprising many employees feel pressured to cut corners, break rules, and engage in other questionable practices.

Increasingly they face **ethical dilemmas and ethical choices**, in which they are required to identify right and wrong conduct. Should they "blow the whistle" if they uncover illegal activities in their company? Do they follow orders with which they don't personally agree? Should they give an inflated performance evaluation to an employee they like, knowing it could save that employee's job? Do they "play politics" to advance their career?

What constitutes good ethical behavior has never been clearly defined, and, in recent years, the line differentiating right from wrong has blurred. Employees see people all around them engaging in unethical practices—elected officials pad expense accounts or take bribes; corporate executives inflate profits so they can cash in lucrative stock options; and university administrators look the other way when winning coaches encourage scholarship athletes to take easy courses. When caught, these people give excuses such as "Everyone does it" or "You have to seize every advantage nowadays." Determining the ethically correct way to behave is especially difficult in a global economy because different cultures have different perspectives on certain ethical issues.[25] Fair treatment of employees in an economic downturn varies considerably across cultures, for instance. As we'll see in Chapter 2, perceptions of religious, ethnic, and gender diversity differ across countries. Is it any wonder employees are expressing decreased confidence in management and increasing uncertainty about what is appropriate ethical behavior in their organizations?[26]

Managers and their organizations are responding to the problem of unethical behavior in a number of ways.[27] They're writing and distributing codes of ethics to guide employees through ethical dilemmas. They're offering seminars, workshops, and other training programs to try to improve ethical behaviors. They're providing in-house advisors who can be contacted, in many cases anonymously, for assistance in dealing with ethical issues, and they're creating protection mechanisms for employees who reveal internal unethical practices.

Today's manager must create an ethically healthy climate for his or her employees, where they can do their work productively with minimal ambiguity about what right and wrong behaviors are. Companies that promote a strong ethical mission, encourage employees to behave with integrity, and provide strong ethical leadership can influence employee decisions to behave ethically.[28] In upcoming chapters, we'll discuss the actions managers can take to create an ethically healthy climate and help employees sort through ethically ambiguous situations. We'll also present ethical-dilemma exercises at the end of each chapter that allow you to think through ethical issues and assess how you would handle them.

Coming Attractions: Developing an OB Model

8 Compare the three levels of analysis in this book's OB model.

We conclude this chapter by presenting a general model that defines the field of OB, stakes out its parameters, and identifies inputs, processes, and outcomes. The result will be "coming attractions" of the topics in the remainder of this book.

An Overview

A **model** is an abstraction of reality, a simplified representation of some real-world phenomenon. Exhibit 1-4 presents the skeleton on which we will construct our OB model. It proposes three types of variables (inputs, processes, and

---

positive organizational scholarship *An area of OB research that concerns how organizations develop human strength, foster vitality and resilience, and unlock potential.*

ethical dilemmas and ethical choices *Situations in which individuals are required to define right and wrong conduct.*

model *An abstraction of reality. A simplified representation of some real-world phenomenon.*

Can You Learn from Failure?

Mistakes happen in business all the time, but most people have a powerful motivation to try to cover up their errors as much as possible. However, not recognizing and learning from failures might be the most dangerous failure of all because it means the problem is likely to occur again. This means that, even though it might be hard to admit it, doing the right thing often means admitting when you've done the wrong thing. Most people would say that we have an ethical obligation to learn from mistakes, but how can we do that? In a recent special issue in *Harvard Business Review* on failures, experts argued that learning from mistakes relies on several strategies, which include:

1. **Heed pressure.** High pressure often provokes faulty thinking. BP faced enormous pressure from cost overruns—roughly $1 million a day—in its deepwater oil explorations. This led its managers to miss warning signs that led to the catastrophic explosion in the Gulf of Mexico in 2010. Similar time and cost pressures precipitated the ill-fated Challenger and Columbia space shuttle launches. In high-pressure situations, ask yourself,

"If I had more time and resources, would I make the same decision?"

2. **Recognize that failure is not always bad.** Most of us would agree that we have learned more in life from our mistakes than from our successes. So, we need to realize that while we don't want to fail, it does have a hidden gift if we're willing to receive—a chance to learn something important. Eli Lilly holds "failure parties" to honor drug trials and experiments that fail to achieve the desired results. The rationale for these parties is to recognize that when little is ventured, little is lost, but little is gained too. Procter & Gamble CEO A. G. Lafley argues that very high success rates show incremental innovation—but what he wants are game changers. He has celebrated P&G's 11 most expensive product failures, focusing on what the company learned from each. So don't be afraid to admit mistakes—and ask "What can I learn" from each.

3. **Understand and address the root cause.** When Apple introduced the iPhone 4 in 2010, many customers complained about dropped calls. Apple first responded by suggesting the problem lay in the way customers held the phones, suggested

they "avoid gripping [the phone] in the lower left corner." Steve Jobs called the problem a "non-issue." Only later did Apple address the root cause of the problem—and fix it. When you make an error, try to understand what caused it.

4. **Reward owning up.** If you make a mistake, be willing to speak up and admit it. Too often we dig ourselves deeper into a hole by being defensive about mistakes. That also keeps us from learning from our failures. If we all make mistakes, what are we being so defensive about?

Given the complexity of human behavior, we'll never avoid making mistakes entirely. Indeed, a healthy appreciation for how mistake-prone we are is one of the points of this chapter (and of Chapter 6). But we *can* do a better job of admitting our mistakes and learning from them when they occur.

Sources: A. C. Edmondson, "Strategies for Learning from Failure," *Harvard Business Review* 89, no. 4 (2011), pp. 48–55; R. G. Mcgrath, "Failing by Design," *Harvard Business Review* 89, no. 4 (2011), pp. 76–83; C. H. Tinsley, R. L. Dillon, and P. M. Madsen, "How to Avoid Catastrophe," *Harvard Business Review* 89, no. 4 (2011), pp. 90–97.

outcomes) at three levels of analysis (individual, group, and organizational). The model proceeds from left to right, with inputs leading to processes and processes leading to outcomes. Notice that the model also shows that outcomes can influence inputs in the future.

Inputs

Inputs are the variables like personality, group structure, and organizational culture that lead to processes. These variables set the stage for what will occur in an organization later. Many are determined in advance of the employment relationship. For example, individual diversity characteristics, personality, and values are shaped by a combination of an individual's genetic inheritance and childhood environment. Group structure, roles, and team responsibilities are

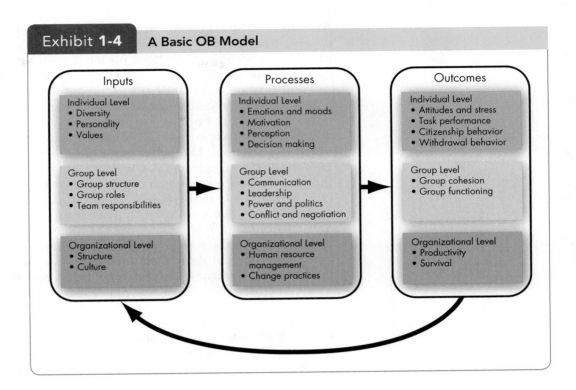

Exhibit **1-4**   **A Basic OB Model**

typically assigned immediately before or after a group is formed. Finally, organizational structure and culture are usually the result of years of development and change as the organization adapts to its environment and builds up customs and norms.

Processes

If inputs are like the nouns in organizational behavior, processes are like verbs. **Processes** are actions that individuals, groups, and organizations engage in as a result of inputs and that lead to certain outcomes. At the individual level, processes include emotions and moods, motivation, perception, and decision making. At the group level, they include communication, leadership, power and politics, and conflict and negotiation. Finally, at the organizational level, processes include human resource management and change practices.

Outcomes

Outcomes are the key variables that you want to explain or predict, and that are affected by some other variables. What are the primary outcomes in OB? Scholars have emphasized individual-level outcomes like attitudes and satisfaction, task performance, citizenship behavior, and withdrawal behavior. At the group level, cohesion and functioning are the dependent variables. Finally, at the organizational level we look at overall profitability and survival. Because these outcomes will be covered in all the chapters, we'll briefly discuss each here so you can understand what the "goal" of OB will be.

input   *Variables that lead to processes.*

processes   *Actions that individuals, groups, and organizations engage in as a result of inputs and that lead to certain outcomes.*

outcomes   *Key factors that are affected by some other variables.*

Attitudes and Stress   Employee attitudes are the evaluations employees make, ranging from positive to negative, about objects, people, or events. For example, the statement, "I really think my job is great," is a positive job attitude, and "My job is boring and tedious" is a negative job attitude. Stress is an unpleasant psychological process that occurs in response to environmental pressures.

Some people might think that influencing employee attitudes and stress is purely soft stuff, and not the business of serious managers, but as we will show, attitudes often have behavioral consequences that directly relate to organizational effectiveness. The belief that satisfied employees are more productive than dissatisfied employees has been a basic tenet among managers for years, though only now has research begun to support it. Ample evidence shows that employees who are more satisfied and treated fairly are more willing to engage in the above-and-beyond citizenship behavior so vital in the contemporary business environment. A study of more than 2,500 business units also found that those scoring in the top 25 percent on the employee opinion survey were, on average, 4.6 percent above their sales budget for the year, while those scoring in the bottom 25 percent were 0.8 percent below budget. In real numbers, this was a difference of $104 million in sales per year between the two groups.

Task Performance   The combination of effectiveness and efficiency at doing your core job tasks is a reflection of your level of **task performance**. If we think about the job of a factory worker, task performance could be measured by the number and quality of products produced in an hour. The task performance of a teacher would be the level of education that students obtain. The task performance of a consultant might be measured by the timeliness and quality of the presentations they offer to the client firm. All these types of performance relate to the core duties and responsibilities of a job and are often directly related to the functions listed on a formal job description.

Obviously task performance is the most important human output contributing to organizational effectiveness, so in every chapter we devote considerable time to detailing how task performance is affected by the topic in question.

Task performance is one of the primary individual-level outcomes in organizational behavior. For these women who install wiring in car doors at the General Motors' assembly plant in Lordstown, Ohio, task performance is measured by the number and quality of the work they produce. Their level of task performance is related to the duties of their job and how effectively and efficiently they perform them. Task performance is the most important human output contributing to organizational effectiveness.

Source: AP Photo/Mark Duncan

Citizenship Behavior The discretionary behavior that is not part of an employee's formal job requirements, and that contributes to the psychological and social environment of the workplace, is called **citizenship behavior**. Successful organizations need employees who will do more than their usual job duties—who will provide performance *beyond* expectations. In today's dynamic workplace, where tasks are increasingly performed by teams and flexibility is critical, employees who engage in "good citizenship" behaviors help others on their team, volunteer for extra work, avoid unnecessary conflicts, respect the spirit as well as the letter of rules and regulations, and gracefully tolerate occasional work-related impositions and nuisances.

Organizations want and need employees who will do things that aren't in any job description. Evidence indicates organizations that have such employees outperform those that don't. As a result, OB is concerned with citizenship behavior as an outcome variable.

Withdrawal Behavior We've already mentioned behavior that goes above and beyond task requirements, but what about behavior that in some way is below task requirements? **Withdrawal behavior** is the set of actions that employees take to separate themselves from the organization. There are many forms of withdrawal, ranging from showing up late or failing to attend meetings to absenteeism and turnover.

Employee withdrawal can have a very negative effect on an organization. The cost of employee turnover alone has been estimated to run into the thousands of dollars, even for entry-level positions. Absenteeism also costs organizations significant amounts of money and time every year. For instance, a recent survey found the average direct cost to U.S. employers of unscheduled absences is 8.7 percent of payroll.[29] In Sweden, an average of 10 percent of the country's workforce is on sick leave at any given time.[30]

It's obviously difficult for an organization to operate smoothly and attain its objectives if employees fail to report to their jobs. The work flow is disrupted, and important decisions may be delayed. In organizations that rely heavily on assembly-line production, absenteeism can be considerably more than a disruption; it can drastically reduce the quality of output or even shut down the facility. Levels of absenteeism beyond the normal range have a direct impact on any organization's effectiveness and efficiency. A high rate of turnover can also disrupt the efficient running of an organization when knowledgeable and experienced personnel leave and replacements must be found to assume positions of responsibility.

All organizations, of course, have some turnover. The U.S. national turnover rate averages about 3 percent per month, about a 36 percent turnover per year. This average varies a lot by occupation, of course; the monthly turnover rate for government jobs is less than 1 percent, versus 5 to 7 percent in the construction industry.[31] If the "right" people are leaving the organization—the marginal and submarginal employees—turnover can actually be positive. It can create an opportunity to replace an underperforming individual with someone who has higher skills or motivation, open up increased opportunities for promotions,

---

task performance *The combination of effectiveness and efficiency at doing your core job tasks.*

citizenship behavior *Discretionary behavior that contributes to the psychological and social environment of the workplace.*

withdrawal behavior *The set of actions employee take to separate themselves from the organization.*

and bring new and fresh ideas to the organization.[32] In today's changing world of work, reasonable levels of employee-initiated turnover improve organizational flexibility and employee independence, and they can lessen the need for management-initiated layoffs.

So why do employees withdraw from work? As we will show later in the book, reasons include negative job attitudes, emotions and moods, and negative interactions with co-workers and supervisors.

Group Cohesion   Although many outcomes in our model can be conceptualized as individual level phenomena, some relate to how groups operate. **Group cohesion** is the extent to which members of a group support and validate one another at work. In other words, a cohesive group is one that sticks together. When employees trust one another, seek common goals, and work together to achieve these common ends, the group is cohesive; when employees are divided among themselves in terms of what they want to achieve and have little loyalty to one another, the group is not cohesive.

There is ample evidence showing that cohesive groups are more effective.[33] These results are found both for groups that are studied in highly controlled laboratory settings and also for work teams observed in field settings. This fits with our intuitive sense that people tend to work harder in groups that have a common purpose. Companies attempt to increase cohesion in a variety of ways ranging from brief icebreaker sessions to social events like picnics, parties, and outdoor adventure-team retreats. Throughout the book we will try to assess whether these specific efforts are likely to result in increases in group cohesiveness. We'll also consider ways that picking the right people to be on the team in the first place might be an effective way to enhance cohesion.

Group Functioning   In the same way that positive job attitudes can be associated with higher levels of task performance, group cohesion should lead to positive group functioning. **Group functioning** refers to the quantity and quality of a group's work output. In the same way that the performance of a sports team is more than the sum of individual players' performance, group functioning in work organizations is more than the sum of individual task performances.

What does it mean to say that a group is functioning effectively? In some organizations, an effective group is one that stays focused on a core task and achieves its ends as specified. Other organizations look for teams that are able to work together collaboratively to provide excellent customer service. Still others put more of a premium on group creativity and the flexibility to adapt to changing situations. In each case, different types of activities will be required to get the most from the team.

Productivity   The highest level of analysis in organizational behavior is the organization as a whole. An organization is productive if it achieves its goals by transforming inputs into outputs at the lowest cost. Thus **productivity** requires both **effectiveness** and **efficiency**.

A hospital is *effective* when it successfully meets the needs of its clientele. It is *efficient* when it can do so at a low cost. If a hospital manages to achieve higher output from its present staff by reducing the average number of days a patient is confined to bed or increasing the number of staff–patient contacts per day, we say the hospital has gained productive efficiency. A business firm is effective when it attains its sales or market share goals, but its productivity also depends on achieving those goals efficiently. Popular measures of organizational efficiency include return on investment, profit per dollar of sales, and output per hour of labor.

Service organizations must include customer needs and requirements in assessing their effectiveness. Why? Because a clear chain of cause and effect runs

Exhibit 1-5	The Plan of the Book

The Individual

Inputs
- Diversity in Organizations (ch.2)
- Personality and Values (ch. 5)

Processes
- Emotions and moods (ch. 4)
- Motivation (Ch. 7 and 8)
- Perception and decision making (Ch. 6)

Outcomes
- Attitudes (ch. 3) & stress (ch. 18)
- Task performance (all)
- Citizenship behavior (all)
- Withdrawal behavior (all)

The Group

Inputs
- Group structures (Ch. 9 & 10)
- Group roles (Ch. 9 & 10)
- Team responsibilities (Ch. 9 & 10)

Processes
- Communication (Ch. 11)
- Leadership (Ch. 12)
- Power and politics (Ch. 13)
- Conflict and negotiation (Ch. 14)

Outcomes
- Group collesion (Ch. 9 & 10)
- Group functioning (Ch. 9 & 10)

The Organization

Inputs
- Structure (Ch. 15)
- Culture (Ch. 16)

Processes
- Human resource management (Ch. 17)
- Change practices (Ch. 18)

Outcomes
- Profitability (Ch. 16 & 17)
- Survival (Ch. 16 & 17)

from employee attitudes and behavior to customer attitudes and behavior to a service organization's productivity. Sears has carefully documented this chain.[34] The company's management found that a 5 percent improvement in employee attitudes leads to a 1.3 percent increase in customer satisfaction, which in turn translates into a 0.5 percent improvement in revenue growth. By training employees to improve the employee–customer interaction, Sears was able to improve customer satisfaction by 4 percent over a 12-month period, generating an estimated $200 million in additional revenues.

Survival   The final outcome we will consider is **organizational survival**, which is simply evidence that the organization is able to exist and grow over the long term. The survival of an organization depends not just on how productive the organization is, but also on how well it fits with its environment. A company that is very productively making goods and services of little value to the market is unlikely to survive for long, so survival factors in things like perceiving the market successfully, making good decisions about how and when to pursue opportunities, and engaging in successful change management to adapt to new business conditions.

Having reviewed the input, process, and outcome model, we're going to change the figure up a little bit by grouping topics together based on whether we study them at the individual, group, or organizational level. As you can seen in Exhibit 1-5, we will deal with inputs, processes, and outcomes at all three levels of

group cohesion   The extent to which members of a group support and validate one another while at work.

group functioning   The quantity and quality of a work group's output.

productivity   The combination of the effectiveness and efficiency of an organization.

effectiveness   The degree to which an organization meets the needs of its clientele or customers.

efficiency   The degree to which an organization can achieve its ends at a low cost.

organizational survival   The degree to which an organization is able to exist and grow over the long term.

Does National Culture Affect Organizational Practices?

Companies that operate in more than one country face a challenging dilemma: how much should they tailor organizational practices like leadership style, rewards, and communication to each country's culture? To some extent, it is necessary to change the way a company does business because of differences in regulations, institutions, and labor force characteristics. For example, a U.S. company that operates in Germany will have to contend with laws requiring greater worker participation in decision making, and an Australian company operating in China will have to match the knowledge and skills found in the Chinese workforce. Despite certain limitations imposed by law and situational factors, managers still need to make many decisions about adjusting their organizational culture to match the culture of the countries in which they operate.

There are no simple responses to this dilemma. Some researchers propose that managers need to make a concerted effort to adapt their organizational culture to match the culture of the countries in which they operate. These authors note that within any country, there is a great deal of similarity in management practices that is likely the result of culture or values. If a country's basic outlook is highly individualistic, then organizational culture should also emphasize individual contributions and efforts. Conversely, if national culture values collectivism, then organizational culture should emphasize group contributions and cohesiveness. From this perspective, successful international management is all about tailoring management practices and values to fit with the cultural values of each country in which the company operates.

On the other hand, some propose that national culture should not, and does not, make much difference in shaping organizational culture. These researchers note that even within a single country, there can be a great deal of variation in values and norms. The development of practices to match a culture is fraught with problems of stereotyping and over-generalizing about the degree to which everyone in a given country shares the same values. These authors also note that in tailoring practices to each country, a firm loses the potential value of having a unifying organizational culture. From this perspective, companies should try as much as possible to create a strong culture that operates across borders to create a unified global workforce.

Sources: Based on B. Gerhart, "How Much Does National Culture Constrain Organizational Culture," *Management and Organization Review 5*, no. 2 (2009), pp. 241–259; A. S. Tsui, S. S. Nifadkar, and A. Y. Ou, "Cross-national, Cross-cultural Organizational Behavior Research: Advances, Gaps, and Recommendations," *Journal of Management 33*, no. 3 (2007), pp. 426–478; G. Johns, "The Essential Impact of Context on Organizational Behavior," *Academy of Management Review* 31, no. 2 (2006), pp. 386–408.

analysis, but we group the chapters as shown here to correspond with the typical ways that research has been done in these areas. It is easier to understand one unified presentation about how personality leads to motivation which leads to performance, than to jump around levels of analysis. Because each level builds on the one that precedes it, after going through them in sequence you will have a good idea of how the human side of organizations functions.

Summary and Implications for Managers

Managers need to develop their interpersonal, or people, skills to be effective in their jobs. Organizational behavior (OB) investigates the impact that individuals, groups, and structure have on behavior within an organization, and it applies that knowledge to make organizations work more effectively. Specifically, OB focuses on how to improve productivity; reduce absenteeism,

Lost in Translation?

POINT

Walk into your nearest major bookstore. You'll undoubtedly find a large selection of books devoted to management and managing. Consider the following recent titles:

- *Tough Cookies: What 100 Years of the Girl Scouts Can Teach You* (Wiley, 2011)
- *From Wags to Riches: How Dogs Teach Us to Succeed in Business & Life* (BenBella Books, 2011)
- *All I Know About Management I Learned from My Dog: The Real Story of Angel, a Rescued Golden Retriever, Who Inspired the New Four Golden Rules of Management* (Skyhorse Publishing, 2011)
- *Mother Teresa, CEO: Unexpected Principles for Practical Leadership* (Berrett-Koehler Publishers, 2011)
- *Polar Bear Pirates and Their Quest to Engage the Sleepwalkers: Motivate Everyday People to Deliver Extraordinary Results* (Capstone, 2011)
- *Winnie-the-Pooh on Management: In Which a Very Important Bear and His Friends Are Introduced to a Very Important Subject* (Penguin, 2011)
- *Chicken Lips, Wheeler-Dealer, and the Beady-Eyed M.B.A.: An Entrepreneurs Wild Adventures on the New Silk Road* (Wiley, 2011)
- *Bodybuilders in Tutus: and 35 Other Obscure Business-Boosting Observations* (Robinwood Press, 2011)
- *I'll Make You an Offer You Can't Refuse: Insider Business Tips from a Former Mob Boss* (Thomas Nelson, 2011)
- *The Art of War from SmarterComics: How to be Successful in Any Competition* (Writers of The Round Table Press, 2011)

Popular books on organizational behavior often have cute titles and are fun to read, but they make the job of managing people seem much simpler than it is. Most are based on the author's opinions rather than substantive research, and it is doubtful that one person's experience translates into effective management practice for everyone. Why do we waste our time on "fluff" when, with a little effort, we can access knowledge produced from thousands of scientific studies on human behavior in organizations?

Organizational behavior is a complex subject. Few, if any, simple statements about human behavior are generalizable to all people in all situations. Should you really try to apply leadership insights you got from a book about Geronimo or Tony Soprano to managing software engineers in the twenty-first century?

COUNTERPOINT

Organizations are always looking for leaders, and managers and manager-wannabes are continually looking for ways to hone their leadership skills. Publishers respond to this demand by offering hundreds of titles that promise insights into managing people. Books like these can provide people with the secrets to management that others know about. Moreover, isn't it better to learn about management from people in the trenches, as opposed to the latest esoteric musings from the "Ivory Tower"? Many of the most important insights we gain from life aren't necessarily the product of careful empirical research studies.

It is true there are some bad books out there. But do they outnumber the esoteric research studies published every year? For example, a couple of recent management and organizational behavior studies were published in 2011 with the following titles:

- *Training for Fostering Knowledge Co-Construction from Collaborative Inference-Drawing*
- *The Factor Structure and Cross-Test Convergence of the Mayer–Salovey–Caruso Model of Emotional Intelligence*
- *Refining Value-Based Differentiation in Business Relationships: A Study of the Higher Order Relationship Building Blocks that Influence Behavioural Intentions*
- *A Dialogical Approach to the Creation of New Knowledge in Organizations*

We don't mean to poke fun at these studies. Rather, our point is that you can't judge a book by its cover any more than you can a research study by its title.

There is no one right way to learn the science and art of managing people in organizations. The most enlightened managers are those who gather insights from multiple sources: their own experience, research findings, observations of others, and, yes, business press books, too. If great management were produced by carefully gleaning results from research studies, academicians would make the best managers. How often do we see that?

Research and academics have an important role to play in understanding effective management. But it isn't fair to condemn all business books by citing the worst (or, at least, the worse-sounding ones).

turnover, and deviant workplace behavior; and increase organizational citizenship behavior and job satisfaction. Here are a few specific implications for managers:

- Some generalizations provide valid insights into human behavior, but many are erroneous. Organizational behavior uses systematic study to improve predictions of behavior over intuition alone.
- Because people are different, we need to look at OB in a contingency framework, using situational variables to explain cause-and-effect relationships.
- Organizational behavior offers specific insights to improve a manager's people skills.
- It helps managers to see the value of workforce diversity and practices that may need to be changed in different countries.
- It can improve quality and employee productivity by showing managers how to empower their people, design and implement change programs, improve customer service, and help employees balance work–life conflicts.
- It can help managers cope in a world of temporariness and learn how to stimulate innovation.
- Finally, OB can guide managers in creating an ethically healthy work climate.

MyManagementLab

Now that you have finished this chapter, go back to **www.pearsonglobaleditions.com/ mymanagementlab** to continue practicing and applying the concepts you've learned.

QUESTIONS FOR REVIEW

1 What is the importance of interpersonal skills?

2 What do managers do in terms of functions, roles, and skills?

3 What is organizational behavior (OB)?

4 Why is it important to complement intuition with systematic study?

5 What are the major behavioral science disciplines that contribute to OB?

6 Why are there few absolutes in OB?

7 What are the challenges and opportunities for managers in using OB concepts?

8 What are the three levels of analysis in this book's OB model?

EXPERIENTIAL EXERCISE Workforce Diversity

Purpose
To learn about the different needs of a diverse workforce.

Time Required
Approximately 40 minutes.

Participants and Roles
Divide the class into six groups of approximately equal size. Assign each group one of the following roles:

Nancy is 28 years old. The divorced mother of three children ages 3, 5, and 7, she is the department head.

She earns $40,000 per year at her job and receives another $3,600 per year in child support from her ex-husband.

Ethel is a 72-year-old widow. She works 25 hours per week at an hourly wage of $8.50 to supplement her $8,000 annual pension and earns a total of $19,000 per year.

John is a 34-year-old born in Trinidad who is now a U.S. resident. He is married and the father of two small children. John attends college at night and is within a year of earning his bachelor's degree. His salary is $27,000 per year. His wife is an attorney and earns approximately $50,000 per year.

Lu is 26 years old and single with a master's degree in education. He is paralyzed and confined to a wheelchair as a result of an auto accident. He earns $32,000 per year.

Maria is a single, 22-year-old woman born and raised in Mexico. She came to the United States only 3 months ago, and her English needs considerable improvement. She earns $20,000 per year.

Mike is a 16-year-old high school sophomore who works 15 hours per week after school and during vacations. He earns $7.20 per hour, or approximately $5,600 per year.

The members of each group are to assume the character consistent with their assigned role.

Background

The six participants work for a company that has recently installed a flexible benefits program. Instead of the traditional "one benefit package fits all," the company is allocating an additional 25 percent of each employee's annual pay to be used for discretionary benefits. Those benefits and their annual cost are as follows:

- Supplementary health care for employee:
  Plan A (no deductible and pays 90 percent) = $3,000
  Plan B ($200 deductible and pays 80 percent) = $2,000
  Plan C ($1,000 deductible and pays 70 percent) = $500
- Supplementary health care for dependents (same deductibles and percentages as above):
  Plan A = $2,000
  Plan B = $1,500
  Plan C = $500
- Supplementary dental plan = $500

- Life insurance:
  Plan A ($25,000 coverage) = $500
  Plan B ($50,000 coverage) = $1,000
  Plan C ($100,000 coverage) = $2,000
  Plan D ($250,000 coverage) = $3,000
- Mental health plan = $500
- Prepaid legal assistance = $300
- Vacation = 2 percent of annual pay for each week, up to 6 weeks a year
- Pension at retirement equal to approximately 50 percent of final annual earnings = $1,500
- 4-day workweek during the 3 summer months (available only to full-time employees) = 4 percent of annual pay
- Day care services (after company contribution) = $2,000 for all of an employee's children, regardless of number
- Company-provided transportation to and from work = $750
- College tuition reimbursement = $1,000
- Language class tuition reimbursement = $500

The Task

1. Each group has 15 minutes to develop a flexible benefits package that consumes 25 percent (and no more!) of its character's pay.

2. After completing step 1, each group appoints a spokesperson who describes to the entire class the benefits package the group has arrived at for its character.

3. The entire class then discusses the results. How did the needs, concerns, and problems of each participant influence the group's decision? What do the results suggest for trying to motivate a diverse workforce?

Source: Special thanks to Professor Penny Wright (San Diego State University) for her suggestions during the development of this exercise.

ETHICAL DILEMMA Jekyll and Hyde

Let's assume you have been offered a job by Jekyll Corporation, a company in the consumer products industry. The job is in your chosen career path.

Jekyll Corporation has offered you a position that would begin 2 weeks after you graduate. The job responsibilities are appealing to you, make good use of your training, and are intrinsically interesting. The company seems well positioned financially, and you have met the individual who would be your supervisor, who assures you that the future prospects for your position and career are

bright. Several other graduates of your program work at Jekyll Corporation, and they speak quite positively of the company and promise to socialize and network with you once you start.

As a company, Jekyll Corporation promotes itself as a fair-trade and sustainable organization. Fair trade is a trading partnership—based on dialogue, transparency, and respect—that seeks greater equity in international trade. It contributes to sustainable development by offering better trading conditions to, and securing the rights of, local producers and businesses. Fair-trade organizations are actively engaged in supporting producers and sustainable environmental farming practices, and fair-trade practices prohibit child or forced labor.

Yesterday, Gabriel Utterson—a human resources manager at Jekyll Corporation—called you to discuss initial terms of the offer, which seemed reasonable and standard for the industry. However, one aspect was not mentioned, your starting salary. Gabriel said Jekyll is an internally transparent organization—there are no secrets. While the firm very much wants to hire you, there are limits to what it can afford to offer, and before it makes a formal offer, it was reasonable to ask what you would expect. Gabriel wanted you to think about this and call back tomorrow.

Before calling Gabriel, you thought long and hard about what it would take to accept Jekyll Corporation's offer. You have a number in mind, which may or may not be the same number you give Gabriel. What starting salary would it take for you to accept Jekyll Corporation's offer?

Questions

1. What starting salary will you give Gabriel? What salary represents the minimum offer you would accept? If these two numbers are different, why? Does giving Gabriel a different number than your "internal" number violate Jekyll Corporation's transparent culture? Why or why not?

2. Assume you've received another offer, this one from Hyde Associates. Like the Jekyll job, this position is on your chosen career path and in the consumer products industry. Assume, however, that you've read in the news that *"Hyde Associates has been criticized for unsustainable manufacturing practices that may be harmful to the environment. It has further been criticized for unfair trade practices and for employing underage children."* Would that change whether you'd be willing to take the job? Why or why not?

3. These scenarios are based on studies of Corporate Social Responsibility (CSR) practices that show consumers generally charge a kind of rent to companies that do not practice CSR. In other words, they generally expect a substantial discount in order to buy a product from Hyde rather than from Jekyll. For example, if Jekyll and Hyde sold coffee, people would pay a premium of $1.40 to buy coffee from Jekyll and demand a discount of $2.40 to buy Hyde coffee. Do you think this preference translates into job choice decisions? Why or why not?

CASE INCIDENT 1 "Lessons for 'Undercover' Bosses"

Executive offices in major corporations are often far removed from the day-to-day work that most employees perform. While top executives might enjoy the perquisites found in the executive suite, and separation from workday concerns can foster a broader perspective on the business, the distance between management and workers can come at a real cost: top managers often fail to understand the ways most employees do their jobs every day. The dangers of this distant approach are clear. Executives sometimes make decisions without recognizing how difficult or impractical they are to implement. Executives can also lose sight of the primary challenges their employees face.

The practice of "management by walking around" (MBWA) works against the insularity of the executive suite. To practice MBWA, managers reserve time to walk through departments regularly, form networks of acquaintances in the organization, and get away from their desks to talk to individual employees. The practice was exemplified by Bill Hewlett and Dave Packard, who used this management style at HP to learn more about the challenges and opportunities their employees were encountering. Many other organizations followed suit and found that this style of management had advantages over a typical desk-bound approach to management. A recent study of successful Swedish organizations revealed that MBWA was an approach common to several firms that received national awards for being great places to work.

The popular television program *Undercover Boss* took MBWA to the next level by having top executives from companies like Chiquita Brands, DirectTV, Great Wolf Resorts, and NASCAR work incognito among line employees. Executives reported that this process taught them how difficult many of the jobs in their organizations were, and just how much skill was required to perform even the lowest-level tasks. They also said the experience taught them a lot about the core business in their organizations and sparked ideas for improvements.

Although MBWA has long had its advocates, it does present certain problems. First, the time managers spend directly observing the workforce is time they are not doing their core job tasks like analysis, coordination, and strategic planning. Second, management based on subjective impressions gathered by walking around runs counter to a research and data-based approach to making managerial decisions. Third, it is also possible that executives who wander about will be seen as intruders and overseers. Implementing the MBWA style requires a great deal of foresight to avoid these potential pitfalls.

Questions

1. What are some of the things managers can learn by walking around and having daily contact with line employees that they might not be able to learn from looking at data and reports?

2. As an employee, would you appreciate knowing your supervisor regularly spent time with workers? How would knowing top executives routinely interact with line employees affect your attitudes toward the organization?

3. What ways can executives and other organizational leaders learn about day-to-day business operations besides going "undercover?"

4. Are there any dangers in the use of a management by walking around strategy? Could this strategy lead employees to feel they are being spied on? What actions on the part of managers might minimize these concerns?

Sources: Based on T. Peters and N. Austin, "Management by Walking About," *Economist* (September 8, 2008), www.economist.com; F. Aguirre, M. White, K. Schaefer, and S. Phelps, "Secrets of an Undercover Boss," *Fortune* (August 27, 2010), pp. 41–44; J. Larsson, I. Backstrom, and H. Wiklund, "Leadership and Organizational Behavior: Similarities between Three Award-Winning Organizations," *International Journal of Management Practice 3* (2009), pp. 327–345.

CASE INCIDENT 2 Era of the Disposable Worker?

The great global recession has claimed many victims. In many countries, unemployment is at near-historic highs, and even those who have managed to keep their jobs have often been asked to accept reduced work hours or pay cuts. Another consequence of the current business and economic environment is an increase in the number of individuals employed on a temporary or contingent basis.

The statistics on U.S. temporary workers are grim. Many, like single mother Tammy Smith, have no health insurance, no retirement benefits, no vacation, no severance, and no access to unemployment insurance. Increases in layoffs mean that many jobs formerly considered safe have become "temporary" in the sense that they could disappear at any time with little warning. Forecasts suggest that the next 5 to 10 years will be similar, with small pay increases, worse working conditions, and low levels of job security. As Peter Cappelli of the University of Pennsylvania's Wharton School notes, "Employers are trying to get rid of all fixed costs. First they did it with employment benefits. Now they're doing it with the jobs themselves. Everything is variable."

We might suppose these corporate actions are largely taking place in an era of diminishing profitability. However, data from the financial sector is not consistent with this explanation. Among *Fortune* 500 companies, 2009 saw the second-largest jump in corporate earnings in the list's 56-year history. Moreover, many of these gains do not appear to be the result of increases in revenue. Rather, they reflect dramatic decreases in labor costs. One equity market researcher noted, "The largest part of the gain came from lower payrolls rather than the sluggish rise in sales . . ." Wages also rose only slightly during this period of rapidly increasing corporate profitability.

Some observers suggest the very nature of corporate profit monitoring is to blame for the discrepancy between corporate profitability and outcomes for workers. Some have noted that teachers whose evaluations are based on standardized test scores tend to "teach to the test," to the detriment of other areas of learning. In the same way, when a company is judged primarily by the single metric of a stock price, executives naturally try their best to increase this number, possibly to the detriment of other concerns like employee well-being or corporate culture. On the other hand, others defend corporate actions that increase the degree to which they can treat labor flexibly, noting that in an increasingly competitive global marketplace, it might be necessary to sacrifice some jobs to save the organization as a whole.

The issues of how executives make decisions about workforce allocation, how job security and corporate loyalty influence employee behavior, and how emotional reactions come to surround these issues are all core components of organizational behavior research.

Questions

1. To what extent can individual business decisions (as opposed to economic forces) explain deterioration in working conditions for many workers?

2. Do business organizations have a responsibility to ensure that employees have secure jobs with good

working conditions, or is their primary responsibility to shareholders?

3. What alternative measures of organizational performance, besides share prices, do you think might change the focus of business leaders?

4. What do you think the likely impact of the growth of temporary employment relationships will be for employee attitudes and behaviors? How would you develop a measurement system to evaluate the impact of corporate downsizing and temporary job assignments on employees?

Sources: Based on P. Coy, M. Conlin, and M. Herbst, "The Disposable Worker," *Bloomberg Businessweek* (January 7, 2010), www.businessweek.com; S. Tully, "Fortune 500: Profits Bounce Back," *Fortune* (May 3, 2010), pp. 140–144; D. Ariely, "You Are What You Measure," *Harvard Business Review* (June 2010), p. 38.

ENDNOTES

1. Cited in R. Alsop, "Playing Well with Others," *Wall Street Journal* (September 9, 2002).
2. See, for instance, C. Penttila, "Hiring Hardships," *Entrepreneur* (October 2002), pp. 34–35.
3. S. E. Humphrey, J. D. Nahrgang, and F. P. Morgeson, "Integrating Motivational, Social, and Contextual Work Design Features: A Meta-Analytic Summary and Theoretical Extension of the Work Design Literature," *Journal of Applied Psychology* 92, no. 5 (2007), pp. 1332–1356.
4. I. S. Fulmer, B. Gerhart, and K. S. Scott, "Are the 100 Best Better? An Empirical Investigation of the Relationship Between Being a 'Great Place to Work' and Firm Performance," *Personnel Psychology* (Winter 2003), pp. 965–993.
5. H. Fayol, *Industrial and General Administration* (Paris: Dunod, 1916).
6. A. I. Kraut, P. R. Pedigo, D. D. McKenna, and M. D. Dunnette, "The Role of the Manager: What's Really Important in Different Management Jobs," *Academy of Management Executive* 19, no. 4 (2005), pp. 122–129.
7. H. Mintzberg, *The Nature of Managerial Work* (Upper Saddle River, NJ: Prentice Hall, 1973).
8. R. L. Katz, "Skills of an Effective Administrator," *Harvard Business Review* (September–October 1974), pp. 90–102; D. Bartram, "The Great Eight Competencies: A Criterion-Centric Approach to Validation," *Journal of Applied Psychology* 90, no. 6 (2005), pp. 1185–1203; and S. E. Scullen, M. K. Mount, and T. A. Judge, "Evidence of the Construct Validity of Developmental Ratings of Managerial Performance," *Journal of Applied Psychology* 88, no. 1 (2003), pp. 50–66.
9. F. Luthans, "Successful vs. Effective Real Managers," *Academy of Management Executive* (May 1988), pp. 127–132; and F. Luthans, R. M. Hodgetts, and S. A. Rosenkrantz, *Real Managers* (Cambridge, MA: Ballinger, 1988). See also F. Shipper and J. Davy, "A Model and Investigation of Managerial Skills, Employees' Attitudes, and Managerial Performance," *Leadership Quarterly* 13 (2002), pp. 95–120.
10. P. Wu, M. Foo, and D. B. Turban, "The Role of Personality in Relationship Closeness, Developer Assistance, and Career Success," *Journal of Vocational Behavior* 73, no. 3 (2008), pp. 440–448; and A. M. Konrad, R. Kashlak, I. Yoshioka, R. Waryszak, and N. Toren, "What Do Managers Like to Do? A Five-Country Study," *Group & Organization Management* (December 2001), pp. 401–433.
11. A. S. Tsui, S. J. Ashford, L. St. Clair, and K. R. Xin, "Dealing with Discrepant Expectations: Response Strategies and Managerial Effectiveness," *Academy of Management Journal* (December 1995), pp. 1515–1543.
12. See, for instance, C. Heath and S. B. Sitkin, "Big-B Versus Big-O: What Is *Organizational* about Organizational Behavior?" *Journal of Organizational Behavior* (February 2001), pp. 43–58. For a review of what one eminent researcher believes *should* be included in organizational behavior, based on survey data, see J. B. Miner, "The Rated Importance, Scientific Validity, and Practical Usefulness of Organizational Behavior Theories: A Quantitative Review," *Academy of Management Learning & Education* (September 2003), pp. 250–268.
13. D. M. Rousseau and S. McCarthy, "Educating Managers from an Evidence-Based Perspective," *Academy of Management Learning & Education* 6, no. 1 (2007), pp. 84–101; and S. L. Rynes, T. L. Giluk, and K. G. Brown, "The Very Separate Worlds of Academic and Practitioner Periodicals in Human Resource Management: Implications for Evidence-Based Management," *Academy of Management Journal* 50, no. 5 (2007), pp. 987–1008.
14. J. Surowiecki, "The Fatal-Flaw Myth," *The New Yorker* (July 31, 2006), p. 25.
15. C. Tuna, "No-Layoff Policies Crumble," *The Wall Street Journal* (December 29, 2008), p. B2.
16. See, for instance, S. D. Pugh, J. Dietz, J. W. Wiley, and S. M. Brooks, "Driving Service Effectiveness through Employee-Customer Linkages," *Academy of Management Executive* (November 2002), pp. 73–84; and H. Liao and A. Chuang, "A Multilevel Investigation of Factors Influencing Employee Service Performance and Customer Outcomes," *Academy of Management Journal* (February 2004), pp. 41–58.
17. See www.patagonia.com/jobs/retail_asst_mgr.shtml; and "Patagonia Sets the Pace for Green Business," *Grist Magazine* (October 22, 2004), www.grist.org.
18. See, for instance, M. Workman and W. Bommer, "Redesigning Computer Call Center Work: A Longitudinal Field Experiment," *Journal of Organizational Behavior* (May 2004), pp. 317–337.
19. See, for instance, V. S. Major, K. J. Klein, and M. G. Ehrhart, "Work Time, Work Interference with Family, and Psychological Distress," *Journal of Applied Psychology* (June 2002), pp. 427–436; D. Brady, "Rethinking the Rat Race," *BusinessWeek* (August 26, 2002), pp. 142–143; J. M. Brett and L. K. Stroh, "Working 61

Plus Hours a Week: Why Do Managers Do It?" *Journal of Applied Psychology* (February 2003), pp. 67–78.

20. See, for instance, *The 2002 National Study of the Changing Workforce* (New York: Families and Work Institute, 2002); and W. J. Casper and L. C. Buffardi, "Work-Life Benefits and Job Pursuit Intentions: The Role of Anticipated Organizational Support," *Journal of Vocational Behavior* 65, no. 3 (2004), pp. 391–410.

21. Cited in S. Armour, "Workers Put Family First Despite Slow Economy, Jobless Fear" (citation number 21) is: S. Armour, "Workers Put Family First Despite Slow Economy, Jobless Fears," USA Today, (June 6, 2002), p. 38.

22. S. Shellenbarger, "What Job Candidates Really Want to Know: Will I Have a Life?" *The Wall Street Journal* (November 17, 1999), p. B1; and "U.S. Employers Polish Image to Woo a Demanding New Generation," *Manpower Argus* (February 2000), p. 2.

23. F. Luthans and C. M. Youssef, "Emerging Positive Organizational Behavior," *Journal of Management* (June 2007), pp. 321–349; C. M. Youssef and F. Luthans, "Positive Organizational Behavior in the Workplace: The Impact of Hope, Optimism, and Resilience," *Journal of Management* 33, no. 5 (2007), pp. 774–800; and J. E. Dutton and S. Sonenshein, "Positive Organizational Scholarship," in C. Cooper and J. Barling (eds.), *Encyclopedia of Positive Psychology* (Thousand Oaks, CA: Sage, 2007).

24. L. M. Roberts, G. Spreitzer, J. Dutton, R. Quinn, E. Heaphy, and B. Barker, "How to Play to Your Strengths," *Harvard Business Review* (January 2005), pp. 1–6; and L. M. Roberts, J. E. Dutton, G. M. Spreitzer, E. D. Heaphy, and R. E. Quinn, "Composing the Reflected Best-Self Portrait: Becoming Extraordinary in Work Organizations," *Academy of Management Review* 30, no. 4 (2005), pp. 712–736.

25. W. Bailey and A. Spicer, "When Does National Identity Matter? Convergence and Divergence in International Business Ethics," *Academy of Management Journal* 50, no. 6 (2007), pp. 1462–1480; and A. B. Oumlil and J. L. Balloun,

"Ethical Decision-Making Differences between American and Moroccan Managers," *Journal of Business Ethics* 84, no. 4 (2009), pp. 457–478.

26. J. Merritt, "For MBAs, Soul-Searching 101," *Business Week* (September 16, 2002), pp. 64–66; and S. Greenhouse, "The Mood at Work: Anger and Anxiety," *The New York Times* (October 29, 2002), p. E1.

27. See, for instance, G. R. Weaver, L. K. Trevino, and P. L. Cochran, "Corporate Ethics Practices in the Mid-1990's: An Empirical Study of the Fortune 1000," *Journal of Business Ethics* (February 1999), pp. 283–294; and C. De Mesa Graziano, "Promoting Ethical Conduct: A Review of Corporate Practices," *Strategic Investor Relations* (Fall 2002), pp. 29–35.

28. D. M. Mayer, M. Kuenzi, R. Greenbaum, M. Bardes, and R. Salvador, "How Low Does Ethical Leadership Flow? Test of a Trickle-Down Model," *Organizational Behavior and Human Decision Processes* 108, no. 1 (2009), pp. 1–13; and A. Ardichvili, J. A. Mitchell, and D. Jondle, "Characteristics of Ethical Business Cultures," *Journal of Business Ethics* 85, no. 4 (2009), pp. 445–451.

29. "Unplanned Absence Costs Organizations 8.7 Percent of Payroll, Mercer/Kronos Study" (June 28, 2010), www .mercer.com/press-releases/1383785.

30. W. Hoge, "Sweden's Cradle-to-Grave Welfare Starts to Get Ill," *International Herald Tribune* (September 25, 2002), p. 8.

31. See www.bls.gov/data (May 11, 2005).

32. See, for example, M. C. Sturman and C. O. Trevor, "The Implications of Linking the Dynamic Performance and Turnover Literatures," *Journal of Applied Psychology* (August 2001), pp. 684–696.

33. M. Casey-Campbell and M. L. Martens, "Sticking It All Together: A Critical Assessment of the Group Cohesion-Performance Literature," *International Journal of Management Reviews* 11, (2008), pp. 223–246.

34. A. J. Rucci, S. P. Kirn, and R. T. Quinn, "The Employee–Customer–Profit Chain at Sears," *Harvard Business Review* (January–February 1998), pp. 83–97.

LEARNING OBJECTIVES

After studying this chapter, you should be able to:

1. Describe the two major forms of workforce diversity.

2. Recognize stereotypes and understand how they function in organizational settings.

3. Identify the key biographical characteristics and describe how they are relevant to OB.

4. Define *intellectual ability* and demonstrate its relevance to OB.

5. Contrast intellectual and physical ability.

6. Describe how organizations manage diversity effectively.

MyManagementLab

Access a host of interactive learning aids to help strengthen your understanding of the chapter concepts at **www.pearsonglobaleditions .com/mymanagementlab**.

DIVERSITY IN SINGAPORE

Singapore is a remarkable country in many respects. Economically, Singapore has been one of the fastest growing countries in the world over the past four decades. For example, gross domestic product (GDP) per capita in Singapore has grown from 55 percent of U.S. GDP per capita in 1980 to 120 percent of US GDP per capita in 2010.* Moreover, the country has grown by 7 percent on average in the years from 1960 to 2010 and by an impressive 17.9 percent in the first half of 2010.

At the same time, Singapore is one of the most diverse countries in the world—more than 35 percent of the population are non-natives, and more than half of the population was born outside Singapore. And indeed, the Singaporean population and workforce could not be much more diverse, including Malayans; first-, second-, and third-generation Chinese immigrants from different Chinese provinces; Indians; and Caucasians, among many others. Not only do these ethnic groups speak different languages, they also subscribe to different religions, customs, and values. As such, Singapore is home to a number of large, distinct subgroups, whose members value their cultural and intellectual heritage.

At the same time, Singapore has one of the highest population densities in the world, which requires people to share tight spaces throughout the day, whether this is in public housing, public transport, office space, or on Orchard Road, the main shopping road of the city state. Given the scarcity of space, dealing with different ethnic or religious groups takes on a totally different meaning. Overall, the question arises whether Singapore has experienced such a remarkable growth in spite of its diversity or whether Singapore's diversity has been one of the driving factors in Singapore's transition from a third-world to a first-world country. Restated, is diversity good for business, or does it detract from the bottom line?

We all realize that diversity can sometimes cause conflicts, misunderstandings, and reduce productivity. But Singaporean businesses are experts at dealing with diversity, turning a nuisance into a competitive advantage. To understand this, let's take a closer look at muvee Technologies, a Singapore-based software company that produces automated video editing software for the consumer PC market. Muvee has 50 employees from 13 different countries. One of the key values of muvee is an appreciation of diversity. This manifests itself in a number of ways, some of them more readily observable than others. For example, muvee assists foreign employees in finding accommodation and uses a buddy system to help newcomers with their integration. Departments are allocated money for social events, which

*Controlled for purchasing power parity.

Diversity in Organizations

I think that God in creating Man somewhat overestimated his ability.

— Oscar Wilde

Photo: Singapore Ochard Road. Source: © Henny Westheim Photography/Alamy

promotes a more collegiate work atmosphere and ensures that employees socialize with employees from different backgrounds. Unlike many other companies, however, muvee does not stop here; it has also changed the very nature of work. For example, muvee employs an open-office concept, where all employees, including the CEO, sit in an open office with workspaces without partition walls. Moreover, individuals work in teams that are designed with the purpose of bringing together people with diverse cultural and functional backgrounds. Most importantly, however, the muvee culture makes the biggest difference: recognizing that diversity can increase the number of different viewpoints and valuing diversity shifts the focus from the differences between employees to the goals that muvee wants to accomplish as a company.

Sources: World Bank, World Development Indicators, www.google.com.sg/publicdata/explore?ds=d5bncppjof8f9_&met_y=ny_gdp_pcap_cd&idim=country:SGP&dl=en&hl=en&q=gdp+per+capita, accessed November 2011; Department of Statistics Singapore, www.singstat.gov.sg/stats/keyind.html, accessed November 2011; Managing Workplace Diversity, Ministry of Manpower, http://www.mom.gov.sg/employment-practices/Pages/WDM.aspx, accessed November 2011.

In this chapter, we look at how organizations work to maximize the potential contributions of a diverse workforce. We also show how demographic characteristics such as ethnicity and individual differences in the form of ability affect employee performance and satisfaction.

But first check out the following Self-Assessment Library, where you can assess your views on one of the characteristics we'll discuss in this chapter: age.

SELF-ASSESSMENT LIBRARY

What's My Attitude Toward Older People?

In the Self-Assessment Library (available on CD or online), take assessment IV.C.1 (What's My Attitude Toward Older People?) and answer the following questions:

1. Are you surprised by your results?
2. How do your results compare to those of others?

Diversity

1 Describe the two major forms of workforce diversity.

We aren't all the same. This is obvious enough, but managers sometimes forget that they need to recognize and capitalize on these differences to get the most from their employees. Effective diversity management increases an organization's access to the widest possible pool of skills, abilities, and ideas. Managers also need to recognize that differences among people can lead to miscommunication, misunderstanding, and conflict. In this chapter, we'll learn about how individual characteristics like age, gender, race, ethnicity, and abilities can influence employee performance. We'll also see how managers can develop awareness about these characteristics and manage a diverse workforce effectively.

Demographic Characteristics of the U.S. Workforce

In the past, OB textbooks noted that rapid change was about to occur as the predominantly white, male managerial workforce gave way to a gender-balanced, multiethnic workforce. Today, that change is no longer happening: it has happened, and it is increasingly reflected in the makeup of managerial and professional jobs. Compared to 1976, women today are much more likely to be employed full-time, have more education, and earn wages comparable to those of men.[1] In addition, over the past 50 years the earnings gap between Whites and other racial and ethnic groups has decreased significantly; past differences between Whites and Asians have disappeared or been reversed.[2] Workers over the age of 55 are an increasingly large portion of the workforce as well. This permanent shift toward a diverse workforce means organizations need to make diversity management a central component of their policies and practices. At the same time, however, differences in wages across genders and racial and ethnic groups persist, and executive positions in *Fortune* 500 corporations continue to be held by white males in numbers far beyond their representation in the workforce in general.

A survey by the Society for Human Resources Management shows some major employer concerns and opportunities resulting from the demographic makeup of the U.S. workforce.[3] The aging of the workforce was consistently the most significant concern of HR managers. The loss of skills resulting from the retirement of many baby boomers, increased medical costs due to an aging workforce, and many employees' needs to care for elderly relatives topped the list of issues. Other issues include developing multilingual training materials and providing work–life benefits for dual-career couples.

Progress Energy reflects the demographic characteristics of the U.S. workforce today. It is gender balanced, multiethnic, and engaged in learning about diversity issues and putting them into practice. Progress, which recently merged with Duke Energy, encourages employees to participate in various network groups, diversity councils, and training workshops, such as the one shown here. The company believes that recognizing and embracing diversity maximize employee potential, customer satisfaction, and business success.

Source: Robert Willett / Raleigh News & Observer/Newscom

Levels of Diversity

Although much has been said about diversity in age, race, gender, ethnicity, religion, and disability status, experts now recognize that these demographic characteristics are just the tip of the iceberg.[4] Demographics mostly reflect **surface-level diversity**, not thoughts and feelings, and can lead employees to perceive one another through stereotypes and assumptions. However, evidence has shown that as people get to know one another, they become less concerned about demographic differences if they see themselves as sharing more important characteristics, such as personality and values, that represent **deep-level diversity**.[5]

To understand this difference between surface- and deep-level diversity, consider a few examples. Luis and Carol are co-workers who seem to have little in common at first glance. Luis is a young, recently hired male college graduate with a business degree, raised in a Spanish-speaking neighborhood in Miami. Carol is an older, long-tenured woman raised in rural Kansas, who achieved her current level in the organization by starting as a high school graduate and working her way through the hierarchy. At first, these co-workers may experience some differences in communication based on their surface-level differences in education, ethnicity, regional background, and gender. However, as they get to know one another, they may find they are both deeply committed to their families, share a common way of thinking about important work problems, like to work collaboratively, and are interested in international assignments in the future. These deep-level similarities will overshadow the more superficial differences between them, and research suggests they will work well together.

On the other hand, Steve and Dave are two unmarried white male college graduates from Oregon who recently started working together. Superficially, they seem well matched. But Steve is highly introverted, prefers to avoid risks, solicits the opinions of others before making decisions, and likes the office quiet, while Dave is extroverted, risk-seeking, and assertive and likes a busy, active, and energetic work environment. Their surface-level similarity will not necessarily lead to positive interactions because they have such fundamental, deep-level differences. It will be a challenge for them to collaborate regularly at work, and they'll have to make some compromises to get things done together.

Throughout this book, we will encounter differences between deep- and surface-level diversity in various contexts. Individual differences in personality and culture shape preferences for rewards, communication styles, reactions to leaders, negotiation styles, and many other aspects of behavior in organizations.

Discrimination

2 Recognize stereotypes and understand how they function in organizational settings.

Although diversity does present many opportunities for organizations, effective diversity management also means working to eliminate unfair **discrimination**. To discriminate is to note a difference between things, which in itself isn't necessarily bad. Noticing one employee is more qualified is necessary for making hiring decisions; noticing another is taking on leadership responsibilities exceptionally well is necessary for making promotion decisions. Usually when we talk about discrimination, though, we mean allowing our behavior to be influenced by stereotypes about *groups* of people. Rather than looking at individual characteristics, unfair discrimination assumes everyone in a group is the same. This discrimination is often very harmful to organizations and employees.

Exhibit 2-1 provides definitions and examples of some forms of discrimination in organizations. Although many of these actions are prohibited by law, and therefore aren't part of almost any organization's official policies, thousands of cases of employment discrimination are documented every year, and many more go unreported. As discrimination has increasingly come under both

Exhibit **2-1**	Forms of Discrimination	
Type of Discrimination	**Definition**	**Examples from Organizations**
Discriminatory policies or practices	Actions taken by representatives of the organization that deny equal opportunity to perform or unequal rewards for performance	Older workers may be targeted for layoffs because they are highly paid and have lucrative benefits.
Sexual harassment	Unwanted sexual advances and other verbal or physical conduct of a sexual nature that create a hostile or offensive work environment	Salespeople at one company went on company-paid visits to strip clubs, brought strippers into the office to celebrate promotions, and fostered pervasive sexual rumors.
Intimidation	Overt threats or bullying directed at members of specific groups of employees	African-American employees at some companies have found nooses hanging over their work stations.
Mockery and insults	Jokes or negative stereotypes; sometimes the result of jokes taken too far	Arab-Americans have been asked at work whether they were carrying bombs or were members of terrorist organizations.
Exclusion	Exclusion of certain people from job opportunities, social events, discussions, or informal mentoring; can occur unintentionally	Many women in finance claim they are assigned to marginal job roles or are given light workloads that don't lead to promotion.
Incivility	Disrespectful treatment, including behaving in an aggressive manner, interrupting the person, or ignoring his or her opinions	Female lawyers note that male attorneys frequently cut them off or do not adequately address their comments.

Sources: J. Levitz and P. Shishkin, "More Workers Cite Age Bias after Layoffs," *The Wall Street Journal* (March 11, 2009), pp. D1–D2; W. M. Bulkeley, "A Data-Storage Titan Confronts Bias Claims," *The Wall Street Journal* (September 12, 2007), pp. A1, A16; D. Walker, "Incident with Noose Stirs Old Memories," *McClatchy-Tribune Business News* (June 29, 2008); D. Solis, "Racial Horror Stories Keep EEOC Busy," *Knight-Ridder Tribune Business News*, July 30, 2005, p. 1; H. Ibish and A. Stewart, *Report on Hate Crimes and Discrimination Against Arab Americans: The Post-September 11 Backlash, September 11, 2001—October 11, 2001* (Washington, DC: American-Arab Anti-Discrimination Committee, 2003); A. Raghavan, "Wall Street's Disappearing Women," *Forbes* (March 16, 2009), pp. 72–78; and L. M. Cortina, "Unseen Injustice: Incivility as Modern Discrimination in Organizations," *Academy of Management Review* 33, no. 1 (2008), pp. 55–75.

legal scrutiny and social disapproval, most overt forms have faded, which may have resulted in an increase in more covert forms like incivility or exclusion.[6]

As you can see, discrimination can occur in many ways, and its effects can be just as varied depending on the organizational context and the personal biases of its members. Some forms, like exclusion or incivility, are especially hard to root out because they are impossible to observe and may occur simply because the actor isn't aware of the effects of his or her actions. Whether intentional or not, discrimination can lead to serious negative consequences for employers, including reduced productivity and citizenship behavior, negative conflicts, and increased turnover. Unfair discrimination also leaves qualified job candidates out of initial hiring and promotions. Even if an employment discrimination lawsuit is never filed, a strong business case can be made for aggressively working to eliminate unfair discrimination.

Diversity is a broad term, and the phrase *workplace diversity* can refer to any characteristic that makes people different from one another. The following section covers some important surface-level characteristics that differentiate members of the workforce.

surface-level diversity *Differences in easily perceived characteristics, such as gender, race, ethnicity, age, or disability, that do not necessarily reflect the ways people think or feel but that may activate certain stereotypes.*

deep-level diversity *Differences in values, personality, and work preferences that become progressively more important for determining similarity as people get to know one another better.*

discrimination *Noting of a difference between things; often we refer to unfair discrimination, which means making judgments about individuals based on stereotypes regarding their demographic group.*

Biographical Characteristics

3 Identify the key biographical characteristics and describe how they are relevant to OB.

Biographical characteristics such as age, gender, race, disability, and length of service are some of the most obvious ways employees differ. As discussed in Chapter 1, this textbook is essentially concerned with finding and analyzing the variables that affect employee productivity, absence, turnover, deviance, citizenship, and satisfaction (refer back to Exhibit 1-4). Many organizational concepts—motivation, say, or power and politics or organizational culture—are hard to assess. Let's begin, then, by looking at factors that are easily definable and readily available—data that can be obtained, for the most part, from an employee's human resources (HR) file. Variations in these surface-level characteristics may be the basis for discrimination against classes of employees, so it is worth knowing how closely related they actually are to important work outcomes. Many are not as important as people believe, and far more variation occurs *within* groups sharing biographical characteristics than between them.

Age

The relationship between age and job performance is likely to be an issue of increasing importance during the next decade for at least three reasons. First, belief is widespread that job performance declines with increasing age. Regardless of whether this is true, a lot of people believe it and act on it. Second, as noted in Chapter 1, the workforce is aging. Many employers recognize that older workers represent a huge potential pool of high-quality applicants. Companies such as Borders and the Vanguard Group have sought to increase their attractiveness to older workers by providing targeted training that meets their needs, and by offering flexible work schedules and part-time work to draw in those who are semi-retired.[7] The third reason is U.S. legislation that, for all intents and purposes, outlaws mandatory retirement. Most U.S. workers today no longer have to retire at age 70.

Older employees are an integral part of the workforce at Publix Supermarkets, where one in five employees is over the age of 50. The company values the work ethic and maturity of its senior associates like the man shown here preparing salmon pinwheels for customers to sample. Publix is known for its employment of senior citizens and actively recruits older workers as part of its corporate philosophy of providing a diverse work place. The company believes that older workers have a strong work ethic, many skills, and job knowledge that they can share with younger co-workers.

Source: s70/ZUMA Press/Newscom

What is the perception of older workers? Employers hold mixed feelings.[8] They see a number of positive qualities older workers bring to their jobs, such as experience, judgment, a strong work ethic, and commitment to quality. But older workers are also perceived as lacking flexibility and resisting new technology. And when organizations are actively seeking individuals who are adaptable and open to change, the negatives associated with age clearly hinder the initial hiring of older workers and increase the likelihood they will be let go during cutbacks.

Now let's take a look at the evidence. What effect does age actually have on turnover, absenteeism, productivity, and satisfaction? The older you get, the less likely you are to quit your job. That conclusion is based on studies of the age–turnover relationship.[9] Of course, this shouldn't be too surprising. As workers get older, they have fewer alternative job opportunities as their skills have become more specialized to certain types of work. Their long tenure also tends to provide them with higher wage rates, longer paid vacations, and more attractive pension benefits.

It's tempting to assume that age is also inversely related to absenteeism. After all, if older workers are less likely to quit, won't they also demonstrate higher stability by coming to work more regularly? Not necessarily. Most studies do show an inverse relationship, but close examination finds it is partially a function of whether the absence is avoidable or unavoidable.[10] In general, older employees have lower rates of avoidable absence than do younger employees. However, they have equal rates of unavoidable absence, such as sickness absences.

How does age affect productivity? Many believe productivity declines with age. It is often assumed that skills like speed, agility, strength, and coordination decay over time and that prolonged job boredom and lack of intellectual stimulation contribute to reduced productivity. The evidence, however, contradicts those assumptions. During a 3-year period, a large hardware chain staffed one of its stores solely with employees over age 50 and compared its results with those of five stores with younger employees. The store staffed by the over-50 employees was significantly more productive (in terms of sales generated against labor costs) than two of the stores and held its own against the other three.[11] Other reviews of the research find that age and job task performance are unrelated and that older workers are more likely to engage in citizenship behavior.[12]

Our final concern is the relationship between age and job satisfaction, where the evidence is mixed. A review of more than 800 studies found that older workers tend to be more satisfied with their work, report better relationships with co-workers, and are more committed to their employing organizations.[13] Other studies, however, have found a U-shaped relationship.[14] Several explanations could clear up these results, the most plausible being that these studies are intermixing professional and nonprofessional employees. When we separate the two types, satisfaction tends to continually increase among professionals as they age, whereas it falls among nonprofessionals during middle age and then rises again in the later years.

biographical characteristics   *Personal characteristics—such as age, gender, race, and length of tenure—that are objective and easily obtained from personnel records. These characteristics are representative of surface-level diversity.*

What are the effects of discrimination against individuals on the basis of age? One large-scale study of more than 8,000 employees in 128 companies found that an organizational climate favoring age discrimination was associated with lower levels of commitment to the company. This lower commitment was, in turn, related to lower levels of organizational performance.[15] Such results suggest that combating age discrimination may be associated with higher levels of organizational performance.

Sex

Few issues initiate more debates, misconceptions, and unsupported opinions than whether women perform as well on jobs as men do.

The best place to begin to consider this is with the recognition that few, if any, important differences between men and women affect job performance. There are no consistent male–female differences in problem-solving ability, analytical skills, competitive drive, motivation, sociability, or learning ability.[16] Psychological studies have found women are more agreeable and willing to conform to authority, whereas men are more aggressive and more likely to have expectations of success, but those differences are minor. Given the significantly increased female participation in the workforce over the past 40 years and the rethinking of what constitutes male and female roles, we can assume no significant difference in job productivity between men and women.[17]

Unfortunately, sex roles still affect our perceptions. For example, women who succeed in traditionally male domains are perceived as less likable, more hostile, and less desirable as supervisors.[18] Interestingly, research also suggests that women believe sex-based discrimination is more prevalent than do male employees, and these beliefs are especially pronounced among women who work with a large proportion of men.[19]

One issue that does seem to differ between men and women, especially when the employee has preschool-age children, is preference for work schedules.[20] Working mothers are more likely to prefer part-time work, flexible work schedules, and telecommuting in order to accommodate their family responsibilities. Women also prefer jobs that encourage work–life balance, which has the effect of limiting their options for career advancement. An interview study showed many of the work–life issues found in U.S. business contexts are also common in France, despite government subsidies for child care.[21]

What about absence and turnover rates? Are women less stable employees than men? First, evidence from a study of nearly 500,000 professional employees indicates significant differences, with women more likely to turn over than men.[22] Women also have higher rates of absenteeism than men do.[23] The most logical explanation is that the research was conducted in North America, and North American culture has historically placed home and family responsibilities on women. When a child is ill or someone needs to stay home to wait for a plumber, the woman has traditionally taken time from work. However, this research is also undoubtedly time-bound.[24] The role of women has definitely changed over the past generation. Men are increasingly sharing responsibility for child care, and an increasing number report feeling a conflict between their home responsibilities and their work lives.[25] One interesting finding is that regardless of sex, parents were rated lower in job commitment, achievement striving, and dependability than individuals without children, but mothers were rated especially low in competence.[26]

Again, it is worth asking what the implications of sex discrimination are for individuals. Research has shown that workers who experience sexual harassment

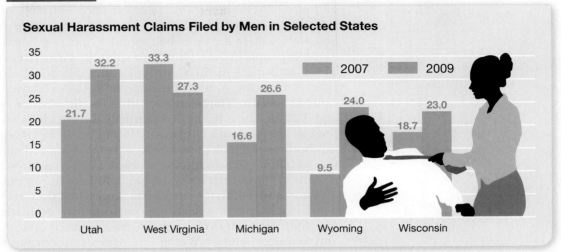

OB Poll   Sexual Harassment Claims by Men

Sexual Harassment Claims Filed by Men in Selected States

Legend: 2007, 2009

- Utah: 21.7 (2007), 32.2 (2009)
- West Virginia: 33.3 (2007), 27.3 (2009)
- Michigan: 16.6 (2007), 26.6 (2009)
- Wyoming: 9.5 (2007), 24.0 (2009)
- Wisconsin: 18.7 (2007), 23.0 (2009)

Sources: Equal Employment Opportunity Commission; D. Mattioli, "More Men Make Harassment Claims," *The Wall Street Journal* (March 23, 2010), p. D4.

have higher levels of psychological stress, and these feelings in turn are related to lower levels of organizational commitment and job satisfaction, and higher intentions to turn over.[27] As with age discrimination, the evidence suggests that combating sex discrimination may be associated with better performance for the organization as a whole.

Myth or Science?

"Dual-Career Couples Divorce Less"

This statement is mostly false.

A recent large-scale study of married couples in the United States, the United Kingdom, and Germany found that in all three countries whether a wife worked outside the home, and what she earned if she did, had no effect on divorce rates. The authors of this study conclude: "In no country did a wife's employment or relative earnings significantly increase the risk of dissolution." Thus, it appears that social critics on both the left (dual-career couples have healthier, happier marriages) and the right (a traditional male working, wife at home family structure is best) are wrong. Still,

this is a complex issue, and research on it continues.

What about whether the *husband* works outside the home? Historically, this was quite unusual, but it is becoming increasingly common— wives are now the primary breadwinner in 22 percent of U.S. couples, up from 7 percent in 1970. There is some evidence that men are less healthy and marriages are more likely to fail when men do not work outside the home, or when they become unemployed while their wives continue to work. As one researcher noted, many married men ask themselves, "What is my value here if I'm not bringing in money?" One

Canadian working mother, the primary breadwinner in her family, says, "There is a part of me that wonders if I can trust, if it's safe for me to take my foot off the gas, to hold back and relax, not be thinking and working all the time."

Sources: L. P. P. Cooke, "Wives' Part-time Employment and Marital Stability in Great Britain, West Germany and the United States," *Sociology* 44, no. 6 (2010), pp. 1091–1108; T. Parker-Pope, "She Works. They're Happy." *The New York Times* (January 24, 2010), pp. ST1, ST10; and S. Proudfoot, "More Women Bringing Home the Bacon, More Men Cooking It," *National Post* (October 7, 2010), www.canada.com/.

Race and Ethnicity

Race is a controversial issue. In many cases, even bringing up the topic of race and ethnicity is enough to create an uncomfortable silence. Indeed, evidence suggests that some people find interacting with other racial groups uncomfortable unless there are clear behavioral scripts to guide their behavior.[28]

Most people in the United States identify themselves according to racial group. The U.S. Bureau of the Census classifies individuals according to seven broad racial categories: American Indian and Alaska Native, Asian, Black or African American, Native Hawaiian and Other Pacific Islander, Some Other Race, White, and Two or More Races. An ethnicity distinction is also made between native English speakers and Hispanics: Hispanics can be of any race. We define *race* in this book as the biological heritage people use to identify themselves; *ethnicity* is the additional set of cultural characteristics that often overlaps with race. This definition allows each individual to define his or her race and ethnicity.

Race and ethnicity have been studied as they relate to employment outcomes such as hiring decisions, performance evaluations, pay, and workplace discrimination. Most research has concentrated on the differences in outcomes and attitudes between Whites and African Americans, with little study of issues relevant to Asian, Native American, and Hispanic populations. Doing justice to all this research isn't possible here, so let's summarize a few points.

First, in employment settings, individuals tend to slightly favor colleagues of their own race in performance evaluations, promotion decisions, and pay raises, although such differences are not found consistently, especially when highly structured methods of decision making are employed.[29] Second, substantial racial differences exist in attitudes toward affirmative action, with African Americans approving of such programs to a greater degree than Whites.[30] This difference may reflect the fact that African Americans and Hispanics perceive discrimination to be more prevalent in the workplace.[31] Third, African Americans generally fare worse than Whites in employment decisions. They receive lower ratings in employment interviews, receive lower job performance ratings, are paid less, and are promoted less frequently.[32] Yet there are no statistically significant differences between African Americans and Whites in observed absence rates, applied social skills at work, or accident rates. African Americans and Hispanics also have higher turnover rates than Whites.

Employers' major concern about using mental-ability tests for selection, promotion, training, and similar employment decisions is that they may have a negative impact on racial and ethnic groups.[33] However, evidence suggests that "despite group differences in mean test performance, there is little convincing evidence that well-constructed tests are more predictive of educational, training, or occupational performance for members of the majority group than for members of minority groups."[34] Observed differences in IQ test scores by racial or ethnic group are smaller in more recent samples.[35] The issue of racial differences in general mental-ability tests continues to be hotly debated.[36]

Does racial and ethnic discrimination lead to negative workplace outcomes? As noted earlier, most research shows that members of racial and ethnic minorities report higher levels of discrimination in the workplace.[37] Some research suggests that having a positive climate for diversity overall can lead to increased sales.[38]

Disability

With the passage of the Americans with Disabilities Act (ADA) in 1990, the representation of individuals with disabilities in the U.S. workforce rapidly increased.[39] According to the ADA, employers are required to make reasonable

Microsoft views employees with disabilities as valuable assets because they help ensure that the company's products and services meet all customer needs. At the Microsoft Accessibility Lab, employees can experience assistive technologies and ergonomic hardware designs that enable them to be more productive. Kelly Ford, who has been blind since birth, is shown here in the lab testing accessibility features of the Windows operating system. Ford also manages a team that is working on improving Web page browsing for all users, not just for people with disabilities.

Source: AP Photo/Ted S. Warren

accommodations so their workplaces will be accessible to individuals with physical or mental disabilities.

Making inferences about the relationship between disability and employment outcomes is difficult because the term *disability* is so broad. The U.S. Equal Employment Opportunity Commission classifies a person as disabled who has any physical or mental impairment that substantially limits one or more major life activities. Examples include missing limbs, seizure disorder, Down Syndrome, deafness, schizophrenia, alcoholism, diabetes, and chronic back pain. These conditions share almost no common features, so there's no generalization about how each condition is related to employment. Some jobs obviously cannot be accommodated to some disabilities—the law and common sense recognize that a blind person could not be a bus driver, a person with severe cerebral palsy could not be a surgeon, and a person with profound mobility constraints probably could not be a police patrol officer. However, the increasing presence of computer technology and other adaptive devices is shattering many traditional barriers to employment.

One of the most controversial aspects of the ADA is the provision that requires employers to make reasonable accommodations for people with psychiatric disabilities.[40] Most people have very strong biases against those with mental illnesses, who are therefore reluctant to disclose this information to employers. Many who do, report negative consequences.

The impact of disabilities on employment outcomes has been explored from a variety of perspectives. On the one hand, a review of the evidence suggests workers with disabilities receive higher performance evaluations. However, this same review found that despite their higher performance, individuals with disabilities tend to encounter lower performance expectations and are less likely to be hired.[41] These negative effects are much stronger for individuals with mental disabilities, and there is some evidence to suggest mental disabilities may impair performance more than physical disabilities: Individuals with such common mental health issues as depression and anxiety are significantly more likely to be absent from work.[42]

Several studies have examined participants who received résumés that were identical, except that some mentioned a disability. The résumés that mentioned mental illness or a physical disability were associated with much lower ratings for perceived employability, especially in jobs requiring a great deal of personal contact with the public.[43] Employability ratings for individuals with mental illnesses were especially low. Similarly, when given randomly manipulated academic portfolios, students preferred not to work with individuals who had a learning disability even though there were no effects of disability on performance ratings or expectations.[44]

Contrast these selection-oriented results with studies showing that the accomplishments of those with disabilities are often rated as more impressive than the same accomplishments in people without disabilities. Participants watched three individuals completing a carpentry task, one of whom was described as having recently been hospitalized for a debilitating mental illness.[45] The raters consistently gave that person higher performance ratings. In this case, it may be that disabled individuals were being treated as an outgroup in need of special help. Similarly, when disability status is randomly manipulated among hypothetical candidates, disabled individuals are rated as having superior personal qualities like dependability and potency.[46]

Other Biographical Characteristics: Tenure, Religion, Sexual Orientation, and Gender Identity

The last set of biographical characteristics we'll look at includes tenure, religion, sexual orientation, and gender identity.

Tenure   Except for gender and racial differences, few issues are more subject to misconceptions and speculations than the impact of seniority on job performance.

Extensive reviews have been conducted of the seniority–productivity relationship.[47] If we define *seniority* as time on a particular job, the most recent evidence demonstrates a positive relationship between seniority and job productivity. So *tenure,* expressed as work experience, appears to be a good predictor of employee productivity.

The research relating tenure to absence is quite straightforward. Studies consistently show seniority to be negatively related to absenteeism.[48] In fact, in terms of both frequency of absence and total days lost at work, tenure is the single most important explanatory variable.[49]

Tenure is also a potent variable in explaining turnover. The longer a person is in a job, the less likely he or she is to quit.[50] Moreover, consistent with research suggesting past behavior is the best predictor of future behavior, evidence indicates tenure at an employee's previous job is a powerful predictor of that employee's future turnover.[51]

Evidence indicates tenure and job satisfaction are positively related.[52] In fact, when age and tenure are treated separately, tenure appears a more consistent and stable predictor of job satisfaction than age.

Religion   Not only do religious and nonreligious people question each other's belief systems; often people of different religious faiths conflict. As the war in Iraq and the past conflict in Northern Ireland demonstrate, violent differences can erupt among sects of the same religion. U.S. federal law prohibits employers from discriminating against employees based on their religion, with very few exceptions. However, that doesn't mean religion is a nonissue in OB.

Perhaps the greatest religious diversity issue in the United States today revolves around Islam. There are nearly 2 million Muslims in the United States,

Religious Tattoos

Considering the following situation . . .

Edward practices the Kemetic religion, based on ancient Egyptian faith, and affiliates himself with a tribe numbering fewer than ten members. He states that he believes in various deities and follows the faith's concept of Ma'at, a guiding principle regarding truth and order that represents physical and moral balance in the universe. During a religious ceremony he received small tattoos encircling his wrist, written in the Coptic language, which express his servitude to Ra, the Egyptian god of the sun. When his employer asks him to cover the tattoos, he explains

that it is a sin to cover them intentionally because doing so would signify a rejection of Ra.

If you were Edward's employer, how would you respond to his request? If several valued customers objected to Edward's tattoos, would it affect your response?

It may surprise you to learn that the Equal Employment Opportunity Commission (EEOC), the chief regulatory agency that enforces laws against workplace discrimination, holds that Edward's employer may not ask him to cover his tattoos. The seeming strangeness of Edward's religious views is not legally relevant. The EEOC notes,

"These can be religious beliefs and practices even if no one else or few other people subscribe to them." If Edward's tattoos did not emanate from sincere religious beliefs, however, the employer could ask him to cover them.

The upshot: Diversity, ethics, and legal compliance are not always the same thing. Sometimes what is legal is not what you might do, and sometimes what you might do is not legal.

Source: N. C. Earp, "Unique Belief Can Be Religious," *EEOC Compliance Manual* (downloaded April 27, 2011), www.eeoc.gov/policy/docs/religion.html.

and across the world Islam is one of the most popular religions. There are a wide variety of perspectives on Islam. As one Islamic scholar has noted, "There is no such thing as a single American Muslim community, much as there is no single Christian community. Muslims vary hugely by ethnicity, faith, tradition, education, income, and degree of religious observance."[53] For the most part, U.S. Muslims have attitudes similar to those of other U.S. citizens (though the differences tend to be greater for younger U.S. Muslims). Still, there are both perceived and real differences. Nearly four in ten U.S. adults admit they harbor negative feelings or prejudices toward U.S. Muslims, and 52 percent believe U.S. Muslims are not respectful of women. Some take these general biases a step further. Motaz Elshafi, a 28-year-old software engineer for Cisco Systems, born and raised in New Jersey, received an e-mail from a co-worker addressed "Dear Terrorist." Research has shown that job applicants in Muslim-identified religious attire who applied for hypothetical retail jobs in the United States had shorter, more interpersonally negative interviews than applicants who did not wear Muslim-identified attire.[54]

Faith can be an employment issue when religious beliefs prohibit or encourage certain behaviors. Based on their religious beliefs, some pharmacists refuse to hand out RU-486, the "morning after" abortion pill. Many Christians do not believe they should work on Sundays, and many conservative Jews believe they should not work on Saturdays. Religious individuals may also believe they have an obligation to express their beliefs in the workplace, and those who do not share those beliefs may object. Perhaps as a result of different perceptions of religion's role in the workplace, religious discrimination claims have been a growing source of discrimination claims in the United States.

Sexual Orientation and Gender Identity   Employers differ widely in their treatment of sexual orientation. Federal law does not prohibit discrimination against employees based on sexual orientation, though many states and municipalities do. In general, observers note that even in the absence of federal legislation requiring nondiscrimination, many organizations have implemented policies and procedures protecting employees on the basis of sexual orientation.[55]

Raytheon, builder of Tomahawk cruise missiles and other defense systems, offers domestic-partner benefits, supports a wide array of gay rights groups, and wants to be an employer of choice for gays. The firm believes these policies give it an advantage in the ever-competitive market for engineers and scientists. Raytheon is not alone. More than half the *Fortune* 500 companies offer domestic-partner benefits for gay couples, including American Express, IBM, Intel, Morgan Stanley, Motorola, and Walmart. Some companies oppose domestic-partner benefits or nondiscrimination clauses for gay employees. Among these are Alltel, ADM, ExxonMobil, H. J. Heinz, Nissan, Nestlé, and Rubbermaid.[56] Despite some gains, many lesbian, gay, and bisexual employees keep their gender identity from their co-workers for fear of being discriminated against.[57]

As for gender identity, companies are increasingly putting in place policies to govern how their organization treats employees who change genders (often called *transgender employees*). In 2001, only eight companies in the *Fortune* 500 had policies on gender identity. By 2006, that number had swelled to 124. IBM is one of them. Brad Salavich, a diversity manager for IBM, says, "We believe that having strong transgender and gender identification policies is a natural extension of IBM's corporate culture." Dealing with transgender employees requires some special considerations, such as for bathrooms, employee names, and so on.[58]

Ability

We've so far covered surface characteristics unlikely, on their own, to directly relate to job performance. Now we turn to deep-level abilities that *are* closely related to job performance. Contrary to what we were taught in grade school, we weren't all created equal in our abilities. Most people are to the left or the right of the median on some normally distributed ability curve. For example, regardless of how motivated you are, it's unlikely you can act as well as Scarlett Johansson, play basketball as well as LeBron James, write as well as J. K. Rowling, or play the guitar as well as Pat Metheny. Of course, just because we aren't all equal in abilities does not imply that some individuals are inherently inferior. Everyone has strengths and weaknesses that make him or her relatively superior or inferior to others in performing certain tasks or activities. From management's standpoint, the issue is not whether people differ in terms of their abilities. They clearly do. The issue is using the knowledge that people differ to increase the likelihood an employee will perform his or her job well.

What does *ability* mean? As we use the term, **ability** is an individual's current capacity to perform the various tasks in a job. Overall abilities are essentially made up of two sets of factors: intellectual and physical.

Intellectual Abilities

4 Define *intellectual ability* and demonstrate its relevance to OB.

Intellectual abilities are abilities needed to perform mental activities—thinking, reasoning, and problem solving. Most societies place a high value on intelligence, and for good reason. Smart people generally earn more money and attain higher levels of education. They are also more likely to emerge as leaders of

Exhibit **2-2**	Dimensions of Intellectual Ability	
Dimension	**Description**	**Job Example**
Number aptitude	Ability to do speedy and accurate arithmetic	Accountant: Computing the sales tax on a set of items
Verbal comprehension	Ability to understand what is read or heard and the relationship of words to each other	Plant manager: Following corporate policies on hiring
Perceptual speed	Ability to identify visual similarities and differences quickly and accurately	Fire investigator: Identifying clues to support a charge of arson
Inductive reasoning	Ability to identify a logical sequence in a problem and then solve the problem	Market researcher: Forecasting demand for a product in the next time period
Deductive reasoning	Ability to use logic and assess the implications of an argument	Supervisor: Choosing between two different suggestions offered by employees
Spatial visualization	Ability to imagine how an object would look if its position in space were changed	Interior decorator: Redecorating an office
Memory	Ability to retain and recall past experiences	Salesperson: Remembering the names of customers

groups. Intelligence quotient (IQ) tests, for example, are designed to ascertain a person's general intellectual abilities. So, too, are popular college admission tests, such as the SAT and ACT and graduate admission tests in business (GMAT), law (LSAT), and medicine (MCAT). Testing firms don't claim their tests assess intelligence, but experts know they do.[59] The seven most frequently cited dimensions making up intellectual abilities are number aptitude, verbal comprehension, perceptual speed, inductive reasoning, deductive reasoning, spatial visualization, and memory.[60] Exhibit 2-2 describes these dimensions.

Intelligence dimensions are positively related, so if you score high on verbal comprehension, for example, you're more likely to also score high on spatial visualization. The correlations aren't perfect, meaning people do have specific abilities that predict important work-related outcomes when considered individually.[61] However, they are high enough that researchers also recognize a general factor of intelligence, **general mental ability (GMA)**. Evidence strongly supports the idea that the structures and measures of intellectual abilities generalize across cultures. Thus, someone in Venezuela or Sudan does not have a different set of mental abilities than a U.S. or Czech worker. There is some evidence that IQ scores vary to some degree across cultures, but those differences are much smaller when we take into account educational and economic differences.[62]

Jobs differ in the demands they place on intellectual abilities. The more complex a job in terms of information-processing demands, the more general intelligence and verbal abilities will be necessary to perform successfully.[63]

ability *An individual's capacity to perform the various tasks in a job.*

intellectual abilities *The capacity to do mental activities—thinking, reasoning, and problem solving.*

general mental ability (GMA) *An overall factor of intelligence, as suggested by the positive correlations among specific intellectual ability dimensions.*

Images of Diversity from Around the Globe

As economic globalization continues to expand, the very idea of diversity management must expand to include a diversity of cultures and situations. Attitudes toward diversity programs range greatly across countries, with the idea of what constitutes a "diverse" workforce differing by culture and the demography of the country. The role of women in the workplace also varies, with some countries valuing sexual equality more than others. Other categories of diversity, like sexual orientation, are not recognized in some countries but are important elements of the diversity picture in others. A consideration of three international examples helps illustrate how diverse diversity programs can be.

In Singapore, diversity has become part of the national agenda. On "Racial Harmony Day," street carnivals are held to celebrate the nation's unique status as a crossroads of Chinese, Malay, Indian, and other cultures. Besides applauding these distinct national identities, the country's leaders have also prioritized these celebrations as a moment to emphasize the shared identity of being Singaporean. Brazil is a similarly diverse country; the major demographic groups addressed by Brazilian diversity policies include African descendant, European descendant, and Asian descendant, as well as disability status. Research suggests that diversity programs are relatively new to Brazil compared to Europe and North America, but companies are coming to see diversity management as a major component of their human resources systems. In India, diversity management often means addressing differences in social class and caste that do not arise in other countries, with affirmative action programs mandating the number of individuals from lower castes who must be included in management positions for some types of organizations.

Multinational organizations will have to carefully consider how to create diversity strategies given the variety of perspectives on diversity across countries. Many countries require specific targets and quotas for achieving affirmative action goals, whereas the legal framework in the United States specifically forbids their use. Some countries have strong prohibitions on sexual harassment, whereas in other countries behavior unacceptable in U.S. workplaces is common. Effectively managing diversity in multinational organizations is clearly a challenge of the global marketplace.

Sources: Based on D. P. S. Goh, "State Carnivals and the Subvention of Multiculturalism in Singapore," *The British Journal of Sociology* 62 (2011), pp. 111–133; C. J. C. Jabbour, F. S. Gordono, J. H. C. de Olivera, J. C. Martinez, and R. A. G. Battistelle, "Diversity Management: Challenges, Benefits, and the Role of Human Resource Management in Brazilian Organizations," *Equality, Diversity, and Inclusion: An International Journal* 30 (2011), pp. 58–74; and F. L. Cooke and D. S. Saini, "Diversity Management in India: A Study of Organizations in Different Ownership Forms and Industrial Sectors," *Human Resource Management* 49 (2010), pp. 477–500.

Where employee behavior is highly routine and there are few or no opportunities to exercise discretion, a high IQ is not as important to performing well. However, that does not mean people with high IQs cannot have an impact on traditionally less complex jobs.

It might surprise you that the most widely used intelligence test in hiring decisions takes only 12 minutes to complete. It's the Wonderlic Cognitive Ability Test. There are different forms, and each has 50 questions. Here are a few examples:

- When rope is selling at $0.10 a foot, how many feet can you buy for $0.60?
- Assume the first two statements are true. Is the final one:
    1. True.
    2. False.
    3. Not certain.
        a. The boy plays baseball.
        b. All baseball players wear hats.
        c. The boy wears a hat.

The Wonderlic measures both speed (almost nobody has time to answer every question) and power (questions get harder as you go along), so the average score is pretty low—about 21/50. And because it is able to provide valid information cheaply (for $5 to $10/applicant), more companies are using the Wonderlic in hiring decisions. The Factory Card & Party Outlet, with 182 stores nationwide, uses it. So do Subway, Peoples Flowers, Security Alarm, Workforce Employment Solutions, and many others. Most of these companies don't give up other hiring tools, such as application forms or interviews. Rather, they add the Wonderlic for its ability to provide valid data on applicants' intelligence levels.

Interestingly, while intelligence is a big help in performing a job well, it doesn't make people happier or more satisfied with their jobs. The correlation between intelligence and job satisfaction is about zero. Why? Research suggests that although intelligent people perform better and tend to have more interesting jobs, they are also more critical when evaluating their job conditions. Thus, smart people have it better, but they also expect more.[64]

Physical Abilities

5   Contrast intellectual and physical ability.

Though the changing nature of work suggests intellectual abilities are increasingly important for many jobs, **physical abilities** have been and will remain valuable. Research on hundreds of jobs has identified nine basic abilities needed in the performance of physical tasks.[65] These are described in Exhibit 2-3. Individuals differ in the extent to which they have each of these abilities. Not surprisingly, there is also little relationship among them: a high score on one is no assurance of a high score on others. High employee performance is likely to be achieved when management has ascertained the extent to which a job requires each of the nine abilities and then ensures that employees in that job have those abilities.

Exhibit **2-3**	Nine Basic Physical Abilities
Strength Factors	
1. Dynamic strength	Ability to exert muscular force repeatedly or continuously over time
2. Trunk strength	Ability to exert muscular strength using the trunk (particularly abdominal) muscles
3. Static strength	Ability to exert force against external objects
4. Explosive strength	Ability to expend a maximum of energy in one or a series of explosive acts
Flexibility Factors	
5. Extent flexibility	Ability to move the trunk and back muscles as far as possible
6. Dynamic flexibility	Ability to make rapid, repeated flexing movements
Other Factors	
7. Body coordination	Ability to coordinate the simultaneous actions of different parts of the body
8. Balance	Ability to maintain equilibrium despite forces pulling off balance
9. Stamina	Ability to continue maximum effort requiring prolonged effort over time

physical abilities *The capacity to do tasks that demand stamina, dexterity, strength, and similar characteristics.*

The Role of Disabilities

The importance of ability at work obviously creates problems when we attempt to formulate workplace policies that recognize diversity in terms of disability status. As we have noted, recognizing that individuals have different abilities that can be taken into account when making hiring decisions is not problematic. However, it is discriminatory to make blanket assumptions about people on the basis of a disability. It is also possible to make accommodations for disabilities.

Implementing Diversity Management Strategies

Having discussed a variety of ways in which people differ, we now look at how a manager can and should manage these differences. **Diversity management** makes everyone more aware of and sensitive to the needs and differences of others. This definition highlights the fact that diversity programs include and are meant for everyone. Diversity is much more likely to be successful when we see it as everyone's business than if we believe it helps only certain groups of employees.

Attracting, Selecting, Developing, and Retaining Diverse Employees

One method of enhancing workforce diversity is to target recruiting messages to specific demographic groups underrepresented in the workforce. This means placing advertisements in publications geared toward specific demographic groups; recruiting at colleges, universities, and other institutions with significant numbers of underrepresented minorities; and forming partnerships with associations like the Society for Women Engineers or the Graduate Minority Business Association. These efforts can be successful, and research has shown that women and minorities do have greater interest in employers that make special efforts to highlight a commitment to diversity in their recruiting materials. Advertisements depicting groups of diverse employees are seen as more attractive to women and racioethnic minorities, which is probably why most organizations depict workforce diversity prominently in their recruiting materials. Diversity advertisements that fail to show women and minorities in positions of organizational leadership send a negative message about the diversity climate at an organization.[66]

The selection process is one of the most important places to apply diversity efforts. Managers who hire need to value fairness and objectivity in selecting employees and focus on the productive potential of new recruits. Fortunately, ensuring that hiring is bias-free does appear to work. Where managers use a well-defined protocol for assessing applicant talent and the organization clearly prioritizes nondiscrimination policies, qualifications become far more important in determining who gets hired than demographic characteristics.[67] Organizations that do not discourage discriminatory behavior are more likely to see problems.

Similarity in personality appears to affect career advancement. Those whose personality traits are similar to those of their co-workers are more likely to be promoted than those whose personalities are different.[68] There's an important qualifier to these results: in collectivistic cultures, similarity to supervisors is more important for predicting advancement, whereas in individualistic cultures,

In Japan, Nissan Motor Company is helping female employees develop their careers at the firm's manufacturing plants and car dealerships. Nissan provides women, such as the assembly-line worker shown here, with training programs to develop skills and the one-on-one counseling services of career advisors. Nissan also posts career interviews on its corporate intranet with women who have made significant contributions to the company and serve as role models for other female employees. For Nissan, developing the talents of women is a strategic imperative for its business success.

Source: AP Photo/Katsumi Kasahara

similarity to peers is more important. Once again, deep-level diversity factors appear to be more important in shaping people's reactions to one another than surface-level characteristics.

Evidence from a study of more than 6,000 workers in a major retail organization indicated that in stores with a less supportive diversity climate, African Americans or Hispanics made significantly fewer sales than White employees, but when the diversity climate was positive, Hispanics and Whites sold about the same amount and African Americans made more sales than Whites.[69] Whites sold about the same amount whether there was a positive diversity climate or not, but African Americans and Hispanics sold far more when there was. There are obvious bottom-line implications of this research: stores that fostered a positive diversity climate were able to capitalize on their diverse workforce and make more money.

Some data suggest individuals who are demographically different from their co-workers are more likely to feel low commitment and to turn over: women are more likely to turn over from predominantly male work groups and men from predominantly female work groups; non-Whites are more likely to turn over from predominantly White work groups and Whites from predominantly non-White work groups.[70] However, this behavior is more prominent among new hires. After people become better acquainted with one another, demographic differences are less consistently related to turnover. One very large-scale study showed a positive diversity climate was related to higher organizational commitment and lower turnover intentions among African-American, Hispanic, *and* White managers.[71] In other words, all workers appeared to prefer an organization that values diversity.

diversity management   *The process and programs by which managers make everyone more aware of and sensitive to the needs and differences of others.*

Diversity in Groups

Most contemporary workplaces require extensive work in group settings. When people work in groups, they need to establish a common way of looking at and accomplishing the major tasks, and they need to communicate with one another often. If they feel little sense of membership and cohesion in their groups, all these group attributes are likely to suffer.

Does diversity help or hurt group performance? The answer is "yes." In some cases, diversity in traits can hurt team performance, whereas in others it can facilitate it.[72] Whether diverse or homogeneous teams are more effective depends on the characteristic of interest. Demographic diversity (in gender, race, and ethnicity) does not appear to either help or hurt team performance in general. On the other hand, teams of individuals who are highly intelligent, conscientious, and interested in working in team settings are more effective. Thus diversity on these variables is likely to be a bad thing—it makes little sense to try to form teams that mix in members who are lower in intelligence, conscientiousness, and uninterested in teamwork. In other cases, differences can be a strength. Groups of individuals with different types of expertise and education are more effective than homogeneous groups. Similarly, a group made entirely of assertive people who want to be in charge, or a group whose members all prefer to follow the lead of others, will be less effective than a group that mixes leaders and followers.

Regardless of the composition of the group, differences can be leveraged to achieve superior performance. The most important way is to emphasize the higher-level similarities among members.[73] In other words, groups of diverse individuals will be much more effective if leaders can show how members have a common interest in the group's success. Evidence also shows transformational leaders (who emphasize higher-order goals and values in their leadership style) are more effective in managing diverse teams.[74]

Effective Diversity Programs

6   Describe how organizations manage diversity effectively.

Organizations use a variety of efforts to capitalize on diversity, including the recruiting and selection policies we have already discussed, as well as training and development practices. Effective, comprehensive workforce programs encouraging diversity have three distinct components. First, they teach managers about the legal framework for equal employment opportunity and encourage fair treatment of all people regardless of their demographic characteristics. Second, they teach managers how a diverse workforce will be better able to serve a diverse market of customers and clients. Third, they foster personal development practices that bring out the skills and abilities of all workers, acknowledging how differences in perspective can be a valuable way to improve performance for everyone.[75]

Much concern about diversity has to do with fair treatment.[76] Most negative reactions to employment discrimination are based on the idea that discriminatory treatment is unfair. Regardless of race or gender, people are generally in favor of diversity-oriented programs, including affirmative action, if they believe the policies ensure everyone a fair opportunity to show their skills and abilities.

A major study of the consequences of diversity programs came to what might seem a surprising conclusion.[77] Organizations that provided diversity training were not consistently more likely to have women and minorities in upper management positions than organizations that did not. On closer examination though, these results are not surprising. Experts have long known that one-shot training sessions without strategies to encourage effective diversity management back on the job are not likely to be very effective. Some diversity programs

NASCAR, an American sport with a worldwide following, promotes diversity within its organization and throughout the motorsports industry. Through its Drive to Diversity program, NASCAR ensures that everyone is given a fair opportunity to show and develop his or her skills and abilities. The program seeks to develop minority and female drivers and crew members as shown in this photo. Drivers participate in a scouting combine and earn the chance to compete with an established NASCAR team for a full season. And after completing their training, crew member trainees can compete with a racing team.

Source: Chuck Burton/AP Images

are truly effective in improving representation in management. They include strategies to measure the representation of women and minorities in managerial positions, and they hold managers accountable for achieving more demographically diverse management teams. Researchers also suggest that diversity experiences are more likely to lead to positive adaptation for all parties if (1) the diversity experience undermines stereotypical attitudes, (2) if the perceiver is motivated and able to consider a new perspective on others, (3) if the perceiver engages in stereotype suppression and generative thought in response to the diversity experience, and (4) if the positive experience of stereotype undermining is repeated frequently.[78] Diversity programs based on these principles are likely to be more effective than traditional classroom learning.

Organizational leaders should examine their workforce to determine whether target groups have been underutilized. If groups of employees are not proportionally represented in top management, managers should look for any hidden barriers to advancement. They can often improve recruiting practices, make selection systems more transparent, and provide training for those employees who have not had adequate exposure to certain material in the past. The organization should also clearly communicate its policies to employees so they can understand how and why certain practices are followed. Communications should focus as much as possible on qualifications and job performance; emphasizing certain groups as needing more assistance could well backfire. A case study of the multinational Finnish company TRANSCO found it was possible to develop a consistent global philosophy for diversity management. However, differences in legal and cultural factors across nations forced TRANSCO to develop unique policies to match the cultural and legal frameworks of each country in which it operated.[79]

To ensure the top-level management team represents the diversity of its workforce and client base, Safeway implemented the Retail Leadership Development (RLD) Program, a formal career development program. This program is open to all employees, so it is inclusive, but women and underrepresented racial or ethnic groups are particularly encouraged to participate. Interested individuals take a series of examinations to determine whether they have management potential. Those who perform well on the tests are provided with work in roles that expose them to managerial opportunities. The program's comprehensive nature is underscored by its additional support activities: All managers attend workshops that help them bring diversity concerns front and center in their staff meetings. They are also charged with providing promising RLD participants with additional training and development opportunities to ensure they have the skills needed for advancement. The program incorporates the type of accountability we have said is crucial to the success of diversity efforts; performance bonuses are provided to managers who meet concrete diversity goals. This program has shown real success: the number of White women store managers has increased by 31 percent since its inception, and the number of women-of-color store managers has increased by 92 percent.[80]

MyManagementLab

Now that you have finished this chapter, go back to **www.pearsonglobaleditions.com/ mymanagementlab** to continue practicing and applying the concepts you've learned.

Summary and Implications for Managers

This chapter looked at diversity from many perspectives. We paid particular attention to three variables—biographical characteristics, ability, and diversity programs. Let's summarize what we found and consider its importance for a manager trying to understand organizational behavior.

- We can readily observe biographical characteristics, but that doesn't mean we should explicitly use them in management decisions. Most research shows fairly minimal effects of biographical characteristics on job performance. We also need to be aware of implicit biases we or other managers may have.
- An effective selection process will improve the fit between employees and job requirements. A job analysis will provide information about jobs currently being done and the abilities individuals need to perform the jobs adequately. Applicants can then be tested, interviewed, and evaluated on the degree to which they possess the necessary abilities.
- Promotion and transfer decisions affecting individuals already in the organization's employ should reflect candidates' abilities. As with new employees, care should be taken to assess critical abilities incumbents will need in the job and match those with the organization's human resources.
- To accommodate employees with disabilities, managers can improve the fit by fine-tuning the job to better match an incumbent's abilities. Often, modifications with no significant impact on the job's basic activities, such as changing equipment or reorganizing tasks within a group, can better adapt work to the specific talents of a given employee.
- Diversity management must be an ongoing commitment that crosses all levels of the organization. Group management, recruiting, hiring, retention, and development practices can all be designed to leverage diversity for the organization's competitive advantage.
- Policies to improve the climate for diversity can be effective, so long as they are designed to acknowledge all employees' perspectives. One-shot diversity training sessions are less likely to be effective than comprehensive programs that address the climate for diversity at multiple levels.

Men Have More Mathematical Ability Than Women

Harvard's Larry Summers was forced to resign from his job as president of the university for claiming that women have different abilities than men, but there is some truth to the claim. Evidence reliability indicates significant gender differences in mathematical test scores.

To be sure, there are many, many women whose mathematical and scientific prowess far surpasses that of many men. The distributions overlap to a considerable degree.

It is also true that most research shows that overall intelligence doesn't differ between genders: women are as smart as men. But the fact of the matter is, the *way* in which men and women are smart is, on average, different. Women tend to have significantly higher scores on verbal ability measures and men tend to have significantly higher scores on measures of mathematical ability.

Many sociologists and educational psychologists argue that these differences are explained by socialization: boys are socialized toward and rewarded for mathematical prowess, whereas girls are pointed toward and expected to excel in writing and reading.

These socialization arguments, however, ignore some cold, hard truths that have been uncovered in the latest research. We know from neural imaging research that men's and women's brains differ. Men tend to show higher activation in the area of the brain responsible for mathematical and for spatial operations. Women, in contrast, tend to have better bilateral communication (the right and left sides of their brain communicate better), which is vital to reading comprehension and written and oral expression. Do we really think a child's third-grade teacher caused these differences?

No reasonable person suggests that boys and girls should be steered into different occupations based on these findings. Men and women should pursue the occupations that suit their abilities and that they will find rewarding. But should our pursuit of egalitarianism blind us to scientific findings that suggest the obvious: men and women are not exactly alike?

Women make up about half the new entrants in the professions of law, medicine, and dentistry. They are the vast majority of veterinarians. Yet they remain woefully underrepresented in science, mathematics, and technology positions. For example, only about one in five of recent entrants into engineering graduate programs are women, and in natural sciences and computer science departments at the top universities, fewer than one in ten tenured professors are women. If women are at such a disadvantage in terms of math and science abilities, why are they better represented in some occupations than others? Differing motivations produced by teacher and parent expectations are the answer. If we think women aren't natural engineers, then we learn to steer girls away from such career choices.

It is true there are gender differences in math test scores, but those differences are not large. And often ignored is a widely documented phenomenon: among the very young, girls *outperform* boys on math (as well as on other) tests. By adolescence, this advantage reverses and boys outperform girls. If socialization and school experiences do not explain this result, what does?

Moreover, we know that a large part of the reason fewer women enter science, technology, engineering, and mathematical (STEM) positions is not ability but motivation. Research indicates that women perceive careers in STEM fields to be less interpersonally fulfilling, and this explains their gravitation toward other fields. If we are concerned about sex differences in participation in these fields, we need to be concerned with the motivational effects of these perceptions, not with any presumed differences in male and female abilities.

Sources: Based on A. B. Diekman, E. R. Brown, A. M. Johnston, and E. K. Clark, "Seeking Congruity between Goals and Roles: A New Look at Why Women Opt Out of Science, Technology, Engineering, and Mathematics Careers," *Psychological Science* 21, no. 8 (2010), pp. 1051–1057; S. J. Ceci and W. Williams, "Sex Differences in Math-Intensive Fields," *Current Directions in Psychological Science* 19, no. 5 (2010), pp. 275–279; and J. Tierney, "Legislation Won't Close Gender Gap in Sciences," *The New York Times* (June 14, 2010), pp. 1–4.

QUESTIONS FOR REVIEW

1 What are the two major forms of workforce diversity?

2 What are stereotypes and how do they function in organizational settings?

3 What are the key biographical characteristics and how are they relevant to OB?

4 What is *intellectual ability* and how is it relevant to OB?

5 How can you contrast intellectual and physical ability?

6 How do organizations manage diversity effectively?

EXPERIENTIAL EXERCISE Feeling Excluded

This six-step exercise takes approximately 20 minutes.

Individual Work (Steps 1 and 2)

1. All participants are asked to recall a time when they have felt uncomfortable or targeted because of their demographic status. Ideally, situations at work should be used, but if no work situations come to mind, any situation will work. Encourage students to use any demographic characteristic they think is most appropriate, so they can write about feeling excluded on the basis of race, ethnicity, gender, age, disability status, religion, or any other characteristic. They should briefly describe the situation, what precipitated the event, how they felt at the time, how they reacted, and how they believe the other party could have made the situation better.

2. The instructor asks the students to then think about a time when they might have either deliberately or accidentally done something that made someone else feel excluded or targeted because of their demographic status. Once again, they should briefly describe the situation, what precipitated the event, how they felt at the time, how the other person reacted, and how they could have made the situation better.

Small Groups (Steps 3 and 4)

3. Once everyone has written their descriptions, divide the class into small groups of not more than four people. If at all possible, try to compose groups that are somewhat demographically diverse, to avoid intergroup conflicts in the class review discussion. Students should be encouraged to discuss their situations and consider how their experiences were similar or different.

4. After reading through everyone's reactions, each group should develop a short list of principles for how they personally can avoid excluding or targeting people in the future. Encourage them to be as specific as possible, and also ask each group to find solutions that work for everyone. Solutions should focus on both avoiding these situations in the first place and resolving them when they do occur.

Class Review (Steps 5 and 6)

5. Members of each group are invited to provide a very brief summary of the major principles of how they've felt excluded or targeted, and then to describe their groups' collective decisions regarding how these situations can be minimized in the future.

6. The instructor should lead a discussion on how companies might be able to develop comprehensive policies that will encourage people to be sensitive in their interactions with one another.

ETHICAL DILEMMA Board Quotas

That women are underrepresented on boards of directors is an understatement. In the United States, only 15 percent of board members among the *Fortune* 500 are women. Among the 100 largest companies in Great Britain, women hold approximately 12 percent of board seats, a representation that has changed little over the past 5 years. In the European Union (EU) more generally, only 9.7 percent of the directors of the 300 largest companies are women. In China and India, the figure is roughly half that.

In response to such underrepresentation, many EU countries—including France, Spain, and Norway—have instituted compulsory quotas for female representation on boards. Great Britain has guidelines and recommendations. A 2011 official British government report recommended that women make up at least 25 percent of the boards of the largest British companies. Under the recommended guidelines, companies would be required to announce their board composition goals to their shareholders and state clearly how they plan on meeting them. France passed a law in 2011 that requires large companies to fill at least 40 percent of board seats with female members within the next six years. Spain has a similar quota in place.

Questions

1. Given that women participate in the labor force in roughly the same proportion as men, why do you think women occupy so few seats on boards of directors?

2. Do you agree with the quotas established in many EU countries? Why or why not?

3. Beyond legal remedies, what do you think can be done to increase women's representations on boards of directors?

4. One recent study found no link between female representation on boards of directors and these companies' corporate sustainability or environmental policies. The study's author expressed surprise at the findings. Do the findings surprise you? Why or why not?

Sources: J. Werdigier, "In Britain, a Push for More Women on Boards of Large Companies," *The New York Times* (February 25, 2011), p. B3; and J. Galbreath, "Are There Gender-Related Influences on Corporate Sustainability? A Study of Women on Boards of Directors," *Journal of Management & Organization* 17, no. 1 (2011), pp. 17–38.

CASE INCIDENT 1 The Flynn Effect

Given that a substantial amount of intellectual ability is inherited, it might surprise you to learn that intelligence test scores are rising. In fact, scores have risen so dramatically that today's great-grandparents seem mentally deficient by comparison. First, let's review the evidence for rising test scores. Then we'll review explanations for the results.

On an IQ scale where 100 is the average, scores have been rising about 3 points per decade, meaning if your grandparent scored 100, the average score for your generation would be around 115. That's a pretty big difference—about a standard deviation, meaning someone from your grandparent's generation whose score was at the 84th percentile would be only average (50th percentile) by today's norms.

James Flynn is a New Zealand researcher credited with first documenting the rising scores. He reported the results in 1984, when he found that almost everyone who took a well-validated IQ test in the 1970s did better than those who took one in the 1940s. The results appear to hold up across cultures. Test scores are rising not only in the United States but in most other countries in which the effect has been tested, too.

What explains the Flynn effect? Researchers are not entirely sure, but some of the explanations offered are these:

1. **Education.** Students today are better educated than their ancestors, and education leads to higher test scores.

2. **Smaller families.** In 1900, the average couple had four children; today the number is fewer than two. We know firstborns tend to have higher IQs than other children, probably because they receive more attention than their later-born siblings.

3. **Test-taking savvy.** Today's children have been tested so often that they are test-savvy: they know how to take tests and how to do well on them.

4. **Genes.** Although smart couples tend to have fewer, not more, children (which might lead us to expect intelligence in the population to drop over time), it's possible that due to better education, tracking, and testing, those who do have the right genes are better able to exploit those advantages. Some genetics researchers also have argued that if genes for intelligence carried by both parents are dominant, they win out, meaning the child's IQ will be as high as or higher than those of the parents.

Despite the strong heritability of IQ, researchers continue to pursue mechanisms that might raise IQ scores. Factors like brain exercises (even video games) and regular physical exercise seem to at least temporarily boost brain power. Other recent research in neuroscience has had difficulty pinpointing physical mechanisms that can lead to a boost in IQ, although researchers propose that a focus on brain chemicals like dopamine may lead, in time, to drugs that can boost IQ chemically.

Questions

1. Do you believe people are really getting smarter? Why or why not?

2. Which of the factors explaining the Flynn effect do you accept?

3. If the Flynn effect is true, does this undermine the theory that IQ is mostly inherited? Why or why not?

Sources: Based on S. Begley, "Sex, Race, and IQ: Off Limits?" *Newsweek* (April 20, 2009), www.newsweek.com; M. A. Mingroni, "Resolving the IQ Paradox: Heterosis as a Cause of the Flynn Effect and Other Trends," *Psychological Review* (July 2007), pp. 806–829; and S. Begley, "Can You Build a Better Brain?" *Newsweek* (January 10, 2011), www.newsweek.com.

CASE INCIDENT 2 Diversity at Work: Nestlé Malaysia

Nestlé, a Swiss company, was founded by Henri Nestlé in 1866 but today, the company operates in 86 countries worldwide, and employs more than 280,000 people. Nestlé's commitment to providing quality products to Malaysians dates back almost 100 years ago. Nestlé began in Malaysia in 1912 as the Anglo-Swiss Condensed Milk Company in Penang and after its success moved to the capital Kuala Lumpur in 1939. The most popular Nestlé brands in Malaysia include Nescafé coffee, Kit Kat chocolate bar, and the drink MILO®.

Apart from the company's popularity among consumers, Nestlé in Malaysia is viewed as an attractive organization to work for which provides exciting new opportunities, benefits, and promising careers to its employees. As Nestlé continues to expand, the company realizes that effective diversity management increases the organization's access to the widest possible pool of skills, abilities, and ideas. Taking advantage of Malaysia's multiethinic backgrounds and its employees' demographic profiles, the company strives to create products to suit local tastes and cultural flavors. Diversity is even incorporated in the company's corporate values to ensure that the employees understand how diversity is essential to the success of Nestlé in Malaysia. The fact that its top management is comprised of people from various ethnic backgrounds and nationalities further enhances the company's ability to promote creativity in its practices and product developments.

One of the initiatives made by Nestlé in Malaysia, demonstrating the organization's commitment to diversity, was to voluntarily obtain the *Halal* Certification, awarded by JAKIM (the Department of Islamic Development Malaysia), for all of its food products manufactured in Malaysia. This has played a significant role in charting Nestlé's position in the Malaysian *halal* market. Moreover, Nestlé in Malaysia has managed to tap into the local tastes through the development of products such as Maggi 2-Minute Noodles Curry, Asam Laksa, and Tom Yam flavors.

Questions

1. Identify the key characteristics that Nestlé in Malaysia considered to be crucial in maintaining its leading position in countries like Malaysia.

2. Discuss other effective diversity programs that Nestlé in Malaysia can apply to ensure the company's continuous improvement.

Sources: Nestlé Malaysia Berhad, http://www.nestle.com.my/Pages/Nestle.aspx, accessed October and November 2011; D. Zawawi, Values and Job Performance: A Malaysian Study, Thesis (PhD), University of Reading (2007).

ENDNOTES

1. M. DiNatale and S. Boraas, "The Labor Force Experience of Women from Generation X," *Monthly Labor Review* (March 2002), pp. 1–15.

2. See, for example, F. Welch, "Catching Up: Wages of Black Men," *The American Economic Review* 93, no. 2 (2003), pp. 320–325; A. Sakamoto, H. Wu, and J. M. Tzeng, "The Declining Significance of Race Among American Men During the Latter Half of the Twentieth Century," *Demography* 37 (January 2000), pp. 41–51; and A Sakomoto, K. A. Goyette, and C. Kim, "Socioeconomic Attainments of Asian Americans," *Annual Review of Sociology* 35, (2009), pp. 255–276.

3. J. Schram, *SHRM Workplace Forecast* (Alexandria, VA: Society for Human Resource Management, 2006).

4. D. A. Harrison, K. H. Price, J. H. Gavin, and A. T. Florey, "Time, Teams, and Task Performance: Changing Effects of Surface- and Deep-Level Diversity on Group Functioning," *Academy of Management Journal* 45, no. 5 (2002), pp. 1029–1045; and A. H. Eagly and J. L. Chin, "Are Memberships in Race, Ethnicity, and Gender Categories Merely Surface Characteristics?" *American Psychologist* 65 (2010), pp. 934–935.

5. P. Chattopadhyay, M. Tluchowska, and E. George, "Identifying the Ingroup: A Closer Look at the Influence of Demographic Dissimilarity on Employee Social Identity," *Academy of Management Review* 29, no. 2 (2004), pp. 180–202; and P. Chattopadhyay, "Beyond Direct and Symmetrical Effects: The Influence of Demographic Dissimilarity on Organizational Citizenship Behavior," *Academy of Management Journal* 42, no. 3 (1999), pp. 273–287.

6. L. M. Cortina, "Unseen Injustice: Incivility as Modern Discrimination in Organizations," *Academy of Management Review* 33, no. 1 (2008), pp. 55–75.

7. R. J. Grossman, "Keep Pace with Older Workers," *HR Magazine* (May 2008), pp. 39–46.

8. K. A. Wrenn and T. J. Maurer, "Beliefs About Older Workers' Learning and Development Behavior in Relation to Beliefs About Malleability of Skills, Age-Related Decline, and Control," *Journal of Applied Social Psychology* 34, no. 2 (2004), pp. 223–242; and R. A. Posthuma and M. A. Campion, "Age Stereotypes in the Workplace: Common Stereotypes,

Moderators, and Future Research Directions," *Journal of Management* 35 (2009), pp. 158–188.

9. T. W. H. Ng and D. C. Feldman, "Re-examining the Relationship Between Age and Voluntary Turnover," *Journal of Vocational Behavior* 74 (2009), pp. 283–294.

10. T. W. H. Ng and D. C. Feldman, "The Relationship of Age to Ten Dimensions of Job Performance," *Journal of Applied Psychology* 93 (2008), pp. 392–423.

11. Cited in K. Labich, "The New Unemployed," *Fortune* (March 8, 1993), p. 43.

12. See Ng and Feldman, "The Relationship of Age to Ten Dimensions of Job Performance."

13. T. W. H. Ng and D. C. Feldman, "The Relationship of Age with Job Attitudes: A Meta-Analysis," *Personnel Psychology* 63 (2010), pp. 677–718.

14. K. M. Kacmar and G. R. Ferris, "Theoretical and Methodological Considerations in the Age–Job Satisfaction Relationship," *Journal of Applied Psychology* (April 1989), pp. 201–207; and W. A. Hochwarter, G. R. Ferris, P. L. Perrewe, L. A. Witt, and C. Kiewitz, "A Note on the Nonlinearity of the Age–Job Satisfaction Relationship," *Journal of Applied Social Psychology* (June 2001), pp. 1223–1237.

15. F. Kunze, S. A. Boehm, and H. Bruch, "Age Diversity, Age Discrimination Climate and Performance Consequences—A Cross Organizational Study," *Journal of Organizational Behavior* 32 (2011), pp. 264–290.

16. See E. M. Weiss, G. Kemmler, E. A. Deisenhammer, W. W. Fleischhacker, and M. Delazer, "Sex Differences in Cognitive Functions," *Personality and Individual Differences* (September 2003), pp. 863–875; and A. F. Jorm, K. J. Anstey, H. Christensen, and B. Rodgers, "Gender Differences in Cognitive Abilities: The Mediating Role of Health State and Health Habits," *Intelligence* (January 2004), pp. 7–23.

17. See M. M. Black and E. W. Holden, "The Impact of Gender on Productivity and Satisfaction Among Medical School Psychologists," *Journal of Clinical Psychology in Medical Settings* (March 1998), pp. 117–131.

18. M. E. Heilman and T. G. Okimoto, "Why Are Women Penalized for Success at Male Tasks? The Implied Communality Deficit," *Journal of Applied Psychology* 92, no. 1 (2007), pp. 81–92.

19. D. R. Avery, P. F. McKay, and D. C. Wilson "What are the Odds? How Demographic Similarity Affects the Prevalence of Perceived Employment Discrimination," *Journal of Applied Psychology* 93 (2008), pp. 235–249.

20. C. Kirchmeyer, "The Different Effects of Family on Objective Career Success Across Gender: A Test of Alternative Explanations," *Journal of Vocational Behavior* 68, no. 2 (2006), pp. 323–346; and C. Guillaume and S. Pochic, "What Would You Sacrifice? Access to Top Management and the Work-Life Balance," *Gender, Work & Organization* 16, no. 1 (2009), pp. 14–36.

21. Guillaume and Pochic, "What Would You Sacrifice? Access to Top Management and the Work-Life Balance."

22. P. W. Hom, L. Roberson, and A. D. Ellis, "Challenging Conventional Wisdom About Who Quits: Revelations from Corporate America," *Journal of Applied Psychology* 93, no. 1 (2008), pp. 1–34.

23. See, for instance, K. D. Scott and E. L. McClellan, "Gender Differences in Absenteeism," *Public Personnel Management* (Summer 1990), pp. 229–253; and A. VandenHeuvel and M. Wooden, "Do Explanations of Absenteeism Differ for Men and Women?" *Human Relations* (November 1995), pp. 1309–1329.

24. See, for instance, M. Tait, M. Y. Padgett, and T. T. Baldwin, "Job and Life Satisfaction: A Reevaluation of the Strength of the Relationship and Gender Effects as a Function of the Date of the Study," *Journal of Applied Psychology* (June 1989), pp. 502–507; and M. B. Grover, "Daddy Stress," *Forbes* (September 6, 1999), pp. 202–208.

25. S. Halrynjo, "Men's Work-Life Conflict: Career, Care and Self-Realization: Patterns of Privileges and Dilemmas," *Gender, Work & Organization* 16, no. 1 (2009), pp. 98–125; and S. Jayson, "Gender Roles See a 'Conflict' Shift," *USA Today* (March 26, 2009), p. 1A.

26. M. E. Heilman and T. G. Okimoto, "Motherhood: A Potential Source of Bias in Employment Decisions," *Journal of Applied Psychology* 93, no. 1 (2008), pp. 189–198.

27. J. L. Raver and L. H. Nishii, "Once, Twice, or Three Times as Harmful? Ethnic Harassment, Gender Harassment, and Generalized Workplace Harassment," *Journal of Applied Psychology* 95 (2010), pp. 236–254.

28. D. R. Avery, J. A. Richeson, M R. Hebl, and N. Ambady, "It Does Not Have to Be Uncomfortable: The Role of Behavioral Scripts in Black-White Interracial Interactions," *Journal of Applied Psychology* 94 (2009), pp. 1382–1393.

29. J. M. McCarthy, C. H. Van Iddekinge, and M. A. Campion, "Are Highly Structured Job Interviews Resistant to Demographic Similarity Effects?" *Personnel Psychology* 63 (2010), pp. 325–359; and G. N. Powell and D. A. Butterfield, "Exploring the Influence of Decision Makers' Race and Gender on Actual Promotions to Top Management," *Personnel Psychology* 55, no. 2 (2002), pp. 397–428.

30. D. A. Kravitz, D. M. Mayer, L. M. Leslie, and D. Lev-Arey, "Understanding Attitudes Toward Affirmative Action Programs in Employment: Summary and Meta-Analysis of 35 Years of Research," *Journal of Applied Psychology* 91 (2006), pp. 1013–1036.

31. D. R. Avery, P F. McKay, and D. C. Wilson "What Are the Odds? How Demographic Similarity Affects the Prevalence of Perceived Employment Discrimination," *Journal of Applied Psychology* 93 (2008), pp. 235–249.

32. J. M. Sacco, C. R. Scheu, A. M. Ryan, and N. Schmitt, "An Investigation of Race and Sex Similarity Effects in Interviews: A Multilevel Approach to Relational Demography," *Journal of Applied Psychology* 88, no. 5 (2003), pp. 852–865; and P. F. McKay and M. A. McDaniel, "A Reexamination of Black-White Mean Differences in Work Performance: More Data, More Moderators," *Journal of Applied Psychology* 91, no. 3 (2006), pp. 538–554.

33. P. Bobko, P. L. Roth, and D. Potosky, "Derivation and Implications of a Meta-Analytic Matrix Incorporating Cognitive Ability, Alternative Predictors, and Job Performance," *Personnel Psychology* (Autumn 1999), pp. 561–589.

34. M. J. Ree, T. R. Carretta, and J. R. Steindl, "Cognitive Ability," in N. Anderson, D. S. Ones, H. K. Sinangil, and C. Viswesvaran (eds.), *Handbook of Industrial, Work, and Organizational Psychology*, vol. 1 (London: Sage Publications, 2001), pp. 219–232.

35. W. T. Dickens and J. R. Flynn, "Black Americans Reduce the Racial IQ Gap: Evidence from Standardization Samples,"

Psychological Science 17 (2006), pp. 913–920; and C. Murray, "The Magnitude and Components of Change in the Black-White IQ Difference from 1920 to 1991: A Birth Cohort Analysis of the Woodcock-Johnson Standardizations," *Intelligence* 35, no. 44 (2007), pp. 305–318.

36. See J. P. Rushton and A. R. Jenson, "Thirty Years of Research on Race Differences in Cognitive Ability," *Psychology, Public Policy, and the Law* 11, no. 2 (2005), pp. 235–295; and R. E. Nisbett, "Heredity, Environment, and Race Differences in IQ: A Commentary on Rushton and Jensen (2005)," *Psychology, Public Policy, and the Law* 11, no. 2 (2005), pp. 302–310.

37. Avery, McKay, and Wilson, "What Are the Odds? How Demographic Similarity Affects the Prevalence of Perceived Employment Discrimination"; and Raver and Nishii, "Once, Twice, or Three Times as Harmful? Ethnic Harassment, Gender Harassment, and Generalized Workplace Harassment."

38. P. F. McKay, D. R. Avery, and M. A. Morris, "Mean Racial-Ethnic Differences in Employee Sales Performance: The Moderating Role of Diversity Climate," *Personnel Psychology* 61, no. 2 (2008), pp. 349–374.

39. *Americans with Disabilities Act,* 42 U.S.C. § 12101, et seq. (1990).

40. S. G. Goldberg, M. B. Killeen, and B. O'Day, "The Disclosure Conundrum: How People with Psychiatric Disabilities Navigate Employment," *Psychology, Public Policy, and Law* 11, no. 3 (2005), pp. 463–500; M. L. Ellison, Z. Russinova, K. L. MacDonald-Wilson, and A. Lyass, "Patterns and Correlates of Workplace Disclosure Among Professionals and Managers with Psychiatric Conditions," *Journal of Vocational Rehabilitation* 18, no. 1 (2003), pp. 3–13.

41. L. R. Ren, R. L. Paetzold, and A. Colella, "A Meta-Analysis of Experimental Studies on the Effects of Disability on Human Resource Judgments," *Human Resource Management Review* 18, no. 3 (2008), pp. 191–203.

42. S. Almond and A. Healey, "Mental Health and Absence from Work: New Evidence from the UK Quarterly Labour Force Survey," *Work, Employment, and Society* 17, no. 4 (2003), pp. 731–742.

43. E. Louvet, "Social Judgment Toward Job Applicants with Disabilities: Perception of Personal Qualities and Competences," *Rehabilitation Psychology* 52, no. 3 (2007), pp. 297–303; and W. D. Gouvier, S. Sytsma-Jordan, and S. Mayville, "Patterns of Discrimination in Hiring Job Applicants with Disabilities: The Role of Disability Type, Job Complexity, and Public Contact," *Rehabilitation Psychology* 48, no. 3 (2003), pp. 175–181.

44. A. Colella, A. S. DeNisi, and A. Varma, "The Impact of Ratee's Disability on Performance Judgments and Choice as Partner: The Role of Disability-Job Fit Stereotypes and Interdependence of Rewards," *Journal of Applied Psychology* 83, no. 1 (1998), pp. 102–111.

45. J. M. Czajka and A. S. DeNisi, "Effects of Emotional Disability and Clear Performance Standards on Performance Ratings," *Academy of Management Journal* 31, no. 2 (1988), pp. 394–404.

46. B. S. Bell and K. J. Klein, "Effect of Disability, Gender, and Job Level on Ratings of Job Applicants," *Rehabilitation Psychology* 46, no. 3 (2001), pp. 229–246; and Louvet, "Social Judgment Toward Job Applicants with Disabilities: Perception of Personal Qualities and Competences."

47. T. W. H. Ng and D. C. Feldman, "Organizational Tenure and Job Performance," *Journal of Management* 36, (2010), pp. 1220–1250.

48. I. R. Gellatly, "Individual and Group Determinants of Employee Absenteeism: Test of a Causal Model," *Journal of Organizational Behavior* (September 1995), pp. 469–485.

49. P. O. Popp and J. A. Belohlav, "Absenteeism in a Low Status Work Environment," *Academy of Management Journal* (September 1982), p. 681.

50. R. W. Griffeth, P. W. Hom, and S. Gaertner, "A Meta-analysis of Antecedents and Correlates of Employee Turnover: Update, Moderator Tests, and Research Implications for the Next Millennium," *Journal of Management* 26, no. 3 (2000), pp. 463–488.

51. M. R. Barrick and R. D. Zimmerman, "Hiring for Retention and Performance," *Human Resource Management* 48 (2009), pp. 183–206.

52. W. van Breukelen, R. van der Vlist, and H. Steensma, "Voluntary Employee Turnover: Combining Variables from the 'Traditional' Turnover Literature with the Theory of Planned Behavior," *Journal of Organizational Behavior* 25, no. 7 (2004), pp. 893–914.

53. M. Elias, "USA's Muslims Under a Cloud," *USA Today* (August 10, 2006), pp. 1D, 2D; and R. R. Hastings, "Muslims Seek Acknowledgement of Mainstream Americans," *HRWeek* (May 11, 2007), p. 1.

54. E. B. King and A. S. Ahmad, "An Experimental Field Study of Interpersonal Discrimination Toward Muslim Job Applicants," *Personnel Psychology* 63 (2010), pp. 881–906.

55. See, for example, E. B. King and J. M. Cortina, "The Social and Economic Imperative of Lesbian, Gay, Bisexual, and Transgendered Supportive Organizational Policies," *Industrial and Organizational Psychology: Perspectives on Science and Practice* 3 (2010), pp. 69–78.

56. *HRC Corporate Equality Index,* 2011, www.hrc.org/documents/HRC-CEI-2011-Final.pdf; and R. R. Hastings, "Necessity Breeds Inclusion: Reconsidering 'Don't Ask, Don't Tell,'" *HRWeek* (January 2007), pp. 1–2.

57. B. R. Ragins, "Disclosure Disconnects: Antecedents and Consequences of Disclosing Invisible Stigmas Across Life Domains," *Academy of Management Review* 33 (2008), pp. 194–215.

58. B. Leonard, "Transgender Issues Test Diversity Limits," *HRMagazine* (June 2007), pp. 32–34.

59. L. S. Gottfredson, "The Challenge and Promise of Cognitive Career Assessment," *Journal of Career Assessment* 11, no. 2 (2003), pp. 115–135.

60. M. D. Dunnette, "Aptitudes, Abilities, and Skills," in M. D. Dunnette (ed.), *Handbook of Industrial and Organizational Psychology* (Chicago: Rand McNally, 1976), pp. 478–483.

61. J. W. B. Lang, M. Kersting, U. R. Hülscheger, and J. Lang, "General Mental Ability, Narrower Cognitive Abilities, and Job Performance: The Perspective of the Nested-Factors Model of Cognitive Abilities" *Personnel Psychology* 63 (2010), pp. 595–640.

62. N. Barber, "Educational and Ecological Correlates of IQ: A Cross-National Investigation," *Intelligence* (May–June 2005), pp. 273–284.

63. J. F. Salgado, N. Anderson, S. Moscoso, C. Bertua, F. de Fruyt, and J. P. Rolland, "A Meta-analytic Study of General Mental

Ability Validity for Different Occupations in the European Community," *Journal of Applied Psychology* (December 2003), pp. 1068–1081; and F. L. Schmidt and J. E. Hunter, "Select on Intelligence," in E. A. Locke (ed.), *Handbook of Principles of Organizational Behavior* (Malden, MA: Blackwell, 2004).

64. Y. Ganzach, "Intelligence and Job Satisfaction," *Academy of Management Journal* 41, no. 5 (1998), pp. 526–539; and Y. Ganzach, "Intelligence, Education, and Facets of Job Satisfaction," *Work and Occupations* 30, no. 1 (2003), pp. 97–122.

65. E. A. Fleishman, "Evaluating Physical Abilities Required by Jobs," *Personnel Administrator* (June 1979), pp. 82–92.

66. D. R. Avery, "Reactions to Diversity in Recruitment Advertising: Are the Differences Black and White?" *Journal of Applied Psychology* 88, no. 4 (2003), pp. 672–679; P. F. McKay and D. R. Avery, "What Has Race Got to Do with It? Unraveling the Role of Racioethnicity in Job Seekers' Reactions to Site Visits," *Personnel Psychology* 59, no. 2 (2006), pp. 395–429; and D. R. Avery and P. F. McKay, "Target Practice: An Organizational Impression Management Approach to Attracting Minority and Female Job Applicants," *Personnel Psychology* 59, no. 1 (2006), pp. 157–187.

67. M. R. Buckley, K. A. Jackson, M. C. Bolino, J. G. Veres, and H. S. Field, "The Influence of Relational Demography on Panel Interview Ratings: A Field Experiment," *Personnel Psychology* 60 (2007), pp. 627–646; J. M. Sacco, C. R. Scheu, A. M. Ryan, and N. Schmitt, "An Investigation of Race and Sex Similarity Effects in Interviews: A Multilevel Approach to Relational Demography," *Journal of Applied Psychology* 88 (2003), pp. 852–865; and J. C. Ziegert and P. J. Hanges, "Employment Discrimination: The Role of Implicit Attitudes, Motivation, and a Climate for Racial Bias," *Journal of Applied Psychology* 90 (2005), pp. 553–562.

68. J. Schaubroeck and S. S. K. Lam, "How Similarity to Peers and Supervisor Influences Organizational Advancement in Different Cultures," *Academy of Management Journal* 45 (2002), pp. 1120–1136.

69. P. F. McKay, D. R. Avery, and M. A. Morris, "Mean Racial-Ethnic Differences in Employee Sales Performance: The Moderating Role of Diversity Climate," *Personnel Psychology* 61, no. 2 (2008), pp. 349–374.

70. A. S. Tsui, T. D. Egan, and C. A. O'Reilly, "Being Different: Relational Demography and Organizational Attachment," *Administrative Science Quarterly* 37 (1992), pp. 547–579; and J. M. Sacco and N. Schmitt, "A Dynamic Multilevel Model of Demographic Diversity and Misfit Effects," *Journal of Applied Psychology* 90 (2005), pp. 203–231.

71. P. F. McKay, D. R. Avery, S. Tonidandel, M. A. Morris, M. Hernandez, and M. R. Hebl, "Racial Differences in Employee Retention: Are Diversity Climate Perceptions the Key?" *Personnel Psychology* 60, no. 1 (2007), pp. 35–62.

72. S. T. Bell, "Deep-Level Composition Variables as Predictors of Team Performance: A Meta–Analysis," *Journal of Applied Psychology* 92, no. 3 (2007), pp. 595–615; S. K. Horwitz and I. B. Horwitz, "The Effects of Team Diversity on Team Outcomes: A Meta-Analytic Review of Team Demography," *Journal of Management* 33, no. 6 (2007), pp. 987–1015; G. L. Stewart, "A Meta-Analytic Review of Relationships Between Team Design Features and Team Performance," *Journal of Management* 32, no. 1 (2006), pp. 29–54; and A. Joshi and H. Roh, "The Role of Context in Work Team Diversity Research: A Meta-Analytic Review," *Academy of Management Journal* 52, no. 3 (2009), pp. 599–627.

73. A. C. Homan, J. R. Hollenbeck, S. E. Humphrey, D. Van Knippenberg, D. R. Ilgen, and G. A. Van Kleef, "Facing Differences with an Open Mind: Openness to Experience, Salience of Intragroup Differences, and Performance of Diverse Work Groups," *Academy of Management Journal* 51, no. 6 (2008), pp. 1204–1222.

74. E. Kearney and D. Gebert, "Managing Diversity and Enhancing Team Outcomes: The Promise of Transformational Leadership," *Journal of Applied Psychology* 94, no. 1 (2009), pp. 77–89.

75. C. L. Holladay and M. A. Quiñones, "The Influence of Training Focus and Trainer Characteristics on Diversity Training Effectiveness," *Academy of Management Learning and Education* 7, no. 3 (2008), pp. 343–354; and R. Anand and M. Winters, "A Retrospective View of Corporate Diversity Training from 1964 to the Present," *Academy of Management Learning and Education* 7, no. 3 (2008), pp. 356–372.

76. Q. M. Roberson and C. K. Stevens, "Making Sense of Diversity in the Workplace: Organizational Justice and Language Abstraction in Employees' Accounts of Diversity-Related Incidents," *Journal of Applied Psychology* 91 (2006), pp. 379–391; and D. A. Harrison, D. A. Kravitz, D. M. Mayer, L. M. Leslie, and D. Lev-Arey, "Understanding Attitudes Toward Affirmative Action Programs in Employment: Summary and Meta-Analysis of 35 Years of Research," *Journal of Applied Psychology* 91 (2006), pp. 1013–1036.

77. A. Kalev, F. Dobbin, and E. Kelly, "Best Practices or Best Guesses? Assessing the Efficacy of Corporate Affirmative Action and Diversity Policies," *American Sociological Review* 71, no. 4 (2006), pp. 589–617.

78. R. J. Crisp and R. N. Turner, "Cognitive Adaptation to the Experience of Social and Cultural Diversity," *Psychological Bulletin* 137 (2011), pp. 242–266.

79. A. Sippola and A. Smale, "The Global Integration of Diversity Management: A Longitudinal Case Study," *International Journal of Human Resource Management* 18, no. 11 (2007), pp. 1895–1916.

80. A. Pomeroy, "Cultivating Female Leaders," *HR Magazine* (February 2007), pp. 44–50.

TANNOURINE GOVM HOSPITAL

LEARNING OBJECTIVES

After studying this chapter, you should be able to:

1 Contrast the three components of an attitude.

2 Summarize the relationship between attitudes and behavior.

3 Compare and contrast the major job attitudes.

4 Define *job satisfaction* and show how we can measure it.

5 Summarize the main causes of job satisfaction.

6 Identify four employee responses to dissatisfaction.

TANNOURINE HOSPITAL: THE ULTIMATE CHALLENGE!

Tannourine Government Hospital is located in Tannourine El-Tahta, Lebanon, 900 meters above sea level. The Kuwaiti government donated the funds and actually built the 5,000-square-meter hospital in 1997. The first patient was accepted in November 1999, and Dr. Walid Harb has served as CEO and president of the board of directors since then.

The employee-friendly culture has instilled in employees a positive attitude because Harb uses a micromanagement style, where every department head has delegated responsibilities and authority. Open channels of communication make employees feel comfortable.

Harb presented his staff with three overall aims and long-term goals: (1) offer vital help to patients in the mountainous areas who are now closer to medical treatment; (2) establish a successful hospital to offer regional employment opportunities (95 percent of staff are from the region); and (3) implement policies to enhance the relationship among management, the staff, and the patients.

Management also focused on the hospital community by getting them involved in activities and asking for their feedback. This has all created an attractive workplace where individuals feel like partners. Bonds have also been established with expatriates in Australia, and task forces are supporting the hospital by sending medical equipment and delegations of specialized physicians.

These developments have given the employees more trust in the decisions of the CEO. Employees are satisfied, motivated, and feel they belong; consequently, they are more committed, and performance and productivity levels are higher. Employees anonymously evaluate the performance of the CEO just as their supervisors evaluate them, according to job descriptions and how they implement policy. Evaluations are discussed, and employees have the opportunity to make suggestions for improvements.

Harb stresses quality control and this assures employees that management is following norms and standards, giving them a more positive outlook. Harb also offers training and support for employees who are struggling to meet the quality control standards.

In general, Harb has created a family atmosphere where all employees treat each other with respect, and the fact that he is from the region has facilitated this task. Employees feel respected by top management and feel their personal and professional welfare is valued.

Source: Interview with Dr. Walid Harb, CEO and president of the board of directors, Tannourine Government Hospital, Tannourine El-Tahta, Lebanon (October 2011).

Attitudes and Job Satisfaction

Attitude isn't everything, but it's close.

—*New York Times* headline, August 6, 2006

ike Tannourine Government Hospital, many organizations are very concerned with the attitudes of their employees. In this chapter, we look at attitudes, their link to behavior, and how employees' satisfaction or dissatisfaction with their jobs affects the workplace.

What are your attitudes toward your job? Use the following Self-Assessment Library to determine your level of satisfaction with your current or past jobs.

SELF-ASSESSMENT LIBRARY

How Satisfied Am I with My Job?

In the Self-Assessment Library (available on CD or online), take assessment I.B.3 (How Satisfied Am I with My Job?) and then answer the following questions. If you currently do not have a job, answer the questions for your most recent job.

1. How does your job satisfaction compare to that of others in your class who have taken the assessment?
2. Why do you think your satisfaction is higher or lower than average?

Attitudes

1 Contrast the three components of an attitude.

Attitudes are evaluative statements—either favorable or unfavorable—about objects, people, or events. They reflect how we feel about something. When I say "I like my job," I am expressing my attitude about work.

Attitudes are complex. If you ask people about their attitude toward religion, Lady Gaga, or the organization they work for, you may get a simple response, but the reasons underlying it are probably complicated. In order to fully understand attitudes, we must consider their fundamental properties or components.

What Are the Main Components of Attitudes?

Typically, researchers have assumed that attitudes have three components: cognition, affect, and behavior.[1] Let's look at each.

The statement "My pay is low" is the **cognitive component** of an attitude—a description of or belief in the way things are. It sets the stage for the more critical part of an attitude—its **affective component**. Affect is the emotional or feeling segment of an attitude and is reflected in the statement "I am angry over how little I'm paid." Finally, affect can lead to behavioral outcomes. The **behavioral component** of an attitude describes an intention to behave in a certain way toward someone or something—to continue the example, "I'm going to look for another job that pays better."

Viewing attitudes as having three components—cognition, affect, and behavior—is helpful in understanding their complexity and the potential

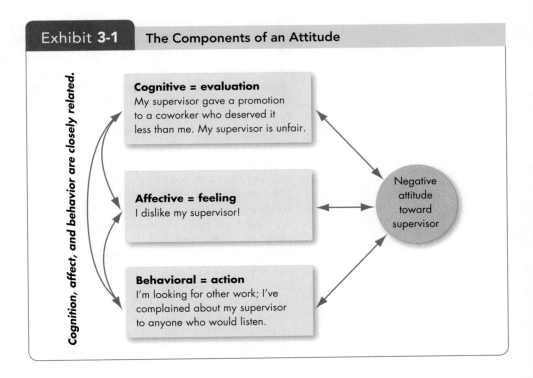

Exhibit 3-1   **The Components of an Attitude**

Cognition, affect, and behavior are closely related.

Cognitive = evaluation
My supervisor gave a promotion to a coworker who deserved it less than me. My supervisor is unfair.

Affective = feeling
I dislike my supervisor!

Behavioral = action
I'm looking for other work; I've complained about my supervisor to anyone who would listen.

Negative attitude toward supervisor

relationship between attitudes and behavior. Keep in mind that these components are closely related, and cognition and affect in particular are inseparable in many ways. For example, imagine you realized that someone has just treated you unfairly. Aren't you likely to have feelings about that, occurring virtually instantaneously with the realization? Thus, cognition and affect are intertwined.

Exhibit 3-1 illustrates how the three components of an attitude are related. In this example, an employee didn't get a promotion he thought he deserved; a co-worker got it instead. The employee's attitude toward his supervisor is illustrated as follows: the employee thought he deserved the promotion (cognition), he strongly dislikes his supervisor (affect), and he is looking for another job (behavior). As we've noted, although we often think cognition causes affect, which then causes behavior, in reality these components are often difficult to separate.

In organizations, attitudes are important for their behavioral component. If workers believe, for example, that supervisors, auditors, bosses, and time-and-motion engineers are all in conspiracy to make employees work harder for the same or less money, it makes sense to try to understand how these attitudes formed, how they relate to actual job behavior, and how they might be changed.

Does Behavior Always Follow from Attitudes?

2 Summarize the relationship between attitudes and behavior.

Early research on attitudes assumed they were causally related to behavior—that is, the attitudes people hold determine what they do. Common sense, too, suggests a relationship. Isn't it logical that people watch television programs they like, or that employees try to avoid assignments they find distasteful?

---

attitudes *Evaluative statements or judgments concerning objects, people, or events.*

cognitive component *The opinion or belief segment of an attitude.*

affective component *The emotional or feeling segment of an attitude.*

behavioral component *An intention to behave in a certain way toward someone or something.*

However, in the late 1960s, a review of the research challenged this assumed effect of attitudes on behavior.[2] One researcher—Leon Festinger—argued that attitudes *follow* behavior. Did you ever notice how people change what they say so it doesn't contradict what they do? Perhaps a friend of yours has consistently argued that the quality of U.S. cars isn't up to that of imports and that he'd never own anything but a Japanese or German car. But his dad gives him a late-model Ford Mustang, and suddenly he says U.S. cars aren't so bad. Festinger proposed that cases of attitude following behavior illustrate the effects of **cognitive dissonance**,[3] any incompatibility an individual might perceive between two or more attitudes or between behavior and attitudes. Festinger argued that any form of inconsistency is uncomfortable and that individuals will therefore attempt to reduce it. They will seek a stable state, which is a minimum of dissonance.

Research has generally concluded that people do seek consistency among their attitudes and between their attitudes and their behavior.[4] They either alter the attitudes or the behavior, or they develop a rationalization for the discrepancy. Tobacco executives provide an example.[5] How, you might wonder, do these people cope with the continuing revelations about the health dangers of smoking? They can deny any clear causation between smoking and cancer. They can brainwash themselves by continually articulating the benefits of tobacco. They can acknowledge the negative consequences of smoking but rationalize that people are going to smoke and that tobacco companies merely promote freedom of choice. They can accept the evidence and make cigarettes less dangerous or reduce their availability to more vulnerable groups, such as teenagers. Or they can quit their job because the dissonance is too great.

No individual, of course, can completely avoid dissonance. You know cheating on your income tax is wrong, but you fudge the numbers a bit every year and hope you're not audited. Or you tell your children to floss their teeth, but you don't do it yourself. Festinger proposed that the desire to reduce dissonance depends on moderating factors, including the *importance* of the elements creating it and the degree of *influence* we believe we have over them. Individuals

Marriott International strives for consistency between employee attitudes and behavior through its motto "Spirit to Serve." CEO and chairman J. W. Marriott, Jr., models the behavior of service by visiting hotel employees throughout the year. "I want our associates to know that there really is a guy named Marriott who cares about them," he says. The company honors employees with job excellence awards for behavior that exemplifies an attitude of service to customers and co-workers.

Source: Bill Greenblat/UPI/Newscom

will be more motivated to reduce dissonance when the attitudes or behavior are important or when they believe the dissonance is due to something they can control. A third factor is the *rewards* of dissonance; high rewards accompanying high dissonance tend to reduce the tension inherent in the dissonance.

While Festinger argued that attitudes follow behavior, other researchers asked whether there was any relationship at all. More recent research shows that attitudes predict future behavior and confirmed Festinger's idea that "moderating variables" can strengthen the link.[6]

Moderating Variables   The most powerful moderators of the attitudes relationship are the *importance* of the attitude, its *correspondence to behavior*, its *accessibility*, the presence of *social pressures*, and whether a person has *direct experience* with the attitude.[7]

Important attitudes reflect our fundamental values, self-interest, or identification with individuals or groups we value. These attitudes tend to show a strong relationship to our behavior.

Specific attitudes tend to predict specific behaviors, whereas general attitudes tend to best predict general behaviors. For instance, asking someone about her intention to stay with an organization for the next 6 months is likely to better predict turnover for that person than asking her how satisfied she is with her job overall. On the other hand, overall job satisfaction would better predict a general behavior, such as whether the individual was engaged in her work or motivated to contribute to her organization.[8]

Attitudes that our memories can easily access are more likely to predict our behavior. Interestingly, you're more likely to remember attitudes you frequently express. So the more you talk about your attitude on a subject, the more likely you are to remember it, and the more likely it is to shape your behavior.

Discrepancies between attitudes and behavior tend to occur when social pressures to behave in certain ways hold exceptional power, as in most organizations. This may explain why an employee who holds strong anti-union attitudes attends pro-union organizing meetings, or why tobacco executives, who are not smokers themselves and who tend to believe the research linking smoking and cancer, don't actively discourage others from smoking.

Finally, the attitude–behavior relationship is likely to be much stronger if an attitude refers to something with which we have direct personal experience. Asking college students with no significant work experience how they would respond to working for an authoritarian supervisor is far less likely to predict actual behavior than asking that same question of employees who have actually worked for such an individual.

What Are the Major Job Attitudes?

3   Compare and contrast the major job attitudes.

We each have thousands of attitudes, but OB focuses our attention on a very limited number of work-related attitudes. These tap positive or negative evaluations that employees hold about aspects of their work environment. Most of the research in OB has looked at three attitudes: job satisfaction, job involvement, and organizational commitment.[9] A few other important attitudes are perceived organizational support and employee engagement; we'll also briefly discuss these.

cognitive dissonance   *Any incompatibility between two or more attitudes or between behavior and attitudes.*

Do Employers Owe Workers More Satisfying Jobs?

Research by the Conference Board suggests that job satisfaction for U.S. employees is at a 23-year low. This appears to be occurring in the midst of a dramatic growth in information technology that was supposed to make work easier for employees. What is going on here? Are employers failing to consider an ethical responsibility to employees by providing a satisfying, fulfilling experience at work?

When Professor James Heskett of Harvard posted information about these low job satisfaction rates on his blog, respondents provided a variety of different explanations for why U.S. workers are less satisfied than they were in the past. They included economic pressures, instability in the business environment, and increased competition to get the best jobs. Others believe businesses have

become so focused on stock prices and profitability that the personal relationship that used to exist between employers and employees has been lost. Still others proposed that in a poor economic environment, employees who wanted to switch to a new job aren't always able to find alternatives, leaving them "hostages" to a dissatisfying work situation.

Whatever the explanation, there is cause for concern. Survey data from Towers Watson's global workforce study of 20,000 employees in 22 markets around the world found that employees are especially concerned about job security and feel they are entirely responsible for ensuring their long-term career prospects work out. In the current economic environment, it seems that in employers' minds, employee well-being and

security have taken a back seat to coping with workplace realities.

What can managers do to ensure they are making ethical decisions about protecting the quality of the workplace in their organizations? As we have shown, managers can enact a variety of concrete steps—including improving working conditions and providing a positive social environment—that will make work more enjoyable for employees. Employers may also want to think about whether their efforts to achieve efficiency and productivity are creating a work environment that is not very satisfying for employees.

Sources: Based on J. Heskett, "Why Are Fewer and Fewer U.S. Employees Satisfied with Their Jobs?" *Harvard Business School Working Knowledge* (April 2, 2010), hbswk .hbs.edu; and Towers Watson, *2010 Global Workforce Study* (New York: Author, 2010).

Job Satisfaction   When people speak of employee attitudes, they usually mean **job satisfaction**, which describes a positive feeling about a job, resulting from an evaluation of its characteristics. A person with a high level of job satisfaction holds positive feelings about his or her job, while a person with a low level holds negative feelings. Because OB researchers give job satisfaction high importance, we'll review this attitude in detail later in the chapter.

Job Involvement   Related to job satisfaction is **job involvement**,[10] which measures the degree to which people identify psychologically with their job and consider their perceived performance level important to self-worth.[11] Employees with a high level of job involvement strongly identify with and really care about the kind of work they do. Another closely related concept is **psychological empowerment**, employees' beliefs in the degree to which they influence their work environment, their competence, the meaningfulness of their job, and their perceived autonomy.[12] One study of nursing managers in Singapore found that good leaders empower their employees by involving them in decisions, making them feel their work is important, and giving them discretion to "do their own thing."[13]

High levels of both job involvement and psychological empowerment are positively related to organizational citizenship and job performance.[14] High job involvement is also related to reduced absences and lower resignation rates.[15]

Organizational Commitment   In **organizational commitment**, an employee identifies with a particular organization and its goals and wishes to remain a

At Veterinary Cancer Group in Tustin, California, employees are committed to their company because they identify with their organization and its goals and want to remain part of the small business. The client care specialists shown in this photo and their co-workers share the cancer clinic's goal of improving the quality of life for patients and giving support to the families of patients. Veterinarian Mona Rosenberg, who founded the practice, has created a positive work environment at the clinic by hiring kind and compassionate people and by valuing the work of each employee, resulting in the favorable employee attitude of organizational commitment.

Source: 044/Zums Press/Newscom

member. Most research has focused on emotional attachment to an organization and belief in its values as the "gold standard" for employee commitment.[16]

A positive relationship appears to exist between organizational commitment and job productivity, but it is a modest one.[17] A review of 27 studies suggested the relationship between commitment and performance is strongest for new employees and considerably weaker for more experienced employees.[18] Interestingly, research indicates that employees who feel their employers fail to keep promises to them feel less committed, and these reductions in commitment, in turn, lead to lower levels of creative performance.[19] And, as with job involvement, the research evidence demonstrates negative relationships between organizational commitment and both absenteeism and turnover.[20]

Theoretical models propose that employees who are committed will be less likely to engage in work withdrawal even if they are dissatisfied, because they have a sense of organizational loyalty. On the other hand, employees who are not committed, who feel less loyal to the organization, will tend to show lower levels of attendance at work across the board. Research confirms this theoretical proposition.[21] It does appear that even if employees are not currently happy with their work, they are willing to make sacrifices for the organization if they are committed enough.

job satisfaction   *A positive feeling about one's job resulting from an evaluation of its characteristics.*

job involvement   *The degree to which a person identifies with a job, actively participates in it, and considers performance important to self-worth.*

psychological empowerment
Employees' belief in the degree to which they affect their work environment, their competence, the meaningfulness of their job, and their perceived autonomy in their work.

organizational commitment   *The degree to which an employee identifies with a particular organization and its goals and wishes to maintain membership in the organization.*

Culture and Work–Life Balance

The increased time pressures of the always-connected workplace are eroding the boundary between work life and personal life, and many individuals in postindustrial economies struggle to balance the two. Is this striving for work–life balance unique to the North American and European context, or is it a global phenomenon?

One possible reason for variations in work–life balance across countries is differences in the structure and functioning of the family. Some research suggests that countries with stronger differences in expectations for men and women have different levels and types of work–life conflict. Other research suggests that work–life balance will be different in an individualistic country like the United States than in a country that is more collectivist in its orientation. In individualist countries, employers might expect more sacrifice from their employees in terms of their family lives, whereas collectivist nations where family has a higher priority will have fewer work–life balance issues. Conversely, collectivists' higher value on family may mean they feel more conflicted if there are competing demands from the workplace and home.

There are other reasons to suspect that research based on the U.S. context will not generalize to other countries. Data from a study by Harvard and McGill University researchers found that work–life balance policies like paid maternity leave, paternity leave, and paid time off in the United States are far less generous than in other wealthy nations. The study's lead author, Jody Heymann, notes, "More countries are providing the workplace protections that millions of Americans can only dream of." The research interest in work–life balance may at least partially be a reflection of an unusually strong conflict between work and family life in the United States.

At the same time, many of the same issues that contribute to work–life imbalance *are* present in other countries. Globally, the rise of the dual-earner couple has meant that both partners now have family responsibilities that must be met. Always-connected technology that blurs the line between personal and work time have become standard for managers in every part of the world. The institution of "siesta," or a midday break, used to be much more common in Hispanic cultures than it is today as the globalized workplace puts greater demands on workers. Concerns about overwork have also become very prevalent in the rapidly growing economic sphere of East Asia. The Japanese even have a term, *karoshi*, referring to death from overwork.

Research to date does suggest that work–life concerns are present in other cultures. For example, most studies find that feelings of conflict between work and personal life are related to lower levels of satisfaction and higher levels of psychological strain. The magnitude of these relationships varies across countries, but it appears that concerns about work interfering with family are present around the world. There is also evidence that translated U.S. surveys about work–life conflicts are equally good measures of work–life conflicts in Europe and East Asia.

Even with the growth of international research, most studies to date have been designed and conducted entirely within the United States, and many others have been conducted in cultures with marked similarities to the United States, like Canada and Great Britain. As the number of international studies continues to increase, we will develop a better understanding of how different cultures relate to work–life challenges.

Sources: Based on G. N. Powell, A. M. Francesco, and Y. Ling, "Toward Culture-Sensitive Theories of the Work–Family Interface," *Journal of Organizational Behavior* 30 (2009), pp. 597–616; "Survey: U.S. Workplace Not Family-Oriented." *MSNBC.com*, (May 22, 2007), www .msnbc.msn.com/id/16907584/; and J. Lu, O. Siu, P. E. Spector, and K. Shi, "Antecedents and Outcomes of a Fourfold Taxonomy of Work-Family Balance in Chinese Employed Parents," *Journal of Occupational Health Psychology* 14 (2009), pp. 182–192.

Perceived Organizational Support   Perceived organizational support (POS) is the degree to which employees believe the organization values their contribution and cares about their well-being (for example, an employee believes his organization would accommodate him if he had a child care problem or would forgive an honest mistake on his part). Research shows that people perceive their organization as supportive when rewards are deemed fair, when employees have a voice in decisions, and when they see their supervisors as supportive.[22] Employees with strong POS perceptions have been found more likely to have higher levels of organizational citizenship behaviors, lower levels of tardiness, and better customer

Employee engagement is high at Genentech, a biotechnology firm where employees share a serious commitment to science and patients and are passionate about the work they do. Genentech employees discover, develop, manufacture, and commercialize medicines that treat patients with serious or life-threatening medical conditions. Feeling that their contributions are important and meaningful, employees cite the chance to make a difference in the lives of patients as the number one reason they enjoy working at Genentech.

Source: Paul Sakuma/AP Images

service.[23] Though little cross-cultural research has been done, one study found POS predicted only the job performance and citizenship behaviors of untraditional or low power-distance Chinese employees—in short, those more likely to think of work as an exchange rather than a moral obligation.[24]

Employee Engagement A new concept is **employee engagement**, an individual's involvement with, satisfaction with, and enthusiasm for, the work she does. We might ask employees whether they have access to resources and the opportunities to learn new skills, whether they feel their work is important and meaningful, and whether their interactions with co-workers and supervisors are rewarding.[25] Highly engaged employees have a passion for their work and feel a deep connection to their company; disengaged employees have essentially checked out—putting time but not energy or attention into their work. A study of nearly 8,000 business units in 36 companies found that those whose employees had high-average levels of engagement had higher levels of customer satisfaction, were more productive, brought in higher profits, and had lower levels of turnover and accidents than at other companies.[26] Molson Coors found engaged employees were five times less likely to have safety incidents, and when one did occur it was much less serious and less costly for the engaged employee than for a disengaged one ($63 per incident versus $392). Engagement becomes a real concern for most organizations because surveys indicate that few employees—between 17 percent and 29 percent—are highly engaged by their work. Caterpillar set out to increase employee engagement and recorded a resulting 80 percent drop in grievances and a 34 percent increase in highly satisfied customers.[27]

perceived organizational support (POS) *The degree to which employees believe an organization values their contribution and cares about their well-being.*

employee engagement *An individual's involvement with, satisfaction with, and enthusiasm for the work he or she does.*

Such promising findings have earned employee engagement a following in many business organizations and management consulting firms. However, the concept is relatively new and still generates active debate about its usefulness. One review of the literature concluded, "The meaning of employee engagement is ambiguous among both academic researchers and among practitioners who use it in conversations with clients." Another reviewer called engagement "an umbrella term for whatever one wants it to be."[28] More recent research has set out to clarify the dimensions of employee engagement. This work has demonstrated that engagement is distinct from job satisfaction and job involvement and incrementally predicts job behaviors after we take these traditional job attitudes into account.

SELF-ASSESSMENT LIBRARY

Am I Engaged?

In the Self-Assessment Library (available on CD or online), take assessment IV.B.1 (Am I Engaged?). (Note: If you do not currently have a job, answer the questions for your most recent job.)

Are These Job Attitudes Really All That Distinct?   You might wonder whether these job attitudes are really distinct. If people feel deeply engaged by their job (high job involvement), isn't it probable they like it too (high job satisfaction)? Won't people who think their organization is supportive (high perceived organizational support) also feel committed to it (strong organizational commitment)?

Evidence suggests these attitudes *are* highly related, perhaps to a troubling degree. For example, the correlation between perceived organizational support and affective commitment is very strong.[29] That means the variables may be redundant—if you know someone's affective commitment, you know her perceived organizational support. Why is redundancy troubling? Because it is inefficient and confusing. Why have two steering wheels on a car when you need only one? Why have two concepts—going by different labels—when you need only one?

Although we OB researchers like proposing new attitudes, often we haven't been good at showing how they compare and contrast with each other. There is some distinctiveness among them, but they overlap greatly, for various reasons including the employee's personality. Some people are predisposed to be positive or negative about almost everything. If someone tells you she loves her company, it may not mean a lot if she is positive about everything else in her life. Or the overlap may mean some organizations are just all-around better places to work than others. Then if you as a manager know someone's level of job satisfaction, you know most of what you need to know about how that person sees the organization.

Job Satisfaction

4 Define *job satisfaction* and show how we can measure it.

We have already discussed job satisfaction briefly. Now let's dissect the concept more carefully. How do we measure job satisfaction? What causes an employee to have a high level of job satisfaction? How do dissatisfied and satisfied employees affect an organization?

Measuring Job Satisfaction

Our definition of job satisfaction—a positive feeling about a job resulting from an evaluation of its characteristics—is clearly broad.[30] Yet that breadth is appropriate. A job is more than just shuffling papers, writing programming code, waiting on customers, or driving a truck. Jobs require interacting with co-workers and bosses, following organizational rules and policies, meeting performance standards, living with less than ideal working conditions, and the like.[31] An employee's assessment of his satisfaction with the job is thus a complex summation of many discrete elements. How, then, do we measure it?

Two approaches are popular. The single global rating is a response to one question, such as "All things considered, how satisfied are you with your job?" Respondents circle a number between 1 and 5 on a scale from "highly satisfied" to "highly dissatisfied." The second method, the summation of job facets, is more sophisticated. It identifies key elements in a job such as the nature of the work, supervision, present pay, promotion opportunities, and relationships with co-workers.[32] Respondents rate these on a standardized scale, and researchers add the ratings to create an overall job satisfaction score.

Is one of these approaches superior? Intuitively, summing up responses to a number of job factors seems likely to achieve a more accurate evaluation of job satisfaction. Research, however, doesn't support the intuition.[33] This is one of those rare instances in which simplicity seems to work as well as complexity, making one method essentially as valid as the other. The best explanation is that the concept of job satisfaction is so broad a single question captures its essence. The summation of job facets may also leave out some important data. Both methods are helpful. The single global rating method isn't very time consuming, thus freeing time for other tasks, and the summation of job facets helps managers zero in on problems and deal with them faster and more accurately.

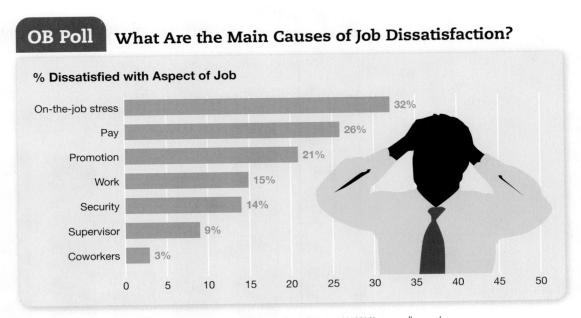

OB Poll   **What Are the Main Causes of Job Dissatisfaction?**

% Dissatisfied with Aspect of Job

On-the-job stress	32%
Pay	26%
Promotion	21%
Work	15%
Security	14%
Supervisor	9%
Coworkers	3%

Source: L. Saad, "On-the-Job Stress Is U.S. Workers' Biggest Complaint," *Gallup Poll* (August 30, 2010), www.gallup.com/.

How Satisfied Are People in Their Jobs?

Are most people satisfied with their jobs? The answer seems to be a qualified "yes" in the United States and most other developed countries. Independent studies conducted among U.S. workers over the past 30 years generally indicate more workers are satisfied with their jobs than not. But a caution is in order. Recent data show a dramatic drop-off in average job satisfaction levels during the economic contraction that started in late 2007, so much so that only about half of workers report being satisfied with their jobs now.[34]

Research also shows satisfaction levels vary a lot, depending on which facet of job satisfaction you're talking about. As shown in Exhibit 3-2, people have typically been more satisfied with their jobs overall, with the work itself, and with their supervisors and co-workers than they have been with their pay and with promotion opportunities. It's not really clear why people dislike their pay and promotion possibilities more than other aspects of their jobs.[35]

Although job satisfaction appears relevant across cultures, that doesn't mean there are no cultural differences in job satisfaction. Evidence suggests employees in Western cultures have higher levels of job satisfaction than those in Eastern cultures.[36] Exhibit 3-3 provides the results of a global study of job satisfaction levels of workers in 15 countries. (This study included 23 countries, but for presentation purposes we report the results for only the largest.) As the exhibit shows, the highest levels appear in the United States and western Europe. Do employees in Western cultures have better jobs? Or are they simply more positive (and less self critical)? Although both factors are probably at play, evidence suggests that individuals in Eastern cultures find negative emotions less aversive more than do individuals in Western cultures, who tend to emphasize positive emotions and individual happiness.[37] That may be why employees in Western cultures such as the United States and Scandinavia are more likely to have higher levels of satisfaction.

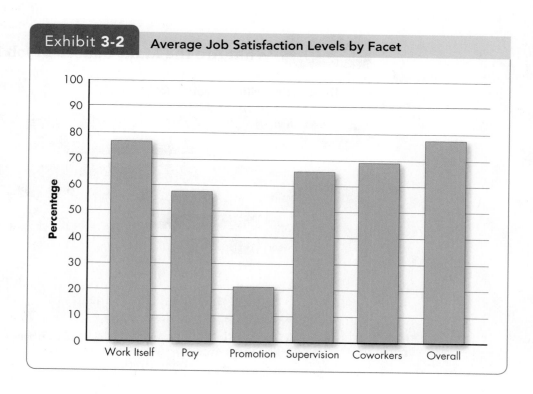

Exhibit 3-2   Average Job Satisfaction Levels by Facet

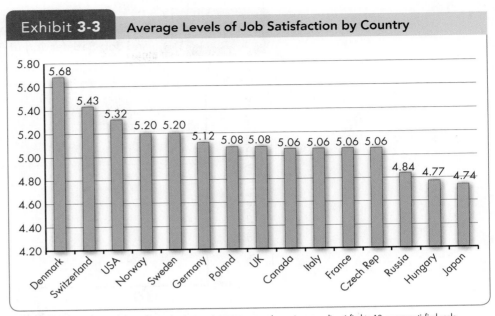

Exhibit 3-3 — Average Levels of Job Satisfaction by Country

Note: Scores represent average job-satisfaction levels in each country as rated on a 1 = very dissatisfied to 10 = very satisfied scale.

Source: M. Benz and B. S. Frey, "The Value of Autonomy: Evidence from the Self-Employed in 23 Countries," working paper 173, Institute for Empirical Research in Economics, University of Zurich, November 2003 (ssrn.com/abstract=475140).

What Causes Job Satisfaction?

5   Summarize the main causes of job satisfaction.

Think about the best job you've ever had. What made it so? Chances are you liked the work you did and the people with whom you worked. Interesting jobs that provide training, variety, independence, and control satisfy most employees.[38] There is also a strong correspondence between how well people enjoy the social context of their workplace and how satisfied they are overall. Interdependence, feedback, social support, and interaction with co-workers outside the workplace are strongly related to job satisfaction even after accounting for characteristics of the work itself.[39]

You've probably noticed that pay comes up often when people discuss job satisfaction. For people who are poor or who live in poor countries, pay does correlate with job satisfaction and overall happiness. But once an individual reaches a level of comfortable living (in the United States, that occurs at about $40,000 a year, depending on the region and family size), the relationship between pay and job satisfaction virtually disappears. People who earn $80,000 are, on average, no happier with their jobs than those who earn closer to $40,000. Take a look at Exhibit 3-4. It shows the relationship between the average pay for a job and the average level of job satisfaction. As you can see, there isn't much of a relationship there. Handsomely compensated jobs have average satisfaction levels no higher than those that pay much less. One researcher even found no significant difference when he compared the overall well-being of the richest people on the *Forbes* 400 list with that of Maasai herders in East Africa.[40]

Money does motivate people, as we will discover in Chapter 6. But what motivates us is not necessarily the same as what makes us happy. A recent poll by UCLA and the American Council on Education found that entering college freshmen rated becoming "very well off financially" first on a list of 19 goals, ahead of choices such as helping others, raising a family, or becoming proficient in an academic pursuit. Maybe your goal isn't to be happy. But if it is, money's probably not going to do much to get you there.[41]

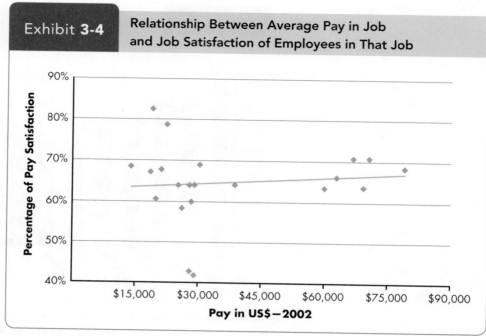

| Exhibit **3-4** | Relationship Between Average Pay in Job and Job Satisfaction of Employees in That Job |

Source: T. A. Judge, R. F. Piccolo, N. P. Podsakoff, J. C. Shaw, and B. L. Rich, "Can Happiness Be 'Earned'? The Relationship Between Pay and Job Satisfaction," working paper, University of Florida, 2005.

Job satisfaction is not just about job conditions. Personality also plays a role. Research has shown that people who have positive **core self-evaluations**—who believe in their inner worth and basic competence—are more satisfied with their jobs than those with negative core self-evaluations. Not only do they see their work as more fulfilling and challenging, they are more likely to gravitate toward challenging jobs in the first place. Those with negative core self-evaluations set less ambitious goals and are more likely to give up when confronting difficulties. Thus, they're more likely to be stuck in boring, repetitive jobs than those with positive core self-evaluations.[42]

The Impact of Satisfied and Dissatisfied Employees on the Workplace

6 Identify four employee responses to dissatisfaction.

What happens when employees like their jobs, and when they dislike their jobs? One theoretical model—the exit–voice–loyalty–neglect framework—is helpful in understanding the consequences of dissatisfaction. Exhibit 3-5 illustrates the framework's four responses, which differ along two dimensions: constructive/destructive and active/passive. The responses are as follows:[43]

- **Exit.** The **exit** response directs behavior toward leaving the organization, including looking for a new position as well as resigning.
- **Voice.** The **voice** response includes actively and constructively attempting to improve conditions, including suggesting improvements, discussing problems with superiors, and undertaking some forms of union activity.
- **Loyalty.** The **loyalty** response means passively but optimistically waiting for conditions to improve, including speaking up for the organization in the face of external criticism and trusting the organization and its management to "do the right thing."
- **Neglect.** The **neglect** response passively allows conditions to worsen and includes chronic absenteeism or lateness, reduced effort, and increased error rate.

| Exhibit **3-5** | Responses to Dissatisfaction |

	Constructive	Destructive
Active	VOICE	EXIT
Passive	LOYALTY	NEGLECT

Myth or Science?

"Favorable Job Attitudes Make Organizations More Profitable"

This statement appears to be true. A recent study of 2,178 business units suggested that job attitudes measured at one point in time predicted organizational financial performance roughly six months later. In the study, job attitudes were measured through employees' responses to 12 questions (such as, "At work, my opinions seem to count") and financial performance was measured in terms of revenue and profit margin.

Why does employee job satisfaction appear to pay off? The authors of this study uncovered two explanations:

satisfied employees are less likely to quit, and they engender stronger customer loyalty. Low turnover and high customer loyalty both helped make organizations more profitable.

This study also found some evidence for what might be called a virtuous cycle: having satisfied employees tends to improve subsequent financial performance, which tends to improve later employee satisfaction even further.

No organization can be all things to all employees, but this study does suggest that attention to improving employee attitudes is well rewarded.

The authors of this study conclude, "Improving employee work perceptions can improve business competitiveness while positively impacting the well-being of employees."

Sources: Based on Anonymous, "Happy Employees May Be the Key to Success for Organizations," *Science Daily* (August 4, 2010), www.sciencedaily.com; J. K. Harter and F. L. Schmidt, "What Really Drives Financial Success?" *Gallup Management Journal* (September 2, 2010), http://gmj.gallup.com/content/142733/really-drives-financial-success.aspx.

core self-evaluations *Bottom-line conclusions individuals have about their capabilities, competence, and worth as a person.*

exit *Dissatisfaction expressed through behavior directed toward leaving the organization.*

voice *Dissatisfaction expressed through active and constructive attempts to improve conditions.*

loyalty *Dissatisfaction expressed by passively waiting for conditions to improve.*

neglect *Dissatisfaction expressed through allowing conditions to worsen.*

Exit and neglect behaviors encompass our performance variables—productivity, absenteeism, and turnover. But this model expands employee response to include voice and loyalty—constructive behaviors that allow individuals to tolerate unpleasant situations or revive satisfactory working conditions. It helps us understand situations, such as we sometimes find among unionized workers, for whom low job satisfaction is coupled with low turnover.[44] Union members often express dissatisfaction through the grievance procedure or formal contract negotiations. These voice mechanisms allow them to continue in their jobs while convincing themselves they are acting to improve the situation.

As helpful as this framework is, it's quite general. We now discuss more specific outcomes of job satisfaction and dissatisfaction in the workplace.

Job Satisfaction and Job Performance   As several studies have concluded, happy workers are more likely to be productive workers. Some researchers used to believe the relationship between job satisfaction and job performance was a myth. But a review of 300 studies suggested the correlation is pretty strong.[45] As we move from the individual to the organizational level, we also find support for the satisfaction–performance relationship.[46] When we gather satisfaction and productivity data for the organization as a whole, we find organizations with more satisfied employees tend to be more effective than organizations with fewer.

Job Satisfaction and OCB   It seems logical to assume job satisfaction should be a major determinant of an employee's organizational citizenship behavior (OCB).[47] Satisfied employees would seem more likely to talk positively about the organization, help others, and go beyond the normal expectations in their job, perhaps because they want to reciprocate their positive experiences. Consistent with this thinking, evidence suggests job satisfaction *is* moderately correlated with OCBs; people who are more satisfied with their jobs are more likely to engage in OCBs.[48] Why? Fairness perceptions help explain the relationship.[49] Those who feel their co-workers support them are more likely to engage in helpful behaviors, whereas those who have antagonistic relationships with co-workers are less likely to do so.[50] Individuals with certain personality traits are

Customers of CSN Stores appreciate the excellent service provided by the online retailer's customer representatives shown here at the company's offices in Boston. Service firms like CSN understand that satisfied employees increase customer satisfaction and loyalty. CSN believes that customers deserve exceptional service and is dedicated to hiring people who are friendly and willing to help others. The company helps shape a positive on-the-job attitude by giving employees product knowledge training and teaching them how to assess customer needs and how to guide buyers in making well-informed decisions.

Source: Melanie Stetson Freeman/CSM/Newscom

also more satisfied with their work, which in turn leads them to engage in more OCBs.[51] Finally, research shows that when people are in a good mood, they are more likely to engage in OCBs.[52]

Job Satisfaction and Customer Satisfaction   As we noted in Chapter 1, employees in service jobs often interact with customers. Because service organization managers should be concerned with pleasing those customers, it is reasonable to ask, Is employee satisfaction related to positive customer outcomes? For front-line employees who have regular customer contact, the answer is "yes." Satisfied employees increase customer satisfaction and loyalty.[53]

A number of companies are acting on this evidence. The first core value of online retailer Zappos, "Deliver WOW through service," seems fairly obvious, but the way in which Zappos does it is not. Employees are encouraged to "create fun and a little weirdness" and are given unusual discretion in making customers satisfied; they are encouraged to use their imaginations, including sending flowers to disgruntled customers, and Zappos even offers a $2,000 bribe to quit the company after training (to weed out the half-hearted).[54] Other organizations seem to work the other end of the spectrum. Two independent reports—one on the Transportation Security Administration (TSA) and the other on airline passenger complaints—argue that low employee morale was a major factor undermining passenger satisfaction. At US Airways, employees have posted comments on blogs such as "Our planes (sic) smell filthy" and, from another, "How can I take pride in this product?"[55]

Job Satisfaction and Absenteeism   We find a consistent negative relationship between satisfaction and absenteeism, but it is moderate to weak.[56] While it certainly makes sense that dissatisfied employees are more likely to miss work, other factors affect the relationship. Organizations that provide liberal sick leave benefits are encouraging all their employees—including those who are highly satisfied—to take days off. You can find work satisfying yet still want to enjoy a 3-day weekend if those days come free with no penalties. When numerous alternative jobs are available, dissatisfied employees have high absence rates, but when there are few they have the same (low) rate of absence as satisfied employees.[57]

Job Satisfaction and Turnover   The relationship between job satisfaction and turnover is stronger than between satisfaction and absenteeism.[58] The satisfaction–turnover relationship also is affected by alternative job prospects. If an employee is presented with an unsolicited job offer, job dissatisfaction is less predictive of turnover because the employee is more likely leaving in response to "pull" (the lure of the other job) than "push" (the unattractiveness of the current job). Similarly, job dissatisfaction is more likely to translate into turnover when employment opportunities are plentiful because employees perceive it is easy to move. Finally, when employees have high "human capital" (high education, high ability), job dissatisfaction is more likely to translate into turnover because they have, or perceive, many available alternatives.[59]

Job Satisfaction and Workplace Deviance   Job dissatisfaction and antagonistic relationships with co-workers predict a variety of behaviors organizations find undesirable, including unionization attempts, substance abuse, stealing at work, undue socializing, and tardiness. Researchers argue these behaviors are indicators of a broader syndrome called *deviant behavior in the workplace* (or *counterproductive behavior* or *employee withdrawal*).[60] If employees don't like their work environment, they'll respond somehow, though it is not always easy to forecast exactly *how*. One worker might quit. Another might use work time to

When employees do not like their work environment, they will respond in some way. An attempt to form a union is one specific behavior that may stem from job dissatisfaction. At several different Wal-Mart locations throughout the United States, dissatisfied employees have tried, unsuccessfully, to organize a union as a way to receive better pay and more affordable health insurance. Joined by supporters, the employees shown here from a Wal-Mart warehouse and distribution center in California are protesting low wages and no health care or other benefits.

Source: Robyn Beck/Getty Images

surf the Internet or take work supplies home for personal use. In short, workers who don't like their jobs "get even" in various ways—and because those ways can be quite creative, controlling only one behavior, such as with an absence control policy, leaves the root cause untouched. To effectively control the undesirable consequences of job dissatisfaction, employers should attack the source of the problem—the dissatisfaction—rather than try to control the different responses.

Managers Often "Don't Get It" Given the evidence we've just reviewed, it should come as no surprise that job satisfaction can affect the bottom line. One study by a management consulting firm separated large organizations into high morale (more than 70 percent of employees expressed overall job satisfaction) and medium or low morale (fewer than 70 percent). The stock prices of companies in the high-morale group grew 19.4 percent, compared with 10 percent for the medium- or low-morale group. Despite these results, many managers are unconcerned about employee job satisfaction. Still others overestimate how satisfied employees are with their jobs, so they don't think there's a problem when there is. In one study of 262 large employers, 86 percent of senior managers believed their organization treated its employees well, but only 55 percent of employees agreed. Another study found 55 percent of managers thought morale was good in their organization, compared to only 38 percent of employees.[61]

Regular surveys can reduce gaps between what managers *think* employees feel and what they *really* feel. Jonathan McDaniel, manager of a KFC restaurant in Houston, surveys his employees every 3 months. Some results led him to make changes, such as giving employees greater say about which workdays they have off. However, McDaniel believes the process itself is valuable. "They really love giving their opinions," he says. "That's the most important part of it—that they have a voice and that they're heard." Surveys are no panacea, but if job attitudes are as important as we believe, organizations need to find out where they can be improved.[62]

Employer–Employee Loyalty Is an Outdated Concept

The word *loyalty* is so outdated it is practically laughable. Long gone are the days when an employer would keep an employee for life, as are the days when an employee would work for a single company for his or her entire career.

Workplace guru Linda Gratton says, "Loyalty is dead—killed off through shortening contracts, outsourcing, automation and multiple careers. Faced with what could be 50 years of work, who honestly wants to spend that much time with one company? Serial monogamy is the order of the day."

Right or wrong, the commitment on each side of the equation is weak. Take the example of Renault. The company ended the 31-year career of employee Michel Balthazard (and two others) on charges of espionage. The problem? The charges were proved false. When the falseness of the charges became public, Renault halfheartedly offered the employees their jobs back and a lame apology: "Renault thanks them for the quality of their work at the group and wishes them every success in the future."

As for employee's loyalty to their employers, that too is worth little nowadays. One manager with Deloitte says the current employee attitude is, "I'm leaving, I had a great experience, and I'm taking that with me."

Employers tend to cut commitments to an employee, and reduce his or her benefits, the minute they perceive they can do so. Employees tend to jump at the best available job offer as soon as they see it.

The sooner we see the employment experience for what it is (mostly transactional, mostly short to medium term), the better off we'll be. The workplace is no place for fantasies.

There are employers and employees who show little regard for each other. That each side can be uncaring or cavalier is hardly a revelation. No doubt such cynical attitudes are as old as the employment relationship itself.

But is that the norm? And is it desirable? The answer to both these questions is "no."

Says management guru Tom Peters, "Bottom line: loyalty matters. A lot. Yesterday. Today. Tomorrow." University of Michigan's Dave Ulrich says, "Leaders who encourage loyalty want employees who are not only committed to and engaged in their work but who also find meaning from it."

It is true that the employer–employee relationship has changed. For example, (largely) gone are the days when employers provide guaranteed payout pensions to which employees contribute nothing. But is that such a bad thing? There is a big difference between asking employees to contribute to their pension plans and abandoning plans altogether (or firing without cause).

Moreover, it's not that loyalty is dead, but rather that employers are loyal to a different kind of employee. Gone are the days when an employer would refuse to fire a long-tenured but incompetent employee. But is that the kind of loyalty most employees expect today anyway? Companies are loyal to employees who do their jobs well, and that too is as it should be.

In short, employees still expect certain standards of decency and loyalty from their employers, and employers want engaged, committed employees in return. That is a good thing—and not so different from yesterday. Says workplace psychologist Binna Kandola, "Workplaces may have changed but loyalty is not dead—the bonds between people are too strong."

Sources: P. Korkki, "The Shifting Definition of Worker Loyalty," *The New York Times* (April 24, 2011), p. BU8; "Is Workplace Loyalty an Outmoded Concept?" *Financial Times* (March 8, 2011), www.ft.com/; and O. Gough and S. Arkani, "The Impact of the Shifting Pensions Landscape on the Psychological Contract," *Personnel Review* 40, no. 2 (2011), pp. 173–184.

Summary and Implications for Managers

Managers should be interested in their employees' attitudes because attitudes give warnings of potential problems and influence behavior. Creating a satisfied workforce is hardly a guarantee of successful organizational performance, but evidence strongly suggests that whatever managers can do to improve employee attitudes will likely result in heightened organizational effectiveness. Some take-away lessons from the study of attitudes include the following:

- Satisfied and committed employees have lower rates of turnover, absenteeism, and withdrawal behaviors. They also perform better on the job. Given that managers want to keep resignations and absences down—especially among their most productive employees—they'll want to do things that generate positive job attitudes.
- Managers will also want to measure job attitudes effectively so they can tell how employees are reacting to their work. As one review put it, "A sound measurement of overall job attitude is one of the most useful pieces of information an organization can have about its employees."[63]
- The most important thing managers can do to raise employee satisfaction is focus on the intrinsic parts of the job, such as making the work challenging and interesting.
- Although paying employees poorly will likely not attract high-quality employees to the organization or keep high performers, managers should realize that high pay alone is unlikely to create a satisfying work environment.

QUESTIONS FOR REVIEW

1 What are the main components of attitudes? Are these components related or unrelated?

2 Does behavior always follow from attitudes? Why or why not? Discuss the factors that affect whether behavior follows from attitudes.

3 What are the major job attitudes? In what ways are these attitudes alike? What is unique about each?

4 How do we measure job satisfaction?

5 What causes job satisfaction? For most people, is pay or the work itself more important?

6 What outcomes does job satisfaction influence? What implications does this have for management?

EXPERIENTIAL EXERCISE What Factors Are Most Important to Your Job Satisfaction?

Most of us probably want a job we think will satisfy us. But because no job is perfect, we often have to trade off job attributes. One job may pay well but provide limited opportunities for advancement or skill development. Another may offer work we enjoy but have poor benefits. The following is a list of 21 job factors or attributes:

- Autonomy and independence.
- Benefits.
- Career advancement opportunities.
- Career development opportunities.
- Compensation/pay.
- Communication between employees and management.
- Contribution of work to organization's business goals.
- Feeling safe in the work environment.
- Flexibility to balance life and work issues.
- Job security.
- Job-specific training.
- Management recognition of employee job performance.
- Meaningfulness of job.
- Networking.
- Opportunities to use skills/abilities.
- Organization's commitment to professional development.
- Overall corporate culture.
- Relationship with co-workers.
- Relationship with immediate supervisor.
- The work itself.
- The variety of work.

On a sheet of paper, rank-order these job factors from top to bottom so number 1 is the job factor you think is most important to your job satisfaction, number 2 is the second most important factor to your job satisfaction, and so on.

Next, gather in teams of three or four people and try the following:

1. Appoint a spokesperson who will take notes and report the answers to the following questions, on behalf of your group, back to the class.
2. Averaging across all members in your group, generate a list of the top five job factors.
3. Did most people in your group seem to value the same job factors? Why or why not?
4. Your instructor will provide you the results of a study of a random sample of 600 employees conducted by the Society for Human Resource Management (SHRM). How do your group's rankings compare with the SHRM results?
5. The chapter says pay doesn't correlate all that well with job satisfaction, but in the SHRM survey, people say it is relatively important. Can your group suggest a reason for the apparent discrepancy?
6. Now examine your own list again. Does your list agree with the group list? Does your list agree with the SHRM study?

ETHICAL DILEMMA Bounty Hunters

His SUV carefully obscured behind a row of trees, Rick Raymond, private investigator, was on another case. This case was not to catch the unfaithful spouse or petty criminal in action. Instead, Raymond was tracking an employee, at the request of an employer, to determine whether an Orlando repairman was sick as he claimed today and as he had claimed to be several times recently.

As we have seen, absenteeism is a huge problem for organizations that has left them desperate for solutions. One solution is to investigate. In the typical routine, when an employee calls in sick, the employer asks for the reason. If the reason is illness, and illness has been the reason for an

abnormal number of times in the past, the employer hires a P.I. to follow the employee and photograph or videotape his or her activity outside the house. Private investigators also are used to ascertain whether individuals filing injury claims (and drawing worker's compensation benefits) are in fact injured.

It may surprise you to learn that a recent court decision indicated hiring a private investigator to follow an employee is legal. In this particular case, Diana Vail was fired by Raybestos Products, an automotive parts manufacturer in Crawfordsville, Indiana, after an off-duty police officer hired by Raybestos produced evidence that she was abusing her sick-leave benefits. The U.S. Court of Appeals ruled that such investigations were legal.

Despite their legality, such investigations are controversial. Oracle and Hewlett-Packard have reportedly used private investigators to follow managers or uncover the source of leaks. Both actions spawned negative media coverage.

There is no doubt, though, that some employees do abuse their sick-leave benefits. In an earlier case, Raymond investigated an employee who called in sick with the flu for 3 days. Raymond discovered that she actually visited Orlando theme parks on each of those days. When Raymond showed her three time-stamped pictures of herself on rides, the employee's first response was, "That's not me!" In another case, Raymond caught a worker

constructing an elaborate scheme to call in sick and go on a cruise. "When he was shown the video surveillance I'd done, he actually said to his boss, 'I can't believe you'd be so sneaky.'" Raymond said. "The hypocrisy is amazing."

Questions

1. If you had reason to believe someone was lying about an absence from work, do you think it would be appropriate to investigate?

2. If excessive absenteeism is a real problem in an organization, are there alternatives to surveillance? If so, what are they, and do they have any limitations of their own?

Sources: E. Spitznagel, "The Sick-Day Bounty Hunters," *Businessweek* (December 6, 2010), pp. 93–95; D. Levine, "Oracle Enlists Private Eyes to Find HP CEO," *Reuters* (November 9, 2010), http://in.reuters.com/; and K. Gullo, "HP's Apotheker, Like Carmen Sandiego, Focus at Trial," *Businessweek* (November 10, 2010), www.businessweek.com/.

CASE INCIDENT 1 Long Hours, Hundreds of E-Mails, and No Sleep: Does This Sound Like a Satisfying Job?

In the 1970s, futurists were predicting that increases in technology would dramatically shorten the workweek for most people. But in the wired work world of today, where employees can reach "the office" from wherever they are, many managers are finding it extremely difficult to get away from their jobs. In fact, one employment firm estimated that 30 percent of professionals take less than their allotted vacation time, and 42 percent said they have to cancel vacation plans regularly. Consider a few examples:

- Gian Paolo Lombardo might work for a firm that manufactures luggage for luxury travel, but he's had precious little time for vacationing himself. During his last "faux-cation" 3 years ago, he spent most of the time in his hotel room in the resort town of Carmel, California, with his BlackBerry, while his wife Ellen chatted with other guests, hoping he'd finally finish with work. Ellen notes that no meal or movie goes by without her husband being hunched over his smartphone. She says, "I think he needs to go into rehab." He agrees.

- Irene Tse heads the government bond-trading division at Goldman Sachs. For 10 years, she has seen the stock market go from all-time highs to recession levels. Such fluctuations can mean millions of dollars in either profits or losses. "There are days when you can make a lot, and other days where you lose so much you're just stunned by what you've done," says Tse. She says she

hasn't slept through the night in years and often wakes up several times to check the global market status. Her average workweek? Eighty hours. "I've done this for 10 years, and I can count on the fingers of one hand the number of days in my career when I didn't want to come to work. Every day I wake up and I can't wait to get here."

- Tony Kurz is a managing director at Capital Alliance Partners, and he raises funds for real estate investments. However, these are not your average properties. Kurz often flies to exotic locations such as Costa Rica and Hawaii to woo prospective clients. He travels more than 300,000 miles per year, often sleeping on planes and coping with jet lag. Kurz is not the only one he knows with such a hectic work schedule. His girlfriend, Avery Baker, logs around 400,000 miles a year as the senior vice president of marketing for Tommy Hilfiger. "It's not easy to maintain a relationship like this," says Kurz. But do Kurz and Baker like their jobs? You bet.

- David Clark is the vice president of global marketing for MTV. His job often consists of traveling around the globe to promote the channel as well as to keep up with the global music scene. If he is not traveling (Clark typically logs 200,000 miles a year), a typical day consists of waking at 6:30 A.M. and immediately responding to numerous messages that have accumulated over the course of the night. He then goes to his office, where throughout the day he responds to another 500 or so messages from clients around the world. If he's lucky, he gets to spend an hour a day with his son, but then it's back to work until he finally goes to bed around midnight. Says Clark, "There are plenty of people who would love to have this job. They're knocking on the door all the time. So that's motivating."

Many individuals would balk at the prospect of a 60-hour or more workweek with constant traveling and little time for anything else. Some individuals are exhilarated by it. But the demands of such jobs are clearly not for everyone. Many quit, with turnover levels at 55 percent for consultants and 30 percent for investment bankers, according to Vault.com. However, clearly such jobs, while time-consuming and often stressful, can be satisfying to some individuals.

Sources: Based on L. Golden, "A Brief History of Long Work Time and the Contemporary Sources of Overwork," *Journal of Business Ethics* 84, (2009), pp. 217–227; L. Tischler, "Extreme Jobs (And the People Who Love Them)," *Fast Company*, April 2005, pp. 55–60, www.glo-jobs.com/article.php?article_no=87; M. Conlin, "Do Us a Favor, Take a Vacation," *Bloomberg Businessweek*, May 21, 2007, www.businessweek.com.

Questions

1. Do you think only certain individuals are attracted to these types of jobs, or is it the characteristics of the jobs themselves that are satisfying?

2. What characteristics of these jobs might contribute to increased levels of job satisfaction?

3. Given that the four individuals we just read about tend to be satisfied with their jobs, how might this satisfaction relate to their job performance, citizenship behavior, and turnover?

4. Recall David Clark's statement that "There are plenty of people who would love to have this job. They're knocking on the door all the time." How might Clark's perceptions that he has a job many others desire contribute to his job satisfaction?

CASE INCIDENT 2 Crafting a Better Job

Consider for a moment a midlevel manager at a multinational foods company, Fatima, who would seem to be at the top of her career. She's consistently making her required benchmarks and goals, she has built successful relationships with colleagues, and senior management have identified her as "high potential." But she isn't happy with her work. She'd be much more interested in understanding how her organization can use social media in marketing efforts. Ideally, she'd like to quit and find something that better suits her passions, but in the current economic environment this may not be an option. So she has decided to proactively reconfigure her current job.

Fatima is part of a movement toward job "crafting," which is the process of deliberately reorganizing your job so that it better fits your motives, strengths, and passions. The core of job crafting is creating diagrams of day-to-day activities with a coach. Then you and the coach collaboratively identify which tasks fit with your personal passions, and which tend to drain motivation and satisfaction. Next the client and coach work together to imagine ways to emphasize preferred activities and de-emphasize those that are less interesting. Many people engaged in job crafting find that upon deeper consideration, they have more control over their work than they thought.

So how did Fatima craft her job? She first noticed that she was spending too much of her time monitoring her team's performance and answering team questions, and not enough time working on the creative projects that inspire her. She then considered how to modify her relationship with the team so that these activities incorporated her passion for social media strategies, with team activities more centered around developing new marketing. She also identified members of her team who might be able to help her implement these new strategies and directed her interactions with these individuals toward her new goals. As a result, not only has her engagement in her work increased, but she has also developed new ideas that are being recognized and advanced within the organization. In sum, she has found that by actively and creatively examining her work, she has been able to craft her current job into one that is truly satisfying.

Questions

1. Why do you think many people are in jobs that are not satisfying? Do organizations help people craft satisfying and motivating jobs, and if not, why not?

2. Think about how you might reorient yourself to your own job. Are the principles of job crafting described above relevant to your work? Why or why not?

3. Some contend that job crafting sounds good in principle but is not necessarily available to everyone. What types of jobs are probably not amenable to job crafting activities?

4. Are there any potential drawbacks to the job crafting approach? How can these concerns be minimized?

Sources: Based on A. Wrzesniewski, J. M. Berg, and J. E. Dutton, "Turn the Job You Have into the Job You Want," *Harvard Business Review* (June 2010), pp. 114–117; A. Wrzesniewski and J. E. Dutton, "Crafting a Job: Revisioning Employees as Active Crafters of Their Work," *Academy of Management Review* 26 (2010), pp. 179–201; and J. Caplan, "Hate Your Job? Here's How to Reshape It," *Time* (December 4, 2009), www.time.com.

ENDNOTES

1. S. J. Breckler, "Empirical Validation of Affect, Behavior, and Cognition as Distinct Components of Attitude," *Journal of Personality and Social Psychology* (May 1984), pp. 1191–1205.

2. A. W. Wicker, "Attitude Versus Action: The Relationship of Verbal and Overt Behavioral Responses to Attitude Objects," *Journal of Social Issues* (Autumn 1969), pp. 41–78.

3. L. Festinger, *A Theory of Cognitive Dissonance* (Stanford, CA: Stanford University Press, 1957).

4. See, for instance, L. R. Fabrigar, R. E. Petty, S. M. Smith, and S. L. Crites, "Understanding Knowledge Effects on Attitude-Behavior Consistency: The Role of Relevance, Complexity, and Amount of Knowledge," *Journal of Personality and Social Psychology* 90, no. 4 (2006), pp. 556–577; and D. J. Schleicher, J. D. Watt, and G. J. Greguras, "Reexamining the Job Satisfaction-Performance Relationship: The Complexity of Attitudes," *Journal of Applied Psychology* 89, no. 1 (2004), pp. 165–177.

5. See, for instance, J. Nocera, "If It's Good for Philip Morris, Can It Also Be Good for Public Health?" *The New York Times* (June 18, 2006).

6. See L. R. Glasman and D. Albarracín, "Forming Attitudes That Predict Future Behavior: A Meta-Analysis of the Attitude–Behavior Relation," *Psychological Bulletin* (September 2006), pp. 778–822; I. Ajzen, "Nature and Operation of Attitudes," in S. T. Fiske, D. L. Schacter, and C. Zahn-Waxler (eds.), *Annual Review of Psychology*, vol. 52 (Palo Alto, CA: Annual Reviews, Inc., 2001), pp. 27–58; and M. Riketta, "The Causal Relation Between Job Attitudes and Performance: A Meta-Analysis of Panel Studies," *Journal of Applied Psychology*, 93, no. 2 (2008), pp. 472–481.

7. Ibid.

8. D. A. Harrison, D. A. Newman, and P. L. Roth, "How Important Are Job Attitudes? Meta-Analytic Comparisons of Integrative Behavioral Outcomes and Time Sequences," *Academy of Management Journal* 49, no. 2 (2006), pp. 305–325.

9. D. P. Moynihan and S. K. Pandey, "Finding Workable Levers Over Work Motivation: Comparing Job Satisfaction, Job Involvement, and Organizational Commitment," *Administration & Society* 39, no. 7 (2007), pp. 803–832.

10. See, for example, J. M. Diefendorff, D. J. Brown, and A. M. Kamin, "Examining the Roles of Job Involvement and Work Centrality in Predicting Organizational Citizenship Behaviors and Job Performance," *Journal of Organizational Behavior* (February 2002), pp. 93–108.

11. Based on G. J. Blau and K. R. Boal, "Conceptualizing How Job Involvement and Organizational Commitment Affect Turnover and Absenteeism," *Academy of Management Review* (April 1987), p. 290.

12. G. Chen and R. J. Klimoski, "The Impact of Expectations on Newcomer Performance in Teams as Mediated by Work Characteristics, Social Exchanges, and Empowerment," *Academy of Management Journal* 46, no. 5 (2003), pp. 591–607; A. Ergeneli, G. Saglam, and S. Metin, "Psychological Empowerment and Its Relationship to Trust in Immediate Managers," *Journal of Business Research* (January 2007), pp. 41–49; and S. E. Seibert, S. R. Silver, and W. A. Randolph, "Taking Empowerment to the Next Level: A Multiple-Level Model of Empowerment, Performance, and Satisfaction," *Academy of Management Journal* 47, no. 3 (2004), pp. 332–349.

13. B. J. Avolio, W. Zhu, W. Koh, and P. Bhatia, "Transformational Leadership and Organizational Commitment: Mediating Role of Psychological Empowerment and Moderating Role of Structural Distance," *Journal of Organizational Behavior* 25, no. 8 (2004), pp. 951–968.

14. J. M. Diefendorff, D. J. Brown, A. M. Kamin, and R. G. Lord, "Examining the Roles of Job Involvement and Work Centrality in Predicting Organizational Citizenship Behaviors and Job Performance," *Journal of Organizational Behavior* (February 2002), pp. 93–108.

15. M. R. Barrick, M. K. Mount, and J. P. Strauss, "Antecedents of Involuntary Turnover Due to a Reduction in Force," *Personnel Psychology* 47, no. 3 (1994), pp. 515–535.

16. O. N. Solinger, W. van Olffen, and R. A. Roe, "Beyond the Three-Component Model of Organizational Commitment," *Journal of Applied Psychology* 93 (2008), pp. 70–83.

17. B. J. Hoffman, C. A. Blair, J. P. Meriac, and D. J. Woehr, "Expanding the Criterion Domain? A Quantitative Review of the OCB Literature," *Journal of Applied Psychology* 92, no. 2 (2007), pp. 555–566.

18. T. A. Wright and D. G. Bonett, "The Moderating Effects of Employee Tenure on the Relation Between Organizational Commitment and Job Performance: A Meta-Analysis," *Journal of Applied Psychology* (December 2002), pp. 1183–1190.

19. T. W. H. Ng, D. C. Feldman, and S. S. K. Lam, "Psychological Contract Breaches, Organizational Commitment, and Innovation-Related Behaviors: A Latent Growth Modeling

Approach," *Journal of Applied Psychology* 95 (2010), pp. 744–751.

20. See, for instance, K. Bentein, C. Vandenberghe, R. Vandenberg, and F. Stinglhamber, "The Role of Change in the Relationship between Commitment and Turnover: A Latent Growth Modeling Approach," *Journal of Applied Psychology* 90 (2005), pp. 468–482; and J. D. Kammeyer-Mueller, C. R. Wanberg, T. M. Glomb, and D. Ahlburg, "The Role of Temporal Shifts in Turnover Processes: It's About Time." *Journal of Applied Psychology* 90 (2005), pp. 644–658.

21. J. P. Hausknecht, N. J. Hiller, and R. J. Vance, "Work-Unit Absenteeism: Effects of Satisfaction, Commitment, Labor Market Conditions, and Time," *Academy of Management Journal* 51 (2008), pp. 1223–1245.

22. L. Rhoades, R. Eisenberger, and S. Armeli, "Affective Commitment to the Organization: The Contribution of Perceived Organizational Support," *Journal of Applied Psychology* 86, no. 5 (2001), pp. 825–836.

23. C. Vandenberghe, K. Bentein, R. Michon, J. Chebat, M. Tremblay, and J. Fils, "An Examination of the Role of Perceived Support and Employee Commitment in Employee–Customer Encounters," *Journal of Applied Psychology* 92, no. 4 (2007), pp. 1177–1187; and P. Eder and R. Eisenberger, "Perceived Organizational Support: Reducing the Negative Influence of Coworker Withdrawal Behavior," *Journal of Management* 34, no. 1 (2008), pp. 55–68.

24. J. Farh, R. D. Hackett, and J. Liang, "Individual-Level Cultural Values as Moderators of Perceived Organizational Support—Employee Outcome Relationships in China: Comparing the Effects of Power Distance and Traditionality," *Academy of Management Journal* 50, no. 3 (2007), pp. 715–729.

25. B. L. Rich, J. A. Lepine, and E. R. Crawford, "Job Engagement: Antecedents and Effects on Job Performance," *Academy of Management Journal* 53 (2010), pp. 617–635.

26. J. K. Harter, F. L. Schmidt, and T. L. Hayes, "Business-Unit-Level Relationship Between Employee Satisfaction, Employee Engagement, and Business Outcomes: A Meta-Analysis," *Journal of Applied Psychology* 87, no. 2 (2002), pp. 268–279.

27. N. R. Lockwood, *Leveraging Employee Engagement for Competitive Advantage* (Alexandria, VA: Society for Human Resource Management, 2007); and R. J. Vance, *Employee Engagement and Commitment* (Alexandria, VA: Society for Human Resource Management, 2006).

28. W. H. Macey and B. Schneider, "The Meaning of Employee Engagement," *Industrial and Organizational Psychology* 1 (2008), pp. 3–30; A. Saks, "The Meaning and Bleeding of Employee Engagement: How Muddy Is The Water?" *Industrial and Organizational Psychology* 1 (2008), pp. 40–43.

29. L. Rhoades and R. Eisenberger, "Perceived Organizational Support: A Review of the Literature," *Journal of Applied Psychology* 87, no. 4 (2002), pp. 698–714; and R. L. Payne and D. Morrison, "The Differential Effects of Negative Affectivity on Measures of Well-Being Versus Job Satisfaction and Organizational Commitment," *Anxiety, Stress & Coping: An International Journal* 15, no. 3 (2002), pp. 231–244.

30. For problems with the concept of job satisfaction, see R. Hodson, "Workplace Behaviors," *Work and Occupations* (August 1991), pp. 271–290; and H. M. Weiss and R. Cropanzano, "Affective Events Theory: A Theoretical Discussion of the Structure, Causes and Consequences of Affective Experiences at Work," in B. M. Staw and L. L. Cummings (eds.), *Research in Organizational Behavior*, vol. 18 (Greenwich, CT: JAI Press, 1996), pp. 1–3.

31. The Wyatt Company's 1989 national WorkAmerica study identified 12 dimensions of satisfaction: Work organization, working conditions, communications, job performance and performance review, co-workers, supervision, company management, pay, benefits, career development and training, job content and satisfaction, and company image and change.

32. See E. Spector, *Job Satisfaction: Application, Assessment, Causes, and Consequences* (Thousand Oaks, CA: Sage, 1997), p. 3.

33. J. Wanous, A. E. Reichers, and M. J. Hudy, "Overall Job Satisfaction: How Good Are Single-Item Measures?" *Journal of Applied Psychology* (April 1997), pp. 247–252.

34. A. F. Chelte, J. Wright, and C. Tausky, "Did Job Satisfaction Really Drop During the 1970s?" *Monthly Labor Review* (November 1982), pp. 33–36; "Job Satisfaction High in America, Says Conference Board Study," *Monthly Labor Review* (February 1985), p. 52; K. Bowman, "Attitudes About Work, Chores, and Leisure in America," *AEI Opinion Studies* (August 25, 2003); and J. Pepitone, "U.S. Job Satisfaction Hits 22-Year Low," *CNNMoney.com* (January 5, 2010).

35. W. K. Balzer, J. A. Kihm, P. C. Smith, J. L. Irwin, P. D. Bachiochi, C. Robie, E. F. Sinar, and L. F. Parra, *Users' Manual for the Job Descriptive Index (JDI; 1997 Revision) and the Job in General Scales* (Bowling Green, OH: Bowling Green State University, 1997).

36. M. J. Gelfand, M. Erez, and Z. Aycan, "Cross-Cultural Organizational Behavior," *Annual Review of Psychology* 58 (2007), pp. 479–514; and A. S. Tsui, S. S. Nifadkar, and A. Y. Ou, "Cross-National, Cross-Cultural Organizational Behavior Research: Advances, Gaps, and Recommendations," *Journal of Management* (June 2007), pp. 426–478.

37. M. Benz and B. S. Frey, "The Value of Autonomy: Evidence from the Self-Employed in 23 Countries," working paper 173, Institute for Empirical Research in Economics, University of Zurich, November 2003 (ssrn.com/abstract=475140); and P. Warr, *Work, Happiness, and Unhappiness* (Mahwah, NJ: Laurence Erlbaum, 2007).

38. J. Barling, E. K. Kelloway, and R. D. Iverson, "High-Quality Work, Job Satisfaction, and Occupational Injuries," *Journal of Applied Psychology* 88, no. 2 (2003), pp. 276–283; and F. W. Bond and D. Bunce, "The Role of Acceptance and Job Control in Mental Health, Job Satisfaction, and Work Performance," *Journal of Applied Psychology* 88, no. 6 (2003), pp. 1057–1067.

39. S. E. Humphrey, J. D. Nahrgang, and F. P. Morgeson, "Integrating Motivational, Social, and Contextual Work Design Features: A Meta-Analytic Summary and Theoretical Extension of the Work Design Literature," *Journal of Applied Psychology* 92, no. 5 (2007), pp. 1332–1356; and D. S. Chiaburu and D. A. Harrison, "Do Peers Make the Place? Conceptual Synthesis and Meta-Analysis of Coworker Effect

on Perceptions, Attitudes, OCBs, and Performance," *Journal of Applied Psychology* 93, no. 5 (2008), pp. 1082–1103.

40. E. Diener, E. Sandvik, L. Seidlitz, and M. Diener, "The Relationship Between Income and Subjective Well-Being: Relative or Absolute?" *Social Indicators Research* 28 (1993), pp. 195–223.

41. E. Diener and M. E. P. Seligman, "Beyond Money: Toward an Economy of Well-Being," *Psychological Science in the Public Interest* 5, no. 1 (2004), pp. 1–31; and A. Grant, "Money = Happiness? That's Rich: Here's the Science Behind the Axiom," *The (South Mississippi) Sun Herald* (January 8, 2005).

42. T. A. Judge and C. Hurst, "The Benefits and Possible Costs of Positive Core Self-Evaluations: A Review and Agenda for Future Research," in D. Nelson and C. L. Cooper (eds.), *Positive Organizational Behavior* (London, UK: Sage Publications, 2007), pp. 159–174.

43. See D. Farrell, "Exit, Voice, Loyalty, and Neglect as Responses to Job Dissatisfaction: A Multidimensional Scaling Study," *Academy of Management Journal* (December 1983), pp. 596–606; C. E. Rusbult, D. Farrell, G. Rogers, and A. G. Mainous III, "Impact of Exchange Variables on Exit, Voice, Loyalty, and Neglect: An Integrative Model of Responses to Declining Job Satisfaction," *Academy of Management Journal* (September 1988), pp. 599–627; M. J. Withey and W. H. Cooper, "Predicting Exit, Voice, Loyalty, and Neglect," *Administrative Science Quarterly* (December 1989), pp. 521–539; J. Zhou and J. M. George, "When Job Dissatisfaction Leads to Creativity: Encouraging the Expression of Voice," *Academy of Management Journal* (August 2001), pp. 682–696; J. B. Olson-Buchanan and W. R. Boswell, "The Role of Employee Loyalty and Formality in Voicing Discontent," *Journal of Applied Psychology* (December 2002), pp. 1167–1174; and A. Davis-Blake, J. P. Broschak, and E. George, "Happy Together? How Using Nonstandard Workers Affects Exit, Voice, and Loyalty Among Standard Employees," *Academy of Management Journal* 46, no. 4 (2003), pp. 475–485.

44. R. B. Freeman, "Job Satisfaction as an Economic Variable," *American Economic Review* (January 1978), pp. 135–141.

45. T. A. Judge, C. J. Thoresen, J. E. Bono, and G. K. Patton, "The Job Satisfaction–Job Performance Relationship: A Qualitative and Quantitative Review," *Psychological Bulletin* (May 2001), pp. 376–407.

46. C. Ostroff, "The Relationship Between Satisfaction, Attitudes, and Performance: An Organizational Level Analysis," *Journal of Applied Psychology* (December 1992), pp. 963–974; A. M. Ryan, M. J. Schmit, and R. Johnson, "Attitudes and Effectiveness: Examining Relations at an Organizational Level," *Personnel Psychology* (Winter 1996), pp. 853–882; and J. K. Harter, F. L. Schmidt, and T. L. Hayes, "Business-Unit Level Relationship Between Employee Satisfaction, Employee Engagement, and Business Outcomes: A Meta-Analysis," *Journal of Applied Psychology* (April 2002), pp. 268–279.

47. See P. Podsakoff, S. B. MacKenzie, J. B. Paine, and D. G. Bachrach, "Organizational Citizenship Behaviors: A Critical Review of the Theoretical and Empirical Literature and Suggestions for Future Research," *Journal of Management* 26, no. 3 (2000), pp. 513–563.

48. B. J. Hoffman, C. A. Blair, J. P. Maeriac, and D. J. Woehr, "Expanding the Criterion Domain? A Quantitative Review of the OCB Literature," *Journal of Applied Psychology* 92, no. 2 (2007), pp. 555–566.

49. S. L. Blader and T. R. Tyler, "Testing and Extending the Group Engagement Model: Linkages Between Social Identity, Procedural Justice, Economic Outcomes, and Extrarole Behavior," *Journal of Applied Psychology* 94, no. 2 (2009), pp. 445–464.

50. D. S. Chiaburu and D. A. Harrison, "Do Peers Make the Place? Conceptual Synthesis and Meta-Analysis of Coworker Effect on Perceptions, Attitudes, OCBs, and Performance," *Journal of Applied Psychology* 93, no. 5 (2008), pp. 1082–1103.

51. R. Ilies, I. S. Fulmer, M. Spitzmuller, and M. D. Johnson, "Personality and Citizenship Behavior: The Mediating Role of Job Satisfaction," *Journal of Applied Psychology* 94 (2009), pp. 945–959.

52. R. Ilies, B. A. Scott, and T. A. Judge, "The Interactive Effects of Personal Traits and Experienced States on Intraindividual Patterns of Citizenship Behavior," *Academy of Management Journal* 49 (2006), pp. 561–575.

53. See, for instance, D. J. Koys, "The Effects of Employee Satisfaction, Organizational Citizenship Behavior, and Turnover on Organizational Effectiveness: A Unit-Level, Longitudinal Study," *Personnel Psychology* (Spring 2001), pp. 101–114; and C. Vandenberghe, K. Bentein, R. Michon, J. Chebat, M. Tremblay, and J. Fils, "An Examination of the Role of Perceived Support and Employee Commitment in Employee-Customer Encounters," *Journal of Applied Psychology* 92, no. 4 (2007), pp. 1177–1187; and M. Schulte, C. Ostroff, S. Shmulyian, and A. Kinicki, "Organizational Climate Configurations: Relationships to Collective Attitudes, Customer Satisfaction, and Financial Performance," *Journal of Applied Psychology* 94 (2009), pp. 618–634.

54. J. M. O'Brien, "Zappos Knows How to Kick It," *Fortune* (February 2, 2009), pp. 55–60.

55. T. Frank, "Report: Low Morale May Hurt Airport Security," *USA Today* (June 25, 2008), p. 3A; and J. Bailey, "Fliers Fed Up? The Employees Feel the Same," *The New York Times* (December 22, 2007), pp. A1, A18.

56. E. A. Locke, "The Nature and Causes of Job Satisfaction," in M. D. Dunnette (ed.), *Handbook of Industrial and Organizational Psychology* (Chicago: Rand McNally, 1976), p. 1331; K. D. Scott and G. S. Taylor, "An Examination of Conflicting Findings on the Relationship Between Job Satisfaction and Absenteeism: A Meta-Analysis," *Academy of Management Journal* (September 1985), pp. 599–612; and R. Steel and J. R. Rentsch, "Influence of Cumulation Strategies on the Long-Range Prediction of Absenteeism," *Academy of Management Journal* (December 1995), pp. 1616–1634.

57. J. P. Hausknecht, N. J. Hiller, and R. J. Vance, "Work-Unit Absenteeism: Effects of Satisfaction, Commitment, Labor Market Conditions, and Time," *Academy of Management Journal* 51, no. 6 (2008), pp. 1123–1245.

58. W. Hom and R. W. Griffeth, *Employee Turnover* (Cincinnati, OH: South-Western Publishing, 1995); R. W. Griffeth, P. W. Hom, and S. Gaertner, "A Meta-Analysis of Antecedents and Correlates of Employee Turnover: Update, Moderator

Tests, and Research Implications for the Next Millennium," *Journal of Management* 26, no. 3 (2000), p. 479.

59. T. H. Lee, B. Gerhart, I. Weller, and C. O. Trevor, "Understanding Voluntary Turnover: Path-Specific Job Satisfaction Effects and the Importance of Unsolicited Job Offers," *Academy of Management Journal* 51, no. 4 (2008), pp. 651–671.

60. P. E. Spector, S. Fox, L. M. Penney, K. Bruursema, A. Goh, and S. Kessler, "The Dimensionality of Counterproductivity: Are All Counterproductive Behaviors Created Equal?" *Journal of Vocational Behavior* 68, no. 3 (2006), pp. 446–460; and D. S. Chiaburu and D. A. Harrison, "Do Peers Make the Place? Conceptual Synthesis and Meta-Analysis of Coworker

Effect on Perceptions, Attitudes, OCBs, and Performance," *Journal of Applied Psychology* 93, no. 5 (2008), pp. 1082–1103.

61. K. Holland, "Inside the Minds of Your Employees," *The New York Times* (January 28, 2007), p. B1; "Study Sees Link Between Morale and Stock Price," *Workforce Management* (February 27, 2006), p. 15; and "The Workplace as a Solar System," *The New York Times* (October 28, 2006), p. B5.

62. E. White, "How Surveying Workers Can Pay Off," *The Wall Street Journal* (June 18, 2007), p. B3.

63. Harrison, D. A., Newman, D. A., & Roth, P. L., How important are job attitudes?: Meta-analytic comparisons for integrative behavioral outcomes and time sequences. *Academy of Management Journal*, no. 49 (2006), pp. 320–321.

Getting his test result was the best—and the worst—thing that could happen to James. The 18-year-old science stream student scored nine A's and one B in the Malaysian high school examination. He was very happy with his outstanding results. He thought he was on his way to university, especially being a native. Born to an Iban father and a Chinese mother, James's life was turned upside down when his application to undertake a university matriculation program was turned down by the Ministry of Higher Education. The ministry did not recognize James's native status.

Dissatisfied, James made an appeal to the ministry but was puzzled with the reply he got. His appeal was rejected because "the candidate is categorized as a non-native" based on a definition used by the Constitution, which states for his village that both parents have to be native for a child to be deemed native.

James's dreams were crushed, and in the process he lost a part of his identity and the drive that made him a top student. "I am very sad that I can't pursue my university education." The disappointment in him was obvious. In addition, James soon learned that many students from his village had experienced a similar situation. James worried for his future and that of others. "If I get good test results, what difference does it make?"

Emotions and Moods

Time cools, time clarifies; no mood can be maintained quite unaltered through the course of hours. —Mark Twain

Photo: Uni lecture hall. Source: © Tengku Mohd Yusof/Alamy

As James's experience shows, life brings unexpected situations that cause people to have complex emotional reactions. Given the obvious role emotions play in our lives, it might surprise you that, until recently, the field of OB has given the topic of emotions little attention.[1] Why? We offer two possible explanations.

First is the *myth of rationality*.[2] Until very recently, the protocol of the work world kept a damper on emotions. A well-run organization didn't allow employees to express frustration, fear, anger, love, hate, joy, grief, or similar feelings thought to be the antithesis of rationality. Though researchers and managers knew emotions were an inseparable part of everyday life, they tried to create organizations that were emotion-free. Of course, that wasn't possible.

The second explanation is that many believed emotions of any kind were disruptive.[3] Researchers looked at strong negative emotions—especially anger— that interfered with an employee's ability to work effectively. They rarely viewed emotions as constructive or contributing to enhanced performance.

Certainly some emotions, particularly exhibited at the wrong time, can hinder performance. But employees do bring their emotions to work every day, and no study of OB would be comprehensive without considering their role in workplace behavior.

SELF-ASSESSMENT LIBRARY

How Are You Feeling Right Now?

In the Self-Assessment Library (available on CD or online), take assessment IV.D.1 (How Are You Feeling Right Now?) and answer the following questions.

1. What was higher—your positive mood score or negative mood score? How do these scores compare with those of your classmates?
2. Did your score surprise you? Why or why not?
3. What sorts of things influence your positive moods, your negative moods?

What Are Emotions and Moods?

1 Differentiate emotions from moods and list the basic emotions and moods.

In our analysis, we'll need three terms that are closely intertwined: *affect, emotions,* and *moods.*

Affect is a generic term that covers a broad range of feelings people experience, including both emotions and moods.[4] **Emotions** are intense feelings directed at someone or something.[5] **Moods** are less intense feelings than emotions and often (though not always) arise without a specific event acting as a stimulus.[6]

Most experts believe emotions are more fleeting than moods.[7] For example, if someone is rude to you, you'll feel angry. That intense feeling probably comes and goes fairly quickly, maybe even in a matter of seconds. When you're in a bad mood, though, you can feel bad for several hours.

Emotions are reactions to a person (seeing a friend at work may make you feel glad) or an event (dealing with a rude client may make you feel frustrated). You show your emotions when you're "happy about something, angry at someone, afraid of something."[8] Moods, in contrast, aren't usually directed at a person or an event. But emotions can turn into moods when you lose focus on the event or object that started the feeling. And, by the same token, good or bad moods can make you more emotional in response to an event. So when a colleague criticizes how you spoke to a client, you might show emotion (anger) toward a specific object (your colleague). But as the specific emotion dissipates, you might just feel generally dispirited. You can't attribute this feeling to any single event; you're just not your normal self. You might then overreact to other events. This affect state describes a mood. Exhibit 4-1 shows the relationships among affect, emotions, and mood.

First, as the exhibit shows, affect is a broad term that encompasses emotions and moods. Second, there are differences between emotions and moods. Some of these differences—that emotions are more likely to be caused by a specific event, and emotions are more fleeting than moods—we just discussed. Other differences are subtler. For example, unlike moods, emotions like anger and disgust tend to be more clearly revealed by facial expressions. Also, some researchers speculate that emotions may be more action-oriented—they may lead us to some immediate action—while moods may be more cognitive, meaning they may cause us to think or brood for a while.[9]

Finally, the exhibit shows that emotions and moods are closely connected and can influence each other. Getting your dream job may generate the emotion of joy, which can put you in a good mood for several days. Similarly, if you're in a good or bad mood, it might make you experience a more intense positive or negative emotion than otherwise. In a bad mood, you might blow up in response to a co-worker's comment that would normally have generated only a mild reaction.

Affect, emotions, and moods are separable in theory; in practice the distinction isn't always crystal-clear. In some areas, researchers have studied mostly moods, in other areas mainly emotions. So, when we review the OB topics on emotions and moods, you may see more information about emotions in one area and about moods in another. This is simply the state of the research.

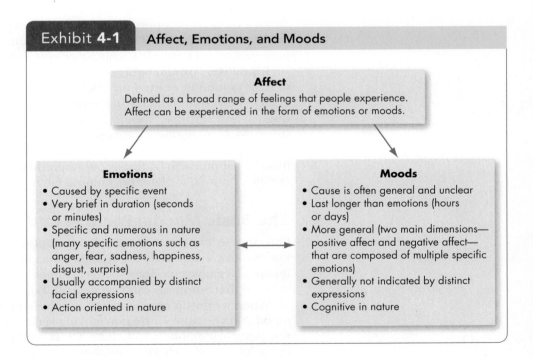

Exhibit 4-1   Affect, Emotions, and Moods

Affect

Defined as a broad range of feelings that people experience. Affect can be experienced in the form of emotions or moods.

Emotions
- Caused by specific event
- Very brief in duration (seconds or minutes)
- Specific and numerous in nature (many specific emotions such as anger, fear, sadness, happiness, disgust, surprise)
- Usually accompanied by distinct facial expressions
- Action oriented in nature

Moods
- Cause is often general and unclear
- Last longer than emotions (hours or days)
- More general (two main dimensions—positive affect and negative affect—that are composed of multiple specific emotions)
- Generally not indicated by distinct expressions
- Cognitive in nature

affect   *A broad range of feelings that people experience.*

emotions   *Intense feelings that are directed at someone or something.*

moods   *Feelings that tend to be less intense than emotions and that lack a contextual stimulus.*

The Basic Emotions

How many emotions are there? There are dozens, including anger, contempt, enthusiasm, envy, fear, frustration, disappointment, embarrassment, disgust, happiness, hate, hope, jealousy, joy, love, pride, surprise, and sadness. Numerous researchers have tried to limit them to a fundamental set.[10] But some argue that it makes no sense to think in terms of "basic" emotions because even emotions we rarely experience, such as shock, can have a powerful effect on us.[11] Other researchers, even philosophers, say there are universal emotions common to all. René Descartes, often called the founder of modern philosophy, identified six "simple and primitive passions"—wonder, love, hatred, desire, joy, and sadness—and argued that "all the others are composed of some of these six or are species of them."[12] Although other philosophers like Hume, Hobbes, and Spinoza identified categories of emotions, proof of the existence of a basic set of emotions still waits for contemporary researchers.

Psychologists have tried to identify basic emotions by studying facial expressions.[13] One problem is that some emotions are too complex to be easily represented on our faces. Many think of love as the most universal of all emotions,[14] for example, yet it's not easy to express it through only a facial expression. Cultures also have norms that govern emotional expression, so the way we *experience* an emotion isn't always the same as the way we *show* it. People in the United States and the Middle East recognize a smile as indicating happiness, but in the Middle East a smile is also more likely to be seen as a sign of sexual attraction, so women have learned not to smile at men.[15] In collectivist countries people are more likely to believe another's emotional displays have something to do with the relationship between them, while people in individualistic cultures don't think others' emotional expressions are directed at them. French retail clerks, in contrast, are infamous for being surly toward customers (as a report from the French government itself confirmed). Serious German shoppers have reportedly been turned off by Walmart's friendly greeters and helpful staff.[16] And many companies today offer anger-management programs to teach people to contain or even hide their inner feelings.[17]

It's unlikely psychologists or philosophers will ever completely agree on a set of basic emotions, or even on whether there is such a thing. Still, many researchers agree on six essentially universal emotions—anger, fear, sadness, happiness, disgust, and surprise.[18] Some even plot them along a continuum: happiness—surprise—fear—sadness—anger—disgust.[19] The closer two emotions are to each other on this continuum, the more likely people will confuse them. We sometimes mistake happiness for surprise, but rarely do we confuse happiness and disgust. In addition, as we'll see later on, cultural factors can also influence interpretations.

The Basic Moods: Positive and Negative Affect

One way to classify emotions is by whether they are positive or negative.[20] Positive emotions—such as joy and gratitude—express a favorable evaluation or feeling. Negative emotions—such as anger or guilt—express the opposite. Keep in mind that emotions can't be neutral. Being neutral is being nonemotional.[21]

When we group emotions into positive and negative categories, they become mood states because we are now looking at them more generally instead of isolating one particular emotion. In Exhibit 4-2, excited is a pure marker of high positive affect, while boredom is a pure marker of low positive affect. Nervous is a pure marker of high negative affect; relaxed is a pure marker of low negative affect. Finally, some emotions—such as contentment (a mixture of high positive affect and low negative affect) and sadness (a mixture of low positive affect and high negative affect)—are in between. You'll notice this model does not include all emotions. Some, such as surprise, don't fit well because they're not as clearly positive or negative.

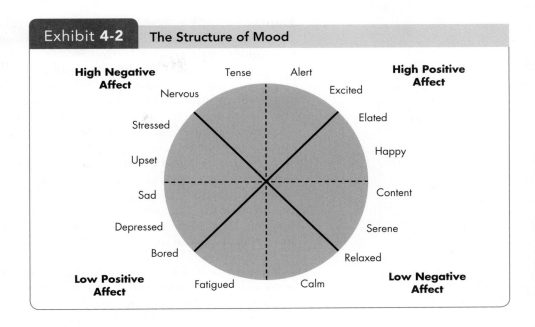

Exhibit 4-2   The Structure of Mood

So, we can think of **positive affect** as a mood dimension consisting of positive emotions such as excitement, self-assurance, and cheerfulness at the high end and boredom, sluggishness, and tiredness at the low end. **Negative affect** is a mood dimension consisting of nervousness, stress, and anxiety at the high end and relaxation, tranquility, and poise at the low end. (*Note:* Positive and negative affect *are* moods. We're using these labels, rather than *positive mood* and *negative mood*, because that's how researchers label them.)

Positive affect and negative affect play out at work and beyond in that they color our perceptions, and these perceptions can become their own reality. One flight attendant posted an anonymous blog on the Web that said, "I work in a pressurized aluminum tube and the environment outside my 'office' cannot sustain human life. That being said, the human life inside is not worth sustaining sometimes . . . in fact, the passengers can be jerks, and idiots. I am often treated with no respect, nobody listens to me . . . until I threaten to kick them off the plane."[22] Clearly, if a flight attendant is in a bad mood, it's going to influence his perceptions of passengers, which will, in turn, influence his behavior.

Negative emotions are likely to translate into negative moods. People think about events that created strong negative emotions five times as long as they do about events that created strong positive ones.[23] So, we should expect people to recall negative experiences more readily than positive ones. Perhaps one reason is that, for most of us, negative experiences also are more unusual. Indeed, research finds a **positivity offset**, meaning that at zero input (when nothing in particular is going on), most individuals experience a mildly positive mood.[24] So, for most people, positive moods are somewhat more common than negative moods. The positivity offset also appears to operate at work. One study of

---

positive affect *A mood dimension that consists of specific positive emotions such as excitement, self-assurance, and cheerfulness at the high end and boredom, sluggishness, and tiredness at the low end.*

negative affect *A mood dimension that consists of emotions such as nervousness, stress, and anxiety at the high end and relaxation, tranquility, and poise at the low end.*

positivity offset *The tendency of most individuals to experience a mildly positive mood at zero input (when nothing in particular is going on).*

customer-service representatives in a British call center (a job where it's probably pretty difficult to feel positive) revealed people reported experiencing positive moods 58 percent of the time.[25]

Does the degree to which people experience these positive and negative emotions vary across cultures? Yes. In China, people report experiencing fewer positive and negative emotions than people in other cultures, and the emotions they experience are less intense. Compared with Mainland Chinese, Taiwanese are more like U.S. workers in their experience of emotions: on average, they report more positive and fewer negative emotions than their Chinese counterparts.[26] People in most cultures appear to experience certain positive and negative emotions, but the frequency and intensity varies to some degree.[27] Despite these differences, people from all over the world interpret negative and positive emotions in much the same way. We all view negative emotions, such as hate, terror, and rage, as dangerous and destructive, and we desire positive emotions, such as joy, love, and happiness. However, some cultures value certain emotions more than others. U.S. culture values enthusiasm, while the Chinese consider negative emotions more useful and constructive than do people in the United States. Pride is generally a positive emotion in Western individualistic cultures such as the United States, but Eastern cultures such as China and Japan view pride as undesirable.[28]

The Function of Emotions

2 Discuss whether emotions are rational and what functions they serve.

Do Emotions Make Us Irrational?   How often have you heard someone say "Oh, you're just being emotional"? You might have been offended. The famous astronomer Carl Sagan once wrote, "Where we have strong emotions, we're liable to fool ourselves." These observations suggest rationality and emotion are in conflict, and that if you exhibit emotion you are likely to act irrationally. One team of authors argues that displaying emotions such as sadness to the point of crying is so toxic to a career that we should leave the room rather than allow others to witness it.[29] These perspectives suggest the demonstration or even experience of emotions can make us seem weak, brittle, or irrational. However, research is increasingly showing that emotions are actually critical to rational thinking.[30] There has been evidence of such a link for a long time.

Consider Phineas Gage, a railroad worker in Vermont. One September day in 1848, while Gage was setting an explosive charge at work, a 3-foot 7-inch iron bar flew into his lower-left jaw and out through the top of his skull. Remarkably, Gage survived his injury. He was still able to read and speak, and he performed well above average on cognitive ability tests. However, it became clear he had lost his ability to experience emotion; he was emotionless at even the saddest misfortunes or the happiest occasions. Gage's inability to express emotion eventually took away his ability to reason. He started making irrational choices about his life, often behaving erratically and against his self-interests. Despite being an intelligent man whose intellectual abilities were unharmed by the accident, Gage drifted from job to job, eventually taking up with a circus. In commenting on Gage's condition, one expert noted, "Reason may not be as pure as most of us think it is or wish it were . . . emotions and feelings may not be intruders in the bastion of reason at all: they may be enmeshed in its networks, for worse *and* for better."[31]

The example of Phineas Gage and many other brain injury studies show emotions are critical to rational thinking. We must have the ability to experience emotions to be rational. Why? Because our emotions provide important

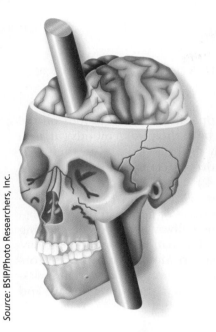

By studying brain injuries, such as the one experienced by Phineas Gage and whose skull is illustrated here, researchers discovered an important link between emotions and rational thinking. They found that losing the ability to emote led to loss of the ability to reason. From this discovery, researchers learned that our emotions provide us with valuable information that helps our thinking process.

3   Identify the sources of emotions and moods.

information about how we understand the world around us. Would we really want a manager to make a decision about firing an employee without regarding either his or the employee's emotions? The key to good decision making is to employ both thinking *and* feeling in our decisions.

Do Emotions Make Us Ethical?   A growing body of research has begun to examine the relationship between emotions and moral attitudes.[32] It was previously believed that, like decision making in general, most ethical decision making was based on higher-order cognitive processes, but research on moral emotions increasingly questions this perspective. Examples of moral emotions include sympathy for the suffering of others, guilt about our own immoral behavior, anger about injustice done to others, contempt for those who behave unethically, and disgust at violations of moral norms. Numerous studies suggest that these reactions are largely based on feelings rather than cold cognition.

You can think about this research in your own life to see how the emotional model of ethics operates. Consider the massive earthquake that struck Japan in 2011. When you heard about it, did you feel emotionally upset about the suffering of others, or did you make more of a rational calculation about their unfortunate situation? Consider a time when you have done something that hurt someone else. Did you feel angry or upset with yourself? Or think about a time when you have seen someone else treated unfairly. Did you feel contempt for the person acting unfairly, or did you engage in a cool rational calculation of the justice of the situation? Most people who think about these situations do have at least some sense of an emotional stirring that might prompt them to engage in ethical actions like donating money to help others, apologizing and attempting to make amends, or intervening on behalf of those who have been mistreated. In sum, we can conclude that people who are behaving ethically are at least partially making decisions based on their emotions and feelings, and this emotional reaction will often be a good thing.

Sources of Emotions and Moods

Have you ever said "I got up on the wrong side of the bed today"? Have you ever snapped at a co-worker or family member for no particular reason? If you have, it probably makes you wonder where emotions and moods come from. Here we discuss some of the primary influences.

Personality   Moods and emotions have a trait component: most people have built-in tendencies to experience certain moods and emotions more frequently than others do. People also experience the same emotions with different intensities. Contrast Texas Tech basketball coach Bobby Knight to Microsoft CEO Bill Gates. The first is easily moved to anger, while the other is relatively distant and unemotional. Knight and Gates probably differ in **affect intensity**, or how strongly they experience their emotions.[33] Affectively intense people experience both positive and negative emotions more deeply: when they're sad, they're really sad, and when they're happy, they're really happy.

affect intensity   *Individual differences in the strength with which individuals experience their emotions.*

What's My Affect Intensity?

In the Self-Assessment Library (available on CD or online), take assessment IV.D.2 (What's My Affect Intensity?).

Day of the Week and Time of the Day   Are people in their best moods on the weekends? As Exhibit 4-3 shows, people tend to be in their worst moods (highest negative affect and lowest positive affect) early in the week, and in their best moods (highest positive affect and lowest negative affect) late in the week.[34]

What about time of the day? (See Exhibit 4-4.) We often think we are either "morning" or "evening" people. However, most of us actually follow the same pattern. Regardless of what time we go to bed at night or get up in the morning, levels of positive affect tend to peak at around the halfway point between waking and sleeping. Negative affect, however, shows little fluctuation throughout the day.

What does this mean for organizational behavior? Monday morning is probably not the best time to ask someone for a favor or convey bad news. Our workplace interactions will probably be more positive from midmorning onward and also later in the week.

Weather   When do you think you would be in a better mood—when it's 70 degrees and sunny, or on a gloomy, cold, rainy day? Many people believe their mood is tied to the weather. However, a fairly large and detailed body of evidence conducted by multiple researchers suggests weather has little effect on mood.[35] One expert concluded, "Contrary to the prevailing cultural view, these data indicate that people do not report a better mood on bright and sunny days (or, conversely, a worse mood on dark and rainy days)."[36] **Illusory correlation** explains why people tend to *think* nice weather improves their mood. It occurs when people associate two events that in reality have no connection.

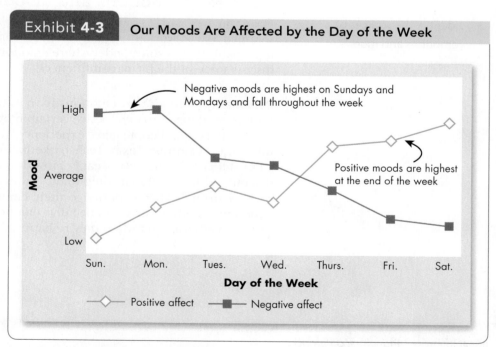

Exhibit **4-3**   **Our Moods Are Affected by the Day of the Week**

Source: "Our Moods Are Affected by the Day of the Week" from Mood and Temperament, *by D. Watson. Reprinted by permission of Guilford Publications, Inc.*

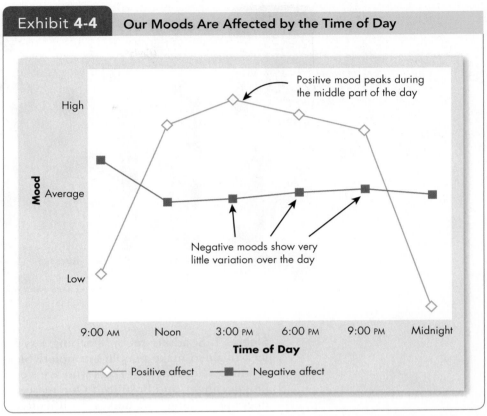

| Exhibit **4-4** | Our Moods Are Affected by the Time of Day |

Positive mood peaks during the middle part of the day

Negative moods show very little variation over the day

Time of Day

◇ Positive affect   ■ Negative affect

Source: "Our Moods Are Affected by the Day of the Week" from Mood and Temperament, by D. Watson. Reprinted by permission of Guilford Publications, Inc.

Stress   As you might imagine, stressful daily events at work (a nasty e-mail, an impending deadline, the loss of a big sale, a reprimand from the boss) negatively affect moods. The effects of stress also build over time. As the authors of one study note, "a constant diet of even low-level stressful events has the potential to cause workers to experience gradually increasing levels of strain over time."[37] Mounting levels of stress can worsen our moods, and we experience more negative emotions. Consider the following entry from a worker's blog: "I'm in a bit of a blah mood today . . . physically, I feel funky, though, and the weather out combined with the amount of personal and work I need to get done are getting to me." Although sometimes we thrive on stress, most of us, like this blogger, find stress takes a toll on our mood.[38]

Social Activities   Do you tend to be happiest when out with friends? For most people, social activities increase positive mood and have little effect on negative mood. But do people in positive moods seek out social interactions, or do social interactions cause people to be in good moods? It seems both are true.[39] Does the *type* of social activity matter? Indeed it does. Research suggests activities that are physical (skiing or hiking with friends), informal (going to a party), or epicurean (eating with others) are more strongly associated with increases in positive mood than events that are formal (attending a meeting) or sedentary (watching TV with friends).[40]

illusory correlation   *The tendency of people to associate two events when in reality there is no connection.*

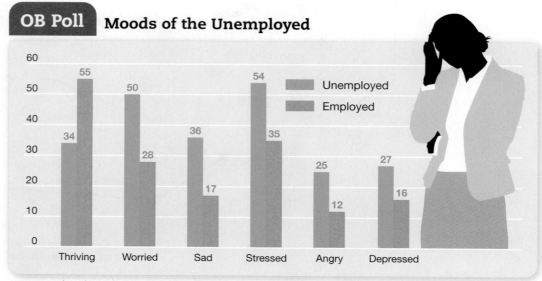

OB Poll **Moods of the Unemployed**

Legend:
- Unemployed
- Employed

	Thriving	Worried	Sad	Stressed	Angry	Depressed
Unemployed	34	50	36	54	25	27
Employed	55	28	17	35	12	16

Source: E. Mendes and L. Saad, "For Unemployed, Length, Scale of Job Search Affects Well Being, Life Ratings," *Gallup News* (February 25, 2011), http://www.gallup.com/. Reprinted with permission.

Sleep   U.S. adults report sleeping less than adults a generation ago.[41] Does lack of sleep make people grumpier? Sleep quality does affect mood. Undergraduates and adult workers who are sleep-deprived report greater feelings of fatigue, anger, and hostility.[42] One reason is that poor or reduced sleep impairs decision making and makes it difficult to control emotions.[43] A recent study suggests poor sleep also impairs job satisfaction because people feel fatigued, irritable, and less alert.[44]

Exercise and social activities are two of the primary sources of emotions and moods. For most people, working out and participating in social activities that are informal and physical increase positive moods. Shown here are employees of Blizzard Entertainment taking a break from work to play volleyball. Blizzard, a developer of entertainment software, offers employees yoga classes, a sand volleyball court, basketball court, bike track, and fitness center where they can exercise and socialize. Like many other organizations, Blizzard believes these activities result in happier, healthier, and more productive employees.

Source: 044/ZUMA Press/Newscomm

We Are Better Judges of When Others Are Happy Than When They Are Sad

This statement is generally true. Consider the following scenario: Assume you work with three other people: Jane, Blake, and Morgan. Jane received several calls from customers unhappy with a product made by her company. Blake broke up with his fiancé. Morgan has had a recurrence of depression. Yet at lunch today all three seemed pretty happy. There were smiles, laughter, and in general good humor for all to see. Yet each person, in his or her own way, is weathering tough times. If you had to gauge the moods of Jane, Blake, and Morgan, you might say they were in relatively good moods. If you asked each of them, however, they might attribute their seeming good humor to impression management, "putting on a good face," or the effects of the social environment.

This hypothetical scenario reflects a phenomenon recent research supports: we typically underestimate the negative emotions experienced by others. In other words, people often feel worse than we believe they do. To some extent, the same is true of positive emotions: We estimate people to experience more positive emotions than they do. Why do we think people are in better moods than they really are, and what are the implications?

There are two reasons we see others as experiencing more positive and fewer negative emotions than they do:

1. People generally experience more negative emotions when they are by themselves than when they are in the company of others. So we tend to see others not at their lowest, but at their highest.
2. Most people are reluctant to divulge negative feelings in social situations. Thus, when we're feeling low, we tend to avoid showing others how bad we feel.

The upshot? First, we should appreciate that in social situations like work, people probably feel less happy than they appear. Second, we should be less afraid to disclose negative emotions to friends, close coworkers, and significant others, given the costs of "keeping it all in." Often the strongest emotional links we form with others occur when someone reports experiencing something negative that we too have experienced.

Sources: Based on: A. H. Jordan, B. Monin, C. S. Dweck, B. J. Lovett, O. P. John, and J. J. Gross, "Misery Has More Company Than People Think: Underestimating the Prevalence of Others' Negative Emotions," *Personality and Social Psychology Bulletin* 37, no. 1 (2011), pp. 120–135; M. Szalavitz, "Misery Has More Company Than You Think, Especially on Facebook," *Time* (January 27, 2011), http://healthland.time.com; and C. Jarrett, "Other People May Experience More Misery Than You Realize," *Research Digest* (January 24, 2011), http://bps-research-digest.blogspot.com.

Exercise You often hear people should exercise to improve their mood. Does "sweat therapy" really work? It appears so. Research consistently shows exercise enhances peoples' positive mood.[45] While not terribly strong overall, the effects are strongest for those who are depressed. So exercise may help put you in a better mood, but don't expect miracles.

Age Do young people experience more extreme positive emotions (so-called youthful exuberance) than older people? If you answered "yes," you were wrong. One study of people ages 18 to 94 revealed that negative emotions seem to occur less as people get older. Periods of highly positive moods lasted longer for older individuals, and bad moods faded more quickly.[46] The study implies emotional experience improves with age; as we get older, we experience fewer negative emotions.

Sex Many believe women are more emotional than men. Is there any truth to this? Evidence does confirm women are more emotionally expressive than men;[47] they experience emotions more intensely, they tend to "hold onto" emotions longer than men, and they display more frequent expressions of both positive and negative emotions, except anger.[48] Evidence from a study of participants from 37 different countries found that men consistently report higher levels of powerful emotions like anger, whereas women report more powerless emotions like sadness and fear. Thus, there are some sex differences in the experience and expression of emotions.[49]

Should You Expect "Service with a Smile" All Around the World?

In most customer service jobs in the United States, there is a strong social pressure for employees to display an upbeat demeanor at all times, demonstrating happy and friendly emotions in an effort to make customers feel pleasant and at ease. Experts on emotional labor have found that these rules encouraging "service with a smile" are also found in many other countries, but that doesn't mean they are followed to the same extent everywhere.

One study examined international differences in emotional displays by having participants from Israel, France, Singapore, and the United States explain how they would behave in a variety of emotionally charged situations as customer service agents. Their results showed that although there was a strongly consistent tendency for respondents to report they would try to show happiness and suppress anger toward customers, there were differences in the extent to which people would engage in these forms of emotional labor. Respondents from Singapore were especially negatively disposed toward expressing anger at customers, while the French found it more acceptable. U.S. respondents were especially likely to display happiness toward customers, while French respondents were most reserved in their expressions of happiness.

This is not to say there aren't cross-cultural similarities in customer service expectations and customer reactions. There are no cultures in which smiling is seen as an expression of hostility or in which a grimace or frown is seen as a sign of friendliness. There also appear to be consistently positive reactions to others who display positive emotions. However, companies that operate in multiple markets should expect to see differences in the types of emotions customer service employees will display.

Sources: A. Grandey, A Rafaeli, S. Ravid, J. Wirtz, and D. D. Steiner, "Emotion Display Rules at Work in the Global Service Economy: The Special Case of the Customer," *Journal of Service Management* 21, (2010), pp. 388–412; and D. Matsumoto, "Culture and Emotional Expression," in R. S. Wyer, C. Chiu, and Y. Hong (Eds.), *Understanding Culture: Theory, Research, and Application* (New York: Taylor and Francis, 2009), pp. 271–288.

People also tend to attribute men's and women's emotions in ways that might be based on stereotypes of what typical emotional reactions are. One study showed that experimental participants who read about emotional expressions interpreted women's reactions as being dispositional (related to personality), whereas men's reactions were interpreted as being due to the situation around them.[50] For example, a picture of a sad woman led observers to believe she was acting consistently with an emotional personality type, whereas a picture of a sad man was more likely to be attributed to his having a bad day. Another study showed that participants were faster at detecting angry expressions on male faces and happy expressions on female faces; neutral faces in men were attributed as more angry and neutral faces in women were interpreted as happy.[51]

Emotional Labor

4 Show the impact emotional labor has on employees.

If you've ever had a job in retail sales or waited on tables in a restaurant, you know the importance of projecting a friendly demeanor and smiling. Even though there were days when you didn't feel cheerful, you knew management expected you to be upbeat when dealing with customers. So you faked it. Every employee expends physical and mental labor by putting body and mind, respectively, into the job. But jobs also require **emotional labor**, an employee's expression of organizationally desired emotions during interpersonal transactions at work.

In addition to physical and mental labor, jobs also require emotional labor. Emerging from studies of service jobs, the concept of emotional labor involves an employee's expression of emotions that an organization requires during interpersonal transactions. Employees of this new Apple store in Scottsdale, Arizona, greeted shoppers standing in line and waiting to get into the store with a warm reception. Employees' smiles and high fives are expressions of emotional labor that Apple requires and considers appropriate for their jobs.

Source: K94/ZUMA Press/Newscom

The concept of emotional labor emerged from studies of service jobs. Airlines expect their flight attendants to be cheerful; we expect funeral directors to be sad and doctors emotionally neutral. But emotional labor is relevant to almost every job. At the least your managers expect you to be courteous, not hostile, in your interactions with co-workers. The true challenge arises when employees have to project one emotion while feeling another.[52] This disparity is **emotional dissonance**, and it can take a heavy toll. Bottled-up feelings of frustration, anger, and resentment can eventually lead to emotional exhaustion and burnout.[53] It's from the increasing importance of emotional labor as a key component of effective job performance that we have come to understand the relevance of emotion within the field of OB.

Emotional labor creates dilemmas for employees. There are people with whom you have to work that you just plain don't like. Maybe you consider their personality abrasive. Maybe you know they've said negative things about you behind your back. Regardless, your job requires you to interact with these people on a regular basis. So you're forced to feign friendliness.

It can help you, on the job especially, if you separate emotions into *felt* or *displayed emotions*.[54] **Felt emotions** are an individual's actual emotions. In contrast, **displayed emotions** are those that the organization requires workers to show and considers appropriate in a given job. They're not innate; they're learned. "The ritual look of delight on the face of the first runner-up as the new Miss America is announced is a product of the display rule that losers should mask their sadness with an expression of joy for the winner."[55] Similarly, most of us know we're expected to act sad at funerals, regardless of whether we consider the person's death a loss, and to appear happy at weddings even if we don't feel like celebrating.

---

emotional labor *A situation in which an employee expresses organizationally desired emotions during interpersonal transactions at work.*

emotional dissonance *Inconsistencies between the emotions people feel and the emotions they project.*

felt emotions *An individual's actual emotions.*

displayed emotions *Emotions that are organizationally required and considered appropriate in a given job.*

Research suggests that at U.S. workplaces, it is expected that we should typically display positive emotions like happiness and excitement and suppress negative emotions like fear, anger, disgust, and contempt.[56] Effective managers have learned to be serious when giving an employee a negative performance evaluation and to hide their anger when they've been passed over for promotion. A salesperson who hasn't learned to smile and appear friendly, despite his or her true feelings at the moment, typically won't last long in the job. How we *experience* an emotion isn't always the same as how we *show* it.[57]

Displaying fake emotions requires us to suppress real ones. **Surface acting** is hiding inner feelings and forgoing emotional expressions in response to display rules. A worker who smiles at a customer even when he doesn't feel like it is surface acting. **Deep acting** is trying to modify our true inner feelings based on display rules. A health care provider trying to genuinely feel more empathy for her patients is deep acting.[58] Surface acting deals with *displayed* emotions, and deep acting deals with *felt* emotions. Research shows that surface acting is more stressful to employees because it entails denying their true emotions.[59] Displaying emotions we don't really feel is exhausting, so it is important to give employees who engage in surface displays a chance to relax and recharge. A study that looked at how cheerleading instructors spent their breaks from teaching found those who used their breaks to rest and relax were more effective instructors after their breaks.[60] Instructors who did chores during their breaks were only about as effective after their break as they were before. Another study found that in hospital work groups where there were heavy emotional display demands, burnout was higher than in other hospital work groups.[61]

Affective Events Theory

5 Describe affective events theory and identify its applications.

We've seen that emotions and moods are an important part of our lives and our work lives. But how do they influence our job performance and satisfaction? A model called **affective events theory (AET)** demonstrates that employees react emotionally to things that happen to them at work, and this reaction influences their job performance and satisfaction.[62]

Exhibit 4-5 summarizes AET. The theory begins by recognizing that emotions are a response to an event in the work environment. The work environment includes everything surrounding the job—the variety of tasks and degree of autonomy, job demands, and requirements for expressing emotional labor. This environment creates work events that can be hassles, uplifting events, or both. Examples of hassles are colleagues who refuse to carry their share of work, conflicting directions from different managers, and excessive time pressures. Uplifting events include meeting a goal, getting support from a colleague, and receiving recognition for an accomplishment.[63]

These work events trigger positive or negative emotional reactions, to which employees' personalities and moods predispose them to respond with greater or lesser intensity. People who score low on emotional stability are more likely to react strongly to negative events. And our emotional response to a given event can change depending on mood. Finally, emotions influence a number of performance and satisfaction variables, such as organizational citizenship behavior, organizational commitment, level of effort, intention to quit, and workplace deviance.

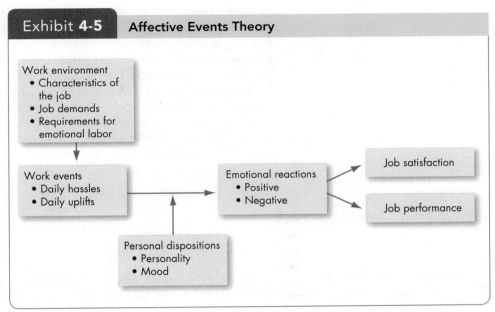

Exhibit **4-5**   **Affective Events Theory**

Source: Based on N. M. Ashkanasy and C. S. Daus, "Emotion in the Workplace: The New Challenge for Managers," *Academy of Management Executive* (February 2002), p. 77.

Tests of affective events theory suggest the following:

1. An emotional episode is actually a series of emotional experiences, precipitated by a single event and containing elements of both emotions and mood cycles.
2. Current emotions influence job satisfaction at any given time, along with the history of emotions surrounding the event.
3. Because moods and emotions fluctuate over time, their effect on performance also fluctuates.
4. Emotion-driven behaviors are typically short in duration and of high variability.
5. Because emotions, even positive ones, tend to be incompatible with behaviors required to do a job, they typically have a negative influence on job performance.[64]

Consider an example.[65] Say you work as an aeronautical engineer for Boeing. Because of the downturn in demand for commercial jets, you've just learned the company is considering laying off 10,000 employees, possibly including you. This event is likely to make you feel negative emotions, especially fear that you might lose your primary source of income. And because you're prone to worry a lot and obsess about problems, this event increases your feelings of insecurity. The layoff also sets in motion a series of smaller events that create an episode: you talk with your boss and he assures you your job is safe; you hear rumors your department is high on the list to be eliminated; and you run into a former colleague who was laid off 6 months ago and still hasn't found work. These events,

surface acting   *Hiding one's inner feelings and forgoing emotional expressions in response to display rules.*

deep acting   *Trying to modify one's true inner feelings based on display rules.*

affective events theory (AET)   *A model that suggests that workplace events cause emotional reactions on the part of employees, which then influence workplace attitudes and behaviors.*

in turn, create emotional ups and downs. One day, you're feeling upbeat that you'll survive the cuts. The next, you might be depressed and anxious. These emotional swings take your attention away from your work and lower your job performance and satisfaction. Finally, your response is magnified because this is the fourth-largest layoff Boeing has initiated in the past 3 years.

In summary, AET offers two important messages.[66] First, emotions provide valuable insights into how workplace hassles and uplifting events influence employee performance and satisfaction. Second, employees and managers shouldn't ignore emotions or the events that cause them, even when they appear minor, because they accumulate.

Emotional Intelligence

6 Contrast the evidence for and against the existence of emotional intelligence.

Diane Marshall is an office manager. Her awareness of her own and others' emotions is almost nil. She's moody and unable to generate much enthusiasm or interest in her employees. She doesn't understand why employees get upset with her. She often overreacts to problems and chooses the most ineffectual responses to emotional situations.[67] Diane has low emotional intelligence. **Emotional intelligence (EI)** is a person's ability to (1) perceive emotions in the self and others, (2) understand the meaning of these emotions, and (3) regulate one's emotions accordingly in a cascading model, as shown in Exhibit 4-6. People who know their own emotions and are good at reading emotional cues—for instance, knowing why they're angry and how to express themselves without violating norms—are most likely to be effective.[68]

Several studies suggest EI plays an important role in job performance. One study that used functional magnetic resonance imaging (fMRI) technology found executive MBA students who performed best on a strategic decision making task were more likely to incorporate emotion centers of the brain into their choice process. The students also de-emphasized the use of the more cognitive parts of their brains.[69] Another study looked at the successes and failures of 11 U.S. presidents—from Franklin Roosevelt to Bill Clinton—and evaluated them on six qualities: communication, organization, political skill, vision, cognitive style, and emotional intelligence. The key quality that differentiated

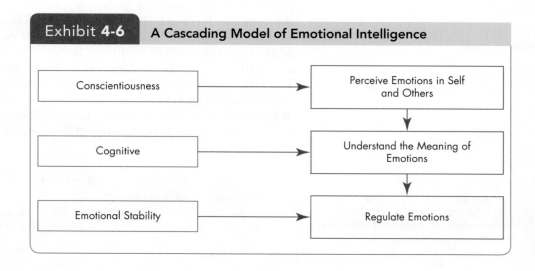

Exhibit 4-6 **A Cascading Model of Emotional Intelligence**

Conscientiousness → Perceive Emotions in Self and Others

Cognitive → Understand the Meaning of Emotions

Emotional Stability → Regulate Emotions

Diane Hoskins, a top leader at Gensler, a global architectural firm, has high emotional intelligence. She is one of three executive directors who operate the firm along with the management committee. Hoskins is a star performer in a job that demands interacting with employees and developing their careers to ensure that Gensler has the talent it needs to serve clients. Hoskins is shown here discussing a new internship program that could help Gensler build its global business.

Source: Daniel Rosen baum/The New York Times/Redux Pictures

the successful (such as Roosevelt, Kennedy, and Reagan) from the unsuccessful (such as Johnson, Carter, and Nixon) was emotional intelligence.[70] One simulation study also showed that students who were good at identifying and distinguishing among their own feelings were able to make more profitable investment decisions.[71]

EI has been a controversial concept in OB, with supporters and detractors. In the following sections, we review the arguments for and against its viability.

The Case for EI

The arguments in favor of EI include its intuitive appeal, the fact that it predicts criteria that matter, and the idea that it is biologically based.

Intuitive Appeal   Almost everyone agrees it is good to possess social intelligence. Intuition suggests people who can detect emotions in others, control their own emotions, and handle social interactions well have a powerful leg up in the business world. Partners in a multinational consulting firm who scored above the median on an EI measure delivered $1.2 million more in business than did the other partners.[72]

EI Predicts Criteria That Matter   Evidence suggests a high level of EI means a person will perform well on the job. One study found EI predicted the performance of employees in a cigarette factory in China.[73] Another study found the

emotional intelligence (EI)   *The ability to detect and to manage emotional cues and information.*

ability to recognize emotions in others' facial expressions and to emotionally "eavesdrop" (pick up subtle signals about peoples' emotions) predicted peer ratings of how valuable people were to their organization.[74] Finally, a review of studies indicated that, overall, EI weakly but consistently correlated with job performance, even after researchers took cognitive ability, conscientiousness, and neuroticism into account.[75]

EI Is Biologically Based   In one study, people with damage to the brain area that governs emotional processing (part of the prefrontal cortex) scored no lower on standard measures of intelligence than people without similar damage. But they scored significantly lower on EI tests and were impaired in normal decision making, as demonstrated by their poor performance in a card game with monetary rewards. This study suggests EI is neurologically based in a way that's unrelated to standard measures of intelligence.[76] There is also evidence EI is genetically influenced, further supporting the idea that it measures a real underlying biological factor.[77]

The Case Against EI

For all its supporters, EI has just as many critics who say it is vague and impossible to measure, and they question its validity.

EI Researchers Do Not Agree on Definitions   To many researchers, it's not clear what EI is because researchers use different definitions of the construct.[78] Some researchers have focused on emotional intelligence via tests with right and wrong answers, scoring the ability to recognize and control emotions. This is the ability-based perspective on EI. Others focus on emotional intelligence as a broad variety of constructs that can be measured by self-reports and are connected primarily by the fact that they are not redundant with cognitive intelligence. Not only are these two definitions different, but the measures used by each perspective are barely correlated with one another.[79]

EI Can't Be Measured   Many critics have raised questions about measuring EI. Because EI is a form of intelligence, they argue, there must be right and wrong answers for it on tests. Some tests do have right and wrong answers, although the validity of some questions is doubtful. One measure asks you to associate feelings with colors, as if purple always makes us feel cool and not warm. Other measures are self-reported, such as "I'm good at 'reading' other people," and have no right or wrong answers. However, these self-report measures could reflect a variety of non-ability related constructs like general self-esteem or self-efficacy. The measures of EI are diverse, and researchers have not subjected them to as much rigorous study as they have measures of personality and general intelligence.[80]

EI Is Nothing but Personality with a Different Label   Some critics argue that because EI is so closely related to intelligence and personality, once you control for these factors, it has nothing unique to offer. There is some foundation to this argument. EI appears to be correlated with measures of personality, especially emotional stability.[81] If this is true, then the evidence for a biological component to EI is spurious, and biological markers like brain activity and heritability are attributable to other well-known and much better researched psychological constructs. To some extent, researchers have resolved this issue by noting that EI is a construct partially determined by traits like cognitive intelligence, conscientiousness, and neuroticism, as shown in Exhibit 4-6, so it makes sense that EI is correlated with these characteristics.[82]

Although the field is progressing in its understanding of EI, many questions have not been answered. Still, EI is wildly popular among consulting firms and in the popular press. One company's promotional materials for an EI measure claimed, "EI accounts for more than 85 percent of star performance in top leaders."[83] To say the least, it's difficult to validate this statement with the research literature.

Emotion Regulation

Have you ever tried to cheer yourself up when you're feeling down, or calm yourself when you're feeling angry? If so, you have engaged in *emotion regulation,* which is part of the EI literature but has also been studied as an independent concept.[84] The central idea behind emotion regulation is to identify and modify the emotions you feel. Strategies to change your emotions include thinking about more pleasant things, suppressing negative thoughts, distracting yourself, reappraising the situation, or engaging in relaxation techniques.

As you might suspect based on our discussion up to this point, not everyone is equally good at regulating their emotions. Individuals who are higher in the personality trait of neuroticism have more trouble doing so and often find their moods are beyond their ability to control. Individuals who have lower levels of self-esteem are also less likely to try to improve their sad moods, perhaps because they are less likely than others to feel like they deserve to be in a good mood.[85]

While it might seem in some ways desirable to regulate your emotions, research suggests there is a downside to trying to change the way you feel. Changing your emotions takes effort, and this effort can be exhausting. Sometimes attempts to change an emotion actually make the emotion stronger; for example, trying to talk yourself out of being afraid can make you focus more on what scares you, which makes you more afraid.[86] Emotion suppression appears to be especially difficult to do effectively and can lead to more negative emotions; reappraising situations is usually more effective in increasing positive emotions and limiting negative emotions.[87] From another perspective, research suggests that avoiding negative emotional experiences is less likely to lead to positive moods than seeking out positive emotional experiences.[88] For example, you're more likely to experience a positive mood if you have a pleasant conversation with a friend than you would be if you avoided an unpleasant conversation with a hostile co-worker.

SELF-ASSESSMENT LIBRARY

What's My Emotional Intelligence Score?

In the Self-Assessment Library (available on CD or online), take assessment I.E.1 (What's My Emotional Intelligence Score?).

OB Applications of Emotions and Moods

7 Identify strategies for emotion regulation and their likely effects.

In this section, we assess how an understanding of emotions and moods can improve our ability to explain and predict the selection process in organizations, decision making, creativity, motivation, leadership, interpersonal conflict, negotiation, customer service, job attitudes, and deviant workplace behaviors. We also look at how managers can influence our moods.

Hiring employees with high emotional intelligence is important for companies such as Starbucks, whose baristas have frequent social interactions with customers. In keeping with Starbucks mission "to inspire and nurture the human spirit," the company selects baristas who relate well to customers, connect with them, and uplift their lives. At Starbucks, emotional intelligence plays an important role in job performance, as the company enjoys a loyal customer base and a reputation as one of the most admired companies in America.

Source: C.W. McKeen/Syracuse Newspapers/The Image Works

Selection

One implication from the evidence on EI to date is that employers should consider it a factor in hiring employees, especially in jobs that demand a high degree of social interaction. In fact, more employers *are* starting to use EI measures to hire people. A study of U.S. Air Force recruiters showed that top-performing recruiters exhibited high levels of EI. Using these findings, the Air Force revamped its selection criteria. A follow-up investigation found future hires who had high EI scores were 2.6 times more successful than those who didn't. At L'Oreal, salespersons selected on EI scores outsold those hired using the company's old selection procedure. On an annual basis, salespeople selected for their emotional competence sold $91,370 more than other salespeople did, for a net revenue increase of $2,558,360.[89]

Decision Making

As you will see in Chapter 6, traditional approaches to the study of decision making in organizations have emphasized rationality. But OB researchers are increasingly finding that moods and emotions have important effects on decision making.

Positive moods and emotions seem to help. People in good moods or experiencing positive emotions are more likely than others to use heuristics, or rules of thumb,[90] to help make good decisions quickly. Positive emotions also enhance problem-solving skills, so positive people find better solutions to problems.[91]

OB researchers continue to debate the role of negative emotions and moods in decision making. Although one often-cited study suggested depressed people reach more accurate judgments,[92] more recent evidence hints they make poorer decisions. Why? Because depressed people are slower at processing information and tend to weigh all possible options rather than the most likely ones.[93] They search for the perfect solution, when there rarely is one.

Creativity

People in good moods tend to be more creative than people in bad moods.[94] They produce more ideas and more options, and others think their ideas are original.[95] It seems people experiencing positive moods or emotions are more flexible and open in their thinking, which may explain why they're more creative.[96] Supervisors should actively try to keep employees happy because doing so creates more good moods (employees like their leaders to encourage them and provide positive feedback on a job well done), which in turn leads people to be more creative.[97]

Some researchers, however, do not believe a positive mood makes people more creative. They argue that when people are in positive moods, they may relax ("If I'm in a good mood, things must be going okay, and I must not need to think of new ideas") and not engage in the critical thinking necessary for some forms of creativity.[98] The answer may lie in thinking of moods somewhat differently. Rather than looking at positive or negative affect, it's possible to conceptualize moods as active feelings like anger, fear, or elation and contrast these with deactivating moods like sorrow, depression, or serenity. All the activating moods, whether positive *or* negative, seem to lead to more creativity, whereas deactivating moods lead to less.[99]

Motivation

Several studies have highlighted the importance of moods and emotions on motivation. One study set two groups of people to solving word puzzles. The first group saw a funny video clip, intended to put the subjects in a good mood first. The other group was not shown the clip and started working on the puzzles right away. The results? The positive-mood group reported higher expectations of being able to solve the puzzles, worked harder at them, and solved more puzzles as a result.[100]

The second study found that giving people performance feedback—whether real or fake—influenced their mood, which then influenced their motivation.[101] So a cycle can exist in which positive moods cause people to be more creative, which leads to positive feedback from those observing their work. This positive feedback further reinforces the positive mood, which may make people perform even better, and so on.

Another study looked at the moods of insurance sales agents in Taiwan.[102] Agents in a good mood were more helpful toward their co-workers and also felt better about themselves. These factors in turn led to superior performance in the form of higher sales and better supervisor reports of performance.

Leadership

Effective leaders rely on emotional appeals to help convey their messages.[103] In fact, the expression of emotions in speeches is often the critical element that makes us accept or reject a leader's message. "When leaders feel excited, enthusiastic, and active, they may be more likely to energize their subordinates and convey a sense of efficacy, competence, optimism, and enjoyment."[104] Politicians, as a case in point, have learned to show enthusiasm when talking about their chances of winning an election, even when polls suggest otherwise.

Corporate executives know emotional content is critical if employees are to buy into their vision of the company's future and accept change. When higher-ups offer new visions, especially with vague or distant goals, it is often difficult for employees to accept the changes they'll bring. By arousing emotions and linking them to an appealing vision, leaders increase the likelihood that managers and employees alike will accept change.[105] Leaders who focus on inspirational goals also generate greater optimism and enthusiasm in employees, leading to more positive social interactions with co-workers and customers.[106]

Negotiation

Negotiation is an emotional process; however, we often say a skilled negotiator has a "poker face." The founder of Britain's Poker Channel, Crispin Nieboer, stated, "It is a game of bluff and there is fantastic human emotion and tension,

The general manager of a professional sports team is the organizational leader responsible for developing a winning team. As general manager of the Los Angeles Dodgers, Ned Colletti is shown here delivering an inspirational talk to employees right before a game between the Dodgers and the San Diego Padres. Colletti relies on emotional appeals to employees of all the individual divisions of the team, from administrative affairs to public relations, to work well together in achieving a victorious season.

Source: Chris Williams/Icon SMIP/Newscomm

seeing who can bluff the longest."[107] Several studies have shown that a negotiator who feigns anger has an advantage over the opponent. Why? Because when a negotiator shows anger, the opponent concludes the negotiator has conceded all she can and so gives in.[108] Anger should be used selectively in negotiation: angry negotiators who have less information or less power than their opponents have significantly worse outcomes.[109] It appears that a powerful, better-informed individual will be less willing to share information or meet an angry opponent halfway.

Displaying a negative emotion (such as anger) can be effective, but feeling bad about your performance appears to impair future negotiations. Individuals who do poorly in a negotiation experience negative emotions, develop negative perceptions of their counterpart, and are less willing to share information or be cooperative in future negotiations.[110] Interestingly, then, while moods and emotions have benefits at work, in negotiation—unless we're putting up a false front like feigning anger—emotions may impair negotiator performance. A 2005 study found people who suffered damage to the emotional centers of their brains (the same part that was injured in Phineas Gage) may be the *best* negotiators, because they're not likely to overcorrect when faced with negative outcomes.[111]

Customer Service

A worker's emotional state influences customer service, which influences levels of repeat business and of customer satisfaction.[112] Providing high-quality customer service makes demands on employees because it often puts them in a state of emotional dissonance. Over time, this state can lead to job burnout, declines in job performance, and lower job satisfaction.[113]

Employees' emotions can transfer to the customer. Studies indicate a matching effect between employee and customer emotions called **emotional contagion**—the "catching" of emotions from others.[114] How does it work? The primary explanation is that when someone experiences positive emotions and laughs and smiles at you, you tend to respond positively. Emotional contagion is important because customers who catch the positive moods or emotions of employees shop longer. But are negative emotions and moods contagious, too? Absolutely. When an employee feels unfairly treated by a customer, for example, it's harder for him to display the positive emotions his organization expects of him.[115]

Job Attitudes

Ever hear the advice "Never take your work home with you," meaning you should forget about work once you go home? That's easier said than done. Several studies have shown people who had a good day at work tend to be in a better mood at home that evening, and vice versa.[116] People who have a stressful day at work also have trouble relaxing after they get off work.[117] One study had married couples describing their moods when responding to timed cell-phone surveys through the course of the day. As most married readers might suspect, if one member of the couple was in a negative mood during the workday, that mood spilled over to the spouse at night.[118] In other words, if you've had a bad day at work, your spouse is likely to have an unpleasant evening. Even though people do emotionally take their work home with them, however, by the next day the effect is usually gone.[119]

Deviant Workplace Behaviors

Anyone who has spent much time in an organization realizes people often behave in ways that violate established norms and threaten the organization, its members, or both. As we saw in Chapter 1, these actions are called *workplace deviant behaviors*.[120] Many can be traced to negative emotions.

For instance, envy is an emotion that occurs when you resent someone for having something you don't have but strongly desire—such as a better work assignment, larger office, or higher salary.[121] It can lead to malicious deviant behaviors. An envious employee could backstab another employee, negatively distort others' successes, and positively distort his own accomplishments.[122] Angry people look for other people to blame for their bad mood, interpret other people's behavior as hostile, and have trouble considering others' point of view.[123] It's not hard to see how these thought processes, too, can lead directly to verbal or physical aggression.

Evidence suggests people who feel negative emotions, particularly anger or hostility, are more likely than others to engage in deviant behavior at work.[124] Once aggression starts, it's likely that other people will become angry and aggressive, so the stage is set for a serious escalation of negative behavior.

Safety and Injury at Work

Research relating negative affectivity to increased injuries at work suggests employers might improve health and safety (and reduce costs) by ensuring workers aren't engaged in potentially dangerous activities when they're in a bad mood. Bad moods can contribute to injury at work in several ways.[125] Individuals in negative moods tend to be more anxious, which can make them less able to cope effectively with hazards. A person who is always scared will be more pessimistic about the effectiveness of safety precautions because she feels she'll just get hurt anyway, or she might panic or freeze up when confronted with a threatening

emotional contagion *The process by which peoples' emotions are caused by the emotions of others.*

Schadenfreude

English may be a robust language, but sometimes a word from another language expresses something that English misses. Such is the case with a particular and interesting emotional sentiment known by a German name.

"Taking delight in the misery of others," or *schadenfreude,* has recently been studied by psychologists whose findings have implications for work. Neuropsychological research shows that when we experience *schadenfreude,* it is the pleasure centers of our brains that light up, similar to what happens when we enjoy good food or win a contest. It may explain why we take a special interest in reading about the misfortunes of Bernie Madoff, Lindsay Lohan, Charlie Sheen, and others.

As you might experience, we are more likely to experience *schadenfreude* when the misfortune happens to someone we envy or dislike, or, as a recent study showed, to someone we see as a rival, such as a co-worker with whom we have a competitive relationship. This effect persisted even when researchers controlled for how much the person liked the other.

What are the ethical and work implications of *schadenfreude?*

1. Don't judge yourself too harshly for experiencing *schadenfreude.* As one review noted, "it seems almost inherent to social being." If we expect ourselves to never experience *schadenfreude* toward a disliked co-worker, it's a standard we're bound to fail to meet.
2. At the same time, try to recognize that while social comparisons are natural, they're not particularly healthy. As eminent psychologist Susan Fiske noted, "Comparison emotions can corrupt the comparer." Perhaps we can't avoid some comparisons to our coworkers or friends, but we can control how much we do it. *Schadenfreude* can keep us from empathizing not only with one individual, but with those experiencing misfortune more generally.

Sources: W. van Dijk, J. W. Ouwerkerk, Y. M. Wesseling, and G. M. van Koningsbruggen, "Towards Understanding Pleasure at the Misfortunes of Others: The Impact of Self-Evaluation Threat on Schadenfreude," *Cognition and Emotion* 25, no. 2 (2011), pp. 360–368; R. H. Smith, C. A. Powell, D. J. Combs, and D. R. Schurtz, "Exploring the When and Why of Schadenfreude," *Social and Personality Psychology Compass* 3, no. 4 (2009), pp. 530–546; S. T. Fiske, "Envy Up, Scorn Down: How Comparison Divides Us," *American Psychologist* 65, no. 8 (2010), pp. 698–706; and D. Rakoff, "When Bad Things Happen To Do-Good People," *The New York Times* (May 1, 2011), p. WK12.

situation. Negative moods also make people more distractable, and distractions can obviously lead to careless behaviors.

How Managers Can Influence Moods

8   Apply concepts about emotions and moods to specific OB issues.

You can usually improve a friend's mood by sharing a funny video clip, giving the person a small bag of candy, or even offering a pleasant beverage.[126] But what can companies do to improve employees' moods? Managers can use humor and give their employees small tokens of appreciation for work well done. Also, when leaders themselves are in good moods, group members are more positive, and as a result they cooperate more.[127]

Finally, selecting positive team members can have a contagion effect because positive moods transmit from team member to team member. One study of professional cricket teams found players' happy moods affected the moods of their team members and positively influenced their performance.[128] It makes sense, then, for managers to select team members predisposed to experience positive moods.

MyManagementLab

Now that you have finished this chapter, go back to **www.pearsonglobaleditions.com/ mymanagementlab** to continue practicing and applying the concepts you've learned.

Summary and Implications for Managers

Emotions and moods are similar in that both are affective in nature. But they're also different—moods are more general and less contextual than emotions. And events do matter. The time of day and day of the week, stressful events, social activities, and sleep patterns are some of the factors that influence emotions and moods. Emotions and moods have proven relevant for virtually every OB topic we study, and they have implications for managerial practice.

- Increasingly, organizations are selecting employees they believe have high levels of emotional intelligence. Research has helped to refine theory related to emotional intelligence in recent years, which should lead to superior tools for assessing ability-based EI.
- Emotions and positive moods appear to facilitate effective decision making and creativity.
- Recent research suggests mood is linked to motivation, especially through feedback.
- Leaders rely on emotions to increase their effectiveness.
- The display of emotions is important to social behavior like negotiation and customer service.
- The experience of emotions is closely linked to job attitudes and behaviors that follow from attitudes, such as deviant workplace behavior.
- Our final managerial implication is a question: can managers control colleagues' and employees' emotions and moods? Certainly there are limits, practical and ethical. Emotions and moods are a natural part of an individual's makeup. Where managers err is in ignoring co-workers' and employees' emotions and assessing others' behavior as if it were completely rational. As one consultant aptly put it, "You can't divorce emotions from the workplace because you can't divorce emotions from people."[129] Managers who understand the role of emotions and moods will significantly improve their ability to explain and predict their co-workers' and employees' behavior.

QUESTIONS FOR REVIEW

1 What is the difference between emotions and moods? What are the basic emotions and moods?

2 Are emotions rational? What functions do they serve?

3 What are the sources of emotions and moods?

4 What impact does emotional labor have on employees?

5 What is affective events theory? What are its applications?

6 What is the evidence for and against the existence of emotional intelligence?

7 What are some strategies for emotion regulation and their likely effects?

8 How do you apply concepts about emotions and moods to specific OB issues?

Sometimes Blowing Your Top Is a Good Thing

POINT

Anger is discussed throughout this chapter for a reason: it's an important emotion. However, what about our responses to feeling anger? Work cultures teach us to avoid showing any anger at all, lest we be seen as poor service providers or, worse, unprofessional or even deviant or violent. While, of course, there *are* times when the expression of anger is harmful or unprofessional, we've taken this view so far that we now teach people to suppress perfectly normal emotions. It is inappropriate to ask people to behave in abnormal ways, and there is even more evidence about the organizational and personal costs of such suppression.

Emerging research shows that suppressing anger takes a terrible toll on individuals. One Stanford University study showed, for example, that when individuals were asked to wear a poker face during the showing of the atomic bombings of Japan during World War II, they were much more stressful conversation partners once the video was over. Other research shows that college students who suppress emotions like anger have more trouble making friends and are more likely to be depressed, and that employees who suppress anger feel more stressed by work.

There is a better way. One recent study showed that even when employees displayed anger deemed inappropriate by co-workers, if co-workers responded supportively to the anger (for example, by listening to the angry employee), favorable responses such as constructive work changes were the result.

Yes, managers must work to maintain a positive, respectful, and nonviolent culture. However, asking employees to suppress their anger not only is an ineffective and costly strategy, it ultimately may backfire if appropriate ways to express and release anger are blocked.

COUNTERPOINT

Yes, anger is a common emotion. But it's also a toxic one. The experience of anger and its close correlate, hostility, is linked to many counterproductive behaviors in organizations. That is why many organizations have developed anger management programs—to blunt the harmful effects of anger in the workplace.

The Bureau of Labor Statistics estimates that 16 percent of fatal workplace injuries resulted from workplace violence. Do we think the individuals who committed these acts were feeling joyful and contented?

To reduce anger in the workplace, many companies develop policies that govern conduct such as yelling, shouting profanities, and making hostile gestures. Others institute anger management programs. For example, one organization conducted mandatory in-house workshops that showed individuals how to deal with conflicts in the workplace before they boil over. The director who instituted the training said it "gave people specific tools for opening a dialogue to work things out." MTS Systems, an Eden Prairie, Minnesota, engineering firm, engages an outside consulting firm to conduct anger management programs for its organization. Typically, MTS holds an eight-hour seminar that discusses sources of anger, conflict resolution techniques, and organizational policies. This is followed by one-on-one sessions with individual employees that focus on cognitive behavioral techniques to manage their anger. The outside trainer charges $7,000–$10,000 for the seminar and one-on-one sessions. "You want people to get better at communicating with each other," says MTS manager Karen Borre.

In the end, everyone wins when organizations seek to diminish both the experience and, yes, the expression of anger at work. The work environment is less threatening and stressful to employees and customers. Employees are likely to feel safer. And the angry employee is often helped as well.

Sources: B. Carey, "The Benefits of Blowing Your Top," *The New York Times* (July 6, 2010), p. D1; R. Y. Cheung and I. J. Park, "Anger Suppression, Interdependent Self-Construal, and Depression Among Asian American and European American College Students," *Cultural Diversity and Ethnic Minority Psychology* 16, no. 4 (2010), pp. 517–525; D. Geddes and L. T. Stickney, "The Trouble with Sanctions: Organizational Responses to Deviant Anger Displays at Work," *Human Relations* 64, no. 2 (2011), pp. 201–230; and J. Fairley, "Taking Control of Anger Management," *Workforce Management* (October 2010), p. 10.

EXPERIENTIAL EXERCISE Who Can Catch a Liar?

We mentioned earlier in the chapter that emotion researchers are highly interested in facial expressions as a window into individuals' emotional worlds. Research has also studied whether people can tell someone is lying based on signs of guilt or nervousness in their facial expressions. Let's see who is good at catching liars.

Split up into teams and follow these instructions.

1. Randomly choose someone to be the team organizer. Have this person write down on a piece of paper "T" for truth and "L" for lie. If there are, say, six people in the group (other than the organizer), then three people will get a slip with a "T" and three a slip with an "L." It's important that all team members keep what's on their paper a secret.

2. Each team member who holds a T slip needs to come up with a true statement, and each team member who holds an L slip needs to come up with a false statement. Try not to make the statement so outrageous that no one would believe it (for example, "I have flown to the moon").

3. The organizer will have each member make his or her statement. Group members should then examine the person making the statement closely to try to determine whether he or she is telling the truth or lying. Once each person has made his or her statement, the organizer will ask for a vote and record the tallies.

4. Each person should now indicate whether the statement was the truth or a lie.

5. How good was your group at catching the liars? Were some people good liars? What did you look for to determine whether someone was lying?

ETHICAL DILEMMA Happiness Coaches for Employees

We know there is considerable spillover from personal unhappiness to negative emotions at work. Moreover, those who experience negative emotions in life and at work are more likely to engage in counterproductive behaviors with customers, clients, or fellow employees.

Increasingly, organizations such as American Express, UBS, and KPMG are turning to happiness coaches to address this spillover from personal unhappiness to work emotions and behaviors.

Srikumar Rao is a former college professor who has the nickname, "the happiness guru." Rao teaches people to analyze negative emotions to prevent them from becoming overwhelming. If your job is restructured, for example, Rao suggests avoiding negative thoughts and feelings about it. Instead, he advises, tell yourself it could turn out well in the long run, and there is no way to know at present.

Beyond reframing the emotional impact of work situations, some happiness coaches attack the negative emotional spillover from life to work (and from work to life). A working mother found that a happiness talk by Shawn Actor helped her stop focusing on her stressed-out life and instead look for chances to smile, laugh, and be grateful.

In some cases, the claims made by happiness coaches seem a bit trite. Jim Smith, who labels himself "The Executive Happiness Coach," asks: "What if I told you that there are secrets nobody told you as a kid—or as an adult, for that matter—that can unlock for you all sorts of positive emotional experiences? What if the only thing that gets in the way of you feeling more happiness is—YOU?! What if you can change your experience of the world by shifting a few simple things in your life, and then practicing them until they become second nature?"

Then again, if employees leave their experiences with a happiness coach feeling happier about their jobs and their lives, is that not better for everyone? Says one individual, Ivelisse Rivera, who felt she benefitted from a happiness coach, "If I assume a negative attitude and complain all the time, whoever is working with me is going to feel the same way."

Questions

1. Do you think happiness coaches are effective? How might you assess their effectiveness?

2. Would you welcome happiness training in your workplace? Why or why not?

3. Some argue that happiness coaches are a way for organizations to avoid solving real work problems—a diversion, if you will. How might we make this determination?

4. Under what circumstances—if any—is it ethically appropriate for a supervisor to suggest a happiness coach for a subordinate?

Sources: S. Shellenbarger, "Thinking Happy Thoughts at Work," *The Wall Street Journal* (January 27, 2010), p. D2; S. Sharma and D. Chatterjee, "Cos Are Keenly Listening to 'Happiness Coach'," *Economic Times* (July 16, 2010), http://articles.economictimes.indiatimes.com; and J. Smith, *The Executive Happiness Coach,* www.lifewithhappiness.com/ (Downloaded May 3, 2011).

CASE INCIDENT 1 Is It Okay to Cry at Work?

As this chapter has shown, emotions are an inevitable part of people's behavior at work. At the same time, it's not entirely clear that we've reached a point where people feel comfortable expressing *all* emotions at work. The reason might be that business culture and etiquette remain poorly suited to handling overt emotional displays. The question is, can organizations become more intelligent about emotional management? Is it ever appropriate to yell, laugh, or cry at work?

Some people are skeptical about the virtues of more emotional displays at the workplace. As the chapter notes, emotions are automatic physiological responses to the environment, and as such, they can be difficult to control appropriately. One 22-year-old customer service representative named Laura who was the subject of a case study noted that fear and anger were routinely used as methods to control employees, and employees deeply resented this use of emotions to manipulate them. In another case, the chairman of a major television network made a practice of screaming at employees whenever anything went wrong, leading to badly hurt feelings and a lack of loyalty to the organization. Like Laura, workers at this organization were hesitant to show their true reactions to these emotional outbursts for fear of being branded as "weak" or "ineffectual." It might seem like these individuals worked in heavily emotional workplaces, but in fact, only a narrow range of emotions was deemed acceptable. Anger appears to be more acceptable than sadness in many organizations, and anger can have serious maladaptive consequences.

Others believe organizations that recognize and work with emotions effectively are more creative, satisfying, and productive. For example, Laura noted that if she could

express her hurt feelings without fear, she would be much more satisfied with her work. In other words, the problem with Laura's organization is not that emotions are displayed, but that emotional displays are handled poorly. Others note that use of emotional knowledge, like being able to read and understand the reactions of others, is crucial for workers ranging from salespeople and customer service agents all the way to managers and executives. One survey even found that 88 percent of workers feel being sensitive to the emotions of others is an asset. Management consultant Erika Anderson notes, "Crying at work is transformative and can open the door to change." The question then is, can organizations take specific steps to become better at allowing emotional displays without opening a Pandora's Box of outbursts?

Questions

1. What factors do you think make some organizations ineffective at managing emotions?

2. Do you think the strategic use and display of emotions serve to protect employees, or does covering your true emotions at work lead to more problems than it solves?

3. Have you ever worked where emotions were used as part of a management style? Describe the advantages and disadvantages of this approach in your experience.

4. Research shows that acts of co-workers (37 percent) and management (22 percent) cause more negative emotions for employees than do acts of customers (7 percent).[130] What can Laura's company do to change its emotional climate?

Sources: A. Kreamer, "Go Ahead—Cry at Work," *Time* (April 4, 2010), www.time.com; J. S. Lerner and K. Shonk, "How Anger Poisons Decision Making," *Harvard Business Review* (September 2010), p. 26; and J. Perrone and M. H. Vickers, "Emotions as Strategic Game in a Hostile Workplace: An Exemplar Case," *Employee Responsibilities and Rights Journal* 16, no. 3 (2004), pp. 167–178.

CASE INCIDENT 2 Can You Read Emotions from Faces?

We mentioned previously that some researchers—the psychologist Paul Ekman is the best known—have studied whether facial expressions reveal true emotions. These researchers have distinguished real smiles (so-called Duchenne smiles, named after French physician Guillaume Duchenne) from "fake" smiles. Duchenne found genuine smiles raised not only the corners of the mouth (easily faked) but also cheek and eye muscles (much more difficult to fake). So, one way to determine whether someone is genuinely happy or amused is to look at the muscles

around the upper cheeks and eyes—if the person's eyes are smiling or twinkling, the smile is genuine. Ekman and his associates have developed similar methods to detect other emotions, such as anger, disgust, and distress. According to Ekman, the key to identifying real emotions is to focus on micro-expressions, or those facial muscles we cannot easily manipulate.

Dan Hill has used these techniques to study the facial expressions of CEOs and found they vary dramatically not only in their Duchenne smiles but also in the degree to which they display positive versus negative facial expressions. The accompanying table shows Hill's analysis of the facial expressions of some prominent male executives:

Jeff Bezos, Amazon	51% positive
Warren Buffet, Berkshire Hathaway	69% positive
Michael Dell, Dell Computers	47% positive
Larry Ellison, Oracle	0% positive
Bill Gates, Microsoft	73% positive
Steve Jobs, Apple	48% positive
Phil Knight, Nike	67% positive
Donald Trump, The Trump Organization	16% positive

It's interesting to note that these individuals, all of whom are successful in various ways, have such different levels of positive facial expressions. It also raises the question: is a smile from Larry Ellison worth more than a smile from Bill Gates?

Questions

1. Most research suggests we are not very good at detecting fake emotions, and we think we're much better at it than we are. Do you believe training would improve your ability to detect emotional displays in others?

2. Do you think the information in this case could help you tell whether someone's smile is genuine?

3. Is your own impression of the facial expressions of the eight business leaders consistent with what the researcher found? If not, why do you think your views might be at odds with his?

4. One research study found people's ratings of the positive affect displayed in CEO's faces had very little correlation to their company's profits. Does that suggest to you that Hill's analysis is immaterial?

5. Assuming you could become better at detecting the real emotions in facial expressions, do you think it would help your career? Why or why not?

Sources: Based on P. Ekman, *Telling Lies: Clues to Deceit in the Marketplace, Politics, and Marriage* (New York: W. W. Norton & Co., 2009); D. Jones, "It's Written All Over Their Faces," *USA Today* (February 25, 2008), pp. 1B–2B; and N. O. Rule and N. Ambady, "The Face of Success," *Psychological Science* 19, no. 2 (2008), pp. 109–111.

ENDNOTES

1. See, for instance, C. D. Fisher and N. M. Ashkanasy, "The Emerging Role of Emotions in Work Life: An Introduction," *Journal of Organizational Behavior,* Special Issue 2000, pp. 123–129; N. M. Ashkanasy, C. E. J. Hartel, and W. J. Zerbe (eds.), *Emotions in the Workplace: Research, Theory, and Practice* (Westport, CT: Quorum Books, 2000); N. M. Ashkanasy and C. S. Daus, "Emotion in the Workplace: The New Challenge for Managers," *Academy of Management Executive* (February 2002), pp. 76–86; and N. M. Ashkanasy, C. E. J. Hartel, and C. S. Daus, "Diversity and Emotion: The New Frontiers in Organizational Behavior Research," *Journal of Management* 28, no. 3 (2002), pp. 307–338.

2. See, for example, L. L. Putnam and D. K. Mumby, "Organizations, Emotion and the Myth of Rationality," in S. Fineman (ed.), *Emotion in Organizations* (Thousand Oaks, CA: Sage, 1993), pp. 36–57; and J. Martin, K. Knopoff, and C. Beckman, "An Alternative to Bureaucratic Impersonality and Emotional Labor: Bounded Emotionality at the Body Shop," *Administrative Science Quarterly* (June 1998), pp. 429–469.

3. B. E. Ashforth and R. H. Humphrey, "Emotion in the Workplace: A Reappraisal," *Human Relations* (February 1995), pp. 97–125.

4. S. G. Barsade and D. E. Gibson, "Why Does Affect Matter in Organizations?" *Academy of Management Perspectives* (February 2007), pp. 36–59.

5. See N. H. Frijda, "Moods, Emotion Episodes and Emotions," in M. Lewis and J. M. Haviland (eds.), *Handbook of Emotions* (New York: Guilford Press, 1993), pp. 381–403.

6. H. M. Weiss and R. Cropanzano, "Affective Events Theory: A Theoretical Discussion of the Structure, Causes and Consequences of Affective Experiences at Work," in B. M. Staw and L. L. Cummings (eds.), *Research in Organizational Behavior,* vol. 18 (Greenwich, CT: JAI Press, 1996), pp. 17–19.

7. See P. Ekman and R. J. Davidson (eds.), *The Nature of Emotions: Fundamental Questions* (Oxford, UK: Oxford University Press, 1994).

8. Frijda, "Moods, Emotion Episodes and Emotions," p. 381.

9. See Ekman and Davidson (eds.), *The Nature of Emotions.*

10. See, for example, P. Ekman, "An Argument for Basic Emotions," *Cognition and Emotion* (May/July 1992), pp. 169–200; C. E. Izard, "Basic Emotions, Relations Among Emotions, and Emotion–Cognition Relations," *Psychological Bulletin* (November 1992), pp. 561–565; and J. L. Tracy and R. W. Robins, "Emerging Insights into the Nature and Function of Pride," *Current Directions in Psychological Science* 16, no. 3 (2007), pp. 147–150.

11. R. C. Solomon, "Back to Basics: On the Very Idea of 'Basic Emotions,'" *Journal for the Theory of Social Behaviour* 32, no. 2 (June 2002), pp. 115–144.

12. R. Descartes, *The Passions of the Soul* (Indianapolis: Hackett, 1989).

13. P. Ekman, *Emotions Revealed: Recognizing Faces and Feelings to Improve Communication and Emotional Life* (New York: Times Books/Henry Holt and Co., 2003).

14. P. R. Shaver, H. J. Morgan, and S. J. Wu, "Is Love a 'Basic' Emotion?" *Personal Relationships* 3, no. 1 (March 1996), pp. 81–96.

15. Ibid.

16. Ashforth and Humphrey, "Emotion in the Workplace," p. 104; B. Plasait, "Accueil des Touristes Dans les Grands Centres de Transit Paris," *Rapport du Bernard Plasait* (October 4, 2004), www.tourisme.gouv.fr/fr/navd/presse/dossiers/att00005767/dp_ plasait.pdf; B. Mesquita, "Emotions in Collectivist and Individualist Contexts," *Journal of Personality and Social Psychology* 80, no. 1 (2001), pp. 68–74; and D. Rubin, "Grumpy German Shoppers Distrust the Wal-Mart Style," *Seattle Times* (December 30, 2001), p. A15.

17. Solomon, "Back to Basics."

18. Weiss and Cropanzano, "Affective Events Theory," pp. 20–22.

19. Cited in R. D. Woodworth, *Experimental Psychology* (New York: Holt, 1938).

20. D. Watson, L. A. Clark, and A. Tellegen, "Development and Validation of Brief Measures of Positive and Negative Affect: The PANAS Scales," *Journal of Personality and Social Psychology* (1988), pp. 1063–1070.

21. A. Ben-Ze'ev, *The Subtlety of Emotions* (Cambridge, MA: MIT Press, 2000), p. 94.

22. "Flight Attendant War Stories . . . Stewardess," AboutMyJob .com, www.aboutmyjob.com/?p=2111.

23. A. Ben-Ze'ev, *The Subtlety of Emotions*, p. 99.

24. J. T. Cacioppo and W. L. Gardner, "Emotion," in *Annual Review of Psychology*, vol. 50 (Palo Alto, CA: Annual Reviews, 1999), pp. 191–214.

25. D. Holman, "Call Centres," in D. Holman, T. D. Wall, C. Clegg, P. Sparrow, and A. Howard (eds.), *The Essentials of the New Work Place: A Guide to the Human Impact of Modern Working Practices* (Chichester, UK: Wiley, 2005), pp. 111–132.

26. M. Eid and E. Diener, "Norms for Experiencing Emotions in Different Cultures: Inter- and International Differences," *Journal of Personality & Social Psychology* 81, no. 5 (2001), pp. 869–885.

27. S. Oishi, E. Diener, and C. Napa Scollon, "Cross-Situational Consistency of Affective Experiences Across Cultures," *Journal of Personality & Social Psychology* 86, no. 3 (2004), pp. 460–472.

28. Eid and Diener, "Norms for Experiencing Emotions in Different Cultures."

29. L. M. Poverny and S. Picascia, "There Is No Crying in Business," *Womensmedia.com*, October 20, 2009, www .womensmedia.com/new/Crying-at-Work.shtml.

30. A. R. Damasio, *Descartes' Error: Emotion, Reason, and the Human Brain* (New York: Quill, 1994).

31. Ibid.

32. J. Haidt, "The New Synthesis in Moral Psychology," *Science* 316 (May 18, 2007), pp. 998, 1002; I. E. de Hooge, R. M. A. Nelissen, S. M. Breugelmans, and M. Zeelenberg, "What is Moral about Guilt? Acting 'Prosocially' at the Disadvantage of Others," *Journal of Personality and Social Psychology* 100 (2011), pp. 462–473; and C. A. Hutcherson and J. J. Gross, "The Moral Emotions: A Social-Functionalist Account of Anger, Disgust, and Contempt," *Journal of Personality and Social Psychology* 100 (2011), pp. 719–737.

33. R. J. Larsen and E. Diener, "Affect Intensity as an Individual Difference Characteristic: A Review," *Journal of Research in Personality* 21 (1987), pp. 1–39.

34. D. Watson, *Mood and Temperament* (New York: Guilford Press, 2000).

35. J. J. A. Denissen, L. Butalid, L. Penke, and M. A. G. van Aken, "The Effects of Weather on Daily Mood: A Multilevel Approach," *Emotion* 8, no. 5 (2008), pp. 662–667; M. C. Keller, B. L. Fredrickson, O. Ybarra, S. Côté, K. Johnson, J. Mikels, A. Conway, and T. Wagner, "A Warm Heart and a Clear Head: The Contingent Effects of Weather on Mood and Cognition," *Psychological Science* 16 (2005) pp. 724–731; and Watson, *Mood and Temperament.*

36. Watson, *Mood and Temperament*, p. 100.

37. J. A. Fuller, J. M. Stanton, G. G. Fisher, C. Spitzmüller, S. S. Russell, and P. C. Smith, "A Lengthy Look at the Daily Grind: Time Series Analysis of Events, Mood, Stress, and Satisfaction," *Journal of Applied Psychology* 88, no. 6 (December 2003), pp. 1019–1033.

38. See "Monday Blahs," May 16, 2005, www.ashidome.com/blogger/housearrest.asp?c=809&m=5&y=2005.

39. A. M. Isen, "Positive Affect as a Source of Human Strength," in L. G. Aspinwall and U. Staudinger (eds.), *The Psychology of Human Strengths* (Washington, DC: American Psychological Association, 2003), pp. 179–195.

40. Watson, *Mood and Temperament.*

41. *Sleep in America Poll* (Washington, DC: National Sleep Foundation, 2005), www.kintera.org/atf/cf/%7Bf6bf2668-a1b4-4fe8-8d1a-a5d39340d9cb%7D/2005_summary_of_findings.pdf.

42. M. Lavidor, A. Weller, and H. Babkoff, "How Sleep Is Related to Fatigue," *British Journal of Health Psychology* 8 (2003), pp. 95–105; and J. J. Pilcher and E. Ott, "The Relationships Between Sleep and Measures of Health and Well-Being in College Students: A Repeated Measures Approach," *Behavioral Medicine* 23 (1998), pp. 170–178.

43. E. K. Miller and J. D. Cohen, "An Integrative Theory of Prefrontal Cortex Function," *Annual Review of Neuroscience* 24 (2001), pp. 167–202.

44. B. A. Scott and T. A. Judge, "Insomnia, Emotions, and Job Satisfaction: A Multilevel Study," *Journal of Management* 32, no. 5 (2006), pp. 622–645.

45. P. R. Giacobbi, H. A. Hausenblas, and N. Frye, "A Naturalistic Assessment of the Relationship Between Personality, Daily Life Events, Leisure-Time Exercise, and Mood," *Psychology of Sport & Exercise* 6, no. 1 (January 2005), pp. 67–81.

46. L. L. Carstensen, M. Pasupathi, M. Ulrich, and J. R. Nesselroade, "Emotional Experience in Everyday Life Across the Adult Life Span," *Journal of Personality and Social Psychology* 79, no. 4 (2000), pp. 644–655.

47. M. LaFrance and M. Banaji, "Toward a Reconsideration of the Gender–Emotion Relationship," in M. Clark (ed.), *Review of Personality and Social Psychology*, vol. 14 (Newbury Park, CA: Sage, 1992), pp. 178–197; and A. M. Kring and A. H. Gordon, "Sex Differences in Emotion: Expression, Experience, and Physiology," *Journal of Personality and Social Psychology* (March 1998), pp. 686–703.

48. M. G. Gard and A. M. Kring, "Sex Differences in the Time Course of Emotion," *Emotion* 7, no. 2 (2007), pp. 429–437; M. Jakupcak, K. Salters, K. L. Gratz, and L. Roemer, "Masculinity and Emotionality: An Investigation of Men's Primary and Secondary Emotional Responding," *Sex Roles* 49 (2003), pp. 111–120; and M. Grossman and W. Wood, "Sex Differences in Intensity of Emotional Experience: A Social Role Interpretation," *Journal of Personality and Social Psychology* (November 1992), pp. 1010–1022.

49. A. H. Fischer, P. M. Rodriguez Mosquera, A. E. M. van Vianen, and A. S. R. Manstead, "Gender and Culture Differences in Emotion," *Emotion* 4 (2004), pp. 84–87.

50. L. F. Barrett and E. Bliss-Moreau, "She's Emotional. He's Having a Bad Day: Attributional Explanations for Emotion Stereotypes," *Emotion* 9 (2009), pp. 649–658.

51. D. V. Becker, D. T. Kenrick, S. L. Neuberg, K. C. Blackwell, and D. M. Smith, "The Confounded Nature of Angry Men and Happy Women," *Journal of Personality and Social Psychology* 92 (2007), pp. 179–190.

52. P. Ekman, W. V. Friesen, and M. O'Sullivan, "Smiles When Lying," in P. Ekman and E. L. Rosenberg (eds.), *What the Face Reveals: Basic and Applied Studies of Spontaneous Expression Using the Facial Action Coding System (FACS)* (London: Oxford University Press, 1997), pp. 201–216.

53. A. Grandey, "Emotion Regulation in the Workplace: A New Way to Conceptualize Emotional Labor," *Journal of Occupational Health Psychology* 5, no. 1 (2000), pp. 95–110; and R. Cropanzano, D. E. Rupp, and Z. S. Byrne, "The Relationship of Emotional Exhaustion to Work Attitudes, Job Performance, and Organizational Citizenship Behavior," *Journal of Applied Psychology* (February 2003), pp. 160–169.

54. A. R. Hochschild, "Emotion Work, Feeling Rules, and Social Structure," *American Journal of Sociology* (November 1979), pp. 551–575; W.-C. Tsai, "Determinants and Consequences of Employee Displayed Positive Emotions," *Journal of Management* 27, no. 4 (2001), pp. 497–512; M. W. Kramer and J. A. Hess, "Communication Rules for the Display of Emotions in Organizational Settings," *Management Communication Quarterly* (August 2002), pp. 66–80; and J. M. Diefendorff and E. M. Richard, "Antecedents and Consequences of Emotional Display Rule Perceptions," *Journal of Applied Psychology* (April 2003), pp. 284–294.

55. B. M. DePaulo, "Nonverbal Behavior and Self-Presentation," *Psychological Bulletin* (March 1992), pp. 203–243.

56. J. M. Diefendorff and G. J. Greguras, "Contextualizing Emotional Display Rules: Examining the Roles of Targets and Discrete Emotions in Shaping Display Rule Perceptions," *Journal of Management* 35 (2009), pp. 880–898.

57. Solomon, "Back to Basics."

58. C. M. Brotheridge and R. T. Lee, "Development and Validation of the Emotional Labour Scale," *Journal of Occupational & Organizational Psychology* 76 (2003), pp. 365–379.

59. A. A. Grandey, "When 'The Show Must Go On': Surface Acting and Deep Acting as Determinants of Emotional Exhaustion and Peer-Rated Service Delivery," *Academy of Management Journal* (February 2003), pp. 86–96; and A. A. Grandey, D. N. Dickter, and H. Sin, "The Customer Is Not Always Right: Customer Aggression and Emotion Regulation of Service Employees," *Journal of Organizational Behavior* 25 (2004), pp. 397–418.

60. J. P. Trougakos, D. J. Beal, S. G. Green, and H. M. Weiss, "Making the Break Count: An Episodic Examination of Recovery Activities, Emotional Experiences, and Positive Affective Displays," *Academy of Management Journal* 51 (2008), pp. 131–146.

61. J. M. Diefendorff, R. J. Erickson, A. A. Grandey, and J. J. Dahling, "Emotional Display Rules as Work Unit Norms: A Multilevel Analysis of Emotional Labor among Nurses," *Journal of Occupational Health Psychology* 16 (2011), pp. 170–186.

62. H. M. Weiss and R. Cropanzano, "An Affective Events Approach to Job Satisfaction," *Research in Organizational Behavior* 18 (1996), pp. 1–74.

63. J. Basch and C. D. Fisher, "Affective Events–Emotions Matrix: A Classification of Work Events and Associated Emotions," in N. M. Ashkanasy, C. E. J. Hartel, and W. J. Zerbe (eds.), *Emotions in the Workplace* (Westport, CT: Quorum Books, 2000), pp. 36–48.

64. See, for example, H. M. Weiss and R. Cropanzano, "Affective Events Theory"; and C. D. Fisher, "Antecedents and Consequences of Real-Time Affective Reactions at Work," *Motivation and Emotion* (March 2002), pp. 3–30.

65. Based on Weiss and Cropanzano, "Affective Events Theory," p. 42.

66. N. M. Ashkanasy, C. E. J. Hartel, and C. S. Daus, "Diversity and Emotion: The New Frontiers in Organizational Behavior Research," *Journal of Management* 28, no. 3 (2002), p. 324.

67. Based on D. R. Caruso, J. D. Mayer, and P. Salovey, "Emotional Intelligence and Emotional Leadership," in R. E. Riggio, S. E. Murphy, and F. J. Pirozzolo (eds.), *Multiple Intelligences and Leadership* (Mahwah, NJ: Lawrence Erlbaum, 2002), p. 70.

68. This section is based on Daniel Goleman, *Emotional Intelligence* (New York: Bantam, 1995); P. Salovey and D. Grewal, "The Science of Emotional Intelligence," *Current Directions in Psychological Science* 14, no. 6 (2005), pp. 281–285; M. Davies, L. Stankov, and R. D. Roberts, "Emotional Intelligence: In Search of an Elusive Construct," *Journal of Personality and Social Psychology* (October 1998), pp. 989–1015; D. Geddes and R. R. Callister, "Crossing the Line(s): A Dual Threshold Model of Anger in Organizations," *Academy of Management Review* 32, no. 3 (2007), pp. 721–746.

69. R. Gilkey, R. Caceda, and C. Kilts, "When Emotional Reasoning Trumps IQ," *Harvard Business Review* (September 2010), p. 27.

70. F. I. Greenstein, *The Presidential Difference: Leadership Style from FDR to Clinton* (Princeton, NJ: Princeton University Press, 2001).

71. M. Seo and L. F. Barrett, "Being Emotional During Decision Making—Good or Bad? An Empirical Investigation," *Academy of Management Journal* 50, no. 4 (2007), pp. 923–940.

72. C. Cherniss, "The Business Case for Emotional Intelligence," *Consortium for Research on Emotional Intelligence in Organizations*, 1999, www.eiconsortium.org/reports/business_case_for_ei.html.

73. K. S. Law, C. Wong, and L. J. Song, "The Construct and Criterion Validity of Emotional Intelligence and Its Potential Utility for Management Studies," *Journal of Applied Psychology* 89, no. 3 (2004), pp. 483–496.

74. H. A. Elfenbein and N. Ambady, "Predicting Workplace Outcomes from the Ability to Eavesdrop on Feelings," *Journal of Applied Psychology* 87, no. 5 (October 2002), pp. 963–971.

75. D. L. Joseph and D. A. Newman, "Emotional Intelligence: An Integrative Meta-Analysis and Cascading Model," *Journal of Applied Psychology* 95 (2010), pp. 54–78.

76. R. Bar-On, D. Tranel, N. L. Denburg, and A. Bechara, "Exploring the Neurological Substrate of Emotional and Social Intelligence," *Brain* 126, no. 8 (August 2003), pp. 1790–1800.

77. P. A. Vernon, K. V. Petrides, D. Bratko, and J. A. Schermer, "A Behavioral Genetic Study of Trait Emotional Intelligence," *Emotion* 8, no. 5 (2008), pp. 635–642.

78. E. A. Locke, "Why Emotional Intelligence Is an Invalid Concept," *Journal of Organizational Behavior* 26, no. 4 (June 2005), pp. 425–431.

79. J. D. Mayer, R. D. Roberts, and S. G. Barsade, "Human Abilities: Emotional Intelligence," *Annual Review of Psychology* 59 (2008), pp. 507–536; H. A. Elfenbein, "Emotion in Organizations: A Review and Theoretical Integration," *Academy of Management Annals* 1 (2008), pp. 315–386; and D. L. Joseph and D. A. Newman, "Emotional Intelligence: An Integrative Meta-Analysis and Cascading Model," *Journal of Applied Psychology* 95 (2010), pp. 54–78.

80. J. M. Conte, "A Review and Critique of Emotional Intelligence Measures," *Journal of Organizational Behavior* 26, no. 4 (June 2005), pp. 433–440; and M. Davies, L. Stankov, and R. D. Roberts, "Emotional Intelligence," pp. 989–1015.

81. T. Decker, "Is Emotional Intelligence a Viable Concept?" *Academy of Management Review* 28, no. 2 (April 2003), pp. 433–440; and Davies, Stankov, and Roberts, "Emotional Intelligence."

82. D. L. Joseph and D. A. Newman, "Emotional Intelligence: An Integrative Meta-Analysis and Cascading Model," *Journal of Applied Psychology* 95 (2010), pp. 54–78.

83. F. J. Landy, "Some Historical and Scientific Issues Related to Research on Emotional Intelligence," *Journal of Organizational Behavior* 26, no. 4 (June 2005), pp. 411–424.

84. S. L. Koole, "The Psychology of Emotion Regulation: An Integrative Review," *Cognition and Emotion* 23 (2009), pp. 4–41; H. A. Wadlinger and D. M. Isaacowitz, "Fixing Our Focus: Training Attention to Regulate Emotion," *Personality and Social Psychology Review* 15 (2011), pp. 75–102.

85. J. V. Wood, S. A. Heimpel, L. A. Manwell, and E. J. Whittington, "This Mood Is Familiar and I Don't Deserve to Feel Better Anyway: Mechanisms Underlying Self-Esteem Differences in Motivation to Repair Sad Moods," *Journal of Personality and Social Psychology* 96 (2009), pp. 363–380.

86. S. L. Koole, "The Psychology of Emotion Regulation: An Integrative Review," *Cognition and Emotion* 23 (2009), pp. 4–41.

87. S. Srivastava, M. Tamir, K. M. McGonigal, O. P. John, and J. J. Gross, "The Social Costs of Emotional Suppression: A Prospective Study of the Transition to College," *Journal of Personality and Social Psychology* 96 (2009), pp. 883–897; Y. Liu, L. M. Prati, P. L. Perrewé, and R. A. Brymer, "Individual Differences in Emotion Regulation, Emotional Experiences at Work, and Work-Related Outcomes: A Two-Study Investigation," *Journal of Applied Social Psychology* 40 (2010), pp. 1515–1538; and H. A. Wadlinger and D. M. Isaacowitz, "Fixing our Focus: Training Attention to Regulate Emotion," *Personality and Social Psychology Review* 15 (2011), pp. 75–102.

88. L. K. Barber, P. G. Bagsby, and D. C. Munz, "Affect Regulation Strategies for Promoting (or Preventing) Flourishing Emotional Health," *Personality and Individual Differences* 49 (2010), pp. 663–666.

89. L. M. J. Spencer, D. C. McClelland, and S. Kelner, *Competency Assessment Methods: History and State of the Art* (Boston: Hay/McBer, 1997).

90. J. Park and M. R. Banaji, "Mood and Heuristics: The Influence of Happy and Sad States on Sensitivity and Bias in Stereotyping," *Journal of Personality and Social Psychology* 78, no. 6 (2000), pp. 1005–1023.

91. See A. M. Isen, "Positive Affect and Decision Making," in M. Lewis and J. M. Haviland-Jones (eds.), *Handbook of Emotions,* 2nd ed. (New York: Guilford, 2000), pp. 261–277.

92. L. B. Alloy and L. Y. Abramson, "Judgment of Contingency in Depressed and Nondepressed Students: Sadder but Wiser?" *Journal of Experimental Psychology: General* 108 (1979), pp. 441–485.

93. N. Ambady and H. M. Gray, "On Being Sad and Mistaken: Mood Effects on the Accuracy of Thin-Slice Judgments," *Journal of Personality and Social Psychology* 83, no. 4 (2002), pp. 947–961.

94. S. Lyubomirsky, L. King, and E. Diener, "The Benefits of Frequent Positive Affect: Does Happiness Lead to Success?" *Psychological Bulletin* 131, no. 6 (2005), pp. 803–855; and M. Baas, C. K. W. De Dreu, and B. A. Nijstad, "A Meta-Analysis of 25 Years of Mood-Creativity Research: Hedonic Tone, Activation, or Regulatory Focus," *Psychological Bulletin* 134 (2008), pp. 779–806.

95. M. J. Grawitch, D. C. Munz, and E. K. Elliott, "Promoting Creativity in Temporary Problem-Solving Groups: The Effects of Positive Mood and Autonomy in Problem Definition on Idea-Generating Performance," *Group Dynamics* 7, no. 3 (September 2003), pp. 200–213.

96. S. Lyubomirsky, L. King, and E. Diener, "The Benefits of Frequent Positive Affect: Does Happiness Lead to Success?" *Psychological Bulletin* 131, no. 6 (2005), pp. 803–855.

97. N. Madjar, G. R. Oldham, and M. G. Pratt, "There's No Place Like Home? The Contributions of Work and Nonwork Creativity Support to Employees' Creative Performance," *Academy of Management Journal* 45, no. 4 (2002), pp. 757–767.

98. J. M. George and J. Zhou, "Understanding When Bad Moods Foster Creativity and Good Ones Don't: The Role of Context and Clarity of Feelings," *Journal of Applied Psychology* 87, no. 4 (August 2002), pp. 687–697; and J. P. Forgas and J. M. George, "Affective Influences on Judgments and Behavior in Organizations: An Information Processing Perspective," *Organizational Behavior and Human Decision Processes* 86, no. 1 (2001), pp. 3–34.

99. C. K. W. De Dreu, M. Baas, and B. A. Nijstad, "Hedonic Tone and Activation Level in the Mood-Creativity Link: Toward a Dual Pathway to Creativity Model," *Journal of Personality and Social Psychology* 94, no. 5 (2008), pp. 739–756; J. M. George and J. Zhou, "Dual Tuning in a Supportive Context: Joint Contributions of Positive Mood, Negative Mood, and Supervisory Behaviors to Employee Creativity," *Academy of Management Journal* 50, no. 3 (2007), pp. 605–622.

100. A. Erez and A. M. Isen, "The Influence of Positive Affect on the Components of Expectancy Motivation," *Journal of Applied Psychology* 87, no. 6 (2002), pp. 1055–1067.

101. R. Ilies and T. A. Judge, "Goal Regulation Across Time: The Effect of Feedback and Affect," *Journal of Applied Psychology* 90, no. 3 (May 2005), pp. 453–467.

102. W. Tsai, C. Chen, and H. Liu, "Test of a Model Linking Employee Positive Moods and Task Performance," *Journal of Applied Psychology* 92, no. 6 (2007), pp. 1570–1583.

103. K. M. Lewis, "When Leaders Display Emotion: How Followers Respond to Negative Emotional Expression of Male and Female Leaders," *Journal of Organizational Behavior,*

March 2000, pp. 221–234; and J. M. George, "Emotions and Leadership: The Role of Emotional Intelligence," *Human Relations* (August 2000), pp. 1027–1055.

104. J. M. George, "Trait and State Affect," In K. Murphy (ed.), *Individual Differences and Behavior in Organizations* (San Francisco: Jossey Bass, 1996), pp. 145–171.

105. Ashforth and Humphrey, "Emotion in the Workplace," p. 116.

106. J. E. Bono, H. J. Foldes, G. Vinson, and J. P. Muros, "Workplace Emotions: The Role of Supervision and Leadership," *Journal of Applied Psychology* 92, no. 5 (2007), pp. 1357–1367.

107. N. Reynolds, "Whiz-Kids Gamble on TV Channel for Poker," *telegraph.co.uk* (April 16, 2005), www.telegraph .co.uk/news/uknews/1487949/Whiz-kids-gamble-on-TV-channel-for-poker.html.

108. G. A. Van Kleef, C. K. W. De Dreu, and A. S. R. Manstead, "The Interpersonal Effects of Emotions in Negotiations: A Motivated Information Processing Approach," *Journal of Personality and Social Psychology* 87, no. 4 (2004), pp. 510–528; and G. A. Van Kleef, C. K. W. De Dreu, and A. S. R. Manstead, "The Interpersonal Effects of Anger and Happiness in Negotiations," *Journal of Personality and Social Psychology* 86, no. 1 (2004), pp. 57–76.

109. E. van Dijk, G. A. Van Kleef, W. Steinel, and I. van Beest, "A Social Functional Approach to Emotions in Bargaining: When Communicating Anger Pays and When It Backfires," *Journal of Personality and Social Psychology* 94, no. 4 (2008), pp. 600–614.

110. K. M. O'Connor and J. A. Arnold, "Distributive Spirals: Negotiation Impasses and the Moderating Role of Disputant Self-Efficacy," *Organizational Behavior and Human Decision Processes* 84, no. 1 (2001), pp. 148–176.

111. B. Shiv, G. Loewenstein, A. Bechara, H. Damasio, and A. R. Damasio, "Investment Behavior and the Negative Side of Emotion," *Psychological Science* 16, no. 6 (2005), pp. 435–439.

112. W.-C. Tsai and Y.-M. Huang, "Mechanisms Linking Employee Affective Delivery and Customer Behavioral Intentions," *Journal of Applied Psychology* (October 2002), pp. 1001–1008.

113. Grandey, "When 'The Show Must Go On.'"

114. See P. B. Barker and A. A. Grandey, "Service with a Smile and Encounter Satisfaction: Emotional Contagion and Appraisal Mechanisms," *Academy of Management Journal* 49, no. 6 (2006), pp. 1229–1238; and S. D. Pugh, "Service with a Smile: Emotional Contagion in the Service Encounter," *Academy of Management Journal* (October 2001), pp. 1018–1027.

115. D. E. Rupp and S. Spencer, "When Customers Lash Out: The Effects of Customer Interactional Injustice on Emotional Labor and the Mediating Role of Emotions," *Journal of Applied Psychology* 91, no. 4 (2006), pp. 971–978; and Tsai and Huang, "Mechanisms Linking Employee Affective Delivery and Customer Behavioral Intentions."

116. R. Ilies and T. A. Judge, "Understanding the Dynamic Relationships Among Personality, Mood, and Job Satisfaction: A Field Experience Sampling Study," *Organizational Behavior and Human Decision Processes* 89 (2002), pp. 1119–1139.

117. R. Rau, "Job Strain or Healthy Work: A Question of Task Design," *Journal of Occupational Health Psychology* 9, no. 4 (October 2004), pp. 322–338; and R. Rau and A. Triemer, "Overtime in Relation to Blood Pressure and Mood During Work, Leisure, and Night Time," *Social Indicators Research* 67, no. 1–2 (June 2004), pp. 51–73.

118. Z. Song, M. Foo, and M. A. Uy, "Mood Spillover and Crossover Among Dual-Earner Couples: A Cell Phone Event Sampling Study," *Journal of Applied Psychology* 93, no. 2 (2008), pp. 443–452.

119. T. A. Judge and R. Ilies, "Affect and Job Satisfaction: A Study of Their Relationship at Work and at Home," *Journal of Applied Psychology* 89 (2004), pp. 661–673.

120. See R. J. Bennett and S. L. Robinson, "Development of a Measure of Workplace Deviance," *Journal of Applied Psychology*, June 2000, pp. 349–360; see also P. R. Sackett and C. J. DeVore, "Counterproductive Behaviors at Work," in N. Anderson, D. S. Ones, H. K. Sinangil, and C. Viswesvaran (eds.), *Handbook of Industrial, Work & Organizational Psychology*, vol. 1 (Thousand Oaks, CA: Sage, 2001), pp. 145–164.

121. A. G. Bedeian, "Workplace Envy," *Organizational Dynamics* (Spring 1995), p. 50; and Ben-Ze'ev, *The Subtlety of Emotions*, pp. 281–326.

122. Bedeian, "Workplace Envy," p. 54.

123. S. C. Douglas, C. Kiewitz, M. Martinko, P. Harvey, Y. Kim, and J. U. Chun, "Cognitions, Emotions, and Evaluations: An Elaboration Likelihood Model for Workplace Aggression," *Academy of Management Review* 33, no. 2 (2008), pp. 425–451.

124. K. Lee and N. J. Allen, "Organizational Citizenship Behavior and Workplace Deviance: The Role of Affect and Cognition," *Journal of Applied Psychology* 87, no. 1 (2002), pp. 131–142; T. A. Judge, B. A. Scott, and R. Ilies, "Hostility, Job Attitudes, and Workplace Deviance: Test of a Multilevel Model," *Journal of Applied Psychology* 91, no. 1 (2006), 126–138; and S. Kaplan, J. C. Bradley, J. N. Luchman, and D. Haynes, "On the Role of Positive and Negative Affectivity in Job Performance: A Meta-Analytic Investigation," *Journal of Applied Psychology* 94, no. 1 (2009), pp. 162–176.

125. R. D. Iverson and P. J. Erwin, "Predicting Occupational Injury: The Role of Affectivity," *Journal of Occupational and Organizational Psychology* 70, no. 2 (1997), pp. 113–128; and Kaplan, Bradley, Luchman, and Haynes, "On the Role of Positive and Negative Affectivity in Job Performance: A Meta-Analytic Investigation."

126. A. M. Isen, A. A. Labroo, and P. Durlach, "An Influence of Product and Brand Name on Positive Affect: Implicit and Explicit Measures," *Motivation & Emotion* 28, no. 1 (March 2004), pp. 43–63.

127. T. Sy, S. Côté, and R. Saavedra, "The Contagious Leader: Impact of the Leader's Mood on the Mood of Group Members, Group Affective Tone, and Group Processes," *Journal of Applied Psychology* 90, no. 2 (2005), pp. 295–305.

128. P. Totterdell, "Catching Moods and Hitting Runs: Mood Linkage and Subjective Performance in Professional Sports Teams," *Journal of Applied Psychology* 85, no. 6 (2000), pp. 848–859.

129. S. Nelton, "Emotions in the Workplace," *Nation's Business* (February 1996), p. 25.

130. Kruml and Geddes, "Catching Fire Without Burning Out."

LEARNING OBJECTIVES

After studying this chapter, you should be able to:

1 Define *personality,* describe how it is measured, and explain the factors that determine an individual's personality.

2 Describe the Myers-Briggs Type Indicator personality framework and assess its strengths and weaknesses.

3 Identify the key traits in the Big Five personality model.

4 Demonstrate how the Big Five traits predict behavior at work.

5 Identify other personality traits relevant to OB.

6 Define *values,* demonstrate the importance of values, and contrast terminal and instrumental values.

7 Compare generational differences in values and identify the dominant values in today's workforce.

8 Identify Hofstede's five value dimensions of national culture.

MyManagementLab

Access a host of interactive learning aids to help strengthen your understanding of the chapter concepts at **www.pearsonglobaleditions .com/mymanagementlab**.

CHANGING OF THE GUARD IN JAPAN: IS IT THE ECONOMY, OR THE VALUES?

Among the world's largest economies, none has been more frustratingly stuck in neutral than Japan. Until 2010, when it was surpassed by China, Japan was the world's second-largest economy (after the United States). However, it has now experienced two "lost decades" in a row, spanning 1990 to 2010, and many recent college graduates have no memory of the halcyon days of the 1980s, when Japan was the most envied economy in the world. The horrendous aftermath of the earthquake and tsunami that struck in March 2011, sending Japan into another recession, has only added to the misery. Many now fear the Japanese economy will forever remain stuck in the doldrums.

Perhaps it will rebound sooner than expected; Japan has been underestimated before. However, two decades of stagnant economic growth seem to have had a permanent effect on new entrants' work values.

At one time, Japan was famous for the close psychological and behavioral bond between company and worker. Most employees expected to remain with their employer for their entire career, based on the belief that if they took care of their company, their company would take care of them. To these individuals, quitting, or taking a side job, would be an unthinkable act of disloyalty.

How things have changed. While unemployment in Japan remains low in comparison to the United States, it is at historic highs. Moreover, earnings continue to shrink—down more than 12 percent over the past decade. The Japanese Ministry of Health, Labor and Welfare estimates that 56 percent of workers age 15 to 34 need another form of income to pay living expenses.

Hiroko Yokogawa, 32, makes one-third of her income from her second job. "It's not that I hate my main job, but I want to have a stable income without being completely dependent on the company," she said.

At first, Kirito Nakano, 28, followed the traditional career path, expecting to remain forever in his job as a Web engineer with a large Japanese multinational. Soon, however, he found that his salary, and lack of salary growth, began to crimp his lifestyle. He began moonlighting, developing affiliate marketing programs. As his side job grew, Kirito quit his main job. He felt he was left with little choice. "The Japanese economy is not just stagnant, it's in retreat," he said. "When people believe the future is going to be better than the present, they are happy. But if they think that the future holds no hope, then they become unhappy. It's that unhappiness that people are trying to negate with side jobs."

Personality and Values

I am driven by fear of failure.
It is a strong motivator for me.

—Dennis Manning, CEO of Guardian Life Insurance Co.

Photo: University students at a job fair in Koto Ward, Tokyo. *Source:* The Yomiuri Shimbun via AP Images.

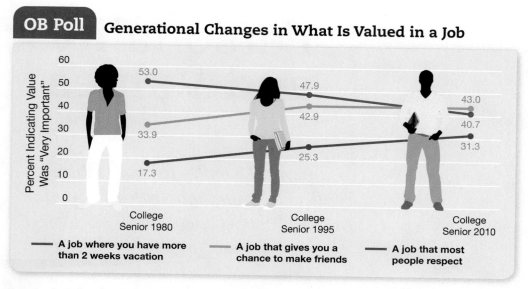

OB Poll **Generational Changes in What Is Valued in a Job**

Source: Based on "What Millennial Workers Want: How to Attract and Retain Gen Y Employees," Robert Half International web interviews of 1,007 individuals age 21–28, 2008.

The choice of young Japanese employees to work more hours is an interesting contrast to workers in the United States and Europe, who express a preference to work fewer hours. As for the hours she works—generally her side job takes 25 hours a week— Hiroko Yokogawa remains undeterred. "I wouldn't say I want to leave my main job—rather, I'd like to have a couple of different jobs at once."

As the opening vignette indicates, employees with different values may enact different behaviors to achieve their work goals, and these differences can be a reflection of culture. In the first half of this chapter, we review the research on personality and its relationship to behavior. In the latter half, we look at how values shape many of our work-related behaviors.

Although we focus much of our discussion on the Big Five personality traits, they are not the only traits that describe people. One of the others we'll discuss is narcissism. Check out the Self-Assessment Library to see how you score on narcissism (remember: be honest!).

SELF-ASSESSMENT LIBRARY

Am I a Narcissist?

In the Self-Assessment Library (available on CD or online), take assessment IV.A.1 (Am I a Narcissist?) and answer the following questions.

1. How did you score? Did your scores surprise you? Why or why not?
2. On which facet of narcissism did you score highest? Lowest?
3. Do you think this measure is accurate? Why or why not?

Personality

1 Define *personality,* describe how it is measured, and explain the factors that determine an individual's personality.

MyManagementLab
For an interactive application of this topic, check out this chapter's simulation activity at **www.pearsonglobaleditions.com/ mymanagementlab**.

Why are some people quiet and passive, while others are loud and aggressive? Are certain personality types better adapted than others for certain job types? Before we can answer these questions, we need to address a more basic one: What is personality?

What Is Personality?

When we talk of personality, we don't mean a person has charm, a positive attitude toward life, or a constantly smiling face. When psychologists talk of personality, they mean a dynamic concept describing the growth and development of a person's whole psychological system.

Defining Personality   The definition of *personality* we most frequently use was produced by Gordon Allport nearly 70 years ago. Allport said personality is "the dynamic organization within the individual of those psychophysical systems that determine his unique adjustments to his environment."[1] For our purposes, you should think of **personality** as the sum total of ways in which an individual reacts to and interacts with others. We most often describe it in terms of the measurable traits a person exhibits.

Measuring Personality   The most important reason managers need to know how to measure personality is that research has shown personality tests are useful in hiring decisions and help managers forecast who is best for a job.[2] The most common means of measuring personality is through self-report surveys, with which individuals evaluate themselves on a series of factors, such as "I worry a lot about the future." Though self-report measures work well when well constructed, one weakness is that the respondent might lie or practice impression management to create a good impression. When people know their personality scores are going to be used for hiring decisions, they rate themselves as about half a standard deviation more conscientious and emotionally stable than if they are taking the test just to learn more about themselves.[3] Another problem is accuracy. A perfectly good candidate could have been in a bad mood when taking the survey, and that will make the scores less accurate.

Observer-ratings surveys provide an independent assessment of personality. Here, a co-worker or another observer does the rating (sometimes with the subject's knowledge and sometimes not). Though the results of self-report surveys and observer-ratings surveys are strongly correlated, research suggests observer-ratings surveys are a better predictor of success on the job.[4] However, each can tell us something unique about an individual's behavior in the workplace. An analysis of a large number of observer-reported personality studies shows that a combination of self-report and observer-reports predicts performance better than any one type of information. The implication is clear: use both observer ratings and self-report ratings of personality when making important employment decisions.

personality   *Enduring characteristics that describe an individual's behavior.*

Personality Determinants   An early debate in personality research centered on whether an individual's personality was the result of heredity or of environment. It appears to be a result of both. However, it might surprise you that research tends to support the importance of heredity over the environment.

Heredity refers to factors determined at conception. Physical stature, facial attractiveness, gender, temperament, muscle composition and reflexes, energy level, and biological rhythms are generally considered to be either completely or substantially influenced by who your parents are—that is, by their biological, physiological, and inherent psychological makeup. The heredity approach argues that the ultimate explanation of an individual's personality is the molecular structure of the genes, located in the chromosomes.

Researchers in many different countries have studied thousands of sets of identical twins who were separated at birth and raised separately.[5] If heredity played little or no part in determining personality, you would expect to find few similarities between the separated twins. But twins raised apart have much in common, and a significant part of the behavioral similarity between them turns out to be associated with genetic factors. One set of twins separated for 39 years and raised 45 miles apart were found to drive the same model and color car. They chain-smoked the same brand of cigarette, owned dogs with the same name, and regularly vacationed within three blocks of each other in a beach community 1,500 miles away. Researchers have found that genetics accounts for about 50 percent of the personality similarities between twins and more than 30 percent of the similarities in occupational and leisure interests.

Interestingly, twin studies have suggested parents don't add much to our personality development. The personalities of identical twins raised in different households are more similar to each other than to the personalities of siblings with whom the twins were raised. Ironically, the most important contribution our parents may make to our personalities is giving us their genes!

This is not to suggest that personality never changes. People's scores on measures of dependability tend to increase over time, as when young adults take on roles like starting a family and establishing a career that require great responsibility. However, strong individual differences in dependability remain;

Personality traits are enduring characteristics that describe an individual's behavior. British entrepreneur Richard Branson, chairman of Virgin Group, is described as energetic, enthusiastic, charismatic, decisive, ambitious, adaptable, courageous, and industrious. These traits helped Branson build one of the most recognized and respected global brands for products and services in the areas of business travel, entertainment, and lifestyle. In this photo Branson is joined by his daughter Holly during the promotional launch of a new venture—the Marussia Virgin racing partnership with Disney's *Cars 2* film. Identifying personality traits helps organizations select employees and match workers to job.

Source: Eric Best/Landmark Media Landmark Media/Newscom.

everyone tends to change by about the same amount, so their rank order stays roughly the same.[6] An analogy to intelligence may make this clearer. Children become smarter as they age, so nearly everyone is smarter at age 20 than at age 10. Still, if Madison is smarter than Blake at age 10, she is likely to be so at age 20, too. Consistent with the notion that the teenage years are periods of great exploration and change, research has shown that personality is more changeable in adolescence and more stable among adults.[7]

Early work on the structure of personality tried to identify and label enduring characteristics that describe an individual's behavior, including shy, aggressive, submissive, lazy, ambitious, loyal, and timid. When someone exhibits these characteristics in a large number of situations, we call them **personality traits** of that person.[8] The more consistent the characteristic over time, and the more frequently it occurs in diverse situations, the more important that trait is in describing the individual.

Early efforts to identify the primary traits that govern behavior[9] often resulted in long lists that were difficult to generalize from and provided little practical guidance to organizational decision makers. Two exceptions are the Myers-Briggs Type Indicator and the Big Five Model, now the dominant frameworks for identifying and classifying traits.

The Myers-Briggs Type Indicator

2 Describe the Myers-Briggs Type Indicator personality framework and assess its strengths and weaknesses.

The **Myers-Briggs Type Indicator (MBTI)** is the most widely used personality-assessment instrument in the world.[10] It is a 100-question personality test that asks people how they usually feel or act in particular situations. Respondents are classified as extraverted or introverted (E or I), sensing or intuitive (S or N), thinking or feeling (T or F), and judging or perceiving (J or P). These terms are defined as follows:

- *Extraverted (E) versus Introverted (I)*. Extraverted individuals are outgoing, sociable, and assertive. Introverts are quiet and shy.
- *Sensing (S) versus Intuitive (N)*. Sensing types are practical and prefer routine and order. They focus on details. Intuitives rely on unconscious processes and look at the "big picture."
- *Thinking (T) versus Feeling (F)*. Thinking types use reason and logic to handle problems. Feeling types rely on their personal values and emotions.
- *Judging (J) versus Perceiving (P)*. Judging types want control and prefer their world to be ordered and structured. Perceiving types are flexible and spontaneous.

These classifications together describe 16 personality types, identifying every person by one trait from each of the four pairs. For example, Introverted/Intuitive/Thinking/Judging people (INTJs) are visionaries with original minds and great drive. They are skeptical, critical, independent, determined, and often stubborn. ESTJs are organizers. They are realistic, logical, analytical, and decisive and have a natural head for business or mechanics. The ENTP type is a conceptualizer, innovative, individualistic, versatile, and attracted to entrepreneurial ideas. This person tends to be resourceful in solving challenging problems but may neglect routine assignments.

The MBTI has been widely used by organizations including Apple Computer, AT&T, Citigroup, GE, 3M Co., many hospitals and educational institutions, and

---

heredity   *Factors determined at conception; one's biological, physiological, and inherent psychological makeup.*

personality traits   *Enduring characteristics that describe an individual's behavior.*

Myers-Briggs Type Indicator (MBTI)   *A personality test that taps four characteristics and classifies people into 1 of 16 personality types.*

even the U.S. Armed Forces. Evidence is mixed about its validity as a measure of personality, however; most of the evidence is against it.[11] One problem is that it forces a person into one type or another; that is, you're either introverted or extraverted. There is no in-between, though in reality people can be both extraverted and introverted to some degree. The best we can say is that the MBTI can be a valuable tool for increasing self-awareness and providing career guidance. But because results tend to be unrelated to job performance, managers probably shouldn't use it as a selection test for job candidates.

The Big Five Personality Model

3 Identify the key traits in the Big Five personality model.

The MBTI may lack strong supporting evidence, but an impressive body of research supports the thesis of the **Big Five Model**—that five basic dimensions underlie all others and encompass most of the significant variation in human personality.[12] Moreover, test scores of these traits do a very good job of predicting how people behave in a variety of real-life situations.[13] The following are the Big Five factors:

- *Extraversion.* The **extraversion** dimension captures our comfort level with relationships. Extraverts tend to be gregarious, assertive, and sociable. Introverts tend to be reserved, timid, and quiet.
- *Agreeableness.* The **agreeableness** dimension refers to an individual's propensity to defer to others. Highly agreeable people are cooperative, warm, and trusting. People who score low on agreeableness are cold, disagreeable, and antagonistic.
- *Conscientiousness.* The **conscientiousness** dimension is a measure of reliability. A highly conscientious person is responsible, organized, dependable, and persistent. Those who score low on this dimension are easily distracted, disorganized, and unreliable.
- *Emotional stability.* The **emotional stability** dimension—often labeled by its converse, neuroticism—taps a person's ability to withstand stress. People with positive emotional stability tend to be calm, self-confident, and secure. Those with high negative scores tend to be nervous, anxious, depressed, and insecure.
- *Openness to experience.* The **openness to experience** dimension addresses range of interests and fascination with novelty. Extremely open people are creative, curious, and artistically sensitive. Those at the other end of the category are conventional and find comfort in the familiar.

Source: Kristin Callahan/Photoshot.

Andrea Jung, chairman and CEO of Avon, scores high on all personality dimensions of the Big Five Model. She is sociable, agreeable, conscientious, emotionally stable, and open to experiences. These personality traits have contributed to Jung's high job performance and career success. Since joining Avon in 1994, Jung has led a dramatic turnaround of a company that had a poor image, slow growth, and decline in sales to one of the world's top cosmetics companies and the world's leading direct sales brand. She transformed Avon by developing and executing growth strategies, launching new brand initiatives, and developing earnings opportunities for women worldwide.

How Do the Big Five Traits Predict Behavior at Work?   Research has found relationships between these personality dimensions and job performance.[14] As the authors of the most-cited review put it, "The preponderance of evidence shows that individuals who are dependable, reliable, careful, thorough, able to plan, organized, hardworking, persistent, and achievement-oriented tend to have higher job performance in most if not all occupations."[15] In addition, employees who score higher in conscientiousness develop higher levels of job knowledge, probably because highly conscientious people learn more (a review of 138 studies revealed conscientiousness was rather strongly related to GPA).[16] Higher levels of job knowledge then contribute to higher levels of job performance. Conscientious individuals who are more interested in learning than in just performing on the job are also exceptionally good at maintaining performance in the face of negative feedback.[17] There can be "too much of a good thing," however, as extremely conscientious individuals typically do not perform better than those who are simply above average in conscientiousness.[18]

Exhibit **5-1**	**Traits That Matter Most to Business Success at Buyout Companies**

Most Important	**Less Important**
Persistence	Strong oral communication
Attention to detail	Teamwork
Efficiency	Flexibility/adaptability
Analytical skills	Enthusiasm
Setting high standards	Listening skills

Conscientiousness is as important for managers as for front-line employees. As Exhibit 5-1 shows, a study of the personality scores of 313 CEO candidates in private equity companies (of whom 225 were hired, and their company's performance later correlated with their personality scores) found conscientiousness—in the form of persistence, attention to detail, and setting of high standards—was more important than other traits. These results attest to the importance of conscientiousness to organizational success.

Interestingly, conscientious people live longer because they take better care of themselves (they eat better and exercise more) and engage in fewer risky behaviors like smoking, drinking and drugs, and risky sexual or driving behavior.[19] Still, probably because they're so organized and structured, conscientious people don't adapt as well to changing contexts. They are generally performance oriented and have more trouble learning complex skills early in the training process because their focus is on performing well rather than on learning. Finally, they are often less creative than less conscientious people, especially artistically.[20]

Although conscientiousness is most consistently related to job performance, the other Big Five traits are also related to aspects of performance and have other implications for work and for life. Let's look at them one at a time. Exhibit 5-2 summarizes.

Of the Big Five traits, emotional stability is most strongly related to life satisfaction, job satisfaction, and low stress levels. This is probably true because high scorers are more likely to be positive and optimistic and experience fewer negative emotions. They are happier than those who score low. People low on emotional stability are hypervigilant (looking for problems or impending signs of danger) and are especially vulnerable to the physical and psychological effects of stress. Extraverts tend to be happier in their jobs and in their lives as a whole. They experience more positive emotions than do introverts, and they more freely express these feelings. They also tend to perform better in jobs that require significant interpersonal interaction, perhaps because they have more social skills—they usually have more friends and spend more time in social

4 Demonstrate how the Big Five traits predict behavior at work.

Big Five Model   *A personality assessment model that taps five basic dimensions.*

extraversion   *A personality dimension describing someone who is sociable, gregarious, and assertive.*

agreeableness   *A personality dimension that describes someone who is good natured, cooperative, and trusting.*

conscientiousness   *A personality dimension that describes someone who is responsible, dependable, persistent, and organized.*

emotional stability   *A personality dimension that characterizes someone as calm, self-confident, secure (positive) versus nervous, depressed, and insecure (negative).*

openness to experience   *A personality dimension that characterizes someone in terms of imagination, sensitivity, and curiosity.*

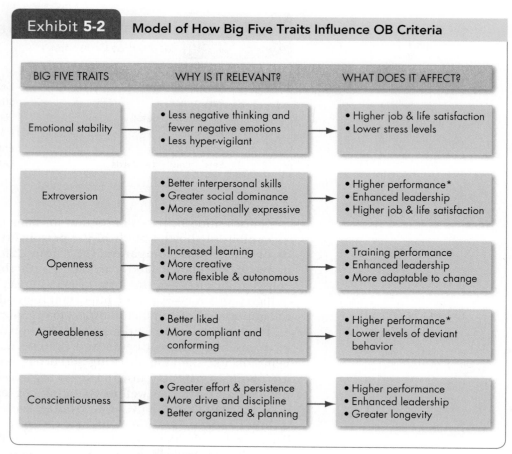

Exhibit **5-2** | Model of How Big Five Traits Influence OB Criteria

BIG FIVE TRAITS	WHY IS IT RELEVANT?	WHAT DOES IT AFFECT?
Emotional stability	• Less negative thinking and fewer negative emotions • Less hyper-vigilant	• Higher job & life satisfaction • Lower stress levels
Extroversion	• Better interpersonal skills • Greater social dominance • More emotionally expressive	• Higher performance* • Enhanced leadership • Higher job & life satisfaction
Openness	• Increased learning • More creative • More flexible & autonomous	• Training performance • Enhanced leadership • More adaptable to change
Agreeableness	• Better liked • More compliant and conforming	• Higher performance* • Lower levels of deviant behavior
Conscientiousness	• Greater effort & persistence • More drive and discipline • Better organized & planning	• Higher performance • Enhanced leadership • Greater longevity

* In jobs requiring significant teamwork or frequent interpersonal interactions.

situations than introverts. Finally, extraversion is a relatively strong predictor of leadership emergence in groups; extraverts are more socially dominant, "take charge" sorts of people, and they are generally more assertive than introverts.[21] One downside is that extraverts are more impulsive than introverts; they are more likely to be absent from work and engage in risky behavior such as unprotected sex, drinking, and other impulsive or sensation-seeking acts.[22] One study also found extraverts were more likely than introverts to lie during job interviews.[23]

Individuals who score high on openness to experience are more creative in science and art than those who score low. Because creativity is important to leadership, open people are more likely to be effective leaders, and more comfortable with ambiguity and change. They cope better with organizational change and are more adaptable in changing contexts. Recent evidence also suggests, however, that they are especially susceptible to workplace accidents.[24]

You might expect agreeable people to be happier than disagreeable people. They are, but only slightly. When people choose romantic partners, friends, or organizational team members, agreeable individuals are usually their first choice. Agreeable individuals are better liked than disagreeable people, which explains why they tend to do better in interpersonally oriented jobs such as customer service. They also are more compliant and rule abiding and less likely to get into accidents as a result. People who are agreeable are more satisfied in their jobs and contribute to organizational performance by engaging in citizenship behavior.[25] They are also less likely to engage in organizational deviance. One downside is that agreeableness is associated with lower levels of career success (especially earnings).

The five personality factors identified in the Big Five model appear in almost all cross-cultural studies.[26] These studies have included a wide variety of diverse cultures—such as China, Israel, Germany, Japan, Spain, Nigeria, Norway, Pakistan, and the United States. Differences are complex but tend to be primarily about whether countries are predominantly individualistic or collectivistic. Chinese managers use the category of conscientiousness more often and agreeableness less often than do U.S. managers. And the Big Five appear to predict a bit better in individualistic than in collectivist cultures.[27] But there is a surprisingly high amount of agreement, especially across individuals from developed countries. A comprehensive review of studies covering people from what was then the 15-nation European Community found conscientiousness a valid predictor of performance across jobs and occupational groups.[28] This is exactly what U.S. studies have found.

Other Personality Traits Relevant to OB

5   Identify other personality traits relevant to OB.

Although the Big Five traits have proven highly relevant to OB, they don't exhaust the range of traits that can describe someone's personality. Now we'll look at other, more specific, attributes that are powerful predictors of behavior in organizations. The first relates to our core self-evaluation. The others are Machiavellianism, narcissism, self-monitoring, propensity for risk taking, proactive personality, and other-orientation.

Core Self-Evaluation   People who have positive **core self-evaluations** like themselves and see themselves as effective, capable, and in control of their environment. Those with negative core self-evaluations tend to dislike themselves, question their capabilities, and view themselves as powerless over their environment.[29] We discussed in Chapter 3 that core self-evaluations relate to job satisfaction because people positive on this trait see more challenge in their job and actually attain more complex jobs.

But what about job performance? People with positive core self-evaluations perform better than others because they set more ambitious goals, are more committed to their goals, and persist longer in attempting to reach these goals. One study of life insurance agents found core self-evaluations were critical predictors of performance. Ninety percent of life insurance sales calls end in rejection, so an agent has to believe in him- or herself to persist. In fact, this study showed the majority of successful salespersons did have positive core self-evaluations.[30] Such people also provide better customer service, are more popular co-workers, and have careers that both begin on better footing and ascend more rapidly over time.[31] Some evidence suggests that individuals high in core self-evaluations perform especially well if they also feel their work provides meaning and is helpful to others.[32]

Can we be *too* positive? What happens when someone thinks he is capable but is actually incompetent? One study of *Fortune* 500 CEOs showed that many are overconfident, and their perceived infallibility often causes them to make bad decisions.[33] Teddy Forstmann, chairman of the sports marketing giant

Source: Ric Francis/AP Images.

The personality trait of positive core self-evaluation helps Satoru Iwata meet the challenges and complexity of his job as CEO of Nintendo. Confident and capable, Iwata has applied his years of experience and innovation as a game developer to introducing new products, such as the Wii gaming console and the 3DS portable console. Iwata views his job as an opportunity to cultivate new customers by widening the appeal of video games to new market segments in developed nations and by introducing products to developing countries.

core self-evaluation   *Bottom-line conclusions individuals have about their capabilities, competence, and worth as a person.*

IMG, said of himself, "I know God gave me an unusual brain. I can't deny that. I have a God-given talent for seeing potential."[34] We might say people like Forstmann are overconfident, but very often we humans sell ourselves short and are less happy and effective than we could be because of it. If we decide we can't do something, for example, we won't try, and not doing it only reinforces our self-doubts.

Machiavellianism   Kuzi is a young bank manager in Taiwan. He's had three promotions in the past 4 years and makes no apologies for the aggressive tactics he's used to propel his career upward. "I'm prepared to do whatever I have to do to get ahead," he says. Kuzi would properly be called Machiavellian.

The personality characteristic of **Machiavellianism** (often abbreviated *Mach*) is named after Niccolo Machiavelli, who wrote in the sixteenth century on how to gain and use power. An individual high in Machiavellianism is pragmatic, maintains emotional distance, and believes ends can justify means. "If it works, use it" is consistent with a high-Mach perspective. A considerable amount of research has found high Machs manipulate more, win more, are persuaded less, and persuade others more than do low Machs.[35] They like their jobs less, are more stressed by their work, and engage in more deviant work behaviors.[36] Yet high-Mach outcomes are moderated by situational factors. High Machs flourish (1) when they interact face to face with others rather than indirectly; (2) when the situation has minimal rules and regulations, allowing latitude for improvisation; and (3) when emotional involvement with details irrelevant to winning distracts low Machs.[37] Thus, in jobs that require bargaining skills (such as labor negotiation) or that offer substantial rewards for winning (such as commissioned sales), high Machs will be productive. But if ends can't justify the means, there are absolute standards of behavior, or the three situational factors we noted are not in evidence, our ability to predict a high Mach's performance will be severely curtailed.

Narcissism   Hans likes to be the center of attention. He looks at himself in the mirror a lot, has extravagant dreams, and considers himself a person of many talents. Hans is a narcissist. The term is from the Greek myth of Narcissus, a man so vain and proud he fell in love with his own image. In psychology, **narcissism** describes a person who has a grandiose sense of self-importance, requires excessive admiration, has a sense of entitlement, and is arrogant. Evidence suggests that narcissists are more charismatic and thus more likely to emerge as leaders, and they may even display better psychological health (at least as they self-report).[38]

Despite having some advantages, most evidence suggests that narcissism is undesirable. A study found that while narcissists thought they were *better* leaders than their colleagues, their supervisors actually rated them as *worse*. An Oracle executive described that company's CEO Larry Ellison as follows: "The difference between God and Larry is that God does not believe he is Larry."[39] Because narcissists often want to gain the admiration of others and receive affirmation of their superiority, they tend to "talk down" to those who threaten them, treating others as if they were inferior. Narcissists also tend to be selfish and exploitive and believe others exist for their benefit.[40] Their bosses rate them as less effective at their jobs than others, particularly when it comes to helping people.[41] Subsequent research using data compiled over 100 years has shown that narcissistic CEOs of baseball organizations tend to generate higher levels of manager turnover, although curiously, members of external organizations see them as more influential.[42]

Self-Monitoring   Joyce McIntyre is always in trouble at work. Though she's competent, hardworking, and productive, in performance reviews she is rated no better than average, and she seems to have made a career of irritating bosses. Joyce's problem is that she's politically inept. She's unable to adjust her behavior to fit changing situations. As she puts it, "I'm true to myself. I don't remake myself to please others." We would describe Joyce as a low self-monitor.

Self-monitoring refers to an individual's ability to adjust his or her behavior to external, situational factors.[43] Individuals high in self-monitoring show considerable adaptability in adjusting their behavior to external situational factors. They are highly sensitive to external cues and can behave differently in different situations, sometimes presenting striking contradictions between their public persona and their private self. Low self-monitors, like Joyce, can't disguise themselves in that way. They tend to display their true dispositions and attitudes in every situation; hence, there is high behavioral consistency between who they are and what they do.

Evidence indicates high self-monitors pay closer attention to the behavior of others and are more capable of conforming than are low self-monitors.[44] They also receive better performance ratings, are more likely to emerge as leaders, and show less commitment to their organizations.[45] In addition, high self-monitoring managers tend to be more mobile in their careers, receive more promotions (both internal and cross-organizational), and are more likely to occupy central positions in an organization.[46]

Risk Taking   Donald Trump stands out for his willingness to take risks. He started with almost nothing in the 1960s. By the mid-1980s, he had made a fortune by betting on a resurgent New York City real estate market. Then, trying to capitalize on his successes, Trump overextended himself. By 1994, he had a *negative* net worth of $850 million. Never fearful of taking chances, "The Donald" leveraged the few assets he had left on several New York, New Jersey, and Caribbean real estate ventures and hit it big again. In 2011, when Trump was contemplating a presidential run, *The Atlantic* estimated his net worth at more than $7 billion.[47]

People differ in their willingness to take chances, a quality that affects how much time and information they need to make a decision. For instance, 79 managers worked on simulated exercises that required them to make hiring decisions.[48] High risk-taking managers made more rapid decisions and used less information than did the low risk takers. Interestingly, decision accuracy was the same for both groups.

Although previous studies have shown managers in large organizations to be more risk averse than growth-oriented entrepreneurs who actively manage small businesses, recent findings suggest managers in large organizations may actually be more willing to take risks than entrepreneurs.[49] The work population as a whole also differs in risk propensity.[50] It makes sense to recognize these differences and even consider aligning them with specific job demands. A high risk-taking propensity may lead to more effective performance for a stock trader in a brokerage firm because that type of job demands rapid decision

---

Machiavellianism   *The degree to which an individual is pragmatic, maintains emotional distance, and believes that ends can justify means.*

narcissism   *The tendency to be arrogant, have a grandiose sense of self-importance, require excessive admiration, and have a sense of entitlement.*

self-monitoring   *A personality trait that measures an individual's ability to adjust his or her behavior to external, situational factors.*

making. On the other hand, a willingness to take risks might prove a major obstacle to an accountant who performs auditing activities.

Proactive Personality   Did you ever notice that some people actively take the initiative to improve their current circumstances or create new ones? These are proactive personalities.[51] Those with a **proactive personality** identify opportunities, show initiative, take action, and persevere until meaningful change occurs, compared to others who passively react to situations. Proactives create positive change in their environment, regardless of, or even in spite of, constraints or obstacles.[52] Not surprisingly, they have many desirable behaviors that organizations covet. They are more likely than others to be seen as leaders and to act as change agents.[53] Proactive individuals are more likely to be satisfied with work and help others more with their tasks, largely because they build more relationships with others.[54]

Proactives are also more likely to challenge the status quo or voice their displeasure when situations aren't to their liking.[55] If an organization requires people with entrepreneurial initiative, proactives make good candidates; however, they're also more likely to leave an organization to start their own business.[56] As individuals, proactives are more likely than others to achieve career success.[57] They select, create, and influence work situations in their favor. They seek out job and organizational information, develop contacts in high places, engage in career planning, and demonstrate persistence in the face of career obstacles.

Other-orientation   Some people just naturally seem to think about other people a lot, being concerned about their well-being and feelings. Others behave like "economic actors," primarily rational and self-interested. These differences

---

Myth or Science?

Personality Predicts the Performance of Entrepreneurs

This statement is true.

Studies of identical twins reared apart suggest striking career similarities—if one twin became an entrepreneur, the other twin was more likely to do the same. The explanation may lie in personality.

One recent analysis of 60 studies linked individuals' personalities to their intentions to undertake an entrepreneurial career, and to the performance of their ventures once they made that decision. The Big Five personality traits—except agreeableness, which didn't matter—significantly predicted entrepreneurial

intentions and, more significantly, entrepreneurial firm performance. Especially important were openness to experience and conscientiousness, both of which also predicted firm growth over time. Interestingly, risk propensity—the tendency to take and be comfortable with taking risks—was not associated with entrepreneurial performance.

What are the implications of these findings? Traditionally, people who saw themselves as risk averse were steered away from entrepreneurship. However, these results suggest it is more important to steer low scorers on openness

and conscientiousness away. The best entrepreneurs appear not to be the swashbuckling risk-takers, but rather the methodical ones who have the discipline to turn their open thinking and creative ideas into reality.

Sources: H. Zhao, S. E. Seibert, and G. T. Lumpkin, "The Relationship of Personality to Entrepreneurial Intentions and Performance: A Meta-Analytic Review," *Journal of Management* 36, no. 2 (2010), pp. 381–404; M. Herper, "Could We Invent an Antibody to Make You an Entrepreneur?" *Forbes* (May 5, 2011), downloaded on May 23, 2011, from http://blogs.forbes.com/.

glOBalization!

The Right Personality for a Global Workplace

As work becomes increasingly international in focus, successful managers need to be able to operate across cultures easily. Obviously, expatriate managers working in other countries will need personality traits that make them better able to work overseas, but managers at home who order parts and services from overseas or prepare marketing plans for other countries, for example, will also conduct cross-cultural communications. In the workforce of the future, everyone from mechanics to customer service representatives to advertisers will need to understand the global market. What is the right personality for a global workplace?

You might suspect that, of the Big Five traits, openness to experience would be most important to effectiveness in international assignments. Open people are more likely to be culturally flexible—to "go with the flow" when things are different in another country. Research is not fully consistent on the issue, but most does suggest that managers who score high on openness perform better than others in international assignments. Other evidence suggests that employees who are more agreeable and extraverted have an easier time with international assignments. They may be better at establishing new relationships and developing social networks in unfamiliar contexts.

What do these results imply for organizations? Given continuing globalization in the future, organizations should select employees with traits related to better performance in international assignments. Managers will need to foster an open-minded perspective about other cultures among their employees.

Sources: Based on M. A. Shaffer, D. A. Harrison, and H. Gregersen, "You Can Take It with You: Individual Differences and Expatriate Effectiveness," _Journal of Applied Psychology_ 91, no. 1 (2006), pp. 109–125; M. van Woerkom and R. S. M. de Reuver, "Predicting Excellent Management Performance in an Intercultural Context: A Study of the Influence of Multicultural Personality on Transformational Leadership and Performance," _International Journal of Human Resource Management_ 20, no. 10 (2009), pp. 2013–2029; and M. Downes, I. I. Varner, and M. Hemmasi, "Individual Profiles as Predictors of Expatriate Effectiveness," _Competitiveness Review_ 20, no. 3 (2010), pp. 235–247.

reflect varying levels of other-orientation, a personality trait that reflects the extent to which decisions are affected by social influences and concerns vs. our own well-being and outcomes.[58]

What are the consequences of having a high level of other-orientation? Those who are other-oriented feel more obligated to help others who have helped them (pay me back), whereas those who are more self-oriented will help others when they expect to be helped in the future (pay me forward).[59] Employees high in other-orientation also exert especially high levels of effort when engaged in helping work or prosocial behavior.[60] In sum, it appears that having a strong orientation toward helping others does affect some behaviors that actually matter for organizations. However, research is still needed to clarify this emerging construct and its relationship with agreeableness.

Having discussed personality traits—the enduring characteristics that describe a person's behavior—we now turn to values. Values are often very specific and describe belief systems rather than behavioral tendencies. Some beliefs or values don't say much about a person's personality, and we don't always act consistently with our values.

proactive personality _People who identify opportunities, show initiative, take action, and persevere until meaningful change occurs._

Values

6 Define *values*, demonstrate the importance of values, and contrast terminal and instrumental values.

Is capital punishment right or wrong? If a person likes power, is that good or bad? The answers to these questions are value laden. Some might argue capital punishment is right because it is an appropriate retribution for crimes such as murder and treason. Others might argue, just as strongly, that no government has the right to take anyone's life.

Values represent basic convictions that "a specific mode of conduct or end-state of existence is personally or socially preferable to an opposite or converse mode of conduct or end-state of existence."[61] They contain a judgmental element in that they carry an individual's ideas as to what is right, good, or desirable. Values have both content and intensity attributes. The content attribute says a mode of conduct or end-state of existence is *important*. The intensity attribute specifies *how important* it is. When we rank an individual's values in terms of their intensity, we obtain that person's **value system**. All of us have a hierarchy of values that forms our value system. We find it in the relative importance we assign to values such as freedom, pleasure, self-respect, honesty, obedience, and equality.

Are values fluid and flexible? Generally speaking, no. They tend to be relatively stable and enduring.[62] A significant portion of the values we hold is established in our early years—by parents, teachers, friends, and others. As children, we are told certain behaviors or outcomes are *always* desirable or *always* undesirable, with few gray areas. You were never taught to be just a little bit honest or a little bit responsible, for example. It is this absolute, or "black-or-white," learning of values that ensures their stability and endurance. If we question our values, of course, they may change, but more often they are reinforced. There is also evidence linking personality to values, implying our values may be partly determined by our genetically transmitted traits.[63]

The Importance of Values

Values lay the foundation for our understanding of people's attitudes and motivation and influence our perceptions. We enter an organization with preconceived notions of what "ought" and "ought not" to be. These notions are not value-free; on the contrary, they contain our interpretations of right and wrong and our preference for certain behaviors or outcomes over others. As a result, values cloud objectivity and rationality; they influence attitudes and behavior.[64]

Suppose you enter an organization with the view that allocating pay on the basis of performance is right, while allocating pay on the basis of seniority is wrong. How will you react if you find the organization you've just joined rewards seniority and not performance? You're likely to be disappointed—and this can lead to job dissatisfaction and a decision not to exert a high level of effort because "It's probably not going to lead to more money anyway." Would your attitudes and behavior be different if your values aligned with the organization's pay policies? Most likely.

Terminal versus Instrumental Values

Can we classify values? Yes. In this section, we review two approaches to developing value typologies.

Rokeach Value Survey Milton Rokeach created the Rokeach Value Survey (RVS).[65] It consists of two sets of values, each containing 18 individual value items. One set, called **terminal values**, refers to desirable end-states. These are the goals a person would like to achieve during his or her lifetime. The other set, called **instrumental values**, refers to preferable modes of behavior, or means of achieving the terminal values. Some examples of terminal values in the Rokeach Value Survey are: Prosperity and economic success, Freedom, Health and well-being, World peace, Social recognition, and Meaning in life. The types of instrumental values illustrated in RVS are Self-improvement, Autonomy and self-reliance, Personal discipline, kindness, Ambition, and Goal-orientation.

Several studies confirm that RVS values vary among groups.[66] People in the same occupations or categories (corporate managers, union members, parents, students) tend to hold similar values. One study compared corporate executives, members of the steelworkers' union, and members of a community activist group. Although there was a good deal of overlap among them,[67] there were also significant differences (see Exhibit 5-3). The activists ranked "equality" as their most important terminal value; executives and union members ranked this value 12 and 13, respectively. Activists ranked "helpful" as their second-highest instrumental value. The other two groups both ranked it 14. Because executives, union members, and activists all have a vested interest in what corporations do, these differences can create serious conflicts when groups contend with each other over an organization's economic and social policies.[68]

7 Compare generational differences in values and identify the dominant values in today's workforce.

Generational Values

Contemporary Work Cohorts Researchers have integrated several recent analyses of work values into four groups that attempt to capture the unique values

---

| Exhibit **5-3** | Mean Value Ranking Executives, Union Members, and Activisits (Top Five Only) |

EXECUTIVES		UNION MEMBERS		ACTIVISTS	
Terminal	Instrumental	Terminal	Instrumental	Terminal	Instrumental
1. Self-respect	1. Honest	1. Family security	1. Responsible	1. Equality	1. Honest
2. Family security	2. Responsible	2. Freedom	2. Honest	2. A world of peace	2. Helpful
3. Freedom	3. Capable	3. Happiness	3. Courageous	3. Family security	3. Courageous
4. A sense of accomplishment	4. Ambitious	4. Self-respect	4. Independent	4. Self-respect	4. Responsible
5. Happiness	5. Independent	5. Mature love	5. Capable	5. Freedom	5. Capable

Source: Based on W. C. Frederick and J. Weber, "The Values of Corporate Managers and Their Critics: An Empirical Description and Normative Implications," in W. C. Frederick and L. E. Preston (eds.), Business Ethics: Research Issues and Empirical Studies (Greenwich, CT: JAI Press, 1990), pp. 123–144.

---

values *Basic convictions that a specific mode of conduct or end-state of existence is personally or socially preferable to an opposite or converse mode of conduct or end-state of existence.*

value system *A hierarchy based on a ranking of an individual's values in terms of their intensity.*

terminal values *Desirable end-states of existence; the goals a person would like to achieve during his or her lifetime.*

instrumental values *Preferable modes of behavior or means of achieving one's terminal values.*

Exhibit 5-4		Dominant Work Values in Today's Workforce	
Cohort	Entered the Workforce	Approximate Current Age	Dominant Work Values
Boomers	1965–1985	Mid-40s to mid-60s	Success, achievement, ambition, dislike of authority; loyalty to career
Xers	1985–2000	Late 20s to early 40s	Work/life balance, team-oriented, dislike of rules; loyalty to relationships
Nexters	2000 to present	Under 30	Confident, financial success, self-reliant but team-oriented; loyalty to both self and relationships

of different cohorts or generations in the U.S. workforce.[69] Exhibit 5-4 segments employees by the era during which they entered the workforce. Because most people start work between the ages of 18 and 23, the eras also correlate closely with employee age.

Let's start with some limitations of this analysis. First, we make no assumption that the framework applies across all cultures. Second, despite a steady stream of press coverage, there is very little rigorous research on generational values, so we have to rely on an intuitive framework. Finally, these are imprecise categories. There is no law that someone born in 1985 can't have values similar to those of someone born in 1955. Despite these limitations, values do change over generations,[70] and we can gain some useful insights from analyzing values this way.

Boomers (*Baby Boomers*) are a large cohort born after World War II when veterans returned to their families and times were good. Boomers entered the workforce from the mid-1960s through the mid-1980s. They brought with them a large measure of the "hippie ethic" and distrust of authority. But they place a great deal of emphasis on achievement and material success. Pragmatists who believe ends can justify means, they work hard and want to enjoy the fruits of their labors. Boomers see the organizations that employ them merely as vehicles for their careers. Terminal values such as a sense of accomplishment and social recognition rank high with them.

The lives of *Xers* (*Generation Xers*) have been shaped by globalization, two-career parents, MTV, AIDS, and computers. Xers value flexibility, life options, and the achievement of job satisfaction. Family and relationships are very important. Xers are skeptical, particularly of authority. They also enjoy team-oriented work. In search of balance in their lives, Xers are less willing to make personal sacrifices for the sake of their employer than previous generations were. On the RVS, they rate high on true friendship, happiness, and pleasure.

The most recent entrants to the workforce, the *Millennials* (also called *Netters, Nexters, Generation Yers,* and *Generation Nexters*) grew up during prosperous times. They have high expectations and seek meaning in their work. Millennials have life goals more oriented toward becoming rich (81 percent) and famous (51 percent) than do Generation Xers (62 percent and 29 percent, respectively), but they also see themselves as socially responsible. At ease with diversity, Millennials are the first generation to take technology for granted. More than other generations, they tend to be questioning, electronically networked, and entrepreneurial. At the same time, some have described Millennials as entitled and needy. They may clash

Should You Try to Change Someone's Personality?

As we have noted, individuals differ in terms of their personality scores, and these differences contribute to effective performance. It isn't always possible to identify personality traits successfully during the hiring process, and sometimes there simply aren't enough people with the "right" personality traits available. So should organizations try to shape their employees to make them more conscientious, agreeable, open, emotionally stable, and extraverted? Is there a potential ethical problem with exercising this type of control over workers?

Some evidence suggests that people's basic temperament is largely fixed by biology, and in this case, attempts to change personality will mostly lead to frustration and dissatisfaction. An employee who tends to see things negatively is unlikely to suddenly become an optimist just because a manager pushes him or her to read self-help books and

take up meditation. Moreover, such efforts may send a strong message of disapproval—who would want a manager saying, "We don't like you the way you are, you need to change!" Employees who are forced into working environments that don't fit their dispositions will also likely experience high levels of psychological strain.

On the other hand, it *is* possible to change the way personality is expressed. Biological anthropologist Helen Fisher notes that despite the importance of biology, "the environment always molds your biology." Someone who isn't particularly open to experience might be comfortable with new work assignments if they're framed appropriately, and someone who isn't very conscientious can display organization and dutifulness if the right environmental supports like checklists and formalized goal-setting are in place. And personality does change somewhat over time. As people age, their scores on conscientiousness and

agreeableness increase rather dramatically, and neuroticism decreases substantially (the results for openness and extraversion are more complex).

So what might employers do to accommodate employee personality differences while still obtaining maximum performance? One strategy is to focus on outcomes and allow employees to determine their own way to achieve them. An extrovert and an introvert might both be able to produce a very high quality report, even if the extrovert will want to collaborate and discuss during the process of writing whereas the introvert will prefer to work out problems alone. Employers can also try to assign employees to activities that best match their personality types.

Sources: B. W. Roberts and D. Mroczek, "Personality Trait Change in Adulthood," *Current Directions in Psychological Science,* no. 1, Vol. 17 (2008), pp. 31–35; "Five Ways to Change Your Personality," *CBS News* (August 21, 2010), www.cbsnews.com.

EBay's young employees rank their employer as one of the best places to work for millennials. The company's culture of fun, casual dress, and flexible work schedules that provide for a work/life balance appeal to Generation Y employees like those shown here at eBay's offices in San Jose, California. Young employees say that eBay managers give them job responsibility quickly, generous recognition for their achievements, and learning opportunities to advance their careers. They also admire eBay's "Social Venture" initiatives such as WorldofGood.com, eBay Giving Works, and MicroPlace that make a positive difference in the lives of people throughout the world.

with other generations over work attire and communication. They also like feedback. An Ernst & Young survey found that 85 percent of Millennials want "frequent and candid performance feedback," compared to only half of Boomers.[71]

Though it is fascinating to think about generational values, remember these classifications lack solid research support. Recent reviews suggest many of the generalizations are either overblown or incorrect.[72] Studies that have found differences across generations do not support the popular conceptions of how generations differ, and most are plagued with methodological problems that make it difficult to assess whether differences actually exist. One study that used an appropriate longitudinal design did find the value placed on leisure increased over generations from the Baby Boomers to the Millennials and work centrality has declined, but it did not find that Millennials had higher altruistic work values as expected.[73] Generational classifications may help us understand our own and other generations better, but we must also appreciate their limits.

Linking an Individual's Personality and Values to the Workplace

Thirty years ago, organizations were concerned only with personality because their primary focus was to match individuals to specific jobs. That concern has expanded to include how well the individual's personality *and* values match the organization. Why? Because managers today are less interested in an applicant's ability to perform a *specific* job than with his or her *flexibility* to meet changing situations and commitment to the organization.

We'll now discuss person–job fit and person–organization fit in more detail.

Person–Job Fit

The effort to match job requirements with personality characteristics is best articulated in John Holland's **personality–job fit theory**.[74] Holland presents six personality types and proposes that satisfaction and the propensity to leave a position depend on how well individuals match their personalities to a job. Exhibit 5-5 describes the six types, their personality characteristics, and examples of the congruent occupations for each.

Holland developed the Vocational Preference Inventory questionnaire, which contains 160 occupational titles. Respondents indicate which they like or dislike, and their answers form personality profiles. Research strongly supports the resulting hexagonal diagram shown in Exhibit 5-6.[75] The closer two fields or orientations are in the hexagon, the more compatible they are. Adjacent categories are quite similar, whereas diagonally opposite ones are highly dissimilar.

What does all this mean? The theory argues that satisfaction is highest and turnover lowest when personality and occupation are in agreement. A realistic person in a realistic job is in a more congruent situation than a realistic person in an investigative job. A realistic person in a social job is in the most incongruent situation possible. The key points of this model are that (1) there do appear to

Exhibit 5-5	Holland's Typology of Personality and Congruent Occupations	
Type	**Personality Characteristics**	**Congruent Occupations**
Realistic: Prefers physical activities that require skill, strength, and coordination	Shy, genuine, persistent, stable, conforming, practical	Mechanic, drill press operator, assembly-line worker, farmer
Investigative: Prefers activities that involve thinking, organizing, and understanding	Analytical, original, curious, independent	Biologist, economist, mathematician, news reporter
Social: Prefers activities that involve helping and developing others	Sociable, friendly, cooperative, understanding	Social worker, teacher, counselor, clinical psychologist
Conventional: Prefers rule-regulated, orderly, and unambiguous activities	Conforming, efficient, practical, unimaginative, inflexible	Accountant, corporate manager, bank teller, file clerk
Enterprising: Prefers verbal activities in which there are opportunities to influence others and attain power	Self-confident, ambitious, energetic, domineering	Lawyer, real estate agent, public relations specialist, small business manager
Artistic: Prefers ambiguous and unsystematic activities that allow creative expression	Imaginative, disorderly, idealistic, emotional, impractical	Painter, musician, writer, interior decorator

be intrinsic differences in personality among individuals, (2) there are different types of jobs, and (3) people in jobs congruent with their personality should be more satisfied and less likely to voluntarily resign than people in incongruent jobs. Evidence supports the value of assessing vocational interests in the selection process, with a match between interests and job requirements predicting job knowledge, performance, and low likelihood of turnover.[76]

Exhibit 5-6	Relationships Among Occupational Personality Types

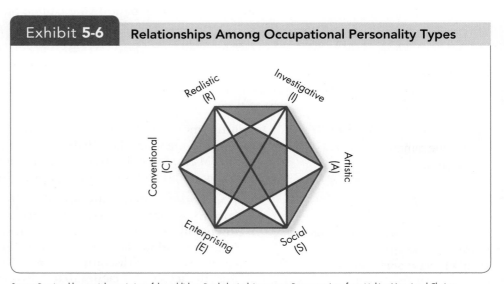

personality–job fit theory   *A theory that identifies six personality types and proposes that the fit between personality type and occupational environment determines satisfaction and turnover.*

As you might expect, Holland types relate to personality scales. One study found individuals higher in openness to experience as children were more likely to take jobs high on the investigative and artistic dimensions as adults, and those higher in conscientiousness as children were more likely to work in conventional jobs as adults.[77]

Person–Organization Fit

We've noted that researchers have looked at matching people to organizations as well as to jobs. If an organization faces a dynamic and changing environment and requires employees able to readily change tasks and move easily between teams, it's more important that employees' personalities fit with the overall organization's culture than with the characteristics of any specific job.

The person–organization fit essentially argues that people are attracted to and selected by organizations that match their values, and they leave organizations that are not compatible with their personalities.[78] Using the Big Five terminology, for instance, we could expect that people high on extraversion fit well with aggressive and team-oriented cultures, that people high on agreeableness match up better with a supportive organizational climate than one focused on aggressiveness, and that people high on openness to experience fit better in organizations that emphasize innovation rather than standardization.[79] Following these guidelines at the time of hiring should identify new employees who fit better with the organization's culture, which should, in turn, result in higher employee satisfaction and reduced turnover. Research on person–organization fit has also looked at whether people's values match the organization's culture. This match predicts job satisfaction, commitment to the organization, and low turnover.[80] Interestingly, some research found that person-organization fit was more important in predicting turnover in a collectivistic nation (India) than in a more individualistic nation (the United States).[81]

International Values

8 Identify Hofstede's five value dimensions of national culture.

MyManagementLab
For an interactive application of this topic, check out this chapter's simulation activity at **www.pearsonglobaleditions.com/ mymanagementlab**.

One of the most widely referenced approaches for analyzing variations among cultures was done in the late 1970s by Geert Hofstede.[82] He surveyed more than 116,000 IBM employees in 40 countries about their work-related values and found that managers and employees vary on five value dimensions of national culture:

- *Power distance.* **Power distance** describes the degree to which people in a country accept that power in institutions and organizations is distributed unequally. A high rating on power distance means that large inequalities of power and wealth exist and are tolerated in the culture, as in a class or caste system that discourages upward mobility. A low power distance rating characterizes societies that stress equality and opportunity.
- *Individualism versus collectivism.* **Individualism** is the degree to which people prefer to act as individuals rather than as members of groups and believe in individual rights above all else. **Collectivism** emphasizes a tight social framework in which people expect others in groups of which they are a part to look after them and protect them.
- *Masculinity versus femininity.* Hofstede's construct of **masculinity** is the degree to which the culture favors traditional masculine roles such as achievement, power, and control, as opposed to viewing men and women as equals. A high masculinity rating indicates the culture has separate roles

for men and women, with men dominating the society. A high **femininity** rating means the culture sees little differentiation between male and female roles and treats women as the equals of men in all respects.

- *Uncertainty avoidance.* The degree to which people in a country prefer structured over unstructured situations defines their **uncertainty avoidance**. In cultures that score high on uncertainty avoidance, people have an increased level of anxiety about uncertainty and ambiguity and use laws and controls to reduce uncertainty. People in cultures low on uncertainty avoidance are more accepting of ambiguity, are less rule oriented, take more risks, and more readily accept change.

- *Long-term versus short-term orientation.* This newest addition to Hofstede's typology measures a society's devotion to traditional values. People in a culture with **long-term orientation** look to the future and value thrift, persistence, and tradition. In a **short-term orientation**, people value the here and now; they accept change more readily and don't see commitments as impediments to change.

How do different countries score on Hofstede's dimensions? Exhibit 5-7 shows the ratings for the countries for which data are available. For example, power distance is higher in Malaysia than in any other country. The United States is very individualistic; in fact, it's the most individualistic nation of all (closely followed by Australia and Great Britain). The United States also tends to be short term in orientation and low in power distance (people in the United States tend not to accept built-in class differences between people). It is also relatively low on uncertainty avoidance, meaning most adults are relatively tolerant of uncertainty and ambiguity. The United States scores relatively high on masculinity; most people emphasize traditional gender roles (at least relative to countries such as Denmark, Finland, Norway, and Sweden).

You'll notice regional differences. Western and northern nations such as Canada and the Netherlands tend to be more individualistic. Poorer countries such as Mexico and the Philippines tend to be higher on power distance. South American nations tend to be higher than other countries on uncertainty avoidance, and Asian countries tend to have a long-term orientation.

Hofstede's culture dimensions have been enormously influential on OB researchers and managers. Nevertheless, his research has been criticized. First, although the data have since been updated, the original work is more than 30 years old and was based on a single company (IBM). A lot has happened on the world scene since then. Some of the most obvious changes include the fall of the Soviet Union, the transformation of central and eastern Europe, the end of apartheid in South Africa, and the rise of China as a global power. Second, few researchers have read the details of Hofstede's methodology closely and are

---

power distance *A national culture attribute that describes the extent to which a society accepts that power in institutions and organizations is distributed unequally.*

individualism *A national culture attribute that describes the degree to which people prefer to act as individuals rather than as members of groups.*

collectivism *A national culture attribute that describes a tight social framework in which people expect others in groups of which they are a part to look after them and protect them.*

masculinity *A national culture attribute that describes the extent to which the culture favors traditional masculine work roles of achievement, power, and control. Societal values are characterized by assertiveness and materialism.*

femininity *A national culture attribute that indicates little differentiation between male and female roles; a high rating indicates that women are treated as the equals of men in all aspects of the society.*

uncertainty avoidance *A national culture attribute that describes the extent to which a society feels threatened by uncertain and ambiguous situations and tries to avoid them.*

long-term orientation *A national culture attribute that emphasizes the future, thrift, and persistence.*

short-term orientation *A national culture attribute that emphasizes the past and present, respect for tradition, and fulfillment of social obligations.*

Exhibit **5-7** | Hofstede's Cultural Values by Nation

Country	Power Distance		Individualism versus Collectivism		Masculinity versus Femininity		Uncertainty Avoidance		Long- versus Short-Term Orientation	
	Index	Rank	Index	Rank	Index	Rank	Index	Rank	Index	Rank
Argentina	49	35–36	46	22–23	56	20–21	86	10–15		
Australia	36	41	90	2	61	16	51	37	31	22–24
Austria	11	53	55	18	79	2	70	24–25	31	22–24
Belgium	65	20	75	8	54	22	94	5–6	38	18
Brazil	69	14	38	26–27	49	27	76	21–22	65	6
Canada	39	39	80	4–5	52	24	48	41–42	23	30
Chile	63	24–25	23	38	28	46	86	10–15		
Colombia	67	17	13	49	64	11–12	80	20		
Costa Rica	35	42–44	15	46	21	48–49	86	10–15		
Denmark	18	51	74	9	16	50	23	51	46	10
Ecuador	78	8–9	8	52	63	13–14	67	28		
El Salvador	66	18–19	19	42	40	40	94	5–6		
Finland	33	46	63	17	26	47	59	31–32	41	14
France	68	15–16	71	10–11	43	35–36	86	10–15	39	17
Germany	35	42–44	67	15	66	9–10	65	29	31	22–24
Great Britain	35	42–44	89	3	66	9–10	35	47–48	25	28–29
Greece	60	27–28	35	30	57	18–19	112	1		
Guatemala	95	2–3	6	53	37	43	101	3		
Hong Kong	68	15–16	25	37	57	18–19	29	49–50	96	2
India	77	10–11	48	21	56	20–21	40	45	61	7
Indonesia	78	8–9	14	47–48	46	30–31	48	41–42		
Iran	58	29–30	41	24	43	35–36	59	31–32		
Ireland	28	49	70	12	68	7–8	35	47–48	43	13
Israel	13	52	54	19	47	29	81	19		
Italy	50	34	76	7	70	4–5	75	23	34	19
Jamaica	45	37	39	25	68	7–8	13	52		
Japan	54	33	46	22–23	95	1	92	7	80	4
Korea (South)	60	27–28	18	43	39	41	85	16–17	75	5
Malaysia	104	1	26	36	50	25–26	36	46		
Mexico	81	5–6	30	32	69	6	82	18		
The Netherlands	38	40	80	4–5	14	51	53	35	44	11–12
New Zealand	22	50	79	6	58	17	49	39–40	30	25–26
Norway	31	47–48	69	13	8	52	50	38	44	11–12
Pakistan	55	32	14	47–48	50	25–26	70	24–25	0	34
Panama	95	2–3	11	51	44	34	86	10–15		
Peru	64	21–23	16	45	42	37–38	87	9		
Philippines	94	4	32	31	64	11–12	44	44	19	31–32
Portugal	63	24–25	27	33–35	31	45	104	2	30	25–26
Singapore	74	13	20	39–41	48	28	8	53	48	9
South Africa	49	35–36	65	16	63	13–14	49	39–40		
Spain	57	31	51	20	42	37–38	86	10–15	19	31–32
Sweden	31	47–48	71	10–11	5	53	29	49–50	33	20
Switzerland	34	45	68	14	70	4–5	58	33	40	15–16
Taiwan	58	29–30	17	44	45	32–33	69	26	87	3
Thailand	64	21–23	20	39–41	34	44	64	30	56	8
Turkey	66	18–19	37	28	45	32–33	85	16–17		
United States	40	38	91	1	62	15	46	43	29	27
Uruguay	61	26	36	29	38	42	100	4		
Venezuela	81	5–6	12	50	73	3	76	21–22		
Yugoslavia	76	12	27	33–35	21	48–49	88	8		
Regions:										
Arab countries	80	7	38	26–27	53	23	68	27		
East Africa	64	21–23	27	33–35	41	39	52	36	25	28–29
West Africa	77	10–11	20	39–41	46	30–31	54	34	16	33

Scores range from 0 5 extremely low on dimension to 100 5 extremely high.

Note: 1 5 highest rank. LTO ranks: 1 5 China; 15–16 5 Bangladesh; 21 5 Poland; 34 5 lowest.

Source: Copyright Geert Hofstede BV, hofstede@bart.nl. Reprinted with permission.

Understanding differences in values across cultures helps explain the behavior of employees from different countries. According to Hofstede's framework for assessing cultures, China, like all Asian nations, ranks high in long-term orientation. China also ranks high in power distance, where the inequality of power and wealth within the country is accepted by citizens as part of their cultural heritage. Ranking low in individualism, China has a strong collectivist culture that fosters relationships where everyone takes responsibility for group members. Using these and other ratings can help organizations considering doing business in China to predict the behavior of employees shown here at a glassware factory.

Source: Imaginechina via AP Images.

therefore unaware of the many decisions and judgment calls he had to make (for example, reducing the number of cultural values to just five). Some results are unexpected. Japan, which is often considered a highly collectivist nation, is considered only average on collectivism under Hofstede's dimensions.[83] Despite these concerns, Hofstede has been one of the most widely cited social scientists ever, and his framework has left a lasting mark on OB.

Recent research across 598 studies with more than 200,000 respondents has investigated the relationship of cultural values and a variety of organizational criteria at both the individual and national level of analysis.[84] Overall, the four original culture dimensions were equally strong predictors of relevant outcomes, meaning researchers and practicing managers need to think about culture holistically and not just focus on one or two dimensions. Cultural values were more strongly related to organizational commitment, citizenship behavior, and team-related attitudes than were personality scores. On the other hand, personality was more strongly related to behavioral criteria like performance, absenteeism, and turnover. The researchers also found that individual scores were much better predictors of most outcomes than assigning all people in a country the same cultural values. In sum, this research suggests that Hofstede's value framework may be a valuable way of thinking about differences among people, but we should be cautious about assuming all people from a country have the same values.

The GLOBE Framework for Assessing Cultures Begun in 1993, the Global Leadership and Organizational Behavior Effectiveness (GLOBE) research program is an ongoing cross-cultural investigation of leadership and national culture. Using data from 825 organizations in 62 countries, the GLOBE team identified nine dimensions on which national cultures differ.[85] Some—such as power distance, individualism/collectivism, uncertainty avoidance, gender differentiation (similar to masculinity versus femininity), and future orientation (similar to long-term versus short-term orientation)—resemble the Hofstede dimensions. The main difference is that the GLOBE framework added dimensions, such as humane orientation (the degree to which a society rewards individuals for being altruistic, generous, and kind to others) and performance orientation (the degree to which a society encourages and rewards group members for performance improvement and excellence).

Which framework is better? That's hard to say, and each has its adherents. We give more emphasis to Hofstede's dimensions here because they have stood the test of time and the GLOBE study confirmed them. However, researchers continue to debate the differences between them, and future studies may favor the more nuanced perspective of the GLOBE study.[86]

MyManagementLab

Now that you have finished this chapter, go back to **www.pearsonglobaleditions.com/ mymanagementlab.** to continue practicing and applying the concepts you've learned.

Summary and Implications for Managers

Personality   What value, if any, does the Big Five model provide to managers? From the early 1900s through the mid-1980s, researchers sought a link between personality and job performance. "The outcome of those 80-plus years of research was that personality and job performance were not meaningfully related across traits or situations."[87] However, the past 20 years have been more promising, largely due to the findings about the Big Five.

- Screening job candidates for high conscientiousness—as well as the other Big Five traits, depending on the criteria an organization finds most important—should pay dividends. Of course, managers still need to take situational factors into consideration.[88]
- Factors such as job demands, the degree of required interaction with others, and the organization's culture are examples of situational variables that moderate the personality–job performance relationship.
- You need to evaluate the job, the work group, and the organization to determine the optimal personality fit.
- Other traits, such as core self-evaluation or narcissism, may be relevant in certain situations, too.
- Although the MBTI has been widely criticized, it may have a place in organizations. In training and development, it can help employees better understand themselves, help team members better understand each other, and open up communication in work groups and possibly reduce conflicts.

Values   Why is it important to know an individual's values? Values often underlie and explain attitudes, behaviors, and perceptions. So knowledge of an individual's value system can provide insight into what makes the person "tick."

- Employees' performance and satisfaction are likely to be higher if their values fit well with the organization. The person who places great importance on imagination, independence, and freedom is likely to be poorly matched with an organization that seeks conformity from its employees.

Millennials Are More Narcissistic

POINT

Those in college today have many good qualities: they are more technologically savvy, more socially tolerant, and more balanced in their work and family priorities than previous generations. Thus, those poised to enter the workforce today do so with some important virtues. Humility, however, is not one of them.

A large-scale, longitudinal study found that those graduating from college in 2010 were more likely than those from previous generations to have seemingly inflated views of themselves. The 2010 graduates were more likely than 1980 graduates to agree they would be "very good" spouses (56 percent of 2010 graduates, compared to 37 percent among 1980 graduates), parents (54 percent of 2010 graduates, 36 percent among 1980 graduates), and workers (65 percent of 2010 graduates, 49 percent among 1980 graduates).

Studies measuring narcissism suggests that scores are rising, especially among younger generations. For example, by presenting a choice between two statements—"I try not to be a show-off" versus "I will usually show off if I get the chance"—psychologists have found that narcissism has been growing since the early 1980s.

A 2011 study by University of Kentucky researcher Dr. Nathan DeWall even found that popular songs are becoming more narcissistic. Analyzing the lyrics of songs on the *Billboard Hot 100 Chart* from 1980 to 2007, DeWall found a clear trend toward narcissism. The words "I" and "me" have replaced "we" and "us." Two recent examples: *"I'm bringing sexy back. Yeah. Them other boys don't know how to act. Yeah"* (Justin Timberlake), and *"I am the greatest man that ever lived. I was born to give and give and give"* (Weezer).

Narcissism's rise is all around us. The sooner we admit it, the sooner we can begin to address the problem in families, in education, and at work.

COUNTERPOINT

Speaking of music, this argument is like a broken record that seems to play over and over: "THE YOUTH OF TODAY ARE LOST!" Every generation tends to think the new generation is without values, and the new generation thinks the older generation is hopelessly judgmental and out of touch. Wasn't the "Me generation" supposedly a generation ago? Let's send the broken record to the recycling bin and review the evidence.

One recent study that tracked nearly half a million young people on measures of egotistic traits such as self-perceived intelligence, self-esteem, and self-enhancement found little evidence to suggest changes since the 1970s. In short, Millennials aren't any more narcissistic than young people were in the 1970s or 1980s. The authors of this study conclude, "Today's youth seem no more egotistical than previous generations . . . In fact, today's youth seem to have psychological profiles that are remarkably similar to youth from the past 30 years."

Another study offered an interesting explanation for why people *think* Millennials are more narcissistic. Specifically, young people in general are more self-focused, but as people age, they become more "other" focused. So we think young people are different when in fact they're just the way older folks were when *they* were younger. As these authors conclude, "Every generation is Generation Me." Our level of narcissism appears to be one of the many things that change as we get older.

More broadly, narcissistic folks exist in every generation. We need to be careful when generalizing about entire groups (whether one sex, one race, one culture, or one generation). While generalizations have caused no small amount of trouble, we still like to simplify the world, sometimes for good reason. In this case, however, the good reason isn't there, especially considering the latest evidence.

Sources: N. Wolchover, "Song Lyrics Suggest Narcissism Is on the Rise," *LiveScience* (April, 26, 2011), downloaded May 16, 2011, from www.livescience.com; M. Norris, "Study: Narcissism on Rise in Pop Lyrics," *All Things Considered* (April 26, 2011), downloaded May 15 from www.npr.org/; K. H. Trzesniewski and M. B. Donnellan, "Rethinking 'Generation Me': A Study of Cohort Effects from 1976–2006," *Perspectives on Psychological Science* 5, no. 1 (2010), pp. 58–75; and B. W. Roberts, G. Edmonds, and E. Grijalva, "It Is Developmental Me, Not Generation Me: Developmental Changes Are More Important Than Generational Changes in Narcissism—Comment on Trzesniewski & Donnellon (2010)," *Perspectives on Psychological Science* 5, No. 1 (2010), pp. 97–102.

> ● Managers are more likely to appreciate, evaluate positively, and allocate rewards to employees who fit in, and employees are more likely to be satisfied if they perceive they do fit in. This argues for management to seek job candidates who have not only the ability, experience, and motivation to perform but also a value system compatible with the organization's.

QUESTIONS FOR REVIEW

1 What is personality? How do we typically measure it? What factors determine personality?

2 What is the Myers-Briggs Type Indicator (MBTI), and what does it measure?

3 What are the Big Five personality traits?

4 How do the Big Five traits predict work behavior?

5 Besides the Big Five, what other personality traits are relevant to OB?

6 What are values, why are they important, and what is the difference between terminal and instrumental values?

7 Do values differ across generations? How so?

8 Do values differ across cultures? How so?

EXPERIENTIAL EXERCISE What Organizational Culture Do You Prefer?

The Organizational Culture Profile (OCP) can help assess whether an individual's values match the organization's.[89] The OCP helps individuals sort their characteristics in terms of importance, which indicates what a person values.

1. Working on your own, complete the OCP found at www.jstor.org/stable/256404.

2. Your instructor may ask you the following questions individually or as a group of three or four students (with a spokesperson appointed to speak to the class for each group):

a. What were your most preferred and least preferred values? Do you think your most preferred and least preferred values are similar to those of other class or group members?

b. Do you think there are generational differences in the most preferred and least preferred values?

c. Research has shown that individuals tend to be happier, and perform better, when their OCP values match those of their employer. How important do you think a "values match" is when you're deciding where you want to work?

ETHICAL DILEMMA Personal Values and Ethics in the Workplace

Sipho Dlamini was born in a small rural village in Swaziland. He spent his childhood years looking after his family's livestock. The community upheld high values, such as honesty and respect, but the people were desperately poor. He realized that he would have to go to South Africa and apply for a job at a gold mine.

As a young man Sipho left his village in the mountains and took on the difficult job of getting to South Africa. He went in search of one of his distant family members who was working for a gold mine near Johannesburg. He managed to find his relative, who was engaged as a personnel assistant. Sipho's relative managed to find him a job as a general mine worker and accommodation in one of the mine hostels.

Sipho was dedicated to his work, and time passed quickly. Every month, he forwarded most of his wages to his family in Swaziland. One day Sipho's family member called Sipho into his office and informed him that he was due for promotion. He also told Sipho that he would be required to pay him R500.00 (about $60) for his "efforts." This arrangement seemed strange to Sipho since he knew that it was not in line with company procedures. When Sipho asked about this, the personnel assistant replied that he had the authority to do so and that Sipho would not be promoted should he not pay the R500.00.

Sipho returned to his room and battled in his mind that night with the options before him. He had grown up with strong personal values that included honesty and hard work, but his family needed the extra income. What was he to do? After a restless night, he returned the next day to the personnel assistant's office and handed him the R500.00.

He was immediately promoted and returned to his room with a troubled mind. A few weeks later, the personnel assistant was reported and investigated for fraudulent behavior. He was suspended from work, and the investigation revealed all his corrupt activities. The record he had kept on all employees who paid bribes to him was also found. All employees on this list were called in and charged with fraud. Sipho's name was on the list, and he was found guilty and dismissed from the service of the company, along with all the others.

Questions

1. Was it fair of the mine to dismiss Sipho from service?
2. What should Sipho have done differently?
3. In what way could the mine management have provided support to him, prior to his wrongful act?
4. How would you have acted had you been in a similar situation?
5. What should you do when your personal values are in conflict with a certain work ethic?

CASE INCIDENT 1 Is There a Price for Being Too Nice?

Agreeable people tend to be kinder and more accommodating in social situations, which you might think could add to their success in life. However, we've already noted that one downside of agreeableness is potentially lower earnings. We're not sure why this is so, but agreeable individuals may be less aggressive in negotiating starting salaries and pay raises.

Yet there is clear evidence that agreeableness is something employers value. Several recent books argue in favor of "leading with kindness" (Baker & O'Malley, 2008) and "capitalizing on kindness" (Tillquist, 2008). Other articles in the business press have argued that the sensitive, agreeable CEO—such as GE's Jeffrey Immelt and Boeing's James McNerney—signals a shift in business culture (Brady, 2007). In many circles, individuals desiring success in their careers are exhorted to be "complimentary," "kind," and "good" (for example, Schillinger, 2007).

Take the example of 500-employee Lindblad Expeditions. It emphasizes agreeableness in its hiring decisions. The VP of HR commented, "You can teach people any technical skill, but you can't teach them how to be a kindhearted, generous-minded person with an open spirit."

So, while employers want agreeable employees, agreeable employees are not better job performers, and they are *less* successful in their careers. We might explain this apparent contradiction by noting that employers value agreeable employees for other reasons: they are more pleasant to be around, and they may help others in ways that aren't reflected in their job performance. Most evidence suggests that agreeable people like agreeable people, which you might expect because people like those who are similar to themselves. However, even disagreeable people like agreeable people, perhaps because they are easier to manipulate than individuals who are lower in agreeableness. Perhaps everyone wants to hire agreeable people just because everyone likes to be around them.

Moreover, a 2008 study of CEO and CEO candidates revealed that this contradiction applies to organizational leaders as well. Using ratings made by an executive search firm, researchers studied the personalities and abilities of 316 CEO candidates for companies involved in buyout and venture capital transactions. They found that what gets a CEO candidate hired is not what makes him or her effective. Specifically, CEO candidates who were rated high on "nice" traits such as respecting others, developing others, and teamwork were more likely to be hired. However, these same characteristics—especially teamwork and respecting others for venture capital CEOs—made the organizations they led less successful.

Questions

1. Do you think there is a contradiction between what employers want in employees (agreeable employees) and what employees actually do best (disagreeable employees)? Why or why not?
2. Often, the effects of personality depend on the situation. Can you think of some job situations in which agreeableness is an important virtue? And in which it is harmful?
3. In some research we've conducted, we've found that the negative effects of agreeableness on earnings is stronger for men than for women (that is, being agreeable hurt men's earnings more than women's). Why do you think this might be the case?

Sources: T. A. Judge, B. A. Livingston, and C. Hurst, "Do Nice Guys—and Gals—Really Finish Last? The Joint Effects of Sex and Agreeableness on Earnings," working paper, University of Florida (2009); S. N. Kaplan, M. M. Klebanov, and M. Sorensen, "Which CEO Characteristics and Abilities Matter?"

working paper, University of Chicago Graduate School of Business (2008), faculty.chicagobooth.edu/steven .kaplan/research/kks.pdf; W. F. Baker and M. O'Malley, *Leading with Kindness: How Good People Consistently Get Superior Results* (New York: AMACOM, 2008); K. Tillquist, *Capitalizing on Kindness: When 21st Century Professionals Need to Be Nice* (Pompton Plains, NJ: Career Press, 2008); D. Brady, "Being Mean Is So Last Millennium," *BusinessWeek* (January 15, 2007), p. 61; and L. Schillinger, "Nice and Ambitious: Either, Neither, or Both?" *The New York Times* (January 14, 2007), p. 1.

CASE INCIDENT 2 Personal Space

In business life, personal space is a very underestimated and even considered an unknown phenomena. As a manager, work consists mainly of dealing with people. Recognizing personal space and the differences among people can improve every business setting.

Personal space is the space or territory valued around oneself in which others are not welcome. This space can be subdivided into several components. Edward Hall (1966) divided personal space into five zones:

1. The *intimate zone*, which ranges from 0 to 18 inches, is only accessible for family and loved ones.

2. The *close personal zone* is the "bubble" that extends 1.5 to 2 feet from a person. Friends are allowed in this zone.

3. The *far personal zone* extends 4 to 12 feet and encompasses some direct communication and some proximity.

4. The *social zone* extends 4 to 12 feet beyond the person. This personal space exists between individuals in normal business life or between new contacts.

5. The *public zone* is everything beyond the social zone. This area is a consideration during public speaking.

As can be determined from Hall's work, personal space differs based on the person and the type of communication. When dealing with more familiar people—family or friends—the bubble of personal space is smaller than when talking to new contacts or engaging in formal conversations.

Personal space is determined by several factors. Personality traits, such as extraversion, are one key determinant. Gender also plays a role, and it has been found that men maintain a larger overall personal space. Culture also plays a dominant role.

In daily life, most people by nature adapt to the personal space of other individuals. When adaptation is not done appropriately, body language can indicate the unease of the other individual. When crossing national borders (or sometimes even regions), the concept becomes more difficult to grasp. Even within countries that might look similar in terms of Hofstede's model, significant differences appear. As the business world becomes increasingly international, the concept of personal space becomes more relevant. International managers who overlook subtle differences in personal space can encounter major hurdles.

Consider, for example, a formal meeting between a Dutch and a Swedish subsidiary. The Dutch manager welcomes the foreign managers and embraces them. The body language of the Swedes says something is not right. The meeting continues, and all relevant business is discussed. However, both parties leave the meeting feeling misunderstood.

Questions

1. Considering Hofstede's model, Sweden and The Netherlands appear similar. What went wrong in the preceding situation? And from what do these differences stem?

2. What can the Dutch manager do to resolve the disturbance in his relation with the Swedes?

3. How can "invasion" of personal space be identified?

4. Describe some experiences of personal space in your life. Consider study abroad, internships, and so on.

Sources: Based on E. Hall, (1966), *The Hidden Dimension.* Garden City, NY: Doubleday; C. Kinsey Goman, (2009), "Keep Your Distance." *Office Pro* 69, no. 7, p. 6.

ENDNOTES

1. G. W. Allport, *Personality: A Psychological Interpretation* (New York: Holt, Rinehart & Winston, 1937), p. 48. For a brief critique of current views on the meaning of personality, see R. T. Hogan and B. W. Roberts, "Introduction: Personality and Industrial and Organizational Psychology," in B. W. Roberts and R. Hogan (eds.), *Personality Psychology in the Workplace* (Washington, DC: American Psychological Association, 2001), pp. 11–12.

2. K. I. van der Zee, J. N. Zaal, and J. Piekstra, "Validation of the Multicultural Personality Questionnaire in the Context of Personnel Selection," *European Journal of Personality* 17, Supl. 1 (2003), pp. S77–S100.

3. S. A. Birkeland, T. M. Manson, J. L. Kisamore, M. T. Brannick, and M. A. Smith, "A Meta-Analytic Investigation of Job Applicant Faking on Personality Measures," *International Journal of Selection and Assessment* 14, no. 14 (2006), pp. 317–335.

4. T. A. Judge, C. A. Higgins, C. J. Thoresen, and M. R. Barrick, "The Big Five Personality Traits, General Mental Ability, and Career Success Across the Life Span," *Personnel Psychology* 52, no. 3 (1999), pp. 621–652; I. Oh, G. Wang, and M. K. Mount, "Validity of Observer Ratings of the Five-Factor Model of Personality Traits: A Meta-Analysis," *Journal of Applied Psychology* 96, No. 4 (2011), pp. 762-773.

5. See R. Illies, R. D. Arvey, and T. J. Bouchard, "Darwinism, Behavioral Genetics, and Organizational Behavior: A Review and Agenda for Future Research," *Journal of Organizational Behavior* 27, no. 2 (2006), pp. 121–141; and W. Johnson, E. Turkheimer, I. I. Gottesman, and T. J. Bouchard, Jr., "Beyond Heritability: Twin Studies in Behavioral Research," *Current Directions in Psychological Science* 18, no. 4 (2009), pp. 217–220.

6. S. Srivastava, O. P. John, and S. D. Gosling, "Development of Personality in Early and Middle Adulthood: Set Like Plaster or Persistent Change?" *Journal of Personality and Social Psychology* 84, no. 5 (2003), pp. 1041–1053; and B. W. Roberts, K. E. Walton, and W. Viechtbauer, "Patterns of Mean-Level Change in Personality Traits Across the Life Course: A Meta-Analysis of Longitudinal Studies," *Psychological Bulletin* 132, no. 1 (2006), pp. 1–25.

7. S. E. Hampson and L. R. Goldberg, "A First Large Cohort Study of Personality Trait Stability Over the 40 Years Between Elementary School and Midlife," *Journal of Personality and Social Psychology* 91, no. 4 (2006), pp. 763–779.

8. See A. H. Buss, "Personality as Traits," *American Psychologist* 44, no. 11 (1989), pp. 1378–1388; R. R. McCrae, "Trait Psychology and the Revival of Personality and Culture Studies," *American Behavioral Scientist* 44, no. 1 (2000), pp. 10–31; and L. R. James and M. D. Mazerolle, *Personality in Work Organizations* (Thousand Oaks, CA: Sage, 2002).

9. See, for instance, G. W. Allport and H. S. Odbert, "Trait Names, A Psycholexical Study," *Psychological Monographs*, no. 47 (1936); and R. B. Cattell, "Personality Pinned Down," *Psychology Today* (July 1973), pp. 40–46.

10. R. B. Kennedy and D. A. Kennedy, "Using the Myers-Briggs Type Indicator in Career Counseling," *Journal of Employment Counseling* 41, no. 1 (2004), pp. 38–44.

11. See, for instance, D. J. Pittenger, "Cautionary Comments Regarding the Myers-Briggs Type Indicator," *Consulting Psychology Journal: Practice and Research* 57, no. 3 (2005), pp. 10–221; L. Bess and R. J. Harvey, "Bimodal Score Distributions and the Myers-Briggs Type Indicator: Fact or Artifact?" *Journal of Personality Assessment* 78, no. 1 (2002), pp. 176–186; R. M. Capraro and M. M. Capraro, "Myers-Briggs Type Indicator Score Reliability Across Studies: A Meta-Analytic Reliability Generalization Study," *Educational & Psychological Measurement* 62, no. 4 (2002), pp. 590–602; and R. C. Arnau, B. A. Green, D. H. Rosen, D. H. Gleaves, and J. G. Melancon, "Are Jungian Preferences Really Categorical? An Empirical Investigation Using Taxometric Analysis," *Personality & Individual Differences* 34, no. 2 (2003), pp. 233–251.

12. See, for example, I. Oh, G. Wang, and M. K. Mount, "Validity of Observer Ratings of the Five-Factor Model of Personality Traits: A Meta-Analysis," *Journal of Applied Psychology* 96, No. 4 (2011), pp. 762–773; and M. R. Barrick and M. K. Mount, "Yes, Personality Matters: Moving On to More Important Matters," *Human Performance* 18, no. 4 (2005), pp. 359–372.

13. W. Fleeson and P. Gallagher, "The Implications of Big Five Standing for the Distribution of Trait Manifestation in Behavior: Fifteen Experience-Sampling Studies and a Meta-Analysis," *Journal of Personality and Social Psychology* 97, no. 6 (2009), pp. 1097–1114.

14. See, for instance, I. Oh and C. M. Berry, "The Five-Factor Model of Personality and Managerial Performance: Validity Gains Through the Use of 360 Degree Performance Ratings," *Journal of Applied Psychology* 94, no. 6 (2009), pp. 1498–1513; G. M. Hurtz and J. J. Donovan, "Personality and Job Performance: The Big Five Revisited," *Journal of Applied Psychology* 85, no. 6 (2000), pp. 869–879; J. Hogan and B. Holland, "Using Theory to Evaluate Personality and Job-Performance Relations: A Socioanalytic Perspective," *Journal of Applied Psychology* 88, no. 1 (2003), pp. 100–112; and M. R. Barrick and M. K. Mount, "Select on Conscientiousness and Emotional Stability," in E. A. Locke (ed.), *Handbook of Principles of Organizational Behavior* (Malden, MA: Blackwell, 2004), pp. 15–28.

15. M. K. Mount, M. R. Barrick, and J. P. Strauss, "Validity of Observer Ratings of the Big Five Personality Factors," *Journal of Applied Psychology* 79, no. 2 (1994), p. 272. Additionally confirmed by G. M. Hurtz and J. J. Donovan, "Personality and Job Performance: The Big Five Revisited"; and Oh and Berry, "The Five-Factor Model of Personality and Managerial Performance."

16. A. E. Poropat, "A Meta-Analysis of the Five-Factor Model of Personality and Academic Performance," *Psychological Bulletin* 135, no. 2 (2009), pp. 322–338.

17. A. M. Cianci, H. J. Klein, and G. H. Seijts, "The Effect of Negative Feedback on Tension and Subsequent Performance: The Main and Interactive Effects of Goal Content and Conscientiousness," *Journal of Applied Psychology* 95, no. 4 (2010), pp. 618–630.

18. H. Le, I. Oh, S. B. Robbins, R. Ilies, E. Holland, and P. Westrick, "Too Much of a Good Thing: Curvilinear Relationships

Between Personality Traits and Job Performance," *Journal of Applied Psychology* 96, no. 1 (2011), pp. 113–133.

19. T. Bogg and B. W. Roberts, "Conscientiousness and Health-Related Behaviors: A Meta-Analysis of the Leading Behavioral Contributors to Mortality," *Psychological Bulletin* 130, no. 6 (2004), pp. 887–919.

20. G. J. Feist, "A Meta-Analysis of Personality in Scientific and Artistic Creativity," *Personality and Social Psychology Review* 2, no. 4 (1998), pp. 290–309; C. Robert and Y. H. Cheung, "An Examination of the Relationship Between Conscientiousness and Group Performance on a Creative Task," *Journal of Research in Personality* 44, no. 2 (2010), pp. 222–231; and M. Batey, T. Chamorro-Premuzic, and A. Furnham, "Individual Differences in Ideational Behavior. Can the Big Five and Psychometric Intelligence Predict Creativity Scores?" *Creativity Research Journal* 22, no. 1 (2010), pp. 90-97.

21. R. J. Foti and M. A. Hauenstein, "Pattern and Variable Approaches in Leadership Emergence and Effectiveness," *Journal of Applied Psychology* 92, no. 2 (2007), pp. 347–355.

22. L. I. Spirling and R. Persaud, "Extraversion as a Risk Factor," *Journal of the American Academy of Child & Adolescent Psychiatry* 42, no. 2 (2003), p. 130.

23. B. Weiss, and R. S. Feldman, "Looking Good and Lying to Do It: Deception as an Impression Management Strategy in Job Interviews," *Journal of Applied Social Psychology* 36, no. 4 (2006), pp. 1070–1086.

24. J. A. LePine, J. A. Colquitt, and A. Erez, "Adaptability to Changing Task Contexts: Effects of General Cognitive Ability, Conscientiousness, and Openness to Experience," *Personnel Psychology* 53, no. 3 (2000), pp. 563–595; S. Clarke and I. Robertson, "An Examination of the Role of Personality in Accidents Using Meta-Analysis," *Applied Psychology: An International Review* 57, no. 1 (2008), pp. 94–108; M. Baer, "The Strength-of-Weak-Ties Perspective on Creativity: A Comprehensive Examination and Extension," *Journal of Applied Psychology* 95, no. 3 (2010), pp. 592–601.

25. R. Ilies, I. S. Fulmer, M. Spitzmuller, and M. D. Johnson, "Personality and Citizenship Behavior: The Mediating Role of Job Satisfaction," *Journal of Applied Psychology* 94, no. 4 (2009), pp. 945–959.

26. See, for instance, S. Yamagata, A. Suzuki, J. Ando, Y. Ono, K. Yutaka, N. Kijima, et al., "Is the Genetic Structure of Human Personality Universal? A Cross-Cultural Twin Study from North America, Europe, and Asia," *Journal of Personality and Social Psychology* 90, no. 6 (2006), pp. 987–998; H. C. Triandis and E. M. Suh, "Cultural Influences on Personality," *Annual Review of Psychology* 53, no. 1 (2002), pp. 133–160; and R. R. McCrae, P. T. Costa Jr., T. A. Martin, V. E. Oryol, A. A. Rukavishnikov, I. G. Senin, et al., "Consensual Validation of Personality Traits Across Cultures," *Journal of Research in Personality* 38, no. 2 (2004), pp. 179–201.

27. A. T. Church and M. S. Katigbak, "Trait Psychology in the Philippines," *American Behavioral Scientist* 44, no. 1, (2000), pp. 73–94.

28. J. F. Salgado, "The Five Factor Model of Personality and Job Performance in the European Community," *Journal of Applied Psychology* 82, no. 1 (1997), pp. 30–43.

29. T. A. Judge and J. E. Bono, "A Rose by Any Other Name . . . Are Self-Esteem, Generalized Self-Efficacy, Neuroticism, and Locus of Control Indicators of a Common Construct?" in B. W. Roberts and R. Hogan (eds.), *Personality Psychology in the Workplace* (Washington, DC: American Psychological Association, 2001), pp. 93–118.

30. A. Erez and T. A. Judge, "Relationship of Core Self-Evaluations to Goal Setting, Motivation, and Performance," *Journal of Applied Psychology* 86, no. 6 (2001), pp. 1270–1279.

31. A. N. Salvaggio, B. Schneider, L. H. Nishi, D. M. Mayer, A. Ramesh, and J. S. Lyon, "Manager Personality, Manager Service Quality Orientation, and Service Climate: Test of a Model," *Journal of Applied Psychology* 92, no. 6 (2007), pp. 1741–1750; B. A. Scott and T. A. Judge, "The Popularity Contest at Work: Who Wins, Why, and What Do They Receive?" *Journal of Applied Psychology* 94, no. 1 (2009), pp. 20–33; and T. A. Judge and C. Hurst, "How the Rich (and Happy) Get Richer (and Happier): Relationship of Core Self-Evaluations to Trajectories in Attaining Work Success," *Journal of Applied Psychology* 93, no. 4 (2008), pp. 849–863.

32. A. M. Grant and A. Wrzesniewksi, "I Won't Let You Down . . . or Will I? Core Self-Evaluations, Other-Orientation, Anticipated Guilt and Gratitude, and Job Performance," *Journal of Applied Psychology* 95, no. 1 (2010), pp. 108–121.

33. U. Malmendier and G. Tate, "CEO Overconfidence and Corporate Investment," *Journal of Finance* 60, no. 6 (2005), pp. 2661–2700.

34. R. Sandomir, "Star Struck," *The New York Times* (January 12, 2007), pp. C10, C14.

35. R. Christie and F. L. Geis, *Studies in Machiavellianism* (New York: Academic Press, 1970), p. 312; and S. R. Kessler, A. C. Bandelli, P. E. Spector, W. C. Borman, C. E. Nelson, L. M. Penney, "Re-Examining Machiavelli: A Three-Dimensional Model of Machiavellianism in the Workplace," *Journal of Applied Social Psychology* 40, no. 8 (2010), pp. 1868–1896.

36. J. J. Dahling, B. G. Whitaker, and P. E. Levy, "The Development and Validation of a New Machiavellianism Scale," *Journal of Management* 35, no. 2 (2009), pp. 219–257.

37. Christie and Geis, *Studies in Machiavellianism.*

38. P. Cramer and C. J. Jones, "Narcissism, Identification, and Longitudinal Change in Psychological Health: Dynamic Predictions," *Journal of Research in Personality* 42, no. 5 (2008), pp. 1148–1159; B. M. Galvin, D. A. Waldman, and P. Balthazard, "Visionary Communication Qualities as Mediators of the Relationship between Narcissism and Attributions of Leader Charisma," *Personnel Psychology* 63, no. 3 (2010), pp. 509–537; and T. A. Judge, R. F. Piccolo, and T. Kosalka, "The Bright and Dark Sides of Leader Traits: A Review and Theoretical Extension of the Leader Trait Paradigm," *The Leadership Quarterly* 20, no. 6 (2009), pp. 855–875.

39. M. Maccoby, "Narcissistic Leaders: The Incredible Pros, the Inevitable Cons," *The Harvard Business Review* (January–February 2000), pp. 69–77, www.maccoby.com/Articles/NarLeaders.shtml.

40. W. K. Campbell and C. A. Foster, "Narcissism and Commitment in Romantic Relationships: An Investment Model Analysis," *Personality and Social Psychology Bulletin* 28, no. 4 (2002), pp. 484–495.

41. T. A. Judge, J. A. LePine, and B. L. Rich, "The Narcissistic Personality: Relationship with Inflated Self-Ratings of Leadership and with Task and Contextual Performance," *Journal of Applied Psychology* 91, no. 4 (2006), pp. 762–776.

42. C. J. Resick, D. S. Whitman, S. M. Weingarden, and N. J. Hiller, "The Bright-Side and Dark-Side of CEO Personality: Examining Core Self-Evaluations, Narcissism, Transformational Leadership, and Strategic Influence," *Journal of Applied Psychology* 94, no. 6 (2009), pp. 1365–1381.

43. See M. Snyder, *Public Appearances/Private Realities: The Psychology of Self-Monitoring* (New York: W. H. Freeman, 1987); and S. W. Gangestad and M. Snyder, "Self-Monitoring: Appraisal and Reappraisal," *Psychological Bulletin* 126, no. 4 (2000), pp. 530–555.

44. F. J. Flynn and D. R. Ames, "What's Good for the Goose May Not Be as Good for the Gander: The Benefits of Self-Monitoring for Men and Women in Task Groups and Dyadic Conflicts," *Journal of Applied Psychology* 91, no. 2 (2006), pp. 272–281; and Snyder, *Public Appearances/ Private Realities*.

45. D. V. Day, D. J. Shleicher, A. L. Unckless, and N. J. Hiller, "Self-Monitoring Personality at Work: A Meta-Analytic Investigation of Construct Validity," *Journal of Applied Psychology* 87, no. 2 (2002), pp. 390–401.

46. H. Oh and M. Kilduff, "The Ripple Effect of Personality on Social Structure: Self-monitoring Origins of Network Brokerage," *Journal of Applied Psychology* 93, no. 5 (2008), pp. 1155–1164; and A. Mehra, M. Kilduff, and D. J. Brass, "The Social Networks of High and Low Self-Monitors: Implications for Workplace Performance," *Administrative Science Quarterly* 46, no. 1 (2001), pp. 121–146.

47. E. Reeve, "A History of Donald Trump's Net Worth Publicity," The Atlantic, (April 21, 2011), www.theatlanticwire.com.

48. R. N. Taylor and M. D. Dunnette, "Influence of Dogmatism, Risk-Taking Propensity, and Intelligence on Decision-Making Strategies for a Sample of Industrial Managers," *Journal of Applied Psychology* 59, no. 4 (1974), pp. 420–423.

49. I. L. Janis and L. Mann, *Decision Making: A Psychological Analysis of Conflict, Choice, and Commitment* (New York: The Free Press, 1977); W. H. Stewart Jr. and L. Roth, "Risk Propensity Differences Between Entrepreneurs and Managers: A Meta-Analytic Review," *Journal of Applied Psychology* 86, no. 1 (2001), pp. 145–153; J. B. Miner and N. S. Raju, "Risk Propensity Differences Between Managers and Entrepreneurs and Between Low- and High-Growth Entrepreneurs: A Reply in a More Conservative Vein," *Journal of Applied Psychology* 89, no. 1 (2004), pp. 3–13; and W. H. Stewart Jr. and P. L. Roth, "Data Quality Affects Meta-Analytic Conclusions: A Response to Miner and Raju (2004) Concerning Entrepreneurial Risk Propensity," *Journal of Applied Psychology* 89, no. 1 (2004), pp. 14–21.

50. J. K. Maner, J. A. Richey, K. Cromer, M. Mallott, C. W. Lejuez, T. E. Joiner, and N. B. Schmidt, "Dispositional Anxiety and Risk-Avoidant Decision Making," *Personality and Individual Differences* 42, no. 4 (2007), pp. 665–675.

51. J. M. Crant, "Proactive Behavior in Organizations," *Journal of Management* 26, no. 3 (2000), p. 436.

52. S. E. Seibert, M. L. Kraimer, and J. M. Crant, "What Do Proactive People Do? A Longitudinal Model Linking Proactive Personality and Career Success," *Personnel Psychology* 54, no. 4 (2001), pp. 845–874.

53. T. S. Bateman and J. M. Crant, "The Proactive Component of Organizational Behavior: A Measure and Correlates," *Journal of Organizational Behavior* 14, no. 2 (1993), pp. 103–118; and J. M. Crant and T. S. Bateman, "Charismatic Leadership Viewed from Above: The Impact of Proactive Personality," *Journal of Organizational Behavior* 21, no. 1 (2000), pp. 63–75.

54. N. Li, J. Liang, and J. M. Crant, "The Role of Proactive Personality in Job Satisfaction and Organizational Citizenship Behavior: A Relational Perspective," *Journal of Applied Psychology* 95, no. 2 (2010), pp. 395–404.

55. Crant, "Proactive Behavior in Organizations," p. 436.

56. See, for instance, R. C. Becherer and J. G. Maurer, "The Proactive Personality Disposition and Entrepreneurial Behavior Among Small Company Presidents," *Journal of Small Business Management* 37, no. 1 (1999), pp. 28–36.

57. S. E. Seibert, J. M. Crant, and M. L. Kraimer, "Proactive Personality and Career Success," *Journal of Applied Psychology* 84, no. 3 (1999), pp. 416–427; Seibert, Kraimer, and Crant, "What Do Proactive People Do?" p. 850; D. J. Brown, R. T. Cober, K. Kane, P. E. Levy, and J. Shalhoop, "Proactive Personality and the Successful Job Search: A Field Investigation with College Graduates," *Journal of Applied Psychology* 91, no. 3 (2006), pp. 717–726; and J. D. Kammeyer-Mueller and C. R. Wanberg, "Unwrapping the Organizational Entry Process: Disentangling Multiple Antecedents and Their Pathways to Adjustment," *Journal of Applied Psychology* 88, no. 5 (2003), pp. 779–794.

58. B. M. Meglino and M. A. Korsgaard, "Considering Situational and Dispositional Approaches to Rational Self-Interest: An Extension and Response to De Dreu (2006)," *Journal of Applied Psychology* 91, no. 6 (2006), pp. 1253-1259; and B. M. Meglino and M. A. Korsgaard, "Considering Rational Self-Interest as a Disposition: Organizational Implications of Other Orientation," *Journal of Applied Psychology* 89, no. 6 (2004), pp. 946–959.

59. M. A. Korsgaard, B. M. Meglino, S. W. Lester, and S. S. Jeong, "Paying You Back or Paying Me Forward: Understanding Rewarded and Unrewarded Organizational Citizenship Behavior," *Journal of Applied Psychology* 95, no. 2 (2010), pp. 277–290.

60. Grant and Wrzesniewski, "I Won't Let You Down . . . Or Will I?; C. K. W. De Dreu, "Self-Interest and Other-Orientation in Organizational Behavior: Implications for Job Performance, Prosocial Behavior, and Personal Initiative," *Journal of Applied Psychology* 94, no. 4 (2009), pp. 913–926.

61. M. Rokeach, *The Nature of Human Values* (New York: The Free Press, 1973), p. 5.

62. M. Rokeach and S. J. Ball-Rokeach, "Stability and Change in American Value Priorities, 1968–1981," *American Psychologist* 44, no. 5 (1989), pp. 775–784; and A. Bardi, J. A. Lee, N. Hofmann-Towfigh, and G. Soutar, "The Structure of Intraindividual Value Change," *Journal of Personality and Social Psychology* 97, no. 5 (2009), pp. 913–929.

63. S. Roccas, L. Sagiv, S. H. Schwartz, and A. Knafo, "The Big Five Personality Factors and Personal Values," *Personality and Social Psychology Bulletin* 28, no. 6 (2002), pp. 789–801.

64. See, for instance, B. M. Meglino and E. C. Ravlin, "Individual Values in Organizations: Concepts, Controversies, and Research," *Journal of Management* 24, no. 3 (1998), p. 355.

65. Rokeach, *The Nature of Human Values*, p. 6.

66. J. M. Munson and B. Z. Posner, "The Factorial Validity of a Modified Rokeach Value Survey for Four Diverse Samples," *Educational and Psychological Measurement* 40, no. 4 (1980), pp. 1073–1079; and W. C. Frederick and J. Weber, "The Values of Corporate Managers and Their Critics: An Empirical Description and Normative Implications," in W. C. Frederick and L. E. Preston (eds.), *Business Ethics: Research Issues and Empirical Studies* (Greenwich, CT: JAI Press, 1990), pp. 123–144.

67. Frederick and Weber, "The Values of Corporate Managers and Their Critics," pp. 123–144.

68. Ibid., p. 132.

69. See, for example, N. R. Lockwood, F. R. Cepero, and S. Williams, *The Multigenerational Workforce* (Alexandria, VA: Society for Human Resource Management, 2009).

70. K. W. Smola and C. D. Sutton, "Generational Differences: Revisiting Generational Work Values for the New Millennium," *Journal of Organizational Behavior* 23, Special Issue (2002), pp. 363–382; and R. F. Inglehart, "Changing Values Among Western Publics from 1970 to 2006," *West European Politics* 31, no. 1 & 2 (2008), pp. 130–146.

71. B. Hite, "Employers Rethink How They Give Feedback," *The Wall Street Journal* (October 13, 2008), p. B5.

72. E. Parry and P. Urwin, "Generational Differences in Work Values: A Review of Theory and Evidence," *International Journal of Management Reviews* 13, no. 1 (2011), pp. 79–96.

73. J. M. Twenge, S. M. Campbell, B. J. Hoffman, and C. E. Lance, "Generational Differences in Work Values: Leisure and Extrinsic Values Increasing, Social and Intrinsic Values Decreasing," *Journal of Management* 36, no. 5 (2010), pp. 1117–1142.

74. J. L. Holland, *Making Vocational Choices: A Theory of Vocational Personalities and Work Environments* (Odessa, FL: Psychological Assessment Resources, 1997).

75. See, for example, J. L. Holland and G. D. Gottfredson, "Studies of the Hexagonal Model: An Evaluation (or, The Perils of Stalking the Perfect Hexagon)," *Journal of Vocational Behavior* 40, no. 2 (1992), pp. 158–170; and T. J. Tracey and J. Rounds, "Evaluating Holland's and Gati's Vocational-Interest Models: A Structural Meta-Analysis," *Psychological Bulletin* 113, no. 2 (1993), pp. 229–246.

76. C. H. Van Iddekinge, D. J. Putka, and J. P. Campbell, "Reconsidering Vocational Interests for Personnel Selection: The Validity of an Interest-Based Selection Test in Relation to Job Knowledge, Job Performance, and Continuance Intentions," *Journal of Applied Psychology* 96, no. 1 (2011), pp. 13–33.

77. S. A. Woods and S. E. Hampson, "Predicting Adult Occupational Environments from Gender and Childhood Personality Traits," *Journal of Applied Psychology* 95, no. 6 (2010), pp. 1045–1057.

78. See B. Schneider, H. W. Goldstein, and D. B. Smith, "The ASA Framework: An Update," *Personnel Psychology* 48, no. 4 (1995), pp. 747–773; B. Schneider, D. B. Smith, S. Taylor, and J. Fleenor, "Personality and Organizations: A Test of the Homogeneity of Personality Hypothesis," *Journal of Applied Psychology* 83, no. 3 (1998), pp. 462–470; W. Arthur Jr., S. T. Bell, A. J. Villado, and D. Doverspike, "The Use of Person-Organization Fit in Employment Decision-Making: An Assessment of Its Criterion-Related Validity," *Journal of Applied Psychology* 91, no. 4 (2006), pp. 786–801; and J. R. Edwards, D. M. Cable, I. O. Williamson, L. S. Lambert, and A. J. Shipp, "The Phenomenology of Fit: Linking the Person and Environment to the Subjective Experience of Person–Environment Fit," *Journal of Applied Psychology* 91, no. 4 (2006), pp. 802–827.

79. Based on T. A. Judge and D. M. Cable, "Applicant Personality, Organizational Culture, and Organization Attraction," *Personnel Psychology* 50, no. 2 (1997), pp. 359–394.

80. M. L. Verquer, T. A. Beehr, and S. E. Wagner, "A Meta-Analysis of Relations Between Person–Organization Fit and Work Attitudes," *Journal of Vocational Behavior* 63, no. 3 (2003), pp. 473–489; and J. C. Carr, A. W. Pearson, M. J. Vest, and S. L. Boyar, "Prior Occupational Experience, Anticipatory Socialization, and Employee Retention, *Journal of Management* 32, no. 32 (2006), pp. 343–359.

81. A. Ramesh and M. J. Gelfand, "Will They Stay or Will They Go? The Role of Job Embeddedness in Predicting Turnover in Individualistic and Collectivistic Cultures," *Journal of Applied Psychology* 95, no. 5 (2010), pp. 807–823.

82. G. Hofstede, *Cultures and Organizations: Software of the Mind* (London: McGraw-Hill, 1991); G. Hofstede, "Cultural Constraints in Management Theories," *Academy of Management Executive* 7, no. 1 (1993), pp. 81–94; G. Hofstede and M. F. Peterson, "National Values and Organizational Practices," in N. M. Ashkanasy, C. M. Wilderom, and M. F. Peterson (eds.), *Handbook of Organizational Culture and Climate* (Thousand Oaks, CA: Sage, 2000), pp. 401–416; and G. Hofstede, *Culture's Consequences: Comparing Values, Behaviors, Institutions, and Organizations Across Nations*, 2nd ed. (Thousand Oaks, CA: Sage, 2001). For criticism of this research, see B. McSweeney, "Hofstede's Model of National Cultural Differences and Their Consequences: A Triumph of Faith—A Failure of Analysis," *Human Relations* 55, no. 1 (2002), pp. 89–118.

83. G. Ailon, "Mirror, Mirror on the Wall: *Culture's Consequences* in a Value Test of Its Own Design," *Academy of Management Review* 33, no. 4 (2008), pp. 885–904; M. H. Bond, "Reclaiming the Individual from Hofstede's Ecological Analysis—A 20-Year Odyssey: Comment on Oyserman et al. (2002), *Psychological Bulletin* 128, no. 1 (2002), pp. 73–77; and G. Hofstede, "The Pitfalls of Cross-National Survey Research: A Reply to the Article by Spector et al. on the Psychometric Properties of the Hofstede Values Survey Module 1994," *Applied Psychology: An International Review* 51, no. 1 (2002), pp. 170–178.

84. V. Taras, B. L. Kirkman, and P. Steel, "Examining the Impact of Culture's Consequences: A Three-Decade, Multilevel,

Meta-Analytic Review of Hofstede's Cultural Value Dimensions," *Journal of Applied Psychology* 95, no. 5 (2010), pp. 405–439.

85. M. Javidan and R. J. House, "Cultural Acumen for the Global Manager: Lessons from Project GLOBE," *Organizational Dynamics* 29, no. 4 (2001), pp. 289–305; and R. J. House, P. J. Hanges, M. Javidan, and P. W. Dorfman (eds.), *Leadership, Culture, and Organizations: The GLOBE Study of 62 Societies* (Thousand Oaks, CA: Sage, 2004).

86. P. C. Early, "Leading Cultural Research in the Future: A Matter of Paradigms and Taste," *Journal of International Business Studies* 37, no. 6 (2006), pp. 922–931; G. Hofstede, "What Did GLOBE Really Measure? Researchers' Minds Versus Respondents' Minds," *Journal of International Business Studies* 37, no. 6 (2006), pp. 882–896; and M. Javidan, R. J. House, P. W. Dorfman, P. J. Hanges, and M. S. de Luque, "Conceptualizing and Measuring Cultures and Their Consequences: A Comparative Review of GLOBE's and Hofstede's Approaches,"

Journal of International Business Studies 37, no. 6 (2006), pp. 897–914.

87. L. A. Witt, "The Interactive Effects of Extraversion and Conscientiousness on Performance," *Journal of Management* 28, no. 6 (2002), p. 836.

88. R. P. Tett and D. D. Burnett, "A Personality Trait–Based Interactionist Model of Job Performance," *Journal of Applied Psychology* 88, no. 3 (2003), pp. 500–517.

89. B. Adkins and D. Caldwell, "Firm or Subgroup Culture: Where Does Fitting in Matter Most?" *Journal of Organizational Behavior* 25, no. 8 (2004), pp. 969–978; H. D. Cooper-Thomas, A. van Vianen, and N. Anderson, "Changes in Person–Organization Fit: The Impact of Socialization Tactics on Perceived and Actual P–O Fit," *European Journal of Work & Organizational Psychology* 13, no. 1 (2004), pp. 52–78; and C. A. O'Reilly, J. Chatman, and D. F. Caldwell, "People and Organizational Culture: A Profile Comparison Approach to Assessing Person–Organization Fit," *Academy of Management Journal* 34, no. 3 (1991), pp. 487–516.

DO MACHINES MAKE BETTER DECISIONS?

Hedge fund managers are unlike other people in ways that are fairly obvious. Typically, they are unusually quantitatively oriented and not made uncomfortable with the thought of losing thousands or even millions of dollars on a bet gone bad. Their careers may rise or fall based on factors over which they have little control.

Even in this unusual group, Spencer Greenberg is unusual. Only 27, he is chief executive and co-chair of a Manhattan investment firm. After graduating from Columbia Business School, Greenberg founded Rebellion Research Technologies with two other recent Amherst College graduates (Alexander Fleiss and Jonathan Sturges) and another partner (Jeremy Newton) who was still in college. Greenberg and his compatriots are, of course, very young to be leading a New York investment firm. What is even more interesting is the way they're doing it.

All investment bankers and hedge fund managers are comfortable with analytics. What makes Rebellion unusual is the degree to which the firm has taken them. The firm uses computers to actually make buy, sell, or hold decisions and to learn from its mistakes. "It's pretty clear that human beings aren't improving," says Greenberg. "But computers and algorithms are only getting more robust."

Based on the returns Rebellion has been able to generate, other companies, including Cerebellum Capital and RGM Advisors, have followed suit. The computers outperform humans, their advocates say, because they can crunch numbers more quickly, "learn" what works, and adapt more readily and objectively. Rebellion's program analyzes more than a decade of financial activity and the latest market results to evaluate stocks. When buy, sell, or hold decisions stop working, the computer adjusts by automatically incorporating new information. Rebellion's leaders have faith in their artificial intelligence (AI). "I've learned not to question the AI," says Fleiss.

Machines are not only taking over financial decision making. From flying airplanes to making medical decisions to running nuclear power plants, computers are gradually supplanting and even replacing human judgment.

Not everyone is convinced that AI always improves on human judgment and decision making. Some argue that reliance on computers makes complex systems more susceptible to errors because no computer can anticipate every scenario, and humans function less well as the passive monitors

Perception and Individual Decision Making

*Indecision may or may not
be my problem.*

—Jimmy Buffett

into which AI makes them. Says an observer of one complex system—airline piloting, "When the person has no role in the task, there's a much greater risk of complacency."

Sources: A. Shell, "Wall Street Traders Mine Tweets to Gain a Trading Edge," *USA Today* (May 4, 2011), downloaded May 23, 2011, from www.usatoday.com/money/; "Soon, Your Computer Will Have Emotions Like You," *The Economic Times* (April 20, 2011), downloaded May 23, 2011, from http://articles.economictimes.indiatimes.com; S. Patterson, "Letting the Machines Decide," *The Wall Street Journal* (July 14, 2010), p. C1; and C. Negroni, "As Attention Wanders, Second Thoughts About the Autopilot," *The New York Times* (May 18, 2010), pp. B1, B5.

The preceding example illustrates some of the issues that arise when people look for techniques to improve their decision making. One reason some like computerized decision making is that human decision makers can be incorrect or biased in many ways. This chapter will review some of these biases in human decision making, but it also explores how human decision makers can outperform machines, especially in the area of creativity.

In the following Self-Assessment Library, consider one perception—that of appropriate gender roles.

SELF-ASSESSMENT LIBRARY

What Are My Gender Role Perceptions?

In the Self-Assessment Library (available on CD or online), take assessment IV.C.2 (What Are My Gender Role Perceptions?) and answer the following questions.

1. Did you score as high as you thought you would?
2. Do you think a problem with measures like this is that people aren't honest in responding?
3. If others, such as friends, classmates, and family members, rated you, would they rate you differently? Why or why not?
4. Research has shown that people's gender role perceptions are becoming less traditional over time. Why do you suppose this is so?

What Is Perception?

1 Define *perception* and explain the factors that influence it.

Perception is a process by which individuals organize and interpret their sensory impressions in order to give meaning to their environment. However, what we perceive can be substantially different from objective reality. For example, all employees in a firm may view it as a great place to work—favorable working conditions, interesting job assignments, good pay, excellent benefits, understanding and responsible management—but, as most of us know, it's very unusual to find such agreement.

Why is perception important in the study of OB? Simply because people's behavior is based on their perception of what reality is, not on reality itself. *The world as it is perceived is the world that is behaviorally important.*

Factors That Influence Perception

How do we explain the fact that individuals may look at the same thing yet perceive it differently? A number of factors operate to shape and sometimes distort perception. These factors can reside in the *perceiver;* in the object, or *target,* being perceived; or in the context of the *situation* in which the perception is made (see Exhibit 6-1).

When you look at a target and attempt to interpret what you see, your interpretation is heavily influenced by your personal characteristics—your attitudes, personality, motives, interests, past experiences, and expectations. For instance, if you expect police officers to be authoritative or young people to be lazy, you may perceive them as such, regardless of their actual traits.

Characteristics of the target also affect what we perceive. Loud people are more likely to be noticed in a group than quiet ones. So, too, are extremely attractive or unattractive individuals. Because we don't look at targets in isolation, the relationship of a target to its background also influences perception, as does our tendency to group close things and similar things together. We often perceive women, men, Whites, African Americans, Asians, or members of any other group that has clearly distinguishable characteristics as alike in other, unrelated ways as well.

Context matters too. The time at which we see an object or event can influence our attention, as can location, light, heat, or any number of situational factors. At a nightclub on Saturday night, you may not notice a young guest "dressed to the nines." Yet that same person so attired for your Monday morning management class would certainly catch your attention (and that of the rest of the class). Neither the perceiver nor the target has changed between Saturday night and Monday morning, but the situation is different.

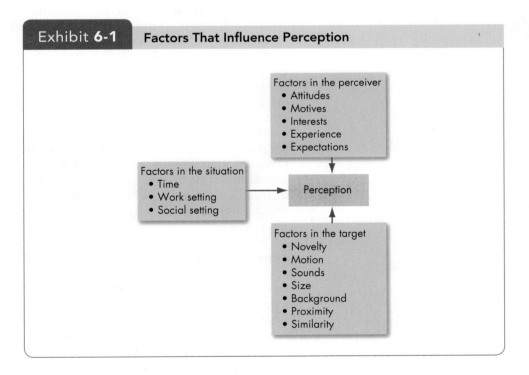

| Exhibit **6-1** | Factors That Influence Perception |

perception *A process by which individuals organize and interpret their sensory impressions in order to give meaning to their environment.*

Person Perception: Making Judgments About Others

Now we turn to the application of perception concepts most relevant to OB—*person perception,* or the perceptions people form about each other.

Attribution Theory

2   Explain attribution theory and list the three determinants of attribution.

Nonliving objects such as desks, machines, and buildings are subject to the laws of nature, but they have no beliefs, motives, or intentions. People do. That's why when we observe people, we attempt to explain why they behave in certain ways. Our perception and judgment of a person's actions, therefore, will be significantly influenced by the assumptions we make about that person's internal state.

Attribution theory tries to explain the ways in which we judge people differently, depending on the meaning we attribute to a given behavior.[1] It suggests that when we observe an individual's behavior, we attempt to determine whether it was internally or externally caused. That determination, however, depends largely on three factors: (1) distinctiveness, (2) consensus, and (3) consistency. First, let's clarify the differences between internal and external causation, and then we'll elaborate on each of the three determining factors.

Internally caused behaviors are those we believe to be under the personal control of the individual. *Externally* caused behavior is what we imagine the situation forced the individual to do. If one of your employees is late for work, you might attribute that to his partying into the wee hours and then oversleeping. This is an internal attribution. But if you attribute lateness to an automobile accident that tied up traffic, you are making an external attribution.

Now let's discuss the three determining factors. *Distinctiveness* refers to whether an individual displays different behaviors in different situations. Is the employee who arrives late today also one who regularly "blows off" commitments? What we want to know is whether this behavior is unusual. If it is, we are likely to give it an external attribution. If it's not, we will probably judge the behavior to be internal.

If everyone who faces a similar situation responds in the same way, we can say the behavior shows *consensus.* The behavior of our tardy employee meets this criterion if all employees who took the same route were also late. From an attribution perspective, if consensus is high, you would probably give an external attribution to the employee's tardiness, whereas if other employees who took the same route made it to work on time, you would attribute his lateness to an internal cause.

Finally, an observer looks for *consistency* in a person's actions. Does the person respond the same way over time? Coming in 10 minutes late for work is not perceived in the same way for an employee who hasn't been late for several months as it is for an employee who is late two or three times a week. The more consistent the behavior, the more we are inclined to attribute it to internal causes.

Exhibit 6-2 summarizes the key elements in attribution theory. It tells us, for instance, that if an employee, Kim Randolph, generally performs at about the same level on related tasks as she does on her current task (low distinctiveness), other employees frequently perform differently—better or worse—than Kim on that task (low consensus), and Kim's performance on this current task is consistent over time (high consistency), anyone judging Kim's work will likely hold her primarily responsible for her task performance (internal attribution).

Exhibit 6-2   Attribution Theory

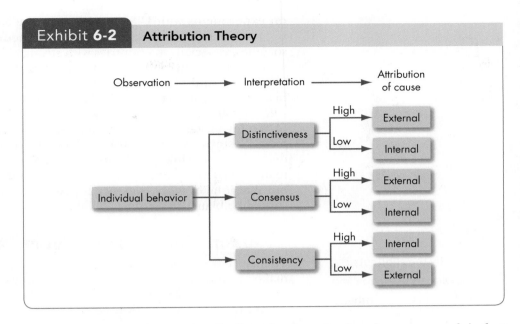

One of the most interesting findings from attribution theory research is that errors or biases distort attributions. When we make judgments about the behavior of other people, we tend to underestimate the influence of external factors and overestimate the influence of internal or personal factors.[2] This **fundamental attribution error** can explain why a sales manager is prone to attribute the poor performance of her sales agents to laziness rather than to the innovative product line introduced by a competitor. Individuals and organizations also tend to attribute their own successes to internal factors such as ability or effort, while blaming failure on external factors such as bad luck or unproductive co-workers. People also tend to attribute ambiguous information as relatively flattering and accept positive feedback while rejecting negative feedback. This is the **self-serving bias**.[3] A *U.S. News & World Report* study showed its power. Researchers asked one group of people "If someone sues you and you win the case, should he pay your legal costs?" Eighty-five percent responded "yes." Another group was asked "If you sue someone and lose the case, should you pay his costs?" Only 44 percent answered "yes."[4]

The evidence on cultural differences in perception is mixed, but most suggest there *are* differences across cultures in the attributions people make.[5] One study found Korean managers less likely to use the self-serving bias—they tended to accept responsibility for group failure "because I was not a capable leader" instead of attributing failure to group members.[6] On the other hand, Asian managers are more likely to blame institutions or whole organizations, whereas Western observers believe individual managers should get blame or praise.[7] That probably explains why U.S. newspapers prominently report the names of individual executives when firms do poorly, whereas Asian media cover how the firm as a whole has failed. This tendency to make group-based attributions also explains why individuals from Asian cultures are more likely to make group-based stereotypes.[8] Attribution theory was developed largely based

---

attribution theory   *An attempt to determine whether an individual's behavior is internally or externally caused.*

fundamental attribution error   *The tendency to underestimate the influence of external factors and overestimate the influence of internal factors when making judgments about the behavior of others.*

self-serving bias   *The tendency for individuals to attribute their own successes to internal factors and put the blame for failures on external factors.*

on experiments with U.S. and Western European workers. But these studies suggest caution in making attribution theory predictions in non-Western societies, especially in countries with strong collectivist traditions.

Differences in attribution tendencies don't mean the basic concepts of attribution and blame completely differ across cultures, though. Self-serving biases may be less common in East Asian cultures, but evidence suggests they still operate across cultures.[9] Recent studies indicate Chinese managers assess blame for mistakes using the same distinctiveness, consensus, and consistency cues Western managers use.[10] They also become angry and punish those deemed responsible for failure, a reaction shown in many studies of Western managers. This means the basic process of attribution applies across cultures, but that it takes more evidence for Asian managers to conclude someone else should be blamed.

Common Shortcuts in Judging Others

3 Identify the shortcuts individuals use in making judgments about others.

The shortcuts we use in judging others are frequently valuable: they allow us to make accurate perceptions rapidly and provide valid data for making predictions. However, they are not foolproof. They can and do get us into trouble when they result in significant distortions.

Selective Perception   Any characteristic that makes a person, an object, or an event stand out will increase the probability we will perceive it. Why? Because it is impossible for us to assimilate everything we see; we can take in only certain stimuli. This explains why you're more likely to notice cars like your own, or why a boss may reprimand some people and not others doing the same thing. Because we can't observe everything going on about us, we engage in **selective perception**. A classic example shows how vested interests can significantly influence which problems we see.

Dearborn and Simon asked 23 business executives (6 in sales, 5 in production, 4 in accounting, and 8 in miscellaneous functions) to read a comprehensive case describing the organization and activities of a steel company.[11] Each manager was asked to write down the most important problem in the case. Eighty-three percent of the sales executives rated sales important; only 29 percent of the others did so. The researchers concluded that participants perceived as important the aspects of a situation specifically related to their own unit's activities and goals. A group's perception of organizational activities is selectively altered to align with the vested interests the group represents.

Because we cannot assimilate all that we observe, we take in bits and pieces. But we don't choose randomly; rather, we select according to our interests, background, experience, and attitudes. Selective perception allows us to speed-read others, but not without the risk of drawing an inaccurate picture. Seeing what we want to see, we can draw unwarranted conclusions from an ambiguous situation.

We find another example of selective perception in financial analysis. From 2007 to 2009, the U.S. stock market lost roughly half its value. Yet during that time, analysts' sell ratings (typically, analysts rate a company's stock with three recommendations: buy, sell, or hold) actually *decreased* slightly. Although there are several reasons analysts are reluctant to put sell ratings on stocks, one is selective perception. When prices are going down, analysts often attend to the past (saying the stock is a bargain relative to its prior price), rather than the future (the downward trend may well continue). As one money manager noted, "Each time the market went down was a new opportunity to buy the stock even cheaper."[12] That much is true, of course, but it shows the dangers of selective perception: by looking only at the past price, analysts were relying on a false reference point and failing to recognize that what has fallen can fall further still.

Chinese Time, North American Time

We realize just how much we take our perceptions of the world for granted when we try to see through the eyes of someone who grew up in a culture totally different from our own.

For instance, people see the passage of time quite differently in different cultures. Some cultures tend to focus more on the past, others on the future. Li-Jun Ji and colleagues investigated how Chinese perceive events relative to Canadians' perceptions. Participants read a description of a theft, along with descriptions of events that occurred in the distant past, recent past, or present. When attempting to solve the case, Chinese participants were more likely to rely on events from the distant past and recent past, whereas Canadians were more attentive to recent events.

Even the way we visualize the passage of time differs across cultures. Lera Boroditsky, Orly Fuhrman, and Kelly McCormick from Stanford University examined how American English speakers and Mandarin (Chinese) speakers differed in their perception of time. Because English uses phrases like "looking forward to" events or "putting the past behind us," English speakers tend to think about time as a horizontal timeline. Mandarin however uses words like *shàng* (up) and *xià* (down) to refer to time, so events accumulate in a stack. Could this difference in language structure explain why Chinese speakers pay more attention to history when thinking about events? Do Chinese think more about events "piling up" on top of one another (making them more

relevant), whereas North Americans think about events moving away in time so that what is in the past is over and done? Further research will have to examine whether this is the case, but it remains an interesting possibility.

Sources: L. Ji, Z. Zhang, and D. Messervey, "Looking Into the Past: Cultural Differences in Perception and Representation of Past Information," *Journal of Personality and Social Psychology* 96, no. 4 (2009), pp. 761–769; L. Boroditsky, O. Fuhrman, and K. McCormick, "Do English and Mandarin Speakers Think about Time Differently?" *Cognition* 118, no. 1 (2011), pp. 123–129; and A. J. Shipp, J. R. Edwards, and L. S. Lambert, "Conceptualization and Measurement of Temporal Focus: The Subjective Experience of Past, Present, and Future," *Organizational Behavior and Human Decision Processes* 110, no. 1 (2009), pp. 1–22.

Halo Effect   When we draw a general impression about an individual on the basis of a single characteristic, such as intelligence, sociability, or appearance, a **halo effect** is operating.[13] If you're a critic of President Obama, try listing 10 things you admire about him. If you're an admirer, try listing 10 things you dislike about him. No matter which group describes you, odds are you won't find this an easy exercise! That's the halo effect: our general views contaminate our specific ones.

The reality of the halo effect was confirmed in a classic study in which subjects were given a list of traits such as intelligent, skillful, practical, industrious, determined, and warm and asked to evaluate the person to whom those traits applied.[14] Subjects judged the person to be wise, humorous, popular, and imaginative. When the same list was modified to include "cold" instead of "warm," a completely different picture emerged. Clearly, the subjects were allowing a single trait to influence their overall impression of the person they were judging.

Contrast Effects   An old adage among entertainers is "Never follow an act that has kids or animals in it." Why? Audiences love children and animals so much that you'll look bad in comparison. This example demonstrates how a **contrast effect** can distort perceptions. We don't evaluate a person in isolation. Our reaction is influenced by other persons we have recently encountered.

---

selective perception *The tendency to selectively interpret what one sees on the basis of one's interests, background, experience, and attitudes.*

halo effect *The tendency to draw a general impression about an individual on the basis of a single characteristic.*

contrast effect *Evaluation of a person's characteristics that is affected by comparisons with other people recently encountered who rank higher or lower on the same characteristics.*

In a series of job interviews, for instance, interviewers can make distortions in any given candidate's evaluation as a result of his or her place in the interview schedule. A candidate is likely to receive a more favorable evaluation if preceded by mediocre applicants and a less favorable evaluation if preceded by strong applicants.

Stereotyping   When we judge someone on the basis of our perception of the group to which he or she belongs, we are using the shortcut called **stereotyping**.[15]

We rely on generalizations every day because they help us make decisions quickly; they are a means of simplifying a complex world. It's less difficult to deal with an unmanageable number of stimuli if we use *heuristics* or stereotypes. For example, it does make sense to assume that Tre, the new employee from accounting, is going to know something about budgeting, or that Allie from finance will be able to help you figure out a forecasting problem. The problem occurs, of course, when we generalize inaccurately or too much. In organizations, we frequently hear comments that represent stereotypes based on gender, age, race, religion, ethnicity, and even weight (see Chapter 2):[16] "Men aren't interested in child care," "Older workers can't learn new skills," "Asian immigrants are hardworking and conscientious." A growing body of research suggests stereotypes operate emotionally and often below the level of conscious awareness, making them particularly hard to challenge and change.[17]

Stereotypes can be deeply ingrained and powerful enough to influence life-and-death decisions. One study, controlling for a wide array of factors (such as aggravating or mitigating circumstances), showed that the degree to which black defendants in murder trials looked "stereotypically black" essentially doubled their odds of receiving a death sentence if convicted.[18] Another experimental study found that students who read scenarios describing leaders tended to assign higher scores for leadership potential and effective leadership to Whites than to minorities even though the content of the scenarios was equivalent, supporting the idea of a stereotype of Whites as better leaders.[19]

These young women are taking part in a running test for employment in a police force in Peshawar, Pakistan. But women in America and European, Eastern European, Asian, and Latin American countries report that gender stereotyping makes it difficult for them to enter the profession because it is largely regarded as a job strictly for men. Even in countries like the United States where the law requires hiring police officers without regard to gender, the stereotypical view of women inaccurately generalizes them as lacking the mental, physical, and emotional fitness required to perform police work. But women who want to do police work contend that they satisfy the fitness requirements and even bring special qualities to the job such as compassion and good communication skills.

Source: Pakistan Press International Photo/Newscom

One problem of stereotypes is that they *are* widespread and often useful generalizations, though they may not contain a shred of truth when applied to a particular person or situation. So we constantly have to check ourselves to make sure we're not unfairly or inaccurately applying a stereotype in our evaluations and decisions. Stereotypes are an example of the warning "The more useful, the more danger from misuse."

Specific Applications of Shortcuts in Organizations

People in organizations are always judging each other. Managers must appraise their employees' performances. We evaluate how much effort our co-workers are putting into their jobs. Team members immediately "size up" a new person. In many cases, our judgments have important consequences for the organization. Let's look at the most obvious applications.

Employment Interview   Few people are hired without an interview. But interviewers make perceptual judgments that are often inaccurate[20] and draw early impressions that quickly become entrenched. Research shows we form impressions of others within a tenth of a second, based on our first glance.[21] If these first impressions are negative, they tend to be more heavily weighted in the interview than if that same information came out later.[22] Most interviewers' decisions change very little after the first 4 or 5 minutes of an interview. As a result, information elicited early in the interview carries greater weight than does information elicited later, and a "good applicant" is probably characterized more by the absence of unfavorable characteristics than by the presence of favorable ones.

Performance Expectations   People attempt to validate their perceptions of reality even when these are faulty.[23] The terms **self-fulfilling prophecy** and *Pygmalion effect* describe how an individual's behavior is determined by others' expectations. If a manager expects big things from her people, they're not likely to let her down. Similarly, if she expects only minimal performance, they'll likely meet those low expectations. Expectations become reality. The self-fulfilling prophecy has been found to affect the performance of students, soldiers, and even accountants.[24]

Performance Evaluation   We'll discuss performance evaluations more fully in Chapter 17, but note for now that they very much depend on the perceptual process.[25] An employee's future is closely tied to the appraisal—promotion, pay raises, and continuation of employment are among the most obvious outcomes. Although the appraisal can be objective (for example, a sales-person is appraised on how many dollars of sales he generates in his territory), many jobs are evaluated in subjective terms. Subjective evaluations, though often necessary, are problematic because all the errors we've discussed thus far—selective perception, contrast effects, halo effects, and so on—affect them. Ironically, sometimes performance ratings say as much about the evaluator as they do about the employee!

---

stereotyping   *Judging someone on the basis of one's perception of the group to which that person belongs.*

self-fulfilling prophecy   *A situation in which a person inaccurately perceives a second person, and the resulting expectations cause the second person to behave in ways consistent with the original perception.*

The Link Between Perception and Individual Decision Making

4   Explain the link between perception and decision making.

MyManagementLab
For an interactive application of this topic, check out this chapter's simulation activity at **www.pearsonglobaleditions.com/ mymanagementlab**.

Individuals in organizations make **decisions**, choices from among two or more alternatives. Top managers determine their organization's goals, what products or services to offer, how best to finance operations, or where to locate a new manufacturing plant. Middle- and lower-level managers set production schedules, select new employees, and decide how to allocate pay raises. Nonmanagerial employees decide how much effort to put forth at work and whether to comply with a boss's request. Organizations have begun empowering their nonmanagerial employees with decision-making authority historically reserved for managers alone. Individual decision making is thus an important part of organizational behavior. But the way individuals make decisions and the quality of their choices are largely influenced by their perceptions.

Decision making occurs as a reaction to a **problem**.[26] That is, a discrepancy exists between the current state of affairs and some desired state, requiring us to consider alternative courses of action. If your car breaks down and you rely on it to get to work, you have a problem that requires a decision on your part. Unfortunately, most problems don't come neatly labeled "problem." One person's *problem* is another person's *satisfactory state of affairs*. One manager may view her division's 2 percent decline in quarterly sales to be a serious problem requiring immediate action on her part. In contrast, her counterpart in another division, who also had a 2 percent sales decrease, might consider that quite acceptable. So awareness that a problem exists and that a decision might or might not be needed is a perceptual issue.

Every decision requires us to interpret and evaluate information. We typically receive data from multiple sources and need to screen, process, and interpret them. Which data are relevant to the decision, and which are not? Our perceptions will answer that question. We also need to develop alternatives and evaluate their strengths and weaknesses. Again, our perceptual

Delta Airlines management made a decision in reaction to the problem of negative publicity resulting from a growing number of customer complaints about poor service. To improve service, Delta reinstated the personal assistance of its elite Red Coat airport agents that it started in the 1960s but eliminated in 2005 due to budget cuts. The primary mission of the Red Coats, such as Charmaine Gordon shown here helping customers at Kennedy International Airport in New York, is to fix customer problems. Today, Delta has about 800 Red Coats who walk around airports and use hand-held devices to give one-on-one, on-the-spot help to customers in everything ranging from printing boarding passes to directing passengers to the right concourse.

Source: Jessica Ebelhar / The New York Times / Redux Pictures

process will affect the final outcome. Finally, throughout the entire decision-making process, perceptual distortions often surface that can bias analysis and conclusions.

Decision Making in Organizations

5 Apply the rational model of decision making and contrast it with bounded rationality and intuition.

Business schools generally train students to follow rational decision-making models. While models have considerable merit, they don't always describe how people actually make decisions. This is where OB enters the picture: to improve the way we make decisions in organizations, we must understand the decision-making errors people commit (in addition to the perception errors we've discussed). Next we describe these errors, beginning with a brief overview of the rational decision-making model.

The Rational Model, Bounded Rationality, and Intuition

Rational Decision Making   We often think the best decision maker is **rational** and makes consistent, value-maximizing choices within specified constraints.[27] These decisions follow a six-step **rational decision-making model**.[28] The six steps are listed in Exhibit 6-3.

The rational decision-making model relies on a number of assumptions, including that the decision maker has complete information, is able to identify all the relevant options in an unbiased manner, and chooses the option with the highest utility.[29] As you might imagine, most decisions in the real world don't follow the rational model. People are usually content to find an acceptable or reasonable solution to a problem rather than an optimal one. Choices tend to be limited to the neighborhood of the problem symptom and the current alternative. As one expert in decision making put it, "Most significant decisions are made by judgment, rather than by a defined prescriptive model."[30] What's more, people are remarkably unaware of making suboptimal decisions.[31]

Exhibit **6-3**	Steps in the Rational Decision-Making Model

1. Define the problem.
2. Identify the decision criteria.
3. Allocate weights to the criteria.
4. Develop the alternatives.
5. Evaluate the alternatives.
6. Select the best alternative.

---

decisions   *Choices made from among two or more alternatives.*

problem   *A discrepancy between the current state of affairs and some desired state.*

rational   *Characterized by making consistent, value-maximizing choices within specified constraints.*

rational decision-making model   *A decision-making model that describes how individuals should behave in order to maximize some outcome.*

Bounded Rationality   Our limited information-processing capability makes it impossible to assimilate and understand all the information necessary to optimize.[32] So most people respond to a complex problem by reducing it to a level at which they can readily understand it. Also many problems don't have an optimal solution because they are too complicated to fit the rational decision-making model. So people *satisfice;* they seek solutions that are satisfactory and sufficient.

When you considered which college to attend, did you look at every viable alternative? Did you carefully identify all the criteria that were important in your decision? Did you evaluate each alternative against the criteria in order to find the optimal college? The answers are probably "no." Well, don't feel bad. Few people made their college choice this way. Instead of optimizing, you probably satisficed.

Because the human mind cannot formulate and solve complex problems with full rationality, we operate within the confines of **bounded rationality**. We construct simplified models that extract the essential features from problems without capturing all their complexity.[33] We can then behave rationally within the limits of the simple model.

How does bounded rationality work for the typical individual? Once we've identified a problem, we begin to search for criteria and alternatives. But the criteria are unlikely to be exhaustive. We identify choices that are easy to find and highly visible and that usually represent familiar criteria and tried-and-true solutions. Next, we begin reviewing them, focusing on alternatives that differ little from the choice currently in effect until we identify one that is "good enough"—that meets an acceptable level of performance. That ends our search. So the solution represents a satisficing choice—the first *acceptable* one we encounter—rather than an optimal one.

Satisficing is not always a bad idea—a simple process may frequently be more sensible than the traditional rational decision-making model.[34] To use the rational model in the real world, you need to gather a great deal of information about all the options, compute applicable weights, and then calculate values across a huge number of criteria. All these processes can cost time, energy,

Top managers of Nike, Inc. operated within the confines of bounded rationality in making a decision about its operations in China. To reinforce its future development and rapid growth in China, Nike decided to invest $99 million to build the China Logistics Center, a new distribution facility in Jiangsu for the company's footwear, apparel, and equipment products. With China overtaking Japan as Nike's second largest market after the United States, the new distribution center is expected to reduce product delivery times by up to 14 percent to the more than 3,000 Nike retail stores in China.

Source: Imagechina/AP Images

and money. And if there are many unknown weights and preferences, the fully rational model may not be any more accurate than a best guess. Sometimes a fast-and-frugal process of solving problems might be your best option. Returning to your college choice, would it really be smarter to fly around the country to visit dozens of potential campuses, paying application fees for all these options? Can you really even know what type of college is "best" for you when you're just graduating from high school, or is there a lot of unknown information about how your interests are going to develop over time? Maybe you won't major in the same subject you started with. It might be much smarter to find a few colleges that match most of your preferences and then focus your attention on differentiating between those.

Intuition   Perhaps the least rational way of making decisions is **intuitive decision making**, an unconscious process created from distilled experience.[35] It occurs outside conscious thought; it relies on holistic associations, or links between disparate pieces of information; it's fast; and it's *affectively charged,* meaning it usually engages the emotions.[36]

While intuition isn't rational, it isn't necessarily wrong. Nor does it always contradict rational analysis; rather, the two can complement each other. But nor is intuition superstition, or the product of some magical or paranormal sixth sense. As one recent review noted, "Intuition is a highly complex and highly developed form of reasoning that is based on years of experience and learning."[37]

For most of the twentieth century, experts believed decision makers' use of intuition was irrational or ineffective. That's no longer the case.[38] We now recognize that rational analysis has been overemphasized and, in certain instances, relying on intuition can improve decision making.[39] But we can't rely on it too much. Because it is so unquantifiable, it's hard to know when our hunches are right or wrong. The key is neither to abandon nor rely solely on intuition, but to supplement it with evidence and good judgment.

Common Biases and Errors in Decision Making

6   List and explain the common decision biases or errors.

Decision makers engage in bounded rationality, but they also allow systematic biases and errors to creep into their judgments.[40] To minimize effort and avoid difficult trade-offs, people tend to rely too heavily on experience, impulses, gut feelings, and convenient rules of thumb. These shortcuts can be helpful. However, they can also distort rationality. Following are the most common biases in decision making. Exhibit 6-4 provides some suggestions for how to avoid falling into these biases and errors.

Overconfidence Bias   It's been said that "no problem in judgment and decision making is more prevalent and more potentially catastrophic than overconfidence."[41] When we're given factual questions and asked to judge the probability that our answers are correct, we tend to be far too optimistic. When people say they're 90 percent confident about the range a certain number might take, their estimated ranges contain the correct answer only about 50 percent of the time—and experts are no more accurate in setting up confidence intervals than are

---

bounded rationality   *A process of making decisions by constructing simplified models that extract the essential features from problems without capturing all their complexity.*

intuitive decision making   *An unconscious process created out of distilled experience.*

Exhibit **6-4**	**Reducing Biases and Errors**

Focus on Goals. Without goals, you can't be rational, you don't know what information you need, you don't know which information is relevant and which is irrelevant, you'll find it difficult to choose between alternatives, and you're far more likely to experience regret over the choices you make. Clear goals make decision making easier and help you eliminate options that are inconsistent with your interests.

Look for Information That Disconfirms Your Beliefs. One of the most effective means for counteracting overconfidence and the confirmation and hindsight biases is to actively look for information that contradicts your beliefs and assumptions. When we overtly consider various ways we could be wrong, we challenge our tendencies to think we're smarter than we actually are.

Don't Try to Create Meaning out of Random Events. The educated mind has been trained to look for cause-and-effect relationships. When something happens, we ask why. And when we can't find reasons, we often invent them. You have to accept that there are events in life that are outside your control. Ask yourself if patterns can be meaningfully explained or whether they are merely coincidence. Don't attempt to create meaning out of coincidence.

Increase Your Options. No matter how many options you've identified, your final choice can be no better than the best of the option set you've selected. This argues for increasing your decision alternatives and for using creativity in developing a wide range of diverse choices. The more alternatives you can generate, and the more diverse those alternatives, the greater your chance of finding an outstanding one.

Source: S. P. Robbins, Decide & Conquer: *Making Winning Decisions and Taking Control of Your Life* (Upper Saddle River, NJ: Financial Times/Prentice Hall, 2004), pp. 164–168.

novices.[42] When people say they're 100 percent sure of an outcome, they tend to be 70 to 85 percent correct.[43] Here's another interesting example. In one random-sample national poll, 90 percent of U.S. adults said they expected to go to heaven. But in another random-sample national poll, only 86 percent thought Mother Teresa was in heaven. Talk about an overconfidence bias!

Individuals whose intellectual and interpersonal abilities are *weakest* are most likely to overestimate their performance and ability.[44] There's also a negative relationship between entrepreneurs' optimism and the performance of their new ventures: the more optimistic, the less successful.[45] The tendency to be too confident about their ideas might keep some from planning how to avoid problems that arise.

Investor overconfidence operates in a variety of ways.[46] Finance professor Terrance Odean says "people think they know more than they do, and it costs them." Investors, especially novices, overestimate not just their own skill in processing information, but also the quality of the information they're working with. Test your own confidence level with investments: compare the long-term returns of your stock market picks relative to index funds. You'll find an overall index performs as well as, or better than, carefully hand-picked stocks. The main reason many people resist index funds is that they think they're better at picking stocks than the average person, but most investors will actually do only as well as or only slightly better than the market as a whole.

Anchoring Bias   The **anchoring bias** is a tendency to fixate on initial information and fail to adequately adjust for subsequent information.[47] It occurs because our mind appears to give a disproportionate amount of emphasis to the first information it receives. Anchors are widely used by people in professions in which persuasion skills are important—advertising, management, politics, real estate, and law. Assume two pilots—Jason and Glenda—have been laid off their current jobs, and after an extensive search their best offers are from Delta Airlines. Each would earn the average annual pay of Delta's narrow-body jet pilots: $126,000. Jason was a pilot for Pinnacle, a regional airline where the average annual salary is $82,000. Glenda was a pilot for FedEx, where the average annual salary is $200,000. Which pilot is most likely to accept, or be happiest with, Delta's offer? Obviously Jason, because he is anchored by the lower salary.[48]

Any time a negotiation takes place, so does anchoring. When a prospective employer asks how much you made in your prior job, your answer typically anchors the employer's offer. (Remember this when you negotiate your salary, but set the anchor only as high as you realistically can.) Finally, the more precise your anchor, the smaller the adjustment. Some research suggests people think of making an adjustment after an anchor is set as rounding off a number. If you suggest a target salary of $55,000, your boss will consider $50,000 to $60,000 a reasonable range for negotiation, but if you mention $55,650, your boss is more likely to consider $55,000 to $56,000 the range of likely values.[49]

Confirmation Bias   The rational decision-making process assumes we objectively gather information. But we don't. We *selectively* gather it. The **confirmation bias** represents a specific case of selective perception: we seek out information that reaffirms our past choices, and we discount information that contradicts them.[50] We also tend to accept at face value information that confirms our preconceived views, while we are critical and skeptical of information that challenges them. Therefore, the information we gather is typically biased toward supporting views we already hold. We even tend to seek sources most likely to tell us what we want to hear, and we give too much weight to supporting information and too little to contradictory. Interestingly, we are most prone to the confirmation bias when we believe we have good information and strongly believe in our opinions. Fortunately, those who feel there is a strong need to be accurate in making a decision are less prone to the confirmation bias.

Availability Bias   More people fear flying than fear driving in a car. But if flying on a commercial airline really were as dangerous as driving, the equivalent of two 747s filled to capacity would crash every week, killing all aboard. Because the media give much more attention to air accidents, we tend to overstate the risk of flying and understate the risk of driving.

The **availability bias** is our tendency to base judgments on information readily available.[51] Events that evoke emotions, are particularly vivid, or are more recent tend to be more available in our memory, leading us to overestimate the chances of unlikely events such as an airplane crash. The availability bias can also explain why managers doing performance appraisals give more weight to recent employee behaviors than to behaviors of 6 or 9 months earlier, or why credit-rating agencies such as Moody's or Standard & Poor's may issue overly positive ratings by relying on information presented by debt issuers, who have an incentive to offer data favorable to their case.[52]

---

anchoring bias   *A tendency to fixate on initial information, from which one then fails to adequately adjust for subsequent information.*

confirmation bias   *The tendency to seek out information that reaffirms past choices and to discount information that contradicts past judgments.*

availability bias   *The tendency for people to base their judgments on information that is readily available to them.*

Escalation of Commitment   Another distortion that creeps into decisions is a tendency to escalate commitment.[53] **Escalation of commitment** refers to staying with a decision even when there is clear evidence it's wrong. Consider a friend who has been dating someone for several years. Although he admits things aren't going too well, he says he is still going to marry her. His justification: "I have a lot invested in the relationship!"

Individuals escalate commitment to a failing course of action when they view themselves as responsible for the failure.[54] They "throw good money after bad" to demonstrate their initial decision wasn't wrong and to avoid admitting they made a mistake.[55] In fact, people who carefully gather and consider information consistent with the rational decision-making model are *more* likely to engage in escalation of commitment than those who spend less time thinking about their choices.[56] Perhaps they have invested so much time and energy in making their decisions that they have convinced themselves they're taking the right course of action and don't update their knowledge in the face of new information. Many an organization has suffered because a manager determined to prove his or her original decision right continued to commit resources to a lost cause.

Randomness Error   Most of us like to think we have some control over our world and our destiny. Our tendency to believe we can predict the outcome of random events is the **randomness error**.

Decision making suffers when we try to create meaning in random events, particularly when we turn imaginary patterns into superstitions.[57] These can be completely contrived ("I never make important decisions on Friday the 13th") or can evolve from a reinforced past pattern of behavior (Tiger Woods often wears a red shirt during a golf tournament's final round because he won many junior tournaments wearing red shirts). Superstitious behavior can be debilitating when it affects daily judgments or biases major decisions.

Risk Aversion   Mathematically, we should find a 50–50 flip of the coin for $100 to be worth as much as a sure promise of $50. After all, the expected value of the gamble over a number of trials is $50. However, nearly everyone but committed gamblers would rather have the sure thing than a risky prospect.[58] For many people, a 50–50 flip of a coin even for $200 might not be worth as much as a sure promise of $50, even though the gamble is mathematically worth twice as much! This tendency to prefer a sure thing over a risky outcome is **risk aversion**.

Risk aversion has important implications. To offset the risks inherent in a commission-based wage, companies pay commissioned employees considerably more than they do those on straight salaries. Risk-averse employees will stick with the established way of doing their jobs, rather than taking a chance on innovative or creative methods. Sticking with a strategy that has worked in the past does minimize risk, but in the long run it will lead to stagnation. Ambitious people with power that can be taken away (most managers) appear to be especially risk averse, perhaps because they don't want to lose on a gamble everything they've worked so hard to achieve.[59] CEOs at risk of being terminated are also exceptionally risk averse, even when a riskier investment strategy is in their firms' best interests.[60]

Because people are less likely to escalate commitment where there is a great deal of uncertainty, the implications of risk aversion aren't all bad.[61] When a risky investment isn't paying off, most people would rather play it safe and cut their losses, but if they think the outcome is a sure thing, they'll keep escalating.

Risk preference is sometimes reversed: people prefer to take their chances when trying to prevent a negative outcome.[62] They would rather take a 50–50 gamble on

Creative Decision Making Is a Right-Brain Activity

One article of faith in creativity research and practice is that whereas the left brain governs analytical, rational thinking, the right brain underlies creative thinking. However, judging from a recent review of neuropsychology research, this accepted wisdom is false.

Neuropsychologists study creativity by asking people to engage in creative thinking, which they measure in different ways. In the Remote Associates Test, individuals indicate what word links a series of three words (such as Falling Actor Dust; Salt Deep Foam). Other tests ask individuals to compose creative stories, write captions for cartoons, or provide unique solutions to unusual hypothetical problems. While participants are thinking creatively, the researchers assess their brain activity using various techniques, including MRI.

A recent review of 72 studies found right brain activity was *not* associated with creative thinking. The authors conclude, "Creativity, or any alleged stage of it, is not particularly associated with the right brain or any part of the right brain." Indeed, the review showed it was difficult to isolate creative thinking in any one region of the brain.

Another review of 45 studies reached the same conclusion, noting that the diverse ways in which creativity and brain activity were measured made generalizations difficult.

These results do not discourage all neuropsychologists. One neuroscientist, Oshin Vartanian, summed up the literature as follows: "Initially, a lot of people were looking for the holy grail. They were searching for the creativity module in the brain. Now we know it is more complicated."

Sources: A. Dietrich and R. Kanso, "A Review of EEG, ERP, and Neuroimaging Studies of Creativity and Insight," *Psychological Bulletin* 136, no. 5 (2010), pp. 822–848; R. Ardena, R. S. Chavez, R. Grazioplene, & R. E. Jung, "Neuroimaging Creativity: A Psychometric View," *Behavioural Brain Research* 214, no. 2 (2010), pp. 143–156; and A. McIlroy, "Neuroscientists Try to Unlock the Origins of Creativity," *Globe and Mail* (January 28, 2011), downloaded May 20, 2011, from www.theglobeandmail.com/.

losing $100 than accept the certain loss of $50. Thus they will risk losing a lot of money at trial rather than settle out of court. Trying to cover up wrongdoing instead of admitting a mistake, despite the risk of truly catastrophic press coverage or even jail time, is another example. Stressful situations can make these risk preferences stronger. People will more likely engage in risk-seeking behavior for negative outcomes, and risk-averse behavior for positive outcomes, when under stress.[63]

Hindsight Bias The **hindsight bias** is the tendency to believe falsely, after the outcome is known, that we'd have accurately predicted it.[64] When we have accurate feedback on the outcome, we seem pretty good at concluding it was obvious.

Over the past 10 years, the home video rental industry has been collapsing fast as online distribution outlets have eaten away at the market.[65] Hollywood Video declared bankruptcy in May 2010 and began liquidating its assets; Blockbuster filed for bankruptcy in September 2010. Some have suggested that if only these organizations had leveraged their brand and distribution resources

---

escalation of commitment *An increased commitment to a previous decision in spite of negative information.*

randomness error *The tendency of individuals to believe that they can predict the outcome of random events.*

risk aversion *The tendency to prefer a sure gain of a moderate amount over a riskier outcome, even if the riskier outcome might have a higher expected payoff.*

hindsight bias *The tendency to believe falsely, after an outcome of an event is actually known, that one would have accurately predicted that outcome.*

effectively and sooner to develop web-based delivery, as Netflix does, and low-cost distribution in grocery and convenience stores, which Redbox offers, they could have been avoided failure. While that might seem obvious now, many experts with good information failed to see these two major trends that would upend the industry.

Of course, after the fact, it is easy to see that a combination of automated and mail-order distribution would outperform the traditional brick-and-mortar movie rental business. Similarly, former Merrill Lynch CEO John Thain—and many other Wall Street executives—took blame for failing to see what now seems obvious (that housing prices were inflated, too many risky loans were made, and the values of many "securities" were based on fragile assumptions). Though the criticisms may have merit, things are often all too clear in hindsight. As Malcolm Gladwell, author of *Blink* and *The Tipping Point,* writes, "What is clear in hindsight is rarely clear before the fact."[66]

The hindsight bias reduces our ability to learn from the past. It lets us think we're better predictors than we are and can make us falsely confident. If your actual predictive accuracy is only 40 percent but you think it's 90, you're likely to be less skeptical about your predictive skills.

Application: Financial Decision Making   This discussion of decision making errors may have you thinking about how organizations and individuals make financial decisions. Did decision errors influence capital markets and even lead to crises like the financial meltdown of 2008? How are financial decisions affected by errors and biases? Experts have identified several ways this can occur.[67]

One of the core problems that created the financial crisis was that large loans were made to individuals who could not repay them, and finance companies purchased these bad debts without realizing how poor the prospects of repayment were. Thus, overconfidence bias by both lenders and borrowers

When the U.S.-based global financial services firm Lehman Brothers failed, many people blamed Richard Fuld, the company's chief executive, accusing him of overconfidence, confirmation, and anchoring biases and a lack of knowledge about complicated financial investment instruments. Even as Lehman Brothers continued to post billion-dollar losses, Fuld exuded confidence that the investment bank was sound, and he rebuffed criticism of the bank's failure to value its assets accurately. Comments by former employees and passersby blaming Fuld for the bankruptcy were recorded on an artists' rendering of him placed in front of Lehman's offices in New York City.

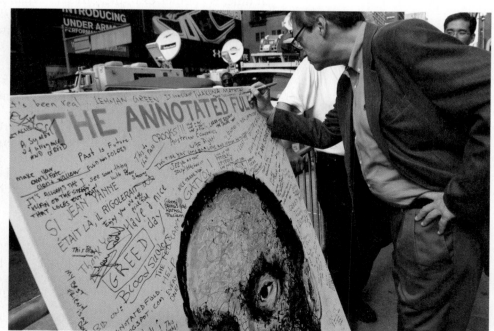

Source: Louis Lanzanop/AP Images

OB Poll   Gloomy Perceptions Return

Percent Indicating Economy Is in Recession or Depression

Depression
Recession

February, 2008 — Recession 33%, Depression 12%

September, 2008 — Recession 36%, Depression 33%

April, 2011 — Recession 26%, Depression 29%

Source: Based on C. Merkle and M. Weber, "True Overconfidence—The Inability of Rational Information Processing to Account for Apparent Overconfidence" (March 2009). Available at SSRN: http://ssrn.com/abstract=1373675

about the ability to pay back loans was clearly a major factor. Most studies suggest that people are more willing to buy on credit and spend more money when they feel confident. Although experts were no more accurate at predicting financial outcomes than were people without knowledge or skills in finance, they *were* more confident in their predictions. Unfortunately, as confidence decreases in the face of poor economic data, businesses and consumers become more conservative in their spending. This further decreases demand for products and services, which deepens the economic crisis in a vicious cycle.

Overconfidence isn't the only decision error implicated in the financial crisis. Investors deliberately avoid negative information about investments, an example of the confirmation bias. Lenders may have overlooked potential problems with borrowers' accounts when making loans, and stock traders may have ignored information about potential problems with complex derivatives when making purchasing decisions. Once a loan has been paid off, lenders also selectively ignore the negative effects of debt, making them more likely to make unwise loans in the future.

What might prevent these situations from occurring in the future? Both investors and consumers may need to more carefully consider whether their confidence level is aligned with their actual future ability to pay. It is also always a good idea to seek information that goes against your initial inclinations, to ensure you're getting the whole picture. Be careful not to commit the hindsight bias and conclude after financial crises have dissipated that it should have been obvious problems were about to occur.

SELF-ASSESSMENT LIBRARY

Am I A Deliberate Decision Maker?

In the Self-Assessment Library (available on CD or online), take assessment IV.A.2 (Am I a Deliberate Decision Maker?). Would it be better to be a more deliberate decision maker? Why or why not?

Influences on Decision Making: Individual Differences and Organizational Constraints

We turn here to factors that influence how people make decisions and the degree to which they are susceptible to errors and biases. We discuss individual differences and organizational constraints.

Individual Differences

7 Explain how individual differences and organizational constraints affect decision making.

Decision making in practice is characterized by bounded rationality, common biases and errors, and the use of intuition. In addition, individual differences create deviations from the rational model. In this section, we look at two such differences: personality and gender.

Personality   The little research so far conducted on personality and decision making suggests personality does influence our decisions. Let's look at conscientiousness and self-esteem (both discussed in Chapter 5).

Specific facets of conscientiousness—rather than the broad trait itself—may affect escalation of commitment (above).[68] Two such facets—achievement striving and dutifulness—actually had opposite effects. Achievement-striving people were more likely to escalate their commitment, whereas dutiful people were less likely. Why? Generally, achievement-oriented people hate to fail, so they escalate their commitment, hoping to forestall failure. Dutiful people, however, are more inclined to do what they see as best for the organization. Second, achievement-striving individuals appear more susceptible to the hindsight bias, perhaps because they have a greater need to justify their actions.[69] Unfortunately, we don't have evidence on whether dutiful people are immune to this bias.

Finally, people with high self-esteem are strongly motivated to maintain it, so they use the self-serving bias to preserve it. They blame others for their failures while taking credit for successes.[70]

Gender   Research on rumination offers insights into gender differences in decision making.[71] *Rumination* refers to reflecting at length. In terms of decision making, it means overthinking problems. Twenty years of study find women spend much more time than men analyzing the past, present, and future. They're more likely to overanalyze problems before making a decision and to rehash a decision once made. This can lead to more careful consideration of problems and choices. However, it can make problems harder to solve, increase regret over past decisions, and increase depression. Women are nearly twice as likely as men to develop depression.[72]

Why women ruminate more than men is not clear. One view is that parents encourage and reinforce the expression of sadness and anxiety more in girls than in boys. Another theory is that women, more than men, base their self-esteem and well-being on what others think of them. A third idea is that women are more empathetic and more affected by events in others' lives, so they have more to ruminate about.

By age 11, girls are ruminating more than boys. But this gender difference seems to lessen with age. Differences are largest during young adulthood and smallest after age 65, when both men and women ruminate the least.[73]

Whose Ethical Standards to Follow?

As we note in the chapter, different standards identify ethical behavior in different cultures. Managers who work in international contexts frequently run into complex problems when behavior acceptable for the home office is unacceptable in local cultures, and vice versa.

How difficult is it to arrive at a global policy for ethical decision making? Consider these examples. Individuals from countries higher in Hofstede's dimension of power distance, like those in Latin America, were more likely to report that bribery was acceptable than were individuals from lower power distance countries, like the United States and much of Europe. An international scandal ensued after German corporation Siemens set aside money for

bribes when working in Africa, but company executives initially defended the actions as consistent with business practices in those countries. Such differences don't mean business ethics are "higher" or "lower" in different countries. Although U.S. executives might frown on bribery, they may view it as ethical and necessary to lay workers off during poor economic times, whereas other cultures view layoffs as a betrayal of the relationship between workers and employers.

So how are managers to decide which ethical standards to observe? Is it better to act consistently with your own culture, or adopt the ethical standards of the countries where you operate? This question isn't easy to answer. Ethics experts suggest

leaders should adhere to universal values of human life and welfare as the core of their international codes of ethics, and they note there are few cases where values are directly in conflict (no culture actively encourages bribery as moral; it's just that some societies view it as less of a problem than others do).

Source: Based on L. J. Thompson, "The Global Moral Compass for Business Leaders," *Journal of Business Ethics* 93, no. S1 (2010), pp. 15–32; C. Baughn, N. L. Bodie, M. A. Buchanan, and M. B. Bixby, "Bribery in International Business Transactions," *Journal of Business Ethics* 92, no. 1 (2010), pp. 15–32; and T. Patel and A. Schaefer, "Making Sense of the Diversity of Ethical Decision Making in Business: An Illustration of the Indian Context," *Journal of Business Ethics* 90, no. 2 (2009), pp. 171–186.

Mental Ability   We know people with higher levels of mental ability are able to process information more quickly, solve problems more accurately, and learn faster, so you might expect them also to be less susceptible to common decision errors. However, mental ability appears to help people avoid only some of these.[74] Smart people are just as likely to fall prey to anchoring, overconfidence, and escalation of commitment, probably because just being smart doesn't alert you to the possibility you're too confident or emotionally defensive. That doesn't mean intelligence never matters. Once warned about decision-making errors, more intelligent people learn more quickly to avoid them. They are also better able to avoid logical errors like false syllogisms or incorrect interpretation of data.

Cultural Differences   The rational model makes no acknowledgment of cultural differences, nor does the bulk of OB research literature on decision making. But Indonesians, for instance, don't necessarily make decisions the same way Australians do. Therefore, we need to recognize that the cultural background of a decision maker can significantly influence the selection of problems, the depth of analysis, the importance placed on logic and rationality, and whether organizational decisions should be made autocratically by an individual manager or collectively in groups.[75]

Cultures differ in their time orientation, the importance of rationality, their belief in the ability of people to solve problems, and their preference for collective decision making. Differences in time orientation help us understand why managers in Egypt make decisions at a much slower and more deliberate pace than their U.S. counterparts. While rationality is valued in North America, that's not true elsewhere in the world. A North American manager might make an important decision intuitively but know it's important to appear to proceed in a rational fashion because rationality is highly valued in the West. In countries such as Iran, where rationality is not as paramount as other factors, efforts to appear rational are not necessary.

Some cultures emphasize solving problems, while others focus on accepting situations as they are. The United States falls in the first category; Thailand and Indonesia are examples of the second. Because problem-solving managers believe they can and should change situations to their benefit, U.S. managers might identify a problem long before their Thai or Indonesian counterparts would choose to recognize it as such. Decision making by Japanese managers is much more group-oriented than in the United States. The Japanese value conformity and cooperation. So before Japanese CEOs make an important decision, they collect a large amount of information, which they use in consensus-forming group decisions. In short, there are probably important cultural differences in decision making, but unfortunately not yet much research to identify them.

Organizational Constraints

Organizations can constrain decision makers, creating deviations from the rational model. For instance, managers shape their decisions to reflect the organization's performance evaluation and reward system, to comply with its formal regulations, and to meet organizationally imposed time constraints. Precedent can also limit decisions.

Performance Evaluation   Managers are strongly influenced by the criteria on which they are evaluated. If a division manager believes the manufacturing plants under his responsibility are operating best when he hears nothing negative, we shouldn't be surprised to find his plant managers spending a good part of their time ensuring that negative information doesn't reach him.

Reward Systems   The organization's reward system influences decision makers by suggesting which choices have better personal payoffs. If the organization rewards risk aversion, managers are more likely to make conservative decisions. From the 1930s through the mid-1980s, General Motors consistently gave promotions and bonuses to managers who kept a low profile and avoided controversy. These executives became adept at dodging tough issues and passing controversial decisions on to committees.

Formal Regulations   David Gonzalez, a shift manager at a Taco Bell restaurant in San Antonio, Texas, describes constraints he faces on his job: "I've got rules and regulations covering almost every decision I make—from how to make a burrito to how often I need to clean the restrooms. My job doesn't come with much freedom of choice." David's situation is not unique. All but the smallest organizations create rules and policies to program decisions and get individuals to act in the intended manner. And of course, in so doing, they limit decision choices.

System-Imposed Time Constraints   Almost all important decisions come with explicit deadlines. A report on new-product development may have to be ready for executive committee review by the first of the month. Such conditions often make it difficult, if not impossible, for managers to gather all the information they might like before making a final choice.

Historical Precedents   Decisions aren't made in a vacuum; they have a context. In fact, individual decisions are points in a stream of choice. Those made in the

Formal regulations shape employee decisions at McDonald's restaurants throughout the world. McDonald's standardizes the behavior of restaurant crew members such as the employee shown here preparing the company's specialty coffee, McCafe Mocha. McDonald's requires employees to follow rules and regulations for food preparation and service to meet the company's high standards of food quality and safety and reliable and friendly service. For example, McDonald's requires 72 safety protocols to be conducted every day in each restaurant as part of a daily monitoring routine for restaurant managers.

Source: Newscom

past are like ghosts that haunt and constrain current choices. It's common knowledge that the largest determinant of the size of any given year's budget is last year's budget.[76] Choices made today are largely a result of choices made over the years.

What About Ethics in Decision Making?

8 Contrast the three ethical decision criteria.

Ethical considerations should be an important criterion in all organizational decision making. In this section, we present three ways to frame decisions ethically.[77]

Three Ethical Decision Criteria

The first ethical yardstick is **utilitarianism**, which proposes making decisions solely on the basis of their *outcomes*, ideally to provide the greatest good for the greatest number. This view dominates business decision making. It is consistent with goals such as efficiency, productivity, and high profits.

Another ethical criterion is to make decisions consistent with fundamental liberties and privileges, as set forth in documents such as the Bill of Rights. An emphasis on *rights* in decision making means respecting and protecting the basic rights of individuals, such as the right to privacy, free speech, and due process. This criterion protects **whistle-blowers** when they reveal an organization's unethical practices to the press or government agencies, using their right to free speech.

utilitarianism   *A system in which decisions are made to provide the greatest good for the greatest number.*

whistle-blowers   *Individuals who report unethical practices by their employer to outsiders.*

A third criterion is to impose and enforce rules fairly and impartially to ensure *justice* or an equitable distribution of benefits and costs. Union members typically favor this view. It justifies paying people the same wage for a given job regardless of performance differences and using seniority as the primary determination in layoff decisions.

Each criterion has advantages and liabilities. A focus on utilitarianism promotes efficiency and productivity, but it can sideline the rights of some individuals, particularly those with minority representation. The use of rights protects individuals from injury and is consistent with freedom and privacy, but it can create a legalistic environment that hinders productivity and efficiency. A focus on justice protects the interests of the underrepresented and less powerful, but it can encourage a sense of entitlement that reduces risk taking, innovation, and productivity.

Decision makers, particularly in for-profit organizations, feel comfortable with utilitarianism. The "best interests" of the organization and its stockholders can justify a lot of questionable actions, such as large layoffs. But many critics feel this perspective needs to change.[78] Public concern about individual rights and social justice suggests managers should develop ethical standards based on nonutilitarian criteria. This presents a challenge because satisfying individual rights and social justice creates far more ambiguities than utilitarian effects on efficiency and profits. However, while raising prices, selling products with questionable effects on consumer health, closing down inefficient plants, laying off large numbers of employees, and moving production overseas to cut costs can be justified in utilitarian terms, that may no longer be the single measure by which good decisions are judged.

Improving Creativity in Decision Making

9 Define *creativity* and discuss the three-component model of creativity.

Although the rational decision-making model will often improve decisions, a rational decision maker also needs **creativity**, the ability to produce novel and useful ideas.[79] These are different from what's been done before but appropriate to the problem presented.

Creativity allows the decision maker to more fully appraise and understand the problem, including seeing problems others can't see. L'Oréal puts its managers through creative exercises such as cooking or making music, and the University of Chicago requires MBA students to make short movies about their experiences.

Creative Potential   Most people have useful creative potential. But to unleash it, they have to escape the psychological ruts many of us fall into and learn how to think about a problem in divergent ways.

Exceptional creativity is scarce. We all know of creative geniuses in science (Albert Einstein), art (Pablo Picasso), and business (Steve Jobs). But what about the typical individual? Intelligent people and those who score high on openness to experience (see Chapter 5) are more likely to be creative.[80] Other traits of creative people are independence, self-confidence, risk taking, an internal locus of control, tolerance for ambiguity, a low need for structure, and perseverance.[81] Exposure to a variety of cultures can also improve creativity.[82] So taking an international assignment, or even an international vacation, could jump-start your creative process.

A study of the lifetime creativity of 461 men and women found fewer than 1 percent were exceptionally creative.[83] But 10 percent were highly creative and about 60 percent were somewhat creative. This reinforces that most of us have creative potential; we just need to learn to unleash it.

Three-Component Model of Creativity What can individuals and organizations do to stimulate employee creativity? The best answer lies in the **three-component model of creativity**,[84] which proposes that individual creativity essentially requires expertise, creative thinking skills, and intrinsic task motivation. Studies confirm that the higher the level of each, the higher the creativity.

Expertise is the foundation for all creative work. Film writer, producer, and director Quentin Tarantino spent his youth working in a video rental store, where he built up an encyclopedic knowledge of movies. The potential for creativity is enhanced when individuals have abilities, knowledge, proficiencies, and similar expertise in their field of endeavor. You wouldn't expect someone with minimal knowledge of programming to be very creative as a software engineer.

The second component is *creative-thinking skills*. This encompasses personality characteristics associated with creativity, the ability to use analogies, and the talent to see the familiar in a different light.

A meta-analysis of 102 studies found positive moods increase creativity, but it depends on what sort of positive mood was considered.[85] Moods such as happiness that encourage interaction with the world are more conducive to creativity than passive moods such as calm. This means the common advice to relax and clear your mind to develop creative ideas may be misplaced. It would be better to get in an upbeat mood and then frame your work as an opportunity to have fun and experiment. Negative moods also don't always have the same effects on creativity. Passive negative moods such as sadness doesn't seem to have much effect, but avoidance-oriented negative moods such as fear and anxiety decrease creativity. Feeling threatened reduces your desire to try new activities; risk aversion increases when you're scared. Active negative moods, such as anger, however, do appear to enhance creativity, especially if you are taking your task seriously.

Being around creative others can make us more inspired, especially if we're creatively "stuck."[86] One study found that having "weak ties" to creative people—knowing them but not well—facilitates creativity because the people are there as a resource if we need them but not so close as to stunt our own independent thinking.[87]

Analogies allow decision makers to apply an idea from one context to another. One of the most famous examples was Alexander Graham Bell's observation that it might be possible to apply the way the ear operates to his "talking box." Bell noticed the bones in the ear are operated by a delicate, thin membrane. He wondered why a thicker and stronger membrane shouldn't be able to move a piece of steel. From that analogy, the telephone was conceived. Thinking in terms of analogies is a complex intellectual skill, which helps explain why cognitive ability is related to creativity. Demonstrating this effect, one study found children who got high scores on cognitive ability tests at age 13 were significantly more likely to have made creative achievements in their professional lives 25 years later.[88]

Some people develop creative skills because they see problems in a new way. They're able to make the strange familiar and the familiar strange.[89] For instance, most of us think of hens laying eggs. But how many of us have considered that a hen is only an egg's way of making another egg?

---

creativity   *The ability to produce novel and useful ideas.*

three-component model of creativity   *The proposition that individual creativity requires expertise, creative thinking skills, and intrinsic task motivation.*

Creative people often love their work, to the point of seeming obsession. The final component in the three-component model of creativity is *intrinsic task motivation*. This is the desire to work on something because it's interesting, involving, exciting, satisfying, or personally challenging. It's what turns creativity *potential* into *actual* creative ideas. Environmental stimulants that foster creativity include a culture that encourages the flow of ideas; fair and constructive judgment of ideas; rewards and recognition for creative work; sufficient financial, material, and information resources; freedom to decide what work is to be done and how to do it; a supervisor who communicates effectively, shows confidence in others, and supports the work group; and work group members who support and trust each other.[90]

International Differences   There are no global ethical standards,[91] as contrasts between Asia and the West illustrate.[92] Because bribery is commonplace in countries such as China, a Canadian working in China might face a dilemma: should I pay a bribe to secure business if it is an accepted part of that country's culture? A manager of a large U.S. company operating in China once caught an employee stealing. Following company policy, she fired him and turned him over to the local authorities. Later, she was horrified to learn the employee had been summarily executed.[93]

Although ethical standards may seem ambiguous in the West, criteria defining right and wrong are actually much clearer there than in Asia, where few issues are black and white and most are gray. Global organizations must establish ethical principles for decision makers in countries such as India and China and modify them to reflect cultural norms if they want to uphold high standards and consistent practices.

SELF-ASSESSMENT LIBRARY

How Creative Am I?

In the Self-Assessment Library (available on CD or online), take assessment I.A.5 (How Creative Am I?).

MyManagementLab

Now that you have finished this chapter, go back to **www.pearsonglobaleditions.com/ mymanagementlab** to continue practicing and applying the concepts you've learned.

Summary and Implications for Managers

Perception   Individuals base their behavior not on the way their external environment actually is but rather on what they see or believe it to be.

- Whether a manager successfully plans and organizes the work of employees and actually helps them to structure their work more efficiently and effectively is far less important than how employees perceive the manager's efforts.
- Employees judge issues such as fair pay, performance appraisals, and working conditions in very individual ways. To influence productivity, we need to assess how workers perceive their jobs.

Checklists Lead to Better Decisions

POINT   **COUNTERPOINT**

While life and lives sometimes turn on the basis of big decisions, it's often the little ones that matter more. Our failure to follow routine, everyday protocols makes the world a more dangerous place for ourselves, and for others. A few examples . . .

Nearly 100,000 U.S. patients are killed every year by the failure of doctors and nurses to follow simple instructions. Really. Hospital-acquired infections kill that many people every year, and nearly all those deaths are entirely preventable.

Most airline crashes occur because pilots ignore the rules. Pilot failure to follow protocols is a primary contributing factor to the majority of incidents and accidents.

An important way of attacking these errors is to use checklists.

Support for a checklist approach is provided by a new book, *The Checklist Manifesto.* In it, the author, Harvard Medical School surgeon Atul Gawande notes, "The volume and complexity of what we know has exceeded our ability to deliver its benefits correctly, safely, or reliably." Unless, of course, we use checklists.

Dr. Peter Pronovost, a critical care specialist at Johns Hopkins, developed his own operating room checklist, which included some "no brainers" such as wash your hands with soap, put drapes over entire patient, and put sterile dressing over incisions. Within 1 year of the checklist's adoption at Johns Hopkins, the post-op infection rate went from 11 percent to zero.

According to Gawande, in using checklists to improve decisions, we should keep the following guidelines in mind:

- Include all "stupid but critical" tasks so they're not overlooked.
- Make it mandatory for team members to inform others when an item on the list is completed (or not).
- Empower team members to question superiors about the checklist.
- Allow for improvisation in unusual circumstances.
- Thoroughly test-drive the checklist before implementing it.

Gawande notes that checklists aren't important only for medical decision making. Engineering, business, technology, safety, and transportation are all industries that would benefit from greater development and use of checklists in everyday decision making.

As a project manager noted, "Successful checklists detail both the sequence of necessary activities as well as the communication checkpoints to ensure dialog among project participants."

Checklists work well, except when they don't.

Checklists have a paradox that makes them of dubious usefulness: the more complex the decision making, ostensibly the more important the checklist. But the more complex the decision making, the less likely that a checklist can or should be followed. Checklists can take an impractical amount of time to follow. Driving an automobile is a routine but complex process. Do you keep a checklist in your car for every time you get behind the wheel?

Moreover, by their very nature, complex tasks can pose problems that fall outside the scope of the checklist. The last thing we need to solve unanticipated or complicated problems is rote allegiance to a checklist that is poorly suited to the problem at hand.

Indeed, a problem with many poor decisions is that heuristics are too often followed, with little thought to whether the assumptions behind them still hold true. If we have learned anything from the financial crisis, it is that a model or heuristic is only as good as its assumptions. Assume housing prices are properly valued and likely to continue to increase, and it makes all the sense in the world to be aggressive in making loans. Countrywide and Fannie Mae had all sorts of rules, protocols, and checklists they followed in making catastrophically bad loan decisions.

As for the medical decision making, as another physician and author, Sandeep Jauhar, noted, advocates of checklists often ignore the unintended consequences. Insurers compensate doctors for ticking off boxes on checklists—like prescribing antibiotics—even when there is no evidence they are warranted. Because this protocol encourages the growth of antibiotic-resistant bacteria, we all are endangered by this checklist-adhering behavior.

We want to think we live in a world where decision-making errors can be easily solved. We can mitigate some decisions by learning more about decision-making errors, but one of the main learning points is that we need a healthier respect for the degree to which we're susceptible to errors. Checklists provide a false sense of security and an ignorance about when they cause more problems than they solve.

Sources: S. Jauhar, "One Thing After Another," *New York Times Book Review* (January 24, 2010), p. 7; C. Arnst, "Make a List. Check it Twice," *Bloomberg Businessweek* (February 22, 2010), pp. 78–79; J. Ross, "The Checklist Manifesto and the Digital Divide," *Forbes* (July 27, 2010), downloaded on May 7, 2011, from www.forbes.com.

- Absenteeism, turnover, and job satisfaction are also reactions to an individual's perceptions. Dissatisfaction with working conditions and the belief that an organization lacks promotion opportunities are judgments based on attempts to create meaning in the job.
- The employee's conclusion that a job is good or bad is an interpretation. Managers must spend time understanding how each individual interprets reality and, when there is a significant difference between what someone sees and what exists, try to eliminate the distortions.

Individual Decision Making   Individuals think and reason before they act. This is why an understanding of how people make decisions can be helpful for explaining and predicting their behavior. In some decision situations, people follow the rational decision-making model. But few important decisions are simple or unambiguous enough for the rational model's assumptions to apply. So we find individuals looking for solutions that satisfice rather than optimize, injecting biases and prejudices into the decision process, and relying on intuition.

What can managers do to improve their decision making? We offer four suggestions.

- Analyze the situation. Adjust your decision-making approach to the national culture you're operating in and to the criteria your organization evaluates and rewards. If you're in a country that doesn't value rationality, don't feel compelled to follow the rational decision-making model or to try to make your decisions appear rational. Similarly, organizations differ in the importance they place on risk, the use of groups, and the like. Adjust your decision approach to ensure it's compatible with the organization's culture.
- Second, be aware of biases. Then try to minimize their impact. Exhibit 6-4 offers some suggestions.
- Third, combine rational analysis with intuition. These are not conflicting approaches to decision making. By using both, you can actually improve your decision-making effectiveness. As you gain managerial experience, you should feel increasingly confident in imposing your intuitive processes on top of your rational analysis.
- Finally, try to enhance your creativity. Actively look for novel solutions to problems, attempt to see problems in new ways, and use analogies. Try to remove work and organizational barriers that might impede your creativity.

QUESTIONS FOR REVIEW

1 What is perception, and what factors influence our perception?

2 What is attribution theory? What are the three determinants of attribution? What are its implications for explaining organizational behavior?

3 What shortcuts do people frequently use in making judgments about others?

4 What is the link between perception and decision making? How does one affect the other?

5 What is the rational model of decision making? How is it different from bounded rationality and intuition?

6 What are some of the common decision biases or errors that people make?

7 What are the influences of individual differences, organizational constraints, and culture on decision making?

8 Are unethical decisions more a function of an individual decision maker or the decision maker's work environment? Explain.

9 What is creativity, and what is the three-component model of creativity?

EXPERIENTIAL EXERCISE Biases in Decision Making

Step 1
Answer each of the following problems.

1. *Fortune* magazine ranked the following 10 corporations among the 500 largest U.S.–based firms according to sales volume for 2008:
   Group A: Apple Computer, Hershey Foods, Kellogg, McDonald's, U.S. Airways
   Group B: Altria Group, AmerisourceBergen, Cardinal Health, McKesson, Valero Energy
   Which group would you say had the larger total sales volume—A or B? By what percentage—10 percent, 50 percent, 100 percent?

2. The best student in your introductory MBA class this past semester writes poetry and is rather shy and small in stature. What was the student's undergraduate major—Chinese studies or psychology?

3. Which of the following causes more deaths in the United States each year?
   a. Stomach cancer
   b. Motor vehicle accidents

4. Which would you choose?
   a. A sure gain of $240
   b. A 25 percent chance of winning $1,000 and a 75 percent chance of winning nothing

5. Which would you choose?
   a. A sure loss of $750
   b. A 75 percent chance of losing $1,000 and a 25 percent chance of losing nothing

6. Which would you choose?
   a. A sure loss of $3,000
   b. An 80 percent chance of losing $4,000 and a 20 percent chance of losing nothing

Step 2
Break into groups of three to five students. Compare your answers. Explain why you chose the answers you did.

Step 3
Your instructor will give you the correct answers to each problem. Now discuss the accuracy of your decisions, the biases evident in the decisions you reached, and how you might improve your decision making to make it more accurate.

Source: These problems are based on examples provided in M. H. Bazerman, *Judgment in Managerial Decision Making*, 3rd ed. (New York: Wiley, 1994).

ETHICAL DILEMMA Max's Burger: The Dollar Value of Ethics

In July 2011, Nassar Group, a well-diversified conglomerate operating in Dubai, bought the rights to manage Max's Burger network of franchised outlets in Dubai. Max's Burger is an emerging American fast-food chain with franchised outlets across the globe. The move was a personal project of Houssam Nassar, the Group's managing director—and a businessman with an excellent reputation.

Dubai's fast-food market is overwhelmed with franchised restaurants. Meat quality at Max's Burger, however, was lower than the standards set by franchisors. This was all about to change, because Nassar did not intend to jeopardize his reputation and image. Accordingly, as the new operator of Max's Burger outlets, he issued a directive instructing the warehouse manager to decline any frozen meat shipment that did not comply with the franchisor's set standards.

A few weeks after Nassar Group took over the management of Max's Burger, a frozen meat shipment was delivered to the Max's Burger main warehouse. Upon measuring the temperature of the meat, the warehouse manager found that it was few degrees outside acceptable limits. In terms of governmental regulations, a couple of degrees' difference in temperature would present no risk to customers' health; however, such a difference could have a minimal effect on the taste and texture of the meat.

Prior to the change of management, and for many years before, the warehouse manager had no second thoughts about accepting such a shipment: no food poisoning claim was ever filed against Max's Burger, and taste inconsistencies never bothered anyone enough to complain. Also, the company supplying the meat to Max's Burger is owned by a relative of the warehouse manager.

With the new directive in place, however, the warehouse manager was unsure about his decision. Even though he knew that Nassar would have no way of finding out that the received meat was noncompliant, he wasn't as sure about his decision this time around.

Questions

1. Does the decision to accept or refuse the frozen meat shipment call for ethical or legal considerations? Why?

2. Identify the stakeholders who will be influenced by the decision to accept or refuse the frozen meat shipment?

3. What type of decision-making framework would you advise the warehouse manager to adopt in order to help him reach an optimal decision? How will your suggestion help?

Sources: Charbel Aoun and Hasan Shahin, "The Dollar Value of Ethics!," Meapro Consulting, www .meapro.com. The case was adapted to provide materials for class discussions. The authors do not intend to illustrate either effective or ineffective handling of a situation. To protect confidentiality, the authors may have disguised certain names and other identifying information, without jeopardizing the fundamentals of the situation.

CASE INCIDENT 1 Decision-Making Processes at Steel Inc.

John Pieterson and Jack Gack are both employees of Steel Incorporated. The company counts more than 5,000 employees and has a presence in almost all European countries. Steel Inc. transforms bulk steel into smaller components, ready to be used in consumer products. Products range from toy parts to food cans. Like most steel companies, Steel Inc. is a traditional company characterized by a low level of flexibility and high levels of bureaucracy. The company has several branches and subsidiaries located all over Europe in order to stay close to its customers.

The decision-making processes at Steel Inc. are crucial to the company's operations. Once a customer (new or existing) approaches the firm, decision making has to happen at a quick pace. Obviously, decisions with regard to level of customization speed of manufacturing, and prices determine which of the competing companies gets the order. When making a proposal, a huge number of factors must be considered. Not only does all internal information have to be considered, but external information such as competitors' proposals also must be taken into account. If Steel Inc. takes too long to deliver a clear proposal, cannot deliver the demanded products fast enough, or bids too high, competitors will seal the deal.

Although Steel Inc. has gone through some changes, the bureaucratic structure still has a big impact on the jobs of both Pieterson and Gack. John Pieterson is a manager at a subsidiary in The Netherlands. In formulating a proposal or bid for a customer's order, he can be characterized as a

very rational person. Although he takes somewhat longer than his colleagues to do similar work, he has always secured a lot of customer orders and is therefore considered a very successful manager within the company. However, Steel Inc.'s success in recent years has affected his decision making. He now drafts a proposal faster, but he also considers less information. In some cases, he even takes competitor prices as a starting point and simply adapts those a little. Still, the change doesn't seem to harm his performance, and orders keep coming in.

Jack Gack, located at a branch in Finland, performs the same job as Pieterson. However, Gack is very unsuccessful lately. Of course he makes rational decisions, but he also includes a fair share of intuition. Although often criticized, Gack is not willing to let go of his intuition. He truly believes that external factors contributed to his bad performance. Subordinates have also started to talk about Gack's possible incompetence. Top management has looked at Pieterson's success and now wonders whether to impose that style on Jack.

Questions

1. Which biases in decision making can be identified in the performances of both Pieterson and Gack?

2. How can the identified biases be overcome?

3. Is rational decision making better than intuitive decision making? If so, when?

4. Should top management change Gack's decision-making style?

CASE INCIDENT 2 Career Promotion at Emox: Rationalizing under Uncertainty

When Kareem left the office of Emox CEO Naji Haddad, all he felt was pride and joy at being considered as a potential Website manager for Emox's star search engine Araboo. While driving back home, however, these feelings of satisfaction were giving way to thoughts of worry and hesitation.

Emox was the first company in the Arab region to create, develop, and manage country-based search engines. When Emox was established in 2000, search engines like Yahoo! and Altavista were the "Facebooks" of that era. At that time, people in the region had no local search engines or guides to satisfy their Internet search needs. Sensing the opportunity, Naji Haddad, co-founder and current CEO of Emox, developed the company's first search engine, LebWeb.com, which only returned Lebanese-related content. It was a huge success.

Since the natural growth target of most Lebanese businesses is the wider Middle East region, it was only natural that within few months, Emox would develop a number of country-dedicated search engines for practically every country in the region. Currently, Emox manages close to 45 regional and international Websites, search engines, and portals.

Kareem's journey at Emox started in 2003 when he joined the company as a research analyst. Three years later, he was promoted to content manager of LebWeb, where he rejuvenated LebWeb's image and increased traffic to the Website by a yearly average of 17 percent and advertisement revenues by 20 percent.

When Emox needed to recruit a new Website manager for its biggest search engine Araboo, Kareem's success at LebWeb made him a prime candidate for the position. Kareem began to worry about his ability to be in charge of the whole Website because, although the new job would be a big career advancement, the job of a Website manager entails much more than that of a content manager. In addition, Araboo's team is based in Saudi Arabia, and Kareem is very satisfied with his lifestyle in Lebanon.

It seems that Kareem has a lot of thinking to do; Emox's CEO was expecting Kareem's decision early the next day.

Questions

1. Using the rational choice theory model of decision making, identify the decision-making criteria that come into play in Kareem's decision whether to accept or refuse the suggested promotion.

2. Based on the criteria identified in question 1, what do you think Kareem's decision should be?

3. Assume the outcome of a rational decision-making process is for Kareem to accept the offer. However, Kareem declines the promotion. How would you explain such a decision?

Sources: Charbel Aoun and Hasan Shahin, "Rationalizing under Uncertainty," Meapro Consulting, www .meapro.com. The case was adapted to provide materials for class discussions. The authors do not intend to illustrate either effective or ineffective handling of a situation. To protect confidentiality, the authors may have disguised certain names and other identifying information, without jeopardizing the essence of the situation.

ENDNOTES

1. H. H. Kelley, "Attribution in Social Interaction," in E. Jones et al. (eds.), *Attribution: Perceiving the Causes of Behavior* (Morristown, NJ: General Learning Press, 1972); and M. J. Martinko, P. Harvey, and M. T. Dasborough, "Attribution Theory in the Organizational Sciences: A Case of Unrealized Potential," *Journal of Organizational Behavior 32,* no. 1 (2011), pp. 144–149.

2. See L. Ross, "The Intuitive Psychologist and His Shortcomings," in L. Berkowitz (ed.), *Advances in Experimental Social Psychology,* vol. 10 (Orlando, FL: Academic Press, 1977), pp. 174–220; and A. G. Miller and T. Lawson, "The Effect of an Informational Option on the Fundamental Attribution Error," *Personality and Social Psychology Bulletin* 15, no. 2 (1989), pp. 194–204.

3. See, for instance, N. Epley and D. Dunning, "Feeling 'Holier Than Thou': Are Self-Serving Assessments Produced by Errors in Self- or Social Prediction?" *Journal of Personality and Social Psychology* 76, no. 6 (2000), pp. 861–875; M. Goerke, J. Moller, S. Schulz-Hardt, U. Napiersky, and D. Frey, "'It's Not My Fault—But Only I Can Change It': Counterfactual and Prefactual Thoughts of Managers," *Journal of Applied Psychology* 89, no. 2 (2004), pp. 279–292; and E. G. Hepper, R. H. Gramzow, and C. Sedikides, "Individual Differences in Self-Enhancement and Self-Protection Strategies: An Integrative Analysis," *Journal of Personality* 78, no. 2 (2010), pp. 781–814.

4. See D. M. Cain and A. S. Little, "Everyone's a Little Bit Biased (even Physicians)," *JAMA: Journal of the American Medical Association* 299, no. 24 (2008), pp. 2893–2895.

5. See, for instance, A. H. Mezulis, L. Y. Abramson, J. S. Hyde, and B. L. Hankin, "Is There a Universal Positivity

Bias in Attributions: A Meta-Analytic Review of Individual, Developmental, and Cultural Differences in the Self-Serving Attributional Bias," *Psychological Bulletin* 130, no. 5 (2004), pp. 711–747; C. F. Falk, S. J. Heine, M. Yuki, and K. Takemura, "Why Do Westerners Self-Enhance More than East Asians?" *European Journal of Personality* 23, no. 3 (2009), pp. 183–203; and F. F. T. Chiang and T. A. Birtch, "Examining the Perceived Causes of Successful Employee Performance: An East–West Comparison," *International Journal of Human Resource Management* 18, no. 2 (2007), pp. 232–248.

6. S. Nam, "Cultural and Managerial Attributions for Group Performance," unpublished doctoral dissertation, University of Oregon. Cited in R. M. Steers, S. J. Bischoff, and L. H. Higgins, "Cross-Cultural Management Research," *Journal of Management Inquiry,* December 1992, pp. 325–326.

7. T. Menon, M. W. Morris, C. Y. Chiu, and Y. Y. Hong, "Culture and the Construal of Agency: Attribution to Individual Versus Group Dispositions," *Journal of Personality and Social Psychology* 76, no. 5 (1999), pp. 701–717; and R. Friedman, W. Liu, C. C. Chen, and S. S. Chi, "Causal Attribution for Interfirm Contract Violation: A Comparative Study of Chinese and American Commercial Arbitrators," *Journal of Applied Psychology* 92, no. 3 (2007), pp. 856–864.

8. J. Spencer-Rodgers, M. J. Williams, D. L. Hamilton, K. Peng, and L. Wang, "Culture and Group Perception: Dispositional and Stereotypic Inferences about Novel and National Groups," *Journal of Personality and Social Psychology* 93, no. 4 (2007), pp. 525–543.

9. J. D. Brown, "Across the (Not So) Great Divide: Cultural Similarities in Self-Evaluative Processes," *Social and Personality Psychology Compass* 4, no. 5 (2010), pp. 318–330.

10. A. Zhang, C. Reyna, Z. Qian, and G. Yu, "Interpersonal Attributions of Responsibility in the Chinese Workplace: A Test of Western Models in a Collectivistic Context," *Journal of Applied Social Psychology* 38, no. 9 (2008), pp. 2361–2377; and A. Zhang, F. Xia, and C. Li, "The Antecedents of Help Giving in Chinese Culture: Attribution, Judgment of Responsibility, Expectation Change and the Reaction of Affect," *Social Behavior and Personality* 35, no. 1 (2007), pp. 135–142.

11. D. C. Dearborn and H. A. Simon, "Selective Perception: A Note on the Departmental Identification of Executives," *Sociometry* 21, no. 2 (1958), pp. 140–144. Some of the conclusions in this classic study have recently been challenged in J. Walsh, "Selectivity and Selective Perception: An Investigation of Managers' Belief Structures and Information Processing," *Academy of Management Journal* 31, no. 4 (1988), pp. 873–896; M. J. Waller, G. Huber, and W. H. Glick, "Functional Background as a Determinant of Executives' Selective Perception," *Academy of Management Journal* 38, no. 4 (1995), pp. 943–974; and J. M. Beyer, P. Chattopadhyay, E. George, W. H. Glick, D. T. Ogilvie, and D. Pugliese, "The Selective Perception of Managers Revisited," *Academy of Management Journal* 40, no. 3 (1997), pp. 716–737.

12. J. Healy and M. M. Grynbaum, "Why Analysts Keep Telling Investors to Buy," *The New York Times* (February 9, 2009), pp. B1, B7.

13. See P. Rosenzweig, *The Halo Effect* (New York: The Free Press, 2007); I. Dennis, "Halo Effects in Grading Student Projects,"

Journal of Applied Psychology 92, no. 4 (2007), pp. 1169–1176; C. E. Naquin and R. O. Tynan, "The Team Halo Effect: Why Teams Are Not Blamed for Their Failures," *Journal of Applied Psychology* 88, no. 2 (2003), pp. 332–340; and T. M. Bechger, G. Maris, and Y. P. Hsiao, "Detecting Halo Effects in Performance-Based Evaluations," *Applied Psychological Measurement* 34, no. 8 (2010), pp. 607–619.

14. S. E. Asch, "Forming Impressions of Personality," *Journal of Abnormal and Social Psychology* 41, no. 3 (1946), pp. 258–290.

15. J. L. Hilton and W. von Hippel, "Stereotypes," *Annual Review of Psychology* 47 (1996), pp. 237–271.

16. See, for example, C. Ostroff and L. E. Atwater, "Does Whom You Work with Matter? Effects of Referent Group Gender and Age Composition on Managers' Compensation," *Journal of Applied Psychology* 88, no. 4 (2003), pp. 725–740; M. E. Heilman, A. S. Wallen, D. Fuchs, and M. M. Tamkins, "Penalties for Success: Reactions to Women Who Succeed at Male Gender-Typed Tasks," *Journal of Applied Psychology* 89, no. 3 (2004), pp. 416–427; V. K. Gupta, D. B. Turban, and N. M. Bhawe, "The Effect of Gender Stereotype Activation on Entrepreneurial Intentions," *Journal of Applied Psychology* 93, no. 5 (2008), pp. 1053–1061; and R. A. Posthuma and M. A. Campion, "Age Stereotypes in the Workplace: Common Stereotypes, Moderators, and Future Research Directions," *Journal of Management* 35, no. 1 (2009), pp. 158–188.

17. See, for example, N. Dasgupta, D. DeSteno, L. A. Williams, and M. Hunsinger, "Fanning the Flames of Prejudice: The Influence of Specific Incidental Emotions on Implicit Prejudice," *Emotion* 9, no. 4 (2009), pp. 585–591; and J. C. Ziegert and P. C. Hanges, "Strong Rebuttal for Weak Criticisms: Reply to Blanton et al. (2009)," *Journal of Applied Psychology* 94, no. 3 (2009), pp. 590–597.

18. J. L. Eberhardt, P. G. Davies, V. J. Purdie-Vaughns, and S. L. Johnson, "Looking Deathworthy: Perceived Stereotypicality of Black Defendants Predicts Capital-Sentencing Outcomes," *Psychological Science* 17, no. 5 (2006), pp. 383–386.

19. A. S. Rosette, G. J. Leonardelli, and K. W. Phillips, "The White Standard: Racial Bias in Leader Categorization," *Journal of Applied Psychology* 93, no. 4 (2008), pp. 758–777.

20. H. G. Heneman III, T. A. Judge, and J. D. Kammeyer-Mueller *Staffing Organizations* (Middleton, WI: Mendota House, 2012).

21. J. Willis and A. Todorov, "First Impressions: Making Up Your Mind after a 100ms Exposure to a Face," *Psychological Science* 17, no. 7 (2006), pp. 592–598.

22. See, for example, E. C. Webster, *Decision Making in the Employment Interview* (Montreal: McGill University, Industrial Relations Center, 1964).

23. See, for example, D. B. McNatt, "Ancient Pygmalion Joins Contemporary Management: A Meta-Analysis of the Result," *Journal of Applied Psychology* 85, no. 2 (2000), pp. 314–322; O. B. Davidson and D. Eden, "Remedial Self-Fulfilling Prophecy: Two Field Experiments to Prevent Golem Effects among Disadvantaged Women," *Journal of Applied Psychology* 85, no. 3 (2000), pp. 386–398; and G. Natanovich and D. Eden, "Pygmalion Effects among Outreach Supervisors and Tutors: Extending Sex Generalizability," *Journal of Applied Psychology* 93, no. 6 (2008), pp. 1382–1389.

24. D. Eden and A. B. Shani, "Pygmalion Goes to Boot Camp: Expectancy, Leadership, and Trainee Performance," *Journal*

of Applied Psychology (April 1982), pp. 194–199; D. B. McNatt and T. A. Judge, "Boundary Conditions of the Galatea Effect: A Field Experiment and Constructive Replication," *Academy of Management Journal* (August 2004), pp. 550–565; and X. M. Bezuijen, P. T. van den Berg, K. van Dam, and H. Thierry, "Pygmalion and Employee Learning: The Role of Leader Behaviors," *Journal of Management* 35, (2009), pp. 1248–1267.

25. See, for example, K. F. E. Wong and J. Y. Y. Kwong, "Effects of Rater Goals on Rating Patterns: Evidence from an Experimental Field Study," *Journal of Applied Psychology* 92, no. 2 (2007), pp. 577–585; and S. E. DeVoe and S. S. Iyengar, "Managers' Theories of Subordinates: A Cross-Cultural Examination of Manager Perceptions of Motivation and Appraisal of Performance," *Organizational Behavior and Human Decision Processes* (January 2004), pp. 47–61.

26. R. Sanders, *The Executive Decisionmaking Process: Identifying Problems and Assessing Outcomes* (Westport, CT: Quorum, 1999).

27. See H. A. Simon, "Rationality in Psychology and Economics," *Journal of Business* (October 1986), pp. 209–224; and E. Shafir and R. A. LeBoeuf, "Rationality," *Annual Review of Psychology* 53 (2002), pp. 491–517.

28. For a review of the rational decision-making model, see M. H. Bazerman and D. A. Moore, *Judgment in Managerial Decision Making*, 7th ed. (Hoboken, New Jersey: Wiley, 2008).

29. J. G. March, *A Primer on Decision Making* (New York: The Free Press, 2009); and D. Hardman and C. Harries, "How Rational Are We?" *Psychologist* (February 2002), pp. 76–79.

30. Bazerman and Moore, *Judgment in Managerial Decision Making.*

31. J. E. Russo, K. A. Carlson, and M. G. Meloy, "Choosing an Inferior Alternative," *Psychological Science* 17, no. 10 (2006), pp. 899–904.

32. D. Kahneman, "Maps of Bounded Rationality: Psychology for Behavioral Economics," *The American Economic Review* 93, no. 5 (2003), pp. 1449–1475; and J. Zhang, C. K. Hsee, and Z. Xiao, "The Majority Rule in Individual Decision Making," *Organizational Behavior and Human Decision Processes* 99 (2006), pp. 102–111.

33. See H. A. Simon, *Administrative Behavior*, 4th ed. (New York: The Free Press, 1997); and M. Augier, "Simon Says: Bounded Rationality Matters," *Journal of Management Inquiry* (September 2001), pp. 268–275.

34. G. Gigerenzer, "Why Heuristics Work," *Perspectives on Psychological Science* 3, no. 1 (2008), pp. 20–29; and A. K. Shah and D. M. Oppenheimer, "Heuristics Made Easy: An Effort-Reduction Framework," *Psychological Bulletin* 134, no. 2 (2008), pp. 207–222.

35. See A. W. Kruglanski and G. Gigerenzer, "Intuitive and Deliberate Judgments Are Based on Common Principles," *Psychological Review* 118 (2011), pp. 97–109.

36. E. Dane and M. G. Pratt, "Exploring Intuition and Its Role in Managerial Decision Making," *Academy of Management Review* 32, no. 1 (2007), pp. 33–54; and J. A. Hicks, D. C. Cicero, J. Trent, C. M. Burton, and L. A. King, "Positive Affect, Intuition, and Feelings of Meaning," *Journal of Personality and Social Psychology* 98 (2010), pp. 967–979.

37. P. D. Brown, "Some Hunches About Intuition," *The New York Times* (November 17, 2007), p. B5.

38. See, for instance, L. A. Burke and M. K. Miller, "Taking the Mystery Out of Intuitive Decision Making," *Academy of Management Executive* (November 1999), pp. 91–99; J. A. Andersen, "Intuition in Managers: Are Intuitive Managers More Effective?" *Journal of Managerial Psychology* 15, no. 1–2 (2000), pp. 46–63; and Y. Ibar, J. Cone, and T. Gilovich, "People's Intuitions about Intuitive Insight and Intuitive Choice," *Journal of Personality and Social Psychology* 99 (2010), pp. 232–247.

39. See, for instance, A. W. Kruglanski and G. Gigerenzer, "Intuitive and Deliberate Judgments are Based on Common Principles," *Psychological Review* 118 (2011), pp. 97–109.

40. S. P. Robbins, *Decide & Conquer: Making Winning Decisions and Taking Control of Your Life* (Upper Saddle River, NJ: Financial Times/Prentice Hall, 2004), p. 13.

41. S. Plous, *The Psychology of Judgment and Decision Making* (New York: McGraw-Hill, 1993), p. 217.

42. C. R. M. McKenzie, M. J. Liersch, and I. Yaniv, "Overconfidence in Interval Estimates: What Does Expertise Buy You," *Organizational Behavior and Human Decision Processes* 107 (2008), pp. 179–191.

43. B. Fischhoff, P. Slovic, and S. Lichtenstein, "Knowing with Certainty: The Appropriateness of Extreme Confidence," *Journal of Experimental Psychology: Human Perception and Performance* (November 1977), pp. 552–564.

44. J. Kruger and D. Dunning, "Unskilled and Unaware of It: How Difficulties in Recognizing One's Own Incompetence Lead to Inflated Self-Assessments," *Journal of Personality and Social Psychology* (November 1999), pp. 1121–1134; and R. P. Larrick, K. A. Burson, and J. B. Soll, "Social Comparison and Confidence: When Thinking You're Better than Average Predicts Overconfidence (and When It Does Not)" *Organizational Behavior and Human Decision Processes* 102 (2007), pp. 76–94.

45. K. M. Hmieleski and R. A. Baron, "Entrepreneurs' Optimism and New Venture Performance: A Social Cognitive Perspective," *Academy of Management Journal* 52, no. 3 (2009), pp. 473–488.

46. R. Frick and A. K. Smith, "Overconfidence Game," *Kiplinger's Personal Finance* 64, no. 3 (2010), p. 23.

47. See, for instance, J. P. Simmons, R. A. LeBoeuf, and L. D. Nelson, "The Effect of Accuracy Motivation on Anchoring and Adjustment: Do People Adjust from Their Provided Anchors?" *Journal of Personality and Social Psychology* 99 (2010), pp. 917–932.

48. J. Bailey, "Dreams Fly Into Reality," *The New York Times* (April 10, 2008), pp. B1, B4.

49. C. Janiszewski and D. Uy, "Precision of the Anchor Influences the Amount of Adjustment," *Psychological Science* 19, no. 2 (2008), pp. 121–127.

50. See E. Jonas, S. Schultz-Hardt, D. Frey, and N. Thelen, "Confirmation Bias in Sequential Information Search after Preliminary Decisions," *Journal of Personality and Social Psychology* (April 2001), pp. 557–571; and W. Hart, D. Albarracín, A. H. Eagly, I. Brechan, M. Lindberg, and L. Merrill, "Feeling Validated Versus Being Correct: A Meta-Analysis of Selective Exposure to Information," *Psychological Bulletin* 135 (2009), pp. 555–588.

51. See A. Tversky and D. Kahneman, "Availability: A Heuristic for Judging Frequency and Probability," in D. Kahneman,

P. Slovic, and A. Tversky (eds.), *Judgment Under Uncertainty: Heuristics and Biases* (Cambridge, UK: Cambridge University Press, 1982), pp. 163–178; and B. J. Bushman and G. L. Wells, "Narrative Impressions of Literature: The Availability Bias and the Corrective Properties of Meta-Analytic Approaches," *Personality and Social Psychology Bulletin* (September 2001), pp. 1123–1130.

52. G. Morgenson, "Debt Watchdogs: Tamed or Caught Napping?" *The New York Times* (December 7, 2009), pp. 1, 32.

53. See B. M. Staw, "The Escalation of Commitment to a Course of Action," *Academy of Management Review* (October 1981), pp. 577–587; K. Fai, E. Wong, M. Yik, and J. Y. Y. Kwong, "Understanding the Emotional Aspects of Escalation of Commitment: The Role of Negative Affect," *Journal of Applied Psychology* 91, no. 2 (2006), pp. 282–297; and A. Zardkoohi, "Do Real Options Lead to Escalation of Commitment? Comment," *Academy of Management Review* (January 2004), pp. 111–119.

54. B. M. Staw, "Knee-Deep in the Big Muddy: A Study of Escalating Commitment to a Chosen Course of Action," *Organizational Behavior and Human Performance* 16 (1976), pp. 27–44; and S. Schulz-Hardt, B. Thurow Kröning, and D. Frey, "Preference-Based Escalation: A New Interpretation for the Responsibility Effect in Escalating Commitment and Entrapment," *Organizational Behavior and Human Decision Processes* 108 (2009), pp. 175–186.

55. K. F. E. Wong and J. Y. Y. Kwong, "The Role of Anticipated Regret in Escalation of Commitment," *Journal of Applied Psychology* 92, no. 2 (2007), pp. 545–554.

56. K. F. E. Wong, J. Y. Y. Kwong, and C. K. Ng, "When Thinking Rationally Increases Biases: The Role of Rational Thinking Style in Escalation of Commitment," *Applied Psychology: An International Review* 57, no. 2 (2008), pp. 246–271.

57. See, for instance, A. James and A. Wells, "Death Beliefs, Superstitious Beliefs and Health Anxiety," *British Journal of Clinical Psychology* (March 2002), pp. 43–53; and U. Hahn and P. A. Warren, "Perceptions of Randomness: Why Three Heads Are Better than One," *Psychological Review* 116 (2009), pp. 454–461.

58. See, for example, D. J. Keys and B. Schwartz, "Leaky Rationality: How Research on Behavioral Decision Making Challenges Normative Standards of Rationality," *Psychological Science* 2, no. 2 (2007), pp. 162–180; and U. Simonsohn, "Direct Risk Aversion: Evidence from Risky Prospects Valued Below Their Worst Outcome," *Psychological Science* 20, no. 6 (2009), pp. 686–692.

59. J. K. Maner, M. T. Gailliot, D. A. Butz, and B. M. Peruche, "Power, Risk, and the Status Quo: Does Power Promote Riskier or More Conservative Decision Making," *Personality and Social Psychology Bulletin* 33, no. 4 (2007), pp. 451–462.

60. A. Chakraborty, S. Sheikh, and N. Subramanian, "Termination Risk and Managerial Risk Taking," *Journal of Corporate Finance* 13 (2007), pp. 170–188.

61. X. He and V. Mittal, "The Effect of Decision Risk and Project Stage on Escalation of Commitment," *Organizational Behavior and Human Decision Processes* 103, no. 2 (2007), pp. 225–237.

62. D. Kahneman and A. Tversky, "Prospect Theory: An Analysis of Decisions Under Risk," *Econometrica* 47, no. 2 (1979), pp. 263–291; and P. Bryant and R. Dunford, "The Influence of Regulatory Focus on Risky Decision-Making,"

Applied Psychology: An International Review 57, no. 2 (2008), pp. 335–359.

63. A. J. Porcelli and M. R. Delgado, "Acute Stress Modulates Risk Taking in Financial Decision Making," *Psychological Science* 20, no. 3 (2009), pp. 278–283.

64. R. L. Guilbault, F. B. Bryant, J. H. Brockway, and E. J. Posavac, "A Meta-Analysis of Research on Hindsight Bias," *Basic and Applied Social Psychology* (September 2004), pp. 103–117; and L. Werth, F. Strack, and J. Foerster, "Certainty and Uncertainty: The Two Faces of the Hindsight Bias," *Organizational Behavior and Human Decision Processes* (March 2002), pp. 323–341.

65. J. Bell, "The Final Cut?" *Oregon Business* 33, no. 5 (2010), p. 27.

66. E. Dash and J. Creswell, "Citigroup Pays for a Rush to Risk," *The New York Times* (November 20, 2008), pp. 1, 28; S. Pulliam, S. Ng, and R. Smith, "Merrill Upped Ante as Boom in Mortgage Bonds Fizzled," *The Wall Street Journal* (April 16, 2008), pp. A1, A14; and M. Gladwell, "Connecting the Dots," *The New Yorker* (March 10, 2003).

67. This section is based on T. Gärling, E. Kirchler, A. Lewis, and F. van Raaij, "Psychology, Financial Decision Making, and Financial Crises," *Psychological Science in the Public Interest* 10 (2009), pp.1–47; T. Zaleskiewicz, "Financial Forecasts During the Crisis: Were Experts More Accurate than Laypeople?" *Journal of Economic Psychology* 32 (2011), pp. 384–390; and G. A. Akerlof and R. J. Shiller, *Animal Spirits: How Human Psychology Drives the Economy and Why It Matters for Global Capitalism* (Princeton, NJ: Princeton University Press, 2009).

68. H. Moon, J. R. Hollenbeck, S. E. Humphrey, and B. Maue, "The Tripartite Model of Neuroticism and the Suppression of Depression and Anxiety within an Escalation of Commitment Dilemma," *Journal of Personality* 71 (2003), pp. 347–368; and H. Moon, "The Two Faces of Conscientiousness: Duty and Achievement Striving in Escalation of Commitment Dilemmas," *Journal of Applied Psychology* 86 (2001), pp. 535–540.

69. J. Musch, "Personality Differences in Hindsight Bias," *Memory* 11 (2003), pp. 473–489.

70. W. K. Campbell and C. Sedikides, "Self-Threat Magnifies the Self-Serving Bias: A Meta-Analytic Integration," *Review of General Psychology* 3 (1999), pp. 23–43.

71. This section is based on S. Nolen-Hoeksema, J. Larson, and C. Grayson, "Explaining the Gender Difference in Depressive Symptoms," *Journal of Personality & Social Psychology* (November 1999), pp. 1061–1072; and J. S. Hyde, A. H. Mezulis, and L. Y. Abramson, "The ABCs of Depression: Integrating Affective, Biological, and Cognitive Models to Explain the Emergence of the Gender Difference in Depression," *Psychological Review* 115, no. 2 (2008), pp. 291–313.

72. H. Connery and K. M. Davidson, "A Survey of Attitudes to Depression in the General Public: A Comparison of Age and Gender Differences," *Journal of Mental Health* 15, no. 2 (April 2006), pp. 179–189.

73. M. Elias, "Thinking It Over, and Over, and Over," *USA Today* (February 6, 2003), p. 10D.

74. K. E. Stanovich and R. F. West, "On the Relative Independence of Thinking Biases and Cognitive Ability,"

Journal of Personality and Social Psychology 94, no. 4 (2008), pp. 672–695.

75. N. J. Adler, *International Dimensions of Organizational Behavior,* 4th ed. (Cincinnati, OH: South-Western Publishing, 2002), pp. 182–189.

76. A. Wildavsky, *The Politics of the Budgetary Process* (Boston: Little, Brown, 1964).

77. G. F. Cavanagh, D. J. Moberg, and M. Valasquez, "The Ethics of Organizational Politics," *Academy of Management Journal* (June 1981), pp. 363–374.

78. See, for example, T. Machan, ed., *Commerce and Morality* (Totowa, NJ: Rowman and Littlefield, 1988).

79. T. M. Amabile, "A Model of Creativity and Innovation in Organizations," in B. M. Staw and L. L. Cummings (eds.), *Research in Organizational Behavior,* vol. 10 (Greenwich, CT: JAI Press, 1988), p. 126; and J. E. Perry-Smith and C. E. Shalley, "The Social Side of Creativity: A Static and Dynamic Social Network Perspective," *Academy of Management Review* (January 2003), pp. 89–106.

80. G. J. Feist and F. X. Barron, "Predicting Creativity from Early to Late Adulthood: Intellect, Potential, and Personality," *Journal of Research in Personality* (April 2003), pp. 62–88.

81. R. W. Woodman, J. E. Sawyer, and R. W. Griffin, "Toward a Theory of Organizational Creativity," *Academy of Management Review* (April 1993), p. 298; J. M. George and J. Zhou, "When Openness to Experience and Conscientiousness Are Related to Creative Behavior: An Interactional Approach," *Journal of Applied Psychology* (June 2001), pp. 513–524; and E. F. Rietzschel, C. K. W. de Dreu, and B. A. Nijstad, "Personal Need for Structure and Creative Performance: The Moderating Influence of Fear of Invalidity," *Personality and Social Psychology Bulletin* (June 2007), pp. 855–866.

82. A. K. Leung, W. W. Maddux, A. D. Galinsky, and C. Chiu, "Multicultural Experience Enhances Creativity," *American Psychologist* 63, no. 3 (2008), pp. 169–180.

83. Cited in C. G. Morris, *Psychology: An Introduction,* 9th ed. (Upper Saddle River, NJ: Prentice Hall, 1996), p. 344.

84. This section is based on T. M. Amabile, "Motivating Creativity in Organizations: On Doing What You Love and Loving What You Do," *California Management Review* 40, no. 1 (Fall 1997), pp. 39–58.

85. M. Baas, C. K. W. De Dreu, and B. A. Nijstad, "A Meta-Analysis of 25 Years of Mood-Creativity Research: Hedonic Tone, Activation, or Regulatory Focus?" *Psychological Bulletin* 134, no. 6 (2008), pp. 779–806.

86. J. Zhou, "When the Presence of Creative Coworkers Is Related to Creativity: Role of Supervisor Close Monitoring, Developmental Feedback, and Creative Personality," *Journal of Applied Psychology* 88, no. 3 (June 2003), pp. 413–422.

87. J. E. Perry-Smith, "Social yet Creative: The Role of Social Relationships in Facilitating Individual Creativity," *Academy of Management Journal* 49, no. 1 (2006), pp. 85–101.

88. G. Park, D. Lubinski, and C. P. Benbow, "Contrasting Intellectual Patterns Predict Creativity in the Arts and Sciences," *Psychological Science* 18, no. 11 (2007), pp. 948–952.

89. W. J. J. Gordon, *Synectics* (New York: Harper & Row, 1961).

90. See C. E. Shalley, J. Zhou, and G. R. Oldham, "The Effects of Personal and Contextual Characteristics on Creativity: Where Should We Go from Here?" *Journal of Management* (November 2004), pp. 933–958; G. Hirst, D. Van Knippenberg, and J. Zhou, "A Cross-Level Perspective on Employee Creativity: Goal Orientation, Team Learning Behavior, and Individual Creativity," *Academy of Management Journal* 52, no. 2 (2009), pp. 280–293; and C. E. Shalley, L. L. Gilson, and T. C. Blum, "Interactive Effects of Growth Need Strength, Work Context, and Job Complexity on Self-Reported Creative Performance," *Academy of Management Journal* 52, no. 3 (2009), pp. 489–505.

91. T. Jackson, "Cultural Values and Management Ethics: A 10-Nation Study," *Human Relations* (October 2001), pp. 1267–1302; see also J. B. Cullen, K. P. Parboteeah, and M. Hoegl, "Cross-National Differences in Managers' Willingness to Justify Ethically Suspect Behaviors: A Test of Institutional Anomie Theory," *Academy of Management Journal* (June 2004), pp. 411–421.

92. W. Chow Hou, "To Bribe or Not to Bribe?" *Asia, Inc.* (October 1996), p. 104.

93. P. Digh, "Shades of Gray in the Global Marketplace," *HRMagazine* (April 1997), p. 91.

LEARNING OBJECTIVES

After studying this chapter, you should be able to:

1 Describe the three key elements of motivation.

2 Identify early theories of motivation and evaluate their applicability today.

3 Apply the predictions of self-determination theory to intrinsic and extrinsic rewards.

4 Understand the implications of employee engagement for management.

5 Compare and contrast goal-setting theory and management by objectives.

6 Contrast reinforcement theory and goal-setting theory.

7 Demonstrate how organizational justice is a refinement of equity theory.

8 Apply the key tenets of expectancy theory to motivating employees.

9 Compare contemporary theories of motivation.

MyManagementLab

Access a host of interactive learning aids to help strengthen your understanding of the chapter concepts at **www.pearsonglobaleditions .com/mymanagementlab**.

THE MOTIVATIONS OF THE 99ERS

While the economy shows signs of improving, the sluggish nature of the recovery has left behind more long-term unemployed than anyone has seen since the Great Depression.

Typically, unemployment insurance lasts 6 months. As the great recession continued, Congress extended these benefits—up to 99 weeks for those in 27 states hit hardest by the recession.

The 99ers are those who have been unemployed more than 99 weeks. They number about 2 million, and millions more are underemployed or have withdrawn from the labor market altogether. Among the hardest hit are older workers who struggle to convince employers to hire them.

St. Louis resident Peter Gordon, 53, has been unemployed more than a year. Once he becomes a 99er, his unemployment check will run out. "I will be OK for another 20 weeks," Gordon said. "But I'm going crazy." Akron's Susan Harrell has been jobless more than 2 years and has exhausted her unemployment benefits. Laid off from her $60,000/year telecommunications job, she finds employers unwilling to hire her because she is unemployed, 58, or both. "They look at me and say, 'How long are you really going to work?' "

Should the government help those in need by extending unemployment benefits further? The question is complicated and divides Republicans and Democrats. But put aside ideology for a moment, and consider the motivational dynamics at play. Many have lost their jobs through no fault of their own. Not only are unemployment benefits compassionate, they provide an opportunity for people to retrain for a new occupation. Benefits thus motivate them to move into more viable occupations.

On the other hand, many economists argue that extending benefits provides disincentives for finding employment. One concludes, "Unemployment insurance is not free: It results in less employment and less output, not more." Paying people not to work gives them incentives not to work, this argument goes.

Our nation will probably never agree on the motivational effects of unemployment insurance. However, with or without insurance, there is troubling evidence that some individuals like Peter Gordon and Susan Harrell will remain out of work for a very long time. "This is horrible," says Harrell. "It's embarrassing and humiliating."

Sources: W. M. Welch, "Long-Term Unemployed See Benefits Rolled Back," *USA Today* (May 17, 2011), p. A1; D. Hunsinger, Long-Term Unemployed Face Stigmas in Job Search," *USA Today* (January 23, 2011), downloaded May 2, 2011, from www.usatoday.com/money/; M. Thornton, "99ers and the Long-term Unemployed Are the Elephants in the Economic Recovery Room," *Huffington Post* (May 15, 2011), downloaded May 25, 2011, from www.huffingtonpost.com/; C. B. Mulligan, "Do Jobless Benefits Discourage People From Finding Jobs?" *New York Times* (March 17, 2010), downloaded May 2, 2011, from http://economix.blogs.nytimes.com/.

7 Motivation Concepts

Luke: "I don't believe it."
Yoda: "That is why you fail."
—The Empire Strikes Back

Photo: Anne Strauss speaks at a protest and rally by '99ers. *Source:* b09/ZUMA Press/Newscom

Debates about motivation can occupy a central role in important public policy debates, and as we will see, they also rank among the most important questions managers need to answer.

However, motivation is not simply about working hard—it also reflects your view of your own abilities. Try a self-assessment of your confidence in your ability to succeed.

Motivation is one of the most frequently researched topics in OB.[1] A recent Gallup poll revealed one reason—a majority of U.S. employees (54 percent) are not actively engaged in their work, and another portion (17 percent) are actively disengaged.[2] In another study, workers reported wasting roughly 2 hours per day, not counting lunch and scheduled breaks (usually Internet surfing and talking with co-workers).[3] Clearly, motivation is an issue. The good news is that all this research provides useful insights into how to improve it.

In this chapter, we'll review the basics of motivation, assess motivation theories, and provide an integrative model that fits the best of these theories together.

SELF-ASSESSMENT LIBRARY

How Confident Am I in My Abilities to Succeed?

In the Self-Assessment Library (available on CD or online), take assessment IV.A.3 (How Confident Am I in My Abilities to Succeed?) and answer the following questions.

1. How did you score relative to other class members? Does that surprise you?
2. Do you think self-confidence is critical to success? Can a person be too confident?

Defining Motivation

1 Describe the three key elements of motivation.

Some individuals seem driven to succeed. But the same student who struggles to read a textbook for more than 20 minutes may devour a *Harry Potter* book in a day. The difference is the situation. So as we analyze the concept of motivation, keep in mind that the level of motivation varies both between individuals and within individuals at different times.

We define **motivation** as the processes that account for an individual's intensity, direction, and persistence of effort toward attaining a goal.[4] While general motivation is concerned with effort toward *any* goal, we'll narrow the focus to *organizational* goals in order to reflect our singular interest in work-related behavior.

The three key elements in our definition are intensity, direction, and persistence. *Intensity* describes how hard a person tries. This is the element most of us focus on when we talk about motivation. However, high intensity is unlikely to lead to favorable job-performance outcomes unless the effort is channeled in a *direction* that benefits the organization. Therefore, we consider the quality of effort as well as its intensity. Effort directed toward, and consistent with, the organization's goals is the kind of effort we should be seeking. Finally, motivation has a *persistence* dimension. This measures how long a person can maintain effort. Motivated individuals stay with a task long enough to achieve their goal.

2   Identify early theories of
       motivation and evaluate
       their applicability today.

Four theories of employee motivation formulated during the 1950s, although now of questionable validity, are probably still the best known. We discuss more valid explanations later, but these four represent a foundation on which they have grown, and practicing managers still use them and their terminology.

Hierarchy of Needs Theory

The best-known theory of motivation is Abraham Maslow's **hierarchy of needs**.[5] Maslow hypothesized that within every human being, there exists a hierarchy of five needs:

1. **Physiological.** Includes hunger, thirst, shelter, sex, and other bodily needs.
2. **Safety.** Security and protection from physical and emotional harm.
3. **Social.** Affection, belongingness, acceptance, and friendship.
4. **Esteem.** Internal factors such as self-respect, autonomy, and achievement, and external factors such as status, recognition, and attention.
5. **Self-actualization.** Drive to become what we are capable of becoming; includes growth, achieving our potential, and self-fulfillment.

Although no need is ever fully gratified, a substantially satisfied need no longer motivates. Thus as each becomes substantially satisfied, the next one becomes dominant. So if you want to motivate someone, according to Maslow, you need to understand what level of the hierarchy that person is currently on and focus on satisfying needs at or above that level, moving up the steps in Exhibit 7-1.

Maslow separated the five needs into higher and lower orders. Physiological and safety needs, where the theory says people start, were **lower-order needs**,

| Exhibit **7-1** | Maslow's Hierarchy of Needs |

Self-actualization
Esteem
Social
Safety
Physiological

Source: A. H. Maslow, Motivation and Personality, 3rd ed., R. D. Frager and J. Fadiman (eds.). © 1997. Adapted by permission of Pearson Education, Inc., Upper Saddle River, New Jersey.

---

motivation *The processes that account for an individual's intensity, direction, and persistence of effort toward attaining a goal.*

hierarchy of needs *Abraham Maslow's hierarchy of five needs—physiological, safety, social, esteem, and self-actualization—in which, as each need is substantially satisfied, the next need becomes dominant.*

lower-order needs *Needs that are satisfied externally, such as physiological and safety needs.*

"The Support of Others Improves Our Chances of Accomplishing Our Goals"

Surprisingly, this statement appears to be false.

There is some research on how team goals facilitate team performance. However, until recently, we knew very little about whether others help or hinder our individual chances of meeting a goal.

Generally, whether it's reaching a weight loss goal, successfully completing an undergraduate course, or completing a work task, help and support from others actually appears to hinder our chances and make us feel worse rather than better.

Why? First, research has found that help is often, well, unhelpful. Advice

and direction from others is seldom well suited for accomplishing our goal. If you're trying to meet a work deadline using your approach, it's not often useful for a co-worker to advise you to use his or her method instead. Second, such advice and assistance generally makes us feel less confident and positive about achieving the goal. The more help is offered, the more negative feelings and stress we have about the goal.

The upshot? Generally, you'll do a better job of meeting your individual work goals if you "just do it" by yourself. Of course, sometimes you do

need the help of others. But keep that help focused on specific questions and not on advice for attaining the general goal.

Sources: H. B. Kappes and P. E. Shrout, "When Goal Sharing Produces Support That Is Not Caring," *Personality and Social Psychology Bulletin* 37, no. 5 (2011), pp. 662–673; P. E. Shrout, N. Bolger, M. Iida, C. Burke, M. E. Gleason, and S. P. Lane, "The Effects of Daily Support Transactions During Acute Stress: Results from a Diary Study of Bar Exam Preparation," in K. Sullivan and J. Davila (Eds.), *Support Processes in Intimate Relationships* (New York: Oxford University Press, 2010), pp. 175–199.

---

and social, esteem, and **self-actualization** were **higher-order needs**. Higher-order needs are satisfied internally (within the person), whereas lower-order needs are predominantly satisfied externally (by things such as pay, union contracts, and tenure).

The hierarchy, if it applies at all, aligns with U.S. culture. In Japan, Greece, and Mexico, where uncertainty-avoidance characteristics are strong, security needs would be on top of the hierarchy. Countries that score high on nurturing characteristics—Denmark, Sweden, Norway, the Netherlands, and Finland—would have social needs on top.[6] Group work will motivate employees more when the country's culture scores high on the nurturing criterion.

Maslow's theory has received wide recognition, particularly among practicing managers. It is intuitively logical and easy to understand. When introduced, it provided a compelling alternative to behaviorist theories that posited only physiological and safety needs as important. Unfortunately, however, research does not validate it. Maslow provided no empirical substantiation, and several studies that sought to validate it found no support for it.[7] There is little evidence that need structures are organized as Maslow proposed, that unsatisfied needs motivate, or that a satisfied need activates movement to a new need level.[8] But old theories, especially intuitively logical ones, apparently die hard.

Some researchers have attempted to revive components of the need hierarchy concept, using principles from evolutionary psychology.[9] They propose that lower-level needs are the chief concern of immature animals or those with primitive nervous systems, whereas higher needs are more frequently observed in mature animals with more developed nervous systems. They also note distinct underlying biological systems for different types of needs. Time will tell whether these revisions to Maslow's hierarchy will be useful to practicing managers.

Theory X and Theory Y

Douglas McGregor proposed two distinct views of human beings: one basically negative, labeled Theory X, and the other basically positive, labeled Theory Y.[10] After studying managers' dealings with employees, McGregor concluded that their views of the nature of human beings are based on certain assumptions that mold their behavior.

Under **Theory X**, managers believe employees inherently dislike work and must therefore be directed or even coerced into performing it. Under **Theory Y**, in contrast, managers assume employees can view work as being as natural as rest or play, and therefore the average person can learn to accept, and even seek, responsibility.

To understand more fully, think in terms of Maslow's hierarchy. Theory Y assumes higher-order needs dominate individuals. McGregor himself believed Theory Y assumptions were more valid than Theory X. Therefore, he proposed such ideas as participative decision making, responsible and challenging jobs, and good group relations to maximize an employee's job motivation.

Unfortunately, no evidence confirms that *either* set of assumptions is valid or that acting on Theory Y assumptions will lead to more motivated workers. OB theories need empirical support before we can accept them. Theory X and Theory Y lack such support as much as the hierarchy of needs.

Two-Factor Theory

Believing an individual's relationship to work is basic, and that attitude toward work can determine success or failure, psychologist Frederick Herzberg wondered, "What do people want from their jobs?" He asked people to describe, in detail, situations in which they felt exceptionally *good* or *bad* about their jobs. The responses differed significantly and led Hertzberg to his **two-factor theory**—also called *motivation-hygiene theory*.[11]

As shown in Exhibit 7-2, intrinsic factors such as advancement, recognition, responsibility, and achievement seem related to job satisfaction. Respondents who felt good about their work tended to attribute these factors to themselves, while dissatisfied respondents tended to cite extrinsic factors, such as supervision, pay, company policies, and working conditions.

To Hertzberg, the data suggest that the opposite of satisfaction is not dissatisfaction, as was traditionally believed. Removing dissatisfying characteristics from a job does not necessarily make the job satisfying. As illustrated in Exhibit 7-3, Herzberg proposed a dual continuum: The opposite of "satisfaction" is "no satisfaction," and the opposite of "dissatisfaction" is "no dissatisfaction."

According to Herzberg, the factors that lead to job satisfaction are separate and distinct from those that lead to job dissatisfaction. Therefore, managers who seek to eliminate factors that can create job dissatisfaction may bring about peace, but not necessarily motivation. They will be placating rather than motivating their workers. As a result, Herzberg characterized conditions such as quality of supervision, pay, company policies, physical working conditions, relationships with others, and job security as **hygiene factors**. When they're

self-actualization *The drive to become what a person is capable of becoming.*

higher-order needs *Needs that are satisfied internally, such as social, esteem, and self-actualization needs.*

Theory X *The assumption that employees dislike work, are lazy, dislike responsibility, and must be coerced to perform.*

Theory Y *The assumption that employees like work, are creative, seek responsibility, and can exercise self-direction.*

two-factor theory *A theory that relates intrinsic factors to job satisfaction and associates extrinsic factors with dissatisfaction. Also called motivation-hygiene theory.*

hygiene factors *Factors—such as company policy and administration, supervision, and salary—that, when adequate in a job, placate workers. When these factors are adequate, people will not be dissatisfied.*

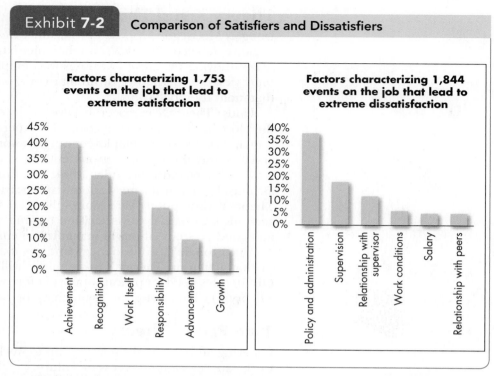

| Exhibit **7-2** | **Comparison of Satisfiers and Dissatisfiers** |

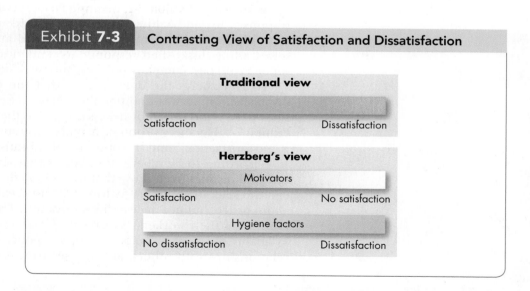

| Exhibit **7-3** | **Contrasting View of Satisfaction and Dissatisfaction** |

adequate, people will not be dissatisfied; neither will they be satisfied. If we want to *motivate* people on their jobs, Herzberg suggested emphasizing factors associated with the work itself or with outcomes directly derived from it, such as promotional opportunities, personal growth opportunities, recognition, responsibility, and achievement. These are the characteristics people find intrinsically rewarding.

The two-factor theory has not been well supported in the literature, and it has many detractors.[12] Criticisms include the following:

1. Herzberg's methodology is limited because it relies on self-reports. When things are going well, people tend to take credit. Contrarily, they blame failure on the extrinsic environment.
2. The reliability of Herzberg's methodology is questionable. Raters have to make interpretations, so they may contaminate the findings by interpreting one response in one manner while treating a similar response differently.
3. No overall measure of satisfaction was utilized. A person may dislike part of a job yet still think the job is acceptable overall.
4. Herzberg assumed a relationship between satisfaction and productivity, but he looked only at satisfaction. To make his research relevant, we must assume a strong relationship between satisfaction and productivity.

Regardless of the criticisms, Herzberg's theory has been widely read, and few managers are unfamiliar with its recommendations.

McClelland's Theory of Needs

You have one beanbag and five targets set up in front of you, each farther away than the last. Target A sits almost within arm's reach. If you hit it, you get $2. Target B is a bit farther out, but about 80 percent of the people who try can hit it. It pays $4. Target C pays $8, and about half the people who try can hit it. Very few people can hit Target D, but the payoff is $16 for those who do. Finally, Target E pays $32, but it's almost impossible to achieve. Which would you try for? If you selected C, you're likely to be a high achiever. Why? Read on.

McClelland's theory of needs was developed by David McClelland and his associates.[13] It looks at three needs:

- **Need for achievement (nAch)** is the drive to excel, to achieve in relationship to a set of standards.
- **Need for power (nPow)** is the need to make others behave in a way they would not have otherwise.
- **Need for affiliation (nAff)** is the desire for friendly and close interpersonal relationships.

McClelland and subsequent researchers focused most of their attention on nAch. High achievers perform best when they perceive their probability of success as 0.5—that is, a 50–50 chance. They dislike gambling with high odds because they get no achievement satisfaction from success that comes by pure chance. Similarly, they dislike low odds (high probability of success) because then there is no challenge to their skills. They like to set goals that require stretching themselves a little.

Relying on an extensive amount of research, we can predict some relationships between achievement need and job performance. First, when jobs have a high degree of personal responsibility and feedback and an intermediate degree of risk, high achievers are strongly motivated. They are successful in

Source: Seth Wenig/AP Images

As a high achiever, Patricia Woertz is motivated by work that demands a high degree of personal responsibility. Today, she is the CEO, president, and chair of Archer Daniels Midland, an agricultural food processing business. She started her career as a certified public accountant but was attracted to the complexity and opportunity of global energy. For the next 30 years she worked for Gulf Oil and Chevron in refining, marketing, strategic planning, and finance positions. Since joining ADM, Woertz continues to shift company resources toward fuel production in a drive to accelerate ADM's global leadership in bioenergy and has led the company to record financial results.

McClelland's theory of needs   *A theory that states achievement, power, and affiliation are three important needs that help explain motivation.*

need for achievement (nAch)   *The drive to excel, to achieve in relationship to a set of standards, and to strive to succeed.*

need for power (nPow)   *The need to make others behave in a way in which they would not have behaved otherwise.*

need for affiliation (nAff)   *The desire for friendly and close interpersonal relationships.*

entrepreneurial activities such as running their own businesses, for example, and managing self-contained units within large organizations.[14] Second, a high need to achieve does not necessarily make someone a good manager, especially in large organizations. People with a high achievement need are interested in how well they do personally, and not in influencing others to do well. High-nAch salespeople do not necessarily make good sales managers, and the good general manager in a large organization does not typically have a high need to achieve.[15] Third, needs for affiliation and power tend to be closely related to managerial success. The best managers are high in their need for power and low in their need for affiliation.[16] In fact, a high power motive may be a requirement for managerial effectiveness.[17]

The view that a high achievement need acts as an internal motivator presupposes two U.S. cultural characteristics—willingness to accept a moderate degree of risk (which excludes countries with strong uncertainty-avoidance characteristics) and concern with performance (which applies to countries with strong achievement characteristics). This combination is found in Anglo-American countries such as the United States, Canada, and Great Britain[18] and much less in Chile and Portugal.

Among the early theories of motivation, McClelland's has had the best research support. Unfortunately, it has less practical effect than the others. Because McClelland argued that the three needs are subconscious—we may rank high on them but not know it—measuring them is not easy. In the most common approach, a trained expert presents pictures to individuals, asks them to tell a story about each, and then scores their responses in terms of the three needs. However, the process is time consuming and expensive, and few organizations have been willing to invest in measuring McClelland's concept.

Contemporary Theories of Motivation

Early theories of motivation either have not held up under close examination or have fallen out of favor. In contrast, contemporary theories have one thing in common: each has a reasonable degree of valid supporting documentation. This doesn't mean they are unquestionably right. We call them "contemporary theories" because they represent the current state of thinking in explaining employee motivation.

Self-Determination Theory

3 Apply the predictions of self-determination theory to intrinsic and extrinsic rewards.

"It's strange," said Marcia. "I started work at the Humane Society as a volunteer. I put in 15 hours a week helping people adopt pets. And I loved coming to work. Then, 3 months ago, they hired me full-time at $11 an hour. I'm doing the same work I did before. But I'm not finding it nearly as much fun."

Does Marcia's reaction seem counterintuitive? There's an explanation for it. It's called **self-determination theory**, which proposes that people prefer to feel they have control over their actions, so anything that makes a previously enjoyed task feel more like an obligation than a freely chosen activity will undermine motivation.[19] Much research on self-determination theory in OB has focused on **cognitive evaluation theory**, which hypothesizes that extrinsic rewards will reduce intrinsic interest in a task. When people are paid for work, it feels less like something they *want* to do and more like something they *have* to do. Self-determination theory also proposes that in addition to being driven

Motivated to Behave Unethically

The popular press often reports about ethical lapses in business by focusing on employees and managers who are "loose cannons," deviating from organizational rules and norms to produce bad consequences for society and business. However, sometimes unethical behavior is not just ignored by organizational leaders but actively encouraged by the company's motivational structures. In fact, one survey found that 56 percent of U.S. workers experience pressure from their superiors to behave in an unethical manner. Craig E. Johnson sums up the problem, noting, "Examine nearly any corporate scandal—AIG Insurance, Arthur Andersen, Enron, Health South, Sotheby's Auction House, Fannie Mae, Hollinger International, Marsh & McLennan, Quest—and you'll find leaders who engaged in immoral behavior and encouraged their followers to do the same."

How do managers create pressure to behave unethically? Management scholar Ben Tepper notes that structures in place in organizations often encourage unethical behavior. Incentives might go to individuals who maximize sales without regard to whether they achieved these ends honestly. Lawyers often are paid in such a way that tacitly encourages them to overbill their clients. Or perhaps rewards might be offered for producing products at low cost without considering the social and environmental impacts of production decisions. In all these cases, the reward systems in place in organizations can serve to motivate unethical behavior.

So what can you do as a manager or employee to confront these powerful motivations to behave unethically? First and foremost, decision makers should consider the unintended consequences of reward systems. Second, top management should foster an organizational culture of honesty and fair dealing and disseminate it through all levels of the organizational hierarchy. Finally, organizations might even consider finding ways to explicitly reward those employees who engage in "above and beyond" instances of ethical behavior.

Sources: B. J. Tepper, "When Managers Pressure Employees to Behave Badly: Toward a Comprehensive Response," *Business Horizons* 53, no. 6 (2010), pp. 591–598; C. E. Johnson, *Meeting the Ethical Challenges of Leadership: Casting Light or Shadow*, 3rd ed. (San Francisco: Sage, 2009).

by a need for autonomy, people seek ways to achieve competence and positive connections to others. A large number of studies support self-determination theory.[20] As we'll show, its major implications relate to work rewards.

When organizations use extrinsic rewards as payoffs for superior performance, employees feel they are doing a good job less because of their own intrinsic desire to excel than because that's what the organization wants. Eliminating extrinsic rewards can also shift an individual's perception of why she works on a task from an external to an internal explanation. If you're reading a novel a week because your English literature instructor requires you to, you can attribute your reading behavior to an external source. However, if you find yourself continuing to read a novel a week after the course is over, your natural inclination is to say, "I must enjoy reading novels because I'm still reading one a week."

Studies examining how extrinsic rewards increased motivation for some creative tasks suggest we might need to place cognitive evaluation theory's predictions in a broader context.[21] Goal-setting is more effective in improving

self-determination theory *A theory of motivation that is concerned with the beneficial effects of intrinsic motivation and the harmful effects of extrinsic motivation.*

cognitive evaluation theory *A version of self-determination theory which holds that allocating extrinsic rewards for behavior that had been previously intrinsically rewarding tends to decrease the overall level of motivation if the rewards are seen as controlling.*

Autonomy Needs Around the Globe

Much of the research we have presented on needs for autonomy and self-determination has been conducted in the United States and Canada, two countries that place a high value on personal independence and freedom of choice. But some researchers question whether a need for autonomy is universal or whether some cultures foster a greater need for relatedness.

Some research does suggest universal needs for autonomy, while other studies find that different cultures see autonomy differently. In a survey of 40 nations, collectivistic countries valued social order, obedience, and respect for tradition more, and within cultures, individuals who value autonomy tend to put less value on social connectedness and vice versa.

In a study with Chinese Canadian and European Canadian participants, those from Chinese culture expressed lower levels of autonomy, but autonomy was related to well-being for both Chinese and European respondents. Although different cultures view their autonomy differently, it appears people across cultures are higher in well-being when they perceive they have freedom of choice.

Sources: C. Vauclair, K. Hanke, R. Fischer, and J. Fontaine, "The Structure of Human Values at the Culture Level: A Meta-Analytical Replication of Schwartz's Value Orientations Using the Rokeach Value Survey," _Journal of Cross-Cultural Psychology_ 42, no. 2 (2011), pp. 186–205; and D. Rudy, K. M. Sheldon, T. Awong, and H. H. Tan, "Autonomy, Culture, and Well-Being: The Benefits of Inclusive Autonomy," _Journal of Research in Personality_ 41, no. 5 (2007), pp. 983–1007.

motivation, for instance, when we provide rewards for achieving the goals. The original authors of self-determination theory acknowledge that extrinsic rewards such as verbal praise and feedback about competence can improve even intrinsic motivation under specific circumstances. Deadlines and specific work standards do, too, if people believe they are in control of their behavior.[22] This is consistent with the central theme of self-determination theory: rewards and deadlines diminish motivation if people see them as coercive.

What does self-determination theory suggest for providing rewards? If a senior sales representative really enjoys selling and making the deal, a commission indicates she's been doing a good job and increases her sense of competence by providing feedback that could improve intrinsic motivation. On the other hand, if a computer programmer values writing code because she likes to solve problems, a reward for working to an externally imposed standard she does not accept, such as writing a certain number of lines of code every day, could feel coercive, and her intrinsic motivation would suffer. She would be less interested in the task and might reduce her effort.

A recent outgrowth of self-determination theory is **self-concordance**, which considers how strongly peoples' reasons for pursuing goals are consistent with their interests and core values. If individuals pursue goals because of an intrinsic interest, they are more likely to attain their goals and are happy even if they do not. Why? Because the process of striving toward them is fun. In contrast, people who pursue goals for extrinsic reasons (money, status, or other benefits) are less likely to attain their goals and less happy even when they do. Why? Because the goals are less meaningful to them.[23] OB research suggests that people who pursue work goals for intrinsic reasons are more satisfied with their jobs, feel they fit into their organizations better, and may perform better.[24]

What does all this mean? For individuals, it means choose your job for reasons other than extrinsic rewards. For organizations, it means managers should provide intrinsic as well as extrinsic incentives. They need to make the work interesting, provide recognition, and support employee growth and development. Employees who feel what they do is within their control and a result of free choice are likely to be more motivated by their work and committed to their employers.[25]

Job Engagement

When nurse Melissa Jones comes to work, it seems that everything else in her life goes away, and she becomes completely absorbed in what she is doing. Her emotions, her thoughts, and her behavior are all directed toward patient care. In fact, she can get so caught up in her work that she isn't even aware of how long she's been there. As a result of this total commitment, she is more effective in providing patient care and feels uplifted by her time at work.

Melissa has a high level of **job engagement**, the investment of an employee's physical, cognitive, and emotional energies into job performance.[26] Practicing managers and scholars alike have lately become interested in facilitating job engagement, believing something deeper than liking a job or finding it interesting drives performance. Many studies attempt to measure this deeper level of commitment.

The Gallup organization has been using 12 questions to assess the extent to which employee engagement is linked to positive work outcomes for millions of employees over the past 30 years.[27] There are far more engaged employees in highly successful than in average organizations, and groups with more engaged employees have higher levels of productivity, fewer safety incidents, and lower turnover. Academic studies have also found positive outcomes. One examined multiple business units for their level of engagement and found a

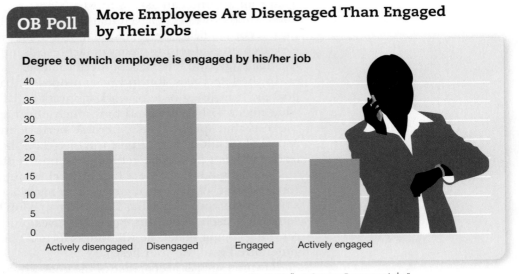

OB Poll **More Employees Are Disengaged Than Engaged by Their Jobs**

Degree to which employee is engaged by his/her job

Source: A. Fox, "Raising Engagement," *HR Magazine* (May 2010), pp. 35–40; "Gallup's Customer Engagement Index" (March 11, 2010), www.smartKPIs.com.

self-concordance *The degree to which peoples' reasons for pursuing goals are consistent with their interests and core values.*

job engagement *The investment of an employee's physical, cognitive, and emotional energies into job performance.*

positive relationship with a variety of practical outcomes.[28] Another reviewed 91 distinct investigations and found higher levels of engagement associated with task performance and citizenship behavior.[29]

What makes people more likely to be engaged in their jobs? One key is the degree to which an employee believes it is meaningful to engage in work. This is partially determined by job characteristics and access to sufficient resources to work effectively.[30] Another factor is a match between the individual's values and those of the organization.[31] Leadership behaviors that inspire workers to a greater sense of mission also increase employee engagement.[32]

One of the critiques of engagement is that the construct is partially redundant with job attitudes like satisfaction or stress.[33] However, engagement questionnaires usually assess motivation and absorption in a task, quite unlike job satisfaction questionnaires. Engagement may also predict important work outcomes better than traditional job attitudes.[34] Other critics note there may be a "dark side" to engagement, as evidenced by positive relationships between engagement and work–family conflict.[35] Individuals might grow so engaged in their work roles that family responsibilities become an unwelcome intrusion. Further research exploring how engagement relates to these negative outcomes may help clarify whether some highly engaged employees might be getting "too much of a good thing."

Goal-Setting Theory

4 Understand the implications of employee engagement for management.

Gene Broadwater, coach of the Hamilton High School cross-country team, gave his squad these last words before they approached the starting line for the league championship race: "Each one of you is physically ready. Now, get out there and do your best. No one can ever ask more of you than that."

You've heard the sentiment a number of times yourself: "Just do your best. That's all anyone can ask." But what does "do your best" mean? Do we ever know whether we've achieved that vague goal? Would the cross-country runners have recorded faster times if Coach Broadwater had given each a specific goal? Research on **goal-setting theory** in fact reveals impressive effects of goal specificity, challenge, and feedback on performance.

In the late 1960s, Edwin Locke proposed that intentions to work toward a goal are a major source of work motivation.[36] That is, goals tell an employee what needs to be done and how much effort is needed.[37] Evidence strongly suggests that specific goals increase performance; that difficult goals, when accepted, result in higher performance than do easy goals; and that feedback leads to higher performance than does nonfeedback.[38]

Specific goals produce a higher level of output than the generalized goal "do your best." Why? Specificity itself seems to act as an internal stimulus. When a trucker commits to making 12 round-trip hauls between Toronto and Buffalo, New York, each week, this intention gives him a specific objective to attain. All things being equal, he will outperform a counterpart with no goals or the generalized goal "do your best."

If factors such as acceptance of the goals are held constant, the more difficult the goal, the higher the level of performance. Of course, it's logical to assume easier goals are more likely to be accepted. But once a hard task is accepted, we can expect the employee to exert a high level of effort to try to achieve it.

But why are people motivated by difficult goals?[39] First, challenging goals get our attention and thus tend to help us focus. Second, difficult goals energize us because we have to work harder to attain them. Do you study as hard for an easy exam as you do for a difficult one? Probably not. Third, when goals are difficult, people persist in trying to attain them. Finally, difficult goals lead us to discover strategies that help us perform the job or task more effectively. If we

Chung Mong-koo, chairman of Hyundai Motor Company, is well known for articulating difficult and specific goals as a potent motivating force. For example, although Hyundai was a latecomer in the development of a hybrid vehicle, the South Korean automaker launched its first U.S. hybrid in 2010, with annual sales set at 50,000 units. By 2018, the company expects hybrid sales to balloon to 500,000 units worldwide. Challenging employees to reach high goals has helped Hyundai experience tremendous growth in recent years.

Source: Ahn Young-joon/AP Images

have to struggle to solve a difficult problem, we often think of a better way to go about it.

People do better when they get feedback on how well they are progressing toward their goals, because it helps identify discrepancies between what they have done and what they want to do—that is, feedback guides behavior. But all feedback is not equally potent. Self-generated feedback—with which employees are able to monitor their own progress—is more powerful than externally generated feedback.[40]

If employees can participate in the setting of their own goals, will they try harder? The evidence is mixed.[41] In some cases, participatively set goals yielded superior performance; in others, individuals performed best when assigned goals by their boss. But a major advantage of participation may be that it increases acceptance of the goal as a desirable one toward which to work.[42] Commitment is important. Without participation, the individual assigning the goal needs to clearly explain its purpose and importance.[43]

In addition to feedback, three other factors influence the goals–performance relationship: goal commitment, task characteristics, and national culture.

Goal-setting theory assumes an individual is committed to the goal and determined not to lower or abandon it. The individual (1) believes he or she can achieve the goal and (2) wants to achieve it.[44] Goal commitment is most likely to occur when goals are made public, when the individual has an internal locus of control (see Chapter 4), and when the goals are self-set rather than assigned.[45] Goals themselves seem to affect performance more strongly when tasks are simple rather than complex, well learned rather than novel, and independent rather than interdependent.[46] On interdependent tasks, group goals are preferable.

Finally, setting specific, difficult, individual goals may have different effects in different cultures. Most goal-setting research has been done in the United States and Canada, where individual achievement and performance are most highly valued. To date, research has not shown that group-based

goal-setting theory *A theory that says that specific and difficult goals, with feedback, lead to higher performance.*

goals are more effective in collectivists than in individualist cultures. In collectivistic and high-power-distance cultures, achievable moderate goals can be more highly motivating than difficult ones.[47] Finally, assigned goals appear to generate greater goal commitment in high than in low power-distance cultures.[48] More research is needed to assess how goal constructs might differ across cultures.

Although goal-setting has positive outcomes, some goals may be *too* effective.[49] When learning something is important, goals related to performance undermine adaptation and creativity because people become too focused on outcomes and ignore changing conditions. In this case, a goal to learn and generate alternative solutions will be more effective than a goal to perform. Some authors argue that goals can lead employees to focus on a single standard and exclude all others. Consider the narrow focus on boosting short-term stock prices in many businesses—it may have led organizations to ignore long-term success and even to engage in such unethical behavior as accounting fraud or excessively risky investments. (Of course, organizations can establish goals for ethical performance.) Other studies show that employees low in conscientiousness and emotional stability experience greater emotional exhaustion when their leaders set goals.[50] Despite differences of opinion, most researchers do agree that goals are powerful in shaping behavior. Managers should make sure they are actually aligned with the company's objectives.

Research has begun to examine subconscious goals—that is, goals we are not even aware of setting.[51] One study primed people to think about goals by having them assemble scrambled words into sentences with achievement themes, while other people assembled sentences without achievement themes. The people who made the achievement sentences were subconsciously primed. That might not sound like a very strong manipulation, but this group performed more effectively in a brainstorming task than those given easier goals. Another study found similar results when a picture of a woman winning a race was the subconscious prime rather than assembling sentences. Interestingly, these studies do not find that conscious and subconscious goal-setting are related.

SELF-ASSESSMENT LIBRARY

What Are My Course Performance Goals?

In the Self-Assessment Library (available on CD or online), take assessment I.C.5 (What Are My Course Performance Goals?).

Implementing Goal-Setting   As a manager, how do you make goal-setting theory operational? That's often left up to the individual. Some managers set aggressive performance targets—what General Electric called "stretch goals." Some CEOs, such as Procter & Gamble's A. G. Lafley and SAP AG's Hasso Plattner, are known for the demanding performance goals they set. But many managers don't set goals. When asked whether their job had clearly defined goals, only a minority of employees in a recent survey said yes.[52]

A more systematic way to utilize goal-setting is with **management by objectives (MBO)**, which emphasizes participatively set goals that are tangible, verifiable, and measurable. As in Exhibit 7-4, the organization's overall objectives are translated into specific objectives for each level (divisional,

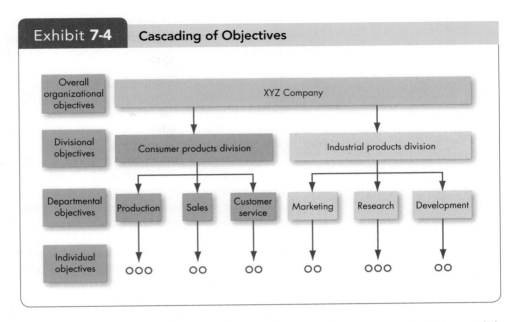

Exhibit 7-4   **Cascading of Objectives**

departmental, individual). But because lower-unit managers jointly participate in setting their own goals, MBO works from the bottom up as well as from the top down. The result is a hierarchy that links objectives at one level to those at the next. And for the individual employee, MBO provides specific personal performance objectives.

Four ingredients are common to MBO programs: goal specificity, participation in decision making (including the setting of goals or objectives), an explicit time period, and performance feedback.[53] Many elements in MBO programs match propositions of goal-setting theory. For example, having an explicit time period to accomplish objectives matches goal-setting theory's emphasis on goal specificity. Similarly, we noted earlier that feedback about goal progress is a critical element of goal-setting theory. The only area of possible disagreement between MBO and goal-setting theory is participation: MBO strongly advocates it, whereas goal-setting theory demonstrates that managers' assigned goals are usually just as effective.

You'll find MBO programs in many business, health care, educational, government, and nonprofit organizations.[54] Their popularity does not mean they always work.[55] When MBO fails, the culprits tend to be unrealistic expectations, lack of commitment by top management, and inability or unwillingness to allocate rewards based on goal accomplishment.

Self-Efficacy Theory

Self-efficacy (also known as *social cognitive theory* or *social learning theory*) refers to an individual's belief that he or she is capable of performing a task.[56] The higher your self-efficacy, the more confidence you have in your ability to succeed. So, in difficult situations, people with low self-efficacy are more likely to lessen their effort or give up altogether, while those with high self-efficacy will

---

management by objectives (MBO)   *A program that encompasses specific goals, participatively set, for an explicit time period, with feedback on goal progress.*

self-efficacy   *An individual's belief that he or she is capable of performing a task.*

try harder to master the challenge.[57] Self-efficacy can create a positive spiral in which those with high efficacy become more engaged in their tasks and then, in turn, increase performance, which increases efficacy further.[58] Changes in self-efficacy over time are related to changes in creative performance as well.[59] Individuals high in self-efficacy also seem to respond to negative feedback with increased effort and motivation, while those low in self-efficacy are likely to lessen their effort after negative feedback.[60] How can managers help their employees achieve high levels of self- efficacy? By bringing goal-setting theory and self-efficacy theory together.

Goal-setting theory and self-efficacy theory don't compete; they complement each other. As Exhibit 7-5 shows, employees whose manager sets difficult goals for them will have a higher level of self-efficacy and set higher goals for their own performance. Why? Setting difficult goals for people communicates your confidence in them. Imagine you learn your boss sets a higher goal for you than for your co-workers. How would you interpret this? As long as you didn't feel you were being picked on, you would probably think, "Well, I guess my boss thinks I'm capable of performing better than others." This sets in motion a psychological process in which you're more confident in yourself (higher self-efficacy) and you set higher personal goals, performing better both inside and outside the workplace.

The researcher who developed self-efficacy theory, Albert Bandura, proposes four ways self-efficacy can be increased:[61]

1. Enactive mastery.
2. Vicarious modeling.
3. Verbal persuasion.
4. Arousal.

According to Bandura, the most important source of increasing self-efficacy is *enactive mastery*—that is, gaining relevant experience with the task or job. If you've been able to do the job successfully in the past, you're more confident you'll be able to do it in the future.

Exhibit 7-5	Joint Effects of Goals and Self-Efficacy on Performance

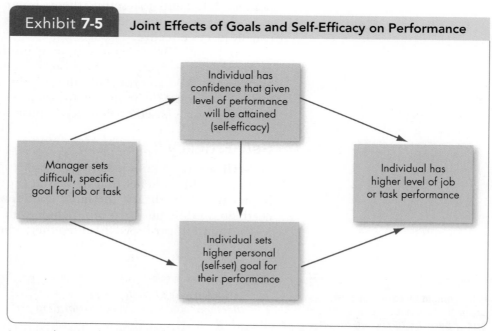

Source: Based on E. A. Locke and G. P. Latham, "Building a Practically Useful Theory of Goal Setting and Task Motivation: A 35-Year Odyssey," American Psychologist (September 2002), pp. 705–717.

The second source is *vicarious modeling*—becoming more confident because you see someone else doing the task. If your friend slims down, it increases your confidence that you can lose weight, too. Vicarious modeling is most effective when you see yourself as similar to the person you are observing. Watching Tiger Woods play a difficult golf shot might not increase your confidence in being able to play the shot yourself, but if you watch a golfer with a handicap similar to yours, it's persuasive.

The third source is *verbal persuasion:* becoming more confident because someone convinces you that you have the skills necessary to be successful. Motivational speakers use this tactic.

Finally, Bandura argues that *arousal* increases self-efficacy. Arousal leads to an energized state, so the person gets "psyched up" and performs better. But if the task requires a steady, lower-key perspective (say, carefully editing a manuscript), arousal may in fact hurt performance.

What are the OB implications of self-efficacy theory? Well, it's a matter of applying Bandura's sources of self-efficacy to the work setting. Training programs often make use of enactive mastery by having people practice and build their skills. In fact, one reason training works is that it increases self-efficacy.[62] Individuals with higher levels of self-efficacy also appear to reap more benefits from training programs and are more likely to use their training on the job.[63]

The best way for a manager to use verbal persuasion is through the *Pygmalion effect* or the *Galatea effect*. As discussed in Chapter 5, the Pygmalion effect is a form of self-fulfilling prophecy in which believing something can make it true. In some studies, teachers were told their students had very high IQ scores when, in fact, they spanned a range from high to low. Consistent with the Pygmalion effect, the teachers spent more time with the students they *thought* were smart, gave them more challenging assignments, and expected more of them—all of which led to higher student self-efficacy and better grades.[64] This strategy also has been used in the workplace.[65] Sailors who were told convincingly that they would not get seasick were in fact much less likely to do so.[66]

Intelligence and personality are absent from Bandura's list, but they can increase self-efficacy.[67] People who are intelligent, conscientiousness, and

Toyota Motor Corporation applies social learning theory in teaching employees skills they need to meet the company's high standards of quality and efficiency. At its Global Production Center training facilities in Japan, England, and the United States, workers and managers from factories around the world learn production techniques through observation and direct experience. Trainees first watch computerized visual manuals to learn basic skills. Then, under the tutelage of an experienced production master, they practice the skills. In this photo, a trainee practices the skill of bolt tightening at Toyota's training center in Toyota City, Japan.

Source: Toru Yamanaka/AFP/Getty Images/Newscom

emotionally stable are so much more likely to have high self-efficacy that some researchers argue self-efficacy is less important than prior research would suggest.[68] They believe it is partially a by-product in a smart person with a confident personality. Although Bandura strongly disagrees with this conclusion, more research is needed.

Reinforcement Theory

5   Compare and contrast goal-setting theory and management by objectives.

Goal-setting is a cognitive approach, proposing that an individual's purposes direct his action. **Reinforcement theory**, in contrast, takes a behavioristic view, arguing that reinforcement conditions behavior. The two theories are clearly at odds philosophically. Reinforcement theorists see behavior as environmentally caused. You need not be concerned, they would argue, with internal cognitive events; what controls behavior is reinforcers—any consequences that, when immediately following responses, increase the probability that the behavior will be repeated.

Reinforcement theory ignores the inner state of the individual and concentrates solely on what happens when he or she takes some action. Because it does not concern itself with what initiates behavior, it is not, strictly speaking, a theory of motivation. But it does provide a powerful means of analyzing what controls behavior, and this is why we typically consider it in discussions of motivation.[69]

Operant conditioning theory, probably the most relevant component of reinforcement theory for management, argues that people learn to behave to get something they want or to avoid something they don't want. Unlike reflexive or unlearned behavior, operant behavior is influenced by the reinforcement or lack of reinforcement brought about by its consequences. Therefore, reinforcement strengthens a behavior and increases the likelihood it will be repeated.[70] B. F. Skinner, one of the most prominent advocates of operant conditioning, argued that creating pleasing consequences to follow specific forms of behavior would increase the frequency of that behavior. He demonstrated that people will most likely engage in desired behaviors if they are positively reinforced for doing so; that rewards are most effective if they immediately follow the desired response; and that behavior that is not rewarded, or is punished, is less likely to be repeated. We know a professor who places a mark by a student's name each time the student makes a contribution to class discussions. Operant conditioning would argue this practice is motivating because it conditions a student to expect a reward (earning class credit) each time she demonstrates a specific behavior (speaking up in class). The concept of operant conditioning was part of Skinner's broader concept of **behaviorism**, which argues that behavior follows stimuli in a relatively unthinking manner. Skinner's form of radical behaviorism rejects feelings, thoughts, and other states of mind as causes of behavior. In short, people learn to associate stimulus and response, but their conscious awareness of this association is irrelevant.[71]

You can see illustrations of operant conditioning everywhere that reinforcements are contingent on some action on your part. Your instructor says if you want a high grade in the course, you must supply correct answers on the test. A commissioned salesperson wanting to earn a sizable income finds doing so is contingent on generating high sales in her territory. Of course, the linkage can also teach individuals to engage in behaviors that work against the best interests of the organization. Assume your boss says if you work overtime during the next 3-week busy season you'll be compensated for it at your next performance appraisal. However, when performance-appraisal time comes, you are given no positive reinforcement for your overtime work. The next time your boss asks you to work overtime, what will you do? You'll probably decline! Your behavior can be explained by operant conditioning: if a behavior fails to be positively reinforced, the probability it will be repeated declines.

Although reinforcers such as pay can motivate people, the process is much more complicated than stimulus–response. In its pure form, reinforcement theory ignores feelings, attitudes, expectations, and other cognitive variables known to affect behavior. In fact, some researchers look at the same experiments reinforcement theorists use to support their position and interpret the findings in a *cognitive* framework.[72]

Reinforcement is undoubtedly an important influence on behavior, but few scholars are prepared to argue it is the only one. The behaviors you engage in at work and the amount of effort you allocate to each task are affected by the consequences that follow. If you're consistently reprimanded for outproducing your colleagues, you'll likely reduce your productivity. But we might also explain your lower productivity in terms of goals, inequity, or expectancies.

Individuals can learn by being told or by observing what happens to other people, as well as through direct experiences. Much of what we have learned comes from watching models—parents, teachers, peers, film and television performers, bosses, and so forth. This view that we can learn through both observation and direct experience is called **social-learning theory**.[73]

Although social-learning theory is an extension of operant conditioning—that is, it assumes behavior is a function of consequences—it also acknowledges the effects of observational learning and perception. People respond to the way they perceive and define consequences, not to the objective consequences themselves.

Models are central to the social-learning viewpoint. Four processes determine their influence on an individual:

1. **Attentional processes.**   People learn from a model only when they recognize and pay attention to its critical features. We tend to be most influenced by models that are attractive, repeatedly available, important to us, or similar to us in our estimation.
2. **Retention processes.**   A model's influence depends on how well the individual remembers the model's action after the model is no longer readily available.
3. **Motor reproduction processes.**   After a person has seen a new behavior by observing the model, watching must be converted to doing. This process demonstrates that the individual can perform the modeled activities.
4. **Reinforcement processes.**   Individuals are motivated to exhibit the modeled behavior if positive incentives or rewards are provided. Positively reinforced behaviors are given more attention, learned better, and performed more often.

Equity Theory/Organizational Justice

6 Contrast reinforcement theory and goal-setting theory.

Jane Pearson graduated from State University last year with a degree in accounting. After interviews with a number of organizations on campus, she accepted a position with a top public accounting firm and was assigned to its Boston office. Jane was very pleased with the offer she received: challenging work with a prestigious firm, an excellent opportunity to gain valuable experience, and

---

reinforcement theory   *A theory that says that behavior is a function of its consequences.*

behaviorism   *A theory that argues that behavior follows stimuli in a relatively unthinking manner.*

social-learning theory   *The view that we can learn through both observation and direct experience.*

the highest salary any accounting major at State was offered last year—$4,550 per month—but Jane was the top student in her class; she was articulate and mature, and she fully expected to receive a commensurate salary.

Twelve months have passed. The work has proved to be as challenging and satisfying as Jane had hoped. Her employer is extremely pleased with her performance; in fact, Jane recently received a $200-per-month raise. However, her motivational level has dropped dramatically in the past few weeks. Why? Jane's employer has just hired a fresh graduate out of State University who lacks the year of experience Jane has gained, for $4,600 per month—$50 more than Jane now makes! Jane is irate. She is even talking about looking for another job.

Jane's situation illustrates the role that equity plays in motivation. Employees perceive what they get from a job situation (salary levels, raises, recognition) in relationship to what they put into it (effort, experience, education, competence), and then they compare their outcome–input ratio with that of relevant others. This is shown in Exhibit 7-6. If we perceive our ratio to be equal to that of the relevant others with whom we compare ourselves, a state of equity exists; we perceive that our situation is fair and justice prevails. When we see the ratio as unequal and we feel underrewarded, we experience equity tension that creates anger. When we see ourselves as overrewarded, tension creates guilt. J. Stacy Adams proposed that this negative state of tension provides the motivation to do something to correct it.[74]

The referent an employee selects adds to the complexity of **equity theory**.[75] There are four referent comparisons:

1. **Self–inside.** An employee's experiences in a different position inside the employee's current organization.
2. **Self–outside.** An employee's experiences in a situation or position outside the employee's current organization.
3. **Other–inside.** Another individual or group of individuals inside the employee's organization.
4. **Other–outside.** Another individual or group of individuals outside the employee's organization.

Employees might compare themselves to friends, neighbors, co-workers, or colleagues in other organizations or compare their present job with past jobs. Which referent an employee chooses will be influenced by the information the employee holds about referents as well as by the attractiveness of the referent. Four moderating variables are gender, length of tenure, level in the organization, and amount of education or professionalism.[76]

Exhibit **7-6**	Equity Theory

Ratio Comparisons*	Perception
$\frac{O}{I_A} < \frac{O}{I_B}$	Inequity due to being underrewarded
$\frac{O}{I_A} = \frac{O}{I_B}$	Equity
$\frac{O}{I_A} > \frac{O}{I_B}$	Inequity due to being overrewarded

*Where $\frac{O}{I_A}$ represents the employee; and $\frac{O}{I_B}$ represents relevant others

Women are typically paid less than men in comparable jobs and have lower pay expectations than men for the same work.[77] So a woman who uses another woman as a referent tends to calculate a lower comparative standard. Of course, employers' stereotypes about women (for example, the belief that women are less committed to the organization or that "women's work" is less valuable) also may contribute to the pay gap.[78] While both men and women prefer same-sex comparisons, employees in jobs that are not sex segregated will likely make more cross-sex comparisons than those in jobs that are male or female dominated.

Employees with short tenure in their current organizations tend to have little information about others inside the organization, so they rely on their personal experiences. Employees with long tenure rely more heavily on co-workers for comparison. Upper-level employees, those in the professional ranks, and those with higher amounts of education tend to have better information about people in other organizations and will make more other–outside comparisons.

Based on equity theory, employees who perceive inequity will make one of six choices:[79]

1. Change inputs (exert less effort if underpaid or more if overpaid).
2. Change outcomes (individuals paid on a piece-rate basis can increase their pay by producing a higher quantity of units of lower quality).
3. Distort perceptions of self ("I used to think I worked at a moderate pace, but now I realize I work a lot harder than everyone else.").
4. Distort perceptions of others ("Mike's job isn't as desirable as I thought.").
5. Choose a different referent ("I may not make as much as my brother-in-law, but I'm doing a lot better than my Dad did when he was my age.").
6. Leave the field (quit the job).

In perceiving inequity in pay, these American Airline pilots used an "other-inside" referent comparison when comparing their pay to that of the airline's managers. The pilots agreed to accept wage and benefit cuts after the airline reported an $8 billion loss. When they returned to profitability, the CEO and other top managers received stock bonuses. Marching in protest, the pilots argued that their sacrifices in pay and benefits helped save the airline from bankruptcy and that they deserved to be rewarded with pay increases.

Source: LM Otero/AP Images

equity theory   *A theory that says that individuals compare their job inputs and outcomes with those of others and then respond to eliminate any inequities.*

Some of these propositions have been supported, but others haven't.[80] First, inequities created by overpayment do not seem to significantly affect behavior in most work situations. Apparently, people have more tolerance of overpayment inequities than of underpayment inequities or are better able to rationalize them. It's pretty damaging to a theory when half the equation falls apart. Second, not all people are equity sensitive.[81] A few actually prefer outcome–input ratios lower than the referent comparisons. Predictions from equity theory are not likely to be very accurate about these "benevolent types."

While most research on equity theory has focused on pay, some employees also look for equity in the distribution of other organizational rewards like high-status job titles and large and lavishly furnished offices.[82]

Finally, recent research has expanded the meaning of *equity*, or *fairness*.[83] Historically, equity theory focused on **distributive justice**, the employee's perceived fairness of the *amount* rewards among individuals and who received them. But **organizational justice** draws a bigger picture. Employees perceive their organizations as just when they believe rewards and the *way* they are distributed are fair. In other words, fairness or equity can be subjective; what one person sees as unfair, another may see as perfectly appropriate. In general, people see allocations or procedure favoring themselves as fair.[84] In a recent poll, 61 percent of respondents said they pay their fair share of taxes, but an almost equal number (54 percent) felt the system as a whole is unfair, saying some people skirt it.[85]

Most of the equity theory research we've described proposes a fairly rational, calculative way of estimating what is fair and unfair. But few people really make mathematical calculations of their inputs relative to the outcomes of others. Instead, they base distributive judgments on a feeling or an emotional reaction to how they think they are treated relative to others, and their reactions are often emotional as well.[86] Our discussion has also focused on reactions to personal mistreatment. However, people also react emotionally to injustices committed against others, prompting them to take retributive actions.[87]

Beyond perceptions of fairness, the other key element of organizational justice is the view that justice is multidimensional. How much we get paid relative to what we think we should be paid (distributive justice) is obviously important. But, according to researchers, *how* we get paid is just as important. Thus, the model of organizational justice in Exhibit 7-7 includes **procedural justice**—the perceived fairness of the *process* used to determine the distribution of rewards. Two key elements of procedural justice are process control and explanations. *Process control* is the opportunity to present your point of view about desired outcomes to decision makers. *Explanations* are clear reasons management gives for the outcome. Thus, for employees to see a process as fair, they need to feel they have some control over the outcome and that they were given an adequate explanation about why the outcome occurred. It's also important that a manager is *consistent* (across people and over time), is *unbiased,* makes decisions based on *accurate information,* and is *open to appeals.*[88]

The effects of procedural justice become more important when distributive justice is lacking. This makes sense. If we don't get what we want, we tend to focus on *why*. If your supervisor gives a cushy office to a co-worker instead of to you, you're much more focused on your supervisor's treatment of you than if you had gotten the office. Explanations are beneficial when they take the form of post hoc excuses ("I know this is bad, and I wanted to give you the office, but it wasn't my decision") rather than justifications ("I decided to give the office to Sam, but having it isn't a big deal.").[89]

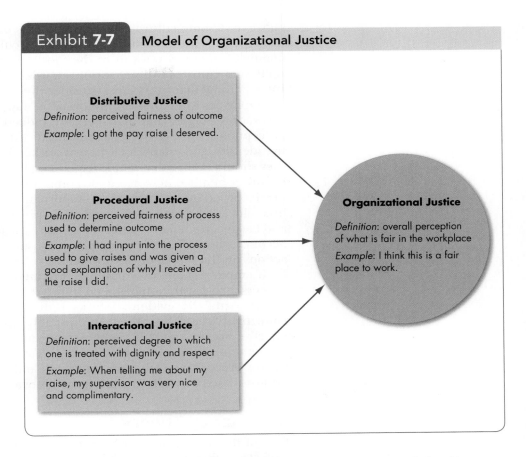

Exhibit 7-7 Model of Organizational Justice

Distributive Justice

Definition: perceived fairness of outcome

Example: I got the pay raise I deserved.

Procedural Justice

Definition: perceived fairness of process used to determine outcome

Example: I had input into the process used to give raises and was given a good explanation of why I received the raise I did.

Interactional Justice

Definition: perceived degree to which one is treated with dignity and respect

Example: When telling me about my raise, my supervisor was very nice and complimentary.

Organizational Justice

Definition: overall perception of what is fair in the workplace

Example: I think this is a fair place to work.

Interactional justice describes an individual's perception of the degree to which she is treated with dignity, concern, and respect. When people are treated in an unjust manner (at least in their own eyes), they retaliate (for example, badmouthing a supervisor).[90] Because people intimately connect interactional justice or injustice to the conveyer of the information, we would expect perceptions of injustice to be more closely related to the supervisor. Generally, that's what the evidence suggests.[91]

Of these three forms of justice, distributive justice is most strongly related to organizational commitment and satisfaction with outcomes such as pay. Procedural justice relates most strongly to job satisfaction, employee trust, withdrawal from the organization, job performance, and citizenship behaviors. There is less evidence about interactional justice.[92]

Equity theory has gained a strong following in the United States because U.S.-style reward systems assume workers are highly sensitive to equity in reward allocations. And in the United States, equity is meant to closely tie pay to performance. However, in collectivist cultures employees expect rewards to reflect their individual needs as well as their performance.[93] Other research suggests that inputs and outcomes are valued differently in various

---

distributive justice *Perceived fairness of the amount and allocation of rewards among individuals.*

organizational justice *An overall perception of what is fair in the workplace, composed of distributive, procedural, and interactional justice.*

procedural justice *The perceived fairness of the process used to determine the distribution of rewards.*

interactional justice *The perceived degree to which an individual is treated with dignity, concern, and respect.*

cultures.[94] Some cultures emphasize status over individual achievement as a basis for allocating resources. Materialistic cultures are more likely to see cash compensation and rewards as the most relevant outcomes of work, whereas relational cultures will see social rewards and status as important outcomes. International managers must consider the cultural preferences of each group of employees when determining what is "fair" in different contexts.

Studies suggest that managers are indeed motivated to foster employees' perceptions of justice because they wish to ensure compliance, maintain a positive identity, and establish fairness at work.[95] To enhance perceptions of justice, they should realize that employees are especially sensitive to unfairness in procedures when bad news has to be communicated (that is, when distributive justice is low). Thus, it's especially important to openly share information about how allocation decisions are made, follow consistent and unbiased procedures, and engage in similar practices to increase the perception of procedural justice. Second, when addressing perceived injustices, managers need to focus their actions on the source of the problem.

If employees feel they have been treated unjustly, having opportunities to express their frustration has been shown to reduce their desire for retribution.[96]

Meta-analytic evidence shows individuals in both individualistic and collectivistic cultures prefer an equitable distribution of rewards (the most effective workers get paid the most) over an equal division (everyone gets paid the same regardless of performance).[97] Across nations, the same basic principles of procedural justice are respected, and workers around the world prefer rewards based on performance and skills over rewards based on seniority.[98]

Expectancy Theory

7 Demonstrate how organizational justice is a refinement of equity theory.

One of the most widely accepted explanations of motivation is Victor Vroom's **expectancy theory**.[99] Although it has its critics, most of the evidence supports it.[100]

Expectancy theory argues that the strength of our tendency to act a certain way depends on the strength of our expectation of a given outcome and its attractiveness. In more practical terms, employees will be motivated to exert a high level of effort when they believe it will lead to a good performance appraisal; that a good appraisal will lead to organizational rewards such as bonuses, salary increases, or promotions; and that the rewards will satisfy the employees' personal goals. The theory, therefore, focuses on three relationships (see Exhibit 7-8):

1. **Effort–performance relationship.** The probability perceived by the individual that exerting a given amount of effort will lead to performance.
2. **Performance–reward relationship.** The degree to which the individual believes performing at a particular level will lead to the attainment of a desired outcome.

MyManagementLab
For an interactive application of this topic, check out this chapter's simulation activity at **www.pearsonglobaleditions.com/mymanagementlab**.

Exhibit 7-8 **Expectancy Theory**

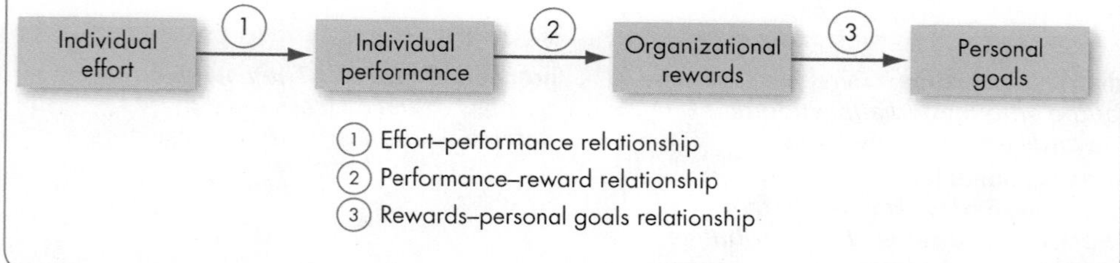

1. Effort–performance relationship
2. Performance–reward relationship
3. Rewards–personal goals relationship

3. **Rewards–personal goals relationship.** The degree to which organizational rewards satisfy an individual's personal goals or needs and the attractiveness of those potential rewards for the individual.[101]

Expectancy theory helps explain why a lot of workers aren't motivated on their jobs and do only the minimum necessary to get by. Let's frame the theory's three relationships as questions employees need to answer in the affirmative if their motivation is to be maximized.

First, *if I give a maximum effort, will it be recognized in my performance appraisal?* For many employees, the answer is "no." Why? Their skill level may be deficient, which means no matter how hard they try, they're not likely to be high performers. The organization's performance appraisal system may be designed to assess nonperformance factors such as loyalty, initiative, or courage, which means more effort won't necessarily result in a higher evaluation. Another possibility is that employees, rightly or wrongly, perceive the boss doesn't like them. As a result, they expect a poor appraisal, regardless of effort. These examples suggest one possible source of low motivation is employees' belief that, no matter how hard they work, the likelihood of getting a good performance appraisal is low.

Second, *if I get a good performance appraisal, will it lead to organizational rewards?* Many organizations reward things besides performance. When pay is based on factors such as having seniority, being cooperative, or "kissing up" to the boss, employees are likely to see the performance–reward relationship as weak and demotivating.

Finally, *if I'm rewarded, are the rewards attractive to me?* The employee works hard in the hope of getting a promotion but gets a pay raise instead. Or the employee wants a more interesting and challenging job but receives only a few words of praise. Unfortunately, many managers are limited in the rewards they can distribute, which makes it difficult to tailor rewards to individual employee needs. Some incorrectly assume all employees want the same thing, thus overlooking the motivational effects of differentiating rewards. In either case, employee motivation is submaximized.

As a vivid example of how expectancy theory can work, consider stock analysts. They make their living trying to forecast a stock's future price; the accuracy of their buy, sell, or hold recommendations is what keeps them in work or gets them fired. But it's not quite that simple. Analysts place few sell ratings on stocks, although in a steady market, by definition, as many stocks are falling as are rising. Expectancy theory provides an explanation: analysts who place a sell rating on a company's stock have to balance the benefits they receive by being accurate against the risks they run by drawing that company's ire. What are these risks? They include public rebuke, professional blackballing, and exclusion from information. When analysts place a buy rating on a stock, they face no such trade-off because, obviously, companies love it when analysts recommend that investors buy their stock. So the incentive structure suggests the expected outcome of buy ratings is higher than the expected outcome of sell ratings, and that's why buy ratings vastly outnumber sell ratings.[102]

expectancy theory *A theory that says that the strength of a tendency to act in a certain way depends on the strength of an expectation that the act will be followed by a given outcome and on the attractiveness of that outcome to the individual.*

At Mary Kay Cosmetics, the performance-reward relationship is strong. The company offers a generous rewards and recognition program based on the achievement of personal goals set by each employee. Mary Kay also understands the motivational effects of differentiating rewards. For some employees, the best reward is the opportunity to work from home, while other employees are motivated by the opportunity to win a trip, jewelry, or the use of a pink Cadillac. In this photo, a Mary Kay sales director explains career opportunities at a job fair to women interested in joining the company.

Source: Eric Risberg/AP Images

Does expectancy theory work? Some critics suggest it has only limited use and is more valid where individuals clearly perceive effort–performance and performance–reward linkages.[103] Because few individuals do, the theory tends to be idealistic. If organizations actually rewarded individuals for performance rather than seniority, effort, skill level, and job difficulty, expectancy theory might be much more valid. However, rather than invalidating it, this criticism can explain why a significant segment of the workforce exerts low effort on the job.

Integrating Contemporary Theories of Motivation

8 Apply the key tenets of expectancy theory to motivating employees.

9 Compare contemporary theories of motivation.

Things might be simpler if, after presenting a half dozen theories, we could say only one was found valid. But many of the theories in this chapter are complementary. We now tie them together to help you understand their interrelationships.[104]

Exhibit 7-9 integrates much of what we know about motivation. Its basic foundation is the expectancy model shown in Exhibit 7-8. Let's walk through Exhibit 7-9. (We will look at job design closely in Chapter 8.)

We begin by explicitly recognizing that opportunities can either aid or hinder individual effort. The individual effort box on the left also has another arrow leading into it, from the person's goals. Consistent with goal-setting theory, the goals–effort loop is meant to remind us that goals direct behavior.

Expectancy theory predicts employees will exert a high level of effort if they perceive a strong relationship between effort and performance, performance and rewards, and rewards and satisfaction of personal goals. Each of these relationships is, in turn, influenced by other factors. For

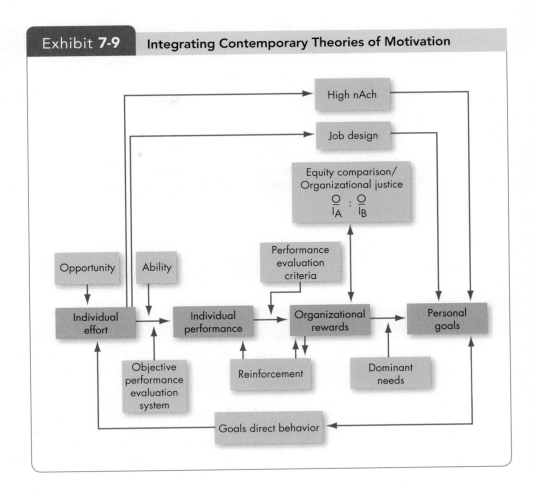

Exhibit 7-9   **Integrating Contemporary Theories of Motivation**

effort to lead to good performance, the individual must have the ability to perform and perceive the performance appraisal system as fair and objective. The performance–reward relationship will be strong if the individual perceives that performance (rather than seniority, personal favorites, or other criteria) is rewarded. If cognitive evaluation theory were fully valid in the actual workplace, we would predict here that basing rewards on performance should decrease the individual's intrinsic motivation. The final link in expectancy theory is the rewards–goals relationship. Motivation is high if the rewards for high performance satisfied the dominant needs consistent with individual goals.

A closer look at Exhibit 7-9 also reveals that the model considers achievement motivation, job design, reinforcement, and equity theories/organizational justice. A high achiever is not motivated by an organization's assessment of performance or organizational rewards, hence the jump from effort to personal goals for those with a high nAch. Remember, high achievers are internally driven as long as their jobs provide them with personal responsibility, feedback, and moderate risks. They are not concerned with the effort–performance, performance–rewards, or rewards–goal linkages.

Reinforcement theory enters the model by recognizing that the organization's rewards reinforce the individual's performance. If employees see a reward system as "paying off" for good performance, the rewards will reinforce and encourage good performance. Rewards also play the key part in organizational justice research. Individuals will judge the favorability of their outcomes (for example, their pay) relative to what others receive but also with respect to how they are treated: when people are disappointed in their rewards, they are likely to be sensitive to the perceived fairness of the procedures used and the consideration given to them by their supervisor.

MyManagementLab

Now that you have finished this chapter, go back to **www.pearsonglobaleditions.com/ mymanagementlab** to continue practicing and applying the concepts you've learned.

Summary and Implications for Managers

The motivation theories in this chapter differ in their predictive strength. Here, we (1) review the most established to determine their relevance in explaining turnover, productivity, and other outcomes and (2) assess the predictive power of each.[105]

- **Need theories.** Maslow's hierarchy, McClelland's needs, and the two-factor theory focus on needs. None has found widespread support, although McClelland's is the strongest, particularly regarding the relationship between achievement and productivity. In general, need theories are not very valid explanations of motivation.
- **Self-determination theory and cognitive evaluation theory.** As research on the motivational effects of rewards has accumulated, it increasingly appears extrinsic rewards can undermine motivation if they are seen as coercive. They can increase motivation if they provide information about competence and relatedness.
- **Goal-setting theory.** Clear and difficult goals lead to higher levels of employee productivity, supporting goal-setting theory's explanation of this dependent variable. The theory does not address absenteeism, turnover, or satisfaction, however.
- **Reinforcement theory.** This theory has an impressive record for predicting quality and quantity of work, persistence of effort, absenteeism, tardiness, and accident rates. It does not offer much insight into employee satisfaction or the decision to quit.
- **Equity theory/organizational justice.** Equity theory deals with productivity, satisfaction, absence, and turnover variables. However, its strongest legacy is that it provided the spark for research on organizational justice, which has more support in the literature.
- **Expectancy theory.** Expectancy theory offers a powerful explanation of performance variables such as employee productivity, absenteeism, and turnover. But it assumes employees have few constraints on decision making, such as bias or incomplete information, and this limits its applicability. Expectancy theory has some validity because, for many behaviors, people consider expected outcomes.

Fear Is a Powerful Motivator

This is a "dark side" topic that no one likes to discuss, but fear works as a motivator. Few of us like the idea of feeling fearful in the workplace. But what we like and what motivates us are not the same.

Ever studied harder for an exam for fear of doing poorly, or worried about doing something that would draw your parents' ire? If you answer "yes," you're on your way to admitting this essential truth: we engage in a lot of behaviors, and refrain from others, out of fear.

Too often in organizational behavior we sing this happy song that when employees are happy, they will give their best effort and the company will sail along in smooth seas.

The truth is that when a manager adopts this philosophy, people often relax. They take off early. They "shoot the breeze" more and work a little less. George Cloutier, founder of American Management Services, is realistic about this. "The concept that if you love your employees they'll perform is on the edge of insanity," he says. "Fear is the best motivator."

Employees should realize that in today's competitive environment, they have to bring their A-game to work each and every day. And managers need to closely monitor them to make sure that's the case. Instilling in employees a fear that if they shirk, they'll lose their jobs, is one way to accomplish that monitoring. Without fear, people would do as they wish, and that rarely includes working hard if they feel they don't have to. Like it or not, that's the cold, hard truth about employee motivation.

How cynical! Fear is a natural emotion, but it generally serves a purpose only in crisis situations. Those unfortunate enough to work under a manager who consciously uses fear to "motivate" behavior will leave as soon as they can or get even in some hidden way. Fear never works as a motivational tool. Various areas of research in psychology and organizational behavior prove the point.

Fear generates a "fight-flight-freeze" response, in which an individual (or animal) experiencing fear or extreme stress is forced to choose one of these behaviors. Any sane manager wants none of them. Imagine supervising Chris, who flees work when fearful or stressed, Sanjay, who fights with others when he feels cornered, and Mercedes, who locks up whenever she is chastised. Does effective management mean eliciting these behaviors?

One workplace expert noted, "Fear motivation always results in inner anger and resentment against the person using the fear tactics . . . Fear motivation is the lowest form of motivation and usually results in 'when the cat is away, the mice will play.'" So, ironically, fear actually undermines performance monitoring, because employees will get even when they know they can't be caught. And they will never go out of their way to help the organization.

As one Canadian manager noted, "Exercising unilateral power [through fear] can be effective for those leaders whose modest ambitions are matched by the modest successes that such tactics bring." Zappos founder Tony Hsieh, who tries to create a happy work environment at Zappos by giving employees the sense that they are part of something bigger, argues that inspiration is a much better motivator than fear.

Fear may motivate short-term performance, but in the long run, it is always a losing motivational tool.

Sources: K. Pattison, "Fire Your Relatives. Scare Your Employees. And Stop Whining," *The New York Times* (February 11, 2010), p. B8; L. Mignone, "How to Build an Army of Happy, Busy Worker Bees," *Fortune* (May 23, 2011), downloaded May 25, 2011, from www.fortune.com; TTI Performance Systems, "Provide a Climate for Motivation," downloaded May 25, 2011, from www.nielsongroup.com/; and J. Wood, "Stories, Not Data, At Heart of Human Motivation," *Vancouver Sun* (May 20, 2011), downloaded May 25, 2011, from www.vancouversun.com/.

QUESTIONS FOR REVIEW

1 What are the three key elements of motivation?

2 What are some early theories of motivation? How applicable are they today?

3 How do the predictions of self-determination theory apply to intrinsic and extrinsic rewards?

4 What are the implications of employee engagement for management?

5 What are the similarities and differences between goal-setting theory and management by objectives?

6 What are the similarities and differences between reinforcement theory and goal-setting theory?

7 How is organizational justice a refinement of equity theory?

8 What are the key tenets of expectancy theory?

9 What are some contemporary theories of motivation and how do they compare to one another?

EXPERIENTIAL EXERCISE Goal-Setting Task

Purpose

This exercise will help you learn how to write tangible, verifiable, measurable, and relevant goals that might evolve from an MBO program.

Time

Approximately 20 to 30 minutes.

Instructions

1. Break into groups of three to five.

2. Spend a few minutes discussing your class instructor's job. What does he or she do? What defines good performance? What behaviors lead to good performance?

3. Each group is to develop a list of five goals that, although not established participatively with your instructor, you believe might be developed in an MBO program at your college. Try to select goals that seem most critical to the effective performance of your instructor's job.

4. Each group will select a leader who will share the group's goals with the entire class. For each group's goals, class discussion should focus on the goals' (a) specificity, (b) ease of measurement, (c) importance, and (d) motivational properties.

ETHICAL DILEMMA The Big Easy?

As you know, college is an expensive proposition. Students, parents, donors, and the government invest millions of dollars every year. Thus, there may be an incumbent responsibility on students to ensure they are learning. However, consider the following results from a recent study of time use by more than 3,000 undergraduates:

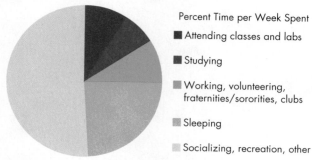

Undergraduate Use of Time per Week

Questions

1. One article commented that college students are "frittering away their time at an astonishing rate." Do you agree this is what the data show? Why or why not?

2. Do you think students have an ethical responsibility to spend more time studying? Why or why not?

3. One study suggested that full-time students in 1961 studied an average of 40 hours per week, compared to 27 hours now. Does this apparent trend concern you? Do you think that, as some experts have claimed, our economic competitiveness would increase if college students studied more?

Sources: M. Burns, "What Happened to Academic Rigor?" *Miller-McCune* (March 8, 2011), pp. 47–49; and R. Arum, *Academically Adrift: Limited Learning on College Campuses* (Chicago: University of Chicago Press, 2011).

CASE INCIDENT 1 Motivation in the Hong Kong Police Force

Believing that success should be driven by other factors beyond the incentive of money, the Hong Kong Police Force has harnessed a strong culture of excellent performance. It embodies the use of comprehensive talent development programs, performance management, and honors and awards systems. In particular, receipt of the last is so highly regarded as the culmination of a police officer's life that it serves as a strong motivational tool.

The vigorous pursuit of an excellent performance is a goal that is aimed for early among new police recruits. Upon graduating from training, the candidate who attains the highest exam score is awarded with the Commissioner of Police's Certificate of Academic Merit. Also, the Brian Slevin Trophy, the Baton of Honor, and a silver plaque are presented to the best all-round probationary inspector who gets excellent results in all aspects of policing. Similarly, gold and silver whistles are awarded to the best all-round recruit police officers.

Furthermore, high morale among police officers is actively supported by internal and external award schemes that emphasize positive reinforcement instead of punishment. Internally, compliments or letters of appreciation are given to police officers who show courage, leadership, ability, or devotion to duty above and beyond what is expected according to the excellence or complexity of the cases resolved. Commissioner of Police Commendations and the Commanding Officer Commendations are also awarded and draw publicity. All awards are recorded in the recipients' dossiers.

Prestigious external awards also may be granted. In particular, the Chief Executive's Commendations have drawn much public attention. They may be given in the form of Bravery awards (Gold, Silver, and Bronze Medals) as well as Disciplined Services Awards for Police Officers. The yearly award presentation is conducted by the Chief Executive and held in Government House. Widespread media coverage is received.

The effect of such motivational tools is far more enduring than money. A recent newspaper article reports that a retired police constable, Mr. Lee, still proudly told his story and presented his red lanyard 紅銀雞繩 and Certificate of Commendation to the reporters when he received the Chief Executive's Commendation for Government Service more than 20 years ago. In 1984 he arrested an infamous gangster, Mr. Yip Kai Foon, 葉繼歡 whose gang specialized in robbing jewelry stores with assault rifles.

Questions

1. Would you be interested in working as a Hong Kong police officer? Why or why not?

2. How many examples in this case can you apply motivation theories to?

3. One may argue that the recipients of the honors and awards are only a fraction of all police officers. Suggest other effective ways to motivate the police officers.

4. Are there any positive motivational consequences of tying compensation pay closely to firm performance?

Sources: Anonymous interviews with police officers; "Arresting Yip Kai Foon by Hand: A Police's Description." *Apple Daily* (October 2, 2009).

CASE INCIDENT 2 Bullying Bosses

After a long weekend, Kara stared at her computer with a sick feeling in her stomach: her boss had added her as a friend on Facebook. Kara did not feel particularly close to her boss, nor did she like the idea of mixing her social life with her work. Still, it was her boss. Kara reluctantly accepted her boss as a Facebook friend. Little did she know her troubles were only beginning.

Kara's boss soon began using her online information to manipulate her work life. It began with inappropriate innuendos regarding Facebook photos. Eventually, Kara's boss manipulated her work hours, confronted her both on and off Facebook, and repeatedly called Kara's cell phone questioning her whereabouts. "My boss was a gossiping, domineering, contriving megalomaniac, and her behavior dramatically intensified when she used Facebook to pry," Kara said. Eventually, Kara was forced to quit. "I feel like I got my freedom back and can breathe again," she said.

Although many individuals recall bullies from elementary school days, some are realizing bullies can exist in the workplace, too. In a recent poll, 37 percent of employees report being victims of a bullying boss. And these bullies don't pick on just the weakest in the group; any subordinate may fall prey. As Kara found, bullying is not limited to male bosses: 40 percent of bullies are women, and women are their targets 70 percent of the time.

How does bullying affect employee motivation and behavior? Surprisingly, though victims may feel less motivated to go to work every day, they continue performing their required job duties. However, some are less motivated to perform extra-role or citizenship behaviors. Helping others, speaking positively about the organization, and going beyond the call of duty are reduced as a result of bullying. According to Dr. Bennett Tepper, fear may be the reason many workers continue to perform. And not all individuals reduce their citizenship behaviors. Some continue to engage in extra-role behaviors to make themselves look better than their colleagues. Other victims of bullying may be motivated to actively retaliate against their bullying supervisor, or engage in acts of workplace withdrawal.

What should you do if your boss is bullying you? Don't necessarily expect help from co-workers. As Emelise Aleandri, an actress and producer from New York who left her job after being bullied, stated, "Some people were afraid to do anything. But others didn't mind what was happening at all, because they wanted my job." Moreover, according to Dr. Michelle Duffy of the University of Kentucky, co-workers often blame victims of bullying in order to resolve their own guilt. "They do this by wondering whether maybe the person deserved the treatment, that

he or she has been annoying, or lazy, [or] did something to earn it," she says.

Questions

1. How does workplace bullying violate the rules of organizational justice?

2. What aspects of motivation might workplace bullying reduce? For example, are there likely to be effects on an employee's self-efficacy? If so, what might those effects be? Do you think bullying would motivate you to retaliate?

3. If you were a victim of workplace bullying, what steps would you take to try to reduce its occurrence? What strategies would be most effective? Least effective? What would you do if one of your colleagues were a victim?

4. What factors do you believe contribute to workplace bullying? Are bullies a product of the situation, or do they have flawed personalities? What situations and what personality factors might contribute to the presence of bullies?

Sources: Based on M. Wilding, "Is Your Boss Your Friend or Foe?" *Sydney Morning Herald* (May 19, 2009), pp. 1–3; C. Benedict, "The Bullying Boss," *The New York Times* (June 22, 2004), p. F1; and S. Thau and M. S. Mitchell, "Self-Gain or Self-Regulation Impairment? Tests of Competing Explanations of the Supervisor Abuse and Employee Deviance Relationship Through Perceptions of Distributive Justice," *Journal of Applied Psychology* 95, (2010), pp. 1009–1031.

ENDNOTES

1. See, for example, G. P. Latham and C. C. Pinder, "Work Motivation Theory and Research at the Dawn of the Twenty-First Century," *Annual Review of Psychology* 56 (2005), pp. 485–516; and C. Pinder, *Work Motivation in Organizational Behavior,* 2nd ed. (London, UK: Psychology Press, 2008).

2. R. Wagner and J. K. Harter, *12: The Elements of Great Managing* (Washington, DC: Gallup Press, 2006).

3. "The 2008 Wasting Time at Work Survey Reveals a Record Number of People Waste Time at Work," Salary.com (2008), www.salary.com.

4. See, for instance, Pinder, *Work Motivation in Organizational Behavior.*

5. A. Maslow, *Motivation and Personality* (New York: Harper & Row, 1954).

6. G. Hofstede, "Motivation, Leadership, and Organization: Do American Theories Apply Abroad?" *Organizational Dynamics* (Summer 1980), p. 55.

7. See, for example, E. E. Lawler III and J. L. Suttle, "A Causal Correlation Test of the Need Hierarchy Concept," *Organizational Behavior and Human Performance* 7, no. 2 (1972), pp. 265–287; D. T. Hall and K. E. Nougaim, "An Examination of Maslow's Need Hierarchy in an Organizational Setting," *Organizational Behavior and Human Performance* 3, no. 1 (1968), pp. 12–35; and J. Rauschenberger, N. Schmitt, and

J. E. Hunter, "A Test of the Need Hierarchy Concept by a Markov Model of Change in Need Strength," *Administrative Science Quarterly* 25, no. 4 (1980), pp. 654–670.

8. M. A. Wahba and L. G. Bridwell, "Maslow Reconsidered: A Review of Research on the Need Hierarchy Theory," *Organizational Behavior and Human Performance* 15, no. 2 (1976), pp. 212–240.

9. D. T. Kenrick, V. Griskevicius, S. L. Neuberg, and M. Schaller, "Renovating the Pyramid of Needs: Contemporary Extensions Built on Ancient Foundations," *Perspectives on Psychological Science* 5, no. 3 (2010), pp. 292–314.

10. D. McGregor, *The Human Side of Enterprise* (New York: McGraw-Hill, 1960). For an updated analysis of Theory X and Theory Y constructs, see R. E. Kopelman, D. J. Prottas, and D. W. Falk, "Construct Validation of a Theory X/Y Behavior Scale," *Leadership and Organization Development Journal* 31, no. 2 (2010), pp. 120–135.

11. F. Herzberg, B. Mausner, and B. Snyderman, *The Motivation to Work* (New York: Wiley, 1959).

12. R. J. House and L. A. Wigdor, "Herzberg's Dual-Factor Theory of Job Satisfaction and Motivations: A Review of the Evidence and Criticism," *Personnel Psychology* 20, no. 4 (1967), pp. 369–389; D. P. Schwab and L. L. Cummings, "Theories of Performance and Satisfaction: A Review," *Industrial Relations* 9, no. 4 (1970), pp. 403–430; and J. Phillipchuk

and J. Whittaker, "An Inquiry into the Continuing Relevance of Herzberg's Motivation Theory," *Engineering Management Journal* 8 (1996), pp. 15–20.

13. D. C. McClelland, *The Achieving Society* (New York: Van Nostrand Reinhold, 1961); J. W. Atkinson and J. O. Raynor, *Motivation and Achievement* (Washington, DC: Winston, 1974); D. C. McClelland, *Power: The Inner Experience* (New York: Irvington, 1975); and M. J. Stahl, *Managerial and Technical Motivation: Assessing Needs for Achievement, Power, and Affiliation* (New York: Praeger, 1986).

14. D. C. McClelland and D. G. Winter, *Motivating Economic Achievement* (New York: The Free Press, 1969); and J. B. Miner, N. R. Smith, and J. S. Bracker, "Role of Entrepreneurial Task Motivation in the Growth of Technologically Innovative Firms: Interpretations from Follow-up Data," *Journal of Applied Psychology* 79, no. 4 (1994), pp. 627–630.

15. McClelland, *Power;* D. C. McClelland and D. H. Burnham, "Power Is the Great Motivator," *Harvard Business Review* (March–April 1976), pp. 100–110; and R. E. Boyatzis, "The Need for Close Relationships and the Manager's Job," in D. A. Kolb, I. M. Rubin, and J. M. McIntyre, *Organizational Psychology: Readings on Human Behavior in Organizations,* 4th ed. (Upper Saddle River, NJ: Prentice Hall, 1984), pp. 81–86.

16. D. G. Winter, "The Motivational Dimensions of Leadership: Power, Achievement, and Affiliation," in R. E. Riggio, S. E. Murphy, and F. J. Pirozzolo (eds.), *Multiple Intelligences and Leadership* (Mahwah, NJ: Lawrence Erlbaum, 2002), pp. 119–138.

17. J. B. Miner, *Studies in Management Education* (New York: Springer, 1965).

18. Ibid.

19. E. Deci and R. Ryan (eds.), *Handbook of Self-Determination Research* (Rochester, NY: University of Rochester Press, 2002); R. Ryan and E. Deci, "Self-Determination Theory and the Facilitation of Intrinsic Motivation, Social Development, and Well-Being," *American Psychologist* 55, no. 1 (2000), pp. 68–78; and M. Gagné and E. L. Deci, "Self-Determination Theory and Work Motivation," *Journal of Organizational Behavior* 26, no. 4 (2005), pp. 331–362.

20. See, for example, E. L. Deci, R. Koestner, and R. M. Ryan, "A Meta-Analytic Review of Experiments Examining the Effects of Extrinsic Rewards on Intrinsic Motivation," *Psychological Bulletin* 125, no. 6 (1999), pp. 627–668; G. J. Greguras and J. M. Diefendorff, "Different Fits Satisfy Different Needs: Linking Person-Environment Fit to Employee Commitment and Performance Using Self-Determination Theory," *Journal of Applied Psychology* 94, no. 2 (2009), pp. 465–477; and D. Liu, X. Chen, and X. Yao, "From Autonomy to Creativity: A Multilevel Investigation of the Mediating Role of Harmonious Passion," *Journal of Applied Psychology* 96, no. 2 (2011), pp. 294–309.

21. R. Eisenberger and L. Rhoades, "Incremental Effects of Reward on Creativity," *Journal of Personality and Social Psychology* 81, no. 4 (2001), 728–741; and R. Eisenberger, W. D. Pierce, and J. Cameron, "Effects of Reward on Intrinsic Motivation—Negative, Neutral, and Positive: Comment on Deci, Koestner, and Ryan (1999)," *Psychological Bulletin* 125, no. 6 (1999), pp. 677–691.

22. M. Burgess, M. E. Enzle, and R. Schmaltz, "Defeating the Potentially Deleterious Effects of Externally Imposed Deadlines: Practitioners' Rules-of-Thumb," *Personality and Social Psychology Bulletin* 30, no. 7 (2004), pp. 868–877.

23. K. M. Sheldon, A. J. Elliot, and R. M. Ryan, "Self-Concordance and Subjective Well-being in Four Cultures," *Journal of Cross-Cultural Psychology* 35, no. 2 (2004), pp. 209–223.

24. J. E. Bono and T. A. Judge, "Self-Concordance at Work: Toward Understanding the Motivational Effects of Transformational Leaders," *Academy of Management Journal* 46, no. 5 (2003), pp. 554–571.

25. J. P. Meyer, T. E. Becker, and C. Vandenberghe, "Employee Commitment and Motivation: A Conceptual Analysis and Integrative Model," *Journal of Applied Psychology* 89, no. 6 (2004), pp. 991–1007.

26. W. A. Kahn, "Psychological Conditions of Personal Engagement and Disengagement at Work," *Academy of Management Journal* 33, no. 4 (1990), pp. 692–724.

27. www.gallup.com/consulting/52/Employee-Engagement.aspx

28. J. K. Harter, F. L. Schmidt, and T. L. Hayes, "Business-Unit-Level Relationship Between Employee Satisfaction, Employee Engagement, and Business Outcomes: A Meta-Analysis," *Journal of Applied Psychology* 87, no. 2 (2002), pp. 268–279.

29. M. S. Christian, A. S. Garza, and J. E. Slaughter, "Work Engagement: A Quantitative Review and Test of Its Relations with Task and Contextual Performance," *Personnel Psychology* 64, no. 1 (2011), pp. 89–136.

30. W. B. Schaufeli, A. B. Bakker, and W. van Rhenen, "How Changes in Job Demands and Resources Predict Burnout, Work Engagement, and Sickness Absenteeism," *Journal of Organizational Behavior* 30, no. 7 (2009), pp. 893–917; E. R. Crawford, J. A. LePine, and B. L. Rich, "Linking Job Demands and Resources to Employee Engagement and Burnout: A Theoretical Extension and Meta-Analytic Test," *Journal of Applied Psychology* 95, no. 5 (2010), pp. 834–848; and D. Xanthopoulou, A. B. Bakker, E. Demerouti, and W. B. Schaufeli, "Reciprocal Relationships Between job Resources, Personal Resources, and Work Engagement," *Journal of Vocational Behavior* 74, no. 3 (2009), pp. 235–244.

31. B. L. Rich, J. A. LePine, and E. R. Crawford, "Job Engagement: Antecedents and Effects on Job Performance," *Academy of Management Journal* 53, no. 3 (2010), pp. 617–635.

32. M. Tims, A. B. Bakker, and D. Xanthopoulou, "Do Transformational Leaders Enhance Their Followers' Daily Work Engagement?" *Leadership Quarterly* 22, no. 1 (2011), pp. 121–131; and F. O. Walumbwa, P. Wang, H. Wang, J. Schaubroeck, and B. J. Avolio, "Psychological Processes Linking Authentic Leadership to Follower Behaviors," *Leadership Quarterly* 21, no. 5 (2010), pp. 901–914.

33. D. A. Newman and D. A. Harrison, "Been There, Bottled That: Are State and Behavioral Work Engagement New and Useful Construct 'Wines?'" *Industrial and Organizational Psychology* 1, no. 1 (2008), pp. 31–35; A. J. Wefald and R. G. Downey, "Job Engagement in Organizations: Fad, Fashion, or Folderol," *Journal of Organizational Behavior* 30, no. 1 (2009), pp. 141–145.

34. See, for example, Rich, LePine, and Crawford, "Job Engagement: Antecedents and Effects on Job Performance;"

and Christian, Garza, and Slaughter, "Work Engagement: A Quantitative Review and Test of Its Relations with Task and Contextual Performance."

35. J. M. George, "The Wider Context, Costs, and Benefits of Work Engagement," *European Journal of Work and Organizational Psychology* 20, no. 1 (2011), pp. 53–59; and J. R. B. Halbesleben, J. Harvey, and M. C. Bolino, "Too Engaged? A Conservation of Resources View of the Relationship Between Work Engagement and Work Interference with Family," *Journal of Applied Psychology* 94, no. 6 (2009), pp. 1452–1465.

36. E. A. Locke, "Toward a Theory of Task Motivation and Incentives," *Organizational Behavior and Human Performance* 3, no. 2 (1968), pp. 157–189.

37. P. C. Earley, P. Wojnaroski, and W. Prest, "Task Planning and Energy Expended: Exploration of How Goals Influence Performance," *Journal of Applied Psychology* 72, no. 1 (1987), pp. 107–114.

38. See M. E. Tubbs, "Goal Setting: A Meta-Analytic Examination of the Empirical Evidence," *Journal of Applied Psychology* 71, no. 3 (1986), pp. 474–483; and E. A. Locke and G. P. Latham, "New Directions in Goal-Setting Theory," *Current Directions in Psychological Science* 15, no. 5 (2006), pp. 265–268.

39. E. A. Locke and G. P. Latham, "Building a Practically Useful Theory of Goal Setting and Task Motivation," *American Psychologist* 57, no. 2 (2002), pp. 705–717.

40. J. M. Ivancevich and J. T. McMahon, "The Effects of Goal Setting, External Feedback, and Self-Generated Feedback on Outcome Variables: A Field Experiment," *Academy of Management Journal* 25, no. 2 (1982), pp. 359–372; and E. A. Locke, "Motivation Through Conscious Goal Setting," *Applied and Preventive Psychology* 5, no. 2 (1996), pp. 117–124.

41. See, for example, G. P. Latham, M. Erez, and E. A. Locke, "Resolving Scientific Disputes by the Joint Design of Crucial Experiments by the Antagonists: Application to the Erez-Latham Dispute Regarding Participation in Goal Setting," *Journal of Applied Psychology* 73, no. 4 (1988), pp. 753–772; T. D. Ludwig and E. S. Geller, "Assigned Versus Participative Goal Setting and Response Generalization: Managing Injury Control among Professional Pizza Deliverers," *Journal of Applied Psychology* 82, no. 2 (1997), pp. 253–261; and S. G. Harkins and M. D. Lowe, "The Effects of Self-Set Goals on Task Performance," *Journal of Applied Social Psychology* 30, no. 1 (2000), pp. 1–40.

42. M. Erez, P. C. Earley, and C. L. Hulin, "The Impact of Participation on Goal Acceptance and Performance: A Two-Step Model," *Academy of Management Journal* 28, no. 1 (1985), pp. 50–66.

43. E. A. Locke, "The Motivation to Work: What We Know," *Advances in Motivation and Achievement* 10 (1997), pp. 375–412; and Latham, Erez, and Locke, "Resolving Scientific Disputes by the Joint Design of Crucial Experiments by the Antagonists," pp. 753–772.

44. Ibid.

45. J. R. Hollenbeck, C. R. Williams, and H. J. Klein, "An Empirical Examination of the Antecedents of Commitment to Difficult Goals," *Journal of Applied Psychology* 74, no. 1 (1989), pp. 18–23. See also J. C. Wofford, V. L. Goodwin, and S. Premack, "Meta-Analysis of the Antecedents of Personal Goal Level and of the Antecedents and Consequences of Goal Commitment," *Journal of Management* 18, no. 3 (1992), pp. 595–615; M. E. Tubbs, "Commitment as a Moderator of the Goal-Performance Relation: A Case for Clearer Construct Definition," *Journal of Applied Psychology* 78, no. 1 (1993), pp. 86–97; and J. E. Bono and A. E. Colbert, "Understanding Responses to Multi-Source Feedback: The Role of Core Self-evaluations," *Personnel Psychology* 58, no. 1 (2005), pp. 171–203.

46. See R. E. Wood, A. J. Mento, and E. A. Locke, "Task Complexity as a Moderator of Goal Effects: A Meta-Analysis," *Journal of Applied Psychology* 72, no. 3 (1987), pp. 416–425; R. Kanfer and P. L. Ackerman, "Motivation and Cognitive Abilities: An Integrative/Aptitude-Treatment Interaction Approach to Skill Acquisition," *Journal of Applied Psychology* 74, no. 4 (1989), pp. 657–690; T. R. Mitchell and W. S. Silver, "Individual and Group Goals When Workers Are Interdependent: Effects on Task Strategies and Performance," *Journal of Applied Psychology* 75, no. 2 (1990), pp. 185–193; and A. M. O'Leary-Kelly, J. J. Martocchio, and D. D. Frink, "A Review of the Influence of Group Goals on Group Performance," *Academy of Management Journal* 37, no. 5 (1994), pp. 1285–1301.

47. D. F. Crown, "The Use of Group and Groupcentric Individual Goals for Culturally Heterogeneous and Homogeneous Task Groups: An Assessment of European Work Teams," *Small Group Research* 38, no. 4 (2007), pp. 489–508; J. Kurman, "Self-Regulation Strategies in Achievement Settings: Culture and Gender Differences," *Journal of Cross-Cultural Psychology* 32, no. 4 (2001), pp. 491–503; and M. Erez and P. C. Earley, "Comparative Analysis of Goal-Setting Strategies Across Cultures," *Journal of Applied Psychology* 72, no. 4 (1987), pp. 658–665.

48. C. Sue-Chan and M. Ong, "Goal Assignment and Performance: Assessing the Mediating Roles of Goal Commitment and Self-Efficacy and the Moderating Role of Power Distance," *Organizational Behavior and Human Decision Processes* 89, no. 2 (2002), pp. 1140–1161.

49. G. P. Latham and E. A. Locke, "Enhancing the Benefits and Overcoming the Pitfalls of Goal Setting," *Organizational Dynamics* 35, no. 6, pp. 332–340; L. D. Ordóñez, M. E. Schweitzer, A. D. Galinsky, and M. Bazerman, "Goals Gone Wild: The Systematic Side Effects of Overprescribing Goal Setting," *Academy of Management Perspectives* 23, no. 1 (2009), pp. 6–16; and E. A. Locke and G. P. Latham, "Has Goal Setting Gone Wild, or Have Its Attackers Abandoned Good Scholarship?" *Academy of Management Perspectives* 23, no. 1 (2009), pp. 17–23.

50. S. J. Perry, L. A. Witt, L. M. Penney, and L. Atwater, "The Downside of Goal-Focused Leadership: The Role of Personality in Subordinate Exhaustion," *Journal of Applied Psychology* 95, no. 6 (2010), pp. 1145–1153.

51. See, for example, A. D. Sajkovic, E. A. Locke, and E. S. Blair, "A First Examination of the Relationships Between Primed Subconscious Goals, Assigned Conscious Goals, and Task Performance," *Journal of Applied Psychology* 91, no. 5 (2006), pp. 1172–1180; G. P. Latham, A. D. Stajkovic, and E. A. Locke, "The Relevance and Viability of Subconscious Goals in the Workplace," *Journal of Management* 36, no. 1 (2010), pp. 234–255; and A. Schantz

and G. P. Latham, "An Exploratory Field Experiment on the Effect of Subconscious and Conscious Goals on Employee Performance," *Organizational Behavior and Human Decision Processes* 109, no. 1 (2009), pp. 9–17.

52. "KEYGroup Survey Finds Nearly Half of All Employees Have No Set Performance Goals," *IPMA-HR Bulletin* (March 10, 2006), p. 1; S. Hamm, "SAP Dangles a Big, Fat Carrot," *BusinessWeek* (May 22, 2006), pp. 67–68; and "P&G CEO Wields High Expectations but No Whip," *USA Today* (February 19, 2007), p. 3B.

53. See, for instance, S. J. Carroll and H. L. Tosi, *Management by Objectives: Applications and Research* (New York: Macmillan, 1973); and R. Rodgers and J. E. Hunter, "Impact of Management by Objectives on Organizational Productivity," *Journal of Applied Psychology* 76, no. 2 (1991), pp. 322–336.

54. See, for instance, T. H. Poister and G. Streib, "MBO in Municipal Government: Variations on a Traditional Management Tool," *Public Administration Review* (January/February 1995), pp. 48–56; C. Garvey, "Goalsharing Scores," *HRMagazine* (April 2000), pp. 99–106; E. Lindberg and T. L. Wilson, "Management by Objectives: The Swedish Experience in Upper Secondary Schools," *Journal of Educational Administration* 49, no. 1 (2011), pp. 62–75; and A. C. Spaulding, L. D. Gamm, and J. M. Griffith, "Studer Unplugged: Identifying Underlying Managerial Concepts," *Hospital Topics* 88, no. 1 (2010), pp. 1–9.

55. See, for instance, R. Rodgers, J. E. Hunter, and D. L. Rogers, "Influence of Top Management Commitment on Management Program Success," *Journal of Applied Psychology* 78, no. 1 (1993), pp. 151–155; M. Tanikawa, "Fujitsu Decides to Backtrack on Performance-Based Pay," *New York Times* (March 22, 2001), p. W1; and W. F. Roth, "Is Management by Objectives Obsolete?" *Global Business and Organizational Excellence* 28 (May/June 2009), pp. 36–43.

56. A. Bandura, *Self-Efficacy: The Exercise of Control* (New York: Freeman, 1997).

57. A. D. Stajkovic and F. Luthans, "Self-Efficacy and Work-Related Performance: A Meta-Analysis," *Psychological Bulletin* 124, no. 2 (1998), pp. 240–261; and A. Bandura, "Cultivate Self-Efficacy for Personal and Organizational Effectiveness," in E. Locke (ed.), *Handbook of Principles of Organizational Behavior* (Malden, MA: Blackwell, 2004), pp. 120–136.

58. M. Salanova, S. Llorens, and W. B. Schaufeli, "Yes I Can, I Feel Good, and I Just Do It! On Gain Cycles and Spirals of Efficacy Beliefs, Affect, and Engagement," *Applied Psychology* 60, no. 2 (2011), pp. 255–285.

59. P. Tierney and S. M. Farmer, "Creative Self-Efficacy Development and Creative Performance Over Time," *Journal of Applied Psychology* 96, no. 2 (2011), pp. 277–293.

60. A. Bandura and D. Cervone, "Differential Engagement in Self-Reactive Influences in Cognitively-Based Motivation," *Organizational Behavior and Human Decision Processes* 38, no. 1 (1986), pp. 92–113.

61. Bandura, *Self-Efficacy.*

62. C. L. Holladay and M. A. Quiñones, "Practice Variability and Transfer of Training: The Role of Self-Efficacy Generality," *Journal of Applied Psychology* 88, no. 6 (2003), pp. 1094–1103.

63. E. C. Dierdorff, E. A. Surface, and K. G. Brown, "Frame-of-Reference Training Effectiveness: Effects of Goal Orientation and Self-Efficacy on Affective, Cognitive, Skill-Based, and Transfer Outcomes," *Journal of Applied Psychology* 95, no. 6 (2010), pp. 1181–1191; and R. Grossman, and E. Salas, "The Transfer of Training: What Really Matters," *International Journal of Training and Development* 15, no. 2 (2011), pp. 103–120.

64. R. C. Rist, "Student Social Class and Teacher Expectations: The Self-Fulfilling Prophecy in Ghetto Education," *Harvard Educational Review* 70, no. 3 (2000), pp. 266–301.

65. D. Eden, "Self-Fulfilling Prophecies in Organizations," in J. Greenberg (ed.), *Organizational Behavior: The State of the Science,* 2nd ed. (Mahwah, NJ: Lawrence Erlbaum, 2003), pp. 91–122.

66. Ibid.

67. T. A. Judge, C. L. Jackson, J. C. Shaw, B. Scott, and B. L. Rich, "Self-Efficacy and Work-Related Performance: The Integral Role of Individual Differences," *Journal of Applied Psychology* 92, no. 1 (2007), pp. 107–127.

68. Ibid.

69. J. L. Komaki, T. Coombs, and S. Schepman, "Motivational Implications of Reinforcement Theory," in R. M. Steers, L. W. Porter, and G. Bigley (eds.), *Motivation and Work Behavior,* 6th ed. (New York: McGraw-Hill, 1996), pp. 87–107.

70. B. F. Skinner, *Contingencies of Reinforcement* (East Norwalk, CT: Appleton-Century-Crofts, 1971).

71. J. A. Mills, *Control: A History of Behavioral Psychology* (New York: New York University Press, 2000).

72. E. A. Locke, "Latham vs. Komaki: A Tale of Two Paradigms," *Journal of Applied Psychology* 65, no. 1 (1980), pp. 16–23.

73. A. Bandura, *Social Learning Theory* (Upper Saddle River, NJ: Prentice Hall, 1977).

74. J. S. Adams, "Inequity in Social Exchanges," in L. Berkowitz (ed.), *Advances in Experimental Social Psychology* (New York: Academic Press, 1965), pp. 267–300.

75. P. S. Goodman, "An Examination of Referents Used in the Evaluation of Pay," *Organizational Behavior and Human Performance* 12, no. 2 (1974), pp. 170–195; W. Scholl, E. A. Cooper, and J. F. McKenna, "Referent Selection in Determining Equity Perception: Differential Effects on Behavioral and Attitudinal Outcomes," *Personnel Psychology* 40, no. 1 (1987), pp. 113–127; and M. L. Williams, M. A. McDaniel, and N. T. Nguyen, "A Meta-Analysis of the Antecedents and Consequences of Pay Level Satisfaction," *Journal of Applied Psychology* 91, no. 2 (2006), pp. 392–413.

76. C. T. Kulik and M. L. Ambrose, "Personal and Situational Determinants of Referent Choice," *Academy of Management Review* 17, no. 2 (1992), pp. 212–237.

77. C. Ostroff and L. E. Atwater, "Does Whom You Work with Matter? Effects of Referent Group Gender and Age Composition on Managers' Compensation," *Journal of Applied Psychology* 88, no. 4 (2003), pp. 725–740.

78. Ibid.

79. See, for example, E. Walster, G. W. Walster, and W. G. Scott, *Equity: Theory and Research* (Boston: Allyn & Bacon, 1978); and J. Greenberg, "Cognitive Reevaluation of Outcomes in Response to Underpayment Inequity," *Academy of Management Journal,* March 1989, pp. 174–184.

80. P. S. Goodman and A. Friedman, "An Examination of Adams' Theory of Inequity," *Administrative Science Quarterly* 16, no. 3 (1971), pp. 271–288; R. P. Vecchio, "An Individual-Differences Interpretation of the Conflicting Predictions Generated by Equity Theory and Expectancy Theory," *Journal of Applied Psychology* 66, no. 4 (1981), pp. 470–481; R. T. Mowday, "Equity Theory Predictions of Behavior in Organizations," in R. Steers, L. W. Porter, and G. Bigley (eds.), *Motivation and Work Behavior*, 6th ed. (New York: McGraw-Hill, 1996), pp. 111–131; R. W. Griffeth and S. Gaertner, "A Role for Equity Theory in the Turnover Process: An Empirical Test," *Journal of Applied Social Psychology* 31, no. 5 (2001), pp. 1017–1037; and L. K. Scheer, N. Kumar, and J.-B. E. M. Steenkamp, "Reactions to Perceived Inequity in U.S. and Dutch Interorganizational Relationships," *Academy of Management* 46, no. 3 (2003), pp. 303–316.

81. See, for example, R. C. Huseman, J. D. Hatfield, and E. W. Miles, "A New Perspective on Equity Theory: The Equity Sensitivity Construct," *Academy of Management Journal* 12, no. 2 (1987), pp. 222–234; K. S. Sauley and A. G. Bedeian, "Equity Sensitivity: Construction of a Measure and Examination of Its Psychometric Properties," *Journal of Management* 26, no. 5 (2000), pp. 885–910; and J. A. Colquitt, "Does the Justice of One Interact with the Justice of Many? Reactions to Procedural Justice in Teams," *Journal of Applied Psychology* 89, no. 4 (2004), pp. 633–646.

82. J. Greenberg and S. Ornstein, "High Status Job Title as Compensation for Underpayment: A Test of Equity Theory," *Journal of Applied Psychology* 68, no. 2 (1983), pp. 285–297; and J. Greenberg, "Equity and Workplace Status: A Field Experiment," *Journal of Applied Psychology* 73, no. 4 (1988), pp. 606–613.

83. See, for instance, J. A. Colquitt, D. E. Conlon, M. J. Wesson, C. O. L. H. Porter, and K. Y. Ng, "Justice at the Millennium: A Meta-Analytic Review of the 25 Years of Organizational Justice Research," *Journal of Applied Psychology* 86, no. 3 (2001), pp. 425–445; T. Simons and Q. Roberson, "Why Managers Should Care About Fairness: The Effects of Aggregate Justice Perceptions on Organizational Outcomes," *Journal of Applied Psychology* 88, no. 3 (2003), pp. 432–443; and B. C. Holtz and C. M. Harold, "Fair Today, Fair Tomorrow? A Longitudinal Investigation of Overall Justice Perceptions," *Journal of Applied Psychology* 94, no. 5 (2009), pp. 1185–1199.

84. K. Leung, K. Tong, and S. S. Ho, "Effects of Interactional Justice on Egocentric Bias in Resource Allocation Decisions," *Journal of Applied Psychology* 89, no. 3 (2004), pp. 405–415; and L. Francis-Gladney, N. R. Manger, and R. B. Welker, "Does Outcome Favorability Affect Procedural Fairness as a Result of Self-Serving Attributions," *Journal of Applied Social Psychology* 40, no. 1 (2010), pp. 182–194.

85. "Americans Feel They Pay Fair Share of Taxes, Says Poll," NaturalNews.com, May 2, 2005, www.naturalnews.com/007297.html.

86. See, for example, R. Cropanzano, J. H. Stein, and T. Nadisic, *Social Justice and the Experience of Emotion* (New York: Routledge/Taylor and Francis Group, 2011).

87. D. P. Skarlicki and D. E. Rupp, "Dual Processing and Organizational Justice: The Role of Rational Versus Experiential Processing in Third-Party Reactions to Workplace Mistreatment," *Journal of Applied Psychology* 95, no. 5 (2010), pp. 944–952.

88. G. S. Leventhal, "What Should Be Done with Equity Theory? New Approaches to the Study of Fairness in Social Relationships," in K. Gergen, M. Greenberg, and R. Willis (eds.), *Social Exchange: Advances in Theory and Research* (New York: Plenum, 1980), pp. 27–55.

89. J. C. Shaw, E. Wild, and J. A. Colquitt, "To Justify or Excuse? A Meta-Analytic Review of the Effects of Explanations," *Journal of Applied Psychology* 88, no. 3 (2003), pp. 444–458.

90. D. P. Skarlicki and R. Folger, "Retaliation in the Workplace: The Roles of Distributive, Procedural, and Interactional Justice," *Journal of Applied Psychology* 82, no. 3 (1997), pp. 434–443; and D. A. Jones, "Getting Even with One's Supervisor and One's Organization: Relationships Among Types of Injustice, Desires for Revenge, and Counterproductive Work Behavior," *Journal of Organizational Behavior* 30, no. 4 (2009), pp. 525–542.

91. R. Cropanzano, C. A. Prehar, and P. Y. Chen, "Using Social Exchange Theory to Distinguish Procedural from Interactional Justice," *Group & Organization Management* 27, no. 3 (2002), pp. 324–351; and S. G. Roch and L. R. Shanock, "Organizational Justice in an Exchange Framework: Clarifying Organizational Justice Dimensions," *Journal of Management* 32, no. 2 (2006), pp. 299–322.

92. Colquitt, Conlon, Wesson, Porter, and Ng, "Justice at the Millennium," pp. 425–445.

93. J. K. Giacobbe-Miller, D. J. Miller, and V. I. Victorov, "A Comparison of Russian and U.S. Pay Allocation Decisions, Distributive Justice Judgments, and Productivity Under Different Payment Conditions," *Personnel Psychology* 51, no. 1 (1998), pp. 137–163.

94. M. C. Bolino and W. H. Turnley, "Old Faces, New Places: Equity Theory in Cross-Cultural Contexts," *Journal of Organizational Behavior* 29, no. 1 (2008), pp. 29–50.

95. B. A. Scott, J. A. Colquitt, and E. L. Paddock, "An Actor-Focused Model of Justice Rule Adherence and Violation: The Role of Managerial Motives and Discretion," *Journal of Applied Psychology* 94, no. 3 (2009), pp. 756–769.

96. L. J. Barlcay and D. P. Skarlicki, "Healing the Wounds of Organizational Injustice: Examining the Benefits of Expressive Writing," *Journal of Applied Psychology* 94, no. 2 (2009), pp. 511–523.

97. R. Fischer and P. B. Smith, "Reward Allocation and Culture: A Meta-Analysis," *Journal of Cross-Cultural Psychology* 34, no. 3 (2003), pp. 251–268.

98. F. F. T. Chiang and T. Birtch, "The Transferability of Management Practices: Examining Cross-National Differences in Reward Preferences," *Human Relations* 60, no. 9 (2007), pp. 1293–1330; A. E. Lind, T. R. Tyler, and Y. J. Huo, "Procedural Context and Culture: Variation in the Antecedents of Procedural Justice Judgments," *Journal of Personality and Social Psychology* 73, no. 4 (1997), pp. 767–780; M. J. Gelfand, M. Erez, and Z. Aycan, "Cross-Cultural Organizational Behavior," *Annual Review of Psychology* 58, (2007), pp. 479–514.

99. V. H. Vroom, *Work and Motivation* (New York: Wiley, 1964).

100. For criticism, see H. G. Heneman III and D. P. Schwab, "Evaluation of Research on Expectancy Theory Prediction of Employee Performance," *Psychological Bulletin* 78, no. 1 (1972), pp. 1–9; T. R. Mitchell, "Expectancy Models of Job Satisfaction, Occupational Preference and Effort: A Theoretical, Methodological and Empirical Appraisal," *Psychological Bulletin* 81, no. 12 (1974), pp. 1053–1077; and W. Van Eerde and H. Thierry, "Vroom's Expectancy Models and Work-Related Criteria: A Meta-Analysis," *Journal of Applied Psychology* 81, no. 5 (1996), pp. 575–586. For support, see L. W. Porter and E. E. Lawler III, *Managerial Attitudes and Performance* (Homewood, IL: Irwin, 1968); and J. J. Donovan, "Work Motivation," in N. Anderson et al. (eds.), *Handbook of Industrial, Work & Organizational Psychology*, vol. 2 (Thousand Oaks, CA: Sage, 2001), pp. 56–59.

101. Vroom refers to these three variables as expectancy, instrumentality, and valence, respectively.

102. J. Nocera, "The Anguish of Being an Analyst," *The New York Times* (March 4, 2006), pp. B1, B12.

103. R. J. House, H. J. Shapiro, and M. A. Wahba, "Expectancy Theory as a Predictor of Work Behavior and Attitudes: A Re-evaluation of Empirical Evidence," *Decision Sciences* 5, no. 3 (1974), pp. 481–506.

104. For other examples of models that seek to integrate motivation theories, see H. J. Klein, "An Integrated Control Theory Model of Work Motivation," *Academy of Management Review* 14, no. 2 (1989), pp. 150–172; E. A. Locke, "The Motivation Sequence, the Motivation Hub, and the Motivation Core," *Organizational Behavior and Human Decision Processes* 50, no. 2 (1991), pp. 288–299; and T. R. Mitchell, "Matching Motivational Strategies with Organizational Contexts," pp. 60–62.

105. This section is based on F. J. Landy and W. S. Becker, "Motivation Theory Reconsidered," in L. L. Cummings and B. M. Staw (eds.), *Research in Organizational Behavior,* vol. 9 (Greenwich, CT: JAI Press, 1987), pp. 24–35.

MOTIVATION MINUS THE MOOLAH

When Nancy Jackson hired a new full-time salesperson for a company she co-owns, Architectural Systems, she was caught off guard by protests from her 19 employees. "I couldn't believe their reactions," she says. The employees had seen their work hours reduced or their pay trimmed. Why was she hiring someone new amid the retrenchments? "There's been a lot of emotional hand-holding here that we've never had to do before," Jackson says.

Christopher Mills, co-owner of Prime Debt Services, a debt management firm in Dallas, has found it helpful to meet with employees one-on-one more often. "I found the more I listened, the better they pepped up," he says. Mills even has taken to cooking them a breakfast of waffles, bacon, and coffee every Wednesday.

Beyond expressing support and appreciation for their efforts, some employers are being more creative in their approaches to motivation. Elise Lelong, owner of a New York consulting firm, decided to upgrade her employees' job titles. "It doesn't cost anything and it makes them feel good," Lelong says. "You've got to think outside the money box when it comes to motivating your employees in this economic environment." Lelong took other steps too, including giving her employees increased chances to work remotely and with flexible hours. Atlassian, an Australian software company, motivated its employees by allowing them to devote 20 percent of their time to any software idea they liked.

When pay raises aren't possible, sometimes even smaller monetary awards can make a difference. Though Intuit human resource manager Jennifer Lepird spent several weeks working long hours on a big one-time project, she still pulled several "all nighters" toward the end. When the project was finished, what was her reward? The acquisitions team leader sent her a gift certificate worth several hundred dollars. Jennifer was thrilled. "The fact that somebody took the time to recognize the effort," she said, "made the long hours just melt away."

Eric Mosley, founder and CEO of Boston-based Globoforce, is a big fan of this approach. "Even higher earners can appreciate a small award if it is unexpected," he said. "Even billionaires appreciate a Christmas sweater from their mom."

Sources: S. E. Needleman, "Business Owners Try to Motivate Employees," *The Wall Street Journal* (January 14, 2010), p. B5; P. D. Broughton, "More Than a Paycheck," *The Wall Street Journal* (February 2, 2010), p. A17; and T. Demos, "Motivate Without Spending Millions," *Fortune* (April 12, 2010), pp. 37–38.

Motivation: From Concepts to Applications

Money is better than poverty,
if only for financial reasons.

—Woody Allen

Employee of the Month
Certificate of Excellence

is hereby granted to
Richard Lopez

Though pay is one central means of motivation we consider in this chapter—what we call extrinsic motivation—it's not the only one. The other is intrinsic. The following self-assessment will provide some information about how intrinsically motivating *your* job might be.

In Chapter 7, we focused on motivation theories. In this chapter, we start applying motivation concepts to practices such as employee involvement and skill-based pay. Why? Because it's one thing to know specific theories; it's quite another to see how, as a manager, you can use them.

SELF-ASSESSMENT LIBRARY

What's My Job'S Motivating Potential?

In the Self-Assessment Library (available on CD or online), take assessment I.C.9 (What's My Job's Motivating Potential?) and answer the following questions. If you currently do not have a job, answer the questions for your most recent job.

1. How did you score relative to your classmates?
2. Did your score surprise you? Why or why not?
3. How might your results affect your career path?

Motivating by Job Design: The Job Characteristics Model

1 Describe the job characteristics model and evaluate the way it motivates by changing the work environment.

Increasingly, research on motivation focuses on approaches that link motivational concepts to changes in the way work is structured.

Research in **job design** suggests the way the elements in a job are organized can increase or decrease effort and also suggests what those elements are. We'll first review the job characteristics model and then discuss some ways jobs can be redesigned. Finally, we'll explore alternative work arrangements.

The Job Characteristics Model

Developed by J. Richard Hackman and Greg Oldham, the **job characteristics model (JCM)** says we can describe any job in terms of five core job dimensions:[1]

1. **Skill variety** is the degree to which a job requires a variety of different activities so the worker can use a number of different skills and talent. The work of a garage owner-operator who does electrical repairs, rebuilds engines, does bodywork, and interacts with customers scores high on skill variety. The job of a bodyshop worker who sprays paint 8 hours a day scores low on this dimension.
2. **Task identity** is the degree to which a job requires completion of a whole and identifiable piece of work. A cabinetmaker who designs a piece of furniture, selects the wood, builds the object, and finishes it to perfection has a job that scores high on task identity. A job scoring low on this dimension is operating a factory lathe solely to make table legs.
3. **Task significance** is the degree to which a job affects the lives or work of other people. The job of a nurse handling the diverse needs of patients in a hospital intensive care unit scores high on task significance; sweeping floors in a hospital scores low.
4. **Autonomy** is the degree to which a job provides the worker freedom, independence, and discretion in scheduling work and determining the procedures in carrying it out. A salesperson who schedules his or her own

work each day and decides on the most effective sales approach for each customer without supervision has a highly autonomous job. A salesperson who is given a set of leads each day and is required to follow a standardized sales script with each potential customer has a job low on autonomy.

5. **Feedback** is the degree to which carrying out work activities generates direct and clear information about your own performance. A job with high feedback is assembling iPads and testing them to see whether they operate properly. A factory worker who assembles iPads but then routes them to a quality-control inspector for testing and adjustments receives low feedback from his or her activities.

Exhibit 8-1 presents the job characteristics model (JCM). Note how the first three dimensions—skill variety, task identity, and task significance—combine to create meaningful work the incumbent will view as important, valuable, and worthwhile. Note, too, that jobs with high autonomy give incumbents a feeling of personal responsibility for the results and that, if a job provides feedback, employees will know how effectively they are performing. From a motivational standpoint, the JCM proposes that individuals obtain internal rewards when they learn (knowledge of results) that they personally (experienced responsibility)

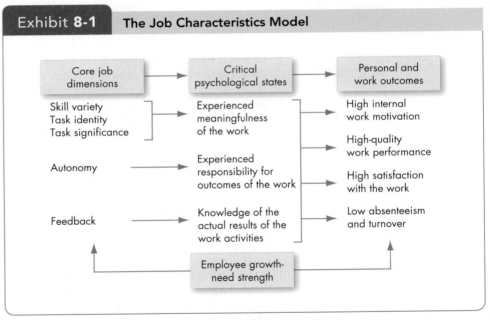

Exhibit 8-1   The Job Characteristics Model

Source: Adaptation of Job Characteristics Model, pp. 78–80 from J. Richard Hackman & Greg R. Oldham, *Work Redesign*, 1st Edition, © 1980. Adapted by permission of Pearson Education, Inc., Upper Saddle River, NJ.

job design   *The way the elements in a job are organized.*

job characteristics model (JCM)   *A model that proposes that any job can be described in terms of five core job dimensions: skill variety, task identity, task significance, autonomy, and feedback.*

skill variety   *The degree to which a job requires a variety of different activities.*

task identity   *The degree to which a job requires completion of a whole and identifiable piece of work.*

task significance   *The degree to which a job has a substantial impact on the lives or work of other people.*

autonomy   *The degree to which a job provides substantial freedom and discretion to the individual in scheduling the work and in determining the procedures to be used in carrying it out.*

feedback   *The degree to which carrying out the work activities required by a job results in the individual obtaining direct and clear information about the effectiveness of his or her performance.*

have performed well on a task they care about (experienced meaningfulness).[2] The more these three psychological states are present, the greater will be employees' motivation, performance, and satisfaction, and the lower their absenteeism and likelihood of leaving. As Exhibit 8-1 also shows, individuals with a high growth need are more likely to experience the critical psychological states when their jobs are enriched—and respond to them more positively—than are their counterparts with low growth need.

We can combine the core dimensions into a single predictive index, called the **motivating potential score (MPS)**, and calculated as follows:

$$\text{MPS} = \frac{\text{Skill variety} + \text{Task identity} + \text{Task significance}}{3} \times \text{Autonomy} \times \text{Feedback}$$

To be high on motivating potential, jobs must be high on at least one of the three factors that lead to experienced meaningfulness and high on both autonomy and feedback. If jobs score high on motivating potential, the model predicts motivation, performance, and satisfaction will improve and absence and turnover will be reduced.

Much evidence supports the JCM concept that the presence of a set of job characteristics—variety, identity, significance, autonomy, and feedback—does generate higher and more satisfying job performance.[3] But apparently we can better calculate motivating potential by simply adding the characteristics rather than using the formula.[4] Think about your job. Do you have the opportunity to work on different tasks, or is your day pretty routine? Are you able to work independently, or do you constantly have a supervisor or co-worker looking over your shoulder? What do you think your answers to these questions say about your job's motivating potential? Revisit your answers to the self-assessment at the beginning of this chapter, and then calculate your MPS from the job characteristics model. You might try computing your MPS score two ways: using the traditional MPS formula, or simply adding the dimensions. Then compare.

A few studies have tested the job characteristics model in different cultures, but the results aren't very consistent. One study suggested that when employees are "other oriented" (concerned with the welfare of others at work), the relationship between intrinsic job characteristics and job satisfaction was weaker. The fact that the job characteristics model is relatively individualistic (considering the relationship between the employee and his or her work) suggests job enrichment strategies may not have the same effects in collectivistic cultures as in individualistic cultures (such as the United States).[5] However, another study suggested the degree to which jobs had intrinsic job characteristics predicted job satisfaction and job involvement equally well for U.S., Japanese, and Hungarian employees.[6]

How Can Jobs Be Redesigned?

2 Compare and contrast the main ways jobs can be redesigned.

"Every day was the same thing," Frank Greer said. "Stand on that assembly line. Wait for an instrument panel to be moved into place. Unlock the mechanism and drop the panel into the Jeep Liberty as it moved by on the line. Then I plugged in the harnessing wires. I repeated that for eight hours a day. I don't care that they were paying me twenty-four dollars an hour. I was going crazy. I did it for almost a year and a half. Finally, I just said to my wife that this isn't going to be the way I'm going to spend the rest of my life. My brain was turning to JELL-O on that Jeep assembly line. So I quit. Now I work in a print shop and I make less than fifteen dollars an hour. But let me tell you, the work I do is really interesting. The job changes all the time, I'm continually learning new things, and the work really challenges me! I look forward every morning to going to work again."

"CEO Pay Can't Be Measured"

Anything can be measured. The question is whether it can be measured *well*. As for CEO pay, it seems it can't be measured well, or at least in a way experts agree upon. There is nearly as much disagreement among compensation experts about how to measure CEO pay as about whether CEOs are paid too much.

You may have read that the Dodd-Frank Act of 2010 included "say on pay" rules, whereby shareholders have a vote on executive compensation. But what pay? There is often a big difference between expected pay (bonus targets and value of options at the time granted) and realized pay (bonuses actually received and realized value of options).

Eli Lilly announced the pay of its CEO John Lechleiter as $15.9 million, up 10 percent from the year before. However, independent experts calculated his pay as $20.9 million, a 45 percent increase over the prior year. Occidental Petroleum CEO Ray Irani's expected pay was $58.3 million. His realized pay was $222.6 million.

Says one expert, even if the pay for two CEOs is reported to be the same,

"you can pretty much bet they are not the same."

Why is it so difficult to get an accurate read on CEO pay? A big part of the answer is that, for some time, a CEO's pay has been tied to the company's financial performance, and an organization's finances are quite complex. CEO pay might be based on any number of important financial indicators: stock appreciation, profitability, market share, earnings per share, and equity per share. Many CEOs are granted stocks at a current price, providing an incentive to make the stock price grow. The main principal at play here is to align the CEO's interests with the company's interests, so the CEO's motivation is in line with the company's best interests.

Another complicating factor is time: the value of CEO incentives often depends on measures, like stock price, that are time-sensitive. The worth of a stock option thus depends on when that option is exercised. Timing is everything. When Apple granted CEO Steve Jobs 7.5 million stock options, someone falsified records so the stock was priced low, as if at an earlier time

than when the options were actually granted. This "backdating" allowed Jobs to sell his options at a greater profit when he cashed them in.

Because this type of compensation is complicated, so are the motivational dynamics involved. CEOs have an incentive to "manage to the metric"—such as by making decisions that maximize short-term stock price (and thus increase the value of stock options) at the expense of the long-term interests of the company. Not all CEOs do this, of course, but the incentive is often there.

As one expert concluded, "Assessing CEO compensation is a bit of a black art."

Sources: S. Thurm, "For CEO Pay, A Single Number Never Tells the Whole Story," *The Wall Street Journal* (March 6, 2010), p. A2; B. McClure, "A Guide To CEO Compensation," *San Francisco Chronicle* (May 2, 2011), downloaded May 25, 2011, from www.investopedia.com/; and R. Gopalan, T. Milbourn, F. Song, and A. V. Thakor, "The Optimal Duration of Executive Compensation: Theory and Evidence," Working paper, April 15, 2011, Washington University in St. Louis, http://apps.olin.wustl.edu/faculty/milbourn/duration_ver_apr15.pdf.

The repetitive tasks in Frank Greer's job at the Jeep plant provided little variety, autonomy, or motivation. In contrast, his job in the print shop is challenging and stimulating. Let's look at some of the ways to put JCM into practice to make jobs more motivating.

Job Rotation If employees suffer from overroutinization of their work, one alternative is **job rotation**, or the periodic shifting of an employee from one task to another with similar skill requirements at the same organizational level (also called *cross-training*). At Singapore Airlines, a ticket agent may take on the duties of a baggage handler. Extensive job rotation is among the reasons Singapore Airlines is rated one of the best airlines in the world and a highly desirable place to work. Many manufacturing firms have adopted job rotation as a means

motivating potential score (MPS) *A predictive index that suggests the motivating potential in a job.*

job rotation *The periodic shifting of an employee from one task to another.*

of increasing flexibility and avoiding layoffs.[7] Managers at Apex Precision Technologies, a custom-machine shop in Indiana, train workers on all the company's equipment so they can move around as needed in response to incoming orders. Although job rotation has often been conceptualized as an activity for assembly line and manufacturing employees, many organizations use job rotation for new managers to help them get a picture of the whole business as well.[8]

The strengths of job rotation are that it reduces boredom, increases motivation, and helps employees better understand how their work contributes to the organization. An indirect benefit is that employees with a wider range of skills give management more flexibility in scheduling work, adapting to changes, and filling vacancies.[9] International evidence from Italy, Britain, and Turkey does show that job rotation is associated with higher levels of organizational performance in manufacturing settings.[10] However, job rotation has drawbacks. Training costs increase, and moving a worker into a new position reduces productivity just when efficiency at the prior job is creating organizational economies. Job rotation also creates disruptions when members of the work group have to adjust to the new employee. And supervisors may also have to spend more time answering questions and monitoring the work of recently rotated employees.

Job Enrichment   Job enrichment expands jobs by increasing the degree to which the worker controls the planning, execution, and evaluation of the work. An enriched job organizes tasks to allow the worker to do a complete activity, increases the employee's freedom and independence, increases responsibility, and provides feedback so individuals can assess and correct their own performance.[11]

How does management enrich an employee's job? Exhibit 8-2 offers suggested guidelines based on the job characteristics model. *Combining tasks* puts fractionalized tasks back together to form a new and larger module of work. *Forming natural work units* makes an employee's tasks create an identifiable and meaningful whole. *Establishing client relationships* increases the direct relationships between workers and their clients (clients can be internal as well as outside the organization). *Expanding jobs vertically* gives employees responsibilities and control formerly reserved for management. *Opening feedback channels* lets employees know how well they are doing and whether their performance is improving, deteriorating, or remaining constant.

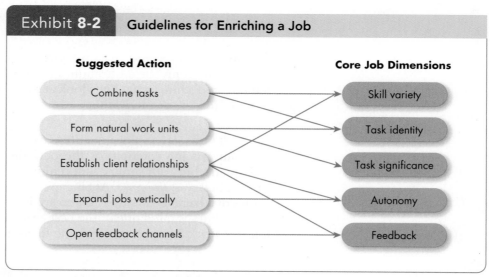

Exhibit 8-2   Guidelines for Enriching a Job

Suggested Action	Core Job Dimensions
Combine tasks	Skill variety
Form natural work units	Task identity
Establish client relationships	Task significance
Expand jobs vertically	Autonomy
Open feedback channels	Feedback

Source: "Guidelines for Enriching a Job" Source: J. R. Hackman and J. L. Suttle (eds.), *Improving Life at Work* (Glenview, IL: Scott Foresman, 1977), p. 138. Reprinted by permission of Richard Hackman and J. Lloyd Suttle.

Some newer versions of job enrichment concentrate specifically on improving the meaningfulness of work. One method is to relate employee experiences to customer outcomes, by providing employees with stories from customers who benefited from the company's products or services. The medical device manufacturer Medtronic invites people to describe how Medtronic products have improved, or even saved, their lives and shares these stories with employees during annual meetings, providing a powerful reminder of the impact of their work. Researchers recently found that when university fund-raisers briefly interacted with the undergraduates who would receive the scholarship money they raised, they persisted 42 percent longer, and raised nearly twice as much money, as those who didn't interact with potential recipients.[12]

Another method for improving the meaningfulness of work is providing employees with mutual assistance programs.[13] Employees who can help each other directly through their work come to see themselves, and the organizations for which they work, in more positive, pro-social terms. This, in turn, can increase employee affective commitment.

Many organizations provide job enrichment through cross-training to learn new skills, and through job rotation to perform new tasks in another position. Employees typically work with managers to set job enrichment goals, identify desired competencies, and find appropriate placement. For example, an employee who usually works in handling client records might receive cross-training to learn about the organization's purchasing and accounting systems. Then an accounting employee might learn about client data processes. These two employees could then rotate through one another's jobs, allowing them to cover for one another and prepare for possible future promotions.

The evidence on job enrichment shows it reduces absenteeism and turnover costs and increases satisfaction, but not all programs are equally effective.[14] A review of 83 organizational interventions designed to improve performance management showed that frequent, specific feedback related to solving problems was linked to consistently higher performance, but infrequent feedback that focused more on past problems than future solutions was much less effective.[15] Some recent evidence suggests job enrichment works best when it compensates for poor feedback and reward systems.[16] Work design may also not affect everyone in the same way. One recent study showed employees with a higher preference for challenging work experienced larger reductions in stress following job redesign than individuals who did not prefer challenging work.[17]

Alternative Work Arrangements

3 Identify three alternative work arrangements and show how they might motivate employees.

Another approach to motivation is to alter work arrangements with flextime, job sharing, or telecommuting. These are likely to be especially important for a diverse workforce of dual-earner couples, single parents, and employees caring for a sick or aging relative.

Flextime   Susan Ross is the classic "morning person." She rises at 5:00 A.M. sharp each day, full of energy. However, as she puts it, "I'm usually ready for bed right after the 7:00 P.M. news."

job enrichment   *The vertical expansion of jobs, which increases the degree to which the worker controls the planning, execution, and evaluation of the work.*

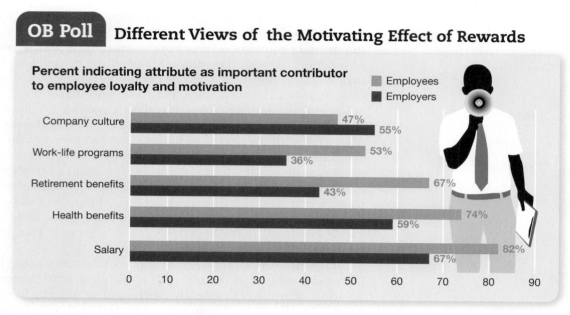

OB Poll Different Views of the Motivating Effect of Rewards

Sources: Survey of 1,503 employers and 1,305 full-time employees. MetLife, www.metlife.com; and "Loyalty Drivers," *Workforce Management* (October 2010), p. 18.

Susan's work schedule as a claims processor at The Hartford Financial Services Group is flexible. Her office opens at 6:00 A.M. and closes at 7:00 P.M. It's up to her how she schedules her 8-hour day within this 13-hour period. Because Susan is a morning person and also has a 7-year-old son who gets out of school at 3:00 P.M. every day, she opts to work from 6:00 A.M. to 3:00 P.M. "My work hours are perfect. I'm at the job when I'm mentally most alert, and I can be home to take care of my son after he gets out of school."

Susan's schedule is an example of **flextime**, short for "flexible work time." Employees must work a specific number of hours per week but are free to vary their hours of work within certain limits. As in Exhibit 8-3, each day consists of a common core, usually 6 hours, with a flexibility band surrounding it. The core may be 9:00 A.M. to 3:00 P.M., with the office actually opening at 6:00 A.M. and closing at 6:00 P.M. All employees are required to be at their jobs during the common core period, but they may accumulate their other 2 hours before, after, or before *and* after that. Some flextime programs allow employees to accumulate extra hours and turn them into a free day off each month.

Flextime has become extremely popular; according to the Bureau of Labor Statistics, nearly 26 percent of working women with children have flexible work schedules, compared to just 14 percent in 1991.[18] And this is not just a U.S. phenomenon. In Germany, for instance, 29 percent of businesses offer flextime, and such practices are becoming more widespread in Japan as well.[19]

Claimed benefits include reduced absenteeism, increased productivity, reduced overtime expenses, reduced hostility toward management, reduced traffic congestion around work sites, elimination of tardiness, and increased autonomy and responsibility for employees—any of which may increase employee job satisfaction.[20] But what's flextime's actual record?

Most of the evidence stacks up favorably. Flextime tends to reduce absenteeism and frequently improves worker productivity,[21] probably for several reasons. Employees can schedule their work hours to align with personal

Exhibit **8-3**	**Possible Flextime Staff Schedules**

Schedule 1

Percent Time:	100% = 40 hours per week
Core Hours:	9:00 A.M.–5:00 P.M., Monday through Friday (1 hour lunch)
Work Start Time:	Between 8:00 A.M. and 9:00 A.M.
Work End Time:	Between 5:00 P.M. and 6:00 P.M.

Schedule 2

Percent Time:	100% = 40 hours per week
Work Hours:	8:00 A.M.–6:30 P.M., Monday through Thursday (1/2 hour lunch)
	Friday off
Work Start Time:	8:00 A.M.
Work End Time:	6:30 P.M.

Schedule 3

Percent Time:	90% = 36 hours per week
Work Hours:	8:30 A.M.–5:00 P.M., Monday through Thursday (1/2 hour lunch)
	8:00 A.M.–Noon Friday (no lunch)
Work Start Time:	8:30 A.M. (Monday–Thursday); 8:00 A.M. (Friday)
Work End Time:	5:00 P.M. (Monday–Thursday); Noon (Friday)

Schedule 4

Percent Time:	80% = 32 hours per week
	8:00 A.M.–6:00 P.M., Monday through Wednesday (1/2 hour lunch)
Work Hours:	8:00 A.M.–11:30 A.M. Thursday (no lunch)
	Friday off
Work Start Time:	Between 8:00 A.M. and 9:00 A.M.
Work End Time:	Between 5:00 P.M. and 6:00 P.M.

demands, reducing tardiness and absences, and they can work when they are most productive. Flextime can also help employees balance work and family lives; it is a popular criterion for judging how "family friendly" a workplace is.

Flextime's major drawback is that it's not applicable to every job or every worker. It works well with clerical tasks for which an employee's interaction with people outside his or her department is limited. It is not a viable option for receptionists, sales personnel in retail stores, or people whose service jobs require them to be at their workstations at predetermined times. It also appears that people who have a stronger desire to separate their work and family lives are less prone to take advantage of opportunities for flextime.[22] Overall, employers need to consider the appropriateness of both the work and the workers before implementing flextime schedules.

Job Sharing   Job sharing allows two or more individuals to split a traditional 40-hour-a-week job. One might perform the job from 8:00 A.M. to noon and the other from 1:00 P.M. to 5:00 P.M., or the two could work full but alternate

flextime   *Flexible work hours.*

job sharing   *An arrangement that allows two or more individuals to split a traditional 40-hour-a-week job.*

Accounting firm Ernst & Young has created a supportive culture of flexibility that allows employees to control where, when, and how their work gets accomplished. The company encourages employees to utilize flexible work hours to meet their personal and professional goals while still providing the highest quality of service to customers. Employees value their flexible work options that include shorter workweeks, working from home, and varying start and finish times of their work days. Giving employees freedom in scheduling their work helps Ernst & Young attract and retain a satisfied, motivated, and loyal work force. In this photo, Ernst & Young employees work on the process of tabulating ballots for the Golden Globe Awards.

Source: AP Photo/Reed Saxon

days. For example, top Ford engineers Julie Levine and Julie Rocco engage in a job-sharing program that allows both of them to spend time with their families while working on the time-intensive job of redesigning the Explorer crossover. Typically, one of the pair will work late afternoons and evenings while the other works mornings. They both agree that the program has worked well, although making such a relationship work requires a great deal of time and preparation.[23]

Approximately 19 percent of large organizations now offer job sharing.[24] Reasons it is not more widely adopted are likely the difficulty of finding compatible partners to share a job and the historically negative perceptions of individuals not completely committed to their job and employer.

Job sharing allows an organization to draw on the talents of more than one individual in a given job. A bank manager who oversees two job sharers describes it as an opportunity to get two heads but "pay for one."[25] It also opens the opportunity to acquire skilled workers—for instance, women with young children and retirees—who might not be available on a full-time basis.[26] Many Japanese firms are increasingly considering job sharing—but for a very different reason.[27] Because Japanese executives are extremely reluctant to fire people, job sharing is seen as a potentially humanitarian means of avoiding layoffs due to overstaffing.

From the employee's perspective, job sharing increases flexibility and can increase motivation and satisfaction when a 40-hour-a-week job is just not practical. But the major drawback is finding compatible pairs of employees who can successfully coordinate the intricacies of one job.[28]

Telecommuting   It might be close to the ideal job for many people. No commuting, flexible hours, freedom to dress as you please, and few or no interruptions from colleagues. It's called **telecommuting**, and it refers to working at home at least 2 days a week on a computer linked to the employer's office.[29] (A closely related term—the *virtual office*—describes working from home on a relatively permanent basis.)

The U.S. Department of the Census estimated there had been a 25 percent increase in self-employed home-based workers from 1999 to 2005, and a 20 percent increase in employed workers who work exclusively from home.[30] One recent survey of more than 5,000 HR professionals found that 35 percent of organizations allowed employees to telecommute at least part of the time, and 21 percent allowed employees to telecommute full-time.[31] Well-known organizations that actively encourage telecommuting include AT&T, IBM, American Express, Sun Microsystems, and a number of U.S. government agencies.[32]

What kinds of jobs lend themselves to telecommuting? There are three categories: routine information-handling tasks, mobile activities, and professional and other knowledge-related tasks.[33] Writers, attorneys, analysts, and employees who spend the majority of their time on computers or the telephone—such as telemarketers, customer-service representatives, reservation agents, and product-support specialists—are natural candidates. As telecommuters, they can access information on their computers at home as easily as in the company's office.

The potential pluses of telecommuting include a larger labor pool from which to select, higher productivity, less turnover, improved morale, and reduced office-space costs. A positive relationship exists between telecommuting and supervisor performance ratings, but any relationship between telecommuting and potentially lower turnover intentions has not been substantiated in research to date.[34] The major downside for management is less direct supervision of employees. In today's team-focused workplace, telecommuting may make it more difficult to coordinate teamwork and can reduce knowledge transfer in organizations.[35] From the employee's standpoint, telecommuting can offer a considerable increase in flexibility and job satisfaction—but not without costs.[36] For employees with a high social need, telecommuting can increase feelings of isolation and reduce job satisfaction. And all telecommuters are vulnerable to the "out of sight, out of mind" effect.[37] Employees who aren't at their desks, who miss meetings, and who don't share in day-to-day informal workplace interactions may be at a disadvantage when it comes to raises and promotions.

The Social and Physical Context of Work

Robin and Chris both graduated from college a couple years ago with degrees in elementary education and became first-grade teachers in different school districts. Robin immediately confronted a number of obstacles: several long-term employees were hostile to her hiring, there was tension between administrators and teachers, and students had little interest in learning. Chris had a colleague who was excited to work with a new graduate, students who were excited about academics, and a highly supportive principal. Not surprisingly, at the end of the first year, Chris had been a considerably more effective teacher than Robin.

The job characteristics model shows most employees are more motivated and satisfied when their intrinsic work tasks are engaging. However, having the most interesting workplace characteristics in the world may not always lead to satisfaction if you feel isolated from your co-workers, and having good social relationships can make even the most boring and onerous tasks more fulfilling.

telecommuting   *Working from home at least two days a week on a computer that is linked to the employer's office.*

FedEx provides two services: the physical transportation and distribution of packages and the information systems that identify and track the location of packages at any time. Jobs involved in physically transporting packages, such as the employee shown here serving a customer at a FedEx office, are not suitable candidates for telecommuting. But in operating one of the world's largest computer and telecommunications networks for recording and tracking shipments, FedEx provides many computer-based jobs for telecommuters who help the firm process more than 20 million transactions daily.

Source: Russell Gordon / DanitaDelimont.com "Danita Delimont Photography" / Newscom

Research demonstrates that social aspects and work context are as important as other job design features.[38] Policies such as job rotation, worker empowerment, and employee participation have positive effects on productivity, at least partially because they encourage more communication and a positive social environment.

Some social characteristics that improve job performance include interdependence, social support, and interactions with other people outside work. Social interactions are strongly related to positive moods and give employees more opportunities to clarify their work role and how well they are performing. Social support gives employees greater opportunities to obtain assistance with their work. Constructive social relationships can bring about a positive feedback loop as employees assist one another in a "virtuous circle."

The work context is also likely to affect employee satisfaction. Hot, loud, and dangerous work is less satisfying than work conducted in climate-controlled, relatively quiet, and safe environments. This is probably why most people would rather work in a coffee shop than a metalworking foundry. Physical demands make people physically uncomfortable, which is likely to show up in lower levels of job satisfaction.

To assess why an employee is not performing to his or her best level, see whether the work environment is supportive. Does the employee have adequate tools, equipment, materials, and supplies? Does the employee have favorable working conditions, helpful co-workers, supportive work rules and procedures, sufficient information to make job-related decisions, and adequate time to do a good job? If not, performance will suffer.

Employee Involvement

Employee involvement is a participative process that uses employees' input to increase their commitment to the organization's success. The logic is that if we engage workers in decisions that affect them and increase their autonomy and control over their work lives, they will become more motivated, more committed to the organization, more productive, and more satisfied with their jobs.[39]

Employee involvement programs differ among countries.[40] A study of four countries, including the United States and India, confirmed the importance of modifying practices to reflect national culture.[41] While U.S. employees readily accepted employee involvement programs, managers in India who tried to empower their employees were rated low by those employees. These reactions are consistent with India's high power–distance culture, which accepts and expects differences in authority. Similarly, Chinese workers who were very accepting of traditional Chinese values showed few benefits from participative decision making, but workers who were less traditional were more satisfied and had higher performance ratings under participative management.[42]

Examples of Employee Involvement Programs

Let's look at two major forms of employee involvement—participative management and representative participation—in more detail.

Participative Management   Common to all **participative management** programs is joint decision making, in which subordinates share a significant degree of decision-making power with their immediate superiors. Participative management has, at times, been promoted as a panacea for poor morale and low productivity. But for it to work, employees must be engaged in issues relevant to their interests so they'll be motivated, they must have the competence and knowledge to make a useful contribution, and trust and confidence must exist among all parties.[43]

Studies of the participation–performance relationship have yielded mixed findings.[44] Organizations that institute participative management do have higher stock returns, lower turnover rates, and higher estimated labor productivity, although these effects are typically not large.[45] A careful review of research at the individual level shows participation typically has only a modest influence on employee productivity, motivation, and job satisfaction. Of course, this doesn't mean participative management can't be beneficial under the right conditions. However, it is not a sure means for improving performance.

Representative Participation   Almost every country in western Europe requires companies to practice **representative participation**, called "the most widely legislated form of employee involvement around the world."[46] Its goal is to redistribute power within an organization, putting labor on a more equal footing with the interests of management and stockholders by letting workers be represented by a small group of employees who actually participate.

The two most common forms are works councils and board representatives.[47] Works councils are groups of nominated or elected employees who must be consulted when management makes decisions about employees. Board representatives are employees who sit on a company's board of directors and represent employees' interests.

Empowerment is a corporate value at Wegmans Food Markets Inc., a regional supermarket chain that involves its employees in making decisions that affect their work and please their customers. This family-run company empowers employees, such as the chef shown here at a café within a Wegmans store, to make on-the-spot decisions without consulting their immediate supervisors. For example, if a customer wants a product that Wegmans doesn't stock, any employee can initiate the process of procuring the item for the customer. Wegmans believes that empowering employees leads to higher job satisfaction and productivity.

4   Give examples of employee involvement measures and show how they can motivate employees.

---

employee involvement   *A participative process that uses the input of employees and is intended to increase employee commitment to an organization's success.*

participative management   *A process in which subordinates share a significant degree of decision-making power with their immediate superiors.*

representative participation   *A system in which workers participate in organizational decision making through a small group of representative employees.*

The influence of representative participation on working employees seems to be minimal.[48] Works councils are dominated by management and have little impact on employees or the organization. While participation might increase the motivation and satisfaction of employee representatives, there is little evidence this trickles down to the employees they represent. Overall, "the greatest value of representative participation is symbolic. If one is interested in changing employee attitudes or in improving organizational performance, representative participation would be a poor choice."[49]

Linking Employee Involvement Programs and Motivation Theories

Employee involvement draws on a number of the motivation theories we discussed in Chapter 7. Theory Y is consistent with participative management and Theory X with the more traditional autocratic style of managing people. In terms of two-factor theory, employee involvement programs could provide intrinsic motivation by increasing opportunities for growth, responsibility, and involvement in the work itself. The opportunity to make and implement decisions—and then see them work out—can help satisfy an employee's needs for responsibility, achievement, recognition, growth, and enhanced self-esteem. And extensive employee involvement programs clearly have the potential to increase employee intrinsic motivation in work tasks.

Using Rewards to Motivate Employees

5 Demonstrate how the different types of variable-pay programs can increase employee motivation.

As we saw in Chapter 3, pay is not a primary factor driving job satisfaction. However, it does motivate people, and companies often underestimate its importance in keeping top talent. A 2006 study found that while 45 percent of employers thought pay was a key factor in losing top talent, 71 percent of top performers called it a top reason.[50]

Given that pay is so important, will the organization lead, match, or lag the market in pay? How will individual contributions be recognized? In this section, we consider (1) what to pay employees (decided by establishing a pay structure), (2) how to pay individual employees (decided through variable pay plans and skill-based pay plans), (3) what benefits and choices to offer (such as flexible benefits), and (4) how to construct employee recognition programs.

What to Pay: Establishing a Pay Structure

There are many ways to pay employees. The process of initially setting pay levels entails balancing *internal equity*—the worth of the job to the organization (usually established through a technical process called job evaluation)—and *external equity*—the external competitiveness of an organization's pay relative to pay elsewhere in its industry (usually established through pay surveys). Obviously, the best pay system pays what the job is worth (internal equity) while also paying competitively relative to the labor market.

Some organizations prefer to pay above the market, while some may lag the market because they can't afford to pay market rates, or they are willing to bear the costs of paying below market (namely, higher turnover as people are lured to better-paying jobs). Walmart, for example, pays less than its competitors and often outsources jobs overseas. Chinese workers in Shenzhen earn $120 a month (that's $1,440 per year) to make stereos for Walmart. Of the 6,000 factories that are worldwide suppliers to Walmart, 80 percent are located in China. In fact, one-eighth of all Chinese exports to the United States go to Walmart.[51]

Pay more, and you may get better-qualified, more highly motivated employees who will stay with the organization longer. A study covering 126 large organizations found employees who believed they were receiving a competitive pay level had higher morale and were more productive, and customers were more satisfied as well.[52] But pay is often the highest single operating cost for an organization, which means paying too much can make the organization's products or services too expensive. It's a strategic decision an organization must make, with clear trade-offs.

How to Pay: Rewarding Individual Employees Through Variable-Pay Programs

"Why should I put any extra effort into this job?" asked Anne Garcia, a fourth-grade elementary schoolteacher in Denver, Colorado. "I can excel or I can do the bare minimum. It makes no difference. I get paid the same. Why do anything above the minimum to get by?" Comments like Anne's have been voiced by schoolteachers for decades because pay increases were tied to seniority. Recently, however, a number of states have revamped their compensation systems to motivate people like Anne by tying teacher pay levels to results in the classroom in various ways, and other states are considering such programs.[53]

A number of organizations are moving away from paying solely on credentials or length of service. Piece-rate plans, merit-based pay, bonuses, profit sharing, gainsharing, and employee stock ownership plans are all forms of a **variable-pay program**, which bases a portion of an employee's pay on some individual and/or organizational measure of performance. Earnings therefore fluctuate up and down.[54]

First grade teacher Kim Hemmis at Will Rogers Elementary School in Houston, Texas, is eligible to receive a bonus when her students make progress on state and national achievement tests. The city's school board adopted a merit pay "Teacher Performance Plan" that rewards teachers who work hard and whose students show academic improvement. The plan motivates teachers by basing part of their pay on performance rather than only on seniority or degrees. The move toward rewarding teachers with bonuses for individual performance follows the widespread adoption of variable-pay plans in many businesses and government agencies.

Source: AP Photo/David J. Phillip

variable-pay program   *A pay plan that bases a portion of an employee's pay on some individual and/or organizational measure of performance.*

Variable-pay plans have long been used to compensate salespeople and executives. Some estimates suggest more than 70 percent of U.S. companies have some form of variable-pay plan, up from only about 5 percent in 1970.[55] Moreover, recent research shows that 26 percent of U.S. companies have either increased or plan to increase the proportion of variable pay in employee pay programs, and another 40 percent have already recently increased the proportion of variable pay.[56] Unfortunately, most employees still don't see a strong connection between pay and performance. Only 29 percent say their performance is rewarded when they do a good job.[57]

The fluctuation in variable pay is what makes these programs attractive to management. It turns part of an organization's fixed labor costs into a variable cost, thus reducing expenses when performance declines. When the U.S. economy encountered a recession in 2001 and 2008, companies with variable pay were able to reduce their labor costs much faster than others.[58] When pay is tied to performance, the employee's earnings also recognize contribution rather than being a form of entitlement. Over time, low performers' pay stagnates, while high performers enjoy pay increases commensurate with their contributions.

Let's examine the different types of variable-pay programs in more detail.

Piece-Rate Pay   The **piece-rate pay plan** has long been popular as a means of compensating production workers with a fixed sum for each unit of production completed. A pure piece-rate plan provides no base salary and pays the employee only for what he or she produces. Ballpark workers selling peanuts and soda are frequently paid this way. If they sell 40 bags of peanuts at $1 each, their take is $40. The harder they work and the more peanuts they sell, the more they earn. The limitation of these plans is that they're not feasible for many jobs. Surgeons earn significant salaries regardless of their patients' outcomes. Would it be better to pay them only if their patients fully recover? It seems unlikely that most would accept such a deal, and it might cause unanticipated consequences as well (such as surgeons avoiding patients with complicated or terminal conditions). So, although incentives are motivating and relevant for some jobs, it is unrealistic to think they can constitute the only piece of some employees' pay.

Merit-Based Pay   A **merit-based pay plan** pays for individual performance based on performance appraisal ratings. A main advantage is that people thought to be high performers can get bigger raises. If designed correctly, merit-based plans let individuals perceive a strong relationship between their performance and their rewards.[59]

Most large organizations have merit pay plans, especially for salaried employees. IBM increases employees' base salary based on annual performance evaluations. Since the 1990s, when the economy stumbled badly, an increasing number of Japanese companies have abandoned seniority-based pay in favor of merit-based pay. Koichi Yanashita of Takeda Chemical Industries, commented, "The merit-based salary system is an important means to achieve goals set by the company's top management, not just a way to change wages."[60]

To motivate and retain the best, more companies are increasing the differential between top and bottom performers. The consulting firm Hewitt Associates found that in 2006, employers gave their best performers roughly 10 percent raises, compared to 3.6 percent for average performers and 1.3 percent for below-average performers. These differences have increased over time. Martyn Fisher of Imperial Chemical in the United Kingdom said his company widened the merit pay gap between top and average performers because "as much as we would regret our average performers leaving, we regret more an above-target performer leaving."[61]

Despite their intuitive appeal, merit pay plans have several limitations. One is that they are typically based on an annual performance appraisal and thus are only as valid as the performance ratings. Another limitation is that the pay-raise pool fluctuates on economic or other conditions that have little to do with individual performance. One year, a colleague at a top university who performed very well in teaching and research was given a pay raise of $300. Why? Because the pay-raise pool was very small. Yet that is hardly pay-for-performance. Finally, unions typically resist merit pay plans. Relatively few teachers are covered by merit pay for this reason. Instead, seniority-based pay, where all employees get the same raises, predominates.

Bonuses   An annual **bonus** is a significant component of total compensation for many jobs. Among *Fortune* 100 CEOs, the bonus (mean of $1.01 million) generally exceeds the base salary (mean of $863,000). But bonus plans increasingly include lower-ranking employees; many companies now routinely reward production employees with bonuses in the thousands of dollars when profits improve. The incentive effects of performance bonuses should be higher than those of merit pay because, rather than paying for performance years ago (that was rolled into base pay), bonuses reward recent performance. When times are bad, firms can cut bonuses to reduce compensation costs. Steel company Nucor, for example, guarantees employees only about $10 per hour, but bonuses can be substantial. In 2006, the average Nucor worker made roughly $91,000. When the recession hit, bonuses were cut dramatically: in 2009, total pay had dropped 40 percent.[62]

This example also highlights the downside of bonuses: employees' pay is more vulnerable to cuts. This is problematic when bonuses are a large percentage of

Walmart is an organization that includes hourly workers in the company's bonus plan. In this photo, a Walmart manager distributes bonus checks to store employees. The bonus amount for employees depends on their full- or part-time status and on the amount of profit individual stores earn each year. Hourly workers also have the potential to receive additional quarterly bonuses based on their store's performance. Employees who go above and beyond in helping customers are also eligible for customer satisfaction bonuses. Bonuses give Walmart employees an incentive to increase sales and improve customer service.

Source: s70/ZUMA Press/Newscom

---

piece-rate pay plan   *A pay plan in which workers are paid a fixed sum for each unit of production completed.*

merit-based pay plan   *A pay plan based on performance appraisal ratings.*

bonus   *A pay plan that rewards employees for recent performance rather than historical performance.*

total pay or when employees take bonuses for granted. "People have begun to live as if bonuses were not bonuses at all but part of their expected annual income," said Jay Lorsch, a Harvard Business School professor. KeySpan Corp., a 9,700-employee utility company in New York, tried to combine yearly bonuses with a smaller merit-pay raise. Elaine Weinstein, KeySpan's senior vice president of HR, credits the plan with changing the culture from "entitlement to meritocracy."[63]

Skill-Based Pay   **Skill-based pay** (also called *competency-based* or *knowledge-based pay*) is an alternative to job-based pay that bases pay levels on how many skills employees have or how many jobs they can do.[64] For employers, the lure of skill-based pay plans is increased flexibility of the workforce: staffing is easier when employee skills are interchangeable. Skill-based pay also facilitates communication across the organization because people gain a better understanding of each other's jobs. One study found that across 214 different organizations, skill-based pay was related to higher levels of workforce flexibility, positive attitudes, membership behaviors, and productivity.[65] Another study found that over 5 years, a skill-based pay plan was associated with higher levels of individual skill change and skill maintenance.[66] These results suggest that skill-based pay plans are effective in achieving their stated goals.

What about the downsides? People can "top out"—that is, they can learn all the skills the program calls for them to learn. This can frustrate employees after they've been challenged by an environment of learning, growth, and continual pay raises. IDS Financial Services[67] found itself paying people more even though there was little immediate use for their new skills. IDS eventually dropped its skill-based pay plan for one that equally balances individual contribution and gains in work-team productivity. Finally, skill-based plans don't address level of performance but only whether someone can perform the skill. Perhaps reflecting these weaknesses, one study of 97 U.S. companies using skill-based pay plans found that 39 percent had switched to a more traditional market-based pay plan 7 years later.[68]

Profit-Sharing Plans   A **profit-sharing plan** distributes compensation based on some established formula designed around a company's profitability. Compensation can be direct cash outlays or, particularly for top managers, allocations of stock options. When you read about executives like Oracle's Larry Ellison earning $75.33 million in pay, it almost all (88.8 percent in Ellison's case) comes from cashing in stock options previously granted based on company profit performance. Not all profit-sharing plans are so grand in scale. Jacob Luke, age 13, started his own lawn-mowing business after getting a mower from his uncle. Jacob employs his brother, Isaiah, and friend, Marcel Monroe, and pays them each 25 percent of the profits he makes on each yard. Profit-sharing plans at the organizational level appear to have positive impacts on employee attitudes; employees report a greater feeling of psychological ownership.[69]

Gainsharing   **Gainsharing**[70] is a formula-based group incentive plan that uses improvements in group productivity from one period to another to determine the total amount of money allocated. Its popularity seems narrowly focused among large manufacturing companies, although some health care organizations have experimented with it as a cost-saving mechanism. Gainsharing differs from profit sharing in tying rewards to productivity gains rather than profits, so employees can receive incentive awards even when the organization isn't profitable. Because the benefits accrue to groups of workers, high performers pressure weaker ones to work harder, improving performance for the group as a whole.[71]

Employee Stock Ownership Plans   An **employee stock ownership plan (ESOP)** is a company-established benefit plan in which employees acquire stock, often at below-market prices, as part of their benefits. Companies as varied as Publix Supermarkets and W. L. Gore & Associates are now more than 50 percent employee-owned.[72] But most of the 10,000 or so ESOPs in the United States are in small, privately held companies.[73]

Research on ESOPs indicates they increase employee satisfaction and innovation.[74] But their impact on performance is less clear. ESOPs have the potential to increase employee job satisfaction and work motivation, but employees need to psychologically experience ownership.[75] That is, in addition to their financial stake in the company, they need to be kept regularly informed of the status of the business and have the opportunity to influence it in order to significantly improve the organization's performance.[76]

ESOP plans for top management can reduce unethical behavior. CEOs are more likely to manipulate firm earnings reports to make themselves look good in the short run when they don't have an ownership share, even though this manipulation will eventually lead to lower stock prices. However, when CEOs own a large amount of stock, they report earnings accurately because they don't want the negative consequences of declining stock prices.[77]

Evaluation of Variable Pay   Do variable-pay programs increase motivation and productivity? Studies generally support the idea that organizations with profit-sharing plans have higher levels of profitability than those without them.[78] Profit-sharing plans have also been linked to higher levels of employee affective commitment, especially in small organizations.[79] Similarly, gainsharing has been found to improve productivity in a majority of cases and often has a positive impact on employee attitudes.[80] Another study found that whereas piece-rate pay-for-performance plans stimulated higher levels of productivity, this positive affect was not observed for risk-averse employees. Thus, economist Ed Lazear seems generally right when he says, "Workers respond to prices just as economic theory predicts. Claims by sociologists and others that monetizing incentives may actually reduce output are unambiguously refuted by the data." But that doesn't mean everyone responds positively to variable-pay plans.[81]

You'd probably think individual pay systems such as merit pay or pay-for-performance work better in individualistic cultures such as the United States or that group-based rewards such as gainsharing or profit sharing work better in collectivistic cultures. Unfortunately, there isn't much research on the issue. One recent study did suggest that employee beliefs about the fairness of a group incentive plan were more predictive of pay satisfaction in the United States than in Hong Kong. One interpretation is that U.S. employees are more critical in appraising a group pay plan, and therefore, it's more critical that the plan be communicated clearly and administered fairly.[82]

Flexible Benefits: Developing a Benefits Package

6 Show how flexible benefits turn benefits into motivators.

Todd Evans is married and has three young children; his wife is at home full-time. His Citigroup colleague Allison Murphy is married too, but her husband has a high-paying job with the federal government, and they have no children.

---

skill-based pay   *A pay plan that sets pay levels on the basis of how many skills employees have or how many jobs they can do.*

profit-sharing plan   *An organization-wide program that distributes compensation based on some established formula designed around a company's profitability.*

gainsharing   *A formula-based group incentive plan.*

employee stock ownership plan (ESOP)   *A company-established benefits plan in which employees acquire stock, often at below-market prices, as part of their benefits.*

Identifying Conflicts of Interest

Managers often find themselves needing to take multiple perspectives at the same time, and sometimes they are motivated by rewards to take actions that are unethical. Financial auditors, actuaries, and accountants have a legal responsibility to accurately report on clients' records, but they might also be tempted to present an overly positive picture to please a client and secure commissions for future work. Leading up to the financial collapse of 2008, credit rating agencies gave AAA ratings to collateralized mortgage securities that were of dubious value, possibly because they were paid by the very companies they were supposed to regulate.

It's sometimes tough to recognize conflicts of interest when they occur. Max Bazerman from Harvard University and his colleagues have been exploring the psychological processes that lead to "motivated blindness"—a tendency to only see what you want to see. For example, a car salesperson motivated by a commission to sell as much as possible might subconsciously overlook evidence that a customer won't be able to afford payments. A pharmaceutical researcher might fudge data from clinical trials in hopes of securing a bonus for bringing a new drug to market. In cases like these, financial rewards may amplify conflicts of interest.

What helps minimize conflicts of interest? The most important step is to beware of motivated blindness and be honest about where conflicts exist. Be aware of biases that might creep into your perceptions when money is at stake. Another possibility is to provide explicit rewards for behaviors like producing critical reports or detecting problems with organizational systems, especially if the responsible party has a motivation to obtain a positive result.

Sources: S. Gunz and S. van der Laan, "Actuaries, Conflicts of Interest and Professional Independence: The Case of James Hardie Industries Limited," *Journal of Business Ethics* 98, no. 4 (2011), pp. 583–596; M. H. Bazerman and A. E. Tenbrunsel, "Ethical Breakdowns," *Harvard Business Review* (April 2011), pp. 58–65; and D. A. Moore, L. Tanlu, and M. H. Bazerman, "Conflict of Interest and the Intrusion of Bias," *Judgment and Decision Making* 5, no. 1 (2010), pp. 37–53.

Todd is concerned about having a good medical plan and enough life insurance to support his family in case it's needed. In contrast, Allison's husband already has her medical needs covered on his plan, and life insurance is a low priority. Allison is more interested in extra vacation time and long-term financial benefits such as a tax-deferred savings plan.

A standardized benefits package would be unlikely to meet the needs of Todd and Allison well. Citigroup could, however, cover both sets of needs with flexible benefits.

Consistent with expectancy theory's thesis that organizational rewards should be linked to each individual employee's goals, **flexible benefits** individualize rewards by allowing each employee to choose the compensation package that best satisfies his or her current needs and situation. These plans replace the "one-benefit-plan-fits-all" programs designed for a male with a wife and two children at home that dominated organizations for more than 50 years.[83] Fewer than 10 percent of employees now fit this image: about 25 percent are single, and one-third are part of two-income families with no children. Flexible benefits can accommodate differences in employee needs based on age, marital status, spouses' benefit status, and number and age of dependents.

The three most popular types of benefits plans are modular plans, core-plus options, and flexible spending accounts.[84] *Modular plans* are predesigned packages or modules of benefits, each of which meets the needs of a specific group of employees. A module designed for single employees with no dependents might include only essential benefits. Another, designed for single parents, might have additional life insurance, disability insurance, and expanded health coverage. *Core-plus plans* consist of a core of essential benefits and a menulike selection of others

Source: Owen Brewer / Sacramento Bee /Newscom

Employees of software developer Oracle Corporation, shown here in the company's cafeteria, receive a basic benefits package and may also choose coverage levels and additional benefits that meet their specific individual needs and the needs of their dependents. The OracleFlex plan gives employees flex credits they can use to purchase benefits so they can control the amount they spend for each benefit option. Employees with remaining credits may direct them to taxable income or to their 401(k) savings, health care reimbursement, or dependent care reimbursement accounts.

7   Identify the motivational benefits of intrinsic rewards.

from which employees can select. Typically, each employee is given "benefit credits," which allow the purchase of additional benefits that uniquely meet his or her needs. *Flexible spending plans* allow employees to set aside pretax dollars up to the dollar amount offered in the plan to pay for particular benefits, such as health care and dental premiums. Flexible spending accounts can increase take-home pay because employees don't pay taxes on the dollars they spend from these accounts.

Today, almost all major corporations in the United States offer flexible benefits. And they're becoming the norm in other countries, too. A recent survey of 211 Canadian organizations found that 60 percent offer flexible benefits, up from 41 percent in 2005.[85] And a similar survey of firms in the United Kingdom found that nearly all major organizations were offering flexible benefits programs, with options ranging from private supplemental medical insurance to holiday trading, discounted bus travel, and childcare vouchers.[86]

Intrinsic Rewards: Employee Recognition Programs

Laura Schendell makes only $8.50 per hour working at her fast-food job in Pensacola, Florida, and the job isn't very challenging or interesting. Yet Laura talks enthusiastically about the job, her boss, and the company that employs her. "What I like is the fact that Guy [her supervisor] appreciates the effort I make. He compliments me regularly in front of the other people on my shift, and I've been chosen Employee of the Month twice in the past six months. Did you see my picture on that plaque on the wall?"

Organizations are increasingly recognizing what Laura knows: important work rewards can be both intrinsic and extrinsic. Rewards are intrinsic in the form of employee recognition programs and extrinsic in the form of compensation systems. In this section, we deal with ways in which managers can reward and motivate employee performance.

Employee recognition programs range from a spontaneous and private thank-you to widely publicized formal programs in which specific types of behavior are encouraged and the procedures for attaining recognition are clearly identified. Some research suggests financial incentives may be more motivating in the short term, but in the long run it's nonfinancial incentives.[87]

A few years ago, 1,500 employees were surveyed in a variety of work settings to find out what they considered the most powerful workplace motivator. Their response? Recognition, recognition, and more recognition. As illustrated in Exhibit 8-4, Phoenix Inn, a West Coast chain of small hotels, encourages employees to smile by letting customers identify this desirable behavior and then recognizing winning employees with rewards and publicity.

An obvious advantage of recognition programs is that they are inexpensive, since praise is free![88] As companies and government organizations face tighter budgets, nonfinancial incentives become more attractive. Everett Clinic in Washington State uses a combination of local and centralized initiatives to encourage managers to recognize employees.[89] Employees and managers give "Hero Grams" and "Caught in the Act" cards to colleagues for exceptional accomplishments at work. Part of the incentive is simply to receive recognition, but there are also drawings for prizes based on the number of cards a person receives. Managers are trained to use the programs frequently and effectively to reward good performance. Multinational corporations like Symantec

flexible benefits   *A benefits plan that allows each employee to put together a benefits package individually tailored to his or her own needs and situation.*

Exhibit 8-4

PHOENIX INN SUITES

I GOT CAUGHT SMILING!

WHO WAS THE PHOENIX INN SUITES EMPLOYEE THAT MADE YOUR STAY <u>EXCEPTIONAL</u>?

EMPLOYEE NAME_____

GUEST NAME _____

ROOM # _____

DATE OF STAY _____

PLEASE EITHER LEAVE THIS IN YOUR ROOM OR DROP OFF AT THE FRONT DESK

---

glOBalization!

Motivated by Individual Goals or Relational Goals?

In previous chapters, we discussed differences between cultures in terms of the level of individualism or collectivism. Do these differences extend to motivation? Most research suggests they do, and differences between self-oriented and collectivistic cultures will affect behavior in meaningful ways.

Psychologists have consistently demonstrated differences in the ways personal or group-based achievements are valued. In cultures that emphasize collective orientation, people strive to achieve goals that benefit the whole group and find processes that isolate individual performance and achievement. People from these cultures admire "team players" and those who help and support one another. Cultures that emphasize individual orientation are marked by striving to achieve personal goals and a lack of attention to what benefits the group as a whole. People from these cultures are more likely to admire "star performers" and those who accomplish their ends independently.

These differences in individual or relational motivation might even affect the type of practices found in organizations and the ways that people behave. Some authors propose that human resource systems can influence whether individualistic or collectivistic motivation is stronger. Collective bargaining structures and group-based decision making are more prevalent in collectivistic countries, whereas more individualistic societies like the United States are noted for individual performance rating and individual rewards. Thus, management systems might well support or even enhance the individualistic or collectivistic nature of a culture.

Sources: C. K. W. De Dreu and A. Nauta, "Self-Interest and Other-Orientation in Organizational Behavior: Implications for Job Performance, Prosocial Behavior, and Personal Initiative," *Journal of Applied Psychology* 94, no. 4 (2009), pp. 913–926; J. S. Gore, S. E. Cross, and C. Kanagawa, "Acting in Our Interests: Relational Self-Construal and Goal Motivation Across Cultures," *Motivation and Emotion* 33, no. 1 (2009), pp. 75–87; and K. W. Mossholder, H. A. Richardson, and R. P. Settoon, "Human Resource Systems and Helping in Organizations: A Relational Perspective," *Academy of Management Review* 36, no. 1 (2011), pp. 33–52.

Corporation have also increased their use of recognition programs. Centralized programs across multiple offices in different countries can help ensure that all employees, regardless of where they work, can be recognized for their contribution to the work environment.[90] Another study found that recognition programs are common in both Canadian and Australian firms as well.[91]

Despite the increased popularity of employee recognition programs, critics argue they are highly susceptible to political manipulation by management. When applied to jobs for which performance factors are relatively objective, such as sales, recognition programs are likely to be perceived by employees as fair. However, in most jobs, the criteria for good performance aren't self-evident, which allows managers to manipulate the system and recognize their favorites. Abuse can undermine the value of recognition programs and demoralize employees.

MyManagementLab

Now that you have finished this chapter, go back to **www.pearsonglobaleditions.com/ mymanagementlab** to continue practicing and applying the concepts you've learned.

Summary and Implications for Managers

Although it's always dangerous to synthesize a large number of complex ideas, the following suggestions summarize what we know about motivating employees in organizations.

- **Recognize individual differences.** Managers should be sensitive to individual differences. For example, employees from Asian cultures prefer not to be singled out as special because it makes them uncomfortable. Spend the time necessary to understand what's important to each employee. This allows you to individualize goals, level of involvement, and rewards to align with individual needs. Design jobs to align with individual needs and maximize their motivation potential.
- **Use goals and feedback.** Employees should have firm, specific goals, and they should get feedback on how well they are faring in pursuit of those goals.
- **Allow employees to participate in decisions that affect them.** Employees can contribute to setting work goals, choosing their own benefits packages, and solving productivity and quality problems. Participation can increase employee productivity, commitment to work goals, motivation, and job satisfaction.
- **Link rewards to performance.** Rewards should be contingent on performance, and employees must perceive the link between the two. Regardless of how strong the relationship is, if individuals perceive it to be weak, the results will be low performance, a decrease in job satisfaction, and an increase in turnover and absenteeism.
- **Check the system for equity.** Employees should perceive that experience, skills, abilities, effort, and other obvious inputs explain differences in performance and hence in pay, job assignments, and other obvious rewards.

"If Money Doesn't Make You Happy, You Aren't Spending It Right"

POINT

As was noted in Chapter 3, some research suggests the relationship between pay and happiness isn't very strong. But pay can be a powerful motivator. It's simply that sometimes we're motivated to pursue things that have a limited ability to make us happy.

However, the story doesn't end there. New research suggests it's what we want to *do* with money that is most important. Specifically, spending money on experiences makes us happier than spending it on possessions. That is, vacations, entertainment, and sports make people happier. Extra money spent on material objects—clothes, jewelry, cars, furniture—did not make these people happier.

One study found that $30,000 spent on leisure over several seasons had as positive an effect on life satisfaction as did getting married.

One of the reasons spending on experiences is money well spent is that experiences build relationships, and evidence reliably shows that relationships make people happier. Other research shows that people tend to look back on experiences sentimentally (you tend to forget that dirty hotel room in Prague and instead remember fondly the Charles Bridge at night); they don't attach this same sentimentality when thinking about their possessions.

One researcher has even calibrated that, in terms of the happiness produced by spending money on something, experiences beat possessions three-to-one.

Thus, it's OK to be motivated by money. Just pay attention to how you spend what you earn.

COUNTERPOINT

Money doesn't do much to improve happiness after existence needs (food, clothing, and shelter) are met. Why worry about what aspects of spending money make us happy when money doesn't appear to matter much at all? Research should instead be directed toward understanding why such a powerful motivator is such a pitiful satisfier.

What should motivate us? We know social relationships are important to happiness and well-being. Keeping in touch with friends, spending meaningful time with family, building positive and supportive relationships at work—those are what really matter, and none of them have a thing to do with making money.

Activity also contributes to happiness—not only physical activity like exercise, but being proactive too. When people reflect back on their lives, they are much more likely to regret actions they never took, as opposed to the ones they did.

Money is not evil. We need it to acquire the basic elements of survival. But after those basic needs are met, we should realize our pursuit of money to make us happy is a fallacy. We can recall an inexpensive camping trip as fondly as a stay at a five-star hotel. Thus, we should take jobs that have interesting and meaningful work, not those that command the highest wages. In managing others, we should create a culture that motivates by building relationships, giving others autonomy and input, and pursing work people see as important and challenging.

Source: S. Rosenbloom, "But Will It Make You Happy?" *The New York Times* (August 8, 2010), pp. B1, B4; J. Axelrod, "Want to Be Happy? Don't Just Sit There," *CBS News* (March 3, 2011), downloaded May 10, 2011, from www.cbsnews.com/; and J. Quoidbach, E. W. Dunn, K. V. Petrides, and M. Mikolajczak, "Money Giveth, Money Taketh Away: The Dual Effect of Wealth on Happiness," *Psychological Science*, in press.

QUESTIONS FOR REVIEW

1 What is the job characteristics model? How does it motivate employees?

2 What are the three major ways that jobs can be redesigned? In your view, in what situations would one of the methods be favored over the others?

3 What are the three alternative work arrangements of flextime, job sharing, and telecommuting? What are the advantages and disadvantages of each?

4 What are employee involvement programs? How might they increase employee motivation?

5 What is variable pay? What are the variable-pay programs that are used to motivate employees? What are their advantages and disadvantages?

6 How can flexible benefits motivate employees?

7 What are the motivational benefits of intrinsic rewards?

EXPERIENTIAL EXERCISE Assessing Employee Motivation and Satisfaction Using the Job Characteristics Model

Purpose
This exercise will help you examine outcomes of the job characteristics model for different professions.

Time
Approximately 30 to 45 minutes.

Background
Data were collected on 6,930 employees in 56 different organizations in the United States, using the Job Diagnostic Survey. The following table contains data on the five core job dimensions of the job characteristics model for several professions. Also included are growth-needs strength, internal motivation, and pay satisfaction for each profession. The values are averages based on a 7-point scale.

Instructions
1. Break into groups of three to five.
2. Calculate the MPS score for each of the professions and compare them. Discuss whether you think these scores accurately reflect your perceptions of the motivating potential of these professions.
3. Graph the relationship between each profession's core job dimensions and its corresponding value for internal motivation and for pay satisfaction, using the core job dimensions as independent variables. What conclusions can you draw about motivation and satisfaction of employees in these professions?

Job Characteristics Averages for Six Professions

	Profession					
Variable	*Professional/ Technical*	*Managerial*	*Sales*	*Service*	*Clerical*	*Machine Trades*
Skill variety	5.4	5.6	4.8	5.0	4.0	5.1
Task identity	5.1	4.7	4.4	4.7	4.7	4.9
Task significance	5.6	5.8	5.5	5.7	5.3	5.6
Autonomy	5.4	5.4	4.8	5.0	4.5	4.9
Feedback	5.1	5.2	5.4	5.1	4.6	4.9
Growth-needs strength	5.6	5.3	5.7	5.4	5.0	4.8
Internal motivation	5.8	5.8	5.7	5.7	5.4	5.6
Pay satisfaction	4.4	4.6	4.2	4.1	4.0	4.2

Source: Adaptation of Job Characteristics Model, pp. 78–80 from J. Richard Hackman & Greg R. Oldham, *Work Redesign*, 1st Edition, © 1980. Adapted by permission of Pearson Education, Inc., Upper Saddle River, NJ.

ETHICAL DILEMMA Spitting Mad

How would you like to be spat at? The answer to that question is pretty obvious, but what may surprise you is that spit is an occupational hazard of New York City bus drivers. The outcomes of these incidents are even more interesting.

In a typical 1-year period, roughly 80 New York City bus drivers are spat upon by disgruntled passengers. These spitting incidents (no other injury was involved) generate an average of 64 days off work—the equivalent of 3 months' pay. In 2009, one spat-upon driver took 191 days of paid leave. The union representing the bus drivers said the leave was justified because being spat upon "is a physically and psychologically traumatic experience."

The causes of passenger spitting are varied, ranging from the MetroCard not working to perceived delays in schedules.

Driver Raul Morales was spat upon by a passenger irate over the fare. After the incident, Morales stopped at a nearby McDonald's, cleaned himself off, then finished his shift. "I just kept on going," he says.

As any watcher of the TV series *World's Toughest Jobs* knows, there is a lot of dangerous work out there, and bus drivers face their own hazards. Some bus drivers have been assaulted by passengers, including one New York City bus driver who was stabbed to death by a passenger in 2008.

Nancy Shevell, chair of the New York City transit authority, questions whether the time off is justified by the injury. "You have to wonder if you can go home and shower off, take a nap, take off the rest of the day and maybe the next day," she said. "When it gets strung out over months, you start to wonder."

Questions

1. Do you think bus drivers should be able to take time off in return for being spit at? If so, how long do you think they should have?

2. People react differently to stressful situations. One of the flight attendants on US Airways Flight 1549 that Captain Chesley "Sully" Sullenberger landed on the Hudson River has not been able to go back to work 3 years after the incident. Yet her two fellow flight attendants have. How do you judge ethical responsibilities and develop policy in situations where different people react differently?

3. What ethical responsibility does New York City's Transit Authority have toward its bus drivers?

Sources: M. M. Grynbaum, "When Angry Passengers Spit, Bus Drivers Take Months Off," *The New York Times* (May 25, 2010), pp. A1, A20; and V. Bishop and H. Hoel, "The Customer Is Always Right?" *Journal of Consumer Culture* 8, no. 3 (2008), pp. 341–367.

CASE INCIDENT 1 Multitasking: A Good Use of Your Time?

Multitasking—doing two or more things at once, or rapidly switching from one task to another—is a characteristic of the Millennial generation. One recent study revealed that during a typical week, 81 percent of young people report "media multitasking" at least some of the time.

Multitasking nicely illustrates our point that motivation is not just effort but also the way you direct your efforts. However, is the direction of efforts in multitasking efficient or inefficient?

Many people who multitask say it makes them more efficient: "Why not do two things at once if I can accomplish about as much as if I only did one thing?" they ask. Research, however, suggests multitasking is inefficient, that it actually takes longer to do two things at once than to do one thing first and then turn to the other. David Meyer, a University of Michigan psychologist who has studied multitasking, argues, "You wind up needing to use the same sorts of mental and physical resources for performing each of the tasks. You're having to switch back and forth between the two tasks as opposed to really doing them simultaneously."

Multitasking appears to result in adverse outcomes beyond inefficiency. Another study found multitaskers absorb material more superficially; they notice more things in their environment but are able to learn material less deeply. "It's not that they can't focus," says one researcher. "It's that they focus on everything. They hear everything—even things they would normally be able to block out—because they are now so used to attending to many things at once." Others note that multitasking can damage productivity and social relationships as individuals devote less concentrated time and attention to the tasks they are working on and conversations they are having. This scattered attention is especially damaging for tasks that require deep insight or creativity.

Questions

1. One expert who has studied multitasking calls it "a big illusion," arguing that multitaskers think they are more motivated and productive even when they aren't. Do you consider yourself a multitasker? If

so, does this case make you reconsider whether multitasking makes you more motivated or productive?

2. The effects of multitasking have been found to be more negative when the tasks are complex. Why do you think this is the case?

3. You might think multitasking makes you happy. While there is less research on this topic, some evidence suggests multitaskers feel more stress in their work. Multitaskers "feel a constant low-level panic." Do you agree? Why or why not?

4. One expert recommends we "recreate boundaries" by training ourselves, while doing something, not to look at other devices like cell phone or television for increasing periods of time. Do you think you could do that? For how long?

Sources: R. A. Clay, "Mini-Multitaskers," *Monitor on Psychology* 40, no. 2 (2009), pp. 38–40; D. Crenshaw, *The Myth of Multitasking: How "Doing It All" Gets Nothing Done* (San Francisco: Jossey Bass, 2008), and A. Tugend, "Multitasking Can Make You Lose . . . Um . . . Focus," *The New York Times* (October 25, 2008), p. B7.

CASE INCIDENT 2 Bonuses Can Backfire

It might seem obvious that people will be motivated by bonuses, but many scholars question this premise. Alfie Kohn has long suggested that workers are "punished by rewards" and urges that organizations avoid tying rewards to performance because of the negative consequences that can result. As an alternative to rewards, some experts recommend that managers foster a positive, upbeat work environment in hopes that enthusiasm will translate into motivation.

Although rewards *can* be motivating, they can reduce employees' intrinsic interest in the tasks they are doing. Along these lines, Mark Lepper of Stanford University found that children rewarded for drawing with felt-tip pens no longer wished to use the pens at all when rewards were removed, whereas children who were not rewarded for using the pens were eager to use them. Similar experiments in which children completed puzzles have also shown that increasing rewards can decrease interest in the rewarded task. Some have questioned the extent to which these results generalize to working adults, but concern about rewards diminishing intrinsic motivation persists.

Rewards can also lead to misbehavior by workers. Psychologist Edward Deci notes, "Once you start making people's rewards dependent on outcomes rather than behaviors, the evidence is people will take the shortest route to those outcomes." Consider factory workers paid purely based on the number of units they produce. Because only quantity is rewarded, workers may neglect quality. Executives rewarded strictly on the basis of quarterly stock price will tend to ignore the long-term profitability and survival of the firm; they might even engage in illegal or unethical behavior to increase their compensation. A review of research on pay-for-performance in medicine found that doctors who were rewarded for treatment outcomes were reluctant to take on the most serious cases, where success was less likely.

Although there might be some problems with providing incentives, the great majority of research cited in this and the previous chapter shows that individuals given rewards for behavior will be more likely to engage in the rewarded behaviors. It is also unlikely that individuals engaged in very boring, repetitive tasks will lose their intrinsic motivation if the task is rewarded, because they never had any intrinsic motivation to begin with. The real issue for managers is finding an appropriate way to reward behaviors so desired behavior is increased while less-desired behavior is reduced.

QUESTIONS

1. Do you think that, as a manager, you would use bonuses regularly? Why or why not?

2. Can you think of a time in your own life when being evaluated and rewarded on a specific goal lead you to engage in negative or unproductive behavior?

3. Do you think providing group bonuses instead of individual bonuses would be more effective or less effective? Why or why not?

4. How would you design a bonus/reward program to avoid the problems mentioned in this case?

Sources: Based on N. Fleming, "The Bonus Myth" *New Scientist* 210 (2011), pp. 40–43; D. Woodward, "Perking Up the Workplace," *Director* (February 2011), pp. 33–34; and G. G. Scott, "How to Create a Motivating Environment," *Nonprofit World* 28 (September/October 2010), p. 9.

ENDNOTES

1. J. R. Hackman and G. R. Oldham, "Motivation Through the Design of Work: Test of a Theory," *Organizational Behavior and Human Performance* 16, no. 2 (1976), pp. 250–279; and J. R. Hackman and G. R. Oldham, *Work Redesign* (Reading, MA: Addison-Wesley, 1980).

2. J. R. Hackman, "Work Design," in J. R. Hackman and J. L. Suttle (eds.), *Improving Life at Work* (Santa Monica, CA: Goodyear, 1977), p. 129.

3. See B. T. Loher, R. A. Noe, N. L. Moeller, and M. P. Fitzgerald, "A Meta-Analysis of the Relation of Job Characteristics to Job Satisfaction," *Journal of Applied Psychology* 70, no. 2 (1985), pp. 280–289; S. J. Zaccaro and E. F. Stone, "Incremental Validity of an Empirically Based Measure of Job Characteristics," *Journal of Applied Psychology* 73, no. 2 (1988), pp. 245–252; J. R. Rentsch and R. P. Steel, "Testing the Durability of Job Characteristics as Predictors of Absenteeism over a Six-Year Period," *Personnel Psychology* 51, no. 2 (1998), pp. 165–190; S. J. Behson, E. R. Eddy, and S. J. Lorenzet, "The Importance of the Critical Psychological States in the Job Characteristics Model: A Meta-Analytic and Structural Equations Modeling Examination," *Current Research in Social Psychology* 51, no. 12 (2000), pp. 170–189; and S. E. Humphrey, J. D. Nahrgang, and F. P. Morgeson, "Integrating Motivational, Social, and Contextual Work Design Features: A Meta-Analytic Summary and Theoretical Extension of the Work Design Literature," *Journal of Applied Psychology* 92, no. 5 (2007), pp. 1332–1356.

4. T. A. Judge, S. K. Parker, A. E. Colbert, D. Heller, and R. Ilies, "Job Satisfaction: A Cross-Cultural Review," in N. Anderson, D. S. Ones (eds.), *Handbook of Industrial, Work and Organizational Psychology,* vol. 2 (Thousand Oaks, CA: Sage Publications, 2002), pp. 25–52.

5. B. M. Meglino and A. M. Korsgaard, "The Role of Other Orientation in Reactions to Job Characteristics," *Journal of Management* 33, no. 1 (2007), pp. 57–83.

6. M. F. Peterson and S. A. Ruiz-Quintanilla, "Cultural Socialization as a Source of Intrinsic Work Motivation," *Group & Organization Management* 28, no. 2 (2003), pp. 188–216.

7. C. Ansberry, "In the New Workplace, Jobs Morph to Suit Rapid Pace of Change," *The Wall Street Journal* (March 22, 2002), p. A1.

8. T. Silver, "Rotate Your Way to Higher Value," *Baseline* (March/April 2010), p. 12; and J. J. Salopek, "Coca-Cola Division Refreshes Its Talent with Diversity Push on Campus," *Workforce Management Online* (March 2011), www.workforce.com.

9. J. Ortega, "Job Rotation as a Learning Mechanism," *Management Science* 47, no. 10 (2001), pp. 1361–1370.

10. A. Christini and D. Pozzoli, "Workplace Practices and Firm Performance in Manufacturing: A Comparative Study of Italy and Britain," *International Journal of Manpower* 31, no. 7 (2010), pp. 818–842; K. Kaymaz, "The Effects of Job Rotation Practices on Motivation: A Research on Managers in the Automotive Organizations," *Business and Economics Research Journal* 1, no. 3 (2010), pp. 69–86.

11. Hackman and Oldham, *Work Redesign.*

12. A. M. Grant, E. M. Campbell, G. Chen, K. Cottone, D. Lapedis, and K. Lee, "Impact and the Art of Motivation Maintenance: The Effects of Contact with Beneficiaries on Persistence Behavior," *Organizational Behavior and Human Decision Processes* 103, no. 1 (2007), pp. 53–67.

13. A. M. Grant, J. E. Dutton, and B. D. Rosso, "Giving Commitment: Employee Support Programs and the Prosocial Sensemaking Process," *Academy of Management Journal* 51, no. 5 (2008), pp. 898–918.

14. See, for example, R. W. Griffin, "Effects of Work Redesign on Employee Perceptions, Attitudes, and Behaviors: A Long-Term Investigation," *Academy of Management Journal* 34, no. 2 (1991), pp. 425–435; and M. Subramony, "A Meta-Analytic Investigation of the Relationship between HRM Bundles and Firm Performance," *Human Resource Management* 48, no. 5 (2009), pp. 745–768.

15. R. D. Pritchard, M. M. Harrell, D. DiazGrandos, and M. J. Guzman, "The Productivity Measurement and Enhancement System: A Meta-Analysis," *Journal of Applied Psychology* 93, no. 3 (2008), pp. 540–567.

16. F. P. Morgeson, M. D. Johnson, M. A. Campion, G. J. Medsker, and T. V. Mumford, "Understanding Reactions to Job Redesign: A Quasi-Experimental Investigation of the Moderating Effects of Organizational Contact on Perceptions of Performance Behavior," *Personnel Psychology* 59, no. 2 (2006), pp. 333–363.

17. F. W. Bond, P. E. Flaxman, and D. Bunce, "The Influence of Psychological Flexibility on Work Redesign: Mediated Moderation of a Work Reorganization Intervention," *Journal of Applied Psychology* 93, no. 3 (2008), pp. 645–654.

18. Cited in K. Palmer, "The New Mommy Track," *U.S. News and World Report* (September 3, 2007), pp. 40–45.

19. Cited in "Flextime Gains in Popularity in Germany," *Manpower Argus* (September 2000), p. 4; and Y. Yanadori and T. Kato, "Work and Family Practices in Japanese Firms: Their Scope, Nature, and Impact on Employee Turnover," *International Journal of Human Resource Management* 20, no. 2 (2009), pp. 439–456.

20. 20 S. Westcott, "Beyond Flextime: Trashing the Workweek," *Inc.* (August 2008), p. 30.

21. See, for example, D. A. Ralston and M. F. Flanagan, "The Effect of Flextime on Absenteeism and Turnover for Male and Female Employees," *Journal of Vocational Behavior* 26, no. 2 (1985), pp. 206–217; B. B. Baltes, T. E. Briggs, J. W. Huff, J. A. Wright, and G. A. Neuman, "Flexible and Compressed Workweek Schedules: A Meta-Analysis of Their Effects on Work-Related Criteria," *Journal of Applied Psychology* 84, no. 4 (1999), pp. 496–513; K. M. Shockley, and T. D. Allen, "When Flexibility Helps: Another Look at the Availability of Flexible Work Arrangements and Work–Family Conflict," *Journal of Vocational Behavior* 71, no. 3 (2007), pp. 479–493; J. G. Grzywacz, D. S. Carlson, and S. Shulkin, "Schedule Flexibility and Stress: Linking Formal Flexible Arrangements and Perceived Flexibility to Employee Health." *Community, Work, and Family* 11, no. 2 (2008), pp. 199–214; and L. A. McNall, A. D. Masuda, and J. M. Nicklin "Flexible Work Arrangements, Job Satisfaction, and Turnover Intentions: The Mediating Role of Work-to-Family Enrichment," *Journal of Psychology* 144, no. 1 (2010), pp. 61–81.

22. K. M. Shockley and T. D. Allen, "Investigating the Missing Link in Flexible Work Arrangement Utilization: An Individual Difference Perspective," *Journal of Vocational Behavior* 76, no. 1 (2010), pp. 131–142.

23. J. LaReau, "Ford's 2 Julies Share Devotion—and Job," *Automotive News* (October 25, 2010), p. 4.

24. Society for Human Resource Management, *2008 Employee Benefits* (Alexandria, VA: Author, 2008).

25. S. Shellenbarger, "Two People, One Job: It Can Really Work," *The Wall Street Journal* (December 7, 1994), p. B1.

26. "Job-Sharing: Widely Offered, Little Used," *Training* (November 1994), p. 12.

27. C. Dawson, "Japan: Work-Sharing Will Prolong the Pain," *BusinessWeek* (December 24, 2001), p. 46.

28. Shellenbarger, "Two People, One Job," p. B1.

29. See, for example, E. J. Hill, M. Ferris, and V. Martinson, "Does It Matter Where You Work? A Comparison of How Three Work Venues (Traditional Office, Virtual Office, and Home Office) Influence Aspects of Work and Personal/Family Life," *Journal of Vocational Behavior* 63, no. 2 (2003), pp. 220–241; B. Williamson, "Managing Virtual Workers," *Bloomberg Businessweek* (July 16, 2009), www.businessweek.com, and B. A. Lautsch and E. E. Kossek, "Managing a Blended Workforce: Telecommuters and Non-Telecommuters," *Organizational Dynamics* 40, no. 1 (2010), pp. 10–17.

30. J. Tozzi, "Home-Based Businesses Increasing," *Bloomberg Businessweek* (January 25, 2010), www.businessweek.com.

31. Society for Human Resource Management, *2008 Employee Benefits*.

32. See, for instance, M. Conlin, "The Easiest Commute of All," *BusinessWeek* (December 12, 2005), p. 78; S. Shellenbarger, "Telework Is on the Rise, but It Isn't Just Done from Home Anymore," *The Wall Street Journal* (January 23, 2001), p. B1; and E. O'Keefe, "Teleworking Grows But Still a Rarity," *The Washington Post* (February 22, 2011), p. B3.

33. Conlin, "The Easiest Commute of All."

34. E. E. Kossek, B. A. Lautsch, S. C. Eaton, "Telecommuting, Control, and Boundary Management: Correlates of Policy Use and Practice, Job Control, and Work-Family Effectiveness," *Journal of Vocational Behavior* 68, no. 2 (2006), pp. 347–367.

35. J. M. Stanton and J. L. Barnes-Farrell, "Effects of Electronic Performance Monitoring on Personal Control, Task Satisfaction, and Task Performance," *Journal of Applied Psychology* 81, no. 6 (1996), pp. 738–745; and L. Taskin and F. Bridoux, "Telework: A Challenge to Knowledge Transfer in Organizations," *International Journal of Human Resource Management* 21, no. 13 (2010), pp. 2503–2520.

36. See, for example, P. Brotherton, "For Teleworkers, Less Is Definitely More," *T+D* 65 (March 2011), p. 29; and M. Virick, N. DaSilva, and K. Arrington, "Moderators of the Curvilinear Relation Between Extent of Telecommuting and Job and Life Satisfaction: The Role of Performance Outcome Orientation and Worker Type," *Human Relations* 63, no. 1 (2010), pp. 137–154.

37. J. Welch and S. Welch, "The Importance of Being There," *BusinessWeek* (April 16, 2007), p. 92; Z. I. Barsness, K. A. Diekmann, and M. L. Seidel, "Motivation and Opportunity: The Role of Remote Work, Demographic Dissimilarity, and Social Network Centrality in Impression Management," *Academy of Management Journal* 48, no. 3 (2005), pp. 401–419.

38. F. P. Morgeson and S. E. Humphrey, "The Work Design Questionnaire (WDQ): Developing and Validating a Comprehensive Measure for Assessing Job Design and the Nature of Work," *Journal of Applied Psychology* 91, no. 6 (2006), pp. 1321–1339; S. E. Humphrey, J. D. Nahrgang, and F. P. Morgeson, "Integrating Motivational, Social, and Contextual Work Design Features: A Meta-Analytic Summary and Theoretical Extension of the Work Design Literature," *Journal of Applied Psychology* 92, no. 5 (2007), pp. 1332–1356; and R. Takeuchi, D. P. Lepak, H. Wang, and K. Takeuchi, "An Empirical Examination of the Mechanisms Mediating Between High-Performance Work Systems and the Performance of Japanese Organizations," *Journal of Applied Psychology* 92, no. 4 (2007), pp. 1069–1083.

39. See, for example, the increasing body of literature on empowerment, such as D. P. Ashmos, D. Duchon, R. R. McDaniel Jr., and J. W. Huonker, "What a Mess! Participation as a Simple Managerial Rule to 'Complexify' Organizations," *Journal of Management Studies* 39, no. 2 (2002), pp. 189–206; S. E. Seibert, S. R. Silver, and W. A. Randolph, "Taking Empowerment to the Next Level: A Multiple-Level Model of Empowerment, Performance, and Satisfaction," *Academy of Management Journal* 47, no. 3 (2004), pp. 332–349; M. M. Butts, R. J. Vandenberg, D. M. DeJoy, B. S. Schaffer, and M. G. Wilson, "Individual Reactions to High Involvement Work Processes: Investigating the Role of Empowerment and Perceived Organizational Support," *Journal of Occupational Health Psychology* 14, no. 2 (2009), pp. 122–136; R. Park, E. Applebaum, and D. Kruse, "Employee Involvement and Group Incentives in Manufacturing Companies: A Multi-Level Analysis," *Human Resource Management Journal* 20, no. 3 (2010), pp. 227–243; and D. C. Jones, P. Kalmi, and A. Kauhanen, "How Does Employee Involvement Stack Up? The Effects of Human Resource Management Policies in a Retail Firm," *Industrial Relations* 49, no. 1 (2010), pp. 1–21.

40. See, for instance, A. Sagie and Z. Aycan, "A Cross-Cultural Analysis of Participative Decision-Making in Organizations," *Human Relations* 56, no. 4 (2003), pp. 453–473; and J. Brockner, "Unpacking Country Effects: On the Need to Operationalize the Psychological Determinants of Cross-National Differences," in R. M. Kramer and B. M. Staw (eds.), *Research in Organizational Behavior*, vol. 25 (Oxford, UK: Elsevier, 2003), pp. 336–340.

41. C. Robert, T. M. Probst, J. J. Martocchio, R. Drasgow, and J. J. Lawler, "Empowerment and Continuous Improvement in the United States, Mexico, Poland, and India: Predicting Fit on the Basis of the Dimensions of Power Distance and Individualism," *Journal of Applied Psychology* 85, no. 5 (2000), pp. 643–658.

42. Z. X. Chen and S. Aryee, "Delegation and Employee Work Outcomes: An Examination of the Cultural Context of Mediating Processes in China," *Academy of Management Journal* 50, no. 1 (2007), pp. 226–238.

43. F. Heller, E. Pusic, G. Strauss, and B. Wilpert, *Organizational Participation: Myth and Reality* (Oxford, UK: Oxford University Press, 1998).

44. See, for instance, K. L. Miller and P. R. Monge, "Participation, Satisfaction, and Productivity: A Meta-Analytic Review," *Academy of Management Journal* (December 1986), pp. 727–753; J. A. Wagner III, "Participation's Effects on Performance and Satisfaction: A Reconsideration of Research Evidence," *Academy of Management Review* 19, no. 2 (1994), pp. 312–330; C. Doucouliagos, "Worker Participation and Productivity in

Labor-Managed and Participatory Capitalist Firms: A Meta-Analysis," *Industrial and Labor Relations Review* 49, no. 1 (1995), pp. 58–77; J. A. Wagner III, C. R. Leana, E. A. Locke, and D. M. Schweiger, "Cognitive and Motivational Frameworks in U.S. Research on Participation: A Meta-Analysis of Primary Effects," *Journal of Organizational Behavior* 18, no. 1 (1997), pp. 49–65; A. Pendleton and A. Robinson, "Employee Stock Ownership, Involvement, and Productivity: An Interaction-Based Approach," *Industrial and Labor Relations Review* 64, no. 1 (2010), pp. 3–29.

45. D. K. Datta, J. P. Guthrie, and P. M. Wright, "Human Resource Management and Labor Productivity: Does Industry Matter?" *Academy of Management Journal* 48, no. 1 (2005), pp. 135–145; C. M. Riordan, R. J. Vandenberg, and H. A. Richardson, "Employee Involvement Climate and Organizational Effectiveness." *Human Resource Management* 44, no. 4 (2005), pp. 471–488; and J. Kim, J. P. MacDuffie, and F. K. Pil, "Employee Voice and Organizational Performance: Team Versus Representative Influence," *Human Relations 63*, no. 3 (2010), pp. 371-394.

46. Cotton, *Employee Involvement*, p. 114.

47. See, for example, M. Gilman and P. Marginson, "Negotiating European Works Council: Contours of Constrained Choice," *Industrial Relations Journal 33*, no. 1 (2002), pp. 36–51; J. T. Addison and C. R. Belfield, "What Do We Know About the New European Works Council? Some Preliminary Evidence from Britain," *Scottish Journal of Political Economy* 49, no. 4 (2002), pp. 418–444; and B. Keller, "The European Company Statute: Employee Involvement—and Beyond," *Industrial Relations Journal* 33, no. 5 (2002), pp. 424–445.

48. Cotton, *Employee Involvement*, pp. 129–130, 139–140.

49. Ibid., p. 140.

50. E. White, "Opportunity Knocks, and It Pays a Lot Better," *The Wall Street Journal* (November 13, 2006), p. B3.

51. P. S. Goodman and P. P. Pan, "Chinese Workers Pay for Wal-Mart's Low Prices," *Washington Post* (February 8, 2004), p. A1.

52. M. Sabramony, N. Krause, J. Norton, and G. N. Burns "The Relationship Between Human Resource Investments and Organizational Performance: A Firm-Level Examination of Equilibrium Theory," *Journal of Applied Psychology* 93, no. 4 (2008), pp. 778–788.

53. See, for example, B. Martinez, "Teacher Bonuses Emerge in Newark," *The Wall Street Journal*, (April 21, 2011), p. A.15; and D. Weber, "Seminole Teachers to Get Bonuses Instead of Raises," *Orlando Sentinel* (January 19, 2011), www.orlandosentinel.com.

54. Based on J. R. Schuster and P. K. Zingheim, "The New Variable Pay: Key Design Issues," *Compensation & Benefits Review* (March–April 1993), p. 28; K. S. Abosch, "Variable Pay: Do We Have the Basics in Place?" *Compensation & Benefits Review* (July–August 1998), pp. 12–22; and K. M. Kuhn and M. D. Yockey, "Variable Pay as a Risky Choice: Determinants of the Relative Attractiveness of Incentive Plans," *Organizational Behavior and Human Decision Processes* 90, no. 2 (2003), pp. 323–341.

55. L. Wiener, "Paycheck Plus," *U.S. News & World Report* (February 24/March 3, 2003), p. 58.

56. Hay Group, "Hay Group Research Finds Increased Use of Variable Pay for Employees," *Investment Weekly News*, (July 24, 2010), p. 269.

57. Cited in "Pay Programs: Few Employees See the Pay-for-Performance Connection," *Compensation & Benefits Report*, (June 2003), p. 1.

58. B. Wysocki Jr., "Chilling Reality Awaits Even the Employed," *The Wall Street Journal* (November 5, 2001), p. A1; and J. C. Kovac, "Sour Economy Presents Compensation Challenges," *Employee Benefit News* (July 1, 2008), p. 18.

59. G. D. Jenkins Jr., N. Gupta, A. Mitra, and J. D. Shaw, "Are Financial Incentives Related to Performance? A Meta-Analytic Review of Empirical Research," *Journal of Applied Psychology* 83, no. 5 (1998), pp. 777–787; and S. L. Rynes, B. Gerhart, and L. Parks, "Personnel Psychology: Performance Evaluation and Pay for Performance," *Annual Review of Psychology* 56, no. 1 (2005), pp. 571–600.

60. E. Arita, "Teething Troubles Aside, Merit-Based Pay Catching On," *Japan Times* (April 23, 2004), search.japantimes.co.jp/cgi-bin/nb20040423a3.html.

61. E. White, "The Best vs. the Rest," *The Wall Street Journal* (January 30, 2006), pp. B1, B3.

62. N. Byrnes, "Pain, But No Layoffs at Nucor," *BusinessWeek* (March 26, 2009), www.businessweek.com.

63. E. White, "Employers Increasingly Favor Bonuses to Raises," *The Wall Street Journal* (August 28, 2006), p. B3; and J. S. Lublin, "Boards Tie CEO Pay More Tightly to Performance," *The Wall Street Journal* (February 21, 2006), pp. A1, A14.

64. G. E. Ledford Jr., "Paying for the Skills, Knowledge, and Competencies of Knowledge Workers," *Compensation & Benefits Review*, (July–August 1995), pp. 55–62; B. Murray and B. Gerhart, "An Empirical Analysis of a Skill-Based Pay Program and Plant Performance Outcomes," *Academy of Management Journal* 41, no. 1 (1998), pp. 68–78; J. R. Thompson and C. W. LeHew, "Skill-Based Pay as an Organizational Innovation," *Review of Public Personnel Administration* 20, no. 1 (2000), pp. 20–40; and J. D. Shaw, N. Gupta, A. Mitra, and G. E. Ledford, Jr., "Success and Survival of Skill-Based Pay Plans," *Journal of Management* 31, no. 1 (2005), pp. 28–49.

65. A. Mitra, N. Gupta, and J. D. Shaw, "A Comparative Examination of Traditional and Skill-Based Pay Plans," *Journal of Managerial Psychology* 26, no. 4 (2011), pp. 278–296.

66. E. C. Dierdorff and E. A. Surface, "If You Pay for Skills, Will They Learn? Skill Change and Maintenance under a Skill-Based Pay System," *Journal of Management* 34, no.4 (2008), pp. 721–743.

67. "Tensions of a New Pay Plan," *The New York Times* (May 17, 1992), p. F5.

68. F. Giancola, "Skill-based Pay—Issues for Consideration," *Benefits and Compensation Digest* 44, no. 5 (2007), pp. 1–15.

69. N. Chi and T. Han, "Exploring the Linkages Between Formal Ownership and Psychological Ownership for the Organization: The Mediating Role of Organizational Justice," *Journal of Occupational and Organizational Psychology* 81, no. 4 (2008), pp. 691–711.

70. See, for instance, D. O. Kim, "Determinants of the Survival of Gainsharing Programs," *Industrial & Labor Relations Review* 53, no. 1 (1999), pp. 21–42; "Why Gainsharing Works Even Better Today Than in the Past," *HR Focus* (April 2000), pp. 3–5; L. R. Gomez-Mejia, T. M. Welbourne, and R. M. Wiseman, "The Role of Risk Sharing and Risk Taking Under Gainsharing," *Academy of Management Review* 25, no. 3 (2000),

pp. 492–507; M. Reynolds, "A Cost-Reduction Strategy That May Be Back," *Healthcare Financial Management* (January 2002), pp. 58–64; and M. R. Dixon, L. J. Hayes, and J. Stack, "Changing Conceptions of Employee Compensation," *Journal of Organizational Behavior Management* 23, no. 2–3 (2003), pp. 95–116; I. M. Leitman, R. Levin, M. J. Lipp, L. Sivaprasad, C. J. Karalakulasingam, D. S. Bernard, P. Friedmann, and D. J. Shulkin, "Quality and Financial Outcomes from Gainsharing for Inpatient Admissions: A Three-Year Experience," *Journal of Hospital Medicine* 5, no. 9 (2010), pp. 501–517.

71. T. M. Welbourne and C. J. Ferrante, "To Monitor or Not to Monitor: A Study of Individual Outcomes from Monitoring One's Peers under Gainsharing and Merit Pay," *Group & Organization Management* 33, no. 2 (2008), pp. 139–162.

72. National Center for Employee Ownership, *The Employee Ownership 100* (July 2003), www.nceo.org.

73. Cited in K. Frieswick, "ESOPs: Split Personality," *CFO* (July 7, 2003), p. 1.

74. A. A. Buchko, "The Effects of Employee Ownership on Employee Attitudes: A Test of Three Theoretical Perspectives," *Work and Occupations* 19, no. 1 (1992), 59–78; and R. P. Garrett, "Does Employee Ownership Increase Innovation?" *New England Journal of Entrepreneurship* 13, no. 2, (2010), pp. 37–46.

75. D. McCarthy, E. Reeves, and T. Turner, "Can Employee Share-Ownership Improve Employee Attitudes and Behaviour?" *Employee Relations* 32, no. 4 (2010), pp. 382–395.

76. A. Pendleton and A. Robinson, "Employee Stock Ownership, Involvement, and Productivity: An Interaction-Based Approach," *Industrial and Labor Relations Review* 64, no. 1 (2010), pp. 3–29.

77. X. Zhang, K. M. Bartol, K. G. Smith, M. D. Pfarrer, and D. M. Khanin, "CEOs on the Edge: Earnings Manipulation and Stock-Based Incentive Misalignment," *Academy of Management Journal* 51, no. 2 (2008), pp. 241–258.

78. D. D'Art and T. Turner, "Profit Sharing, Firm Performance, and Union Influence in Selected European Countries," *Personnel Review* 33, no. 3 (2004), pp. 335–350; and D. Kruse, R. Freeman, and J. Blasi, *Shared Capitalism at Work: Employee Ownership, Profit and Gain Sharing, and Broad-Based Stock Options* (Chicago: University of Chicago Press, 2010).

79. A. Bayo-Moriones and M. Larraza-Kintana, "Profit-Sharing Plans and Affective Commitment: Does the Context Matter?" *Human Resource Management* 48, no. 2 (2009), pp. 207–226.

80. T. M. Welbourne and L. R. Gomez-Mejia, "Gainsharing: A Critical Review and a Future Research Agenda," *Journal of Management* 21, no. 3 (1995), pp. 559–609.

81. C. B. Cadsby, F. Song, and F. Tapon, "Sorting and Incentive Effects of Pay for Performance: An Experimental Investigation," *Academy of Management Journal* 50, no. 2 (2007), pp. 387–405.

82. S. C. L. Fong and M. A. Shaffer, "The Dimensionality and Determinants of Pay Satisfaction: A Cross-Cultural Investigation of a Group Incentive Plan," *International Journal of Human Resource Management* 14, no. 4 (2003), pp. 559–580.

83. See, for instance, M. W. Barringer and G. T. Milkovich, "A Theoretical Exploration of the Adoption and Design of Flexible Benefit Plans: A Case of Human Resource Innovation," *Academy of Management Review* 23, no. 2 (1998), pp. 305–324; D. Brown, "Everybody Loves Flex," *Canadian HRReporter* (November 18, 2002), p. 1; J. Taggart, "Putting Flex Benefits Through Their Paces," *Canadian HR Reporter* (December 2, 2002), p. G3; and N. D. Cole and D. H. Flint, "Perceptions of Distributive and Procedural Justice in Employee Benefits: Flexible Versus Traditional Benefit Plans," *Journal of Managerial Psychology* 19, no. 1 (2004), pp. 19–40.

84. D. A. DeCenzo and S. P. Robbins, *Fundamentals of Human Resource Management,* 10th ed. (New York: Wiley, 2009).

85. P. Stephens, "Flex Plans Gain in Popularity," *CA Magazine* (January/February 2010), p. 10.

86. D. Lovewell, "Flexible Benefits: Benefits on Offer," *Employee Benefits* (March 2010), p. S15.

87. S. E. Markham, K. D. Scott, and G. H. McKee, "Recognizing Good Attendance: A Longitudinal, Quasi-Experimental Field Study," *Personnel Psychology* 55, no. 3 (2002), p. 641; and S. J. Peterson and F. Luthans, "The Impact of Financial and Nonfinancial Incentives on Business Unit Outcomes over Time," *Journal of Applied Psychology* 91, no. 1 (2006), pp. 156–165.

88. A. D. Stajkovic and F. Luthans, "Differential Effects of Incentive Motivators on Work Performance," *Academy of Management Journal* 4, no. 3 (2001), p. 587. See also F. Luthans and A. D. Stajkovic, "Provide Recognition for Performance Improvement," in E. A. Locke (ed.), *Handbook of Principles of Organizational Behavior* (Malden, MA: Blackwell, 2004), pp. 166–180.

89. L. Shepherd, "Special Report on Rewards and Recognition: Getting Personal," *Workforce Management* (September 2010), pp. 24–29.

90. L. Shepherd, "On Recognition, Multinationals Think Globally," *Workforce Management* (September 2010), p. 26.

91. R. J. Long and J. L. Shields, "From Pay to Praise? Non-Case Employee Recognition in Canadian and Australian Firms," *International Journal of Human Resource Management* 21, no. 8 (2010), pp. 1145–1172.

LEARNING OBJECTIVES

After studying this chapter, you should be able to:

1 Define *group* and distinguish the different types of groups.

2 Identify the five stages of group development.

3 Show how role requirements change in different situations.

4 Demonstrate how norms and status exert influence on an individual's behavior.

5 Show how group size affects group performance.

6 Contrast the benefits and disadvantages of cohesive groups.

7 Understand the implications of diversity for group effectiveness.

8 Contrast the strengths and weaknesses of group decision making.

9 Compare the effectiveness of interacting, brainstorming, nominal, and electronic meeting groups.

MyManagementLab

Access a host of interactive learning aids at to help strengthen your understanding of the chapter concepts at **www.pearsonglobaleditions .com/mymanagementlab**.

TO THE CLICKERS GO THE SPOILS

"Ability to function well in groups" is often near the top of employer lists of desired skills in new hires. New evidence suggests that being popular or able to "click" with colleagues is more important than we have realized.

Take Heather Moseley. When Heather started her job as an accounting associate, her cubicle was right outside the office of one of her organization's top managers, Kelly McVickers. McVickers mostly kept to herself, but that didn't deter Heather. Over the next few months, Heather struck up a friendship with Kelly and found out they both admired Stevie Wonder.

"I do an accountant's job, which is really administrative," said Heather. "Because of my relationship with Kelly, I now get invited to events, meetings, and conferences that I'd have no business going to as an accountant." Even though she is above Heather in the organization, Kelly finds her friendship with Heather pays benefits, too. "Knowing Heather, I find out what's on people's minds," Kelly said. "As supervisor this is crucial information."

What Heather did was find a way to click with Kelly. Research has emerged that shows other "clickers" have experiences similar to Heather's: they advance further and more quickly in their careers. That is the nature of groups—some people seem to have a natural ability to do well in groups, and they benefit as a result.

One study of health care administrators had employees list co-workers in terms of how popular they thought their co-workers were. Popularity of each worker was measured by summing how often each person was mentioned. Interestingly, not only did popular employees receive more help from their co-workers, they were also subject to less uncivil behaviors at work.

What do you have to do to be a "clicker" and be popular with others in a group? To some degree, it's personality. Those who are agreeable, have high core self-evaluations, and are self-monitors just click more readily in groups. Geographically, clickers also tend to be centrally located. One study of dorm locations found that each dorm room down from the center of the hall decreased popularity by 50 percent.

If you can't change your personality or your office, you might be able to do something else. Harvard researchers found that when someone asks others questions requiring more intimate self-revelation, respondents later feel closer to the person who asked the question. So, without becoming too personal, try to deepen conversations with others. Move beyond, "What did you do this weekend?"

Foundations of Group Behavior

9

*Madness is the exception in individuals
but the rule in groups.*

—Friedrich Nietzsche

Photo: Stock photo. *Source:* Daniel laflor/istockphoto.com.

Being popular in groups and "clicking" with others seems to be as important at work as in school. The more things change, the more they stay the same.

Sources: O. Brafman and R. Brafman, "To the Vulnerable Go the Spoils," *Bloomberg Businessweek* (June 20, 2010), pp. 71–73; and B. A. Scott and T. A. Judge, "The Popularity Contest at Work: Who Wins, Why, and What Do They Receive?" *Journal of Applied Psychology* 94, no. 1 (2009), pp. 20–33.

Groups have their place—and their pitfalls. Before we discuss them, examine your own attitude toward working in groups. Take the following self-assessment and answer the accompanying questions.

The objectives of this chapter and Chapter 10 are to introduce you to basic group concepts, provide you with a foundation for understanding how groups work, and show you how to create effective teams. Let's begin by defining *group* and explaining why people join groups.

SELF-ASSESSMENT LIBRARY

Do I Have a Negative Attitude Toward Working in Groups?

In the Self-Assessment Library (available on CD or online), take assessment IV.E.1 (Do I Have a Negative Attitude Toward Working in Groups?) and answer the following questions.

1. Are you surprised by your results? If yes, why? If not, why not?
2. Do you think it is important to always have a positive attitude toward working in groups? Why or why not?

Defining and Classifying Groups

1 Define *group* and distinguish the different types of groups.

We define a **group** as two or more individuals, interacting and interdependent, who have come together to achieve particular objectives. Groups can be either formal or informal. By a **formal group**, we mean one defined by the organization's structure, with designated work assignments establishing tasks. In formal groups, the behaviors team members should engage in are stipulated by and directed toward organizational goals. The six members of an airline flight crew are a formal group. In contrast, an **informal group** is neither formally structured nor organizationally determined. Informal groups are natural formations in the work environment that appear in response to the need for social contact. Three employees from different departments who regularly have lunch or coffee together are an informal group. These types of interactions among individuals, though informal, deeply affect their behavior and performance.

Why Do People Form Groups?

Why do people form groups, and why do they feel so strongly about them? Consider the celebrations that follow a sports team's winning a national championship. Fans have staked their own self-image on the performance of someone else. The winner's supporters are elated, and sales of team-related shirts, jackets, and hats declaring support for the team skyrocket. Fans of the losing team feel dejected, even embarrassed. Our tendency to take personal pride or offense for the accomplishments of a group is the territory of **social identity theory**.

The employees of the Swedish transportation company Scania shown here exercising at a sports complex comprise an informal group. At different company locations, Scania offers employees free access to sports facilities during working hours. The company puts a high priority on employee health and offers employees many opportunities to reinforce an active lifestyle. The informal groups that participate in sports and exercise activities are neither formally structured nor organizationally determined. However, informal groups like these can fulfill employee desires for social interaction at work.

Source: Soren andersson/Afp/Getty/Newscom.

Social identity theory proposes that people have emotional reactions to the failure or success of their group because their self-esteem gets tied into the group's performance.[1] When your group does well, you bask in reflected glory, and your own self-esteem rises. When your group does poorly, you might feel bad about yourself, or you might even reject that part of your identity, like "fair weather fans." Social identities also help people reduce uncertainty about who they are and what they should do.[2]

People develop a lot of identities through the course of their lives. You might define yourself in terms of the organization you work for, the city you live in, your profession, your religious background, your ethnicity, or your gender. A U.S. expatriate working in Rome might be very aware of being from the United States but won't give this national identity a second thought when transferring from Tulsa to Tucson.[3]

Social identities help us understand who we are and where we fit in with other people, but they can have a negative side as well. **Ingroup favoritism** means we see members of our ingroup as better than other people, and people not in our group as all the same. This obviously paves the way for stereotyping.

When do people develop a social identity? Several characteristics make a social identity important to a person:

- **Similarity.** Not surprisingly, people who have the same values or characteristics as other members of their organization have higher levels of group identification.[4] Demographic similarity can also lead to stronger

group *Two or more individuals, interacting and interdependent, who have come together to achieve particular objectives.*

formal group *A designated work group defined by an organization's structure.*

informal group *A group that is neither formally structured nor organizationally determined; such a group appears in response to the need for social contact.*

social identity theory *Perspective that considers when and why individuals consider themselves members of groups.*

ingroup favoritism *Perspective in which we see members of our ingroup as better than other people, and people not in our group as all the same.*

Social identities help Bal Seal Engineering employees interact with co-workers. The company's Spanish-speaking employees gather at the home of a co-worker to participate in an English-as-a-second-language program. Bal Seal, which buys the training materials for the program, reports that it has improved the company's communications, cooperation among fellow workers, and customer service. As social identity theory proposes, program graduates identify with the high performance of a winning team. As a result, graduates who ruled out the option of going back to school are motivated to continue their education by enrolling in GED, community college, and citizenship classes.

Source: O44/Zuma Press/Newscom.

identification for new hires, while those who are demographically different may have a hard time identifying with the group as a whole.[5]

- **Distinctiveness.**   People are more likely to notice identities that show how they are different from other groups. Respondents in one study identified more strongly with those in their work group with whom they shared uncommon or rare demographic characteristics.[6] For example, veterinarians who work in veterinary medicine (where everyone is a veterinarian) identify with their organization, and veterinarians in nonveterinary medicine fields such as animal research or food inspection (where being a veterinarian is a more distinctive characteristic) identify with their profession.[7]

- **Status.**   Because people use identities to define themselves and increase self-esteem, it makes sense that they are most interested in linking themselves to high-status groups. Graduates of prestigious universities will go out of their way to emphasize their links to their alma maters and are also more likely to make donations.[8] People are likely to not identify with a low-status organization and will be more likely to quit in order to leave that identity behind.[9]

- **Uncertainty reduction.**   Membership in a group also helps some people understand who they are and how they fit into the world.[10] One study showed how the creation of a spin-off company created questions about how employees should develop a unique identity that corresponded more closely to what the division was becoming.[11] Managers worked to define and communicate an idealized identity for the new organization when it became clear employees were confused.

Stages of Group Development

2 Identify the five stages of group development.

Groups generally pass through a predictable sequence in their evolution. Although not all groups follow this five-stage model,[12] it is a useful framework for understanding group development. In this section, we describe the five-stage model and an alternative for temporary groups with deadlines.

The Five-Stage Model

As shown in Exhibit 9-1, the **five-stage group-development model** characterizes groups as proceeding through the distinct stages of forming, storming, norming, performing, and adjourning.[13]

The first stage, **forming stage**, is characterized by a great deal of uncertainty about the group's purpose, structure, and leadership. Members "test the waters" to determine what types of behaviors are acceptable. This stage is complete when members have begun to think of themselves as part of a group.

The **storming stage** is one of intragroup conflict. Members accept the existence of the group but resist the constraints it imposes on individuality. There is conflict over who will control the group. When this stage is complete, there will be a relatively clear hierarchy of leadership within the group.

In the third stage, close relationships develop and the group demonstrates cohesiveness. There is now a strong sense of group identity and camaraderie. This **norming stage** is complete when the group structure solidifies and the group has assimilated a common set of expectations of what defines correct member behavior.

The fourth stage is **performing**. The structure at this point is fully functional and accepted. Group energy has moved from getting to know and understand each other to performing the task at hand.

For permanent work groups, performing is the last stage in development. However, for temporary committees, teams, task forces, and similar groups that have a limited task to perform, the **adjourning stage** is for wrapping up activities and preparing to disband. Some group members are upbeat, basking in the group's accomplishments. Others may be depressed over the loss of camaraderie and friendships gained during the work group's life.

Many interpreters of the five-stage model have assumed a group becomes more effective as it progresses through the first four stages. Although this may be generally true, what makes a group effective is actually more complex.[14] First, groups proceed through the stages of group development at different rates. Those with a strong sense of purpose and strategy rapidly achieve high performance and improve over time, whereas those with less sense of purpose actually see their performance worsen over time. Similarly, groups that begin with a positive social focus appear to achieve the "performing" stage more

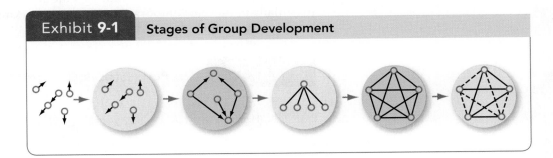

Exhibit 9-1   **Stages of Group Development**

rapidly. Nor do groups always proceed clearly from one stage to the next. Storming and performing can occur simultaneously, and groups can even regress to previous stages.

An Alternative Model for Temporary Groups with Deadlines

Temporary groups with deadlines don't seem to follow the usual five-stage model. Studies indicate they have their own unique sequencing of actions (or inaction): (1) their first meeting sets the group's direction, (2) this first phase of group activity is one of inertia, (3) a transition takes place exactly when the group has used up half its allotted time, (4) this transition initiates major changes, (5) a second phase of inertia follows the transition, and (6) the group's last meeting is characterized by markedly accelerated activity.[15] This pattern, called the **punctuated-equilibrium model**, is shown in Exhibit 9-2.

The first meeting sets the group's direction, and then a framework of behavioral patterns and assumptions through which the group will approach its project emerges, sometimes in the first few seconds of the group's existence. Once set, the group's direction is solidified and is unlikely to be reexamined throughout the first half of its life. This is a period of inertia—the group tends to stand still or become locked into a fixed course of action even if it gains new insights that challenge initial patterns and assumptions.

One of the most interesting discoveries[16] was that each group experienced its transition precisely halfway between its first meeting and its official deadline—whether members spent an hour on their project or 6 months. The midpoint appears to work like an alarm clock, heightening members' awareness that their time is limited and they need to get moving. This transition ends phase 1 and is characterized by a concentrated burst of changes, dropping of old patterns, and adoption of new perspectives. The transition sets a revised direction for phase 2, a new equilibrium or period of inertia in which the group executes plans created during the transition period.

The group's last meeting is characterized by a final burst of activity to finish its work. In summary, the punctuated-equilibrium model characterizes groups as exhibiting long periods of inertia interspersed with brief revolutionary changes triggered primarily by members' awareness of time and deadlines. Keep in mind, however, that this model doesn't apply to all groups. It's essentially limited to temporary task groups working under a time-constrained completion deadline.[17]

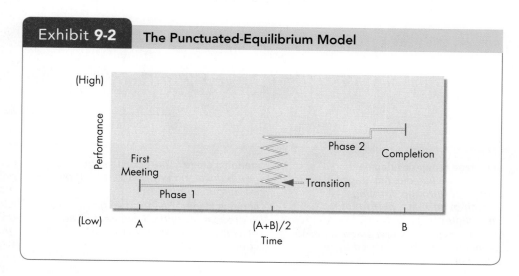

Exhibit **9-2**   The Punctuated-Equilibrium Model

3   Show how role requirements change in different situations.

Work groups are not unorganized mobs; they have properties that shape members' behavior and help explain and predict individual behavior within the group as well as the performance of the group itself. Some of these properties are roles, norms, status, size, cohesiveness, and diversity.

Group Property 1: Roles

Shakespeare said, "All the world's a stage, and all the men and women merely players." Using the same metaphor, all group members are actors, each playing a **role**. By this term, we mean a set of expected behavior patterns attributed to someone occupying a given position in a social unit. Our understanding of role behavior would be dramatically simplified if each of us could choose one role and play it regularly and consistently. Instead, we are required to play a number of diverse roles, both on and off our jobs. As we'll see, one of the tasks in understanding behavior is grasping the role a person is currently playing.

Bill Patterson is a plant manager with EMM Industries, a large electrical equipment manufacturer in Phoenix. He fulfills a number of roles—EMM employee, member of middle management, electrical engineer, and primary company spokesperson in the community. Off the job, Bill Patterson finds himself in still more roles: husband, father, Catholic, tennis player, member of the Thunderbird Country Club, and president of his homeowners' association. Many of these roles are compatible; some create conflicts. How does Bill's religious commitment influence his managerial decisions regarding layoffs, expense account padding, and provision of accurate information to government agencies? A recent offer of promotion requires Bill to relocate, yet his family wants to stay in Phoenix. Can the role demands of his job be reconciled with the demands of his husband and father roles?

Like Bill Patterson, we are all required to play a number of roles, and our behavior varies with each. So different groups impose different role requirements on individuals.

Role Perception   Our view of how we're supposed to act in a given situation is a **role perception**. We get role perceptions from stimuli all around us—for example, friends, books, films, television, as when we form an impression of the work of doctors from watching *Grey's Anatomy*. Of course, the primary reason apprenticeship programs exist in many trades and professions is to allow beginners to watch an expert so they can learn to act as they should.

---

punctuated-equilibrium model   *A set of phases that temporary groups go through that involves transitions between inertia and activity.*

role   *A set of expected behavior patterns attributed to someone occupying a given position in a social unit.*

role perception   *An individual's view of how he or she is supposed to act in a given situation.*

Green Bay Packers football player Donald Driver plays a variety of roles. As a wide receiver for the Packers, his principal role is to catch passes from the quarterback and then run the ball downfield. Driver is also a husband, father, author of a children's books series, the host of a statewide TV show in Wisconsin called Inside the Huddle, and a volunteer for Children's Hospital of Wisconsin and Goodwill Industries. Along with his wife, he created the Donald Driver Foundation that offers assistance to ill children with unmanageable hospital bills and provides housing for the homeless. Each of these positions imposes different role requirements on Driver. This photo shows him diving for a first down in his role as a wide receiver.

Source: David Maialetti/Mct/Newscom.

Role Expectations   **Role expectations** are the way others believe you should act in a given context. The role of a U.S. federal judge is viewed as having propriety and dignity, while a football coach is seen as aggressive, dynamic, and inspiring to his players.

In the workplace, we look at role expectations through the perspective of the **psychological contract**: an unwritten agreement that exists between employees and employer. This agreement sets out mutual expectations: what management expects from workers and vice versa.[18] Management is expected to treat employees justly, provide acceptable working conditions, clearly communicate what is a fair day's work, and give feedback on how well an employee is doing. Employees are expected to respond by demonstrating a good attitude, following directions, and showing loyalty to the organization.

What happens if management is derelict in keeping its part of the bargain? We can expect negative effects on employee performance and satisfaction. One study among restaurant managers found that psychological contact violations were related to greater intentions to quit the job, while another study of a variety of different industries found they were associated with lower levels of productivity, higher levels of theft, and greater work withdrawal.[19]

Role Conflict   When compliance with one role requirement may make it difficult to comply with another, the result is **role conflict**.[20] At the extreme, two or more role expectations are mutually contradictory.

Bill Patterson had to deal with role conflicts, such as his attempt to reconcile the expectations placed on him as a husband and father with those placed on him as an executive with EMM Industries. Bill's wife and children want to remain in Phoenix, while EMM expects its employees to be responsive to the company's needs and requirements. Although it might be in Bill's financial and career interests to accept a relocation, the conflict comes down to choosing between family and career role expectations. Indeed, a great deal of research demonstrates that conflict between the work and family roles is one of the most significant sources of stress for most employees.[21]

Most employees are simultaneously in occupations, work groups, divisions, and demographic groups, and these different identities can come into conflict when the expectations of one clash with the expectations of another.[22] During mergers and acquisitions, employees can be torn between their identities as members of their original organization and of the new parent company.[23] Organizations structured around multinational operations also have been shown to lead to dual identification, with employees distinguishing between the local division and the international organization.[24]

Zimbardo's Prison Experiment   One of the most illuminating role and identity experiments was done a number of years ago by Stanford University psychologist Philip Zimbardo and his associates.[25] They created a "prison" in the basement of the Stanford psychology building; hired at $15 a day two dozen emotionally stable, physically healthy, law-abiding students who scored "normal average" on extensive personality tests; randomly assigned them the role of either "guard" or "prisoner"; and established some basic rules.

It took the "prisoners" little time to accept the authority positions of the "guards" or for the mock guards to adjust to their new authority roles. Consistent with social identity theory, the guards came to see the prisoners as a negative outgroup, and their comments to researchers showed they had developed stereotypes about the "typical" prisoner personality type. After the guards crushed a rebellion attempt on the second day, the prisoners became increasingly passive. Whatever the guards "dished out," the prisoners took. The prisoners actually began to believe and act as if they were inferior and powerless, as the guards constantly reminded them. And every guard, at some time during the simulation, engaged in abusive, authoritative behavior. One said, "I was surprised at myself. . . . I made them call each other names and clean the toilets out with their bare hands. I practically considered the prisoners cattle, and I kept thinking: 'I have to watch out for them in case they try something.'" Surprisingly, during the entire experiment—even after days of abuse—not one prisoner said, "Stop this. I'm a student like you. This is just an experiment!"

The simulation actually proved *too successful* in demonstrating how quickly individuals learn new roles. The researchers had to stop it after only 6 days because of the participants' pathological reactions. And remember, these were individuals chosen precisely for their normalcy and emotional stability.

What can we conclude from this prison simulation? Like the rest of us, the participants had learned stereotyped conceptions of guard and prisoner roles from the mass media and their own personal experiences in power and powerlessness relationships gained at home (parent–child), in school (teacher–student), and in other situations. This background allowed them easily and rapidly to assume roles very different from their inherent personalities and, with no prior personality pathology or training in the parts they were playing, execute extreme forms of behavior consistent with those roles.

A follow-up reality television show conducted by the BBC that used a lower-fidelity simulated prison setting provides some insights into these results.[26] The

role expectations   *How others believe a person should act in a given situation.*

psychological contract   *An unwritten agreement that sets out what management expects from an employee and vice versa.*

role conflict   *A situation in which an individual is confronted by divergent role expectations.*

results were dramatically different from those of the Stanford experiment. The "guards" were far more careful in their behavior and limited the aggressive treatment of "prisoners." They often described their concerns about how their actions might be perceived. In short, they did not fully take on their roles, possibly because they knew their behavior was being observed by millions of viewers. As shared identity increased among "prisoners," they provided higher levels of social support to one another, and an egalitarian system developed between them and the guards. Philip Zimbardo has contended that the BBC study is not a replication of his study for several reasons, but he acknowledges the results demonstrate how both guards and prisoners act differently when closely monitored. These results suggest abuse of roles can be limited when people are made conscious of their behavior.

SELF-ASSESSMENT LIBRARY

Do I Trust Others?

In the Self-Assessment Library (available on CD or online), take assessment II.B.3 (Do I Trust Others?). You can also check out assessment II.B.4 (Do Others See Me as Trusting?).

Group Property 2: Norms

4   Demonstrate how norms and status exert influence on an individual's behavior.

Did you ever notice that golfers don't speak while their partners are putting on the green or that employees don't criticize their bosses in public? Why not? The answer is norms.

All groups have established **norms**—acceptable standards of behavior shared by their members that express what they ought and ought not to do under certain circumstances. When agreed to and accepted by the group, norms influence members' behavior with a minimum of external controls. Different groups, communities, and societies have different norms, but they all have them.[27]

Norms can cover virtually any aspect of group behavior.[28] Probably the most common is a *performance norm*, providing explicit cues about how hard members should work, what the level of output should be, how to get the job done, what level of tardiness is appropriate, and the like. These norms are extremely powerful and are capable of significantly modifying a performance prediction based solely on ability and level of personal motivation. Other norms include *appearance norms* (dress codes, unspoken rules about when to look busy), *social arrangement norms* (with whom to eat lunch, whether to form friendships on and off the job), and *resource allocation norms* (assignment of difficult jobs, distribution of resources like pay or equipment).

The Hawthorne Studies   Full-scale appreciation of the influence of norms on worker behavior did not occur until the early 1930s, following studies undertaken between 1924 and 1932 at the Western Electric Company's Hawthorne Works in Chicago.[29]

The Hawthorne researchers began by examining the relationship between the physical environment and productivity. As they increased the light level for the experimental group of workers, output rose for that unit and the control group. But to their surprise, as they dropped the light level in the experimental group, productivity continued to increase in both groups. In fact, productivity in the experimental group decreased only when the light intensity had been reduced to that of moonlight.

As a follow-up, the researchers began a second set of experiments at Western Electric. A small group of women assembling telephone relays was isolated from the main work group so their behavior could be more carefully observed. Observations covering a multiyear period found this small group's

From the Hawthorne Studies, researchers gained valuable insights into how individual behavior is influenced by group norms. They observed that a group of workers determined the level of fair output and established norms for individual work rates that conformed to the output. To enforce the group norms, workers used sarcasm, ridicule, and even physical force to influence individual behaviors that were not acceptable to the group. Researchers also learned that money was less a factor in determining worker output than were group standards, sentiments, and security.

Source: Hawthorne Works Factory of Morton College.

output increased steadily. The number of personal and out-sick absences was approximately one-third that recorded by women in the regular production department. It became evident this group's performance was significantly influenced by its status as "special." The members thought being in the experimental group was fun, that they were in an elite group, and that management showed concern about their interests by engaging in such experimentation. In essence, workers in both the illumination and assembly-test-room experiments were really reacting to the increased attention they received.

A third study, in the bank wiring observation room, was introduced to study the effect of a sophisticated wage incentive plan. The most important finding was that employees did not individually maximize their outputs. Rather, their output became controlled by a group norm that determined what was a proper day's work. Interviews determined the group was operating well below its capability and was leveling output to protect itself. Members were afraid that if they significantly increased their output, the unit incentive rate would be cut, the expected daily output would be increased, layoffs might occur, or slower workers would be reprimanded. So the group established its idea of a fair output—neither too much nor too little. Members helped each other ensure their reports were nearly level.

The norms the group established included a number of "don'ts." *Don't* be a rate-buster, turning out too much work. *Don't* be a chiseler, turning out too little work. *Don't* squeal on any of your peers. How did the group enforce these norms? The methods included sarcasm, name-calling, ridicule, and even punches to the upper arm of any member who violated the group's norms. Members also ostracized individuals whose behavior was against the group's interest.

norms   *Acceptable standards of behavior within a group that are shared by the group's members.*

Conformity   As a member of a group, you desire acceptance by the group. Thus you are susceptible to conforming to the group's norms. Considerable evidence suggests that groups can place strong pressures on individual members to change their attitudes and behaviors to conform to the group's standard.[30] There are numerous reasons for conformity, with recent research highlighting the importance of a desire to form accurate perceptions of reality based on group consensus, to develop meaningful social relationships with others, and to maintain a favorable self-concept.

The impact that group pressures for **conformity** can have on an individual member's judgment was demonstrated in now-classic studies by Solomon Asch.[31] Asch made up groups of seven or eight people who were asked to compare two cards held by the experimenter. One card had one line, and the other had three lines of varying length, one of which was identical to the line on the one-line card, as Exhibit 9-3 shows. The difference in line length was quite obvious; in fact, under ordinary conditions, subjects made fewer than 1 percent errors in announcing aloud which of the three lines matched the single line. But what happens if members of the group begin giving incorrect answers? Will pressure to conform cause an unsuspecting subject (USS) to alter an answer? Asch arranged the group so only the USS was unaware the experiment was rigged. The seating was prearranged so the USS was one of the last to announce a decision.

The experiment began with several sets of matching exercises. All the subjects gave the right answers. On the third set, however, the first subject gave an obviously wrong answer—for example, saying "C" in Exhibit 9-3. The next subject gave the same wrong answer, and so did the others. Now the dilemma confronting the USS was this: publicly state a perception that differs from the announced position of the others in the group, or give an incorrect answer in order to agree with the others.

The results over many experiments and trials showed 75 percent of subjects gave at least one answer that conformed—that they knew was wrong but was consistent with the replies of other group members—and the average conformer gave wrong answers 37 percent of the time. What meaning can we draw from these results? They suggest group norms press us toward conformity. We desire to be one of the group and therefore avoid being visibly different.

This research was conducted more than 50 years ago. Has time altered the conclusions' validity? And should we consider them generalizable across cultures? Evidence indicates levels of conformity have steadily declined since Asch's studies in the early 1950s, and his findings *are* culture-bound.[32] Conformity to social norms is higher in collectivist cultures, but it is still a powerful force in groups in individualistic countries.

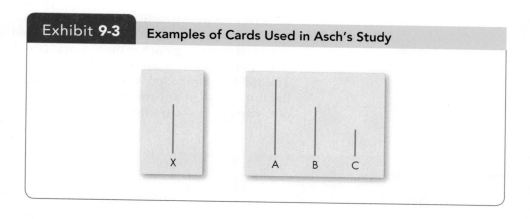

Exhibit 9-3   **Examples of Cards Used in Asch's Study**

Do individuals conform to the pressures of all the groups to which they belong? Obviously not, because people belong to many groups, and their norms vary and sometimes are contradictory. So what do people do? They conform to the important groups to which they belong or hope to belong. These important groups are **reference groups**, in which a person is aware of other members, defines himself or herself as a member or would like to be a member, and feels group members are significant to him or her. The implication, then, is that all groups do not impose equal conformity pressures on their members.

Deviant Workplace Behavior   LeBron Hunt is frustrated by a co-worker who constantly spreads malicious and unsubstantiated rumors about him. Debra Hundley is tired of a member of her work team who, when confronted with a problem, takes out his frustration by yelling and screaming at her and other members. And Mi-Cha Kim recently quit her job as a dental hygienist after being constantly sexually harassed by her employer.

What do these three episodes have in common? They represent employees exposed to acts of deviant workplace behavior.[33] **Deviant workplace behavior** (also called *antisocial behavior* or *workplace incivility*) is voluntary behavior that violates significant organizational norms and, in doing so, threatens the well-being of the organization or its members. Exhibit 9-4 provides a typology of deviant workplace behaviors, with examples of each.

Few organizations will admit to creating or condoning conditions that encourage and maintain deviant norms. Yet they exist. Employees report an increase in rudeness and disregard toward others by bosses and co-workers in recent years. And nearly half of employees who have suffered this incivility say

---

Exhibit 9-4   Typology of Deviant Workplace Behavior

Category	Examples
Production	Leaving early Intentionally working slowly Wasting resources
Property	Sabotage Lying about hours worked Stealing from the organization
Political	Showing favoritism Gossiping and spreading rumors Blaming co-workers
Personal aggression	Sexual harassment Verbal abuse Stealing from co-workers

Source: Based on S. L. Robinson and R. J. Bennett, "A Typology of Deviant Workplace Behaviors: A Multidimensional Scaling Study," *Academy of Management Journal*, April 1995, p. 565. Copyright 1995 by Academy of Management (NY); S. H. Appelbaum, G. D. Iaconi and A. Matousek, "Positive and Negative Deviant Workplace Behaviors: Causes, Impacts, and Solutions," *Corporate Governance* 7, no. 5 (2007), pp. 586–598; and R. W. Griffin, and A. O'Leary-Kelly, *The Dark Side of Organizational Behavior.* (Wiley, New York: 2004).

---

conformity   *The adjustment of one's behavior to align with the norms of the group.*

reference groups   *Important groups to which individuals belong or hope to belong and with whose norms individuals are likely to conform.*

deviant workplace behavior   *Voluntary behavior that violates significant organizational norms and, in so doing, threatens the well-being of the organization or its members. Also called antisocial behavior or workplace incivility.*

it has led them to think about changing jobs; 12 percent actually quit because of it.[34] A study of nearly 1,500 respondents found that in addition to increasing turnover intentions, incivility at work increased reports of psychological stress and physical illness.[35]

Like norms in general, individual employees' antisocial actions are shaped by the group context within which they work. Evidence demonstrates deviant workplace behavior is likely to flourish where it's supported by group norms.[36] Workers who socialize either at or outside work with people who are frequently absent from work are more likely to be absent themselves.[37] What this means for managers is that when deviant workplace norms surface, employee cooperation, commitment, and motivation are likely to suffer.

What are the consequences of workplace deviance for teams? Some research suggests a chain reaction occurs in a group with high levels of dysfunctional behavior.[38] The process begins with negative behaviors like shirking, undermining co-workers, or being generally uncooperative. As a result of these behaviors, the team collectively starts to have negative moods. These negative moods then result in poor coordination of effort and lower levels of group performance, especially when there is a lot of nonverbal negative communication between members.

One study suggests those working in a group are more likely to lie, cheat, and steal than individuals working alone. As shown in Exhibit 9-5, in this study, no individual working alone lied, but 22 percent of those working in groups did. They also were more likely to cheat on a task (55 percent versus 23 percent of individuals working alone) and steal (29 percent compared to 10 percent working alone).[39] Groups provide a shield of anonymity, so someone who might ordinarily be afraid of getting caught can rely on the fact that other group members had the same opportunity, creating a false sense of confidence that may result in more aggressive behavior. Thus, deviant behavior depends on the accepted norms of the group—or even whether an individual is part of a group.[40]

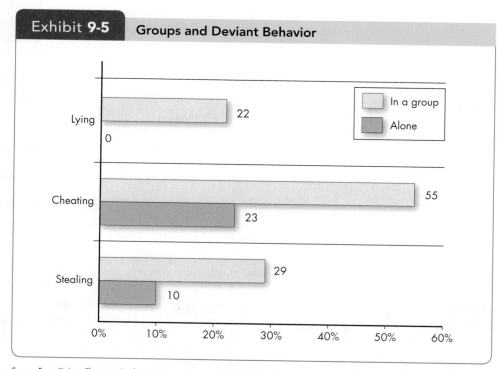

Exhibit 9-5   Groups and Deviant Behavior

Source: From "Lying, Cheating, Stealing: It Happens More in Groups" by A. Erez, H. Elms and E. Fong, paper presented at the European Business Ethics Network Annual Conference, Budapest, August 30, 2003. Reprinted by permission of the author.

Group Property 3: Status

Status   Status—a socially defined position or rank given to groups or group members by others—permeates every society. Even the smallest group will develop roles, rights, and rituals to differentiate its members. Status is a significant motivator and has major behavioral consequences when individuals perceive a disparity between what they believe their status is and what others perceive it to be.

What Determines Status?   According to **status characteristics theory**, status tends to derive from one of three sources:[41]

1. **The power a person wields over others.**   Because they likely control the group's resources, people who control the outcomes tend to be perceived as high status.
2. **A person's ability to contribute to a group's goals.**   People whose contributions are critical to the group's success tend to have high status. Some thought NBA star Kobe Bryant had more say over player decisions than his coaches (though not as much as Bryant wanted!).
3. **An individual's personal characteristics.**   Someone whose personal characteristics are positively valued by the group (good looks, intelligence, money, or a friendly personality) typically has higher status than someone with fewer valued attributes.

Status and Norms   Status has some interesting effects on the power of norms and pressures to conform. High-status individuals are often given more freedom to deviate from norms than are other group members.[42] Physicians actively resist administrative decisions made by lower-ranking insurance company

Earning a brown apron as a winner in Starbucks' Ambassador Cup competitions is a symbol of high status. The company holds Ambassador Cup contests throughout the world, with some contests regional and others countrywide, to determine which employees are the best coffee experts, or "ambassadors." The competitions involve making coffee drinks, identifying coffees in blind taste tests, and testing contestants' knowledge about Starbucks and different aspects of the coffee industry such as growing regions, roasting, purchasing, and fair trade practices. Winning a brown apron signifies achieving the highest level of coffee knowledge. This photo shows coffee ambassadors who won brown aprons during a competition at Starbucks' headquarters.

Source: Erika Schultz/MCT/Newscom.

status   *A socially defined position or rank given to groups or group members by others.*

status characteristics theory   *A theory that states that differences in status characteristics create status hierarchies within groups.*

employees.[43] High-status people are also better able to resist conformity pressures than their lower-status peers. An individual who is highly valued by a group but doesn't need or care about the group's social rewards is particularly able to disregard conformity norms.[44]

These findings explain why many star athletes, celebrities, top-performing salespeople, and outstanding academics seem oblivious to appearance and social norms that constrain their peers. As high-status individuals, they're given a wider range of discretion as long as their activities aren't severely detrimental to group goal achievement.[45]

Status and Group Interaction   High-status people tend to be more assertive group members.[46] They speak out more often, criticize more, state more commands, and interrupt others more often. But status differences actually inhibit diversity of ideas and creativity in groups, because lower-status members tend to participate less actively in group discussions. When they possess expertise and insights that could aid the group, failure to fully utilize them reduces the group's overall performance.

Status Inequity   It is important for group members to believe the status hierarchy is equitable. Perceived inequity creates disequilibrium, which inspires various types of corrective behavior. Hierarchical groups can lead to resentment among those at the lower end of the status continuum. Large differences in status within groups are also associated with poorer individual performance, lower health, and higher intentions to leave the group.[47]

The concept of equity we presented in Chapter 6 applies to status. People expect rewards to be proportionate to costs incurred. If Dana and Anne are the two finalists for the head nurse position in a hospital, and Dana clearly has more seniority and better preparation, Anne will view the selection of Dana as equitable. However, if Anne is chosen because she is the daughter-in-law of the hospital director, Dana will believe an injustice has been committed.

Groups generally agree within themselves on status criteria; hence, there is usually high concurrence in group rankings of individuals. Managers who occupy central positions in their social networks are typically seen as higher in status by their subordinates, and this position translates into greater influence over the group's functioning.[48] However, individuals can find themselves in conflicts when they move between groups whose status criteria are different, or when they join groups whose members have heterogeneous backgrounds. Business executives may use personal income or the growth rate of their companies as determinants of status. Government bureaucrats may use the size of their budgets, and blue-collar workers years of seniority. When groups are heterogeneous or when heterogeneous groups must be interdependent, status differences may initiate conflict as the group attempts to reconcile the differing hierarchies. As we'll see in Chapter 10, this can be a problem when management creates teams of employees from varied functions.

Do cultural differences affect status and the criteria that create it? The answer is a resounding "yes."[49] The French are highly status conscious. Latin Americans and Asians derive status from family position and formal roles in organizations. In the United States and Australia, status is more often conferred for accomplishments.[50]

Group Property 4: Size

5   Show how group size affects group performance.

Does the size of a group affect the group's overall behavior? Yes, but the effect depends on what dependent variables we look at. Smaller groups are faster at completing tasks than larger ones, and individuals perform better in smaller groups.[51] However, in problem solving, large groups consistently get better marks than their smaller counterparts.[52] Translating these results into specific numbers is a bit more hazardous, but groups with a dozen or more members are good for gaining diverse input. So if the goal is fact-finding, larger groups should be more effective. Smaller groups of about seven members are better at doing something productive with that input.

One of the most important findings about the size of a group concerns **social loafing**, the tendency for individuals to expend less effort when working collectively than alone.[53] It directly challenges the assumption that the productivity of the group as a whole should at least equal the sum of the productivity of the individuals in it.

Does team spirit spur individual effort and enhance the group's overall productivity? In the late 1920s, German psychologist Max Ringelmann compared the results of individual and group performance on a rope-pulling task.[54] He expected that three people pulling together should exert three times as much pull on the rope as one person, and eight people eight times as much. But one person pulling on a rope alone exerted an average of 63 kilograms of force. In groups of three, the per-person force dropped to 53 kilograms. And in groups of eight, it fell to only 31 kilograms per person.

Replications of Ringelmann's research with similar tasks have generally supported his findings.[55] Group performance increases with group size, but the addition of new members has diminishing returns on productivity. So more may be better in that total productivity of a group of four is greater than that of three, but the individual productivity of each member declines.

What causes social loafing? It may be a belief that others in the group are not carrying their fair share. If you see others as lazy or inept, you can reestablish equity by reducing your effort. Another explanation is the dispersion of responsibility. Because group results cannot be attributed to any single person, the relationship between an individual's input and the group's output is clouded. Individuals may then be tempted to become free riders and coast on the group's efforts. The implications for OB are significant. When managers use collective work situations to enhance morale and teamwork, they must also be able to identify individual efforts. Otherwise, they must weigh the potential losses in productivity from using groups against the possible gains in worker satisfaction.[56]

Social loafing appears to have a Western bias. It's consistent with individualistic cultures, such as the United States and Canada, that are dominated by self-interest. It is *not* consistent with collective societies, in which individuals are motivated by in-group goals. In studies comparing U.S. employees with employees from the People's Republic of China and Israel (both collectivist societies), the Chinese and Israelis showed no propensity to engage in social loafing and actually performed better in a group than alone.

There are several ways to prevent social loafing: (1) Set group goals, so the group has a common purpose to strive toward; (2) increase intergroup competition, which again focuses on the shared outcome; (3) engage in peer evaluation so each person evaluates each other person's contribution; (4) select members who have high motivation and prefer to work in groups, and (5) if possible, base group rewards in part on each member's unique contributions.[57] Although no magic bullet will prevent social loafing in all cases, these steps should help minimize its effect.

social loafing   *The tendency for individuals to expend less effort when working collectively than when working individually.*

Social loafing is the tendency for individuals to put forth less of an effort when working in a group than when working alone. Studies indicate that the employees shown here producing Spice handsets at a factory in China do not show any propensity to engage in social loafing. In collectivist societies such as China and Israel, employees actually prefer working in a group and are motivated by in-group goals. But in individualistic societies such as the United States and Canada that are dominated by self-interest, social loafing is more likely.

Source: Str/Stringer/Getty Images.

6   Contrast the benefits and disadvantages of cohesive groups.

Group Property 5: Cohesiveness

Groups differ in their **cohesiveness**—the degree to which members are attracted to each other and motivated to stay in the group. Some work groups are cohesive because the members have spent a great deal of time together, or the group's small size facilitates high interaction, or external threats have brought members close together.

Cohesiveness affects group productivity.[58] Studies consistently show that the relationship between cohesiveness and productivity depends on the group's performance-related norms.[59] If norms for quality, output, and cooperation with outsiders, for instance, are high, a cohesive group will be more productive than will a less cohesive group. But if cohesiveness is high and performance norms are low, productivity will be low. If cohesiveness is low and performance norms are high, productivity increases, but less than in the high-cohesiveness/high-norms situation. When cohesiveness and performance-related norms are both low, productivity tends to fall into the low-to-moderate range. These conclusions are summarized in Exhibit 9-6.

What can you do to encourage group cohesiveness? (1) Make the group smaller, (2) encourage agreement with group goals, (3) increase the time members spend together, (4) increase the group's status and the perceived difficulty of attaining membership, (5) stimulate competition with other groups, (6) give rewards to the group rather than to individual members, and (7) physically isolate the group.[60]

Group Property 6: Diversity

The final property of groups we consider is **diversity** in the group's membership, the degree to which members of the group are similar to, or different from, one another. A great deal of research is being done on how diversity influences group performance. Some looks at cultural diversity and some at racial, gender, and other differences. Overall, studies identify both benefits and costs from group diversity.

Diversity appears to increase group conflict, especially in the early stages of a group's tenure, which often lowers group morale and raises dropout rates. One study compared groups that were culturally diverse (composed of people from different countries) and homogeneous (composed of people from the

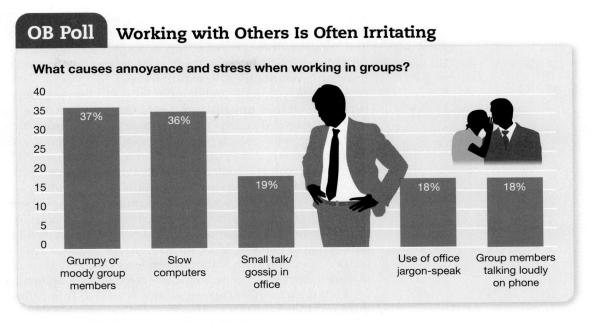

OB Poll Working with Others Is Often Irritating

What causes annoyance and stress when working in groups?

- Grumpy or moody group members — 37%
- Slow computers — 36%
- Small talk/gossip in office — 19%
- Use of office jargon-speak — 18%
- Group members talking loudly on phone — 18%

National sample of 1,836 adults working in an office in the United Kingdom.

Source: "The Office--An Annoying Workplace," Opinium Research LLP (February 24, 2010), downloaded May 26, 2011 from http://news.opinium.co.uk. Reprinted with permission from The Gallup Organization.

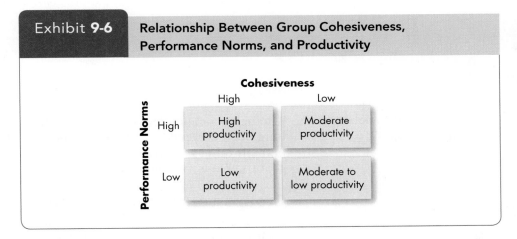

Exhibit 9-6   Relationship Between Group Cohesiveness, Performance Norms, and Productivity

	Cohesiveness	
Performance Norms	High	Low
High	High productivity	Moderate productivity
Low	Low productivity	Moderate to low productivity

same country). On a wilderness survival exercise (not unlike the Experiential Exercise at the end of this chapter), the groups performed equally well, but the diverse groups were less satisfied with their groups, were less cohesive, and had more conflict.[61] Another study examined the effect of differences in tenure on the performance of 67 engineering research and development groups.[62] When most people had roughly the same level of tenure, performance was high, but as tenure diversity increased, performance dropped off. There was an important qualifier: higher levels of tenure diversity were not related to lower performance for groups when there were effective team-oriented human resources practices. Teams in which members' values or opinions differ tend

cohesiveness   *The degree to which group members are attracted to each other and are motivated to stay in the group.*

diversity   *The extent to which members of a group are similar to, or different from, one another.*

to experience more conflict, but leaders who can get the group to focus on the task at hand and encourage group learning are able to reduce these conflicts and enhance discussion of group issues.[63] It seems diversity can be bad for performance even in creative teams, but appropriate organizational support and leadership might offset these problems.

However, culturally and demographically diverse groups may perform better over time—if they can get over their initial conflicts. Why might this be so?

Surface-level diversity—in observable characteristics such as national origin, race, and gender—alerts people to possible deep-level diversity—in underlying attitudes, values, and opinions. One researcher argues, "The mere presence of diversity you can see, such as a person's race or gender, actually cues a team that there's likely to be differences of opinion."[64] Although those differences can lead to conflict, they also provide an opportunity to solve problems in unique ways.

One study of jury behavior found diverse juries more likely to deliberate longer, share more information, and make fewer factual errors when discussing evidence. Two studies of MBA student groups found surface-level diversity led to greater openness even without deep-level diversity. Here, surface-level diversity may subconsciously cue team members to be more open-minded in their views.[65]

The impact of diversity on groups is mixed. It is difficult to be in a diverse group in the short term. However, if members can weather their differences, over time diversity may help them be more open-minded and creative and to do better. But even positive effects are unlikely to be especially strong. As one review stated, "The business case (in terms of demonstrable financial results) for diversity remains hard to support based on the extant research."[66]

Group Decision Making

7 Understand the implications of diversity for group effectiveness.

The belief—characterized by juries—that two heads are better than one has long been accepted as a basic component of the U.S. legal system and those of many other countries. Today, many decisions in organizations are made by groups, teams, or committees.[67]

Groups versus the Individual

Decision-making groups may be widely used in organizations, but are group decisions preferable to those made by an individual alone? The answer depends on a number of factors. Let's begin by looking at the strengths and weaknesses of group decision making.[68]

Strengths of Group Decision Making Groups generate *more complete information and knowledge.* By aggregating the resources of several individuals, groups bring more input as well as heterogeneity into the decision process. They offer *increased diversity of views.* This opens up the opportunity to consider more approaches and alternatives. Finally, groups lead to increased *acceptance of a solution.* Group members who participated in making a decision are more likely to enthusiastically support and encourage others to accept it.

Weaknesses of Group Decision Making Group decisions are time consuming because groups typically take more time to reach a solution. There are *conformity pressures.* The desire by group members to be accepted and considered an asset to the group can squash any overt disagreement. Group discussion can be *dominated*

Forming International Teams in a Virtual World

As more organizations become global entities, the need for work groups that can collaborate across national boundaries grows. Advances in technology that have accompanied globalization lead us to a new type of working relationship: *global virtual teams*. These are groups of individuals working together across national boundaries through electronic communication media. Engineers in Germany might communicate with production teams in China to produce components for assembly and marketing by team members in Canada. Although some global teams occasionally meet in person, geographically dispersed managers often must collaborate virtually.

Virtual global teams have certain liabilities. Traditional teams offer multiple opportunities to work closely with colleagues and develop close personal relationships that can facilitate performance. To be effective, virtual teams need to facilitate these relationships despite numerous barriers. It's easy to misinterpret messages without cues like facial expression and tone of voice. These problems can be even more pronounced among individuals with different cultural backgrounds.

So how can virtual global teams be more effective? Alcoa found it was important to develop regular meeting routines to facilitate collaboration. Groups were also encouraged to review the progress of their own and other teams to identify "best practices" that worked in a variety of situations. Not surprisingly, higher levels of communication and cohesion among members of global virtual teams are associated with shared performance goals, which

in turn lead to higher performance. More surprisingly, leaders' efforts to build personal, inspirational relationships can help even teams that don't meet face to face.

Although global virtual teams face many challenges, companies that implement them effectively can realize tremendous rewards through the diverse knowledge they gain.

Sources: Based on A. Joshi, M. B. Lazarova, and H. Liao, "Getting Everyone on Board: The Role of Inspirational Leadership in Geographically Dispersed Teams," *Organization Science* 20, no. 1 (2009), pp. 240–252; J. Cordery, C. Soo, B. Kirkman, B. Rosen, and J. Mathieu, "Leading Parallel Global Virtual Teams: Lessons from Alcoa," *Organizational Dynamics* 38, no. 3 (2009), pp. 204–216; and R. L. Algesheimer, U. M. Dholakia, and C. Gurau, "Virtual Team Performance in a Highly Competitive Environment," *Group and Organization Management* 36, no. 2 (2011), pp. 161–190.

by one or a few members. If they're low- and medium-ability members, the group's overall effectiveness will suffer. Finally, group decisions suffer from *ambiguous responsibility*. In an individual decision, it's clear who is accountable for the final outcome. In a group decision, the responsibility of any single member is diluted.

Effectiveness and Efficiency   Whether groups are more effective than individuals depends on how you define effectiveness. Group decisions are generally more *accurate* than the decisions of the average individual in a group, but less accurate than the judgments of the most accurate.[69] In terms of *speed*, individuals are superior. If *creativity* is important, groups tend to be more effective. And if effectiveness means the degree of *acceptance* the final solution achieves, the nod again goes to the group.[70]

But we cannot consider effectiveness without also assessing efficiency. With few exceptions, group decision making consumes more work hours than an individual tackling the same problem alone. The exceptions tend to be the instances in which, to achieve comparable quantities of diverse input, the single decision maker must spend a great deal of time reviewing files and talking to other people. In deciding whether to use groups, then, managers must assess whether increases in effectiveness are more than enough to offset the reductions in efficiency.

Summary   In summary, groups are an excellent vehicle for performing many steps in the decision-making process and offer both breadth and depth of input for information gathering. If group members have diverse backgrounds, the alternatives generated should be more extensive and the analysis more critical.

"Asians Have Less Ingroup Bias Than Americans"

This statement is true. But first let's review what in-group bias means.

When they form groups, members characteristically exhibit an *ingroup bias*—they tend to favor members of their group regardless of whether they deserve it. Race, gender, and nationality are commonly investigated causes of ingroup bias. However, nearly any identity can activate ingroup bias, even when individuals are randomly assigned to groups and given a group identity ("lions," "bears," and so on).

Ingroup bias happens because when group identity is salient to people—which it often is—they tend to simplify; they see themselves as more similar to other group members, and less similar to outgroup members, than is really the case.

Recent research suggests that Asians exhibit less ingroup bias than

Americans. One study asked Chinese students at Peking University and U.S. students at University of California–Berkeley to describe the degree to which a set of 16 favorable–unfavorable characteristics (intelligent/foolish, loyal/undependable) described the family member they were closest to. Chinese students described their closest family members significantly less favorably than did the U.S. students. In another study, when Chinese and Americans were asked to evaluate cultural stereotypes of Chinese and Americans in general (intelligent, hard-working, leaderlike, and so on), Americans were more likely to favor their group than were the Chinese.

Why do Asians appear to demonstrate less ingroup bias? One likely explanation is that Asians score higher on *dialecticism*—the tendency to be more comfortable with contradiction

(yin and yang), change (nothing is permanent), and holism (everything has both good and bad). As one Chinese student noted, "If you ask me about Chinese politics, the culture, the people, I can go on for hours talking about everything that's negative. But I still love that place." This tendency may help Asians see both the good and bad sides of their own ingroups.

Sources: C. Ma-Kellams, J. Spencer-Rodgers, and K. Peng, "I Am Against Us? Unpacking Cultural Differences in Ingroup Favoritism Via Dialecticism," *Personality and Social Psychology Bulletin* 37, no. 1 (2011), pp. 15–27; A. E. Giannakakis and I. Fritsche, "Social Identities, Group Norms, and Threat: On the Malleability of Ingroup Bias," *Personality and Social Psychology Bulletin* 37, no. 1 (2011), pp. 82–93; and T. E. DiDonato, J. Ullrich, and J. I. Krueger, "Social Perception as Induction and Inference: An Integrative Model of Intergroup Differentiation, Ingroup Favoritism, and Differential Accuracy," *Journal of Personality and Social Psychology* 100, no. 1 (2011), pp. 66–83.

When the final solution is agreed on, there are more people in a group decision to support and implement it. These pluses, however, can be more than offset by the time consumed by group decisions, the internal conflicts they create, and the pressures they generate toward conformity. In some cases, therefore, we can expect individuals to make better decisions than groups.

Groupthink and Groupshift

Two by-products of group decision making have the potential to affect a group's ability to appraise alternatives objectively and arrive at high-quality solutions.

The first, called **groupthink**, relates to norms. It describes situations in which group pressures for conformity deter the group from critically appraising unusual, minority, or unpopular views. Groupthink is a disease that attacks many groups and can dramatically hinder their performance. The second phenomenon is **groupshift**, which describes the way group members tend to exaggerate the initial positions they hold when discussing a given set of alternatives and arriving at a solution. In some situations, caution dominates and there is a conservative shift, while in other situations groups tend toward a risky shift. Let's look at each phenomenon in detail.

Groupthink   Have you ever felt like speaking up in a meeting, a classroom, or an informal group but decided against it? One reason may have been shyness. Or you may have been a victim of groupthink, which occurs when the norm for consensus overrides the realistic appraisal of alternative courses and the full expression of deviant, minority, or unpopular views. The individual's mental efficiency, reality testing, and moral judgment deteriorate as a result of group pressures.[71]

We have all seen the symptoms of groupthink:

1. Group members rationalize any resistance to the assumptions they've made. No matter how strongly the evidence may contradict their basic assumptions, they behave so as to reinforce them.
2. Members apply direct pressures on those who momentarily express doubts about any of the group's shared views, or who question the validity of arguments supporting the alternative favored by the majority.
3. Members who have doubts or differing points of view seek to avoid deviating from what appears to be group consensus by keeping silent about misgivings and even minimizing to themselves the importance of their doubts.
4. There is an illusion of unanimity. If someone doesn't speak, it's assumed he or she is in full accord. Abstention becomes a "yes" vote.[72]

Groupthink appears closely aligned with the conclusions Solomon Asch drew in his experiments with a lone dissenter. Individuals who hold a position different from that of the dominant majority are under pressure to suppress, withhold, or modify their true feelings and beliefs. As members of a group, we find it more pleasant to be in agreement—to be a positive part of the group—than to be a disruptive force, even if disruption is necessary to improve the effectiveness of the group's decisions. Groups that are more focused on performance than on learning are especially likely to fall victim to groupthink and to suppress the opinions of those who do not agree with the majority.[73]

Does groupthink attack all groups? No. It seems to occur most often when there is a clear group identity, when members hold a positive image of their group that they want to protect, and when the group perceives a collective threat to this positive image.[74] So groupthink is not a dissenter-suppression mechanism as much as it's a means for a group to protect its positive image. One study also showed that those influenced by groupthink were more confident about their course of action early on.[75] Groups that believe too strongly in the correctness of their course of action are more likely to suppress dissent and encourage conformity than are groups that are more skeptical about their course of action.

What can managers do to minimize groupthink?[76] First, they can monitor group size. People grow more intimidated and hesitant as group size increases, and although there is no magic number that will eliminate groupthink, individuals are likely to feel less personal responsibility when groups get larger than about 10 members. Managers should also encourage group leaders to play an impartial role. Leaders should actively seek input from all members and avoid expressing their own opinions, especially in the early stages of deliberation. In addition, managers should appoint one group member to play the role of devil's advocate, overtly challenging the majority position and offering divergent perspectives. Still another suggestion is to use exercises that stimulate active discussion of diverse alternatives without threatening the group or intensifying identity protection. Have group members delay discussion of possible gains so they can first talk about the dangers or risks inherent in a decision. Requiring

groupthink *A phenomenon in which the norm for consensus overrides the realistic appraisal of alternative courses of action.*

groupshift *A change between a group's decision and an individual decision that a member within the group would make; the shift can be toward either conservatism or greater risk but it generally is toward a more extreme version of the group's original position.*

An Ethical Choice

Should You Use Group Peer Pressure?

We've all experienced peer pressure, and it can be hard to behave differently from your friends and co-workers. As more work in organizations is performed in groups and teams, the possibilities and pitfalls of such pressure have become an increasingly important ethical issue for managers.

Peer pressure can be a positive force in some ways. If one member of a group or team is not performing to full potential, pressure from co-workers can encourage better performance. A team with a norm toward behaving ethically might even use peer pressure directly to minimize negative

behavior. Peer pressure can increase all sorts of ethical behavior ranging from donating to charity to working for the Salvation Army.

However, as the chapter has shown, peer pressure can also be more destructive. It can create a feeling of exclusion in those who do not go along with group norms and can be very stressful and hurtful for those who don't see eye-to-eye with the rest of the group. Peer pressure itself might become an unethical practice that unduly influences workers' behavior and thoughts.

So should you use group peer pressure? It depends on what type and why. If you are using peer pressure to

encourage individuals to work toward team goals and behave consistently with organizational values, it can enhance ethical performance. But it should emphasize acceptance and rewarding of positive behavior, rather than rejection and exclusion, as a means of getting everyone to behave consistently in a group.

Sources: Based on: A. Verghese, "The Healing Power of Peer Pressure," *Newsweek* (March 14, 2011), www .newsweek.com; T. Rosenberg, *Join the Club: How Peer Pressure Can Transform the World* (New York: W. W. Norton & Company, 2011); and J. Meer, "Brother, Can You Spare a Dime? Peer Pressure in Charitable Solicitation," *Journal of Public Economics* 95, no. 7–8 (2011), pp. 926–941.

members to first focus on the negatives of an alternative makes the group less likely to stifle dissenting views and more likely to gain an objective evaluation.

Group Shift or Group Polarization   There are differences between group decisions and the individual decisions of group members.[77] What appears to happen in groups is that the discussion leads members toward a more extreme view of the position they already held. Conservatives become more cautious, and more aggressive types take on more risk. The group discussion tends to exaggerate the initial position of the group.

We can view group polarization as a special case of groupthink. The group's decision reflects the dominant decision-making norm that develops during discussion. Whether the shift in the group's decision is toward greater caution or more risk depends on the dominant pre-discussion norm.

The shift toward polarization has generated several explanations.[78] It's been argued, for instance, that discussion makes the members more comfortable with each other and, thus, more willing to express extreme versions of their original positions. Another argument is that the group diffuses responsibility. Group decisions free any single member from accountability for the group's final choice, so a more extreme position can be taken. It's also likely that people take on extreme positions because they want to demonstrate how different they are from the outgroup.[79] People on the fringes of political or social movements take on ever-more extreme positions just to prove they are really committed to the cause, whereas those who are more cautious tend to take exceptionally moderate positions to demonstrate how reasonable they are.

So how should you use the findings on groupshift? Recognize that group decisions exaggerate the initial position of the individual members, that the shift has been shown more often to be toward greater risk, and that which way a group will shift is a function of the members' pre-discussion inclinations.

We now turn to the techniques by which groups make decisions. These reduce some of the dysfunctional aspects of group decision making.

Group Decision-Making Techniques

8   Contrast the strengths and weaknesses of group decision making.

The most common form of group decision making takes place in **interacting groups**. Members meet face to face and rely on both verbal and nonverbal interaction to communicate. But as our discussion of groupthink demonstrated, interacting groups often censor themselves and pressure individual members toward conformity of opinion. Brainstorming, the nominal group technique, and electronic meetings can reduce problems inherent in the traditional interacting group.

Brainstorming can overcome the pressures for conformity that dampen creativity [80] by encouraging any and all alternatives while withholding criticism. In a typical brainstorming session, a half-dozen to a dozen people sit around a table. The group leader states the problem in a clear manner so all participants understand. Members then freewheel as many alternatives as they can in a given length of time. To encourage members to "think the unusual," no criticism is allowed, even of the most bizarre suggestions, and all ideas are recorded for later discussion and analysis.

Brainstorming may indeed generate ideas—but not in a very efficient manner. Research consistently shows individuals working alone generate more ideas than a group in a brainstorming session. One reason for this is "production blocking." When people are generating ideas in a group, many are talking at once, which blocks the thought process and eventually impedes the sharing of ideas.[81] The following two techniques go further than brainstorming by helping groups arrive at a preferred solution.[82]

The **nominal group technique** restricts discussion or interpersonal communication during the decision-making process, hence the term *nominal*. Group members are all physically present, as in a traditional committee meeting, but they operate independently. Specifically, a problem is presented and then the group takes the following steps:

1. Before any discussion takes place, each member independently writes down ideas on the problem.
2. After this silent period, each member presents one idea to the group. No discussion takes place until all ideas have been presented and recorded.
3. The group discusses the ideas for clarity and evaluates them.
4. Each group member silently and independently rank-orders the ideas. The idea with the highest aggregate ranking determines the final decision.

The chief advantage of the nominal group technique is that it permits a group to meet formally but does not restrict independent thinking, as does an interacting group. Research generally shows nominal groups outperform brainstorming groups.[83]

The most recent approach to group decision making blends the nominal group technique with sophisticated computer technology.[84] It's called a computer-assisted group, or an **electronic meeting**. Once the required technology is in

---

interacting groups   *Typical groups in which members interact with each other face to face.*

brainstorming   *An idea-generation process that specifically encourages any and all alternatives while withholding any criticism of those alternatives.*

nominal group technique   *A group decision-making method in which individual members meet face to face to pool their judgments in a systematic but independent fashion.*

electronic meeting   *A meeting in which members interact on computers, allowing for anonymity of comments and aggregation of votes.*

Exhibit **9-7**	Evaluating Group Effectiveness			

| Effectiveness Criteria | Type of Group | | | |
	Interacting	Brainstorming	Nominal	Electronic
Number and quality of ideas	Low	Moderate	High	High
Social pressure	High	Low	Moderate	Low
Money costs	Low	Low	Low	High
Speed	Moderate	Moderate	Moderate	Moderate
Task orientation	Low	High	High	High
Potential for interpersonal conflict	High	Low	Moderate	Low
Commitment to solution	High	Not applicable	Moderate	Moderate
Development of group cohesiveness	High	High	Moderate	Low

place, the concept is simple. Up to 50 people sit around a horseshoe-shaped table, empty except for a series of networked laptops. Issues are presented to them, and they type their responses into their computers. These individual but anonymous comments, as well as aggregate votes, are displayed on a projection screen. This technique also allows people to be brutally honest without penalty. And it's fast because chitchat is eliminated, discussions don't digress, and many participants can "talk" at once without stepping on one another's toes. Early evidence, however, suggests electronic meetings don't achieve most of their proposed benefits. They actually lead to *decreased* group effectiveness, require *more* time to complete tasks, and result in *reduced* member satisfaction compared with face-to-face groups.[85] Nevertheless, current enthusiasm for computer-mediated communications suggests this technology is here to stay and is likely to increase in popularity in the future.

9 Compare the effectiveness of interacting, brainstorming, nominal, and electronic meeting groups.

Each of the four group-decision techniques has its own set of strengths and weaknesses. The choice depends on what criteria you want to emphasize and the cost–benefit trade-off. As Exhibit 9-7 indicates, an interacting group is good for achieving commitment to a solution, brainstorming develops group cohesiveness, the nominal group technique is an inexpensive means for generating a large number of ideas, and electronic meetings minimize social pressures and conflicts.

MyManagementLab

Now that you have finished this chapter, go back to **www.pearsonglobaleditions.com/ mymanagementlab** to continue practicing and applying the concepts you've learned.

Summary and Implications for Managers

Several implications can be drawn from our discussion of groups. The next chapter will explore several of these in greater depth.

- Role perception and an employee's performance evaluation are positively related.[86] The degree of congruence between the employee's and the boss's perception of the employee's job influences the degree to which the boss will judge that employee effective. An employee whose role perception fulfills the boss's role expectations will receive a higher performance evaluation.

- Norms control behavior by establishing standards of right and wrong. The norms of a given group can help explain members' behaviors for managers. When norms support high output, managers can expect markedly higher individual performance than when they aim to restrict output. Norms that support antisocial behavior increase the likelihood that individuals will engage in deviant workplace activities.

- Status inequities create frustration and can adversely influence productivity and willingness to remain with an organization. Incongruence is likely to reduce motivation and motivate a search for ways to bring about fairness (say, by taking another job). Because lower-status people tend to participate less in group discussions, groups with high status differences are likely to inhibit input from lower-status members and reduce their potential.

- The impact of size on a group's performance depends on the type of task. Larger groups are more effective at fact-finding activities, smaller groups at action-taking tasks. Our knowledge of social loafing suggests that managers using larger groups should also provide measures of individual performance.

- Cohesiveness can influence a group's level of productivity or not, depending on the group's performance-related norms.

- Diversity appears to have a mixed impact on group performance, with some studies suggesting that diversity can help performance and others suggesting it can hurt it. It appears the situation makes a difference in whether positive or negative results predominate.

- High congruence between a boss's and an employee's perception of the employee's job correlates strongly with high employee satisfaction.[87] Role conflict is associated with job-induced tension and job dissatisfaction.[88]

- Most people prefer to communicate with others at their own status level or a higher one rather than with those below them.[89] As a result, we should expect satisfaction to be greater among employees whose job minimizes interaction with individuals lower in status than themselves.

- The group size–satisfaction relationship is what we would intuitively expect: larger groups are associated with lower satisfaction.[90] As size increases, opportunities for participation and social interaction decrease, as does the ability of members to identify with the group's accomplishments. At the same time, having more members also prompts dissension, conflict, and the formation of subgroups, which all act to make the group a less pleasant entity of which to be a part.

QUESTIONS FOR REVIEW

1 Define *group*. What are the different types of groups?

2 What are the five stages of group development?

3 Do role requirements change in different situations? If so, how?

4 How do group norms and status influence an individual's behavior?

5 How does group size affect group performance?

6 What are the advantages and limitations of cohesive groups?

7 What are the implications of diversity for group effectiveness?

8 What are the strengths and weaknesses of group (versus individual) decision making?

9 How effective are interacting, brainstorming, nominal, and electronic meeting groups?

Affinity Groups Fuel Business Success

Employee resource groups (ERGs), also known as affinity groups, have become part of nearly all large organizations' cultures. ERGs are voluntary networking groups that provide forums for employees to gather socially and share ideas outside their particular business units. Many ERGs are organized around surface characteristics such as gender, age, disability, sexual orientation, race, and ethnic background. However, they can be formed around any issue.

The rationale for ERGs is obvious. Large organizations often are very decentralized, leading many employees to feel disconnected and isolated. That's especially true for employees who are or feel different. So large companies such as Best Buy, Ford, Intuit, Prudential, Wells Fargo, Johnson & Johnson, and Macy's have found that their ERGs lead to greater feelings of inclusiveness. When employees of a large organization realize they're hardly alone, ERGs are a great way to foster commitment by joining employees to others in the organization, often in a way that's independent of their work unit. Why not tie employees to one another in as many ways as possible?

Finally, many ERGs solve organizational problems in unique ways. Cisco's Asian Affinity Network played a key role in forging a bond between Cisco and Shui On Group, the largest publicly traded real estate company in China, by proposing that Cisco hold a business development event during a Silicon Valley visit by Shui On Group's founder and chairman.

Many thought the decline in the economy and the growth of social networking sites would spell the end for ERGs. However, it seems the opposite is true. ERGs are growing. When a company like Northrop Grumman has 125,000 employees spread across 25 countries and all 50 states, it needs a way to join them together. That's exactly what ERGs do best.

ERGs make great business sense. Ford executive Rosalind Cox says of Ford's ERGs: "At the end of the day, we want to build a diverse and inclusive culture that drives business results."

ERGs may sound like a good idea with few drawbacks, but that's not the case. They have some real problems, few of which you'll hear about in the rah-rah press generated about them, much of it put forth by companies' PR departments.

First, there's cost. These affinity groups can cost a lot of money. One study estimated that the budget for affinity groups was $7,203 for each 100 group members. That doesn't even include the cost of technology, facilities, and staff support (on average, about 1.5 staff employees for each group). Costlier still is the time ERG members spend on their groups, coaching, training, meeting, and planning events oriented around a very small slice of the company's workforce—on average, only 8 percent of an organization's employees. In these competitive times, that doesn't sound like the most efficient and fair use of an organization's resources.

Then there are the legal issues. Affinity groups have been subject to significant legal action, often by excluded employees. Most employers also don't realize that ERGs can be viewed as "sweetheart unions" by the National Labor Relations Board. "The National Labor Relations Act controls collective actions between employers and employees whether a union is present or not," says one employment law expert. Most companies resist unions trying to organize their employees. Why do they form them by their own hand?

Organizations should do everything they can to encourage all employees to feel they are included and heard. Networking is a wonderful way to do that. But organizations that endorse, establish, and fund segmented groups that exclude some employees are asking for trouble. The best way to fight feelings of isolation is by drawing employees in and giving them a voice. It's not by slicing the organizations into groups, including some and excluding others.

Sources: R. R. Hastings, "Employee Resource Groups Drive Business Results," *HR Magazine* (February 15, 2011), downloaded June 10, 2011, from www.shrm.org/; R. R. Hastings, "Employee Resource Groups Can Create Labor Issues, "*HR Magazine* (June 25, 2009), downloaded June 10, 2011, from www.shrm.org/; and "Affinity and Networking Groups," *The New York Times*, downloaded June 11, 2011 from www.nytimes.com/.

EXPERIENTIAL EXERCISE Wilderness Survival

You are a member of a hiking party. After reaching base camp on the first day, you decide to take a quick sunset hike by yourself. After a few exhilarating miles, you decide to return to camp. On your way back, you realize you are lost. You have shouted for help, to no avail. It is now dark. And getting cold.

Your Task

Without communicating with anyone else in your group, read the following scenarios and choose the best answer. Keep track of your answers on a sheet of paper. You have 10 minutes to answer the 10 questions.

1. The first thing you decide to do is to build a fire. However, you have no matches, so you use the bow-and-drill method. What is the bow-and-drill method?
   a. A dry, soft stick is rubbed between the hands against a board of supple green wood.
   b. A soft green stick is rubbed between the hands against a hardwood board.
   c. A straight stick of wood is quickly rubbed back and forth against a dead tree.
   d. Two sticks (one being the bow, the other the drill) are struck to create a spark.

2. It occurs to you that you can also use the fire as a distress signal. How do you form the international distress signal with fire?
   a. 2 fires
   b. 4 fires in a square
   c. 4 fires in a cross
   d. 3 fires in a line

3. You are very thirsty. You go to a nearby stream and collect some water in the small metal cup you have in your backpack. How long should you boil the water?
   a. 15 minutes
   b. A few seconds
   c. 1 hour
   d. It depends on the altitude.

4. You are very hungry, so you decide to eat what appear to be edible berries. When performing the universal edibility test, what should you do?
   a. Do not eat for 2 hours before the test.
   b. If the plant stings your lip, confirm the sting by holding it under your tongue for 15 minutes.
   c. If nothing bad has happened 2 hours after digestion, eat half a cup of the plant and wait again.
   d. Separate the plant into its basic components and eat each component, one at a time.

5. Next, you decide to build a shelter for the evening. In selecting a site, what do you *not* have to consider?
   a. It must contain material to make the type of shelter you need.
   b. It must be free of insects, reptiles, and poisonous plants.

c. It must be large enough and level enough for you to lie down comfortably.
   d. It must be on a hill so you can signal rescuers and keep an eye on your surroundings.

6. In the shelter that you built, you notice a spider. You heard from a fellow hiker that black widow spiders populate the area. How do you identify a black widow spider?
   a. Its head and abdomen are black; its thorax is red.
   b. It is attracted to light.
   c. It runs away from light.
   d. It is a dark spider with a red or orange marking on the female's abdomen.

7. After getting some sleep, you notice that the night sky has cleared, so you decide to try to find your way back to base camp. You believe you should travel north and can use the North Star for navigation. How do you locate the North Star?
   a. Hold your right hand up as far as you can and look between your index and middle fingers.
   b. Find Sirius and look 60 degrees above it and to the right.
   c. Look for the Big Dipper and follow the line created by its cup end.
   d. Follow the line of Orion's belt.

8. You come across a fast-moving stream. What is the best way to cross it?
   a. Find a spot downstream from a sandbar, where the water will be calmer.
   b. Build a bridge.
   c. Find a rocky area, as the water will be shallow and you will have hand- and footholds.
   d. Find a level stretch where it breaks into a few channels.

9. After walking for about an hour, you feel several spiders in your clothes. You don't feel any pain, but you know some spider bites are painless. Which of these spider bites is painless?
   a. Black widow
   b. Brown recluse
   c. Wolf spider
   d. Harvestman (daddy longlegs)

10. You decide to eat some insects. Which insects should you avoid?
    a. Adults that sting or bite
    b. Caterpillars and insects that have a pungent odor
    c. Hairy or brightly colored ones
    d. All the above

Group Task

Break into groups of five or six people. Now imagine that your whole group is lost. Answer each question as a group, employing a consensus approach to reach each decision. Once the group comes to an agreement, write down the decision on the same sheet of paper that you used for your individual answers. You will have approximately 20 minutes for the group task.

Scoring Your Answers

Your instructor will provide you with the correct answers, which are based on expert judgments in these situations. Once you have received the answers, calculate (A) your individual score; (B) your group's score; (C) the average individual score in the group; and (D) the best individual score in the group. Write these down and consult with your group to ensure that these scores are accurate.

A. Your individual score _____

B. Your group's score _____

C. Average individual score in group _____

D. Best individual score in group _____

Discussion Questions

1. How did your group (B) perform relative to yourself (A)?

2. How did your group (B) perform relative to the average individual score in the group (C)?

3. How did your group (B) perform relative to the best individual score in the group (D)?

4. Compare your results with those of other groups. Did some groups do a better job of outperforming individuals than others?

5. What do these results tell you about the effectiveness of group decision making?

6. What can groups do to make group decision making more effective?

ETHICAL DILEMMA Is Social Loafing Shirking?

As you now know, social loafing is one disadvantage of working in groups. Regardless of the type of task—from games of Tug of War to working on a group projects—research suggests that when working in a group, most individuals contribute less than if they were working on their own. We might call those who do social loafing "shirkers" because they are not living up to their responsibilities as group members.

Most of us have experienced social loafing, or shirking, in groups. And we may even admit to times when we shirked ourselves. We discussed earlier in this chapter some ways of discouraging social loafing, such as limiting group size, holding individuals responsible for their contributions, setting group goals, and providing "hybrid" incentives that reward both individual and group performance. While these tactics may be effective, in our experience many students simply work around shirkers. "We just did it ourselves—it was easier that way," says one group member.

Questions

1. If group members end up "working around" shirkers, do you think this information should be communicated to the instructor so that each individual's contribution to the project is judged more fairly? If so, does the group have an ethical responsibility to communicate this to the shirking group member?

2. Do you think social loafing is always shirking (failing to live up to one's responsibilities)? Is social loafing always unethical? Why or why not?

3. Social loafing has been found to be higher in Western, more individualist, nations than in other countries. Do you think this means we should tolerate shirking on the part of U.S. students and workers to a greater degree than if it occurred with someone from Asia?

CASE INCIDENT 1 Third Circle Asset Management

Third Circle is an asset management company that operates in the financial services industry in South Africa. The company has a vast knowledge of psychometrics and is constantly refining its psychometric models. It works on the premise that there are three main groups of individuals: dolphins, puffer fish, and sharks.

According to Third Circle's approach, "dolphins" are group players and extremely sociable. They will always look out for the safety of the others in the group and their behavior is always focused to benefit the group. Dolphin people like to strategize, focus on opportunities, and work together in harmony. They operate mostly as a clan and understand the rules of interdependence. By working together they know that they don't have to know everything.

Each of them has certain abilities and by working together they can unlock more opportunities.

The "puffer fish" operate on the sidelines; they don't get involved in the mainstream activities and will hardly ever air their opinions. If you get too close to them, they will blow themselves up and have a very poisonous sting.

The "sharks" are big and strong and are known as the bullies of the ocean. They are seen as threatening and predatory. Shark personality people are sharp and opportunistic. They see opportunities where there are none. This is why we need these thick skinned bullies from time to time to shake up our world.

The natural reaction is to always only want dolphins on your team. However, that isn't healthy because the group's approach could be narrow and the business could ultimately lose out on many opportunities. Puffer fish are important in a team—they make life difficult for team members, forcing them to rethink their strategies, which can lead to solutions that the team would never have come up with if not for the persistent and painful "stings!" Sharks also play a critical role in challenging teams to consider all the inherent risks of their approach or strategy because a shark will not hesitate to attack at the opportune time to destroy an initiative.

Third Circle walks a fine balance by having all three of these behaviors found on its team. It understands that by harnessing all three of these behaviors, the end business will be considerably stronger, although the journey is not always a pleasant one!

Questions

1. People have different roles to play—do you think they all can contribute?

2. What is the value in having different personalities as part of your team?

3. How do you ensure that you have a balanced team in your working environment ensuring true harmony for effectiveness while allowing puffer and shark personalities to stimulate and challenge the team?

4. What is your personal profile and would you deliberately invite other personality profiles into your work group? Do you have the same view about inviting other personalities into your social groups?

Sources: Third Circle Asset Management, www.thirdcircle.co.za, accessed October 2011; Johnson, D. W. *Joining Together: Group Theory and Group Skills,* 2009. Upper Saddel River. N. J. Pearson Education; Rita Putatunda, *Puffer Fish,* http://sites.google.com/site/biologybfinalproject/animalia/pufferfish-arthron-hispidus, accessed October 2011.

CASE INCIDENT 2 Herd Behavior and the Housing Bubble (and Collapse)

It is sometimes easy to forget that humans are not unlike other animals. Economist John Maynard Keynes recognized this when he commented, "Most, probably, of our decisions to do something positive, the full consequences of which will be drawn out over many days to come, can only be taken as the result of animal spirits—a spontaneous urge to action rather than inaction, and not as the outcome of a weighted average of quantitative benefits multiplied by quantitative probabilities."

Such "animal spirits" are particularly dangerous at the collective level. One animal's decision to charge over a cliff is a tragedy for the animal, but it may also lead the entire herd over the cliff.

You may be wondering how this is applicable to organizational behavior. Consider the recent housing bubble and its subsequent and enduring collapse, or the dot-com implosion of the turn of the century. As housing prices rose ever higher, people discounted risk. Homeowners and investors rushed to buy properties because everyone else was doing it. Banks rushed to provide loans with little due diligence because, well, everyone else was doing it. "Banks didn't want to get left behind. Everybody lowered their underwriting standards, no matter who they are," said Regions Bank executive Michael Menk. "As bankers that's who we are; we follow the herd." Similar problems led to a run up in prices for internet-based companies during the early twenty-first century, and some wonder whether the current valuations of social networking sites are following a similar trend of overpricing.

Yale Economist Robert Shiller called this "herd behavior" and cited research showing people often rely heavily on the behavior of groups in formulating decisions about what they should do. A recent study in behavioral finance confirmed herd behavior in investment decisions and showed that analysts were especially likely to follow other analysts' behavior when they had private information that was less accurate or reliable.

Questions

1. Some research suggests herd behavior increases as the size of the group increases. Why do you think this might be the case?

2. One researcher argues that "pack behavior" comes about because it has benefits. What is the upside of such behavior?

3. Shiller argues that herd behavior can go both ways: It explains the housing bubble, but it also explains the bust. As he notes, "Rational individuals become excessively pessimistic as they see others bidding down home prices to abnormally low levels." Do you agree with Shiller?

4. How might organizations combat the problems resulting from herd behavior?

Sources: Based on R. J. Shiller, "How a Bubble Stayed Under the Radar," *The New York Times* (March 2, 2008), p. BU6; W. Hobson, "Reversal of Fortune," *Panama City News Herald* (March 22, 2009), www.newsherald.com; P. Leoni, "Pack Behavior," *Journal of Mathematical Psychology* 52, no. 6 (2008), pp. 348–351; and J. Reiczigel, Z. Lang, L. Rózsa, and B. Tóthmérész, "Measures of Sociality: Two Different Views of Group Size," *Animal Behaviour* 75, no. 2 (2008), pp. 715–721.

ENDNOTES

1. B. E. Ashforth and F. Mael, "Social Identity Theory and the Organization," *Academy of Management Review* 14, no. 1 (1989), pp. 20–39; and M. A. Hogg and D. J. Terry, "Social Identity and Self-Categorization Processes in Organizational Contexts," *Academy of Management Review* 25, no. 1 (2000), pp. 121–140.

2. M. A. Hogg and B. A. Mullin, "Joining Groups to Reduce Uncertainty: Subjective Uncertainty Reduction and Group Identification," in D. Abrams and M. A. Hogg (eds.), *Social Identity and Social Cognition* (Maiden MA: Blackwell, 1999), pp. 249–279.

3. O. Yakushko, M. M. Davidson, and E. N. Williams, "Identity Salience Model: A Paradigm for Integrating Multiple Identities in Clinical Practice." *Psychotherapy* 46, no. 2 (2009), pp. 180-192; and S. M. Toh and A. S. Denisi, "Host Country Nationals as Socializing Agents: A Social Identity Approach," *Journal of Organizational Behavior* 28, no. 3 (2007), pp. 281–301.

4. D. M. Cable and D. S. DeRue, "The Convergent and Discriminant Validity of Subjective Fit Perceptions," *Journal of Applied Psychology* 87, no. 5 (2002), pp. 875–884; E. George and P. Chattopadhyay, "One Foot in Each Camp: The Dual Identification of Contract Workers," *Administrative Science Quarterly* 50, no. 1 (2005), pp. 68–99; and D. M. Cable and J. R. Edwards, "Complementary and Supplementary Fit: A Theoretical and Empirical Integration," *Journal of Applied Psychology* 89, no. 5 (2004), pp. 822–834.

5. P. F. McKay and D. R. Avery, "What Has Race Got to Do with It? Unraveling the Role of Racioethnicity in Job Seekers' Reactions to Site Visits," *Personnel Psychology* 59, no. 2 (2006), pp. 395–429; A. S. Leonard, A. Mehra, and R. Katerberg, "The Social Identity and Social Networks of Ethnic Minority Groups in Organizations: A Crucial Test of Distinctiveness Theory," *Journal of Organizational Behavior* 29, no. 5 (2008), pp. 573–589.

6. A. Mehra, M. Kilduff, and D. J. Brass, "At the Margins: A Distinctiveness Approach to the Social Identity and Social Networks of Underrepresented Groups," *Academy of Management Journal* 41, no. 4 (1998), pp. 441–452.

7. M. D. Johnson, F. P. Morgeson, D. R. Ilgen, C. J. Meyer, and J. W. Lloyd, "Multiple Professional Identities: Examining Differences in Identification Across Work-Related Targets," *Journal of Applied Psychology* 91, no. 2 (2006), pp. 498–506.

8. F. Mael and B. E. Ashforth, "Alumni and Their Alma Mater: A Partial Test of the Reformulated Model of Organizational Identification," *Journal of Organizational Behavior* 13, no. 2 (1992), pp. 103–123.

9. K. Mignonac, O. Herrbach, and S. Guerrero, "The Interactive Effects of Perceived External Prestige and Need for Organizational Identification on Turnover Intentions," *Journal of Vocational Behavior* 69, no. 3 (2006), pp. 477–493; A. Carmeli, and A. Shteigman, "Top Management Team Behavioral Integration in Small-Sized Firms: A Social Identity Perspective," *Group Dynamics* 14, no. 4 (2010), pp. 318–331.

10. M. Hogg and D. Abrams, "Towards A Single-Process Uncertainty-Reduction Model of Social Motivation in Groups," In M. Hogg and D. Abrams (eds.), *Group Motivation: Social Psychological Perspectives* (New York: Harvester-Wheatsheaf, 1993), pp. 173–190.

11. D. A. Gioia, K. N. Price, A. L. Hamilton, and J. B. Thomas, "Change Reference to Forging An Identity: An Insider-Outsider Study of Processes Involved in the Formation of Organizational Identity." *Administrative Science Quarterly* 55, no. 1 (2010), pp. 1–46.

12. J. F. McGrew, J. G. Bilotta, and J. M. Deeney, "Software Team Formation and Decay: Extending the Standard Model for Small Groups," *Small Group Research* 30, no. 2 (1999), pp. 209–234.

13. B. W. Tuckman, "Developmental Sequences in Small Groups," *Psychological Bulletin,* June 1965, pp. 384–399; B. W. Tuckman and M. C. Jensen, "Stages of Small-Group Development Revisited," *Group and Organizational Studies,* December 1977, pp. 419–427; M. F. Maples, "Group Development: Extending Tuckman's Theory," *Journal for Specialists in Group Work* (Fall 1988), pp. 17–23; and K. Vroman and J. Kovacich, "Computer-Mediated Interdisciplinary Teams: Theory and Reality," *Journal of Interprofessional Care* 16, no. 2 (2002), pp. 159–170.

14. J. E. Mathieu and T. L. Rapp, "Laying the Foundation for Successful Team Performance Trajectories: The Roles of Team Charters and Performance Strategies," *Journal of Applied Psychology* 94, no. 1 (2009), pp. 90–103; and E. C. Dierdorff, S. T. Bell, and J. A. Belohlav, "The Power of 'We': Effects of Psychological Collectivism on Team Performance Over Time," *Journal of Applied Psychology* 96, no. 2 (2011), pp. 247–262.

15. C. J. G. Gersick, "Time and Transition in Work Teams: Toward a New Model of Group Development," *Academy of Management Journal* (March 1988), pp. 9–41; C. J. G. Gersick, "Marking Time: Predictable Transitions in Task Groups," *Academy of Management Journal* (June 1989), pp. 274–309; M. J. Waller, J. M. Conte, C. B. Gibson, and M. A. Carpenter, "The Effect of Individual Perceptions of Deadlines on Team Performance," *Academy of Management Review* (October 2001), pp. 586–600; and A. Chang, P. Bordia, and J. Duck, "Punctuated Equilibrium and Linear Progression: Toward a New Understanding of Group Development," *Academy of Management Journal* (February 2003), pp. 106–117.

16. Gersick, "Time and Transition in Work Teams"; and Gersick, "Marking Time."

17. A. Seers and S. Woodruff, "Temporal Pacing in Task Forces: Group Development or Deadline Pressure?" *Journal of Management* 23, no. 2 (1997), pp. 169–187.

18. See D. M. Rousseau, *Psychological Contracts in Organizations: Understanding Written and Unwritten Agreements* (Thousand Oaks, CA: Sage, 1995); E. W. Morrison and S. L. Robinson, "When Employees Feel Betrayed: A Model of How Psychological Contract Violation Develops," *Academy of Management Review* (April 1997), pp. 226–256; L. Sels, M. Janssens, and I. Van den Brande, "Assessing the Nature of Psychological Contracts: A Validation of Six Dimensions," *Journal of Organizational Behavior* (June 2004), pp. 461–488; and C. Hui, C. Lee, and D. M. Rousseau, "Psychological Contract and Organizational Citizenship Behavior in China: Investigating Generalizability and Instrumentality," *Journal of Applied Psychology* (April 2004), pp. 311–321.

19. M. D. Collins, "The Effect of Psychological Contract Fulfillment on Manager Turnover Intentions and Its Role As a Mediator in a Casual, Limited-Service Restaurant Environment," *International Journal of Hospitality Management* 29, no. 4 (2010), pp. 736–742; J. M. Jensen, R. A. Opland, and A. M. Ryan, "Psychological Contracts and Counterproductive Work Behaviors: Employee Responses to Transactional and

Relational Breach," *Journal of Business and Psychology* 25, no. 4 (2010), pp. 555–568.

20. See M. F. Peterson et al., "Role Conflict, Ambiguity, and Overload: A 21-Nation Study," *Academy of Management Journal* (April 1995), pp. 429–452; and I. H. Settles, R. M. Sellers, and A. Damas Jr., "One Role or Two? The Function of Psychological Separation in Role Conflict," *Journal of Applied Psychology* (June 2002), pp. 574–582.

21. See, for example, F. T. Amstad, L L. Meier, U. Fasel, A. Elfering, and N. K. Semmer, "A Meta-Analysis of Work-Family Conflict and Various Outcomes with a Special Emphasis on Cross-Domain Versus Matching-Domain Relations," *Journal of Occupational Health Psychology* 16, no. 2 (2011), pp. 151–169.

22. M. A. Hogg and D. J. Terry, "Social Identity and Self-Categorization Processes in Organizational Contexts," *Academy of Management Review* 25, no. 1 (2000), pp. 121–140.

23. D. Vora and T. Kostova. "A Model of Dual Organizational Identification in the Context of the Multinational Enterprise," *Journal of Organizational Behavior* 28 (2007), pp. 327–350.

24. C. Reade, "Dual Identification in Multinational Corporations: Local Managers and Their Psychological Attachment to the Subsidiary Versus the Global Organization," *International Journal of Human Resource Management,* 12, no. 3 (2001), pp. 405–424.

25. P. G. Zimbardo, C. Haney, W. C. Banks, and D. Jaffe, "The Mind Is a Formidable Jailer: A Pirandellian Prison," *The New York Times* (April 8, 1973), pp. 38–60; and C. Haney and P. G. Zimbardo, "Social Roles and Role-Playing: Observations from the Stanford Prison Study," *Behavioral and Social Science Teacher* (January 1973), pp. 25–45.

26. S. A. Haslam and S. Reicher, "Stressing the Group: Social Identity and the Unfolding Dynamics of Responses to Stress," *Journal of Applied Psychology* 91, no. 5 (2006), pp. 1037–1052; S. Reicher and S. A. Haslam, "Rethinking the Psychology of Tyranny: The BBC Prison Study," *British Journal of Social Psychology* 45, no. 1 (2006), pp. 1–40; and P. G. Zimbardo, "On Rethinking the Psychology of Tyranny: The BBC Prison Study," *British Journal of Social Psychology* 45, no. 1 (2006), pp. 47–53.

27. For a review of the research on group norms, see J. R. Hackman, "Group Influences on Individuals in Organizations," in M. D. Dunnette and L. M. Hough (eds.), *Handbook of Industrial & Organizational Psychology,* 2nd ed., vol. 3 (Palo Alto, CA: Consulting Psychologists Press, 1992), pp. 235–250. For a more recent discussion, see M. G. Ehrhart and S. E. Naumann, "Organizational Citizenship Behavior in Work Groups: A Group Norms Approach," *Journal of Applied Psychology* (December 2004), pp. 960–974.

28. Adapted from P. S. Goodman, E. Ravlin, and M. Schminke, "Understanding Groups in Organizations," in L. L. Cummings and B. M. Staw (eds.), *Research in Organizational Behavior,* vol. 9 (Greenwich, CT: JAI Press, 1987), p. 159.

29. E. Mayo, *The Human Problems of an Industrial Civilization* (New York: Macmillan, 1933); and F. J. Roethlisberger and W. J. Dickson, *Management and the Worker* (Cambridge, MA: Harvard University Press, 1939).

30. C. A. Kiesler and S. B. Kiesler, *Conformity* (Reading, MA: Addison-Wesley, 1969); R. B. Cialdini and N. J. Goldstein, "Social Influence: Compliance and Conformity," *Annual Review of Psychology* 55 (2004), pp. 591–621.

31. S. E. Asch, "Effects of Group Pressure upon the Modification and Distortion of Judgments," in H. Guetzkow (ed.), *Groups, Leadership and Men* (Pittsburgh: Carnegie Press, 1951), pp. 177–190; and S. E. Asch, "Studies of Independence and Conformity: A Minority of One Against a Unanimous Majority," *Psychological Monographs: General and Applied* 70, no. 9 (1956), pp. 1–70.

32. R. Bond and P. B. Smith, "Culture and Conformity: A Meta-Analysis of Studies Using Asch's (1952, 1956) Line Judgment Task," *Psychological Bulletin* (January 1996), pp. 111–137.

33. See S. L. Robinson and A. M. O'Leary-Kelly, "Monkey See, Monkey Do: The Influence of Work Groups on the Antisocial Behavior of Employees," *Academy of Management Journal* (December 1998), pp. 658–672; R. J. Bennett and S. L. Robinson, "The Past, Present, and Future of Workplace Deviance," in J. Greenberg (ed.), *Organizational Behavior: The State of the Science,* 2nd ed. (Mahwah, NJ: Erlbaum, 2003), pp. 237–271; and C. M. Berry, D. S. Ones, and P. R. Sackett, "Interpersonal Deviance, Organizational Deviance, and Their Common Correlates: A Review and Meta-Analysis," *Journal of Applied Psychology* 92, no. 2 (2007), pp. 410–424.

34. C. M. Pearson, L. M. Andersson, and C. L. Porath, "Assessing and Attacking Workplace Civility," *Organizational Dynamics* 29, no. 2 (2000), p. 130; see also C. Pearson, L. M. Andersson, and C. L. Porath, "Workplace Incivility," in S. Fox and P. E. Spector (eds.), *Counterproductive Work Behavior: Investigations of Actors and Targets* (Washington, DC: American Psychological Association, 2005), pp. 177–200.

35. S. Lim, L. M. Cortina, V. J. Magley, "Personal and Workgroup Incivility: Impact on Work and Health Outcomes," *Journal of Applied Psychology* 93, no. 1 (2008), pp. 95–107.

36. Robinson and O'Leary-Kelly, "Monkey See, Monkey Do"; and T. M. Glomb and H. Liao, "Interpersonal Aggression in Workgroups: Social Influence, Reciprocal, and Individual Effects," *Academy of Management Journal* 46 (2003), pp. 486–496.

37. P. Bamberger and M. Biron, "Group Norms and Excessive Absenteeism: The Role of Peer Referent Others," *Organizational Behavior and Human Decision Processes* 103, no. 2 (2007), pp. 179–196; and A. Väänänen, N. Tordera, M. Kivimäki, A. Kouvonen, J. Pentti, A. Linna, and J. Vahtera, "The Role of Work Group in Individual Sickness Absence Behavior," *Journal of Health & Human Behavior* 49, no. 4 (2008), pp. 452–467.

38. M. S. Cole, F. Walter, and H. Bruch, "Affective Mechanisms Linking Dysfunctional Behavior to Performance in Work Teams: A Moderated Mediation Study," *Journal of Applied Psychology* 93, no. 5 (2008), pp. 945–958.

39. A. Erez, H. Elms, and E. Fong, "Lying, Cheating, Stealing: It Happens More in Groups," paper presented at the European Business Ethics Network Annual Conference, Budapest, Hungary, August 30, 2003.

40. S. L. Robinson and M. S. Kraatz, "Constructing the Reality of Normative Behavior: The Use of Neutralization Strategies by Organizational Deviants," in R. W. Griffin and A. O'Leary-Kelly (eds.), *Dysfunctional Behavior in Organizations: Violent and Deviant Behavior* (Greenwich, CT: JAI Press, 1998), pp. 203–220.

41. See J. Berger, M. H. Fisek, R. Z. Norman, and M. Zelditch, *Status Characteristics and Social Interaction: An Expected States Approach* (New York: Elsevier, 1977).

42. Cited in Hackman, "Group Influences on Individuals in Organizations," p. 236.

43. R. R. Callister and J. A. Wall Jr., "Conflict Across Organizational Boundaries: Managed Care Organizations Versus Health Care Providers," *Journal of Applied Psychology* 86, no. 4 (2001), pp. 754–763; and P. Chattopadhyay, W. H. Glick, and G. P. Huber, "Organizational Actions in Response to Threats and Opportunities," *Academy of Management Journal* 44, no. 5 (2001), pp. 937–955.

44. P. F. Hewlin, "Wearing the Cloak: Antecedents and Consequences of Creating Facades of Conformity," *Journal of Applied Psychology* 94, no. 3 (2009), pp. 727–741.

45. J. A. Wiggins, F. Dill, and R. D. Schwartz, "On 'Status-Liability,'" *Sociometry* (April–May 1965), pp. 197–209.

46. See J. M. Levine and R. L. Moreland, "Progress in Small Group Research," in J. T. Spence, J. M. Darley, and D. J. Foss (eds.), *Annual Review of Psychology*, vol. 41 (Palo Alto, CA: Annual Reviews, 1990), pp. 585–634; S. D. Silver, B. P. Cohen, and J. H. Crutchfield, "Status Differentiation and Information Exchange in Face-to-Face and Computer-Mediated Idea Generation," *Social Psychology Quarterly* (1994), pp. 108–123; and J. M. Twenge, "Changes in Women's Assertiveness in Response to Status and Roles: A Cross-Temporal Meta-Analysis, 1931–1993," *Journal of Personality and Social Psychology* (July 2001), pp. 133–145.

47. A. M. Christie and J. Barling, "Beyond Status: Relating Status Inequality to Performance and Health in Teams," *Journal of Applied Psychology* 95, no. 5 (2010), pp. 920–934; and L. H. Nishii and D. M. Mayer, "Do Inclusive Leaders Help to Reduce Turnover in Diverse Groups? The Moderating Role of Leader-Member Exchange in the Diversity to Turnover Relationship," *Journal of Applied Psychology* 94, no. 6 (2009), pp. 1412–1426.

48. V. Venkataramani, S. G. Green, and D. J. Schleicher, "Well-Connected Leaders: The Impact of Leaders' Social Network Ties on LMX and Members' Work Attitudes," *Journal of Applied Psychology* 95, no. 6 (2010), pp. 1071–1084.

49. See G. Hofstede, *Cultures and Organizations: Software of the Mind* (New York: McGraw-Hill, 1991).

50. This section is based on P. R. Harris and R. T. Moran, *Managing Cultural Differences*, 5th ed. (Houston: Gulf Publishing, 1999).

51. G. H. Seijts and G. P. Latham, "The Effects of Goal Setting and Group Size on Performance in a Social Dilemma," *Canadian Journal of Behavioural Science* 32, no. 2 (2000), pp. 104–116.

52. M. E. Shaw, *Group Dynamics: The Psychology of Small Group Behavior*, 3rd ed. (New York: McGraw-Hill, 1981).

53. See, for instance, D. R. Comer, "A Model of Social Loafing in Real Work Groups," *Human Relations* (June 1995), pp. 647–667; S. M. Murphy, S. J. Wayne, R. C. Liden, and B. Erdogan, "Understanding Social Loafing: The Role of Justice Perceptions and Exchange Relationships," *Human Relations* (January 2003), pp. 61–84; and R. C. Liden, S. J. Wayne, R. A. Jaworski, and N. Bennett, "Social Loafing: A Field Investigation," *Journal of Management* (April 2004), pp. 285–304.

54. W. Moede, "Die Richtlinien der Leistungs-Psychologie," *Industrielle Psychotechnik* 4 (1927), pp. 193–207. See also D. A. Kravitz and B. Martin, "Ringelmann Rediscovered: The Original Article," *Journal of Personality and Social Psychology* (May 1986), pp. 936–941.

55. See, for example, J. A. Shepperd, "Productivity Loss in Performance Groups: A Motivation Analysis," *Psychological Bulletin* (January 1993), pp. 67–81; and S. J. Karau and

K. D. Williams, "Social Loafing: A Meta-Analytic Review and Theoretical Integration," *Journal of Personality and Social Psychology* (October 1993), pp. 681–706.

56. S. G. Harkins and K. Szymanski, "Social Loafing and Group Evaluation," *Journal of Personality and Social Psychology* (December 1989), pp. 934–941.

57. A. Gunnthorsdottir and A. Rapoport, "Embedding Social Dilemmas in Intergroup Competition Reduces Free-Riding," *Organizational Behavior and Human Decision Processes* 101 (2006), pp. 184–199; and E. M. Stark, J. D. Shaw, and M. K. Duffy, "Preference for Group Work, Winning Orientation, and Social Loafing Behavior in Groups," *Group and Organization Management* 32, no. 6 (2007), pp. 699–723.

58. B. Mullen and C. Cooper, "The Relation Between Group Cohesiveness and Performance: An Integration," *Psychological Bulletin* (March 1994), pp. 210–227; P. M. Podsakoff, S. B. MacKenzie, and M. Ahearne, "Moderating Effects of Goal Acceptance on the Relationship Between Group Cohesiveness and Productivity," *Journal of Applied Psychology* (December 1997), pp. 974–983; and D. J. Beal, R. R. Cohen, M. J. Burke, and C. L. McLendon, "Cohesion and Performance in Groups: A Meta-Analytic Clarification of Construct Relations," *Journal of Applied Psychology* (December 2003), pp. 989–1004.

59. Ibid.

60. Based on J. L. Gibson, J. M. Ivancevich, and J. H. Donnelly Jr., *Organizations*, 8th ed. (Burr Ridge, IL: Irwin, 1994), p. 323.

61. D. S. Staples and L. Zhao, "The Effects of Cultural Diversity in Virtual Teams Versus Face-to-Face Teams," *Group Decision and Negotiation* (July 2006), pp. 389–406.

62. N. Chi, Y. Huang, and S. Lin, "A Double-Edged Sword? Exploring the Curvilinear Relationship Between Organizational Tenure Diversity and Team Innovation: The Moderating Role of Team-Oriented HR Practices," *Group and Organization Management* 34, no. 6 (2009), pp. 698–726.

63. K. J. Klein, A. P. Knight, J. C. Ziegert, B. C. Lim, and J. L. Saltz, "When Team Members' Values Differ: The Moderating Role of Team Leadership," *Organizational Behavior and Human Decision Processes* 114, no. 1 (2011), pp. 25–36; and G. Park and R. P. DeShon, "A Multilevel Model of Minority Opinion Expression and Team Decision-Making Effectiveness," *Journal of Applied Psychology* 95, no. 5 (2010), pp. 824–833.

64. M. Rigoglioso, "Diverse Backgrounds and Personalities Can Strengthen Groups," *Standford Knowledgebase*, (August 15, 2006), http://www.stanford.edu/group/knowledgebase/

65. K. W. Phillips and D. L. Loyd, "When Surface and Deep-Level Diversity Collide: The Effects on Dissenting Group Members," *Organizational Behavior and Human Decision Processes* 99 (2006), pp. 143–160; and S. R. Sommers, "On Racial Diversity and Group Decision Making: Identifying Multiple Effects of Racial Composition on Jury Deliberations," *Journal of Personality and Social Psychology* (April 2006), pp. 597–612.

66. E. Mannix and M. A. Neale, "What Differences Make a Difference? The Promise and Reality of Diverse Teams in Organizations," *Psychological Science in the Public Interest* (October 2005), pp. 31–55.

67. N. Foote, E. Matson, L. Weiss, and E. Wenger, "Leveraging Group Knowledge for High-Performance Decision-Making," *Organizational Dynamics* 31, no. 2 (2002), pp. 280–295.

68. See N. R. F. Maier, "Assets and Liabilities in Group Problem Solving: The Need for an Integrative Function," *Psychological*

Review (April 1967), pp. 239–249; G. W. Hill, "Group Versus Individual Performance: Are *N*+1 Heads Better Than One?" *Psychological Bulletin* (May 1982), pp. 517–539; M. D. Johnson and J. R. Hollenbeck, "Collective Wisdom as an Oxymoron: Team-Based Structures as Impediments to Learning," in J. Langan-Fox, C. L. Cooper, and R. J. Klimoski (eds), *Research Companion to the Dysfunctional Workplace: Management Challenges and Symptoms* (Northampton, MA: Edward Elgar Publishing, 2007), pp. 319–331; and R. F. Martell and M. R. Borg, "A Comparison of the Behavioral Rating Accuracy of Groups and Individuals," *Journal of Applied Psychology* (February 1993), pp. 43–50.

69. D. Gigone and R. Hastie, "Proper Analysis of the Accuracy of Group Judgments," *Psychological Bulletin* (January 1997), pp. 149–167; and B. L. Bonner, S. D. Sillito, and M. R. Baumann, "Collective Estimation: Accuracy, Expertise, and Extroversion as Sources of Intra-Group Influence," *Organizational Behavior and Human Decision Processes* 103 (2007), pp. 121–133.

70. See, for example, W. C. Swap and Associates, *Group Decision Making* (Newbury Park, CA: Sage, 1984).

71. I. L. Janis, *Groupthink* (Boston: Houghton Mifflin, 1982); W. Park, "A Review of Research on Groupthink," *Journal of Behavioral Decision Making* (July 1990), pp. 229–245; J. N. Choi and M. U. Kim, "The Organizational Application of Groupthink and Its Limits in Organizations," *Journal of Applied Psychology* (April 1999), pp. 297–306; and W. W. Park, "A Comprehensive Empirical Investigation of the Relationships Among Variables of the Groupthink Model," *Journal of Organizational Behavior* (December 2000), pp. 873–887.

72. Janis, *Groupthink*.

73. G. Park and R. P. DeShon, "A Multilevel Model of Minority Opinion Expression and Team Decision-Making Effectiveness," *Journal of Applied Psychology* 95, no. 5 (2010), pp. 824–833.

74. M. E. Turner and A. R. Pratkanis, "Mitigating Groupthink by Stimulating Constructive Conflict," in C. De Dreu and E. Van de Vliert (eds.), *Using Conflict in Organizations* (London: Sage, 1997), pp. 53–71.

75. J. A. Goncalo, E. Polman, and C. Maslach, "Can Confidence Come Too Soon? Collective Efficacy, Conflict, and Group Performance over Time," *Organizational Behavior and Human Decision Processes* 113, no. 1 (2010), pp. 13–24.

76. See N. R. F. Maier, *Principles of Human Relations* (New York: Wiley, 1952); I. L. Janis, *Groupthink: Psychological Studies of Policy Decisions and Fiascoes*, 2nd ed. (Boston: Houghton Mifflin, 1982); N. Richardson Ahlfinger and J. K. Esser, "Testing the Groupthink Model: Effects of Promotional Leadership and Conformity Predisposition," *Social Behavior & Personality* 29, no. 1 (2001), pp. 31–41; and S. Schultz-Hardt, F. C. Brodbeck, A. Mojzisch, R. Kerschreiter, and D. Frey, "Group Decision Making in Hidden Profile Situations: Dissent as a Facilitator for Decision Quality," *Journal of Personality and Social Psychology* 91, no. 6 (2006), pp. 1080–1093.

77. See D. J. Isenberg, "Group Polarization: A Critical Review and Meta-Analysis," *Journal of Personality and Social Psychology* (December 1986), pp. 1141–1151; J. L. Hale and F. J. Boster, "Comparing Effect Coded Models of Choice Shifts," *Communication Research Reports* (April 1988), pp. 180–186; and P. W. Paese, M. Bieser, and M. E. Tubbs, "Framing Effects and Choice Shifts in Group Decision Making,"

Organizational Behavior and Human Decision Processes (October 1993), pp. 149–165.

78. R. D. Clark III, "Group-Induced Shift Toward Risk: A Critical Appraisal," *Psychological Bulletin* (October 1971), pp. 251–270; M. Brauer and C. M. Judd, "Group Polarization and Repeated Attitude Expression: A New Take on an Old Topic," *European Review of Social Psychology* 7, (1996), pp. 173–207; and M. P. Brady and S. Y. Wu, "The Aggregation of Preferences in Groups: Identity, Responsibility, and Polarization," *Journal of Economic Psychology* 31, no. 6 (2010), pp. 950–963.

79. Z. Krizan and R. S. Baron, "Group Polarization and Choice-Dilemmas: How Important Is Self-Categorization?" *European Journal of Social Psychology* 37, no. 1 (2007), pp. 191–201.

80. A. F. Osborn, *Applied Imagination: Principles and Procedures of Creative Thinking*, 3rd ed. (New York: Scribner, 1963). See also R. P. McGlynn, D. McGurk, V. S. Effland, N. L. Johll, and D. J. Harding, "Brainstorming and Task Performance in Groups Constrained by Evidence," *Organizational Behavior and Human Decision Processes* (January 2004), pp. 75–87; and R. C. Litchfield, "Brainstorming Reconsidered: A Goal-Based View," *Academy of Management Review* 33, no. 3 (2008), pp. 649–668.

81. N. L. Kerr and R. S. Tindale, "Group Performance and Decision-Making," *Annual Review of Psychology* 55 (2004), pp. 623–655.

82. See A. L. Delbecq, A. H. Van deVen, and D. H. Gustafson, *Group Techniques for Program Planning: A Guide to Nominal and Delphi Processes* (Glenview, IL: Scott Foresman, 1975); and P. B. Paulus and H.-C. Yang, "Idea Generation in Groups: A Basis for Creativity in Organizations," *Organizational Behavior and Human Decision Processing* (May 2000), pp. 76–87.

83. C. Faure, "Beyond Brainstorming: Effects of Different Group Procedures on Selection of Ideas and Satisfaction with the Process," *Journal of Creative Behavior* 38 (2004), pp. 13–34.

84. See, for instance, A. B. Hollingshead and J. E. McGrath, "Computer-Assisted Groups: A Critical Review of the Empirical Research," in R. A. Guzzo and E. Salas (eds.), *Team Effectiveness and Decision Making in Organizations* (San Francisco: Jossey-Bass, 1995), pp. 46–78.

85. B. B. Baltes, M. W. Dickson, M. P. Sherman, C. C. Bauer, and J. LaGanke, "Computer-Mediated Communication and Group Decision Making: A Meta-Analysis," *Organizational Behavior and Human Decision Processes* (January 2002), pp. 156–179.

86. T. P. Verney, "Role Perception Congruence, Performance, and Satisfaction," in D. J. Vredenburgh and R. S. Schuler (eds.), *Effective Management: Research and Application*, Proceedings of the 20th Annual Eastern Academy of Management, Pittsburgh, PA (May 1983), pp. 24–27.

87. Ibid.

88. A. G. Bedeian and A. A. Armenakis, "A Path-Analytic Study of the Consequences of Role Conflict and Ambiguity," *Academy of Management Journal* (June 1981), pp. 417–424; and P. L. Perrewe, K. L. Zellars, G. R. Ferris, A. M. Rossi, C. J. Kacmar, and D. A. Ralston, "Neutralizing Job Stressors: Political Skill as an Antidote to the Dysfunctional Consequences of Role Conflict," *Academy of Management Journal* (February 2004), pp. 141–152.

89. Shaw, *Group Dynamics*.

90. B. Mullen, C. Symons, L. Hu, and E. Salas, "Group Size, Leadership Behavior, and Subordinate Satisfaction," *Journal of General Psychology* (April 1989), pp. 155–170.

KILLING BIN LADEN

The decision by the U.S. government on May 1, 2011, to send SEAL Team Six to hunt and capture or kill Osama bin Laden was, by all accounts, not an easy one. Appreciating the team dynamics of this decision helps us understand how teams make key decisions.

The decision of a government to deploy military force to capture or kill is obviously among the most serious, and often controversial, decisions leaders and teams can make. Keep in mind that our focus here is not on the merits of the decision, but on how the decision was made.

In 2010, U.S. intelligence identified and located a man whom captured al Qaeda operatives had named as Osama bin Laden's courier. After spending months tracking him and analyzing the compound in Pakistan, Central Intelligence Agency (CIA) analysts were convinced there was a "strong possibility" that bin Laden was also hiding there. At that point, Navy SEAL teams began training to take the compound. But no one knew for sure whether bin Laden was actually there.

The mission carried considerable risk. The members of the administration's national security team brought up past failed missions: the U.S. Army battle in Mogadishu, Somalia (depicted in the movie, *Black Hawk Down*), and the attempted rescue of U.S. hostages in Iran. "There wasn't a meeting when someone didn't mention 'Black Hawk Down,'" said one team member. The United States might be sending troops into hostile territory with no proof that the target of their efforts was even there. The president later said military commanders put the odds of a successful mission at 55–45.

Over the next 2 months, the administration's national security team met at least six times. Some members were against the operation, pending more definitive proof that bin Laden was actually there. None came. After a final meeting between the president and his national security team at 2 P.M. on Sunday, May 1, the 40 elite SEAL Team Six commandos departed in four helicopters from an undisclosed location in Afghanistan, the eastern border of which is about 120 miles west of bin Laden's compound. A White House photo shows Obama and his national security team anxiously watching as the mission played out on the situation room monitor. Obama is tieless and grim-faced, his eyes fixed on the screen. Hillary Clinton, holding a hand to her mouth, and Robert Gates, his arms folded across his chest, gaze at the same point. After the "minutes passed like days," the team received confirmation that the mission was over. "Geronimo"—the code name given bin Laden—was dead.

That many members of the decision-making team were willing to voice their reservations probably aided the decision-making process. President Obama later told *60 Minutes*: "The fact that there were some who voiced doubts about this approach was invaluable, because it meant the plan was

Understanding Work Teams

*We're going to turn this team around
360 degrees.* —Jason Kidd

Photo: Official White House photograph shows U.S. President Barack Obama, Vice President Joe Biden, US Secretary of Defense Robert Gates and US Secretary of State Hillary Clinton as they receive an update on the mission against Osama bin Laden. Source: Pete Souza/AFP/Getty Images/Newscom.

sharper, it meant that we had thought through all of our options, it meant that when I finally did make the decision, I was making it based on the very best information."

Sources: A. Kruglanski, "Obama's Choice and the Social Psychology of Group Decision Making," _Huffington Post_ (May 12, 2011), downloaded June 1, 2011, from www.huffingtonpost.com/; B. Steiden, "Bin Laden Dead," _The Atlanta Journal-Constitution_ (May 3, 2011), downloaded June 2, 2011, from www.ajc.com/; and M. Mazzetti, H. Cooper, and P. Baker, "Behind the Hunt for Bin Laden," _The New York Times_ (May 2, 2011), downloaded June 2, 2011, from www.nytimes.com/.

T eams are increasingly the primary means for organizing work in contemporary business firms. In fact, there are few more damaging insults than "not a team player." Do you think you're a team player? Take the following self-assessment to find out.

SELF-ASSESSMENT LIBRARY

How Good Am I at Building and Leading a Team?

In the Self-Assessment Library (available on CD or online), take assessment II.B.6 (How Good Am I at Building and Leading a Team?) and answer the following questions.

1. Did you score as high as you thought you would? Why or why not?
2. Do you think you can improve your score? If so, how? If not, why not?
3. Do you think there is such a thing as team players? If yes, what are their behaviors?

Why Have Teams Become So Popular?

1 Analyze the growing popularity of teams in organizations.

Decades ago, when companies such as W. L. Gore, Volvo, and General Foods introduced teams into their production processes, it made news because no one else was doing it. Today, it's just the opposite. The organization that _doesn't_ use teams has become newsworthy. Teams are everywhere.

How do we explain the current popularity of teams? As organizations have restructured themselves to compete more effectively and efficiently, they have turned to teams as a better way to use employee talents. Teams are more flexible and responsive to changing events than traditional departments or other forms of permanent groupings. They can quickly assemble, deploy, refocus, and disband. But don't overlook the motivational properties of teams. Consistent with our discussion in Chapter 7 of employee involvement as a motivator, teams facilitate employee participation in operating decisions. So another explanation for their popularity is that they are an effective means for management to democratize organizations and increase employee motivation.

The fact that organizations have turned to teams doesn't necessarily mean they're always effective. Decision makers, as humans, can be swayed by fads and herd mentality. Are teams truly effective? What conditions affect their potential? How do members work together? These are some of the questions we'll answer in this chapter.

Differences Between Groups and Teams

2 Contrast groups and teams.

Groups and teams are not the same thing. In this section, we define and clarify the difference between work groups and work teams.[1]

In Chapter 9, we defined a *group* as two or more individuals, interacting and interdependent, who have come together to achieve particular objectives. A **work group** is a group that interacts primarily to share information and make decisions to help each member perform within his or her area of responsibility.

Work groups have no need or opportunity to engage in collective work that requires joint effort. So their performance is merely the summation of each group member's individual contribution. There is no positive synergy that would create an overall level of performance greater than the sum of the inputs.

A **work team**, on the other hand, generates positive synergy through coordinated effort. The individual efforts result in a level of performance greater than the sum of those individual inputs. Exhibit 10-1 highlights the differences between work groups and work teams.

These definitions help clarify why so many organizations have recently restructured work processes around teams. Management is looking for positive synergy that will allow the organizations to increase performance. The extensive use of teams creates the *potential* for an organization to generate greater outputs with no increase in inputs. Notice, however, that we said *potential*. There is nothing inherently magical that ensures the achievement of positive synergy in the creation of teams. Merely calling a *group* a *team* doesn't automatically improve its performance. As we show later in this chapter, effective teams have certain common characteristics. If management hopes to gain increases in organizational performance through the use of teams, its teams must possess these.

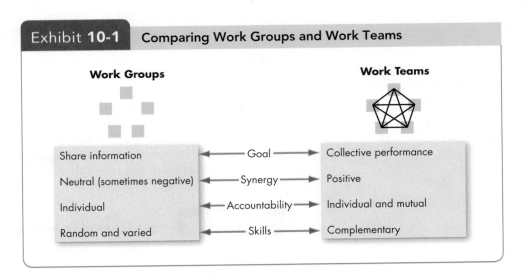

Exhibit 10-1   Comparing Work Groups and Work Teams

Work Groups		Work Teams
Share information	←— Goal —→	Collective performance
Neutral (sometimes negative)	←— Synergy —→	Positive
Individual	←— Accountability —→	Individual and mutual
Random and varied	←— Skills —→	Complementary

work group *A group that interacts primarily to share information and to make decisions to help each group member perform within his or her area of responsibility.*

work team *A group whose individual efforts result in performance that is greater than the sum of the individual inputs.*

Types of Teams

3   Compare and contrast four types of teams.

Teams can make products, provide services, negotiate deals, coordinate projects, offer advice, and make decisions.[2] In this section, we describe the four most common types of teams in an organization: *problem-solving teams, self-managed work teams, cross-functional teams,* and *virtual teams* (see Exhibit 10-2).

Problem-Solving Teams

In the past, teams were typically composed of 5 to 12 hourly employees from the same department who met for a few hours each week to discuss ways of improving quality, efficiency, and the work environment.[3] These **problem-solving teams** rarely have the authority to unilaterally implement any of their suggestions. Merrill Lynch created a problem-solving team to figure out ways to reduce the number of days it took to open a new cash management account.[4] By suggesting cutting the number of steps from 46 to 36, the team reduced the average number of days from 15 to 8.

Self-Managed Work Teams

Problem-solving teams only make recommendations. Some organizations have gone further and created teams that not only solve problems but implement solutions and take responsibility for outcomes.

Self-managed work teams are groups of employees (typically 10 to 15 in number) who perform highly related or interdependent jobs and take on many of the responsibilities of their former supervisors.[5] Typically, these tasks are planning and scheduling work, assigning tasks to members, making operating decisions, taking action on problems, and working with suppliers and customers. Fully self-managed work teams even select their own members and evaluate each other's performance. Supervisory positions take on decreased importance and are sometimes even eliminated.

But research on the effectiveness of self-managed work teams has not been uniformly positive.[6] Self-managed teams do not typically manage conflicts well. When disputes arise, members stop cooperating and power struggles ensue, which leads to lower group performance.[7] Moreover, although individuals on these teams report higher levels of job satisfaction than other individuals, they also sometimes have higher absenteeism and turnover rates. One large-scale study of labor productivity in British establishments found that although using teams in general does improve labor productivity, no evidence supported the

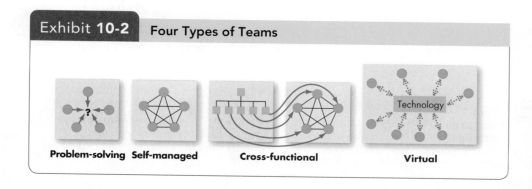

Exhibit 10-2   Four Types of Teams

Problem-solving   Self-managed   Cross-functional   Virtual

Sprig Toys, Inc. uses cross-functional teamwork in creating toys that are made of recycled products to keep the planet healthy and kids off the couch. The Sprig Dream Team includes toy designers and toy industry-specific expertise in the areas of product design, patent development, supply chain strategy, market research, vendor sourcing, merchandising, branding, packaging, and marketing. Team members are dedicated to Sprig's mission of creating fun toys that encourage active play for kids and are battery-free, eco-friendly, and paint-free. Shown here with some Sprig toys are chief executive Craig Storey (standing, left) and the firm's co-founders.

Source: AP Photo/The Coloradoan, V. Richard Haro.

claim that self-managed teams performed better than traditional teams with less decision-making authority.[8]

Cross-Functional Teams

Starbucks created a team of individuals from production, global PR, global communications, and U.S. marketing to develop its Via brand of instant coffee. The team's suggestions resulted in a product that would be cost-effective to produce and distribute and that was marketed through a tightly integrated, multifaceted strategy.[9] This example illustrates the use of **cross-functional teams**, made up of employees from about the same hierarchical level but different work areas, who come together to accomplish a task.

Many organizations have used horizontal, boundary-spanning groups for decades. In the 1960s, IBM created a large task force of employees from across departments to develop its highly successful System 360. Today cross-functional teams are so widely used it is hard to imagine a major organizational undertaking without one. All the major automobile manufacturers—Toyota, Honda, Nissan, BMW, GM, Ford, and Chrysler—currently use this form of team to coordinate complex projects. Cisco relies on specific cross-functional teams to identify and capitalize on new trends in several areas of the software market. The teams are the equivalent of social-networking groups that collaborate in real time to identify new business opportunities in the field and then implement them from the bottom up.[10]

problem-solving teams *Groups of 5 to 12 employees from the same department who meet for a few hours each week to discuss ways of improving quality, efficiency, and the work environment.*

self-managed work teams *Groups of 10 to 15 people who take on responsibilities of their former supervisors.*

cross-functional teams *Employees from about the same hierarchical level, but from different work areas, who come together to accomplish a task.*

Cross-functional teams are an effective means of allowing people from diverse areas within or even between organizations to exchange information, develop new ideas, solve problems, and coordinate complex projects. Of course, cross-functional teams are no picnic to manage. Their early stages of development are often long, as members learn to work with diversity and complexity. It takes time to build trust and teamwork, especially among people from different backgrounds with different experiences and perspectives.

Virtual Teams

The teams described in the preceding section do their work face to face. **Virtual teams** use computer technology to unite physically dispersed members and achieve a common goal.[11] They collaborate online—using communication links such as wide-area networks, videoconferencing, or e-mail—whether they're a room away or continents apart. Virtual teams are so pervasive, and technology has advanced so far, that it's probably a bit of a misnomer to call them "virtual." Nearly all teams today do at least some of their work remotely.

Despite their ubiquity, virtual teams face special challenges. They may suffer because there is less social rapport and direct interaction among members. Evidence from 94 studies entailing more than 5,000 groups found that virtual teams are better at sharing unique information (information held by individual members but not the entire group), but they tend to share less information overall.[12] As a result, low levels of virtuality in teams results in higher levels of information sharing, but high levels of virtuality hinder it. For virtual teams to be effective, management should ensure that (1) trust is established among members (one inflammatory remark in an e-mail can severely undermine team trust), (2) team progress is monitored closely (so the team doesn't lose sight of its goals and no team member "disappears"), and (3) the efforts and products of the team are publicized throughout the organization (so the team does not become invisible).[13]

Creating Effective Teams

4 Identify the characteristics of effective teams.

Many have tried to identify factors related to team effectiveness.[14] However, some studies have organized what was once a "veritable laundry list of characteristics"[15] into a relatively focused model.[16] Exhibit 10-3 summarizes what we currently know about what makes teams effective. As you'll see, it builds on many of the group concepts introduced in Chapter 9.

The following discussion is based on the model in Exhibit 10-3. Keep in mind two points. First, teams differ in form and structure. The model attempts to generalize across all varieties of teams, but avoid rigidly applying its predictions to all teams.[17] Use it as a guide. Second, the model assumes teamwork is preferable to individual work. Creating "effective" teams when individuals can do the job better is like perfectly solving the wrong problem.

We can organize the key components of effective teams into three general categories. First are the resources and other *contextual* influences that make teams effective. The second relates to the team's *composition*. Finally, *process* variables are events within the team that influence effectiveness. What does *team effectiveness* mean in this model? Typically, it has included objective measures of the team's productivity, managers' ratings of the team's performance, and aggregate measures of member satisfaction.

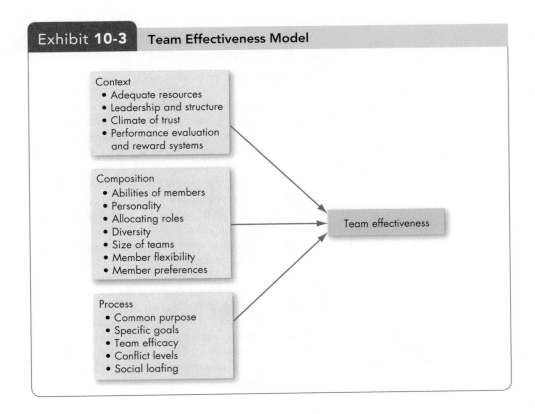

Exhibit 10-3   **Team Effectiveness Model**

Context
- Adequate resources
- Leadership and structure
- Climate of trust
- Performance evaluation and reward systems

Composition
- Abilities of members
- Personality
- Allocating roles
- Diversity
- Size of teams
- Member flexibility
- Member preferences

Process
- Common purpose
- Specific goals
- Team efficacy
- Conflict levels
- Social loafing

Team effectiveness

Context: What Factors Determine Whether Teams Are Successful

The four contextual factors most significantly related to team performance are adequate resources, effective leadership, a climate of trust, and a performance evaluation and reward system that reflects team contributions.

Adequate Resources   Teams are part of a larger organization system; every work team relies on resources outside the group to sustain it. A scarcity of resources directly reduces the ability of a team to perform its job effectively and achieve its goals. As one study concluded, after looking at 13 factors related to group performance, "perhaps one of the most important characteristics of an effective work group is the support the group receives from the organization."[18] This support includes timely information, proper equipment, adequate staffing, encouragement, and administrative assistance.

Leadership and Structure   Teams can't function if they can't agree on who is to do what and ensure all members share the workload. Agreeing on the specifics of work and how they fit together to integrate individual skills requires leadership and structure, either from management or from the team members themselves. It's true in self-managed teams that team members absorb many of the

virtual teams   *Teams that use computer technology to tie together physically dispersed members in order to achieve a common goal.*

glOBalization!

Group Cohesiveness across Cultures

As you might suspect, researchers have paid a great deal of attention to the differences between individualists and collectivists in terms of team orientation. As we learned from Chapter 5 on personality and values, people from collectivist societies—like those found in much of East Asia, Latin America, and Africa—are generally more prone to look toward group goals as important and to emphasize collaborative processes. Individualist cultures like the United States, Canada, and the UK, on the other hand, emphasize individual achievement and performance.

Individualist cultures may have greater difficulty implementing team-based work processes for a variety of reasons. Collectivists appear more sensitive to the moods of their coworkers, so the motivation and positive mood of one group member is likely to spill over to increase motivation and positive moods in others. Collectivist teams also already have a strong predisposition to work together as a group, so there's less need for increased teamwork. Other research suggests that collectively oriented teams are better able to pool resources and correct one another's errors than are individually oriented teams.

What's the lesson for managers? Managers in individualist cultures may need to work harder to increase team cohesiveness. One way to do this is to give teams more challenging assignments and provide them with more independence. Alternatively, managers may find it useful to promote a collectivist orientation for team processes even when working with groups of individualists.

Sources: Based on R. Ilies, D. T. Wagner, and F. P. Morgeson, "Explaining Affective Linkages in Teams: Individual Differences in Susceptibility to Contagion and Individualism-Collectivism," _Journal of Applied Psychology_ 92, no. 4 (2007), pp. 1140–1148; E. C. Dierdorff, S. T. Bell, and J. A. Belohlav, "The Power of 'We': Effects of Psychological Collectivism on Team Performance Over Time," _Journal of Applied Psychology_ 96, no. 2 (2011), pp. 247–262; and J. E. Driskell, E. Salas, and S. Hughes, "Collective Orientation and Team Performance: Development of an Individual Differences Measure," _Human Factors_ 52, no. 2 (2010), pp. 316–328.

duties typically assumed by managers. However, a manager's job then becomes managing *outside* (rather than inside) the team.

Leadership is especially important in **multiteam systems**, in which different teams coordinate their efforts to produce a desired outcome. Here, leaders need to empower teams by delegating responsibility to them, and they play the role of facilitator, making sure the teams work together rather than against one another.[19] Teams that establish shared leadership by effectively delegating it are more effective than teams with a traditional single-leader structure.[20]

Climate of Trust   Members of effective teams trust each other. They also exhibit trust in their leaders.[21] Interpersonal trust among team members facilitates cooperation, reduces the need to monitor each others' behavior, and bonds members around the belief that others on the team won't take advantage of them. Team members are more likely to take risks and expose vulnerabilities when they believe they can trust others on their team. And, as we will discuss in Chapter 12, trust is the foundation of leadership. It allows a team to accept and commit to its leader's goals and decisions.

Performance Evaluation and Reward Systems   How do you get team members to be both individually and jointly accountable? Individual performance evaluations and incentives may interfere with the development of high-performance teams. So, in addition to evaluating and rewarding employees for their individual contributions, management should modify the traditional, individually oriented evaluation and reward system to reflect team performance and focus on hybrid systems that recognize individual members for their exceptional

Using Global Virtual Teams as an Environmental Choice

Many teams in geographically dispersed organizations have turned to electronic media to improve communication across locations. However, there may be an equally strong *ethical* argument for using global virtual teams: it may be a more environmentally responsible choice than having team members travel internationally when they need to communicate. A very large proportion of airline, rail, and car transport is for business purposes and contributes greatly to global carbon dioxide emissions. When teams are able to meet virtually rather than face-to-face, they dramatically reduce the amount of energy consumed.

In a globally connected world, what sorts of actions might you take to minimize your organization's environmental impact from business travel? Several tips might help to get you started thinking about ways that global virtual teams can be harnessed for greater sustainability:

1. Encourage all team members to think about whether a face-to-face meeting is really necessary, and to try to utilize alternative communication methods whenever possible.
2. Communicate as much information as possible through virtual means, including e-mail, telephone calls, and teleconferencing.
3. When traveling to team meetings, choose the most environmentally responsible methods possible, such as flying in coach rather than business class. Also, check the environmental profile of hotels prior to booking rooms.
4. Make the business case for sustainable business travel alternatives. Most experts agree that teleconferencing and environmentally responsible travel arrangements not only help the environment but are more cost-effective as well.

Sources: P. Tilstone, "Cut Carbon... and Bills," *Director* (May 2009), p. 54; and L. C. Latimer, "6 Strategies for Sustainable Business Travel," *Greenbiz* (February 11, 2011), www.greenbiz.com.

contributions and reward the entire group for positive outcomes.[22] Group-based appraisals, profit sharing, gainsharing, small-group incentives, and other system modifications can reinforce team effort and commitment.

Team Composition

The team composition category includes variables that relate to how teams should be staffed—the ability and personality of team members, allocation of roles and diversity, size of the team, and members' preference for teamwork.

Abilities of Members   Part of a team's performance depends on the knowledge, skills, and abilities of its individual members.[23] It's true we occasionally read about an athletic team of mediocre players who, because of excellent coaching, determination, and precision teamwork, beat a far more talented group. But such cases make the news precisely because they are unusual. A team's performance is not merely the summation of its individual members' abilities. However, these abilities set limits on what members can do and how effectively they will perform on a team.

Research reveals some insights into team composition and performance. First, when the task entails considerable thought (solving a complex problem

multiteam systems   *Systems in which different teams need to coordinate their efforts to produce a desired outcome.*

such as reengineering an assembly line), high-ability teams—composed of mostly intelligent members—do better than lower-ability teams, especially when the workload is distributed evenly. That way, team performance does not depend on the weakest link. High-ability teams are also more adaptable to changing situations; they can more effectively apply existing knowledge to new problems.

Finally, the ability of the team's leader also matters. Smart team leaders help less-intelligent team members when they struggle with a task. But a less intelligent leader can neutralize the effect of a high-ability team.[24]

Personality of Members   We demonstrated in Chapter 5 that personality significantly influences individual employee behavior. Many of the dimensions identified in the Big Five personality model are also relevant to team effectiveness; a review of the literature identified three.[25] Specifically, teams that rate higher on mean levels of conscientiousness and openness to experience tend to perform better, and the minimum level of team member agreeableness also matters: teams did worse when they had one or more highly disagreeable members. Perhaps one bad apple *can* spoil the whole bunch!

Research has also provided us with a good idea about why these personality traits are important to teams. Conscientious people are good at backing up other team members, and they're also good at sensing when their support is truly needed. One study found that specific behavioral tendencies such as personal organization, cognitive structuring, achievement orientation, and endurance were all related to higher levels of team performance.[26] Open team members communicate better with one another and throw out more ideas, which makes teams composed of open people more creative and innovative.[27]

Suppose an organization needs to create 20 teams of 4 people each and has 40 highly conscientious people and 40 who score low on conscientiousness. Would the organization be better off (1) forming 10 teams of highly conscientious people and 10 teams of members low on conscientiousness, or

British Chief Inspector of Nuclear Installations Mike Weightman is the leader of an 18-member global team created by the International Atomic Energy Commission to study the Fukushima nuclear power station accident triggered by the 2011 earthquake in Japan. This high-ability team with members from 12 countries includes experts with experience across a wide range of nuclear specialties. Team members apply their technical expertise, problem-solving and decision-making skills, and interpersonal skills to their mission of identifying lessons learned from the accident that can help improve nuclear safety around the world. In this photo, Weightman (left) shakes hands with the Fukushima plant chief after the team inspected the crippled nuclear power plant.

Source: HO/AFP/Getty Images/Newscom.

(2) "seeding" each team with 2 people who scored high and 2 who scored low on conscientiousness? Perhaps surprisingly, evidence suggests option 1 is the best choice; performance across the teams will be higher if the organization forms 10 highly conscientious teams and 10 teams low in conscientiousness.[28]

Allocation of Roles   Teams have different needs, and members should be selected to ensure all the various roles are filled. A study of 778 major league baseball teams over a 21-year period highlights the importance of assigning roles appropriately.[29] As you might expect, teams with more experienced and skilled members performed better. However, the experience and skill of those in core roles who handle more of the workflow of the team, and who are central to all work processes (in this case, pitchers and catchers), were especially vital. In other words, put your most able, experienced, and conscientious workers in the most central roles in a team.

We can identify nine potential team roles (see Exhibit 10-4). Successful work teams have selected people to play all these roles based on their skills and preferences.[30] (On many teams, individuals will play multiple roles.) To increase the likelihood the team members will work well together, managers need to understand the individual strengths each person can bring to a team, select members with their strengths in mind, and allocate work assignments that fit with members' preferred styles.

Diversity of Members   In Chapter 9, we discussed research on the effect of diversity on groups. How does *team* diversity affect *team* performance? The degree to which members of a work unit (group, team, or department) share a common demographic attribute, such as age, sex, race, educational level, or

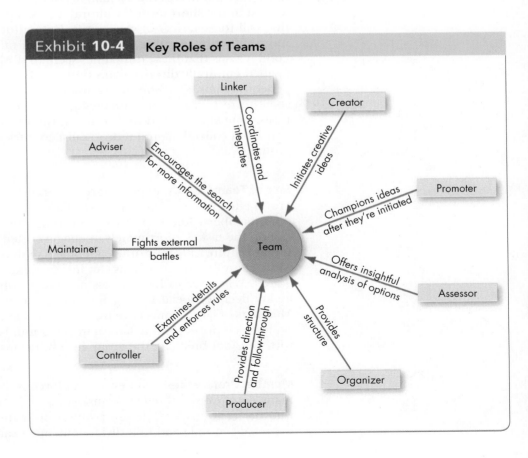

Exhibit 10-4   Key Roles of Teams

length of service in the organization, is the subject of **organizational demography**. Organizational demography suggests that attributes such as age or the date of joining should help us predict turnover. The logic goes like this: turnover will be greater among those with dissimilar experiences because communication is more difficult and conflict is more likely. Increased conflict makes membership less attractive, so employees are more likely to quit. Similarly, the losers in a power struggle are more apt to leave voluntarily or be forced out.[31]

Many of us hold the optimistic view that diversity should be a good thing—diverse teams should benefit from differing perspectives. Two meta-analytic reviews of the research literature show, however, that demographic diversity is essentially unrelated to team performance overall, while a third actually suggests that race and gender diversity are negatively related to team performance.[32] One qualifier is that gender and ethnic diversity have more negative effects in occupations dominated by white or male employees, but in more demographically balanced occupations, diversity is less of a problem. Diversity in function, education, and expertise are positively related to group performance, but these effects are quite small and depend on the situation.

Proper leadership can also improve the performance of diverse teams.[33] When leaders provide an inspirational common goal for members with varying types of education and knowledge, teams are very creative. When leaders don't provide such goals, diverse teams fail to take advantage of their unique skills and are actually *less* creative than teams with homogeneous skills. Even teams with diverse values can perform effectively, however, if leaders provide a focus on work tasks rather than leading based on personal relationships.

We have discussed research on team diversity in race or gender. But what about diversity created by national differences? Like the earlier research, evidence here indicates these elements of diversity interfere with team processes, at least in the short term.[34] Cultural diversity does seem to be an asset for tasks that call for a variety of viewpoints. But culturally heterogeneous teams have more difficulty learning to work with each other and solving problems. The good news is that these difficulties seem to dissipate with time. Although newly formed culturally diverse teams underperform newly formed culturally homogeneous teams, the differences disappear after about 3 months.[35] Fortunately, some team performance-enhancing strategies seem to work well in many cultures. One study found that teams in the European Union made up of members from collectivist and individualist countries benefited equally from having group goals.[36]

Size of Teams   Most experts agree, keeping teams small is a key to improving group effectiveness.[37] Generally speaking, the most effective teams have five to nine members. And experts suggest using the smallest number of people who can do the task. Unfortunately, managers often err by making teams too large. It may require only four or five members to develop diversity of views and skills, while coordination problems can increase exponentially as team members are added. When teams have excess members, cohesiveness and mutual accountability decline, social loafing increases, and more people communicate less. Members of large teams have trouble coordinating with one another, especially under time pressure. If a natural working unit is larger and you want a team effort, consider breaking the group into subteams.[38]

Member Preferences   Not every employee is a team player. Given the option, many employees will select themselves *out* of team participation. When people who prefer to work alone are required to team up, there is a direct threat to the team's morale and to individual member satisfaction.[39] This result suggests

Members of Wells Fargo's ethnography teams are diversified in function and expertise. Working in the bank's strategic account-management group, team members possess a variety of banking experiences and skills in treasury management, investments, credit cards, and relationship management. The teams visit clients to interview their key managers and observe how employees perform various financial workflows such as payroll and accounts payable. From these studies, the ethnography teams help clients improve their work processes and use of technology. Wells Fargo benefits by gaining a deeper understanding of customer needs and improving customer responsiveness.

Source: Cindy Charles / PhotoEdit

that, when selecting team members, managers should consider individual preferences along with abilities, personalities, and skills. High-performing teams are likely to be composed of people who prefer working as part of a group.

Team Processes

The final category related to team effectiveness is process variables such as member commitment to a common purpose, establishment of specific team goals, team efficacy, a managed level of conflict, and minimized social loafing. These will be especially important in larger teams and in teams that are highly interdependent.[40]

Why are processes important to team effectiveness? Let's return to the topic of social loafing. We found that $1 + 1 + 1$ doesn't necessarily add up to 3. When each member's contribution is not clearly visible, individuals tend to decrease their effort. Social loafing, in other words, illustrates a process loss from using teams. But teams should create outputs greater than the sum of their inputs, as when a diverse group develops creative alternatives. Exhibit 10-5 illustrates how group processes can have an impact on a group's actual effectiveness.[41] Teams are often used in research laboratories because they can draw on the diverse skills of various individuals to produce more meaningful research than researchers working independently—that is, they produce positive synergy, and their process gains exceed their process losses.

Common Plan and Purpose   Effective teams begin by analyzing the team's mission, developing goals to achieve that mission, and creating strategies for

organizational demography   *The degree to which members of a work unit share a common demographic attribute, such as age, sex, race, educational level, or length of service in an organization, and the impact of this attribute on turnover.*

"Teams Work Best Under Angry Leaders"

This statement is false as a general rule. However, there *are* situations when teams perform their best when their leader is angry.

If you have ever seen an episode of one of celebrity chef Gordon Ramsay's reality television shows (*Hell's Kitchen, The F Word, Kitchen Nightmares*)—where Ramsay regularly terrorizes culinary teams with outbursts, threats, and intimidation—you have seen how angry leaders motivate. But does this approach really get results? Many of us would be skeptical. A harsh, temperamental approach to leading teams would seem to be reliably counterproductive. Who would want to work for such a leader?

As it turns out, the angry team leader may, in fact, have his or her place. A recent study found that whereas teams filled with relatively agreeable members were the most motivated and performed the best when their leader showed happiness, teams filled with relatively disagreeable members were the most motivated and did best when their leader expressed anger.

Why do disagreeable teams do their best when their leader is angry? If you recall our discussion of agreeableness in Chapter 5, disagreeable individuals are more direct, more argumentative, and less conflict-averse than their more agreeable counterparts. Disagreeable teams may react better to an angry leader because the leader is speaking a language the team can understand, or the disagreeable team members may be less sensitive to inconsiderate behavior (of which the display of anger is a prime example).

Asked to reflect on his angry approach to leading teams, Ramsay said, "When there's no adrenaline flying high and there's very little pressure created, you don't get results." For some types of teams (those filled with team members as disagreeable as their leader), it appears he is right. Tough love seems to work best with tough teams.

Sources: G. A. Van Kleef, A. C. Homan, B. Beersma, and D. van Knippenberg, "On Angry Leaders and Agreeable Followers: How Leaders' Emotions and Followers' Personalities Shape Motivation and Team Performance," *Psychological Science* 21, no. 12 (2010), pp. 1827–1834; G. A. Van Kleef, A. C. Homan, B. Beersma, D. van Knippenberg, B. van Knippenberg, and F. Damen, "Searing Sentiment or Cold Calculation? The Effects of Leader Emotional Displays on Team Performance Depend on Follower Epistemic Motivation," *Academy of Management Journal* 52, no. 3 (2009), pp. 562–580; and S. Lyall, "The Terrible-Tempered Star Chef of London," *The New York Times* (February 23, 2005), downloaded June 3, 2011, from http://select.nytimes.com/.

achieving the goals. Teams that consistently perform better have established a clear sense of what needs to be done and how.[42]

Members of successful teams put a tremendous amount of time and effort into discussing, shaping, and agreeing on a purpose that belongs to them both collectively and individually. This common purpose, when accepted by the team, becomes what celestial navigation is to a ship captain: it provides direction and guidance under any and all conditions. Like a ship following the wrong course, teams that don't have good planning skills are doomed; perfectly executing the wrong plan is a lost cause.[43] Teams should also agree on whether their goal is to learn about and master a task or simply to perform the task; evidence suggest that different perspectives on learning versus performance goals lead to lower levels of team performance overall.[44] It appears that these differences in goal orientation have their effects by reducing discussion and sharing

Exhibit 10-5   Effects of Group Processes

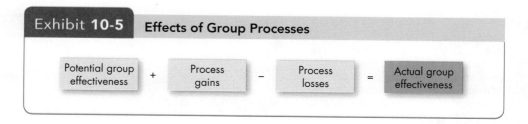

Team members of NASCAR race car driver Danica Patrick's pit crew shown here work toward the common goal of winning the race. Providing direction, momentum, and commitment, the pit crew's plan is to function at top speed with no errors in checking the car, fixing parts, changing tires, and pumping gas. Each member of the pit crew has a specific job and a clear sense of what needs to be done. And each member continuously fine-tunes his job to shave time off the pit stops, which are so important because they may win or lose a race.

Source: Brandon Wade/MCT/Newscom.

of information. In sum, having all employees on a team strive for the same *type* of goal is important.

Effective teams also show **reflexivity**, meaning they reflect on and adjust their master plan when necessary. A team has to have a good plan, but it also has to be willing and able to adapt when conditions call for it.[45] Interestingly, some evidence does suggest that teams high in reflexivity are better able to adapt to conflicting plans and goals among team members.[46]

Specific Goals   Successful teams translate their common purpose into specific, measurable, and realistic performance goals. Specific goals facilitate clear communication. They also help teams maintain their focus on getting results.

Consistent with the research on individual goals, team goals should also be challenging. Difficult but achievable goals raise team performance on those criteria for which they're set. So, for instance, goals for quantity tend to raise quantity, goals for accuracy raise accuracy, and so on.[47]

Team Efficacy   Effective teams have confidence in themselves; they believe they can succeed. We call this *team efficacy*.[48] Teams that have been successful raise their beliefs about future success, which, in turn, motivates them to work harder. What can management do to increase team efficacy? Two options are helping the team achieve small successes that build confidence and providing training to improve members' technical and interpersonal skills. The greater the abilities of team members, the more likely the team will develop confidence and the ability to deliver on that confidence.

Mental Models   Effective teams share accurate **mental models**—organized mental representations of the key elements within a team's environment that team members share.[49] If team members have the wrong mental models, which is particularly likely with teams under acute stress, their performance suffers.[50]

reflexivity   *A team characteristic of reflecting on and adjusting the master plan when necessary.*

mental models   *Team members' knowledge and beliefs about how the work gets done by the team.*

In the Iraq War, for instance, many military leaders said they underestimated the power of the insurgency and the infighting among Iraqi religious sects. The similarity of team members' mental models matters, too. If team members have different ideas about how to do things, the team will fight over methods rather than focus on what needs to be done.[51] One review of 65 independent studies of team cognition found that teams with shared mental models engaged in more frequent interactions with one another, were more motivated, had more positive attitudes toward their work, and had higher levels of objectively rated performance.[52]

Conflict Levels   Conflict on a team isn't necessarily bad. As we discuss in Chapter 15, conflict has a complex relationship with team performance. Relationship conflicts—those based on interpersonal incompatibilities, tension, and animosity toward others—are almost always dysfunctional. However, when teams are performing nonroutine activities, disagreements about task content (called *task conflicts*) stimulate discussion, promote critical assessment of problems and options, and can lead to better team decisions. A study conducted in China found that moderate levels of task conflict during the initial phases of team performance were positively related to team creativity, but both very low and very high levels of task conflict were negatively related to team performance.[53] In other words, both too much and too little disagreement about how a team should initially perform a creative task can inhibit performance.

The way conflicts are resolved can also make the difference between effective and ineffective teams. A study of ongoing comments made by 37 autonomous work groups showed that effective teams resolved conflicts by explicitly discussing the issues, whereas ineffective teams had conflicts focused more on personalities and the way things were said.[54]

Social Loafing   As we noted earlier, individuals can engage in social loafing and coast on the group's effort because their particular contributions can't be identified. Effective teams undermine this tendency by making members individually and jointly accountable for the team's purpose, goals, and approach.[55] Therefore, members should be clear on what they are individually responsible for and what they are jointly responsible for on the team.

SELF-ASSESSMENT LIBRARY

What Is My Team Efficacy?

In the Self-Assessment Library (available on CD or online), take assessment IV.E.2 (What Is My Team Efficacy?).

Turning Individuals into Team Players

5   Show how organizations can create team players.

We've made a strong case for the value and growing popularity of teams. But many people are not inherently team players, and many organizations have historically nurtured individual accomplishments. Finally, teams fit well in countries that score high on collectivism. But what if an organization wants

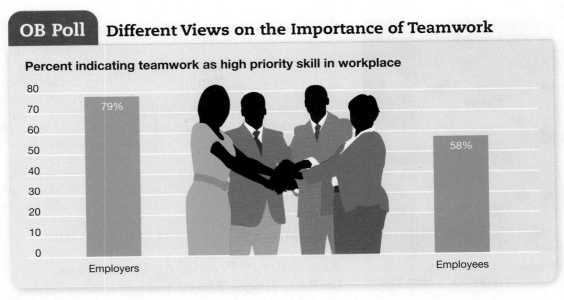

OB Poll | **Different Views on the Importance of Teamwork**

Percent indicating teamwork as high priority skill in workplace

Employers 79%
Employees 58%

Source: Based on "New Study Sheds Light on Chicago's Employment Landscape," PR Newswire (May 4, 2011). Reprinted with permission from The Gallup Organization.

to introduce teams into a work population of individuals born and raised in an individualistic society? A veteran employee of a large company, who had done well working in an individualistic company in an individualist country, described the experience of joining a team: "I'm learning my lesson. I just had my first negative performance appraisal in 20 years."[56]

So what can organizations do to enhance team effectiveness—to turn individual contributors into team members? Here are options for managers trying to turn individuals into team players.

Selecting: Hiring Team Players

Some people already possess the interpersonal skills to be effective team players. When hiring team members, be sure candidates can fulfill their team roles as well as technical requirements.[57]

When faced with job candidates who lack team skills, managers have three options. First, don't hire them. If you have to hire them, assign them to tasks or positions that don't require teamwork. If that is not feasible, the candidates can undergo training to make them into team players. In established organizations that decide to redesign jobs around teams, some employees will resist being team players and may be untrainable. Unfortunately, they typically become casualties of the team approach.

Creating teams often means resisting the urge to hire the best talent no matter what. The Los Angeles Galaxy professional soccer team paid enormously for British star David Beckham's talents, seemingly without considering whether he was a team player.[58] The result was low levels of coordination and cooperation with the team. Personal traits also appear to make some people better candidates for working in diverse teams. Teams made up of members who like to work through difficult mental puzzles also seem more effective and capitalizing on the multiple points of view that arise from diversity in age and education.[59]

Employees of Cigna, a global health services corporation, learn how to become team players by participating in WhirlyBall competitions. Organizations like Cigna use the team sport as a team-building exercise in which two teams maneuver WhirlyBugs on a court while using scoops to toss a ball back and forth among team members in trying to score a goal. WhirlyBall is one of many team-building activities that employees participate in to build their teamwork skills and experience the satisfaction that teamwork can provide.

MyManagementLab

For an interactive application of this topic, check out this chapter's simulation activity at **www.pearsonglobaleditions.com/ mymanagementlab.**

Training: Creating Team Players

Training specialists conduct exercises that allow employees to experience the satisfaction teamwork can provide. Workshops help employees improve their problem-solving, communication, negotiation, conflict-management, and coaching skills. L'Oréal, for example, found that successful sales teams required much more than being staffed with high-ability salespeople: management had to focus much of its efforts on team building. "What we didn't account for was that many members of our top team in sales had been promoted because they had excellent technical and executional skills," said L'Oréal's senior VP of sales, David Waldock. As a result of the focus on team training, Waldock says, "We are no longer a team just on paper, working independently. We have a real group dynamic now, and it's a good one."[60] Employees also learn the five-stage group development model described in Chapter 9. Developing an effective team doesn't happen overnight—it takes time.

Rewarding: Providing Incentives to Be a Good Team Player

An organization's reward system must be reworked to encourage cooperative efforts rather than competitive ones.[61] Hallmark Cards Inc. added to its basic individual-incentive system an annual bonus based on achievement of team goals. Whole Foods directs most of its performance-based rewards toward team performance. As a result, teams select new members carefully so they will contribute to team effectiveness (and thus team bonuses).[62] It is usually best to set a cooperative tone as soon as possible in the life of a team. As we already noted, teams that switch from a competitive to a cooperative system do not immediately share information, and they still tend to make rushed, poor-quality decisions.[63] Apparently, the low trust typical of the competitive group will not be readily replaced by high trust with a quick change in reward systems. These problems are not seen in teams that have consistently cooperative systems.

Promotions, pay raises, and other forms of recognition should be given to individuals who work effectively as team members by training new colleagues, sharing information, helping resolve team conflicts, and mastering needed new skills. This doesn't mean individual contributions should be ignored; rather, they should be balanced with selfless contributions to the team.

Finally, don't forget the intrinsic rewards, such as camaraderie, that employees can receive from teamwork. It's exciting and satisfying to be part of a successful team. The opportunity for personal development of self and teammates can be a very satisfying and rewarding experience.

Beware! Teams Aren't Always the Answer

6 Decide when to use individuals instead of teams.

Teamwork takes more time and often more resources than individual work. Teams have increased communication demands, conflicts to manage, and meetings to run. So, the benefits of using teams have to exceed the costs, and that's not always the case.[64] Before you rush to implement teams, carefully assess whether the work requires or will benefit from a collective effort.

How do you know whether the work of your group would be better done in teams? You can apply three tests.[65] First, can the work be done better by more than one person? A good indicator is the complexity of the work and the need for different perspectives. Simple tasks that don't require diverse input are probably better left to individuals. Second, does the work create a common purpose or set of goals for the people in the group that is more than the aggregate of individual goals? Many service departments of new-vehicle dealers have introduced teams that link customer-service people, mechanics, parts specialists, and sales representatives. Such teams can better manage collective responsibility for ensuring customer needs are properly met.

The final test is to determine whether the members of the group are interdependent. Using teams makes sense when there is interdependence among tasks—the success of the whole depends on the success of each one, *and* the success of each one depends on the success of the others. Soccer, for instance, is an obvious *team* sport. Success requires a great deal of coordination between interdependent players. Conversely, except possibly for relays, swim teams are not really teams. They're groups of individuals performing individually, whose total performance is merely the aggregate summation of their individual performances.

MyManagementLab

Now that you have finished this chapter, go back to **www.pearsonglobaleditions.com/ mymanagementlab** to continue practicing and applying the concepts you've learned.

Summary and Implications for Managers

7 Show how our understanding of teams differs in a global context.

Few trends have influenced jobs as much as the massive movement to introduce teams into the workplace. The shift from working alone to working on teams requires employees to cooperate with others, share information, confront differences, and sublimate personal interests for the greater good of the team.

- Effective teams have common characteristics. They have adequate resources, effective leadership, a climate of trust, and a performance evaluation and reward system that reflects team contributions. These teams have individuals with technical expertise as well as problem-solving, decision-making, and interpersonal skills and the right traits, especially conscientiousness and openness.
- Effective teams also tend to be small—with fewer than 10 people, preferably of diverse backgrounds. They have members who fill role demands and who prefer to be part of a group. And the work that members do provides freedom and autonomy, the opportunity to use different skills and talents, the ability to complete a whole and identifiable task or product, and work that has a substantial impact on others.
- Finally, effective teams have members who believe in the team's capabilities and are committed to a common plan and purpose, an accurate shared mental model of what is to be accomplished, specific team goals, a manageable level of conflict, and a minimal degree of social loafing.
- Because individualistic organizations and societies attract and reward individual accomplishments, it can be difficult to create team players in these environments. To make the conversion, management should try to select individuals who have the interpersonal skills to be effective team players, provide training to develop teamwork skills, and reward individuals for cooperative efforts.

We Can Learn Much About Work Teams from Studying Sports Teams

POINT

In nearly every nation on earth, sports teams are looked upon as examples of teamwork and collective achievement. We celebrate when our favorite teams win and commiserate with others when they lose. Individual sports like golf or singles tennis can be enjoyable to play and, depending on your taste, to watch, but nothing compares to the exhilaration of seeing teams—whether it is football (soccer or American football), basketball, or baseball—band together and succeed.

Of course, it only stands to reason that we seek to draw leadership lessons from these teams. After all, they won at the highest levels of competition, and sometimes they can provide a unique window into team dynamics because their actions are so visible. There is nothing wrong in seeing what we can learn from these teams in terms of making our teams at work more effective. We learn from examples, and if the examples are good ones, the learning is good, too.

Interestingly, some research suggests that, more than those in other cultures, U.S. individuals tend to use team metaphors rather than references to family, the military, or other institutions. Hewlett-Packard's Susie Wee writes:

> Every so often someone asks me what I learned in grad school that helped me in the working world. I can say that many of my most important learnings from school came from playing team sports. My school had a women's club ice hockey team that I played on for 10 years (as an undergrad and grad student). Over these 10 years, my role on the team evolved from a benchwarmer . . . to a player . . . to a captain . . . back to a player . . . and to an assistant coach. Many of my everyday experiences with the team turned into learnings that stayed with me and help me at work.

> A perhaps more subtle learning comes from how you make yourself a part of the team when you are the "worst skilled" player or a bench warmer. You can still make important contributions by having a great attitude, [and] by working hard to improve your skills. This directly carries over to the working world, as no matter what your skill or experience level, you can always find a way to make an important contribution to your team.

> My advice to people? Students—get involved in a team sport! Workers—treat your career like a team sport!

COUNTERPOINT

Susie Wee's story is a nice one, but that fact that she found her athletic experience helpful doesn't prove much, because that experience may be specific to Susie Wee. A lot of mischief is created in our understanding of organizational behavior when folks try to over-generalize from their past experience.

There certainly is no shortage of athletes and coaches hawking books they propose have organizational implications. In fact, such books are a veritable cottage industry for current and former NFL coaches. Tony Dungy can tell you how to be a "mentor leader" of your team. Rex Ryan can tell you how to use passion and humor to lead teams. Even Bill Walsh (who died in 2007) has a 2010 team leadership book whose theme is "the score takes care of itself." Vince Lombardi (who died in 1970) seems to have a book on team leadership published every year. In all these books, the coaches spend a lot of time discussing how their approach is relevant in the business world. These are all good coaches, some of them are great coaches, but there is little reason to believe athletic teams function like work teams. How many coaches go on to successful careers in organizations outside the athletic context?

In fact, some in-depth reporting on the 2010 U.S. Winter Olympic Team, which won more medals in Vancouver than have ever been won by a U.S. team, demonstrate it was not really a team. The hockey team didn't have much to do with the figure skating team, which didn't have much interaction with the curling team. However, even within the teams organized by sport, there often was no team effort in any real sense of the word. Speedskater Shani Davis, winner of a gold and a silver medal, neither lived nor practiced with the team. He didn't even allow his biography to be posted on the team's Web site. Skier Lindsey Vonn, snowboarder Shaun White, and many others were similarly and rather defiantly "on their own."

There are not many organizations in which a member of a team could get by with that kind of behavior. It often happens, and in fact may be the norm, in sports teams where winning is the only thing that matters. That is one of many differences between sports teams and work teams.

Source: G. B. Gibson and D. M. McDaniel, "Moving Beyond Conventional Wisdom: Advancements in Cross-Cultural Theories of Leadership, Conflict, and Teams," *Perspectives on Psychological Science* 5, no. 4 (2010), pp. 450–462; K. Thomas, "U.S. Olympic Glory, From Stars Hardly on Team," *The New York Times* (February 28, 2010), pp. 1, 4; and S. Schomer, "HP's Susie Wee and the "Wall of Touch," *Fast Company* (May 1, 2010), downloaded June 3, 2011, from www.fastcompany.com/.

QUESTIONS FOR REVIEW

1 How do you explain the growing popularity of teams in organizations?

2 What is the difference between a group and a team?

3 What are the four types of teams?

4 What conditions or context factors determine whether teams are effective?

5 How can organizations create team players?

6 When is work performed by individuals preferred over work performed by teams?

7 What are three ways in which our understanding of teams differs in a global context?

EXPERIENTIAL EXERCISE Fixed Versus Variable Flight Crews

Break into teams of five. Assume that you've been hired by AJet, a startup airline based in St. Louis. Your team has been formed to consider the pros and cons of using variable flight crews and to arrive at a recommendation on whether to follow this industry practice at AJet.

Variable flight crews are crews formed when pilots, co-pilots, and flight attendants typically bid for schedules on specific planes (for instance, Boeing 737s, 757s, or 767s) based on seniority. Then they're given a monthly schedule made up of 1- to 4-day trips. Thus, any given flight crew on a plane is rarely together for more than a few days at a time. A complicated system is required to complete the schedules. Because of this system, it's not unusual for a senior pilot at a large airline to fly with a different co-pilot on every trip during any given month. And a pilot and co-pilot who work together for 3 days in

January may never work together again the rest of the year. (In contrast, a fixed flight crew consists of the same group of pilots and attendants who fly together for a period of time.)

In considering whether to use variable flight crews, your team is to answer the following questions:

1. What are the primary advantages of variable flight crews?

2. If you were to recommend some version of fixed flight crews, drawing from the material in this chapter, on what criteria would you assign AJet crews?

When your team has considered the advantages and disadvantages of variable flight crews and answered these questions, be prepared to present to the class your recommendations and justification.

ETHICAL DILEMMA Unethical Teams

We often think of unethical behavior as individual behavior. However, in many cases, unethical behavior is a team effort. The Enron, Adelphia, and WorldCom corporate scandals were brewed by members of the top management teams in these organizations. The BP oil disaster implicated several teams that failed to ensure construction and safety guidelines were followed. Do these examples show that team unethical behavior is limited to top management teams, or can it also occur with "ordinary" work teams?

A study of 126 three-member teams of undergraduates suggests that unethical team behavior can occur beyond top management teams. In this study, teams were given a problem on which to work, with the following instructions:

You are assigned a team project in one of your finance courses. Your team waits until the last minute to being working. To save time, a friend suggests using an old project out of his fraternity files. Does your team go along with this plan?

How many of the teams decided to cheat? About 37 percent decided to use the old project.

Because this exercise was hypothetical, the authors also studied team cheating in another way—by allowing teams to self-grade a "decoy" assignment (an aspect of their assignment that did not in reality exist) that counted as 2 percent of their course grade. How many teams cheated here? About one in four.

This study found that team cheating was greater when a team was composed of utilitarian members (those who think the ends justify the means). However, utilitarian attitudes were more likely to translate into team cheating when team members felt interpersonally "safe"—when they felt there was little risk within the team of being attacked or ridiculed for propositions or arguments they made.

The upshot? It appears that in the right circumstances, all types of teams are capable of behaving unethically.

By holding individual team members accountable, and by providing a climate of "voice" where dissenting team members feel free to speak up, managers can discourage team unethical behavior.

Questions

1. Do you know for certain that you would have refused to agree to the unethical behavior in the experiment?

2. Do you think the team nature of the decision makes it more likely or less likely that individuals will choose to behave unethically?

3. In this study, all team members were required to sign a response form indicating they agreed with the decision. Do you think the results would change if consensus or a signature was not required?

Sources: M. J. Pearsall and A. P. J. Ellis, "Thick as Thieves: The Effects of Ethical Orientation and Psychological Safety on Unethical Team Behavior," *Journal of Applied Psychology* 96, no. 2 (2011), pp. 401–411; and D. W. White and E. Lean, "The Impact of Perceived Leader Integrity on Subordinates in a Work Team Environment," *Journal of Business Ethics* 81, no. 4 (2008), pp. 765–778.

CASE INCIDENT 1 Why Don't Teams Work Like They're Supposed to?

Despite years of promises that teamwork will serve as a cure-all for the problems of business, many managers have found that even teams with highly motivated, skilled, and committed members can fail to achieve the expected results. Professor Richard Hackman from Harvard University has been studying teams for years and believes that more often than not, failing to establish the groundwork for effective team performance leads teams to be less effective than if the leader simply divided up tasks and had each individual work on his or her assigned part. As Hackman notes, "I have no question that a team can generate magic. But don't count on it."

What are the main factors Hackman has identified that lead to effective teams? Teams should be kept small and have consistent membership to minimize the types of co-ordination tasks that take up valuable time. Too often, organizations set up project-based teams and then reconfigure them, without considering the stages of group development that might have to occur before the team can achieve full performance. Supports need to be in place, like group-based rewards and clearly defined group responsibilities. Surprisingly, in his study of 120 senior management teams, Hackman found fewer than 10 percent of members agreed about who was even on the team!

Successful teams also have assertive, courageous leaders who can invoke authority even when the team resists direction. Similar lessons were derived from the failure of Ghana Airways, a state-run organization that experienced frequent changes in top management that were disruptive to establishing a consistent leadership team. As a result of excessive turbulence and lack of strategic vision, the 40-year-old air carrier that was once an emblem for the country went bankrupt.

Do these weaknesses mean teams are never the answer to a business problem? Obviously, it is often necessary to bring together and coordinate individuals with a diverse set of skills and abilities to solve a problem. It would be impossible for all the management tasks of a complex organization like Ghana Airways to be done by disconnected individuals. And often there is more work to be done in a compressed time period than any one individual can possibly accomplish. In these cases, it is wise to consider how to best heed the advice provided above and ensure your team isn't less than the sum of its parts.

Questions

1. What do you think of the elements of successful teamwork Hackman has identified? Do you believe these elements are necessary for effective team performance?

2. Can you think of other conditions necessary for teams to be effective?

3. Imagine you've been asked to assemble and lead a team of high-potential new hires to work on the development of an international marketing campaign. What specific steps might you take early in the team's life to ensure that the new team is able to avoid some of the problems Hackman identified? Is there any way to break down the overall group goal into subtasks so individual accountability can be enhanced?

Sources: D. Coutu, "Why Teams Don't Work" *Harvard Business Review* (May 2009), pp. 99–105; G. Gregory, "Why All-Star Teams Fail," *Lab Manager Magazine* (January 11, 2011), www.labmanager.com; and J. Amankwah-Amoah and Y. A. Debrah, "The Protracted Collapse of Ghana Airways: Lessons in Organizational Failure," *Group and Organization Management* 35, no. 5 (2010), pp. 636–665.

CASE INCIDENT 2 Multicultural Multinational Teams at IBM

When many people think of a traditional, established company, they think of IBM. IBM has been famous for its written and unwritten rules—such as its no-layoff policy, its focus on individual promotions and achievement, the expectation of lifetime service at the company, and its requirement of suits and white shirts at work. The firm was one of the mainstays of the "man in a gray flannel suit" corporate culture in the United States.

Times have certainly changed.

IBM has clients in 170 countries and now does two-thirds of its business outside the United States. As a result, it has overturned virtually all aspects of its old culture. One relatively new focus is on teamwork. While IBM uses work teams extensively, like almost all large organizations, the way it does so is unique.

To foster appreciation of a variety of cultures and open up emerging markets, IBM sends hundreds of its employees to month-long volunteer project teams in regions of the world where most big companies don't do business. Al Chakra, a software development manager located in Raleigh, North Carolina, was sent to join GreenForest, a furniture manufacturing team in Timisoara, Romania. With Chakra were IBM employees from five other countries. Together, the team helped GreenForest become more computer-savvy to increase its business. In return for the IBM team's assistance, GreenForest was charged nothing.

This is hardly altruism at work. IBM firmly believes these multicultural, multinational teams are good investments. First, they help lay the groundwork for uncovering business in emerging economies, many of which might be expected to enjoy greater future growth than mature markets. Stanley Litow, the IBM VP who oversees the program, also thinks it helps IBMers develop multicultural team skills and an appreciation of local markets. He notes, "We want to build a leadership cadre that learns about these places and also learns to exchange their diverse backgrounds and skills." Among the countries where IBM has sent its multicultural teams are Turkey, Tanzania, Vietnam, Ghana, and the Philippines.

As for Chakra, he was thrilled to be selected for the team. "I felt like I won the lottery," he said. He advised GreenForest on how to become a paperless company in 3 years and recommended computer systems to boost productivity and increase exports to western Europe.

Another team member, Bronwyn Grantham, an Australian who works at IBM in London, advised GreenForest about sales strategies. Describing her team experience, Grantham said, "I've never worked so closely with a team of IBMers from such a wide range of competencies."

Questions

1. If you calculate the person-hours devoted to IBM's team projects, they amount to more than 180,000 hours of management time each year. Do you think this is a wise investment of IBM's human resources? Why or why not?

2. Why do you think IBM's culture changed from formal, stable, and individualistic to informal, impermanent, and team-oriented?

3. Would you like to work on one of IBM's multicultural, multinational project teams? Why or why not?

4. Multicultural project teams often face problems with communication, expectations, and values. How do you think some of these challenges can be overcome?

Sources: Based on C. Hymowitz, "IBM Combines Volunteer Service, Teamwork to Cultivate Emerging Markets," *The Wall Street Journal* (August 4, 2008), p. B6; S. Gupta, "Mine the Potential of Multicultural Teams," *HR Magazine* (October 2008), pp. 79–84; and H. Aguinis and K. Kraiger, "Benefits of Training and Development for Individuals and Teams, Organizations, and Society," *Annual Review of Psychology* 60, no. 1 (2009), pp. 451–474.

ENDNOTES

1. This section is based on J. R. Katzenbach and D. K. Smith, *The Wisdom of Teams* (Cambridge, MA: Harvard University Press, 1993), pp. 21, 45, 85; and D. C. Kinlaw, *Developing Superior Work Teams* (Lexington, MA: Lexington Books, 1991), pp. 3–21.

2. J. Mathieu, M. T. Maynard, T. Rapp, and L. Gilson, "Team Effectiveness 1997–2007: A Review of Recent Advancements and a Glimpse into the Future," *Journal of Management* 34, no. 3 (2008), pp. 410–476.

3. J. H. Shonk, *Team-Based Organizations* (Homewood, IL: Business One Irwin, 1992); and M. A. Verespej, "When Workers Get New Roles," *IndustryWeek* (February 3, 1992), p. 11.

4. G. Bodinson and R. Bunch, "AQP's National Team Excellence Award: Its Purpose, Value and Process," *The Journal for Quality and Participation* (Spring 2003), pp. 37–42.

5. See, for example, A. Erez, J. A. LePine, and H. Elms, "Effects of Rotated Leadership and Peer Evaluation on the Functioning and Effectiveness of Self-Managed Teams: A Quasi-experiment," *Personnel Psychology* (Winter 2002), pp. 929–948.

6. See, for instance, C. W. Langfred, "Too Much of a Good Thing? Negative Effects of High Trust and Individual Autonomy in Self-Managing Teams," *Academy of Management Journal* (June 2004), pp. 385–399.

7. C. W. Langfred, "The Downside of Self-Management: A Longitudinal Study of the Effects of Conflict on Trust, Autonomy, and Task Interdependence in Self-Managing Teams," *Academy of Management Journal* 50, no. 4 (2007), pp. 885–900.

8. J. Devaro, "The Effects of Self-Managed and Closely Managed Teams on Labor Productivity and Product Quality: An Empirical Analysis of a Cross-Section of Establishments," *Industrial Relations* 47, no. 4 (2008), pp. 659–698.

9. A. Shah, "Starbucks Strives for Instant Gratification with Via Launch," *PRWeek* (December 2009), p. 15.

10. B. Freyer and T. A. Stewart, "Cisco Sees the Future," *Harvard Business Review* (November 2008), pp. 73–79.

11. See, for example, L. L. Martins, L. L. Gilson, and M. T. Maynard, "Virtual Teams: What Do We Know and Where Do We Go from Here?" *Journal of Management* (November 2004), pp. 805–835; and B. Leonard, "Managing Virtual Teams," *HRMagazine* (June 2011), pp. 39–42.

12. J. R. Mesmer-Magnus, L. A. DeChurch, M. Jimenez-Rodriguez, J. Wildman, and M. Shuffler, "A Meta-Analytic Investigation of Virtuality and Information Sharing in Teams," *Organizational Behavior and Human Decision Processes* 115, no. 2 (2011), pp. 214–225.

13. A. Malhotra, A. Majchrzak, and B. Rosen, "Leading Virtual Teams," *Academy of Management Perspectives* (February 2007), pp. 60–70; and J. M. Wilson, S. S. Straus, and B. McEvily, "All in Due Time: The Development of Trust in Computer-Mediated and Face-to-Face Teams," *Organizational Behavior and Human Decision Processes* 19 (2006), pp. 16–33.

14. See, for instance, J. R. Hackman, "The Design of Work Teams," in J. W. Lorsch (ed.), *Handbook of Organizational Behavior* (Upper Saddle River, NJ: Prentice Hall, 1987), pp. 315–342; and M. A. Campion, G. J. Medsker, and C. A. Higgs, "Relations Between Work Group Characteristics and Effectiveness: Implications for Designing Effective Work Groups," *Personnel Psychology* (Winter 1993), pp. 823–850.

15. D. E. Hyatt and T. M. Ruddy, "An Examination of the Relationship Between Work Group Characteristics and Performance: Once More into the Breech," *Personnel Psychology* (Autumn 1997), p. 555.

16. This model is based on M. A. Campion, E. M. Papper, and G. J. Medsker, "Relations Between Work Team Characteristics and Effectiveness: A Replication and Extension," *Personnel Psychology* (Summer 1996), pp. 429–452; Hyatt and Ruddy, "An Examination of the Relationship Between Work Group Characteristics and Performance," pp. 553–585; S. G. Cohen and D. E. Bailey, "What Makes Teams Work: Group Effectiveness Research from the Shop Floor to the Executive Suite," *Journal of Management* 23, no. 3 (1997),

pp. 239–290; L. Thompson, *Making the Team* (Upper Saddle River, NJ: Prentice Hall, 2000), pp. 18–33; and J. R. Hackman, *Leading Teams: Setting the Stage for Great Performance* (Boston: Harvard Business School Press, 2002).

17. See G. L. Stewart and M. R. Barrick, "Team Structure and Performance: Assessing the Mediating Role of Intrateam Process and the Moderating Role of Task Type," *Academy of Management Journal* (April 2000), pp. 135–148.

18. Hyatt and Ruddy, "An Examination of the Relationship Between Work Group Characteristics and Performance," p. 577.

19. P. Balkundi and D. A. Harrison, "Ties, Leaders, and Time in Teams: Strong Inference About Network Structure's Effects on Team Viability and Performance," *Academy of Management Journal* 49, no. 1 (2006), pp. 49–68; G. Chen, B. L. Kirkman, R. Kanfer, D. Allen, and B. Rosen, "A Multilevel Study of Leadership, Empowerment, and Performance in Teams," *Journal of Applied Psychology* 92, no. 2 (2007), pp. 331–346; L. A. DeChurch and M. A. Marks, "Leadership in Multiteam Systems," *Journal of Applied Psychology* 91, no. 2 (2006), pp. 311–329; A. Srivastava, K. M. Bartol, and E. A. Locke, "Empowering Leadership in Management Teams: Effects on Knowledge Sharing, Efficacy, and Performance," *Academy of Management Journal* 49, no. 6 (2006), pp. 1239–1251; and J. E. Mathieu, K. K. Gilson, and T. M. Ruddy, "Empowerment and Team Effectiveness: An Empirical Test of an Integrated Model," *Journal of Applied Psychology* 91, no. 1 (2006), pp. 97–108.

20. J. B. Carson, P. E. Tesluk, and J. A. Marrone, "Shared Leadership in Teams: An Investigation of Antecedent Conditions and Performance," *Academy of Management Journal* 50, no. 5 (2007), pp. 1217–1234.

21. K. T. Dirks, "Trust in Leadership and Team Performance: Evidence from NCAA Basketball," *Journal of Applied Psychology* (December 2000), pp. 1004–1012; M. Williams, "In Whom We Trust: Group Membership as an Affective Context for Trust Development," *Academy of Management Review* (July 2001), pp. 377–396; and J. Schaubroeck, S. S. K. Lam, and A. C. Peng, "Cognition-Based and Affect-Based Trust as Mediators of Leader Behavior Influences on Team Performance," *Journal of Applied Psychology*, Online First Publication (February 7, 2011), doi: 10.1037/a0022625.

22. See F. Aime, C. J. Meyer, and S. E. Humphrey, "Legitimacy of Team Rewards: Analyzing Legitimacy as a Condition for the Effectiveness of Team Incentive Designs," *Journal of Business Research* 63, no. 1 (2010), pp. 60–66; and P. A. Bamberger and R. Levi, "Team-Based Reward Allocation Structures and the Helping Behaviors of Outcome-Interdependent Team Members," *Journal of Managerial Psychology* 24, no. 4 (2009), pp. 300–327; and M. J. Pearsall, M. S. Christian, and A. P. J. Ellis, "Motivating Interdependent Teams: Individual Rewards, Shared Rewards, or Something in Between?" *Journal of Applied Psychology* 95, no. 1 (2010), pp. 183–191.

23. R. R. Hirschfeld, M. H. Jordan, H. S. Feild, W. F. Giles, and A. A. Armenakis, "Becoming Team Players: Team Members' Mastery of Teamwork Knowledge as a Predictor of Team Task Proficiency and Observed Teamwork Effectiveness,"

Journal of Applied Psychology 91, no. 2 (2006), pp. 467–474; and K. R. Randall, C. J. Resick, and L. A. DeChurch, "Building Team Adaptive Capacity: The Roles of Sensegiving and Team Composition," *Journal of Applied Psychology* 96, no. 3 (2011), pp. 525–540.

24. H. Moon, J. R. Hollenbeck, and S. E. Humphrey, "Asymmetric Adaptability: Dynamic Team Structures as One-Way Streets," *Academy of Management Journal* 47, no. 5 (October 2004), pp. 681–695; A. P. J. Ellis, J. R. Hollenbeck, and D. R. Ilgen, "Team Learning: Collectively Connecting the Dots," *Journal of Applied Psychology* 88, no. 5 (October 2003), pp. 821–835; C. L. Jackson and J. A. LePine, "Peer Responses to a Team's Weakest Link: A Test and Extension of LePine and Van Dyne's Model," *Journal of Applied Psychology* 88, no. 3 (June 2003), pp. 459–475; and J. A. LePine, "Team Adaptation and Postchange Performance: Effects of Team Composition in Terms of Members' Cognitive Ability and Personality," *Journal of Applied Psychology* 88, no. 1 (February 2003), pp. 27–39.

25. S. T. Bell, "Deep-Level Composition Variables as Predictors of Team Performance: A Meta-Analysis," *Journal of Applied Psychology* 92, no. 3 (2007), pp. 595–615; and M. R. Barrick, G. L. Stewart, M. J. Neubert, and M. K. Mount, "Relating Member Ability and Personality to Work-Team Processes and Team Effectiveness," *Journal of Applied Psychology* (June 1998), pp. 377–391.

26. T. A. O'Neill and N. J. Allen, "Personality and the Prediction of Team Performance," *European Journal of Personality* 25, no. 1 (2011), pp. 31–42.

27. Ellis, Hollenbeck, and Ilgen, "Team Learning"; C. O. L. H. Porter, J. R. Hollenbeck, and D. R. Ilgen, "Backing Up Behaviors in Teams: The Role of Personality and Legitimacy of Need," *Journal of Applied Psychology* 88, no. 3 (June 2003), pp. 391–403; A. Colquitt, J. R. Hollenbeck, and D. R. Ilgen, "Computer-Assisted Communication and Team Decision-Making Performance: The Moderating Effect of Openness to Experience," *Journal of Applied Psychology* 87, no. 2 (April 2002), pp. 402–410; J. A. LePine, J. R. Hollenbeck, D. R. Ilgen, and J. Hedlund, "The Effects of Individual Differences on the Performance of Hierarchical Decision Making Teams: Much More Than G," *Journal of Applied Psychology* 82 (1997), pp. 803–811; Jackson and LePine, "Peer Responses to a Team's Weakest Link"; and LePine, "Team Adaptation and Postchange Performance."

28. Barrick, Stewart, Neubert, and Mount, "Relating Member Ability and Personality to Work-Team Processes and Team Effectiveness," p. 388; and S. E. Humphrey, J. R. Hollenbeck, C. J. Meyer, and D. R. Ilgen, "Trait Configurations in Self-Managed Teams: A Conceptual Examination of the Use of Seeding for Maximizing and Minimizing Trait Variance in Teams," *Journal of Applied Psychology* 92, no. 3 (2007), pp. 885–892.

29. S. E. Humphrey, F. P. Morgeson, and M. J. Mannor, "Developing a Theory of the Strategic Core of Teams: A Role Composition Model of Team Performance," *Journal of Applied Psychology* 94, no. 1 (2009), pp. 48–61.

30. C. Margerison and D. McCann, *Team Management: Practical New Approaches* (London: Mercury Books, 1990).

31. K. Y. Williams and C. A. O'Reilly III, "Demography and Diversity in Organizations: A Review of 40 Years of Research," in B. M. Staw and L. L. Cummings (eds.), *Research in Organizational Behavior*, vol. 20, (Stamford, CT: Jai Press, 1998) pp. 77–140; and A. Joshi, "The Influence of Organizational Demography on the External Networking Behavior of Teams," *Academy of Management Review* (July 2006), pp. 583–595.

32. A. Joshi and H. Roh, "The Role of Context in Work Team Diversity Research: A Meta-Analytic Review," *Academy of Management Journal* 52, no. 3 (2009), pp. 599–-627; S. K. Horwitz and I. B. Horwitz, "The Effects of Team Diversity on Team Outcomes: A Meta-Analytic Review of Team Demography," *Journal of Management* 33, no. 6 (2007), pp. 987–1015; and S. T. Bell, A. J. Villado, M. A. Lukasik, L. Belau, and A. L. Briggs, "Getting Specific about Demographic Diversity Variable and Team Performance Relationships: A Meta-Analysis," *Journal of Management* 37, no. 3 (2011), pp. 709–743.

33. S. J. Shin and J. Zhou, "When Is Educational Specialization Heterogeneity Related to Creativity in Research and Development Teams? Transformational Leadership as a Moderator," *Journal of Applied Psychology* 92, no. 6 (2007), pp. 1709–1721; and K. J. Klein, A. P. Knight, J. C. Ziegert, B. C. Lim, and J. L. Saltz, "When Team Members' Values Differ: The Moderating Role of Team Leadership," *Organizational Behavior and Human Decision Processes* 114, no. 1 (2011), pp. 25–36.

34. W. E. Watson, K. Kumar, and L. K. Michaelsen, "Cultural Diversity's Impact on Interaction Process and Performance: Comparing Homogeneous and Diverse Task Groups," *Academy of Management Journal* (June 1993), pp. 590–602; P. C. Earley and E. Mosakowski, "Creating Hybrid Team Cultures: An Empirical Test of Transnational Team Functioning," *Academy of Management Journal* (February 2000), pp. 26–49; and S. Mohammed and L. C. Angell, "Surface- and Deep-Level Diversity in Workgroups: Examining the Moderating Effects of Team Orientation and Team Process on Relationship Conflict," *Journal of Organizational Behavior* (December 2004), pp. 1015–1039.

35. Watson, Kumar, and Michaelsen, "Cultural Diversity's Impact on Interaction Process and Performance."

36. D. F. Crown, "The use of Group and Groupcentric Individual Goals for Culturally Heterogeneous and Homogeneous Task Groups: An Assessment of European Work Teams," *Small Group Research* 38, no. 4 (2007), pp. 489–508.

37. D. Coutu, "Why Teams Don't Work" *Harvard Business Review* (May 2009), pp. 99–105. The evidence in this section is described in Thompson, *Making the Team*, pp. 65–67. See also L. A. Curral, R. H. Forrester, and J. F. Dawson, "It's What You Do and the Way That You Do It: Team Task, Team Size, and Innovation-Related Group Processes," *European Journal of Work & Organizational Psychology* 10, no. 2 (June 2001), pp. 187–204; R. C. Liden, S. J. Wayne, and R. A. Jaworski, "Social Loafing: A Field Investigation," *Journal of Management* 30, no. 2 (2004), pp. 285–304; and J. A. Wagner, "Studies of Individualism–Collectivism: Effects on Cooperation in Groups," *Academy of Management Journal* 38, no. 1 (February 1995), pp. 152–172.

38. "Is Your Team Too Big? Too Small? What's the Right Number? *Knowledge@Wharton* (June 14, 2006), pp. 1–5.

39. Hyatt and Ruddy, "An Examination of the Relationship Between Work Group Characteristics and Performance"; J. D. Shaw, M. K. Duffy, and E. M. Stark, "Interdependence and Preference for Group Work: Main and Congruence Effects on the Satisfaction and Performance of Group Members," *Journal of Management* 26, no. 2 (2000), pp. 259–279; and S. A. Kiffin-Peterson and J. L. Cordery, "Trust, Individualism, and Job Characteristics of Employee Preference for Teamwork," *International Journal of Human Resource Management* (February 2003), pp. 93–116.

40. J. A. LePine, R. F. Piccolo, C. L. Jackson, J. E. Mathieu, and J. R. Saul, "A Meta-Analysis of Teamwork Processes: Tests of a Multidimensional Model and Relationships with Team Effectiveness Criteria," *Personnel Psychology* 61 (2008), pp. 273–307.

41. I. D. Steiner, *Group Processes and Productivity* (New York: Academic Press, 1972).

42. J. A. LePine, R. F. Piccolo, C. L. Jackson, J. E. Mathieu, and J. R. Saul, "A Meta-Analysis of Teamwork Processes: Tests of a Multidimensional Model and Relationships with Team Effectiveness Criteria"; and J. E. Mathieu and T. L. Rapp, "Laying the Foundation for Successful Team Performance Trajectories: The Roles of Team Charters and Performance Strategies," *Journal of Applied Psychology* 94, no. 1 (2009), pp. 90–103.

43. J. E. Mathieu and W. Schulze, "The Influence of Team Knowledge and Formal Plans on Episodic Team Process—Performance Relationships," *Academy of Management Journal* 49, no. 3 (2006), pp. 605–619.

44. A. N. Pieterse, D. van Knippenberg, and W. P. van Ginkel, "Diversity in Goal Orientation, Team Reflexivity, and Team Performance," *Organizational Behavior and Human Decision Processes* 114, no. 2 (2011), pp. 153–164.

45. A. Gurtner, F. Tschan, N. K. Semmer, and C. Nagele, "Getting Groups to Develop Good Strategies: Effects of Reflexivity Interventions on Team Process, Team Performance, and Shared Mental Models," *Organizational Behavior and Human Decision Processes* 102 (2007), pp. 127–142; M. C. Schippers, D. N. Den Hartog, and P. L. Koopman, "Reflexivity in Teams: A Measure and Correlates," *Applied Psychology: An International Review* 56, no. 2 (2007), pp. 189–211; and C. S. Burke, K. C. Stagl, E. Salas, L. Pierce, and D. Kendall, "Understanding Team Adaptation: A Conceptual Analysis and Model," *Journal of Applied Psychology* 91, no. 6 (2006), pp. 1189–1207.

46. A. N. Pieterse, D. van Knippenberg, and W. P. van Ginkel, "Diversity in Goal Orientation, Team Reflexivity, and Team Performance," *Organizational Behavior and Human Decision Processes* 114, no. 2 (2011), pp. 153–164.

47. E. Weldon and L. R. Weingart, "Group Goals and Group Performance," *British Journal of Social Psychology* (Spring 1993), pp. 307–334. See also R. P. DeShon, S. W. J. Kozlowski, A. M. Schmidt, K. R. Milner, and D. Wiechmann, "A Multiple-Goal, Multilevel Model of Feedback Effects on the Regulation of Individual and Team Performance," *Journal of Applied Psychology* (December 2004), pp. 1035–1056.

48. K. Tasa, S. Taggar, and G. H. Seijts, "The Development of Collective Efficacy in Teams: A Multilevel and Longitudinal Perspective," *Journal of Applied Psychology* 92, no. 1 (2007),

pp. 17–27; D. I. Jung and J. J. Sosik, "Group Potency and Collective Efficacy: Examining Their Predictive Validity, Level of Analysis, and Effects of Performance Feedback on Future Group Performance," *Group & Organization Management* (September 2003), pp. 366–391; and R. R. Hirschfeld and J. B. Bernerth, "Mental Efficacy and Physical Efficacy at the Team Level: Inputs and Outcomes Among Newly Formed Action Teams," *Journal of Applied Psychology* 93, no. 6 (2008), pp. 1429–1437.

49. S. Mohammed, L. Ferzandi, and K. Hamilton, "Metaphor No More: A 15-Year Review of the Team Mental Model Construct," *Journal of Management* 36, no. 4 (2010), pp. 876–910.

50. A. P. J. Ellis, "System Breakdown: The Role of Mental Models and Transactive Memory on the Relationships Between Acute Stress and Team Performance," *Academy of Management Journal* 49, no. 3 (2006), pp. 576–589.

51. S. W. J. Kozlowski and D. R. Ilgen, "Enhancing the Effectiveness of Work Groups and Teams," *Psychological Science in the Public Interest* (December 2006), pp. 77–124; and B. D. Edwards, E. A. Day, W. Arthur Jr., and S. T. Bell, "Relationships Among Team Ability Composition, Team Mental Models, and Team Performance," *Journal of Applied Psychology* 91, no. 3 (2006), pp. 727–736.

52. L. A. DeChurch and J. R. Mesmer-Magnus, "The Cognitive Underpinnings of Effective Teamwork: A Meta-Analysis," *Journal of Applied Psychology* 95, no. 1 (2010), pp. 32–53.

53. J. Farh, C. Lee, and C.I.C. Farh, "Task Conflict and Team Creativity: A Question of How Much and When," *Journal of Applied Psychology* 95, no. 6 (2010), pp. 1173–1180.

54. K. J. Behfar, R. S. Peterson, E. A. Mannix, and W. M. K. Trochim, "The Critical Role of Conflict Resolution in Teams: A Close Look at the Links Between Conflict Type, Conflict Management Strategies, and Team Outcomes," *Journal of Applied Psychology* 93, no. 1 (2008), pp. 170–188.

55. K. H. Price, D. A. Harrison, and J. H. Gavin, "Withholding Inputs in Team Contexts: Member Composition, Interaction Processes, Evaluation Structure, and Social Loafing," *Journal of Applied Psychology* 91, no. 6 (2006), pp. 1375–1384.

56. See, for instance, B. L. Kirkman and D. L. Shapiro, "The Impact of Cultural Values on Employee Resistance to Teams: Toward a Model of Globalized Self-Managing Work Team Effectiveness," *Academy of Management Review*, July 1997, pp. 730–757; and B. L. Kirkman, C. B. Gibson, and D. L. Shapiro, "'Exporting' Teams: Enhancing the Implementation and Effectiveness of Work Teams in Global Affiliates," *Organizational Dynamics* 30, no. 1 (2001), pp. 12–29.

57. G. Hertel, U. Konradt, and K. Voss, "Competencies for Virtual Teamwork: Development and Validation of a Web-Based Selection Tool for Members of Distributed Teams," *European Journal of Work and Organizational Psychology* 15, no. 4 (2006), pp. 477–504.

58. I. Galarcep, "Beckham Loan Makes No Sense for the Galaxy," *ESPNsoccernet* (October 24, 2008), soccernet.espn.go.com.

59. E. Kearney, D. Gebert, and S. C. Voelpel, "When and How Diversity Benefits Teams: The Importance of Team Members' Need for Cognition," *Academy of Management Journal* 52, no. 3 (2009), pp. 581–598.

60. H. M. Guttman, "The New High-Performance Player," *The Hollywood Reporter* (October 27, 2008), www.hollywoodreporter.com.

61. J. S. DeMatteo, L. T. Eby, and E. Sundstrom, "Team-Based Rewards: Current Empirical Evidence and Directions for Future Research," in B. M. Staw and L. L. Cummings (eds.), *Research in Organizational Behavior,* vol. 20, (Stamford CT: JAI Press), pp. 141–183 (1998).

62. T. Erickson and L. Gratton, "What It Means to Work Here," *BusinessWeek* (January 10, 2008), www.businessweek.com.

63. M. D. Johnson, J. R. Hollenbeck, S. E. Humphrey, D. R. Ilgen, D. Jundt, and C. J. Meyer, "Cutthroat Cooperation: Asymmetrical Adaptation to Changes in Team Reward Structures," *Academy of Management Journal* 49, no. 1 (2006), pp. 103–119.

64. C. E. Naquin and R. O. Tynan, "The Team Halo Effect: Why Teams Are Not Blamed for Their Failures," *Journal of Applied Psychology,* April 2003, pp. 332–340.

65. A. B. Drexler and R. Forrester, "Teamwork—Not Necessarily the Answer," *HRMagazine* (January 1998), pp. 55–58.

LEARNING OBJECTIVES

After studying this chapter, you should be able to:

1 Identify the main functions of communication.

2 Describe the communication process and distinguish between formal and informal communication.

3 Contrast downward, upward, and lateral communication, and provide examples of each.

4 Contrast oral, written, and nonverbal communication.

5 Analyze the advantages and challenges of electronic communication.

6 Show how channel richness underlies the choice of communication channel.

7 Differentiate between automatic and controlled processing of persuasive messages.

8 Identify common barriers to effective communication.

9 Show how to overcome the potential problems in cross-cultural communication.

MyManagementLab

Access a host of interactive learning aids to help strengthen your understanding of the chapter concepts at **www.pearsonglobaleditions.com/mymanagementlab**.

GOLDMAN RULES

Large organizations have policies governing many aspects of employee behavior, including e-mail communication. But few have e-mail rules more elaborate than Goldman Sachs.

Goldman is one of the oldest, largest, and most respected U.S. investment banks. While some of its competitors either went bankrupt during the recent subprime mortgage meltdown (Lehman Brothers, Bear Stearns) or required massive government assistance (especially Citigroup, Bank of America, JPMorgan Chase, and Wells Fargo), Goldman fared better. It did take $10 billion from the government's Troubled Asset Relief Program (TARP), but it paid the money back (with 23 percent interest) before any other investment bank.

What makes Goldman great? One factor surely is management. *BusinessWeek* ranked Goldman sixth on its 2010 list of best places to start a career. One review commented, "MBAs perennially rank Goldman Sachs as one of the most desired places to work, and it's foremost among financial services firms. Once in the door, people still love the firm."

But do they love its e-mail policies? Goldman's e-mail manual, ominously titled *United States Policies for the Preparation, Supervision, Distribution and Retention of Written and Electronic Communications*, is so intricate that it has two rules for the uses of "and."

Some of the more interesting e-mail rules are:

- "The level of detail or explanation necessary to make a communication clear, accurate, and understandable will depend, in part, on the breadth and sophistication of the intended audience . . . the lack of financial sophistication of the recipient will often warrant a more detailed presentation."
- "All sales correspondence from or to employees working from home offices must be routed through regional offices for purposes of review, approval, distribution, and retention."
- "Each individual's correspondence must be sampled no less often than annually."

As elaborate as Goldman's rules are, they didn't keep the company out of hot water when it came to light that Goldman was recommending clients make mortgage investments while the company itself was betting against— "shorting"—those very same mortgage obligations. Several e-mails were particularly damning, calling the strategy "The Big Short." Another e-mail string showed that while being instructed to "be aggressive distributing these things" (positive mortgage positions), a Goldman manager wrote to his girlfriend, "That business is dead, and the poor little subprime borrowers will not last long."

Communication

Constantly talking isn't necessarily communicating. —Joel in *Eternal Sunshine of the Spotless Mind*

Photo: Goldman Sachs booth, New York Stock Exchange. *Source:* AP Photo/Richard Drew.

369

It's unlikely these messages would be consistent with Goldman's elaborate e-mail policies. But the firm did make some serious profit.

Source: M. Abelson and C. Winter, "The Goldman Rules," *Bloomberg Businessweek* (April 25, 2011), pp. 90–91; L Lavelle, "Best Places to Launch a Career," *Bloomberg Businessweek* (June 2010), downloaded June 10, 2011, from http://images.businessweek.com/; and L. Story and S. Chan, "Goldman Cited 'Serious' Profit on Mortgages," *The New York Times* (April 25, 2010), pp. Y1, Y25.

This example illustrates the profound consequences of communication. In this chapter, we'll analyze the power of communication and ways in which it can be more effective. One of the topics we'll discuss is gossip. Consider the following self-assessment, and see how you score on your attitudes toward gossip at work.

Poor communication is probably the most frequently cited source of interpersonal conflict.[1] Because individuals spend nearly 70 percent of their waking hours communicating—writing, reading, speaking, listening—it seems reasonable that one of the biggest inhibitors of group performance is lack of effective communication. Good communication skills are critical to career success. Polls of recruiters nearly always show communication skills among the most desired characteristics.[2]

No individual, group, or organization can exist without sharing meaning among its members. It is only thus that we can convey information and ideas. Communicating, however, is more than merely imparting meaning; that meaning must also be understood. If one group member speaks only German and the others do not know the language, the German speaker will not be fully understood. Therefore, **communication** must include both the *transfer and the understanding of meaning*.

Perfect communication, if it existed, would occur when a thought or idea was transmitted so the receiver perceived exactly the same mental picture as the sender. Though it sounds elementary, perfect communication is never achieved in practice, for reasons we shall see later in this chapter.

First let's briefly review the functions communication performs and describe the communication process.

SELF-ASSESSMENT LIBRARY

Am I A Gossip?

In the Self-Assessment Library (available on CD or online), take assessment IV.E.3 (Am I a Gossip?) and answer the following questions.

1. How did you score relative to your classmates?
2. Do you think gossiping is morally wrong? Why or why not?

Functions of Communication

1 Identify the main functions of communication.

Communication serves four major functions within a group or organization: control, motivation, emotional expression, and information.[3]

Communication acts to *control* member behavior in several ways. Organizations have authority hierarchies and formal guidelines employees

Many communication interactions that take place in an organization perform the function of providing for the emotional expression of feelings and fulfillment of social needs. In this photo, Rene Brookbank, marketing consultant and director of client relations at Cummins & White law firm, jokes with her co-workers during a corporate fashion event. The law firm staged a show for female lawyers and staffers as a fun way for them to view fashion trends in business attire and then treated them all to new outfits. Throughout the social event, cheerful communication among employees allowed them to express their emotions of happiness and gratitude.

Source: o44/ZUMA Press/Newscom.

are required to follow. When employees must communicate any job-related grievance to their immediate boss, follow their job description, or comply with company policies, communication is performing a control function. Informal communication controls behavior too. When work groups tease or harass a member who produces too much (and makes the rest of the group look bad), they are informally communicating, and controlling, the member's behavior.

Communication fosters *motivation* by clarifying to employees what they must do, how well they are doing it, and how they can improve if performance is subpar. We saw this operating in our review of goal-setting theory in Chapter 7. The formation of specific goals, feedback on progress toward the goals, and reward for desired behavior all stimulate motivation and require communication.

Their work group is a primary source of social interaction for many employees. Communication within the group is a fundamental mechanism by which members show their satisfaction and frustrations. Communication, therefore, provides for the *emotional expression* of feelings and fulfillment of social needs.

The final function of communication is to facilitate decision making. Communication provides the *information* individuals and groups need to make decisions by transmitting the data needed to identify and evaluate choices.

Almost every communication interaction that takes place in a group or organization performs one or more of these functions, and none of the four is more important than the others. To perform effectively, groups need to maintain some form of control over members, stimulate members to perform, allow emotional expression, and make decision choices.

communication *The transfer and understanding of meaning.*

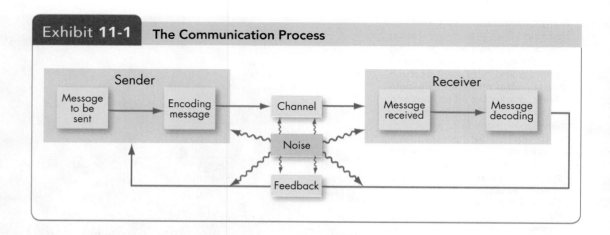

Exhibit 11-1   The Communication Process

The Communication Process

2 Describe the communication process and distinguish between formal and informal communication.

Before communication can take place it needs a purpose, a message to be conveyed between a sender and a receiver. The sender encodes the message (converts it to a symbolic form) and passes it through a medium (channel) to the receiver, who decodes it. The result is transfer of meaning from one person to another.[4]

Exhibit 11-1 depicts this **communication process**. The key parts of this model are (1) the sender, (2) encoding, (3) the message, (4) the channel, (5) decoding, (6) the receiver, (7) noise, and (8) feedback.

The *sender* initiates a message by encoding a thought. The *message* is the actual physical product of the sender's *encoding*. When we speak, the speech is the message. When we write, the writing is the message. When we gesture, the movements of our arms and the expressions on our faces are the message. The *channel* is the medium through which the message travels. The sender selects it, determining whether to use a formal or informal channel. **Formal channels** are established by the organization and transmit messages related to the professional activities of members. They traditionally follow the authority chain within the organization. Other forms of messages, such as personal or social, follow **informal channels**, which are spontaneous and emerge as a response to individual choices.[5] The *receiver* is the person(s) to whom the message is directed, who must first translate the symbols into understandable form. This step is the *decoding* of the message. *Noise* represents communication barriers that distort the clarity of the message, such as perceptual problems, information overload, semantic difficulties, or cultural differences. The final link in the communication process is a feedback loop. *Feedback* is the check on how successful we have been in transferring our messages as originally intended. It determines whether understanding has been achieved.

Direction of Communication

3 Contrast downward, upward, and lateral communication, and provide examples of each.

Communication can flow vertically or laterally. We further subdivide the vertical dimension into downward and upward directions.[6]

Downward Communication

Communication that flows from one level of a group or organization to a lower level is *downward communication.* Group leaders and managers use it to assign goals, provide job instructions, explain policies and procedures, point out problems that need attention, and offer feedback about performance.

When engaging in downward communication, managers must explain the reasons *why* a decision was made. One study found employees were twice as likely to be committed to changes when the reasons behind them were fully explained. Although this may seem like common sense, many managers feel they are too busy to explain things or that explanations will "open up a big can of worms." Evidence clearly indicates, though, that explanations increase employee commitment and support of decisions.[7] Moreover, although managers might think that sending a message one time is enough to get through to lower-level employees, most research suggests managerial communications must be repeated several times and through a variety of different media to be truly effective.[8]

Another problem in downward communication is its one-way nature; generally, managers inform employees but rarely solicit their advice or opinions. A study revealed that nearly two-thirds of employees say their boss rarely or never asks their advice. The study noted, "Organizations are always striving for higher employee engagement, but evidence indicates they unnecessarily create fundamental mistakes. People need to be respected and listened to." Companies like cell phone maker Nokia actively listen to employee's suggestions, a practice the company thinks is especially important to innovation.[9]

The best communicators explain the reasons behind their downward communications but also solicit communication from the employees they supervise. That leads us to the next direction: upward communication.

Upward Communication

Upward communication flows to a higher level in the group or organization. It's used to provide feedback to higher-ups, inform them of progress toward goals, and relay current problems. Upward communication keeps managers aware of how employees feel about their jobs, co-workers, and the organization in general. Managers also rely on upward communication for ideas on how conditions can be improved.

Given that most managers' job responsibilities have expanded, upward communication is increasingly difficult because managers are overwhelmed and easily distracted. To engage in effective upward communication, try to reduce distractions (meet in a conference room if you can, rather than your boss's office or cubicle), communicate in headlines not paragraphs (your goal is to get your boss's attention, not to engage in a meandering discussion), support your headlines with actionable items (what you believe should happen), and prepare an agenda to make sure you use your boss's attention well.[10]

Lateral Communication

When communication takes place among members of the same work group, members of work groups at the same level, managers at the same level, or any other horizontally equivalent workers, we describe it as *lateral communication.*

communication process *The steps between a source and a receiver that result in the transfer and understanding of meaning.*

formal channels *Communication channels established by an organization to transmit messages related to the professional activities of members.*

informal channels *Communication channels that are created spontaneously and that emerge as responses to individual choices.*

As president of Home Depot's southern division, Ann-Marie Campbell demonstrates the text concept of downward communication when speaking with the manager and employees of a store in St. Petersburg, Florida. Serving as a member of Home Depot's senior leadership team, Campbell oversees 100,000 workers at 640 stores in 15 states, Puerto Rico, and the Virgin Islands. During her store visits, Campbell communicates the retailer's goals of focusing on clean warehouses, stocked shelves, and excellent customer service. Her personal, face-to-face meetings with employees give her the opportunity to solicit upward communication from them.

Source: s70/ZUMA Press/Newscom.

Why is lateral communication needed if a group or an organization's vertical communications are effective? Lateral communication saves time and facilitates coordination. Some lateral relationships are formally sanctioned. More often, they are informally created to short-circuit the vertical hierarchy and expedite action. So from management's viewpoint, lateral communications can be good or bad. Because strictly adhering to the formal vertical structure for all communications can be inefficient, lateral communication occurring with management's knowledge and support can be beneficial. But it can create dysfunctional conflicts when the formal vertical channels are breached, when members go above or around their superiors to get things done, or when bosses find actions have been taken or decisions made without their knowledge.

Interpersonal Communication

4   Contrast oral, written, and nonverbal communication.

How do group members transfer meaning between and among each other? They essentially rely on oral, written, and nonverbal communication.

Oral Communication

The chief means of conveying messages is oral communication. Speeches, formal one-on-one and group discussions, and the informal rumor mill or grapevine are popular forms of oral communication.

The advantages of oral communication are speed and feedback. We can convey a verbal message and receive a response in minimal time. If the receiver is unsure of the message, rapid feedback allows the sender to quickly detect and correct it. As one professional put it, "Face-to-face communication on a consistent basis is still the best way to get information to and from employees."[11]

The major disadvantage of oral communication surfaces whenever a message has to pass through a number of people: the more people, the greater the potential distortion. If you've ever played the game "Telephone," you know the problem. Each person interprets the message in his or her own way. The message's content, when it reaches its destination, is often very different from the original. In an organization, where decisions and other communiqués are verbally passed up and down the authority hierarchy, considerable opportunities arise for messages to become distorted.

Written Communication

Written communications include memos, letters, fax transmissions, e-mail, instant messaging, organizational periodicals, notices placed on bulletin boards (including electronic ones), and any other device that transmits via written words or symbols.

Why would a sender choose written communication? It's often tangible and verifiable. Both the sender and receiver have a record of the communication; and the message can be stored for an indefinite period. If there are questions about its content, the message is physically available for later reference. This feature is particularly important for complex and lengthy communications. The marketing plan for a new product, for instance, is likely to contain a number of tasks spread out over several months. By putting it in writing, those who have to initiate the plan can readily refer to it over its lifespan. A final benefit of all written communication comes from the process itself. People are usually forced to think more thoroughly about what they want to convey in a written message than in a spoken one. Thus, written communications are more likely to be well thought out, logical, and clear.

Of course, written messages have drawbacks. They're time consuming. You could convey far more information to a college instructor in a 1-hour oral exam than in a 1-hour written exam. In fact, what you can say in 10 to 15 minutes might take you an hour to write. The other major disadvantage is lack of a built-in feedback mechanism. Oral communication allows the receiver to respond rapidly to what he thinks he hears. But emailing a memo or sending an instant message provides no assurance it has been received or that the recipient will interpret it as the sender intended.

Nonverbal Communication

Every time we deliver a verbal message, we also impart a nonverbal message.[12] Sometimes the nonverbal component may stand alone. In a singles bar, a glance, a stare, a smile, a frown, and a provocative body movement all convey meaning. No discussion of communication would thus be complete without consideration of *nonverbal communication*—which includes body movements, the intonations or emphasis we give to words, facial expressions, and the physical distance between the sender and receiver.

We could argue that every *body movement* has meaning, and no movement is accidental (though some are unconscious). Through body language, we say, "Help me, I'm lonely"; "Take me, I'm available"; and "Leave me alone, I'm depressed." We act out our state of being with nonverbal body language. We lift one eyebrow for disbelief. We rub our noses for puzzlement. We clasp our arms to isolate ourselves or to protect ourselves. We shrug our shoulders for indifference, wink for intimacy, tap our fingers for impatience, slap our forehead for forgetfulness.[13]

The two most important messages body language conveys are (1) the extent to which we like another and are interested in his or her views and (2) the perceived status between a sender and receiver.[14] We're more likely to position ourselves closer to people we like and touch them more often. Similarly, if you feel you're of higher status than another, you're more likely to display body movements—such as crossed legs or a slouched seated position—that reflect a casual and relaxed manner.[15]

| Exhibit **11-2** | Intonations: It's the Way You Say It! |

Change your tone and you change your meaning:

Placement of the Emphasis	What It Means
Why don't I take **you** to dinner tonight?	I was going to take someone else.
Why don't **I** take you to dinner tonight?	Instead of the guy you were going with.
Why **don't** I take you to dinner tonight?	I'm trying to find a reason why I **shouldn't** take you.
Why don't I take you to dinner tonight?	Do you have a problem with me?
Why don't I **take** you to dinner tonight?	Instead of going on your own.
Why don't I take you to **dinner** tonight?	Instead of lunch tomorrow.
Why don't I take you to dinner **tonight**?	Not tomorrow night.

Source: Based on M. Kiely, "when 'No' Means 'Yes,'" *Marketing* (October 1993), pp. 7–9. Reproduced in A. Huczynski and D. Buchanan, *Organizational Behavior,* 4th ed. (Essex, UK: Pearson Education, 2001), p. 194.

Body language adds to, and often complicates, verbal communication. A body position or movement can communicate something of the emotion behind a message, but when it is linked with spoken language, it gives fuller meaning to a sender's message.

If you read the verbatim minutes of a meeting, you wouldn't grasp the impact of what was said the same way as if you had been there or could see the meeting on video. Why? There is no record of nonverbal communication. The emphasis given to words or phrases is missing. Exhibit 11-2 illustrates how *intonations* can change the meaning of a message. *Facial expressions* also convey meaning. A snarling face says something different from a smile. Facial expressions, along with intonations, can show arrogance, aggressiveness, fear, shyness, and other characteristics.

Physical distance also has meaning. What is considered proper spacing between people largely depends on cultural norms. A businesslike distance in some European countries feels intimate in many parts of North America. If someone stands closer to you than is considered appropriate, it may indicate aggressiveness or sexual interest; if farther away, it may signal disinterest or displeasure with what is being said.

It's important to be alert to these nonverbal aspects of communication and look for nonverbal cues as well as the literal meaning of a sender's words. You should particularly be aware of contradictions between the messages. Someone who frequently glances at her wristwatch is giving the message that she would prefer to terminate the conversation no matter what she actually says. We misinform others when we express one message verbally, such as trust, but nonverbally communicate a contradictory message that reads, "I don't have confidence in you."

Organizational Communication

5 Analyze the advantages and challenges of electronic communication.

In this section, we move from interpersonal communication to organizational communication. Our first focus will be to describe and distinguish formal networks and the grapevine. Then we discuss technological innovations in communication.

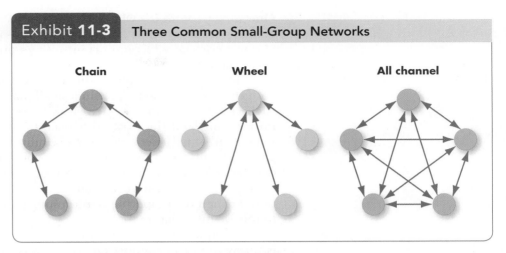

Exhibit **11-3**   Three Common Small-Group Networks

Chain   Wheel   All channel

Formal Small-Group Networks

Formal organizational networks can be very complicated, including hundreds of people and a half-dozen or more hierarchical levels. To simplify our discussion, we've condensed these networks into three common small groups of five people each (see Exhibit 11-3): chain, wheel, and all channel.

The *chain* rigidly follows the formal chain of command; this network approximates the communication channels you might find in a rigid three-level organization. The *wheel* relies on a central figure to act as the conduit for all the group's communication; it simulates the communication network you would find on a team with a strong leader. The *all-channel* network permits all group members to actively communicate with each other; it's most often characterized in practice by self-managed teams, in which all group members are free to contribute and no one person takes on a leadership role.

As Exhibit 11-4 demonstrates, the effectiveness of each network depends on the dependent variable that concerns you. The structure of the wheel facilitates the emergence of a leader, the all-channel network is best if you desire high member satisfaction, and the chain is best if accuracy is most important. Exhibit 11-4 leads us to the conclusion that no single network will be best for all occasions.

The Grapevine

The informal communication network in a group or organization is called the **grapevine**.[16] Although the rumors and gossip transmitted through the grapevine may be informal, it's still an important source of information.

Exhibit **11-4**   Small-Group Networks and Effective Criteria

		Networks	
Criteria	Chain	Wheel	All Channel
Speed	Moderate	Fast	Fast
Accuracy	High	High	Moderate
Emergence of a leader	Moderate	High	None
Member satisfaction	Moderate	Low	High

grapevine *An organization's informal communication network.*

One survey found it's where 75 percent of employees hear news first.[17] A recent report shows that grapevine or word-of-mouth information from peers about a company has important effects on whether job applicants join an organization.[18]

One of the most famous studies of the grapevine investigated communication patterns among 67 managers in a small manufacturing firm.[19] The study asked each communication recipient how he or she first received a given piece of information and then traced it back to its source. While the grapevine was important, only 10 percent of the executives acted as liaison individuals (that is, passed the information to more than one other person). When one executive decided to resign to enter the insurance business, 81 percent of the others knew about it, but only 11 percent told someone else. This lack of spreading information through the grapevine is interesting in light of how often individuals claim to receive information that way.

It's frequently assumed rumors start because they make good gossip. This is rarely the case. Rumors emerge as a response to situations that are *important* to us, when there is *ambiguity,* and under conditions that arouse *anxiety.*[20] The fact that work situations frequently contain these three elements explains why rumors flourish in organizations. The secrecy and competition that typically prevail in large organizations—around the appointment of new bosses, the relocation of offices, downsizing decisions, or the realignment of work assignments—encourage and sustain rumors on the grapevine. A rumor will persist until either the wants and expectations creating the uncertainty are fulfilled or the anxiety has been reduced.

What can we conclude about the grapevine? Certainly it's an important part of any group or organization communication network and is well worth understanding. It gives managers a feel for the morale of their organization, identifies issues employees consider important, and helps tap into employee anxieties. The grapevine also serves employees' needs: small talk creates a sense of closeness and friendship among those who share information, although research suggests it often does so at the expense of those in the "out" group.[21] There is also evidence that gossip is driven largely by employee social networks that managers can study to learn more about how positive and negative information is flowing through their organization.[22] Thus, while the grapevine may not be sanctioned or controlled by the organization, it can be understood.

Can managers entirely eliminate rumors? no. What they should do, however, is minimize the negative consequences of rumors by limiting their range and impact. Exhibit 11-5 offers a few practical suggestions.

Exhibit **11-5**	**Suggestions for Reducing the Negative Consequences of Rumors**

1. **Provide** information—in the long run, the best defense against rumors is a good offense (in other words, rumors tend to thrive in the absence of formal communication).
2. **Explain** actions and decisions that may appear inconsistent, unfair, or secretive.
3. **Refrain** from shooting the messenger—rumors are a natural fact of organizational life, so respond to them calmly, rationally, and respectfully.
4. **Maintain** open communication channels—constantly encourage employees to come to you with concerns, suggestions, and ideas.

Source: Based on L. Hirschhorn, "Managing Rumors," in L. Hirschhorn (ed.), **Cutting Back** (San Francisco: Jossey-Bass, 1983), pp. 54–56.

The Ethics of Gossip at Work

Experts define gossip as "the exchange of information between two people about a third, absent person." It's tempting to gossip about others at work. We all want to know about what's going on with our co-workers, even if it isn't necessarily our concern. But there is a real possibility that gossip can change from harmless chat about other people's lives to truly destructive words that can spread animosity and anger.

So is gossip necessarily bad? Not according to Joe Labianca at the University of Kentucky. He notes, "If a few people know what's really going on, gossip becomes the means of spreading that information to everyone else. What's more, research shows that gossip often reduces individuals'

anxiety and helps them cope with uncertainty." How? Labianca and colleagues have found that gossip allows people to make personal connections with co-workers and facilitates social support. Managers tend not to like gossip because it subverts their authority, but at the same time, it can level the playing field for those who do not otherwise have access to power. Gossip can also be a means to identify individuals who are free riders, bullies, or difficult to work with. In this way, gossip can even facilitate productive performance.

Does this mean that anything goes when it comes to gossip? Hardly. There are several guidelines for keeping gossip a positive source of information. First, don't pass on any information without checking that it's

accurate. Second, don't share personally sensitive information about someone else that violates that person's privacy. Finally, whenever possible, let the person you are talking about to have a chance to enter the discussion at some later point so his or her view can be explicitly taken into account.

Sources: Based on G. Michelson, A. van Iterson, and K. Waddington, "Gossip in Organizations: Contexts, Consequences, and Controversies," *Group and Organization Management* 35, no. 4 (2010), pp. 371–390; K. M. Kniffin and D. S. Wilson, "Evolutionary Perspectives on Workplace Gossip: Why and How Gossip Can Serve Groups," *Group and Organization Management* 35, no. 2 (2010), pp. 150–176; and J. Labianca, "It's Not 'Unprofessional' to Gossip at Work," *Harvard Business Review* (September 2010), pp. 28–29.

Electronic Communications

An indispensable—and in about 71 percent of cases, the primary—medium of communication in today's organizations is electronic. Electronic communications include e-mail, text messaging, networking software, blogs, and video conferencing. Let's discuss each.

E-mail   E-mail uses the Internet to transmit and receive computer-generated text and documents. Its growth has been spectacular, and its use is now so pervasive it's hard to imagine life without it. E-mail messages can be quickly written, edited, and stored. They can be distributed to one person or thousands with a click of a mouse. And the cost of sending formal e-mail messages to employees is a fraction of the cost of printing, duplicating, and distributing a comparable letter or brochure.[23]

E-mail is not without drawbacks. The following are some of its most significant limitations and what organizations should do to reduce or eliminate them:

- **Risk of misinterpreting the message.**   It's true we often misinterpret verbal messages, but the potential to misinterpret e-mail is even greater. One research team at New York University found we can accurately decode an e-mail's intent and tone only 50 percent of the time, yet most of us vastly overestimate our ability to send and interpret clear messages. If you're sending an important message, make sure you reread it for clarity.[24]
- **Drawbacks for communicating negative messages.**   E-mail may not be the best way to communicate negative information. When Radio Shack

decided to lay off 400 employees, it drew an avalanche of scorn inside and outside the company by doing it via e-mail. Employees need to be careful when communicating negative messages via e-mail, too. Justen Deal, 22, wrote an e-mail critical of some strategic decisions made by his employer, pharmaceutical giant Kaiser Permanente, and questioned the financing of several information technology projects. Within hours, Deal's computer was seized; he was later fired.[25]

- **Time-consuming nature.**   An estimated 62 trillion e-mails are sent every year, of which approximately 60 percent, or 36 trillion, are non-spam messages that someone has to answer![26] Some people, such as venture capitalist and Dallas Mavericks owner Mark Cuban, receive more than a thousand messages a day (Cuban says 10 percent are of the "I want" variety). Although you probably don't receive *that* many, most of us have trouble keeping up with all e-mail, especially as we advance in our career. Experts suggest the following strategies:
  - **Don't check e-mail in the morning.**   Take care of important tasks before getting ensnared in e-mails. Otherwise, you may never get to those tasks.
  - **Check e-mail in batches.**   Don't check e-mail continually throughout the day. Some experts suggest twice a day. "You wouldn't want to do a new load of laundry every time you have a dirty pair of socks," says one expert.
  - **Unsubscribe.**   Stop newsletters and other subscriptions you don't really need.
  - **Stop sending e-mail.**   The best way to receive lots of e-mail is to send lots of e-mail, so send less. Shorter e-mails garner shorter responses. "A well-written message can and should be as concise as possible," says one expert.
  - **Declare e-mail bankruptcy.**   Some people, like recording artist Moby and venture capitalist Fred Wilson, become so overwhelmed by e-mail they declare "e-mail bankruptcy." They wipe out their entire inbox and start over.

  Although some of these steps may not work for you, keep in mind that e-mail can be less productive than it seems: we often seem busy but get less accomplished through e-mail than we might think.[27]

- **Limited expression of emotions.**   We tend to think of e-mail as a sort of sterile, faceless form of communication. Some researchers say the lack of visual and vocal cues means emotionally positive messages, like those including praise, will be seen as more emotionally neutral than the sender intended.[28] But as you no doubt know, e-mails are often highly emotional. E-mail tends to have a disinhibiting effect on people; without the recipient's facial expression to temper their emotional expression, senders write things they'd never be comfortable saying in person. When others send flaming messages, remain calm and try not to respond in kind. And, as hard as it might sometimes be, try to see the flaming message from the other party's point of view. That in itself may calm your nerves.[29]

- **Privacy concerns.**   There are two privacy issues with e-mail.[30] First, your e-mails may be, and often are, monitored. You can't always trust the recipient of your e-mail to keep it confidential, either. For these reasons, you shouldn't write anything you wouldn't want made public. Second, you need to exercise caution in forwarding e-mail from your company's e-mail account to a personal or "public" e-mail account (for example, Gmail, Yahoo!, MSN). These accounts often aren't as secure as corporate accounts, so when you forward a company e-mail to them, you may be violating your organization's policy or unintentionally disclosing confidential data. Many employers hire vendors to sift through e-mails, using software to catch not only obvious key words ("insider trading") but also the vague ("that thing we talked about") or the guilt-ridden ("regret"). Another survey revealed nearly 40 percent of companies have employees whose only job is to read other employees' e-mail.[31]

Instant Messaging and Text Messaging Like e-mail, instant messaging (IM) and text messaging (TM) use electronic media. Unlike e-mail, though, IM and TM either occur in real time (IM) or use portable communication devices (TM). In just a few years, IM and TM have become pervasive. As you no doubt know from experience, IM is usually sent via computer, whereas TM is transmitted via cellphones or handheld devices such as BlackBerrys and iPhones.

Despite their advantages, IM and TM aren't going to replace e-mail. E-mail is still probably a better device for conveying long messages that must be saved. IM is preferable for one- or two-line messages that would just clutter up an e-mail inbox. On the downside, some IM and TM users find the technology intrusive and distracting. Its continual presence can make it hard for employees to concentrate and stay focused. A survey of managers revealed that in 86 percent of meetings, at least some participants checked TM, and another survey revealed 20 percent of managers report having been scolded for using wireless devices during meetings.[32] Finally, because instant messages can be intercepted easily, many organizations are concerned about the security of IM and TM.[33]

One other point: it's important to not let the informality of text messaging ("omg! r u serious? brb") spill over into business e-mails. Many prefer to keep business communication relatively formal. A survey of employers revealed that 58 percent rate grammar, spelling, and punctuation as "very important" in e-mail messages.[34] By making sure your professional communications are, well, professional, you'll show yourself to be mature and serious. Avoid jargon and slang, use formal titles, use formal e-mail addresses for yourself (lose thatpartygirl@yahoo.com), and take care to make your message concise and well written. None of this means, of course, that you have to give up TM or IM; you just need to maintain the differences between the way you communicate with your friends and the way you communicate professionally.

Social Networking Nowhere has communication been more transformed than in the rise of social networking. You are doubtless familiar with and perhaps a user of social networking platforms such as Facebook and LinkedIn. Rather than being one huge site, Facebook, which has more than 600 million active users, is actually composed of separate networks based on schools, companies, or regions. Individuals older than age 25 are now its fastest-growing group of users. In a desire to maintain control over employee use of social networking for professional purposes, many organizations have developed their own in-house social networking applications. The research and advisory firm Gartner Inc. estimates that social networking will soon replace e-mail as the primary form of business communication for 20 percent or more of business users.[35]

To get the most from social networks and avoid irritating your contacts, reserve them for high-value items only—not as an everyday or even every-week tool. Remember that a prospective employer might check your Facebook entries. Some entrepreneurs have developed software that mines such Web sites on behalf of companies (or individuals) that want to check up on a job applicant

Source: Teh Eng Koon/AP Images.

Malaysia's airline AirAsia is taking advantage of the flexibility of text messaging to make it more convenient for travelers to book flights. AirAsia flight attendants are shown here with a mobile phone billboard during the launch of the world's first airline booking through a short messaging service (SMS) on cell phones. The SMS makes it easier for travelers to book their seats as the service allows them to choose their flights, confirm their booking, and pay for their seats by text messaging from the convenience of their mobile phone wherever they are.

OB Poll | Rising Risks of Social Networking at Work

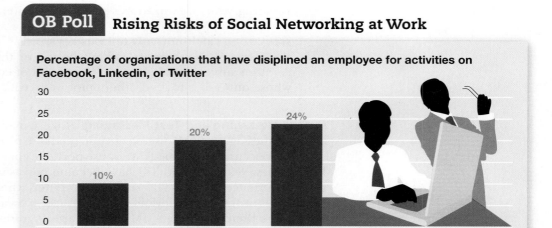

Percentage of organizations that have disiplined an employee for activities on Facebook, Linkedin, or Twitter

- 2009: 10%
- 2010: 20%
- 2011: 24%

Source: Based on Studylogic poll for Starwood Hotels and Resorts/Sheraton.

Sunita Williams, a NASA astronaut commander and the woman who has spent the longest time in space, used videoconferencing to speak to students and journalists at The American Center in Kolkata, India. The videoconferencing technology allowed the students and journalists to interact with Williams as she discussed her experiences aboard the Space Station Atlantis. The interactive meeting gave Williams the opportunity to answer questions about her job as a U.S. Navy experimental test pilot and as a helicopter pilot during the Gulf War.

(or potential date). So keep in mind that what you post may be read by people other than your intended contacts.[36]

Blogs   A **blog (Web log)** is a Web site about a single person or company. Experts estimate that more than 156 million blogs now exist. Millions of U.S. workers have blogs. And, of course, many organizations and organizational leaders have blogs that speak for the organization.

Twitter is a hybrid social networking service that allows users to post "microblog" entries to their subscribers about any topic, including work. Many organizational leaders send Twitter messages ("tweets"), but they can also come from any employee about any work topic, leaving organizations with less control over the communication of important or sensitive information.

Although some companies have policies governing the content of blogs and Twitter feeds, many don't, and many posters say they have blogged or tweeted comments that could be construed as harmful to their company's reputation. Many think their personal blogs are outside their employer's purview, but if someone else in the company happens to read a critical or negative blog entry or post, there is nothing to keep him or her from sharing that information with others, and the employee could be dismissed as a result.

One legal expert notes, "Employee bloggers mistakenly believe the First Amendment gives them the right to say whatever they want on their personal blogs. Wrong!" Also, beware of posting personal blog entries from work. More than three-quarters of employers actively monitor employees' Web site connections. In short, if you are going to have a personal blog, maintain a strict work–personal "firewall."[37]

Video Conferencing   *Video conferencing* permits employees in an organization to have real-time meetings with people at different locations. Live audio and video images let participants see, hear, and talk with each other without being physically in the same location.

Peter Quirk, a program manager with EMC Corporation, uses video conferencing to hold monthly meetings of employees at various locations and many other meetings as well. Doing so saves travel expenses and time. However, Quirk notes it's especially important to stimulate questions and involve all participants in order to avoid someone who is linked in but disengaged. Sun Microsystem's Karen Rhode agrees special efforts must be made to engage remote participants, suggesting, "You can poll people, people can ask questions, you can do an engaging presentation."[38]

Managing Information

We all have more information at our disposal than ever. It brings us many benefits, but also two important challenges: information overload and threats to information security. We consider each in turn.

Dealing with Information Overload   Do you find yourself bombarded with information—from e-mail, blogs, Internet surfing, IMs, cell phones, and televisions? You're not alone. Basex, a company that looks at worker efficiency, found the largest part of an average worker's day—43 percent—is spent on matters that are neither important nor urgent, such as responding to noncrucial e-mails and surfing the Web. (In fairness to e-mail, Basex also found 25 percent of an employee's time was spent composing and responding to *important* e-mail.)

Intel designed an 8-month experiment to see how limiting this **information overload** might aid productivity. One group of employees was told to limit both digital and in-person contact for 4 hours on Tuesdays, while another group followed its usual routine. The first group was more productive, and 75 percent of its members suggested the program be expanded. "It's huge. We were expecting less," remarked Nathan Zeldes, an Intel engineer who led the experiments. "When people are uninterrupted they can sit back and design chips and really think."[39]

We have already reviewed some ways of reducing the time sunk into e-mails. More generally, as the Intel study shows, it may make sense to connect to technology less frequently, to, in the words of one article, "avoid letting the drumbeat of digital missives constantly shake up and reorder to-do lists." Lynaia Lutes, an account supervisor for a small Texas company, was able to think much more strategically by taking a break from digital information each day. In the past, she said, "I basically completed an assignment" but didn't approach it strategically. By creating such breaks for yourself, you may be better able to prioritize, think about the big picture, and thereby be more effective.[40]

As information technology and immediate communication have become a more prevalent component of modern organizational life, more employees find they are never able to get offline. Some business travelers were disappointed when airlines began offering wireless Internet connections in flight because they could no longer use their travel time as a rare opportunity to relax without a constant barrage of organizational communications. The negative impacts of these communication devices can spill over into employees' personal lives as well. Both workers and their spouses relate the use of electronic communication technologies outside work to higher levels of work–life conflict.[41] Employees must balance the need for constant communication with their own

---

blog (Web log)   *A Web site where entries are written, and generally displayed in reverse chronological order, about news, events, and personal diary entries.*

Twitter   *A free blogging and networking service where users send and read messages known as tweets, many of which concern OB issues.*

information overload   *A condition in which information inflow exceeds an individual's processing capacity.*

personal need for breaks from work, or they risk burnout from being on call 24 hours a day.

Threats to Information Security   Security is a huge concern for nearly all organizations with private or proprietary information about clients, customers, and employees. A Merrill Lynch survey of 50 executives found 52 percent rated leaks of company information as their number-one information security concern, topping viruses and hackers. Most companies actively monitor employee Internet use and e-mail records, and some even use video surveillance and record phone conversations. Necessary though they may be, such practices can seem invasive to employees. An organization can relieve employee concerns by engaging them in the creation of information-security policies and giving them some control over how their personal information is used.[42]

Choice of Communication Channel

6   Show how channel richness underlies the choice of communication channel.

Why do people choose one channel of communication over another—say, a phone call instead of a face-to-face talk? A model of media richness helps explain channel selection among managers.[43]

Channels differ in their capacity to convey information. Some are *rich* in that they can (1) handle multiple cues simultaneously, (2) facilitate rapid feedback, and (3) be very personal. Others are *lean* in that they score low on these factors. As Exhibit 11-6 illustrates, face-to-face conversation scores highest in **channel richness** because it transmits the most information per communication episode—multiple information cues (words, postures, facial expressions, gestures, intonations), immediate feedback (both verbal and nonverbal), and

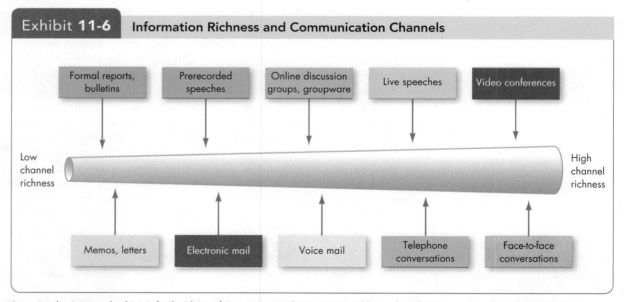

| Exhibit **11-6** | **Information Richness and Communication Channels** |

Source: Based on R. H. Lengel and R. L. Daft, "The Selection of Communication Media as an Executive Skill," *Academy of Management Executive* (August 1988), pp. 225–232; and R. L. Daft and R. H. Lengel, "Organizational Information Requirements, Media Richness, and Structural Design," *Managerial Science* (May 1996), pp. 554–572. Reproduced from R. L. Daft and R. A. Noe, *Organizational Behavior* (Fort Worth, TX: Harcourt, 2001), p. 311.

the personal touch of being present. Impersonal written media such as formal reports and bulletins rate lowest in richness.

The choice of channel depends on whether the message is routine. Routine messages tend to be straightforward and have minimal ambiguity; channels low in richness can carry them efficiently. Nonroutine communications are likely to be complicated and have the potential for misunderstanding. Managers can communicate them effectively only by selecting rich channels.

When tough times hit Manpower Business Solutions during the recent economic contraction, the company elected to communicate with employees daily in a variety of media to ensure that everyone remained informed.[44] Employees were given updates about the company's plans for dealing with economic problems, including advance warning before layoffs. The company believes its strategy of using rich communication channels for nonroutine information has paid off by reducing employee anxiety and increasing engagement with the organization.

Persuasive Communications

7 Differentiate between automatic and controlled processing of persuasive messages.

We've discussed a number of methods for communication up to this point. Now we turn our attention to one of the functions of communication and the features that might make messages more or less persuasive to an audience.

Automatic and Controlled Processing

To understand the process of communication, it is useful to consider two relatively different ways that we process information.[45] Think about the last time you bought a can of soda. Did you carefully research brands and engage in your own double-blind taste test to see which types you actually prefer? Or did you reach for the can that had the most appealing advertising images? If we're honest, we'll admit glitzy ads and catchy slogans do indeed have an influence on our choices as consumers. We often rely on **automatic processing**, a relatively superficial consideration of evidence and information making use of heuristics like those we discussed in Chapter 6. Automatic processing takes little time and low effort, so it makes sense to use it for processing persuasive messages related to topics you don't care much about. The disadvantage is that it lets us be easily fooled by a variety of tricks, like a cute jingle or glamorous photo.

Now consider the last time you chose a place to live. For this more important decision, you probably did do some independent research among experts who know something about the area, gathered information about prices from a variety of sources, and considered the costs and benefits of renting versus buying. Here, you're relying on more effortful **controlled processing**, a detailed consideration of evidence and information relying on facts, figures, and logic. Controlled processing requires effort and energy, but it's harder to fool

channel richness *The amount of information that can be transmitted during a communication episode.*

automatic processing *A relatively superficial consideration of evidence and information making use of heuristics.*

controlled processing *A detailed consideration of evidence and information relying on facts, figures, and logic.*

someone who has taken the time and effort to engage in it. So what makes someone engage in either shallow or deep processing? There are a few rules of thumb for determining what types of processing an audience will use.

Interest Level

One of the best predictors of whether people will use an automatic or controlled process for reacting to a persuasive message is their level of interest in it.[46] Interest levels reflect the impact a decision is going to have on your life. When people are very interested in the outcome of a decision, they're more likely to process information carefully. That's probably why people look for so much more information when deciding about something important (like where to live) than something relatively unimportant (like which soda to drink).

Prior Knowledge

People who are very well informed about a subject area are also more likely to use controlled processing strategies. They have already thought through various arguments for or against a specific course of action, and therefore they won't readily change their position unless very good, thoughtful reasons are provided. On the other hand, people who are poorly informed about a topic can change their minds more readily, even in the face of fairly superficial arguments presented without a great deal of evidence. In other words, a better informed audience is likely to be much harder to persuade.

Personality

Are you the type of person who always likes to read at least five reviews of a movie before deciding whether to see it? Do you carefully consider several movies before making a choice? Perhaps you even research recent films by the same stars and director. If so, you are probably high in *need for cognition,* a personality trait of individuals who are most likely to be persuaded by evidence and facts.[47] Those who are lower in need for cognition are more likely to use automatic processing strategies, relying on intuition and emotion to guide their evaluation of persuasive messages.

Message Characteristics

Another factor that influences whether people use an automatic or controlled processing strategy is the characteristics of the message itself. Messages provided through relatively lean communication channels, with little opportunity for users to interact with the content of the message, tend to encourage automatic processing. For example, most television advertisements go by too fast for really deliberative thought; we automatically process these. Conversely, messages provided through richer communication channels, like a long magazine article, tend to encourage more deliberative processing.

The most important implication of all this research is to match your persuasive message to the type of processing your audience is likely to use. When the audience is not especially interested in a persuasive message topic, when they are poorly informed, when they are low in need for cognition, and when information is transmitted through relatively lean channels, they'll be more likely to use automatic processing. In these cases, use messages that are more emotion-laden and associate positive images with your preferred outcome. On the other hand, when the audience is interested in a topic, when they are high in need for cognition, or when the information is transmitted through rich channels, then it is a better idea to focus on rational arguments and evidence to make your case.

Barriers to Effective Communication

8 Identify common barriers to effective communication.

A number of barriers can retard or distort effective communication. In this section, we highlight the most important.

Filtering

Filtering refers to a sender's purposely manipulating information so the receiver will see it more favorably. A manager who tells his boss what he feels the boss wants to hear is filtering information.

The more vertical levels in the organization's hierarchy, the more opportunities there are for filtering. But some filtering will occur wherever there are status differences. Factors such as fear of conveying bad news and the desire to please the boss often lead employees to tell their superiors what they think they want to hear, thus distorting upward communications.

Selective Perception

We have mentioned selective perception before in this book. It appears again here because the receivers in the communication process selectively see and hear based on their needs, motivations, experience, background, and other personal characteristics. Receivers also project their interests and expectations into communications as they decode them. An employment interviewer who expects a female job applicant to put her family ahead of her career is likely to see that in all female applicants, regardless of whether they actually feel that way. As we said in Chapter 6, we don't see reality; we interpret what we see and call it reality.

Information Overload

Individuals have a finite capacity for processing data. When the information we have to work with exceeds our processing capacity, the result is information overload. We've seen that dealing with it has become a huge challenge for individuals and for organizations. It's a challenge you can manage—to some degree—by following the steps outlined earlier in this chapter.

What happens when individuals have more information than they can sort and use? They tend to select, ignore, pass over, or forget. Or they may put off further processing until the overload situation ends. In any case, lost information and less effective communication results, making it all the more important to deal well with overload.

Emotions

You may interpret the same message differently when you're angry or distraught than when you're happy. For example, individuals in positive moods are more confident about their opinions after reading a persuasive message, so well-crafted arguments have stronger impacts on their opinions.[48] People in negative moods are more likely to scrutinize messages in greater detail, whereas those in positive moods tend to accept communications at face value.[49] Extreme

filtering *A sender's manipulation of information so that it will be seen more favorably by the receiver.*

Managers of Hochtief, Germany's largest construction firm, relied on controlled processing when addressing employees during a supervisory board meeting at company headquarters in Essen, Germany, shown here. In response to a takeover bid by the Spanish construction firm Actividades de Construccion & Servicios (ACS), Hochtief management focused on rational evidence and arguments in presenting its defense against the takeover bid and its plans to fend off the bid. Employees' level of interest in the takeover attempt is high, because they fear that an ACS takeover would result in a major downsizing of Hochtief's workforce and would put their jobs at risk.

Source: Bernd Thissen/dpa/picture-alliance/Newscom.

emotions such as jubilation or depression are most likely to hinder effective communication. In such instances, we are most prone to disregard our rational and objective thinking processes and substitute emotional judgments.

Language

Even when we're communicating in the same language, words mean different things to different people. Age and context are two of the biggest factors that influence such differences.

When Michael Schiller, a business consultant, was talking with his 15-year-old daughter about where she was going with her friends, he told her, "You need to recognize your KPIs and measure against them." Schiller said that in response, his daughter "looked at him like he was from outer space." (For the record, KPI stands for key performance indicators.) Those new to corporate lingo may find acronyms such as *KPI*, words such as *deliverables* (verifiable outcomes of a project), and phrases such as *get the low-hanging fruit* (deal with the easiest parts first) bewildering, in the same way parents may be mystified by teen slang.[50]

In short, our use of language is far from uniform. If we knew how each of us modified the language, we could minimize communication difficulties, but we usually don't know. Senders tend to assume the words and terms they use mean the same to the receiver as to them. This assumption is often incorrect.

Silence

It's easy to ignore silence or lack of communication, precisely because it is defined by the absence of information. However, research suggests silence and withholding communication are both common and problematic.[51] One survey found that more than 85 percent of managers reported remaining silent about at least one issue of significant concern.[52] Employee silence means managers lack information about ongoing operational problems. And silence regarding discrimination, harassment, corruption, and misconduct means top management cannot take action to eliminate this behavior. Finally, employees who are silent about important issues may also experience psychological stress.

Silence is less likely where minority opinions are treated with respect, workgroup identification is high, and high procedural justice prevails.[53] Practically, this means managers must make sure they behave in a supportive manner when employees voice divergent opinions or concerns, and they must take these under advisement. One act of ignoring or belittling an employee for expressing concerns may well lead the employee to withhold important future communication.

Communication Apprehension

An estimated 5 to 20 percent of the population suffers debilitating **communication apprehension**, or social anxiety.[54] These people experience undue tension and anxiety in oral communication, written communication, or both.[55] They may find it extremely difficult to talk with others face-to-face or may become extremely anxious when they have to use the phone, relying on memos or e-mails when a phone call would be faster and more appropriate.

Studies show oral-communication apprehensives avoid situations, such as teaching, for which oral communication is a dominant requirement.[56] But almost all jobs require *some* oral communication. Of greater concern is evidence that high oral-communication apprehensives distort the communication demands of their jobs in order to minimize the need for communication. So be aware that some people severely limit their oral communication and rationalize their actions by telling themselves communicating isn't necessary for them to do their job effectively.

Lying

The final barrier to effective communication is outright misrepresentation of information, or lying. People differ in their definition of what constitutes a lie. For example, is deliberately withholding information about a mistake you made a lie, or do you have to actively deny your role in the mistake to pass the threshold of deceit? While the definition of a lie will continue to befuddle both ethicists and social scientists, there is no denying the prevalence of lying. In one diary study, the average person reported telling one to two lies per day, with some individuals telling considerably more.[57] Compounded across a large organization, this is an enormous amount of deception happening every single day! Evidence also shows that people are more comfortable lying over the phone than face-to-face and more comfortable lying in e-mails than when they have to write with pen and paper.[58]

Can you detect liars? Despite a great deal of investigation, research generally suggests most people are not very good at detecting deception in others.[59] The problem is, there are no nonverbal or verbal cues unique to lying—averting your gaze, pausing, and shifting your posture can also be signals of nervousness, shyness, or doubt. Moreover, most people who lie take a number of steps to guard against being detected, so they might deliberately look a person in the eye when lying because they know that direct eye contact is (incorrectly) assumed to be a sign of truthfulness. Finally, many lies are embedded in truths; liars usually give a somewhat true account with just enough details changed to avoid detection.

In sum, the frequency of lying and the difficulty in detecting liars makes this an especially strong barrier to effective communication in organizations.

communication apprehension   *Undue tension and anxiety about oral communication, written communication, or both.*

Myth or Science?

"We Know What Makes Good Liars Good"

This statement is true, though we still have more to learn about the characteristics of proficient liars.

As we have noted in this chapter, it is not easy to detect whether liars are telling the truth. We have reviewed some of the reasons for this, but recent research has uncovered an obvious but only recently tested explanation for why it's hard to catch a liar: some people are just good at lying, and we're beginning to understand why.

What causes people to be good liars? A major review of the literature identified six features of good liars:

1. Their natural behavior is disarming—they smile, make eye contact, mimic the gestures of their target, and avoid "ums" and "ehs."

2. They do their homework—they have thought up plausible cover stories before they are demanded.

3. They don't let their emotions get in the way—good liars are unusually calm and composed when lying.

4. They are good-looking—good liars are physically attractive; we are more likely to trust stories told by attractive people.

5. They have good insights into others' thought processes.

6. They tend to believe their own lies—this has been established by studies that ask people to lie and later find many of them believe their original lies to be true.

A sad truth of organizational behavior is that people are better liars than we think, and we are worse at unveiling them than we realize.

Sources: A. Vrij, P. A. Granhag, and S. Porter, "Pitfalls and Opportunities in Nonverbal and Verbal Lie Detection," *Psychological Science in the Public Interest* 11, no. 3 (2010), pp. 89–121; E. F. Loftus, "Catching Liars," *Psychological Science in the Public Interest* 11, no. 3 (2010), pp. 87–88; and A. Vrij, P. A. Granhag, and S. Mann, "Good Liars," Unpublished manuscript, University of Portsmouth, 2011, www.port.ac.uk/departments/academic/psychology/staff/downloads/filetodownload,89132,en.pdf.

Global Implications

9 Show how to overcome the potential problems in cross-cultural communication.

Effective communication is difficult under the best of conditions. Cross-cultural factors clearly create the potential for increased communication problems. A gesture that is well understood and acceptable in one culture can be meaningless or lewd in another. Only 18 percent of companies have documented strategies for communicating with employees across cultures, and only 31 percent require that corporate messages be customized for consumption in other cultures. Procter & Gamble seems to be an exception; more than half the company's employees don't speak English as their first language, so the company focuses on simple messages to make sure everyone knows what's important.[60]

Cultural Barriers

Researchers have identified a number of problems related to language difficulties in cross-cultural communications.[61]

First are *barriers caused by semantics*. Words mean different things to different people, particularly people from different national cultures. Some words don't translate between cultures. The Finnish word *sisu* means something akin to "guts" or "dogged persistence" but is essentially untranslatable into English. The new capitalists in Russia may have difficulty communicating with British or Canadian counterparts because English terms such as *efficiency, free market,* and *regulation* have no direct Russian equivalents.

Second are *barriers caused by word connotations*. Words imply different things in different languages. Negotiations between U.S. and Japanese executives can be difficult because the Japanese word *hai* translates as "yes," but its connotation is "Yes, I'm listening" rather than "Yes, I agree."

Third are *barriers caused by tone differences.* In some cultures, language is formal; in others, it's informal. In some cultures, the tone changes depending on the context: People speak differently at home, in social situations, and at work. Using a personal, informal style when a more formal style is expected can be embarrassing.

Fourth are *differences in tolerance for conflict and methods for resolving conflicts.* Individuals from individualist cultures tend to be more comfortable with direct conflicts and will make the source of their disagreements overt. Collectivists are more likely to acknowledge conflict only implicitly and avoid emotionally charged disputes. They may attribute conflicts to the situation more than to the individuals and therefore may not require explicit apologies to repair relationships, whereas individualists prefer explicit statements accepting responsibility for conflicts and public apologies to restore relationships.

Cultural Context

Cultures tend to differ in the degree to which context influences the meaning individuals take from communication.[62] In **high-context cultures** such as China, Korea, Japan, and Vietnam, people rely heavily on nonverbal and subtle situational cues in communicating with others, and a person's official status, place in society, and reputation carry considerable weight. What is *not* said may be more significant than what *is* said. In contrast, people from Europe and North America reflect their **low-context cultures**. They rely essentially on spoken and written words to convey meaning; body language and formal titles are secondary (see Exhibit 11-7).

These contextual differences actually mean quite a lot in terms of communication. Communication in high-context cultures implies considerably more trust by both parties. What may appear to be casual and insignificant conversation in fact reflects the desire to build a relationship and create trust. Oral agreements imply strong commitments in high-context cultures. And who you are—your age, seniority, rank in the organization—is highly valued and heavily influences your credibility. But in low-context cultures, enforceable contracts tend to be in writing, precisely worded, and highly legalistic. Similarly, low-context cultures value directness. Managers are expected to be explicit and precise in conveying intended meaning. It's quite different in high-context cultures, in which managers tend to "make suggestions" rather than give orders.

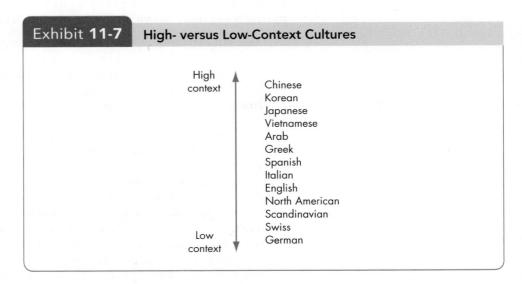

Exhibit 11-7 | **High- versus Low-Context Cultures**

High context

- Chinese
- Korean
- Japanese
- Vietnamese
- Arab
- Greek
- Spanish
- Italian
- English
- North American
- Scandinavian
- Swiss
- German

Low context

---

high-context cultures   *Cultures that rely heavily on nonverbal and subtle situational cues in communication.*

low-context cultures   *Cultures that rely heavily on words to convey meaning in communication.*

How Direct Should You Be?

Those who have traveled or done business internationally are often advised to be careful about how directly they communicate with people from different cultures. The popular advice suggests that U.S. citizens prefer upbeat, positive communication; the English prefer formal communication; central Europeans are more interested in direct communication even if information is negative; and East Asians prefer to minimize disagreements and emphasize shared perspectives. Although there is more advice than research on this particular issue, some preliminary work does suggest some reliable differences in how cultures value direct and indirect communication.

One study examined cultural differences in values, beliefs, and personality data to see whether any consistent patterns in communication could be found. A group of East Asian countries, including China, Taiwan, Singapore, and Japan, were marked by a bias for low levels of both agreement *and* disagreement in communication, preferring moderate discussions with respondents not taking strong sides on an issue. Conversely, countries like Morocco, Iraq, Israel, and Saudi Arabia prefer high levels of both agreement and disagreement in their communications; in these countries, the preferred communication style meant directly taking a stand on issues whether positive or negative. "Dissent" cultures like Germany, the United Kingdom, Sweden, and Greece favored high levels of disagreement in communication with relatively low levels of agreement. Nigeria, India, and Vietnam were found to be high in agreement and low in disagreement in communication.

The results of studies of this nature should always be considered carefully in light of the large differences we also find within cultures. Some individuals from India may well value negative opinions and active disagreement from others, whereas some Germans might prefer to focus on areas of shared values. However, some patterning of responses across cultures does indicate a real difference in preferences for communication styles.

Sources: P. B. Smith, "Communication Styles as Dimensions of National Culture," *Journal of Cross-Cultural Psychology* 42, no. 2 (2011), pp. 216–233; and M. G. Kittler, D. Rygl, and A. Mackinnon, "Beyond Culture or Beyond Control? Reviewing the Use of Hall's High-/Low-Context Concept," *International Journal of Cross Cultural Management* 11, no. 1 (2011), pp. 63–82.

A Cultural Guide

When communicating with people from a different culture, what can you do to reduce misinterpretations? Begin by trying to assess the cultural context. You're likely to have fewer difficulties if it's similar to yours. The following rules can be helpful:[63]

1. **Assume differences until similarity is proven.** Most of us assume others are more similar to us than they actually are. You are less likely to err if you assume they are different from you until proven otherwise.

2. **Emphasize description rather than interpretation or evaluation.** Interpreting or evaluating what someone has said or done draws more on your own culture and background than on the observed situation. So delay judgment until you've had sufficient time to observe and interpret the situation from the differing perspectives of all concerned.

3. **Practice empathy.** Before sending a message, put yourself in the recipient's shoes. What are his or her values, experiences, and frames of reference? What do you know about his or her education, upbringing, and background that can give you added insight? Try to see the other person as he or she really is.

4. **Treat your interpretations as a working hypothesis.** Once you've developed an explanation for a new situation or think you empathize with someone from a foreign culture, treat your interpretation as a hypothesis that needs further testing rather than as a certainty. Carefully assess the feedback recipients provide you, to see whether it confirms your hypothesis. For important decisions or communiqués, check with other foreign and home-country colleagues to make sure your interpretations are on target.

Social Networking Is Good Business

POINT ▸◂ **COUNTERPOINT**

Facebook has passed a half a billion users for a reason. It's an inspired idea that serves many useful purposes for organizations and employees alike. Other social networking and media sites like Twitter are not far behind.

Employers can learn a lot about prospective hires by examining their Facebook (or other social networking) page. UPS recently ramped up its use of social networking to recruit. "Our reason for using social media is because that's where we think the applicants are," says a UPS manager in charge of recruitment. Applicants likewise can learn a lot about an organization by analyzing its online presence.

Facebook and other social networks are also great ways for employees to communicate with one another, particularly when they work in geographically dispersed locales and do an increasing amount of their work remotely. Banning or discouraging employees from using social media needlessly places each employee in a communications silo. One social media expert said the Millennial generation "is horrified at how unconnected people in many organizations are." Many firms, like UPS, are embracing social networking, though. IBM developed its own social networking software—called w3—to link its 400,000 employees across the world. IBM manager John Rooney says the software "contributes to the integration of our company on a global basis. It's seen as part of our ability to succeed."

In some companies, teams create Facebook groups around their projects to foster teamwork and open the lines of communication. Pushed to its full potential, social networking can even change a company's culture given its open, democratic, and transparent nature. "You better believe it can democratize a company," said one workplace expert. Isn't that what we want?"

There's no doubt social networking has exploded. There is significant doubt, however, that this explosion is beneficial to employees and to organizations. Although there are many dangers in social networking, let's focus on three.

First, companies can get into legal hot water by looking into applicants' social networking profiles. Equal Employment Opportunity laws require companies to hire without respect to race, sex, age, religion, national origin, or disability. Yet you can learn all these things from someone's profile. And that's not the only legal minefield. Recently, when a Chicago-area employee was reprimanded for posting her frustrations with her boss on her Facebook page, the National Labor Relations Board ruled against the company.

Second, social networks are risky for employees and applicants too. They were originally established to connect friends—and that remains their primary purpose. When employers snoop into an employee or applicant's Facebook page, fairly or not, they won't judge the information and its informality as dialogue among friends. Rather, they'll use it to draw the wrong conclusions. As one employment expert says, "While employers shouldn't use affiliations with social networks or your personal posts as reasons not to hire you, why take the risk?"

Finally, and perhaps most important, today nearly all of us suffer from communication overload, and social networking only adds to it. "There are so many things coming at you," says 29-year-old manager Jose Huitron. "Sometimes it can be so overwhelming," says George Washington University student Ben Yarmis. Scores of research studies show that the growth in social networking has limited people's attention spans and increased distractions. Says one neuroscientist who has studied the effect of social networking on how the mind works: "We are exposing our brains to an environment and asking them to do things we weren't necessarily evolved to do. We know already there are consequences."

Sources: J. A. Segal, "Dancing on the Edge of a Volcano," *HR Magazine* (April 2011), pp. 83–86; T. L. Griffith, "Tapping Into Social-Media Smarts," *The Wall Street Journal* (April 25, 2011), p. R6; L. Petrecca, "More Grads Use Social Media to Job Hunt," *USA Today* (April 5, 2011), p. B1; J. Swartz, "Communications Overload," *USA Today* (February 2, 2011), pp. 1B–2B; S. Ladika, "Socially Evolved," *Workforce Management* (September 2010), pp. 18–22; M. Richtel, "Hooked on Gadgets, and Paying a Mental Price," *The New York Times* (June 6, 2010), pp. A1, A12, A13; and A. Clark, "Watch What You're Posting: Your Boss May Be Watching," *Gainesville Sun* (February 19, 2011), pp. 1B, 5B.

SELF-ASSESSMENT LIBRARY

How Good Are My Listening Skills?

In the Self-Assessment Library (available on CD or online), take assessment II.A.2 (How Good Are My Listening Skills?).

MyManagementLab

Now that you have finished this chapter, go back to **www.pearsonglobaleditions.com/ mymanagementlab** to continue practicing and applying the concepts you've learned.

Summary and Implications for Managers

You've probably discovered the link between communication and employee satisfaction in this chapter: the less uncertainty, the greater the satisfaction. Distortions, ambiguities, and incongruities between verbal and nonverbal messages all increase uncertainty and reduce satisfaction.[64]

- The less distortion, the more employees will receive goals, feedback, and other management messages as intended.[65] This, in turn, should reduce ambiguities and clarify the group's task.
- Extensive use of vertical, lateral, and informal channels also increases communication flow, reduces uncertainty, and improves group performance and satisfaction.
- Perfect communication is unattainable. Yet a positive relationship exists between effective communication and worker productivity.[66] Choosing the correct channel, being an effective listener, and using feedback can make for more effective communication.
- Whatever the sender's expectations, the message as decoded in the receiver's mind represents his or her reality. And this reality will determine performance, along with the individual's level of motivation and degree of satisfaction.
- Because we gather so much meaning from the way a message is communicated, the potential for misunderstanding in electronic communication is great despite its advantages .
- We sometimes process messages relatively automatically, while at other times we use a more effortful, controlled process. Make sure you use communication strategies appropriate to your audience and the type of message you're sending.
- Finally, by keeping in mind communication barriers such as gender and culture, we can overcome them and increase our communication effectiveness.

QUESTIONS FOR REVIEW

1 What are the primary functions of the communication process in organizations?

2 What are the key parts of the communication process, and how do you distinguish formal and informal communication?

3 What are the differences among downward, upward, and lateral communication?

4 What are the unique challenges to oral, written, and nonverbal communication?

5 What are the advantages and challenges of electronic communication?

6 What are the main forms of electronic communication? What are their unique benefits and challenges?

7 What is the difference between automatic and controlled processing of persuasive messages?

8 What are some common barriers to effective communication?

9 What unique problems underlie cross-cultural communication?

EXPERIENTIAL EXERCISE An Absence of Nonverbal Communication

This exercise will help you to see the value of nonverbal communication to interpersonal relations.

1. The class is to split up into pairs (party A and party B).
2. Party A is to select a topic from the following list:
   a. Managing in the Middle East is significantly different from managing in North America.
   b. Employee turnover in an organization can be functional.
   c. Some conflict in an organization is good.
   d. Whistle-blowers do more harm than good for an organization.
   e. An employer has a responsibility to provide every employee with an interesting and challenging job.
   f. Everyone should register to vote.
   g. Organizations should require all employees to undergo regular drug tests.
   h. Individuals who have majored in business or economics make better employees than those who have majored in history or English.
   i. The place where you get your college degree is more important in determining your career success than what you learn while you're there.
   j. It's unethical for a manager to purposely distort communications to get a favorable outcome.
3. Party B is to choose a position on this topic (for example, arguing *against* the view "Some conflict in an organization is good"). Party A now must automatically take the opposite position.
4. The two parties have 10 minutes in which to debate their topic. The catch is that the individuals can only communicate verbally. They may *not* use gestures, facial movements, body movements, or any other nonverbal communication. It may help for each party to sit on their hands to remind them of their restrictions and to maintain an expressionless look.
5. After the debate is over, form groups of six to eight and spend 15 minutes discussing the following:
   a. How effective was communication during these debates?
   b. What barriers to communication existed?
   c. What purposes does nonverbal communication serve?
   d. Relate the lessons learned in this exercise to problems that might occur when communicating on the telephone or through e-mail.

ETHICAL DILEMMA Pitfalls of E-Mail

Jacob, the sales manager at JOB, realized that he had forgotten to send out a reminder to his sales team to complete their appraisal forms. It was Friday and their appraisals were on Monday morning. He asked his secretary Salma, to send an e-mail reminder to all his team. Salma decided to only send the e-mail to those who had not sent in their forms, rather than the whole team. She copied in her boss and marked it as high importance. Jacob responded copying in the whole team to say he had already received half of the forms. Salma was a bit annoyed as it made her look incompetent. There were various replies from members of the sales team, some of them replied to all, others to Salma, a few to Jacob. On Monday morning, Jacob had some of the appraisal forms but was not sure whether to proceed—there is a human resource policy that states he needs that documentation prior to the appraisal.

Questions
1. What issues may arise when we use "cc," "bcc," "mailing lists," "reply all," and "high importance" in e-mails?
2. Considering the Goldman rules at the beginning of the chapter, consider what rules there should be in an organization relating to the use of the issues in question 1.

CASE INCIDENT 1   Using Social Media to Your Advantage

As you know, social media have transformed the way we interact. The transparent, rapid-fire communication they make possible means people can spread information about companies more rapidly than ever.

Do organizations understand yet how to use social media effectively? Perhaps not. As recently as 2010, only 19 of the top 50 chief executives in the world had Facebook accounts, only 6 had LinkedIn pages, and only 2 regularly used Twitter or blogs to communicate. Many executives are wary of these new technologies because they cannot always control the outcomes of their communications. However, whether they are directly involved with social media or not, companies should recognize that these messages are out there, so it behooves them to make their voices heard. And social media can be an important way to learn about emerging trends. André Schneider, chief operating officer of the World Economic Forum, uses feedback from LinkedIn discussion groups and Facebook friends to discover emerging trends and issues worldwide. Padmasree Warrior, chief technology officer of Cisco, has used social media to refine her presentations before a "test" audience.

The first step in developing a social media strategy is establishing a brand for your communications—define what you want your social media presence to express. Experts recommend that companies begin their social media strategy by leveraging their internal corporate networks to test their strategy in a medium that's easier to control. Most companies already have the technology to use social media through their corporate Web sites. Begin by using these platforms for communicating with employees and facilitating social networks for general information sharing.

As social networking expert Soumitra Dutta from Insead notes, "My advice is to build your audience slowly and be selective about your contacts."

Despite the potential advantages, companies also need to be aware of significant drawbacks to social media. First, it's very difficult to control social media communications. Microsoft found this out when the professional blogger it hired spent more time promoting himself than getting positive information out about the company. Second, important intellectual capital might leak out. Companies need to establish very clear policies and procedures to ensure that sensitive information about ongoing corporate strategies is not disseminated via social media. Finally, managers should maintain motivation and interest beyond their initial forays into social media. A site that's rarely updated can send a very negative message about the organization's level of engagement with the world.

Questions

1. Do you think organizations need to have a social media presence today? Are the drawbacks sufficient to make you think it's better for them to avoid certain media?

2. What features would you look for in a social media outlet? What types of information would you avoid making part of your social media strategy?

3. Which social media sources do you think are most useful for organizations to send communications to external stakeholders, like stockholders or customers? Are different social media more appropriate for communicating with employees?

4. What do you think is the future direction of social media? How might emerging technologies change them?

Sources: S. Dutta, "What's Your Personal Social Media Strategy," *Harvard Business Review* (November 2010), pp. 127–130; and G. Connors, "10 Social Media Commandments for Employers," *Workforce Management Online* (February 2010), www.workforce.com.

CASE INCIDENT 2   An Underwater Meeting

On Saturday October 17, 2009, forty-two year old, democratically elected President Mohammad Nasheed of the Maldives invited his 13 officials to a cabinet meeting: the world's first underwater governmental meeting. The meeting "room" was in a lagoon off Girifushi, in the North Male atoll, and the ministers dove 20 feet (6 meters) to meet around a horseshoe-shaped table on the sea floor.

The Maldives, located southwest of Sri Lanka, is an Indian Ocean archipelago, whose 1,192 islands stretch for 850 kilometers (530 miles). The Maldivian islands are on

average only 2 meters (7 feet) above sea level, and they comprise the lowest-lying nation on the planet.

The meeting agenda highlighted how global warming was threatening the disappearance of the Maldives within a century. In 2007, data about this threat were confirmed by the United Nation (UN) Intergovernmental Panel on Climate Change, warning that a rise in sea levels of 18 to 59 centimeters (7 to 23 inches) by 2100 would be enough to make the Maldives virtually uninhabitable. The decision made at the meeting was to sign off on an agreement for carbon emission cuts: "We must unite in a global effort to halt further temperature rises." The meeting took place prior to the United Nations climate change conference in December, in anticipation of the renegotiation of the Kyoto Protocol.

The safety of the ministers was well considered; they held a dress rehearsal the day before; coral on the reef was checked for harmful creatures; participants communicated via hand signals to indicate they were okay. Instead of dressing in business suits, though, the 14 government ministers donned scuba diving gear and also wore name tags. Just as in every meeting, discussion took place, but here it was through writing on a special white board. The meeting was broadcast live on television. Inhabitants on Kuda Huvadhoo island built a sealed box, put their television in it, and, following their

governments' lead, dove to the depths to view the underwater meeting—underwater.

Back on dry land, the cabinet ministers were to sign their wet suits for auctioning on the www.protectthemaldives.com Web site in a bid to raise money for protecting coral reefs. President Nasheed used the meeting venue as a publicity exercise to push for action so that his people can continue to live in the Maldives well into the future.

Questions

1. Identify the main function of the meeting.

2. Describe the communication process and distinguish between its formality and informality.

3. Identify barriers to effective communication in this meeting.

Sources: Based on: AFP, (October 17, 2009), "Maldives Officials Hold Underwater Meeting to Highlight Threat of Global Warming," *Gulf News,* p. 21, accessed October 23, 2009 at gulfnews.com/news/world/other-world/maldives-officialshold-underwater-meeting-to-highlight-threat-of-globalwarming-1.515739; AFP, (October 16, 2009), "Maldives Cabinet Rehearses Underwater Meeting," *Canwest* News Service, accessed October 23, 2009 at www.canada.com/technology/Maldives+cabinet+rehearses+underwater+meeting/2111098/story.html; O. Lang, (October 17, 2009), "Maldives Leader in Climate Change Stunt," *BBC News,* accessed October 23, 2009 at news.bbc.co.uk/2/hi/south_asia/8312320.stm.

ENDNOTES

1. See, for example, R. S. Lau and A. T. Cobb, "Understanding the Connections between Relationship Conflict and Performance: The Intervening Roles of Trust and Exchange," *Journal of Organizational Behavior* 31, no. 6 (2010), pp. 898–917; and M. Olekalns, L. L. Putnam, L. R. Weingart, and L. Metcalf, "Communication Processes and Conflict Management: The Psychology of Conflict and Conflict Management in Organizations," in C. K. W. De Dreu and M. J. Gelfand, (eds.), *The Psychology of Conflict and Conflict Management in Organizations.* (New York: Taylor & Francis Group, 2008) pp. 81–114.

2. "Employers Cite Communication Skills, Honesty/Integrity as Key for Job Candidates," *IPMA-HR Bulletin* (March 23, 2007), p. 1.

3. W. G. Scott and T. R. Mitchell, *Organization Theory: A Structural and Behavioral Analysis* (Homewood, IL: Irwin, 1976).

4. D. K. Berlo, *The Process of Communication* (New York: Holt, Rinehart & Winston, 1960), pp. 30–32; see also K. Byron, "Carrying Too Heavy a Load? The Communication and Miscommunication of Emotion by Email," *The Academy of Management Review* 33, no. 2 (2008), pp. 309–327.

5. J. Langan-Fox, "Communication in Organizations: Speed, Diversity, Networks, and Influence on Organizational Effectiveness, Human Health, and Relationships," in N. Anderson, D. S. Ones, H. K. Sinangil, and C. Viswesvaran (Eds.), *Handbook of Industrial, Work and Organizational Psychology,* vol. 2 (Thousand Oaks, CA: Sage, 2001), p. 190.

6. R. L. Simpson, "Vertical and Horizontal Communication in Formal Organizations," *Administrative Science Quarterly* (September 1959), pp. 188–196; A. G. Walker and J. W. Smither, "A Five-Year Study of Upward Feedback: What Managers Do with Their Results Matter," *Personnel Psychology* (Summer 1999), pp. 393–424; and J. W. Smither and A. G. Walker, "Are the Characteristics of Narrative Comments Related to Improvement in Multirater Feedback Ratings Over Time?" *Journal of Applied Psychology* 89, no. 3 (June 2004), pp. 575–581.

7. P. Dvorak, "How Understanding the 'Why' of Decisions Matters," *The Wall Street Journal* (March 19, 2007), p. B3.

8. T. Neeley and P. Leonardi, "Effective Managers Say the Same Thing Twice (or More)," *Harvard Business Review* (May 2011), pp. 38–39.

9. J. Ewing, "Nokia: Bring on the Employee Rants," *BusinessWeek* (June 22, 2009), p. 50.

10. E. Nichols, "Hyper-Speed Managers," *HRMagazine* (April 2007), pp. 107–110.

11. L. Dulye, "Get Out of Your Office," *HRMagazine* (July 2006), pp. 99–101.

12. L. S. Rashotte, "What Does That Smile Mean? The Meaning of Nonverbal Behaviors in Social Interaction," *Social Psychology Quarterly* (March 2002), pp. 92–102.

13. J. Fast, *Body Language* (Philadelphia: M. Evan, 1970), p. 7.

14. A. Mehrabian, *Nonverbal Communication* (Chicago: Aldine-Atherton, 1972).

15. N. M. Henley, "Body Politics Revisited: What Do We Know Today?" in P. J. Kalbfleisch and M. J. Cody (eds.), *Gender, Power, and Communication in Human Relationships* (Hillsdale, NJ: Lawrence Erlbaum, 1995), pp. 27–61.

16. See, for example, N. B. Kurland and L. H. Pelled, "Passing the Word: Toward a Model of Gossip and Power in the Workplace," *Academy of Management Review* (April 2000), pp. 428–438; and G. Michelson, A. van Iterson,

and K. Waddington, "Gossip in Organizations: Contexts, Consequences, and Controversies," *Group and Organization Management* 35, no. 4 (2010), pp. 371–390.

17. Cited in "Heard It Through the Grapevine," *Forbes* (February 10, 1997), p. 22.

18. G. Van Hoye and F. Lievens, "Tapping the Grapevine: A Closer Look at Word-of-Mouth as a Recruitment Source," *Journal of Applied Psychology* 94, no. 2 (2009), pp. 341–352.

19. K. Davis, "Management Communication and the Grapevine," *Harvard Business Review* (September–October 1953), pp. 43–49.

20. R. L. Rosnow and G. A. Fine, *Rumor and Gossip: The Social Psychology of Hearsay* (New York: Elsevier, 1976).

21. J. K. Bosson, A. B. Johnson, K. Niederhoffer, and W. B. Swann, Jr., "Interpersonal Chemistry Through Negativity: Bonding by Sharing Negative Attitudes About Others," *Personal Relationships* 13 (2006), pp. 135–150.

22. T. J. Grosser, V. Lopez-Kidwell, and G. Labianca, "A Social Network Analysis of Positive and Negative Gossip in Organizational Life," *Group and Organization Management* 35, no. 2 (2010), pp. 177–212.

23. B. Gates, "How I Work," *Fortune* (April 17, 2006), money.cnn.com.

24. D. Brady, "*!#?@ the E-mail. Can We Talk?" *BusinessWeek* (December 4, 2006), p. 109.

25. E. Binney, "Is E-mail the New Pink Slip?" *HR Magazine* (November 2006), pp. 32–33; and R. L. Rundle, "Critical Case: How an Email Rant Jolted a Big HMO," *The Wall Street Journal* (April 24, 2007), pp. A1, A16.

26. S. Hourigan, "62 Trillion Spam Emails Cause Huge Carbon Footprint," *Courier Mail* (April 17, 2009), www.news.com.au/couriermail.

27. R. Stross, "The Daily Struggle to Avoid Burial by E-Mail," *New York Times* (April 21, 2008), p. BU5; and H. Rhodes, "You've Got Mail . . . Again," *Gainesville Sun* (September 29, 2008), pp. 1D, 6D.

28. C. Byron, "Carrying Too Heavy a Load? The Communication and Miscommunication of Emotion by Email," *Academy of Management Review* 33, no. 2 (2008), pp. 309–327.

29. D. Goleman, "Flame First, Think Later: New Clues to E-mail Misbehavior," *The New York Times* (February 20, 2007), p. D5; and E. Krell, "The Unintended Word," *HRMagazine* (August 2006), pp. 50–54.

30. J. E. Hall, M. T. Kobata, and M. Denis, "Employees and E-mail Privacy Rights," *Workforce Management* (June 2010), p. 10.

31. R. Zeidner, "Keeping E-mail in Check," *HRMagazine* (June 2007), pp. 70–74; "E-mail May Be Hazardous to Your Career," *Fortune* (May 14, 2007), p. 24; and J. D. Glater, "Open Secrets," *The New York Times* (June 27, 2008), pp. B1, B5.

32. A. Williams, "Mind Your BlackBerry or Mind Your Manners," *The New York Times* (June 21, 2009), www.nytimes.com.

33. "Survey Finds Mixed Reviews on Checking E-mail During Meetings," *IPMA-HR Bulletin* (April 27, 2007), p. 1.

34. K. Gurchiek, "Shoddy Writing Can Trip Up Employees, Organizations," *SHRM Online* (April 27, 2006), pp. 1–2.

35. T. Henneman, "Companies Making Friends with Social Media," *Workforce Management*, (April 2010), p. 4.

36. D. Lidsky, "It's Not Just Who You Know," *Fast Company* (May 2007), p. 56.

37. "Bosses Battle Risk by Firing E-mail, IM & Blog Violators," *IPMA-HR Bulletin* (January 12, 2007), pp. 1–2; G. Krants, "Blogging with a Vendetta," *Workforce Week* 8, no. 25 (June 10,

2007), www.workforce.com/section/quick_takes/49486_3.html; B. Leonard, "Blogs Can Present New Challenges to Employers," *SHRM Online* (March 13, 2006), pp. 1–2; and J. Greenwald, "Monitoring Communications? Know Legal Pitfalls," *Workforce Management Online* (February 2011), www.workforce.com.

38. E. Agnvall, "Meetings Go Virtual," *HR Magazine* (January 2009), pp. 74–77.

39. C. Huff, "Staying Afloat in a Digital Flood," *Workforce Management Online* (July 2008), www.workforce.com.

40. M. Richtel, "Lost in E-mail, Tech Firms Face Self-Made Beast," *The New York Times* (June 14, 2008), pp. A1, A14; and M. Johnson, "Quelling Distraction," *HR Magazine* (August 2008), pp. 43–46.

41. W. R. Boswell and J. B. Olson-Buchanan, "The Use of Communication Technologies After Hours: The Role of Work-Attitudes and Work-Life Conflict," *Journal of Management* 33, no. 4 (2007), pp. 592–610.

42. "At Many Companies, Hunt for Leakers Expands Arsenal of Monitoring Tactics," *The Wall Street Journal* (September 11, 2006), pp. B1, B3; and B. J. Alge, G. A. Ballinger, S. Tangirala, and J. L. Oakley, "Information Privacy in Organizations: Empowering Creative and Extrarole Performance," *Journal of Applied Psychology* 91, No. 1 (2006), pp. 221–232.

43. See R. L. Daft and R. H. Lengel, "Information Richness: A New Approach to Managerial Behavior and Organization Design," in B. M. Staw and L. L. Cummings (eds.), *Research in Organizational Behavior*, vol. 6 (Greenwich, CT: JAI Press, 1984), pp. 191–233; R. L. Daft and R. H. Lengel, "Organizational Information Requirements, Media Richness, and Structural Design," *Managerial Science* (May 1986), pp. 554–572; R. E. Rice, "Task Analyzability, Use of New Media, and Effectiveness," *Organization Science* (November 1992), pp. 475–500; S. G. Straus and J. E. McGrath, "Does the Medium Matter? The Interaction of Task Type and Technology on Group Performance and Member Reaction," *Journal of Applied Psychology* (February 1994), pp. 87–97; L. K. Trevino, J. Webster, and E. W. Stein, "Making Connections: Complementary Influences on Communication Media Choices, Attitudes, and Use," *Organization Science* (March–April 2000), pp. 163–182; and N. Kock, "The Psychobiological Model: Towards a New Theory of Computer-Mediated Communication Based on Darwinian Evolution," *Organization Science* 15, no. 3 (May–June 2004), pp. 327–348.

44. E. Frauenheim, "Communicating For Engagement During Tough Times," *Workforce Management Online* (April 2010), www.workforce.com.

45. R. E. Petty and P. Briñol, "Persuasion: From Single to Multiple to Metacognitive Processes," *Perspectives on Psychological Science* 3, no. 2 (2008), pp. 137–147; F. A. White, M. A. Charles, and J. K. Nelson, "The Role of Persuasive Arguments in Changing Affirmative Action Attitudes and Expressed Behavior in Higher Education," *Journal of Applied Psychology* 93, no. 6 (2008), pp. 1271–1286.

46. B. T. Johnson, and A. H. Eagly, "Effects of Involvement on Persuasion: A Meta-Analysis," *Psychological Bulletin* 106, no. 2 (1989), pp. 290–314; and K. L. Blankenship and D. T. Wegener, "Opening the Mind to Close It: Considering a Message in Light of Important Values Increases Message Processing and Later Resistance to Change," *Journal of Personality and Social Psychology* 94, no. 2 (2008), pp. 196–213.

47. See, for example, Y. H. M. See, R. E. Petty, and L. R. Fabrigar, "Affective and Cognitive Meta-Bases of Attitudes: Unique Effects of Information Interest and Persuasion," *Journal of Personality and Social Psychology* 94, no. 6 (2008), pp. 938–955; M. S. Key, J. E. Edlund, B. J. Sagarin, and G. Y. Bizer, "Individual Differences in Susceptibility to Mindlessness," *Personality and Individual Differences* 46, no. 3 (2009), pp. 261–264 and M. Reinhard and M. Messner, "The Effects of Source Likeability and Need for Cognition on Advertising Effectiveness Under Explicit Persuasion," *Journal of Consumer Behavior* 8, no. 4 (2009), pp. 179–191.

48. P. Briñol, R. E. Petty, and J. Barden, "Happiness Versus Sadness as a Determinant of Thought Confidence in Persuasion: A Self-Validation Analysis," *Journal of Personality and Social Psychology* 93, no. 5 (2007), pp. 711–727.

49. R. C. Sinclair, S. E. Moore, M. M. Mark, A. S. Soldat, and C. A. Lavis, "Incidental Moods, Source Likeability, and Persuasion: Liking Motivates Message Elaboration in Happy People," *Cognition and Emotion* 24, no. 6 (2010), pp. 940–961; and V. Griskevicius, M. N. Shiota, and S. L. Neufeld, "Influence of Different Positive Emotions on Persuasion Processing: A Functional Evolutionary Approach," *Emotion* 10, no. 2 (2010), pp. 190–206.

50. J. Sandberg, "The Jargon Jumble," *The Wall Street Journal* (October 24, 2006), p. B1.

51. E. W. Morrison and F. J. Milliken, "Organizational Silence: A Barrier to Change and Development in a Pluralistic World," *Academy of Management Review* 25, no. 4 (2000), pp. 706–725; and B. E. Ashforth and V. Anand, "The Normalization of Corruption in Organizations," *Research in Organizational Behavior* 25 (2003), pp. 1–52.

52. F. J. Milliken, E. W. Morrison, and P. F. Hewlin, "An Exploratory Study of Employee Silence: Issues That Employees Don't Communicate Upward and Why," *Journal of Management Studies* 40, no. 6 (2003), pp. 1453–1476.

53. S. Tangirala and R. Ramunujam, "Employee Silence on Critical Work Issues: The Cross-Level Effects of Procedural Justice Climate," *Personnel Psychology* 61, no. 1 (2008), pp. 37–68; and F. Bowen and K. Blackmon, "Spirals of Silence: The Dynamic Effects of Diversity on Organizational Voice," *Journal of Management Studies* 40, no. 6 (2003), pp. 1393–1417.

54. B. R. Schlenker and M. R. Leary, "Social Anxiety and Self-Presentation: A Conceptualization and Model," *Psychological Bulletin* 92 (1982), pp. 641–669; and L. A. Withers, and L. L. Vernon, "To Err Is Human: Embarrassment, Attachment, and Communication Apprehension," *Personality and Individual Differences* 40, no. 1 (2006), pp. 99–110.

55. See, for instance, S. K. Opt and D. A. Loffredo, "Rethinking Communication Apprehension: A Myers-Briggs Perspective," *Journal of Psychology* (September 2000), pp. 556–570; and B. D. Blume, G. F. Dreher, and T. T. Baldwin, "Examining the Effects of Communication Apprehension within Assessment Centres," *Journal of Occupational and Organizational Psychology* 83, no. 3 (2010), pp. 663–671.

56. See, for example, J. A. Daly and J. C. McCroskey, "Occupational Desirability and Choice as a Function of Communication Apprehension," *Journal of Counseling Psychology* 22, no. 4 (1975), pp. 309–313; and T. L. Rodebaugh, "I Might Look OK, But I'm Still Doubtful, Anxious, and Avoidant: The Mixed Effects of Enhanced Video Feedback on Social Anxiety Symptoms," *Behaviour Research & Therapy* 42, no. 12 (December 2004), pp. 1435–1451.

57. B. M. Depaulo, D. A. Kashy, S. E. Kirkendol, M. M. Wyer, and J. A. Epstein, "Lying in Everyday Life," *Journal of Personality and Social Psychology* 70, No. 5 (1996), pp. 979–995; and K. B. Serota, T. R. Levine, and F. J. Boster, "The Prevalence of Lying in America: Three Studies of Self-Reported Lies," *Human Communication Research* 36, No. 1. (2010), pp. 2–25.

58. DePaulo, Kashy, Kirkendol, Wyer, and Epstein, "Lying in Everyday Life"; and C. E. Naguin, T. R. Kurtzberg, and L. Y. Belkin, "The Finer Points of Lying Online: E-Mail Versus Pen and Paper," *Journal of Applied Psychology* 95, No. 2 (2010), pp. 387–394.

59. A. Vrij, P. A. Granhag, and S. Porter, "Pitfalls and Opportunities in Nonverbal and Verbal Lie Detection," *Psychological Science in the Public Interest* 11, No. 3 (2010), pp. 89–121.

60. R. E. Axtell, *Gestures: The Do's and Taboos of Body Language Around the World* (New York: Wiley, 1991); Watson Wyatt Worldwide, "Effective Communication: A Leading Indicator of Financial Performance—2005/2006 Communication ROI Study," www.watsonwyatt.com/research/resrender.asp?id=w-868; and A. Markels, "Turning the Tide at P&G," *U.S. News & World Report* (October 30, 2006), p. 69.

61. See M. Munter, "Cross-Cultural Communication for Managers," *Business Horizons* (May–June 1993), pp. 75–76; and H. Ren and B. Gray, "Repairing Relationship Conflict: How Violation Types and Culture Influence the Effectiveness of Restoration Rituals," *Academy of Management Review* 34, no. 1 (2009), pp. 105–126.

62. See E. T. Hall, *Beyond Culture* (Garden City, NY: Anchor Press/Doubleday, 1976); W. L. Adair, "Integrative Sequences and Negotiation Outcome in Same- and Mixed-Culture Negotiations," *International Journal of Conflict Management* 14, no. 3–4 (2003), pp. 1359–1392; W. L. Adair and J. M. Brett, "The Negotiation Dance: Time, Culture, and Behavioral Sequences in Negotiation," *Organization Science* 16, no. 1 (2005), pp. 33–51; E. Giebels and P. J. Taylor, "Interaction Patterns in Crisis Negotiations: Persuasive Arguments and Cultural Differences," *Journal of Applied Psychology* 94, no. 1 (2009), pp. 5–19; and M. G. Kittler, D. Rygl, and A. Mackinnon, "Beyond Culture or Beyond Control? Reviewing the Use of Hall's High-/Low-Context Concept," *International Journal of Cross-Cultural Management* 11, no. 1 (2011), pp. 63–82.

63. N. Adler, *International Dimensions of Organizational Behavior*, 4th ed. (Cincinnati, OH: South-Western Publishing, 2002), p. 94.

64. See, for example. R. S. Schuler, "A Role Perception Transactional Process Model for Organizational Communication-Outcome Relationships," *Organizational Behavior and Human Performance* (April 1979), pp. 268–291.

65. J. P. Walsh, S. J. Ashford, and T. E. Hill, "Feedback Obstruction: The Influence of the Information Environment on Employee Turnover Intentions," *Human Relations* (January 1985), pp. 23–46.

66. S. A. Hellweg and S. L. Phillips, "Communication and Productivity in Organizations: A State-of-the-Art Review," in *Proceedings of the 40th Annual Academy of Management Conference*, Detroit, 1980, pp. 188–192. See also B. A. Bechky, "Sharing Meaning Across Occupational Communities: The Transformation of Understanding on a Production Floor," *Organization Science* 14, no. 3 (May–June 2003), pp. 312–330.

MyManagementLab

Access a host of interactive learning aids to help strengthen your understanding of the chapter concepts at **www.pearsonglobaleditions .com/mymanagementlab**.

VALUE-DRIVEN LEADERSHIP

Before operating their own business, brothers Christian Leeser and Dr. Achim Leeser worked as management consultants with international clients from a broad range of industries. They saw that organizations following traditional management systems were losing huge amounts of energy, and they developed a more "entrepreneurial" kind of organization that followed a value-driven organizational model. Their new type of organization consisted of small groups of independent units that were driven by entrepreneurial people. These groups focused on a common goal and a common set of values but were autonomous in their actions.

Achim and Christian highlighted the following values as important: competence (everyone has the right and obligation to do what he or she is best at); total information; dynamic development (every team member has to teach someone else his or her current task requirements in order to be dispensable and ready for the next task); and fair sharing.

Believing that this organization and leadership model would be a unique success factor—especially for businesses in niche markets that had high innovation rates—in 1993 the brothers bought the nearly bankrupt FRABA (Fabrik elekt. Apparate GmbH), a medium-size, family-owned German company that was active in the field of industrial automation. Managing the turnaround, they introduced their model and soon found people with high leadership potential attracted by the unique options the model offered. By consistently demonstrating their leadership behavior as linked to the organization's values and consequently sharing their own power, the brothers managed to strongly retain these high-achieving employees, some of whom already have been elected as partner.

Today, the brothers' values remain valid. The partners of FRABA have developed a sophisticated set of procedures and processes as a standard management system to be applied in every company within the FRABA group. The group now consists of eight companies located in America, Asia, and Europe, and it successfully operates in three different segments of industrial automation. It is still growing.

Leadership

12

I am more afraid of an army of 100 sheep
led by a lion than an army of 100 lions
led by a sheep. —Talleyrand

Photo: Meeting. Source: © OJO Images Ltd/Alamy.

As in the case of Achim and Christian Leeser, leadership styles differ considerably. So which styles, and which people, are most effective? These are some of the questions we'll tackle in this chapter. To assess yourself on a specific set of qualities that we'll discuss shortly, take the following self-assessment.

In this chapter, we look at what makes an effective leader and what differentiates leaders from nonleaders. First, we present trait theories, which dominated the study of leadership until the late 1940s. Then we discuss behavioral theories, popular until the late 1960s. Next, we introduce contingency and interactive theories. Finally, we discuss the most contemporary approaches: charismatic, transformational, and authentic leadership. Most of the research discussed in this chapter was conducted in English-speaking countries. We know very little about how culture might influence the validity of the theories, particularly in Eastern cultures. However, analysis of the Global Leadership and Organizational Behavior Effectiveness (GLOBE) research project has produced some useful preliminary insights that we discuss throughout.[1] But first, let's clarify what we mean by *leadership*.

SELF-ASSESSMENT LIBRARY

What's My Leadership Style?

In the Self-Assessment Library (available on CD and online) take assessment II.B.1 (What's My Leadership Style?) and answer the following questions.

1. How did you score on the two scales?
2. Do you think a leader can be both task oriented and people oriented? Do you think there are situations in which a leader has to make a choice between the two styles?
3. Do you think your leadership style will change over time? Why or why not?

What Is Leadership?

1 Define *leadership* and contrast leadership and management.

We define **leadership** as the ability to influence a group toward the achievement of a vision or set of goals. The source of this influence may be formal, such as that provided by managerial rank in an organization. But not all leaders are managers, nor, for that matter, are all managers leaders. Just because an organization provides its managers with certain formal rights is no assurance they will lead effectively. Nonsanctioned leadership—the ability to influence that arises outside the formal structure of the organization—is often as important or more important than formal influence. In other words, leaders can emerge from within a group as well as by formal appointment.

Organizations need strong leadership *and* strong management for optimal effectiveness. We need leaders today to challenge the status quo, create visions of the future, and inspire organizational members to want to achieve the visions. We also need managers to formulate detailed plans, create efficient organizational structures, and oversee day-to-day operations.

Trait Theories

2   Summarize the conclusions of trait theories of leadership.

Throughout history, strong leaders—Buddha, Napoleon, Mao, Churchill, Roosevelt, Reagan—have been described in terms of their traits. **Trait theories of leadership** thus focus on personal qualities and characteristics. We recognize leaders like South Africa's Nelson Mandela, Virgin Group CEO Richard Branson, Apple co-founder Steve Jobs, and American Express chairman Ken Chenault as *charismatic, enthusiastic,* and *courageous.* The search for personality, social, physical, or intellectual attributes that differentiate leaders from non-leaders goes back to the earliest stages of leadership research.

Early research efforts to isolate leadership traits resulted in a number of dead ends. A review in the late 1960s of 20 different studies identified nearly 80 leadership traits, but only 5 were common to 4 or more of the investigations.[2] By the 1990s, after numerous studies and analyses, about the best we could say was that most leaders "are not like other people," but the particular traits that characterized them varied a great deal from review to review.[3] It was a pretty confusing state of affairs.

A breakthrough, of sorts, came when researchers began organizing traits around the Big Five personality framework (see Chapter 5).[4] Most of the dozens of traits in various leadership reviews fit under one of the Big Five (ambition and energy are part of extraversion, for instance), giving strong support to traits as predictors of leadership.

The personal qualities and traits of Indra Nooyi make her a great leader. Nooyi is CEO and board chairman of PepsiCo, the second largest food and beverage firm in the world. She is described as fun-loving, sociable, agreeable, conscientious, emotionally stable, and open to experiences. Nooyi's personality traits have contributed to her job performance and career success. She joined PepsiCo in 1994 as head of corporate strategy and was promoted to president and chief financial officer before moving into the firm's top management position. Nooyi has been named one of the most powerful women in business and one of the most powerful women in the world.

Source: PRNewsFoto/PepsiCo, Ray Hand.

leadership   *The ability to influence a group toward the achievement of a vision or set of goals.*

trait theories of leadership   *Theories that consider personal qualities and characteristics that differentiate leaders from nonleaders.*

A comprehensive review of the leadership literature, when organized around the Big Five, has found extraversion to be the most important trait of effective leaders,[5] but it is more strongly related to the way leaders emerge than to their effectiveness. Sociable and dominant people are more likely to assert themselves in group situations, but leaders need to make sure they're not too assertive—one study found leaders who scored very high on assertiveness were less effective than those who were moderately high.[6]

Unlike agreeableness and emotional stability, conscientiousness and openness to experience also showed strong relationships to leadership, though not quite as strong as extraversion. Overall, the trait approach does have something to offer. Leaders who like being around people and are able to assert themselves (extraverted), who are disciplined and able to keep commitments they make (conscientious), and who are creative and flexible (open) do have an apparent advantage when it comes to leadership, suggesting good leaders do have key traits in common.

One reason is that conscientiousness and extraversion are positively related to leaders' self-efficacy, which explained most of the variance in subordinates' ratings of leader performance.[7] People are more likely to follow someone who is confident she's going in the right direction.

Another trait that may indicate effective leadership is emotional intelligence (EI), discussed in Chapter 4. Advocates of EI argue that without it, a person can have outstanding training, a highly analytical mind, a compelling vision, and an endless supply of terrific ideas but still not make a great leader. This may be especially true as individuals move up in an organization.[8] Why is EI so critical to effective leadership? A core component of EI is empathy. Empathetic leaders can sense others' needs, listen to what followers say (and don't say), and read the reactions of others. A leader who effectively displays and manages emotions will find it easier to influence the feelings of followers, by both expressing genuine sympathy and enthusiasm for good performance and by using irritation for those who fail to perform.[9]

The link between EI and leadership effectiveness may be worth investigating in greater detail.[10] Some recent research has demonstrated that people high in EI are more likely to emerge as leaders, even after taking cognitive ability and personality into account, which helps to answer some of the most significant criticisms of this research.[11]

Based on the latest findings, we offer two conclusions. First, contrary to what we believed 20 years ago and thanks to the Big Five, we can say that traits can predict leadership. Second, traits do a better job predicting the emergence of leaders and the appearance of leadership than actually distinguishing between *effective* and *ineffective* leaders.[12] The fact that an individual exhibits the traits and that others consider him or her a leader does not necessarily mean the leader is successful at getting the group to achieve its goals.

Behavioral Theories

3 Identify the central tenets and main limitations of behavioral theories.

The failures of early trait studies led researchers in the late 1940s through the 1960s to wonder whether there was something unique in the way effective leaders *behave*. Trait research provides a basis for *selecting* the right people for leadership. In contrast, **behavioral theories of leadership** implied we could *train* people to be leaders.

Morgan Smith is an employee-oriented leader. As owner and managing partner of Boneheads Restaurant in Lake Forest, California, Smith (left) takes a personal interest in the needs of his employees. Described as generous, kind, and cheerful, he shows respect for his employees and invests a great deal of time in helping them at work and assisting them in their personal lives such as donating food for their weddings. Smith's goal for his employees is for them to reach their full potential. During bi-weekly one-on-one meetings with employees, Smith serves as their leader, trainer, role model, and advisor. He also provides quarterly training for employees and includes them in reviewing the restaurant's profit and loss statement.

Source: o44/ZUMA Press/Newscom.

The most comprehensive theories resulted from the Ohio State Studies in the late 1940s,[13] which sought to identify independent dimensions of leader behavior. Beginning with more than a thousand dimensions, the studies narrowed the list to two that substantially accounted for most of the leadership behavior described by employees: *initiating structure* and *consideration*.

Initiating structure is the extent to which a leader is likely to define and structure his or her role and those of employees in the search for goal attainment. It includes behavior that attempts to organize work, work relationships, and goals. A leader high in initiating structure is someone who "assigns group members to particular tasks," "expects workers to maintain definite standards of performance," and "emphasizes the meeting of deadlines."

Consideration is the extent to which a person's job relationships are characterized by mutual trust, respect for employees' ideas, and regard for their feelings. A leader high in consideration helps employees with personal problems, is friendly and approachable, treats all employees as equals, and expresses appreciation and support. In a recent survey, when asked to indicate what most motivated them at work, 66 percent of employees mentioned appreciation.[14]

Leadership studies at the University of Michigan's Survey Research Center had similar objectives: to locate behavioral characteristics of leaders that appeared related to performance effectiveness. The Michigan group also came up with two behavioral dimensions: the **employee-oriented leader** emphasized

behavioral theories of leadership *Theories proposing that specific behaviors differentiate leaders from nonleaders.*

initiating structure *The extent to which a leader is likely to define and structure his or her role and those of subordinates in the search for goal attainment.*

consideration *The extent to which a leader is likely to have job relationships characterized by mutual trust, respect for subordinates' ideas, and regard for their feelings.*

employee-oriented leader *A leader who emphasizes interpersonal relations, takes a personal interest in the needs of employees, and accepts individual differences among members.*

interpersonal relationships by taking a personal interest in the needs of employees and accepting individual differences among them, and the **production-oriented leader** emphasized the technical or task aspects of the job, focusing on accomplishing the group's tasks. These dimensions are closely related to the Ohio State dimensions. Employee-oriented leadership is similar to consideration, and production-oriented leadership is similar to initiating structure. In fact, most leadership researchers use the terms synonymously.[15]

At one time, the results of testing behavioral theories were thought to be disappointing. However, a more recent review of 160 studies found the followers of leaders high in consideration were more satisfied with their jobs, were more motivated, and had more respect for their leader. Initiating structure was more strongly related to higher levels of group and organization productivity and more positive performance evaluations.

Some research from the GLOBE study suggests there are international differences in preference for initiating structure and consideration.[16] Based on the values of Brazilian employees, a U.S. manager leading a team in Brazil would need to be team oriented, participative, and humane. Leaders high in consideration would succeed best in this culture. As one Brazilian manager said in the GLOBE study, "We do not prefer leaders who take self-governing decisions and act alone without engaging the group. That's part of who we are." Compared to U.S. employees, the French have a more bureaucratic view of leaders and are less likely to expect them to be humane and considerate. A leader high in initiating structure (relatively task-oriented) will do best and can make decisions in a relatively autocratic manner. A manager who scores high on consideration (people oriented) may find that style backfiring in France. According to the GLOBE study, Chinese culture emphasizes being polite, considerate, and unselfish, but it also has a high performance orientation. Thus, consideration and initiating structure may both be important.

Summary of Trait Theories and Behavioral Theories

Leaders who have certain traits and who display consideration and structuring behaviors do appear to be more effective. Perhaps you're wondering whether conscientious leaders (trait) are more likely to be structuring (behavior) and extraverted leaders (trait) to be considerate (behavior). Unfortunately, we can't be sure there is a connection. Future research is needed to integrate these approaches.

Some leaders may have the right traits or display the right behaviors and still fail. As important as traits and behaviors are in identifying effective or ineffective leaders, they do not guarantee success. The context matters, too.

Contingency Theories

4 Assess contingency theories of leadership by their level of support.

Some tough-minded leaders seem to gain a lot of admirers when they take over struggling companies and help lead them out of the doldrums. Home Depot and Chrysler didn't hire former CEO Bob Nardelli for his winning personality. However, such leaders also seem to be quickly dismissed when the situation stabilizes.

The rise and fall of leaders like Bob Nardelli illustrate that predicting leadership success is more complex than isolating a few traits or behaviors. In their cases, what worked in very bad times and in very good times didn't seem to translate into long-term success. When researchers looked at situational influences, it appeared that under condition *a*, leadership style *x* would be appropriate, whereas style *y* was more suitable for condition *b*, and style *z* for condition *c*. But what *were* conditions *a, b, c?* We next consider three approaches to isolating situational variables: the Fiedler model, situational theory, path–goal theory, and the leader-participation model.

The Fiedler Model

Fred Fiedler developed the first comprehensive contingency model for leadership.[17] The **Fiedler contingency model** proposes that effective group performance depends on the proper match between the leader's style and the degree to which the situation gives the leader control.

Identifying Leadership Style   Fiedler believes a key factor in leadership success is the individual's basic leadership style. He created the **least preferred co-worker (LPC) questionnaire** to identify that style by measuring whether a person is task or relationship oriented. The LPC questionnaire asks respondents to think of all the co-workers they have ever had and describe the one they *least enjoyed* working with by rating that person on a scale of 1 to 8 for each of 16 sets of contrasting adjectives (such as pleasant–unpleasant, efficient–inefficient, open–guarded, supportive–hostile). If you describe the person you are least able to work with in favorable terms (a high LPC score), Fiedler would label you *relationship oriented*. If you see your least-preferred co-worker in unfavorable terms (a low LPC score), you are primarily interested in productivity and are *task oriented*. About 16 percent of respondents score in the middle range[18] and thus fall outside the theory's predictions. The rest of our discussion relates to the 84 percent who score in either the high or low range of the LPC questionnaire.

Fiedler assumes an individual's leadership style is fixed. This means if a situation requires a task-oriented leader and the person in the leadership position is relationship oriented, either the situation has to be modified or the leader has to be replaced to achieve optimal effectiveness.

SELF-ASSESSMENT LIBRARY

What's My LPC Score?

In the Self-Assessment Library (available on CD and online) take assessment IV.E.5 (What's My LPC Score?).

Defining the Situation   After assessing an individual's basic leadership style through the LPC questionnaire, we match the leader with the situation. Fiedler has identified three contingency or situational dimensions:

1. **Leader–member relations** is the degree of confidence, trust, and respect members have in their leader.

---

production-oriented leader   *A leader who emphasizes technical or task aspects of the job.*

Fiedler contingency model   *The theory that effective groups depend on a proper match between a leader's style of interacting with subordinates and the degree to which the situation gives control and influence to the leader.*

least preferred co-worker (LPC) questionnaire   *An instrument that purports to measure whether a person is task or relationship oriented.*

leader–member relations   *The degree of confidence, trust, and respect subordinates have in their leader.*

2. **Task structure** is the degree to which the job assignments are procedurized (that is, structured or unstructured).
3. **Position power** is the degree of influence a leader has over power variables such as hiring, firing, discipline, promotions, and salary increases.

The next step is to evaluate the situation in terms of these three variables. Fiedler states that the better the leader–member relations, the more highly structured the job, and the stronger the position power, the more control the leader has. A very favorable situation (in which the leader has a great deal of control) might include a payroll manager who is well respected and whose employees have confidence in her (good leader–member relations); activities that are clear and specific—such as wage computation, check writing, and report filing (high task structure); and provision of considerable freedom to reward and punish employees (strong position power). An unfavorable situation might be that of the disliked chairperson of a volunteer United Way fundraising team. In this job, the leader has very little control.

Matching Leaders and Situations Combining the three contingency dimensions yields eight possible situations in which leaders can find themselves (Exhibit 12-1). The Fiedler model proposes matching an individual's LPC score and these eight situations to achieve maximum leadership effectiveness.[19] Fiedler concluded that task-oriented leaders perform better in situations very favorable to them and very unfavorable. So, when faced with a category I, II, III, VII, or VIII situation, task-oriented leaders perform better. Relationship-oriented leaders, however, perform better in moderately favorable situations—categories IV, V, and VI. In recent years, Fiedler has condensed these eight situations down to three.[20] He now says task-oriented leaders perform best in

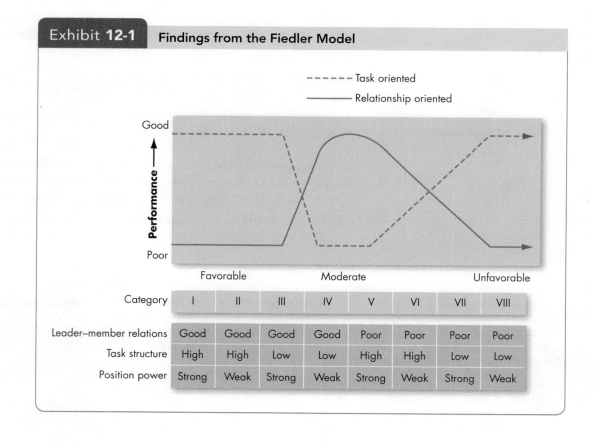

Exhibit 12-1   Findings from the Fiedler Model

	I	II	III	IV	V	VI	VII	VIII
Leader–member relations	Good	Good	Good	Good	Poor	Poor	Poor	Poor
Task structure	High	High	Low	Low	High	High	Low	Low
Position power	Strong	Weak	Strong	Weak	Strong	Weak	Strong	Weak

situations of high and low control, while relationship-oriented leaders perform best in moderate control situations.

How would you apply Fiedler's findings? You would match leaders—in terms of their LPC scores—with the type of situation—in terms of leader–member relationships, task structure, and position power—for which they were best suited. But remember that Fiedler views an individual's leadership style as fixed. Therefore, there are only two ways to improve leader effectiveness.

First, you can change the leader to fit the situation—as a baseball manager puts a right- or left-handed pitcher into the game depending on the hitter. If a group situation rates highly unfavorable but is currently led by a relationship-oriented manager, the group's performance could be improved under a manager who is task-oriented. The second alternative is to change the situation to fit the leader by restructuring tasks or increasing or decreasing the leader's power to control factors such as salary increases, promotions, and disciplinary actions.

Evaluation   Studies testing the overall validity of the Fiedler model find considerable evidence to support substantial parts of it.[21] If we use only three categories rather than the original eight, ample evidence supports Fiedler's conclusions.[22] But the logic underlying the LPC questionnaire is not well understood, and respondents' scores are not stable.[23] The contingency variables are also complex and difficult for practitioners to assess.[24]

Other Contingency Theories

Although LPC theory is the most widely researched contingency theory, three others deserve mention.

When Yahoo's growth and revenues slowed for several years, the company hired Carol Bartz as its new chief executive. Known as a task-oriented leader, Bartz previously led a successful turnaround at software maker Autodesk where, under her leadership, the company's revenues grew from $300 million to more than $1.5 billion. But after two and a half years at Yahoo, Bartz was fired as CEO for failing to revive the company's revenues and stock price. According to Fiedler's contingency model, Bartz's task-oriented style was not effective in improving Yahoo's performance. Observers noted that Bartz failed to provide the visionary leadership and focused strategic direction and execution needed to position the company for growth.

Source: Paul Sakuma/AP Images.

task structure   *The degree to which job assignments are procedurized.*

position power   *Influence derived from one's formal structural position in the organization; includes power to hire, fire, discipline, promote, and give salary increases.*

Situational Leadership Theory   **Situational leadership theory (SLT)** focuses on the followers. It says successful leadership depends on selecting the right leadership style contingent on the followers' *readiness*, or the extent to which they are willing and able to accomplish a specific task. A leader should choose one of four behaviors depending on follower readiness.

If followers are *unable* and *unwilling* to do a task, the leader needs to give clear and specific directions; if they are *unable* and *willing*, the leader needs to display high task orientation to compensate for followers' lack of ability and high relationship orientation to get them to "buy into" the leader's desires. If followers are *able* and *unwilling*, the leader needs to use a supportive and participative style; if they are both *able* and *willing*, the leader doesn't need to do much.

SLT has intuitive appeal. It acknowledges the importance of followers and builds on the logic that leaders can compensate for their limited ability and motivation. Yet research efforts to test and support the theory have generally been disappointing.[25] Why? Possible explanations include internal ambiguities and inconsistencies in the model itself as well as problems with research methodology in tests. So, despite its intuitive appeal and wide popularity, any endorsement must be cautious for now.

Path–Goal Theory   Developed by Robert House, **path–goal theory** extracts elements from the Ohio State leadership research on initiating structure and consideration and the expectancy theory of motivation.[26] It says it's the leader's job to provide followers with the information, support, or other resources necessary to achieve their goals. (The term *path–goal* implies effective leaders clarify followers' paths to their work goals and make the journey easier by reducing roadblocks.)

According to path–goal theory, whether a leader should be directive or supportive or should demonstrate some other behavior depends on complex analysis of the situation. It predicts the following:

- Directive leadership yields greater satisfaction when tasks are ambiguous or stressful than when they are highly structured and well laid out.
- Supportive leadership results in high performance and satisfaction when employees are performing structured tasks.
- Directive leadership is likely to be perceived as redundant among employees with high ability or considerable experience.

Testing path–goal theory has not been easy. A review of the evidence found mixed support for the proposition that removing obstacles is a component of effective leadership. Another review found the lack of support "shocking and disappointing."[27] Others argue that adequate tests of the theory have yet to be conducted.[28] Thus, the jury is still out. Because path–goal theory is so complex to test, that may remain the case for some time.

In a study of 162 workers in a document-processing organization, researchers found workers' conscientiousness was related to higher levels of performance only when supervisors set goals and defined roles, responsibilities, and priorities.[29] Other research has found that goal-focused leadership can lead to higher levels of emotional exhaustion for subordinates who are low in conscientiousness and emotional stability.[30] These studies demonstrate that leaders who set goals enable conscientious followers to achieve higher performance and may cause stress for workers who are low in conscientiousness.

Leader-Participation Model   The final contingency theory we cover argues that *the way* the leader makes decisions is as important as *what* she or he decides.

MyManagementLab
For an interactive application of this topic, check out this chapter's simulation activity at **www.pearsonglobaleditions.com/mymanagementlab.**

Victor Vroom and Phillip Yetton's **leader-participation model** relates leadership behavior and participation in decision making.[31] Like path–goal theory, it says leader behavior must adjust to reflect the task structure. The model is normative—it provides a decision tree of seven contingencies and five leadership styles for determining the form and amount of participation in decision making.

Research testing both the original and revised leader-participation models has not been encouraging, although the revised model rates higher in effectiveness.[32] Criticism focuses on the model's complexity and the variables it omits.[33] Although Vroom and Jago have developed a computer program to guide managers through all the decision branches in the revised model, it's not very realistic to expect practicing managers to consider 12 contingency variables, eight problem types, and five leadership styles to select the decision process for a problem.

As one leadership scholar noted, "Leaders do not exist in a vacuum"; leadership is a symbiotic relationship between leaders and followers.[34] But the theories we've covered to this point assume leaders use a fairly homogeneous style with everyone in their work unit. Think about your experiences in groups. Did leaders often act very differently toward different people? Our next theory considers differences in the relationships leaders form with different followers.

Leader–Member Exchange (LMX) Theory

Think of a leader you know. Did this leader have favorites who made up his or her ingroup? If you answered "yes," you're acknowledging the foundation of leader–member exchange theory.[35] **Leader–member exchange (LMX) theory** argues that, because of time pressures, leaders establish a special relationship with a small group of their followers. These individuals make up the ingroup— they are trusted, get a disproportionate amount of the leader's attention, and are more likely to receive special privileges. Other followers fall into the toutgroup.

The theory proposes that early in the history of the interaction between a leader and a given follower, the leader implicitly categorizes the follower as an "in" or an "out" and that relationship is relatively stable over time. Leaders induce LMX by rewarding those employees with whom they want a closer linkage and punishing those with whom they do not.[36] But for the LMX relationship to remain intact, the leader and the follower must invest in the relationship.

Just how the leader chooses who falls into each category is unclear, but there is evidence ingroup members have demographic, attitude, and personality characteristics similar to those of their leader or a higher level of competence

---

situational leadership theory (SLT) *A contingency theory that focuses on followers' readiness.*

path–goal theory *A theory that states that it is the leader's job to assist followers in attaining their goals and to provide the necessary direction and/or support to ensure that their goals are compatible with the overall objectives of the group or organization.*

leader-participation model *A leadership theory that provides a set of rules to determine the form and amount of participative decision making in different situations.*

leader–member exchange (LMX) theory *A theory that supports leaders' creation of in-groups and out-groups; subordinates with in-group status will have higher performance ratings, less turnover, and greater job satisfaction.*

glOBalization!

Cross-Cultural Leadership Styles

While a great deal has been said about international differences in leadership styles and their effectiveness, another issue probably matters more for most organizations: How can we develop leaders who are effective across cultural boundaries? Is it possible to create a truly global leadership style that will extend across cultures? Some recent forays into the field of cross-cultural leadership highlight possibilities for how global organizations might proceed.

Some of the leadership styles we have described in this chapter do seem to generalize across cultures. For example, research suggests charismatic leadership is effective in a variety of national contexts. In many cultures, terms like *visionary, symbolizer,* and *self-sacrificer* appear as descriptors of effective leaders, and positive leader–member exchanges also are associated with high performance across a variety of cultures. Culturally intelligent leaders are flexible and adaptable, tailoring their leadership styles to the specific and changing needs of the global workforce.

Researchers agree that learning to be a global leader requires gaining active experience in dealing with multiple cultures simultaneously. These experiences give leaders a chance to observe how different leadership styles work with different groups of people and build confidence in working across cultural boundaries. Leadership development programs can also use 360-degree feedback from supervisors, colleagues, and subordinates to help leaders recognize when their behavior is not effective with certain populations of employees. Companies like PepsiCo and Ford have their most effective global leaders provide seminars to emerging leaders so they can describe practices that have been especially effective.

Sources: K. Ng, L. Van Dyne, and S. Ang, "From Experience to Experiential Learning: Cultural Intelligence as a Learning Capacity for Global Leader Development," *Academy of Management Learning and Education* 9, no. 4 (2009), pp. 511–526; C. B. Gibson and D. M. McDaniel, "Moving Beyond Conventional Wisdom: Advancements in Cross-Cultural Theories of Leadership, Conflict, and Teams," *Perspectives on Psychological Science* 5, no. 4 (2010), pp. 450–462; and D. Simmonds and O. Tsui, "Effective Design of a Global Leadership Programme," *Human Resource Development International* 13, no. 5 (2010), pp. 519–540.

than outgroup members[37] (see Exhibit 12-2). Leaders and followers of the same gender tend to have closer (higher LMX) relationships than those of different genders.[38] Even though the leader does the choosing, the follower's characteristics drive the categorizing decision.

Research to test LMX theory has been generally supportive, with substantive evidence that leaders do differentiate among followers; these disparities are far from random; and followers with ingroup status will have higher performance ratings, engage in more helping or "citizenship" behaviors at work, and report greater satisfaction with their superior.[39] One study conducted in both Portugal

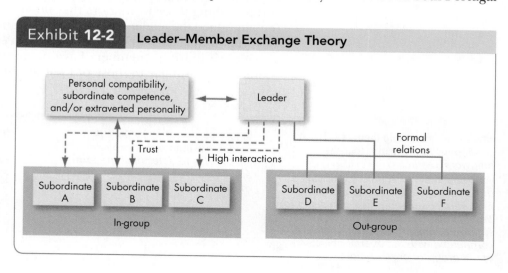

Exhibit 12-2   Leader–Member Exchange Theory

and the United States found that leader–member exchange was associated especially strongly with followers' commitment to the organization when the leaders were seen as embodying the values and identity of the organization.[40] These positive findings for ingroup members shouldn't be surprising, given our knowledge of self-fulfilling prophecy (see Chapter 6). Leaders invest their resources with those they expect to perform best. And believing ingroup members are the most competent, leaders treat them as such and unwittingly fulfill their prophecy. Conversely, a study in Turkey demonstrated that when leaders differentiated strongly among their followers in terms of their relationships (some followers had very positive leader–member exchange, others very poor), employees responded with more negative work attitudes and higher levels of withdrawal behavior.[41] Leader–follower relationships may be stronger when followers have a more active role in shaping their own job performance. Research on 287 software developers and 164 supervisors showed leader–member relationships have a stronger impact on employee performance and attitudes when employees have higher levels of autonomy and a more internal locus of control.[42]

Charismatic Leadership and Transformational Leadership

5 Compare and contrast *charismatic* and *transformational leadership.*

In this section, we present two contemporary leadership theories—charismatic leadership and transformational leadership—with a common theme: they view leaders as individuals who inspire followers through their words, ideas, and behaviors.

Charismatic Leadership

John F. Kennedy, Martin Luther King Jr., Ronald Reagan, Bill Clinton, Mary Kay Ash (founder of Mary Kay Cosmetics), and Steve Jobs (co-founder of Apple Computer) are frequently cited as charismatic leaders. What do they have in common?

What Is Charismatic Leadership? Max Weber, a sociologist, defined *charisma* (from the Greek for "gift") more than a century ago as "a certain quality of an individual personality, by virtue of which he or she is set apart from ordinary people and treated as endowed with supernatural, superhuman, or at least specifically exceptional powers or qualities. These are not accessible to the ordinary person and are regarded as of divine origin or as exemplary, and on the basis of them the individual concerned is treated as a leader."[43] Weber argued that charismatic leadership was one of several ideal types of authority.

The first researcher to consider charismatic leadership in terms of OB was Robert House. According to House's **charismatic leadership theory**, followers attribute heroic or extraordinary leadership abilities when they observe certain behaviors.[44] A number of studies have attempted to identify the characteristics of charismatic leaders: they have a vision, they are willing to take personal

charismatic leadership theory *A leadership theory that states that followers make attributions of heroic or extraordinary leadership abilities when they observe certain behaviors.*

| Exhibit **12-3** | Key Characteristics of a Charismatic Leader |

1. *Vision and articulation.* Has a vision—expressed as an idealized goal—that proposes a future better than the status quo; and is able to clarify the importance of the vision in terms that are understandable to others.

2. *Personal risk.* Willing to take on high personal risk, incur high costs, and engage in self-sacrifice to achieve the vision.

3. *Sensitivity to follower needs.* Perceptive of others' abilities and responsive to their needs and feelings.

4. *Unconventional behavior.* Engages in behaviors that are perceived as novel and counter to norms.

Source: Based on J. A. Conger and R. N. Kanungo, *Charismatic Leadership in Organizations* (Thousand Oaks, CA: Sage, 1998), p. 94.

risks to achieve that vision, they are sensitive to follower needs, and they exhibit extraordinary behaviors[45] (see Exhibit 12-3).

Are Charismatic Leaders Born or Made? Are charismatic leaders born with their qualities? Or can people actually learn to be charismatic leaders? Yes, and yes.

Individuals *are* born with traits that make them charismatic. In fact, studies of identical twins have found they score similarly on charismatic leadership measures, even if they were raised in different households and had never met. Personality is also related to charismatic leadership; charismatic leaders are likely to be extraverted, self-confident, and achievement oriented.[46] Consider Presidents Barack Obama and Ronald Reagan: like them or not, they are often compared because both possess the qualities of charismatic leaders.

Most experts believe individuals can be trained to exhibit charismatic behaviors.[47] After all, just because we inherit certain tendencies doesn't mean we can't learn to change. One set of authors proposes a three-step process.[48] First, develop an aura of charisma by maintaining an optimistic view; using passion as a catalyst for generating enthusiasm; and communicating with the whole body, not just with words. Second, draw others in by creating a bond that inspires them to follow. Third, bring out the potential in followers by tapping into their emotions.

The approach seems to work, according to researchers who have asked undergraduate business students to "play" charismatic.[49] The students were taught to articulate an overarching goal, communicate high performance expectations, exhibit confidence in the ability of followers to meet these expectations, and empathize with the needs of their followers; they learned to project a powerful, confident, and dynamic presence; and they practiced using a captivating and engaging voice. They were also trained to evoke charismatic nonverbal characteristics: they alternated between pacing and sitting on the edges of their desks, leaned toward the subjects, maintained direct eye contact, and had relaxed postures and animated facial expressions. Their followers had higher task performance, task adjustment, and adjustment to the leader and the group than did followers of noncharismatic leaders.

How Charismatic Leaders Influence Followers How do charismatic leaders actually influence followers? Evidence suggests a four-step process.[50] It begins with articulating an appealing **vision**, a long-term strategy for attaining a goal by linking the present with a better future for the organization. Desirable visions fit the times and circumstances and reflect the uniqueness of the organization. Steve Jobs championed the iPod at Apple, noting, "It's as Apple as anything

Apple has ever done." People in the organization must also believe the vision is challenging yet attainable.

Second, a vision is incomplete without an accompanying **vision statement**, a formal articulation of an organization's vision or mission. Charismatic leaders may use vision statements to imprint on followers an overarching goal and purpose. They build followers' self-esteem and confidence with high performance expectations and belief that followers can attain them. Next, through words and actions the leader conveys a new set of values and sets an example for followers to imitate. One study of Israeli bank employees showed charismatic leaders were more effective because their employees personally identified with them. Charismatic leaders also set a tone of cooperation and mutual support. A study of 115 government employees found they had a stronger sense of personal belonging at work when they had charismatic leaders, increasing their willingness to engage in helping and compliance-oriented behavior.[51]

Finally, the charismatic leader engages in emotion-inducing and often unconventional behavior to demonstrate courage and conviction about the vision. Followers "catch" the emotions their leader is conveying.[52]

Does Effective Charismatic Leadership Depend on the Situation? Research shows impressive correlations between charismatic leadership and high performance and satisfaction among followers.[53] People working for charismatic leaders are motivated to exert extra effort and, because they like and respect their leader, express greater satisfaction. Organizations with charismatic CEOs are also more profitable, and charismatic college professors enjoy higher course evaluations.[54] However, charisma appears most successful when the follower's task has an ideological component or the environment includes a high degree of stress and uncertainty.[55] Even in laboratory studies, when people are psychologically aroused, they are more likely to respond to charismatic leaders.[56] This may explain why, when charismatic leaders surface, it's likely to be in politics or religion, or during wartime, or when a business is in its infancy or facing a life-threatening crisis. Franklin D. Roosevelt offered a vision to get the United States out of the Great Depression in the 1930s. In 1997, when Apple Computer was floundering and lacking direction, the board persuaded charismatic co-founder Steve Jobs to return as interim CEO and return the company to its innovative roots.

Another situational factor apparently limiting charisma is level in the organization. Top executives create vision; it's more difficult to utilize a person's charismatic leadership qualities in lower-level management jobs or to align his or her vision with the larger goals of the organization.

Finally, people are especially receptive to charismatic leadership when they sense a crisis, when they are under stress, or when they fear for their lives. Charismatic leaders are able to reduce stress for their employees, perhaps because they help make work seem more meaningful and interesting.[57] And some peoples' personalities are especially susceptible to charismatic leadership.[58] Consider self-esteem. An individual who lacks self-esteem and questions his or her self-worth is more likely to absorb a leader's direction rather than establish his or her own way of leading or thinking.

The Dark Side of Charismatic Leadership Charismatic business leaders like AIG's Hank Greenberg, GE's Jack Welch, Tyco's Dennis Kozlowski, Southwest Airlines' Herb Kelleher, Disney's Michael Eisner, and HP's Carly Fiorina became

---

vision *A long-term strategy for attaining a goal or goals.*

vision statement *A formal articulation of an organization's vision or mission.*

celebrities on the order of David Beckham and Madonna. Every company wanted a charismatic CEO, and to attract them boards of directors gave them unprecedented autonomy and resources—the use of private jets and multimillion-dollar penthouses, interest-free loans to buy beach homes and artwork, security staffs, and similar benefits befitting royalty. One study showed charismatic CEOs were able to leverage higher salaries even when their performance was mediocre.[59]

Unfortunately, charismatic leaders who are larger than life don't necessarily act in the best interests of their organizations.[60] Many have allowed their personal goals to override the goals of the organization. The results at companies such as Enron, Tyco, WorldCom, and HealthSouth were leaders who recklessly used organizational resources for their personal benefit and executives who violated laws and ethical boundaries to inflate stock prices and allow leaders to cash in millions of dollars in stock options. It's little wonder research has shown that individuals who are narcissistic are also higher in some behaviors associated with charismatic leadership.[61]

It's not that charismatic leadership isn't effective; overall, it is. But a charismatic leader isn't always the answer. Success depends, to some extent, on the situation and on the leader's vision. Some charismatic leaders—Hitler, for example—are all too successful at convincing their followers to pursue a vision that can be disastrous.

SELF-ASSESSMENT LIBRARY

How Charismatic Am I?

In the Self-Assessment Library (available on CD and online), take assessment II.B.2 (How Charismatic Am I?).

Transformational Leadership

A stream of research has focused on differentiating transformational from transactional leaders.[62] The Ohio State studies, Fiedler's model, and path–goal theory describe **transactional leaders**, who guide their followers toward established goals by clarifying role and task requirements. **Transformational leaders** inspire followers to transcend their self-interests for the good of the organization and can have an extraordinary effect on their followers. Andrea Jung at Avon, Richard Branson of the Virgin Group, and Jim McNerney of Boeing are all transformational leaders. They pay attention to the concerns and needs of individual followers; they change followers' awareness of issues by helping them look at old problems in new ways; and they excite and inspire followers to put out extra effort to achieve group goals. Exhibit 12-4 briefly identifies and defines the characteristics that differentiate these two types of leaders.

Transactional and transformational leadership complement each other; they aren't opposing approaches to getting things done.[63] Transformational leadership *builds on* transactional leadership and produces levels of follower effort and performance beyond what transactional leadership alone can do. But the reverse isn't true. So if you are a good transactional leader but do not have transformational qualities, you'll likely only be a mediocre leader. The best leaders are transactional *and* transformational.

Full Range of Leadership Model Exhibit 12-5 shows the full range of leadership model. Laissez-faire is the most passive and therefore least effective of leader behaviors.[64] Management by exception—active or passive—is slightly better, but it's still considered ineffective. Management-by-exception leaders tend to be available only when there is a problem, which is often too late. Contingent reward leadership can be an effective style of leadership but will not get employees to go above and beyond the call of duty.

Exhibit 12-4	Characteristics of Transactional and Transformational Leaders

Transactional Leader

Contingent Reward: Contracts exchange of rewards for effort, promises rewards for good performance, recognizes accomplishments.

Management by Exception (active): Watches and searches for deviations from rules and standards, takes correct action.

Management by Exception (passive): Intervenes only if standards are not met.

Laissez-Faire: Abdicates responsibilities, avoids making decisions.

Transformational Leader

Idealized Influence: Provides vision and sense of mission, instills pride, gains respect and trust.

Inspirational Motivation: Communicates high expectations, uses symbols to focus efforts, expresses important purposes in simple ways.

Intellectual Stimulation: Promotes intelligence, rationality, and careful problem solving.

Individualized Consideration: Gives personal attention, treats each employee individually, coaches, advises.

Source: Based on A. H. Eagly, M. C. Johannesen-Schmidt, and M. L. Van Engen, "Transformational, Transactional, and Laissez-faire Leadership Styles: A Meta-Analysis Comparing Women and Men," *Psychological Bulletin* 129, no. 4 (2003), pp. 569–591; and T. A. Judge and J. E. Bono, "Five Factor Model of Personality and Transformational Leadership," *Journal of Applied Psychology* 85, no. 5 (2000), pp. 751–765.

Only with the four remaining styles—all aspects of transformational leadership—are leaders able to motivate followers to perform above expectations and transcend their self-interest for the sake of the organization. Individualized consideration, intellectual stimulation, inspirational motivation, and idealized influence all result in extra effort from workers, higher productivity, higher morale and satisfaction, higher organizational effectiveness, lower turnover, lower absenteeism, and greater organizational adaptability. Based on this model, leaders are generally most effective when they regularly use each of the four transformational behaviors.

How Transformational Leadership Works   Transformational leaders are more effective because they are more creative, but also because they encourage those who follow them to be creative, too.[65] Companies with transformational leaders have greater decentralization of responsibility, managers have more propensity to take risks, and compensation plans are geared toward long-term results—all of which facilitate corporate entrepreneurship.[66] One study of information technology workers in China found empowering leadership behavior led to feelings of positive personal control among workers, which increased their creativity at work.[67]

Companies with transformational leaders also show greater agreement among top managers about the organization's goals, which yields superior organizational performance.[68] The Israeli military has seen similar results, showing

transactional leaders *Leaders who guide or motivate their followers in the direction of established goals by clarifying role and task requirements.*

transformational leaders *Leaders who inspire followers to transcend their own self-interests and who are capable of having a profound and extraordinary effect on followers.*

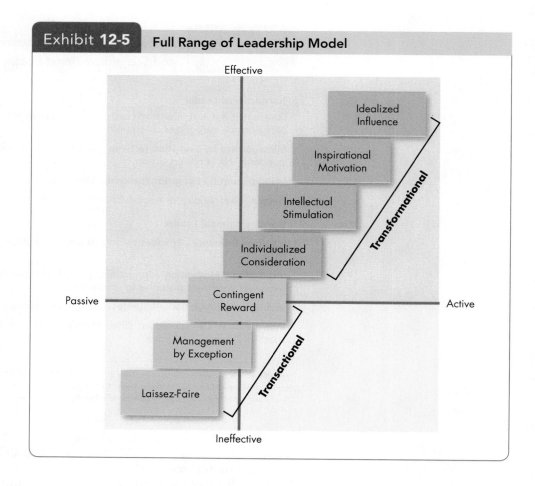

Exhibit 12-5   Full Range of Leadership Model

that transformational leaders improve performance by building consensus among group members.[69] Transformational leaders are able to increase follower self-efficacy, giving the group a "can do" spirit.[70] Followers are more likely to pursue ambitious goals, agree on the strategic goals of the organization, and believe the goals they are pursuing are personally important.[71]

Just as vision helps explain how charismatic leadership works, it also explains part of the effect of transformational leadership. One study found vision was even more important than a charismatic (effusive, dynamic, lively) communication style in explaining the success of entrepreneurial firms.[72] Finally, transformational leadership engenders commitment on the part of followers and instills greater trust in the leader.[73]

Evaluation of Transformational Leadership   Transformational leadership has been impressively supported at diverse job levels and occupations (school principals, teachers, marine commanders, ministers, presidents of MBA associations, military cadets, union shop stewards, sales reps). One study of R&D firms found teams whose project leaders scored high on transformational leadership produced better-quality products as judged 1 year later and higher profits 5 years later.[74] Another study looking at employee creativity and transformational leadership more directly found employees with transformational leaders had more confidence in their ability to be creative at work and higher levels of creative performance.[75] A review of 117 studies testing transformational leadership found it was related to higher levels of individual follower performance, team performance, and organizational performance.[76]

Transformational leadership isn't equally effective in all situations. It has a greater impact on the bottom line in smaller, privately held firms than in more complex organizations.[77] The personal nature of transformational leadership may be most effective when leaders can directly interact with the workforce and make decisions than when they report to an external board of directors or deal with a complex bureaucratic structure. Another study showed transformational leaders were more effective in improving group potency in teams higher in power distance and collectivism.[78] Other recent research using a sample of employees both in China and the United States found that transformational leadership had a more positive relationship with perceived procedural justice among individuals who were lower in power-distance orientation, which in turn related to a stronger transformational leadership-citizenship behavior relationship among those higher in power distance.[79] Transformational leaders also obtain higher levels of trust, which reduces stress for followers.[80] In short, transformational leadership works through a number of different processes.

One study examined how different types of transformational leadership can be effective depending on whether work is evaluated at the team or the individual level.[81] Individual-focused transformational leadership is behavior that empowers individual followers to develop, enhance their abilities, and increase self-efficacy. Team-focused transformational leadership emphasizes group goals, shared values and beliefs, and unified efforts. Evidence from a sample of 203 team members and 60 leaders in a business unit found individual transformational leadership associated with higher individual-level performance, whereas team-focused transformational leadership drew higher group-level performance.

Transformational leadership theory is not perfect. Contingent reward leadership may not characterize transactional leaders only. And contrary to the full range of leadership model, the four I's in transformational leadership are not always superior in effectiveness to transactional leadership (contingent reward leadership sometimes works as well as transformational leadership).

In summary, transformational leadership is more strongly correlated than transactional leadership with lower turnover rates, higher productivity, lower employee stress and burnout, and higher employee satisfaction.[82] Like charisma, it can be learned. One study of Canadian bank managers found branches managed by those who underwent transformational leadership training performed significantly better than branches whose managers did not receive training. Other studies show similar results.[83]

The GLOBE study—of 18,000 leaders from 825 organizations in 62 countries—links a number of elements of transformational leadership with effective leadership, regardless of country.[84] This conclusion is very important because it disputes the contingency view that leadership style needs to adapt to cultural differences.

What elements of transformational leadership appear universal? Vision, foresight, providing encouragement, trustworthiness, dynamism, positiveness, and proactiveness top the list. The GLOBE team concluded that "effective business leaders in any country are expected by their subordinates to provide a powerful and proactive vision to guide the company into the future, strong motivational skills to stimulate all employees to fulfill the vision, and excellent planning skills to assist in implementing the vision."[85]

A vision is important in any culture, then, but the way it is formed and communicated may need to vary by culture. A GE executive who used his U.S. leadership style in Japan recalls, "Nothing happened. I quickly realized that I had to adapt my approach, to act more as a consultant to my colleagues and to adopt a team-based motivational decision-making process rather than the more vocal style which tends to be common in the West. In Japan the silence of a leader means far more than a thousand words uttered by somebody else."[86]

Authentic Leadership: Ethics and Trust

6 Define *authentic leadership* and show why effective leaders exemplify ethics and trust.

Although theories have increased our understanding of effective leadership, they do not explicitly deal with the role of ethics and trust, which some argue is essential to complete the picture. Here, we consider these two concepts under the rubric of authentic leadership.[87]

What Is Authentic Leadership?

Mike Ullman, JCPenney CEO, argues that leaders have to be selfless, listen well, and be honest. Campbell Soup's CEO Douglas R. Conant is decidedly understated. When asked to reflect on the strong performance of Campbell Soup, he says, "We're hitting our stride a little bit more (than our peers)." He regularly admits mistakes and often says, "I can do better." Ullman and Conant appear to be good exemplars of authentic leadership.[88]

Authentic leaders know who they are, know what they believe in and value, and act on those values and beliefs openly and candidly. Their followers consider them ethical people. The primary quality produced by authentic leadership, therefore, is trust. Authentic leaders share information, encourage open communication, and stick to their ideals. The result: people come to have faith in them.

Because the concept is new, there has been little research on authentic leadership. However, it's a promising way to think about ethics and trust in leadership because it focuses on the moral aspects of being a leader. Transformational or charismatic leaders can have a vision and communicate it persuasively, but sometimes the vision is wrong (as in the case of Hitler), or the leader is more concerned with his or her own needs or pleasures, as were Dennis Kozlowski (ex-CEO of Tyco), Jeff Skilling (ex-CEO of Enron), and Raj Rajaratnam (founder of the Galleon Group).[89]

SELF-ASSESSMENT LIBRARY

Am I an Ethical Leader?

In the Self-Assessment Library (available on CD and online), take assessment IV.E.4 (Am I an Ethical Leader?).

Ethics and Leadership

Only recently have researchers begun to consider the ethical implications in leadership.[90] Why now? One reason may be the growing interest in ethics throughout the field of management. Another may be the discovery that many past leaders—such as Martin Luther King Jr., John F. Kennedy, and Thomas Jefferson—suffered ethical shortcomings. Some companies, like Boeing, are tying executive compensation to ethics to reinforce the idea that, in CEO Jim McNerney's words, "there's no compromise between doing things the right way and performance."[91]

Ethics and leadership intersect at a number of junctures. We can think of transformational leaders as fostering moral virtue when they try to change the attitudes and behaviors of followers.[92] Charisma, too, has an ethical component. Unethical leaders use their charisma to enhance power over followers, directed toward self-serving ends. Ethical leaders use it in a socially constructive way to serve others.[93] Leaders who treat their followers with fairness, especially by providing honest, frequent, and accurate information, are seen as more effective.[94] Leaders rated highly ethical tend to have followers who engage in more organizational citizenship behaviors and who are more willing to bring problems to the leaders' attention.[95] Because top executives set the moral tone for an organization, they need to set high ethical standards, demonstrate them through their own behavior, and encourage and reward integrity in others while avoiding abuses of power such as giving themselves large raises and bonuses while seeking to cut costs by laying off longtime employees.

Leadership is not value-free. In assessing its effectiveness, we need to address the *means* a leader uses in trying to achieve goals, as well as the content of those goals. Scholars have tried to integrate ethical and charismatic leadership by advancing the idea of **socialized charismatic leadership**—leadership that conveys other-centered (not self-centered) values by leaders who model ethical conduct.[96] Socialized charismatic leaders are able to bring employee values in line with their own values through their words and actions.[97]

Servant Leadership

Scholars have recently considered ethical leadership from a new angle by examining **servant leadership**.[98] Servant leaders go beyond their own self-interest and focus on opportunities to help followers grow and develop. They don't use power to achieve ends; they emphasize persuasion. Characteristic behaviors include listening, empathizing, persuading, accepting stewardship, and actively developing followers' potential. Because servant leadership focuses on serving the needs of others, research has focused on its outcomes for the well-being of followers.

What are the effects of servant leadership? One study of 123 supervisors found it resulted in higher levels of commitment to the supervisor, self-efficacy, and perceptions of justice, which all were related to organizational citizenship behavior.[99] This relationship between servant leadership and follower OCB appears to be stronger when followers are focused on being dutiful and responsible.[100] Second, servant leadership increases team potency (a belief that one's team has above-average skills and abilities), which in turn leads to higher levels of group performance.[101] Third, a study with a nationally representative sample of 250 workers found higher levels of citizenship associated with a focus on growth and advancement, which in turn was associated with higher levels of creative performance.[102]

Servant leadership may be more prevalent and more effective in certain cultures.[103] When asked to draw images of leaders, U.S. subjects tend to draw them in front of the group, giving orders to followers. Singaporeans tend to draw leaders at the back of the group, acting more to gather a group's opinions together and then unify them from the rear. This suggests the East Asian prototype is more like a servant leader, which might mean servant leadership is more effective in these cultures.

Trust and Leadership

Trust is a psychological state that exists when you agree to make yourself vulnerable to another because you have positive expectations about how things are going to turn out.[104] Even though you aren't completely in control of the

---

authentic leaders   *Leaders who know who they are, know what they believe in and value, and act on those values and beliefs openly and candidly. Their followers would consider them to be ethical people.*

socialized charismatic leadership   *A leadership concept that states that leaders convey values that are other centered versus self centered and who role-model ethical conduct.*

servant leadership   *A leadership style marked by going beyond the leader's own self-interest and instead focusing on opportunities to help followers grow and develop.*

trust   *A positive expectation that another will not act opportunistically.*

Do Leaders Have a Responsibility to Protect Followers?

Leaders are expected to monitor performance and assign work tasks. But do they also have a responsibility to protect their followers as well? Should they "take the heat" so employees can be more productive? Former research and development head at 3M William Coyne felt one of his most significant contributions as a manager of creative employees was to prevent them from being bombarded with questions and suggestions from higher-ups. Especially in creative fields, leaders need to make the environment safe for employees to express their ideas, even if it means generating conflict with upper levels in the organization. Leaders may also need to protect up-and-coming employees from longer-tenured employees who see them as a threat.

Important components of servant leadership include putting subordinates first, helping them grow, and empowering them. We might thus expect servant leaders to protect their followers from negative pressures in the organization. Studies also show that higher levels of servant leadership are associated with more citizenship behavior, higher performance, and greater creativity in work groups. As our review of the literature shows, acting to protect workers has a demonstrated impact on effective performance in the real world.

Still, shielding workers may not be in the organization's best interest all the time. Close personal relationships with subordinates can make it difficult to provide negative feedback when it's needed. A leader might be coddling a poor performer rather than protecting him or her from excess scrutiny. Thus, leaders need to take care when exercising their protecting role and be objective about what function it is serving.

So what should leaders do to effectively protect workers without falling into the trap of protecting the incompetent? Here are a few suggestions:

1. Try to identify barriers to effective performance in the work environment and protect employees from these unnecessary sources of political infighting, distraction, and delay.

2. Assess employee contributions realistically. Try to separate your feelings about an employee from your desire to protect him or her from outside scrutiny.

3. Sometimes the best thing to do is let an employee handle problems independently and wait for him or her to ask for help. This can be surprisingly hard for many leaders who are used to seeing themselves in a proactive role.

Sources: Based on R. I. Sutton, "The Boss as Human Shield," *Harvard Business Review* (September, 2010), pp. 106–109; J. Hu and R. C. Liden, "Antecedents of Team Potency and Team Effectiveness: An Examination of Goal and Process Clarity and Servant Leadership," *Journal of Applied Psychology*, Online first publication (February 14, 2011), doi: 10.1037/a0022465; and F. O. Walumbwa, C. A. Hartnell, and A. Oke, "Servant Leadership, Procedural Justice Climate, Service Climate, Employee Attitudes, and Organizational Citizenship Behavior: A Cross-Level Investigation," *Journal of Applied Psychology* 95, no. 3 (2010), pp. 517–529.

situation, you are willing to take a chance that the other person will come through for you.

Trust is a primary attribute associated with leadership; breaking it can have serious adverse effects on a group's performance.[105] As one author noted, "Part of the leader's task has been, and continues to be, working with people to find and solve problems, but whether leaders gain access to the knowledge and creative thinking they need to solve problems depends on how much people trust them. Trust and trust-worthiness modulate the leader's access to knowledge and cooperation."[106]

Followers who trust a leader are confident their rights and interests will not be abused.[107] Transformational leaders create support for their ideas in part by arguing that their direction will be in everyone's best interests. People are unlikely to look up to or follow someone they perceive as dishonest or likely to take advantage of them. Thus, as you might expect, transformational leaders do generate higher levels of trust from their followers, which in turn is related to higher levels of team confidence and, ultimately, higher levels of team performance.[108]

In a simple contractual exchange of goods and services, your employer is legally bound to pay you for fulfilling your job description. But today's rapid reorganizations, diffusion of responsibility, and collaborative team-based work style mean employment relationships are not stable long-term contracts with explicit terms. Rather, they are more fundamentally based on trusting relationships than ever before. You have to trust that if you show your supervisor a creative project you've been working on, she won't steal the credit behind your back. You have to trust that extra work you've been doing will be recognized in your performance appraisal. In contemporary organizations, where less work is closely documented and specified, voluntary employee contribution based on trust is absolutely necessary. And only a trusted leader will be able to encourage employees to reach beyond themselves to a transformational goal.

How Is Trust Developed?

Trust isn't just about the leader; the characteristics of followers also influence its development. What key characteristics lead us to believe a leader is trustworthy? Evidence has identified three: integrity, benevolence, and ability (see Exhibit 12-6).[109]

Integrity refers to honesty and truthfulness. It seems the most critical characteristic in assessing another's trustworthiness.[110] When 570 white-collar employees were given a list of 28 attributes related to leadership, they rated honesty the most important by far.[111] Integrity also means having consistency between what you do and say. "Nothing is noticed more quickly . . . than a discrepancy between what executives preach and what they expect their associates to practice."[112]

Benevolence means the trusted person has your interests at heart, even if yours aren't necessarily in line with theirs. Caring and supportive behavior is part of the emotional bond between leaders and followers.

Ability encompasses an individual's technical and interpersonal knowledge and skills. Even a highly principled person with the best intentions in the world won't be trusted to accomplish a positive outcome for you if you don't have faith in his or her ability to get the job done. Does the person know what he or she is talking about? You're unlikely to listen to or depend on someone whose abilities you don't respect.

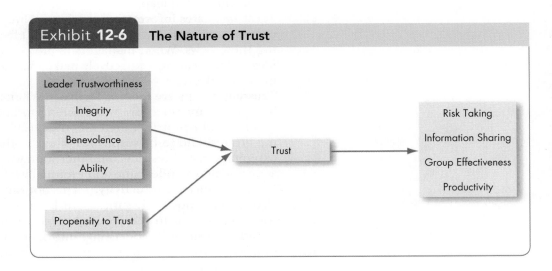

Exhibit 12-6   The Nature of Trust

Trust as a Process

Trust propensity refers to how likely a particular employee is to trust a leader. Some people are simply more likely to believe others can be trusted.[113] Those who carefully document every promise or conversation with their supervisors aren't very high in trust propensity, and they probably aren't going to take a leader's word for anything. Those who think most people are basically honest and forthright will be much more likely to seek out evidence that their leaders have behaved in a trustworthy manner. Trust propensity is closely linked to the personality trait of agreeableness, while people with lower self-esteem are less likely to trust others.[114]

Time is the final ingredient in the recipe for trust. We come to trust people based on observing their behavior over a period of time.[115] Leaders need to demonstrate they have integrity, benevolence, and ability in situations where trust is important—say, where they could behave opportunistically or let employees down but don't. Trust can also be won in the ability domain simply by demonstrating competence.

Leaders who break the psychological contract with workers, demonstrating they aren't trustworthy, will find employees are less satisfied and less committed, have a higher intent toward turnover, engage in less citizenship behavior, and have lower task performance.[116] Leaders who betray trust are especially likely to be evaluated negatively by followers if there is already a low level of leader–member exchange.[117] Once it is violated, trust can be regained, but only in certain situations that depend on the type of violation.[118] If the cause is lack of ability, it's usually best to apologize and recognize you should have done better. When lack of integrity is the problem, though, apologies don't do much good. Regardless of the violation, simply saying nothing or refusing to confirm or deny guilt is never an effective strategy for regaining trust. Trust can be restored when we observe a consistent pattern of trustworthy behavior by the transgressor. However, if the transgressor used deception, trust never fully returns, not even after apologies, promises, or a consistent pattern of trustworthy actions.[119]

What Are the Consequences of Trust?

Trust between supervisors and employees has a number of important advantages. Here are just a few that research has shown:

- **Trust encourages taking risks.** Whenever employees decide to deviate from the usual way of doing things, or to take their supervisors' word on a new direction, they are taking a risk. In both cases, a trusting relationship can facilitate that leap.
- **Trust facilitates information sharing.** One big reason employees fail to express concerns at work is that they don't feel psychologically safe revealing their views. When managers demonstrate they will give employees' ideas a fair hearing and actively make changes, employees are more willing to speak out.[120]
- **Trusting groups are more effective.** When a leader sets a trusting tone in a group, members are more willing to help each other and exert extra effort, which further increases trust. Conversely, members of mistrusting groups tend to be suspicious of each other, constantly guard against exploitation, and restrict communication with others in the group. These actions tend to undermine and eventually destroy the group.
- **Trust enhances productivity.** The bottom-line interest of companies also appears positively influenced by trust. Employees who trust their supervisors tend to receive higher performance ratings.[121] People respond to mistrust by concealing information and secretly pursuing their own interests.

Leading for the Future: Mentoring

7 Demonstrate the role mentoring plays in our understanding of leadership.

Leaders often take responsibility for developing future leaders. Let's consider what makes mentoring valuable as well as its potential pitfalls.

Mentoring

A **mentor** is a senior employee who sponsors and supports a less-experienced employee, a protégé. Successful mentors are good teachers. They present ideas clearly, listen well, and empathize with protégés' problems. Mentoring relationships serve both career functions and psychosocial functions (see Exhibit 12-7).[122]

Traditional informal mentoring relationships develop when leaders identify a less experienced, lower-level employee who appears to have potential for future development.[123] The protégé will often be tested with a particularly challenging assignment. If he or she performs acceptably, the mentor will develop the relationship, informally showing the protégé how the organization *really* works outside its formal structures and procedures.

Why would a leader want to be a mentor?[124] Many feel they have something to share with the younger generation and want to provide a legacy. Mentoring also provides unfiltered access to the attitudes of lower-ranking employees, and protégés can be an excellent source of early warning signals that identify potential organizational problems.

Are all employees in an organization equally likely to participate in a mentoring relationship? Unfortunately, no.[125] In the United States, upper managers in most organizations have traditionally been white males, and because mentors tend to select protégés similar to themselves in background, education, gender,

Exhibit **12-7**	**Career and Psychological Functions of the Mentoring Relationship**

Career Functions	**Psychosocial Functions**
• Lobbying to get the protégé challenging and visible assignments	• Counseling the protégé to bolster his or her self-confidence
• Coaching the protégé to help develop his or her skills and achieve work objectives	• Sharing personal experiences with the protégé
• Providing exposure to influential individuals within the organization	• Providing friendship and acceptance
• Protecting the protégé from possible risks to his or her reputation	• Acting as a role model
• Sponsoring the protégé by nominating him or her for potential advances or promotions	
• Acting as a sounding board for ideas the protégé might be hesitant to share with a direct supervisor	

mentor   *A senior employee who sponsors and supports a less-experienced employee, called a protégé.*

Myth or Science?

"Power Helps Leaders Perform Better"

Somewhat surprisingly, this statement appears to be partly true.

All leaders, of course, have some power (we'll consider power in the next chapter). But how do differences in power between leaders affect how they do their jobs? Most of us probably think that when leaders obtain *more* power, they relax and "rest on their laurels"—or worse, they abuse it.

Several recent studies, however, suggest that this is not quite the case. Power actually can help a leader do his or her job more effectively. In a series of experiments, researchers found that when individuals were given power as leaders, they performed more effectively. Why? Power gives leaders a greater sense of responsibility toward their group—as a result, powerful leaders were more likely to exert effort and make sacrifices than those with less power. If you're powerless (or *think* you're powerless), after all, why bother?

Interestingly, though, the research also suggested that if leaders happen to see a task as beneath them, they will disregard it. Thus, if leaders are given more power, it's important that they don't use it to dismiss as trivial the duties that truly matter.

Of course, we don't really know whether these experimental results generalize to more realistic settings, or whether power has long-term corrupting effects. But the findings do suggest that giving leaders more power is not always a bad idea.

Source: C. N. DeWall, R. F. Baumeister, N. L. Mead, and K. D. Vohs, "How Leaders Self-Regulate Their Task Performance: Evidence That Power Promotes Diligence, Depletion, and Disdain," *Journal of Personality and Social Psychology* 100, no. 1 (2010), pp. 47–65.

race, ethnicity, and religion, minorities and women are less likely to be chosen. "People naturally move to mentor and can more easily communicate with those with whom they most closely identify."[126] Senior male managers may also select male protégés to minimize problems such as sexual attraction or gossip.

Many organizations have created formal programs to ensure mentoring relationships are equally available to minorities and women.[127] Although begun with the best intentions, these formal relationships are not as effective as informal ones.[128]

Poor planning and design may often be the reason. Mentor commitment is critical to a program's effectiveness; mentors must see the relationship as beneficial to themselves and the protégé. The protégé, too, must feel he or she has input into the relationship; someone who feels it's foisted on him or her will just go through the motions.[129] Formal mentoring programs are also most likely to succeed if they appropriately match the work style, needs, and skills of protégé and mentor.[130]

You might assume mentoring is valuable for objective outcomes like compensation and job performance, but research suggests the gains are primarily psychological. One review concluded, "Though mentoring may not be properly labeled an utterly useless concept to careers, neither can it be argued to be as important as the main effects of other influences on career success such as ability and personality."[131] It may *feel* nice to have a mentor, but it doesn't appear that having a good mentor, or any mentor, is critical to your career. Mentors may be effective not because of the functions they provide, but because of the resources they can obtain: a mentor connected to a powerful network can build relationships that will help the protégé advance. Most evidence suggests that network ties, whether built through a mentor or not, are a significant predictor of career success.[132] If a mentor is not well connected or not a very strong performer, the best mentoring advice in the world will not be very beneficial.

Challenges to the Leadership Construct

8 Address challenges to the effectiveness of leadership.

"In the 1500s, people ascribed all events they didn't understand to God. Why did the crops fail? God. Why did someone die? God. Now our all-purpose explanation is leadership."[133] But much of an organization's success or failure is due to factors outside the influence of leadership. Sometimes it's just a matter of being in the right or wrong place at a given time. In this section, we present two perspectives and one technological change that challenge accepted beliefs about the value of leadership.

Leadership as an Attribution

As you may remember from Chapter 6, attribution theory examines how people try to make sense of cause-and-effect relationships. The **attribution theory of leadership** says leadership is merely an attribution people make about other individuals.[134] Thus we attribute to leaders intelligence, outgoing personality, strong verbal skills, aggressiveness, understanding, and industriousness.[135] At the organizational level, we tend to see leaders, rightly or wrongly, as responsible for extremely negative or extremely positive performance.[136]

One longitudinal study of 128 major U.S. corporations found that whereas perceptions of CEO charisma did not lead to objective company performance, company performance did lead to perceptions of charisma.[137] Employee perceptions of their leaders' behaviors are significant predictors of whether they blame the leader for failure, regardless of how the leader assesses him- or

Elements of transformational leadership such as vision and foresight appear to be universal. In China, for example, Wang Jianzhou is the CEO of China Mobile, the world's largest mobile phone operator with more than 600 million subscribers. With vision and foresight, Jianzhou is expanding mobile service throughout China's vast rural areas and plans to expand in emerging markets such as Africa, Asia, and Latin America. Proactive and positive, Jianzhou's leadership draws from his extensive knowledge of and more than 30 years of experience in the telecommunications industry. Jianzhou is shown here during the launch of the firm's OPhone operating system platform.

Source: Bao fan / Imaginechina/AP Images.

attribution theory of leadership   *A leadership theory that says that leadership is merely an attribution that people make about other individuals.*

herself.[138] A study of more than 3,000 employees from western Europe, the United States, and the Middle East found people who tended to "romanticize" leadership in general were more likely to believe their own leaders were transformational.[139]

When Merrill Lynch began to lose billions in 2008 as a result of its investments in mortgage securities, it wasn't long before CEO Stan O'Neal lost his job. He appeared before the House Oversight and Government Reform Committee of the U.S. Congress for what one committee member termed "a public flogging." Some called him a "criminal," and still others suggested Merrill's losses represented "attempted destruction."[140]

Whether O'Neal was responsible for the losses at Merrill or deserved his nine-figure severance package are difficult questions to answer. However, it is not difficult to argue that he probably changed very little between 2004 when *Fortune* described him as a "turnaround genius" and 2009 when he was fired. What did change was the performance of the organization he led. It's not necessarily wrong to terminate a CEO for failing or flagging financial performance. However, O'Neal's story illustrates the power of the attribution approach to leadership: hero and genius when things are going well, villain when they aren't.

We also make demographic assumptions about leaders. Respondents in a study assumed a leader described with no identifying racial information was white at a rate beyond the base rate of white employees in a company. In scenarios where identical leadership situations are described but the leaders' race is manipulated, white leaders are rated as more effective than leaders of other racial groups.[141] One large-scale summary study (a meta-analysis) found that many individuals hold stereotypes of men as having more leader characteristics than women, although as you might expect, this tendency to equate leadership with masculinity has decreased over time.[142] Other data suggest women's perceived success as transformational leaders may be based on demographic characteristics. Teams prefer male leaders when aggressively competing against other teams, but they prefer female leaders when the competition is within teams and calls for improving positive relationships within the group.[143]

Attribution theory suggests what's important is projecting the *appearance* of being a leader rather than focusing on *actual accomplishments*. Leader-wannabes who can shape the perception that they're smart, personable, verbally adept, aggressive, hardworking, and consistent in their style can increase the probability their bosses, colleagues, and employees will view them as effective leaders.

Substitutes for and Neutralizers of Leadership

One theory of leadership suggests that in many situations leaders' actions are irrelevant.[144] Experience and training are among the **substitutes** that can replace the need for a leader's support or ability to create structure. Organizational characteristics such as explicit formalized goals, rigid rules and procedures, and cohesive work groups can also replace formal leadership, while indifference to organizational rewards can neutralize its effects. **Neutralizers** make it impossible for leader behavior to make any difference to follower outcomes (see Exhibit 12-8).

This observation shouldn't be too surprising. After all, we've introduced a number of variables—such as attitudes, personality, ability, and group norms—that affect employee performance and satisfaction. It's simplistic to think employees are guided to goal accomplishments solely by the actions of their leader. Leadership is simply another independent variable in our overall OB model.

Sometimes the difference between substitutes and neutralizers is fuzzy. If I'm working on a task that's intrinsically enjoyable, theory predicts leadership

Exhibit 12-8	Substitutes for and Neutralizers of Leadership		

Defining Characteristics	Relationship-Oriented Leadership	Task-Oriented Leadership
Individual		
Experience/training	No effect on	Substitutes for
Professionalism	Substitutes for	Substitutes for
Indifference to rewards	Neutralizes	Neutralizes
Job		
Highly structured task	No effect on	Substitutes for
Provides its own feedback	No effect on	Substitutes for
Intrinsically satisfying	Substitutes for	No effect on
Organization		
Explicit formalized goals	No effect on	Substitutes for
Rigid rules and procedures	No effect on	Substitutes for
Cohesive work groups	Substitutes for	Substitutes for

Source: Based on S. Kerr and J. M. Jermier, "Substitutes for Leadership: Their Meaning and Measurement," *Organizational Behavior and Human Performance* (December 1978), p. 378.

will be less important because the task itself provides enough motivation. But does that mean intrinsically enjoyable tasks neutralize leadership effects, or substitute for them, or both? Another problem is that while substitutes for leadership (such as employee characteristics, the nature of the task, and so forth) matter to performance, that doesn't necessarily mean leadership doesn't.[145]

Online Leadership

How do you lead people who are physically separated from you and with whom you communicate electronically? This question needs attention from OB researchers.[146] Today's managers and employees are increasingly linked by networks rather than geographic proximity.

We propose that online leaders have to think carefully about what actions they want their digital messages to initiate. They confront unique challenges, the greatest of which appears to be developing and maintaining trust. **Identification-based trust**, based on a mutual understanding of each other's intentions and appreciation of the other's wants and desires, is particularly difficult to achieve without face-to-face interaction.[147] And online negotiations can also be hindered because parties express lower levels of trust.[148]

We tentatively conclude that good leadership skills will soon include the abilities to communicate support, trust, and inspiration through keyboarded words and accurately read emotions in others' messages. In electronic communication, writing skills are likely to become an extension of interpersonal skills.

---

substitutes *Attributes, such as experience and training, that can replace the need for a leader's support or ability to create structure.*

neutralizers *Attributes that make it impossible for leader behavior to make any difference to follower outcomes.*

identification-based trust *Trust based on a mutual understanding of each other's intentions and appreciation of each other's wants and desires.*

Finding and Creating Effective Leaders

Source: Carlos Osorio/AP Images.

Richard Wagoner was fired as CEO and chairman of General Motors. His leadership was faulted for playing a part in the automaker's bankruptcy, with critics saying that he did not force much-needed radical change in reducing debt, cutting costs, and investing in fuel-efficient cars. Wagoner, however, inherited a messy situation and accomplished much in fixing GM during his 9 years as CEO. He cut GM's U.S. workforce from 177,000 to 92,000, closed factories, saved billions of dollars by globalizing engineering, manufacturing, and design, and led a resurgence in quality and performance. But the attribution approach to leadership would suggest a reverse causality: that GM's failures caused people to question his leadership, and not the other way around.

How can organizations find or create effective leaders? Let's try to answer that question.

Selecting Leaders

The entire process organizations go through to fill management positions is essentially an exercise in trying to identify effective leaders. You might begin by reviewing the knowledge, skills, and abilities needed to do the job effectively. Personality tests can identify traits associated with leadership—extraversion, conscientiousness, and openness to experience. High self-monitors are better at reading situations and adjusting their behavior accordingly. Candidates with high emotional intelligence should have an advantage, especially in situations requiring transformational leadership.[149] Experience is a poor predictor of leader effectiveness, but situation-specific experience is relevant.

Because nothing lasts forever, the most important event an organization needs to plan for is a change in leadership. Recently, Apple's board of directors has been very concerned with identifying a successor to Steve Jobs. Other organizations seem to spend no time on leadership succession and are surprised when their picks turn out poorly. University of Kentucky chose its men's basketball coach, Billy Gillispie, within 2 weeks of the departure of Tubby Smith. Yet within 2 years Gillispie had been fired, causing observers to wonder whether Kentucky had done its homework in leadership succession.

Training Leaders

Organizations spend billions of dollars on leadership training and development.[150] These efforts take many forms—from $50,000 executive leadership programs offered by universities such as Harvard to sailing experiences offered by the Outward Bound program. Business schools, including some elite programs such as those at Dartmouth, MIT, and Stanford, are placing renewed emphasis on leadership development. Some companies, too, place a lot of emphasis on leadership development. Goldman Sachs is well known for developing leaders; *BusinessWeek* called it the "Leadership Factory."[151]

How can managers get maximum effect from their leadership-training budgets?[152] First, let's recognize the obvious. Leadership training of any kind is likely to be more successful with high self-monitors. Such individuals have the flexibility to change their behavior.

Second, what can organizations teach that might be related to higher leader effectiveness? Probably not "vision creation" but, likely, implementation skills. We can train people to develop "an understanding about content themes critical to effective visions."[153] We can also teach skills such as trust building and mentoring. And leaders can be taught situational-analysis skills. They can learn how to evaluate situations, modify them to better fit their style, and assess which leader behaviors might be most effective in given situations. BHP Billiton, Best Buy, Nokia, and Adobe have hired coaches to help top executives one on one to improve their interpersonal skills and act less autocratically.[154]

Behavioral training through modeling exercises can increase an individual's ability to exhibit charismatic leadership qualities. Recall the researchers who scripted undergraduate business students to "play" charismatic.[155] Finally, leaders can be trained in transformational leadership skills that have bottom-line results, whether in the financial performance of Canadian banks or the effectiveness of soldiers in the Israeli Defense Forces.[156]

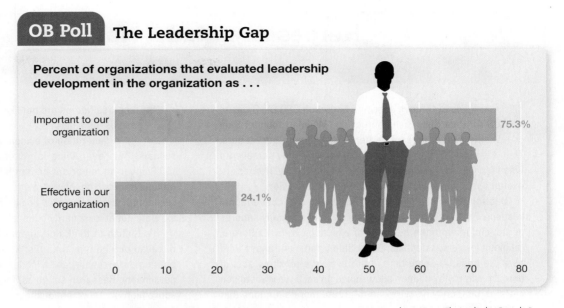

OB Poll   **The Leadership Gap**

Percent of organizations that evaluated leadership development in the organization as . . .

Important to our organization — 75.3%

Effective in our organization — 24.1%

Source: G. Kranz, "Special Report: Leadership Development," *Workforce Management* (May 2011), pp. 28–32; and P. J. Kiger, "The Leadership Formula," *Workforce Management* (May 2010), pp. 25–31.

MyManagementLab

Now that you have finished this chapter, go back to **www.pearsonglobaleditions.com/ mymanagementlab** to continue practicing and applying the concepts you've learned.

Summary and Implications for Managers

9 Assess whether charismatic and transformational leadership generalize across cultures.

Leadership plays a central part in understanding group behavior, because it's the leader who usually directs us toward our goals. Knowing what makes a good leader should thus be valuable in improving group performance.

- The early search for a set of universal leadership traits failed. However, recent efforts using the Big Five personality framework show strong and consistent relationships between leadership and extraversion, conscientiousness, and openness to experience.
- The behavioral approach's major contribution was narrowing leadership into task-oriented (initiating structure) and people-oriented (consideration) styles. By considering the situation in which the leader operates, contingency theories promised to improve on the behavioral approach, but only LPC theory has fared well in leadership research.
- Research on charismatic and transformational leadership has made major contributions to our understanding of leadership effectiveness. Organizations want managers who can exhibit transformational leadership qualities and who have vision and the charisma to carry it out.
- Effective managers must develop trusting relationships with followers because, as organizations have become less stable and predictable, strong bonds of trust are replacing bureaucratic rules in defining expectations and relationships.
- Tests and interviews help identify people with leadership qualities. Managers should also consider investing in leadership training such as formal courses, workshops, rotating job responsibilities, coaching, and mentoring.

Heroes Are Made, Not Born

From Apple CEO Steve Jobs and Microsoft CEO Bill Gates to US Air Pilot Sully Sullenberger and Walmart founder Sam Walton, we often ascribe heroic qualities to our leaders. They are courageous in the face of great risk. They persevered when few would. They take action when most sit by. Heroes are exceptional people who display exceptional behavior.

But some social psychologists question this conventional wisdom. They note that heroism can be found in many spheres of life, including in the behavior of whistleblowers, explorers, religious leaders, scientists, Good Samaritans, and those who beat the odds. At some time in our lives, we all show acts of heroism when the situation allows us to do so. If we want to see more heroic behavior, we need to create more situations that produce it.

Stanford psychologist Phil Zimbardo goes even further to argue that our romantic, inborn, trait-based view of heroic behavior is misplaced:

> "The banality of evil is matched by the banality of heroism. Neither is the consequence of dispositional tendencies. . . . Both emerge in particular situations at particular times, when situational forces play a compelling role in moving individuals across the line from inaction to action."

People exhibit brave behavior every day. The workers who risked their lives to contain Japan's earthquake-ravaged nuclear reactors are a great example. Thus, we err when we think leaders are uniquely positioned to behave heroically. We all can be heroes in the right situation.

Of course heroes are not like everyone else. That's what makes them heroes.

A generation of evidence from behavioral genetics reveals that "everything is genetic," meaning we have yet to discover an important human behavior that does not have genetic origins. Though we're not aware of any such study with respect to heroism, it would be surprising if courageous behavior were not at least partly genetic.

It's foolish to think courageous people aren't exceptional because of who they are. Just as we know there is an entrepreneurial personality and a leader personality, there is a heroic personality. Research suggests, for example, that people who score high on conscientiousness are more likely to engage in courageous behavior.

Not all leaders are heroes, but many have exhibited courageous behavior. When Richard Branson launches his latest attempt to set the world record for an around-the-world balloon flight or sloop sailing, he is the same leader who also exhibits courageous behavior as CEO of Virgin Group. Virgin Group now includes more than 400 companies, including Virgin Galactic, a space tourism company, and Virgin Fuels, whose goal is to revolutionize the industry by providing sustainable fuels for automobiles and aircraft. Same leader, same heroic behavior—in work and in life.

Are we really to believe that Richard Branson and other courageous leaders are just like everyone else?

Sources: Z. E. Franco, K. Blau, and P. G. Zimbardo, "Heroism: A Conceptual Analysis and Differentiation Between Heroic Action and Altruism," *Review of General Psychology* 15, no. 2 (2011), pp. 99–113; O. Dorell, "At Nuke Plant, Heroes Emerge," *USA Today* (March 25, 2011), pp. 1A, 2A; L. J. Walker, J. A. Frimer, and W. L. Dunlop, "Varieties of Moral Personality: Beyond the Banality of Heroism," *Journal of Personality* 78, no. 3 (2010), pp. 907–942; and J. Lehrer, "Are Heroes Born, or Can They Be Made?" *The Wall Street Journal* (December 11, 2010), p. C12.

QUESTIONS FOR REVIEW

1 Are leadership and management different from one another? If so, how?

2 What is the difference between trait and behavioral theories? Are the theories valid?

3 What are the main limitations of behavioral theories of leadership?

4 What is Fiedler's contingency model? Has it been supported in research?

5 How do charismatic and transformational leadership compare and contrast? Are they valid?

6 What is authentic leadership? Why do ethics and trust matter to leadership?

7 How is mentoring valuable to leadership? What are the keys to effective mentoring?

8 How can organizations select and develop effective leaders?

EXPERIENTIAL EXERCISE What Is a Leader?

1. Working on your own, write down 12 adjectives that describe an effective business leader.
2. Break into groups of four or five. Appoint a note-taker and spokesperson. Compare your lists of adjectives, making a new list of those common across two or more persons' lists. (Count synonyms—steadfast and unwavering, for example—as the same.)
3. Each spokesperson should present the group's list to the class.
4. Are there many similarities among the lists? What does this tell you about the nature of leadership?

ETHICAL DILEMMA Undercover Leaders

As you saw in one of the Chapter 1 cases, the television show *Undercover Boss* features a leader working undercover in his or her own company to find out how the organization really works. In Chapter 1, we considered the show as an example of management by walking around (MBWA). Here, we consider the ethical leadership lessons it might offer.

Executives from DirecTV, Hooters, 7-Eleven, NASCAR, Chiquita, and Choice Hotels have been featured on the show. Typically, the executive works undercover for a week. Then the employees with whom and under whom the leader has worked are summoned to company headquarters and rewarded, or punished, for their actions.

In one episode, Waste Management's president Larry O'Donnell, sporting gray stubble and work clothes, works the back of a trash truck. Later, he sorts recyclables from a fast-moving conveyer belt. Under the barking orders of a supervisor, he even cleans a long line of portable toilets.

Some criticize the show for its faux realism. The CEOs know they are on camera, so every word and facial expression is for the cameras. Many employees know they

are on camera too. One critic commented, "Because the series' very existence requires cooperation from the executives that it purports to make suffer for their sins, it has to raise them higher, in the end, than it found them at the start."

Realistic or not, the series continues to be popular. After all, haven't you sometimes wondered what it would be like to do someone else's job?

The idea has moved beyond television too. Recently, the Australian government created a program that places CEOs undercover in their own workplaces. One CEO, Phil Smith of clothing retailer Fletcher Jones, said in tears of the experience, "I learnt a lot from this that I wouldn't have found out any other way."

Questions
1. Do you think it is ethical for a leader to go undercover in his or her organization? Why or why not?

2. Do you think leaders who work undercover are really changed as a result of their experiences?

3. Would you support a government program that gave companies incentives to send leaders undercover?

Sources: K. Jones, "CEOs Go Undercover Over Workplace Safety," *SafetyAtWorkBlog* (February 5, 2011), downloaded June 10, 2011, from http://safetyatworkblog.wordpress.com/; W. Kern, "The Fakery of CEOs Undercover," *Bloomberg Businessweek* (February 15, 2010), pp. 78–79.

CASE INCIDENT 1 Leadership Training in "Job Simulations" at Niederrhein University, Germany

For five years, Niederrhein University of Applied Sciences, housing Europe's largest faculty of textile and clothing technology, has provided case-related leadership training in international bachelor's- and master's-degree courses. Textile, clothing, and related industries are known as very traditional; however, industry leaders in Europe face a variety of cultural and motivational challenges in fast-changing international markets.

During their course work, textile management students are introduced to various leadership scenarios, such as moving to a supervisory role, giving feedback to an under performing employee, or dealing with instances of sexual harassment in the office. In small groups of four to five, students review theories and behavioral alternatives that lead to the students exploring and playing different roles in the situation. Eventually they give a simulated performance of the situation to an audience of industrial and governmental leaders.

In response to the simulations, Diplom-Engineer M. Kleindorp, who is also the CEO of Memminger-IRO GmbH, stated, "Testing out your own image sends a message to the people around you, but even more it gives you the possibility to read the reflection."

Questions
1. Which leadership traits and which interactions can be evaluated by the trainees in the situation of "Job Simulations"?
2. Explain trust in leadership and the consequences of the leadership training on future job behavior.

CASE INCIDENT 2 Healthy Employees are Happy Employees

Teow Boon Ling is the general manager of Cargo Community Network (CCN), a market leader in the logistics industry, that believes that a company's biggest asset is its workforce.

In 2005, he initiated the Workplace Health Promotion (WHP) Program for his 60 employees. He envisioned that employees who possess a healthy mind and body will contribute to the overall growth and productivity of the organization.

Strong management support and participation is pervasive throughout the implementation of the WHP program. A senior manager heads the Company Recreation Committee (CRC), comprised of representatives from different departments. CRC, with support and guidance from the WHP consultant, designs activities that address employees' physical and mental well-being and healthy eating. Annual basic health screenings and health and activities surveys are conducted to collate information on employees' current lifestyles, health practices, and preferred types of activities. To promote healthy eating habits and lifestyle among the staff, the company organized free distribution of fruits on "Friday Fruit Day" as well as regular nutrition talks, healthy cooking demos, and fitness classes.

Despite the initial setback of low staff participation (only 10 percent) in the organized activities, Teow persisted and remained convinced of the intended transformation of the company. He acknowledged, "It was not easy for one to change the habits of the employees and begin an active lifestyle. It's just like training for a marathon—it might seem impossibly difficult at the beginning, but you just need to take that first step. Set small achievable goals from the outset and once you start achieving them, you'll find that you eventually become stronger and faster with less effort."

He leads by example by taking part in all the organized activities. He also continuously works on improving the policies to better integrate workplace health promotion withinthe organization culture. Innovatively, he has included WHP as a component in the performance appraisal that affects the employees' bonus payout. A points system, monetary tokens, and award recognitions were also given to motivate employees who made the effort to lead healthier lifestyles. Flexible working hours are also introduced for staff to take time off to participate in weekly jog and brisk walk sessions.

Four years down the WHP road, Teow proudly commented at the Health Promotion Silver Award ceremony, "Productivity is pretty hard to measure but I see improved team spirit, the atmosphere is more cheery,

Source: Health Promotion Board, SHA 2008 Silver Award.

people are more happy—[they are] more open, engaging in discussions, with increased communication across departments."

Questions

1. Describe Teow's personality and leadership style. How does it foster or hinder his effort to transform CCN into a healthy and productive organization?

2. Based on the description of Teow's personality and leadership style, in your opinion, is he a charismatic leader, a transformational leader, or both? Support your answer.

ENDNOTES

1. M. Javidan, P. W. Dorfman, M. S. de Luque, and R. J. House, "In the Eye of the Beholder: Cross Cultural Lessons in Leadership from Project Globe," *Academy of Management Perspectives* (February 2006), pp. 67–90.
2. J. G. Geier, "A Trait Approach to the Study of Leadership in Small Groups," *Journal of Communication* (December 1967), pp. 316–323.
3. S. A. Kirkpatrick and E. A. Locke, "Leadership: Do Traits Matter?" *Academy of Management Executive* (May 1991), pp. 48–60; and S. J. Zaccaro, R. J. Foti, and D. A. Kenny, "Self-Monitoring and Trait-Based Variance in Leadership: An Investigation of Leader Flexibility Across Multiple Group Situations," *Journal of Applied Psychology* (April 1991), pp. 308–315.
4. See T. A. Judge, J. E. Bono, R. Ilies, and M. W. Gerhardt, "Personality and Leadership: A Qualitative and Quantitative Review," *Journal of Applied Psychology* (August 2002), pp. 765–780.
5. Judge, Bono, Ilies, and Gerhardt, "Personality and Leadership."
6. D. R. Ames and F. J. Flynn, "What Breaks a Leader: The Curvilinear Relation Between Assertiveness and Leadership," *Journal of Personality and Social Psychology* 92, no. 2 (2007), pp. 307–324.
7. K. Ng, S. Ang, and K. Chan, "Personality and Leader Effectiveness: A Moderated Mediation Model of Leadership Self-Efficacy, Job Demands, and Job Autonomy," *Journal of Applied Psychology* 93, no. 4 (2008), pp. 733–743.
8. This section is based on J. M. George, "Emotions and Leadership: The Role of Emotional Intelligence," *Human Relations* (August 2000), pp. 1027–1055; C.-S. Wong and K. S. Law, "The Effects of Leader and Follower Emotional Intelligence on Performance and Attitude: An Exploratory Study," *Leadership Quarterly* (June 2002), pp. 243–274; and J. Antonakis, N. M. Ashkanasy, and M. T. Dasborough, "Does Leadership Need Emotional Intelligence?" *Leadership Quarterly* 20 (2009), pp. 247–261.
9. R. H. Humphrey, J. M. Pollack, and T. H. Hawver, "Leading with Emotional Labor," *Journal of Managerial Psychology* 23 (2008), pp. 151–168.
10. F. Walter, M. S. Cole, and R. H. Humphrey, "Emotional Intelligence: Sine Qua Non of Leadership or Folderol?"

Academy of Management Perspectives (February 2011), pp. 45–59.

11. S. Côté, P. N. Lopez, P. Salovey, and C. T. H. Miners, "Emotional Intelligence and Leadership Emergence in Small Groups," *Leadership Quarterly* 21 (2010), pp. 496–508.

12. R. G. Lord, C. L. DeVader, and G. M. Alliger, "A Meta-Analysis of the Relation Between Personality Traits and Leadership Perceptions: An Application of Validity Generalization Procedures," *Journal of Applied Psychology* (August 1986), pp. 402–410; and J. A. Smith and R. J. Foti, "A Pattern Approach to the Study of Leader Emergence," *Leadership Quarterly* (Summer 1998), pp. 147–160.

13. R. M. Stogdill and A. E. Coons (eds.), *Leader Behavior: Its Description and Measurement*, Research Monograph no. 88 (Columbus: Ohio State University, Bureau of Business Research, 1951). This research is updated in C. A. Schriesheim, C. C. Cogliser, and L. L. Neider, "Is It 'Trustworthy'? A Multiple-Levels-of-Analysis Reexamination of an Ohio State Leadership Study, with Implications for Future Research," *Leadership Quarterly* (Summer 1995), pp. 111–145; and T. A. Judge, R. F. Piccolo, and R. Ilies, "The Forgotten Ones? The Validity of Consideration and Initiating Structure in Leadership Research," *Journal of Applied Psychology* (February 2004), pp. 36–51.

14. D. Akst, "The Rewards of Recognizing a Job Well Done," *The Wall Street Journal* (January 31, 2007), p. D9.

15. Judge, Piccolo, and Ilies, "The Forgotten Ones?"

16. M. Javidan, P. W. Dorfman, M. S. de Luque, and R. J. House, "In the Eye of the Beholder: Cross Cultural Lessons in Leadership from Project GLOBE," *Academy of Management Perspectives* (February 2006), pp. 67–90.

17. F. E. Fiedler, *A Theory of Leadership Effectiveness* (New York: McGraw-Hill, 1967).

18. S. Shiflett, "Is There a Problem with the LPC Score in LEADER MATCH?" *Personnel Psychology* (Winter 1981), pp. 765–769.

19. F. E. Fiedler, M. M. Chemers, and L. Mahar, *Improving Leadership Effectiveness: The Leader Match Concept* (New York: Wiley, 1977).

20. Cited in R. J. House and R. N. Aditya, "The Social Scientific Study of Leadership," *Journal of Management* 23, no. 3 (1997), p. 422.

21. L. H. Peters, D. D. Hartke, and J. T. Pohlmann, "Fiedler's Contingency Theory of Leadership: An Application of the Meta-Analysis Procedures of Schmidt and Hunter," *Psychological Bulletin* (March 1985), pp. 274–285; C. A. Schriesheim, B. J. Tepper, and L. A. Tetrault, "Least Preferred Coworker Score, Situational Control, and Leadership Effectiveness: A Meta-Analysis of Contingency Model Performance Predictions," *Journal of Applied Psychology* (August 1994), pp. 561–573; and R. Ayman, M. M. Chemers, and F. Fiedler, "The Contingency Model of Leadership Effectiveness: Its Levels of Analysis," *Leadership Quarterly* (Summer 1995), pp. 147–167.

22. House and Aditya, "The Social Scientific Study of Leadership."

23. See, for instance, R. W. Rice, "Psychometric Properties of the Esteem for the Least Preferred Coworker (LPC) Scale," *Academy of Management Review* (January 1978), pp. 106–118; C. A. Schriesheim, B. D. Bannister, and W. H. Money, "Psychometric Properties of the LPC Scale: An Extension of Rice's Review," *Academy of Management Review* (April 1979), pp. 287–290; and J. K. Kennedy, J. M. Houston, M. A. Korgaard, and D. D. Gallo, "Construct Space of the Least Preferred Coworker (LPC) Scale," *Educational & Psychological Measurement* (Fall 1987), pp. 807–814.

24. See E. H. Schein, *Organizational Psychology*, 3rd ed. (Upper Saddle River, NJ: Prentice Hall, 1980), pp. 116–117; and B. Kabanoff, "A Critique of Leader Match and Its Implications for Leadership Research," *Personnel Psychology* (Winter 1981), pp. 749–764.

25. See, for instance, Ibid., pp. 67–84; C. L. Graeff, "Evolution of Situational Leadership Theory: A Critical Review," *Leadership Quarterly* 8, no. 2 (1997), pp. 153–170; and R. P. Vecchio and K. J. Boatwright, "Preferences for Idealized Styles of Supervision," *Leadership Quarterly* (August 2002), pp. 327–342.

26. R. J. House, "A Path-Goal Theory of Leader Effectiveness," *Administrative Science Quarterly* (September 1971), pp. 321–338; R. J. House and T. R. Mitchell, "Path-Goal Theory of Leadership," *Journal of Contemporary Business* (Autumn 1974), pp. 81–97; and R. J. House, "Path-Goal Theory of Leadership: Lessons, Legacy, and a Reformulated Theory," *Leadership Quarterly* (Fall 1996), pp. 323–352.

27. J. C. Wofford and L. Z. Liska, "Path-Goal Theories of Leadership: A Meta-Analysis," *Journal of Management* (Winter 1993), pp. 857–876; and P. M. Podsakoff, S. B. MacKenzie, and M. Ahearne, "Searching for a Needle in a Haystack: Trying to Identify the Illusive Moderators of Leadership Behaviors," *Journal of Management* 21 (1995), pp. 423–470.

28. J. R. Villa, J. P. Howell, and P. W. Dorfman, "Problems with Detecting Moderators in Leadership Research Using Moderated Multiple Regression," *Leadership Quarterly* 14 (2003), pp. 3–23; C. A. Schriesheim and L. Neider, "Path-Goal Leadership Theory: The Long and Winding Road," *Leadership Quarterly* 7 (1996), pp. 317–321; and M. G. Evans, "R. J. House's 'A Path-Goal Theory of Leader Effectiveness,'" *Leadership Quarterly* 7 (1996), pp. 305–309.

29. A. E. Colbert and L. A. Witt, "The Role of Goal-Focused Leadership in Enabling the Expression of Conscientiousness," *Journal of Applied Psychology* 94, no. 3 (2009), pp. 790–796.

30. S. J. Perry, L. A. Witt, L. M. Penney, and L. Atwater, "The Downside of Goal-Focused Leadership: The Role of Personality in Subordinate Exhaustion," *Journal of Applied Psychology* 95, no. 6 (2010), pp. 1145–1153.

31. See V. H. Vroom and P. W. Yetton, *Leadership and Decision-Making* (Pittsburgh: University of Pittsburgh Press, 1973); and V. H. Vroom and A. G. Jago, "The Role of the Situation in Leadership," *American Psychologist* (January 2007), pp. 17–24.

32. See, for example, R. H. G. Field, "A Test of the Vroom-Yetton Normative Model of Leadership," *Journal of Applied*

Psychology (October 1982), pp. 523–532; C. R. Leana, "Power Relinquishment Versus Power Sharing: Theoretical Clarification and Empirical Comparison of Delegation and Participation," *Journal of Applied Psychology* (May 1987), pp. 228–233; J. T. Ettling and A. G. Jago, "Participation Under Conditions of Conflict: More on the Validity of the Vroom-Yetton Model," *Journal of Management Studies* (January 1988), pp. 73–83; R. H. G. Field and R. J. House, "A Test of the Vroom-Yetton Model Using Manager and Subordinate Reports," *Journal of Applied Psychology* (June 1990), pp. 362–366; and R. H. G. Field and J. P. Andrews, "Testing the Incremental Validity of the Vroom-Jago Versus Vroom-Yetton Models of Participation in Decision Making," *Journal of Behavioral Decision Making* (December 1998), pp. 251–261.

33. House and Aditya, "The Social Scientific Study of Leadership," p. 428.

34. W. Bennis, "The Challenges of Leadership in the Modern World," *American Psychologist* (January 2007), pp. 2–5.

35. X. Zhou and C. A. Schriesheim, "Supervisor–Subordinate Convergence in Descriptions of Leader–Member Exchange (LMX) Quality: Review and Testable Propositions." *Leadership Quarterly* 20, no. 6 (2009), pp. 920–932; G. B. Graen and M. Uhl-Bien, "Relationship-Based Approach to Leadership: Development of Leader–Member Exchange (LMX) Theory of Leadership Over 25 Years: Applying a Multi-Domain Perspective," *Leadership Quarterly* (Summer 1995), pp. 219–247; R. C. Liden, R. T. Sparrowe, and S. J. Wayne, "Leader–Member Exchange Theory: The Past and Potential for the Future," in G. R. Ferris (ed.), *Research in Personnel and Human Resource Management*, vol. 15 (Greenwich, CT: JAI Press, 1997), pp. 47–119; and C. A. Schriesheim, S. L. Castro, X. Zhou, and F. J. Yammarino, "The Folly of Theorizing 'A' but Testing 'B': A Selective Level-of-Analysis Review of the Field and a Detailed Leader–Member Exchange Illustration," *Leadership Quarterly* (Winter 2001), pp. 515–551.

36. B. Erdogan and T. N. Bauer, "Differentiated Leader–Member Exchanges: The Buffering Role of Justice Climate," *Journal of Applied Psychology* 95, no. 6 (2010), pp. 1104–1120; R. C. Liden, S. J. Wayne, and D. Stilwell, "A Longitudinal Study of the Early Development of Leader–Member Exchanges," *Journal of Applied Psychology* (August 1993), pp. 662–674; S. J. Wayne, L. M. Shore, W. H. Bommer, and L. E. Tetrick, "The Role of Fair Treatment and Rewards in Perceptions of Organizational Support and Leader–Member Exchange," *Journal of Applied Psychology* 87, no. 3 (June 2002), pp. 590–598; and S. S. Masterson, K. Lewis, and B. M. Goldman, "Integrating Justice and Social Exchange: The Differing Effects of Fair Procedures and Treatment on Work Relationships," *Academy of Management Journal* 43, no. 4 (August 2000), pp. 738–748.

37. D. Duchon, S. G. Green, and T. D. Taber, "Vertical Dyad Linkage: A Longitudinal Assessment of Antecedents, Measures, and Consequences," *Journal of Applied Psychology* (February 1986), pp. 56–60; Liden, Wayne, and Stilwell, "A Longitudinal Study on the Early Development of Leader–Member

Exchanges"; and M. Uhl-Bien, "Relationship Development as a Key Ingredient for Leadership Development," in S. E. Murphy and R. E. Riggio (eds.), *Future of Leadership Development* (Mahwah, NJ: Lawrence Erlbaum, 2003) pp. 129–147.

38. R. Vecchio and D. M. Brazil, "Leadership and Sex-Similarity: A Comparison in a Military Setting," *Personnel Psychology* 60 (2007), pp. 303–335.

39. See, for instance, C. R. Gerstner and D. V. Day, "Meta-Analytic Review of Leader–Member Exchange Theory: Correlates and Construct Issues," *Journal of Applied Psychology* (December 1997), pp. 827–844; R. Ilies, J. D. Nahrgang, and F. P. Morgeson, "Leader–Member Exchange and Citizenship Behaviors: A Meta-Analysis," *Journal of Applied Psychology* 92, no. 1 (2007), pp. 269–277; and Z. Chen, W. Lam, and J. A. Zhong, "Leader–Member Exchange and Member Performance: A New Look at Individual-Level Negative Feedback-Seeking Behavior and Team-Level Empowerment Culture," *Journal of Applied Psychology* 92, no. 1 (2007), pp. 202–212.

40. R. Eisenberger, G. Karagonlar, F. Stinglhamber, P. Neves, T. E. Becker, M. G. Gonzalez-Morales, and M. Steiger-Mueller, "Leader-Member Exchange and Affective Organizational Commitment: The Contribution of Supervisor's Organizational Embodiment," *Journal of Applied Psychology* 95, no. 6 (2010), pp. 1085–1103.

41. B. Erdogan and T. N. Bauer, "Differentiated Leader-Member Exchanges: The Buffering Role of Justice Climate," *Journal of Applied Psychology* 95, no. 6 (2010), pp. 1104–1120.

42. M. Ozer, "Personal and Task-Related Moderators of Leader-Member Exchange Among Software Developers," *Journal of Applied Psychology* 93, no. 5 (2008), pp. 1174–1182.

43. M. Weber, *The Theory of Social and Economic Organization*, A. M. Henderson and T. Parsons (trans.) (New York: The Free Press, 1947).

44. J. A. Conger and R. N. Kanungo, "Behavioral Dimensions of Charismatic Leadership," in J. A. Conger, R. N. Kanungo, and Associates (eds.), *Charismatic Leadership* (San Francisco: Jossey-Bass, 1988), p. 79.

45. J. A. Conger and R. N. Kanungo, *Charismatic Leadership in Organizations* (Thousand Oaks, CA: Sage, 1998); and R. Awamleh and W. L. Gardner, "Perceptions of Leader Charisma and Effectiveness: The Effects of Vision Content, Delivery, and Organizational Performance," *Leadership Quarterly* (Fall 1999), pp. 345–373.

46. R. J. House and J. M. Howell, "Personality and Charismatic Leadership," *Leadership Quarterly* 3 (1992), pp. 81–108; D. N. Den Hartog and P. L. Koopman, "Leadership in Organizations," in N. Anderson and D. S. Ones (eds.), *Handbook of Industrial, Work and Organizational Psychology*, vol. 2 (Thousand Oaks, CA: Sage, 2002), pp. 166–187.

47. See J. A. Conger and R. N. Kanungo, "Training Charismatic Leadership: A Risky and Critical Task," *Charismatic Leadership* (San Francisco: Jossey-Bass, 1988), pp. 309–323; A. J. Towler, "Effects of Charismatic Influence Training on Attitudes, Behavior, and Performance," *Personnel Psychology* (Summer 2003), pp. 363–381; and M. Frese, S. Beimel, and S. Schoenborn, "Action Training for Charismatic Leadership: Two Evaluations of Studies of a Commercial

Training Module on Inspirational Communication of a Vision," *Personnel Psychology* (Autumn 2003), pp. 671–697.

48. R. J. Richardson and S. K. Thayer, *The Charisma Factor: How to Develop Your Natural Leadership Ability* (Upper Saddle River, NJ: Prentice Hall, 1993).

49. J. M. Howell and P. J. Frost, "A Laboratory Study of Charismatic Leadership," *Organizational Behavior and Human Decision Processes* (April 1989), pp. 243–269. See also Frese, Beimel, and Schoenborn, "Action Training for Charismatic Leadership."

50. B. Shamir, R. J. House, and M. B. Arthur, "The Motivational Effects of Charismatic Leadership: A Self-Concept Theory," *Organization Science* (November 1993), pp. 577–594.

51. D. N. Den Hartog, A. H. B. De Hoogh, and A. E. Keegan, "The Interactive Effects of Belongingness and Charisma on Helping and Compliance," *Journal of Applied Psychology* 92, no. 4 (2007), pp. 1131–1139.

52. A. Erez, V. F. Misangyi, D. E. Johnson, M. A. LePine, and K. C. Halverson, "Stirring the Hearts of Followers: Charismatic Leadership as the Transferal of Affect," *Journal of Applied Psychology* 93, no. 3 (2008), pp. 602–615. For reviews on the role of vision in leadership, see S. J. Zaccaro, "Visionary and Inspirational Models of Executive Leadership: Empirical Review and Evaluation," in S. J. Zaccaro (ed.), *The Nature of Executive Leadership: A Conceptual and Empirical Analysis of Success* (Washington, DC: American Psychological Association, 2001), pp. 259–278; and M. Hauser and R. J. House, "Lead Through Vision and Values," in E. A. Locke (ed.), *Handbook of Principles of Organizational Behavior* (Malden, MA: Blackwell, 2004), pp. 257–273.

53. D. A. Waldman, B. M. Bass, and F. J. Yammarino, "Adding to Contingent-Reward Behavior: The Augmenting Effect of Charismatic Leadership," *Group & Organization Studies*, December 1990, pp. 381–394; and S. A. Kirkpatrick and E. A. Locke, "Direct and Indirect Effects of Three Core Charismatic Leadership Components on Performance and Attitudes," *Journal of Applied Psychology* (February 1996), pp. 36–51.

54. A. H. B. de Hoogh, D. N. Den Hartog, P. L. Koopman, H. Thierry, P. T. van den Berg, and J. G. van der Weide, "Charismatic Leadership, Environmental Dynamism, and Performance," *European Journal of Work & Organizational Psychology* (December 2004), pp. 447–471; S. Harvey, M. Martin, and D. Stout, "Instructor's Transformational Leadership: University Student Attitudes and Ratings," *Psychological Reports* (April 2003), pp. 395–402; and D. A. Waldman, M. Javidan, and P. Varella, "Charismatic Leadership at the Strategic Level: A New Application of Upper Echelons Theory," *Leadership Quarterly* (June 2004), pp. 355–380.

55. R. J. House, "A 1976 Theory of Charismatic Leadership," in J. G. Hunt and L. L. Larson (eds.), *Leadership: The Cutting Edge* (Carbondale: Southern Illinois University Press, 1977), pp. 189–207; and House and Aditya, "The Social Scientific Study of Leadership," p. 441.

56. J. C. Pastor, M. Mayo, and B. Shamir, "Adding Fuel to Fire: The Impact of Followers' Arousal on Ratings of Charisma," *Journal of Applied Psychology* 92, no. 6 (2007), pp. 1584–1596.

57. A. H. B. De Hoogh and D. N. Den Hartog, "Neuroticism and Locus of Control as Moderators of the Relationships of Charismatic and Autocratic Leadership with Burnout," *Journal of Applied Psychology* 94, no. 4 (2009), pp. 1058–1067.

58. F. Cohen, S. Solomon, M. Maxfield, T. Pyszczynski, and J. Greenberg, "Fatal Attraction: The Effects of Mortality Salience on Evaluations of Charismatic, Task-Oriented, and Relationship-Oriented Leaders," *Psychological Sciences* (December 2004), pp. 846–851; and M. G. Ehrhart and K. J. Klein, "Predicting Followers' Preferences for Charismatic Leadership: The Influence of Follower Values and Personality," *Leadership Quarterly* (Summer 2001), pp. 153–179.

59. H. L. Tosi, V. Misangyi, A. Fanelli, D. A. Waldman, and F. J. Yammarino, "CEO Charisma, Compensation, and Firm Performance," *Leadership Quarterly* (June 2004), pp. 405–420.

60. See, for instance, R. Khurana, *Searching for a Corporate Savior: The Irrational Quest for Charismatic CEOs* (Princeton, NJ: Princeton University Press, 2002); and J. A. Raelin, "The Myth of Charismatic Leaders," *Training & Development* (March 2003), pp. 47–54.

61. B. M. Galvin, D. A. Waldman, and P. Balthazard, "Visionary Communication Qualities as Mediators of the Relationship between Narcissism and Attributions of Leader Charisma," *Personnel Psychology* 63, no. 3 (2010), pp. 509–537.

62. See, for instance, B. M. Bass, B. J. Avolio, D. I. Jung, and Y. Berson, "Predicting Unit Performance by Assessing Transformational and Transactional Leadership," *Journal of Applied Psychology* (April 2003), pp. 207–218; and T. A. Judge and R. F. Piccolo, "Transformational and Transactional Leadership: A Meta-Analytic Test of Their Relative Validity," *Journal of Applied Psychology* (October 2004), pp. 755–768.

63. B. M. Bass, "Leadership: Good, Better, Best," *Organizational Dynamics* (Winter 1985), pp. 26–40; and J. Seltzer and B. M. Bass, "Transformational Leadership: Beyond Initiation and Consideration," *Journal of Management* (December 1990), pp. 693–703.

64. T. R. Hinkin and C. A. Schriescheim, "An Examination of 'Nonleadership': From Laissez-Faire Leadership to Leader Reward Omission and Punishment Omission," *Journal of Applied Psychology* 93, no. 6 (2008), pp. 1234–1248.

65. S. J. Shin and J. Zhou, "Transformational Leadership, Conservation, and Creativity: Evidence from Korea," *Academy of Management Journal* (December 2003), pp. 703–714; V. J. García-Morales, F. J. Lloréns-Montes, and A. J. Verdú-Jover, "The Effects of Transformational Leadership on Organizational Performance Through Knowledge and Innovation," *British Journal of Management* 19, no. 4 (2008), pp. 299–313; and S. A. Eisenbeiss, D. van Knippenberg, and S. Boerner, "Transformational Leadership and Team Innovation: Integrating Team Climate Principles," *Journal of Applied Psychology* 93, no. 6 (2008), pp. 1438–1446.

66. Y. Ling, Z. Simsek, M. H. Lubatkin, and J. F. Veiga, "Transformational Leadership's Role in Promoting Corporate Entrepreneurship: Examining the CEO-TMT Interface," *Academy of Management Journal* 51, no. 3 (2008), pp. 557–576.

67. X. Zhang and K. M. Bartol, "Linking Empowering Leadership and Employee Creativity: The Influence of Psychological Empowerment, Intrinsic Motivation, and Creative Process Engagement," *Academy of Management Journal* 53, no. 1 (2010), pp. 107–128.

68. A. E. Colbert, A. E. Kristof-Brown, B. H. Bradley, and M. R. Barrick, "CEO Transformational Leadership: The Role of Goal Importance Congruence in Top Management Teams," *Academy of Management Journal* 51, no. 1 (2008), pp. 81–96.

69. D. Zohar and O. Tenne-Gazit, "Transformational Leadership and Group Interaction as Climate Antecedents: A Social Network Analysis," *Journal of Applied Psychology* 93, no. 4 (2008), pp. 744–757.

70. F. O. Walumbwa, B. J. Avolio, and W. Zhu, "How Transformational Leadership Weaves Its Influence on Individual Job Performance: The Role of Identification and Efficacy Beliefs," *Personnel Psychology* 61, no. 4 (2008), pp. 793–825.

71. J. E. Bono and T. A. Judge, "Self-Concordance at Work: Toward Understanding the Motivational Effects of Transformational Leaders," *Academy of Management Journal* (October 2003), pp. 554–571; Y. Berson and B. J. Avolio, "Transformational Leadership and the Dissemination of Organizational Goals: A Case Study of a Telecommunication Firm," *Leadership Quarterly* (October 2004), pp. 625–646; and J. Schaubroeck, S. S. K. Lam, and S. E. Cha, "Embracing Transformational Leadership: Team Values and the Impact of Leader Behavior on Team Performance," *Journal of Applied Psychology* 92, no. 4 (2007), pp. 1020–1030.

72. J. R. Baum, E. A. Locke, and S. A. Kirkpatrick, "A Longitudinal Study of the Relation of Vision and Vision Communication to Venture Growth in Entrepreneurial Firms," *Journal of Applied Psychology* (February 2000), pp. 43–54.

73. B. J. Avolio, W. Zhu, W. Koh, and P. Bhatia, "Transformational Leadership and Organizational Commitment: Mediating Role of Psychological Empowerment and Moderating Role of Structural Distance," *Journal of Organizational Behavior* (December 2004), pp. 951–968; and T. Dvir, N. Kass, and B. Shamir, "The Emotional Bond: Vision and Organizational Commitment Among High-Tech Employees," *Journal of Organizational Change Management* 17, no. 2 (2004), pp. 126–143.

74. R. T. Keller, "Transformational Leadership, Initiating Structure, and Substitutes for Leadership: A Longitudinal Study of Research and Development Project Team Performance," *Journal of Applied Psychology* 91, no. 1 (2006), pp. 202–210.

75. Y. Gong, J. Huang, and J. Farh, "Employee Learning Orientation, Transformational Leadership, and Employee Creativity: The Mediating Role of Employee Creative Self-Efficacy," *Academy of Management Journal* 52, no. 4 (2009), pp. 765–778.

76. G. Wang, I. Oh, S. H. Courtright, and A. E. Colbert, "Transformational Leadership and Performance Across Criteria and Levels: A Meta-Analytic Review of 25 Years of Research," *Group and Organization Management* 36, no. 2 (2011), pp. 223–270.

77. Y. Ling, Z. Simsek, M. H. Lubatkin, and J. F. Veiga, "The Impact of Transformational CEOs on the Performance of Small- to Medium-Sized Firms: Does Organizational Context Matter?" *Journal of Applied Psychology* 93, no. 4 (2008), pp. 923–934.

78. Schaubroeck, Lam, and Cha, "Embracing Transformational Leadership."

79. B. L. Kirkman, G. Chen, J. Farh, Z. X. Chen, and K. B. Lowe, "Individual Power Distance Orientation and Follower Reactions to Transformational Leaders: A Cross-Level, Cross-Cultural Examination," *Academy of Management Journal* 52, no. 4 (2009), pp. 744–764.

80. J. Liu, O. Siu, and K. Shi, "Transformational Leadership and Employee Well-Being: The Mediating Role of Trust in the Leader and Self-Efficacy," *Applied Psychology: An International Review* 59, no. 3 (2010), pp. 454–479.

81. X. Wang and J. M. Howell, "Exploring the Dual-Level Effects of Transformational Leadership on Followers," *Journal of Applied Psychology* 95, no. 6 (2010), pp. 1134–1144.

82. H. Hetland, G. M. Sandal, and T. B. Johnsen, "Burnout in the Information Technology Sector: Does Leadership Matter?" *European Journal of Work and Organizational Psychology* 16, no. 1 (2007), pp. 58–75; and K. B. Lowe, K. G. Kroeck, and N. Sivasubramaniam, "Effectiveness Correlates of Transformational and Transactional Leadership: A Meta-Analytic Review of the MLQ Literature," *Leadership Quarterly* (Fall 1996), pp. 385–425.

83. See, for instance, J. Barling, T. Weber, and E. K. Kelloway, "Effects of Transformational Leadership Training on Attitudinal and Financial Outcomes: A Field Experiment," *Journal of Applied Psychology* (December 1996), pp. 827–832; and T. Dvir, D. Eden, and B. J. Avolio, "Impact of Transformational Leadership on Follower Development and Performance: A Field Experiment," *Academy of Management Journal* (August 2002), pp. 735–744.

84. R. J. House, M. Javidan, P. Hanges, and P. Dorfman, "Understanding Cultures and Implicit Leadership Theories Across the Globe: An Introduction to Project GLOBE," *Journal of World Business* (Spring 2002), pp. 3–10.

85. D. E. Carl and M. Javidan, "Universality of Charismatic Leadership: A Multi-Nation Study," paper presented at the National Academy of Management Conference, Washington, DC (August 2001), p. 29.

86. N. Beccalli, "European Business Forum Asks: Do Companies Get the Leaders They Deserve?" *European Business Forum* (2003), www.pwcglobal.com/extweb/pwcpublications.nsf/DocID/D1EC3380F589844585256D7300346A1B.

87. See B. J. Avolio, W. L. Gardner, F. O. Walumbwa, F. Luthans, and D. R. May, "Unlocking the Mask: A Look at the Process by Which Authentic Leaders Impact Follower Attitudes and Behaviors," *Leadership Quarterly* (December 2004), pp. 801–823; W. L. Gardner and J. R. Schermerhorn Jr., "Performance Gains Through Positive Organizational Behavior and Authentic Leadership," *Organizational Dynamics* (August 2004), pp. 270–281; and M. M. Novicevic, M. G. Harvey, M. R. Buckley, J. A. Brown-Radford, and R. Evans, "Authentic Leadership: A Historical Perspective,"

Journal of Leadership and Organizational Behavior 13, no. 1 (2006), pp. 64–76.

88. C. Tan, "CEO Pinching Penney in a Slowing Economy," *The Wall Street Journal* (January 31, 2008), pp. 1–2; and A. Carter, "Lighting a Fire Under Campbell," *BusinessWeek* (December 4, 2006), pp. 96–101.

89. R. Ilies, F. P. Morgeson, and J. D. Nahrgang, "Authentic Leadership and Eudaemonic Wellbeing: Understanding Leader-follower Outcomes," *Leadership Quarterly* 16 (2005), pp. 373–394; B. Levin, "Raj Rajaratnam Did Not Appreciate Rajat Gupta's Attempt to Leave The Goldman Board, Join 'The Billionaire circle,'" *NetNet with John Carney* (March 14, 2011), downloaded July 26, 2011, from http://www.cnbc.com/.

90. This section is based on E. P. Hollander, "Ethical Challenges in the Leader–Follower Relationship," *Business Ethics Quarterly* (January 1995), pp. 55–65; J. C. Rost, "Leadership: A Discussion About Ethics," *Business Ethics Quarterly* (January 1995), pp. 129–142; L. K. Treviño, M. Brown, and L. P. Hartman, "A Qualitative Investigation of Perceived Executive Ethical Leadership: Perceptions from Inside and Outside the Executive Suite," *Human Relations* (January 2003), pp. 5–37; and R. M. Fulmer, "The Challenge of Ethical Leadership," *Organizational Dynamics* 33, no. 3 (2004), pp. 307–317.

91. J. L. Lunsford, "Piloting Boeing's New Course," *The Wall Street Journal* (June 13, 2006), pp. B1, B3.

92. J. M. Burns, *Leadership* (New York: Harper & Row, 1978).

93. J. M. Howell and B. J. Avolio, "The Ethics of Charismatic Leadership: Submission or Liberation?" *Academy of Management Executive* (May 1992), pp. 43–55.

94. D. van Knippenberg, D. De Cremer, and B. van Knippenberg, "Leadership and Fairness: The State of the Art," *European Journal of Work and Organizational Psychology* 16, no. 2 (2007), pp. 113–140.

95. K. M. Kacmar, D. G. Bachrach, K. J. Harris, and S. Zivnuska, "Fostering Good Citizenship Through Ethical Leadership: Exploring the Moderating Role of Gender and Organizational Politics," *Journal of Applied Psychology,* Advance Online Publication (December 13, 2010), doi: 10.1037/a0021872; F. O. Walumbwa and J. Schaubroeck, "Leader Personality Traits and Employee Voice Behavior: Mediating Roles of Ethical Leadership and Work Group Psychological Safety," *Journal of Applied Psychology* 94, no. 5 (2009), pp. 1275–1286.

96. M. E. Brown and L. K. Treviño, "Socialized Charismatic Leadership, Values Congruence, and Deviance in Work Groups," *Journal of Applied Psychology* 91, no. 4 (2006), pp. 954–962.

97. M. E. Brown and L. K. Treviño, "Leader-Follower Values Congruence: Are Socialized Charismatic Leaders Better Able to Achieve It?" *Journal of Applied Psychology* 94, no. 2 (2009), pp. 478–490.

98. D. van Dierendonck, "Servant Leadership: A Review and Synthesis," *Journal of Management* 37, no. 4 (2011), pp. 1228–1261.

99. F. Walumbwa, C. A. Hartnell, and A. Oke, "Servant Leadership, Procedural Justice Climate, Service Climate, Employee Attitudes, and Organizational Citizenship Behavior: A Cross-Level Investigation," *Journal of Applied Psychology* 95, no. 3 (2010), pp. 517–529.

100. D. De Cremer, D. M. Mayer, M. van Dijke, B. C. Schouten, and M. Bardes, "When Does Self-Sacrificial Leadership Motivate Prosocial Behavior? It Depends on Followers' Prevention Focus," *Journal of Applied Psychology* 2009, no. 4 (2009), pp. 887–899.

101. J. Hu and R. C. Liden, "Antecedents of Team Potency and Team Effectiveness: An Examination of Goal and Process Clarity and Servant Leadership," *Journal of Applied Psychology*, Online first publication (February 14, 2011), doi: 10.1037/a0022465.

102. M. J. Neubert, K. M. Kacmar, D. S. Carlson, L. B. Chonko, and J. A. Roberts, "Regulatory Focus as a Mediator of the Influence of Initiating Structure and Servant Leadership on Employee Behavior," *Journal of Applied Psychology* 93, no. 6 (2008), pp. 1220–1233.

103. T. Menon, J. Sim, J. Ho-Ying Fu, C. Chiu, and Y. Hong, "Blazing the Trail Versus Trailing the Group: Culture and Perceptions of the Leader's Position," *Organizational Behavior and Human Decision Processes* 113, no. 1 (2010), pp. 51–61.

104. D. M. Rousseau, S. B. Sitkin, R. S. Burt, and C. Camerer, "Not So Different After All: A Cross-Discipline View of Trust," *Academy of Management Review* (July 1998), pp. 393–404; and J. A. Simpson, "Psychological Foundations of Trust," *Current Directions in Psychological Science* 16, no. 5 (2007), pp. 264–268.

105. See, for instance, K. Dirks and D. Ferrin, "Trust in Leadership: Meta-Analytic Findings and Implications for Research and Practice," *Journal of Applied Psychology* 87, no.4, (2002), pp. 611–628; D. I. Jung and B. J. Avolio, "Opening the Black Box: An Experimental Investigation of the Mediating Effects of Trust and Value Congruence on Transformational and Transactional Leadership," *Journal of Organizational Behavior* (December 2000), pp. 949–964; and A. Zacharatos, J. Barling, and R. D. Iverson, "High-Performance Work Systems and Occupational Safety," *Journal of Applied Psychology* (January 2005), pp. 77–93.

106. D. E. Zand, *The Leadership Triad: Knowledge, Trust, and Power* (New York: Oxford University Press, 1997), p. 89.

107. Based on L. T. Hosmer, "Trust: The Connecting Link Between Organizational Theory and Philosophical Ethics," *Academy of Management Review* (April 1995), p. 393; R. C. Mayer, J. H. Davis, and F. D. Schoorman, "An Integrative Model of Organizational Trust," *Academy of Management Review* (July 1995), pp. 709–734; and F. D. Schoorman, R. C. Mayer, and J. H. Davis, "An Integrative Model of Organizational Trust: Past, Present, and Future," *Academy of Management Review* 32, no. 2 (2007), pp. 344–354.

108. J. Schaubroeck, S. S. K. Lam, and A. C. Peng, "Cognition-Based and Affect-Based Trust as Mediators of Leader

Behavior Influences on Team Performance." *Journal of Applied Psychology*, Advance online publication (February 7, 2011), doi: 10.1037/a0022625.

109. Mayer, Davis, and Schoorman, "An Integrative Model of Organizational Trust"; and J. A. Colquitt, B. A. Scott, and J. A. LePine, "Trust, Trustworthiness, and Trust Propensity: A Meta-Analytic Test of Their Unique Relationships with Risk Taking and Job Performance," *Journal of Applied Psychology* 92, no. 4 (2007), pp. 909–927.

110. H. H. Tan and C. S. F. Tan, "Toward the Differentiation of Trust in Supervisor and Trust in Organization," *Genetic, Social, and General Psychology Monographs* (May 2000), pp. 241–260.

111. Cited in D. Jones, "Do You Trust Your CEO?" *USA Today* (February 12, 2003), p. 7B.

112. B. Nanus, *The Leader's Edge: The Seven Keys to Leadership in a Turbulent World* (Chicago: Contemporary Books, 1989), p. 102.

113. R. C. Mayer and J. H. Davis, "The Effect of the Performance Appraisal System on Trust for Management: A Quasi-Experiment," *Journal of Applied Psychology* 84, no. 1 (1999), pp. 123–136; and R. C. Mayer and M. B. Gavin, "Trust in Management and Performance: Who Minds the Shop While the Employees Watch the Boss?" *Academy of Management Journal* 38 (2005), pp. 874–888.

114. J. A. Simpson, "Foundations of Interpersonal Trust," in A. W. Kruglanski and E. T. Higgins (eds.), *Social Psychology: Handbook of Basic Principles*, 2nd ed. (New York: Guilford, 2007), pp. 587–607.

115. Ibid.

116. H. Zhao, S. J. Wayne, B. C. Glibkowski, and J. Bravo, "The Impact of Psychological Contract Breach on Work-Related Outcomes: A Meta-Analysis," *Personnel Psychology* 60 (2007), pp. 647–680.

117. D. L. Shapiro, A. D. Boss, S. Salas, S. Tangirala, and M. A. Von Glinow, "When Are Transgressing *Leaders* Punitively Judged? An Empirical Test," *Journal of Applied Psychology* 96, no. 2 (2011), pp. 412–422.

118. D. L. Ferrin, P. H. Kim, C. D. Cooper, and K. T. Dirks, "Silence Speaks Volumes: The Effectiveness of Reticence in Comparison to Apology and Denial for Responding to Integrity- and Competence-Based Trust Violations," *Journal of Applied Psychology* 92, no. 4 (2007), pp. 893–908.

119. M. E. Schweitzer, J. C. Hershey, and E. T. Bradlow, "Promises and Lies: Restoring Violated Trust," *Organizational Behavior and Human Decision Processes* 101, no. 1 (2006), pp. 1–19.

120. J. R. Detert and E. R. Burris, "Leadership Behavior and Employee Voice: Is the Door Really Open?" *Academy of Management Journal* 50, no. 4 (2007), pp. 869–884.

121. Colquitt, Scott, and LePine, "Trust, Trustworthiness, and Trust Propensity."

122. See, for example, M. Murray, *Beyond the Myths and Magic of Mentoring: How to Facilitate an Effective Mentoring Process*, rev. ed. (New York: Wiley, 2001); K. E. Kram, "Phases of the Mentor Relationship," *Academy of Management Journal* (December 1983), pp. 608–625; R. A. Noe, "An Investigation of the Determinants of Successful Assigned Mentoring Relationships," *Personnel Psychology* (Fall 1988), pp. 559–580; and L. Eby, M. Butts, and A. Lockwood, "Protégés' Negative Mentoring Experiences: Construct Development and Nomological Validation," *Personnel Psychology* (Summer 2004), pp. 411–447.

123. B. R. Ragins and J. L. Cotton, "Easier Said than Done: Gender Differences in Perceived Barriers to Gaining a Mentor," *Academy of Management Journal* 34, no. 4 (1993), pp. 939–951; C. R. Wanberg, E. T. Welsh, and S. A. Hezlett, "Mentoring Research: A Review and Dynamic Process Model," in G. R. Ferris and J. J. Martocchio (eds.), *Research in Personnel and Human Resources Management*, vol. 22 (Greenwich, CT: Elsevier Science, 2003), pp. 39–124; and T. D. Allen, "Protégé Selection by Mentors: Contributing Individual and Organizational Factors," *Journal of Vocational Behavior* 65, no. 3 (2004), pp. 469–483.

124. T. D. Allen, M. L. Poteet, J. E. A. Russell, and G. H. Dobbins, "A Field Study of Factors Related to Supervisors' Willingness to Mentor Others," *Journal of Vocational Behavior* 50, no. 1 (1997), pp. 1–22; S. Aryee, Y. W. Chay, and J. Chew, "The Motivation to Mentor Among Managerial Employees in the Maintenance Career Stage: An Interactionist Perspective," *Group and Organization Management* 21, no. 3 (1996), pp. 261–277; L. T. Eby, A. L. Lockwood, and M. Butts, "Perceived Support for Mentoring: A Multiple Perspectives Approach," *Journal of Vocational Behavior* 68, no. 2 (2006), pp. 267–291; and T. D. Allen, E. Lentz, and R. Day, "Career Success Outcomes Associated with Mentoring Others: A Comparison of Mentors and Nonmentors," *Journal of Career Development* 32, no. 3 (2006), pp. 272–285.

125. See, for example, K. E. Kram and D. T. Hall, "Mentoring in a Context of Diversity and Turbulence," in E. E. Kossek and S. A. Lobel (eds.), *Managing Diversity* (Cambridge, MA: Blackwell, 1996), pp. 108–136; B. R. Ragins and J. L. Cotton, "Mentor Functions and Outcomes: A Comparison of Men and Women in Formal and Informal Mentoring Relationships," *Journal of Applied Psychology* (August 1999), pp. 529–550; and D. B. Turban, T. W. Dougherty, and F. K. Lee, "Gender, Race, and Perceived Similarity Effects in Developmental Relationships: The Moderating Role of Relationship Duration," *Journal of Vocational Behavior* (October 2002), pp. 240–262.

126. J. A. Wilson and N. S. Elman, "Organizational Benefits of Mentoring," *Academy of Management Executive* 4, no. 4 (1990), p. 90.

127. See, for instance, K. Houston-Philpot, "Leadership Development Partnerships at Dow Corning Corporation," *Journal of Organizational Excellence* (Winter 2002), pp. 13–27.

128. Ragins and Cotton, "Mentor Functions and Outcomes"; and C. M. Underhill, "The Effectiveness of Mentoring Programs in Corporate Settings: A Meta-Analytical Review of the Literature," *Journal of Vocational Behavior* 68, no. 2 (2006), pp. 292–307.

129. T. D. Allen, E. T. Eby, and E. Lentz, "The Relationship Between Formal Mentoring Program Characteristics and

Perceived Program Effectiveness," *Personnel Psychology* 59 (2006), pp. 125–153; T. D. Allen, L. T. Eby, and E. Lentz, "Mentorship Behaviors and Mentorship Quality Associated with Formal Mentoring Programs: Closing the Gap Between Research and Practice," *Journal of Applied Psychology* 91, no. 3 (2006), pp. 567–578; and M. R. Parise and M. L. Forret, "Formal Mentoring Programs: The Relationship of Program Design and Support to Mentors' Perceptions of Benefits and Costs," *Journal of Vocational Behavior* 72, no. 2 (2008), pp. 225–240.

130. L. T. Eby and A. Lockwood, "Protégés' and Mentors' Reactions to Participating in Formal Mentoring Programs: A Qualitative Investigation," *Journal of Vocational Behavior* 67, no. 3 (2005), pp. 441–458; G. T. Chao, "Formal Mentoring: Lessons Learned from Past Practice," *Professional Psychology: Research and Practice* 40, no. 3 (2009), pp. 314–320; and C. R. Wanberg, J. D. Kammeyer-Mueller, and M. Marchese, "Mentor and Protégé Predictors and Outcomes of Mentoring in a Formal Mentoring Program," *Journal of Vocational Behavior* 69 (2006), pp. 410–423.

131. T. D. Allen, L. T. Eby, M. L. Poteet, E. Lentz, and L. Lima, "Career Benefits Associated with Mentoring for Protégés: A Meta-Analysis," *Journal of Applied Psychology* (February 2004), pp. 127–136; and J. D. Kammeyer-Mueller and T. A. Judge, "A Quantitative Review of the Mentoring Literature: Test of a Model," *Journal of Vocational Behavior* 72 (2008), pp. 269–283.

132. M. K. Feeney and B. Bozeman, "Mentoring and Network Ties," *Human Relations* 61, no. 12 (2008), pp. 1651–1676; N. Bozionelos, "Intra-Organizational Network Resources: How They Relate to Career Success and Organizational Commitment," *Personnel Review* 37, no. 3 (2008), pp. 249–263; and S. A. Hezlett and S. K. Gibson, "Linking Mentoring and Social Capital: Implications for Career and Organization Development," *Advances in Developing Human Resources* 9, no. 3 (2007), pp. 384–412.

133. Comment by Jim Collins, cited in J. Useem, "Conquering Vertical Limits," *Fortune* (February 19, 2001), p. 94.

134. See, for instance, J. R. Meindl, "The Romance of Leadership as a Follower-centric Theory: A Social Constructionist Approach," *Leadership Quarterly* (Fall 1995), pp. 329–341; and B. Schyns, J. Felfe, and H. Blank, "Is Charisma Hyper-Romanticism? Empirical Evidence from New Data and a Meta-Analysis," *Applied Psychology: An International Review* 56, no. 4 (2007), pp. 505–527.

135. R. G. Lord, C. L. DeVader, and G. M. Alliger, "A Meta-Analysis of the Relation Between Personality Traits and Leadership Perceptions: An Application of Validity Generalization Procedures," *Journal of Applied Psychology* (August 1986), pp. 402–410.

136. J. R. Meindl, S. B. Ehrlich, and J. M. Dukerich, "The Romance of Leadership," *Administrative Science Quarterly* (March 1985), pp. 78–102; and M. C. Bligh, J. C. Kohles, C. L. Pearce, J. E. Justin, and J. F. Stovall, "When the Romance Is Over: Follower Perspectives of Aversive Leadership," *Applied Psychology: An International Review* 56, no. 4 (2007), pp. 528–557.

137. B. R. Agle, N. J. Nagarajan, J. A. Sonnenfeld, and D. Srinivasan, "Does CEO Charisma Matter?" *Academy of Management Journal* 49, no. 1 (2006), pp. 161–174.

138. Bligh, Kohles, Pearce, Justin, and Stovall, "When the Romance Is Over."

139. Schyns, Felfe, and Blank, "Is Charisma Hyper-Romanticism?"

140. J. Cassidy, "Subprime Suspect: The Rise and Fall of Wall Street's First Black C.E.O.," *The New Yorker* (March 31, 2008), pp. 78–91.

141. A. S. Rosette, G. J. Leonardelli, and K. W. Phillips, "The White Standard: Racial Bias in Leader Categorization," *Journal of Applied Psychology* 93, no. 4 (2008), pp. 758–777.

142. A. M. Koenig, A. H. Eagly, A. A. Mitchell, and T. Ristikari, "Are Leader Stereotypes Masculine? A Meta-Analysis of Three Research Paradigms," *Psychological Bulletin* 137, no. 4 (2011), pp. 616–642.

143. M. Van Vugt and B. R. Spisak, "Sex Differences in the Emergence of Leadership During Competitions Within and Between Groups," *Psychological Science* 19, no. 9 (2008), pp. 854–858.

144. M. Van Vugt and B. R. Spisak, "Sex Differences in the Emergence of Leadership During Competitions Within and Between Groups," *Psychological Science* 19, no. 9 (2008), pp. 854–858.

145. S. D. Dionne, F. J. Yammarino, L. E. Atwater, and L. R. James, "Neutralizing Substitutes for Leadership Theory: Leadership Effects and Common-Source Bias," *Journal of Applied Psychology,* 87 (2002), pp. 454–464; and J. R. Villa, J. P. Howell, P. W. Dorfman, and D. L. Daniel, "Problems with Detecting Moderators in Leadership Research Using Moderated Multiple Regression," *Leadership Quarterly* 14 (2002), pp. 3–23.

146. L. A. Hambley, T. A. O'Neill, and T. J. B. Kline, "Virtual Team Leadership: The Effects of Leadership Style and Communication Medium on Team Interaction Styles and Outcomes," *Organizational Behavior and Human Decision Processes* 103 (2007), pp. 1–20; and B. J. Avolio and S. S. Kahai, "Adding the 'E' to E-Leadership: How It May Impact Your Leadership," *Organizational Dynamics* 31, no. 4 (2003), pp. 325–338.

147. S. J. Zaccaro and P. Bader, "E-Leadership and the Challenges of Leading E-Teams: Minimizing the Bad and Maximizing the Good," *Organizational Dynamics* 31, no. 4 (2003), pp. 381–385.

148. C. E. Naquin and G. D. Paulson, "Online Bargaining and Interpersonal Trust," *Journal of Applied Psychology* (February 2003), pp. 113–120.

149. B. M. Bass, "Cognitive, Social, and Emotional Intelligence of Transformational Leaders," in R. E. Riggio, S. E. Murphy, and F. J. Pirozzolo (eds.), *Multiple Intelligences and Leadership* (Mahwah, NJ: Lawrence Erlbaum, 2002), pp. 113–114.

150. See, for instance, P. Dvorak, "M.B.A. Programs Hone 'Soft Skills,'" *The Wall Street Journal* (February 12, 2007), p. B3.

151. J. Weber, "The Leadership Factor," *BusinessWeek* (June 12, 2006), pp. 60–64.

152. See, for instance, Barling, Weber, and Kelloway, "Effects of Transformational Leadership Training on Attitudinal and Financial Outcomes"; and D. V. Day, "Leadership Development: A Review in Context," *Leadership Quarterly* (Winter 2000), pp. 581–613.

153. M. Sashkin, "The Visionary Leader," in J. A. Conger, R. N. Kanungo, et al. (eds.), *Charismatic Leadership* (San Francisco: Jossey-Bass, 1988), p. 150.

154. D. Brady, "The Rising Star of CEO Consulting" *Bloomberg Businessweek* (November 24, 2010), www .businessweek.com.

155. Howell and Frost, "A Laboratory Study of Charismatic Leadership."

156. Dvir, Eden, and Avolio, "Impact of Transformational Leadership on Follower Development and Performance"; B. J. Avolio and B. M. Bass, *Developing Potential Across a Full Range of Leadership: Cases on Transactional and Transformational Leadership* (Mahwah, NJ: Lawrence Erlbaum, 2002); A. J. Towler, "Effects of Charismatic Influence Training on Attitudes, Behavior, and Performance," *Personnel Psychology* (Summer 2003), pp. 363–381; and Barling, Weber, and Kelloway, "Effects of Transformational Leadership Training on Attitudinal and Financial Outcomes."

LEARNING
OBJECTIVES

After studying this chapter,
you should be able to:

1 Define *power* and contrast
leadership and power.

2 Contrast the five bases
of power.

3 Explain the role of
dependence in power
relationships.

4 Identify nine power or
influence tactics and their
contingencies.

5 Show the connection
between sexual harassment
and the abuse of power.

6 Identify the causes and
consequences of political
behavior.

7 Apply impression
management techniques.

8 Determine whether a
political action is ethical.

MyManagementLab

Access a host of interactive
learning aids to help strengthen
your understanding of the
chapter concepts at
**www.pearsonglobaleditions
.com/mymanagementlab**.

APPEARANCES CAN BE DECEIVING

He led one of the world's most trusted and prestigious consulting firms, McKinsey & Company. As a philanthropist, he raised tens of millions of dollars for health care, education, and AIDS. He was often mentioned as a business executive-to-philanthropist role model in the same breath as Warren Buffett and Bill Gates. He collaborated with some of the world's most famous leaders, including Gates, former President Bill Clinton, and leading CEOs.

He served on the boards of directors of some of the world's most respected companies, including Goldman Sachs, Procter & Gamble, and American Airlines, often as chair. He was advisor to many of the world's leading business schools, including Harvard Business School, Tsinghua University, IIT, MIT Sloan School of Management, Wharton's Lauder Institute, and Northwestern's Kellogg School of Management. When President Obama hosted the Indian Prime minister at a state dinner, he was at the White House.

People described him as "humble" and "egoless." His colleagues at McKinsey admired him for the value he placed on family. He described himself as a "servant leader." *Bloomberg Businessweek* noted that he was "that rare businessman whose integrity was beyond reproach."

Yet this man—Rajat Gupta—appears to have led a double life.

When the FBI and SEC were investigating Galleon Group founder and CEO Raj Rajaratnam (convicted in 2011 on 14 charges of fraud and insider trading), they uncovered a "flurry" of phone conversations between Rajaratnam and Gupta. In wiretapped calls, Gupta appears to have alerted Rajaratnam to an upcoming $5 billion investment in Goldman by Berkshire Hathaway. On another occasion, 23 seconds after hanging up on a Goldman conference call, Gupta called Rajaratnam with news that Goldman would report a quarterly loss. All the while, Gupta was investing in and profiting from Galleon's profits on these and other trades. Rajaratnam also "loaned" Gupta millions so he could increase his investments in Galleon.

When these facts became public in 2010 and 2011, the companies with whom Gupta had a relationship—from McKinsey to Goldman Sachs to Proctor & Gamble—quietly ended their associations with him. By mid-2011, not a single company or university still listed Gupta as an advisor.

As of this writing, Gupta has not yet been convicted of insider trading. Even if he is acquitted, however, the damage has been done. A CEO who once was as powerful, networked, and admired as any whose names aren't Gates, Buffett, or Jobs, Gupta is now a pariah and his power is gone.

Power and Politics

*Power is not revealed by striking hard
or often, but by striking true.*

—Honoré de Balzac

Photo: Rajat Gupta Source: Eric Piermont/AFP/Getty Images/Newscom.

445

Why did a man with such power decide to risk it all? Only Gupta knows for certain.

_____

Source: S. Andrews, "How Gupta Came Undone," _Bloomberg Businessweek_ (May 19, 2011), pp. 56– 63; M. Gordon and L. Neumeister, "Ex-Goldman Sachs Director Rajat Gupta Charged with Insider Trading," _Washington Post_ (March 1, 2011), downloaded June 18, 2011 from www.washingtonpost .com/; W. Pavlo, "Goldman's Boardroom Meetings—Less Proprietary Than Computer Code?" _Forbes_ (March 17, 2011), downloaded June 21, 2011, from http://blogs.forbes.com/.

In both research and practice, _power_ and _politics_ have been described as the last dirty words. It is easier for most of us to talk about sex or money than about power or political behavior. People who have power deny it, people who want it try not to look like they're seeking it, and those who are good at getting it are secretive about how they do so.[1] To see whether you think your work environment is political, take the accompanying self-assessment.

A major theme of this chapter is that power and political behavior are natural processes in any group or organization. Given that, you need to know how power is acquired and exercised if you are to fully understand organizational behavior. Although you may have heard that "Power corrupts, and absolute power corrupts absolutely," power is not always bad. As one author noted, most medicines can kill if taken in the wrong amount, and thousands die each year in automobile accidents, but we don't abandon chemicals or cars because of the dangers associated with them. Rather, we consider danger an incentive to get training and information that will help us to use these forces productively.[2] The same applies to power. It's a reality of organizational life, and it's not going to go away. By learning how power works in organizations, you'll be better able to use your knowledge to become a more effective manager.

SELF-ASSESSMENT LIBRARY

Is My Workplace Political?

In the Self-Assessment Library (available on CD and online), take assessment IV.F.1 (Is My Workplace Political?). If you don't currently have a job, answer for your most recent job. Then answer the following questions.

1. How does your score relate to those of your classmates? Do you think your score is accurate? Why or why not?
2. Do you think a political workplace is a bad thing? If yes, why? If no, why not?
3. What factors cause your workplace to be political?

A Definition of Power

1   Define _power_ and contrast leadership and power.

Power refers to a capacity that _A_ has to influence the behavior of _B_ so _B_ acts in accordance with _A_'s wishes.[3]

Someone can thus have power but not use it; it is a capacity or potential. Probably the most important aspect of power is that it is a function of **dependence**. The greater _B_'s dependence on _A_, the greater _A_'s power in the relationship. Dependence, in turn, is based on alternatives that _B_ perceives and the importance *B* places on the alternative(s) *A* controls. A person can have power over you only if he or she controls something you desire. If you want a college degree and have to pass a certain course to get it, and your current instructor is the only faculty member in the college who teaches that course, he or she has power over you. Your alternatives are highly limited, and you place a high degree of importance on obtaining a passing grade. Similarly, if you're attending college on funds totally provided by your parents, you probably recognize the power they hold over you. You're dependent on them for financial support. But once you're out of school, have a job, and are making a good income, your parents' power is reduced significantly. Who among us, though, has not known or heard of a rich relative who is able to control a large number of family members merely through the implicit or explicit threat of "writing them out of the will"?

One study even suggests that powerful people might be better liars because they are more confident in their status. Researchers gave one group of research subjects bigger offices and more authority, while another group received smaller offices and less authority. Then half the subjects in each condition were told to steal a $100 bill and convince an interviewer they hadn't taken it. If they were able to fool the interviewer, they could keep the money. In the interviews, those in positions of power showed fewer signs of dishonesty and stress like shoulder shrugs and stuttering when lying—perhaps because they felt less dependent on others. Recall that this simulation involved only hypothetical, experimentally manipulated power, so imagine the effects when real power is on the line.[4]

One study investigated how people respond to the poor performance of a subordinate dependent on them in a work context.[5] To study this, a laboratory mockup of a performance review was developed, and participants acted the part of either powerful or unpowerful managers. The result? Powerful managers were more likely to respond to poor performers by either directly confronting them or frankly encouraging them to get training to improve. Less powerful managers enacted strategies not to confront the poor performer, like compensating for poor performance or avoiding the individual altogether. In other words, they were less likely to actively engage in a potential conflict with the subordinate, possibly because they would be more vulnerable if the subordinate wanted to "get revenge" for the negative feedback.

Contrasting Leadership and Power

A careful comparison of our description of power with our description of leadership in Chapter 12 reveals the concepts are closely intertwined. Leaders use power as a means of attaining group goals.

How are the two terms different? Power does not require goal compatibility, merely dependence. Leadership, on the other hand, requires some congruence between the goals of the leader and those being led. A second difference relates to the direction of influence. Leadership focuses on the downward influence on followers. It minimizes the importance of lateral and upward influence patterns. Power does not. In still another difference, leadership research, for the most

power *A capacity that A has to influence the behavior of B so that B acts in accordance with A's wishes.*

dependence *B's relationship to A when A possesses something that B requires.*

part, emphasizes style. It seeks answers to questions such as these: How supportive should a leader be? How much decision making should be shared with followers? In contrast, the research on power focuses on tactics for gaining compliance. It goes beyond the individual as the exerciser of power, because groups as well as individuals can use power to control other individuals or groups.

Bases of Power

2   Contrast the five bases of power.

Where does power come from? What gives an individual or a group influence over others? We answer by dividing the bases or sources of power into two general groupings—formal and personal—and then breaking each of these down into more specific categories.[6]

Formal Power

Formal power is based on an individual's position in an organization. It can come from the ability to coerce or reward, or from formal authority.

Coercive Power   The **coercive power** base depends on fear of the negative results from failing to comply. It rests on the application, or the threat of application, of physical sanctions such as the infliction of pain, frustration through restriction of movement, or the controlling by force of basic physiological or safety needs.

At the organizational level, *A* has coercive power over *B* if *A* can dismiss, suspend, or demote *B*, assuming *B* values his or her job. If *A* can assign *B* work activities *B* finds unpleasant, or treat *B* in a manner *B* finds embarrassing, *A* possesses coercive power over *B*. Coercive power can also come from withholding key information. People in an organization who have data or knowledge others need can make those others dependent on them.

Reward Power   The opposite of coercive power is **reward power**, with which people comply because it produces positive benefits; someone who can distribute rewards others view as valuable will have power over them. These rewards can be either financial—such as controlling pay rates, raises, and bonuses—or nonfinancial, including recognition, promotions, interesting work assignments, friendly colleagues, and preferred work shifts or sales territories.[7]

Legitimate Power   In formal groups and organizations, probably the most common access to one or more of the power bases is through **legitimate power**. It represents the formal authority to control and use organizational resources based on structural position in the organization.

Legitimate power is broader than the power to coerce and reward. Specifically, it includes members' acceptance of the authority of a position. We associate power so closely with the concept of hierarchy that just drawing longer lines in an organization chart leads people to infer the leaders are especially powerful, and when a powerful executive is described, people tend to put the person at a higher position when drawing an organization chart.[8] When school principals, bank presidents, or army captains speak (assuming their directives are viewed as within the authority of their positions), teachers, tellers, and first lieutenants listen and usually comply.

Personal Power

Many of the most competent and productive chip designers at Intel have power, but they aren't managers and have no formal power. What they have is **personal power**, which comes from an individual's unique characteristics. There are two bases of personal power: expertise and the respect and admiration of others.

Expert Power   **Expert power** is influence wielded as a result of expertise, special skill, or knowledge. As jobs become more specialized, we become increasingly dependent on experts to achieve goals. It is generally acknowledged that physicians have expertise and hence expert power: Most of us follow our doctor's advice. Computer specialists, tax accountants, economists, industrial psychologists, and other specialists wield power as a result of their expertise.

Referent Power   **Referent power** is based on identification with a person who has desirable resources or personal traits. If I like, respect, and admire you, you can exercise power over me because I want to please you.

Referent power develops out of admiration of another and a desire to be like that person. It helps explain, for instance, why celebrities are paid millions of dollars to endorse products in commercials. Marketing research shows people such as LeBron James and Tom Brady have the power to influence your choice of athletic shoes and credit cards. With a little practice, you and I could probably deliver as smooth a sales pitch as these celebrities, but the buying public doesn't identify with you and me. Some people who are not in formal leadership positions nonetheless have referent power and exert influence over others because of their charismatic dynamism, likability, and emotional effects on us.

Nike CEO Mark Parker has expert power. Since joining Nike in 1979 as a footwear designer, Parker has been involved in many of Nike's most significant design innovations. His primary responsibilities and leadership positions at Nike have been in product research, design, and development. Nike depends on Parker's expertise in leading the company's innovation initiatives and in setting corporate strategy to achieve the growth of its global business portfolio that includes Converse, Nike Golf, and Cole Haan. Parker is shown here introducing Nike's Considered Design during a news conference about the company's latest products that combine sustainability and innovation.

Source: Mark Lennihan/AP Images.

coercive power   *A power base that is dependent on fear of the negative results from failing to comply.*

reward power   *Compliance achieved based on the ability to distribute rewards that others view as valuable.*

legitimate power   *The power a person receives as a result of his or her position in the formal hierarchy of an organization.*

personal power   *Influence derived from an individual's characteristics.*

expert power   *Influence based on special skills or knowledge.*

referent power   *Influence based on identification with a person who has desirable resources or personal traits.*

Which Bases of Power Are Most Effective?

Of the three bases of formal power (coercive, reward, legitimate) and two bases of personal power (expert, referent), which is most important to have? Research suggests pretty clearly that the personal sources of power are most effective. Both expert and referent power are positively related to employees' satisfaction with supervision, their organizational commitment, and their performance, whereas reward and legitimate power seem to be unrelated to these outcomes. One source of formal power—coercive power—actually can backfire in that it is negatively related to employee satisfaction and commitment.[9]

Consider Steve Stoute's company, Translation, which matches pop-star spokespersons with corporations that want to promote their brands. Stoute has paired Gwen Stefani with HP, Justin Timberlake with McDonald's, Beyoncé Knowles with Tommy Hilfiger, and Jay-Z with Reebok. Stoute's business seems to be all about referent power. His firm's work aims to use the credibility of these artists and performers to reach youth culture.[10] In other words, people buy products associated with cool figures because they wish to identify with and emulate them.

Power and Perceived Justice

Individuals in positions of power tend to be blamed for their failures and credited for their successes to a greater degree than those who have less power. In the same way, studies suggest that leaders and managers in positions of power pay greater costs for unfairness and reap greater benefits for fairness.[11] Specifically, authorities are given greatest trust when they have a lot of power and their organizations are seen as operating fairly, and the least trust when they have a lot of power and their organizations are seen as operating unfairly. Thus, it appears that people think powerful leaders should have the discretion to shape organizational policies and change unfair rules, and if they fail to do so, they will be seen especially negatively.

Dependence: The Key to Power

The most important aspect of power is that it is a function of dependence. In this section, we show how understanding dependence helps us understand power itself.

The General Dependence Postulate

Let's begin with a general postulate: *the greater* B*'s dependence on* A, *the more power* A *has over* B. When you possess anything others require that you alone control, you make them dependent on you, and therefore you gain power over them.[12] If something is plentiful, possessing it will not increase your power. But as the old saying goes, "In the land of the blind, the one-eyed man is king!" Conversely, the more you can expand your own options, the less power you place in the hands of others. This explains why most organizations develop multiple suppliers rather than give their business to only one. It also explains why so many aspire to financial independence. Independence reduces the power others can wield who can limit our access to opportunities and resources.

What Creates Dependence?

Dependence increases when the resource you control is important, scarce, and nonsubstitutable.[13]

Importance   If nobody wants what you have, it's not going to create dependence. Because organizations, for instance, actively seek to avoid uncertainty,[14] we should expect that individuals or groups that can absorb uncertainty will be perceived as controlling an important resource. A study of industrial organizations found their marketing departments were consistently rated the most powerful.[15] The researcher concluded that the most critical uncertainty facing these firms was selling their products, suggesting that engineers, as a group, would be more powerful at technology company Matsushita than at consumer products giant Procter & Gamble. These inferences appear to be generally valid. Matsushita, which is heavily technologically oriented, depends heavily on its engineers to maintain its products' technical advantages and quality, and so they are a powerful group. At Procter & Gamble, marketing is the name of the game, and marketers are the most powerful occupational group.

Scarcity   Ferruccio Lamborghini, who created the exotic supercars that still carry his name, understood the importance of scarcity and used it to his advantage during World War II. Lamborghini was in Rhodes with the Italian army. His superiors were impressed with his mechanical skills, as he demonstrated an almost uncanny ability to repair tanks and cars no one else could fix. After the war, he admitted his ability was largely due to his having been the first person on the island to receive the repair manuals, which he memorized and then destroyed so as to become indispensable.[16]

We see the scarcity–dependence relationship in the power of occupational categories. Where the supply of labor is low relative to demand, workers can negotiate compensation and benefits packages far more attractive than can

Mary Pochobradsky (center) is in a position of power at Procter & Gamble. She is the North American marketing director for P&G's fabric enhancing products that include the Downy brand, one of 24 company brands that each generate more than $1 billion in sales a year. Mary is shown here announcing a new marketing campaign for the 50-year-old Downy brand that includes TV ads, social networks, and a live window display at Macy's retail store featuring comedian Mike Birbiglia. At consumer product firms like P&G, marketers are the most powerful occupational group because they control the important resource of selling products.

Source: AP Photo/Al Behrman.

those in occupations with an abundance of candidates. College administrators have no problem today finding English instructors. The market for network systems analysts, in contrast, is comparatively tight, with demand high and supply limited. The bargaining power of computer-engineering faculty allows them to negotiate higher salaries, lighter teaching loads, and other benefits.

Nonsubstitutability   The fewer viable substitutes for a resource, the more power control over that resource provides. At universities with strong pressures on the faculty to publish, the more recognition the faculty member receives through publication, the more mobile he or she is, because other universities want faculty who are highly published and visible. Although tenure can alter this relationship by restricting the department head's alternatives, faculty members with few or no publications have the least mobility and are subject to the greatest influence from their superiors.

Power Tactics

3 Explain the role of dependence in power relationships.

What **power tactics** do people use to translate power bases into specific action? What options do they have for influencing their bosses, co-workers, or employees? In this section, we review popular tactical options and the conditions that may make one more effective than another.

Research has identified nine distinct influence tactics:[17]

- **Legitimacy.**   Relying on your authority position or saying a request accords with organizational policies or rules.
- **Rational persuasion.**   Presenting logical arguments and factual evidence to demonstrate a request is reasonable.
- **Inspirational appeals.**   Developing emotional commitment by appealing to a target's values, needs, hopes, and aspirations.
- **Consultation.**   Increasing the target's support by involving him or her in deciding how you will accomplish your plan.
- **Exchange.**   Rewarding the target with benefits or favors in exchange for following a request.
- **Personal appeals.**   Asking for compliance based on friendship or loyalty.
- **Ingratiation.**   Using flattery, praise, or friendly behavior prior to making a request.
- **Pressure.**   Using warnings, repeated demands, and threats.
- **Coalitions.**   Enlisting the aid or support of others to persuade the target to agree.

Some tactics are more effective than others. Rational persuasion, inspirational appeals, and consultation tend to be the most effective, especially when the audience is highly interested in the outcomes of a decision process. Pressure tends to backfire and is typically the least effective of the nine tactics.[18] You can also increase your chance of success by using two or more tactics together or sequentially, as long as your choices are compatible.[19] Using both ingratiation and legitimacy can lessen negative reactions to your appearing to dictate outcomes, but only when the audience does not really care about the outcome of a decision process or the policy is routine.[20]

Let's consider the most effective way of getting a raise. You can start with rational persuasion: figure out how your pay compares to that of peers, or land a competing job offer, or show objective results that testify to your performance. Kitty Dunning, a vice president at Don Jagoda Associates, landed a 16 percent raise when she e-mailed her boss numbers showing she had increased sales.[21] You can also make good use of salary calculators such as Salary.com to compare your pay with comparable others.

But the effectiveness of some influence tactics depends on the direction of influence.[22] As Exhibit 13-1 shows, rational persuasion is the only tactic effective across organizational levels. Inspirational appeals work best as a downward-influencing tactic with subordinates. When pressure works, it's generally downward only. Personal appeals and coalitions are most effective as lateral influence. Other factors that affect the effectiveness of influence include the sequencing of tactics, a person's skill in using the tactic, and the organizational culture.

You're more likely to be effective if you begin with "softer" tactics that rely on personal power, such as personal and inspirational appeals, rational persuasion, and consultation. If these fail, you can move to "harder" tactics, such as exchange, coalitions, and pressure, which emphasize formal power and incur greater costs and risks.[23] Interestingly, a single soft tactic is more effective than a single hard tactic, and combining two soft tactics or a soft tactic and rational persuasion is more effective than any single tactic or combination of hard tactics.[24] The effectiveness of tactics depends on the audience.[25] People especially likely to comply with soft power tactics tend to be more reflective and intrinsically motivated; they have high self-esteem and greater desire for control. Those likely to comply with hard power tactics are more action-oriented and extrinsically motivated and are more focused on getting along with others than on getting their own way.

People in different countries prefer different power tactics.[26] Those from individualistic countries tend to see power in personalized terms and as a legitimate means of advancing their personal ends, whereas those in collectivistic countries see power in social terms and as a legitimate means of helping others.[27] A study comparing managers in the United States and China found that U.S. managers prefer rational appeal, whereas Chinese managers preferred coalition tactics.[28] These differences tend to be consistent with the values in these two countries. Reason is consistent with the U.S. preference for direct confrontation and rational persuasion to influence others and resolve differences, while coalition tactics align with the Chinese preference for meeting

Exhibit 13-1	Preferred Power Tactics by Influence Direction	
Upward Influence	**Downward Influence**	**Lateral Influence**
Rational persuasion	Rational persuasion	Rational persuasion
	Inspirational appeals	Consultation
	Pressure	Ingratiation
	Consultation	Exchange
	Ingratiation	Legitimacy
	Exchange	Personal appeals
	Legitimacy	Coalitions

power tactics *Ways in which individuals translate power bases into specific actions.*

Power Distance and Innovation

Throughout this book, you may have noticed a lot of international research into the differences between individualistic and collectivistic countries. Differences in power distance between countries are also likely to affect organizational behavior. *Power distance* is the extent to which people with low levels of power in society accept and expect that power will be distributed unequally. Cultures high in power distance tend to have greater differentiation between leaders and followers in organizations, and less power sharing between employees and upper management.

How does power distance affect the development and implementation of new ideas in organizations? One study that looked at data from 212 Chinese firms found control mechanisms and strict rules in higher power-distance organizations to be associated with lower levels of information exchange and experimentation. This implies fewer opportunities for creation of new knowledge when power distance is great.

Power distance might also restrict the implementation of new workplace practices. A study across 16 European countries with different levels of power distance showed that innovative work practices like job rotation, autonomous teams, job autonomy, and upward communication were less common in countries with higher power distance. Similar results were obtained in a study of 743 workers in Turkey. This tendency toward less empowerment in high power distance cultures probably reflects the stronger preferences among workers and managers alike for hierarchical social relationships. However, it may come with a price, because power sharing and autonomy-enhancing practices are most likely to lead to greater innovation.

Source: Based on A. Ollo-López, A. Bayo-Moriones, and M. Larraza-Kintana, "The Impact of Country Level Factors on the Use of New Work Practices," *Journal of World Business* 46, no. 3 (2011), pp. 394–403; D. Wang, Z. Su, and D. Yang, "Organizational Culture and Knowledge Creation Capability," *Journal of Knowledge Management* 15, no. 3 (2011), pp. 363–373; and N. D. Cakar and A. Ertürk, "Comparing Innovation Capability of Small and Medium-Sized Enterprises: Examining the Effects of Organizational Culture and Empowerment," *Journal of Small Business Management* 48, no. 3 (2010), pp. 325–359.

difficult or controversial requests with indirect approaches. Research also has shown that individuals in Western, individualistic cultures tend to engage in more self-enhancement behaviors (such as self-promotion) than individuals in more collectivistic Eastern cultures.[29]

People differ in their **political skill**, or their ability to influence others to enhance their own objectives. The politically skilled are more effective users of all the influence tactics. Political skill also appears more effective when the stakes are high—such as when the individual is accountable for important organizational outcomes. Finally, the politically skilled are able to exert their influence without others detecting it, a key element in being effective (it's damaging to be labeled political).[30] However, these individuals also appear most able to use their political skills in environments marked by low levels of procedural and distributive justice. When an organization is run with open and fairly applied rules, free of favoritism or biases, political skill is actually negatively related to job performance ratings.[31]

Finally, we know cultures within organizations differ markedly—some are warm, relaxed, and supportive; others are formal and conservative. Some encourage participation and consultation, some encourage reason, and still others rely on pressure. People who fit the culture of the organization tend to obtain more influence.[32] Specifically, extraverts tend to be more influential in team-oriented organizations, and highly conscientious people are more influential in organizations that value working alone on technical tasks. People who fit the culture are influential because they can perform especially well in the domains deemed most important for success. In other words, they are influential because they are competent. Thus, the organization itself will influence which subset of power tactics is viewed as acceptable for use.

Sexual Harassment: Unequal Power in the Workplace

4 Identify nine power or influence tactics and their contingencies.

A federal jury awarded this young woman a $95 million judgment in a sexual harassment lawsuit against her employer Aaron's Rents. She reported that her supervisor, the store's general manager, sexually harassed her with hostile and abusive behavior that included lewd propositions and unwanted physical sexual contact. She alleged that she called a company harassment hotline but that an investigator never contacted her and that she was denied a promotion for complaining about her boss's behavior. In their verdicts, the jurors found the supervisor guilty of assault and battery and the company liable for negligent supervision, sexual harassment, and intentional infliction of emotional distress.

Sexual harassment is wrong. It can also be costly to employers. Just ask executives at Walmart, the World Bank, and the United Nations.[33] Mitsubishi paid $34 million to settle a sexual harassment case. And a former UPS manager won an $80 million suit against UPS on her claims it fostered a hostile work environment when it failed to listen to her complaints of sexual harassment. Of course, it's not only big organizations that run into trouble: A jury awarded Janet Bianco, a nurse at New York's Flushing Hospital, $15 million for harassment she suffered at the hands of Dr. Matthew Miller. After the verdict, Bianco said, "I think that people take it lightly when you say sexual harassment. They don't understand how it affects your life, not only in your job, but in your home, with your friends."[34]

In addition to the legal dangers to sexual harassment, obviously it can have a negative impact on the work environment, too. Sexual harassment negatively affects job attitudes and leads those who feel harassed to withdraw from the organization. In many cases, reporting sexual harassment doesn't improve the situation because the organization responds in a negative or unhelpful way. When organizational leaders make honest efforts to stop the harassment, the outcomes are much more positive.[35]

Sexual harassment is defined as any unwanted activity of a sexual nature that affects an individual's employment and creates a hostile work environment. The U.S. Supreme Court helped to clarify this definition by adding a key test for determining whether sexual harassment has occurred—when comments or behavior in a work environment "would reasonably be perceived, and [are] perceived, as hostile or abusive."[36] But disagreement continues about what *specifically* constitutes sexual harassment. Organizations have generally made progress toward limiting overt forms of sexual harassment. This includes unwanted physical touching, recurring requests for dates when it is made clear the person isn't interested, and coercive threats that a person will lose his or her job for refusing a sexual proposition. Problems today are likely to surface around more subtle forms of sexual harassment—unwanted looks or comments, off-color jokes, sexual artifacts like pinups posted in the workplace, or misinterpretations of where the line between being friendly ends and harassment begins.

A recent review concluded that 58 percent of women report having experienced potentially harassing behaviors, and 24 percent report having experienced sexual harassment at work.[37] Other research suggests that despite increased media attention and training, perceptions of sexual harassment levels have been fairly stable since the 1990s.[38] One problem with reporting is that sexual harassment is, to some degree, in the eye of the beholder. Women are more likely than men to see a given behavior or set of behaviors as constituting sexual harassment. Men are less likely to see harassment in such behaviors as kissing someone, asking for a date, or making sex-stereotyped jokes. As the authors of one study note, "Although progress has been made at defining sexual harassment, it is still unclear as to whose perspective should be taken."[39] Witnesses offering sexual harassment testimony also find that victims who took

political skill   *The ability to influence others in such a way as to enhance one's objectives.*

sexual harassment   *Any unwanted activity of a sexual nature that affects an individual's employment and creates a hostile work environment.*

OB Poll   **Reports of Sexual Harassment Differ by Country**

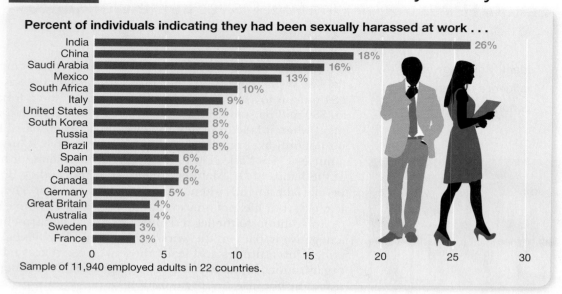

Percent of individuals indicating they had been sexually harassed at work . . .

Country	Percent
India	26%
China	18%
Saudi Arabia	16%
Mexico	13%
South Africa	10%
Italy	9%
United States	8%
South Korea	8%
Russia	8%
Brazil	8%
Spain	6%
Japan	6%
Canada	6%
Germany	5%
Great Britain	4%
Australia	4%
Sweden	3%
France	3%

Sample of 11,940 employed adults in 22 countries.

Note: Sample of 11,940 employed adults in 22 countries.

Source: J. Wright, "Physical Assault and Sexual Harassment in the Workplace" *Ipsos Global @dvisory* (August 12, 2010), downloaded June 20, 2011, from www.ipsos-na.com/.

either an aggressive or a passive tone in making their complaints were seen as less plausible than victims who took a more neutral tone.[40] This research suggests that people may not be able to be entirely objective when listening to sexual harassment complaints, taking the tone of the victim into account when making judgments rather than simply relying on the facts of the case at hand. The best approach is to be careful—refrain from any behavior that may be taken as harassing, even if that was not the intent. Realize that what you see as an innocent joke or hug may be seen as harassment by the other party.

Most studies confirm that the concept of power is central to understanding sexual harassment.[41] This seems true whether the harassment comes from a supervisor, a co-worker, or an employee. And sexual harassment is more likely to occur when there are large power differentials. The supervisor–employee dyad best characterizes an unequal power relationship, where formal power gives the supervisor the capacity to reward and coerce. Because employees want favorable performance reviews, salary increases, and the like, supervisors control resources most employees consider important and scarce. Thus, sexual harassment by the boss typically creates the greatest difficulty for those being harassed. If there are no witnesses, it is the victim's word against the harasser's. Has this boss harassed others, and, if so, will they come forward or fear retaliation? Male respondents in one study in Switzerland who were high in hostile sexism reported higher intentions to sexually harass in organizations that had low levels of justice, suggesting that failure to have consistent policies and procedures for all employees might actually increase levels of sexual harassment.[42]

Women in positions of power in an organization can be subjected to sexual harassment from males who occupy less powerful positions, although this situation doesn't get nearly as much attention as harassment by a supervisor. The employee devalues the woman in power by highlighting traditional gender stereotypes that reflect negatively on her (such as helplessness, passivity, or lack of career commitment), usually in an attempt to gain power over her or minimize power differentials. Increasingly, too, there are cases of women in positions of power harassing male employees.

Should All Sexual Behavior Be Prohibited at Work?

The difficulty in monitoring and defining sexual harassment at work has led some organizations to go beyond discouraging overt sexually harassing behaviors. Companies ranging from Walmart to Staples to Xerox have disciplined employees for workplace romances and upheld policies that ban hierarchical romantic relationships, such as between a supervisor and subordinate. The idea is that such relationships are so fraught with potential for abuse of power that they cannot possibly be consensual for extended periods of time. Surveys by the Society of Human Resource Management suggest that concerns about both potential sexual harassment and lowered productivity have motivated prohibitions on workplace romances. However, ethicists and legal scholars have thrown some "no romance" policies into question on the grounds they are patronizing or invade employee privacy.

What does organizational behavior research have to say about *consensual* sexual behavior at work? One study of more than 1,000 respondents found 40 percent were exposed to sexual behavior in some form in the past year. Counter to the idea that all sexual behavior at work is negative, some female and many male respondents reported enjoying the experience. However, exposure to sexual behavior at work was negatively related to performance and psychological well-being. People may report enjoying it, but it might be hurting their productivity and well-being anyway.

When thinking about a sexual harassment policy for your own organization that might prohibit all workplace romances, consider the following questions:

1. Are there potential problems in monitoring and enforcing such a comprehensive policy on all employees?

2. Does the organization have the right to actively determine what types of behaviors consenting employees engage in outside the work environment?

3. Can the policy be written in a less restrictive manner, such as by prohibiting employees who work together closely from having workplace romances? In this way, the organization might be able to transfer employees who are in a relationship so they don't work directly with one another, and thus they can be retained in the organization and their personal privacy respected.

Source: Based on J. L. Berdahl and K. Aquino, "Sexual Behavior at Work: Fun or Folly?" *Journal of Applied Psychology* 94, no. 1 (2009), pp. 34–47; and C. Boyd, "The Debate over the Prohibition of Romance in the Workplace," *Journal of Business Ethics* 97, no. 2 (2010), pp. 325–338.

A recent review of the literature shows the damage caused by sexual harassment. As you would expect, victims report lower job satisfaction and diminished organizational commitment as a result. Sexual harassment undermines their mental and physical health, as well as lowering productivity in the group in which they work. The authors of this study conclude that sexual harassment "is significantly and substantively associated with a host of harms."[43]

Sexual harassment can wreak havoc on an organization, not to mention on the victims themselves, but it can be avoided. The manager's role is critical. Here are some ways managers can protect themselves and their employees from sexual harassment:

1. Make sure an active policy defines what constitutes sexual harassment, informs employees they can be fired for sexually harassing another employee, and establishes procedures for making complaints.
2. Reassure employees they will not encounter retaliation if they file a complaint.
3. Investigate every complaint, and inform the legal and human resource departments.
4. Make sure offenders are disciplined or terminated.
5. Set up in-house seminars to raise employee awareness of sexual harassment issues.

The bottom line is that managers have a responsibility to protect their employees from a hostile work environment, but they also need to protect themselves. Managers may be unaware that one of their employees is being sexually harassed. But being unaware does not protect them or their organization. If investigators believe a manager could have known about the harassment, both the manager and the company can be held liable.

Politics: Power in Action

5 Show the connection between sexual harassment and the abuse of power.

Source: Kyodo News/AP Images.

After police officer Toshiro Semba (center) blew the whistle on his bosses in the police department, they took his gun away, claiming he was too emotionally unstable to carry a weapon, and reassigned him as a dispatcher. Semba revealed that for decades his superiors wrote false reports to secure public funds and then used the funds for their personal benefit. A district court in Japan ruled that Semba's treatment was retaliation for his exposure of corruption. Traditionally, whistleblowers in Japan have been viewed as traitors, and their exposure of wrongdoing as a betrayal of their superiors. But this perception of whistleblowing as a political behavior is changing as employees like Semba are now being recognized for doing the right thing by exposing illegal, corrupt, or unethical conduct in the workplace.

When people get together in groups, power will be exerted. People want to carve out a niche from which to exert influence, earn rewards, and advance their careers. When employees in organizations convert their power into action, we describe them as being engaged in politics. Those with good political skills have the ability to use their bases of power effectively.[44]

Definition of Organizational Politics

There is no shortage of definitions of *organizational politics*. Essentially, this type of politics focuses on the use of power to affect decision making in an organization, or on self-serving and organizationally unsanctioned behaviors.[45] For our purposes, **political behavior** in organizations consists of activities that are not required as part of an individual's formal role but that influence, or attempt to influence, the distribution of advantages and disadvantages within the organization.[46]

This definition encompasses what most people mean when they talk about organizational politics. Political behavior is outside specified job requirements. It requires some attempt to use power bases. It includes efforts to influence the goals, criteria, or processes used for decision making. Our definition is broad enough to include varied political behaviors such as withholding key information from decision makers, joining a coalition, whistleblowing, spreading rumors, leaking confidential information to the media, exchanging favors with others in the organization for mutual benefit, and lobbying on behalf of or against a particular individual or decision alternative.

The Reality of Politics

Interviews with experienced managers show that most believe political behavior is a major part of organizational life.[47] Many managers report some use of political behavior is both ethical and necessary, as long as it doesn't directly harm anyone else. They describe politics as a necessary evil and believe someone who *never* uses political behavior will have a hard time getting things done. Most also indicate they had never been trained to use political behavior effectively. But why, you may wonder, must politics exist? Isn't it possible for an organization to be politics free? It's *possible*—but unlikely.

Organizations are made up of individuals and groups with different values, goals, and interests.[48] This sets up the potential for conflict over the allocation of limited resources, such as departmental budgets, space, project responsibilities, and salary adjustments.[49] If resources were abundant, then all constituencies within the organization could satisfy their goals. But because they are limited, not everyone's interests can be satisfied. Furthermore, gains by one individual or group are often *perceived* as coming at the expense of others within the organization (whether they are or not). These forces create real competition among members for the organization's limited resources.

Maybe the most important factor leading to politics within organizations is the realization that most of the "facts" used to allocate the limited resources are open to interpretation. What, for instance, is *good* performance? What's an *adequate* improvement? What constitutes an *unsatisfactory* job? One person's "selfless effort to benefit the organization" is seen by another as a "blatant attempt to further one's interest."[50] The manager of any major league baseball team knows a .400 hitter is a high performer and a .125 hitter is a poor performer. You don't need to be a baseball genius to know you should play your .400 hitter and send the .125 hitter back to the minors. But what if you have to choose between players who hit .280 and .290? Then less objective factors come into play: fielding expertise, attitude, potential, ability to perform in a clutch, loyalty to the team, and so on. More managerial decisions resemble the choice between a .280 and a .290 hitter than between a .125 hitter and a .400 hitter. It is in this large and ambiguous middle ground of organizational life—where the facts *don't* speak for themselves—that politics flourish (see Exhibit 13-2).

Exhibit **13-2**	Politics Is in the Eye of the Beholder

A behavior one person labels as "organizational politics" is very likely to seem like "effective management" to another. The fact is not that effective management is necessarily political, although in some cases it might be. Rather, a person's reference point determines what he or she classifies as organizational politics. For example, one experimental study showed that power-oriented behavior performed by a permanent, tenured employee is seen as more legitimate and less harsh than the same behavior performed by a temporary employee.[43] Take a look at the following labels used to describe the same phenomenon. These suggest that politics, like beauty, is in the eye of the beholder.

"Political" Label		"Effective Management" Label
1. Blaming others	vs.	Fixing responsibility
2. "Kissing up"	vs.	Developing working relationships
3. Apple polishing	vs.	Demonstrating loyalty
4. Passing the buck	vs.	Delegating authority
5. Covering your rear	vs.	Documenting decisions
6. Creating conflict	vs.	Encouraging change and innovation
7. Forming coalitions	vs.	Facilitating teamwork
8. Whistle-blowing	vs.	Improving efficiency
9. Scheming	vs.	Planning ahead
10. Overachieving	vs.	Competent and capable
11. Ambitious	vs.	Career minded
12. Opportunistic	vs.	Astute
13. Cunning	vs.	Practical minded
14. Arrogant	vs.	Confident
15. Perfectionist	vs.	Attentive to detail

Source: Based on T. C. Krell, M. E. Mendenhall, and J. Sendry, "Doing Research in the Conceptual Morass of Organizational Politics," paper presented at the Western Academy of Management Conference, Hollywood, CA, April 1987.

political behavior *Activities that are not required as part of a person's formal role in the organization but that influence, or attempt to influence, the distribution of advantages and disadvantages within the organization.*

Finally, because most decisions have to be made in a climate of ambiguity—where facts are rarely fully objective and thus are open to interpretation—people within organizations will use whatever influence they can to taint the facts to support their goals and interests. That, of course, creates the activities we call *politicking*.

Therefore, to answer the question whether it is possible for an organization to be politics-free, we can say "yes"—if all members of that organization hold the same goals and interests, if organizational resources are not scarce, and if performance outcomes are completely clear and objective. But that doesn't describe the organizational world in which most of us live.

Causes and Consequences of Political Behavior

6   Identify the causes and consequences of political behavior.

Factors Contributing to Political Behavior

Not all groups or organizations are equally political. In some organizations, for instance, politicking is overt and rampant, while in others politics plays a small role in influencing outcomes. Why this variation? Recent research and observation have identified a number of factors that appear to encourage political behavior. Some are individual characteristics, derived from the unique qualities of the people the organization employs; others are a result of the organization's culture or internal environment. Exhibit 13-3 illustrates how both individual and organizational factors can increase political behavior and provide favorable outcomes (increased rewards and averted punishments) for both individuals and groups in the organization.

Individual Factors   At the individual level, researchers have identified certain personality traits, needs, and other factors likely to be related to political

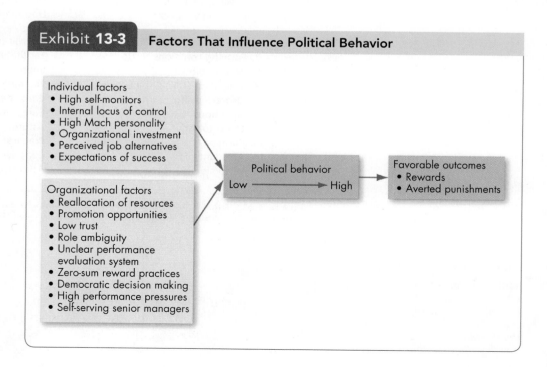

Exhibit 13-3   Factors That Influence Political Behavior

Individual factors
• High self-monitors
• Internal locus of control
• High Mach personality
• Organizational investment
• Perceived job alternatives
• Expectations of success

Organizational factors
• Reallocation of resources
• Promotion opportunities
• Low trust
• Role ambiguity
• Unclear performance evaluation system
• Zero-sum reward practices
• Democratic decision making
• High performance pressures
• Self-serving senior managers

Political behavior
Low ⟶ High

Favorable outcomes
• Rewards
• Averted punishments

behavior. In terms of traits, we find that employees who are high self-monitors, possess an internal locus of control, and have a high need for power are more likely to engage in political behavior.[51] The high self-monitor is more sensitive to social cues, exhibits higher levels of social conformity, and is more likely to be skilled in political behavior than the low self-monitor. Because they believe they can control their environment, individuals with an internal locus of control are more prone to take a proactive stance and attempt to manipulate situations in their favor. Not surprisingly, the Machiavellian personality—characterized by the will to manipulate and the desire for power—is comfortable using politics as a means to further his or her self-interest.

In addition, an individual's investment in the organization, perceived alternatives, and expectations of success influence the degree to which he or she will pursue illegitimate means of political action.[52] The more a person expects increased future benefits from the organization, the more that person has to lose if forced out and the less likely he or she is to use illegitimate means. The more alternative job opportunities an individual has—due to a favorable job market or the possession of scarce skills or knowledge, a prominent reputation, or influential contacts outside the organization—the more likely that individual is to risk illegitimate political actions. Finally, an individual with low expectations of success from illegitimate means is unlikely to use them. High expectations from such measures are most likely to be the province of both experienced and powerful individuals with polished political skills and inexperienced and naïve employees who misjudge their chances.

Organizational Factors   Although we acknowledge the role individual differences can play, the evidence more strongly suggests that certain situations and cultures promote politics. Specifically, when an organization's resources are declining, when the existing pattern of resources is changing, and when there is opportunity for promotions, politicking is more likely to surface.[53] When organizations downsize to improve efficiency, resources must be reduced, and people may engage in political actions to safeguard what they have. But *any* changes, especially those that imply significant reallocation of resources within the organization, are likely to stimulate conflict and increase politicking. The opportunity for promotions or advancement has consistently been found to encourage competition for a limited resource as people try to positively influence the decision outcome.

Cultures characterized by low trust, role ambiguity, unclear performance evaluation systems, zero-sum reward allocation practices, democratic decision making, high pressures for performance, and self-serving senior managers will also create breeding grounds for politicking.[54] The less trust within the organization, the higher the level of political behavior and the more likely it will be of the illegitimate kind. So, high trust should suppress political behavior in general and inhibit illegitimate actions in particular.

Role ambiguity means the prescribed employee behaviors are not clear. There are, therefore, fewer limits to the scope and functions of the employee's political actions. Because political activities are defined as those not required as part of the employee's formal role, the greater the role ambiguity, the more employees can engage in unnoticed political activity.

Performance evaluation is far from a perfect science. The more organizations use subjective criteria in the appraisal, emphasize a single outcome measure, or allow significant time to pass between the time of an action and its appraisal, the greater the likelihood that an employee can get away with politicking. Subjective performance criteria create ambiguity. The use of a single outcome measure encourages individuals to do whatever is necessary to "look good" on

"Corporate Political Activity Pays"

This statement appears to be true. Political influence behavior certainly appears to pay in some situations. According to a recent review of the literature, that applies to *organizational* political influence as well.

Much organizational political activity takes the form of exchange, such as when favorable government treatment is exchanged for political support or donations to political candidates. A different kind of political activity takes place when competitors collude against a common adversary. For example, major league sports team owners often join forces to obtain more favorable labor settlements.

Unions that normally compete for union members may do the same.

A review of 78 studies on the link between organizational political activity and firm performance found a significant positive relationship. The authors conclude that their finding "explains why more business interests are engaged in [political activity] than at any other time in recorded history."

In 2011, it came to light that General Electric (GE) paid no taxes in 2010, despite earning global profits of $14.2 billion, including $5.1 billion from U.S. operations. Although GE disputes the charge, many credited the firm's political activities with its favorable

treatment (GE CEO Jeff Immelt chairs President Obama's Jobs and Competitiveness Council). GE spokesman Gary Sheffer defended the company's political activity, saying, "We want to be sure our voice is heard."

Sources: S. Lux, T. R. Crook, and D. J. Woehr, "Mixing Business with Politics: A Meta-Analysis of the Antecedents and Outcomes of Corporate Political Activity," *Journal of Management* 37, no. 1 (2011), pp. 223–247; J. D. McKinnon, "New Fight Brews Over Corporate Taxes," *The Wall Street Journal* (May 26, 2011), downloaded on June 17, 2011, from http://blogs.wsj.com/; and D. Kocieniewski, "G.E.'s Strategies Let It Avoid Taxes Altogether," *The New York Times* (March 24, 2011), p. A1.

that measure, but that often occurs at the cost of good performance on other important parts of the job that are not being appraised. The longer the time between an action and its appraisal, the more unlikely it is that the employee will be held accountable for political behaviors.

The more an organization's culture emphasizes the zero-sum or win–lose approach to reward allocations, the more employees will be motivated to

Organizations foster politicking when they reduce resources in order to improve performance. As part of a restructuring program, Germany's Allianz AG announced plans to eliminate 5,000 jobs at its insurance operation and 2,500 jobs at its banking subsidiary. Allianz stated that the job cuts were necessary to improve efficiency and to increase its competitiveness and would result in savings of between $600 and $750,000 million. The company's cost-cutting measures stimulated conflict and political activity, as trade union workers joined Allianz employees in staging a token strike to safeguard their jobs.

Source: Winfried Rothermel/AP Images.

engage in politicking. The zero-sum approach treats the reward "pie" as fixed, so any gain one person or group achieves has to come at the expense of another person or group. If $15,000 in annual raises is to be distributed among five employees, any employee who gets more than $3,000 takes money away from one or more of the others. Such a practice encourages making others look bad and increasing the visibility of what you do.

Finally, when employees see the people on top engaging in political behavior, especially doing so successfully and being rewarded for it, a climate is created that supports politicking. Politicking by top management in a sense gives those lower in the organization permission to play politics by implying that such behavior is acceptable.

How Do People Respond to Organizational Politics?

Trish O'Donnell loves her job as a writer on a weekly television comedy series but hates the internal politics. "A couple of the writers here spend more time kissing up to the executive producer than doing any work. And our head writer clearly has his favorites. While they pay me a lot and I get to really use my creativity, I'm sick of having to be on alert for backstabbers and constantly having to self-promote my contributions. I'm tired of doing most of the work and getting little of the credit." Are Trish O'Donnell's comments typical of people who work in highly politicized workplaces? We all know friends or relatives who regularly complain about the politics at their job. But how do people in general react to organizational politics? Let's look at the evidence.

In our earlier discussion in this chapter of factors that contribute to political behavior, we focused on the favorable outcomes. But for most people—who have modest political skills or are unwilling to play the politics game—outcomes tend to be predominantly negative. Exhibit 13-4 summarizes the extensive research (mostly conducted in the United States) on the relationship between organizational politics and individual outcomes.[55] Very strong evidence indicates, for instance, that perceptions of organizational politics are negatively related to job satisfaction.[56] The perception of politics also tends to increase job anxiety and stress, possibly because people believe they may be losing ground

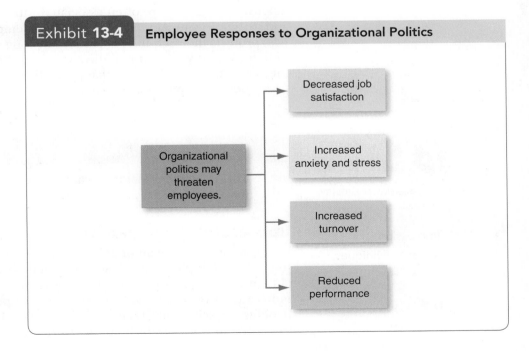

Exhibit 13-4   Employee Responses to Organizational Politics

Organizational politics may threaten employees. →
- Decreased job satisfaction
- Increased anxiety and stress
- Increased turnover
- Reduced performance

to others who are active politickers or, conversely, because they feel additional pressures from entering into and competing in the political arena.[57] Politics may lead to self-reported declines in employee performance, perhaps because employees perceive political environments to be unfair, which demotivates them.[58] Not surprisingly, when politicking becomes too much to handle, it can lead employees to quit.[59]

When employees of two agencies in a recent study in Nigeria viewed their work environments as political, they reported higher levels of job distress and were less likely to help their co-workers. Thus, although developing countries such as Nigeria are perhaps more ambiguous and more political environments in which to work, the negative consequences of politics appear to be the same as in the United States.[60]

Researchers have also noted several interesting qualifiers. First, the politics–performance relationship appears to be moderated by an individual's understanding of the "hows" and "whys" of organizational politics. "An individual who has a clear understanding of who is responsible for making decisions and why they were selected to be the decision makers would have a better understanding of how and why things happen the way they do than someone who does not understand the decision-making process in the organization."[61] When both politics and understanding are high, performance is likely to increase because the individual will see political actions as an opportunity. This is consistent with what you might expect among individuals with well-honed political skills. But when understanding is low, individuals are more likely to see politics as a threat, which can have a negative effect on job performance.[62]

Second, political behavior at work moderates the effects of ethical leadership.[63] One study found that male employees were more responsive to ethical leadership and showed the most citizenship behavior when levels of both politics and ethical leadership were high. Women, on the other hand, appear most likely to engage in citizenship behavior when the environment is consistently ethical and *apolitical*.

Third, when employees see politics as a threat, they often respond with **defensive behaviors**—reactive and protective behaviors to avoid action, blame, or change.[64] (Exhibit 13-5 provides some examples of these behaviors.) And defensive behaviors are often associated with negative feelings toward the job and work environment.[65] In the short run, employees may find that defensiveness protects their self-interest, but in the long run it wears them down. People who consistently rely on defensiveness find that, eventually, it is the only way they know how to behave. At that point, they lose the trust and support of their peers, bosses, employees, and clients.

SELF-ASSESSMENT LIBRARY

How Good Am I at Playing Politics?

In the Self-Assessment Library (available on CD and online), take assessment II.C.3 (How Good Am I at Playing Politics?).

7 Apply impression management techniques.

Impression Management

We know people have an ongoing interest in how others perceive and evaluate them. For example, North Americans spend billions of dollars on diets, health club memberships, cosmetics, and plastic surgery—all intended to make them more attractive to others.[66] Being perceived positively by others should have benefits for people in organizations. It might, for instance, help them initially to get the jobs they want in an organization and, once hired, to get favorable

Exhibit **13-5**	**Defensive Behaviors**

Avoiding Action

Overconforming. Strictly interpreting your responsibility by saying things like "The rules clearly state . . . " or "This is the way we've always done it."

Buck passing. Transferring responsibility for the execution of a task or decision to someone else.

Playing dumb. Avoiding an unwanted task by falsely pleading ignorance or inability.

Stretching. Prolonging a task so that one person appears to be occupied—for example, turning a two-week task into a 4-month job.

Stalling. Appearing to be more or less supportive publicly while doing little or nothing privately.

Avoiding Blame

Buffing. This is a nice way to refer to "covering your rear." It describes the practice of rigorously documenting activity to project an image of competence and thoroughness.

Playing safe. Evading situations that may reflect unfavorably. It includes taking on only projects with a high probability of success, having risky decisions approved by superiors, qualifying expressions of judgment, and taking neutral positions in conflicts.

Justifying. Developing explanations that lessen one's responsibility for a negative outcome and/or apologizing to demonstrate remorse, or both.

Scapegoating. Placing the blame for a negative outcome on external factors that are not entirely blameworthy.

Misrepresenting. Manipulation of information by distortion, embellishment, deception, selective presentation, or obfuscation.

Avoiding Change

Prevention. Trying to prevent a threatening change from occurring.

Self-protection. Acting in ways to protect one's self-interest during change by guarding information or other resources.

evaluations, superior salary increases, and more rapid promotions. In a political context, it might help sway the distribution of advantages in their favor. The process by which individuals attempt to control the impression others form of them is called **impression management (IM)**.[67]

Who might we predict will engage in IM? No surprise here. It's our old friend, the high self-monitor.[68] Low self-monitors tend to present images of themselves that are consistent with their personalities, regardless of the beneficial or detrimental effects for them. In contrast, high self-monitors are good at reading situations and molding their appearances and behavior to fit each situation. If you want to control the impression others form of you, what IM techniques can you use? Exhibit 13-6 summarizes some of the most popular and provides an example of each.

Keep in mind that when people engage in IM, they are sending a false message that might be true under other circumstances.[69] Excuses, for instance, may be offered with sincerity. Referring to the example in Exhibit 13-6, you can *actually* believe that ads contribute little to sales in your region. But misrepresentation can have a high cost. If you "cry wolf" once too often, no one is likely to believe you when the wolf really comes. So the impression manager must be

defensive behaviors *Reactive and protective behaviors to avoid action, blame, or change.*

impression management (IM) *The process by which individuals attempt to control the impression others form of them.*

Exhibit 13-6	Impression Management (IM) Techniques

Conformity

Agreeing with someone else's opinion to gain his or her approval is a *form of ingratiation.*

Example: A manager tells his boss, "You're absolutely right on your reorganization plan for the western regional office. I couldn't agree with you more."

Favors

Doing something nice for someone to gain that person's approval is a *form of ingratiation.*

Example: A salesperson says to a prospective client, "I've got two tickets to the theater tonight that I can't use. Take them. Consider it a thank-you for taking the time to talk with me."

Excuses

Explanations of a predicament-creating event aimed at minimizing the apparent severity of the predicament is a *defensive IM technique.*

Example: A sales manager says to her boss, "We failed to get the ad in the paper on time, but no one responds to those ads anyway."

Apologies

Admitting responsibility for an undesirable event and simultaneously seeking to get a pardon for the action is a *defensive IM technique.*

Example: An employee says to his boss, "I'm sorry I made a mistake on the report. Please forgive me."

Self-Promotion

Highlighting one's best qualities, downplaying one's deficits, and calling attention to one's achievements is a *self-focused IM technique.*

Example: A salesperson tells his boss, "Matt worked unsuccessfully for three years to try to get that account. I sewed it up in six weeks. I'm the best closer this company has."

Enhancement

Claiming that something you did is more valuable than most other members of the organizations would think is a *self-focused IM technique.*

Example: A journalist tells his editor, "My work on this celebrity divorce story was really a major boost to our sales" (even though the story only made it to page 3 in the entertainment section).

Flattery

Complimenting others about their virtues in an effort to make oneself appear perceptive and likeable is an *assertive IM technique.*

Example: A new sales trainee says to her peer, "You handled that client's complaint so tactfully! I could never have handled that as well as you did."

Exemplification

Doing more than you need to in an effort to show how dedicated and hard working you are is an *assertive IM technique.*

Example: An employee sends e-mails from his work computer when he works late so that his supervisor will know how long he's been working.

Source: Based on B. R. Schlenker, Impression Management s(Monterey, CA: Brooks/Cole, 1980); M. C. Bolino, K. M. Kacmar, W. H. Turnley, and J. B. Gilstrap, "A Multi-Level Review of Impression Management Motives and Behaviors," *Journal of Management* 34, no. 6 (2008), pp. 1080–1109; and R. B. Cialdini, "Indirect Tactics of Image Management Beyond Basking," in R. A. Giacalone and P. Rosenfeld (eds.), *Impression Management in the Organization* (Hillsdale, NJ: Lawrence Erlbaum, 1989), pp. 45–71.

cautious not to be perceived as insincere or manipulative.[70] Consider the effect of implausible name-dropping as an example of this principle. Participants in a study in Switzerland disliked an experimental confederate who claimed to be a personal friend of the well-liked Swiss tennis star Roger Federer, but they generally liked confederates who just said they were fans.[71] Another study found that when managers attributed an employee's citizenship behaviors to impression management, they actually felt angry (probably because they felt manipulated) and gave subordinates lower performance ratings. When managers attributed the same behaviors to prosocial values and concern about the organization, they felt happy and gave higher performance ratings.[72] In sum, people don't like to feel others are manipulating them through impression management, so such tactics should be employed with caution.

Are there *situations* in which individuals are more likely to misrepresent themselves or more likely to get away with it? Yes—situations characterized by high uncertainty or ambiguity provide relatively little information for challenging a fraudulent claim and reduce the risks associated with misrepresentation.[73] The increasing use of telework may be increasing the use of IM. Individuals who work remotely from their supervisors engage in high levels of IM relative to those who work closely with their supervisors.[74]

Most of the studies undertaken to test the effectiveness of IM techniques have related it to two criteria: interview success and performance evaluations. Let's consider each of these.

The evidence indicates most job applicants use IM techniques in interviews[75] and that it works.[76] In one study, for instance, interviewers felt applicants for a position as a customer service representative who used IM techniques performed better in the interview, and they seemed somewhat more inclined to hire these people.[77] Moreover, when the researchers considered applicants' credentials, they concluded it was the IM techniques alone that influenced the interviewers—that is, it didn't seem to matter whether applicants were well or poorly qualified. If they used IM techniques, they did better in the interview.

Some IM techniques work better in interviews than others. Researchers have compared applicants whose IM techniques focused on promoting their accomplishments (called *self-promotion*) to those who focused on complimenting the interviewer and finding areas of agreement (referred to as *ingratiation*). In general, applicants appear to use self-promotion more than ingratiation.[78] What's more, self-promotion tactics may be more important to interviewing success. Applicants who work to create an appearance of competence by enhancing their accomplishments, taking credit for successes, and explaining away failures do better in interviews. These effects reach beyond the interview: applicants who use more self-promotion tactics also seem to get more follow-up job-site visits, even after adjusting for grade-point average, gender, and job type. Ingratiation also works well in interviews; applicants who compliment the interviewer, agree with his or her opinions, and emphasize areas of fit do better than those who don't.[79]

In terms of performance ratings, the picture is quite different. Ingratiation is positively related to performance ratings, meaning those who ingratiate with their supervisors get higher performance evaluations. However, self-promotion appears to backfire: those who self-promote actually seem to receive *lower* performance evaluations.[80] There is an important qualifier to this general result. It appears that individuals high in political skill are able to translate IM into higher performance appraisals, whereas those lower in political skill are more likely to be hurt by their IM attempts.[81] Another study of 760 boards of directors found that individuals who ingratiate themselves to current board members (express agreement with the director, point out shared attitudes and opinions, compliment the director) increase their chances of landing on a board.[82]

What explains these results? If you think about them, they make sense. Ingratiating always works because everyone—both interviewers and supervisors—likes to be treated nicely. However, self-promotion may work only in interviews and backfire on the job because, whereas the interviewer has little idea whether you're blowing smoke about your accomplishments, the supervisor knows because it's his or her job to observe you. Thus, if you're going to self-promote, remember that what works in an interview won't always work once you're on the job.

Are our conclusions about responses to politics globally valid? Should we expect employees in Israel, for instance, to respond the same way to workplace politics that employees in the United States do? Almost all our conclusions on employee reactions to organizational politics are based on studies conducted in North America. The few studies that have included other countries suggest some minor modifications.[83] One study of managers in U.S. culture and three Chinese cultures (People's Republic of China, Hong Kong, and Taiwan) found U.S. managers evaluated "gentle persuasion" tactics such as consultation and inspirational appeal as more effective than did their Chinese counterparts.[84] Other research suggests that effective U.S. leaders achieve influence by focusing on personal goals of group members and the tasks at hand (an analytical approach), whereas influential East Asian leaders focus on relationships among group members and meeting the demands of the people around them (a holistic approach).[85]

As another example, Israelis and the British seem to generally respond as do North Americans—that is, their perception of organizational politics relates to decreased job satisfaction and increased turnover.[86] But in countries that are more politically unstable, such as Israel, employees seem to demonstrate greater tolerance of intense political processes in the workplace, perhaps because they are used to power struggles and have more experience in coping with them.[87] This suggests that people from politically turbulent countries in the Middle East or Latin America might be more accepting of organizational politics, and even more willing to use aggressive political tactics in the workplace, than people from countries such as Great Britain or Switzerland.

The Ethics of Behaving Politically

8 Determine whether a political action is ethical.

Although there are no clear-cut ways to differentiate ethical from unethical politicking, there are some questions you should consider. For example, what is the utility of engaging in politicking? Sometimes we do it for little good reason. Major league baseball player Al Martin claimed he played football at USC when in fact he never did. As a baseball player, he had little to gain by pretending to have played football. Outright lies like this may be a rather extreme example of impression management, but many of us have at least distorted information to make a favorable impression. One thing to keep in mind is whether it's really worth the risk. Another question to ask is this: how does the utility of engaging in the political behavior balance out any harm (or potential harm) it will do to others? Complimenting a supervisor on his or her appearance in order to curry favor is probably much less harmful than grabbing credit for a project that others deserve.

Finally, does the political activity conform to standards of equity and justice? Sometimes it is difficult to weigh the costs and benefits of a political action, but its ethicality is clear. The department head who inflates the performance evaluation of a favored employee and deflates the evaluation of a disfavored employee—and then uses these evaluations to justify giving the former a big raise and nothing to the latter—has treated the disfavored employee unfairly.

Unfortunately, powerful people can become very good at explaining self-serving behaviors in terms of the organization's best interests. They can persuasively argue that unfair actions are really fair and just. Our point is that immoral people can justify almost any behavior. Those who are powerful, articulate, and persuasive are most vulnerable to ethical lapses because they are likely to be able to get away with unethical practices successfully. When faced with an ethical dilemma regarding organizational politics, try to consider whether playing politics is worth the risk and whether others might be harmed in the process. If you have a strong power base, recognize the ability of power to corrupt. Remember that it's a lot easier for the powerless to act ethically, if for no other reason than they typically have very little political discretion to exploit.

MyManagementLab

Now that you have finished this chapter, go back to **www.pearsonglobaleditions.com/ mymanagementlab** to continue practicing and applying the concepts you've learned.

Summary and Implications for Managers

If you want to get things done in a group or an organization, it helps to have power. Here are several suggestions for how to deal with power in your own work life:

- As a manager who wants to maximize your power, you will want to increase others' dependence on you. You can, for instance, increase your power in relation to your boss by developing knowledge or a skill she needs and for which she perceives no ready substitute. But you will not be alone in attempting to build your power bases. Others, particularly employees and peers, will be seeking to increase your dependence on them, while you are trying to minimize it and increase their dependence on you. The result is a continual battle.
- Few employees relish being powerless in their job and organization. Try to avoid putting others in a position where they feel they have no power.
- People respond differently to the various power bases. Expert and referent power are derived from an individual's personal qualities. In contrast, coercion, reward, and legitimate power are essentially organizationally derived. Competence especially appears to offer wide appeal, and its use as a power base results in high performance by group members. The message for managers seems to be "Develop and use your expert power base!"
- An effective manager accepts the political nature of organizations. By assessing behavior in a political framework, you can better predict the actions of others and use that information to formulate political strategies that will gain advantages for you and your work unit.
- Some people are significantly more politically astute than others, meaning that they are aware of the underlying politics and can manage impressions. Those who are good at playing politics can be expected to get higher performance evaluations and, hence, larger salary increases and more promotions than the politically naïve or inept. The politically astute are also likely to exhibit higher job satisfaction and be better able to neutralize job stressors.
- Employees who have poor political skills or are unwilling to play the politics game generally relate perceived organizational politics to lower job satisfaction and self-reported performance, increased anxiety, and higher turnover.

Power Corrupts People

POINT · **COUNTERPOINT**

Lord Acton famously wrote: "All power tends to corrupt and absolute power corrupts absolutely." Most of us probably believe that leaders with more power are more likely to abuse their power to the detriment of others and, ultimately, of the entity they lead. For this reason, most organizations—including governments and corporations—put checks and balances in place to keep leaders from amassing too much power. If we look at the history of corruption and malfeasance among government, business, and other organizational leaders, rarely would we conclude that the core reason for corruption was that the leader had *too little* power.

Why is power so toxic? As one expert plainly states, "Power quickly turns us into hypocrites." In one study, researchers found that the more powerful people felt, the more likely they were to see misreporting travel expenses as unethical. But these researchers next studied how these same people self-reported the results of a game of chance, when it was in their self-interest to lie about their results. What did they find? You guessed it: the more powerful the people felt, the more likely they were to self-report results significantly better than chance. Power really does seem to breed hypocrisy. The powerful are more likely to see behavior as unethical, but more likely to behave unethically themselves. Researchers speculate that power allows people to better rationalize away ethical lapses. "They're important people, with important things to do," says one expert.

The study of the corrupting effects of power is not limited to laboratory studies. A fascinating study of 1,000 Supreme Court decisions found that as justices gained power on the court, their opinions tended to become less complex and nuanced. They considered fewer perspectives and possible outcomes. The really bad news is that as their power increased, of course, their opinions were more likely to become majority opinions, and thus the law of the land.

Power may be effective in allowing us to get our way. But that power, while good for the individual getting it, is bad for almost everyone else.

Power may help leaders do some aspects of their jobs more effectively, but that isn't the whole story.

Most of the great deeds in history required great power. Do you really think George Washington would have been of more use to the Continental Army if he was a private rather a general? Would Steven Jobs have had more impact on computer technology innovations if he remained a technician with video-game maker Atari? We want our best and brightest in positions where their qualities can do the most good, and that means we want them to be in power.

When Bill Gates used his wealth and power to start the Bill & Melinda Gates Foundation, and when Warren Buffett announced his intention to give 85 percent of his wealth to the foundation, they were using their wealth and power to do acts of good the rest of us can only dream about. You may not think Gates or Buffett is any better than the rest of us, but can you imagine starting your own philanthropic foundation or giving away 85 percent of your wealth? Yes, it is easier for them to do good because they're rich and powerful, but that's the point: they could still be good without their wealth and power, but they couldn't do as much good.

Yes, power is dangerous. But so is electricity. Just because something can be misused in the wrong hands does not mean we abandon it. Nor should we mistake the real cause of corrupt behavior. The only difference between a petty thief and billion-dollar swindler Bernie Madoff is scale—a petty thief in Madoff's shoes with Madoff's talents would do the same thing Madoff did. Power is therefore a conduit—of both good and bad motives.

Most of the great acts in history were done by people with power. And, yes, many of the most evil acts were done by people with power. But the issue isn't power itself; it's what we do with it.

Sources: J. Lehrer, "The Power Trip," *The Wall Street Journal* (August 14, 2010), pp. W1–2; J. Lehrer, "How Power Corrupts," *The Frontal Cortex* (May 18, 2011), downloaded June 7, 2011, from www.wired.com/; and K. Heim, "The New Gates Foundation Headquarters Reflects Charity's Roots—and Reach," *Seattle Times* (May 21, 2011), downloaded on June 7, 2011, from http://seattletimes.nwsource.com/.

QUESTIONS FOR REVIEW

1 What is *power*? How is leadership different from power?

2 What are the similarities and differences among the five bases of power?

3 What is the role of dependence in power relationships?

4 What are the nine most often identified power or influence tactics and their contingencies?

5 What is the connection between sexual harassment and the abuse of power?

6 What are the causes and consequences of political behavior?

7 What are some examples of impression management techniques?

8 What standards can you use to determine whether a political action is ethical?

EXPERIENTIAL EXERCISE Understanding Power Dynamics

Create Groups

Each student is to turn in a dollar bill (or similar value of currency) to the instructor, and students are then divided into three groups (based on criteria given by the instructor), assigned to their workplaces, and instructed to read the following rules and tasks. The money is divided into thirds, and two-thirds of it is given to the top group, one-third to the middle group, and none to the bottom group.

Conduct Exercise

Groups go to their assigned workplaces and have 30 minutes to complete their tasks.

Rules

Members of the top group are free to enter the space of either of the other groups and to communicate whatever they wish, whenever they wish. Members of the middle group may enter the space of the lower group when they wish but must request permission to enter the top group's space (which the top group can refuse). Members of the lower group may not disturb the top group in any way unless specifically invited by the top. The lower group does have the right to knock on the door of the middle group and request permission to communicate with them (which can also be refused).

The members of the top group have the authority to make any change in the rules that they wish, at any time, with or without notice.

Tasks

- **Top group.** Responsible for the overall effectiveness and learning from the exercise and to decide how to use its money.
- **Middle group.** Assist the top group in providing for the overall welfare of the organization and deciding how to use its money.
- **Bottom group.** Identify the organization's resources and decide how best to provide for learning and the overall effectiveness of the organization.

Debriefing

Each of the three groups chooses two representatives to go to the front of the class and discuss the following:

1. Summarize what occurred within and among the three groups.

2. What are some of the differences between being in the top group and being in the bottom group?

3. What can we learn about power from this experience?

4. How accurate do you think this exercise is in reflecting the reality of resource allocation decisions in large organizations?

Source: Adapted from L. Bolman and T. E. Deal, *Exchange* 3, no. 4 (1979), pp. 38–42. Reprinted by permission of Sage Publications Inc.

ETHICAL DILEMMA Corporate Spying

In a conference call with investors and financial analysts, the chief financial officer (CFO) for a major corporation outlines the company's positive expected earnings for the next quarter despite some serious economic challenges. Unknown to the CFO, party to this conference call is an ex-CIA interrogator trained in "tactical behavioral assessment." The investigator detects nervousness and evasiveness in the CFO's hurried answers to questions. In his report, he concludes that the CFO is probably lying.

Who is the recipient of the report? A hedge fund. Based on the report, the fund shorts the company's stock—selling borrowed shares in anticipation that the price will drop—and when the company's earnings do fall short of expectations, the hedge fund buys the shares back at the lower price and profits greatly.

Whatever trust you may place in the ability of investigators to detect lying, this sort of espionage happens. And it goes further. When Swiss chocolatier Nestlé was trying to sell a chocolate-covered toy in the United States, its U.S. competitor, Mars, covertly used consultants to prod government officials with misinformation that the toy was a safety hazard. The strategy worked. Learning of Mars' activities, Nestlé paid former Secret Service agents to bribe garbage collectors so it could acquire Mars' corporate trash and counterspy.

Chinese companies hacked into Google's website, gaining access to corporate premises using night-vision glasses stolen from a U.S. military contractor. Hewlett-Packard used "pretexting" by investigators who impersonated HP board members in order to obtain their phone records as a means to investigate it own board members.

These stories are all true.

Questions

1. One corporate spy said, "Companies do this in order to stay in front of problems." Can you envision a business problem so dangerous that you would approve a spy mission if you were in charge?

2. Are there ever circumstances in which corporate spying is ethical? If so, what are they?

3. Recently, LinkedIn reposted a tweet that questioned whether Facebook was appropriate for public schools. Is it ever ethical for a company to attempt to undermine another in this way?

Source: J. J. Fialka, "Hugger-Mugger in the Executive Suite," *The Wall Street Journal* (February 5, 2010), p. W10; E. Javers, *Broker, Trader, Lawyer, Spy* (New York: Harper, 2010); and J. Scott, "Is Corporate Spying Legal?" *Forbes* (May 31, 2011), downloaded June 15, 2011, from http://blogs.forbes.com/.

CASE INCIDENT 1 Delegate Power, or Keep It Close?

Samantha Parks is the owner and CEO of Sparks, a small New York agency that develops advertising, promotions, and marketing materials for high-fashion firms. Parks has tended to keep a tight rein on her business, overseeing most projects from start to finish. However, as the firm has grown, she has found it necessary to delegate more and more decisions to her associates. She's recently been approached by a hairstyling chain that wants a comprehensive redefinition of its entire marketing and promotions look. Should Samantha try to manage this project in her traditional way, or should she delegate major parts to her employees?

Most managers confront this question at some point in their careers. Some experts propose that top executives need to stay very close to the creative core of their business, which means that even if their primary responsibility is to manage, CEOs should never cede too much control to committees of creative individuals or they can lose sight of the firm's overall future direction. Moreover, executives who do fall out of touch with the creative process risk being passed over by a new generation of "plugged in" employees who better understand how the business really works.

Others offer the opposite advice, saying it's not a good idea for a CEO to "sweat the small stuff" like managing individual client accounts or projects. These experts advise executives to identify everything they can "outsource" to other employees and to delegate as much as possible. By eliminating trivial tasks, executives will be better able to focus their attention on the most important decision-making and control aspects of their jobs, which will help the business and also ensure that the top executive maintains control over the functions that really matter.

These pieces of advice are not necessarily in conflict with one another. The real challenge is to identify what you can delegate effectively without ceding too much power and control away from the person with the unifying vision. That is certainly easier said than done, though.

Questions

1. If you were Samantha Parks, how would you prioritize which projects or parts of projects to delegate?

2. In explaining what makes her decisions hard, Parks said, "I hire good people, creative people, to run

these projects, and I worry that they will see my over-sight and authority as interfering with their creative process." How can she deal with these concerns with-out giving up too much control?

3. Should executives try to control projects to maintain their position of authority? Do they have a right to

control projects and keep in the loop on important decisions just so they can remain in charge?

4. What are some tasks in an organization that a top executive should never delegate to others?

Source: Based on M. L. Tushman, W. K. Smith, and A. Binns, "The Ambidextrous CEO," *Harvard Business Review* (June 2011), pp. 74–79; and S. Bogan, "Find Your Focus," *Financial Planning* (February 2011), p. 72.

CASE INCIDENT 2 The Persuasion Imperative

At one point in time, bosses gave orders and subordinates followed them without question. Those of you who have seen the AMC series *Mad Men*—based on Madison Avenue marketing executives in the 1960s—will know this image of deference to authority, obedience to those higher up in the hierarchy, and relationships between supervisors and employees that are highly paternalistic.

With time comes change. The male-dominated organization with rampant sexual harassment portrayed in *Mad Men* is far less prevalent than it was in the 1960s. Laws and policies are in place that better protect employees against the sometimes-capricious whims of supervisors.

Another sign of shifting cultural values is the way managers use their power. Commandments are out. Persuasion is in.

When IBM manager Kate Riley Tenant needed to reassign managers and engineers to form a database soft-ware team, she had to persuade IBM employees from all corners of the globe, none of whom directly reported to her. According to Tenant, it's a big change from when she started in the field 20 years ago. "You just decided things, and people went off and executed," she said. Now, "not everybody reports to you, and so there's much more negotiation and influence."

John Churchill, a manager with Florida-based Gerdau Ameristeel Corporation, agrees. The question now, he says, is, "How do I influence this group and gain credibility?"

At IBM, the challenge of persuading employees across reporting relationships has become so significant that the firm developed a 2-hour online course to help managers persuade other employees to help with projects crucial to is business. IBM's tips for managers include the following:

- Build a shared vision.
- Negotiate collaboratively.
- Make trade-offs.
- Build and maintain your network.

Despite meeting initial resistance, after completing the training program, Tenant was able to persuade most IBM managers and engineers to join the team.

This doesn't mean authority has lost all its power. Robert Cialdini, a social psychologist who has studied persuasion for decades, lists authority as one of his keys to influence. Even more important may be "social proof"—Cialdini and others have found that people are often deeply persuaded by observing what others are doing. From his research, no message more effectively got hotel guests to reuse their towels than citing statistics that others were reusing their towels.

So, if you're a manager who needs to persuade, present the vision behind the request and be collaborative, but it also wouldn't hurt to tell those you're trying to persuade about others who have already agreed to your request.

Questions

1. Are the precepts of the IBM training program con-sistent with the concepts in this chapter? Why or why not?

2. Again based on the chapter, are there other keys to persuasion and influence that might be added to the IBM program?

3. If you had a manager who wanted you to do some-thing against your initial inclination, which of IBM's elements would work best on you? Why?

4. Drawing from Chapter 5, do you think generational values explain the changing nature of the employer–employee relationship? Why or why not?

Source: Based on E. White, "Art of Persuasion Becomes Key," *The Wall Street Journal* (May 19, 2008), p. B5; B. Tsui, "Greening with Envy," *The Atlantic* (July/August 2009), www.theatlantic.com; and R. Cialdini, *Influence: The Psychology of Persuasion* (New York: HarperBusiness, 2007).

ENDNOTES

1. R. M. Kanter, "Power Failure in Management Circuits," *Harvard Business Review* (July–August 1979), p. 65.
2. J. Pfeffer, "Understanding Power in Organizations," *California Management Review* (Winter 1992), p. 35.
3. Based on B. M. Bass, *Bass & Stogdill's Handbook of Leadership*, 3rd ed. (New York: The Free Press, 1990).
4. D. Carney, "Powerful People Are Better Liars," *Harvard Business Review* (May 2010), pp. 32–33.
5. A. J. Ferguson, M. E. Ormiston, and H. Moon, "From Approach to Inhibition: The Influence of Power on Responses to Poor Performers," *Journal of Applied Psychology* 95, no. 2 (2010), pp. 305–320.
6. J. R. P. French Jr. and B. Raven, "The Bases of Social Power," in D. Cartwright (ed.), *Studies in Social Power* (Ann Arbor, MI: University of Michigan, Institute for Social Research, 1959), pp. 150–167; B. J. Raven, "The Bases of Power: Origins and Recent Developments," *Journal of Social Issues* (Winter 1993), pp. 227–251; and G. Yukl, "Use Power Effectively," in E. A. Locke (ed.), *Handbook of Principles of Organizational Behavior* (Malden, MA: Blackwell, 2004), pp. 242–247.
7. E. A. Ward, "Social Power Bases of Managers: Emergence of a New Factor," *Journal of Social Psychology* (February 2001), pp. 144–147.
8. S. R. Giessner and T. W. Schubert, "High in the Hierarchy: How Vertical Location and Judgments of Leaders' Power Are Interrelated," *Organizational Behavior and Human Decision Processes* 104, no. 1 (2007), pp. 30–44.
9. P. M. Podsakoff and C. A. Schriesheim, "Field Studies of French and Raven's Bases of Power: Critique, Reanalysis, and Suggestions for Future Research," *Psychological Bulletin* (May 1985), pp. 387–411; T. R. Hinkin and C. A. Schriesheim, "Development and Application of New Scales to Measure the French and Raven (1959) Bases of Social Power," *Journal of Applied Psychology* (August 1989), pp. 561–567; and P. P. Carson, K. D. Carson, and C. W. Roe, "Social Power Bases: A Meta-Analytic Examination of Interrelationships and Outcomes," *Journal of Applied Social Psychology* 23, no. 14 (1993), pp. 1150–1169.
10. S. Perman, "Translation Advertising: Where Shop Meets Hip Hop," *Time* (August 30, 2010), www.time.com.
11. M. van Dijke, D. De Cremer, and D. M. Mayer, "The Role of Authority Power in Explaining Procedural Fairness Effects," *Journal of Applied Psychology* 95, no. 3 (2010), pp. 488–502.
12. R. E. Emerson, "Power–Dependence Relations," *American Sociological Review* (February 1962), pp. 31–41.
13. H. Mintzberg, *Power In and Around Organizations* (Upper Saddle River, NJ: Prentice Hall, 1983), p. 24.
14. R. M. Cyert and J. G. March, *A Behavioral Theory of the Firm* (Upper Saddle River, NJ: Prentice Hall, 1963).
15. C. Perrow, "Departmental Power and Perspective in Industrial Firms," in M. N. Zald (ed.), *Power in Organizations* (Nashville, TN: Vanderbilt University Press, 1970).
16. N. Foulkes, "Tractor Boy," *High Life* (October 2002), p. 90.
17. See, for example, D. Kipnis and S. M. Schmidt, "Upward-Influence Styles: Relationship with Performance Evaluations, Salary, and Stress," *Administrative Science Quarterly* (December 1988), pp. 528–542; G. Yukl and J. B. Tracey, "Consequences of Influence Tactics Used with Subordinates, Peers, and the Boss," *Journal of Applied Psychology* (August 1992), pp. 525–535; G. Blickle, "Influence Tactics Used by Subordinates: An Empirical Analysis of the Kipnis and Schmidt Subscales," *Psychological Reports* (February 2000), pp. 143–154; and G. Yukl, "Use Power Effectively," pp. 249–252.
18. G. Yukl, *Leadership in Organizations*, 5th ed. (Upper Saddle River, NJ: Prentice Hall, 2002), pp. 141–174; G. R. Ferris, W. A. Hochwarter, C. Douglas, F. R. Blass, R. W. Kolodinksy, and D. C. Treadway, "Social Influence Processes in Organizations and Human Resource Systems," in G. R. Ferris and J. J. Martocchio (eds.), *Research in Personnel and Human Resources Management*, vol. 21 (Oxford, UK: JAI Press/Elsevier, 2003), pp. 65–127; and C. A. Higgins, T. A. Judge, and G. R. Ferris, "Influence Tactics and Work Outcomes: A Meta-Analysis," *Journal of Organizational Behavior* (March 2003), pp. 89–106.
19. C. M. Falbe and G. Yukl, "Consequences for Managers of Using Single Influence Tactics and Combinations of Tactics," *Academy of Management Journal* (July 1992), pp. 638–653.
20. R. E. Petty and P. Briñol, "Persuasion: From Single to Multiple to Metacognitive Processes," *Perspectives on Psychological Science* 3, no. 2 (2008), pp. 137–147.
21. J. Badal, "Getting a Raise from the Boss," *The Wall Street Journal* (July 8, 2006), pp. B1, B5.
22. Yukl, *Leadership in Organizations*.
23. Ibid.
24. Falbe and Yukl, "Consequences for Managers of Using Single Influence Tactics and Combinations of Tactics."
25. A. W. Kruglanski, A. Pierro, and E. T. Higgins, "Regulatory Mode and Preferred Leadership Styles: How Fit Increases Job Satisfaction," *Basic and Applied Social Psychology* 29, no. 2 (2007), pp. 137–149; and A. Pierro, L. Cicero, and B. H. Raven, "Motivated Compliance with Bases of Social Power," *Journal of Applied Social Psychology* 38, no. 7 (2008), pp. 1921–1944.
26. P. P. Fu and G. Yukl, "Perceived Effectiveness of Influence Tactics in the United States and China," *Leadership Quarterly* (Summer 2000), pp. 251–266; O. Branzei, "Cultural Explanations of Individual Preferences for Influence Tactics in Cross-Cultural Encounters," *International Journal of Cross Cultural Management* (August 2002), pp. 203–218; G. Yukl, P. P. Fu, and R. McDonald, "Cross-Cultural Differences in Perceived Effectiveness of Influence Tactics for Initiating or Resisting Change," *Applied Psychology: An International Review* (January 2003), pp. 66–82; and P. P. Fu, T. K. Peng, J. C. Kennedy, and G. Yukl, "Examining the Preferences of Influence Tactics in Chinese Societies: A Comparison of Chinese Managers in Hong Kong, Taiwan, and Mainland China," *Organizational Dynamics* 33, no. 1 (2004), pp. 32–46.
27. C. J. Torelli and S. Shavitt, "Culture and Concepts of Power," *Journal of Personality and Social Psychology* 99, no. 4 (2010), pp. 703–723.
28. Fu and Yukl, "Perceived Effectiveness of Influence Tactics in the United States and China."
29. S. J. Heine, "Making Sense of East Asian Self-Enhancement," *Journal of Cross-Cultural Psychology* (September 2003), pp. 596–602.
30. G. R. Ferris, D. C. Treadway, P. L. Perrewé, R. L. Brouer, C. Douglas, and S. Lux, "Political Skill in Organizations,"

Journal of Management (June 2007), pp. 290–320; K. J. Harris, K. M. Kacmar, S. Zivnuska, and J. D. Shaw, "The Impact of Political Skill on Impression Management Effectiveness," *Journal of Applied Psychology* 92, no. 1 (2007), pp. 278–285; W. A. Hochwarter, G. R. Ferris, M. B. Gavin, P. L. Perrewé, A. T. Hall, and D. D. Frink," Political Skill as Neutralizer of Felt Accountability–Job Tension Effects on Job Performance Ratings: A Longitudinal Investigation," *Organizational Behavior and Human Decision Processes* 102 (2007), pp. 226–239; and D. C. Treadway, G. R. Ferris, A. B. Duke, G. L. Adams, and J. B. Tatcher, "The Moderating Role of Subordinate Political Skill on Supervisors' Impressions of Subordinate Ingratiation and Ratings of Subordinate Interpersonal Facilitation," *Journal of Applied Psychology* 92, no. 3 (2007), pp. 848–855.

31. M. C. Andrews, K. M. Kacmar, and K. J. Harris, "Got Political Skill? The Impact of Justice on the Importance of Political Skills for Job Performance." *Journal of Applied Psychology* 94, no. 6 (2009), pp. 1427–1437.

32. C. Anderson, S. E. Spataro, and F. J. Flynn, "Personality and Organizational Culture as Determinants of Influence," *Journal of Applied Psychology* 93, no. 3 (2008), pp. 702–710.

33. S. Stecklow, "Sexual-Harassment Cases Plague U.N.," *The Wall Street Journal* (May 21, 2009), p. A1.

34. N. Bode, "Flushing Hospital Nurse Gets $15 Million Award in Sexual Harassment Suit," *New York Daily News* (February 23, 2009), www.nydailynews.com.

35. L. J. Munson, C. Hulin, and F. Drasgow, "Longitudinal Analysis of Dispositional Influences and Sexual Harassment: Effects on Job and Psychological Outcomes," *Personnel Psychology* (Spring 2000), pp. 21–46; T. M. Glomb, L. J. Munson, C. L. Hulin, M. E. Bergman, and F. Drasgow, "Structural Equation Models of Sexual Harassment: Longitudinal Explorations and Cross-Sectional Generalizations," *Journal of Applied Psychology* (February 1999), pp. 14–28; M. E. Bergman, R. D. Langhout, P. A. Palmieri, L. M. Cortina, and L. F. Fitzgerald, "The (Un)reasonableness of Reporting: Antecedents and Consequences of Reporting Sexual Harassment," *Journal of Applied Psychology* (April 2002), pp. 230–242; and L. R. Offermann and A. B. Malamut, "When Leaders Harass: The Impact of Target Perceptions of Organizational Leadership and Climate on Harassment Reporting and Outcomes," *Journal of Applied Psychology* (October 2002), pp. 885–893.

36. S. Silverstein and S. Christian, "Harassment Ruling Raises Free-Speech Issues," *Los Angeles Times* (November 11, 1993), p. D2.

37. R. Ilies, N. Hauserman, S. Schwochau, and J. Stibal, "Reported Incidence Rates of Work-Related Sexual Harassment in the United States: Using Meta-Analysis to Explain Reported Rate Disparities," *Personnel Psychology* (Fall 2003), pp. 607–631.

38. K. Bursik and J. Gefter, "Still Stable After All These Years: Perceptions of Sexual Harassment in Academic Contexts," *The Journal of Social Psychology* 151, no. 3 (2011), pp. 331–349.

39. M. Rotundo, D. Nguyen, and P. R. Sackett, "A Meta-Analytic Review of Gender Differences in Perceptions of Sexual Harassment," *Journal of Applied Psychology* (October 2001), pp. 914–922.

40. R. L. Weiner, R. Reiter-Palmon, R. J. Winter, E. Richter, A. Humke, and E. Maeder, "Complainant Behavioral Tone, Ambivalent Sexism, and Perceptions of Sexual Harassment," *Psychology, Public Policy, and Law* 16, no. 1 (2010), pp. 56–84.

41. Ilies, Hauserman, Schwochau, and Stibal, "Reported Incidence Rates of Work-Related Sexual Harassment in the United States; A. B. Malamut and L. R. Offermann, "Coping with Sexual Harassment: Personal, Environmental, and Cognitive Determinants," *Journal of Applied Psychology* (December 2001), pp. 1152–1166; L. M. Cortina and S. A. Wasti, "Profiles in Coping: Responses to Sexual Harassment Across Persons, Organizations, and Cultures," *Journal of Applied Psychology* (February 2005), pp. 182–192; and J. W. Kunstman, "Sexual Overperception: Power, Mating Motives, and Biases in Social Judgment," *Journal of Personality and Social Psychology* 100, no. 2 (2011), pp. 282–294.

42. F. Krings and S. Facchin, "Organizational Justice and Men's Likelihood to Sexually Harass: The Moderating Role of Sexism and Personality," *Journal of Applied Psychology* 94, no. 2 (2009), pp. 501–510.

43. C. R. Willness, P. Steel, and K. Lee, "A Meta-Analysis of the Antecedents and Consequences of Workplace Sexual Harassment," *Personnel Psychology* 60 (2007), pp. 127–162.

44. Mintzberg, *Power In and Around Organizations*, p. 26. See also K. M. Kacmar and R. A. Baron, "Organizational Politics: The State of the Field, Links to Related Processes, and an Agenda for Future Research," in G. R. Ferris (ed.), *Research in Personnel and Human Resources Management,* vol. 17 (Greenwich, CT: JAI Press, 1999), pp. 1–39; and G. R. Ferris, D. C. Treadway, R. W. Kolokinsky, W. A. Hochwarter, C. J. Kacmar, and D. D. Frink, "Development and Validation of the Political Skill Inventory," *Journal of Management* (February 2005), pp. 126–152.

45. S. B. Bacharach and E. J. Lawler, "Political Alignments in Organizations," in R. M. Kramer and M. A. Neale (eds.), *Power and Influence in Organizations* (Thousand Oaks, CA: Sage, 1998), pp. 68–69.

46. A. Drory and T. Romm, "The Definition of Organizational Politics: A Review," *Human Relations* (November 1990), pp. 1133–1154; and R. S. Cropanzano, K. M. Kacmar, and D. P. Bozeman, "Organizational Politics, Justice, and Support: Their Differences and Similarities," in R. S. Cropanzano and K. M. Kacmar (eds.), *Organizational Politics, Justice and Support: Managing Social Climate at Work* (Westport, CT: Quorum Books, 1995), pp. 1–18; and G. R. Ferris and W. A. Hochwarter, "Organizational Politics," in S. Zedeck (ed.), *APA Handbook of Industrial and Organizational Psychology,* vol. 3 (Washington, DC: American Psychological Association, 2011), pp. 435–459.

47. D. A. Buchanan, "You Stab My Back, I'll Stab Yours: Management Experience and Perceptions of Organization Political Behavior," *British Journal of Management* 19, no. 1 (2008), pp. 49–64.

48. J. Pfeffer, *Power: Why Some People Have It—And Others Don't* (New York: Harper Collins, 2010).

49. Drory and Romm, "The Definition of Organizational Politics."

50. S. M. Rioux and L. A. Penner, "The Causes of Organizational Citizenship Behavior: A Motivational Analysis," *Journal of Applied Psychology* (December 2001), pp. 1306–1314; M. A. Finkelstein and L. A. Penner, "Predicting Organizational Citizenship Behavior: Integrating the Functional and Role

Identity Approaches," *Social Behavior & Personality* 32, no. 4 (2004), pp. 383–398; and J. Schwarzwald, M. Koslowsky, and M. Allouf, "Group Membership, Status, and Social Power Preference," *Journal of Applied Social Psychology* 35, no. 3 (2005), pp. 644–665.

51. See, for example, G. R. Ferris, G. S. Russ, and P. M. Fandt, "Politics in Organizations," in R. A. Giacalone and P. Rosenfeld (eds.), *Impression Management in the Organization* (Hillsdale, NJ: Lawrence Erlbaum, 1989), pp. 155–156; and W. E. O'Connor and T. G. Morrison, "A Comparison of Situational and Dispositional Predictors of Perceptions of Organizational Politics," *Journal of Psychology* (May 2001), pp. 301–312.

52. Farrell and Petersen, "Patterns of Political Behavior in Organizations," *Academy of Management Review* 7, no. 3 (1982), pp. 403–412.

53. G. R. Ferris and K. M. Kacmar, "Perceptions of Organizational Politics," *Journal of Management* (March 1992), pp. 93–116.

54. See, for example, P. M. Fandt and G. R. Ferris, "The Management of Information and Impressions: When Employees Behave Opportunistically," *Organizational Behavior and Human Decision Processes* (February 1990), pp. 140–158; Ferris, Russ, and Fandt, "Politics in Organizations," p. 147; and J. M. L. Poon, "Situational Antecedents and Outcomes of Organizational Politics Perceptions," *Journal of Managerial Psychology* 18, no. 2 (2003), pp. 138–155.

55. Ferris and Hochwarter, "Organizational Politics."

56. W. A. Hochwarter, C. Kiewitz, S. L. Castro, P. L. Perrewe, and G. R. Ferris, "Positive Affectivity and Collective Efficacy as Moderators of the Relationship Between Perceived Politics and Job Satisfaction," *Journal of Applied Social Psychology* (May 2003), pp. 1009–1035; and C. C. Rosen, P. E. Levy, and R. J. Hall, "Placing Perceptions of Politics in the Context of Feedback Environment, Employee Attitudes, and Job Performance," *Journal of Applied Psychology* 91, no. 1 (2006), pp. 211–230.

57. G. R. Ferris, D. D. Frink, M. C. Galang, J. Zhou, K. M. Kacmar, and J. L. Howard, "Perceptions of Organizational Politics: Prediction, Stress-Related Implications, and Outcomes," *Human Relations* (February 1996), pp. 233–266; and E. Vigoda, "Stress-Related Aftermaths to Workplace Politics: The Relationships Among Politics, Job Distress, and Aggressive Behavior in Organizations," *Journal of Organizational Behavior* (August 2002), pp. 571–591.

58. S. Aryee, Z. Chen, and P. S. Budhwar, "Exchange Fairness and Employee Performance: An Examination of the Relationship Between Organizational Politics and Procedural Justice," *Organizational Behavior & Human Decision Processes* (May 2004), pp. 1–14; and K. M. Kacmar, D. P. Bozeman, D. S. Carlson, and W. P. Anthony, "An Examination of the Perceptions of Organizational Politics Model." *Human Relations* 52, no. 3 (1999), pp. 383–416.

59. C. Kiewitz, W. A. Hochwarter, G. R. Ferris, and S. L. Castro, "The Role of Psychological Climate in Neutralizing the Effects of Organizational Politics on Work Outcomes," *Journal of Applied Social Psychology* (June 2002), pp. 1189–1207; and M. C. Andrews, L. A. Witt, and K. M. Kacmar, "The Interactive Effects of Organizational Politics and Exchange Ideology on Manager Ratings of Retention," *Journal of Vocational Behavior* (April 2003), pp. 357–369.

60. O. J. Labedo, "Perceptions of Organisational Politics: Examination of the Situational Antecedent and Consequences Among Nigeria's Extension Personnel," *Applied Psychology: An International Review* 55, no. 2 (2006), pp. 255–281.

61. Kacmar, Bozeman, Carlson, and Anthony, "An Examination of the Perceptions of Organizational Politics Model," p. 389.

62. Ibid., p. 409.

63. K. M. Kacmar, D. G. Bachrach, K. J. Harris, and S. Zivnuska, "Fostering Good Citizenship Through Ethical Leadership: Exploring the Moderating Role of Gender and Organizational Politics," *Journal of Applied Psychology* 96 (2011), pp. 633–642.

64. B. E. Ashforth and R. T. Lee, "Defensive Behavior in Organizations: A Preliminary Model," *Human Relations* (July 1990), pp. 621–648.

65. M. Valle and P. L. Perrewe, "Do Politics Perceptions Relate to Political Behaviors? Tests of an Implicit Assumption and Expanded Model," *Human Relations* (March 2000), pp. 359–386.

66. M. R. Leary and R. M. Kowalski, "Impression Management: A Literature Review and Two-Component Model," *Psychological Bulletin* (January 1990), pp. 34–47.

67. See, for instance, W. L. Gardner and M. J. Martinko, "Impression Management in Organizations," *Journal of Management* (June 1988), pp. 321–338; M. C. Bolino and W. H. Turnley, "More Than One Way to Make an Impression: Exploring Profiles of Impression Management," *Journal of Management* 29, no. 2 (2003), pp. 141–160; S. Zivnuska, K. M. Kacmar, L. A. Witt, D. S. Carlson, and V. K. Bratton, "Interactive Effects of Impression Management and Organizational Politics on Job Performance," *Journal of Organizational Behavior* (August 2004), pp. 627–640; and M. C. Bolino, K. M. Kacmar, W. H. Turnley, and J. B. Gilstrap, "A Multi-Level Review of Impression Management Motives and Behaviors," *Journal of Management* 34, no. 6 (2008), pp. 1080–1109.

68. M. Snyder and J. Copeland, "Self-monitoring Processes in Organizational Settings," in R. A. Giacalone and P. Rosenfeld (eds.), *Impression Management in the Organization* (Hillsdale, NJ: Lawrence Erlbaum, 1989), p. 11; Bolino and Turnley, "More Than One Way to Make an Impression"; and W. H. Turnley and M. C. Bolino, "Achieved Desired Images While Avoiding Undesired Images: Exploring the Role of Self-Monitoring in Impression Management," *Journal of Applied Psychology* (April 2001), pp. 351–360.

69. Leary and Kowalski, "Impression Management," p. 40.

70. J. Ham and R. Vonk, "Impressions of Impression Management: Evidence of Spontaneous Suspicion of Ulterior Motivation." *Journal of Experimental Social Psychology* 47, no. 2 (2011), pp. 466–471; and W. M. Bowler, J. R. B. Halbesleben, and J. R. B. Paul, "If You're Close with the Leader, You Must Be a Brownnose: The Role of Leader–Member Relationships in Follower, Leader, and Coworker Attributions of Organizational Citizenship Behavior Motives." *Human Resource Management Review* 20, no. 4 (2010), pp. 309–316.

71. C. Lebherz, K. Jonas, and B. Tomljenovic, "Are We Known by the Company We Keep? Effects of Name Dropping on First Impressions," *Social Influence* 4, no. 1 (2009), pp. 62–79.

72. J. R. B. Halbesleben, W. M. Bowler, M. C. Bolino, and W. H Turnley, "Organizational Concern, Prosocial Values, or

Impression Management? How Supervisors Attribute Motives to Organizational Citizenship Behavior," *Journal of Applied Social Psychology* 40, no. 6 (2010), pp. 1450–1489.

73. Ferris, Russ, and Fandt, "Politics in Organizations."

74. Z. I. Barsness, K. A. Diekmann, and M. L. Seidel, "Motivation and Opportunity: The Role of Remote Work, Demographic Dissimilarity, and Social Network Centrality in Impression Management," *Academy of Management Journal* 48, no. 3 (2005), pp. 401–419.

75. A. P. J. Ellis, B. J. West, A. M. Ryan, and R. P. DeShon, "The Use of Impression Management Tactics in Structural Interviews: A Function of Question Type?" *Journal of Applied Psychology* (December 2002), pp. 1200–1208.

76. C. K. Stevens and A. L. Kristof, "Making the Right Impression: A Field Study of Applicant Impression Management During Job Interviews," *Journal of Applied Psychology* 80 (1995), pp. 587– 606; L. A. McFarland, A. M. Ryan, and S. D. Kriska, "Impression Management Use and Effectiveness Across Assessment Methods," *Journal of Management* 29, no. 5 (2003), pp. 641–661; C. A. Higgins and T. A. Judge, "The Effect of Applicant Influence Tactics on Recruiter Perceptions of Fit and Hiring Recommendations: A Field Study," *Journal of Applied Psychology* 89, no. 4 (2004), pp. 622–632; and W. C. Tsai, C. C. Chen, and S. F. Chiu, "Exploring Boundaries of the Effects of Applicant Impression Management Tactics in Job Interviews," *Journal of Management* (February 2005), pp. 108– 125.

77. D. C. Gilmore and G. R. Ferris, "The Effects of Applicant Impression Management Tactics on Interviewer Judgments," *Journal of Management* 15, no. 4 (1989), pp. 557–564

78. Stevens and Kristof, "Making the Right Impression."

79. C. A. Higgins, T. A. Judge, and G. R. Ferris, "Influence Tactics and Work Outcomes: A Meta-Analysis," *Journal of Organizational Behavior* (March 2003), pp. 89–106.

80. Ibid.

81. K. J. Harris, K. M. Kacmar, S. Zivnuska, and J. D. Shaw, "The Impact of Political Skill on Impression Management Effectiveness," *Journal of Applied Psychology* 92, no. 1 (2007), pp. 278–285; and D. C. Treadway, G. R. Ferris, A. B. Duke, G. L. Adams, and J. B. Thatcher, "The Moderating Role of Subordinate Political Skill on Supervisors' Impressions of Subordinate Ingratiation and Ratings of Subordinate Interpersonal Facilitation," *Journal of Applied Psychology* 92, no. 3 (2007), pp. 848–855.

82. J. D. Westphal and I. Stern, "Flattery Will Get You Everywhere (Especially if You Are a Male Caucasian): How Ingratiation, Boardroom Behavior, and Demographic Minority Status Affect Additional Board Appointments of U.S. Companies," *Academy of Management Journal* 50, no. 2 (2007), pp. 267–288.

83. See T. Romm and A. Drory, "Political Behavior in Organizations: A Cross-Cultural Comparison," *International Journal of Value Based Management* 1 (1988), pp. 97–113; and E. Vigoda, "Reactions to Organizational Politics: A Cross-Cultural Examination in Israel and Britain," *Human Relations* (November 2001), pp. 1483–1518.

84. J. L. T. Leong, M. H. Bond, and P. P. Fu, "Perceived Effectiveness of Influence Strategies in the United States and Three Chinese Societies," *International Journal of Cross Cultural Management* (May 2006), pp. 101–120.

85. Y. Miyamoto and B. Wilken, "Culturally Contingent Situated Cognition: Influencing Other People Fosters Analytic Perception in the United States but Not in Japan," *Psychological Science* 21, no. 11 (2010), pp. 1616–1622.

86. E. Vigoda, "Reactions to Organizational Politics," p. 1512.

87. Ibid., p. 1510.

NO CONFLICT AT THE POST OFFICE . . . IS THAT GOOD?

Do you remember a strike of U.S. Postal Service (USPS) workers? You probably don't, because the last one was more than 40 years ago—in 1970. USPS leadership and the unions that represent its employees are proud of their cooperation. In March 2011, the USPS reached an agreement with the American Postal Workers Union (APWU) that, among other things:

- Provides a 3.5 percent annual raise for APWU workers.
- Includes seven uncapped cost-of-living increases.
- Extends the no-layoff provision in the contract.

Both union and management are happy with the contract. "The union and management have reached an agreement that is a 'win–win' proposition," says APWU president Cliff Guffey. Postmaster General Patrick R. Donahoe hailed the agreement as well: "By working together we have created a new contract that serves the best interest of our customers, our employees and the future of the Postal Service."

When two sides cooperate and show few signs of conflict, it is usually a sign of a healthy relationship, right? No, say many experts, including the man assigned to review the USPS, Phillip Herr of the Government Accountability Office (GAO).

The problem, according to these experts, is that the business model for the USPS is fatally flawed. The USPS loses billions nearly every year it operates. It has borrowed $12 billion from the U.S. Treasury and is on the verge of defaulting on a $5.5 billion payment to cover future retirees' health care costs. It is asking Congress to waive its debt obligations. (In 2006, Congress already relieved the USPS of a $27 billion pension obligation, shifting the debt to U.S. taxpayers.) Why is the USPS losing so much money even with heavy subsidies?

One fundamental reason is volume. With the growth of e-mail communication, mail volume is down—way down. It plummeted 20 percent from 2006 to 2010, and nearly everyone expects the downward trend to continue, if not accelerate. In anticipation, many other nations have privatized their mail services, which have been faster to adapt. Sweden's largely privatized postal system gives mail recipients the option to receive their mail by scanned copy, it maintains a digital archive of mail going back seven years, and it recently introduced an app that lets users turn cell phone pictures into postcards. USPS continues to charge the same rate per ounce to deliver anywhere—whether it's down the street or by pack mule to the bottom of the Grand Canyon. The majority of USPS's revenue comes from junk mail, which is, of course, mostly mail no one wants to receive.

Conflict and Negotiation

14

Let us never negotiate out of fear.
But let us never fear to negotiate. —John F. Kennedy

Photo: A postal employee attends to an automated sorting machine. Source: Robyn Beck/AFP/Newscom

479

Finally, USPS is not particularly competitive with Federal Express (FedEx) and United Parcel Service (UPS), its rivals in the lucrative overnight and ground shipping business. Though USPS is much larger—it employs 571,566 full-time workers, making it the nation's largest employer after Walmart—FedEx and UPS hold 84 percent of the express and ground shipping market. One reason USPS is not competitive? More than 80 percent of its budget goes to employee wages and benefits, as opposed to 43 percent for FedEx and 61 percent for UPS.

To be fair, USPS does many things well, it has many dedicated workers, and its leaders continue to talk of changing. But change is rarely easy, and it rarely comes without ruffling some feathers. Meanwhile, USPS continues to follow the path of least resistance. Says one expert: "Pretty soon it's going to be a government-run [junk mail] service. Does that make any sense?"

Sources: D. Leonard, "The End of Mail," *Bloomberg Businessweek* (May 30, 2011), pp. 60–65; G. Easterbrook, "The Post Office—Return to Sender," *Reuters* (June 1, 2011), downloaded June 30, 2011, from http://blogs.reuters.com/; and E. O'Keefe, "Postal Union Contract Ratified," *Washington Post* (May 12, 2011), downloaded on July 10, 2011, from www.washingtonpost.com/.

A s we see in the USPS example, both the presence and the absence of conflict and negotiation are often complex—and controversial— interpersonal processes. While we generally see conflict as a negative topic and negotiation as a positive one, each can generate positive and negative outcomes, and what we deem positive or negative often depends on our perspective. Let's first gauge how you handle conflict. Take the following self-assessment.

SELF-ASSESSMENT LIBRARY

What's My Preferred Conflict-Handling Style?

In the Self-Assessment Library (available on CD and online), take assessment II.C.5 (What's My Preferred Conflict-Handling Style?) and answer the following questions.

1. Judging from your highest score, what's your primary conflict-handling style?
2. Do you think your style varies, depending on the situation?
3. Would you like to change any aspects of your conflict-handling style?

A Definition of Conflict

1 Define *conflict.*

There has been no shortage of definitions of *conflict,*[1] but common to most is the idea that conflict is a perception. If no one is aware of a conflict, then it is generally agreed no conflict exists. Also needed to begin the conflict process are opposition or incompatibility and some form of interaction.

We can define **conflict**, then, as a process that begins when one party perceives another party has or is about to negatively affect something the first party cares about.[2] This definition is purposely broad. It describes that point in any ongoing activity when an interaction crosses over to become an interparty conflict. It encompasses the wide range of conflicts people experience in organizations: incompatibility of goals, differences over interpretations of facts, disagreements based on behavioral expectations, and the like. Finally, our definition is flexible enough to cover the full range of conflict levels—from overt and violent acts to subtle forms of disagreement.

Transitions in Conflict Thought

2 Differentiate among the traditional, interactionist, and managed-conflict views of conflict.

It is entirely appropriate to say there has been conflict over the role of conflict in groups and organizations. One school of thought has argued that conflict must be avoided—that it indicates a malfunctioning within the group. We call this the *traditional* view. Another perspective proposes not only that conflict can be a positive force in a group but that some conflict is absolutely necessary for a group to perform effectively. We label this the *interactionist* view. Finally, recent research argues that instead of encouraging "good" or discouraging "bad" conflict, it's more important to resolve naturally occurring conflicts productively. This perspective is the *managed conflict* view. Let's take a closer look at each view.

The Traditional View of Conflict

The early approach to conflict assumed all conflict was bad and to be avoided. Conflict was viewed negatively and discussed with such terms as *violence, destruction,* and *irrationality* to reinforce its negative connotation. This **traditional view of conflict** was consistent with attitudes about group behavior that prevailed in the 1930s and 1940s. Conflict was a dysfunctional outcome resulting from poor communication, a lack of openness and trust between people, and the failure of managers to be responsive to the needs and aspirations of their employees.

The view that all conflict is bad certainly offers a simple approach to looking at the behavior of people who create conflict. We need merely direct our attention to the causes of conflict and correct those malfunctions to improve group and organizational performance. This view of conflict fell out of favor for a long time as researchers came to realize that some level of conflict was inevitable.

The Interactionist View of Conflict

The **interactionist view of conflict** encourages conflict on the grounds that a harmonious, peaceful, tranquil, and cooperative group is prone to becoming static, apathetic, and unresponsive to needs for change and innovation.[3] The major contribution of this view is recognizing that a minimal level of conflict can help keep a group viable, self-critical, and creative.

The interactionist view does not propose that all conflicts are good. Rather, **functional conflict** supports the goals of the group and improves its performance

---

conflict   *A process that begins when one party perceives that another party has negatively affected, or is about to negatively affect, something that the first party cares about.*

traditional view of conflict   *The belief that all conflict is harmful and must be avoided.*

interactionist view of conflict   *The belief that conflict is not only a positive force in a group but also an absolute necessity for a group to perform effectively.*

functional conflict   *Conflict that supports the goals of the group and improves its performance.*

and is, thus, a constructive form of conflict. A conflict that hinders group performance is a destructive or **dysfunctional conflict**. What differentiates functional from dysfunctional conflict? The evidence indicates we need to look at the *type* of conflict—whether it's connected to task, relationship, or process.[4]

Task conflict relates to the content and goals of the work. **Relationship conflict** focuses on interpersonal relationships. **Process conflict** relates to how the work gets done. Studies demonstrate that relationship conflicts are almost always dysfunctional.[5] Why? It appears that the friction and interpersonal hostilities inherent in relationship conflicts increase personality clashes and decrease mutual understanding, which hinders the completion of organizational tasks. Unfortunately, managers spend a lot of effort resolving personality conflicts among staff members; one survey indicated this task consumes 18 percent of their time.[6]

In contrast, low levels of process conflict and low to moderate levels of task conflict can be functional, but only in very specific cases. Recent reviews have shown that task conflicts are usually just as disruptive as relationship conflicts.[7] For conflict to be productive, it must be kept within certain boundaries. For example, one study in China found that moderate levels of task conflict in the early development stage could increase creativity in groups, but high levels of task conflict decreased team performance, and task conflicts were unrelated to performance once the group was in the later stages of group development.[8] Intense arguments about who should do what become dysfunctional when they create uncertainty about task roles, increase the time to complete tasks, and lead members to work at cross-purposes. Low to moderate levels of task conflict stimulate discussion of ideas. This means task conflicts relate positively to creativity and innovation, but they are not related to routine task performance. Groups performing routine tasks that don't require creativity won't benefit from task conflict. Moreover, if the group is already engaged in active discussion of ideas in a nonconfrontational way, adding conflict will not help generate more ideas. Task conflict is also related to these positive outcomes only when all members share the same goals and have high levels of trust.[9] Another way of saying this is that task conflicts are related to increased performance only when all members believe the team is a safe place for taking risks and that members will not deliberately undermine or reject those who speak up.[10]

Task conflict is often functional, but one of its dangers is that it can escalate and become a battle of wills. For example, as a Target Corporation investor, William Ackman tried, unsuccessfully, for many years to convince the retailer to change its business strategy to improve performance and boost shareholder returns. Ackman sought to bring in new board members with a proxy vote. He asked shareholders to elect candidates who would bring new ideas to Target's board, which he claimed was slow in making critical decisions. After a long battle that cost Target millions of dollars in defending itself, the shareholders voted to keep the current board members. Ackman is shown here meeting with the media after losing the proxy battle in which his candidates received less than 20 percent of the vote.

Resolution-Focused View of Conflict

Researchers, including those who had strongly advocated the interactionist view, have begun to recognize some problems with encouraging conflict.[11] As we will see, there are some very specific cases in which conflict can be beneficial. However, workplace conflicts are not productive, they take time away from job tasks or interacting with customers, and hurt feelings and anger often linger after conflicts appear to be over. People can seldom wall off their feelings into neat categories of "task" or "relationship" disagreements, so task conflicts sometimes escalate into relationship conflicts.[12] A study conducted in Taiwan and Indonesia found that when levels of relationship conflict are high, increases in task conflict are consistently related to lower levels of team performance and team member satisfaction.[13] Conflicts produce stress, which may lead people to become more close minded and adversarial.[14] Studies of conflict in laboratories also fail to take account of the reductions in trust and cooperation that occur even with relationship conflicts. Longer-term studies show that all conflicts reduce trust, respect, and cohesion in groups, which reduces their long-term viability.[15]

In light of these findings, researchers have started to focus more on managing the whole context in which conflicts occur, both before and after the behavioral stage of conflict occurs. A growing body of research, which we review later, suggests we can minimize the negative effects of conflict by focusing on preparing people for conflicts, developing resolution strategies, and facilitating open discussion. Researchers interested in cross-cultural conflicts have also encouraged individuals to recognize impediments to agreement like hidden emotional attachments to a particular course of action and social identities that place people on different "sides" of an issue based on national or cultural variables. Resolving cross-cultural conflicts begins by addressing these emotional and identity-based concerns and building bonds between parties through common interests.[16]

In sum, the traditional view was shortsighted in assuming all conflict should be eliminated. The interactionist view that conflict can stimulate active discussion without spilling over into negative, disruptive emotions is incomplete. The managed conflict perspective does recognize that conflict is probably inevitable in most organizations, and it focuses more on productive conflict resolution. The research pendulum has swung from eliminating conflict, to encouraging limited levels of conflict, and now to finding constructive methods for resolving conflicts productively so their disruptive influence can be minimized.

The Conflict Process

3 Outline the conflict process.

The **conflict process** has five stages: potential opposition or incompatibility, cognition and personalization, intentions, behavior, and outcomes. The process is diagrammed in Exhibit 14-1.

---

dysfunctional conflict *Conflict that hinders group performance.*

task conflict *Conflict over content and goals of the work.*

relationship conflict *Conflict based on interpersonal relationships.*

process conflict *Conflict over how work gets done.*

conflict process *A process that has five stages: potential opposition or incompatibility, cognition and personalization, intentions, behavior, and outcomes.*

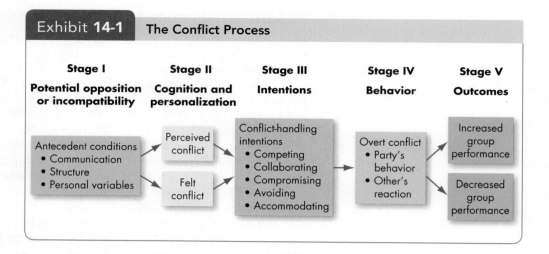

Exhibit **14-1**   The Conflict Process

Stage I	Stage II	Stage III	Stage IV	Stage V
Potential opposition or incompatibility	**Cognition and personalization**	**Intentions**	**Behavior**	**Outcomes**

Stage I: Potential Opposition or Incompatibility

The first step in the conflict process is the appearance of conditions that create opportunities for conflict to arise. These conditions *need not* lead directly to conflict, but one of them is necessary if conflict is to surface. For simplicity's sake, we group the conditions (which we can also look at as causes or sources of conflict) into three general categories: communication, structure, and personal variables.

Communication   Susan had worked in supply chain management at Bristol-Myers Squibb for 3 years. She enjoyed her work in large part because her manager, Harry, was a great boss. Then Harry got promoted, and Chuck took his place. Six months later, Susan says her job is a lot more frustrating. "Harry and I were on the same wavelength. It's not that way with Chuck. He tells me something, and I do it. Then he tells me I did it wrong. I think he means one thing but says something else. It's been like this since the day he arrived. I don't think a day goes by when he isn't yelling at me for something. You know, there are some people you just find it easy to communicate with. Well, Chuck isn't one of those!"

Susan's comments illustrate that communication can be a source of conflict.[17] They represent the opposing forces that arise from semantic difficulties, misunderstandings, and "noise" in the communication channels. Recall our comments on communication in Chapter 11.

A review of the research suggests that differing word connotations, jargon, insufficient exchange of information, and noise in the communication channel are all barriers to communication and potential antecedent conditions to conflict. Research has further demonstrated a surprising finding: the potential for conflict increases when either too little or *too much* communication takes place. Apparently, an increase in communication is functional up to a point, after which it is possible to overcommunicate, with a resultant increase in the potential for conflict.

Structure   Charlotte and Mercedes both work at the Portland Furniture Mart—a large discount furniture retailer. Charlotte is a salesperson on the floor, and Mercedes is the company credit manager. The two women have known each other for years and have much in common: they live within two blocks of each other, and their oldest daughters attend the same middle school and are best friends. If Charlotte and Mercedes had different jobs, they might be best friends themselves, but they are constantly fighting battles with each other. Charlotte's job is to sell furniture, and she does it well. But most of her sales are made on credit. Because Mercedes' job is to make sure the company minimizes credit losses, she regularly has to turn down the credit application of a customer with whom Charlotte has just closed a sale. It's nothing personal between the women; the requirements of their jobs just bring them into conflict.

The conflicts between Charlotte and Mercedes are structural in nature. The term *structure* in this context includes variables such as size of the group, degree of specialization in the tasks assigned to group members, jurisdictional clarity, member–goal compatibility, leadership styles, reward systems, and the degree of dependence between groups.

Size and specialization can stimulate conflict. The larger the group and the more specialized its activities, the greater the likelihood of conflict. Tenure and conflict have been found to be inversely related; the potential for conflict is greatest when group members are younger and when turnover is high.

The greater the ambiguity about where responsibility for actions lies, the greater the potential for conflict to emerge. Such jurisdictional ambiguities increase intergroup fighting for control of resources and territory. Diversity of goals among groups is also a major source of conflict. When groups within an organization seek diverse ends, some of which—like sales and credit at Portland Furniture Mart—are inherently at odds, opportunities for conflict increase. Reward systems, too, create conflict when one member's gain comes at another's expense. Finally, if a group is dependent on another group (in contrast to the two being mutually independent), or if interdependence allows one group to gain at another's expense, opposing forces are stimulated.

Personal Variables   Have you ever met someone for whom you felt an immediate dislike? You disagreed with most of the opinions he expressed. Even insignificant characteristics—the sound of his voice, the smirk when he smiled, his personality—annoyed you. We've all met people like that. When you have to work with such individuals, the potential for conflict arises.

Our last category of potential sources of conflict is personal variables, which include personality, emotions, and values. Personality does appear to play a role in the conflict process: some people just tend to get into conflicts a lot. In particular, people high in the personality traits of disagreeableness, neuroticism, or self-monitoring are prone to tangle with other people more often, and to react poorly when conflicts occur.[18] Emotions can also cause conflict. An employee who shows up to work irate from her hectic morning commute may carry that anger with her to her 9:00 a.m. meeting. The problem? Her anger can annoy her colleagues, which can result in a tension-filled meeting.[19]

Stage II: Cognition and Personalization

If the conditions cited in Stage I negatively affect something one party cares about, then the potential for opposition or incompatibility becomes actualized in the second stage.

As we noted in our definition of conflict, one or more of the parties must be aware that antecedent conditions exist. However, because a conflict is a **perceived conflict** does not mean it is personalized. In other words, "*A* may be aware that *B* and *A* are in serious disagreement . . . but it may not make *A* tense

perceived conflict   *Awareness by one or more parties of the existence of conditions that create opportunities for conflict to arise.*

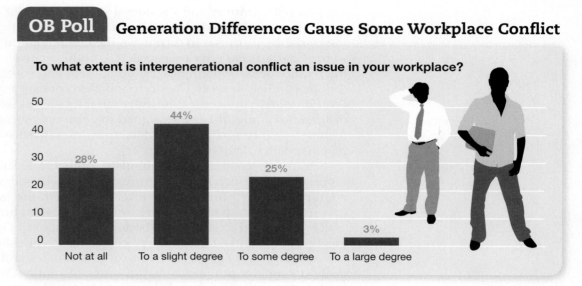

OB Poll — Generation Differences Cause Some Workplace Conflict

To what extent is intergenerational conflict an issue in your workplace?

- Not at all: 28%
- To a slight degree: 44%
- To some degree: 25%
- To a large degree: 3%

Source: Based on "Intergenerational Conflict in the Workplace," SHRM News (April 29, 2011).

or anxious, and it may have no effect whatsoever on *A*'s affection toward *B*."[20] It is at the **felt conflict** level, when individuals become emotionally involved, that they experience anxiety, tension, frustration, or hostility.

Keep in mind two points. First, Stage II is important because it's where conflict issues tend to be defined, where the parties decide what the conflict is about.[21] If I define our salary disagreement as a zero-sum situation (if you get the increase in pay you want, there will be just that amount less for me), I am going to be far less willing to compromise than if I frame the conflict as a potential win–win situation (the dollars in the salary pool might be increased so both of us could get the added pay we want). Thus, the definition of a conflict is important because it typically delineates the set of possible settlements.

Our second point is that emotions play a major role in shaping perceptions.[22] Negative emotions allow us to oversimplify issues, lose trust, and put negative interpretations on the other party's behavior.[23] In contrast, positive feelings increase our tendency to see potential relationships among the elements of a problem, to take a broader view of the situation, and to develop more innovative solutions.[24]

Stage III: Intentions

Intentions intervene between people's perceptions and emotions and their overt behavior. They are decisions to act in a given way.[25]

We separate out intentions as a distinct stage because we have to infer the other's intent to know how to respond to his or her behavior. Many conflicts escalate simply because one party attributes the wrong intentions to the other. There is also typically a great deal of slippage between intentions and behavior, so behavior does not always accurately reflect a person's intentions.

Exhibit 14-2 represents one author's effort to identify the primary conflict-handling intentions. Using two dimensions—*cooperativeness* (the degree to which one party attempts to satisfy the other party's concerns) and *assertiveness*

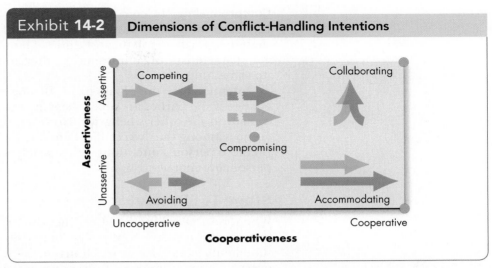

| Exhibit **14-2** | **Dimensions of Conflict-Handling Intentions** |

Source: Figure from "Conflict and Negotiation Processes in Organizations" by K. Thomas in *Handbook of Industrial and Organizational Psychology,* 2/e, Vol. 3, ed. by M. D. Dunnette and L. M. Hough, p. 668 (Palo Alto, CA: Consulting Psychologists Press, 1992). Used with permission.

(the degree to which one party attempts to satisfy his or her own concerns)— we can identify five conflict-handling intentions: *competing* (assertive and unco-operative), *collaborating* (assertive and cooperative), *avoiding* (unassertive and uncooperative), *accommodating* (unassertive and cooperative), and *compromising* (midrange on both assertiveness and cooperativeness).[26]

Competing   When one person seeks to satisfy his or her own interests regard-less of the impact on the other parties to the conflict, that person is **competing**. You compete when you place a bet that only one person can win, for example.

Collaborating   When parties in conflict each desire to fully satisfy the concerns of all parties, there is cooperation and a search for a mutually beneficial out-come. In **collaborating**, the parties intend to solve a problem by clarifying dif-ferences rather than by accommodating various points of view. If you attempt to find a win–win solution that allows both parties' goals to be completely achieved, that's collaborating.

Avoiding   A person may recognize a conflict exists and want to withdraw from or suppress it. Examples of **avoiding** include trying to ignore a conflict and avoiding others with whom you disagree.

Accommodating   A party who seeks to appease an opponent may be willing to place the opponent's interests above his or her own, sacrificing to maintain the relationship. We refer to this intention as **accommodating**. Supporting someone else's opinion despite your reservations about it, for example, is accommodating.

---

felt conflict   *Emotional involvement in a conflict that creates anxiety, tenseness, frustration, or hostility.*
intentions   *Decisions to act in a given way.*

competing   *A desire to satisfy one's interests, regardless of the impact on the other party to the conflict.*
collaborating   *A situation in which the parties to a conflict each desire to satisfy fully the concerns of all parties.*

avoiding   *The desire to withdraw from or suppress a conflict.*
accommodating   *The willingness of one party in a conflict to place the opponent's interests above his or her own.*

Compromising   In **compromising**, there is no clear winner or loser. Rather, there is a willingness to ration the object of the conflict and accept a solution that provides incomplete satisfaction of both parties' concerns. The distinguishing characteristic of compromising, therefore, is that each party intends to give up something.

Intentions are not always fixed. During the course of a conflict, they might change if the parties are able to see the other's point of view or respond emotionally to the other's behavior. However, research indicates people have preferences among the five conflict-handling intentions we just described.[27] We can predict a person's intentions rather well from a combination of intellectual and personality characteristics.

Stage IV: Behavior

When most people think of conflict situations, they tend to focus on Stage IV because this is where conflicts become visible. The behavior stage includes the statements, actions, and reactions made by the conflicting parties, usually as overt attempts to implement their own intentions. As a result of miscalculations or unskilled enactments, overt behaviors sometimes deviate from these original intentions.[28]

It helps to think of Stage IV as a dynamic process of interaction. For example, you make a demand on me, I respond by arguing, you threaten me, I threaten you back, and so on. Exhibit 14-3 provides a way of visualizing conflict behavior. All conflicts exist somewhere along this continuum. At the lower part are conflicts characterized by subtle, indirect, and highly controlled forms of tension, such as a student questioning in class a point the instructor has just made. Conflict intensities escalate as they move upward along the continuum until they become highly destructive. Strikes, riots, and wars clearly fall in this upper range. Conflicts that reach the upper ranges of the continuum are almost always dysfunctional. Functional conflicts are typically confined to the lower range of the continuum.

If a conflict is dysfunctional, what can the parties do to de-escalate it? Or, conversely, what options exist if conflict is too low and needs to be increased? This brings us to techniques of **conflict management**. Exhibit 14-4 lists the major resolution and stimulation techniques that allow managers to control conflict levels. We have already described several as conflict-handling intentions. This shouldn't be surprising. Under ideal conditions, a person's intentions should translate into comparable behaviors.

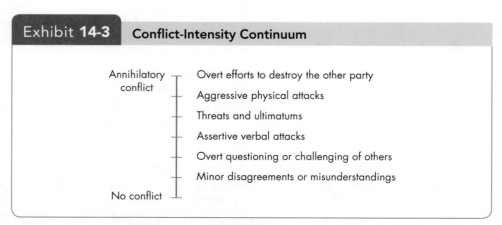

Exhibit **14-3**	Conflict-Intensity Continuum

Annihilatory conflict — Overt efforts to destroy the other party

Aggressive physical attacks

Threats and ultimatums

Assertive verbal attacks

Overt questioning or challenging of others

Minor disagreements or misunderstandings

No conflict

Sources: Based on S. P. Robbins, *Managing Organizational Conflict: A Nontraditional Approach* (Upper Saddle River, NJ: Prentice Hall, 1974), pp. 93–97; and F. Glasi, "The Process of Conflict Escalation and the Roles of Third Parties," in G. B. J. Bomers and R. Peterson (eds.), *Conflict Management and Industrial Relations* (Boston: Kluwer-Nijhoff, 1982), pp. 119–140.

Exhibit **14-4**	**Conflict Management Techniques**

Conflict-Resolution Techniques

Problem solving	Face-to-face meeting of the conflicting parties for the purpose of identifying the problem and resolving it through open discussion.
Superordinate goals	Creating a shared goal that cannot be attained without the cooperation of each of the conflicting parties.
Expansion of resources	When a conflict is caused by the scarcity of a resource (for example, money, promotion, opportunities, office space), expansion of the resource can create a win-win solution.
Avoidance	Withdrawal from or suppression of the conflict.
Smoothing	Playing down differences while emphasizing common interests between the conflicting parties.
Compromise	Each party to the conflict gives up something of value.
Authoritative command	Management uses its formal authority to resolve the conflict and then communicates its desires to the parties involved.
Altering the human variable	Using behavioral change techniques such as human relations training to alter attitudes and behaviors that cause conflict.
Altering the structural variables	Changing the formal organization structure and the interaction patterns of conflicting parties through job redesign, transfers, creation of coordinating positions, and the like.

Conflict-Stimulation Techniques

Communication	Using ambiguous or threatening messages to increase conflict levels.
Bringing in outsiders	Adding employees to a group whose backgrounds, values, attitudes, or managerial styles differ from those of present members.
Restructuring the organization	Realigning work groups, altering rules and regulations, increasing interdependence, and making similar structural changes to disrupt the status quo.
Appointing a devil's advocate	Designating a critic to purposely argue against the majority positions held by the group.

Source: Based on S. P. Robbins, *Managing Organizational Conflict: A Nontraditional Approach* (Upper Saddle River, NJ: Prentice Hall, 1974), pp. 59–89.

Stage V: Outcomes

The action–reaction interplay between the conflicting parties results in consequences. As our model demonstrates (see Exhibit 14-1), these outcomes may be functional, if the conflict improves the group's performance, or dysfunctional, if it hinders performance.

Functional Outcomes   How might conflict act as a force to increase group performance? It is hard to visualize a situation in which open or violent aggression could be functional. But it's possible to see how low or moderate levels of conflict could improve the effectiveness of a group. Let's consider some examples and then review the research evidence. Note that all our examples focus on task and process conflicts and exclude the relationship variety.

Conflict is constructive when it improves the quality of decisions, stimulates creativity and innovation, encourages interest and curiosity among group members, provides the medium through which problems can be aired and tensions released, and fosters an environment of self-evaluation and change. The evidence suggests conflict can improve the quality of decision making by allowing all points to be weighed, particularly those that are unusual or held by a minority.[29] Conflict is an antidote for groupthink. It doesn't allow the group to passively rubber-stamp decisions that may be based on weak assumptions,

compromising   *A situation in which each party to a conflict is willing to give up something.*

conflict management   *The use of resolution and stimulation techniques to achieve the desired level of conflict.*

inadequate consideration of relevant alternatives, or other debilities. Conflict challenges the status quo and therefore furthers the creation of new ideas, promotes reassessment of group goals and activities, and increases the probability that the group will respond to change. An open discussion focused on higher-order goals can make these functional outcomes more likely. Groups that are extremely polarized do not manage their underlying disagreements effectively and tend to accept suboptimal solutions, or they avoid making decisions altogether rather than working out the conflict.[30]

Research studies in diverse settings confirm the functionality of active discussion. Groups whose members have different interests tend to produce higher-quality solutions to a variety of problems than do homogeneous groups.[31] Team members with greater differences in work styles and experience also tend to share more information with one another.[32]

These observations lead us to predict benefits to organizations from the increasing cultural diversity of the workforce. And that's what the evidence indicates, under most conditions. Heterogeneity among group and organization members can increase creativity, improve the quality of decisions, and facilitate change by enhancing member flexibility.[33] Researchers compared decision-making groups composed of all-Caucasian individuals with groups that also contained members from Asian, Hispanic, and Black ethnic groups. The ethnically diverse groups produced more effective and more feasible ideas, and the unique ideas they generated tended to be of higher quality than the unique ideas produced by the all-Caucasian group.

Dysfunctional Outcomes   The destructive consequences of conflict on the performance of a group or an organization are generally well known: uncontrolled opposition breeds discontent, which acts to dissolve common ties and eventually leads to the destruction of the group. And, of course, a substantial body of literature documents how dysfunctional conflicts can reduce group effectiveness.[34] Among the undesirable consequences are poor communication, reductions in group cohesiveness, and subordination of group goals to the primacy

IBM benefits from the diversity of its employees who engage in functional conflict that improves the company's performance. At IBM, diversity drives innovation. Achieving the full potential of its diverse workforce is a business priority fundamental to IBM's competitive success. For innovation to flourish, IBM needs different employee experiences, perspectives, skills, ideas, interests, information, and thinking. It relies on creative tension and opposing ideas that increase creativity, improve the quality of decisions, and facilitate change. IBM employees shown here broaden their diversity experiences and perspectives by participating in overseas assignments in emerging markets.

Source: Chris Seward/MCT/Newscom.

of infighting among members. All forms of conflict—even the functional varieties—appear to reduce group member satisfaction and trust.[35] When active discussions turn into open conflicts between members, information sharing between members decreases significantly.[36] At the extreme, conflict can bring group functioning to a halt and threaten the group's survival.

We noted that diversity can usually improve group performance and decision making. However, if differences of opinion open up along demographic fault lines, harmful conflicts result and information sharing decreases.[37] For example, if differences of opinion in a gender-diverse team line up so that men all hold one opinion and women hold another, group members tend to stop listening to one another. They fall into ingroup favoritism and won't take the other side's point of view into consideration. Managers in this situation need to pay special attention to these fault lines and emphasize the shared goals of the team.

The demise of an organization as a result of too much conflict isn't as unusual as you might think. One of New York's best-known law firms, Shea & Gould, closed down solely because the 80 partners just couldn't get along.[38] As one legal consultant familiar with the organization said, "This was a firm that had basic and principled differences among the partners that were basically irreconcilable." That same consultant also addressed the partners at their last meeting: "You don't have an economic problem," he said. "You have a personality problem. You hate each other!"

Managing Functional Conflict   If managers recognize that in some situations conflict can be beneficial, what can they do to manage conflict effectively in their organizations? Let's look at some approaches organizations are using to encourage their people to challenge the system and develop fresh ideas.

One of the keys to minimizing counterproductive conflicts is recognizing when there really is a disagreement. Many apparent conflicts are due to people using different language to discuss the same general course of action. For example, someone in marketing might focus on "distribution problems," while someone from operations will talk about "supply chain management" to describe essentially the same issue. Successful conflict management recognizes these different approaches and attempts to resolve them by encouraging open, frank discussion focused on interests rather than issues (we'll have more to say about this when we contrast distributive and integrative bargaining styles). Another approach is to have opposing groups pick parts of the solution that are most important to them and then focus on how each side can get its top needs satisfied. Neither side may get exactly what it wants, but both sides will get the most important parts of its agenda.[39]

Groups that resolve conflicts successfully discuss differences of opinion openly and are prepared to manage conflict when it arises.[40] The most disruptive conflicts are those that are never addressed directly. An open discussion makes it much easier to develop a shared perception of the problems at hand; it also allows groups to work toward a mutually acceptable solution. Managers need to emphasize shared interests in resolving conflicts, so groups that disagree with one another don't become too entrenched in their points of view and start to take the conflicts personally. Groups with cooperative conflict styles and a strong underlying identification to the overall group goals are more effective than groups with a competitive style.[41]

Differences across countries in conflict resolution strategies may be based on collectivistic tendencies and motives.[42] Collectivist cultures see people as deeply embedded in social situations, whereas individualist cultures see them as autonomous. As a result, collectivists are more likely to seek to preserve relationships and promote the good of the group as a whole. They will avoid direct expression of conflicts, preferring indirect methods for resolving differences of opinion. Collectivists may also be more interested in demonstrations of concern and working through third parties to resolve disputes, whereas individualists will be more likely to confront differences of opinion directly and openly.

Some research does support this theory. Compared to collectivist Japanese negotiators, their more individualist U.S. counterparts are more likely to see offers from their counterparts as unfair and to reject them. Another study revealed that whereas U.S. managers were more likely to use competing tactics in the face of conflicts, compromising and avoiding are the most preferred methods of conflict management in China.[43] Interview data, however, suggests top management teams in Chinese high-technology firms prefer collaboration even more than compromising and avoiding.[44]

Having considered conflict—its nature, causes, and consequences—we now turn to negotiation, which often resolves conflict.

Negotiation

4 Define *negotiation*.

Negotiation permeates the interactions of almost everyone in groups and organizations. There's the obvious: labor bargains with management. There's the not-so-obvious: managers negotiate with employees, peers, and bosses; salespeople negotiate with customers; purchasing agents negotiate with suppliers. And there's the subtle: an employee agrees to cover for a colleague for a few minutes in exchange for some past or future benefit. In today's loosely structured organizations, in which members work with colleagues over whom they have no direct authority and with whom they may not even share a common boss, negotiation skills become critical.

We can define **negotiation** as a process that occurs when two or more parties decide how to allocate scarce resources.[45] Although we commonly think of the outcomes of negotiation in one-shot economic terms, like negotiating over the price of a car, every negotiation in organizations also affects the relationship between the negotiators and the way the negotiators feel about themselves.[46] Depending on how much the parties are going to interact with one another, sometimes maintaining the social relationship and behaving ethically will be just as important as achieving an immediate outcome of bargaining. Note that we use the terms *negotiation* and *bargaining* interchangeably. In this section, we contrast two bargaining strategies, provide a model of the negotiation process, ascertain the role of moods and personality traits on bargaining, review gender and cultural differences in negotiation, and take a brief look at third-party negotiations.

Bargaining Strategies

5 Contrast distributive and integrative bargaining.

There are two general approaches to negotiation—*distributive bargaining* and *integrative bargaining*.[47] As Exhibit 14-5 shows, they differ in their goal and motivation, focus, interests, information sharing, and duration of relationship. Let's define each and illustrate the differences.

Distributive Bargaining   You see a used car advertised for sale online. It appears to be just what you've been looking to buy. You go out to see the car. It's great, and you want it. The owner tells you the asking price. You don't want to pay that much. The two of you then negotiate. The negotiating strategy you're

---

Exhibit 14-5   Distributive Versus Integrative Bargaining

Bargaining Characteristic	Distributive Bargaining	Integrative Bargaining
Goal	Get as much of the pie as possible	Expand the pie so that both parties are satisfied
Motivation	Win–lose	Win–win
Focus	Positions ("I can't go beyond this point on this issue.")	Interests ("Can you explain why this issue is so important to you?")
Interests	Opposed	Congruent
Information sharing	Low (Sharing information will only allow other party to take advantage)	High (Sharing information will allow each party to find ways to satisfy interests of each party)
Duration of relationship	Short term	Long term

---

engaging in is called **distributive bargaining**. Its identifying feature is that it operates under zero-sum conditions—that is, any gain I make is at your expense and vice versa. Every dollar you can get the seller to cut from the car's price is a dollar you save, and every dollar more the seller can get from you comes at your expense. So the essence of distributive bargaining is negotiating over who gets what share of a fixed pie. By **fixed pie**, we mean a set amount of goods or services to be divvied up. When the pie is fixed, or the parties believe it is, they tend to bargain distributively.

Probably the most widely cited example of distributive bargaining is labor–management negotiations over wages. Typically, labor's representatives come to the bargaining table determined to get as much money as possible from management. Because every cent labor negotiates increases management's costs, each party bargains aggressively and treats the other as an opponent who must be defeated.

The essence of distributive bargaining is depicted in Exhibit 14-6. Parties A and B represent two negotiators. Each has a *target point* that defines what he or she would like to achieve. Each also has a *resistance point,* which marks the lowest acceptable outcome—the point below which the party would break off

Exhibit 14-6   Staking Out the Bargaining Zone

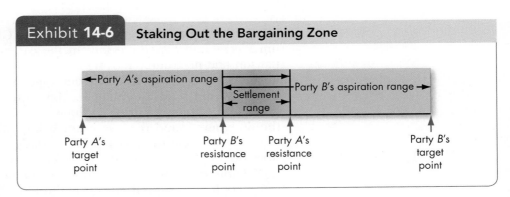

negotiation A process in which two or more parties exchange goods or services and attempt to agree on the exchange rate for them.

distributive bargaining Negotiation that seeks to divide up a fixed amount of resources; a win–lose situation.

fixed pie The belief that there is only a set amount of goods or services to be divvied up between the parties.

negotiations rather than accept a less favorable settlement. The area between these two points makes up each party's aspiration range. As long as there is some overlap between A's and B's aspiration ranges, there exists a settlement range in which each one's aspirations can be met.

When you are engaged in distributive bargaining, research consistently shows one of the best things you can do is make the first offer, and make it an aggressive one. Making the first offer shows power; individuals in power are much more likely to make initial offers, speak first at meetings, and thereby gain the advantage. Another reason this is a good strategy is the anchoring bias, mentioned in Chapter 6. People tend to fixate on initial information. Once that anchoring point is set, they fail to adequately adjust it based on subsequent information. A savvy negotiator sets an anchor with the initial offer, and scores of negotiation studies show that such anchors greatly favor the person who sets them.[48]

Say you have a job offer, and your prospective employer asks you what sort of starting salary you'd want. You've just been given a great gift—you have a chance to set the anchor, meaning you should ask for the highest salary you think the employer could reasonably offer. Asking for a million dollars is only going to make most of us look ridiculous, which is why we suggest being on the high end of what you think is *reasonable*. Too often, we err on the side of caution, afraid of scaring off the employer and thus settling for too little. It *is* possible to scare off an employer, and it's true employers don't like candidates to be assertive in salary negotiations, but liking isn't the same as doing what it takes to hire or retain someone.[49] What happens much more often is that we ask for less than we could have gotten.

Another distributive bargaining tactic is revealing a deadline. Erin is a human resources manager. She is negotiating salary with Ron, who is a highly sought-after new hire. Because Ron knows the company needs him, he decides to play hardball and ask for an extraordinary salary and many benefits. Erin tells Ron the company can't meet his requirements. Ron tells Erin he is going to have to think things over. Worried the company is going to lose Ron to a competitor, Erin decides to tell Ron she is under time pressure and needs to reach an agreement with him immediately, or she will have to offer the job to another candidate. Would you consider Erin to be a savvy negotiator? Well, she is. Why? Negotiators who reveal deadlines speed concessions from their negotiating counterparts, making them reconsider their position. And even though negotiators don't *think* this tactic works, in reality, negotiators who reveal deadlines do better.[50]

Integrative Bargaining   Jake is a 5-year-old Chicago luxury boutique owned by Jim Wetzel and Lance Lawson. In the early days of the business, Wetzel and Lawson had no trouble moving millions of dollars of merchandise from many up-and-coming designers. They developed such a good rapport that many designers would send allotments to Jake without requiring advance payment. When the economy soured in 2008, Jake had trouble selling inventory, and the designers found they were not being paid for what they had shipped to the store. Despite the fact that many designers were willing to work with the store on a delayed payment plan, Wetzel and Lawson stopped returning their calls. Lamented one designer, Doo-Ri Chung, "You kind of feel this familiarity with people who supported you for so long. When they have cash-flow issues, you want to make sure you are there for them as well."[51] Ms. Chung's attitude shows the promise of **integrative bargaining**. In contrast to distributive bargaining, integrative bargaining operates under the assumption that one or more of the possible settlements can create a win–win solution. Of course, as the Jake example shows and we'll highlight later, integrative bargaining takes "two to tango"—both parties must be engaged for it to work.

United Auto Workers officials (left) and Ford Motor Company officials shake hands during a news conference for the start of national negotiations in July 2011. Both UAW and Ford say that they are committed to integrative bargaining in finding mutually acceptable solutions to create a win-win settlement that will help boost their competitiveness with other automakers in the United States and abroad. The negotiations reflect a 70-year history of UAW and Ford working together to share information that will help address difficult business challenges.

Source: AP Photo/Paul Sancya.

In terms of intraorganizational behavior, all things being equal, integrative bargaining is preferable to distributive bargaining because the former builds long-term relationships. Integrative bargaining bonds negotiators and allows them to leave the bargaining table feeling they have achieved a victory. Distributive bargaining, however, leaves one party a loser. It tends to build animosities and deepen divisions when people have to work together on an ongoing basis. Research shows that over repeated bargaining episodes, a "losing" party who feels positive about the negotiation outcome is much more likely to bargain cooperatively in subsequent negotiations. This points to an important advantage of integrative negotiations: even when you "win," you want your opponent to feel good about the negotiation.[52]

Why, then, don't we see more integrative bargaining in organizations? The answer lies in the conditions necessary for it to succeed. These include opposing parties who are open with information and candid about their concerns, are sensitive to the other's needs and trust, and are willing to maintain flexibility.[53] Because these conditions seldom exist in organizations, it isn't surprising that negotiations often take on a win-at-any-cost dynamic.

There are ways to achieve more integrative outcomes. Individuals who bargain in teams reach more integrative agreements than those who bargain individually because more ideas are generated when more people are at the bargaining table. So, try bargaining in teams.[54] Another way to achieve higher joint-gain settlements is to put more issues on the table. The more negotiable issues introduced into a negotiation, the more opportunity for "logrolling," where issues are traded off because people have different preferences. This

integrative bargaining   *Negotiation that seeks one or more settlements that can create a win–win solution.*

"Communicating Well Is More Important in Cross-Cultural Negotiations"

This statement is true.

At no time in human history has the contact between members of different cultures been higher. Supply chains are increasingly multinational networks. Large organizations market their products and services in many nations. Global virtual teams work to make their organizations globally competitive. Most of these supplier/customer/manager/employee relationships include negotiating over something. Only the smallest and most local organization is insulated from the need to negotiate cross-culturally.

Because negotiation is an intense communication process, you might think that globalization has placed a premium on communicating well in negotiations. A recent study supported that view, but it also gave important details about what's necessary to communicate well in cross-cultural negotiations:

Clarity—did each party understand each other?
Responsiveness—did each party respond quickly and smoothly?
Comfort—did each party feel comfortable and trust the other?

The authors found that cross-cultural negotiations did have lower communication quality with respect to all three characteristics than did within-country negotiations. They also found that higher levels of communication quality contributed to success in cross-cultural negotiations—in terms of both the joint gains the parties achieved and their satisfaction with the agreements.

Because communication quality was measured at the end of the negotiation, this study can't determine cause-and-effect (it's possible that negotiation outcomes cause the parties to perceive communication more favorably). However, it does suggest that cross-cultural negotiations need not always result in lower outcomes—if the parties commit themselves to communicating clearly, responsively, and in such a way to make the other side comfortable.

Source: Based on L. A. Liu, C. H. Chua, and G. K. Stahl, "Quality of Communication Experience: Definition, Measurement, and Implications for Intercultural Negotiations," Journal of Applied Psychology 95, No. 3 (2010), pp. 469–487.

creates better outcomes for each side than if they negotiated each issue individually.[55] A final piece of advice is to focus on the underlying interests of both sides rather than on issues. In other words, it is better to concentrate on *why* an employee wants a raise rather than focusing just on the raise amount—some unseen potential for integrative outcomes may arise if both sides concentrate on what they really want rather than on the specific items they're bargaining over. Typically, it's easier to concentrate on underlying interests when parties to a negotiation are focused on broad, overall goals rather than on immediate outcomes of a specific decision.[56] Negotiations that occur when both parties are focused on learning and understanding the other side tend to also yield higher joint outcomes than those in which parties are more interested in their individual bottom-line outcomes.[57]

Finally, recognize that compromise may be your worst enemy in negotiating a win–win agreement. Compromising reduces the pressure to bargain integratively. After all, if you or your opponent caves in easily, it doesn't require anyone to be creative to reach a settlement. Thus, people end up settling for less than they could have obtained if they had been forced to consider the other party's interests, trade off issues, and be creative.[58] Think of the classic example in which two sisters are arguing over who gets an orange. Unknown to them, one sister wants the orange to drink the juice, whereas the other wants the orange peel to bake a cake. If one sister simply capitulates and gives the other sister the orange, they will not be forced to explore their reasons for wanting the orange, and thus they will never find the win–win solution: they could *each* have the orange because they want different parts of it!

The Negotiation Process

6 Apply the five steps of the negotiation process.

Exhibit 14-7 provides a simplified model of the negotiation process. It views negotiation as made up of five steps: (1) preparation and planning, (2) definition of ground rules, (3) clarification and justification, (4) bargaining and problem solving, and (5) closure and implementation.[59]

Preparation and Planning   Before you start negotiating, you need to do your homework. What's the nature of the conflict? What's the history leading up to this negotiation? Who's involved and what are their perceptions of the conflict? What do you want from the negotiation? What are *your* goals? If you're a supply manager at Dell Computer, for instance, and your goal is to get a significant cost reduction from your supplier of keyboards, make sure this goal stays paramount in your discussions and doesn't get overshadowed by other issues. It often helps to put your goals in writing and develop a range of outcomes—from "most hopeful" to "minimally acceptable"—to keep your attention focused.

You also want to assess what you think are the other party's goals. What are they likely to ask? How entrenched is their position likely to be? What intangible or hidden interests may be important to them? On what might they be willing to settle? When you can anticipate your opponent's position, you are better equipped to counter arguments with the facts and figures that support your position.

Relationships will change as a result of a negotiation, so that's another outcome to take into consideration. If you could "win" a negotiation but push the other side into resentment or animosity, it might be wiser to pursue a more compromising style. If preserving the relationship will make you seem weak and easily exploited, you may want to consider a more aggressive style. As an example of how the tone of a relationship set in negotiations matters, consider that people who feel good about the *process* of a job offer negotiation are more satisfied with their jobs and less likely to turn over a year later regardless of their actual *outcomes* from these negotiations.[60]

Once you've gathered your information, use it to develop a strategy. For example, expert chess players know ahead of time how they will respond to

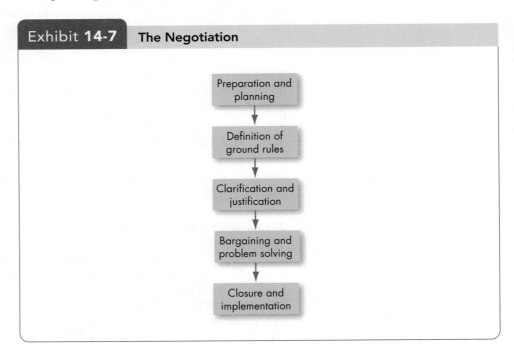

Exhibit 14-7   **The Negotiation**

- Preparation and planning
- Definition of ground rules
- Clarification and justification
- Bargaining and problem solving
- Closure and implementation

any given situation. As part of your strategy, you should determine your and the other side's **best a**lternative **to a n**egotiated **a**greement, or **BATNA**.[61] Your BATNA determines the lowest value acceptable to you for a negotiated agreement. Any offer you receive that is higher than your BATNA is better than an impasse. Conversely, you shouldn't expect success in your negotiation effort unless you're able to make the other side an offer it finds more attractive than its BATNA. If you go into your negotiation having a good idea of what the other party's BATNA is, even if you're not able to meet it you might be able to elicit a change. Think carefully about what the other side is willing to give up. People who underestimate their opponent's willingness to give on key issues before the negotiation even starts end up with lower outcomes from a negotiation.[62]

Definition of Ground Rules   Once you've done your planning and developed a strategy, you're ready to begin defining with the other party the ground rules and procedures of the negotiation itself. Who will do the negotiating? Where will it take place? What time constraints, if any, will apply? To what issues will negotiation be limited? Will you follow a specific procedure if an impasse is reached? During this phase, the parties will also exchange their initial proposals or demands.

Clarification and Justification   When you have exchanged initial positions, both you and the other party will explain, amplify, clarify, bolster, and justify your original demands. This step needn't be confrontational. Rather, it's an opportunity for educating and informing each other on the issues, why they are important, and how you arrived at your initial demands. Provide the other party with any documentation that helps support your position.

Bargaining and Problem Solving   The essence of the negotiation process is the actual give-and-take in trying to hash out an agreement. This is where both parties will undoubtedly need to make concessions.

Closure and Implementation   The final step in the negotiation process is formalizing the agreement you have worked out and developing any procedures necessary for implementing and monitoring it. For major negotiations—from labor–management negotiations to bargaining over lease terms to buying a piece of real estate to negotiating a job offer for a senior management position—this requires hammering out the specifics in a formal contract. For most cases, however, closure of the negotiation process is nothing more formal than a handshake.

Individual Differences in Negotiation Effectiveness

7 Show how individual differences influence negotiations.

Are some people better negotiators than others? The answer is more complex than you might think. Four factors influence how effectively individuals negotiate: personality, mood/emotions, culture, and gender.

Personality Traits in Negotiation   Can you predict an opponent's negotiating tactics if you know something about his or her personality? Because personality and negotiation outcomes are related but only weakly, the answer is, at best, "sort of." Negotiators who are agreeable or extraverted are not very successful in distributive bargaining. Why? Because extraverts are outgoing and friendly, they tend to share more information than they should. And agreeable people are more interested in finding ways to cooperate rather than to butt heads. These traits, while slightly helpful in integrative negotiations, are liabilities when interests are opposed. So the best distributive bargainer appears to be a disagreeable introvert—someone more interested in his or her own outcomes than in pleasing the other party and having a pleasant social exchange. People who are highly interested in having positive relationships with other people, and who are not very concerned about their own outcomes, are especially poor negotiators. These people tend to be very anxious about disagreements and plan to give in quickly to avoid unpleasant conflicts even before negotiations start.[63]

Research also suggests intelligence predicts negotiation effectiveness, but, as with personality, the effects aren't especially strong.[64] In a sense, these weak links are good news because they mean you're not severely disadvantaged, even if you're an agreeable extrovert, when it's time to negotiate. We all can learn to be better negotiators. In fact, people who think so are more likely to do well in negotiations because they persist in their efforts even in the face of temporary setbacks.[65]

Moods/Emotions in Negotiation   Do moods and emotions influence negotiation? They do, but the way they do appears to depend on the type of negotiation. In distributive negotiations, it appears that negotiators in a position of power or equal status who show anger negotiate better outcomes because their anger induces concessions from their opponents. Angry negotiators also feel more focused and assertive in striking a bargain. This appears to hold true even when the negotiators are instructed to show anger despite not being truly angry. On the other hand, for those in a less powerful position, displaying anger leads to worse outcomes. Thus, if you're a boss negotiating with a peer or a subordinate, displaying anger may help you, but if you're an employee negotiating with a boss, it might hurt you.[66] So what happens when two parties have to negotiate and one has shown anger in the past? Does the other try to get revenge and act extra tough, or does this party have some residual fear that the angry negotiator might get angry again? Evidence suggests that being angry has a spillover effect, such that angry negotiators are perceived as "tough" when the parties meet a second time, which leads negotiation partners to give up more concessions again.[67]

Anxiety also appears to have an impact on negotiation. For example, one study found that individuals who experienced more anxiety about a negotiation used more deceptions in dealing with others.[68] Another study found that anxious negotiators expect lower outcomes from negotiations, respond to offers more quickly, and exit the bargaining process more quickly, which leads them to obtain worse outcomes.[69]

All these findings regarding emotions have related to distributive bargains. In integrative negotiations, in contrast, positive moods and emotions appear to lead to more integrative agreements (higher levels of joint gain). This may happen because, as we noted in Chapter 4, positive mood is related to creativity.[70]

Culture in Negotiations   One study compared U.S. and Japanese negotiators and found the generally conflict-avoidant Japanese negotiators tended to communicate indirectly and adapt their behaviors to the situation. A follow-up study showed that, whereas early offers by U.S. managers led to the anchoring effect we noted when discussing distributive negotiation, for Japanese negotiators,

BATNA   *The best alternative to a negotiated agreement; the least the individual should accept.*

early offers led to more information sharing and better integrative outcomes.[71] In another study, managers with high levels of economic power from Hong Kong, which is a high power-distance country, were more cooperative in negotiations over a shared resource than German and U.S. managers, who were lower in power distance.[72] This suggests that in high power-distance countries, those in positions of power might exercise more restraint.

Another study looked at differences between U.S. and Indian negotiators.[73] Indian respondents reported having less trust in their negotiation counterparts than did U.S. respondents. These lower levels of trust were associated with lower discovery of common interests between parties, which occurred because Indian negotiators were less willing to disclose and solicit information. In both cultures, use of question-and-answer methods of negotiation were associated with superior negotiation outcomes, so although there are some cultural differences in negotiation styles, it appears that some negotiation tactics yield superior outcomes across cultures.

Gender Differences in Negotiations   Do men and women negotiate differently? And does gender affect negotiation outcomes? The answer to the first question appears to be no.[74] The answer to the second is a qualified yes.[75]

A popular stereotype is that women are more cooperative and pleasant in negotiations than are men. The evidence doesn't support this belief. However, men have been found to negotiate better outcomes than women, although the difference is relatively small. It's been postulated that men and women place unequal values on outcomes. "It is possible that a few hundred dollars more in salary or the corner office is less important to women than forming and maintaining an interpersonal relationship."[76]

Because women are expected to be "nice" and men "tough," research shows women are penalized when they initiate negotiations.[77] What's more, when women and men actually do conform to these stereotypes—women act "nice" and men "tough"—it becomes a self-fulfilling prophecy, reinforcing the stereotypical gender differences between male and female negotiators.[78] Thus, one of the reasons negotiations favor men is that women are "damned if they do, damned if they don't." Negotiate tough and they are penalized for violating a gender stereotype. Negotiate nice and it only reinforces and lets others take advantage of the stereotype.

In this photo, Japanese labor union leader Hidekazu Kitagawa (right) presents the group's annual wage and benefits demands to Ikuo Mori, president of Fuji Heavy Industries, Ltd., the manufacturer of Subaru automobiles. Studies on how negotiating styles vary across national cultures reveal that the generally conflict-avoidant Japanese negotiators tend to communicate indirectly and use a more polite conversational style. Their style of interaction is less aggressive than other cultures, favoring frequent silent periods and more positive recommendations and commitments and de-emphasizing the use of threats and commands.

*Source: */Kyodo/Newscom.*

glOBalization!

Anger and Conflict Across Cultures

We've discussed anger as a negotiating tactic, but do different cultures view the expression of anger differently? Evidence suggest they do, meaning the use of anger is not a consistently wise negotiation strategy.

One study explicitly compared how U.S. and Chinese negotiators react to an angry counterpart. Chinese negotiators increased their use of distributive negotiating tactics, whereas U.S. negotiators decreased their use of these tactics. That is, Chinese negotiators

began to drive a harder bargain once they saw that their negotiation partner was becoming angry, whereas U.S. negotiators actually capitulate somewhat in the face of angry demands.

Why do East Asian negotiators respond more negatively to angry negotiators? In a second study, researchers found that European Americans tended to give larger concessions when faced with an angry negotiation partner, whereas Asian negotiators again gave smaller ones. This difference may occur because

individuals from East Asian cultures feel that using anger to get your way in a negotiation is not a legitimate tactic, so they respond by refusing to cooperate when their opponents become upset.

Sources: Based on M. Liu, "The Intrapersonal and Interpersonal Effects of Anger on Negotiation Strategies: A Cross-Cultural Investigation," *Human Communication Research* 35, no. 1 (2009), pp. 148–169; and H. Adam, A. Shirako, and W. W. Maddux, "Cultural Variance in the Interpersonal Effects of Anger in Negotiations," *Psychological Science* 21, no. 6 (2010), pp. 882–889.

SELF-ASSESSMENT LIBRARY

What's My Negotiating Style?

In the Self-Assessment Library (available on CD and online), take assessment II.C.6 (What's My Negotiating Style?).

Evidence also suggests women's own attitudes and behaviors hurt them in negotiations. Managerial women demonstrate less confidence than men in anticipation of negotiating and are less satisfied with their performance afterward, even when their performance and the outcomes they achieve are similar to those for men.[79] Women are also less likely than men to see an ambiguous situation as an opportunity for negotiation. It appears that women may unduly penalize themselves by failing to engage in negotiations that would be in their best interests. Some research suggests that women are less aggressive in negotiations because they are worried about backlash from others. There is an interesting qualifier to this result: women are more likely to engage in assertive negotiation when they are bargaining on behalf of someone else than when they are bargaining on their own behalf.[80]

Third-Party Negotiations

8 Assess the roles and functions of third-party negotiations.

To this point, we've discussed bargaining in terms of direct negotiations. Occasionally, however, individuals or group representatives reach a stalemate and are unable to resolve their differences through direct negotiations. In such cases, they may turn to a third party to help them find a solution. There are three basic third-party roles: mediator, arbitrator, and conciliator.

A **mediator** is a neutral third party who facilitates a negotiated solution by using reasoning and persuasion, suggesting alternatives, and the like.

---

mediator *A neutral third party who facilitates a negotiated solution by using reasoning, persuasion, and suggestions for alternatives.*

Using Empathy to Negotiate More Ethically

You may have noticed that much of our advice for negotiating effectively depends on understanding the perspective and goals of the person with whom you are negotiating. Preparing checklists of your negotiation partner's interests, likely tactics, and BATNA have all been shown to improve negotiation outcomes. Can these steps make you a more ethical negotiator as well? Studies suggest that it might.

Researchers asked respondents to indicate how much they tended to think about other people's feelings and emotions and to describe the types of tactics they engaged in during a negotiation exercise. More empathetic individuals consistently engaged in fewer unethical negotiation behaviors like making false promises and manipulating information, and

emotions. To put this in terms familiar to you from personality research, it appears that individuals who are higher in agreeableness will be more ethical negotiators.

When considering how to improve your ethical negotiation behavior, follow these guidelines:

1. Try to understand your negotiation partner's perspective, not just by understanding cognitively what the other person wants, but by empathizing with the emotional reaction he or she will have to the possible outcomes.
2. Be aware of your own emotions, because many moral reactions are fundamentally emotional. One study found that engaging in unethical negotiation strategies increased feelings of guilt, so

by extension, feeling guilty in a negotiation may mean you are engaging in behavior you'll regret later.
3. Beware of empathizing so much that you work against your own interests. Just because you try to understand the motives and emotional reactions of the other side does not mean you have to assume the other person is going to be honest and fair in return. So be on guard.

Sources: Based on T. R. Cohen, "Moral Emotions and Unethical Bargaining: The Differential Effects of Empathy and Perspective Taking in Deterring Deceitful Negotiation," *Journal of Business Ethics* 94, no. 4 (2010), pp. 569–579; and R. Volkema, D. Fleck, and A. Hofmeister, "Predicting Competitive-Unethical Negotiating Behavior and Its Consequences," *Negotiation Journal* 26, no. 3 (2010), pp. 263–286.

Mediators are widely used in labor–management negotiations and in civil court disputes. Their overall effectiveness is fairly impressive. The settlement rate is approximately 60 percent, with negotiator satisfaction at about 75 percent. But the situation is the key to whether mediation will succeed; the conflicting parties must be motivated to bargain and resolve their conflict. In addition, conflict intensity can't be too high; mediation is most effective under moderate levels of conflict. Finally, perceptions of the mediator are important; to be effective, the mediator must be perceived as neutral and noncoercive.

An **arbitrator** is a third party with the authority to dictate an agreement. Arbitration can be voluntary (requested by the parties) or compulsory (forced on the parties by law or contract). The big plus of arbitration over mediation is that it always results in a settlement. Whether there is a negative side depends on how heavy-handed the arbitrator appears. If one party is left feeling overwhelmingly defeated, that party is certain to be dissatisfied and the conflict may resurface at a later time.

A **conciliator** is a trusted third party who provides an informal communication link between the negotiator and the opponent. This role was made famous by Robert Duval in the first *Godfather* film. As Don Corleone's adopted son and a lawyer by training, Duval acted as an intermediary between the Corleones and the other Mafioso families. Comparing conciliation to mediation in terms of effectiveness has proven difficult because the two overlap a great deal. In practice, conciliators typically act as more than mere communication conduits. They also engage in fact-finding, interpret messages, and persuade disputants to develop agreements.

MyManagementLab

Now that you have finished this chapter, go back to **www.pearsonglobaleditions.com/ mymanagementlab** to continue practicing and applying the concepts you've learned.

Summary and Implications for Managers

While many people assume conflict lowers group and organizational performance, this assumption is frequently incorrect. Conflict can be either constructive or destructive to the functioning of a group or unit. As shown in Exhibit 14-8, levels of conflict can be either too high or too low to be constructive. Either extreme hinders performance. An optimal level is one that prevents stagnation, stimulates creativity, allows tensions to be released, and initiates the seeds of change without being disruptive or preventing coordination of activities.

What advice can we give managers faced with excessive conflict and the need to reduce it? Don't assume one conflict-handling strategy will always be best! Select a strategy appropriate for the situation. Here are some guidelines:[81]

- Use *competition* when quick decisive action is needed (in emergencies), when issues are important, when unpopular actions need to be implemented (in cost cutting, enforcement of unpopular rules, discipline), when the issue is vital to the organization's welfare and you know you're right, and when others are taking advantage of noncompetitive behavior.
- Use *collaboration* to find an integrative solution when both sets of concerns are too important to be compromised, when your objective is to learn, when you want to merge insights from people with different perspectives or gain commitment by incorporating concerns into a consensus, and when you need to work through feelings that have interfered with a relationship.
- Use *avoidance* when an issue is trivial or symptomatic of other issues, when more important issues are pressing, when you perceive no chance of satisfying your concerns, when potential disruption outweighs the benefits of resolution, when people need to cool down and regain perspective, when gathering information supersedes immediate decision, and when others can resolve the conflict more effectively.
- Use *accommodation* when you find you're wrong, when you need to learn or show reasonableness, when you should allow a better position to be heard, when issues are more important to others than to yourself, when you want to satisfy others and maintain cooperation, when you can build social credits for later issues, when you are outmatched and losing (to minimize loss), when harmony and stability are especially important, and when employees can develop by learning from mistakes.

arbitrator   *A third party to a negotiation who has the authority to dictate an agreement.*

conciliator   *A trusted third party who provides an informal communication link between the negotiator and the opponent.*

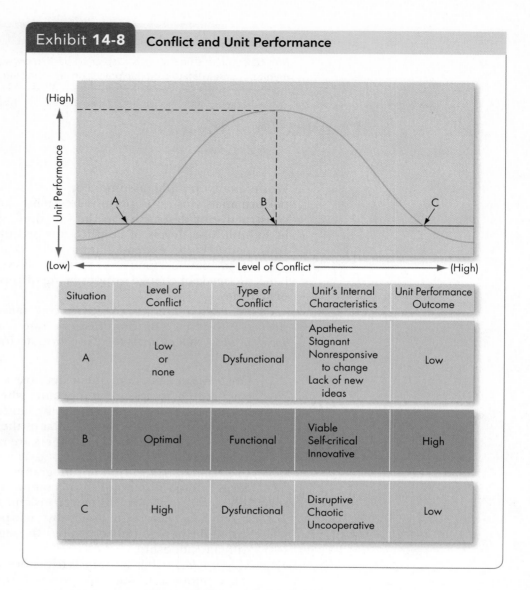

Exhibit 14-8   Conflict and Unit Performance

Situation	Level of Conflict	Type of Conflict	Unit's Internal Characteristics	Unit Performance Outcome
A	Low or none	Dysfunctional	Apathetic Stagnant Nonresponsive to change Lack of new ideas	Low
B	Optimal	Functional	Viable Self-critical Innovative	High
C	High	Dysfunctional	Disruptive Chaotic Uncooperative	Low

- Use *compromise* when goals are important but not worth the effort of potential disruption of more assertive approaches, when opponents with equal power are committed to mutually exclusive goals, when you seek temporary settlements to complex issues, when you need expedient solutions under time pressure, and as a backup when collaboration or competition is unsuccessful.
- Distributive bargaining can resolve disputes, but it often reduces the satisfaction of one or more negotiators because it is confrontational and focused on the short term. Integrative bargaining, in contrast, tends to provide outcomes that satisfy all parties and build lasting relationships.
- Make sure you set aggressive negotiating goals and try to find creative ways to achieve the objectives of both parties, especially when you value the long-term relationship with the other party. That doesn't mean sacrificing your self-interest; rather, it means trying to find creative solutions that give both parties what they really want.

Player–Owner Disputes Are Unnecessary

POINT

It seems there's always a major sports league on the verge of a strike. In the past few years, Major League Baseball (MLB), the National Basketball Association (NBA), the National Hockey League (NHL), and the National Football League (NFL) have had major labor disputes. When greed meets greed, guess who loses? Yes, the fans.

A few years ago, an entire NHL season was canceled due to a labor dispute (NHL owners staged a work stoppage or "lockout" that lasted 311 days). The main issue? How to divide the more than $2 billion in revenues generated by the league. The average NHL player earns an annual salary of $1.35 million, and that doesn't include income from endorsements, appearances, merchandise, and so on. The owners aren't hurting, either. Most are millionaires many times over. Los Angeles Kings owner Philip Anschutz is reported to have a net worth of $7 billion.

The NFL is a variation on the same theme. During the 2011 lockout, during which the player's union temporarily disbanded so it could claim it wasn't a union, the owners and players fought over how to divide $9 billion in revenues. The average player makes $1.9 million a year. The average net worth of an NFL owner is $1.4 billion. And each side squabbles over getting more.

Yes, players get injured. Some lives are permanently damaged. But do you think being a construction worker, farmer, police officer, fisher, or loading-dock worker is a piece of cake? How often do these groups strike? They earn far less than professional athletes (the average fisher earns 2 percent of the average salary of an NHL player!), but they do work year-round, which is much more dangerous.

Meanwhile, ticket prices for sports events continue to soar. In the past 20 years, major league ticket prices have increased at double the rate of inflation. But what are the owners and players focused on? How to line their pockets even further. Was it any surprise when Minnesota Vikings running back Adrian Peterson, fuming over the dispute, called NFL players "modern-day slaves"? (He earns more than $10 million a year.)

Billionaires feuding with millionaires. These are unseemly—and unnecessary—conflicts.

COUNTERPOINT

Sports teams are an easy target.

It's true that most major league players are well rewarded for their exceptional talents and the risks they take. It's also true that owners who are able to invest in teams are wealthy—investors usually are. But do the resources on each side mean their conflict should just melt away? The reason these disputes happen is that real interests and real money is at stake.

The operation of major league sports is a complex business. The owners and players can be caricatured, but if you delve a bit deeper, you can see that their disputes are fairly natural. Let's look at hockey. NHL clubs spent 76 percent of their gross revenues on players' salaries and collectively lost $273 million the year before the lockout. The NHL tried to convince players to accept a wage structure that linked player salaries to league revenues, guaranteeing the clubs "cost certainty." Understandably, the players' union resisted, arguing that "cost certainty" was nothing more than another term for a salary cap. They argued in favor of retaining the "market-based" system in which players individually negotiated contracts with teams, and teams had complete control over how much it spent on players.

The NFL lockout hinged on a number of issues that divided the owners and players, including the owners' desire for an 18-game season (with no increase in player compensation), the way costs are considered in revenue sharing, and pensions for retired players. These aren't trivial issues, and neither are they entirely different from issues that arise in other labor–management disputes.

Finally, it's easy to argue that major league sports have an unusual number of labor disputes, but that's not necessarily accurate. Did you hear about the 2011 Saskatchewan Teachers Federation strike? Sports interest us (which is why there's so much money involved), and thus we're more likely to notice major league sports labor disputes, but that doesn't prove they're more common.

Yes, owners are rich and players make a lot of money. We're the ones who helped them do it, and we shouldn't fault them for wanting more of what we gave them.

Sources: A. Benoit, "2010 Jets: What the Film Revealed," *The New York Times* (April 14, 2011), downloaded on July 1, 2011, from http://fifthdown.blogs.nytimes.com/; D. Farrar, "Adrian Peterson Expresses Frustration on Labor Issues," *Yahoo! Sports* (March 15, 2011), downloaded June 30, 2011, from http://sports.yahoo.com/nfl/; and J. Z. Klein and S. Hackel, "SLAP SHOT; A Labor Dispute Still Shapes the N.H.L.," *The New York Times* (January 3, 2010), downloaded July 2, 2011, from http://query.nytimes.com/.

QUESTIONS FOR REVIEW

1 What is conflict?

2 What are the differences among the traditional, interactionist, and managed-conflict views of conflict?

3 What are the steps of the conflict process?

4 What is negotiation?

5 What are the differences between distributive and integrative bargaining?

6 What are the five steps in the negotiation process?

7 How do the individual differences of personality and gender influence negotiations?

8 What are the roles and functions of third-party negotiations?

EXPERIENTIAL EXERCISE A Negotiation Role-Play

This role-play is designed to help you develop your negotiating skills. The class is to break into pairs. One person will play the role of Alex, the department supervisor. The other person will play C. J., Alex's boss. Both participants should read "The Situation," "The Negotiation," and then their role only.

The Situation

Alex and C. J. work for Nike in Beaverton, Oregon. Alex supervises a research laboratory. C. J. is the manager of research and development. Alex and C. J. are former college runners who have worked for Nike for more than 6 years. C. J. has been Alex's boss for 2 years. One of Alex's employees has greatly impressed Alex. This employee is Lisa Roland. Lisa was hired 11 months ago. She is 24 years old and holds a master's degree in mechanical engineering. Her entry-level salary was $57,500 per year. Alex told her that, in accordance with corporation policy, she would receive an initial performance evaluation at 6 months and a comprehensive review after 1 year. Based on her performance record, Lisa was told she could expect a salary adjustment at the time of the 1-year evaluation.

Alex's evaluation of Lisa after 6 months was very positive. Alex commented on the long hours Lisa was putting in, her cooperative spirit, the fact that others in the lab enjoyed working with her, and that she was making an immediate positive impact on the project assigned to her. Now that Lisa's first anniversary is coming up, Alex has again reviewed Lisa's performance. Alex thinks Lisa may be the best new person the R&D group has ever hired. After only a year, Alex has ranked Lisa as the number-3 performer in a department of 11.

Salaries in the department vary greatly. Alex, for instance, has a base salary of $86,000, plus eligibility for a bonus that might add another $7,000 to $12,000 a year. The salary range of the 11 department members is $48,400 to $76,350. The individual with the lowest salary is a recent hire with a bachelor's degree in physics. The two people whom Alex has rated above Lisa earn base salaries of $69,200 and $76,350. They're both 27 years old and have been at Nike for 3 and 4 years, respectively. The median salary in Alex's department is $64,960.

Alex's Role

You want to give Lisa a big raise. Although she's young, she has proven to be an excellent addition to the department. You don't want to lose her. More importantly, she knows in general what other people in the department are earning, and she thinks she's underpaid. The company typically gives 1-year raises of 5 percent, although 10 percent is not unusual, and 20 to 30 percent increases have been approved on occasion. You'd like to get Lisa as large an increase as C. J. will approve.

C. J.'s Role

All your supervisors typically try to squeeze you for as much money as they can for their people. You understand this because you did the same thing when you were a supervisor, but your boss wants to keep a lid on costs. He wants you to keep raises for recent hires generally in the 5 to 8 percent range. In fact, he's sent a memo to all managers and supervisors saying this. He also said that managers will be evaluated on their ability to maintain budgetary control. However, your boss is also concerned with equity and paying people what they're worth. You feel assured that he will support any salary recommendation you make, as long as it can be justified. Your goal, consistent with cost reduction, is to keep salary increases as low as possible.

The Negotiation

Alex has a meeting scheduled with C. J. to discuss Lisa's performance review and salary adjustment. Take a couple of minutes to think through the facts in this exercise and to prepare a strategy. Then take up to 15 minutes to conduct your negotiation. When your negotiation is complete, the class will compare the various strategies used and pair outcomes.

ETHICAL DILEMMA The Lowball Applicant

Consider this real-life scenario:

A freelance project manager, I was hired to find someone to fill a highly specialized job. When I asked an impressive candidate her pay rate, she named a figure far below the industry standard. I could have rejected her for this lack of sophistication or exploited her low bid. Instead, I coached her to a figure nearly twice her bid yet about 30 percent below my client's budget. I did not inform my client about the discrepancy, and she was hired at the rate I recommended. Did I do wrong by either party?

—*NAME WITHHELD, New York*

Questions

1. In coaching the applicant to request a higher salary, did the project manager work against the interests of the client organization by which he or she is employed? Why or why not?

2. Could the manager have avoided this dilemma by proposing a salary figure that was the industry norm? Would that be in the interests of the client organization?

3. If you were in the project manager's situation, would you have handled this negotiation differently? If so, how so?

Source: R. Cohen, "The Ethicist," *New York Times Magazine* (July 18, 2010), p. 19.

CASE INCIDENT 1 Choosing Your Battles

While much of this chapter has discussed methods for achieving harmonious relationships and getting out of conflicts, it's also important to remember there are situations in which too little conflict can be a problem. As we noted, in creative problem-solving teams, some level of task conflict early in the process of formulating a solution can be an important stimulus to innovation.

However, the conditions must be right for productive conflict. In particular, individuals must feel psychologically safe in bringing up issues for discussion. If people fear that what they say is going to be held against them, they may be reluctant to speak up or rock the boat. Experts suggest that effective conflicts have three key characteristics: they should (1) speak to what is possible, (2) be compelling, and (3) involve uncertainty.

So how should a manager "pick a fight?" First, ensure that the stakes are sufficient to actually warrant a disruption. Second, focus on the future, and on how to resolve the conflict rather than on whom to blame. Third, tie the conflict to fundamental values. Rather than concentrating on winning or losing, encourage both parties to see how successfully exploring and resolving the conflict will lead to optimal outcomes for all. If managed successfully, some degree of open disagreement can be an important way for companies to manage simmering and potentially destructive conflicts.

Do these principles work in real organizations? The answer is yes. Dropping its old ways of handling scheduling and logistics created a great deal of conflict at Burlington Northern Santa Fe railroad, but applying these principles to managing the conflict helped the railroad adopt a more sophisticated system and recover its competitive position in the transportation industry. Doug Conant, CEO of Campbell Soup, increased functional conflicts in his organization by emphasizing a higher purpose to the organization's efforts rather than focusing on whose side was winning a conflict. Thus, a dysfunctional conflict environment changed dramatically and the organization was able to move from one of the world's worst-performing food companies to one that was recognized as a top performer by both the Dow Jones Sustainability Index and *Fortune* 500 data on employee morale.

Questions

1. How would you ensure sufficient discussion of contentious issues in a work group? How can managers bring unspoken conflicts into the open without making them worse?

2. How can negotiators utilize conflict management strategies to their advantage so that differences in interests lead not to dysfunctional conflicts but rather to positive integrative solutions?

3. Can you think of situations in your own life in which silence has worsened a conflict between parties? What might have been done differently to ensure that open communication facilitated collaboration instead?

Sources: Based on S. A. Joni and D. Beyer, "How to Pick a Good Fight," *Harvard Business Review* (December 2009), pp. 48–57; and B. H. Bradley, B. E. Postlewaite, A. C. Klotz, M. R. Hamdani, and K. G. Brown., "Reaping the Benefits of Task Conflict in Teams: The Critical Role of Team Psychological Safety Climate," *Journal of Applied Psychology*, Advance publication (July 4, 2011), doi: 10.1037/a0024200.

CASE INCIDENT 2 Mediation: Master Solution to Employment Disputes?

We typically think of mediation as the province of marital counselors and labor strife. More organizations use mediation to resolve conflicts than you might think. In fact, in the United States, Canada, Great Britain, Ireland, and India, mediation is growing rapidly as a means to settle employment disputes. We introduced mediation in this chapter; let's look at some examples when it has succeeded and when it has failed.

Mediation has often succeeded:

- Many states have experimented with mediation as an alternative to traditional trials to resolve legal disputes. The state of Maryland found in a pilot program that 58 percent of appellate cases could be resolved through mediation and that mediation was both cheaper and faster than a traditional courtroom resolution.

- The Equal Employment Opportunity Commission (EEOC), the federal agency that oversees employment discrimination complaints in the United States, uses mediation extensively. Safeway, the third-largest U.S. supermarket chain, uses the EEOC to mediate numerous employment disputes. Says Donna Gwin, Safeway's Director of Human Resources, "Through mediation, we have had the opportunity to proactively resolve issues and avoid potential charges in the future. We have seen the number of charges filed with EEOC against us actually decline. We believe that our participating in mediation and listening to employees' concerns has contributed to that decline."

However, mediation doesn't always work:

- In 2008, the Screen Actors Guild (SAG) and the Alliance of Motion Picture and Television Producers (AMPTP), representing some 350 studios and production companies, engaged in prolonged negotiations over a new labor agreement. The negotiations failed, and the parties agreed to mediation. However, mediation also failed, and in response SAG asked its members to approve a strike authorization.

- When David Kuchinsky, the former driver for New York Knicks center Eddy Curry, sued Curry for sexual harassment, discrimination, and failure to pay $93,000 in wages and reimbursements, the parties agreed to mediation. However, after the sides failed to reach a settlement during mediation, Kuchinsky reinstated his lawsuit, and Curry filed a $50,000 countersuit.

Questions

1. Drawing from these examples, what factors do you think differentiate occasions when mediation was successful and when it failed?

2. One successful mediator, Boston's Paul Finn, argues that if the disputing parties are seeking justice, "It's best to go somewhere else." Why do you think he says that?

3. Do you think a mediator should find out *why* the parties want what they want? Why or why not?

4. The EEOC reports that whereas 85 percent of employees agree to mediate their charges, employers agree to mediate only 30 percent of the time. Why do you think this disparity exists?

Sources: Based on M. Kapko, "Actors Union Seeks Strike Vote After Federal Mediation Fails," *Forbes* (November 23, 2008), www.forbes.com; K. Tyler, "Mediating a Better Outcome," *HR Magazine* (November 2007), pp. 63–66; K. O'Brien, "The Closer," *Boston Globe* (April 12, 2009), www.boston.com; and S. Lash, "Appealing for Appellate Mediation in Maryland," *The Daily Record* (July 4, 2011), www.thedailyrecord.com.

ENDNOTES

1. See, for instance, D. Tjosvold, "Defining Conflict and Making Choices About Its Management: Lighting the Dark Side of Organizational Life," *International Journal of Conflict Management* 17, no. 2 (2006), pp. 87–95; and M. A. Korsgaard, S. S. Jeong, D. M. Mahony, and A. H. Pitariu, "A Multilevel View of Intragroup Conflict," *Journal of Management* 34, no. 6 (2008), pp. 1222–1252.

2. K. W. Thomas, "Conflict and Negotiation Processes in Organizations," in M. D. Dunnette and L. M. Hough (eds.), *Handbook of Industrial and Organizational Psychology*, 2nd ed.,

vol. 3 (Palo Alto, CA: Consulting Psychologists Press, 1992), pp. 651–717.

3. For a comprehensive review of the interactionist approach, see C. De Dreu and E. Van de Vliert (eds.), *Using Conflict in Organizations* (London: Sage, 1997).

4. See K. A. Jehn, "A Multimethod Examination of the Benefits and Detriments of Intragroup Conflict," *Administrative Science Quarterly* (June 1995), pp. 256–282; K. A. Jehn, "A Qualitative Analysis of Conflict Types and Dimensions in Organizational Groups," *Administrative Science Quarterly* (September 1997), pp. 530–557; K. A. Jehn and E. A. Mannix, "The Dynamic Nature of Conflict: A Longitudinal Study of Intragroup

Conflict and Group Performance," *Academy of Management Journal* (April 2001), pp. 238–251; and C. K. W. De Dreu and L. R. Weingart, "Task Versus Relationship Conflict, Team Performance, and Team Member Satisfaction: A Meta-Analysis," *Journal of Applied Psychology* (August 2003), pp. 741–749.

5. J. Yang and K. W. Mossholder, "Decoupling Task and Relationship Conflict: The Role of Intragroup Emotional Processing," *Journal of Organizational Behavior* 25, no. 5 (August 2004), pp. 589–605; and N. Gamero, V. González-Romá, and J. M. Peiró, "The Influence of Intra-Team Conflict on Work Teams' Affective Climate: A Longitudinal Study," *Journal of Occupational and Organizational Psychology* 81, no. 1 (2008), pp. 47–69.

6. "Survey Shows Managers Have Their Hands Full Resolving Staff Personality Conflicts," *IPMA-HR Bulletin* (November 3, 2006).

7. De Dreu and Weingart, "Task Versus Relationship Conflict, Team Performance, and Team Member Satisfaction."

8. J. Farh, C. Lee, and C. I. C. Farh, "Task Conflict and Team Creativity: A Question of How Much and When," *Journal of Applied Psychology* 95, no. 6 (2010), pp. 1173–1180.

9. C. K.W. De Dreu and M. A. West, "Minority Dissent and Team Innovation: The Importance of Participation in Decision Making," *Journal of Applied Psychology* 86, no. 6 (2001), pp. 1191–1201.

10. B. H. Bradley, B. E. Postlewaite, A. C. Klotz, M. R. Hamdani, and K. G. Brown, "Reaping the Benefits of Task Conflict in Teams: The Critical Role of Team Psychological Safety Climate," *Journal of Applied Psychology,* Advance publication, (July 4, 2011), doi: 10.1037/a0024200.

11. C. K. W. De Dreu, "The Virtue and Vice of Workplace Conflict: Food for (Pessimistic) Thought," *Journal of Organizational Behavior* 29, no. 1 (2008), pp. 5–18.

12. R. S. Peterson and K. J. Behfar, "The Dynamic Relationship Between Performance Feedback, Trust, and Conflict in Groups: A Longitudinal Study," *Organizational Behavior and Human Decision Process* 92, no. 1–2 (2003), pp. 102–112.

13. J. D. Shaw, J. Zhu, M. K. Duffy, K. L. Scott, H. Shih, and E. Susanto, "A Contingency Model of Conflict and Team Effectiveness," *Journal of Applied Psychology* 96, no. 2 (2011), pp. 391–400.

14. L. M. Penny and P. E. Spector, "Job Stress, Incivility, and Counterproductive Work Behavior: The Moderating Role of Negative Affectivity," *Journal of Organizational Behavior* 26, no. 7 (2005), pp. 777–796.

15. K. A. Jehn, L. Greer, S. Levine, and G. Szulanski, "The Effects of Conflict Types, Dimensions, and Emergent States on Group Outcomes," *Group Decision and Negotiation* 17, no. 6 (2008), pp. 465–495.

16. D. A. Shapiro, "Relational Identity Theory: A Systematic Approach for Transforming the Emotional Dimension of Conflict," *American Psychologist* (October 2010), pp. 634–645.

17. R. S. Peterson and K. J. Behfar, "The Dynamic Relationship Between Performance Feedback, Trust, and Conflict in Groups: A Longitudinal Study," *Organizational Behavior & Human Decision Processes* (September–November 2003), pp. 102–112.

18. T. M. Glomb and H. Liao, "Interpersonal Aggression in Work Groups: Social Influence, Reciprocal, and Individual Effects," *Academy of Management Journal* 46, no. 4 (2003), pp. 486–496; and V. Venkataramani and R. S. Dalal, "Who Helps and Harms Whom? Relational Aspects of Interpersonal Helping and Harming in Organizations," *Journal of Applied Psychology* 92, no. 4 (2007), pp. 952–966.

19. R. Friedman, C. Anderson, J. Brett, M. Olekalns, N. Goates, and C. C. Lisco, "The Positive and Negative Effects of Anger on Dispute Resolution: Evidence from Electronically Mediated Disputes," *Journal of Applied Psychology* (April 2004), pp. 369–376.

20. L. R. Pondy, "Organizational Conflict: Concepts and Models," *Administrative Science Quarterly* (September 1967), p. 302.

21. See, for instance, R. L. Pinkley, "Dimensions of Conflict Frame: Disputant Interpretations of Conflict," *Journal of Applied Psychology* (April 1990), pp. 117–126; and R. L. Pinkley and G. B. Northcraft, "Conflict Frames of Reference: Implications for Dispute Processes and Outcomes," *Academy of Management Journal* (February 1994), pp. 193–205.

22. A. M. Isen, A. A. Labroo, and P. Durlach, "An Influence of Product and Brand Name on Positive Affect: Implicit and Explicit Measures," *Motivation & Emotion* (March 2004), pp. 43–63.

23. Ibid.

24. P. J. D. Carnevale and A. M. Isen, "The Influence of Positive Affect and Visual Access on the Discovery of Integrative Solutions in Bilateral Negotiations," *Organizational Behavior and Human Decision Processes* (February 1986), pp. 1–13.

25. Thomas, "Conflict and Negotiation Processes in Organizations."

26. Ibid.

27. See R. A. Baron, "Personality and Organizational Conflict: Effects of the Type A Behavior Pattern and Self-monitoring," *Organizational Behavior and Human Decision Processes* (October 1989), pp. 281–296; R. J. Volkema and T. J. Bergmann, "Conflict Styles as Indicators of Behavioral Patterns in Interpersonal Conflicts," *Journal of Social Psychology* (February 1995), pp. 5–15; and J. A. Rhoades, J. Arnold, and C. Jay, "The Role of Affective Traits and Affective States in Disputants' Motivation and Behavior During Episodes of Organizational Conflict," *Journal of Organizational Behavior* (May 2001), pp. 329–345.

28. Thomas, "Conflict and Negotiation Processes in Organizations."

29. See, for instance, K. A. Jehn, "Enhancing Effectiveness: An Investigation of Advantages and Disadvantages of Value-Based Intragroup Conflict," *International Journal of Conflict Management* (July 1994), pp. 223–238; R. L. Priem, D. A. Harrison, and N. K. Muir, "Structured Conflict and Consensus Outcomes in Group Decision Making," *Journal of Management* 21, no. 4 (1995), pp. 691–710; and K. A. Jehn and E. A. Mannix, "The Dynamic Nature of Conflict: A Longitudinal Study of Intragroup Conflict and Group Performance," *Academy of Management Journal* (April 2001), pp. 238–251.

30. B. A. Nijstad and S. C. Kaps, "Taking the Easy Way Out: Preference Diversity, Decision Strategies, and Decision Refusal in Groups," *Journal of Personality and Social Psychology* 94, no. 5 (2008), pp. 860–870.

31. R. L. Hoffman, "Homogeneity of Member Personality and Its Effect on Group Problem-Solving," *Journal of Abnormal and Social Psychology* (January 1959), pp. 27–32; R. L. Hoffman and N. R. F. Maier, "Quality and Acceptance of Problem Solutions by Members of Homogeneous and Heterogeneous Groups," *Journal of Abnormal and Social Psychology* (March 1961), pp. 401–407; and P. Pitcher and A. D. Smith, "Top Management Team Heterogeneity: Personality, Power, and Proxies," *Organization Science* (January–February 2001), pp. 1–18.

32. M. E. Zellmer-Bruhn, M. M. Maloney, A. D. Bhappu, and R. Salvador, "When and How Do Differences Matter? An Exploration of Perceived Similarity in Teams," *Organizational Behavior and Human Decision Processes* 107, no. 1 (2008), pp. 41–59.

33. See T. H. Cox, S. A. Lobel, and P. L. McLeod, "Effects of Ethnic Group Cultural Differences on Cooperative Behavior on a Group Task," *Academy of Management Journal* (December 1991), pp. 827–847; and D. van Knippenberg, C. K. W. De Dreu, and A. C. Homan, "Work Group Diversity and Group Performance: An Integrative Model and Research Agenda," *Journal of Applied Psychology* (December 2004), pp. 1008–1022.

34. For example, see J. A. Wall Jr. and R. R. Callister, "Conflict and Its Management," *Journal of Management* 21, no. 3 (1995) pp. 523–526, for evidence supporting the argument that conflict is almost uniformly dysfunctional. See also P. J. Hinds and D. E. Bailey, "Out of Sight, Out of Sync: Understanding Conflict in Distributed Teams," *Organization Science* (November–December 2003), pp. 615–632.

35. Jehn, Greer, Levine, and Szulanski, "The Effects of Conflict Types, Dimensions, and Emergent States on Group Outcomes."

36. Zellmer-Bruhn, Maloney, Bhappu, and Salvador, "When and How Do Differences Matter?"

37. K. B. Dahlin, L. R. Weingart, and P. J. Hinds, "Team Diversity and Information Use," *Academy of Management Journal* 48, no. 6 (2005), pp. 1107–1123; and M. J. Pearsall, A. P. J. Ellis, and J. M. Evans, "Unlocking the Effects of Gender Faultlines on Team Creativity: Is Activation the Key?" *Journal of Applied Psychology* 93, no. 1 (2008), pp. 225–234.

38. M. Geyelin and E. Felsenthal, "Irreconcilable Differences Force Shea & Gould Closure," *The Wall Street Journal* (January 31, 1994), p. B1.

39. J. Fried, "I Know You Are, But What Am I?" *Inc.* (July/August 2010), pp. 39–40.

40. K. J. Behfar, R. S. Peterson, E. A. Mannix, and W. M. K. Trochim, "The Critical Role of Conflict Resolution in Teams: A Close Look at the Links Between Conflict Type, Conflict Management Strategies, and Team Outcomes," *Journal of Applied Psychology* 93, no. 1 (2008), pp. 170–188; A. G. Tekleab, N. R. Quigley, and P. E. Tesluk, "A Longitudinal Study of Team Conflict, Conflict Management, Cohesion, and Team Effectiveness," *Group and Organization Management* 34, no. 2 (2009), pp. 170–205; and E. Van de Vliert, M. C. Euwema, and S. E. Huismans, "Managing Conflict with a Subordinate or a Superior: Effectiveness of Conglomerated Behavior," *Journal of Applied Psychology* 80 (1995), pp. 271–281.

41. A. Somech, H. S. Desivilya, and H. Lidogoster, "Team Conflict Management and Team Effectiveness: The Effects of Task Interdependence and Team Identification," *Journal of Organizational Behavior* 30, no. 3 (2009), pp. 359–378.

42. H. R. Markus and S. Kitayama, "Culture and the Self: Implications for Cognition, Emotion, and Motivation," *Psychological Review* 98, no. 2 (1991), pp. 224–253; and H. Ren and B. Gray, "Repairing Relationship Conflict: How Violation Types and Culture Influence the Effectiveness of Restoration Rituals," *Academy of Management Review* 34, no. 1 (2009), pp. 105–126.

43. M. J. Gelfand, M. Higgins, L. H. Nishii, J. L. Raver, A. Dominguez, F. Murakami, S. Yamaguchi, and M. Toyama, "Culture and Egocentric Perceptions of Fairness in Conflict and Negotiation," *Journal of Applied Psychology* (October 2002), pp. 833–845; and Z. Ma, "Chinese Conflict Management Styles and Negotiation Behaviours: An Empirical Test," *International Journal of Cross Cultural Management* (April 2007), pp. 101–119.

44. P. P. Fu, X. H. Yan, Y. Li, E. Wang, and S. Peng, "Examining Conflict-Handling Approaches by Chinese Top Management Teams in IT Firms," *International Journal of Conflict Management* 19, no. 3 (2008), pp. 188–209.

45. M. H. Bazerman, J. R. Curhan, D. A. Moore, and K. L. Valley, "Negotiation," *Annual Review of Psychology* 51 (2000), pp. 279–314.

46. See, for example, D. R. Ames, "Assertiveness Expectancies: How Hard People Push Depends on the Consequences They Predict," *Journal of Personality and Social Psychology* 95, no. 6 (2008), pp. 1541–1557; and J. R. Curhan, H. A. Elfenbein, and H. Xu, "What Do People Value When They Negotiate? Mapping the Domain of Subjective Value in Negotiation," *Journal of Personality and Social Psychology* 91, no. 3 (2006), pp. 493–512.

47. R. Lewicki, D. Saunders, and B. Barry, *Negotiation*, 6th ed. (New York: McGraw-Hill/Irwin, 2009).

48. J. C. Magee, A. D. Galinsky, and D. H. Gruenfeld, "Power, Propensity to Negotiate, and Moving First in Competitive Interactions," *Personality and Social Psychology Bulletin* (February 2007), pp. 200–212.

49. H. R. Bowles, L. Babcock, and L. Lei, "Social Incentives for Gender Differences in the Propensity to Initiative Negotiations: Sometimes It Does Hurt to Ask," *Organizational Behavior and Human Decision Processes* 103 (2007), pp. 84–103.

50. D. A. Moore, "Myopic Prediction, Self-Destructive Secrecy, and the Unexpected Benefits of Revealing Final Deadlines in Negotiation," *Organizational Behavior & Human Decision Processes* (July 2004), pp. 125–139.

51. E. Wilson, "The Trouble with Jake," *The New York Times* (July 15, 2009), www.nytimes.com.

52. J. R. Curhan, H. A. Elfenbein, and H. Xu, "What Do People Value When They Negotiate? Mapping the Domain of Subjective Value in Negotiation," *Journal of Personality and Social Psychology* 91, no. 3 (2006), pp. 493–512.

53. Thomas, "Conflict and Negotiation Processes in Organizations."

54. P. M. Morgan and R. S. Tindale, "Group vs. Individual Performance in Mixed-Motive Situations: Exploring an Inconsistency," *Organizational Behavior & Human Decision Processes* (January 2002), pp. 44–65.

55. C. E. Naquin, "The Agony of Opportunity in Negotiation: Number of Negotiable Issues, Counterfactual Thinking, and Feelings of Satisfaction," *Organizational Behavior & Human Decision Processes* (May 2003), pp. 97–107.

56. M. Giacomantonio, C. K. W. De Dreu, and L. Mannetti, "Now You See It, Now You Don't: Interests, Issues, and Psychological Distance in Integrative Negotiation," *Journal of Personality and Social Psychology* 98, no. 5 (2010), pp. 761–774.

57. F. S. Ten Velden, B. Beersma, and C. K. W. De Dreu, "It Takes One to Tango: The Effect of Dyads' Epistemic Motivation Composition in Negotiation," *Personality and Social Psychology Bulletin* 36, no. 11 (2010), pp. 1454–1466.

58. C. K. W. De Dreu, L. R. Weingart, and S. Kwon, "Influence of Social Motives on Integrative Negotiation: A Meta-Analytic Review and Test of Two Theories," *Journal of Personality & Social Psychology* (May 2000), pp. 889–905.

59. This model is based on R. J. Lewicki, "Bargaining and Negotiation," *Exchange: The Organizational Behavior Teaching Journal* 6, no. 2 (1981), pp. 39–40.

60. J. R. Curhan, H. A. Elfenbein, and G. J. Kilduff, "Getting Off on the Right Foot: Subjective Value Versus Economic Value in Predicting Longitudinal Job Outcomes from Job Offer Negotiations," *Journal of Applied Psychology* 94, no. 2 (2009), pp. 524–534.

61. M. H. Bazerman and M. A. Neale, *Negotiating Rationally* (New York: The Free Press, 1992), pp. 67–68.

62. R. P. Larrick and G. Wu, "Claiming a Large Slice of a Small Pie: Asymmetric Disconfirmation in Negotiation," *Journal of Personality and Social Psychology* 93, no. 2 (2007), pp. 212–233.

63. E. T. Amanatullah, M. W. Morris, and J. R. Curhan, "Negotiators Who Give Too Much: Unmitigated Communion, Relational Anxieties, and Economic Costs in Distributive and Integrative Bargaining," *Journal of Personality and Social Psychology* 95, no. 3 (2008), pp. 723–738; and D. S. DeRue, D. E. Conlon, H. Moon, and H. W. Willaby, "When Is Straightforwardness a Liability in Negotiations? The Role of Integrative Potential and Structural Power," *Journal of Applied Psychology* 94, no. 4 (2009), pp. 1032–1047.

64. B. Barry and R. A. Friedman, "Bargainer Characteristics in Distributive and Integrative Negotiation," *Journal of Personality & Social Psychology* (February 1998), pp. 345–359.

65. L. J. Kray and M. P. Haselhuhn, "Implicit Negotiations Beliefs and Performance: Experimental and Longitudinal Evidence," *Journal of Personality and Social Psychology* 93, no. 1 (2007), pp. 49–64.

66. G. A. Gan Kleef and S. Côté, "Expressing Anger in Conflict: When It Helps and When It Hurts," *Journal of Applied Psychology* 92, no. 6 (2007), pp. 1157–1569; J. M. Brett, M. Olekalns, R. Friedman, N. Goates, C. Anderson, C. C. Lisco, "Sticks and Stones: Language, Face, and Online Dispute Resolution," *Academy of Management Journal* 50, no. 1 (2007), pp. 85–99; and J. R. Overbeck, M. A. Neale, and C. L. Govan, "I Feel, Therefore You Act: Intrapersonal and Interpersonal Effects of Emotion on Negotiations as a Function of Social Power," *Organizational Behavior and Human Decision Processes* 112, no. 2 (2010), pp. 126–139.

67. G. A. Van Kleef and C. K. W. De Dreu, "Longer-Term Consequences of Anger Expression in Negotiation: Retaliation or Spillover?" *Journal of Experimental Social Psychology* 46, no. 5 (2010), pp. 753–760.

68. M. Olekalns and P. L Smith, "Mutually Dependent: Power, Trust, Affect, and the Use of Deception in Negotiation," *Journal of Business Ethics* 85, no. 3 (2009), pp. 347–365.

69. A. W. Brooks and M. E. Schweitzer, "Can Nervous Nellie Negotiate? How Anxiety Causes Negotiators to Make Low First Offers, Exit Early, and Earn Less Profit," *Organizational Behavior and Human Decision Processes* 115, no. 1 (2011), pp. 43–54.

70. S. Kopelman, A. S. Rosette, and L. Thompson, "The Three Faces of Eve: Strategic Displays of Positive, Negative, and Neutral Emotions in Negotiations," *Organizational Behavior and Human Decision Processes* 99 (2006), pp. 81–101.

71. W. L. Adair, T. Okumura, and J. M. Brett, "Negotiation Behavior When Cultures Collide: The United States and Japan," *Journal of Applied Psychology* (June 2001), pp. 371–385; and W. L. Adair, L. Weingart, and J. Brett, "The Timing and Function of Offers in U.S. and Japanese Negotiations," *Journal of Applied Psychology* 92, no. 4 (2007), pp. 1056–1068.

72. S. Kopelman, "The Effect of Culture and Power on Cooperation in Commons Dilemmas: Implications for Global Resource Management," *Organizational Behavior and Human Decision Processes* 108, no. 1 (2009), pp. 153–163.

73. B. C. Gunia, J. M. Brett, A. K. Nandkeolyar, and D. Kamdar, "Paying a Price: Culture, Trust, and Negotiation Consequences," *Journal of Applied Psychology* 96, no. 4 (2010), pp. 774–789.

74. C. Watson and L. R. Hoffman, "Managers as Negotiators: A Test of Power Versus Gender as Predictors of Feelings, Behavior, and Outcomes," *Leadership Quarterly* (Spring 1996), pp. 63–85.

75. A. E. Walters, A. F. Stuhlmacher, and L. L. Meyer, "Gender and Negotiator Competitiveness: A Meta-Analysis," *Organizational Behavior and Human Decision Processes* (October 1998), pp. 1–29; and A. F. Stuhlmacher and A. E. Walters, "Gender Differences in Negotiation Outcome: A Meta-Analysis," *Personnel Psychology* (Autumn 1999), pp. 653–677.

76. Stuhlmacher and Walters, "Gender Differences in Negotiation Outcome," p. 655.

77. Bowles, Babcock, and Lei, "Social Incentives for Gender Differences in the Propensity to Initiative Negotiations."

78. L. J. Kray, A. D. Galinsky, and L. Thompson, "Reversing the Gender Gap in Negotiations: An Exploration of Stereotype Regeneration," *Organizational Behavior & Human Decision Processes* (March 2002), pp. 386–409.

79. D. A. Small, M. Gelfand, L. Babcock, and H. Gettman, "Who Goes to the Bargaining Table? The Influence of Gender and Framing on the Initiation of Negotiation," *Journal of Personality and Social Psychology* 93, no. 4 (2007), pp. 600–613.

80. E. T. Amanatullah and M. W. Morris, "Negotiating Gender Roles: Gender Differences in Assertive Negotiating Are Mediated by Women's Fear of Backlash and Attenuated When Negotiating on Behalf of Others," *Journal of Personality and Social Psychology* 98, no. 2 (2010), pp. 256–267.

81. K. W. Thomas, "Toward Multidimensional Values in Teaching: The Example of Conflict Behaviors," *Academy of Management Review* (July 1977), p. 487.

DISMANTLING A BUREAUCRACY

Though at one time it was the largest, most successful, and most admired company in the world, today General Motors (GM) serves as a reminder to many of a staid company caught in a bureaucratic structure and culture of mediocrity that it created.

The reasons for GM's decline into bankruptcy are many. The company was heavily unionized and negotiated uncompetitive wage and pension structures for its union members. It was caught off-guard by the rise of Japanese automakers and their emphasis on quality. It was similarly blindsided by rising fuel costs and the push for fuel-efficient cars. Whenever a shock or innovation occurred, it seemed GM was poorly prepared and nearly always lagged behind competitors in anticipating, or even reacting to, a rapidly changing environment.

As in any story of organizational decline, we can't trace these missed opportunities to one cause. However, a source as likely as any is GM's organizational structure. That was the point of attack for Terry J. Woychowski.

Woychowski is vice president of the Global Vehicle Program Management at GM. He was promoted shortly after GM emerged from bankruptcy in 2009. In thinking strategically about GM and its future, Woychowski kept coming back to GM's bureaucracy. It led, he felt, to conservative, risk-averse, and analytical reactions rather than to innovative strategic risk taking. "We measured ourselves ten ways from Sunday," Woychowski says. "But as soon as everything is important, nothing is important."

Woychowski was not alone in his perceptions about the stifling effects of GM's bureaucracy. As far back as 1988, when the firm still dominated the world auto market, a GM senior executive sounded a note of caution about GM's bureaucracy that fell on deaf ears: "We have not achieved the success that we must because of severe limitations on our organization's ability to execute in a timely manner."

Woychowski is committed to changing that. In the past, any design alterations to a car required review by as many as 70 managers, with decisions often taking months and even years to wend their way through the bureaucracy. An ally of Woychowski, Jon Lauckner, head of Global Product Planning, significantly streamlined that process. Decisions that used to take months now take a few weeks.

Other aspects of GM's structure have been changed. Previously, managers were required to rate their tasks as green, yellow, or red, depending on whether the job had been completed, needed work, or should be frozen until a major problem was resolved. Mark Reuss, head of GM's global engineering group, says, "If you had a red issue and stood up, it was very punitive." So GM managers developed a risk-averse attitude and carefully sought approval

Foundations of Organization Structure

Every revolution evaporates and leaves behind only the slime of a new bureaucracy. —Franz Kafka

Photo: General Motors employees cheer as the nine-millionth vehicle rolls down the line. *Source: Paul Moseley/MCT/Newscom.*

from as many sources as possible before acting. Woychowski, Lauckner, and Reuss are working hard to make GM less bureaucratic, more informal, and less reactive and risk averse.

Can GM recover? This is not the first transformation it has attempted. Ironically, Reuss' father was dismissed as president of GM in a large restructuring in 1992. "This is an opportunity my dad never had," says Reuss. "I don't want to waste it."

Sources: B. Vlasic, "Culture Shock," *The New York Times* (November 13, 2009), pp. BU1, BU4; P. Brown, "According to Bob: How GM Cars Got Better," *AutoWeek* (May 23, 2011), downloaded June 30, 2011, from www.autoweek.com/; and A. Taylor, "GM vs. Ford: The Hundred-Year War," *Fortune* (March 23, 2011), downloaded June 29, 2011, from http://money.cnn.com/.

Structural decisions like the reconfiguration of GM are arguably the most fundamental ones a leader has to make. Before we delve into the elements of an organization's structure and how they can affect behavior, consider how you might react to one type of organizational structure—the bureaucratic structure—by taking the following self-assessment.

SELF-ASSESSMENT LIBRARY

Do I Like Bureaucracy?

In the Self-Assessment Library (available on CD and online), take assessment IV.F.2 (Do I Like Bureaucracy?) and answer the following questions.

1. Judging from the results, how willing are you to work in a bureaucratic organization?
2. Do you think scores on this measure matter? Why or why not?
3. Do you think people who score very low (or even very high) on this measure should try to adjust their preferences based on where they are working?

What Is Organizational Structure?

1 Identify the six elements of an organization's structure.

An **organizational structure** defines how job tasks are formally divided, grouped, and coordinated. Managers need to address six key elements when they design their organization's structure: work specialization, departmentalization, chain of command, span of control, centralization and decentralization, and formalization.[1] Exhibit 15-1 presents each of these elements as answers to an important structural question, and the following sections describe them.

Work Specialization

Early in the twentieth century, Henry Ford became rich by building automobiles on an assembly line. Every Ford worker was assigned a specific, repetitive task such as putting on the right-front wheel or installing the right-front door. By dividing jobs into small standardized tasks that could be performed over and over, Ford was able to produce a car every 10 seconds, using employees who had relatively limited skills.

| Exhibit **15-1** | Key Design Questions and Answers for Designing the Proper Organizational Structure |

The Key Question	The Answer Is Provided by
1. To what degree are activities subdivided into separate jobs?	Work specialization
2. On what basis will jobs be grouped together?	Departmentalization
3. To whom do individuals and groups report?	Chain of command
4. How many individuals can a manager efficiently and effectively direct?	Span of control
5. Where does decision-making authority lie?	Centralization and decentralization
6. To what degree will there be rules and regulations to direct employees and managers?	Formalization

Ford demonstrated that work can be performed more efficiently if employees are allowed to specialize. Today, we use the term **work specialization**, or *division of labor,* to describe the degree to which activities in the organization are subdivided into separate jobs. The essence of work specialization is to divide a job into a number of steps, each completed by a separate individual. In essence, individuals specialize in doing part of an activity rather than the entirety.

By the late 1940s, most manufacturing jobs in industrialized countries featured high work specialization. Because not all employees in an organization have the same skills, management saw specialization as a means of making the most efficient use of its employees' skills and even successfully improving them through repetition. Less time is spent in changing tasks, putting away tools and equipment from a prior step, and getting ready for another. Equally important, it's easier and less costly to find and train workers to do specific and repetitive tasks, especially in highly sophisticated and complex operations. Could Cessna produce one Citation jet a year if one person had to build the entire plane alone? Not likely! Finally, work specialization increases efficiency and productivity by encouraging the creation of special inventions and machinery.

Thus, for much of the first half of the twentieth century, managers viewed work specialization as an unending source of increased productivity. And they were probably right. When specialization was not widely practiced, its introduction almost always generated higher productivity. But by the 1960s, it increasingly seemed a good thing can be carried too far. Human diseconomies from specialization began to surface in the form of boredom, fatigue, stress, low productivity, poor quality, increased absenteeism, and high turnover, which more than offset the economic advantages (see Exhibit 15-2). Managers could increase productivity now by enlarging, rather than narrowing, the scope of job activities. Giving employees a variety of activities to do, allowing them to do a whole and complete job, and putting them into teams with interchangeable skills often achieved significantly higher output, with increased employee satisfaction.

organizational structure   *The way in which job tasks are formally divided, grouped, and coordinated.*

work specialization   *The degree to which tasks in an organization are subdivided into separate jobs.*

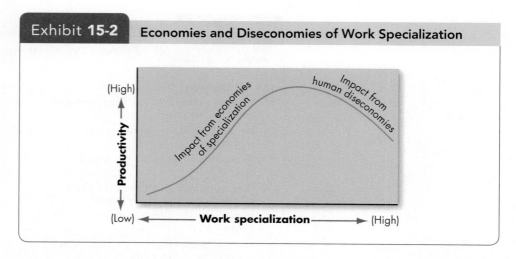

Exhibit 15-2 **Economies and Diseconomies of Work Specialization**

Most managers today recognize the economies specialization provides in certain jobs and the problems when it's carried too far. High work specialization helps McDonald's make and sell hamburgers and fries efficiently and aids medical specialists in most health maintenance organizations. Amazon's Mechanical Turk program, TopCoder, and others like it have facilitated a new trend in microspecialization in which extremely small pieces of programming, data processing, or evaluation tasks are delegated to a global network of individuals by a program manager who then assembles the results.[2] For example, a manager who has a complex but routine computer program to write might send a request for specific subcomponents of the code to be written and tested by dozens of subcontracted individuals in the network (which spans the entire globe), enabling the project to be completed far more quickly than if a single programmer were writing the parts. This emerging trend suggests there still may be advantages to be had in specialization.

Departmentalization

Once jobs have been divided through work specialization, they must be grouped so common tasks can be coordinated. The basis by which jobs are grouped is called **departmentalization**.

One of the most popular ways to group activities is by *functions* performed. A manufacturing manager might organize a plant into engineering, accounting, manufacturing, personnel, and supply specialists departments. A hospital might have departments devoted to research, surgery, intensive care, accounting, and so forth. A professional football franchise might have departments entitled player personnel, ticket sales, and travel and accommodations. The major advantage of this type of functional departmentalization is efficiencies gained from putting like specialists together.

We can also departmentalize jobs by the type of *product* or *service* the organization produces. Procter & Gamble places each major product—such as Tide, Pampers, Charmin, and Pringles—under an executive who has complete global responsibility for it. The major advantage here is increased accountability for performance, because all activities related to a specific product or service are under the direction of a single manager.

When a firm is departmentalized on the basis of *geography*, or territory, the sales function, for instance, may have western, southern, midwestern, and eastern regions, each, in effect, a department organized around geography. This form is valuable when an organization's customers are scattered over a large geographic area and have similar needs based on their location.

At Microsoft, customer departmentalization allows the company to better understand customers and respond to their needs. Microsoft is organized by four customer segments: consumers, software developers, small businesses, and large corporations. Products and services the company designs for consumers include Bing, Windows, Windows Phone 7, Xbox 360, and Microsoft retail stores, which give the company direct contact with consumers. This photo shows a boy playing the Kinect for Xbox 360 at a gaming store. Kinect, which has a full-body sensor, allows consumers to play Xbox games without using a controller and to interact with games in a real physical sense.

Source: AP Photo/Nell Redmond.

Process departmentalization works for processing customers as well as products. If you've ever been to a state motor vehicle office to get a driver's license, you probably went through several departments before receiving your license. In one typical state, applicants go through three steps, each handled by a separate department: (1) validation by motor vehicles division, (2) processing by the licensing department, and (3) payment collection by the treasury department.

A final category of departmentalization uses the particular type of *customer* the organization seeks to reach. Microsoft, for example, is organized around four customer markets: consumers, large corporations, software developers, and small businesses. Customers in each department have a common set of problems and needs best met by having specialists for each.

Chain of Command

While the chain of command was once a basic cornerstone in the design of organizations, it has far less importance today.[3] But contemporary managers should still consider its implications. The **chain of command** is an unbroken line of authority that extends from the top of the organization to the lowest echelon and clarifies who reports to whom.

departmentalization *The basis by which jobs in an organization are grouped together.*

chain of command *The unbroken line of authority that extends from the top of the organization to the lowest echelon and clarifies who reports to whom.*

We can't discuss the chain of command without also discussing *authority* and *unity of command*. **Authority** refers to the rights inherent in a managerial position to give orders and expect them to be obeyed. To facilitate coordination, each managerial position is given a place in the chain of command, and each manager is given a degree of authority in order to meet his or her responsibilities. The principle of **unity of command** helps preserve the concept of an unbroken line of authority. It says a person should have one and only one superior to whom he or she is directly responsible. If the unity of command is broken, an employee might have to cope with conflicting demands or priorities from several superiors.

Times change, and so do the basic tenets of organizational design. A low-level employee today can access information in seconds that was available only to top managers a generation ago. Operating employees are empowered to make decisions previously reserved for management. Add the popularity of self-managed and cross-functional teams and the creation of new structural designs that include multiple bosses, and you can see why authority and unity of command hold less relevance. Many organizations still find they can be most productive by enforcing the chain of command. Indeed, one survey of more than 1,000 managers found that 59 percent of them agreed with the statement, "There is an imaginary line in my company's organizational chart. Strategy is created by people above this line, while strategy is executed by people below the line."[4] However, this same survey found that buy-in to the organization's strategy by lower-level employees was inhibited by too much reliance on hierarchy for decision making.

Span of Control

How many employees can a manager efficiently and effectively direct? This question of **span of control** is important because it largely determines the number of levels and managers an organization has. All things being equal, the wider or larger the span, the more efficient the organization.

Assume two organizations each have about 4,100 operative-level employees. One has a uniform span of four and the other a span of eight. As Exhibit 15-3 illustrates, the wider span will have two fewer levels and approximately 800 fewer managers. If the average manager makes $50,000 a year, the wider span will save

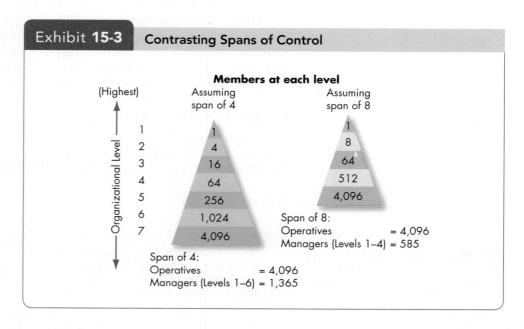

Exhibit 15-3　Contrasting Spans of Control

Members at each level

(Highest)

Organizational level

Assuming span of 4	Assuming span of 8
1	1
4	8
16	64
64	512
256	4,096
1,024	
4,096	

Span of 8:
Operatives = 4,096
Managers (Levels 1–4) = 585

Span of 4:
Operatives = 4,096
Managers (Levels 1–6) = 1,365

$40 million a year in management salaries! Obviously, wider spans are more efficient in terms of cost. However, at some point when supervisors no longer have time to provide the necessary leadership and support, they reduce effectiveness and employee performance suffers.

Narrow or small spans have their advocates. By keeping the span of control to five or six employees, a manager can maintain close control.[5] But narrow spans have three major drawbacks. First, they're expensive because they add levels of management. Second, they make vertical communication in the organization more complex. The added levels of hierarchy slow down decision making and tend to isolate upper management. Third, narrow spans encourage overly tight supervision and discourage employee autonomy.

The trend in recent years has been toward wider spans of control.[6] They're consistent with firms' efforts to reduce costs, cut overhead, speed decision making, increase flexibility, get closer to customers, and empower employees. However, to ensure performance doesn't suffer because of these wider spans, organizations have been investing heavily in employee training. Managers recognize they can handle a wider span best when employees know their jobs inside and out or can turn to co-workers when they have questions.

Centralization and Decentralization

Centralization refers to the degree to which decision making is concentrated at a single point in the organization. In *centralized* organizations, top managers make all the decisions, and lower-level managers merely carry out their directives. In organizations at the other extreme, *decentralized* decision making is pushed down to the managers closest to the action.

The concept of centralization includes only formal authority—that is, the rights inherent in a position. An organization characterized by centralization is inherently different structurally from one that's decentralized. A decentralized organization can act more quickly to solve problems, more people provide input into decisions, and employees are less likely to feel alienated from those who make decisions that affect their work lives.

Management efforts to make organizations more flexible and responsive have produced a recent trend toward decentralized decision making by lower-level managers, who are closer to the action and typically have more detailed knowledge about problems than top managers. Sears and JCPenney have given their store managers considerably more discretion in choosing what merchandise to stock. This allows those stores to compete more effectively against local merchants. Similarly, when Procter & Gamble empowered small groups of employees to make many decisions about new-product development independent of the usual hierarchy, it was able to rapidly increase the proportion of new products ready for market.[7] Research investigating a large number of Finnish organizations demonstrates that companies with decentralized research and development offices in multiple locations were better at producing innovation than companies that centralized all research and development in a single office.[8]

---

authority   *The rights inherent in a managerial position to give orders and to expect the orders to be obeyed.*

unity of command   *The idea that a subordinate should have only one superior to whom he or she is directly responsible.*

span of control   *The number of subordinates a manager can efficiently and effectively direct.*

centralization   *The degree to which decision making is concentrated at a single point in an organization.*

How Willing Am I to Delegate?

In the Self-Assessment Library (available on CD and online), take assessment III.A.2 (How Willing Am I to Delegate?).

Formalization

Formalization refers to the degree to which jobs within the organization are standardized. If a job is highly formalized, the incumbent has a minimal amount of discretion over what to do and when and how to do it. Employees can be expected always to handle the same input in exactly the same way, resulting in a consistent and uniform output. There are explicit job descriptions, lots of organizational rules, and clearly defined procedures covering work processes in organizations in which there is high formalization. Where formalization is low, job behaviors are relatively unprogrammed, and employees have a great deal of freedom to exercise discretion in their work. Standardization not only eliminates the possibility of employees engaging in alternative behaviors, but it even removes the need for employees to consider alternatives.

The degree of formalization can vary widely between and within organizations. Publishing representatives who call on college professors to inform them of their company's new publications have a great deal of freedom in their jobs. They have only a general sales pitch, which they tailor as needed, and rules and procedures governing their behavior may be little more than the requirement to submit a weekly sales report and suggestions on what to emphasize about forthcoming titles. At the other extreme, clerical and editorial employees in the same publishing houses may need to be at their desks by 8:00 a.m. and follow a set of precise procedures dictated by management.

Common Organizational Designs

2 Identify the characteristics of a bureaucracy.

We now turn to three of the more common organizational designs: the *simple structure*, the *bureaucracy*, and the *matrix structure*.

The Simple Structure

What do a small retail store, an electronics firm run by a hard-driving entrepreneur, and an airline's "war room" in the midst of a pilot's strike have in common? They probably all use the **simple structure**.

We can think of the simple structure in terms of what it is *not* rather than what it is. The simple structure is not elaborate.[9] It has a low degree of departmentalization, wide spans of control, authority centralized in a single person, and little formalization. It is a "flat" organization; it usually has only two or three vertical levels, a loose body of employees, and one individual in whom the decision-making authority is centralized.

The simple structure is most widely adopted in small businesses in which the manager and owner are one and the same. Exhibit 15-4 is an organization chart for a retail men's store owned and managed by Jack Gold. Although he employs five full-time salespeople, a cashier, and extra personnel for weekends and holidays, Jack "runs the show." Large companies, in times of crisis, often simplify their structures as a means of focusing their resources. When Anne Mulcahy

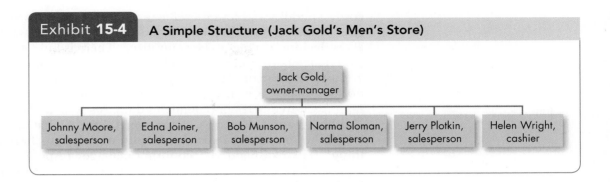

Exhibit 15-4   A Simple Structure (Jack Gold's Men's Store)

Jack Gold, owner-manager

Johnny Moore, salesperson | Edna Joiner, salesperson | Bob Munson, salesperson | Norma Sloman, salesperson | Jerry Plotkin, salesperson | Helen Wright, cashier

took over Xerox, its product mix and management structure were overly complex. She simplified both, cutting corporate overhead by 26 percent. "It's a case of placing your bets in a few areas" she says.[10]

The strength of the simple structure lies in its simplicity. It's fast, flexible, and inexpensive to operate, and accountability is clear. One major weakness is that it becomes increasingly inadequate as an organization grows, because its low formalization and high centralization tend to create information overload at the top. As size increases, decision making typically becomes slower and can eventually come to a standstill as the single executive tries to continue making all the decisions. This proves the undoing of many small businesses. If the structure isn't changed and made more elaborate, the firm often loses momentum and can eventually fail. The simple structure's other weakness is that it's risky—everything depends on one person. One illness can literally destroy the organization's information and decision-making center.

The Bureaucracy

Standardization! That's the key concept that underlies all bureaucracies. Consider the bank where you keep your checking account; the department store where you buy clothes; or the government offices that collect your taxes, enforce health regulations, or provide local fire protection. They all rely on standardized work processes for coordination and control.

The **bureaucracy** is characterized by highly routine operating tasks achieved through specialization, very formalized rules and regulations, tasks grouped into functional departments, centralized authority, narrow spans of control, and decision making that follows the chain of command. As the opening quote to this chapter attests, *bureaucracy* is a dirty word in many people's minds. However, it does have advantages. Its primary strength is its ability to perform standardized activities in a highly efficient manner. Putting like specialties together in functional departments results in economies of scale, minimum duplication of people and equipment, and employees who can speak "the same language" among their peers. Bureaucracies can get by with less talented—and hence less

formalization *The degree to which jobs within an organization are standardized.*

simple structure *An organization structure characterized by a low degree of departmentalization, wide spans of control, authority centralized in a single person, and little formalization.*

bureaucracy *An organization structure with highly routine operating tasks achieved through specialization, very formalized rules and regulations, tasks that are grouped into functional departments, centralized authority, narrow spans of control, and decision making that follows the chain of command.*

costly—middle- and lower-level managers because rules and regulations substitute for managerial discretion. Standardized operations and high formalization allow decision making to be centralized. There is little need for innovative and experienced decision makers below the level of senior executives.

Listen in on a dialogue among four executives in one company: "You know, nothing happens in this place until we *produce* something," said the production executive. "Wrong," commented the research and development manager. "Nothing happens until we *design* something!" "What are you talking about?" asked the marketing executive. "Nothing happens here until we *sell* something!" The exasperated accounting manager responded, "It doesn't matter what you produce, design, or sell. No one knows what happens until we *tally up the results!*" This conversation highlights that bureaucratic specialization can create conflicts in which functional-unit goals override the overall goals of the organization.

The other major weakness of a bureaucracy is something we've all witnessed: obsessive concern with following the rules. When cases don't precisely fit the rules, there is no room for modification. The bureaucracy is efficient only as long as employees confront familiar problems with programmed decision rules.

The Matrix Structure

3 Describe a matrix organization.

You'll find the **matrix structure** in advertising agencies, aerospace firms, research and development laboratories, construction companies, hospitals, government agencies, universities, management consulting firms, and entertainment companies.[11] It combines two forms of departmentalization: functional and product. Companies that use matrix-like structures include ABB, Boeing, BMW, IBM, and Procter & Gamble.

The strength of functional departmentalization is putting like specialists together, which minimizes the number necessary while allowing the pooling and sharing of specialized resources across products. Its major disadvantage is the difficulty of coordinating the tasks of diverse functional specialists on time and within budget. Product departmentalization has exactly the opposite benefits and disadvantages. It facilitates coordination among specialties to achieve on-time completion and meet budget targets. It provides clear responsibility for all

Hospitals benefit from standardized work processes and procedures common to a bureaucratic structure because they help employees perform their jobs efficiently. When faced with financial problems, management at Crouse Hospital in Syracuse, New York, decided that its structure was too bureaucratic and hierarchical. Top managers gathered employees from all levels and areas and asked them to find innovative solutions needed to improve every aspect of the hospital, from creating a new mission statement to designing new work processes. With more employee involvement, Crouse raised its revenues and quality, provided more community services, and improved its relationship with employees such as the registered nurse shown here.

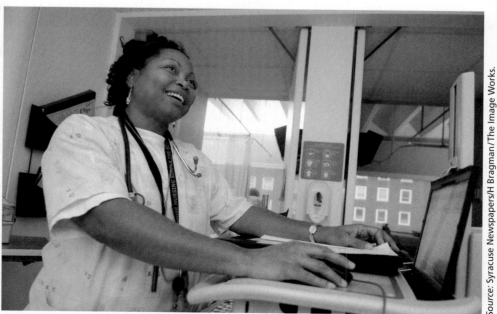

Source: Syracuse Newspapers/H Bragman/The Image Works.

The Global Organization

One of the most significant trends in organizational structure is the emergence of truly global organizations with leadership and development functions located all around the world.

In organizations that offshore many functions, a central office located in one country sends business processes to facilities in another country, like a U.S. computer company (think of Dell or Apple) that designs computers in California, manufactures all the parts in China, and assembles them in Texas. Such companies are global in the sense that their operations span multiple nations, but the central culture of the organization is based in a home country.

In a "stateless" corporation, in contrast, all divisions share a common management culture, and operations are standardized for all locations. Managers are drawn from a variety of national backgrounds and placed wherever their functional expertise will be most valuable. Reckitt Benckiser (maker of Clearasil, Lysol, and Woolite) assigns managers to a variety of global offices to ensure they get a picture of border-spanning trends that might produce innovations in other countries. As a result, an Italian is running the UK business, an American the German business, an Indian the Chinese operation, and a Dutch executive the U.S. business.

Although these international strategies may produce advantages like cost savings and centralization of decision making, some observers feel the future is more likely to belong to truly cosmopolitan organizations that produce and market products and services particular to each country in which they operate. This strategy gives local offices maximal control over their own particular areas and takes the greatest advantage of specialized, local knowledge of markets.

It's not yet clear whether it's better to pursue a strategy based on offshoring, stateless corporations, or cosmopolitan organizations, but it's likely there is no universal best configuration. The best structure is likely to depend heavily on the type of products and market the company is targeting.

Sources: Based on J. Lampel and A. Bhalla, "Living with Offshoring: The Impact of Offshoring on the Evolution of Organizational Configurations," *Journal of World Business* 46, (2011), pp. 346–358; P. Gehmawat, "The Cosmopolitan Corporation," *Harvard Business Review* (May 2011), pp. 92–99; and B. Becht, "Building a Company Without Borders," *Harvard Business Review* (April 2010), pp. 103–106.

activities related to a product, but with duplication of activities and costs. The matrix attempts to gain the strengths of each while avoiding their weaknesses.

The most obvious structural characteristic of the matrix is that it breaks the unity-of-command concept. Employees in the matrix have two bosses: their functional department managers and their product managers.

Exhibit 15-5 shows the matrix form in a college of business administration. The academic departments of accounting, decision and information systems, marketing, and so forth are functional units. Overlaid on them are specific programs (that is, products). Thus, members in a matrix structure have a dual chain of command: to their functional department and to their product groups. A professor of accounting teaching an undergraduate course may report to the director of undergraduate programs as well as to the chairperson of the accounting department.

The strength of the matrix is its ability to facilitate coordination when the organization has a number of complex and interdependent activities. Direct and frequent contacts between different specialties in the matrix can let information permeate the organization and more quickly reach the people who need it. The matrix reduces "bureaupathologies"—the dual lines of authority reduce people's tendency to become so busy protecting their little worlds that

matrix structure *An organization structure that creates dual lines of authority and combines functional and product departmentalization.*

Exhibit 15-5	Matrix Structure for a College of Business Administration

Academic Departments \ Programs	Undergraduate	Master's	Ph.D.	Research	Executive Development	Community Service
Accounting						
Finance						
Decision and Information Systems						
Management						
Marketing						

the organization's goals become secondary. A matrix also achieves economies of scale and facilitates the allocation of specialists by providing both the best resources and an effective way of ensuring their efficient deployment.

The major disadvantages of the matrix lie in the confusion it creates, its tendency to foster power struggles, and the stress it places on individuals.[12] Without the unity-of-command concept, ambiguity about who reports to whom is significantly increased and often leads to conflict. It's not unusual for product managers to fight over getting the best specialists assigned to their products. Bureaucracy reduces the potential for power grabs by defining the rules of the game. When those rules are "up for grabs" in a matrix, power struggles between functional and product managers result. For individuals who desire security and absence from ambiguity, this work climate can be stressful. Reporting to more than one boss introduces role conflict, and unclear expectations introduce role ambiguity. The comfort of bureaucracy's predictability is replaced by insecurity and stress.

New Design Options

Senior managers in a number of organizations have been developing new structural options with fewer layers of hierarchy and more emphasis on opening the boundaries of the organization.[13] In this section, we describe two such designs: the *virtual organization* and the *boundaryless organization*. We'll also discuss how efforts to reduce bureaucracy and increase strategic focus have made downsizing routine.

The Virtual Organization

4 Identify the characteristics of a virtual organization.

Why own when you can rent? That question captures the essence of the **virtual organization** (also sometimes called the *network*, or *modular*, organization), typically a small, core organization that outsources its major business functions.[14] In structural terms, the virtual organization is highly centralized, with little or no departmentalization.

The prototype of the virtual structure is today's movie-making organization. In Hollywood's golden era, movies were made by huge, vertically integrated corporations. Studios such as MGM, Warner Brothers, and 20th Century Fox owned large movie lots and employed thousands of full-time specialists—set designers, camera people, film editors, directors, and even actors. Today, most movies are made by a collection of individuals and small companies who come together and make films project by project.[15] This structural form allows each project to be staffed with the talent best suited to its demands, rather than just the people employed by the studio. It minimizes bureaucratic overhead because there is no lasting organization to maintain. And it lessens long-term risks and their costs because there *is* no long term—a team is assembled for a finite period and then disbanded.

Philip Rosedale runs a virtual company called LoveMachine that lets employees send brief electronic messages to one another to acknowledge a job well done that can be then used to facilitate company bonuses. The company has no full-time software development staff—instead, LoveMachine outsources assignments to freelancers who submit bids for projects like debugging software or designing new features. Programmers come from around the world, including Russia, India, Australia, and the United States.[16] Similarly, Newman's Own, the food products company founded by Paul Newman, sells hundreds of millions of dollars in food every year yet employs only 28 people. This is possible because it outsources almost everything: manufacturing, procurement, shipping, and quality control.

Exhibit 15-6 shows a virtual organization in which management outsources all the primary functions of the business. The core of the organization is a small group of executives whose job is to oversee directly any activities done in-house and to coordinate relationships with the other organizations that manufacture, distribute, and perform other crucial functions for the virtual organization. The dotted lines represent the relationships typically maintained under

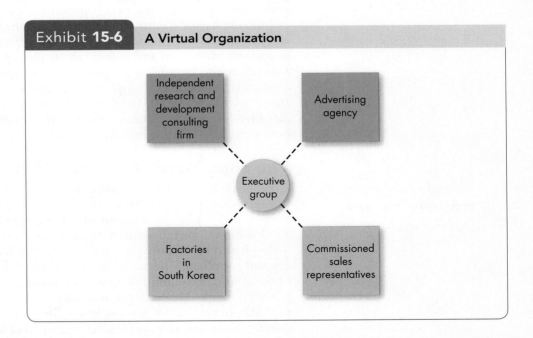

Exhibit **15-6**   A Virtual Organization

Independent research and development consulting firm

Advertising agency

Executive group

Factories in South Korea

Commissioned sales representatives

virtual organization   *A small, core organization that outsources major business functions.*

As a network organization, Boeing outsourced the production of about 70 percent of the components for its new 787 Dreamliner passenger jet aircraft. Boeing used some 100 suppliers at more than 100 sites in different countries, including Alenia Aeronautica of Italy to produce the plane's rear fuselage and Mitsubishi Motors of Japan to create the wings. Although global outsourcing helped Boeing reduce the plane's development and production costs, the extreme complexities of such a structure was also responsible for delays in bringing the cutting-edge aircraft to market. Shown here is the plane's assembly line surrounded by rows of workers at their computers as the planes are built at Boeing's plant in Everett, Washington.

Source: Robert Sorbo/Reuters/Landov Media.

contracts. In essence, managers in virtual structures spend most of their time coordinating and controlling external relations, typically by way of computer network links.

The major advantage of the virtual organization is its flexibility, which allows individuals with an innovative idea and little money to successfully compete against larger, more established organizations. Virtual organizations also save a great deal of money by eliminating permanent offices and hierarchical roles.[17]

Virtual organizations' drawbacks have become increasingly clear as their popularity has grown.[18] They are in a state of perpetual flux and reorganization, which means roles, goals, and responsibilities are unclear, setting the stage for political behavior. Cultural alignment and shared goals can be lost because of the low degree of interaction among members. Team members who are geographically dispersed and communicate infrequently find it difficult to share information and knowledge, which can limit innovation and slow response time. Ironically, some virtual organizations are less adaptable and innovative than those with well-established communication and collaboration networks. A leadership presence that reinforces the organization's purpose and facilitates communication is thus especially valuable.

The Boundaryless Organization

5 Show why managers want to create boundaryless organizations.

General Electric's former chairman, Jack Welch, coined the term **boundaryless organization** to describe what he wanted GE to become: a "family grocery store."[19] That is, in spite of GE's monstrous size (2010 revenues were $150 billion), Welch wanted to eliminate *vertical* and *horizontal* boundaries within it and break down *external* barriers between the company and its customers and suppliers. The boundaryless organization seeks to eliminate the chain of command, have limitless spans of control, and replace departments with empowered teams. Although GE has not yet achieved this boundaryless state—and probably never will—it has made significant progress toward that end. So have other companies, such as Hewlett-Packard, AT&T, Motorola, and 3M. Let's see what a boundaryless organization looks like and what some firms are doing to make it a reality.[20]

By removing vertical boundaries, management flattens the hierarchy and minimizes status and rank. Cross-hierarchical teams (which include top executives, middle managers, supervisors, and operative employees), participative decision-making practices, and the use of 360-degree performance appraisals (in which peers and others above and below the employee evaluate performance) are examples of what GE is doing to break down vertical boundaries. At Oticon A/S, a $160-million-per-year Danish hearing aid manufacturer, all traces of hierarchy have disappeared. Everyone works at uniform mobile workstations, and project teams, not functions or departments, coordinate work.

Functional departments create horizontal boundaries that stifle interaction among functions, product lines, and units. The way to reduce them is to replace functional departments with cross-functional teams and organize activities around processes. Xerox now develops new products through multidisciplinary teams that work on a single process instead of on narrow functional tasks. Some AT&T units prepare annual budgets based not on functions or departments but on processes, such as the maintenance of a worldwide telecommunications network. Another way to lower horizontal barriers is to rotate people through different functional areas using lateral transfers. This approach turns specialists into generalists.

When fully operational, the boundaryless organization also breaks down geographic barriers. Today, most large U.S. companies see themselves as global corporations; many, like Coca-Cola and McDonald's, do as much business overseas as in the United States, and some struggle to incorporate geographic regions into their structure. The boundaryless organization provides one solution because it considers geography more of a tactical, logistical issue than a structural one. In short, the goal is to break down cultural barriers.

BMW Group operates as a boundaryless organization in designing, developing, and producing its BMW, Rolls-Royce, and Mini cars. The automaker uses virtual tools such as computer-aided design and simulation models and a flexible global production network to respond quickly to fluctuations in the market and individual customer preferences. BMW's boundaryless structure drives innovative ideas by eliminating vertical and horizontal barriers among workers and creating an environment of learning and experimentation. From their first day on the job, employees are encouraged to build a network of relationships from all functional areas and across all divisions to speed innovation and problem-solving.

Source: Eckehard Schulz/AP Images.

boundaryless organization *An organization that seeks to eliminate the chain of command, have limitless spans of control, and replace departments with empowered teams.*

One way to do so is through strategic alliances.[21] Firms such as NEC Corporation, Boeing, and Apple each have strategic alliances or joint partnerships with dozens of companies. These alliances blur the distinction between one organization and another as employees work on joint projects. And some companies allow customers to perform functions previously done by management. Some AT&T units receive bonuses based on customer evaluations of the teams that serve them. Finally, telecommuting is blurring organizational boundaries. The security analyst with Merrill Lynch who does her job from her ranch in Montana or the software designer in Boulder, Colorado, who works for a San Francisco firm are just two of the millions of workers operating outside the physical boundaries of their employers' premises.

The Leaner Organization: Downsizing

The goal of the new organizational forms we've described is to improve agility by creating a lean, focused, and flexible organization. *Downsizing* is a systematic effort to make an organization leaner by closing locations, reducing staff, or selling off business units that don't add value.

The radical shrinking of Chrysler and General Motors in recent years was a case of downsizing to survive, due to loss of market share and changes in consumer demand. Other firms, including Research in Motion (makers of the BlackBerry) and Cisco, downsize to direct all their efforts toward their core competencies. After a series of costly acquisitions, VeriSign decided to divest itself of most of its business units and resume its original focus on e-commerce security and online identity protection.[22] Some companies focus on lean management techniques to reduce bureaucracy and speed decision making. Park Nicollet Health Services in Minneapolis eliminated fixed budgets and pushed managers to reduce costs as part of a transformation to lean production; it was able to save at least $15 million per year[23] and adapt to changes in the health care market much more quickly.

Despite the advantages of being a lean organization, the impact of downsizing on organizational performance has been very controversial.[24] Reducing

Foursquare transfers its inputs into outputs by using a location-based mobile platform. The social networking Web site provides a service for consumers and businesses. Founded by Dennis Crowley and Naveen Selvadurai, the service allows people to connect with friends and update their location, and it provides businesses with tools to obtain, engage, and retain customers. Nonroutineness characterizes the work of employees at Foursquare, an organic organization that adapts quickly and flexibly to rapid changes. Foursquare co-founder Selvadurai is shown in this photo presenting an address at an annual digital technology forum in Seoul, South Korea.

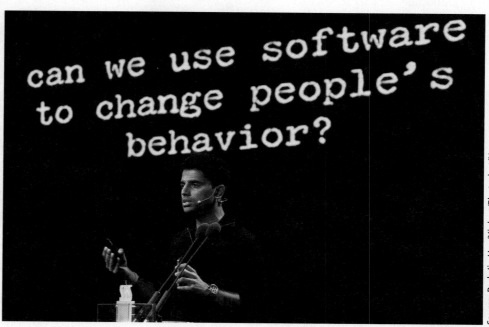

Source: Park Jin Hee/Xinhua/Photoshot/Newscom.

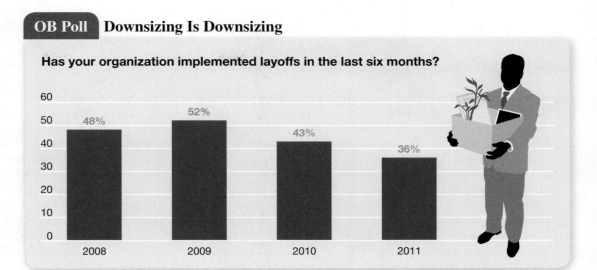

OB Poll   **Downsizing Is Downsizing**

Has your organization implemented layoffs in the last six months?

Source: Based on E. Frauenheim, "The Thought Police?" Workforce Management (March, 2010), pp. 28-31; "Companies Grapple with Viral Vents," Workforce Management (December, 2010), p. 6.

the size of the workforce has an immediately positive outcome in the form of lower wage costs. Companies downsizing to improve strategic focus often see positive effects on stock prices after the announcement. On the other hand, among companies that only cut employees but don't restructure, profits and stock prices usually decline. Part of the problem is the effect of downsizing on employee attitudes. Those who remain often feel worried about future layoffs and may be less committed to the organization.[25] Stress reactions can lead to increased sickness absences, lower concentration on the job, and lower creativity. In companies that don't invest much in their employees, downsizing can also lead to more voluntary turnover, so vital human capital is lost. The result is a company that is more anemic than lean.

Companies can reduce negative impacts by preparing in advance, thus alleviating some employee stress and strengthening support for the new direction.[26] Here are some effective strategies for downsizing. Most are closely linked to the principles for organizational justice we've discussed previously:

- **Investment.**   Companies that downsize to focus on core competencies are more effective when they invest in high-involvement work practices afterward.
- **Communication.**   When employers make efforts to discuss downsizing with employees early, employees are less worried about the outcomes and feel the company is taking their perspective into account.
- **Participation.**   Employees worry less if they can participate in the process in some way. Voluntary early-retirement programs or severance packages can help achieve leanness without layoffs.
- **Assistance.**   Severance, extended health care benefits, and job search assistance demonstrate a company cares about its employees and honors their contributions.

In short, companies that make themselves lean can be more agile, efficient, and productive—but only if they make cuts carefully and help employees through the process.

Downsizing with a Conscience

Especially during economic down times, organizations may have to reduce headcount. The negative effects on those who remain are well documented and include increased sickness absence, withdrawal from work tasks, intentions to sue the organization, stress, dissatisfaction, and loss of commitment.

Do employers have a responsibility to help cushion the blow of downsizing? While ethicists debate how much organizations should help laid-off employees, they generally agree that firms that *can* afford to do something probably should. Indeed, this assistance can work in the organization's self-interest, by increasing commitment among those who remain and reducing stress and strain for all. Managing layoffs with an eye to the

organization's reputation may also be important for hiring new employees when economic prospects improve.

Here are some suggestions to minimize the negative impact of downsizing on employees:

1. Managers are often reticent to give out information about future company plans, but research clearly suggests that ample advance warning about downsizing can reduce employee distress. Open communication makes it much easier for employees to plan how they will respond.
2. Deliver the news about layoffs in a compassionate, personal manner. Let employees know face-to-face they are being let go. This can be hard for managers who would rather

avoid conflict or angry encounters, but most research suggests employees prefer to find out about a job loss in this manner (as opposed to e-mail).
3. Explore ways to help, such as by providing job search assistance or severance pay. This might not always be financially feasible, but it's ethically responsible to do everything you can to help departing employees land on their feet.

Sources: B. Weinstein, "Downsizing 101" *Bloomberg Businessweek* (September 12, 2008), www.businessweek.com; S. Randall, "Attracting Layoff-Wary Millennials," *Workforce Management Online* (February 2010), www.workforce.com; and D. K. Datta, J. P. Guthrie, D. Basuil, and A. Pandey, "Causes and Effects of Employee Downsizing: A Review and Synthesis," *Journal of Management* 36, no. 1 (2010), pp. 281–348.

Why Do Structures Differ?

6   Demonstrate how organizational structures differ, and contrast mechanistic and organic structural models.

We've described organizational designs ranging from the highly structured bureaucracy to the amorphous boundaryless organization. The other designs we discussed exist somewhere in between.

Exhibit 15-7 recaps our discussions by presenting two extreme models of organizational design. One we'll call the **mechanistic model**. It's generally synonymous with the bureaucracy in that it has highly standardized processes for work, high formalization, and more managerial hierarchy. The other extreme, the **organic model**, looks a lot like the boundaryless organization. It's flat, has fewer formal procedures for making decisions, has multiple decision makers, and favors flexible practices.[27]

With these two models in mind, let's ask a few questions: Why are some organizations structured along more mechanistic lines whereas others follow organic characteristics? What forces influence the choice of design? In this section, we present the major causes or determinants of an organization's structure.[28]

Organizational Strategy

Because structure is a means to achieve objectives, and objectives derive from the organization's overall strategy, it's only logical that structure should follow strategy. If management significantly changes the organization's strategy,

Exhibit **15-7**	**Mechanistic versus Organic Models**

The Mechanistic Model

The Organic Model

- High specialization
- Rigid departmentalization
- Clear chain of command
- Narrow spans of control
- Centralization
- High formalization

- Cross-functional teams
- Cross-hierarchical teams
- Free flow of information
- Wide spans of control
- Decentralization
- Low formalization

MyManagementLab

For an interactive application of this topic, check out this chapter's simulation activity at **www.pearsonglobaleditions.com/ mymanagementlab.**

the structure must change to accommodate.[29] Most current strategy frameworks focus on three strategy dimensions—innovation, cost minimization, and imitation—and the structural design that works best with each.[30]

To what degree does an organization introduce major new products or services? An **innovation strategy** strives to achieve meaningful and unique innovations. Obviously, not all firms pursue innovation. Apple and 3M do, but conservative retailer Marks & Spencer doesn't. Innovative firms will use competitive pay and benefits to attract top candidates and motivate employees to take risks. Some degree of mechanistic structure can actually benefit innovation. Well-developed communication channels, policies for enhancing long-term commitment, and clear channels of authority all may make it easier for rapid changes to occur smoothly.

An organization pursuing a **cost-minimization strategy** tightly controls costs, refrains from incurring unnecessary expenses, and cuts prices in selling a basic product. This describes the strategy pursued by Walmart and the makers of generic or store-label grocery products. Cost-minimizing organizations pursue fewer policies meant to develop commitment among their workforce.

Organizations following an **imitation strategy** try to both minimize risk and maximize opportunity for profit, moving new products or entering new markets only after innovators have proven their viability. Mass-market fashion

mechanistic model *A structure characterized by extensive departmentalization, high formalization, a limited information network, and centralization.*

organic model *A structure that is flat, uses cross-hierarchical and cross-functional teams, has low formalization, possesses a comprehensive information network, and relies on participative decision making.*

innovation strategy *A strategy that emphasizes the introduction of major new products and services.*

cost-minimization strategy *A strategy that emphasizes tight cost controls, avoidance of unnecessary innovation or marketing expenses, and price cutting.*

imitation strategy *A strategy that seeks to move into new products or new markets only after their viability has already been proven.*

Exhibit 15-8	The Strategy–Structure Relationship
Strategy	**Structural Option**
Innovation	**Organic:** A loose structure; low specialization, low formalization, decentralized
Cost minimization	**Mechanistic:** Tight control; extensive work specialization, high formalization, high centralization
Imitation	**Mechanistic and organic:** Mix of loose with tight properties; tight controls over current activities and looser controls for new undertakings

manufacturers that copy designer styles follow this strategy, as do firms such as Hewlett-Packard and Caterpillar. They follow smaller and more innovative competitors with superior products, but only after competitors have demonstrated the market is there.

Exhibit 15-8 describes the structural option that best matches each strategy. Innovators need the flexibility of the organic structure, whereas cost minimizers seek the efficiency and stability of the mechanistic structure. Imitators combine the two structures. They use a mechanistic structure to maintain tight controls and low costs in their current activities but create organic subunits in which to pursue new undertakings.

Organization Size

An organization's size significantly affects its structure.[31] Organizations that employ 2,000 or more people tend to have more specialization, more departmentalization, more vertical levels, and more rules and regulations than do small organizations. However, size becomes less important as an organization expands. Why? At around 2,000 employees, an organization is already fairly mechanistic; 500 more employees won't have much impact. But adding 500 employees to an organization of only 300 is likely to significantly shift it toward a more mechanistic structure.

Technology

Technology describes the way an organization transfers inputs into outputs. Every organization has at least one technology for converting financial, human, and physical resources into products or services. Ford Motor Company uses an assembly-line process to make its products. Colleges may use a number of instructional technologies—the ever-popular lecture method, case analysis, the experiential exercise, programmed learning, and online instruction and distance learning. Regardless, organizational structures adapt to their technology.

Numerous studies have examined the technology–structure relationship.[32] What differentiates technologies is their *degree of routineness*. Routine activities are characterized by automated and standardized operations. Examples are injection-mold production of plastic knobs, automated transaction processing of sales transactions, and the printing and binding of this book. Nonroutine activities are customized and require frequent revision and updating. They include furniture restoring, custom shoemaking, genetic research, and the writing and editing of this book. In general, organizations engaged in nonroutine activities tend to prefer organic structures, while those performing routine activities prefer mechanistic structures.

These employees of a restaurant in Urumqi, China, stand in formation while attending a meeting before they start their jobs. It's a common practice in China for employers to gather employees before they begin work to give them a pep talk and instructions for their work day. This daily ritual is acceptable to Chinese employees because power distance is high in China and workers are much more accepting of mechanistic structures than those from lower power-distance cultures. Research suggests that a nation's culture and its employees' preference for structure will influence worker performance and satisfaction.

Source: Li Ziheng /Newscom.

Environment

An organization's **environment** includes outside institutions or forces that can affect its performance, such as suppliers, customers, competitors, government regulatory agencies, and public pressure groups. Dynamic environments create significantly more uncertainty for managers than do static ones. To minimize uncertainty, managers may broaden their structure to sense and respond to threats. For example, most companies, including Pepsi and Southwest Airlines, have added social networking departments to counter negative information posted on blogs. Or companies may form strategic alliances, such as when Microsoft and Yahoo! joined forces to better compete with Google.

Any organization's environment has three dimensions: capacity, volatility, and complexity.[33] *Capacity* refers to the degree to which the environment can support growth. Rich and growing environments generate excess resources, which can buffer the organization in times of relative scarcity.

Volatility describes the degree of instability in the environment. A dynamic environment with a high degree of unpredictable change makes it difficult for management to make accurate predictions. Because information technology changes at such a rapid place, for instance, more organizations' environments are becoming volatile.

Finally, *complexity* is the degree of heterogeneity and concentration among environmental elements. Simple environments—like the tobacco industry—are homogeneous and concentrated. Environments characterized by heterogeneity and dispersion—like the broadband industry—are complex and diverse, with numerous competitors.

technology *The way in which an organization transfers its inputs into outputs.*

environment *Institutions or forces outside an organization that potentially affect the organization's performance.*

"Employees Resent Outsourcing"

Surprisingly, this statement appears to be false.

Two relatively new ways organizations restructure themselves are *outsourcing* (moving work to another domestic company) and *offshoring* (moving work to another country). For example, a Denver-based company that contracts with a call center vendor in Cleveland is outsourcing those operations. If the same company decides to contact with a call center in Bangalore, India, it is offshoring.

Like downsizing, outsourcing and offshoring are restructuring efforts primarily pursued for cost-saving reasons; some companies might undertake all three. All result in job loss for the organization.

Yet, a recent study of 13,683 U.S. employees (all of whom retained their jobs) suggests that employees react differently to these three restructuring efforts. Predictably, where downsizing and offshoring occurred, employees reacted negatively, reporting significantly lower job satisfaction and organizational commitment than in matched organizations where they did not occur. Surprisingly, however, this study found no negative effects of outsourcing on these attitudes.

The authors speculate that employees may view outsourcing less negatively because they see it as less of a threat to their jobs. Future research is needed to test this explanation.

Sources: C. P. Maertz, J. W. Wiley, C. LeRouge, and M. A. Campion, "Downsizing Effects on Survivors: Layoffs, Offshoring, and Outsourcing," *Industrial Relations* 49, no. 2 (2010), pp. 275–285; and L. H. Nishii, D. P. Lepak, and B. Schneider, "Employee Attributions of the 'Why' of HR Practices: Their Effects on Employee Attitudes and Behaviors, and Customer Satisfaction," *Personnel Psychology* 61, no. 3 (2008), pp. 503–545.

Exhibit 15-9 summarizes our definition of the environment along its three dimensions. The arrows indicate movement toward higher uncertainty. Thus, organizations that operate in environments characterized as scarce, dynamic, and complex face the greatest degree of uncertainty because they have high unpredictability, little room for error, and a diverse set of elements in the environment to monitor constantly.

Given this three-dimensional definition of *environment,* we can offer some general conclusions about environmental uncertainty and structural arrangements. The more scarce, dynamic, and complex the environment, the more organic a structure should be. The more abundant, stable, and simple the environment, the more the mechanistic structure will be preferred.

Exhibit **15-9**	Three-Dimensional Model of the Environment

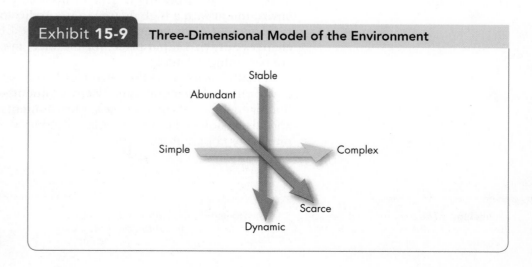

Organizational Designs and Employee Behavior

7 Analyze the behavioral implications of different organizational designs.

We opened this chapter by implying that an organization's structure can have significant effects on its members. What might those effects be?

A review of the evidence leads to a pretty clear conclusion: you can't generalize! Not everyone prefers the freedom and flexibility of organic structures. Different factors stand out in different structures as well. In highly formalized, heavily structured, mechanistic organizations, the level of fairness in formal policies and procedures is a very important predictor of satisfaction. In more personal, individually adaptive organic organizations, employees value interpersonal justice more.[34] Some people are most productive and satisfied when work tasks are standardized and ambiguity minimized—that is, in mechanistic structures. So, any discussion of the effect of organizational design on employee behavior has to address individual differences. To do so, let's consider employee preferences for work specialization, span of control, and centralization.[35]

The evidence generally indicates that *work specialization* contributes to higher employee productivity—but at the price of reduced job satisfaction. However, work specialization is not an unending source of higher productivity. Problems start to surface, and productivity begins to suffer, when the human diseconomies of doing repetitive and narrow tasks overtake the economies of specialization. As the workforce has become more highly educated and desirous of jobs that are intrinsically rewarding, we seem to reach the point at which productivity begins to decline more quickly than in the past.

There is still a segment of the workforce that prefers the routine and repetitiveness of highly specialized jobs. Some individuals want work that makes minimal intellectual demands and provides the security of routine; for them, high work specialization is a source of job satisfaction. The question, of course, is whether they represent 2 percent of the workforce or 52 percent. Given that some self-selection operates in the choice of careers, we might conclude that negative behavioral outcomes from high specialization are most likely to surface in professional jobs occupied by individuals with high needs for personal growth and diversity.

It is probably safe to say no evidence supports a relationship between *span of control* and employee satisfaction or performance. Although it is intuitively attractive to argue that large spans might lead to higher employee performance because they provide more distant supervision and more opportunity for personal initiative, the research fails to support this notion. Some people like to be left alone; others prefer the security of a boss who is quickly available at all times. Consistent with several of the contingency theories of leadership discussed in Chapter 12, we would expect factors such as employees' experiences and abilities and the degree of structure in their tasks to explain when wide or narrow spans of control are likely to contribute to their performance and job satisfaction. However, some evidence indicates that a *manager's* job satisfaction increases as the number of employees supervised increases.

We find fairly strong evidence linking *centralization* and job satisfaction. In general, less centralized organizations have a greater amount of autonomy. And autonomy appears positively related to job satisfaction. But, again, while one employee may value freedom, another may find autonomous environments frustratingly ambiguous.

Our conclusion: to maximize employee performance and satisfaction, managers must take individual differences, such as experience, personality, and the work task, into account. Culture should factor in, too.

We can draw one obvious insight: other things equal, people don't select employers randomly. They are attracted to, are selected by, and stay with organizations that suit their personal characteristics.[36] Job candidates who prefer predictability are likely to seek out and take employment in mechanistic structures, and those who want autonomy are more likely to end up in an organic structure. Thus, the effect of structure on employee behavior is undoubtedly reduced when the selection process facilitates proper matching of individual characteristics with organizational characteristics.

Although research is slim, it does suggest national culture influences the preference for structure.[37] Organizations that operate with people from high power-distance cultures, such as Greece, France, and most of Latin America, find their employees are much more accepting of mechanistic structures than are employees from low power-distance countries. So consider cultural differences along with individual differences when predicting how structure will affect employee performance and satisfaction.

MyManagementLab

Now that you have finished this chapter, go back to **www.pearsonglobaleditions.com/mymanagementlab** to continue practicing and applying the concepts you've learned.

Summary and Implications for Managers

The theme of this chapter is that an organization's internal structure contributes to explaining and predicting behavior. That is, in addition to individual and group factors, the structural relationships in which people work has a bearing on employee attitudes and behavior. What's the basis for this argument? To the degree that an organization's structure reduces ambiguity for employees and clarifies concerns such as "What am I supposed to do?" "How am I supposed to do it?" "To whom do I report?" and "To whom do I go if I have a problem?" it shapes their attitudes and facilitates and motivates them to higher levels of performance. Exhibit 15-10 summarizes what we've discussed. There are a few other take-home messages worth considering:

- Although specialization can bring efficiency, excessive specialization also can breed dissatisfaction and reduced motivation.

Exhibit 15-10   Organization Structure: Its Determinants and Outcomes

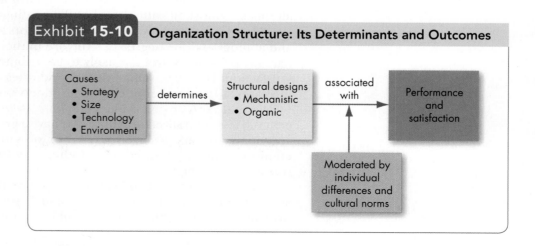

The End of Management

anagement—at least as we know it—is dying. Formal organizational structures are giving way to flatter, less bureaucratic, less formal structures. And that's a good thing.

Today, leaders are celebrated for triumphing *over* structure rather than for working well within it. Innovative companies like Apple, Google, Facebook, Twitter, and Groupon were born and thrive thanks not to a multilayered bureaucracy but to an innovative idea that was creatively executed by a flexible group of people freely collaborating. Management in those companies exists to facilitate, rather than control.

Only 100 of today's *Fortune* 500 companies existed in 1957. Yet management theory and practice continue to hew to a 1957 mode of thinking. As one future-minded expert noted, "The single biggest reason companies fail is that they overinvest in what is, as opposed to what might be." How does a traditional, formal, bureaucratic structure foster "what might be" thinking? It doesn't.

Inertia can cause even innovative companies to become bureaucratized. Google co-founder Larry Page replaced ex-CEO Eric Schmidt when Page's "desire to move quickly on ambitious ideas was stifled by company bureaucracy." Page and co-founder Sergey Brin know traditional, bureaucratic structures are Google's greatest threats.

Some enlightened leaders have learned from their mistakes. Early in his career, says Cristóbal Conde, president and CEO of IT company SunGard, "I was very command-and-control, very top-down. I felt I was smart, and that my decisions would be better." After some of his best people left because they felt constrained, Conde decided to flatten and loosen the structure. He says: "A CEO needs to focus more on the platform that enables collaboration. . . . By having technologies that allow people to see what others are doing, share information, collaborate, brag about their successes—that is what flattens the organization."

here is no "right size fits all" approach to organizational structure. How flat, informal, and collaborative an organization should be depends on many factors. Let's consider two cases.

People lauded how loosely and informally Warren Buffett structured his investment firm, Berkshire Hathaway. Buffett spends most of his day reading and talking informally "with highly gifted people whom he trusts and who trust him." This all sounded wonderful until it was discovered Buffett's CFO and heir apparent David Sokol was on the take. Sokol made $3 million when he successfully lobbied for Berkshire Hathaway to acquire a firm in which he had secretly acquired a significant stake. His insider maneuvers discovered, Sokol was forced to resign. Wouldn't Buffett have known Sokol was compromised if he supervised more closely or had structures in place to check such "freedom"? It's hard to argue with Berkshire Hathaway's past successes, but they don't prove the company is ideally structured.

Berkshire Hathaway is a cautionary example of the perils of a structure that's *too* flat and informal. For the benefits of a formal, complex structure, look no further than Boeing. Boeing's 787 "Dreamliner"—built of composite materials and 20 percent more fuel efficient than comparable passenger planes—is one of the most innovative products in the history of aviation and the fastest-selling ever. How was the Dreamliner invented and produced? Through an enormously complex planning, design, engineering, production, and testing process. To build the Dreamliner, Boeing has contracted with 40 different suppliers at 135 sites around the world—a feat it could not accomplish without an organizational structure to support it. Boeing's organizational structure is quite formal, complex, and even bureaucratic. The Dreamliner proves innovation does not need to come from radical organizational structures.

Sources: A. Bryant, "Structure? The Flatter the Better," *The New York Times* (January 17, 2010), p. BU2; A. R. Sorkin, "Delegator in Chief," *The New York Times* (April 24, 2011), p. B4; A. Murray, "The End of Management," *The Wall Street Journal* (August 21, 2010), p. W3; and A. Efrati and S. Morrison, "Chief Seeks More Agile Google," *The Wall Street Journal* (January 22, 2011), pp. B1, B4.

- Formal hierarchies offer advantages like unification of mission and goals, while employees in excessively rigid hierarchies can feel they have no power or autonomy. As with specialization, the key is striking the right balance.

- Virtual and boundaryless forms are changing the face of many organizations. Contemporary managers should thoroughly understand their implications and recognize advantages and potential pitfalls.

- Organizational downsizing can lead to major cost savings and focus organizations around their core competencies, but it can leave workers dissatisfied and worried about the future of their jobs.

- When determining an appropriate organizational form, managers will need to consider scarcity, dynamism, and complexity of the environment and balance the organic and mechanistic elements appropriate to their organization's environment.

QUESTIONS FOR REVIEW

1 What are the six key elements that define an organization's structure?

2 What is a bureaucracy, and how does it differ from a simple structure?

3 What is a matrix organization?

4 What are the characteristics of a virtual organization?

5 How can managers create a boundaryless organization?

6 Why do organizational structures differ, and what is the difference between a mechanistic structure and an organic structure?

7 What are the behavioral implications of different organizational designs?

EXPERIENTIAL EXERCISE Dismantling a Bureaucracy

Pre-work

In order to understand how to improve an organizational structure, it is important to start with a clear understanding of how an organization is currently structured. For this exercise, you will perform research on the college or university you are attending or another organization that your professor identifies. Using the organization's Web site, find out about different administrative units, paying special attention to different noncore functions like finance, information technology, and human resources. While doing this research, assemble a list of five features that resemble a bureaucracy and five features that you think might be successfully managed by an external partner.

Create Groups

Your instructor will form you into groups of at least four individuals at the start of class.

Assess Bureaucracy

Your initial task will be to share your assessments of the features of the organization that seem bureaucratic in nature. What are the common functions that tend to be run in a bureaucratic manner? Try to identify standardized work practices that enhance coordination and control. In particular, think of systems of rules, regulations, departments, and offices that have highly specific and specialized roles. Collectively, your team will take about 15 minutes to accomplish this task.

Dismantle Bureaucracy

To dismantle a bureaucracy, it is important to consider both the advantages and disadvantages of the current system. Thus, the goal of the second part of the exercise is to employ techniques related to boundaryless and virtual organizations to reduce bureaucracy in a debate format, with one person arguing for why changes can be good, while the other person argues for why changes might be disruptive.

The team will start by dividing into two subgroups and will work in these groups independently for about 10 minutes. One member will have the responsibility to identify alternative mechanisms that might be able to replace the current bureaucratic structure while still keeping all the same functions "in-house" by creating a boundaryless organization. How can the organizations get the same results but with a different set of control systems? Another member will identify reasons it might be difficult to transition from a bureaucracy to the system you advocated in point #2. What are the potential sources of resistance to change? These two members should work together to arrive at a consensus for how bureaucracy might be minimized without damaging organizational productivity and efficiency.

At the same time, the second group of two individuals will work on a different task. One member will consider how each organization can take on elements of a virtual organization as a way to become less bureaucratic. Identify elements of the organization that might be downsized or outsourced. Another member will identify why "going virtual" might be a bad idea, looking to potential loss of control and poor information exchange as possible obstacles. These two members will arrive at a consensus for how the organization can be made as lean as possible without damaging organizational productivity and efficiency.

Finally, all four members of the team will come together to arrive at a consensus for how to limit bureaucracy by either (1) using new systems that are consistent with a boundaryless organization or (2) using elements of a lean, virtual organization to strip off unnecessary bureaucratic layers. This final combination process should take about 10 minutes.

Debriefing

After each group has come to a consensus for how to limit bureaucracy, the instructor will lead an all-class discussion in which each group will describe its eventual approach to minimizing bureaucracy in its organization. Your instructor will provide additional insight into why it may be difficult to change a bureaucracy, as well as suggesting areas where bureaucracy can be effectively limited through either boundarylessness or virtuality.

ETHICAL DILEMMA Directing the Directors

One critical structural element of most corporations is the board of directors. In principle, chief executives report to the directors. In practice, however, boards do not always function as you might expect. Boards were implicated in many corporate scandals of the past decade—either because they actively condoned unethical behavior or because they turned a blind eye to it. Many also blamed lax board oversight for the financial meltdown and ensuing recession. Business media have called boards "absolutely useless" and "a sham."

One of the keys to reforming board behavior is ensuring that boards function independently of the CEO. The Securities and Exchange Commission (SEC) and the New York Stock Exchange (NYSE) have set guidelines for the independence of directors—who should not be otherwise affiliated with, employed by, or connected to the organization they direct. The more independent the structure and composition of the board, the better the corporation will be governed, and the more effective it will be.

One example of nonindependence came to light in 2010. In addition to $225,000 in cash and deferred stock he was paid to function as a member of Citibank's board, Robert Joss earned $350,000 in consulting fees for advising the bank on projects "from time to time." When asked to comment, Joss replied, "I'm comfortable that I can handle that."

Such examples seem egregious violations of independence in board structures. Yet, evidence on the link between board independence and firm performance is surprisingly weak. One recent review concluded, "There is no evidence of systematic relationships between board composition and corporate financial performance."

Another structural issue is how the roles of the CEO and chairperson are filled—for instance, whether these positions are held by different people. Most argue that for the board to function independently, the roles must be separate, and *Bloomberg Businessweek* estimates that 37 percent of the 500 largest U.S. corporations do split them. Yet here, too, the evidence is weak: it doesn't appear that corporations with separate CEOs and chairs perform any better than those where the CEO and chairperson are one and the same.

Questions

1. Do you think Citibank's consulting arrangement with Robert Joss was unethical? Or is it possible to justify the arrangement?

2. Why do you think board structure doesn't appear to matter to corporate performance?

3. Do you think the roles of CEO and chairperson of the board of directors should always be separate? Why or why not?

Sources: D. R. Dalton and C. M. Dalton, "Integration of Micro and Macro Studies in Governance Research: CEO Duality, Board Composition, and Financial Performance," *Journal of Management* 37, no. 2 (2011), pp. 404–411; T. J. Neff and R. Charan, "Separating the CEO and Chairman Roles," *Bloomberg Businessweek* (January 15, 2010), downloaded July 5, 2011, from www.businessweek.com/; B. Keoun, "Citigroup to Pay Director $350,000 for Weeks of Consulting," *Bloomberg News* (May 10, 2010), downloaded July 5, 2011, from www.bloomberg.com/news/.

CASE INCIDENT 1 Creative Deviance: Bucking the Hierarchy?

One of the major functions of an organizational hierarchy is to increase standardization and control for top managers. Using the chain of command, managers can direct the activities of subordinates toward a common purpose. If the right person with a creative vision is in charge of a hierarchy, the results can be phenomenal. Until Steve Jobs' regrettable passing in October of 2011, Apple had used a strongly top-down creative process in which most major decisions and innovations flowed directly through Jobs and then were delegated to sub-teams as specific assignments to complete.

Then there is creative deviance, in which individuals create extremely successful products despite being told by senior management to stop working on them. The electrostatic displays used in more than half of Hewlett-Packard's instruments, the tape slitter that was one of the most important process innovations in 3M's history, and Nichia's development of multi-billion-dollar LED bright lighting technology were all officially rejected by the management hierarchy. In all these cases, an approach like Apple's would have shut down some of the most successful products these companies ever produced. Doing "business as usual" can become such an imperative in a hierarchical organization that new ideas are seen as threats rather than opportunities for development.

It's not immediately apparent why top-down decision making works so well for one highly creative company like Apple, while hierarchy nearly ruined innovations at several other organizations. It may be that Apple's structure is actually quite simple, with relatively few layers and a great deal of responsibility placed on each individual for his or her own outcomes. Or it may be that Apple simply had a very unique leader who was able to rise above the conventional strictures of a CEO to create a culture of constant innovation.

Questions

1. Do you think it's possible for an organization to deliberately create an "anti-hierarchy" to encourage employees to engage in more acts of creative deviance? What steps might a company take to encourage creative deviance?

2. What are the dangers of an approach that encourages creative deviance?

3. Why do you think a company like Apple is able to be creative with a strongly hierarchical structure, whereas other companies find hierarchy limiting?

4. Do you think Apple's success has been entirely dependent upon Steve Jobs' role as head of the hierarchy? What are the potential liabilities of a company that is so strongly connected to the decision-making of a single Individual?

Sources: C. Mainemelis, "Stealing Fire: Creative Deviance in the Evolution of New Ideas," *Academy of Management Review* 35, no. 4 (2010), pp. 558–578; and A. Lashinsky, "Inside Apple," *Fortune* (May 23, 2011), pp. 125–134.

CASE INCIDENT 2 Siemens' Simple Structure—Not

There is perhaps no tougher task for an executive than to restructure a European organization. Ask former Siemens CEO Klaus Kleinfeld.

Siemens—with €76 billion in revenue in financial year 2009/2010, some 405,000 employees, and branches in 190 countries—is one of the largest electronics companies in the world. Although the company has long been respected for its engineering prowess, it's also derided for its sluggishness and mechanistic structure. So when Kleinfeld took over as CEO, he sought to restructure the company, making the structure less bureaucratic so decisions are made more quickly. He spun off underperforming businesses and simplified the company's structure.

One of the challenges of transforming European organizations is the customary participation of employees in executive decisions. Half the seats on the Seimens board of directors are allocated to labor representatives. Not surprisingly, labor did not react positively to Kleinfeld's restructuring efforts, and picket lines became a constant presence outside his corporate offices. In his efforts to speed the restructuring, labor groups alleged, Kleinfeld secretly bankrolled a business-friendly workers' group to try to undermine Germany's main industrial union.

Due to this and other allegations, Kleinfeld was forced out in June 2007 and replaced by Peter Löscher. Löscher has found the same tensions between inertia and the need for restructuring. Only a month after becoming CEO, he faced the decision whether to spin off the firm's underperforming €10 billion auto parts unit, VDO. He had to weigh the forces for stability, which want to protect worker interests, against U.S.-style pressures for financial performance. One of VDO's possible buyers was a U.S. company, TRW, the controlling interest of which is held by Blackstone, a U.S. private equity firm. German labor representatives scorn such firms as "locusts." When Löscher decided to sell VDO to German tire giant Continental Corporation, Continental promptly began to downsize and restructure the unit's operations.

Löscher has continued to restructure Siemens. In mid-2008, he announced elimination of nearly 17,000 jobs worldwide. He also announced plans to consolidate more business units and reorganize the company's operations geographically. "The speed at which business is changing worldwide has increased considerably, and we're orienting Siemens accordingly," Löscher said.

Under Löscher, Siemens has experienced its ups and downs. In 2008, its stock price fell 26 percent on the European stock exchange and 31 percent on the New York Stock Exchange. In 2009, however, Siemens' earnings were up 32 percent, despite an ongoing global recession, and most indicators suggested 2011 would be an equally profitable year.

Though Löscher's restructuring efforts have generated far less controversy than Kleinfeld's, that doesn't mean they went over well with all constituents. Of the 2008 job cuts, Werner Neugebauer, regional director for a union representing many Siemens employees, said, "The planned job cuts are incomprehensible nor acceptable for these reasons, and in this extent, completely exaggerated."

Questions

1. What do Kleinfeld's efforts at Siemens tell you about the difficulties of restructuring organizations?

2. Why do you think Löscher's restructuring decisions have generated less controversy than did Kleinfeld's?

3. Assume a colleague read this case and concluded, "This case proves restructuring efforts do not necessarily improve a company's financial performance." How would you respond?

4. Do you think a CEO who decides to restructure or downsize a company takes the well-being of employees into account? Should he or she do so? Why or why not?

Sources: Based on A. Davidson, "Peter Löscher Makes Siemens Less German," *The Sunday Times* (June 29, 2008), business.timesonline.co.uk; M. Esterl and D. Crawford, "Siemens CEO Put to Early Test," *The Wall Street Journal* (July 23, 2007), p. A8; J. Ewing, "Siemens' Culture Clash," *BusinessWeek* (January 29, 2007), pp. 42–46; and C. C. Williams, "Slimmed-Down Siemens Girds for Growth," *Barron's* (November 29, 2010), pp. 26–27.

ENDNOTES

1. See, for instance, R. L. Daft, *Organization Theory and Design,* 10th ed. (Cincinnati, OH: South-Western Publishing, 2010).

2. T. W. Malone, R. J. Laubacher, and T. Johns, "The Age of Hyperspecialization," *Harvard Business Review* (July–August 2011), pp. 56–65.

3. C. Hymowitz, "Managers Suddenly Have to Answer to a Crowd of Bosses," *The Wall Street Journal* (August 12, 2003), p. B1.

4. See, for instance, "How Hierarchy Can Hurt Strategy Execution," *Harvard Business Review* (July–August 2010), pp. 74–75.

5. See, for instance, J. H. Gittell, "Supervisory Span, Relational Coordination, and Flight Departure Performance: A Reassessment of Postbureaucracy Theory," *Organization Science* (July–August 2001), pp. 468–483.

6. J. Child and R. G. McGrath, "Organizations Unfettered: Organizational Form in an Information-Intensive Economy," *Academy of Management Journal* (December 2001), pp. 1135–1148.

7. B. Brown and S. D. Anthony, "How P&G Tripled Its Innovation Success Rate," *Harvard Business Review* (June 2011), pp. 64–72.

8. A. Leiponen and C. E. Helfat, "Location, Decentralization, and Knowledge Sources for Innovation," *Organization Science* 22, no. 3 (2011), pp. 641–658.

9. H. Mintzberg, *Structure in Fives: Designing Effective Organizations* (Upper Saddle River, NJ: Prentice Hall, 1983), p. 157.

10. W. M. Bulkeley, "Back from the Brink," *The Wall Street Journal* (April 24, 2006), pp. B1, B3.

11. L. R. Burns and D. R. Wholey, "Adoption and Abandonment of Matrix Management Programs: Effects of Organizational Characteristics and Interorganizational Networks," *Academy of Management Journal* (February 1993), pp. 106–138; J. R. Galbraith, *Designing Matrix Organizations that Actually Work: How IBM, Procter & Gamble, and Others Design for Success* (San Francisco: Jossey Bass, 2009); and E. Krell, "Managing the Matrix," *HRMagazine* (April 2011), pp. 69–71.

12. See, for instance, T. Sy and L. S. D'Annunzio, "Challenges and Strategies of Matrix Organizations: Top-Level and Mid-Level Managers' Perspectives," *Human Resource Planning* 28, no. 1 (2005), pp. 39–48; and T. Sy and S. Cote, "Emotional Intelligence: A Key Ability to Succeed in the Matrix Organization," *Journal of Management Development* 23, no. 5 (2004), pp. 437–455.

13. N. Anand and R. L. Daft, "What Is the Right Organization Design?" *Organizational Dynamics* 36, no. 4 (2007), pp. 329–344.

14. See, for instance, R. E. Miles and C. C. Snow, "The New Network Firm: A Spherical Structure Built on Human Investment Philosophy," *Organizational Dynamics* (Spring 1995), pp. 5–18; D. Pescovitz, "The Company Where Everybody's a Temp," *New York Times Magazine* (June 11, 2000), pp. 94–96; B. Hedberg, G. Dahlgren, J. Hansson, and N. Olve, *Virtual Organizations and Beyond* (New York: Wiley, 2001); N. S. Contractor, S. Wasserman, and K. Faust, "Testing Multitheoretical, Multilevel Hypotheses About Organizational Networks: An Analytic Framework and Empirical Example," *Academy of Management Review* 31, no. 3 (2006) pp. 681–703; and Y. Shin, "A Person-Environment Fit Model for Virtual Organizations," *Journal of Management* (October 2004), pp. 725–743.

15. J. Bates, "Making Movies and Moving On," *Los Angeles Times* (January 19, 1998), p. A1.

16. D. Dahl, "Want a Job? Let the Bidding Begin," *Inc.* (March 2011), pp. 94–96.

17. J. Schramm, "At Work in a Virtual World," *HR Magazine* (June 2010), p. 152.

18. C. B. Gibson and J. L. Gibbs, "Unpacking the Concept of Virtuality: The Effects of Geographic Dispersion, Electronic Dependence, Dynamic Structure, and National Diversity on Team Innovation," *Administrative Science Quarterly* 51, no. 3 (2006), pp. 451–495; H. M. Latapie and V. N. Tran, "Subculture Formation, Evolution, and Conflict Between Regional Teams in Virtual Organizations," *The Business Review* (Summer 2007), pp. 189–193; and S. Davenport and U. Daellenbach, "'Belonging' to a Virtual Research Center: Exploring the Influence of Social Capital Formation Processes on Member Identification in a Virtual Organization" *British Journal of Management* 22, no. 1 (2011), pp. 54–76.

19. "GE: Just Your Average Everyday $60 Billion Family Grocery Store," *IndustryWeek* (May 2, 1994), pp. 13–18.

20. The following is based on D. D. Davis, "Form, Function and Strategy in Boundaryless Organizations," in A. Howard (ed.), *The Changing Nature of Work* (San Francisco: Jossey-Bass, 1995), pp. 112–138; R. L. Cross, A. Yan, and M. R. Louis, "Boundary Activities in 'Boundaryless' Organizations: A Case Study of a Transformation to a Team-Based Structure," *Human Relations* (June 2000), pp. 841–868; and R. Ashkenas, D. Ulrich, T. Jick, and S. Kerr, *The Boundaryless Organization: Breaking the Chains of Organizational Structure*, revised and updated (San Francisco: Jossey-Bass, 2002).

21. See, for example, U. Wassmer, "Alliance Portfolios: A Review and Research Agenda," *Journal of Management* 36, no. 1 (2010), pp 141–171; A. M. Hess and F. T. Rothaemel, "When Are Assets Complementary? Star Scientists, Strategic Alliances, and Innovation in the Pharmaceutical Industry," *Strategic Management Journal* 32, no. 8 (2011), pp. 895–909; and J. A. Adegbesan and M. J. Higgins, "The Intra-Alliance Division of Value Created through Collaboration," *Strategic Management Journal* 32, no. 2 (2011), pp. 187–211.

22. B. White, "VeriSign to Slim Down, Sharpen Its Focus," *The Wall Street Journal* (November 14, 2007), p. A12.

23. S. Player, "Leading the Way to Lean," *Business Finance* (May 2007), pp. 13–16.

24. See J. P. Guthrie and D. K. Datta, "Dumb and Dumber: The Impact of Downsizing on Firm Performance as Moderated by Industry Conditions," *Organization Science* 19, no. 1 (2008), pp. 108–123; and K. P. De Meuse, T. J. Bergmann, P. A. Vanderheiden, and C. E. Roraff, "New Evidence Regarding Organizational Downsizing and a Firm's Financial Performance: A Long-Term Analysis," *Journal of Managerial Issues* 16, no. 2 (2004), pp. 155–177.

25. See, for example, C. O. Trevor and A. J. Nyberg, "Keeping Your Headcount When All About You Are Losing Theirs: Downsizing, Voluntary Turnover Rates, and the Moderating Role of HR Practices," *Academy of Management Journal* 51, no. 2 (2008), pp. 259–276; T. M. Probst, S. M. Stewart, M. L. Gruys, and B. W. Tierney, "Productivity, Counterproductivity and Creativity: The Ups and Downs of Job Insecurity," *Journal of Occupational and Organizational Psychology* 80, no. 3 (2007), pp. 479–497; and C. P. Maertz, J. W. Wiley, C. LeRouge, and M. A. Campion, "Downsizing Effects on Survivors: Layoffs, Offshoring, and Outsourcing," *Industrial Relations* 49, no. 2 (2010), pp. 275–285.

26. C. D. Zatzick, and R. D. Iverson, "High-Involvement Management and Workforce Reduction: Competitive Advantage or Disadvantage?" *Academy of Management Journal* 49, no. 5 (2006), pp. 999–1015; A. Travaglione, and B. Cross, "Diminishing the Social Network in Organizations: Does There Need to Be Such a Phenomenon as 'Survivor Syndrome' After Downsizing?" *Strategic Change* 15, no. 1 (2006), pp. 1–13; and J. D. Kammeyer-Mueller, H. Liao, and R. D. Arvey, "Downsizing and Organizational Performance: A Review of the Literature from a Stakeholder Perspective," *Research in Personnel and Human Resources Management* 20 (2001), pp. 269–329.

27. T. Burns and G. M. Stalker, *The Management of Innovation* (London: Tavistock, 1961); and J. A. Courtright, G. T. Fairhurst, and L. E. Rogers, "Interaction Patterns in Organic and Mechanistic Systems," *Academy of Management Journal* (December 1989), pp. 773–802.

28. This analysis is referred to as a contingency approach to organization design. See, for instance, J. M. Pennings, "Structural

Contingency Theory: A Reappraisal," in B. M. Staw and L. L. Cummings (eds.), *Research in Organizational Behavior*, vol. 14 (Greenwich, CT: JAI Press, 1992), pp. 267–309; J. R. Hollenbeck, H. Moon, A. P. J. Ellis, B. J. West, D. R. Ilgen, L. Sheppard, C. O. L. H. Porter, and J. A. Wagner III, "Structural Contingency Theory and Individual Differences: Examination of External and Internal Person-Team Fit," *Journal of Applied Psychology* (June 2002), pp. 599–606; and A. Drach-Zahavy and A. Freund, "Team Effectiveness Under Stress: A Structural Contingency Approach," *Journal of Organizational Behavior* 28, no. 4 (2007), pp. 423–450.

29. The strategy–structure thesis was originally proposed in A. D. Chandler Jr., *Strategy and Structure: Chapters in the History of the Industrial Enterprise* (Cambridge, MA: MIT Press, 1962). For an updated analysis, see T. L. Amburgey and T. Dacin, "As the Left Foot Follows the Right? The Dynamics of Strategic and Structural Change," *Academy of Management Journal* (December 1994), pp. 1427–1452.

30. See R. E. Miles and C. C. Snow, *Organizational Strategy, Structure, and Process* (New York: McGraw-Hill, 1978); D. C. Galunic and K. M. Eisenhardt, "Renewing the Strategy–Structure–Performance Paradigm," in B. M. Staw and L. L. Cummings (eds.), *Research in Organizational Behavior*, vol. 16 (Greenwich, CT: JAI Press, 1994), pp. 215–255; and S. M. Toh, F. P. Morgeson, and M. A. Campion, "Human Resource Configurations: Investigating Fit with the Organizational Context," *Journal of Applied Psychology* 93, no. 4 (2008), pp. 864–882.

31. See, for instance, P. M. Blau and R. A. Schoenherr, *The Structure of Organizations* (New York: Basic Books, 1971); D. S. Pugh, "The Aston Program of Research: Retrospect and Prospect," in A. H. Van de Ven and W. F. Joyce (eds.), *Perspectives on Organization Design and Behavior* (New York: Wiley, 1981), pp. 135–166; R. Z. Gooding and J. A. Wagner III, "A Meta-Analytic Review of the Relationship Between Size and Performance: The Productivity and Efficiency of Organizations and Their Subunits," *Administrative Science Quarterly* (December 1985), pp. 462–481; and A. C. Bluedorn, "Pilgrim's Progress: Trends and Convergence in Research on Organizational Size and Environments," *Journal of Management* (Summer 1993), pp. 163–192.

32. See C. Perrow, "A Framework for the Comparative Analysis of Organizations," *American Sociological Review* (April 1967), pp. 194–208; J. Hage and M. Aiken, "Routine Technology, Social Structure, and Organizational Goals," *Administrative Science Quarterly* (September 1969), pp. 366–377; C. C. Miller, W. H. Glick, Y. Wang, and G. P. Huber, "Understanding Technology-Structure Relationships: Theory Development and Meta-Analytic Theory Testing," *Academy of Management Journal* (June 1991), pp. 370–399; and W. D. Sine, H. Mitsuhashi, and D. A. Kirsch, "Revisiting Burns and Stalker: Formal Structure and New Venture Performance in Emerging Economic Sectors," *Academy of Management Journal* 49, no. 1 (2006), pp. 121–132.

33. G. G. Dess and D. W. Beard, "Dimensions of Organizational Task Environments," *Administrative Science Quarterly* (March 1984), pp. 52–73; E. A. Gerloff, N. K. Muir, and W. D. Bodensteiner, "Three Components of Perceived Environmental Uncertainty: An Exploratory Analysis of the Effects of Aggregation," *Journal of Management* (December 1991), pp. 749–768; and O. Shenkar, N. Aranya, and T. Almor, "Construct Dimensions in the Contingency Model: An Analysis Comparing Metric and Non-metric Multivariate Instruments," *Human Relations* (May 1995), pp. 559–580.

34. C. S. Spell and T. J. Arnold, "A Multi-Level Analysis of Organizational Justice and Climate, Structure, and Employee Mental Health," *Journal of Management* 33, no. 5 (2007), pp. 724–751; and M. L. Ambrose and M. Schminke, "Organization Structure as a Moderator of the Relationship Between Procedural Justice, Interactional Justice, Perceived Organizational Support, and Supervisory Trust," *Journal of Applied Psychology* 88, no. 2 (2003), pp. 295–305.

35. See, for instance, Spell and Arnold, "A Multi-Level Analysis of Organizational Justice Climate, Structure, and Employee Mental Health"; J. D. Shaw and N. Gupta, "Job Complexity, Performance, and Well-Being: When Does Supplies-Values Fit Matter? *Personnel Psychology* 57, no. 4 (2004), 847–879; and C. Anderson and C. E. Brown, "The Functions and Dysfunctions of Hierarchy," *Research in Organizational Behavior* 30 (2010), pp. 55–89.

36. See, for instance, R. E. Ployhart, J. A. Weekley, and K. Baughman, "The Structure and Function of Human Capital Emergence: A Multilevel Examination of the Attraction-Selection-Attrition Model," *Academy of Management Journal* 49, no. 4 (2006), pp. 661–677.

37. See, for example, P. R. Harris and R. T. Moran, *Managing Cultural Differences*, 5th ed. (Houston, TX: Gulf Publishing, 1999).

LEARNING OBJECTIVES

After studying this chapter, you should be able to:

1 Define *organizational culture,* and describe its common characteristics.

2 Compare the functional and dysfunctional effects of organizational culture on people and the organization.

3 Identify the factors that create and sustain an organization's culture.

4 Show how culture is transmitted to employees.

5 Demonstrate how an ethical culture can be created.

6 Describe a positive organizational culture.

7 Identify characteristics of a spiritual culture.

8 Show how national culture may affect the way organizational culture is transported to a different country.

MyManagementLab

Access a host of interactive learning aids to help strengthen your understanding of the chapter concepts at **www.pearsonglobaleditions .com/mymanagementlab**.

URSULA M. BURNS AND THE CULTURE OF XEROX

Ursula M. Burns is not your typical CEO. She is unusually low key, avoiding the limelight many of her fellow CEOs—from Apple's former CEO Steve Jobs to GE's Jeffrey Immelt—seem to relish. When asked what first surprised her about being CEO, she mentioned the flood of attention. "The accolades I get for doing absolutely nothing are amazing. What have I done?" she asked. "The real story is not Ursula Burns. I just happen to be the person standing up at this point representing Xerox."

We respectfully disagree. Burns is indeed notable as the first African American female CEO of an S&P 100 company. But the real story is the way she is quietly reshaping the culture of the industrial giant.

Historically, Xerox was a photocopying company, so successful that its name became a verb. However, in the 1980s and 1990s, as that business model declined, so did Xerox's profits. When Anne Mulcahy took over Xerox in 2001, some said she won the job no one else wanted. She and Burns planned a bold transformation that included job cuts, but also investing in new technologies.

Since Burns took over in 2009, she has pushed forward two major initiatives. One is product focused: getting Xerox into information technology services. In 2011, Xerox rolled out Xerox Cloud, a set of business services that includes mobile printing and business process management.

Burns' other initiative is cultural: she thinks Xerox's culture is getting in its way. Burns wants Xerox's 130,000 employees to embrace risk-taking, initiative, and frankness. "Terminal niceness" is how Burns describes a key tenet of Xerox's old culture, one she thinks is often counterproductive to growth and innovation.

Maybe, says Burns, Xerox needs to function more like a real family. "When we're in the family, you don't have to be as nice as when you're outside of the family," she says. "I want us to stay civil and kind, but we have to be frank—and the reason we can be frank is because we are all in the same family."

This delicate balance between civility and frankness requires humility. After all, one of the key ways to lead others to be frank is to be honest about your own limits. Burns does that. "I cannot be viewed as the solution to all problems in this company," she notes. She does not expect perfection in herself, or in others. "People actually believe that before they come to you that they have to have perfection," Burns laments. She would much prefer people be honest, open, and decisive. "Decide," she implores. "Do things."

Burns grew up in a gang-infested area of New York City without a father in her life and credits her mother with raising her aspirations and inspiring her humility. Her mother would often bluntly tell Burns to try to be better.

Organizational Culture

When I hear the word culture,
I reach for my Browning.

—Hanns Johst

Photo: President and Delegated Advisor of Xerox. Source: Samuel Sanchez El Pais Photos/Newscom.

Like every major CEO, Burns is a millionaire. Yet she still shops for groceries. She drives herself to work. She cleans her own house. "Where you are is not who you are," her mother often told her. Burns appears to have lived that credo. With quiet determination, she's trying to make Xerox's culture, in some ways, reflect who she is.

Sources: A. Bryant, "We're Family, So We Can Disagree," *The New York Times* (February 21, 2010), pp. BU1, BU9; K. Damore, "Burns: Blazing A New Trail," *CRN* (May 23, 2011), downloaded on July 15, 2011, from www.crn.com/; and D. Mattioli, "Xerox Makes Push for Faster Services Growth," *The Wall Street Journal* (May 11, 2011), downloaded on July 15, 2011, from http://online.wsj.com/.

A strong organizational culture provides stability to an organization. But as the chapter-opening example shows, it's not for everyone. And for some organizations, it can also be a major barrier to change. In this chapter, we show that every organization has a culture that, depending on its strength, can have a significant influence on the attitudes and behaviors of organization members. First let's figure out what kind of organizational culture you prefer. Take the self-assessment to find out.

SELF-ASSESSMENT LIBRARY

What's the Right Organizational Culture for Me?

In the Self-Assessment Library (available on CD and online), take assessment III.B.1 (What's the Right Organizational Culture for Me?) and answer the following questions.

1. Judging from your results, do you fit better in a more formal and structured culture or in a more informal and unstructured culture?
2. Did your results surprise you? Why do you think you scored as you did?
3. How might your results affect your career path?

What Is Organizational Culture?

1 Define *organizational culture* and describe its common characteristics.

An executive once was asked what he thought *organizational culture* meant. He gave essentially the same answer a U.S. Supreme Court justice once gave in attempting to define pornography: "I can't define it, but I know it when I see it." We, however, need a basic definition of organizational culture to better understand the phenomenon. In this section we propose one and review several related ideas.

A Definition of *Organizational Culture*

Organizational culture refers to a system of shared meaning held by members that distinguishes the organization from other organizations.[1] Seven primary characteristics seem to capture the essence of an organization's culture:[2]

1. **Innovation and risk taking.** The degree to which employees are encouraged to be innovative and take risks.
2. **Attention to detail.** The degree to which employees are expected to exhibit precision, analysis, and attention to detail.

3. **Outcome orientation.** The degree to which management focuses on results or outcomes rather than on the techniques and processes used to achieve them.
4. **People orientation.** The degree to which management decisions take into consideration the effect of outcomes on people within the organization.
5. **Team orientation.** The degree to which work activities are organized around teams rather than individuals.
6. **Aggressiveness.** The degree to which people are aggressive and competitive rather than easygoing.
7. **Stability.** The degree to which organizational activities emphasize maintaining the status quo in contrast to growth.

Each of these characteristics exists on a continuum from low to high. Appraising the organization on them, then, gives a composite picture of its culture and a basis for the shared understanding members have about the organization, how things are done in it, and the way they are supposed to behave. Exhibit 16-1

Exhibit 16-1   Contrasting Organizational Cultures

Organization A

This organization is a manufacturing firm. Managers are expected to fully document all decisions, and "good managers" are those who can provide detailed data to support their recommendations. Creative decisions that incur significant change or risk are not encouraged. Because managers of failed projects are openly criticized and penalized, managers try not to implement ideas that deviate much from the status quo. One lower-level manager quoted an often-used phrase in the company: "If it ain't broke, don't fix it."

There are extensive rules and regulations in this firm that employees are required to follow. Managers supervise employees closely to ensure there are no deviations. Management is concerned with high productivity, regardless of the impact on employee morale or turnover.

Work activities are designed around individuals. There are distinct departments and lines of authority, and employees are expected to minimize formal contact with other employees outside their functional area or line of command. Performance evaluations and rewards emphasize individual effort, although seniority tends to be the primary factor in the determination of pay raises and promotions.

Organization B

This organization is also a manufacturing firm. Here, however, management encourages and rewards risk taking and change. Decisions based on intuition are valued as much as those that are well rationalized. Management prides itself on its history of experimenting with new technologies and its success in regularly introducing innovative products. Managers or employees who have a good idea are encouraged to "run with it." And failures are treated as "learning experiences." The company prides itself on being market driven and rapidly responsive to the changing needs of its customers.

There are few rules and regulations for employees to follow, and supervision is loose because management believes that its employees are hardworking and trustworthy. Management is concerned with high productivity but believes that this comes through treating its people right. The company is proud of its reputation as being a good place to work.

Job activities are designed around work teams, and team members are encouraged to interact with people across functions and authority levels. Employees talk positively about the competition between teams. Individuals and teams have goals, and bonuses are based on achievement of these outcomes. Employees are given considerable autonomy in choosing the means by which the goals are attained.

---

organizational culture *A system of shared meaning held by members that distinguishes the organization from other organizations.*

demonstrates how these characteristics can be mixed to create highly diverse organizations.

Other research has conceptualized culture into four different types based on competing values:[3] the collaborative and cohesive *clan,* the innovative and adaptable *adhocracy,* the controlled and consistent *hierarchy,* and the competitive and customer focused *market.* A review of 94 studies found that job attitudes were especially positive in clan-based cultures, innovation was especially strong in market cultures, and financial performance was especially good in market cultures.[4] Although the competing values framework received some support in this review, the authors noted that further theoretical work needs to ensure it is consistent with the actual cultural values found in organizations.

Culture Is a Descriptive Term

Organizational culture shows how employees perceive the characteristics of an organization's culture, not whether they like them—that is, it's a descriptive term. This is important because it differentiates culture from job satisfaction.

Research on organizational culture has sought to measure how employees see their organization: Does it encourage teamwork? Does it reward innovation? Does it stifle initiative? In contrast, job satisfaction seeks to measure how employees feel about the organization's expectations, reward practices, and the like. Although the two terms have overlapping characteristics, keep in mind that *organizational culture* is descriptive, whereas *job satisfaction* is evaluative.

Do Organizations Have Uniform Cultures?

Organizational culture represents a common perception the organization's members hold. We should therefore expect individuals with different backgrounds or at different levels in the organization to describe its culture in similar terms.[5]

That doesn't mean, however, that there are no subcultures. Most large organizations have a dominant culture and numerous subcultures.[6] A **dominant culture** expresses the **core values** a majority of members share and that give the organization its distinct personality.[7] **Subcultures** tend to develop in large organizations to reflect common problems or experiences members face in the same department or location. The purchasing department can have a subculture that includes the core values of the dominant culture plus additional values unique to members of that department.

If organizations were composed only of numerous subcultures, organizational culture as an independent variable would be significantly less powerful. It is the "shared meaning" aspect of culture that makes it such a potent device for guiding and shaping behavior. That's what allows us to say, for example, that the Zappos culture values customer care and dedication over speed and efficiency and to use that information to better understand the behavior of Zappos executives and employees.[8] But subcultures can influence members' behavior too.

Strong versus Weak Cultures

It's possible to differentiate between strong and weak cultures.[9] If most employees (responding to management surveys) have the same opinions about the organization's mission and values, the culture is strong; if opinions vary widely, the culture is weak.

In a **strong culture**, the organization's core values are both intensely held and widely shared.[10] The more members who accept the core values and the greater their commitment, the stronger the culture and the greater its influence on member behavior, because the high degree of sharedness and intensity creates a climate of high behavioral control. Nordstrom employees know in no

glOBalization!

Face Culture, Dignity Culture, and Organizational Culture

As we have discussed throughout the book, *culture* can be represented at either the national or the organizational level. Global organizations need to carefully consider the differences in culture across countries to determine which management practices are likely to be most effective with different populations of employees.

Recently, social psychologists have begun to explore the difference between "face" and "dignity" national cultures. In a face culture, individuals use information from others in order to determine who they are, allowing themselves to be defined by social opinions. In a dignity culture, on the other hand, individuals are more eager to define themselves based on their own internal judgments and may be more resistant to outside efforts to define them. Although more research is needed to specify which cultures put more emphasis on social face versus personal dignity in self-definition, most has focused on East Asian countries as face cultures and European countries and the United States and Canada as dignity cultures.

What are the implications of these differences? Individuals from face cultures will be more concerned with the implications of hierarchical judgments on their worth. Thus, organizational cultures in face countries are likely to emphasize roles and titles to give definition to employees and provide them with a secure sense of self. Organizational cultures in dignity countries will be more flexible in providing role definitions, allowing individuals to use self-expression to determine who they are.

Sources: Based on Y. Kim, D. Cohen, and W. Au, "The Jury and Abjury of My Peers: The Self in Face and Dignity Cultures," *Journal of Personality and Social Psychology* 98, no. 6 (2010), pp. 904–916; and Y. Liao and M. H. Bond, "The Dynamics of Face Loss Following Interpersonal Harm for Chinese and Americans," *Journal of Cross-Cultural Psychology* 42, no. 1 (2011), pp. 25–38.

uncertain terms what is expected of them, and these expectations go a long way in shaping their behavior. In contrast, Nordstrom competitor Macy's, which has struggled through an identity crisis, is working to remake its culture.

A strong culture should reduce employee turnover because it demonstrates high agreement about what the organization represents. Such unanimity of purpose builds cohesiveness, loyalty, and organizational commitment. These qualities, in turn, lessen employees' propensity to leave.[11] One study found that the more employees agreed on customer orientation in a service organization, the higher the profitability of the business unit.[12] Another study found that when team managers and team members disagree about perceptions of organizational support, there were more negative moods among team members, and the performance of teams was lower.[13] These negative effects are especially strong when managers believe the organization provides more support than employees think it does.

Culture versus Formalization

We've seen that high formalization creates predictability, orderliness, and consistency. A strong culture achieves the same end without the need for written documentation.[14] Therefore, we should view formalization and culture as two

dominant culture   *A culture that expresses the core values that are shared by a majority of the organization's members.*
core values   *The primary or dominant values that are accepted throughout the organization.*

subcultures   *Minicultures within an organization, typically defined by department designations and geographical separation.*

strong culture   *A culture in which the core values are intensely held and widely shared.*

different roads to a common destination. The stronger an organization's culture, the less management need be concerned with developing formal rules and regulations to guide employee behavior. Those guides will be internalized in employees when they accept the organization's culture.

What Do Cultures Do?

2   Compare the functional and dysfunctional effects of organizational culture on people and the organization.

Let's review the role culture performs and whether it can ever be a liability for an organization.

Culture's Functions

First, culture has a boundary-defining role: it creates distinctions between one organization and others. Second, it conveys a sense of identity for organization members. Third, culture facilitates commitment to something larger than individual self-interest. Fourth, it enhances the stability of the social system. Culture is the social glue that helps hold the organization together by providing standards for what employees should say and do. Finally, it is a sense-making and control mechanism that guides and shapes employees' attitudes and behavior. This last function is of particular interest to us.[15] Culture defines the rules of the game.

Today's trend toward decentralized organizations makes culture more important than ever, but ironically it also makes establishing a strong culture more difficult. When formal authority and control systems are reduced, culture's *shared meaning* can point everyone in the same direction. However, employees organized in teams may show greater allegiance to their team and its values than to the organization as a whole. In virtual organizations, the lack of frequent face-to-face contact makes establishing a common set of norms very difficult. Strong leadership that communicates frequently about common goals and priorities is especially important in innovative organizations.[16]

Individual–organization "fit"—that is, whether the applicant's or employee's attitudes and behavior are compatible with the culture—strongly influences who gets a job offer, a favorable performance review, or a promotion. It's no coincidence that Disney theme park employees appear almost universally attractive, clean, and wholesome with bright smiles. The company selects employees who will maintain that image. On the job, a strong culture supported by formal rules and regulations ensures they will act in a relatively uniform and predictable way.

Source: Jonathan Sprague/Redux.

Facebook describes itself as "a cutting-edge technology company, constantly taking on new challenges in the worlds of milliseconds and terabytes." The vast majority of the company's employees are under 40 and enjoy the excitement of working in a fast-paced environment with considerable change and ambiguity. Facebook encourages employees to interact in a creative climate that encourages experimentation and tolerates conflict and risk. The company fosters a fun-loving, casual, and collegial identity in its employees.

Culture Creates Climate

If you've worked with someone whose positive attitude inspired you to do your best, or with a lackluster team that drained your motivation, you've experienced the effects of climate. **Organizational climate** refers to the shared perceptions organizational members have about their organization and work environment.[17] This aspect of culture is like team spirit at the organizational level. When everyone has the same general feelings about what's important or how well things are working, the effect of these attitudes will be more than the sum of the individual parts. One meta-analysis found that across dozens of different samples, psychological climate was strongly related to individuals' level of job satisfaction, involvement, commitment, and motivation.[18] A positive overall workplace climate has been linked to higher customer satisfaction and financial performance as well.[19]

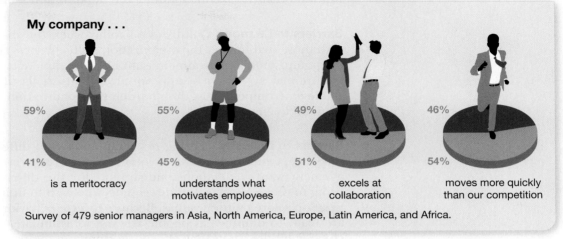

OB Poll — **How Leaders See Their Company's Culture**

My company . . .

59%	55%	49%	46%
41%	45%	51%	54%
is a meritocracy	understands what motivates employees	excels at collaboration	moves more quickly than our competition

Survey of 479 senior managers in Asia, North America, Europe, Latin America, and Africa.

Note: Survey of 479 senior managers in Asia, North America, Europe, Latin America, and Africa.
Source: Based on *Global Firms in 2020* (Economist Intelligence Unit, 2010). Downloaded on July 2, 2011, from www.shrm.org/.

Dozens of dimensions of climate have been studied, including safety, justice, diversity, and customer service.[20] A person who encounters a positive climate for performance will think about doing a good job more often and will believe others support his or her success. Someone who encounters a positive climate for diversity will feel more comfortable collaborating with co-workers regardless of their demographic background. Climates can interact with one another to produce behavior. For example, a positive climate for worker empowerment can lead to higher levels of performance in organizations that also have a climate for personal accountability.[21] Climate also influences the habits people adopt. If the climate for safety is positive, everyone wears safety gear and follows safety procedures even if individually they wouldn't normally think very often about being safe—indeed, many studies have shown that a positive safety climate decreases the number of documented injuries on the job.[22]

Culture as a Liability

Culture can enhance organizational commitment and increase the consistency of employee behavior, clearly benefits to an organization. Culture is valuable to employees too, because it spells out how things are done and what's important. But we shouldn't ignore the potentially dysfunctional aspects of culture, especially a strong one, on an organization's effectiveness.

Institutionalization   When an organization undergoes **institutionalization** and becomes *institutionalized*—that is, it is valued for itself and not for the goods or services it produces—it takes on a life of its own, apart from its founders or members.[23] It doesn't go out of business even if its original goals are no longer relevant. Acceptable modes of behavior become largely self-evident to members,

organizational climate *The shared perceptions organizational members have about their organization and work environment.*

institutionalization *A condition that occurs when an organization takes on a life of its own, apart from any of its members, and acquires immortality.*

and although this isn't entirely negative, it does mean behaviors and habits that should be questioned and analyzed become taken for granted, which can stifle innovation and make maintaining the organization's culture an end in itself.

Barriers to Change   Culture is a liability when the shared values don't agree with those that further the organization's effectiveness. This is most likely when an organization's environment is undergoing rapid change, and its entrenched culture may no longer be appropriate.[24] Consistency of behavior, an asset in a stable environment, may then burden the organization and make it difficult to respond to changes.

Barriers to Diversity   Hiring new employees who differ from the majority in race, age, gender, disability, or other characteristics creates a paradox:[25] management wants to demonstrate support for the differences these employees bring to the workplace, but newcomers who wish to fit in must accept the organization's core cultural values. Because diverse behaviors and unique strengths are likely to diminish as people attempt to assimilate, strong cultures can become liabilities when they effectively eliminate these advantages. A strong culture that condones prejudice, supports bias, or becomes insensitive to people who are different can even undermine formal corporate diversity policies.

Barriers to Acquisitions and Mergers   Historically, when management looked at acquisition or merger decisions, the key factors were financial advantage and product synergy. In recent years, cultural compatibility has become the primary

---

Myth or Science?

"Employees Treat Customers the Same Way the Organization Treats Them"

This statement is true to a significant degree. Two studies using different methods for operationalizing organizational treatment have shown that when employees are treated well, they are likely to treat customers well, but when employees are treated poorly, they treat customers poorly. Thus, a culture that shows positive treatment for employees is likely to create a positive culture for treatment of customers.

The first study collected data from 292 managers, 830 employees, and 1,772 bank customers in Japan. The researchers examined whether companies that provided high-performance work practices like service training, information sharing, self-management teams, and employee autonomy had a superior climate for customer service and whether this climate for service was related to higher levels of organizational performance. The employee-benefiting practices did indeed lead to higher performance through a better climate for customer service.

The second study looked at "internal service," the extent to which employees believe their work unit is treated well by the organization as a whole. More than 600 employees of a Caribbean financial services firm described their internal service, and then quality data were collected from nearly 2,000 customers. The results showed that service climate was more positively related to customer satisfaction when internal service was high, meaning that having a positive climate for service leads to higher levels of customer satisfaction especially when a company provides positive internal service to its employees.

Sources: H. Liao, K. Toya, D. Lepak, and Y. Hong, "Do They See Eye to Eye? Management and Employee Perspectives of High-Performance Work Systems and Influence Processes on Service Quality," *Journal of Applied Psychology* 94, no. 2 (2009), pp. 371–391; and K. H. Ehrhart, L. A. Witt, B. Schneider, and S. J. Perry, "Service Employees Give as They Get: Internal Service as a Moderator of the Service Climate-Service Outcomes Link," *Journal of Applied Psychology* 96, no. 2 (2011), pp. 423–431.

concern.[26] All things being equal, whether the acquisition actually works seems to have more to do with how well the two organizations' cultures match up.

A survey by consulting firm A. T. Kearney revealed that 58 percent of mergers failed to reach their financial goals.[27] As one expert commented, "Mergers have an unusually high failure rate, and it's always because of people issues"—in other words, conflicting organizational cultures. The $183 billion merger between America Online (AOL) and Time Warner in 2001 was the largest in U.S. corporate history. It was also a disaster. Only 2 years later, the stock had fallen an astounding 90 percent, and the new company reported what was then the largest financial loss in U.S. history. To this day, Time Warner stock—trading around $32 per share in late 2011—remains at a fraction of its former price (around $200 per share before the merger). Culture clash is commonly argued to be one of the causes of AOL Time Warner's problems. As one expert noted, "In some ways the merger of AOL and Time Warner was like the marriage of a teenager to a middle-aged banker. The cultures were vastly different. There were open collars and jeans at AOL. Time Warner was more buttoned-down."[28]

Creating and Sustaining Culture

3 Identify the factors that create and sustain an organization's culture.

MyManagementLab
For an interactive application of this topic, check out this chapter's simulation activity at **www.pearsonglobaleditions.com/ mymanagementlab.**

An organization's culture doesn't pop out of thin air, and once established it rarely fades away. What influences the creation of a culture? What reinforces and sustains it once it's in place?

How a Culture Begins

An organization's current customs, traditions, and general way of doing things are largely due to what it has done before and how successful it was in doing it. This leads us to the ultimate source of an organization's culture: its founders.[29] Free of previous customs or ideologies, founders have a vision of what the organization should be, and the firm's small size makes it easy to impose that vision on all members.

Culture creation occurs in three ways.[30] First, founders hire and keep only employees who think and feel the same way they do. Second, they indoctrinate and socialize these employees to their way of thinking and feeling. And finally, the founders' own behavior encourages employees to identify with them and internalize their beliefs, values, and assumptions. When the organization succeeds, the founders' personality becomes embedded in the culture.

The fierce, competitive style and disciplined, authoritarian nature of Hyundai, the giant Korean conglomerate, exhibits the same characteristics often used to describe founder Chung Ju-Yung. Other founders with immeasurable impact on their organization's culture include Bill Gates at Microsoft, Ingvar Kamprad at IKEA, Herb Kelleher at Southwest Airlines, Fred Smith at FedEx, and Richard Branson at the Virgin Group.

Keeping a Culture Alive

Once a culture is in place, practices within the organization maintain it by giving employees a set of similar experiences.[31] The selection process, performance evaluation criteria, training and development activities, and promotion procedures (all discussed in Chapter 17) ensure those hired fit in with the culture, reward those who support it, and penalize (or even expel) those who challenge

Source: Brad Swonetz / Redux.

Tony Hsieh, CEO of Zappos.com, is also the architect of the company's culture. Hsieh invited all employees to participate in creating ten core values that define the culture of Zappos and serve as the framework from which all decisions are made. The core values are: deliver WOW through service; embrace and drive change; create fun and a little weirdness; be adventurous, creative, and open minded; pursue growth and learning; build open and honest relationships with communication; build a positive team and family spirit; do more with less; be passionate and determined; and be humble. Hsieh maintains the culture through the company's hiring process and training programs to ensure that employees are committed to the core values.

it. Three forces play a particularly important part in sustaining a culture: selection practices, the actions of top management, and socialization methods. Let's look at each.

Selection   The explicit goal of the selection process is to identify and hire individuals with the knowledge, skills, and abilities to perform successfully. The final decision, because it's significantly influenced by the decision maker's judgment of how well the candidates will fit into the organization, identifies people whose values are essentially consistent with at least a good portion of the organization's.[32] Selection also provides information to applicants. Those who perceive a conflict between their values and those of the organization can remove themselves from the applicant pool. Selection thus becomes a two-way street, allowing employer or applicant to avoid a mismatch and sustaining an organization's culture by selecting out those who might attack or undermine its core values.

W. L. Gore & Associates, the maker of Gore-Tex fabric used in outerwear, prides itself on its democratic culture and teamwork. There are no job titles at Gore, nor bosses or chains of command. All work is done in teams. In Gore's selection process, teams of employees put job applicants through extensive interviews to ensure they can deal with the level of uncertainty, flexibility, and teamwork that's normal in Gore plants. Not surprisingly, W. L. Gore appears regularly on *Fortune*'s list of "100 Best Companies to Work For" (number 31 in 2011).[33]

Top Management   The actions of top management also have a major impact on the organization's culture.[34] Through words and behavior, senior executives establish norms that filter through the organization about, for instance, whether risk taking is desirable, how much freedom managers give employees, what is appropriate dress, and what actions earn pay raises, promotions, and other rewards.

The culture of supermarket chain Wegmans—which believes driven, happy, and loyal employees are more eager to help one another and provide exemplary customer service—is a direct result of the beliefs of the Wegman family. The chain began in 1930 when brothers John and Walter Wegman opened their first grocery store in Rochester, New York. Its focus on fine foods quickly separated it from other grocers—a focus maintained by the company's employees, many of whom are hired based on their interest in food. In 1950, Walter's son Robert became president and added generous employee benefits such as profit sharing and fully paid medical coverage. Now Robert's son Danny is president, and he has continued the Wegmans tradition of taking care of employees. To date, Wegmans has paid more than $54 million in college scholarships for its employees, both full-time and part-time. Pay is well above market average, making annual turnover for full-time employees a mere 6 percent, according to the Food Marketing Institute. (The industry average is 24 percent). Wegman's regularly appears on *Fortune*'s list as well (number 3 in 2011).

Socialization   No matter how good a job the organization does in recruiting and selection, new employees need help adapting to the prevailing culture. That help is **socialization**.[35] For example, all Marines must go through boot camp, where they prove their commitment and learn the "Marine way." The consulting firm Booz Allen Hamilton begins its process of bringing new employees onboard even before they start their first day of work. New recruits go to an internal Web portal to learn about the company and engage in some activities that help them understand the culture of the organization. After they start work, they continue to learn about the organization through an ongoing social

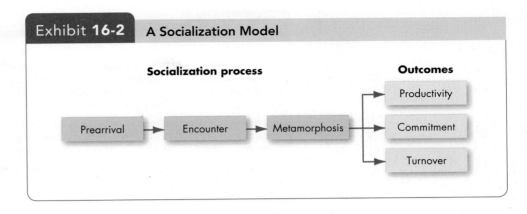

Exhibit **16-2**   A Socialization Model

networking application that links new workers with more established members of the firm and helps ensure that culture is transmitted over time.[36]

We can think of socialization as a process with three stages: prearrival, encounter, and metamorphosis.[37] This process, shown in Exhibit 16-2, has an impact on the new employee's work productivity, commitment to the organization's objectives, and eventual decision to stay with the organization.

The **prearrival stage** recognizes that each individual arrives with a set of values, attitudes, and expectations about both the work and the organization. One major purpose of a business school, for example, is to socialize business students to the attitudes and behaviors business firms want. Newcomers to high-profile organizations with a strong market position will make their own assumptions about what it must be like to work there.[38] Most new recruits will expect Nike to be dynamic and exciting, a prestigious law firm to be high in pressure and rewards, and the Marine Corps to require both discipline and courage. No matter how well managers think they can socialize newcomers, however, the most important predictor of future behavior is past behavior. What people know before they join the organization, and how proactive their personality is, are critical predictors of how well they adjust to a new culture.[39]

One way to capitalize on prehire characteristics in socialization is to use the selection process to inform prospective employees about the organization as a whole. We've also seen how the selection process ensures the inclusion of the "right type"—those who will fit in. "Indeed, the ability of the individual to present the appropriate face during the selection process determines his ability to move into the organization in the first place. Thus, success depends on the degree to which the aspiring member has correctly anticipated the expectations and desires of those in the organization in charge of selection."[40]

On entry into the organization, the new member enters the **encounter stage** and confronts the possibility that expectations—about the job, co-workers, the boss, and the organization in general—may differ from reality. If expectations were fairly accurate, the encounter stage merely cements earlier perceptions. However, this is often not the case. At the extreme, a new member may become disillusioned enough to resign. Proper recruiting and selection should significantly reduce that outcome, along with encouraging friendship ties in the

socialization *A process that adapts employees to the organization's culture.*

prearrival stage *The period of learning in the socialization process that occurs before a new employee joins the organization.*

encounter stage *The stage in the socialization process in which a new employee sees what the organization is really like and confronts the possibility that expectations and reality may diverge.*

| Exhibit 16-3 | Entry Socialization Options |

Formal vs. Informal The more a new employee is segregated from the ongoing work setting and differentiated in some way to make explicit his or her newcomer's role, the more socialization is formal. Specific orientation and training programs are examples. Informal socialization puts the new employee directly into the job, with little or no special attention.

Individual vs. Collective New members can be socialized individually. This describes how it's done in many professional offices. They can also be grouped together and processed through an identical set of experiences, as in military boot camp.

Fixed vs. Variable This refers to the time schedule in which newcomers make the transition from outsider to insider. A fixed schedule establishes standardized stages of transition. This characterizes rotational training programs. It also includes probationary periods, such as the 8- to 10-year "associate" status used by accounting and law firms before deciding on whether or not a candidate is made a partner. Variable schedules give no advance notice of their transition timetable. Variable schedules describe the typical promotion system, in which one is not advanced to the next stage until one is "ready."

Serial vs. Random Serial socialization is characterized by the use of role models who train and encourage the newcomer. Apprenticeship and mentoring programs are examples. In random socialization, role models are deliberately withheld. New employees are left on their own to figure things out.

Investiture vs. Divestiture Investiture socialization assumes that the newcomer's qualities and qualifications are the necessary ingredients for job success, so these qualities and qualifications are confirmed and supported. Divestiture socialization tries to strip away certain characteristics of the recruit. Fraternity and sorority "pledges" go through divestiture socialization to shape them into the proper role.

organization—newcomers are more committed when friends and co-workers help them "learn the ropes."[41]

Finally, to work out any problems discovered during the encounter stage, the new member changes or goes through the **metamorphosis stage**. The options presented in Exhibit 16-3 are alternatives designed to bring about the desired metamorphosis. Most research suggests there are two major "bundles" of socialization practices. The more management relies on formal, collective, sequential, fixed, and serial socialization programs and emphasize divestiture, the more likely newcomers' differences will be stripped away and replaced by standardized predictable behaviors. These *institutional* practices are common in police departments, fire departments, and other organizations that value rule following and order. Programs that are informal, individual, random, variable, and disjunctive and emphasize investiture are more likely to give newcomers an innovative sense of their role and methods of working. Creative fields, such as research and development, advertising, and filmmaking, rely on these *individual* practices. Most research suggests high levels of institutional practices encourage person–organization fit and high levels of commitment, whereas individual practices produce more role innovation.[42]

The three-part entry socialization process is complete when new members have internalized and accepted the norms of the organization and their work group, are confident in their competence, and feel trusted and valued by their peers. They understand the system—not only their own tasks but the rules, procedures, and informally accepted practices as well. Finally, they know what is expected of them and what criteria will be used to measure and evaluate their work. As Exhibit 16-2 showed, successful metamorphosis should have a positive impact on new employees' productivity and their commitment to the organization and reduce their propensity to leave the organization.

Exhibit 16-4   **How Organization Cultures Form**

Researchers have begun to examine how employee attitudes change during socialization by measuring at several points over the first few months. One study has documented patterns of "honeymoons" and "hangovers" for new workers, showing that the period of initial adjustment is often marked by decreases in job satisfaction as their idealized hopes come into contact with the reality of organizational life.[43] Other research suggests that role conflict and role overload for newcomers rise over time, and that workers with the largest increases in these role problems experience the largest decreases in commitment and satisfaction.[44] It may be that the initial adjustment period for newcomers presents increasing demands and difficulties, at least in the short term.

Summary: How Cultures Form

Exhibit 16-4 summarizes how an organization's culture is established and sustained. The original culture derives from the founder's philosophy and strongly influences hiring criteria as the firm grows. Top managers' actions set the general climate, including what is acceptable behavior and what is not. The way employees are socialized will depend both on the degree of success achieved in matching new employees' values to those of the organization in the selection process, and on top management's preference for socialization methods.

How Employees Learn Culture

4   Show how culture is transmitted to employees.

Culture is transmitted to employees in a number of forms, the most potent being stories, rituals, material symbols, and language.

Stories

When Henry Ford II was chairman of Ford Motor Company, you would have been hard pressed to find a manager who hadn't heard how he reminded his executives, when they got too arrogant, "It's my name that's on the building." The message was clear: Henry Ford II ran the company.

metamorphosis stage   *The stage in the socialization process in which a new employee changes and adjusts to the job, work group, and organization.*

A number of senior Nike executives spend much of their time serving as corporate storytellers.[45] When they tell how co-founder (and Oregon track coach) Bill Bowerman went to his workshop and poured rubber into his wife's waffle iron to create a better running shoe, they're talking about Nike's spirit of innovation. When new hires hear tales of Oregon running star Steve Prefontaine's battles to make running a professional sport and attain better performance equipment, they learn of Nike's commitment to helping athletes.

Stories such as these circulate through many organizations, anchoring the present in the past and legitimating current practices. They typically include narratives about the organization's founders, rule breaking, rags-to-riches successes, reductions in the workforce, relocation of employees, reactions to past mistakes, and organizational coping.[46] Employees also create their own narratives about how they came to either fit or not fit with the organization during the process of socialization, including first days on the job, early interactions with others, and first impressions of organizational life.[47]

Rituals

Rituals are repetitive sequences of activities that express and reinforce the key values of the organization—what goals are most important and which people are important and which are expendable.[48] One of the best known rituals is Walmart's company chant. Begun by the company's founder, the late Sam Walton, as a way to motivate and unite his workforce, "Gimme a W, gimme an A, gimme an L, gimme a squiggle, give me an M, A, R, T!" has become a ritual that bonds workers and reinforces Walton's belief in the contribution his employees made to the company's success. Similar corporate chants are used by IBM, Ericsson, Novell, Deutsche Bank, and PricewaterhouseCoopers.[49]

Material Symbols

Alcoa headquarters doesn't look like your typical head-office operation. There are few individual offices, even for senior executives. The space is essentially made up of cubicles, common areas, and meeting rooms. This informality conveys to employees that Alcoa values openness, equality, creativity, and flexibility. Some corporations provide their top executives with chauffeur-driven limousines and a corporate jet. Other CEOs drive the company car themselves and travel in the economy section.

The layout of corporate headquarters, the types of automobiles top executives are given, and the presence or absence of corporate aircraft are a few examples of **material symbols**. Others include the size of offices, the elegance of furnishings, executive perks, and attire.[50] These convey to employees who is important, the degree of egalitarianism top management desires, and the kinds of behavior that are appropriate, such as risk taking, conservative, authoritarian, participative, individualistic, or social.

Language

Many organizations and subunits within them use language to help members identify with the culture, attest to their acceptance of it, and help preserve it. Unique terms describe equipment, officers, key individuals, suppliers, customers, or products that relate to the business. New employees may at first be overwhelmed by acronyms and jargon, that, once assimilated, act as a common denominator to unite members of a given culture or subculture.

At Sermo, it's okay for employees to bring their dogs to work and to include them in company meetings, as shown in this photo. Sermo is an online community for physicians where they can collaborate and improve patient care. Sermo's culture derives from the company's founder and CEO Dr. Daniel Palestrant, who wants employees to love coming to work, to be comfortable, to have fun, and to just be themselves in a space that suits them. Sermo's informal work environment and open office plan conveys to employees that the company values openness, individuality, creativity, and flexibility.

Source: Melanie Stetson Freeman/CSM/Newscom.

Creating an Ethical Organizational Culture

5 Demonstrate how an ethical culture can be created.

The organizational culture most likely to shape high ethical standards among its members is high in risk tolerance, low to moderate in aggressiveness, and focused on means as well as outcomes.[51] This type of culture takes a long-term perspective and balances the rights of multiple stakeholders, including employees, stockholders, and the community. Managers are supported for taking risks and innovating, discouraged from engaging in unbridled competition, and guided to heed not just to *what* goals are achieved but also *how*.

If the culture is strong and supports high ethical standards, it should have a very powerful and positive influence on employee behavior. Examples of organizations that have failed to establish proper codes of ethical conduct can be found in the media nearly every day. Some actively deceive customers or clients. Others produce products that harm consumers or the environment, or they harass or discriminate against certain groups of employees. Others are more subtle and cover up or fail to report wrongdoing. The negative consequences of a systematic culture of unethical behavior can be severe and include customer boycotts, fines, lawsuits, and government regulation of an organization's practices.

rituals *Repetitive sequences of activities that express and reinforce the key values of the organization, which goals are most important, which people are important, and which are expendable.*

material symbols *What conveys to employees who is important, the degree of egalitarianism top management desires, and the kinds of behavior that are appropriate.*

What can managers do to create a more ethical culture? They can adhere to the following principles:[52]

- **Be a visible role model.** Employees will look to the actions of top management as a benchmark for appropriate behavior. Send a positive message.
- **Communicate ethical expectations.** Minimize ethical ambiguities by sharing an organizational code of ethics that states the organization's primary values and ethical rules employees must follow.
- **Provide ethical training.** Set up seminars, workshops, and training programs to reinforce the organization's standards of conduct, clarify what practices are permissible, and address potential ethical dilemmas.
- **Visibly reward ethical acts and punish unethical ones.** Appraise managers on how their decisions measure up against the organization's code of ethics. Review the means as well as the ends. Visibly reward those who act ethically and conspicuously punish those who don't.
- **Provide protective mechanisms.** Provide formal mechanisms so employees can discuss ethical dilemmas and report unethical behavior without fear of reprimand. These might include ethical counselors, ombudsmen, or ethical officers.

The work of setting a positive ethical climate has to start at the top of the organization.[53] A study of 195 managers demonstrated that when top management emphasizes strong ethical values, supervisors are more likely to practice ethical leadership. Positive ethical attitudes transfer down to line employees, who show lower levels of deviant behavior and higher levels of cooperation and assistance. A study involving auditors found perceived pressure from organizational leaders to behave unethically was associated with increased intentions to engage in unethical practices.[54] Clearly the wrong type of organizational

---

An Ethical Choice

Designing a Culture of Ethical Voice

Much research has emphasized how organizations establish ethical principles that employees are supposed to follow. More recent work examines how organizations can harness employees' inherent sense of right and wrong, so employees will speak up when they feel organizational actions are inconsistent with their own ethical principles.

Saying organizations should establish a culture for ethical behavior is easy enough, but developing a culture where employees feel empowered to speak up is considerably trickier. Here are a few suggestions:

1. Overcome the silence. Employees who know something is wrong may still fail to speak up because they fear reprisals. Both official and unofficial measures must encourage people to bring ethical lapses to the attention of upper management and reward them for doing so.
2. Encourage employees to continually investigate whether their behavior is consistent with organizational values. Many ethical lapses are not so much dishonest or malicious acts but failure to even recognize the moral issue at stake.
3. Develop formal roles for ethical compliance officers, who provide oversight and training to ensure employees are aware of the company's core values and can discuss ethical behavior in practice.

Sources: M. Kaptein, "Ethics Programs and Ethical Culture: A Next Step in Unraveling Their Multi-Faceted Relationship," *Journal of Business Ethics* 89, no. 2 (2009), pp. 261–281; P. Verhezen, "Giving Voice in a Culture of Silence. From a Culture of Compliance to a Culture of Integrity," *Journal of Business Ethics* 96, no. 2 (2010), pp. 187–206; and M. Kaptein, "From Inaction to External Whistleblowing: The Influence of Ethical Culture of Organizations on Employee Responses to Observed Wrongdoing," *Journal of Business Ethics* 98, no. 3 (2011), pp. 513–530.

culture can negatively influence employee ethical behavior. Finally, employees whose ethical values are similar to those of their department are more likely to be promoted, so we can think of ethical culture as flowing from the bottom up as well.[55]

Creating a Positive Organizational Culture

6 Describe a positive organizational culture.

At first blush, creating a positive culture may sound hopelessly naïve or like a Dilbert-style conspiracy. The one thing that makes us believe this trend is here to stay, however, are signs that management practice and OB research are converging.

A **positive organizational culture** emphasizes building on employee strengths, rewards more than it punishes, and emphasizes individual vitality and growth.[56] Let's consider each of these areas.

Building on Employee Strengths Although a positive organizational culture does not ignore problems, it does emphasize showing workers how they can capitalize on their strengths. As management guru Peter Drucker said, "Most Americans do not know what their strengths are. When you ask them, they look at you with a blank stare, or they respond in terms of subject knowledge, which is the wrong answer." Wouldn't it be better to be in an organizational culture that helped you discover your strengths and learn how to make the most of them?

Larry Hammond used this approach when you'd least expect it: during his firm's darkest days. Hammond is CEO of Auglaize Provico, an agribusiness company based in Ohio. In the midst of the firm's worst financial struggles, when it had to lay off one-quarter of its workforce, Hammond decided to try a different approach. Rather than dwell on what was wrong, he took advantage of what was right. "If you really want to [excel], you have to know yourself—you have to know what you're good at, and you have to know what you're not so good at," says Hammond. With the help of Gallup consultant Barry Conchie, Hammond focused on discovering and using employee strengths and helped the company turn itself around. "You ask Larry [Hammond] what the difference is, and he'll say that it's individuals using their natural talents," says Conchie.[57]

Rewarding More Than Punishing Although most organizations are sufficiently focused on extrinsic rewards such as pay and promotions, they often forget about the power of smaller (and cheaper) rewards such as praise. Part of creating a positive organizational culture is "catching employees doing something right." Many managers withhold praise because they're afraid employees will coast or because they think praise is not valued. Employees generally don't ask for praise, and managers usually don't realize the costs of failing to give it.

positive organizational culture *A culture that emphasizes building on employee strengths, rewards more than punishes, and emphasizes individual vitality and growth.*

Employees of Pricewaterhouse Coopers work within a positive organizational culture that emphasizes individuals' vitality and growth. One of the largest global accounting firms, PwC offers employees professional and individual learning opportunities on the job, at clients' workplaces, and in formal training programs. PwC's Learning and Education Group provides access to the latest information on industry standards and best practices, and offers classes to help employees develop their technical skills. Company coaches and mentors guide employees in designing a personalized career path. The PwC team, shown here, counts the Oscars ballots for the Academy of Motion Picture Arts and Sciences, a company client for more than 75 years.

Source: Reed Saxon/AP Images.

Consider El´zbieta Górska-Kolodziejczyk, a plant manager for International Paper's facility in Kwidzyn, Poland. Employees work in a bleak windowless basement. Staffing is roughly one-third its prior level, while production has tripled. These challenges had done in the previous three managers. So when Górska-Kolodziejczyk took over, although she had many ideas about transforming the organization, at the top were recognition and praise. She initially found it difficult to give praise to those who weren't used to it, especially men. "They were like cement at the beginning," she said. "Like cement." Over time, however, she found they valued and even reciprocated praise. One day a department supervisor pulled her over to tell her she was doing a good job. "This I do remember, yes," she said.[58]

Emphasizing Vitality and Growth   No organization will get the best from employees who see themselves as mere cogs in the machine. A positive culture recognizes the difference between a job and a career. It supports not only what the employee contributes to organizational effectiveness but also how the organization can make the employee more effective—personally and professionally.

Although it may take more creativity to encourage employee growth in some types of industries, consider the food industry. At Masterfoods in Belgium, Philippe Lescornez leads a team of employees including Didier Brynaert, who works in Luxembourg, nearly 150 miles away. Brynaert was considered a good sales promoter who was meeting expectations when Lescornez decided Brynaert's job could be made more important if he were seen less as just another sales promoter and more as an expert on the unique features of the Luxembourg market. So Lescornez asked Brynaert for information he could share with the home office. He hoped that by raising Brynaert's profile in Brussels, he could create in him a greater sense of ownership for his remote sales territory. "I started to communicate much more what he did to other people [within the company], because there's quite some distance between the Brussels office and the section he's working in. So I started to communicate, communicate, communicate. The more I communicated, the more he started to provide material," says Lescornez. As a result, "Now he's recognized as the specialist for Luxembourg—the guy who is able to build a strong relationship with the Luxembourg clients," says Lescornez. What's good for Brynaert is, of course, also good for Lescornez, who gets credit for helping Brynaert grow and develop.[59]

Limits of Positive Culture   Is a positive culture a cure-all? Though companies such as GE, Xerox, Boeing, and 3M have embraced aspects of a positive organizational culture, it is a new enough idea for us to be uncertain about how and when it works best.

Not all cultures value being positive as much as U.S. culture does, and, even within U.S. culture, there surely are limits to how far we should go to preserve a positive culture. For example, Admiral, a British insurance company, has established a Ministry of Fun in its call centers to organize poem writings, foosball, conker (a British game involving chestnuts), and fancy-dress days. When does the pursuit of a positive culture start to seem coercive or even Orwellian? As one critic notes, "Promoting a social orthodoxy of positiveness focuses on a particular constellation of desirable states and traits but, in so doing, can stigmatize those who fail to fit the template."[60] There may be benefits to establishing a positive culture, but an organization also needs to be objective and not pursue it past the point of effectiveness.

Spirituality and Organizational Culture

What do Southwest Airlines, Hewlett-Packard, Ford, The Men's Wearhouse, Tyson Foods, Wetherill Associates, and Tom's of Maine have in common? They're among a growing number of organizations that have embraced workplace spirituality.

What Is Spirituality?

Workplace spirituality is *not* about organized religious practices. It's not about God or theology. **Workplace spirituality** recognizes that people have an inner life that nourishes and is nourished by meaningful work in the context of community.[61] Organizations that promote a spiritual culture recognize that people seek to find meaning and purpose in their work and desire to connect with other human beings as part of a community. Many of the topics we have discussed—ranging from job design (designing work that is meaningful to employees) to transformational leadership (leadership practices that emphasize a higher-order purpose and self-transcendent goals) are well matched to the concept of organizational spirituality. When a company emphasizes its commitment to paying Third World suppliers a fair (above-market) price for their coffee to facilitate community development—as did Starbucks—or encourages employees to share prayers or inspirational messages through e-mail—as did Interstate Batteries—it is encouraging a more spiritual culture.[62]

workplace spirituality *The recognition that people have an inner life that nourishes and is nourished by meaningful work that takes place in the context of community.*

Steve Baxter, a Target Corporation employee, tries to comfort a child while serving as a volunteer for Project Homeless Connect, a community program that provides housing, dental, medical, employment, child care, and other services for homeless people and others in need. Baxter and other Target employees are inspired by a strong sense of purpose in showing kindness to, promoting the happiness of, and serving customers, fellow workers, and people in the community. Employees experience the joy and satisfaction that comes from helping others by volunteering in social services programs that feed the hungry, prevent family violence, give shelter to the homeless, and provide disaster relief.

ENDING HOMELESSNESS, ONE PERSON AT A TIME.

Source: m42/ZUMA Press/Newscom.

Why Spirituality Now?

As we noted in our discussion of emotions in Chapter 4, the myth of rationality assumed the well-run organization eliminated feelings. Concern about an employee's inner life had no role in the perfectly rational model. But just as we've now come to realize that the study of emotions improves our understanding of organizational behavior, an awareness of spirituality can help us better understand employee behavior in the twenty-first century.

Of course, employees have always had an inner life. So why has the search for meaning and purposefulness in work surfaced now? We summarize the reasons in Exhibit 16-5.

Characteristics of a Spiritual Organization

The concept of workplace spirituality draws on our previous discussions of values, ethics, motivation, and leadership. What differentiates spiritual organizations from their nonspiritual counterparts? Although research remains

Exhibit 16-5   Reasons for the Growing Interest in Spirituality

- Spirituality can counterbalance the pressures and stress of a turbulent pace of life. Contemporary lifestyles—single-parent families, geographic mobility, the temporary nature of jobs, new technologies that create distance between people—underscore the lack of community many people feel and increase the need for involvement and connection.

- Formalized religion hasn't worked for many people, and they continue to look for anchors to replace lack of faith and to fill a growing feeling of emptiness.

- Job demands have made the workplace dominant in many people's lives, yet they continue to question the meaning of work.

- People want to integrate personal life values with their professional life.

- An increasing number of people are finding that the pursuit of more material acquisitions leaves them unfulfilled.

preliminary, several cultural characteristics tend to be evident in spiritual organizations:[63]

- **Benevolence.**   Spiritual organizations value showing kindness toward others and promoting the happiness of employees and other organizational stakeholders.
- **Strong sense of purpose.**   Spiritual organizations build their cultures around a meaningful purpose. Although profits may be important, they're not the primary value of the organization.
- **Trust and respect.**   Spiritual organizations are characterized by mutual trust, honesty, and openness. Employees are treated with esteem and value, consistent with the dignity of each individual.
- **Open-mindedness.**   Spiritual organizations value flexible thinking and creativity among employees.

SELF-ASSESSMENT LIBRARY

How Spiritual Am I?

In the Self-Assessment Library (available on CD and online), take assessment IV.A.4 (How Spiritual Am I?). Note: People's scores on this measure vary from time to time, so take that into account when interpreting the results.

Achieving a Spiritual Organization

Many organizations have grown interested in spirituality but have had difficulty putting its principles into practice. Several types of practices can facilitate a spiritual workplace,[64] including those that support work–life balance. Leaders can demonstrate values, attitudes, and behaviors that trigger intrinsic motivation and a sense of calling through work. Encouraging employees to consider how their work provides a sense of purpose through community building also can help achieve a spiritual workplace; often this is achieved through group counseling and organizational development, a topic we take up in Chapter 18.

Criticisms of Spirituality

7 Identify characteristics of a spiritual culture.

Critics of the spirituality movement in organizations have focused on three issues. First is the question of scientific foundation. What really is workplace spirituality? Is it just a new management buzzword? Second, are spiritual organizations legitimate? Specifically, do organizations have the right to impose spiritual values on their employees? Third is the question of economics: are spirituality and profits compatible?

First, as you might imagine, there is comparatively little research on workplace spirituality. We don't know whether the concept will have staying power. Do the cultural characteristics we just identified really separate spiritual organizations? Spirituality has been defined so broadly in some sources that practices from job rotation to corporate retreats at meditation centers have been identified as spiritual. Questions need to be answered before the concept gains full credibility.

On the second point, an emphasis on spirituality can clearly make some employees uneasy. Critics have argued that secular institutions, especially business firms, have no business imposing spiritual values on employees.[65] This criticism is undoubtedly valid when spirituality is defined as bringing religion and God into the workplace. However, it seems less stinging when the goal is limited to helping employees find meaning and purpose in their work lives. If the concerns listed in Exhibit 16-5 truly characterize a large segment of the workforce, then perhaps organizations can do so.

Finally, whether spirituality and profits are compatible objectives is certainly relevant for managers and investors in business. The evidence, although limited, indicates they are. Organizations that provided their employees with opportunities for spiritual development have outperformed those that didn't.[66] Other studies a report that spirituality in organizations was positively related to creativity, employee satisfaction, job involvement, and organizational commitment.[67]

Global Implications

8 Show how national culture may affect the way organizational culture is transported to a different country.

We considered global cultural values (collectivism–individualism, power distance, and so on) in Chapter 5. Here our focus is a bit narrower: how is organizational culture affected by a global context? Organizational culture is so powerful it often transcends national boundaries. But that doesn't mean organizations should, or could, ignore local culture.

Organizational cultures often reflect national culture. The culture at AirAsia, a Malaysian-based airline, emphasizes informal dress so as not to create status differences. The carrier has lots of parties, participative management, and no private offices, reflecting Malaysia's relatively collectivistic culture. The culture of US Airways does not reflect the same degree of informality. If US Airways were to set up operations in Malaysia or merge with AirAsia, it would need to take these cultural differences into account.

One of the primary things U.S. managers can do is to be culturally sensitive. The United States is a dominant force in business and in culture—and with that influence comes a reputation. "We are broadly seen throughout the world as arrogant people, totally self-absorbed and loud," says one U.S. executive. Companies such as American Airlines, Lowe's, Novell, ExxonMobil, and Microsoft have implemented training programs to sensitize their managers to cultural differences. Some ways in which U.S. managers can be culturally sensitive include talking in a low tone of voice, speaking slowly, listening more, and avoiding discussions of religion and politics.

The management of ethical behavior is one area where national culture can rub up against corporate culture.[68] U.S. managers endorse the supremacy of anonymous market forces and implicitly or explicitly view profit maximization as a moral obligation for business organizations. This worldview sees bribery, nepotism, and favoring personal contacts as highly unethical. Any action that deviates from profit maximization may indicate that inappropriate or corrupt behavior may be occurring. In contrast, managers in developing economies are more likely to see ethical decisions as embedded in a social environment. That means doing special favors for family and friends is not only appropriate but possibly even an ethical responsibility. Managers in many nations also view capitalism skeptically and believe the interests of workers should be put on a par with the interests of shareholders.

U.S. employees are not the only ones who need to be culturally sensitive. Three times a week, employees at the Canadian unit of Japanese videogame maker Koei begin the day by standing next to their desks, facing their boss, and saying "Good morning" in unison. Employees then deliver short speeches on topics that range from corporate principles to 3D game engines. Koei also has employees punch a time clock and asks women to serve tea to top executive guests. Although these practices are consistent with Koei's culture, they do not fit Canadian culture very well. "It's kind of like school," says one Canadian employee.[69]

MyManagementLab

Now that you have finished this chapter, go back to **www.pearsonglobaleditions.com/
mymanagementlab** to continue practicing and applying the concepts you've learned.

Summary and Implications for Managers

Exhibit 16-6 depicts organizational culture as an intervening variable. Employees form an overall subjective perception of the organization based on factors such as degree of risk tolerance, team emphasis, and support of people. This overall perception becomes, in effect, the organization's culture or personality and affects employee performance and satisfaction, with stronger cultures having greater impact.

- Just as people's personalities tend to be stable over time, so too do strong cultures. This makes a strong culture difficult for managers to change if it becomes mismatched to its environment. Changing an organization's culture is a long and difficult process. Thus, at least in the short term, managers should treat their organization's culture as relatively fixed.
- One of the most important managerial implications of organizational culture relates to selection decisions. Hiring individuals whose values don't align with those of the organization is likely to yield employees who lack motivation and commitment and are dissatisfied with their jobs and the organization.[70] Not surprisingly, "misfits" have considerably higher turnover rates.
- An employee's performance also depends to a considerable degree on knowing what to do and not do. Understanding the right way to do a job indicates proper socialization.
- As a manager, you can shape the culture of your work environment, sometimes as much as it shapes you. All managers can especially do their part to create an ethical culture and to consider spirituality and its role in creating a positive organizational culture.

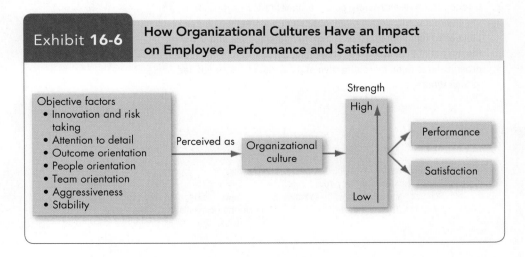

Exhibit **16-6**   **How Organizational Cultures Have an Impact on Employee Performance and Satisfaction**

Organizations Should Strive to Create a Positive Organizational Culture

POINT

COUNTERPOINT

Organizations should do everything they can to establish a positive culture, because it works. Scores of recent studies have shown that individuals who are in positive states of mind at work and in life lead happier, more productive, and more fulfilling lives. Given the accumulating evidence, researchers are now studying ways to make that happen.

In a recent *Harvard Business Review* article, Wharton faculty member Adam Grant discusses an interesting concept: *outsourcing inspiration*. What does he mean by that? Grant writes: "A growing body of research shows that end users—customers, clients, patients, and others who benefit from a company's products and services—are surprisingly effective in motivating people to work harder, smarter, and more productively."

Some tangible examples of how this can work:

- Northwestern University's "buddy program" introduces Alzheimer's patients to scientists working to develop treatments for the disease.

- At a Merrill Lynch branch, weekly team meetings begin with stories about how the team has made a difference in customers' lives.

- "All Medtronic employees have a 'defining moment' in which they come face-to-face with a patient whose story deeply touches them," writes former CEO Bill George.

- At Wells Fargo, managers show bankers videos of people describing how low-interest loans rescued them from severe debt—a vivid reminder to the bankers that they are striving to serve their customers, not their managers.

Of course, there are other ways of creating a positive organizational culture, including building on strengths and rewarding more than punishing.

Creating a positive organizational culture is not magic, but it tends to have extremely positive benefits for organizations which embrace it. *Outsourcing inspiration* is a great way for employees to feel appreciated, to experience empathy, and to see the impact of their work—all motivating outcomes that will lead organizations to be more effective and individuals more fulfilled in their work.

There are many unanswered questions about the merits of using positive organizational scholarship to build positive organizational cultures. Let's focus on three.

What is a positive culture? The employment relationship can be amicable and even mutually beneficial. However, glossing over natural differences in interests with the frosting of positive culture is intellectually dishonest and potentially harmful. From time to time, any organization needs to undertake unpopular actions. Can anyone terminate an employee positively (and honestly), or explain to someone why others received a raise? There's a danger in trying to sugarcoat. Positive relationships will develop—or not—on their own. We'd be better off preaching that people, and organizational cultures, should be honest and fair, rather than unabashedly positive.

Is practice ahead of science? Before we start beseeching organizations to build positive cultures, we should make sure these interventions work as we think they do. Many have unintended consequences, and we simply don't have enough research to support the claims put forth. As one reviewer noted, "Everyone wants to believe they could have greater control over their lives by simply changing the way they think. Research that supports this idea gets promoted loudly and widely." But it's not based on a mountain of evidence.

Is building a positive culture manipulative? Psychologist Lisa Aspinwall writes of "saccharine terrorism," where employees are coerced into positive mindsets by Happiness Coaches. You may think this an exaggeration, but companies like UBS, American Express, KPMG, FedEx, Adobe, and IBM use Happiness Coaches to do exactly that. As one critic noted, "Encouraging people to maintain a happy outlook in the face of less-than-ideal conditions is a good way of keeping citizens under control in spite of severe societal problems, or keeping employees productive while keeping pay and benefits low."

Sources: B. Azar, "Positive Psychology Advances, with Growing Pains," *Monitor on Psychology* (April 2011), pp. 32–36; A. Grant, "How Customers Can Rally Your Troops," *Harvard Business Review* (June 2011), downloaded on July 12, 2011, from http://hbr.org/; and J. McCarthy, "5 Big Problems with Positive Thinking (And Why You Should Do It Anyway)," *Positive Psychology* (October 2010), downloaded on July 10, 2011, from http://psychologyofwellbeing.com/.

QUESTIONS FOR REVIEW

1 What is organizational culture, and what are its common characteristics?

2 What are the functional and dysfunctional effects of organizational culture?

3 What factors create and sustain an organization's culture?

4 How is culture transmitted to employees?

5 How can an ethical culture be created?

6 What is a positive organizational culture?

7 What are the characteristics of a spiritual culture?

8 How does national culture affect how organizational culture is transported to a different country?

EXPERIENTIAL EXERCISE Rate Your Classroom Culture

Listed here are 14 statements. Using the 5-item scale (from strongly agree to strongly disagree), respond to each statement by circling the number that best represents your opinion.

	Strongly Agree	*Agree*	*Neutral*	*Disagree*	*Strongly Disagree*
1. I feel comfortable challenging statements made by my instructor.	1	2	3	4	5
2. My instructor heavily penalizes assignments that are not turned in on time.	1	2	3	4	5
3. My instructor believes that "It's final results that count."	1	2	3	4	5
4. My instructor is sensitive to my personal needs and problems.	1	2	3	4	5
5. A large portion of my grade depends on how well I work with others in the class.	1	2	3	4	5
6. I often feel nervous and tense when I come to class.	1	2	3	4	5
7. My instructor seems to prefer stability over change.	1	2	3	4	5
8. My instructor encourages me to develop new and different ideas.	1	2	3	4	5
9. My instructor has little tolerance for sloppy thinking.	1	2	3	4	5
10. My instructor is more concerned with how I came to a conclusion than with the conclusion itself.	1	2	3	4	5
11. My instructor treats all students alike.	1	2	3	4	5
12. My instructor frowns on class members helping each other with assignments.	1	2	3	4	5
13. Aggressive and competitive people have a distinct advantage in this class.	1	2	3	4	5
14. My instructor encourages me to see the world differently.	1	2	3	4	5

Calculate your total score by adding up the numbers you circled. Your score will fall between 14 and 70.

A high score (49 or above) describes an open, risk-taking, supportive, humanistic, team-oriented, easygoing, growth-oriented culture. A low score (35 or below) describes a closed, structured, task-oriented, individualistic, tense, and stability-oriented culture. Note that differences count, so a score of 60 is a more open culture than one

that scores 50. Also, realize that one culture isn't preferable over another. The "right" culture depends on you and your preferences for a learning environment.

Form teams of five to seven members each. Compare your scores. How closely do they align? Discuss and resolve any discrepancies. Based on your team's analysis, what type of student do you think would perform best in this class?

ETHICAL DILEMMA   Is There a Universal Ethics? HQ–Subsidiary Relations

Marieke van den Berg, an internal auditor of a Dutch multinational retailer X-pander, arrived in China barely 2 weeks ago. She was sent by headquarters to conduct an audit of their Beijing-based subsidiary. Looking through the tonnes of Excel sheets, Marieke noticed a surprisingly high note in the month of December with a mysterious label: "Gratitude."

"What does 'Gratitude' stand for?" Marieke asked Lien, a local finance assistant supporting her throughout the audit process.

"It's a generic name for the 'thank you' gifts we send to our customers at the end of the year," responded Lien.

"What do you mean gifts? The sum we are talking about amounts to more than half a percent of the overall budget," Marieke said, surprised.

Lien delivered a lengthy speech about the power of strong customer–supplier relations, the role of *guanxi* (the personalized, close network of connections) in Chinese business, and the longitudinal nature of any transactional relationship, which, in fact, is never purely transactional.

"Our customers receive great service—that's how strong relations are built. There is no way X-pander is paying for this! We need to work out transparent regulations regarding customer relations," Marieke responded firmly.

"What do you mean by transparent regulations? As you can see, all our expenses are properly accounted for, and every item can be traced back in our budget. This is the established way to work with customers in China. If we make the decision to abandon it, we might lose the majority of our clients," Lien responded timidly. She was already imagining the troublesome year ahead in the Chinese subsidiary of X-pander, in case headquarters' regulations overruled local practices.

Questions

1. What is the difference between a gift and a bribe?

2. What should Marieke do: Impose headquarters' regulations or accept the local, culture-specific way of conducting business?

3. Is there a universal ethics, or do we consider ethical values to be culturally relative? In what way should ethical organizational standards be determined? Should the headquarters' corporate values prevail?

CASE INCIDENT 1   Are Employees Happier Working in Their Own National Cultures?

In 2011, a study was carried out to compare the correlation between employee satisfaction and organizational cultures. The study involved three international hotels in Cairo, Egypt: the Hyatt Regency Hotel, the Semiramis InterContinental, and the Four Seasons Hotel. The study showed that each hotel had a strong organizational culture

in which core values were intensely held and widely shared by employees. However, in two of the hotels, the Egyptian culture was more apparent according to Hofstede's and Trompenaars' cultural dimensions.

The level of job satisfaction of employees in the three hotels was examined in a survey. The organizational cultures of the three hotels as perceived by the employees were also identified in the same survey. In addition, the extent to which the organization was influenced by the national culture was assessed. The employee surveys were distributed equally in the three hotels. When it came to job satisfaction, the Hyatt scored the highest level of employee satisfaction, followed by the Four Seasons Hotel. Analyzing the organizational culture showed that the Hyatt combined a mix of a clan and a market culture, whereas both the Four Seasons and Semiramis InterContinental hotels had a hierarchy culture.

The last section of the survey identified the extent to which national culture was present in each hotel based on Hofstede's and Trompenaars' dimensions—that is, the Egyptian compared to the American (for Hyatt and Semiramis InterContinental hotels) and the Canadian (for the Four Seasons hotel). The Hyatt and the Four Seasons hotels had more of the Egyptian culture apparent in the hotels. For example, the behavior of the employees reflected a higher power distance and more effective relationships between employees (an indicator of the influence of Egyptian culture). However, the Semiramis InterContinental adopted a mix of both the American and the Egyptian cultures. For example, it showed a high power distance mixed with neutral relations, low levels of uncertainty avoidance, and a high consideration of time. Although both the Four Seasons and the Semiramis InterContinental have a hierarchy organizational culture, the levels of satisfaction in both hotels varied widely. Thus, the effect of the organizational culture on employee satisfaction was not evident.

Based on the results of the study and comparing the three hotels, it was concluded that embracing the national culture of the host country, in addition to having a strong organizational culture, had a positive effect on the level of job satisfaction of employees. Therefore, when international hotels open branches in new regions, they need to familiarize themselves with the host country's national culture, especially if they are dependent on hiring local employees. This way, they will be able to adopt many aspects of the host country's culture and will end up with "happier" employees.

Questions

1. How do the Egyptian, American, and Canadian cultures differ according to Hofstede and Trompenaars?

2. The Hyatt and the Semiramis InterContinental should have shown similar results when it comes to cultural assessment. Do you agree or disagree?

Source: Sherif Kamel, dissertation, under the supervision of Dr. Hadia FakhrElDin, the British University in Egypt.

CASE INCIDENT 2 Did Toyota's Culture Cause Its Problems?

You may be familiar with the problems that have recently plagued Toyota. However, you may not know the whole story. First the facts. In 2010 Toyota issued a series of recalls for various models. The most serious was for a defect called "unintended acceleration," which occurs when a car accelerates with no apparent input from the driver. Investigations revealed that unintended acceleration in Toyota cars has been the cause of 37 deaths since 2000. When the problems first surfaced, however, Toyota denied it was the cause. Eventually, Toyota apologized and recalled more than 9 million cars.

To many, the root cause of Toyota's problems was its insular, arrogant culture. *Fortune* argued: "Like GM before it, Toyota has gotten smug. It believes the Toyota Way is the only way." *Time* reported "a Toyota management team that had fallen in love with itself and become too insular to properly handle something like the current crisis." Transportation Secretary Ray LaHood described Toyota's culture as "safety-deaf."

But is this the reality? Increasingly, evidence suggests that Toyota's culture—or even the cars it produces—is not the source of the problem.

A 2011 report released by the U.S. National Highway Traffic Safety Administration (NHTSA) concluded that unintended acceleration was not caused by problems in the electronic circuitry. *The Wall Street Journal* wrote that "safety regulators, human-error experts and auto makers say driver error is the primary cause of sudden acceleration." *Forbes* and *The Atlantic* commented that most of the incidents of sudden acceleration in Toyota cars occurred with elderly drivers, and elderly drivers are known to be more prone to confusing pedals. Many other independent investigations, including ones conducted by automobile experts at *Popular Mechanics* and *Car and Driver*, reached the same conclusion: the main cause of unintended acceleration was drivers mistaking the gas pedal for the brake pedal.

There's a long history of misreporting on this issue. Audi was nearly driven into bankruptcy when *60 Minutes* aired a report, "Out of Control," purportedly proving that defects in the car were behind six fatal sudden-acceleration accidents. As it turns out, *60 Minutes* paid sometime to tamper with the car—filling a canister of compressed air linked to the transmission—to cause the sudden acceleration shown in the segment. Further investigations never uncovered evidence that defects in Audi's cars were behind the incidents.

Does Toyota have an insular and inbred corporate culture? Probably. But it's been that way for a long time, and it's far from clear that the culture, or even the company's cars, is responsible for the sudden acceleration problems.

Questions

1. If Toyota is not the cause of unintended acceleration, why was it blamed for it?

2. Investigations have shown that after stories of unintended acceleration are publicized, report of incidents increase for all automakers. Why is this the case?

3. Is it possible to have a strong—even arrogant—culture and still produce safe and high-quality vehicles?

4. If you were the CEO of Toyota when the story was first publicized, how would you have reacted?

Sources: A. Taylor, "How Toyota Lost Its Way," *Fortune* (July 26, 2010), pp. 108–117; P. Allen, "Anatomy of Toyota's Problem Pedal: Mechanic's Diary," *Popular Mechanics* (March 3, 2010), downloaded July 11, 2011 from www.popularmechanics.com/; B. Saporito, "Behind the Troubles at Toyota," *Time* (February 11, 2010), downloaded July 11, 2011, from www.time.com/; and B. Simon, "LaHood Voices Concerns Over Toyota Culture," *Financial Times* (February 24, 2010), downloaded July 11, 2011, from www.ft.com/.

ENDNOTES

1. See, for example, E. H. Schein, "Culture: The Missing Concept in Organization Studies," *Administrative Science Quarterly* 41, no. 2 (1996), pp. 229–240.

2. This seven-item description is based on C. A. O'Reilly III, J. Chatman, and D. F. Caldwell, "People and Organizational Culture: A Profile Comparison Approach to Assessing Person-Organization Fit," *Academy of Management Journal* (September 1991), pp. 487–516; and J. A. Chatman and K. A. Jehn, "Assessing the Relationship Between Industry Characteristics and Organizational Culture: How Different Can You Be?" *Academy of Management Journal* (June 1994), pp. 522–553.

3. K. S. Cameron, R. E. Quinn, J. DeGraff, and A. V. Thakor, *Competing Values Leadership: Creating Value in Organizations* (Cheltenham, UK and Northampton, MA: Edward Elgar, 2006).

4. C. A. Hartnell, A. Y. Ou, and A. Kinicki, "Organizational Culture and Organizational Effectiveness: A Meta-Analytic Investigation of the Competing Values Framework's Theoretical Suppositions," *Journal of Applied Psychology*, Online first publication (January 17, 2011), doi: 10.1037/a0021987.

5. The view that there will be consistency among perceptions of organizational culture has been called the "integration" perspective. For a review of this perspective and conflicting approaches, see D. Meyerson and J. Martin, "Cultural Change: An Integration of Three Different Views," *Journal of Management Studies* (November 1987), pp. 623–647; and P. J. Frost, L. F. Moore, M. R. Louis, C. C. Lundberg, and J. Martin (eds.), *Reframing Organizational Culture* (Newbury Park, CA: Sage, 1991).

6. See J. M. Jermier, J. W. Slocum Jr., L. W. Fry, and J. Gaines, "Organizational Subcultures in a Soft Bureaucracy: Resistance Behind the Myth and Facade of an Official Culture," *Organization Science* (May 1991), pp. 170–194; and P. Lok, R. Westwood, and J. Crawford, 'Perceptions of Organisational Subculture and their Significance for Organisational Commitment," *Applied Psychology: An International Review* 54, no. 4 (2005), pp. 490–514.

7. D. A. Hoffman and L. M. Jones, "Leadership, Collective Personality, and Performance," *Journal of Applied Psychology* 90, no. 3 (2005), pp. 509–522.

8. T. Hsieh, "Zappos's CEO on Going to Extremes for Customers." *Harvard Business Review* (July/August 2010), pp. 41–45.

9. See, for example, G. G. Gordon and N. DiTomaso, "Predicting Corporate Performance from Organizational Culture," *Journal of Management Studies* (November 1992), pp. 793–798; J. B. Sorensen, "The Strength of Corporate Culture and the Reliability of Firm Performance," *Administrative Science Quarterly* (March 2002), pp. 70–91; and J. Rosenthal and M. A. Masarech, "High-Performance Cultures: How Values Can Drive Business Results," *Journal of Organizational Excellence* (Spring 2003), pp. 3–18.

10. Y. Wiener, "Forms of Value Systems: A Focus on Organizational Effectiveness and Cultural Change and Maintenance," *Academy of Management Review* (October 1988), p. 536; and B. Schneider, A. N. Salvaggio, and M. Subirats, "Climate Strength: A New Direction for Climate Research," *Journal of Applied Psychology* 87 (2002), pp. 220–229.

11. R. T. Mowday, L. W. Porter, and R. M. Steers, *Employee Linkages: The Psychology of Commitment, Absenteeism, and Turnover* (New York: Academic Press, 1982); C. Vandenberghe, "Organizational Culture, Person-Culture Fit, and Turnover: A Replication in the Health Care Industry," *Journal of Organizational Behavior* (March 1999), pp. 175–184; and M. Schulte, C. Ostroff, S. Shmulyian, and A. Kinicki, "Organizational Climate Configurations: Relationships to Collective Attitudes, Customer Satisfaction, and Financial Performance," *Journal of Applied Psychology* 94, no. 3 (2009), pp. 618–634.

12. J. W. Grizzle, A. R. Zablah, T. J. Brown, J. C. Mowen, and J. M. Lee, "Employee Customer Orientation in Context: How the Environment Moderates the Influence of Customer Orientation on Performance Outcomes," *Journal of Applied Psychology* 94, no. 5 (2009), pp. 1227–1242.

13. M. R. Bashshur, A. Hernández, and V. González-Romá, "When Managers and Their Teams Disagree: A Longitudinal Look at the Consequences of Differences in Perceptions of Organizational Support," *Journal of Applied Psychology* 96, no. 3 (2011), pp. 558–573.

14. S. L. Dolan and S. Garcia, "Managing by Values: Cultural Redesign for Strategic Organizational Change at the Dawn of the Twenty-First Century," *Journal of Management Development* 21, no. 2 (2002), pp. 101–117.

15. See C. A. O'Reilly and J. A. Chatman, "Culture as Social Control: Corporations, Cults, and Commitment," in B. M. Staw and L. L. Cummings (eds.), *Research in Organizational Behavior,* vol. 18 (Greenwich, CT: JAI Press, 1996), pp. 157–200. See also M. Pinae Cunha, "The 'Best Place to Be': Managing Control and Employee Loyalty in a Knowledge-Intensive Company," *Journal of Applied Behavioral Science* (December 2002), pp. 481–495.

16. Y. Ling, Z. Simsek, M. H. Lubatkin, and J. F. Veiga, "Transformational Leadership's Role in Promoting Corporate Entrepreneurship: Examining the CEO-TMT Interface," *Academy of Management Journal* 51, no. 3 (2008), pp. 557–576; and A. Malhotra, A. Majchrzak, and B. Rosen, Benson, "Leading Virtual Teams," *Academy of Management Perspectives* 21, no. 1 (2007), pp. 60–70.

17. D. Denison, "What Is the Difference Between Organizational Culture and Organizational Climate? A Native's Point of View on a Decade of Paradigm Wars," *Academy of Management Review* 21 (1996) pp. 519–654; and L. R. James, C. C. Choi, C. E. Ko, P. K. McNeil, M. K. Minton, M. A. Wright, and K. Kim, "Organizational and Psychological Climate: A Review of Theory and Research," *European Journal of Work and Organizational Psychology* 17, no. 1 (2008), pp. 5–32.

18. J. Z. Carr, A. M. Schmidt, J. K. Ford, and R. P. DeShon, "Climate Perceptions Matter: A Meta-Analytic Path Analysis Relating Molar Climate, Cognitive and Affective States, and Individual Level Work Outcomes," *Journal of Applied Psychology* 88, no. (2003), pp. 605–619.

19. Schulte, Ostroff, Shmulyian, and Kinicki, "Organizational Climate Configurations: Relationships to Collective Attitudes, Customer Satisfaction, and Financial Performance."

20. See, for example, Z. S. Byrne, J. Stoner, K. R. Thompson, and W. Hochwarter, "The Interactive Effects of Conscientiousness, Work Effort, and Psychological Climate on Job Performance," *Journal of Vocational Behavior* 66, no. 2 (2005), pp. 326–338; D. S. Pugh, J. Dietz, A. P. Brief, and J. W. Wiley, "Looking Inside and Out: The Impact of Employee and Community Demographic Composition on Organizational Diversity Climate," *Journal of Applied Psychology* 93, no. 6 (2008), pp. 1422–1428; J. C. Wallace, E. Popp, and S. Mondore, "Safety Climate as a Mediator Between Foundation Climates and Occupational Accidents: A Group-Level Investigation," *Journal of Applied Psychology* 91, no. 3 (2006), pp. 681–688; and K. H. Ehrhart, L. A. Witt, B. Schneider, and S. J. Perry, "Service Employees Give as They Get: Internal Service as a Moderator of the Service Climate-Service Outcomes Link," *Journal of Applied Psychology* 96, no. 2 (2011), pp. 423–431.

21. J C. Wallace, P. D. Johnson, K. Mathe, and J. Paul, "Structural and Psychological Empowerment Climates, Performance, and the Moderating Role of Shared Felt Accountability: A Managerial Perspective," *Journal of Applied Psychology* 96, no. 3 (2011), pp. 840–850.

22. J. M. Beus, S. C. Payne, M. E. Bergman, and W. Arthur, "Safety Climate and Injuries: An Examination of Theoretical and Empirical Relationships," *Journal of Applied Psychology* 95, no. 4 (2010), pp. 713–727.

23. R. L. Jepperson, "Institutions, Institutional Effects, and Institutionalism," in W. W. Powell and P. J. DiMaggio (eds.), *The New Institutionalism in Organizational Analysis* (Chicago: University of Chicago Press, 1991), pp. 143–163; G. F. Lanzara and G. Patriotta, "The Institutionalization of Knowledge in an Automotive Factory: Templates, Inscriptions, and the Problems of Durability," *Organization Studies* 28, no. 5 (2007), pp. 635–660; and T. B. Lawrence, M. K. Mauws, B. Dyck, and R. F. Kleysen, "The Politics of Organizational Learning: Integrating Power into the 4I Framework," *Academy of Management Review* (January 2005), pp. 180–191.

24. Sorensen, "The Strength of Corporate Culture and the Reliability of Firm Performance."

25. See T. Cox Jr., *Cultural Diversity in Organizations: Theory, Research & Practice* (San Francisco: Berrett-Koehler, 1993), pp. 162–170; L. Grensing-Pophal, "Hiring to Fit Your Corporate Culture," *HRMagazine* (August 1999), pp. 50–54; and D. L. Stone, E. F. Stone-Romero, and K. M. Lukaszewski, "The Impact of Cultural Values on the Acceptance and Effectiveness of Human Resource Management Policies and Practices," *Human Resource Management Review* 17, no. 2 (2007), pp. 152–165.

26. S. Cartwright and C. L. Cooper, "The Role of Culture Compatibility in Successful Organizational Marriages," *Academy of Management Executive* (May 1993), pp. 57–70; R. A. Weber and C. F. Camerer, "Cultural Conflict and Merger Failure: An Experimental Approach," *Management Science* (April 2003), pp. 400–412; and I. H. Gleibs, A. Mummendey, and P. Noack, "Predictors of Change in Postmerger Identification During a Merger Process: A Longitudinal Study," *Journal of Personality and Social Psychology* 95, no. 5 (2008), pp. 1095–1112.

27. P. Gumbel, "Return of the Urge to Merge," *Time Europe Magazine* (July 13, 2003), www.time.com/time/europe/magazine/article/0,13005,901030721-464418,00.html.

28. S. F. Gale, "Memo to AOL Time Warner: Why Mergers Fail—Case Studies," *Workforce Management* (February 2003),

www.workforce.com; and W. Bock, "Mergers, Bubbles, and Steve Case," *Wally Bock's Monday Memo,* January 20, 2003, www.mondaymemo.net/030120feature.htm.

29. E. H. Schein, "The Role of the Founder in Creating Organizational Culture," *Organizational Dynamics* (Summer 1983), pp. 13–28.

30. E. H. Schein, "Leadership and Organizational Culture," in F. Hesselbein, M. Goldsmith, and R. Beckhard (eds.), *The Leader of the Future* (San Francisco: Jossey-Bass, 1996), pp. 61–62.

31. See, for example, J. R. Harrison and G. R. Carroll, "Keeping the Faith: A Model of Cultural Transmission in Formal Organizations," *Administrative Science Quarterly* (December 1991), pp. 552–582; and D. E. Bowen and C. Ostroff, "The 'Strength' of the HRM System, Organizational Climate Formation, and Firm Performance," *Academy of Management Review* 29 (2004), pp. 203–221.

32. B. Schneider, H. W. Goldstein, and D. B. Smith, "The ASA Framework: An Update," *Personnel Psychology* (Winter 1995), pp. 747–773; D. M. Cable and T. A. Judge, "Interviewers' Perceptions of Person-Organization Fit and Organizational Selection Decisions," *Journal of Applied Psychology* (August 1997), pp. 546–561; M. L. Verquer, T. A. Beehr, and S. H. Wagner, "A Meta-Analysis of Relations Between Person-Organization Fit and Work Attitudes," *Journal of Vocational Behavior* (December 2003), pp. 473–489; and W. Li, Y. Wang, P. Taylor, K. Shi, and D. He, "The Influence of Organizational Culture on Work-Related Personality Requirement Ratings: A Multilevel Analysis," *International Journal of Selection and Assessment* 16, no. 4 (2008), pp. 366–384.

33. R. Levering and M. Moskowitz, "And the Winners Are . . . ," *Fortune* (January 20, 2011), http://money.cnn.com/ magazines/fortune/bestcompanies/2011/full_list/.

34. D. C. Hambrick and P. A. Mason, "Upper Echelons: The Organization as a Reflection of Its Top Managers," *Academy of Management Review* (April 1984), pp. 193–206; M. A. Carpenter, M. A. Geletkanycz, and W. G. Sanders, "Upper Echelons Research Revisited: Antecedents, Elements, and Consequences of Top Management Team Composition," *Journal of Management* 30, no. 6 (2004), pp. 749–778, and H. Wang, A. S. Tsui, and K. R. Xin, "CEO Leadership Behaviors, Organizational Performance, and Employees' Attitudes," *The Leadership Quarterly* 22, no. 1 (2011), pp. 92–105.

35. See, for instance, J. P. Wanous, *Organizational Entry,* 2nd ed. (New York: Addison-Wesley, 1992); D. M. Cable and C. K. Parsons, "Socialization Tactics and Person-Organization Fit," *Personnel Psychology* (Spring 2001), pp. 1–23; and T. N. Bauer, T. Bodner, B. Erdogan, D. M. Truxillo, and J. S. Tucker, "Newcomer Adjustment During Organizational Socialization: A Meta-Analytic Review of Antecedents, Outcomes, and Methods," *Journal of Applied Psychology* 92, no. 3 (2007), pp. 707–721.

36. G. Kranz, "Training That Starts Before the Job Begins," *Workforce Management Online* (July 2009), www .workforce.com.

37. D. C. Feldman, "The Multiple Socialization of Organization Members," *Academy of Management Review* (April 1981), p. 310.

38. C. J. Collins, "The Interactive Effects of Recruitment Practices and Product Awareness on Job Seekers' Employer Knowledge and Application Behaviors," *Journal of Applied Psychology* 92, no. 1 (2007), pp. 180–190.

39. J. D. Kammeyer-Mueller and C. R. Wanberg, "Unwrapping the Organizational Entry Process: Disentangling Multiple Antecedents and Their Pathways to Adjustment," *Journal of Applied Psychology* 88 (2003), pp. 779–794; E. W. Morrison, "Longitudinal Study of the Effects of Information Seeking on Newcomer Socialization," *Journal of Applied Psychology* 78 (2003), pp. 173–183; and M. Wangm Y. Zhan, E. McCune, and D. Truxillo, "Understanding Newcomers' Adaptability and Work-Related Outcomes: Testing the Mediating Roles of Perceived P-E Fit Variables," *Personnel Psychology* 64, no. 1 (2011), pp. 163–189.

40. Van Maanen and Schein, "Career Development," p. 59. J. Van Maanen and E. H. Schein, "Career development." In J. R. Hackman and J. L. Suttle (eds.) *Improving Life at Work.* (Santa Monica, Calif.: Goodyear Publishing, 1977), pp. 30–95.

41. E. W. Morrison, "Newcomers' Relationships: The Role of Social Network Ties During Socialization," *Academy of Management Journal* 45 (2002), pp. 1149–1160.

42. T. N. Bauer, T. Bodner, B. Erdogan, D. M. Truxillo, and J. S. Tucker, "Newcomer Adjustment During Organizational Socialization: A Meta-Analytic Review of Antecedents, Outcomes, and Methods," *Journal of Applied Psychology* 92, no. 3 (2007), pp. 707–721.

43. W. R. Boswell, A. J. Shipp, S. C., Payne, and S. S. Culbertson, "Changes in Newcomer Job Satisfaction Over Time: Examining the Pattern of Honeymoons and Hangovers," *Journal of Applied Psychology* 94, no. 4 (2009), pp. 844–858.

44. C Vandenberghe, A. Panaccio, K. Bentein, K. Mignonac, and P. Roussel, "Assessing Longitudinal Change of and Dynamic Relationships Among Role Stressors, Job Attitudes, Turnover Intention, and Well-Being in Neophyte Newcomers," *Journal of Organizational Behavior* 32, no. 4 (2011), pp. 652–671.

45. E. Ransdell, "The Nike Story? Just Tell It!" *Fast Company* (January–February 2000), pp. 44–46; and A. Muccino, "Exclusive Interview with Chuck Eichten," *Liquid Brand Summit Blog,* (February 4, 2011), http://blog.liquidbrandsummit .com/.

46. D. M. Boje, "The Storytelling Organization: A Study of Story Performance in an Office-Supply Firm," *Administrative Science Quarterly* (March 1991), pp. 106–126; and M. Ricketts and J. G. Seiling, "Language, Metaphors, and Stories: Catalysts for Meaning Making in Organizations," *Organization Development Journal* (Winter 2003), pp. 33–43l.

47. A. J. Shipp and K. J. Jansen, "Reinterpreting Time in Fit Theory: Crafting and Recrafting Narratives of Fit in Medias Res," *Academy of Management Review* 36, no. 1 (2011), pp. 76–101.

48. See G. Islam and M. J. Zyphur, "Rituals in Organizations: A Review and Expansion of Current Theory," *Group and Organization Management* 34, no. 1 (2009), pp. 114–139.

49. V. Matthews, "Starting Every Day with a Shout and a Song," *Financial Times* (May 2, 2001), p. 11; and M. Gimein, "Sam Walton Made Us a Promise," *Fortune* (March 18, 2002), pp. 121–130.

50. M. G. Pratt and A. Rafaeli "Artifacts and Organizations: Understanding Our Objective Reality," in A. Rafaeli and

M. G. Pratt, *Artifacts and Organizations: Beyond Mere Symbolism* (Mahwah, NJ: Lawrence Erlbaum, 2006), pp. 279–288.

51. See B. Victor and J. B. Cullen, "The Organizational Bases of Ethical Work Climates," *Administrative Science Quarterly* (March 1988), pp. 101–125; R. L. Dufresne, "An Action Learning Perspective on Effective Implementation of Academic Honor Codes," *Group & Organization Management* (April 2004), pp. 201–218; and A. Ardichvilli, J. A. Mitchell, and D. Jondle, "Characteristics of Ethical Business Cultures," *Journal of Business Ethics* 85, no. 4 (2009), pp. 445–451.

52. J. P. Mulki, J. F. Jaramillo, and W. B. Locander, "Critical Role of Leadership on Ethical Climate and Salesperson Behaviors," *Journal of Business Ethics* 86, no. 2 (2009), pp. 125–141; M. Schminke, M. L. Ambrose, and D. O. Neubaum, "The Effect of Leader Moral Development on Ethical Climate and Employee Attitudes," *Organizational Behavior and Human Decision Processes* 97, no. 2 (2005), pp. 135–151; and M. E. Brown, L. K. Treviño, and D. A. Harrison, "Ethical Leadership: A Social Learning Perspective for Construct Development and Testing," *Organizational Behavior and Human Decision Processes* 97, no. 2 (2005), pp. 117–134.

53. D. M. Mayer, M. Kuenzi, R. Greenbaum, M. Bardes, and S. Salvador, "How Low Does Ethical Leadership Flow? Test of a Trickle-Down Model," *Organizational Behavior and Human Decision Processes* 108, no. 1 (2009), pp. 1–13.

54. B. Sweeney, D. Arnold, and B. Pierce, "The Impact of Perceived Ethical Culture of the Firm and Demographic Variables on Auditors' Ethical Evaluation and Intention to Act Decisions," *Journal of Business Ethics* 93, no. 4 (2010), pp. 531–551.

55. M. L. Gruys, S. M. Stewart, J. Goodstein, M. N. Bing, and A. C. Wicks, "Values Enactment in Organizations: A Multi-Level Examination," *Journal of Management* 34, no. 4 (2008), pp. 806–843.

56. D. L. Nelson and C. L. Cooper (eds.), *Positive Organizational Behavior* (London: Sage, 2007); K. S. Cameron, J. E. Dutton, and R. E. Quinn (eds.), *Positive Organizational Scholarship: Foundations of a New Discipline* (San Francisco: Berrett-Koehler, 2003); and F. Luthans and C. M. Youssef, "Emerging Positive Organizational Behavior," *Journal of Management* (June 2007), pp. 321–349.

57. J. Robison, "Great Leadership Under Fire," *Gallup Leadership Journal* (March 8, 2007), pp. 1–3.

58. R. Wagner and J. K. Harter, *12: The Elements of Great Managing* (New York: Gallup Press, 2006).

59. R. Wagner and J. K. Harter, "Performance Reviews Without the Anxiety," *Gallup Leadership Journal* (July 12, 2007), pp. 1–4; and Wagner and Harter, *12: The Elements of Great Managing.*

60. S. Fineman, "On Being Positive: Concerns and Counterpoints," *Academy of Management Review* 31, no. 2 (2006), pp. 270–291.

61. D. P. Ashmos and D. Duchon, "Spirituality at Work: A Conceptualization and Measure," *Journal of Management Inquiry* (June 2000), p. 139; and E. Poole, "Organisational

Spirituality: A Literature Review," *Journal of Business Ethics* 84, no. 4 (2009), pp. 577–588.

62. L. W. Fry and J. W. Slocum, "Managing the Triple Bottom Line Through Spiritual Leadership," *Organizational Dynamics* 37, no. 1 (2008), pp. 86–96.

63. This section is based on I. A. Mitroff and E. A. Denton, *A Spiritual Audit of Corporate America: A Hard Look at Spirituality, Religion, and Values in the Workplace* (San Francisco: Jossey-Bass, 1999); E. H. Burack, "Spirituality in the Workplace," *Journal of Organizational Change Management* 12, no. 3 (1999), pp. 280–291; and C. L. Jurkiewicz and R. A. Giacalone, "A Values Framework for Measuring the Impact of Workplace Spirituality on Organizational Performance," *Journal of Business Ethics* 49, no. 2 (2004), pp. 129–142.

64. See, for example, B. S. Pawar, "Workplace Spirituality Facilitation: A Comprehensive Model," *Journal of Business Ethics* 90, no. 3 (2009), pp. 375–386; and L. Lambert, *Spirituality Inc.: Religion in the American Workplace* (New York: New York University Press, 2009).

65. M. Lips-Miersma, K. L. Dean, and C. J. Fornaciari, "Theorizing the Dark Side of the Workplace Spirituality Movement," *Journal of Management Inquiry* 18, no. 4 (2009), pp. 288–300.

66. J.-C. Garcia-Zamor, "Workplace Spirituality and Organizational Performance," *Public Administration Review* (May–June 2003), pp. 355–363; and L. W. Fry, S. T. Hannah, M. Noel, and F. O. Walumbwa, "Impact of Spiritual Leadership on Unit Performance," *Leadership Quarterly* 22, no. 2 (2011), pp. 259–270.

67. A. Rego and M. Pina e Cunha, "Workplace Spirituality and Organizational Commitment: An Empirical Study," *Journal of Organizational Change Management* 21, no. 1 (2008), pp. 53–75; and R. W. Kolodinsky, R. A. Giacalone, and C. L. Jurkiewicz, "Workplace Values and Outcomes: Exploring Personal, Organizational, and Interactive Workplace Spirituality," *Journal of Business Ethics* 81, no. 2 (2008), pp. 465–480.

68. D. J. McCarthy and S. M. Puffer, "Interpreting the Ethicality of Corporate Governance Decision in Russia: Utilizing Integrative Social Contracts Theory to Evaluate the Relevance of Agency Theory Norms," *Academy of Management Review* 33, no. 1 (2008), pp. 11–31.

69. P. Dvorak, "A Firm's Culture Can Get Lost in Translation," *The Wall Street Journal* (April 3, 2006), pp. B1, B3; K. Kranhold, "The Immelt Era, Five Years Old, Transforms GE," *The Wall Street Journal* (September 11, 2006), pp. B1, B3; and S. McCartney, "Teaching Americans How to Behave Abroad," *The Wall Street Journal* (April 11, 2006), pp. D1, D4.

70. J. A. Chatman, "Matching People and Organizations: Selection and Socialization in Public Accounting Firms," *Administrative Science Quarterly* (September 1991), pp. 459–484; and A. E. M. Van Vianen, "Person-Organization Fit: The Match Between Newcomers' and Recruiters' Preferences for Organizational Cultures," *Personnel Psychology* (Spring 2000), pp. 113–149.

HUMAN RESOURCES AT KIMANTRA

KiMantra is a family run spa business, established in Lebanon by Marie-Christine Hachem (CEO and general manager) and her sister Hiba Hachem (guest relations manager). As a flight attendant, Marie-Christine traveled the world and it was whilst on a stop over in Thailand that she decided to open up a spa back home in Lebanon. Thai massages were a relaxing and blissful experience and Marie-Christine wanted women in Lebanon to be pampered and looked after, and so KiMantra was born.

KiMantra employs staff from a wide range of countries including Thailand, Japan, and the United States. Recruitment is done very carefully to ensure that the right people are selected for the right job. This is a business of caring for others, so employees must be compassionate individuals. Despite the ethnic and religious diversity, there is complete harmony among the staff at KiMantra. All new staff meet daily for a whole month to become familiar with one another and understand the corporate culture of KiMantra. At the end of each day, each employee is asked to write down the pros and cons of the day and give suggestions for improvement. The ideas are shared and discussed, encouraging open channels of communication.

Marie-Christine is very transparent with her decisions, and this enhances trust and confidence among KiMantra employees. They understand that comments are given to improve service at KiMantra. Employees are motivated in many ways. Every month, each employee is given a free treatment whilst friends and relatives are also offered a discount on treatments. KiMantra employees are encouraged to sell products and services through incentives and staff discounts. Employees are asked for their input in their area of specialization, and their suggestions are taken seriously. For example, the dermatologist is the only person who can determine which facial cream is the best to use on certain skin types.

Moreover, KiMantra implements flexible working hours, and employees can choose their shifts as long as they work 8-hour days and they coordinate their schedules with prior warning. Most importantly, employees are encouraged to attend self-development programs, and management is ready to support them and fund if necessary. Before the official opening of the spa, Marie-Christine took two employees to Thailand for training, and employees are trained by an expert on any new equipment from overseas.

LEARNING OBJECTIVES

After studying this chapter, you should be able to:

1 Define *initial selection,* and identify the most useful methods.

2 Define *substantive selection,* and identify the most useful methods.

3 Define *contingent selection,* and contrast the arguments for and against drug testing.

4 Compare the four main types of training.

5 Contrast formal and informal training methods.

6 Contrast on-the-job and off-the-job training.

7 Describe the purposes of performance evaluation, and list the methods by which it can be done.

8 Show how managers can improve performance evaluations.

9 Describe how organizations can manage work–family conflicts.

MyManagementLab

Access a host of interactive learning aids to help strengthen your understanding of the chapter concepts at **www.pearsonglobaleditions .com/mymanagementlab**.

Human Resource Policies and Practices

*To manage people well, companies should . . .
elevate HR to a position of power and primacy
in the organization.* —Jack Welch

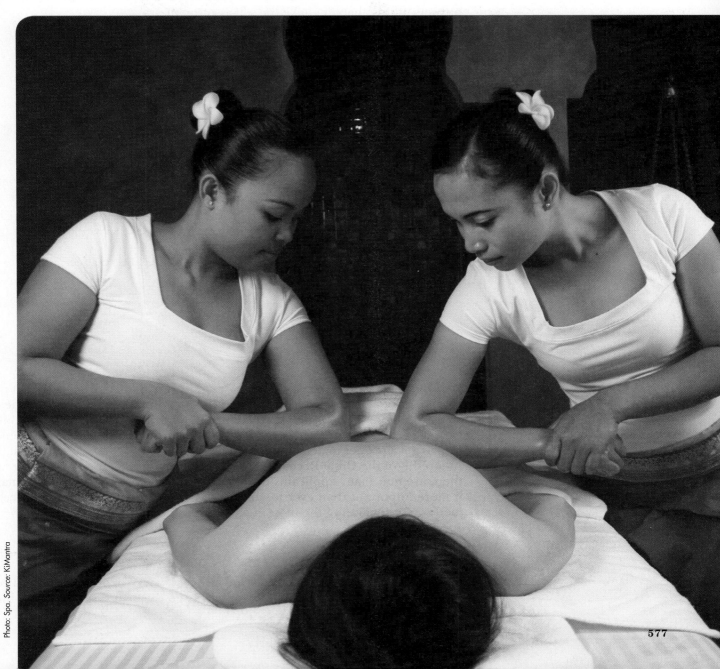

Employee performance evaluations are conducted regularly, and they are discussed by Marie-Christine and Hiba. They also ask for feedback from employees and listen to their comments and recommendations. Guests are also asked for feedback.

Sources: Interview with Hiba Hachem, Guest Relations Manager, KiMantra SPA, Dbayeh, Lebanon, October 2011; KiMantra Web site, www.kimantraspa.com, accessed October 2011.

The message of this chapter is that human resource (HR) policies and practices—such as employee selection, training, and performance management—influence an organization's effectiveness.[1] However, studies show managers—even HR managers—often don't know which HR practices work and which don't. To see how much you know (before learning the right answers in this chapter), take the self-assessment.

SELF-ASSESSMENT LIBRARY

How Much Do I Know About Human Resource Management (HRM)?

In the Self-Assessment Library (available on CD and online), take assessment IV.G.2 (How Much Do I Know About HRM?) and answer the following questions:

1. How did you score compared to your classmates'? Did the results surprise you?
2. How much of effective HRM is common sense?
3. Do you think your score will improve after you read this chapter?

Selection Practices

We just suggested that the most important HR function is hiring the right people. How do you figure out who they are? Identifying the right people is the objective of the selection process, which matches individual characteristics (ability, experience, and so on) with the requirements of the job.[2] When management fails to get a proper match, employee performance and satisfaction both suffer. As a result of the Great Recession and the continued high unemployment rate, there are now many applicants for almost every open job position. This makes it more important than ever to ensure that your organization has an effective method for separating the most qualified candidates from the large number of applicants.

How the Selection Process Works

Exhibit 17-1 shows how the selection process works in most organizations. Having decided to apply for a job, applicants go through several stages—three

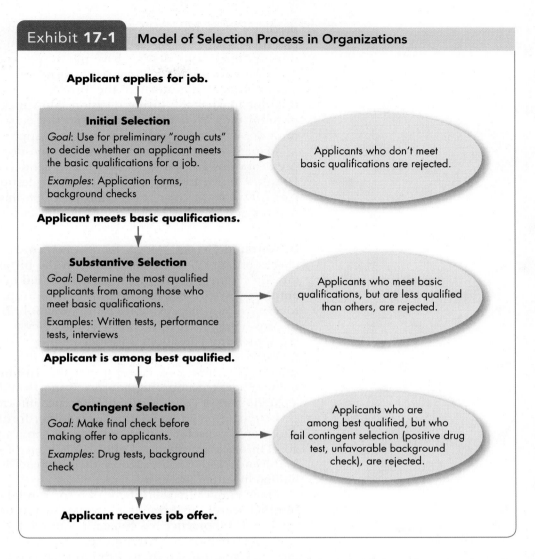

Exhibit 17-1 Model of Selection Process in Organizations

Applicant applies for job.

Initial Selection

Goal: Use for preliminary "rough cuts" to decide whether an applicant meets the basic qualifications for a job.

Examples: Application forms, background checks

Applicants who don't meet basic qualifications are rejected.

Applicant meets basic qualifications.

Substantive Selection

Goal: Determine the most qualified applicants from among those who meet basic qualifications.

Examples: Written tests, performance tests, interviews

Applicants who meet basic qualifications, but are less qualified than others, are rejected.

Applicant is among best qualified.

Contingent Selection

Goal: Make final check before making offer to applicants.

Examples: Drug tests, background check

Applicants who are among best qualified, but who fail contingent selection (positive drug test, unfavorable background check), are rejected.

Applicant receives job offer.

are shown in the exhibit—during which they can be rejected at any time. In practice, some organizations forgo some of these steps in the interests of time. (A meat-packing plant may hire someone who walks in the door, but there is not a long line of people who want to "thread" a pig's intestines for a living.) But most organizations follow a process that looks something like this exhibit. Let's go into a bit more detail about each stage.

Initial Selection

1   Define *initial selection,* and identify the most useful methods.

Initial selection devices are the first information applicants submit and are used for preliminary rough cuts to decide whether the applicant meets the basic qualifications for a job. Application forms (including letters of recommendation) are initial selection devices. We list background checks as either an initial selection device or a contingent selection device, depending on how the organization handles them. Some organizations prefer to look into an applicant's background right away. Others wait until the applicant is about ready to be hired, contingent on everything else checking out.

Application Forms   You've no doubt submitted your fair share of applications. By itself, the information submitted on an application form is not a very useful predictor of performance. However, it can be a good initial screen. For example, there's no sense spending time interviewing an applicant for a registered nurse position if he doesn't have the proper credentials (education, certification, experience). Many organizations encourage applicants to apply online. It takes only a few minutes, and the form can be forwarded to the people responsible for making the hiring decision. Most major corporations have a career page on their Web site where prospective employees can search for available positions by location or job type and then apply online.

Managers must be careful about the questions they ask on applications. It's pretty obvious that questions about race, gender, and nationality are disallowed. However, it might surprise you that other questions also put companies in legal jeopardy. For example, it generally is not permissible to ask about prior arrest records or even convictions unless the answer is job related.

Background Checks   More than 80 percent of employers conduct reference checks on applicants at some point in the hiring process. The reason is obvious: they want to know how an applicant did in past jobs and whether former employers would recommend hiring the person. The problem is that rarely do former employers provide useful information. In fact, nearly two-thirds refuse to provide detailed references because they are afraid of being sued for saying something bad about a former employee. Although this concern is often unfounded (employers are safe as long as they stick to documented facts, and several states have passed laws protecting truthful information provided in reference checks), in our litigious society most employers play it safe. The result is a paradox: most employers want reference information, but few will give it out.

Letters of recommendation are another form of background check. These also aren't as useful as they may seem. Applicants select those who will write good things about them, so almost all letters of recommendation are positive. In the end, readers either ignore them or read "between the lines" to try to find hidden meaning there.

Many employers will now search for candidates online through a general Internet search or through a targeted search on social networking sites. The legality of this practice has come into question, but there is no doubt that many employers include an electronic search to see whether candidates have any history that might make them a dubious choice for employment. For some potential employees, an embarrassing or incriminating photo circulated through Facebook may make it hard to get a job.

Finally, some employers check credit histories or criminal records. A bank hiring tellers, for example, would probably want to know about an applicant's criminal and credit histories. Increasingly, credit checks are being used for nonbanking jobs. Kevin Palmer's offer of a job with a property management company evaporated after the company performed a credit check on him that revealed a bankruptcy in his past.[3] Despite the trend, because of the invasive nature of such checks, employers need to be sure there is a need for them. To further complicate matters, however, *not* checking can carry a legal cost. Manor Park Nursing Home in Texas failed to do a criminal background check of an employee who later sexually assaulted a resident of the home. The jury awarded the plaintiff $1.1 million, concluding the nursing home was negligent for failing to conduct a background check.[4]

Substantive Selection

2   Define *substantive selection,* and identify the most useful methods.

If an applicant passes the initial screens, next are substantive selection methods. These are the heart of the selection process and include written tests, performance tests, and interviews.

Written tests are the heart of the selection process at Cabela's, a specialty retailer of hunting, fishing, camping, and other outdoor merchandise. Job applicants for Cabela's contact center and retail stores are given a difficult 150-question test that measures the depth of their knowledge of outdoor sports. Cabela's management believes that the written tests are helpful in determining who will succeed in providing customers with exceptional service and product knowledge.

Source: William Thomas Cain/Getty Images.

Written Tests   Long popular as selection devices, written tests—called "paper-and-pencil" tests, though most are now available online—declined in use between the late 1960s and mid-1980s, especially in the United States. They were frequently characterized as discriminatory, and many organizations had not validated them as job related. The past 20 years, however, have seen a resurgence, and today more than 60 percent of all U.S. organizations and most of the *Fortune* 1,000 use some type of employment test.[5] Managers recognize that valid tests can help predict who will be successful on the job.[6] Applicants, however, tend to view written tests as less valid and fair than interviews or performance tests.[7] Typical written tests include (1) intelligence or cognitive ability tests, (2) personality tests, (3) integrity tests, and (4) interest inventories.

Tests of intellectual ability, spatial and mechanical ability, perceptual accuracy, and motor ability have long proven valid predictors for many skilled, semiskilled, and unskilled operative jobs organizations.[8] Intelligence tests have proven to be particularly good predictors for jobs that include cognitively complex tasks.[9] Many experts say intelligence tests are the *single best* selection measure across jobs, and that they are at least as valid in the European Union (EU) nations as in the United States.[10]

Personality tests are inexpensive and simple to administer, and in the past decade, their use has grown. The traits that best predict job performance are conscientiousness and positive self-concept.[11] This makes sense in that conscientious people tend to be motivated and dependable, and positive people are "can-do" oriented and persistent. However, concerns about applicant faking remain, because it's fairly easy for applicants to claim they are hard-working, motivated, and dependable when asked in a job application setting.[12] Two reviews of studies comparing self-reported personality to observer-rated personality found that observer ratings are better predictors of job performance and other behaviors.[13] Thus, employers might want to consider asking employment references about applicant personality as part of the screening process.

As ethical problems have increased in organizations, integrity tests have gained popularity. These paper-and-pencil tests measure factors such as dependability, carefulness, responsibility, and honesty; they have proven to be powerful predictors of supervisory ratings of job performance and of theft, discipline problems, and excessive absenteeism.[14]

Performance-Simulation Tests   What better way to find out whether applicants can do a job successfully than by having them do it? That's precisely the logic of performance-simulation tests.

Although they are more complicated to develop and administer than written tests, performance-simulation tests have higher *face validity* (which measures whether applicants perceive the measures to be accurate), and their popularity has increased. The three best-known are work samples, assessment centers, and situational judgment tests.

Work sample tests are hands-on simulations of part or all of the work that applicants for routine jobs must perform. Each work sample element is matched with a job-performance element to measure applicants' knowledge, skills, and abilities with more validity than written aptitude and personality tests.[15] Work samples are widely used in the hiring of skilled workers, such as welders, machinists, carpenters, and electricians. Job candidates for production jobs often have a limited period of time to perform a variety of typical work tasks on a specially built simulated assembly line.[16]

A more elaborate set of performance-simulation tests, specifically designed to evaluate a candidate's managerial potential, is administered in **assessment centers**. Line executives, supervisors, and/or trained psychologists evaluate candidates as they go through one to several days of exercises that simulate real problems they would confront on the job.[17] A candidate might be required to play the role of a manager who must decide how to respond to ten memos in an in-basket within a 2-hour period.

To reduce the costs of job simulations, many organizations have started to use situational judgment tests, which ask applicants how they would perform in a variety of job situations and compare their answers to those of high-performing employees.[18] One study comparing situational judgment tests to assessment centers found the assessment center was a better predictor of job performance, although the difference was not large.[19] Ultimately, the lower cost of the situational judgment test may make it a better choice for some organizations than a more elaborate work sample or assessment center.

Interviews   Of all the selection devices organizations around the globe use to differentiate candidates, the interview remains the most common.[20] It also tends to have a disproportionate amount of influence. Over-reliance on interviews is problematic, because extensive evidence shows that impression management techniques like self-promotion have a strong effect on interviewer preferences even when unrelated to the job.[21] Conversely, the candidate who performs poorly in the employment interview is likely to be cut from the applicant pool regardless of experience, test scores, or letters of recommendation.

These findings are relevant because of the interview's typical nature.[22] The popular unstructured interview—short, casual, and made up of random questions—is simply not a very effective selection device.[23] The data it gathers are typically biased and often only modestly related to future job performance. Still, managers are reluctant to use *structured interviews* in place of their favorite questions, such as "If you could be any animal, what would you be, and why?"[24]

Without structure, interviewers tend to favor applicants who share their attitudes, give undue weight to negative information, and allow the order in which applicants are interviewed to influence their evaluations.[25] To reduce such bias

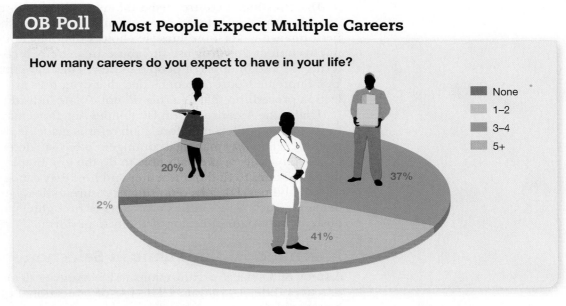

OB Poll | **Most People Expect Multiple Careers**

How many careers do you expect to have in your life?

None
1–2
3–4
5+

2%
20%
37%
41%

Source: Based on J. Yang and A. Gonzalez, "Charles Schwab Survey of 1,000 Adults," *USA Today* (March 9, 2011), p. 1B.

and improve the validity of interviews, managers should adopt a standardized set of questions, a uniform method of recording information, and standardized ratings of applicants' qualifications. Training interviewers to focus on specific dimensions of job performance, practicing evaluation of sample candidates, and giving interviewers feedback on how well they were focused on job-relevant characteristics significantly improves the accuracy of their ratings.[26] Interview effectiveness also improves when employers use *behavioral structured interviews,* probably because these assessments are less influenced by interviewer biases.[27] They require applicants to describe how they handled specific problems and situations in previous jobs, based on the assumption that past behavior offers the best predictor of future behavior. Panel interviews also minimize the influence of individual biases and have higher validity.

In practice, most organizations use interviews as more than a prediction-of-performance device.[28] Companies as diverse as Southwest Airlines, Disney, Bank of America, Microsoft, Procter & Gamble, and Harrah's Entertainment use them to assess applicant–organization fit. So, in addition to evaluating specific, job-related skills, managers are looking at personality characteristics and personal values to find individuals who fit the organization's culture and image.

Contingent Selection

3 Define *contingent selection,* and contrast the arguments for and against drug testing.

If applicants pass the substantive selection methods, they are ready to be hired, contingent on a final check. One common contingent method is a drug test. Publix grocery stores make a tentative offer to applicants contingent on their passing such a test and checking out as drug-free.

work sample tests *Hands-on simulations of part or all of the work that applicants for routine jobs must perform.*

assessment centers *A set of performance-simulation tests designed to evaluate a candidate's managerial potential.*

Drug testing is controversial. Many applicants think testing without reasonable suspicion is invasive or unfair and say they should be tested on job-performance factors, not lifestyle choices that may not be relevant. Employers might counter that drug use and abuse are extremely costly, not just in financial terms but also in terms of people's safety. They have the law on their side. The U.S. Supreme Court has concluded that drug tests are "minimally invasive" selection procedures that as a rule do not violate individuals' rights.

Under the Americans with Disabilities Act, firms may not require employees to pass a medical exam before a job offer is made. However, they can conduct medical exams *after* making a contingent offer—to determine whether an applicant is physically or mentally able to do the job. Employers also sometimes use medical exams to find out whether and how they can accommodate employees with disabilities. For jobs requiring exposure to heavy physical or psychological demands, such as air traffic controllers or firefighters, medical exams are obviously an important indicator of ability to perform.

International Variations in Selection Processes

A study of 300 large organizations in 22 countries demonstrated that selection practices differ by nation.[29] The use of educational qualifications in screening candidates seems to be a universal practice, but aside from this, different countries emphasize different selection techniques. Structured interviews were popular in some countries and nonexistent in others. The study authors suggested that "certain cultures may find structured interviews antithetical to beliefs about how one should conduct an interpersonal interaction or the extent to which one should trust the judgment of the interviewer."[30] Other research shows that across the Netherlands, the United States, France, Spain, Portugal, and Singapore, most applicants prefer interviews and work sample tests and dislike use of personal contacts and integrity tests.[31] There was little variation in preferences across these countries.

Executives of ImageNet Company (in red jackets), a Japanese Internet retailer, conducted job interviews atop Mount Fuji, Japan's highest mountain. Of the 20 candidates who applied for one of four job openings, 11 succeeded in reaching the summit of the 12,388-foot mountain for the interview. ImageNet said that the unique interview was to ensure that job applicants "have what it takes to scale the heights of business" and would identify candidates who are highly motivated, determined to succeed, and prepared for unusual challenges. Requiring applicants to climb a mountain to attend an interview would run afoul of equal employment laws in the United States and most European nations.

Source: Yuriko Nakao/Reuters/Landov Media.

Training and Development Programs

Competent employees don't remain competent forever. Skills deteriorate and can become obsolete, and new skills need to be learned. That's why U.S. corporations with a hundred or more employees spent more than $125 billion on formal training in a recent year.[32]

Types of Training

4 Compare the four main types of training.

Training can include everything from teaching employees basic reading skills to conducting advanced courses in executive leadership. Here we discuss four general skill categories—basic literacy, technical skills, interpersonal skills, and problem-solving skills—and ethics training.

Basic Skills One survey of more than 400 human resources professionals found that 40 percent of employers believe high school graduates lack basic skills in reading comprehension, writing, and math.[33] As work has become more sophisticated, the need for these basic skills has grown significantly, leading to a gap between employer demands for skills and the available skills in the workforce.[34] The challenge isn't unique to the United States. It's a worldwide problem—from the most developed countries to the least.[35] For many undeveloped countries, widespread illiteracy means there is almost no hope of competing in a global economy.

Organizations increasingly have to teach employees basic reading and math skills. A literacy audit showed that employees at gun manufacturer Smith & Wesson needed at least an eighth-grade reading level to do typical workplace tasks.[36] Yet 30 percent of the company's 676 workers with no degree scored below eighth-grade levels in either reading or math. After the first round of basic-skills classes, company-paid and on company time, 70 percent of attendees brought their skills up to the target level, allowing them to do a better job. They displayed increased abilities to use fractions and decimals, better overall communication, greater ease in writing and reading charts, graphs, and bulletin boards—and a significant increase in confidence.

Technical Skills Most training is directed at upgrading and improving an employee's technical skills, increasingly important for two reasons: new technology and new structural designs in the organization.

Indian companies have faced a dramatic increase in demand for skilled workers in areas like engineering for emerging technologies, but many recent engineering graduates lack up-to-date knowledge required to perform these technical tasks.[37] Companies like Tata and Wipro provide new hires with up to 3 months of training to ensure they have the knowledge to perform the technical work demanded. In addition, these organizations are attempting to form partnerships with engineering schools to ensure their curricula meet the needs of contemporary employers.

As organizations flatten their structures, expand their use of teams, and break down traditional departmental barriers, employees need mastery of a wider variety of tasks and increased knowledge of how their organization operates. The restructuring of jobs around empowered teams at Miller Brewing led management to introduce a comprehensive business literacy program to help employees better understand competition, the state of the beer industry, where the company's revenues come from, how costs are calculated, and where employees fit into the company's value chain.[38]

Problem-Solving Skills   Problem-solving training for managers and other employees can include activities to sharpen their logic, reasoning, and problem-defining skills as well as their abilities to assess causation, develop and analyze alternatives, and select solutions. Problem-solving training has become a part of almost every organizational effort to introduce self-managed teams or implement quality-management programs.

Interpersonal Skills   Almost all employees belong to a work unit, and their work performance depends on their ability to effectively interact with their co-workers and boss. Some employees have excellent interpersonal abilities, but others require training to improve listening, communicating, and team-building skills. Although professionals are greatly interested in interpersonal skills training, most evidence suggests that skills learned in such training do not readily transfer back to the workplace.[39]

Civility Training   As human resource managers have become increasingly aware of the effects of social behavior in the workplace, they have paid more attention to the problems of incivility, bullying, and abusive supervision in organizations. Examples of incivility include being ignored, being excluded from social situations, having your reputation undermined in front of others, and experiencing other actions meant to demean or disparage. Researchers have shown that these forms of negative behavior can decrease satisfaction, reduce job performance, increase perceptions of unfair treatment, increase depression, and lead to psychological withdrawal from the workplace.[40]

Is there anything managers can do to minimize incivility, bullying, and abusive supervision? One possibility is training specifically targeted to building civility by having directed conversations about it and supporting the reduction of incivility on an ongoing process. Following a training intervention based on these principles, co-worker civility, respect, job satisfaction, and management trust have increased, while supervisor incivility, cynicism, and absences

There's a heavy focus on teamwork and unit cohesion for this squad of midshipmen during their 18-hour-long Sea Trials training at the U.S. Naval Academy. Learning how to become a team player and recognizing the value of teamwork are part of the interpersonal skills training for cadets who are finishing their freshman year at the academy. Working together to complete a challenge, such as transporting the log shown here, is the objective of the training, because the tasks cannot be completed alone. The training also teaches cadets the skills of encouraging and motivating peers to succeed as part of building unity among squad members.

Source: Damon J. Moritz /MAI /Landov Media.

decreased.[41] Thus, the evidence suggests that deliberate interventions to improve the workplace climate for positive behavior can indeed minimize the problems of incivility.

Ethics Training   A large percentage of employees working in the 1,000 largest U.S. corporations receive ethics training[42] either during new-employee orientation, as part of ongoing developmental programs, or as periodic reinforcement of ethical principles.[43] But the jury is still out on whether you can actually teach ethics.[44]

Critics argue that ethics are based on values, and value systems are learned by example at an early age. By the time employees are hired, their ethical values are fixed. Some research does suggest ethics training does not have a significant long-term effect on participants' values and even that exposure to business and law school programs *decreases* students' level of prosocial ethical values.[45]

Supporters of ethics training say values *can* be learned and changed after early childhood. And even if they couldn't, ethics training helps employees recognize ethical dilemmas and become more aware of the ethical issues underlying their actions. It also reaffirms an organization's expectations that members will act ethically. Individuals who have greater exposure to organizational ethics codes and ethics training do tend to be more satisfied and perceive their organizations as more socially responsible, so ethics training does have some positive effects.[46]

Training Methods

5   Contrast formal and informal training methods.

6   Contrast on-the-job and off-the-job training.

MyManagementLab
For an interactive application of this topic, check out this chapter's simulation activity at **www.pearsonglobaleditions.com/mymanagementlab.**

Historically, *training* meant "formal training," planned in advance and having a structured format. However, evidence indicates 70 percent of workplace learning takes place in *informal training*—unstructured, unplanned, and easily adapted to situations and individuals—for teaching skills and keeping employees current.[47] In reality, most informal training is nothing other than employees helping each other out, sharing information, and solving work-related problems together. Thus, many managers are now supportive of what used to be considered "idle chatter."

On-the-job training methods include job rotation, apprenticeships, understudy assignments, and formal mentoring programs. But because they often disrupt the workplace, organizations also invest in *off-the-job training*. The $125 billion figure we cited for training was largely spent on the formal off-the-job variety, the most popular method being live classroom lectures. But it also encompasses public seminars, self-study programs, Internet courses, Webinars, podcasts, and group activities that use role-plays and case studies.

The fastest-growing training medium is probably computer-based training, or e-training.[48] E-learning systems emphasize learner control over the pace and content of instruction, allow e-learners to interact through online communities, and incorporate other techniques such as simulations and group discussions. Computer-based training that lets learners actively participate in exercises and quizzes was more effective than traditional classroom instruction.[49] Recent research has also highlighted the ways in which computer-based training can be improved by providing learners with regular prompts to set goals for learning, use effective study strategies, and measure progress toward their learning goals.[50]

On the positive side, e-training increases flexibility because organizations can deliver materials anywhere, any time. It also seems fast and efficient. On the other hand, it's expensive to design self-paced online materials, employees miss the social interaction of a classroom, online learners are more susceptible to distractions, and "clicking through" training without engaging in practice activities provides no assurance that employees have actually learned anything.[51]

Videogame training is widely used in the technology industry and is gaining popularity in low-tech firms. Cold Stone Creamery, for example, has developed a proprietary game called "Stone City" to help new employees like the young man shown here learn about products, portion sizes, and customer service. As one element of computerized training, Internet games are intrinsically motivating and result in employees choosing to repeatedly engage in game play and mastering skills. Computer-based training is fast and efficient and gives learners control over the pace and content of instruction.

Source: Abel Uribe/MCT/Newscom.

Evaluating Effectiveness

The *effectiveness* of a training program can refer to the level of student satisfaction, the amount students learn, the extent to which they transfer the material from training to their jobs, or the financial return on investments in training.[52] These results are not always related. Some people who have a positive experience in an upbeat, fun class learn very little; some who learn a great deal have difficulty figuring out how to use their knowledge at work; and changes in employee behavior are often not large enough to justify the expense of training. This means rigorous measurement of multiple training outcomes should be a part of every training effort.

The success of training also depends on the individual. If individuals are unmotivated, they will learn very little. What creates training motivation? Personality is important: those with an internal locus of control, high conscientiousness, high cognitive ability, and high self-efficacy learn more. The climate also is important: when trainees believe there are opportunities and resources to let them apply their newly learned skills, they are more motivated and do better in training programs.[53] Finally, after-training support from supervisors and co-workers has a strong influence on whether employees transfer their learning into new behavior.[54] For a training program to be effective requires not just teaching the skills but also changing the work environment to support the trainees.

Performance Evaluation

7 Describe the purposes of performance evaluation, and list the methods by which it can be done.

Would you study differently or exert a different level of effort for a college course graded on a pass–fail basis than for one that awarded letter grades A to F? Students typically tell us they study harder when letter grades are at stake. When they take a course on a pass–fail basis, they tend to do just enough to ensure a passing grade.

What applies in the college context also applies to employees at work. In this section, we show how the choice of a performance evaluation system and the way it's administered can be an important force influencing employee behavior.

What Is Performance?

In the past, most organizations assessed only how well employees performed the tasks listed on a job description, but today's less hierarchical and more service-oriented organizations require more. Researchers now recognize three major types of behavior that constitute performance at work:

1. **Task performance.** Performing the duties and responsibilities that contribute to the production of a good or service or to administrative tasks. This includes most of the tasks in a conventional job description.
2. **Citizenship.** Actions that contribute to the psychological environment of the organization, such as helping others when not required, supporting organizational objectives, treating co-workers with respect, making constructive suggestions, and saying positive things about the workplace.
3. **Counterproductivity.** Actions that actively damage the organization. These behaviors include stealing, damaging company property, behaving aggressively toward co-workers, and taking avoidable absences.

Most managers believe good performance means doing well on the first two dimensions and avoiding the third.[55] A person who does core job tasks very well but is rude and aggressive toward co-workers is not going to be considered a good employee in most organizations, and even the most pleasant and upbeat worker who can't do the main job tasks well is not going to be a good employee.

Purposes of Performance Evaluation

Performance evaluation serves a number of purposes.[56] One is to help management make general *human resource decisions* about promotions, transfers, and terminations. Evaluations also *identify training and development needs*. They *pinpoint employee skills and competencies* for which remedial programs can be developed. Finally, they *provide feedback to employees* on how the organization views their performance and are often the *basis for reward allocations,* including merit pay increases.

Because our interest is in organizational behavior, here we emphasize performance evaluation as a mechanism for providing feedback and determining reward allocations.

What Do We Evaluate?

The criteria management choose to evaluate will have a major influence on what employees do. The three most popular sets of criteria are individual task outcomes, behaviors, and traits.

Individual Task Outcomes If ends count rather than means, management should evaluate an employee's task on outcomes such as quantity produced, scrap generated, and cost per unit of production for a plant manager or on

task performance *The combination of effectiveness and efficiency at doing your core job tasks.*

citizenship *Actions that contribute to the psychological environment of the organization, such as helping others when not required*

counterproductivity *Actions that actively damage the organization, including stealing, behaving aggressively toward co-workers, or being late or absent*

Behavior is an important element in evaluating the performance of caregivers in nursing homes and retirement facilities. In addition to individual task outcomes, the caregiver shown here attending to a resident at a nursing home for the elderly in Yokohama, Japan, is evaluated on behaviors such as helping others and building caring and trusting relationships with residents and their family members. These subjective factors contribute to the effectiveness of the nursing home and its reputation as a place where older people are treated with love and respect.

overall sales volume in the territory, dollar increase in sales, and number of new accounts established for a salesperson.

Behaviors   It is difficult to attribute specific outcomes to the actions of employees in advisory or support positions or employees whose work assignments are part of a group effort. We may readily evaluate the group's performance, but if it is hard to identify the contribution of each group member, management will often evaluate the employee's behavior. A plant manager might be evaluated on promptness in submitting monthly reports or leadership style, and a salesperson on average number of contact calls made per day or sick days used per year.

Measured behaviors needn't be limited to those directly related to individual productivity. As we pointed out in discussing organizational citizenship behavior (see Chapters 1 and 3), helping others, making suggestions for improvements, and volunteering for extra duties make work groups and organizations more effective and often are incorporated into evaluations of employee performance.

Traits   The weakest criteria, because they're furthest removed from actual job performance, are individual traits.[57] Having a good attitude, showing confidence, being dependable, looking busy, or possessing a wealth of experience may or may not be highly correlated with positive task outcomes, but it's naïve to ignore the reality that organizations still use such traits to assess job performance.

Who Should Do the Evaluating?

Who should evaluate an employee's performance? By tradition, the task has fallen to managers, because they are held responsible for their employees' performance. But others may do the job better.

With many of today's organizations using self-managed teams, telecommuting, and other organizing devices that distance bosses from employees, the immediate superior may not be the most reliable judge of an employee's performance. Peers and even subordinates are being asked to take part in the process, and employees are participating in their own evaluation. One survey found about half of executives and 53 percent of employees now have input into their performance evaluations.[58] As you might expect, self-evaluations often suffer from overinflated assessment and self-serving bias, and they seldom agree with superiors' ratings.[59] They are probably better suited to developmental than evaluative purposes and should be combined with other sources of information to reduce rating errors.

In most situations, in fact, it is highly advisable to use multiple sources of ratings. Any individual performance rating may say as much about the rater as about the person being evaluated. By averaging across raters, we can obtain a more reliable, unbiased, and accurate performance evaluation.

Another popular approach to performance evaluation is 360-degree evaluations.[60] These provide performance feedback from the employee's full circle of daily contacts, from mailroom workers to customers to bosses to peers (see Exhibit 17-2). The number of appraisals can be as few as 3 or 4 or as many as 25; most organizations collect 5 to 10 per employee.

What's the appeal of the 360-degree appraisal? By relying on feedback from co-workers, customers, and subordinates, organizations are hoping to give everyone a sense of participation in the review process and gain more accurate readings on employee performance.

Evidence on the effectiveness of the 360-degree evaluation is mixed.[61] It provides employees with a wider perspective on their performance, but many organizations don't spend the time to train evaluators in giving constructive

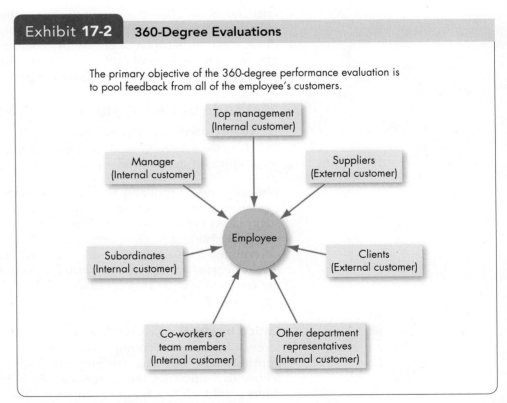

Exhibit 17-2 **360-Degree Evaluations**

The primary objective of the 360-degree performance evaluation is to pool feedback from all of the employee's customers.

Top management (Internal customer)

Manager (Internal customer)

Suppliers (External customer)

Subordinates (Internal customer)

Employee

Clients (External customer)

Co-workers or team members (Internal customer)

Other department representatives (Internal customer)

Source: Adapted from *Personnel Journal* (November 1994), p. 100.

Performance Appraisal Around the World

The process of appraising performance is complicated and requires both assessing what employees are doing and communicating this information back to the employees. These are two highly social, context-dependent processes, so we might expect performance appraisal to vary dramatically depending on the country. Preliminary research suggests that management practices related to performance appraisal do indeed vary across borders.

A structured interview study examined Chinese managers' beliefs about performance appraisal. Most respondents found it a good way to build communication and believed performance levels are a function of each person's individual attributes. These attitudes were fairly similar to those of managers in the United States, where most research on performance appraisal has been performed. However, the Chinese managers believed a person in a position of power and control should run the appraisal meeting, unlike the more informal preferences of U.S. managers.

One larger-scale study compared appraisal practices in the United States, Canada, the United Kingdom, Finland, Sweden, Hong Kong, and Singapore using the dimensions of culture identified in the GLOBE survey. Appraisals were more frequently used for communication and development in countries like Sweden and Finland that were low in assertiveness and power distance. Formal feedback was more frequent in highly assertive, low collectivist, and uncertainty avoidant cultures like the United States, the United Kingdom, and Canada. Finally, appraisals were more collaborative in nature in the United States and Canada, and more formal and top-down in Hong Kong and Singapore.

Source: Based on K. H. C. Cheng and W. Cascio, "Performance-Appraisal Beliefs of Chinese Employees in Hong Kong and the Pearl River Delta," *International Journal of Selection and Assessment* 17, no. 3 (2009), pp. 329–333; and F. F. T. Chiang and T. A. Birtch, "Appraising Performance across Borders: An Empirical Examination of the Purposes and Practices of Performance Appraisal in a Multi-Country Context," *Journal of Management Studies* 47, no. 7 (2010), pp. 1365–1393.

criticism. Some allow employees to choose the peers and subordinates who evaluate them, which can artificially inflate feedback. It's also difficult to reconcile disagreements between rater groups. There is clear evidence that peers tend to give much more lenient ratings that supervisors or subordinates, and peers also tend to make more errors in appraising performance.

Methods of Performance Evaluation

We've discussed *what* we evaluate and *who* should do the evaluating. Now we ask: *How* do we evaluate an employee's performance? What are the specific techniques for evaluation?

Written Essays   Probably the simplest method is to write a narrative describing an employee's strengths, weaknesses, past performance, potential, and suggestions for improvement. The written essay requires no complex forms or extensive training to complete. But, in this method, a useful appraisal may be determined as much by the evaluator's writing skill as by the employee's actual level of performance. It's also difficult to compare essays for different employees (or for the same employees written by different managers) because there is no standardized scoring key.

Critical Incidents   **Critical incidents** focus the evaluator's attention on the difference between executing a job effectively and executing it ineffectively. The appraiser describes what the employee did that was especially effective or ineffective in a situation, citing only specific behaviors. A list of such critical incidents provides a rich set of examples to show the employee desirable behaviors and those that call for improvement.

Graphic Rating Scales One of the oldest and most popular methods of evaluation is **graphic rating scales**. The evaluator goes through a set of performance factors—such as quantity and quality of work, depth of knowledge, cooperation, attendance, and initiative—and rates each on incremental scales. The scales may specify, say, five points, so *job knowledge* might be rated 1 ("is poorly informed about work duties") to 5 ("has complete mastery of all phases of the job"). Although they don't provide the depth of information that essays or critical incidents do, graphic rating scales are less time consuming to develop and administer and allow for quantitative analysis and comparison.

Behaviorally Anchored Rating Scales Behaviorally anchored rating scales **(BARS)** combine major elements from the critical incident and graphic rating scale approaches. The appraiser rates employees on items along a continuum, but the items are examples of actual behavior on the job rather than general descriptions or traits. To develop the BARS, participants first contribute specific illustrations of effective and ineffective behavior, which are translated into a set of performance dimensions with varying levels of quality.

Forced Comparisons **Forced comparisons** evaluate one individual's performance against the performance of another or others. It is a relative rather than an absolute measuring device. The two most popular comparisons are group order ranking and individual ranking.

Group order ranking requires the evaluator to place employees into a particular classification, such as top one-fifth or second one-fifth. If a rater has 20 employees, only 4 can be in the top fifth and, of course, 4 must also be relegated to the bottom fifth. This method is often used in recommending students to graduate schools.

The **individual ranking** approach rank-orders employees from best to worst. If the manager is required to appraise 30 employees, the difference between the 1st and 2nd employee is assumed to be the same as that between the 21st and 22nd. Some employees may be closely grouped, but no ties are permitted. The result is a clear ordering from the highest performer to the lowest.

One parallel to forced ranking is forced distribution of college grades. Why would universities do this? As shown in Exhibit 17-3, average GPAs have gotten much higher over time.[62] In recent years, nearly 43 percent of all letter grades given were A's, whereas there was a decrease in the number of C's. Although it is not exactly clear why this increase has occurred over time, many attribute the rise in high letter grades to the popularity of student evaluations as a means of assessing professor performance. Generous grades might produce

---

critical incidents *A way of evaluating the behaviors that are key in making the difference between executing a job effectively and executing it ineffectively.*

graphic rating scales *An evaluation method in which the evaluator rates performance factors on an incremental scale.*

behaviorally anchored rating scales (BARS) *Scales that combine major elements from the critical incident and graphic rating scale approaches. The appraiser rates the employees based on items along a continuum, but the points are examples of actual behavior on the given job rather than general descriptions or traits.*

forced comparison *Method of performance evaluation where an employee's performance is made in explicit comparison to others (e.g., an employee may rank third out of 10 employees in her work unit.*

group order ranking *An evaluation method that places employees into a particular classification, such as quartiles.*

individual ranking *An evaluation method that rank-orders employees from best to worst.*

| Exhibit **17-3** | Distribution of Grades at American Colleges and Universities as a Function of Time |

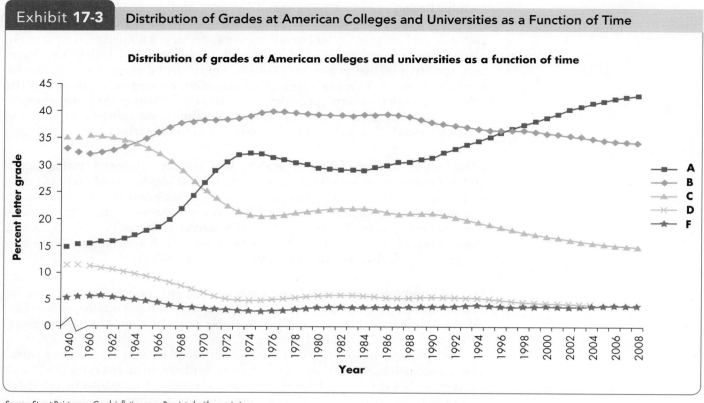

Distribution of grades at American colleges and universities as a function of time

Source: Stuart Rojstaczer, Gradeinflation.com. Reprinted with permission.

higher student evaluations. It's also the case that giving higher grades can help students become more competitive candidates for graduate school and jobs.

In response to grade inflation, some colleges have instituted forced grade distributions, whereby professors must give a certain percentage of A's, B's, and C's. This is exactly what Princeton recently did; each department can now give A's to no more than 35 percent of its students. Natasha Gopaul, a Princeton senior, commented, "You do feel you might be one of the ones they just cut off."

Suggestions for Improving Performance Evaluations

8 Show how managers can improve performance evaluations.

The performance evaluation process is a potential minefield. Evaluators can unconsciously inflate evaluations (positive leniency), understate performance (negative leniency), or allow the assessment of one characteristic to unduly influence the assessment of others (the halo error). Some appraisers bias their evaluations by unconsciously favoring people who have qualities and traits similar to their own (the similarity error). And, of course, some evaluators see the evaluation process as a political opportunity to overtly reward or punish employees they like or dislike. A review of the literature and several studies on performance appraisals demonstrates that many managers deliberately distort performance ratings in order to maintain a positive relationship with their subordinates or to achieve a positive image of themselves by showing that all their

Recruiting the Unemployed

As the economy has continued to perform poorly since the start of the Great Recession, a large number of individuals have joined the ranks of the long-term unemployed. The difficulties of unemployment are compounded because many employers either overtly or covertly prefer candidates who do not have gaps in their work history. For example, *New York Times* reporter Catherine Rampell found in hundreds of job postings on Monster .com, CareerBuilder, and Craigslist that employers prefer people who are either currently employed or only recently laid off. This makes it extremely difficult for qualified individuals to find work because it constitutes a bias against the unemployed.

Although federal regulators in the Equal Employment Opportunity Commission have voiced concerns about the practice, unemployment is not a protected status like age, race, or gender. Due to gaps in the law, some states like New Jersey, New York, and Michigan have considered or implemented laws prohibiting advertisements that discourage unemployed workers from applying.

What can employers do to ensure they are giving qualified individuals who have been unemployed a fair shot at open positions? A few principles can help ensure they are recruiting ethically:

1. Always try to evaluate the whole candidate, including prior experience, ability, and personality. Don't get overly focused on a single detail of their employment history.

2. If you are concerned about an employment gap in the résumé, ask about it directly. Don't assume it reflects a lack of initiative or interest in work.

3. Consider offering additional training to those who may have missed out on certain developments in the field during their spell of unemployment. Although it can add expense, your organization might benefit from securing someone other employers would overlook.

Sources: Based on C. Rampell, "The Help-Wanted Sign Comes with a Frustrating Asterisk," *The New York Times* (July 25, 2011), www.nytimes.com; and S. Kelly, "Unemployed Not Wanted? The EEOC Scrutinizes Whether Companies' Recruiting Only Already Employed Applications Could Be Discrimination." *Treasury and Risk* (April 2011), www.treasuryandrisk.com.

employees are performing well.[63] Although no protections *guarantee* accurate performance evaluations, the following suggestions can make the process more objective and fair.

Use Multiple Evaluators As the number of evaluators increases, the probability of attaining more accurate information increases, as does the likelihood that the employee will accept the feedback as valid.[64] We often see multiple evaluators in competitions in such sports as diving and gymnastics. A set of evaluators judges a performance, the highest and lowest scores are dropped, and the final evaluation is made up of those remaining. The logic of multiple evaluators applies to organizations as well. If an employee has had ten supervisors, nine having rated her excellent and one poor, we can safely discount the one poor evaluation. By moving employees around within the organization to gain a number of evaluations, or by using multiple assessors (as in 360-degree appraisals), we increase the probability of achieving more valid and reliable evaluations.

Evaluate Selectively To increase agreement among them, appraisers should evaluate only where they have some expertise.[65] They should thus be as close as possible, in organizational level, to the individual being evaluated. The more levels that separate them, the less opportunity the evaluator has to observe the individual's behavior and, not surprisingly, the greater the possibility for inaccuracies.

Train Evaluators   If you can't *find* good evaluators, *make* them. Training evaluators can produce more accurate raters.[66] Most rater training courses emphasize changing the raters' frame of reference by teaching them what to look for, so everyone in the organization defines *good performance* in the same way. Another effective training technique is to encourage raters to describe the employee's behavior in as much detail as possible. Providing more detail encourages raters to remember more about the employee's performance, rather than just acting on their feelings about the employee at the moment.

Provide Employees with Due Process   The concept of *due process* can be applied to appraisals to increase the perception that employees are being treated fairly.[67] Three features characterize due process systems: (1) Individuals are provided with adequate notice of what is expected of them; (2) all evidence relevant to a proposed violation is aired in a fair hearing so the individuals affected can respond; and (3) the final decision is based on the evidence and free of bias.

One technique organizations might consider to enhance due process is posting appraisals online so employees can see their own performance scores exactly as the supervisor enters them. One company that did so found employees believed rater accountability and employee participation were higher when appraisal information was available online prior to appraisal interviews.[68] It might be that raters were more sensitive to providing accurate ratings when they knew employees would be able to see their own information directly.

Providing Performance Feedback

Few activities are more unpleasant for many managers than providing performance feedback to employees. In fact, unless pressured by organizational policies and controls, managers are likely to ignore this responsibility.

Why? First, even though almost every employee could stand to improve in some areas, managers fear confrontation when presenting negative feedback. Second, many employees do tend to become defensive when their weaknesses are pointed out. Instead of accepting the feedback as constructive and a basis for improving performance, some criticize the manager or redirect blame to someone else. Finally, employees tend to have an inflated assessment of their own performance. Statistically speaking, half of all employees must be below-average performers. But the average employee's estimate of his or her own performance level generally falls around the 75th percentile.[69] So even when managers are providing good news, employees are likely to perceive it as not good enough.

The solution to the problem is not to ignore it but to train managers to conduct constructive feedback sessions. An effective review—in which the employee perceives the appraisal as fair, the manager as sincere, and the climate as constructive—can leave the employee feeling upbeat, informed about areas needing improvement, and determined to correct them.[70] It probably won't surprise you that employees in a bad mood are much less likely to take advice than employees in a good mood.[71] Appraisals should also be as specific as possible. People are most likely to overrate their own performance when asked about overall job performance, but they can be more objective when feedback is about a specific area.[72] It's also hard to figure out how to improve your performance globally—it's much easier to improve in specific areas. In addition, the performance review should be a counseling activity more than a judgment process, best accomplished by allowing it to evolve from the employee's own self-evaluation.

International Variations in Performance Appraisal

Let's examine performance evaluation globally in the context of four cultural dimensions: individualism/collectivism, a person's relationship to the environment, time orientation, and focus of responsibility.

Individual-oriented cultures such as the United States emphasize formal performance evaluation systems more than informal systems. They advocate written evaluations performed at regular intervals, the results of which managers share with employees and use in the determination of rewards. On the other hand, the collectivist cultures that dominate Asia and much of Latin America are characterized by more informal systems—downplaying formal feedback and disconnecting reward allocations from performance ratings. Some of these differences may be narrowing, however. In Korea, Singapore, and even Japan, the use of performance evaluation has increased dramatically in the past decade, though not always smoothly or without controversy. One survey of Korean employees revealed that a majority questioned the validity of their performance evaluation results.[73]

One recent study focused on the banking industry found significant differences across countries in performance appraisal practices.[74] Formal performance appraisals were used more frequently in countries that were high in assertiveness, high in uncertainty avoidance, and low in in-group collectivism. In other words, assertive countries that see performance as an individual responsibility, and that desire certainty about where people stand, were more likely to use formal performance appraisals. On the other hand, in high uncertainty avoidance cultures performance appraisals were also used more frequently for communication and development purposes (as opposed to being used for rewards and promotion). Another study found that individuals who were high in power distance and high in collectivism tend to give more lenient performance appraisals.[75]

SELF-ASSESSMENT LIBRARY

How Good Am I at Giving Performance Feedback?

In the Self-Assessment Library (available on CD and online), take assessment III.A.3 (How Good Am I at Giving Performance Feedback?).

Managing Work–Life Conflicts in Organizations

9 Describe how organizations can manage work–family conflicts.

We introduced work–life balance in Chapter 1 and discussed the blurring lines between work life and personal life. Here, we specifically focus on what organizations can do to help employees reduce conflicts.

Work–life conflicts grabbed management's attention in the 1980s, largely as a result of the increased entry into the workforce of women with dependent children. In response, most major organizations took actions to make their workplaces more family-friendly.[76] They introduced on-site child care, summer day camps, flextime, job sharing, leaves for school functions, telecommuting, and part-time employment. But organizations quickly realized work–life conflicts were not limited to female employees with children. Male workers and women without children were also facing this problem. Heavy workloads and increased travel demands, for instance, made it increasingly hard for many employees to meet both work and personal responsibilities. A Boston College survey of nearly 1,000 fathers who have professional careers showed that the participants put more importance on job security and flexible, family-friendly working schedules than on high income and advancement opportunities.[77]

Organizations are modifying their workplaces with scheduling options and benefits to accommodate the varied needs of a diverse workforce. Employees at NestléPurina can bring their dogs into the office, SAS Institute has on-site childcare, a health care center, and a fitness center; and other firms offer perks ranging from on-site laundry to food services and free child care.[78] Exhibit 17-4 lists some initiatives to help employees reduce work–life conflicts.

Time pressures aren't the primary problem underlying these conflicts.[79] It's the psychological incursion of work into the family domain—and vice versa—when people are worrying about personal problems at work and thinking about work problems at home. So, dad may make it home in time for dinner, but his mind is elsewhere. This suggests organizations should spend less effort helping employees with time-management issues and more helping them clearly segment their lives. Keeping workloads reasonable, reducing work-related travel,

Myth or Science?

"Work Is Making Us Fat"

This statement is true. Let's explain.

Two-thirds of U.S. adults are overweight or even obese, and the changing nature of work is a major reason. Indeed, it might be the main explanation for why obesity has become the number-one public health problem in the United States and many other advanced economies.

Our work has evolved to be more mental than physical. That tends to make it more interesting, but also more sedentary. Why is that a problem? The changes in work are estimated to mean that, on average, workers burn 120 to 150 fewer calories a day than they did 50 years ago. That may not seem like a lot, but it equates to 25 pounds of potential weight gain per year.

Interestingly, research indicates that our physical activity in leisure time hasn't changed much in the past 50 years. So we burn as many calories in nonwork activities as before—it's work that is killing us.

Fifty years ago, about half of all private-sector jobs included some kind of physical labor (farming, mining, construction, manufacturing). Today, fewer than 20 percent do, thanks to the growth of jobs in retailing, information technology, education, and business.

What is the implication? "We need to encourage physical activity even more, especially given that we sit more during the day than we did 100 years ago," said Keri Gans, a spokesperson for the American Dietetic Association.

Some ways to do that are taking the stairs when you can, parking your car a good distance from work, and going for a walk at lunchtime. And, of course, exercising more off the job. As one expert noted when commenting on the increasingly sedentary nature of work, "We just have to make time for it."

Sources: T. Parker-Hope, "Sedentary Work Cited as Factor in Rising Obesity," *The New York Times* (May 26, 2011), pp. A1, A3; A. Gardner, "Sedentary Jobs Helping to Drive Obesity Epidemic," *US News & World Report* (May 26, 2011), downloaded July 11, 2011, from http://health.usnews.com/; and T. S. Church et al., "Trends Over 5 Decades in U.S. Occupation-Related Physical Activity and Their Associations with Obesity," *PLoS ONE* 6, no. 5 (2011), doi:10.1371/journal.pone.0019657.

Exhibit **17-4**	**Work–Life Initiatives**

Time based strategies	• Flextime • Job sharing • Leave for new parents • Transportation • Telecommuting • Paid time off	At Abbott, 89% of employees held jobs that permitted them to flex their schedules; at Lego 90% of employees do. Cisco provides job-sharing and videoconferencing facilities to minimize needs for travel away from family. Deloitte offers employees 4 unpaid weeks sabbatical, or 3 to 6 partially paid months off to volunteer. Deutsche Bank offers parents 20 days of free backup care per child per year, which they can redeem at local child care centers. At DuPont, 15% of employees telecommute; at Eli Lilly 30% of employees telecommute.
Information based strategies	• Work–life support • Relocation assistance • Elder care resources • Counseling services	Blue Cross Blue Shield of North Carolina provides ParentLife classes and seminars. Capital One provides a networking and counseling group for parents of children with autism. Genetech offers a CareerLab, which provides career counseling, skills workshops, and networking sessions. Hallmark offers employees monthly meetings to talk about career management for women. Johnson and Johnson offers work–life Webinars covering topics like single parenting, fatherhood, and elder care.
Money-based strategies	• Insurance subsidies • Flexible benefits • Adoption assistance • Discounts for child care tuition • Direct financial assistance • Domestic partner benefits • Scholarships, tuition reimbursement	Accenture offers a $5,000 adoption assistance benefit. Carlson companies offers employees scholarships of up to $20,000 to attend the University of Minnesota's Carlson School of Management. Citi employees can save up to $5,000 per year in pretax dependent care accounts, with a match of up to 30% from the company. Colgate-Palmolive provides up to $10,000 per year in annual tuition aid for job-related courses. IBM provides medical testing and therapy for children with special needs, up to a lifetime maximum of $50,000. Prudential employees can receive up to 15% off child care discounts.
Direct services	• On-site child care • Fitness center • Summer child care • On-site conveniences • Concierge services • Free or discounted company products	Allstate and SAS provide on-site child care center at company headquarters. Companies like AOL and Verizon have on-site fitness centers and discounts at gyms nationwide. Bristol-Myers Squibb offers full-time, part-time, and backup care for kids up to age 5, and summer camps for older children. Discovery Communications provides low-cost concierge services to help with to-do lists. Turner Broadcasting has a wellness center at headquarters that provides free exams, vaccinations, allergy shots, and health coaching. REI employees can participate in a program that offers large discounts on company products.
Culture-change strategies	• Establishing work–life balanced culture; training managers to help employees deal with work–life conflicts • Tie manager pay to employee satisfaction • Focus on employees' actual performance, not "face time"	At American Express, 80% of managers received training on how to supervise employees with flexible work arrangements. Bank of America's My Work program allows mothers to log in from home or a satellite office. General Mills has a flexibility manager to enhance work–life balance. Pearson developed a Flexible Work Options. Accountability Guide that trains managers in the use of flextime for their employees.

Sources: "2010 100 Best Companies" *Working Mother* (August 17, 2011), www.workingmother.com; "100 Best Companies to Work For," *CNNMoney*, (August 17, 2011), www.money.cnn.com; and J. Goudreau, "Top Companies for Work-Life Balance," *Forbes* (May 13, 2011), www.forbes.com.

and offering on-site quality child care are examples of practices that can help in this endeavor.

Not surprisingly, people differ in their preference for scheduling options and benefits.[80] Some prefer organizational initiatives that better segment work from their personal lives, as flextime, job sharing, and part-time hours do by allowing employees to schedule work hours less likely to conflict with personal responsibilities. Others prefer ways to integrate work and personal life, such as on-site child care, gym facilities, and company-sponsored family picnics. On average, though, most people do prefer an organization that provides more support for work–life balance. One study even found that potential employees, particularly women, are more attracted to organizations that have a reputation for supporting employee work–life balance.[81]

MyManagementLab

Now that you have finished this chapter, go back to **www.pearsonglobaleditions.com/ mymanagementlab** to continue practicing and applying the concepts you've learned.

Summary and Implications for Managers

An organization's human resource policies and practices create important forces that shape employee behavior and attitudes. In this chapter, we specifically discussed the influence of selection practices, training and development programs, and performance evaluation systems.

- If properly designed, an organization's selection practices will identify competent candidates and accurately match them to the job and the organization. Although employee selection is far from a science, some organizations fail to design a selection system that can achieve the right person–job fit.
- The most obvious effect of training programs is direct improvement in the skills necessary to successfully complete the job. Increased ability thus improves potential, but whether that potential becomes realized is largely an issue of motivation.
- A second benefit of training is that it increases an employee's self-efficacy—that is, a person's expectation that he or she can successfully execute the behaviors required to produce an outcome (see Chapter 7). Employees with high self-efficacy have strong expectations about their abilities to perform in new situations. They're confident and expect to be successful. Training, then, is a means to positively affect self-efficacy because employees may be more willing to undertake job tasks and exert a high level of effort.
- A major goal of performance evaluation is to assess an individual's performance accurately as a basis for allocating rewards. If evaluation is inaccurate or emphasizes the wrong criteria, employees will be over- or underrewarded. As demonstrated in Chapter 7 in our discussion of equity theory, evaluations perceived as unfair can result in reduced effort, increases in absenteeism, or a search for alternative job opportunities.

Social Media Is a Great Source of New Hires

Social media sites such as Facebook, LinkedIn, and Twitter, and job boards like Monster.com, are indispensable in today's marketplace for top talent.

It's true that an online presence with social media sites is a good way to sniff out fraud. Studies reveal that 45 percent of today's résumés contain at least one piece of false information. Mining social media sites is great at gaining a fuller—and more accurate—picture of a candidate.

One survey found that today 63 percent of employers use social media sites in recruitment and hiring decisions. Another revealed that 80 percent of employers plan to increase their presence on Facebook and LinkedIn in the future.

Not only can social media sites help you make a more informed selection decisions, they can be a great help in recruiting more and better candidates to apply in the first place. Dawn Mitchell, a recruiter for business software company Red Hat, says it's about "living where the candidates are." She says that nearly all her recent hires have come from social media contacts.

Increasingly, recruiting firms that link applicants to companies are finding social media critical for their business too. "Social media is the heart of everything we do," said Bill Peppler of Kavaliro Staffing Services. "We make numerous job placements that we never would have been able to do without Facebook," he said.

Accenture—the New York–based consulting firm—has mastered the art of using social media in hiring. John Campagnino, Accenture's global director of recruitment, says it has become "a centerpiece of our talent acquisition strategy." Campagnino says that Accenture interacts with potential hires on Facebook, LinkedIn, and Twitter; posts jobs on these sites daily; and creates "talent communities" by joining professional groups.

Hiring without heavy reliance on social media is backward-looking, and a missed opportunity.

A lot of employers are scaling back their presence on online job boards like Monster.com and social media sites like Facebook and LinkedIn, because there is just too much chaff for the wheat. For example, McLean, Virginia–based Science Applications International Corporate (SAIC) reduced the number of job boards it uses from 15 to 6. SAIC found that it simply wasn't getting to enough of the right candidates early enough to staff its engineering and analyst positions. "We need to reach candidates earlier, before they're being pursued by competitors," the company said.

Paris-owned food services company Sodexo has slashed its online presence in half. Why? Because while recruiting via social media increased the number of applications, nearly all the increase was in unqualified applicants. "Recruiters had to put in all this extra time to read applications but we didn't get benefit from it," said Arie Ball, the company's talent acquisition vice president.

PNC also is scaling back due to the low signal-to-noise ratio. "We used to post everything," said the online banking company. "But you have to think strategically."

There is also the nontrivial issue of mistaken identity. A lot of mistaken hiring decisions have been made because a company used the wrong Facebook or LinkedIn profile. Applicants can post false information on social media sites, too.

Perhaps the biggest issue of all is objectivity. Says one employment expert, "Once an HR recruiter or administrator has been exposed to an applicant's social networking profile, it's difficult to remain objective and consider only the information that is relevant to the job."

Another recruiting manager voiced his skepticism regarding social media: "I'd love to drink the Kool-Aid if it did anything for me."

Sources: J. Light, "Recruiters Rethink Online Playbook," *The Wall Street Journal* (January 18, 2011), p. B7; R. Pyrillis, "The Bait Debate," *Workforce Management* (February 2011), pp. 16–22; and J. Bos, "Five Trends in Employee Screening: Is Your Company Prepared?" *Workforce Management* (March 2010), pp. 28–30.

- The content of the performance evaluation also influences employee performance and satisfaction. Specifically, performance and satisfaction are increased when the evaluation is based on behavioral and results-oriented criteria, when career issues as well as performance issues are discussed, and when the employee has an opportunity to participate in the evaluation.

QUESTIONS FOR REVIEW

1 What is *initial selection*? What are the most useful methods?

2 What is *substantive selection*? What are the most useful methods?

3 What is *contingent selection*? What are the arguments for and against drug testing?

4 What are the similarities and differences among the four main types of training?

5 What are the similarities and differences between formal and informal training methods?

6 What are the similarities and differences between on-the-job and off-the-job training?

7 What are the purposes of performance evaluation? What are the methods by which it can be done?

8 How can managers improve performance evaluations?

9 How can organizations manage work-family conflicts?

EXPERIENTIAL EXERCISE Evaluating Performance and Providing Feedback

Objective

To experience the assessment of performance and observe the provision of performance feedback.

Time

Approximately 30 minutes.

Procedure

Select a class leader—either a volunteer or someone chosen by your instructor. The class leader will preside over the class discussion and perform the role of manager in the evaluation review.

Your instructor will leave the room. The class leader is then to spend up to 15 minutes helping the class to evaluate your instructor. Your instructor understands that this is only a class exercise and is prepared to accept criticism (and, of course, any praise you may want to convey). Your instructor also recognizes that the leader's evaluation is actually a composite of many students' input. So, be open and honest in your evaluation and have confidence that your instructor will not be vindictive.

Research has identified seven performance dimensions to the college instructor's job: (1) instructor knowledge, (2) testing procedures, (3) student–teacher relations, (4) organizational skills, (5) communication skills, (6) subject relevance, and (7) utility of assignments. The discussion of your instructor's performance should focus on these seven dimensions. The leader may want to take notes for personal use but will not be required to give your instructor any written documentation.

When the 15-minute class discussion is complete, the leader will invite the instructor back into the room. The performance review will begin as soon as the instructor walks through the door, with the class leader becoming the manager and the instructor playing himself or herself.

When completed, class discussion will focus on performance evaluation criteria and how well your class leader did in providing performance feedback.

ETHICAL DILEMMA Credit Checking

Is it unethical—or illegal—for a hiring organization to check an applicant's credit history? The Equal Employment Opportunity Commission (EEOC) seems to think so. It is suing Kaplan Higher Education

Corporation for its use of credit checks, alleging that relying on poor credit histories to reject applicants has adverse impact on minority applicants, with no legitimate purpose justifying its use. Justine Lisser, an EEOC spokesperson, said, "Credit histories were not compiled to show responsibility. They were compiled to show whether or not someone was paying the bills, which is not always the same thing."

In its defense, Kaplan maintained that it typically conducted credit checks: "The checks are job-related and necessary for our organization to ensure that staffing handling financial matters, including financial aid, are properly screened."

A 2011 survey of employers revealed that 21 percent conducted credit checks on all applicants. That was up from 15 percent the year before. Two-thirds conduct credit checks on some applicants, up from 61 percent in 2010.

Joey Price, with BL Seamon, thought she had found the perfect candidate for a conference planner position. The candidate was fresh out of college but had experience planning conferences and a good academic record. But when Price found out that the candidate had multiple car repossessions, extremely high credit card bills, and collection agencies after her, she rejected her. "A credit report doesn't lie," Price said.

Questions

1. Do you think organizations should be allowed to investigate applicants' credit histories in the hiring process? Why or why not?

2. Do you think Seamon's Joey Price was within her rights to reject the applicant with the poor credit history? Do you think this candidate's financial problems might be job relevant?

3. Some employers chose to disclose their reasoning to applicants rejected for poor credit. Says one hiring manager, "If a credit check comes back poor, the potential employee has a week to dispute and correct the errors." What are the advantages and disadvantages of such a policy?

Sources: J. Zappe, "Survey Finds More Companies Credit-Checking Candidates," *ERE.net* (May 16, 2011), downloaded on July 11, 2011, from www.ere.net/2011/; S. Greenhouse, "Hiring Suit Takes on Bias Based on Credit," *The New York Times* (December 22, 2010), pp. B1, B4; J. Fairley, "Employers Face Challenges in Screening Candidates," *Workforce Management* (November 2010), pp. 7–9; and B. Roberts, "Close-Up on Screening," *HR Magazine* (February 2011), p. 23–29.

CASE INCIDENT 1 Who Are You?

Today, we all seem to be very concerned with who we are. "Who am I?" Oprah Winfrey asked herself, as she has asked others for years when interviewing. "Who am I?" Donald Trump answers this question on global business channels like CNN or BBC.

We tend to ask this question often as we compete with others 24/7. In fact, the competition seems to have grown fiercer as students try to edge their foot inside the doors of top organizations. This is definitely the case in Beirut, Lebanon, a developing country in the Middle East and North African Area (MENA), where successful companies begin with interview screening, having done an initial background check (sometimes without the applicant's consent) in order to monitor whether the candidates did well in university, were successful in the local/regional market, or had a criminal record.

Today, job applicants are aware of "impression management" and the importance of perception. How important is a candidate's appearance? For instance, the highly competitive local market in Lebanon adheres to the French tradition in terms of mannerism and dress code. Managers and employees alike adhere to a custom that favors bright, attractive, very fashionably dressed personnel. As such, before they went to be interviewed at Byblos Bank, a leading domestic multinational bank, Zeina Samaha spent a small fortune on cosmetic surgery, whereas Josiane El Khoury spent it on her briefcase, suit, shoes, and jewelry. Even though they had both graduated with distinction from university and had shown professional competence in their previous job, they understood that appearance played a crucial role in the business world. These issues also influenced Joseph Boustany, the human resource manager at a trendy clothing shop on the Jounieh shopping strip of Kaslik. Before being interviewed at Zara, the hip Spanish clothes shop at the ABC Mall in Aschrafieh, Joseph went over the company's history and the job description; then he thought through the upcoming interview and mulled over his dress code before he bought a fashionable trendy suit, tie, and jewelry.

Questions

1. People, in general, spend a fortune to improve their image, both physical and on their résumé. Do you think candidates eliminate competition when improving their personal image?

2. What is the extent of candidates' control in terms of "dressing up" their résumé and letters of recommendation? In effect, how much latitude do companies give when they assess candidates' portfolios?

3. Is it ethical that potential employers have the right to carry out an assessment of the candidate's past?

4. When can candidates or employees claim that the company has crossed the line and stepped into their private life?

CASE INCIDENT 2 Fairness and Human Resources Management: What Do Your Employees Want?

The financial sector is the third largest sector in the Australian economy and the banking industry accounts for more than half of the financial sector. Financial services organizations depend on their employees to deliver superior customer service and to maintain successful customer relationships. Treating employees fairly may lead to the operational success of financial services organizations. Fair treatment also communicates that organizations are committed to their employees. Employees assess their work experiences in terms of whether or not organizations show concern for them as individuals and provide fair treatment. When employees perceive that human resources management (HRM) decisions and procedures are fair and satisfactory, they can be expected to repay the organization by forming positive attitudes toward it.

Twenty-nine senior, middle, and lower-level managers from one Australian bank in South Australia were interviewed. All interviewees had direct involvement with HRM practices in the banking organization. Interviewees were asked to name those HRM practices in which fairness would be most important. Options included HR planning, recruiting, selection, compensation, promotion/career development, performance management, and employee relations. The findings indicated that interviewees perceived fairness to be most important in three main HRM areas: compensation (44.8 percent), performance management (27.6 percent), and promotion/career development (27.6 percent).

Compensation and performance management are areas where fairness is most important because these two are linked together. I suppose it is about what you do and how you get rewarded. I think that's where the fairness becomes important—how you actually reward your people. Performance management goes hand in hand with compensation and benefits.

Interviewees claimed that compensation needed to be fair and transparent because employees perceived that if they were exerting as much effort as others but getting fewer rewards, they became de-motivated and their performance declined. Employees expect fair remuneration. It helps them to work better if their organization compensates them according to their contributions and acknowledge them. Moreover, employees with different needs accordingly should be given different benefits.

Interviewees also considered fairness in performance management important as it affected their opportunities for career development and for bonus payments. Performance management, however, has the potential to be subjective because it deals with judgments. For instance, when a superior who acts as an appraiser or reviewer does not believe or does not get along with staff, it may somehow affect employees' performance because their performance do not get on well with the superior, they are unlikely to receive a good report.

Interviewees also perceived that fairness in promotion/career development was important so that employees have goals to work toward and equal chances for promotion. For instance, job candidates must be treated with fairness relative to every other candidate so everyone goes through the same testing procedures, interview procedures, and screening. Each employee expects equal opportunity to progress on his or her career path and to be rewarded for what he or she does.

The interview illustrates how perception of fairness is important in the distribution of HRM practices such as compensation, performance evaluations, and promotion/career development. There is clear evidence that bank employees place emphasis on the issue of fairness in these areas.

Questions

1. What is the link between fairness and HRM?
2. If you were the HR manager, could you explain why Australian bank employees chose compensation and benefits, performance management, and career development as their most important HRM practices?

Sources: Daisy Kee Mui Hung (2006), "A Study of the Relationship Between Perceived Fairness of Compensation and Performance in the Australian Banking Industry," Ph.D. thesis, University of South Australia, Australia.

ENDNOTES

1. See B. Becker and B. Gerhart, "The Impact of Human Resource Management on Organizational Performance: Progress and Prospects," *Academy of Management Journal* (August 1996), pp. 779–801; M. A. Huselid, S. E. Jackson, and R. S. Schuler, "Technical and Strategic Human Resource Management Effectiveness as Determinants of Firm Performance," *Academy of Management Journal* (February 1997), pp. 171–188; C. J. Collins, and K. D. Clark, "Strategic Human Resource Practices, Top Management Team Social Networks, and Firm Performance: The Role of Human Resource Practices in Creating Organizational Competitive Advantage," *Academy of Management Journal* (December 2003), pp. 740–751; D. E. Bowen and C. Ostroff, "Understanding HRM–Firm Performance Linkages: The Role of the 'Strength' of the HRM System," *Academy of Management Review* (April 2004), pp. 203–221; and K. Birdi, C. Clegg, M. Patterson, A. Robinson, C. B. Stride, T. D. Wall, and S. J. Wood, "The Impact of Human Resource and Operational Management Practices on Company Productivity: A Longitudinal Study," *Personnel Psychology* 61, no. 3 (2008), pp. 467–501.

2. See, for instance, A. L. Kristof-Brown, R. D. Zimmerman, and E. C. Johnson, "Consequences of Individual's Fit at Work: A Meta-Analysis of Person-Job, Person-Organization, Person-Group, and Person-Supervisor Fit," *Personnel Psychology* 58, no. 2 (2005), pp. 281–342; and D. S. DeRue and F. P. Morgeson, "Stability and Change in Person-Team and Person-Role Fit over Time: The Effects of Growth Satisfaction, Performance, and General Self-Efficacy," *Journal of Applied Psychology* 92, no. 5 (2007), pp. 1242–1253.

3. J. D. Glater, "Another Hurdle for the Jobless: Credit Inquiries," *The New York Times* (August 6, 2009), www.nytimes.com.

4. C. Lachnit, "The Cost of Not Doing Background Checks," *Workforce Management,* www.workforce.com.

5. Cited in J. H. Prager, "Nasty or Nice: 56-Question Quiz," *The Wall Street Journal* (February 22, 2000), p. A4; see also H. Wessel, "Personality Tests Grow Popular," *Seattle Post–Intelligencer* (August 3, 2003), p. G1; and E. Frauenheim, "Personality Tests Adapt to the Times," *Workforce Management* (February 2010), p. 4.

6. E. Maltby, "To Find Best Hires, Firms Become Creative," *The Wall Street Journal* (November 17, 2009), p. B6.

7. J. P. Hausknecht, D. V. Day, and S. C. Thomas, "Applicant Reactions to Selection Procedures: An Updated Model and Meta-Analysis," *Personnel Psychology* (September 2004), pp. 639–683.

8. E. E. Ghiselli, "The Validity of Aptitude Tests in Personnel Selection," *Personnel Psychology* (Winter 1973), p. 475; J. E. Hunter, "Cognitive Ability, Cognitive Aptitudes, Job Knowledge, and Job Performance," *Journal of Vocational Behavior* 29, no. 3 (1986), pp. 340–362.

9. F. L. Schmidt, and J. Hunter, "General Mental Ability in the World of Work: Occupational Attainment and Job Performance," *Journal of Personality and Social Psychology* 86, no. 1 (2004), pp. 162–173; and F. L. Schmidt, J. A. Shaffer, and I. Oh, "Increased Accuracy for Range Restriction Corrections: Implications for the Role of Personality and General Mental Ability in Job and Training Performance," *Personnel Psychology* 61, no. 4 (2008), pp. 827–868.

10. J. F. Salgado, N. Anderson, S. Moscoso, C. Bertua, F. de Fruyt, and J. P. Rolland, "A Meta-Analytic Study of General Mental Ability Validity for Different Occupations in the European Community," *Journal of Applied Psychology* (December 2003), pp. 1068–1081.

11. M. R. Barrick, M. K. Mount, and T. A. Judge, "Personality and Performance at the Beginning of the New Millennium: What Do We Know and Where Do We Go Next?" *International Journal of Selection & Assessment* (March–June 2001), pp. 9–30; M. R. Barrick, G. L. Stewart, and M. Piotrowski, "Personality and Job Performance: Test of the Mediating Effects of Motivation Among Sales Representatives," *Journal of Applied Psychology* (February 2002), pp. 43–51; and C. J. Thoresen, J. C. Bradley, P. D. Bliese, and J. D. Thoresen, "The Big Five Personality Traits and Individual Job Performance and Growth Trajectories in Maintenance and Transitional Job Stages," *Journal of Applied Psychology* (October 2004), pp. 835–853.

12. R. N. Landers, P. R. Sackett, and K. A. Tuzinski, "Retesting after Initial Failure, Coaching Rumors, and Warnings against Faking in Online Personality Measures for Selection," *Journal of Applied Psychology* 96, no. 1 (2011), pp. 202–210; and J. P. Hausknecht, "Candidate Persistence and Personality Test Practice Effects: Implications for Staffing System Management," *Personnel Psychology* 63, no. 2 (2010), pp. 299–324.

13. I. Oh, G. Wang, and M. K. Mount, "Validity of Observer Ratings of the Five-Factor Model of Personality Traits: A Meta-Analysis," *Journal of Applied Psychology* 96, no. 4 (2011), pp. 762–773; and B. S. Connelly and D. S. Ones, "An Other Perspective on Personality: Meta-Analytic Integration of Observers' Accuracy and Predictive Validity," *Psychological Bulletin* 136, no. 6 (2010), pp. 1092–1122.

14. D. S. Ones, C. Viswesvaran, and F. L. Schmidt, "Comprehensive Meta-Analysis of Integrity Test Validities: Findings and Implications for Personnel Selection and Theories of Job Performance," *Journal of Applied Psychology* (August 1993), pp. 679–703; D. S. Ones, C. Viswesvaran, and F. L. Schmidt, "Personality and Absenteeism: A Meta-Analysis of Integrity Tests," *European Journal of Personality* (March–April 2003), Supplement 1, pp. S19–S38; and C. M. Berry, P. R. Sackett, and S. Wiemann, "A Review of Recent Developments in Integrity Test Research," *Personnel Psychology* 60, no. 2 (2007), pp. 271–301.

15. P. L. Roth, P. Bobko, and L. A. McFarland, "A Meta-Analysis of Work Sample Test Validity: Updating and Integrating Some Classic Literature," *Personnel Psychology* 58, no. 4 (2005), pp. 1009–1037.

16. P. Carbonara, "Hire for Attitude, Train for Skill," *Fast Company*, Greatest Hits, vol. 1 (1997), p. 68.

17. See, for instance, A. C. Spychalski, M. A. Quinones, B. B. Gaugler, and K. Pohley, "A Survey of Assessment Center Practices in Organizations in the United States, *Personnel Psychology* (Spring 1997), pp. 71–90; C. Woodruffe, *Development and Assessment Centres: Identifying and Assessing Competence* (London: Institute of Personnel and Development, 2000); and J. Schettler, "Building Bench Strength," *Training* (June 2002), pp. 55–58.

18. F. Lievens, H. Peeters, and E. Schollaert, "Situational Judgment Tests: A Review of Recent Research," *Personnel Review* 37, no. 4 (2008), pp. 426–441.

19. F. Lievens, and F. Patterson, "The Validity and Incremental Validity of Knowledge Tests, Low-Fidelity Simulations, and High-Fidelity Simulations for Predicting Job Performance in Advanced-Level High-Stakes Selection," *Journal of Applied Psychology,* Online First Publication (April 11, 2011), doi: 10.1037/a0023496.

20. R. A. Posthuma, F. P. Moregeson, and M. A. Campion, "Beyond Employment Interview Validity: A Comprehensive Narrative Review of Recent Research and Trend Over Time," *Personnel Psychology* (Spring 2002), p. 1; and S. L. Wilk and P. Cappelli, "Understanding the Determinants of Employer Use of Selection Methods," *Personnel Psychology* (Spring 2003), p. 111.

21. B. W. Swider, M. R. Barrick, T. B. Harris, and A. C. Stoverink, "Managing and Creating an Image in the Interview; The Role of Interviewee Initial Impressions," *Journal of Applied Psychology,* Online First Publication, (May 30, 2011), doi: 10.1037/a0024005.

22. K. I. van der Zee, A. B. Bakker, and P. Bakker, "Why Are Structured Interviews So Rarely Used in Personnel Selection?" *Journal of Applied Psychology* (February 2002), pp. 176–184.

23. See M. A. McDaniel, D. L. Whetzel, F. L. Schmidt, and S. D. Maurer, "The Validity of Employment Interviews: A Comprehensive Review and Meta-Analysis," *Journal of Applied Psychology* (August 1994), pp. 599–616; M. A. Campion, D. K. Palmer, and J. E. Campion, "A Review of Structure in the Selection Interview," *Personnel Psychology* (Autumn 1997), pp. 655–702; A. I. Huffcutt and D. J. Woehr, "Further Analysis of Employment Interview Validity: A Quantitative Evaluation of Interviewer-Related Structuring Methods," *Journal of Organizational Behavior* (July 1999), pp. 549–560; and M. Ziegler, E. Dietl, E. Danay, M. Vogel, and M. Bühner, "Predicting Training Success with General Mental Ability, Specific Ability Tests, and (Un)Structured Interviews: A Meta-Analysis with Unique Samples," *International Journal of Selection and Assessment* 19, no. 2 (2011), pp. 170–182.

24. van der Zee, Bakker, and Bakker, "Why Are Structured Interviews So Rarely Used in Personnel Selection?"

25. T. W. Dougherty, D. B. Turban, and J. C. Callender, "Confirming First Impressions in the Employment Interview: A Field Study of Interviewer Behavior," *Journal of Applied Psychology* (October 1994), pp. 659–665; and M. R. Barrick, B. W. Swider, and G. L. Stewart, "Initial Evaluations in the Interview: Relationships with Subsequent Interviewer Evaluations and Employment Offers," *Journal of Applied Psychology* 95, no. 6 (2010), pp. 1163–1172.

26. K. G. Melchers, N. Lienhardt, M. von Aarburg, and M. Kleinmann, "Is More Structure Really Better? A Comparison of Frame-of-Reference Training and Descriptively Anchored Rating Scales to Improve Interviewers' Rating Quality," *Personnel Psychology* 64, no. 1 (2011), pp. 53–87.

27. F. L. Schmidt and R. D. Zimmerman, "A Counterintuitive Hypothesis About Employment Interview Validity and Some Supporting Evidence," *Journal of Applied Psychology* 89, no. 3 (2004), pp. 553–561.

28. See G. A. Adams, T. C. Elacqua, and S. M. Colarelli, "The Employment Interview as a Sociometric Selection Technique," *Journal of Group Psychotherapy* (Fall 1994), pp. 99–113; R. L. Dipboye, "Structured and Unstructured Selection Interviews: Beyond the Job-Fit Model," *Research in Personnel Human Resource Management* 12 (1994), pp. 79–123; B. Schneider, D. B. Smith, S. Taylor, and J. Fleenor, "Personality and Organizations: A Test of the Homogeneity of Personality Hypothesis," *Journal of Applied Psychology* (June 1998), pp. 462–470; and M. Burke, "Funny Business," *Forbes* (June 9, 2003), p. 173.

29. A. M. Ryan, L. McFarland, H. Baron, and R. Page, "An International Look at Selection Practices: Nation and Culture as Explanations for Variability in Practice," *Personnel Psychology* (Summer 1999), pp. 359–392.

30. Ibid., p. 386.

31. N. Anderson and C. Witvliet, "Fairness Reactions to Personnel Selection Methods: An International Comparison Between the Netherlands, the United States, France, Spain, Portugal, and Singapore," *International Journal of Selection and Assessment* 16, no. 1 (2008), pp. 1–13.

32. American Society for Training and Development, *2010 State of the Industry Report*, www.astd.org/content/research.

33. T. Minton-Eversole and K. Gurchiek, "New Workers Not Ready for Prime Time," *HR Magazine* (December 2006), pp. 28–34.

34. P. Galagan, "Bridging the Skills Gap: New Factors Compound the Growing Skills Shortage," *T+D*, (February 2010), pp. 44–49.

35. M. Smulian, "England Fails on Numeracy and Literacy," *Public Finance* (February 6, 2009), p. 13; E. K. Sharma, "Growing a New Crop of Talent: India Inc. Is Increasingly Going Rural," *Business Today* (June 28, 2009), http://businesstoday.intoday.in/; and G. Paton, "Almost Half of Employers Forced to Teach Teenagers Basic Literacy and Numeracy Skills," *Telegraph* (May 9, 2011), www.telegraph.com.

36. D. Baynton, "America's $60 Billion Problem," Training, (May 2001) p. 52.

37. G. Anand, "India Graduates Millions, But Few Are Fit to Hire," *The Wall Street Journal* (April 5, 2011), www.online.wsj.com.

38. J. Barbarian, "Mark Spear: Director of Management and Organizational Development, Miller Brewing Co.," *Training* (October 2001), pp. 34–38.

39. See, for example, P. J. Taylor, D. F. Russ-Eft, and H. Taylor, "Transfer of Management Training from Alternative Perspectives," *Journal of Applied Psychology* 94, no. 1 (2009), pp. 104–121.

40. See, for example, S. Lim and A. Lee, "Work and Nonwork Outcomes of Workplace Incivility: Does Family Support Help?" *Journal of Occupational Health Psychology* 16, no. 1 (2011), pp. 95–111; C. L. Porath and C. M. Pearson, "The Cost of Bad Behavior," *Organizational Dynamics* 39, no. 1 (2010), pp. 64–71; and B. Estes and J. Wang, "Workplace Incivility: Impacts on Individual and Organizational Performance," *Human Resource Development Review* 7, no. 2 (2008), pp. 218–240.

41. M. P. Leiter, H. K. S. Laschinger, A. Day, and D. G. Oore, "The Impact of Civility Interventions on Employee Social Behavior, Distress, and Attitudes," *Journal of Applied Psychology*, Advance online publication (July 11, 2011), doi: 10.1037/a0024442.

42. G. R. Weaver, L. K. Trevino, and P. L. Cochran, "Corporate Ethics Practices in the Mid-1990's: An Empirical Study of the Fortune 1000," *Journal of Business Ethics* (February 1999), pp. 283–294.

43. M. B. Wood, *Business Ethics in Uncertain Times* (Upper Saddle River, NJ: Prentice Hall, 2004), p. 61.

44. See, for example, D. Seligman, "Oxymoron 101," *Forbes* (October 28, 2002), pp. 160–164; and R. B. Schmitt, "Companies Add Ethics Training; Will It Work?" *The Wall Street Journal* (November 4, 2002), p. B1; A. Becker, "Can You Teach Ethics to MBAs?" *BNet* (October 19, 2009), www.bnet.com.

45. W. R. Allen, P. Bacdayan, K. B. Kowalski, and M. H. Roy, "Examining the Impact of Ethics Training on Business Student Values," *Education and Training* 47, no. 3 (2005), pp. 170–182; A. Lämsä, M. Vehkaperä, T. Puttonen, and H. Pesonen, "Effect of Business Education on Women and Men Students' Attitudes on Corporate Responsibility in Society," *Journal of Business Ethics* 82, no. 1 (2008), pp. 45–58; and K. M. Sheldon and L. S. Krieger, "Understanding the Negative Effects of Legal Education on Law Students: A Longitudinal Test of Self-Determination Theory," *Personality and Social Psychology Bulletin* 33, no. 6 (2007), pp. 883–897.

46. S. Valentine and G. Fleischman, "Ethics Programs, Perceived Corporate Social Responsibility, and Job Satisfaction," *Journal of Business Ethics* 77, no. 2 (2008), pp. 159–172.

47. K. Dobbs, "The U.S. Department of Labor Estimates That 70 Percent of Workplace Learning Occurs Informally," *Sales & Marketing Management* (November 2000), pp. 94–98.

48. See, for instance, R. E. Derouin, B. A. Fritzsche, and E. Salas, "E-Learning in Organizations," *Journal of Management* 31, no. 3 (2005), pp. 920–940; and K. A. Orvis, S. L. Fisher, and M. E. Wasserman, "Power to the People: Using Learner Control to Improve Trainee Reactions and Learning in Web-Based Instructional Environments," *Journal of Applied Psychology* 94, no 4 (2009), pp. 960–971.

49. T. Sitzman, K. Kraiger, D. Stewart, and R. Wisher, "The Comparative Effectiveness of Web-Based and Classroom Instruction: A Meta-Analysis," *Personnel Psychology* 59, no. 3 (2006), pp. 623–664.

50. T. Sitzmann, B. S. Bell, K. Kraiger, and A. M. Kanar, "A Multilevel Analysis of the Effect of Prompting Self-Regulation in Technology-Delivered Instruction," *Personnel Psychology* 62 no. 4 (2009), pp. 697–734.

51. E. A. Ensher, T. R. Nielson, and E. Grant-Vallone, "Tales from the Hiring Line: Effects of the Internet and Technology on HR Processes," *Organizational Dynamics* 31, no. 3 (2002), pp. 232–233; and J. B. Arbaugh, "Do Undergraduates and MBAs Differ Online? Initial Conclusions from the Literature," *Journal of Leadership and Organizational Studies* 17, no. 2 (2010), pp. 129–142.

52. G. M. Alliger, S. I. Tannenbaum, W. Bennett, H. Traver, and A. Shotland, "A Meta-Analysis of the Relations Among Training Criteria," *Personnel Psychology* 50, no. 2 (1997), pp. 341–358; and T. Sitzmann, K. G. Brown, W. J. Casper, K. Ely, and R. D. Zimmerman, "A Review and Meta-Analysis of the Nomological Network of Trainee Reactions," *Journal of Applied Psychology* 93, no. 2 (2008), pp. 280–295.

53. J. A. Colquitt, J. A. LePine, and R. A. Noe, "Toward an Integrative Theory of Training Motivation: A Meta-Analytic Path Analysis of 20 Years of Research," *Journal of Applied Psychology* (October 2000), pp. 678–707.

54. See L. A. Burke and H. S. Hutchins, "Training Transfer: An Integrative Literature Review," *Human Resource Development Review* 6 (2007), pp. 263–296; and D. S. Chiaburu and S. V. Marinova, "What Predicts Skill Transfer? An Exploratory Study of Goal Orientation, Training Self-Efficacy, and Organizational Supports," *International Journal of Training and Development* 9, no. 2 (2005), pp. 110–123.

55. M. Rotundo and P. R. Sackett, "The Relative Importance of Task, Citizenship, and Counterproductive Performance to Global Ratings of Job Performance: A Policy Capturing Approach," *Journal of Applied Psychology* 87, no. 1 (2002), pp. 66–80; and S. W. Whiting, P. M. Podsakoff, and J. R. Pierce, "Effects of Task Performance, Helping, Voice, and Organizational Loyalty on Performance Appraisal Ratings," *Journal of Applied Psychology* 93, no. 1 (2008), pp. 125–139.

56. W. F. Cascio and H. Aguinis, *Applied Psychology in Human Resource Management*, 7th ed. (Upper Saddle River, NJ: Prentice Hall, 2010).

57. A. H. Locher and K. S. Teel, "Appraisal Trends," *Personnel Journal* (September 1988), pp. 139–145.

58. Cited in S. Armour, "Job Reviews Take on Added Significance in Down Times," *USA Today* (July 23, 2003), p. 4B.

59. D. J. Woehr, M. K. Sheehan, and W. Bennett, "Assessing Measurement Equivalence Across Rating Sources: A Multitrait-Multirater Approach," *Journal of Applied Psychology* 90, no. 3 (2005), pp. 592–600; and H. Heidemeier and K. Moser, "Self–Other Agreement in Job Performance Ratings: A Meta-Analytic Test of a Process Model," *Journal of Applied Psychology* 94, no. 2 (March 2009), pp. 353–370.

60. See, for instance, J. D. Facteau and S. B. Craig, "Are Performance Appraisal Ratings from Different Rating Sources Compatible?" *Journal of Applied Psychology* (April 2001), pp. 215–227; J. F. Brett and L. E. Atwater, "360-Degree Feedback: Accuracy, Reactions, and Perceptions of Usefulness," *Journal of Applied Psychology* (October 2001), pp. 930–942; F. Luthans and S. J. Peterson, "360 Degree Feedback with Systematic Coaching: Empirical Analysis Suggests a Winning Combination," *Human Resource Management* (Fall 2003), pp. 243–256; and B. I. J. M. van der Heijden and A. H. J. Nijhof, "The Value of Subjectivity: Problems and Prospects for 360-Degree Appraisal Systems," *International Journal of Human Resource Management* (May 2004), pp. 493–511.

61. M. K. Mount and S. E. Scullen, "Multisource Feedback Ratings: What Do They Really Measure?" in M. London (Ed.), *How People Evaluate Others in Organizations* (Mahwah, NJ: Lawrence Erlbaum, 2001), pp. 155–176; and K. Ng, C. Koh, S. Ang, J. C. Kennedy, and K. Chan, "Rating Leniency and Halo in Multisource Feedback Ratings: Testing Cultural Assumptions of Power Distance and Individualism-Collectivism," *Journal of Applied Psychology*, Online First Publication (April 11, 2011), doi: 10.1037/a0023368.

62. Catherine Rampell, "A History of College Grade Inflation," The New York Times, July 14, 2011, accessed at http://economix.blogs.nytimes.com/2011/07/14/the-history-of-college-grade-inflation/?scp=1&sq=grade%20inflation&st=cse.

63. X. M. Wang, K. F. E. Wong, and J. Y. Y. Kwong, "The Roles of Rater Goals and Ratee Performance Levels in the Distortion of Performance Ratings," *Journal of Applied Psychology* 95, no. 3 (2010), pp. 546–561; J. R. Spence and L. M. Keeping, "The Impact of Non-Performance Information on Ratings of Job Performance: A Policy-Capturing Approach," *Journal of Organizational Behavior* 31 (2010), pp. 587–608; and J. R Spence and L. Keeping, "Conscious Rating Distortion in Performance Appraisal: A Review, Commentary, and Proposed Framework for Research," *Human Resource Management Review* 21, no. 2 (2011), pp. 85–95.

64. L. E. Atwater, J. F. Brett, and A. C. Charles, "Multisource Feedback: Lessons Learned and Implications for Practice," *Human Resource Management* 46, no. 2 (2007), pp. 285–307; and R. Hensel, F. Meijers, R. van der Leeden, and J. Kessels, "360 Degree Feedback: How Many Raters Are Needed for Reliable Ratings on the Capacity to Develop Competences, with Personal Qualities as Developmental Goals?" *International Journal of Human Resource Management* 21, no. 15 (2010), pp. 2813–2830.

65. See, for instance, J. W. Hedge and W. C. Borman, "Changing Conceptions and Practices in Performance Appraisal," in A. Howard (ed.), *The Changing Nature of Work* (San Francisco, CA: Jossey-Bass, 1995), pp. 453–459.

66. See, for instance, K. L. Uggerslev and L. M. Sulsky, "Using Frame-of-Reference Training to Understand the Implications of Rater Idiosyncrasy for Rating Accuracy," *Journal of Applied Psychology* 93, no. 3 (2008), pp. 711–719; and R. F. Martell and D. P. Evans, "Source-Monitoring Training: Toward Reducing Rater Expectancy Effects in Behavioral Measurement," *Journal of Applied Psychology* 90, no. 5 (2005), pp. 956–963.

67. B. Erdogan, "Antecedents and Consequences of Justice Perceptions in Performance Appraisals," *Human Resource Management Review* 12, no. 4 (2002), pp. 555–578; and I M. Jawahar, "The Mediating Role of Appraisal Feedback Reactions on the Relationship Between Rater Feedback-Related Behaviors and Ratee Performance," *Group and Organization Management* 35, no. 4 (2010), pp. 494–526.

68. S. C. Payne, M. T. Horner, W. R. Boswell, A. N. Schroeder, and K. J. Stine-Cheyne, "Comparison of Online and Traditional Performance Appraisal Systems," *Journal of Managerial Psychology* 24, no. 6 (2009), pp. 526–544.

69. R. J. Burke, "Why Performance Appraisal Systems Fail," *Personnel Administration* (June 1972), pp. 32–40.

70. B. D. Cawley, L. M. Keeping, and P. E. Levy, "Participation in the Performance Appraisal Process and Employee Reactions: A Meta-Analytic Review of Field Investigations," *Journal of Applied Psychology* (August 1998), pp. 615–633; and P. E. Levy and J. R. Williams, "The Social Context of Performance Appraisal: A Review and Framework for the Future," *Journal of Management* 30, no. 6 (2004), pp. 881–905.

71. F. Gino and M. E. Schweitzer, "Blinded by Anger or Feeling the Love: How Emotions Influence Advice Taking," *Journal of Applied Psychology* 93, no. 3 (2008), pp. 1165–1173.

72. Heidemeier and Moser, "Self–Other Agreement in Job Performance Ratings."

73. J. Han, "Does Performance-Based Salary System Suit Korea?" *The Korea Times* (January 15, 2008), www.koreatimes.co.kr.

74. F. F. T. Chiang and T. A. Birtch, "Appraising Performance across Borders: An Empirical Examination of the Purposes and Practices of Performance Appraisal in a Multi-Country Context," *Journal of Management Studies* 47, no. 7 (2010), pp. 1365–1393.

75. K. Ng, C. Koh, S. Ang, J. C. Kennedy, and K. Chan, "Rating Leniency and Halo in Multisource Feedback Ratings: Testing Cultural Assumptions of Power Distance and Individualism-Collectivism," *Journal of Applied Psychology*, Online First Publication (April 11, 2011), doi: 10.1037/a0023368.

76. See, for instance, *Harvard Business Review on Work and Life Balance* (Boston: Harvard Business School Press, 2000); R. Rapoport, L. Bailyn, J. K. Fletcher, and B. H. Pruitt, *Beyond Work-Family Balance* (San Francisco: Jossey-Bass, 2002); and E. E. Kossek, S. Pichler, T. Bodner, and L. B. Hammer, "Workplace Social Support and Work-Family Conflict: A Meta-Analysis Clarifying the Influence of General and Work-Family Specific Supervisor and Organizational Support," *Personnel Psychology* 64, no. 2 (2011), pp. 289–313.

77. B. Harrington, F. Van Deusen, and B. Humberd, *The New Dad: Caring Committed and Conflicted.* (Boston: Boston College Center for Work and Family, 2011).

78. A. Grant, "Top 25 Companies for Work-Life Balance," *US News and World Report* (May 11, 2011), www.money.usnews .com.

79. C. P. Maertz and S. L. Boyar, "Work-Family Conflict, Enrichment, and Balance Under 'Levels' and 'Episodes' Approaches," *Journal of Management* 37, no. 1 (2011), pp. 68–98.

80. J. S. Michel and M. B. Hargis, "Linking Mechanisms of Work-Family Conflict and Segmentation," *Journal of Vocational Behavior* 73, no. 3 (2008), pp. 509–522; G. E. Kreiner, "Consequences of Work-Home Segmentation or Integration: A Person-Environment Fit Perspective," *Journal of Organizational Behavior* 27, no. 4 (2006), pp. 485–507; and C. A. Bulger, R. A. Matthews, and M. E. Hoffman, "Work and Personal Life Boundary Management: Boundary Strength, Work/Personal Life Balance, and the Segmentation-Integration Continuum," *Journal of Occupational Health Psychology* 12, no. 4 (2007), pp. 365–375.

81. D. Catanzaro, H. Moore, and T. R. Marshall, "The Impact of Organizational Culture on Attraction and Recruitment of Job Applicants," *Journal of Business and Psychology* 25, (2010), pp. 649–662.

LEARNING OBJECTIVES

After studying this chapter, you should be able to:

1 Identify forces that act as stimulants to change, and contrast planned and unplanned change.

2 Describe the sources of resistance to change.

3 Compare the four main approaches to managing organizational change.

4 Demonstrate two ways of creating a culture for change.

5 Define *stress,* and identify its potential sources.

6 Identify the consequences of stress.

7 Contrast the individual and organizational approaches to managing stress.

MyManagementLab

Access a host of interactive learning aids to help strengthen your understanding of the chapter concepts at **www.pearsonglobaleditions.com/mymanagementlab**.

SWEET CHANGES AT CADBURY?

Hostile takeovers are never easy, especially for those in the company being acquired. But some takeovers are more hostile than others.

Kraft's acquisition of Cadbury is a case in point. After its initial offer to acquire the UK confectioner was deemed "derisory," Kraft sweetened the deal, and Cadbury's CEO declared it "good value for Cadbury shareholders." Cadbury managers and employees, however, continue to have difficulty adjusting to the change.

One problem was the way Kraft handled the acquisition. Shortly after signing the deal, Kraft reneged on its pledge to keep Cadbury's Somerdale, England, plant open. The British, infuriated, demanded that Kraft CEO Irene Rosenfeld appear before Parliament. Rosenfeld refused, saying, it "was not the best use of my personal time." Members of Parliament, in turn, threatened to bring charges of contempt. Rosenfeld retorted: "The continued assault has been somewhat surprising."

The public relations aspect of the plant closing will probably blow over with time. However, a deeper and potentially more serious issue is the difference in cultures between the two organizations.

Kraft, by far the larger, is known for its formal and relatively hierarchical culture. Its meetings tend to be lengthy, with most decisions requiring the approval of top-level executives.

Cadbury was known for its more informal and more egalitarian culture. Its former CEO was often seen on the shop floor talking informally with workers. Its managers felt they were given the autonomy to be creative. Its marketing team won awards for producing the "Cadbury Gorilla" ad (available on YouTube).

Some employees who had been part of Cadbury have complained of Kraft's "Orwellian" management. Cadbury managers complain that Kraft "runs the show with military precision . . . directives or proposals pass through a hierarchy of layers." Says another anonymous manager: "That more entrepreneurial side of things got quashed because there are so many more layers of input and discussion." And according to a former employee, "Cadbury has a cutting edge understanding of the shopper and its retail customers. We spent years building that at Cadbury, and that's been lost."

The *Financial Times* commented: "The tension reaches all levels of former Cadbury staff, from the commercial division to the factory floor." On the other hand, some argue that Cadbury has reacted in a childish manner. *Bloomberg Businessweek* commented, "For many Brits, complaining is a national sport."

Is this a story of culture clash where a sympathetic, entrepreneurial company is devoured by an arrogant, bureaucratic one? Or is it a case of

Organizational Change and Stress Management

It is not the strongest of the species that survives, nor the most intelligent, but the one most responsive to change. —Charles Darwin

employees of a proud, smaller company refusing to adapt to new business conditions and a new culture?

The answer you favor appears to depend upon which side of the Atlantic you reside on.

Sources: L. Lucas, "Cadbury People Still Chewing on Kraft Culture," *Financial Times* (January 15, 2011), p. 13; L. Lucas and A. Rappeport, "Mergers and Acquisitions: A Bitter Taste," *Financial Times* (May 23, 2011), downloaded on July 19, 2011, from www.ft.com/; and M. Scott, "Why Britain Will Survive Kraft's Takeover of Cadbury," *Bloomberg Businessweek* (January 21, 2010), downloaded on July 8, 2011, from www.businessweek.com/.

This chapter is about change and stress. We describe environmental forces that require firms to change, why people and organizations often resist change, and how this resistance can be overcome. We review processes for managing organizational change. Then we move to the topic of stress and its sources and consequences. In closing, we discuss what individuals and organizations can do to better manage stress levels.

First, see how well you handle change by taking the following self-assessment.

SELF-ASSESSMENT LIBRARY

How Well Do I Respond to Turbulent Change?

In the Self-Assessment Library (available on CD and online), take assessment III.C.1 (How Well Do I Respond to Turbulent Change?) and answer the following questions.

1. How did you score? Are you surprised by your score?
2. During what time of your life have you experienced the most change? How did you deal with it? Would you handle these changes in the same way today? Why or why not?
3. Are there ways you might reduce your resistance to change?

Forces for Change

1   Identify forces that act as stimulants to change, and contrast planned and unplanned change.

No company today is in a particularly stable environment. Even those with dominant market share must change, sometimes radically. Even though Apple has been successful with its iPad, the growing number of competitors in the field of tablet computers suggests that Apple will need to continually update and innovate to keep ahead of the market.

"Change or die!" is thus the rallying cry among today's managers worldwide. Exhibit 18-1 summarizes six specific forces stimulating change.

In a number of places in this book, we've discussed the *changing nature of the workforce*. Almost every organization must adjust to a multicultural environment, demographic changes, immigration, and outsourcing. *Technology* is continually changing jobs and organizations. It is not hard to imagine the very idea of an office becoming an antiquated concept in the near future.

The housing and financial sectors recently have experienced extraordinary *economic shocks*, leading to the elimination, bankruptcy, or acquisition of some of

| Exhibit **18-1** | Forces for Change |

Force	Examples
Nature of the workforce	More cultural diversity
	Aging population
	Increased immigration and outsourcing
Technology	Faster, cheaper, and more mobile computers and handheld devices
	Emergence and growth of social networking sites
	Deciphering of the human genetic code
Economic shocks	Rise and fall of global housing market
	Financial sector collapse
	Global recession
Competition	Global competitors
	Mergers and consolidations
	Increased government regulation of commerce
Social trends	Increased environmental awareness
	Liberalization of attitudes toward gay, lesbian, and transgender employees
	More multitasking and connectivity
World politics	Rising health care costs
	Negative social attitudes toward business and executives
	Opening of markets in China

the best-known U.S. companies, including Bear Stearns, Merrill Lynch, Lehman Brothers, Countrywide Financial, Washington Mutual, and Ameriquest. Tens of thousands of jobs were lost and may never return. After years of declining numbers of bankruptcies, the global recession caused the bankruptcy of auto manufacturers General Motors and Chrysler, retailers Borders and Sharper Image, and myriad other organizations.

Competition is changing. Competitors are as likely to come from across the ocean as from across town. Successful organizations will be fast on their feet, capable of developing new products rapidly and getting them to market quickly. In other words, they'll be flexible and will require an equally flexible and responsive workforce. Increasingly, in the United States and Europe, the government regulates business practices, including executive pay.

Social trends don't remain static either. Consumers who are otherwise strangers now meet and share product information in chat rooms and blogs. Companies must continually adjust product and marketing strategies to be sensitive to changing social trends, as Liz Claiborne did when it sold off fashion brands (such as Ellen Tracy), deemphasized large vendors such as Macy's, and streamlined operations and cut staff. Consumers, employees, and organizational leaders are more sensitive to environmental concerns. "Green" practices are quickly becoming expected rather than optional.

Not even globalization's strongest proponents could have imagined how *world politics* would change in recent years. We've seen a major set of financial crises that have rocked global markets, a dramatic rise in the power and influence of China, and dramatic shakeups in government across the Arab world. Throughout the industrialized world, businesses—particularly in the banking and financial sectors—have come under new scrutiny.

Planned Change

Jeff Bezos is the change agent at Amazon.com. He founded the company as an online bookstore in 1994 and then built it into the largest retailer on the Web that sells everything from groceries to electronics. Amazon changed from a seller of electronics to also become a product developer when it created the Kindle reading device and the Kindle service for downloading books in less than 60 seconds. In his drive for change at Amazon, Bezos combines a long-term orientation with identifying a customer need. Bezos is shown here unveiling the Kindle DX, a large-screen version of the original Kindle designed for reading newspapers, magazines, and textbooks.

Source: Emmanuel Dunand/AFP/Getty Images/Newscom.

A group of housekeeping employees who work for a small hotel confronted the owner: "It's very hard for most of us to maintain rigid 7-to-4 work hours," said their spokeswoman. "Each of us has significant family and personal responsibilities. And rigid hours don't work for us. We're going to begin looking for someplace else to work if you don't set up flexible work hours." The owner listened thoughtfully to the group's ultimatum and agreed to its request. The next day, a flextime plan for these employees was introduced.

A major automobile manufacturer spent several billion dollars to install state-of-the-art robotics. One area that would receive the new equipment was quality control, where sophisticated computers would significantly improve the company's ability to find and correct defects. Because the new equipment would dramatically change the jobs in the quality-control area, and because management anticipated considerable employee resistance to it, executives were developing a program to help people become familiar with it and deal with any anxieties they might be feeling.

Both these scenarios are examples of **change**, or making things different. However, only the second scenario describes a **planned change**. Many changes are like the one that occurred at the hotel: they just happen. Some organizations treat all change as an accidental occurrence. In this chapter, we address change as an intentional, goal-oriented activity.

What are the goals of planned change? First, it seeks to improve the ability of the organization to adapt to changes in its environment. Second, it seeks to change employee behavior.

Who in organizations is responsible for managing change activities? The answer is **change agents**.[1] They see a future for the organization that others have not identified, and they are able to motivate, invent, and implement this vision. Change agents can be managers or nonmanagers, current or new employees, or outside consultants.

DuPont has two primary change agents in CEO Ellen Kullman and Chief Innovation Officer Thomas Connelly.[2] Taking the reins of the company in 2010, Kullman has pushed the organization toward a higher level of achievement by focusing on a principle Connelly calls "launch hard and ramp fast." This means the organization will seek to derive as much of its revenues from new products as possible. The goal is to move DuPont from a comparatively placid culture to one that focuses on market-driven science and delivers products customers need. The process has not always been easy, but it is necessary to keep DuPont ahead of the competitive marketplace.

Many change agents fail because organizational members resist change. In the next section, we discuss resistance to change and what managers can do about it.

Resistance to Change

2 Describe the sources of resistance to change.

Our egos are fragile, and we often see change as threatening. One recent study showed that even when employees are shown data that suggest they need to change, they latch onto whatever data they can find that suggests they are okay and don't need to change.[3] Employees who have negative feelings about a change cope by not thinking about it, increasing their use of sick time, and quitting. All these reactions can sap the organization of vital energy when it is most needed.[4]

Resistance to change can be positive if it leads to open discussion and debate.[5] These responses are usually preferable to apathy or silence and can indicate that members of the organization are engaged in the process, providing change agents an opportunity to explain the change effort. Change agents can also use resistance to modify the change to fit the preferences of other members of the organization. When they treat resistance only as a threat, rather than a point of view to be discussed, they may increase dysfunctional conflict.

Resistance doesn't necessarily surface in standardized ways. It can be overt, implicit, immediate, or deferred. It's easiest for management to deal with overt and immediate resistance, such as complaints, a work slowdown, or a strike threat. The greater challenge is managing resistance that is implicit or deferred. These responses—loss of loyalty or motivation, increased errors or absenteeism—are more subtle and more difficult to recognize for what they are. Deferred actions also cloud the link between the change and the reaction to it and may surface weeks, months, or even years later. Or a single change of little inherent impact may be the straw that breaks the camel's back because resistance to earlier changes has been deferred and stockpiled.

Exhibit 18-2 summarizes major forces for resistance to change, categorized by their sources. Individual sources reside in human characteristics such as perceptions, personalities, and needs. Organizational sources reside in the structural makeup of organizations themselves.

It's worth noting that not all change is good. Speed can lead to bad decisions, and sometimes those initiating change fail to realize the full magnitude of the effects or their true costs. Rapid, transformational change is risky, and

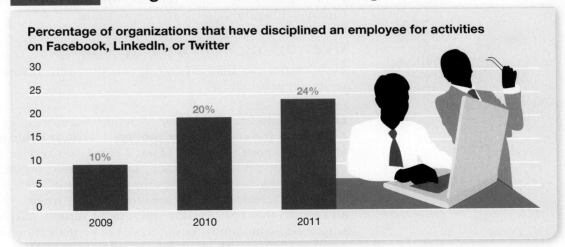

OB Poll **Rising Risks of Social Networking at Work**

Percentage of organizations that have disciplined an employee for activities on Facebook, LinkedIn, or Twitter

2009: 10%
2010: 20%
2011: 24%

Source: Based on J. Yang and P. Trap, "Society for Human Resource Management Survey," *USA Today* (June 2, 2011), p. 1B.

---

change *Making things different.*

planned change *Change activities that are intentional and goal oriented.*

change agents *Persons who act as catalysts and assume the responsibility for managing change activities.*

> **Exhibit 18-2**　**Sources of Resistance to Change**
>
> **Individual Sources**
>
> *Habit*—To cope with life's complexities, we rely on habits or programmed responses. But when confronted with change, this tendency to respond in our accustomed ways becomes a source of resistance.
>
> *Security*—People with a high need for security are likely to resist change because it threatens their feelings of safety.
>
> *Economic factors*—Changes in job tasks or established work routines can arouse economic fears if people are concerned that they won't be able to perform the new tasks or routines to their previous standards, especially when pay is closely tied to productivity.
>
> *Fear of the unknown*—Change substitutes ambiguity and uncertainty for the unknown.
>
> *Selective information processing*—Individuals are guilty of selectively processing information in order to keep their perceptions intact. They hear what they want to hear, and they ignore information that challenges the world they've created.
>
> **Organizational Sources**
>
> *Structural inertia*—Organizations have built-in mechanisms—such as their selection processes and formalized regulations—to produce stability. When an organization is confronted with change, this structural inertia acts as a counterbalance to sustain stability.
>
> *Limited focus of change*—Organizations consist of a number of interdependent subsystems. One can't be changed without affecting the others. So limited changes in subsystems tend to be nullified by the larger system.
>
> *Group inertia*—Even if individuals want to change their behavior, group norms may act as a constraint.
>
> *Threat to expertise*—Changes in organizational patterns may threaten the expertise of specialized groups.
>
> *Threat to established power relationships*—Any redistribution of decision-making authority can threaten long-established power relationships within the organization.

some organizations have collapsed for this reason.[6] Change agents need to carefully think through the full implications.

Overcoming Resistance to Change

Eight tactics can help change agents deal with resistance to change.[7] Let's review them briefly.

Education and Communication　Communicating the logic of a change can reduce employee resistance on two levels. First, it fights the effects of misinformation and poor communication: if employees receive the full facts and clear up misunderstandings, resistance should subside. Second, communication can help "sell" the need for change by packaging it properly.[8] A study of German companies revealed changes are most effective when a company communicates a rationale that balances the interests of various stakeholders (shareholders, employees, community, customers) rather than those of shareholders only.[9] Another study of a changing organization in the Philippines found that formal change information sessions decreased employee anxiety about the change, while providing high-quality information about the change increased commitment to it.[10]

Participation　It's difficult to resist a change decision in which we've participated. Assuming participants have the expertise to make a meaningful contribution, their involvement can reduce resistance, obtain commitment, and increase the quality of the change decision. However, against these advantages are the negatives: potential for a poor solution and great consumption of time.

Building Support and Commitment   When employees' fear and anxiety are high, counseling and therapy, new-skills training, or a short paid leave of absence may facilitate adjustment. When managers or employees have low emotional commitment to change, they favor the status quo and resist it.[11] Employees are also more accepting of changes when they are committed to the organization as a whole.[12] So, firing up employees and emphasizing their commitment to the organization overall can also help them emotionally commit to the change rather than embrace the status quo.

Develop Positive Relationships   People are more willing to accept changes if they trust the managers implementing them.[13] One study surveyed 235 employees from a large housing corporation in the Netherlands that was experiencing a merger. Those who had a more positive relationship with their supervisors, and who felt that the work environment supported development, were much more positive about the change process.[14] Another set of studies found that individuals who were dispositionally resistant to change felt more positive about the change if they trusted the change agent.[15] This research suggests that if managers are able to facilitate positive relationships, they may be able to overcome resistance to change even among those who ordinarily don't like changes.

Implementing Changes Fairly   One way organizations can minimize negative impact is to make sure change is implemented fairly. As we saw in Chapter 7, procedural fairness is especially important when employees perceive an outcome as negative, so it's crucial that employees see the reason for the change and perceive its implementation as consistent and fair.[16]

Manipulation and Cooptation   *Manipulation* refers to covert influence attempts. Twisting facts to make them more attractive, withholding information, and creating false rumors to get employees to accept change are all examples of manipulation. If management threatens to close a manufacturing plant whose employees are resisting an across-the-board pay cut, and if the threat is actually untrue, management is using manipulation. *Cooptation,* on the other hand, combines manipulation and participation. It seeks to "buy off" the leaders of a resistance group by giving them a key role, seeking their advice not to find a better solution but to get their endorsement. Both manipulation and cooptation are relatively inexpensive ways to gain the support of adversaries, but they can backfire if the targets become aware they are being tricked or used. Once that's discovered, the change agent's credibility may drop to zero.

Selecting People Who Accept Change   Research suggests the ability to easily accept and adapt to *change* is related to personality—some people simply have more positive attitudes about change than others.[17] Such individuals are open to experience, take a positive attitude toward change, are willing to take risks, and are flexible in their behavior. One study of managers in the United States, Europe, and Asia found those with a positive self-concept and high risk tolerance coped better with organizational change. A study of 258 police officers found those higher in growth-needs strength, internal locus of control, and internal work motivation had more positive attitudes about organizational change efforts.[18] Individuals higher in general mental ability are also better able to learn and adapt to changes in the workplace.[19] In sum, an impressive body of evidence shows organizations can facilitate change by selecting people predisposed to accept it.

Besides selecting individuals who are willing to accept changes, it is also possible to select teams that are more adaptable. Studies have shown that teams that are strongly motivated by learning about and mastering tasks are better able to adapt to changing environments.[20] This research suggests that it may be necessary to consider not just individual motivation, but also group motivation when trying to implement changes.

Coercion   Last on the list of tactics is *coercion*, the application of direct threats or force on the resisters. If management really is determined to close a manufacturing plant whose employees don't acquiesce to a pay cut, the company is using coercion. Other examples are threats of transfer, loss of promotions, negative performance evaluations, and a poor letter of recommendation. The advantages and drawbacks of coercion are approximately the same as for manipulation and cooptation.

The Politics of Change

No discussion of resistance would be complete without a brief mention of the politics of change. Because change invariably threatens the status quo, it inherently implies political activity.

Politics suggests the impetus for change is more likely to come from outside change agents, employees new to the organization (who have less invested in the status quo), or managers slightly removed from the main power structure. Managers who have spent their entire careers with a single organization and achieved a senior position in the hierarchy are often major impediments to change. It is a very real threat to their status and position. Yet they may be expected to implement changes to demonstrate they're not merely caretakers. By acting as change agents, they can convey to stockholders, suppliers, employees, and customers that they are addressing problems and adapting to a dynamic environment. Of course, as you might guess, when forced to introduce change, these longtime power holders tend to implement incremental changes. Radical change is too threatening. This explains why boards of directors that recognize the imperative for rapid and radical change frequently turn to outside candidates for new leadership.[21]

Approaches to Managing Organizational Change

3 Compare the four main approaches to managing organizational change.

Now we turn to several approaches to managing change: Lewin's classic three-step model of the change process, Kotter's eight-step plan, action research, and organizational development.

Lewin's Three-Step Model

Kurt Lewin argued that successful change in organizations should follow three steps: **unfreezing** the status quo, **movement** to a desired end state, and **refreezing** the new change to make it permanent.[22] (See Exhibit 18-3.)

The status quo is an equilibrium state. To move from equilibrium—to overcome the pressures of both individual resistance and group conformity—unfreezing

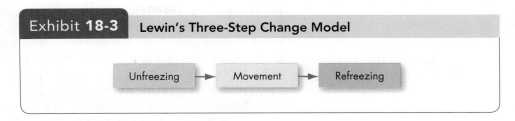

Exhibit **18-3**   Lewin's Three-Step Change Model

Unfreezing → Movement → Refreezing

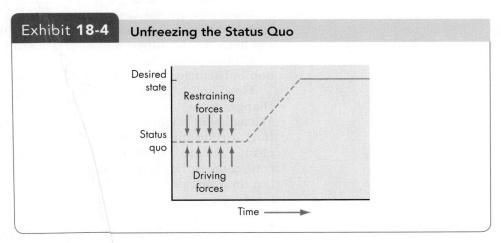

Exhibit **18-4**   Unfreezing the Status Quo

must happen in one of three ways (see Exhibit 18-4.) The **driving forces**, which direct behavior away from the status quo, can be increased. The **restraining forces**, which hinder movement away from equilibrium, can be decreased. A third alternative is to combine the first two approaches. Companies that have been successful in the past are likely to encounter restraining forces because people question the need for change.[23] Similarly, research shows that companies with strong cultures excel at incremental change but are overcome by restraining forces against radical change.[24]

Consider a large oil company that decided to consolidate its three divisional marketing offices in Seattle, San Francisco, and Los Angeles into a single regional San Francisco office. The decision was made in New York and the people affected had no say whatsoever in the choice. The reorganization meant transferring more than 150 employees, eliminating some duplicate managerial positions, and instituting a new hierarchy of command.

The oil company's management could expect employee resistance to the consolidation. Those in Seattle or Los Angeles may not want to transfer to another city, pull youngsters out of school, make new friends, adapt to new coworkers, or undergo the reassignment of responsibilities. Positive incentives such as pay increases, liberal moving expenses, and low-cost mortgage funds for new homes in San Francisco might encourage employees to accept the change. Management might also unfreeze acceptance of the status quo by removing restraining forces. It could counsel employees individually, hearing and clarifying each employee's specific concerns and apprehensions. Assuming most are

unfreezing   *Changing to overcome the pressures of both individual resistance and group conformity.*

movement   *A change process that transforms the organization from the status quo to a desired end state.*

refreezing   *Stabilizing a change intervention by balancing driving and restraining forces.*

driving forces   *Forces that direct behavior away from the status quo.*

restraining forces   *Forces that hinder movement from the existing equilibrium.*

unjustified, the counselor could assure employees there was nothing to fear and offer tangible evidence that restraining forces are unwarranted. If resistance is extremely high, management may have to resort to both reducing resistance and increasing the attractiveness of the alternative if the unfreezing is to be successful.

Research on organizational change has shown that, to be effective, the actual change has to happen quickly.[25] Organizations that build up to change do less well than those that get to and through the movement stage quickly.

Once change has been implemented, to be successful the new situation must be refrozen so it can be sustained over time. Without this last step, change will likely be short-lived and employees will attempt to revert to the previous equilibrium state. The objective of refreezing, then, is to stabilize the new situation by balancing the driving and restraining forces.

How could the oil company's management refreeze its consolidation change? By systematically replacing temporary forces with permanent ones. Management might impose a permanent upward adjustment of salaries. The formal rules and regulations governing behavior of those affected by the change should also be revised to reinforce the new situation. Over time, of course, the work group's own norms will evolve to sustain the new equilibrium. But until that point is reached, management will have to rely on more formal mechanisms.

Kotter's Eight-Step Plan for Implementing Change

John Kotter of the Harvard Business School built on Lewin's three-step model to create a more detailed approach for implementing change.[26] Kotter began by listing common mistakes managers make when trying to initiate change. They may fail to create a sense of urgency about the need for change, to create a coalition for managing the change process, to have a vision for change and effectively communicate it, to remove obstacles that could impede the vision's achievement, to provide short-term and achievable goals, and to anchor the changes into the organization's culture. They may also declare victory too soon.

Kotter then established eight sequential steps to overcome these problems. They're listed in Exhibit 18-5.

Notice how Kotter's first four steps essentially extrapolate Lewin's "unfreezing" stage. Steps 5, 6 and 7 represent "movement," and the final step works on

---

Exhibit 18-5   **Kotter's Eight-Step Plan for Implementing Change**

1. Establish a sense of urgency by creating a compelling reason for why change is needed.
2. Form a coalition with enough power to lead the change.
3. Create a new vision to direct the change and strategies for achieving the vision.
4. Communicate the vision throughout the organization.
5. Empower others to act on the vision by removing barriers to change and encouraging risk taking and creative problem solving.
6. Plan for, create, and reward short-term "wins" that move the organization toward the new vision.
7. Consolidate improvements, reassess changes, and make necessary adjustments in the new programs.
8. Reinforce the changes by demonstrating the relationship between new behaviors and organizational success.

Source: Based on J. P. Kotter, *Leading Change* (Boston: Harvard Business School Press, 1996).

"refreezing." So Kotter's contribution lies in providing managers and change agents with a more detailed guide for successfully implementing change.

Action Research

Action research is a change process based on the systematic collection of data and selection of a change action based on what the analyzed data indicate.[27] Its value is in providing a scientific methodology for managing planned change. Action research consists of five steps (note how they closely parallel the scientific method): diagnosis, analysis, feedback, action, and evaluation.

The change agent, often an outside consultant in action research, begins by gathering information about problems, concerns, and needed changes from members of the organization. This *diagnosis* is analogous to the physician's search to find specifically what ails a patient. In action research, the change agent asks questions, reviews records, and interviews employees and listens to their concerns.

Diagnosis is followed by *analysis*. What problems do people key in on? What patterns do these problems seem to take? The change agent synthesizes this information into primary concerns, problem areas, and possible actions.

Action research requires the people who will participate in any change program to help identify the problem and determine the solution. So the third step—*feedback*—requires sharing with employees what has been found from the first and second steps. The employees, with the help of the change agent, develop action plans for bringing about any needed change.

Now the *action* part of action research is set in motion. The employees and the change agent carry out the specific actions they have identified to correct the problem.

The final step, consistent with the scientific underpinnings of action research, is *evaluation* of the action plan's effectiveness, using the initial data gathered as a benchmark.

Action research provides at least two specific benefits. First, it's problem focused. The change agent objectively looks for problems, and the type of problem determines the type of change action. Although this may seem intuitively obvious, many change activities are not handled this way. Rather, they're solution centered. The change agent has a favorite solution—for example, implementing flextime, teams, or a process reengineering program—and then seeks out problems that the solution fits.

Second, because action research engages employees so thoroughly in the process, it reduces resistance to change. Once employees have actively participated in the feedback stage, the change process typically takes on a momentum of its own under their sustained pressure to bring it about.

Organizational Development

Organizational development (OD) is a collection of change methods that try to improve organizational effectiveness and employee well-being.[28]

OD methods value human and organizational growth, collaborative and participative processes, and a spirit of inquiry.[29] Contemporary OD borrows

action research   *A change process based on systematic collection of data and then selection of a change action based on what the analyzed data indicate.*

organizational development (OD)   *A collection of planned change interventions, built on humanistic–democratic values, that seeks to improve organizational effectiveness and employee well-being.*

These retirement center employees participate in a simulated training program to help them understand the diminishing abilities of the older population that is growing in developing nations worldwide. While wearing glasses that blurred their vision, they collaborated in an activity of devising a driving route.

Called Xtreme Aging, the training program has become a regular part of many nursing and medical school curricula and corporate training programs and is designed to help participants grow in their understanding of and sensitivity to the needs of older customers and fellow workers.

Source: Kirk Irwin/The New York Times/Redux Pictures.

heavily from postmodern philosophy in placing heavy emphasis on the subjective ways in which people see their environment. The focus is on how individuals make sense of their work environment. The change agent may take the lead in OD, but there is a strong emphasis on collaboration. These are the underlying values in most OD efforts:

1. **Respect for people.**   Individuals are perceived as responsible, conscientious, and caring. They should be treated with dignity and respect.
2. **Trust and support.**   An effective and healthy organization is characterized by trust, authenticity, openness, and a supportive climate.
3. **Power equalization.**   Effective organizations deemphasize hierarchical authority and control.
4. **Confrontation.**   Problems should be openly confronted, not swept under the rug.
5. **Participation.**   The more engaged in the decisions they are, the more people affected by a change will be committed to implementing them.

What are some OD techniques or interventions for bringing about change? Here are six.

Sensitivity Training   A variety of names—**sensitivity training**, laboratory training, encounter groups, and T-groups (training groups)—all refer to an early method of changing behavior through unstructured group interaction.[30] Members were brought together in a free and open environment in which participants discuss themselves and their interactive processes, loosely directed by a professional behavioral scientist who created the opportunity to express ideas, beliefs, and attitudes without taking any leadership role. The group was process-oriented, which means individuals learned through observing and participating rather than being told.

Many participants found these unstructured groups intimidating, chaotic, and damaging to work relationships. Although extremely popular in the 1960s, they diminished in use during the 1970s and have essentially disappeared. However, organizational interventions such as diversity training, executive coaching, and team-building exercises are descendants of this early OD intervention technique.

Survey Feedback   One tool for assessing attitudes held by organizational members, identifying discrepancies among member perceptions, and solving these differences is the **survey feedback** approach.[31]

Everyone in an organization can participate in survey feedback, but of key importance is the organizational "family"—the manager of any given unit and the employees who report directly to him or her. All usually complete a questionnaire about their perceptions and attitudes on a range of topics, including decision-making practices; communication effectiveness; coordination among units; and satisfaction with the organization, job, peers, and immediate supervisor.

Data from this questionnaire are tabulated with data pertaining to an individual's specific "family" and to the entire organization and then distributed to employees. These data become the springboard for identifying problems and clarifying issues that may be creating difficulties for people. Particular attention is given to encouraging discussion and ensuring it focuses on issues and ideas and not on attacking individuals. For instance, are people listening? Are new ideas being generated? Can decision making, interpersonal relations, or job assignments be improved? Answers should lead the group to commit to various remedies for the problems identified.

Process Consultation   Managers often sense their unit's performance can be improved but are unable to identify what to improve and how. The purpose of **process consultation (PC)** is for an outside consultant to assist a client, usually a manager, "to perceive, understand, and act upon process events" with which the manager must deal.[32] These events might include work flow, informal relationships among unit members, and formal communication channels.

PC is similar to sensitivity training in assuming we can improve organizational effectiveness by dealing with interpersonal problems and in emphasizing involvement. But PC is more task directed, and consultants are there to "give the client 'insight' into what is going on around him, within him, and between him and other people."[33] They do not solve the organization's problems but rather guide or coach the client to solve his or her own problems after *jointly* diagnosing what needs improvement. The client develops the skill to analyze processes within his or her unit and can continue to call on it long after the consultant is gone. Because the client actively participates in both the diagnosis and the development of alternatives, he or she arrives at greater understanding of the process and the remedy and is less resistant to the action plan chosen.

Team Building   We've noted throughout this book that organizations increasingly rely on teams to accomplish work tasks. **Team building** uses high-interaction group activities to increase trust and openness among team members, improve coordinative efforts, and increase team performance.[34] Here, we emphasize the intragroup level, meaning organizational families (command groups) as well as committees, project teams, self-managed teams, and task groups.

sensitivity training   *Training groups that seek to change behavior through unstructured group interaction.*

survey feedback   *The use of questionnaires to identify discrepancies among member perceptions; discussion follows, and remedies are suggested.*

process consultation (PC)   *A meeting in which a consultant assists a client in understanding process events with which he or she must deal and identifying processes that need improvement.*

team building   *High interaction among team members to increase trust and openness.*

ServiceMaster, a provider of lawn care, cleaning, disaster restoration, and other services, is a sponsoring company of Habitat for Humanity. As a sponsor, ServiceMaster provides employee volunteers and the funds to buy building materials for constructing homes for families in need. For ServiceMaster, the building project also serves as a team-building activity, with employees spending their workdays at the building site rather than on their regular jobs. Serving as a high-interaction group activity, the Habitat build increases trust and openness among employees and translates into better communication and greater cooperation in the workplace.

Source: c51/ZUMA Press/Newscom.

Team building typically includes goal-setting, development of interpersonal relations among team members, role analysis to clarify each member's role and responsibilities, and team process analysis. It may emphasize or exclude certain activities, depending on the purpose of the development effort and the specific problems with which the team is confronted. Basically, however, team building uses high interaction among members to increase trust and openness.

Intergroup Development A major area of concern in OD is dysfunctional conflict among groups. **Intergroup development** seeks to change groups' attitudes, stereotypes, and perceptions about each other. Here, training sessions closely resemble diversity training (in fact, diversity training largely evolved from intergroup development in OD), except rather than focusing on demographic differences, they focus on differences among occupations, departments, or divisions within an organization.

In one company, the engineers saw the accounting department as composed of shy and conservative types and the human resources department as having a bunch of "ultra-liberals more concerned that some protected group of employees might get their feelings hurt than with the company making a profit." Such stereotypes can have an obvious negative impact on coordination efforts among departments.

Among several approaches for improving intergroup relations, a popular one emphasizes problem solving.[35] Each group meets independently to list its perceptions of itself and of the other group and how it believes the other group perceives it. The groups share their lists, discuss similarities and differences, and look for the causes of disparities. Are the groups' goals at odds? Were perceptions distorted? On what basis were stereotypes formulated? Have some differences been caused by misunderstanding of intentions? Have words and concepts been defined differently by each group? Answers to questions like these clarify the exact nature of the conflict.

Once they have identified the causes of the difficulty, the groups move to the integration phase—developing solutions to improve relations between them.

Subgroups can be formed of members from each of the conflicting groups to conduct further diagnosis and formulate alternative solutions.

Appreciative Inquiry   Most OD approaches are problem centered. They identify a problem or set of problems, then look for a solution. **Appreciative inquiry (AI)** instead accentuates the positive.[36] Rather than looking for problems to fix, it seeks to identify the unique qualities and special strengths of an organization, which members can build on to improve performance. That is, AI focuses on an organization's successes rather than its problems.

The AI process consists of four steps—discovery, dreaming, design, and discovery—often played out in a large-group meeting over a 2- or 3-day time period and overseen by a trained change agent. *Discovery* sets out to identify what people think are the organization's strengths. Employees recount times they felt the organization worked best or when they specifically felt most satisfied with their jobs. In *dreaming*, employees use information from the discovery phase to speculate on possible futures, such as what the organization will be like in 5 years. In *design*, participants find a common vision of how the organization will look in the future and agree on its unique qualities. For the fourth step, participants seek to define the organization's *destiny* or how to fulfill their dream, and they typically write action plans and develop implementation strategies.

AI has proven an effective change strategy in organizations such as GTE, Roadway Express, and the U.S. Navy. American Express used AI to revitalize its culture during a lean economy. In workshops, employees described how they already felt proud of working at American Express and were encouraged to create a change vision by describing how it could be better in the future. The efforts led to some very concrete improvements. Senior managers were able to use employees' information to better their methods of making financial forecasts, improve IT investments, and create new performance-management tools for managers. The end result was a renewed culture focused on winning attitudes and behaviors.[37]

Creating a Culture for Change

4 Demonstrate two ways of creating a culture for change.

We've considered how organizations can *adapt* to change. But recently, some OB scholars have focused on a more proactive approach—how organizations can *embrace* change by transforming their cultures. In this section, we review two such approaches: stimulating an innovative culture and creating a learning organization.

Stimulating a Culture of Innovation

How can an organization become more innovative? An excellent model is W. L. Gore, the $2.6-billion-per-year company best known as the maker of Gore-Tex fabric.[38] Gore has developed a reputation as one of the most innovative

intergroup development   *OD efforts to change the attitudes, stereotypes, and perceptions that groups have of each other.*

appreciative inquiry (AI)   *An approach that seeks to identify the unique qualities and special strengths of an organization, which can then be built on to improve performance.*

U.S. companies by developing a stream of diverse products—including guitar strings, dental floss, medical devices, and fuel cells.

What's the secret of Gore's success? What can other organizations do to duplicate its track record for innovation? Although there is no guaranteed formula, certain characteristics surface repeatedly when researchers study innovative organizations. We've grouped them into structural, cultural, and human resource categories. Change agents should consider introducing these characteristics into their organization to create an innovative climate. Before we look at these characteristics, however, let's clarify what we mean by innovation.

Definition of *Innovation*   We said change refers to making things different. **Innovation**, a more specialized kind of change, is a new idea applied to initiating or improving a product, process, or service.[39] So all innovations imply change, but not all changes necessarily introduce new ideas or lead to significant improvements. Innovations can range from small incremental improvements, such as netbook computers, to radical breakthroughs, such as Nissan's electric Leaf car.

Sources of Innovation   *Structural variables* have been the most studied potential source of innovation.[40] A comprehensive review of the structure–innovation relationship leads to the following conclusions:[41]

1. Organic structures positively influence innovation. Because they're lower in vertical differentiation, formalization, and centralization, organic organizations facilitate the flexibility, adaptation, and cross-fertilization that make the adoption of innovations easier.
2. Long tenure in management is associated with innovation. Managerial tenure apparently provides legitimacy and knowledge of how to accomplish tasks and obtain desired outcomes.
3. Innovation is nurtured when there are slack resources. Having an abundance of resources allows an organization to afford to purchase innovations, bear the cost of instituting them, and absorb failures.

Innovation is a specialized kind of change whereby a new idea is applied to initiating or improving a product, process, or service. Twitter, for example, is an innovation in the distribution of information. Twitter's founders Evan Williams (left) and Biz Stone shown in this photo along with Jack Dorsey launched their new communication tool for sending 140-character messages, or tweets, from a computer or mobile device. As a social network, Twitter allows users to have live digital conversations. By using Twitter's search feature, users can have a real-time view into other people's conversations.

Source: Peter DaSilva/The New York Times/Redux.

4. Interunit communication is high in innovative organizations.[42] These organizations are high users of committees, task forces, cross-functional teams, and other mechanisms that facilitate interaction across departmental lines.

Innovative organizations tend to have similar *cultures*. They encourage experimentation. They reward both successes and failures. They celebrate mistakes. Unfortunately, in too many organizations, people are rewarded for the absence of failures rather than for the presence of successes. Such cultures extinguish risk taking and innovation. People will suggest and try new ideas only when they feel such behaviors exact no penalties. Managers in innovative organizations recognize that failures are a natural by-product of venturing into the unknown.

Within the *human resources* category, innovative organizations actively promote the training and development of their members so they keep current, offer high job security so employees don't fear getting fired for making mistakes, and encourage individuals to become champions of change. Once a new idea is developed, **idea champions** actively and enthusiastically promote it, build support, overcome resistance, and ensure it's implemented.[43] Champions have common personality characteristics: extremely high self-confidence, persistence, energy, and a tendency to take risks. They also display characteristics associated with transformational leadership—they inspire and energize others with their vision of an innovation's potential and their strong personal conviction about their mission. Idea champions are good at gaining the commitment of others, and their jobs provide considerable decision-making discretion; this autonomy helps them introduce and implement innovations.[44]

Do successful idea champions do things differently in different cultures? Yes.[45] People in collectivist cultures prefer appeals for cross-functional support for innovation efforts; people in high power distance cultures prefer champions to work closely with those in authority to approve innovative activities before work is begun; and the higher the uncertainty avoidance of a society, the more champions should work within the organization's rules and procedures to develop the innovation. These findings suggest that effective managers will alter their organization's championing strategies to reflect cultural values. So, for instance, although idea champions in Russia might succeed by ignoring budgetary limitations and working around confining procedures, champions in Austria, Denmark, Germany, or other cultures high in uncertainty avoidance will be more effective by closely following budgets and procedures.

Sergio Marcchione, CEO of Fiat-Chrysler, has acted as idea champion for the single objective of updating the pipeline of vehicles for Chrysler. To facilitate this change, he has radically dismantled the bureaucracy, tearing up Chrysler's organization chart and introducing a flatter structure with himself at the lead. As a result, the company introduced a more innovative line of vehicles and planned to redesign or significantly refresh 75 percent of its lineup in 2010 alone.[46]

Creating a Learning Organization

Another way an organization can proactively manage change is to make continuous growth part of its culture—to become a learning organization.[47]

---

innovation   *A new idea applied to initiating or improving a product, process, or service.*

idea champions   *Individuals who take an innovation and actively and enthusiastically promote the idea, build support, overcome resistance, and ensure that the idea is implemented.*

What's a Learning Organization?   Just as individuals learn, so too do organizations. A **learning organization** has developed the continuous capacity to adapt and change. "All organizations learn, whether they consciously choose to or not—it is a fundamental requirement for their sustained existence."[48] Some organizations just do it better than others.

Most organizations engage in **single-loop learning**.[49] When they detect errors, their correction process relies on past routines and present policies. In contrast, learning organizations use **double-loop learning**. They correct errors by *modifying* objectives, policies, and standard routines. Double-loop learning challenges deeply rooted assumptions and norms. It provides opportunities for radically different solutions to problems and dramatic jumps in improvement.

Exhibit 18-6 summarizes the five basic characteristics of a learning organization. It's one in which people put aside their old ways of thinking, learn to be open with each other, understand how their organization really works, form a plan or vision everyone can agree on, and work together to achieve that vision.[50]

Proponents of the learning organization envision it as a remedy for three fundamental problems of traditional organizations: fragmentation, competition, and reactiveness.[51] First, *fragmentation* based on specialization creates "walls" and "chimneys" that separate different functions into independent and often warring fiefdoms. Second, an overemphasis on *competition* often undermines collaboration. Managers compete to show who is right, who knows more, or who is more persuasive. Divisions compete when they ought to cooperate and share knowledge. Team leaders compete to show who the best manager is. And third, *reactiveness* misdirects management's attention to problem solving rather than creation. The problem solver tries to make something go away, while a creator tries to bring something new into being. An emphasis on reactiveness pushes out innovation and continuous improvement and, in its place, encourages people to run around "putting out fires."

Managing Learning   What can managers do to make their firms learning organizations? Here are some suggestions:

- **Establish a strategy.**   Management needs to make explicit its commitment to change, innovation, and continuous improvement.
- **Redesign the organization's structure.**   The formal structure can be a serious impediment to learning. Flattening the structure, eliminating or combining departments, and increasing the use of cross-functional teams reinforces interdependence and reduces boundaries.

Exhibit **18-6**	**Characteristics of a Learning Organization**

1. There exists a shared vision that everyone agrees on.

2. People discard their old ways of thinking and the standard routines they use for solving problems or doing their jobs.

3. Members think of all organizational processes, activities, functions, and interactions with the environment as part of a system of interrelationships.

4. People openly communicate with each other (across vertical and horizontal boundaries) without fear of criticism or punishment.

5. People sublimate their personal self-interest and fragmented departmental interests to work together to achieve the organization's shared vision.

Source: Based on P. M. Senge, *The Fifth Discipline* (New York: Doubleday, 1990).

- **Reshape the organization's culture.** To become a learning organization, managers must demonstrate by their actions that taking risks and admitting failures are desirable. That means rewarding people who take chances and make mistakes. And management needs to encourage functional conflict. "The key to unlocking real openness at work," says one expert on learning organizations, "is to teach people to give up having to be in agreement. We think agreement is so important. Who cares? You have to bring paradoxes, conflicts, and dilemmas out in the open, so collectively we can be more intelligent than we can be individually."[52]

Work Stress and Its Management

5 Define *stress* and identify its potential sources.

Friends say they're stressed from greater workloads and longer hours because of downsizing at their companies. Parents worry about the lack of job stability and reminisce about a time when a job with a large company implied lifetime security. We read surveys in which employees complain about the stress of trying to balance work and family responsibilities.[53] Indeed, as Exhibit 18-7 shows, work is, for most people, the most important source of stress in life. What are the causes and consequences of stress, and what can individuals and organizations do to reduce it?

What Is Stress?

Stress is a dynamic condition in which an individual is confronted with an opportunity, demand, or resource related to what the individual desires and for which the outcome is perceived to be both uncertain and important.[54] This is a complicated definition. Let's look at its components more closely.

Exhibit 18-7	Work Is the Biggest Source of Stress for Most

"What area of your life causes you the most stress on a regular basis?"

Area	Causes Most Stress
My job	26%
My finances	20%
My relationships	21%
My children	10%
School	8%
Fear of a disaster/terror attack	3%
Other	8%

Source: 2009 Stress Management poll of 7,807 individuals, stress.about.com/gi/pages/poll.htm?linkback5&poll_id52213421040&poll 151&poll351&submit15Submit1Vote.

---

learning organization *An organization that has developed the continuous capacity to adapt and change.*

single-loop learning *A process of correcting errors using past routines and present policies.*

double-loop learning *A process of correcting errors by modifying the organization's objectives, policies, and standard routines.*

stress *An unpleasant psychological process that occurs in response to environmental pressures.*

Although stress is typically discussed in a negative context, it is not necessarily bad in and of itself; it also has a positive value.[55] It's an opportunity when it offers potential gain. Consider, for example, the superior performance an athlete or stage performer gives in a "clutch" situation. Such individuals often use stress positively to rise to the occasion and perform at their maximum. Similarly, many professionals see the pressures of heavy workloads and deadlines as positive challenges that enhance the quality of their work and the satisfaction they get from their job.

Recently, researchers have argued that **challenge stressors**—or stressors associated with workload, pressure to complete tasks, and time urgency—operate quite differently from **hindrance stressors**—or stressors that keep you from reaching your goals (for example, red tape, office politics, confusion over job responsibilities). Although research is just starting to accumulate, early evidence suggests challenge stressors produce less strain than hindrance stressors.[56]

Researchers have sought to clarify the conditions under which each type of stress exists. It appears that employees who have a stronger affective commitment to their organization can transfer psychological stress into greater focus and higher sales performance, whereas employees with low levels of commitment perform worse under stress.[57] And when challenge stress increases, those with high levels of organizational support have higher role-based performance, but those with low levels of organizational support do not.[58]

More typically, stress is associated with **demands** and **resources**. Demands are responsibilities, pressures, obligations, and uncertainties individuals face in the workplace. Resources are things within an individual's control that he or she can use to resolve the demands. Let's discuss what this demands–resources model means.[59]

When you take a test at school or undergo your annual performance review at work, you feel stress because you confront opportunities and performance pressures. A good performance review may lead to a promotion, greater responsibilities, and a higher salary. A poor review may prevent you from getting a promotion. An extremely poor review might even result in your being fired. To the extent you can apply resources to the demands on you—such as

"Men Experience More Job Stress Than Women"

This statement is false. One recent review of the literature concluded, "Few, if any, differences exist between the respective amount of occupational stress men and women experience." Another review of 183 studies found that men and women differed to a very small degree on the burnout they experience.

While it doesn't appear that men and women differ in the work stress they report, there is more to the story. Working women tend to report more life stress than men. The reason

may be that, as surveys reliably show, when a husband and wife both work full-time outside the home, the wife carries considerably greater household responsibilities (cleaning, shopping, keeping finances). So if both spouses work the same number of hours, it's likely the wife's total load of paid work and household/family work is greater—and thus more stressful generally, even if her work stress alone is not greater. Says one expert, "A woman's major stressors come from both the work she's paid for and the work

she isn't." The former doesn't differ between the genders, but the latter clearly does.

Sources: S. B. Watson, Y. W. Goh, and S. Sawang, "Gender Influences on the Work-Related Stress Coping Process," *Journal of Individual Differences* 32, no. 1 (2011), pp. 39–46; R. K. Purvanova, and J. P. Muros, "Gender Differences in Burnout: A Meta-Analysis," *Journal of Vocational Behavior* 77, no. 2 (2010), pp. 168–185; and M. Casserly, "Summer Burnout: Avoiding Overload This Season," *Forbes* (May 26, 2011), downloaded on July 20, 2011, from http://blogs.forbes.com/meghancasserly/.

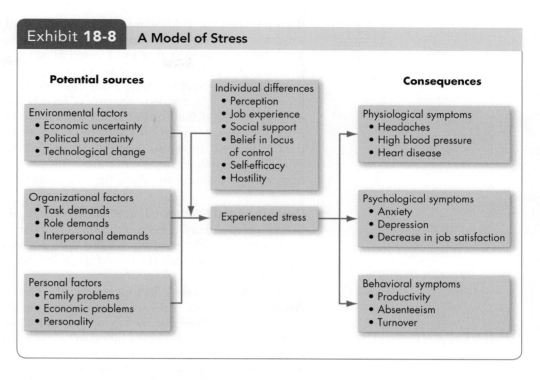

Exhibit 18-8   A Model of Stress

Potential sources

Environmental factors
- Economic uncertainty
- Political uncertainty
- Technological change

Organizational factors
- Task demands
- Role demands
- Interpersonal demands

Personal factors
- Family problems
- Economic problems
- Personality

Individual differences
- Perception
- Job experience
- Social support
- Belief in locus of control
- Self-efficacy
- Hostility

Experienced stress

Consequences

Physiological symptoms
- Headaches
- High blood pressure
- Heart disease

Psychological symptoms
- Anxiety
- Depression
- Decrease in job satisfaction

Behavioral symptoms
- Productivity
- Absenteeism
- Turnover

being prepared, placing the exam or review in perspective, or obtaining social support—you will feel less stress.

Research suggests adequate resources help reduce the stressful nature of demands when demands and resources match. If emotional demands are stressing you, having emotional resources in the form of social support is especially important. If the demands are cognitive—say, information overload—then job resources in the form of computer support or information are more important. Thus, under the demands–resources perspective, having resources to cope with stress is just as important in offsetting it as demands are in increasing it.[60]

Potential Sources of Stress

What causes stress? As the model in Exhibit 18-8 shows, there are three categories of potential stressors: environmental, organizational, and personal. Let's take a look at each.[61]

Environmental Factors   Just as environmental uncertainty influences the design of an organization's structure, it also influences stress levels among employees in that organization. Indeed, uncertainty is the biggest reason people have trouble coping with organizational changes.[62] There are three main types of environmental uncertainty: economic, political, and technological.

Changes in the business cycle create *economic uncertainties*. When the economy is contracting, for example, people become increasingly anxious about

challenge stressors   *Stressors associated with workload, pressure to complete tasks, and time urgency.*
hindrance stressors   *Stressors that keep you from reaching your goals (for example, red tape, office politics, confusion over job responsibilities).*

demands   *Responsibilities, pressures, obligations, and even uncertainties that individuals face in the workplace.*

resources   *Things within an individual's control that can be used to resolve demands.*

their job security. *Political uncertainties* don't tend to create stress among North Americans as they do for employees in countries such as Haiti or Venezuela. The obvious reason is that the United States and Canada have stable political systems, in which change is typically implemented in an orderly manner. Yet political threats and changes, even in countries such as the United States and Canada, can induce stress. Threats of terrorism in developed and developing nations, or the difficulties of East Germany reintegrating with West Germany, lead to political uncertainty that becomes stressful to people in these countries.[63] Because innovations can make an employee's skills and experience obsolete in a very short time, computers, robotics, automation, and similar forms of *technological change* are also a threat to many people and cause them stress.

Organizational Factors   There is no shortage of factors within an organization that can cause stress. Pressures to avoid errors or complete tasks in a limited time, work overload, a demanding and insensitive boss, and unpleasant co-workers are a few examples. We've categorized these factors around task, role, and interpersonal demands.[64]

Task demands relate to a person's job. They include the design of the job (its degrees of autonomy, task variety, degree of automation), working conditions, and the physical work layout. Assembly lines can put pressure on people when they perceive the line's speed to be excessive. Working in an overcrowded room or a visible location where noise and interruptions are constant can increase anxiety and stress.[65] As customer service grows ever more important, emotional labor becomes a source of stress.[66] Imagine being a flight attendant for Southwest Airlines or a cashier at Starbucks. Do you think you could put on a happy face when you're having a bad day?

Role demands relate to pressures placed on a person as a function of the particular role he or she plays in the organization. Role conflicts create expectations that may be hard to reconcile or satisfy. Role overload occurs when the employee is expected to do more than time permits. Role ambiguity means role expectations are not clearly understood and the employee is not sure what to do. Individuals who face high situational constraints (such as fixed work hours or demanding job responsibilities) are also less able to engage in the proactive coping behaviors that reduce stress levels.[67] When faced with hassles at work,

Task demands are organizational factors that can cause stress. These call center employees of Encore Capital Group in Gurgaon, India, have the difficult job of collecting mostly credit card and auto debts of Americans. The nature of their job can cause stress, as the people they call may be abusive, emotional, frustrated, sad, or angry. Encore strives to reduce the on-the-job stress of its call center workers by teaching them how to empathize with the delinquent borrowers and how to handle verbal abuse. Collectors learn that the debtors respond to them when they are very polite and respectful and never raise their voice.

Source: Zack Canepari /The New York Times /Redux Pictures.

they will not only have higher levels of distress at the time, but they'll also be less likely to take steps to eliminate stressors in the future.

Interpersonal demands are pressures created by other employees. Lack of social support from colleagues and poor interpersonal relationships can cause stress, especially among employees with a high social need. A rapidly growing body of research has also shown that negative co-worker and supervisor behaviors, including fights, bullying, incivility, racial harassment, and sexual harassment, are especially strongly related to stress at work.[68]

Personal Factors   The typical individual works about 40 to 50 hours a week. But the experiences and problems people encounter in the other 120-plus can spill over to the job. Our final category, then, is factors in the employee's personal life: family issues, personal economic problems, and inherent personality characteristics.

National surveys consistently show people hold *family* and personal relationships dear. Marital difficulties, the breaking of a close relationship, and discipline troubles with children create stresses employees often can't leave at the front door when they arrive at work.[69]

Regardless of income level—people who make $100,000 per year seem to have as much trouble handling their finances as those who earn $20,000—some people are poor money managers or have wants that exceed their earning capacity. The *economic* problems of overextended financial resources create stress and siphon attention away from work.

Studies in three diverse organizations found that participants who reported stress symptoms before beginning a job accounted for most of the variance in stress symptoms reported 9 months later.[70] The researchers concluded that some people may have an inherent tendency to accentuate negative aspects of the world. If this is true, then a significant individual factor that influences stress is a person's basic disposition. That is, stress symptoms expressed on the job may actually originate in the person's *personality*.

Stressors Are Additive   When we review stressors individually, it's easy to overlook that stress is an additive phenomenon—it builds up.[71] Each new and persistent stressor adds to an individual's stress level. So a single stressor may be relatively unimportant in and of itself, but if added to an already high level of stress, it can be the straw that breaks the camel's back. To appraise the total amount of stress an individual is under, we have to sum up his or her opportunity stresses, constraint stresses, and demand stresses.

Individual Differences

Some people thrive on stressful situations, while others are overwhelmed by them. What differentiates people in terms of their ability to handle stress? What individual variables moderate the relationship between *potential* stressors and *experienced* stress? At least four—perception, job experience, social support, and personality—are relevant.

In Chapter 6, we demonstrated that employees react in response to their perception of reality, rather than to reality itself. *Perception,* therefore, will moderate the relationship between a potential stress condition and an employee's reaction to it. Layoffs may cause one person to fear losing his job, while another sees an opportunity to get a large severance allowance and start her own business. So stress potential doesn't lie in objective conditions; rather, it lies in an employee's interpretation of those conditions.

Experience on the job tends to be negatively related to work stress. Why? Two explanations have been offered.[72] First is selective withdrawal. Voluntary turnover is more probable among people who experience more stress. Therefore, people who remain with an organization longer are those with more stress-resistant traits or those more resistant to the stress characteristics of their organization. Second, people eventually develop coping mechanisms to deal with stress. Because this takes time, senior members of the organization are more likely to be fully adapted and should experience less stress.

Social support—collegial relationships with co-workers or supervisors—can buffer the impact of stress.[73] This is among the best-documented relationships in the stress literature. Social support acts as a palliative, mitigating the negative effects of even high-strain jobs.

Perhaps the most widely studied *personality* trait in stress is neuroticism, which we discussed in Chapter 5. As you might expect, neurotic individuals are more prone to experience psychological strain.[74] Evidence suggests that neurotic individuals are more prone to believe there are stressors in their work environments, so part of the problem is that they believe their environments are more threatening. They also tend to select less adaptive coping mechanisms, relying on avoidance as a way of dealing with problems rather than attempting to resolve them.[75]

Workaholism is another personal characteristic related to stress levels. Workaholics are people obsessed with their work; they put in an enormous number of hours, think about work even when not working, and create additional work responsibilities to satisfy an inner compulsion to work more. In some ways, they might seem like ideal employees. That's probably why when most people are asked in interviews what their greatest weakness is, they reflexively say, "I just work too hard." However, there is a difference between working hard and working compulsively. Workaholics are not necessarily more productive than other employees, despite their extreme efforts. The strain of putting in such a high level of work effort eventually begins to wear on the workaholic, leading to higher levels of work–life conflict and psychological burnout.[76]

Cultural Differences

Research suggests the job conditions that cause stress show some differences across cultures. One study revealed that whereas U.S. employees were stressed by a lack of control, Chinese employees were stressed by job evaluations and lack of training. It doesn't appear that personality effects on stress are different across cultures, however. One study of employees in Hungary, Italy, the United Kingdom, Israel, and the United States found Type A personality traits (see Chapter 5) predicted stress equally well across countries.[77] A study of 5,270 managers from 20 countries found individuals from individualistic countries such as the United States, Canada, and the United Kingdom experienced higher levels of stress due to work interfering with family than did individuals from collectivist countries in Asia and Latin America.[78] The authors proposed that this may occur because, in collectivist cultures, working extra hours is seen as a sacrifice to help the family, whereas in individualistic cultures, work is seen as a means to personal achievement that takes away from the family.

Evidence suggests that stressors are associated with perceived stress and strains among employees in different countries. In other words, stress is equally bad for employees of all cultures.[79]

SELF-ASSESSMENT LIBRARY

How Stressful Is My Life?

In the Self-Assessment Library (available on CD and online), take assessment III.C.2 (How Stressful Is My Life?).

Consequences of Stress

6   Identify the consequences of stress.

Stress shows itself in a number of ways, such as high blood pressure, ulcers, irritability, difficulty making routine decisions, loss of appetite, accident proneness, and the like. These symptoms fit under three general categories: physiological, psychological, and behavioral symptoms.

Physiological Symptoms   Most early concern with stress was directed at physiological symptoms because most researchers were specialists in the health and medical sciences. Their work led to the conclusion that stress could create changes in metabolism, increase heart and breathing rates and blood pressure, bring on headaches, and induce heart attacks.

Evidence now clearly suggests stress may have harmful physiological effects. One study linked stressful job demands to increased susceptibility to upper-respiratory illnesses and poor immune system functioning, especially for individuals with low self-efficacy.[80] A long-term study conducted in the United Kingdom found that job strain was associated with higher levels of coronary heart disease.[81] Still another study conducted with Danish human services workers found that higher levels of psychological burnout at the work-unit level were related to significantly higher levels of sickness absence.[82] Many other studies have shown similar results linking work stress to a variety of indicators of poor health.

Psychological Symptoms   Job dissatisfaction is "the simplest and most obvious psychological effect" of stress.[83] But stress shows itself in other psychological states—for instance, tension, anxiety, irritability, boredom, and procrastination. For example, a study that tracked physiological responses of employees over time found that stress due to high workloads was related to higher blood pressure and lower emotional well-being.[84]

An Ethical Choice

Responsibly Managing Your Own Stress

Although much of the research we've reviewed in this chapter discusses how organizations and managers can relieve stress for employees, employees also have a certain degree of responsibility for managing their own stress. Beyond the fact that high levels of stress are unpleasant, employees who experience them have difficulty concentrating at work, make more mistakes, miss more days of work, and use more health insurance. This suggests that it may be your ethical responsibility as an employee to ensure your stress levels are not high enough to interfere with your ability to work effectively for clients, customers, and co-workers. A few examples of strategies you might want to employ to reduce your level of stress from work include the following:

1. **Take breaks.**   If you're feeling depleted or exhausted at work, taking some time away from your tasks can significantly reduce your level of psychological strain.

2. **Let your supervisor know you're stressed.**   In many cases, managers will want to provide assistance to workers who are experiencing stress, but if they don't know there's a problem, they can't help to address it.

3. **Detach yourself from work in your off-time.**   Try not to take work home with you, and make your time off a period when you can truly recover from the strains of the day. Research shows that workers who can detach themselves from their work in their off-time experience significantly less stress than those who do not.

Sources: Based on M. M. Krischer, L. M. Penney, and E. M. Hunter, "Can Counterproductive Work Behaviors Be Productive? CWB as Emotion-Focused Coping," *Journal of Occupational Health Psychology* 15, no 2 (2010), pp. 154–166; V. C. Hahn, C. Binnewies, S. Sonnentag, and E. J. Mojza, "Learning How to Recover from Job Stress: Effects of a Recovery Training Program on Recovery, Recovery Related Self-Efficacy, and Well-Being," *Journal of Occupational Health Psychology* 16, no. 2 (2011), pp. 202–216; and S. Sonnentag, C. Binnewies, and E. J. Mojza, "Staying Well and Engaged when Demands Are High: The Role of Psychological Detachment," *Journal of Applied Psychology* 95, no. 5 (2010), pp. 965–976.

Jobs that make multiple and conflicting demands or that lack clarity about the incumbent's duties, authority, and responsibilities increase both stress and dissatisfaction.[85] Similarly, the less control people have over the pace of their work, the greater their stress and dissatisfaction. Jobs that provide a low level of variety, significance, autonomy, feedback, and identity appear to create stress and reduce satisfaction and involvement in the job.[86] Not everyone reacts to autonomy in the same way, however. For those with an external locus of control, increased job control increases the tendency to experience stress and exhaustion.[87]

Behavioral Symptoms Research on behavior and stress has been conducted across several countries and over time, and the relationships appear relatively consistent. Behavior-related stress symptoms include reductions in productivity, absence, and turnover, as well as changes in eating habits, increased smoking or consumption of alcohol, rapid speech, fidgeting, and sleep disorders.[88]

A significant amount of research has investigated the stress–performance relationship. The most widely studied pattern of this relationship is the inverted U shown in Exhibit 18-9.[89] The logic underlying the figure is that low to moderate levels of stress stimulate the body and increase its ability to react. Individuals then often perform their tasks better, more intensely, or more rapidly. But too much stress places unattainable demands on a person, which result in lower performance. In spite of the popularity and intuitive appeal of the inverted-U model, it doesn't get a lot of empirical support.[90] So we should be careful of assuming it accurately depicts the stress–performance relationship.

As we mentioned earlier, researchers have begun to differentiate challenge and hindrance stressors, showing that these two forms of stress have opposite effects on job behaviors, especially job performance. A meta-analysis of responses from more than 35,000 individuals showed role ambiguity, role conflict, role overload, job insecurity, environmental uncertainty, and situational constraints were all consistently negatively related to job performance.[91] There is also evidence that challenge stress improves job performance in a supportive work environment, whereas hindrance stress reduces job performance in all work environments.[92]

7 Contrast the individual and organizational approaches to managing stress.

Managing Stress

Because low to moderate levels of stress can be functional and lead to higher performance, management may not be concerned when employees experience

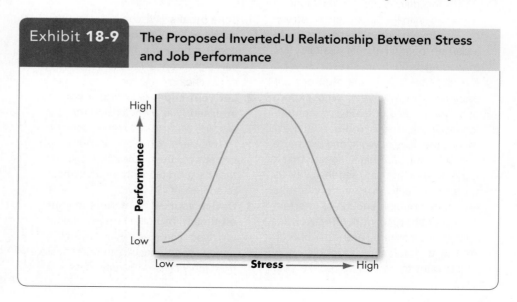

| Exhibit **18-9** | The Proposed Inverted-U Relationship Between Stress and Job Performance |

them. Employees, however, are likely to perceive even low levels of stress as undesirable. It's not unlikely, therefore, for employees and management to have different notions of what constitutes an acceptable level of stress on the job. What management may consider to be "a positive stimulus that keeps the adrenaline running" is very likely to be seen as "excessive pressure" by the employee. Keep this in mind as we discuss individual and organizational approaches toward managing stress.[93]

Individual Approaches   An employee can take personal responsibility for reducing stress levels. Individual strategies that have proven effective include time-management techniques, increased physical exercise, relaxation training, and expanded social support networks. Also see the Ethical Choice box in this chapter for additional suggestions.

Many people manage their time poorly. The well-organized employee, like the well-organized student, can often accomplish twice as much as the person who is poorly organized. So an understanding and utilization of basic time-management principles can help individuals better cope with tensions created by job demands.[94] A few of the best-known time-management principles are (1) making daily lists of activities to be accomplished, (2) prioritizing activities by importance and urgency, (3) scheduling activities according to the priorities set, (4) knowing your daily cycle and handling the most demanding parts of your job when you are most alert and productive, and (5) avoiding electronic distractions like frequently checking e-mail, which can limit attention and reduce efficiency.[95] These time-management skills can help minimize procrastination by focusing efforts on immediate goals and boosting motivation even in the face of tasks that are less desirable.[96]

Physicians have recommended noncompetitive *physical exercise*, such as aerobics, walking, jogging, swimming, and riding a bicycle, as a way to deal with excessive stress levels. These activities increase lung capacity, lower the at-rest heart rate, and provide a mental diversion from work pressures, effectively reducing work-related levels of stress.[97]

Individuals can also teach themselves to reduce tension through *relaxation techniques* such as meditation, hypnosis, and deep breathing. The objective is to reach a state of deep physical relaxation, in which you focus all your energy on release

This group of Chinese working women participate in a yoga class in Beijing as a way to deal with excessive stress levels caused by long working hours and trying to achieve a work/life balance. Working women in China have high levels of stress because in Chinese culture women are expected to take more responsibility for family matters than in other cultures. As an individual approach to managing stress, yoga is a noncompetitive physical exercise that combines stretching, mental imagery, breathing control, physical postures, and meditation. Yoga reduces stress, anxiety, and muscle tension, provides a mental diversion from work pressures, and promotes physical well-being by lowering blood pressure and heart rate.

Source: AFP Photo/Getty Images/Newscom.

Work–Family Stress in Different Cultures

Studies repeatedly show that conflicts between work life and nonwork life, especially conflicts between work and family responsibilities, are significant stressors. Examples of work–life conflicts include nights and weekends spent at work rather than with family, work schedules so full that vacations cannot happen, and work obligations that require arranging for child care at the last minute. As we noted in Chapter 17, many organizations have experimented with policies like flexible scheduling or working from home to reduce work–life conflicts and help employees reduce their levels of stress. The question is, do these policies have the same effects in different cultures, which have different values and norms regarding family and life responsibilities?

Reviewers have critiqued the literature on strain related to work–life conflict for failing to take culture into account. And, in fact, the great majority of studies on stress due to work–life conflict have been conducted entirely within the United States. Research that included multiple cultures suggests that collectivist cultures have lower levels of work–life conflict because collectivists are more likely to obtain social support from others. Differences in cultural expectations for men and women in different cultures also mean that women in some countries will experience greater work–life conflict because they have more responsibilities in the family domain, whereas in more egalitarian cultures men and women will experience similar levels of work–life conflict.

Do these cultural differences mean organizations should use different policies to combat work–life conflicts? One study of nearly 25,000 IBM employees in 75 countries investigated how policies like flexibility about where and when work is performed were related to employee stress levels. The results clearly showed that both forms of flexibility (such as work-at-home arrangements and flexible schedules) were linked to lower levels of work–life conflict in affluent and developing countries in the East and the West. In other words, it appears that flexible scheduling can help reduce employee stress levels around the world. This is good news for organizations attempting to develop policies and procedures that apply equally to all their employees.

Sources: Based on E. J. Hill, J. J. Erickson, E. K. Holmes, and M. Ferris, "Workplace Flexibility, Work Hours, and Work-Life Conflict: Finding an Extra Day or Two," *Journal of Family Psychology* 24, no. 3 (2010), pp. 349–358; and G. N. Powell, A. M. Francesco, and Y. Ling, "Toward Culture-Sensitive Theories of the Work-Family Interface," *Journal of Organizational Behavior* 30, no. 5 (2009), pp. 597–616.

of muscle tension.[98] Deep relaxation for 15 or 20 minutes a day releases strain and provides a pronounced sense of peacefulness, as well as significant changes in heart rate, blood pressure, and other physiological factors. A growing body of research shows that simply taking breaks from work at routine intervals can facilitate psychological recovery and reduce stress significantly and may improve job performance, and these effects are even greater if relaxation techniques are employed.[99]

As we have noted, friends, family, or work colleagues can provide an outlet when stress levels become excessive. Expanding your *social support network* provides someone to hear your problems and offer a more objective perspective on a stressful situation than your own.

Organizational Approaches   Several organizational factors that cause stress—particularly task and role demands—are controlled by management and thus can be modified or changed. Strategies to consider include improved employee selection and job placement, training, realistic goal-setting, redesign of jobs, increased employee involvement, improved organizational communication, employee sabbaticals, and corporate wellness programs.

Certain jobs are more stressful than others but, as we've seen, individuals differ in their response to stressful situations. We know individuals with little experience or an external locus of control tend to be more prone to stress. *Selection and placement* decisions should take these facts into consideration. Obviously, management shouldn't restrict hiring to only experienced individuals with an internal locus, but such individuals may adapt better to high-stress jobs and perform those jobs more effectively. Similarly, *training* can increase an individual's self-efficacy and thus lessen job strain.

We discussed *goal-setting* in Chapter 7. Individuals perform better when they have specific and challenging goals and receive feedback on their progress toward these goals. Goals can reduce stress as well as provide motivation.[100] Employees who are highly committed to their goals and see purpose in their jobs experience less stress because they are more likely to perceive stressors as challenges rather than hindrances. Specific goals perceived as attainable clarify performance expectations. In addition, goal feedback reduces uncertainties about actual job performance. The result is less employee frustration, role ambiguity, and stress.

Redesigning jobs to give employees more responsibility, more meaningful work, more autonomy, and increased feedback can reduce stress because these factors give employees greater control over work activities and lessen dependence on others. But as we noted in our discussion of work design, not all employees want enriched jobs. The right redesign for employees with a low need for growth might be less responsibility and increased specialization. If individuals prefer structure and routine, reducing skill variety should also reduce uncertainties and stress levels.

Role stress is detrimental to a large extent because employees feel uncertain about goals, expectations, how they'll be evaluated, and the like. By giving these employees a voice in the decisions that directly affect their job performance, management can increase employee control and reduce role stress. Thus, managers should consider *increasing employee involvement* in decision making, because evidence clearly shows that increases in employee empowerment reduce psychological strain.[101]

Increasing formal *organizational communication* with employees reduces uncertainty by lessening role ambiguity and role conflict. Given the importance that perceptions play in moderating the stress–response relationship, management can also use effective communications as a means to shape employee perceptions. Remember that what employees categorize as demands, threats, or opportunities at work is an interpretation and that interpretation can be affected by the symbols and actions communicated by management.

Some employees need an occasional escape from the frenetic pace of their work. Companies including Genentech, American Express, Intel, General Mills, Microsoft, Morningstar, DreamWorks Animation, and Adobe Systems have begun to provide extended voluntary leaves.[102] These *sabbaticals*—ranging in length from a few weeks to several months—allow employees to travel, relax, or pursue personal projects that consume time beyond normal vacations. Proponents say they can revive and rejuvenate workers who might otherwise be headed for burnout.

Our final suggestion is organizationally supported **wellness programs**. These typically provide workshops to help people quit smoking, control alcohol use, lose weight, eat better, and develop a regular exercise program; they focus on the employee's total physical and mental condition.[103] Some help employees improve their psychological health as well. A meta-analysis of 36 programs designed to reduce stress (including wellness programs) showed that interventions to help employees reframe stressful situations and use active coping strategies appreciably reduced stress levels.[104] Most wellness programs assume employees need to take personal responsibility for their physical and mental health and that the organization is merely a means to that end.

wellness programs *Organizationally supported programs that focus on the employee's total physical and mental condition.*

Cindy Russell poses with her assembled gear in preparation for a one-month sabbatical to go fly fishing in the South Pacific. Russell is a paralegal with the law firm Alters, Boldt, Brown, Rash, and Culmo in Miami. Like many small companies, the law firm does not have a formal sabbatical program. But Russell approached her boss with the idea, saying that she worked long hours in preparing for trials and desired a longer time away from work than her vacation time allowed. She explained how the fishing trip would help her to decompress and return to work energized and refreshed. Russell was granted the leave, some of it unpaid, after convincing her boss how it would benefit both her and the firm.

Source: C.W. Griffin/Miami Herald/MCT/Newscom.

Most firms that have introduced wellness programs have found significant benefits. A study of eight Canadian organizations found that every dollar spent on comprehensive wellness programs generated a return of $1.64, and for high-risk employees, such as smokers, the return was nearly $4.00.[105]

MyManagementLab

Now that you have finished this chapter, go back to **www.pearsonglobaleditions.com/ mymanagementlab** to continue practicing and applying the concepts you've learned.

Summary and Implications for Managers

The need for change has been implied throughout this text. "A casual reflection on change should indicate that it encompasses almost all of our concepts in the organizational behavior literature."[106] For instance, think about attitudes, motivation, work teams, communication, leadership, organizational structures, human resource practices, and organizational cultures. Change was an integral part in our discussion of each. If environments were perfectly static, if employees' skills and abilities were always up to date and incapable of deteriorating, and if tomorrow were always exactly the same as today, organizational change would have little or no relevance to managers. But the real world is turbulent, requiring organizations and their members to undergo dynamic change if they are to perform at competitive levels.

- Managers are the primary change agents in most organizations. By the decisions they make and their role-modeling behaviors, they shape the organization's change culture.

Responsible Managers Relieve Stress on Their Employees

One of the reasons the economic recovery has been sluggish is that employers have been reluctant to replace those they laid off. If you can produce the same amount or provide the same service with fewer employees, that's efficient, of course. But is it a short-sighted way to manage? Evidence suggests that employees are at their breaking point—and employers will pay a price just like the employees they are stressing.

Employees are really stressed. More work is being done with fewer people. Workers wonder whether they will be the "next shoe to fall" in layoffs. In a recent survey of managers, 81 percent agreed worker stress and fatigue is a greater problem than in the past.

Says one Sacramento, California, employee, "I can't remember the last time I went out for lunch. I bring my lunch and eat at my desk," she says. She can't even complain to her husband, since he's the same boat—working 10-hour days and "coming home late and exhausted."

Some employers are long-sighted enough to address the problem.

Tony Schwartz, CEO of a consulting firm, decided to institute a program he called "Take Back Your Lunch." He encourages his employees to take a lunch break and even urges them to organize midday gatherings with social networking site Meetup .com.

Another company with progressive management is the accounting firm Ernst & Young. Of the company's 23,000 employees, about 10 percent work under flexible arrangements where they can work less or adopt a more flexible schedule during nonpeak times.

These companies have found that taking the long view and emphasizing balance helps good employees be more productive over the long-term—and more likely to stick around. "We listen to our people and they tell us very consistently that flexibility in incredibly important to them and to their family," said James Turley, Ernst & Young's CEO.

It is not hard to find employees who think they're overworked and underpaid. If a company managed according to worker complaints, the squeakiest wheel would always get the grease. Sure, people might work fewer hours and feel less stressed, but that would compromise an organization's ability to be competitive and to reward its hardest-working and most productive employees.

Labor is often the largest single cost for an employer, which means that if it is to be competitive, the firm needs to earn more revenue per employee. It doesn't take a math genius to realize that one way of accomplishing that is to pay attention to the denominator. It's that magical thing we call "productivity," a central metric by which we can measure the organization's performance. Organizations that are productive today enjoy higher earnings later.

Take Deutsche Bank as an example. The number of front-office employees in Deutsche Bank's investment banking division has fallen 12 percent from pre-crisis levels, while net revenue per employee has increased 20 percent. That sounds like a well-managed company, doesn't it? Yet Deutsche Bank employees probably do feel they're working harder. They are. What would you think of a company if the story instead was, "Net revenue per employee has fallen 20 percent, but employees feel much less stressed at work"? We don't live in a world where companies have the luxury of doing less with more.

Managers shouldn't go out of their way to stress out their employees. Nor should they turn a blind eye toward burnout. But realistically, in today's globally competitive business environment, the organizations that will survive are those that can do more with less. If that means employees are stressed by higher workloads, well, it beats the unemployment line, doesn't it?

Sources: S. Greenhouse, "The Retention Bonus? Time," *The New York Times* (January 8, 2011), pp. B1, B7; M. V. Rafter, "The Yawning of a New Era," *Workforce Management* (December 2010), pp. 3–4; and M. Turner, "Deutsche Says It Does More with Less," *Financial News* (June 2, 2011), downloaded on July 19, 2011, from www.efinancialnews.com/.

- Management decisions related to structural design, cultural factors, and human resource policies largely determine the level of innovation within the organization.
- Management policies and practices will determine the degree to which the organization learns and adapts to changing environmental factors.
- The existence of work stress, in and of itself, need not imply lower performance. The evidence indicates that stress can be either a positive or a negative influence on employee performance.
- Low to moderate amounts of stress enable many people to perform their jobs better by increasing their work intensity, alertness, and ability to react. This is especially true if stress arises due to challenges on the job rather than hindrances that prevent employees from doing their jobs effectively.
- However, a high level of stress, or even a moderate amount sustained over a long period, eventually takes its toll, and performance declines.

QUESTIONS FOR REVIEW

1 What forces act as stimulants to change, and what is the difference between planned and unplanned change?

2 What forces act as sources of resistance to change?

3 What are the four main approaches to managing organizational change?

4 How can managers create a culture for change?

5 What is stress, and what are the possible sources of stress?

6 What are the consequences of stress?

7 What are the individual and organizational approaches to managing stress?

EXPERIENTIAL EXERCISE Power and the Changing Environment

Objectives

1. To describe the forces for change influencing power differentials in organizational and interpersonal relationships.

2. To understand the effect of technological, legal/political, economic, and social changes on the power of individuals within an organization.

The Situation

Your organization manufactures golf carts and sells them to country clubs, golf courses, and consumers. Your team is faced with the task of assessing how environmental changes will affect individuals' organizational power. Read each of the five scenarios and then, for each, identify the five members in the organization whose power will increase most in light of the environmental condition(s). [*Note:* m = male, (f) = female.]

Accountant/CPA (m)

Advertising expert (m)

Chemist (m)

Chief financial officer (f)

Computer programmer (f)

Corporate trainer (m)

General manager (m)

Human resource manager (f)

Industrial engineer (m)

In-house counsel (m)

Marketing manager (f)

Operations manager (f)

Product designer (m)

Public relations expert (m)

Securities analyst (m)

1. New computer-aided manufacturing technologies are being introduced in the workplace during the next 2 to 18 months.

2. New federal emission standards are being legislated by the government that will essentially make gas-powered golf carts (40 percent of your current business) obsolete.

3. Sales are way down for two reasons: (a) a decline in the number of individuals playing golf and (b) your competitor was faster to embrace lithium batteries, which allow golf carts to run longer without another charge.

4. Given the growth of golf courses in other places (especially India, China, and Southeast Asia), the company is planning to go international in the next 12 to 18 months.

5. The U.S. Equal Employment Opportunity Commission is applying pressure to balance the male–female population in the organization's upper hierarchy by threatening to publicize the predominance of men in upper management.

The Procedure

1. Divide the class into teams of three to four students each.

2. Teams should read each scenario and identify the five members whose power will increase most in light of the external environmental conditions described.

3. Teams should then address this question: assuming that the five environmental changes are taking place at once, which five members of the organization will now have the most power?

4. After 20 to 30 minutes, representatives of each team will be selected to present and justify their conclusions to the entire class. Discussion will begin with scenario 1 and proceed through scenario 5 and the "all at once" scenario.

Source: Adapted from J. E. Barbuto Jr., "Power and the Changing Environment," *Journal of Management Education* (April 2000), pp. 288–296.

ETHICAL DILEMMA Changes at WPAC

WPAC—a television station based in Yuma, Arizona—had been experiencing a ratings decline for several years. In 2009, the station switched from a CBS to NBC affiliate. That has explained some of the ratings decline. However, in recent months, the ratings have continued to slide. Eventually, the station manager, Lucien Stone, decided he had to make a change to the local newscast.

After meeting with the programming manager, Stone called a meeting of WPAC employees and announced his intention to "spice things up" during the 5 P.M. and 10 P.M. local news. The 30-minute broadcasts would still include the traditional "top stories," "sports," and "weather" segments. However, on slow news days, more attention-getting material would be used. Stone also indicated some programming decisions would probably be revisited. "The days of *Little House on the Prairie* are over," he said.

Madison Devereaux, 29, had been the chief meteorologist for WPAC since 2010. After receiving her degree in meteorology from the University of Oklahoma in 2007, she joined WPAC and quickly worked her way up the ranks, impressing viewers and WPAC management alike with her extension knowledge and articulate, professional, mistake-free delivery.

Though she was Christian, Devereaux never was one to go around "thumping Bibles in the newsroom," as she put it. Most of those at WPAC weren't even aware of Madison's religious views.

Devereaux was troubled by the announced changes to WPAC's programming but didn't speak up at the time. One Monday during a pre-production meeting, she learned that on Thursday of that week, WPAC reporter Sam Berkshow would present a segment called "Dancing Around the Economy," which would focus on how local strip clubs were doing well despite the sluggish economy.

Devereaux didn't think it was appropriate to air the segment during the 5 P.M. newcast and asked both her producer and Stone to reconsider the piece, or at least air it in the 10 P.M. time slot. When they refused, she asked whether she could take the day off when the segment aired. Stone again refused. This was "sweeps week" (when ratings are calculated), Stone wanted to air the story now, and Devereaux's contract prohibited her from taking time off during sweeps week.

When Devereaux didn't show up for work that Thursday, WPAC fired her, arguing she had breached her contract.

For her part, Devereaux said, "I'm not angry with the station, but I am sorry about the changes that have taken place."

Questions

1. Do you think either party behaved unethically in this case?

2. If you shared Devereaux's views, would you have handled the situation differently? How?

3. Drawing on Kotter's eight-step plan for implementing change, how might WPAC have handled its planned change differently?

Sources: Based on C. Edelhart, "Weatherman's Stand Against Story Costs Job," *Californian* (May 16, 2011), downloaded July 7, 2011, from www.bakersfield.com/; and K. T. Phan, "ABC Affiliate Fires Christian over Strip Club Segment," *Fox News* (May 10, 2011), www.nation.foxnews.com.

CASE INCIDENT 1   Starbucks Returns to Its Roots

You are probably so used to seeing Starbucks coffee shops everywhere that you might not realize the company went from just 11 stores in 1987 to 2,600 in the year 2000. This incredibly rapid growth sprang from the company's ability to create a unique experience for customers who wanted to buy its distinct brand of lattes and mochas wherever they found themselves. At Starbucks' core, there was also a culture of treating each customer as a valued guest who should feel comfortable relaxing and taking in the ambience of the store. Whether you were in the company's founding location in Seattle, Washington, or at the other end of the country in Miami, Florida, you knew what to expect when you went to a Starbucks.

This uniform culture was truly put to the test in the face of massive expansion, however, and by 2006 Starbucks' chairman and former CEO Howard Schultz knew something had gone wrong. He noted that "As I visited hundreds of Starbucks stores in cities around the world, the entrepreneurial merchant in me sensed that something intrinsic to Starbucks' brand was missing. An aura. A spirit. The stores were lacking a certain soul." Starbucks' performance had become lackluster, with hundreds of planned store openings being canceled and hundreds more stores being closed.

So, Schultz took the dramatic step of coming back as CEO and engaging in a companywide effort to change the corporate culture back to what it had been before its expansion. All 7,000 Starbucks stores were closed for a single afternoon as part of a training effort of 135,000 baristas. Quality control was a primary mission; baristas were instructed to pour every glass of espresso like honey from a spoon, to preserve the flavor. This emphasis on quality over speed ran counter to the principles of mass production, but it was just what the company needed to ensure it could retain its culture. Espresso machines that obscured the customers' view were replaced with lower-profile machines that allowed baristas to look directly at guests while making beverages. And "assembly-line production," like making several drinks at once, was discouraged in favor of slowly making each drink for each customer.

Schultz is convinced his efforts to take the culture back to its roots as a neighborhood coffee shop—one entranced with the "romance of coffee" and treating every customer as an old friend—has saved the company. Today, Starbucks earns more than $10 billion in annual revenue and serves more than 50 million customers a week around the globe.

Questions

1. What factors are most likely to change when a company grows very rapidly, as Starbucks did? How can these changes threaten the culture of an organization?

2. Why might this type of radical change process be easier for Starbucks to implement than it would be for other companies?

3. A great deal of the return to an original culture has been credited to Howard Schultz, who acted as an idea champion. Explain how Schultz's efforts to change the Starbucks culture fit with our discussion of culture change earlier in the chapter.

4. Schultz's change initiative might succeed at another company that values customization and high levels of customer service, but how would it need to differ at a firm that emphasizes speed and efficiency of service?

Sources: Based on H. Schultz, "How Starbucks Got Its Mojo Back," *Newsweek,* (March 21, 2011), www .newsweek.com; A. Ignatius, "We Had to Own the Mistakes," *Harvard Business Review* (July/August 2010), pp. 108–115; and R. Baker, "Starbucks Demonstrates Power of Brand," *Marketing Week* (April 28, 2011), www.marketingweek.co.uk.

CASE INCIDENT 2   Embracing Change Through Operational Leadership

From a Lebanese family-owned small business to a leading multi-line conglomerate in the Middle East and North Africa (MENA) region, Khalil Fattal & Fils (KFF) Holding (www.kff.com.lb) is the exclusive agent and distributor of many multinational brands within the following categories: food and beverages, home and personal care, beauty and accessories, household and office equipment, consumer electronics, and pharmaceuticals. The corporation now employs more than 2,100 individuals with a turnover of approximately US$650 million.

Over the course of 114 years (1897–2011), the corporation has gone through many successful structural changes that have shaped the business and contributed to its success. At the base of this success is the owners' philosophy, which drove the corporation toward its vision and instilled solid corporate values that have increased performance and created a spirit of unity among its members.

At the beginning of 2002, the owners gathered 30 of their top managers in a retreat to define the corporate culture in the coming years. The team succeeded in drafting a mission that enlarged the scope of the corporation's activities to "reach out to millions of consumers in the Levant and North African countries." (The Levant is comprised of Lebanon, Syria, Jordan, and Iraq.) The team also adopted a set of corporate values that were disseminated to all other employees through workshops and group discussions.

The corporation's core values revolve around trust, respect, sharing, and courage, with a specific set of expected behaviors for each value. Under the value of courage, embracing change was selected as the main behavior for individuals who aspire to succeed in their careers with the group. This is now stated in the corporate manual as "embrace change as an opportunity to grow," and employees are invited to accept rotation in their assignments every four to five years, or whenever needed, not only in Lebanon but also throughout the region where the corporation operates.

To conduct business in the MENA region, it is a legal requirement that local partners and employees be engaged. Hence, to ensure the operation's success, the corporation decided to relocate part of the management team to its subsidiaries in Syria, Jordan, Iraq, Sudan, Algeria, and Egypt. Although these countries share a common language (Arabic) with Lebanon, their social, economic, and political systems differ. As a result, some managers were reluctant to relocate outside their home country. This became a major obstacle that needed to be resolved.

To overcome this impediment, the KFF's CEO took the initiative and moved ahead of everyone else to ensure a satisfactory setup and even asked some members of his family to accept these new foreign assignments, thereby setting the example for others to follow suit, and many managers did. To further motivate these managers, an attractive financial package was offered, including fringe benefits such as housing, schooling for children, expatriate allowances, and longer vacations. This rotational path has since become part of KFF management's recognized fast track for career progression within the group.

KFF's expansion throughout the region exposed the corporation to new kinds of customers, such as hypermarket chains. This necessitated a change in the business model, which required new knowledge and techniques and raised awareness of the need to enhance employee skills. Accordingly, the corporation took the initiative and provided employees with intensive training and workshops aimed at improving the competences and skills of its workforce. As a result, it was better able to meet the expectations of its customers and suppliers alike.

Questions
1. What were the forces that necessitated change in the organization?
2. Why is it so difficult for individuals to accept change?
3. What were the forces that helped make the change process smoother?

Sources: KFF Holding Manual. Special thanks to Samir Messarra for his valuable suggestions.

ENDNOTES
1. See, for instance, J. Birkinshaw, G. Hamel, and M. J. Mol, "Management Innovation," *Academy of Management Review* 33, no. 4 (2008), pp. 825–845; and J. Welch and S. Welch, "What Change Agents Are Made Of," *BusinessWeek* (October 20, 2008), p. 96.
2. C. J. Loomis and D. Burke, "Can Ellen Kullman Make DuPont Great Again?" *Fortune* (May 3, 2010), pp. 156–163.
3. P. G. Audia and S. Brion, "Reluctant to Change: Self-Enhancing Responses to Diverging Performance Measures," *Organizational Behavior and Human Decision Processes* 102 (2007), pp. 255–269.
4. M. Fugate, A. J. Kinicki, and G. E. Prussia, "Employee Coping with Organizational Change: An Examination of Alternative Theoretical Perspectives and Models," *Personnel Psychology* 61, no. 1 (2008), pp. 1–36.
5. J. D. Ford, L. W. Ford, and A. D'Amelio, "Resistance to Change: The Rest of the Story," *Academy of Management Review* 33, no. 2 (2008), pp. 362–377.
6. M. T. Hannan, L. Pólos, and G. R. Carroll, "The Fog of Change: Opacity and Asperity in Organizations," *Administrative Science Quarterly* (September 2003), pp. 399–432.
7. J. P. Kotter and L. A. Schlesinger, "Choosing Strategies for Change," *Harvard Business Review* (March–April 1979), pp. 106–114.
8. J. E. Dutton, S. J. Ashford, R. M. O'Neill, and K. A. Lawrence, "Moves That Matter: Issue Selling and Organizational Change," *Academy of Management Journal* (August 2001), pp. 716–736.
9. P. C. Fiss and E. J. Zajac, "The Symbolic Management of Strategic Change: Sensegiving via Framing and Decoupling," *Academy of Management Journal* 49, no. 6 (2006), pp. 1173–1193.
10. A. E. Rafferty and S. L. D. Restubog, "The Impact of Change Process and Context on Change Reactions and Turnover

During a Merger," *Journal of Management* 36, no. 5 (2010), pp. 1309–1338.

11. Q. N. Huy, "Emotional Balancing of Organizational Continuity and Radical Change: The Contribution of Middle Managers," *Administrative Science Quarterly* (March 2002), pp. 31–69; D. M. Herold, D. B. Fedor, and S. D. Caldwell, "Beyond Change Management: A Multilevel Investigation of Contextual and Personal Influences on Employees' Commitment to Change," *Journal of Applied Psychology* 92, no. 4 (2007), pp. 942–951; and G. B. Cunningham, "The Relationships Among Commitment to Change, Coping with Change, and Turnover Intentions," *European Journal of Work and Organizational Psychology* 15, no. 1 (2006), pp. 29–45.

12. R. Peccei, A. Giangreco, and A. Sebastiano, "The Role of Organizational Commitment in the Analysis of Resistance to Change: Co-predictor and Moderator Effects," *Personnel Review* 40, no. 2 (2011), pp. 185–204.

13. J. P. Kotter, "Leading Change: Why Transformational Efforts Fail," *Harvard Business Review* 85 (January 2007), p. 96–103.

14. K. van Dam, S. Oreg, and B. Schyns, "Daily Work Contexts and Resistance to Organisational Change: The Role of Leader-Member Exchange, Development Climate, and Change Process Characteristics," *Applied Psychology: An International Review* 57, no. 2 (2008), pp. 313–334.

15. S. Oreg and N. Sverdlik, "Ambivalence toward Imposed Change: The Conflict between Dispositional Resistance to Change and the Orientation toward the Change Agent," *Journal of Applied Psychology* 96, no. 2 (2011), pp. 337–349.

16. D. B. Fedor, S. Caldwell, and D. M. Herold, "The Effects of Organizational Changes on Employee Commitment: A Multilevel Investigation," *Personnel Psychology* 59 (2006), pp. 1–29; and R. D. Foster, "Resistance, Justice, and Commitment to Change," *Human Resource Development Quarterly* 21, no. 1 (2010), pp. 3–39.

17. S. Oreg, "Personality, Context, and Resistance to Organizational Change," *European Journal of Work and Organizational Psychology* 15, no. 1 (2006), pp. 73–101.

18. S. M. Elias, "Employee Commitment in Times of Change: Assessing the Importance of Attitudes Toward Organizational Change," *Journal of Management* 35, no. 1 (2009), pp. 37–55.

19. J. W. B. Lang and P. D. Bliese, "General Mental Ability and Two Types of Adaptation to Unforeseen Change: Applying Discontinuous Growth Models to the Task-Change Paradigm," *Journal of Applied Psychology* 94, no. 2 (2009), pp. 411–428.

20. C. O. L. H. Porter, J. W. Webb, and C. I Gogus, "When Goal Orientations Collide: Effects of Learning and Performance Orientation on Team Adaptability in Response to Workload Imbalance," *Journal of Applied Psychology* 95, no. 5 (2010), pp. 935–943.

21. See, for instance, A. Karaevli, "Performance Consequences for New CEO 'Outsiderness': Moderating Effects of Pre- and Post-Succession Contexts," *Strategic Management Journal* 28, no. 7 (2007), pp. 681–706.

22. K. Lewin, *Field Theory in Social Science* (New York: Harper & Row, 1951).

23. P. G. Audia, E. A. Locke, and K. G. Smith, "The Paradox of Success: An Archival and a Laboratory Study of Strategic Persistence Following Radical Environmental Change," *Academy of Management Journal* (October 2000), pp. 837–853; and P. G. Audia and S. Brion, "Reluctant to Change: Self-Enhancing Responses to Diverging Performance Measures,"

Organizational Behavior and Human Decision Processes 102, no. 2 (2007), pp. 255–269.

24. J. B. Sorensen, "The Strength of Corporate Culture and the Reliability of Firm Performance," *Administrative Science Quarterly* (March 2002), pp. 70–91.

25. J. Amis, T. Slack, and C. R. Hinings, "The Pace, Sequence, and Linearity of Radical Change," *Academy of Management Journal* (February 2004), pp. 15–39; and E. Autio, H. J. Sapienza, and J. G. Almeida, "Effects of Age at Entry, Knowledge Intensity, and Imitability on International Growth," *Academy of Management Journal* (October 2000), pp. 909–924.

26. J. P. Kotter, "Leading Changes: Why Transformation Efforts Fail," *Harvard Business Review* (March–April 1995), pp. 59–67; and J. P. Kotter, *Leading Change* (Harvard Business School Press, 1996).

27. See, for example, C. Eden and C. Huxham, "Action Research for the Study of Organizations," in S. R. Clegg, C. Hardy, and W. R. Nord (eds.), *Handbook of Organization Studies* (London: Sage, 1996); and L. S. Lüscher and M. W. Lewis, "Organizational Change and Managerial Sensemaking: Working Through Paradox," *Academy of Management Journal* 51, no. 2 (2008), pp. 221–240.

28. For a sampling of various OD definitions, see H. K. Sinangil and F. Avallone, "Organizational Development and Change," in N. Anderson, D. S. Ones, H. K. Sinangil, and C. Viswesvaran (eds.), *Handbook of Industrial, Work and Organizational Psychology*, vol. 2 (Thousand Oaks, CA: Sage, 2001), pp. 332–335; and R. J. Marshak and D. Grant, "Organizational Discourse and New Organization Development Practices," *British Journal of Management* 19, no. 1 (2008), pp. S7–S19.

29. See, for instance, R. Lines, "Influence of Participation in Strategic Change: Resistance, Organizational Commitment and Change Goal Achievement," *Journal of Change Management* (September 2004), pp. 193–215.

30. S. Highhouse, "A History of the T-Group and Its Early Application in Management Development," *Group Dynamics: Theory, Research, & Practice* (December 2002), pp. 277–290.

31. J. E. Edwards and M. D. Thomas, "The Organizational Survey Process: General Steps and Practical Considerations," in P. Rosenfeld, J. E. Edwards, and M. D. Thomas (eds.), *Improving Organizational Surveys: New Directions, Methods, and Applications* (Newbury Park, CA: Sage, 1993), pp. 3–28.

32. E. H. Schein, *Process Consultation: Its Role in Organizational Development*, 2nd ed. (Reading, MA: Addison-Wesley, 1988), p. 9. See also E. H. Schein, *Process Consultation Revisited: Building Helpful Relationships* (Reading, MA: Addison-Wesley, 1999).

33. Schein, *Process Consultation*.

34. W. W. G. Dyer, W. G. Dyer, and J. H. Dyer, *Team Building: Proven Strategies for Improving Team Performance* (Hoboken, NJ: Jossey-Bass, 2007).

35. U. Wagner, L. Tropp, G. Finchilescu, and C. Tredoux (Eds), *Improving Intergroup Relations* (New York: Wiley-Blackwell, 2008).

36. See, for example, R. Fry, F. Barrett, J. Seiling, and D. Whitney (eds.), *Appreciative Inquiry & Organizational Transformation: Reports from the Field* (Westport, CT: Quorum, 2002); J. K. Barge and C. Oliver, "Working with Appreciation in Managerial Practice," *Academy of Management Review* (January 2003), pp. 124–142; and D. van der Haar and D. M. Hosking, "Evaluating Appreciative Inquiry: A Relational Constructionist Perspective," *Human Relations* (August 2004), pp. 1017–1036.

37. G. Giglio, S. Michalcova, and C. Yates, "Instilling a Culture of Winning at American Express," *Organization Development Journal* 25, no. 4 (2007), pp. P33–P37.

38. A. Harrington, "Who's Afraid of a New Product?" *Fortune* (November 10, 2003), pp. 189–192; C. C. Manz, F. Shipper, and G. L. Stewart, "Everyone a Team Leader: Shared Influence at W. L. Gore and Associates," *Organizational Dynamics* 38, no. 3 (2009), pp. 239–244.

39. See, for instance, R. M. Kanter, "When a Thousand Flowers Bloom: Structural, Collective and Social Conditions for Innovation in Organizations," in B. M. Staw and L. L. Cummings (eds.), *Research in Organizational Behavior*, vol. 10 (Greenwich, CT: JAI Press, 1988), pp. 169–211.

40. F. Damanpour, "Organizational Innovation: A Meta-Analysis of Effects of Determinants and Moderators," *Academy of Management Journal* (September 1991), p. 557.

41. Ibid., pp. 555–590; and G. Westerman, F. W. McFarlan, and M. Iansiti, "Organization Design and Effectiveness over the Innovation Life Cycle," *Organization Science* 17, no. 2 (2006), pp. 230–238.

42. See P. R. Monge, M. D. Cozzens, and N. S. Contractor, "Communication and Motivational Predictors of the Dynamics of Organizational Innovation," *Organization Science* (May 1992), pp. 250–274; P. Schepers and P. T. van den Berg, "Social factors of work-environment creativity," *Journal of Business and Psychology* 21, no. 3 (2007), pp. 407–428.

43. D. L. Day, "Raising Radicals: Different Processes for Championing Innovative Corporate Ventures," *Organization Science* (May 1994), pp. 148–172; and M. E. Mullins, S. W. J. Kozlowski, N. Schmitt, and A. W. Howell, "The Role of the Idea Champion in Innovation: The Case of the Internet in the Mid-1990s," *Computers in Human Behavior* 24, no. 2 (2008), pp. 451–467.

44. Howell and Higgins, "Champions of Change." J. M. Howell and C. A. Higgins "Champions of change: Identifying, understanding, and supporting champions of technological innovations." *Organizational Dynamics* 19, (1990), pp. 40–55.

45. See S. Shane, S. Venkataraman, and I. MacMillan, "Cultural Differences in Innovation Championing Strategies," *Journal of Management* 21, no. 5 (1995), pp. 931–952.

46. A. Taylor, "Chrysler's Speed Merchant," *Fortune* (September 6, 2010), pp. 77–82.

47. See, for example, T. B. Lawrence, M. K. Mauws, B. Dyck, and R. F. Kleysen, "The Politics of Organizational Learning: Integrating Power into the 4I Framework," *Academy of Management Review* (January 2005), pp. 180–191.

48. D. H. Kim, "The Link Between Individual and Organizational Learning," *Sloan Management Review* (Fall 1993), p. 37.

49. C. Argyris and D. A. Schon, *Organizational Learning* (Reading, MA: Addison-Wesley, 1978).

50. B. Dumaine, "Mr. Learning Organization," *Fortune* (October 17, 1994), p. 148.

51. F. Kofman and P. M. Senge, "Communities of Commitment: The Heart of Learning Organizations," *Organizational Dynamics* (Autumn 1993), pp. 5–23.

52. Dumaine, "Mr. Learning Organization," p. 154.

53. See, for instance, S. Armour, "Rising Job Stress Could Affect Bottom Line," *USA Today* (July 29, 2003), p. 1B; and J. Schramm, "Work/Life on Hold," *HRMagazine* 53 (October 2008), p. 120.

54. Adapted from R. S. Schuler, "Definition and Conceptualization of Stress in Organizations," *Organizational Behavior and Human Performance* (April 1980), p. 189. For an updated review of definitions, see C. L. Cooper, P. J. Dewe, and M. P. O'Driscoll, *Organizational Stress: A Review and Critique of Theory, Research, and Applications* (Thousand Oaks, CA: Sage, 2002).

55. See, for instance, M. A. Cavanaugh, W. R. Boswell, M. V. Roehling, and J. W. Boudreau, "An Empirical Examination of Self-Reported Work Stress Among U.S. Managers," *Journal of Applied Psychology* (February 2000), pp. 65–74.

56. N. P. Podsakoff, J. A. LePine, and M. A. LePine, "Differential Challenge-Hindrance Stressor Relationships with Job Attitudes, Turnover Intentions, Turnover, and Withdrawal Behavior: A Meta-Analysis," *Journal of Applied Psychology* 92, no. 2 (2007), pp. 438–454; and J. A. LePine, M. A. LePine, and C. L. Jackson, "Challenge and Hindrance Stress: Relationships with Exhaustion, Motivation to Learn, and Learning Performance," *Journal of Applied Psychology* (October 2004), pp. 883–891.

57. L. W. Hunter and S. M. B. Thatcher, "Feeling the Heat: Effects of Stress, Commitment, and Job Experience on Job Performance," *Academy of Management Journal* 50, no. 4 (2007), pp. 953–968.

58. J. C. Wallace, B. D. Edwards, T. Arnold, M. L. Frazier, and D. M. Finch, "Work Stressors, Role-Based Performance, and the Moderating Influence of Organizational Support," *Journal of Applied Psychology* 94, no. 1 (2009), pp. 254–262.

59. N. W. Van Yperen and O. Janssen, "Fatigued and Dissatisfied or Fatigued but Satisfied? Goal Orientations and Responses to High Job Demands," *Academy of Management Journal* (December 2002), pp. 1161–1171; and N. W. Van Yperen and M. Hagedoorn, "Do High Job Demands Increase Intrinsic Motivation or Fatigue or Both? The Role of Job Control and Job Social Support," *Academy of Management Journal* (June 2003), pp. 339–348.

60. J. de Jonge and C. Dormann, "Stressors, Resources, and Strain at Work: A Longitudinal Test of the Triple-Match Principle," *Journal of Applied Psychology* 91, no. 5 (2006), pp. 1359–1374.

61. This section is adapted from C. L. Cooper and R. Payne, *Stress at Work* (London: Wiley, 1978); S. Parasuraman and J. A. Alutto, "Sources and Outcomes of Stress in Organizational Settings: Toward the Development of a Structural Model," *Academy of Management Journal* 27, no. 2 (June 1984), pp. 330–350; and P. M. Hart and C. L. Cooper, "Occupational Stress: Toward a More Integrated Framework," in N. Anderson, D. S. Ones, H. K. Sinangil, and C. Viswesvaran (eds.), *Handbook of Industrial, Work and Organizational Psychology*, vol. 2 (London: Sage, 2001), pp. 93–114.

62. A. E. Rafferty and M. A. Griffin, "Perceptions of Organizational Change: A Stress and Coping Perspective," *Journal of Applied Psychology* 71, no. 5 (2007), pp. 1154–1162.

63. H. Garst, M. Frese, and P. C. M. Molenaar, "The Temporal Factor of Change in Stressor-Strain Relationships: A Growth Curve Model on a Longitudinal Study in East Germany," *Journal of Applied Psychology* (June 2000), pp. 417–438.

64. See, for example, M. L. Fox, D. J. Dwyer, and D. C. Ganster, "Effects of Stressful Job Demands and Control of Physiological and Attitudinal Outcomes in a Hospital Setting," *Academy of Management Journal* (April 1993), pp. 289–318.

65. T. L. Smith-Jackson and K. W. Klein, "Open-Plan Offices: Task Performance and Mental Workload," *Journal of Environmental Psychology* 29, no. 2 (2009), pp. 279–289.

66. T. M. Glomb, J. D. Kammeyer-Mueller, and M. Rotundo, "Emotional Labor Demands and Compensating Wage Differentials," *Journal of Applied Psychology* (August 2004), pp. 700–714; and A. A. Grandey, "When 'The Show Must Go On': Surface Acting and Deep Acting as Determinants of Emotional Exhaustion and Peer-Rated Service Delivery," *Academy of Management Journal* (February 2003), pp. 86–96.

67. C. Fritz and S. Sonnentag, "Antecedents of Day-Level Proactive Behavior: A Look at Job Stressors and Positive Affect During the Workday," *Journal of Management* 35, no. 1 (2009), pp. 94–111.

68. S. Lim, L. M. Cortina, and V. J. Magley, "Personal and Workgroup Incivility: Impact on Work and Health Outcomes," *Journal of Applied Psychology* 93, no. 1 (2008), pp. 95–107; N. T. Buchanan, and L. F. Fitzgerald, "Effects of Racial and Sexual Harassment on Work and the Psychological Well-Being of African American Women," *Journal of Occupational Health Psychology* 13, no. 2 (2008), pp. 137–151; C. R. Willness, P. Steel, and K. Lee, "A Meta-Analysis of the Antecedents and Consequences of Workplace Sexual Harassment," *Personnel Psychology* 60, no. 1 (2007), pp. 127–162; and B. Moreno-Jiménez, A. Rodríguez-Muñoz, J. C. Pastor, A. I. Sanz-Vergel, and E. Garrosa, "The Moderating Effects of Psychological Detachment and Thoughts of Revenge in Workplace Bullying," *Personality and Individual Differences* 46, no. 3 (2009), pp. 359–364.

69. V. S. Major, K. J. Klein, and M. G. Ehrhart, "Work Time, Work Interference with Family, and Psychological Distress," *Journal of Applied Psychology* (June 2002), pp. 427–436. See also P. E. Spector, C. L. Cooper, S. Poelmans, T. D. Allen, M. O'Driscoll, J. I. Sanchez, et al., "A Cross-National Comparative Study of Work-Family Stressors, Working Hours, and Well-Being: China and Latin America Versus the Anglo World," *Personnel Psychology* (Spring 2004), pp. 119–142.

70. D. L. Nelson and C. Sutton, "Chronic Work Stress and Coping: A Longitudinal Study and Suggested New Directions," *Academy of Management Journal* (December 1990), pp. 859–869.

71. H. Selye, *The Stress of Life*, rev. ed. (New York: McGraw-Hill, 1976); and Q. Hu, W. B. Schaufeli, and T. W. Taris, "The Job Demands–Resources Model: An Analysis of Additive and Joint Effects of Demands and Resources," *Journal of Vocational Behavior* 79, no. 1 (2011), pp. 181–190.

72. S. J. Motowidlo, J. S. Packard, and M. R. Manning, "Occupational Stress: Its Causes and Consequences for Job Performance," *Journal of Applied Psychology* (November 1987), pp. 619–620; and E. R. Crawford, J. A. LePine, and B. L. Rich, "Linking Job Demands and Resources to Employee Engagement and Burnout: A Theoretical Extension and Meta-Analytic test," Journal of Applied Psychology 95, no. 5 (2010), pp. 834–848.

73. See J. B. Halbesleben, "Sources of Social Support and Burnout: A Meta-Analytic Test of the Conservation of Resources Model," *Journal of Applied Psychology* 91, no. 5 (2006), pp. 1134–1145; N. Bolger and D. Amarel, "Effects of Social Support Visibility on Adjustment to Stress: Experimental Evidence," *Journal of Applied Psychology* 92, no. 3 (2007), pp. 458–475; and C. Fernet, M. Gagné and S. Austin, "When Does Quality of Relationships with Coworkers Predict Burnout over Time? The Moderating Role of Work Motivation" *Journal of Organizational Behavior* 31 (2010), pp. 1163–1180.

74. See, for example, C. M. Middeldorp, D. C. Cath, A. L. Beem, G. Willemsen, and D. I. Boomsma, "Life Events, Anxious Depression, and Personality: A Prospective and Genetic Study," *Psychological Medicine* 38, no. 11 (2008), pp. 1557–1565; A. A. Uliaszek, R. E. Zinbarg, S. Mineka, M. G. Craske, J. M. Sutton, J. W. Griffith, R. Rose, A. Waters, and C. Hammen, "The Role of Neuroticism and Extraversion in the Stress-Anxiety and Stress-Depression Relationships," *Anxiety, Stress, and Coping* 23, no. 4 (2010), pp. 363–381.

75. J. D. Kammeyer-Mueller, T. A. Judge, and B. A. Scott, "The Role of Core Self-Evaluations in the Coping Process," *Journal of Applied Psychology* 94, no. 1 (2009), pp. 177–195.

76. R. J. Burke, A. M. Richardson, and M. Mortinussen, "Workaholism Among Norwegian Managers: Work and Well-Being Outcomes," *Journal of Organizational Change Management* 7 (2004), pp. 459–470; and W. B. Schaufeli, T. W. Taris, and W. van Rhenen, "Workaholism, Burnout, and Work Engagement: Three of a Kind or Three Different Kinds of Employee Well-Being," *Applied Psychology: An International Review* 57, no. 2 (2008), pp. 173–203.

77. J. Chen, C. Silverthorne, and J. Hung, "Organization Communication, Job Stress, Organizational Commitment, and Job Performance of Accounting Professionals in Taiwan and America," *Leadership & Organization Development Journal* 27, no. 4 (2006), pp. 242–249; and C. Liu, P. E. Spector, and L. Shi, "Cross-National Job Stress: A Quantitative and Qualitative Study," *Journal of Organizational Behavior* (February 2007), pp. 209–239.

78. P. E. Spector, T. D. Allen, S. A. Y. Poelmans, L. M. Lapierre, C. L. Cooper, M. O'Driscoll, et al., "Cross National Differences in Relationships of Work Demands, Job Satisfaction, and Turnover Intention with Work-Family Conflict," *Personnel Psychology* 60, no. 4 (2007), pp. 805–835.

79. H. M. Addae and X. Wang, "Stress at Work: Linear and Curvilinear Effects of Psychological-, Job-, and Organization-Related Factors: An Exploratory Study of Trinidad and Tobago," *International Journal of Stress Management* (November 2006), pp. 476–493.

80. J. Schaubroeck, J. R. Jones, and J. L. Xie, "Individual Differences in Utilizing Control to Cope with Job Demands: Effects on Susceptibility to Infectious Disease," *Journal of Applied Psychology* (April 2001), pp. 265–278.

81. M. Kivimäki, J. Head, J. E. Ferrie, E. Brunner, M. G. Marmot, J. Vahtera, and M. J. Shipley, "Why Is Evidence on Job Strain and Coronary Heart Disease Mixed? An Illustration of Measurement Challenges in the Whitehall II Study," *Psychosomatic Medicine* 68, no. 3 (2006), pp. 398–401.

82. M. Borritz, K. B. Christensen, U. Bültmann, R. Rugulies, T. Lund, I Andersen, E. Villadsen, F. Didreichsen, and T. S. Krisensen, "Impact on Burnout and Psychosocial Work Characteristics on Future Long-Term Sickness Absence, Prospective Results of the Danish PUMA Study Among Human Service Workers," *Journal of Occupational and Environmental Medicine* 52, no. 10 (2010), pp. 964–970.

83. B. D. Steffy and J. W. Jones, "Workplace Stress and Indicators of Coronary-Disease Risk," *Academy of Management Journal* 31, no. 3 (1988), pp. 686–698.

84. R. Illies, N. Dimotakis, and I. E. DePater, "Psychological and Physiological Reactions to High Workloads: Implications

for Well-Being," *Personnel Psychology* 63, no. 2 (2010), pp. 407–463.

85. D. Örtqvist and J. Wincent, "Prominent Consequences of Role Stress: A Meta-Analytic Review," *International Journal of Stress Management*, 13, no. 4 (2006), pp. 399–422.

86. J. R. Hackman and G. R. Oldham, "Development of the Job Diagnostic Survey," *Journal of Applied Psychology* (April 1975), pp. 159–170; J. J. Hakanen, A. B. Bakker, and M. Jokisaari, "A 35-Year Follow-Up Study on Burnout Among Finnish Employees," *Journal of Occupational Health Psychology* 16, no. 3 (2011), pp. 345–360; Crawford, LePine, and Rich, "Linking Job Demands and Resources to Employee Engagement and Burnout; and G. A. Chung-Yan, "The Nonlinear Effects of Job Complexity and Autonomy on Job Satisfaction, Turnover, and Psychological Well-Being," *Journal of Occupational Health Psychology* 15, no. 3 (2010), pp. 237–251.

87. L. L. Meier, N. K. Semmer, A. Elfering, and N. Jacobshagen, "The Double Meaning of Control: Three-Way Interactions Between Internal Resources, Job Control, and Stressors at Work," *Journal of Occupational Health Psychology* 13, no. 3 (2008), pp. 244–258.

88. E. M. de Croon, J. K. Sluiter, R. W. B. Blonk, J. P. J. Broersen, and M. H. W. Frings-Dresen, "Stressful Work, Psychological Job Strain, and Turnover: A 2-Year Prospective Cohort Study of Truck Drivers," *Journal of Applied Psychology* (June 2004), pp. 442–454; R. Cropanzano, D. E. Rupp, and Z. S. Byrne, "The Relationship of Emotional Exhaustion to Work Attitudes, Job Performance, and Organizational Citizenship Behaviors," *Journal of Applied Psychology* (February 2003), pp. 160–169; and S. Diestel and K. Schmidt, "Costs of Simultaneous Coping with Emotional Dissonance and Self-Control Demands at Work: Results from Two German Samples," *Journal of Applied Psychology* 96, no. 3 (2011), pp. 643–653.

89. See, for instance, S. Zivnuska, C. Kiewitz, W. A. Hochwarter, P. L. Perrewe, and K. L. Zellars, "What Is Too Much or Too Little? The Curvilinear Effects of Job Tension on Turnover Intent, Value Attainment, and Job Satisfaction," *Journal of Applied Social Psychology* (July 2002), pp. 1344–1360.

90. L. A. Muse, S. G. Harris, and H. S. Field, "Has the Inverted-U Theory of Stress and Job Performance Had a Fair Test?" *Human Performance* 16, no. 4 (2003), pp. 349–364.

91. S. Gilboa, A. Shirom, Y. Fried, and C. Cooper, "A Meta-Analysis of Work Demand Stressors and Job Performance: Examining Main and Moderating Effects," *Personnel Psychology* 61, no. 2 (2008), pp. 227–271.

92. J. C. Wallace, B. D. Edwards, T. Arnold, M. L. Frazier, and D. M. Finch, "Work Stressors, Role-Based Performance, and the Moderating Influence of Organizational Support," *Journal of Applied Psychology* 94, no. 1 (2009), pp. 254–262.

93. The following discussion has been influenced J. M. Ivancevich, M. T. Matteson, S. M. Freedman, and J. S. Phillips, "Worksite Stress Management Interventions," *American Psychologist* (February 1990), pp. 252–261; R. Schwarzer, "Manage Stress at Work Through Preventive and Proactive Coping," in E. A. Locke (ed.), *Handbook of Principles of Organizational Behavior* (Malden, MA: Blackwell, 2004), pp. 342–355; and K. M. Richardson and H. R. Rothstein, "Effects of Occupational Stress Management Intervention Programs: A Meta-Analysis," *Journal of Occupational Health Psychology* 13, no. 1 (2008), pp. 69–93.

94. T. H. Macan, "Time Management: Test of a Process Model," *Journal of Applied Psychology* (June 1994), pp. 381–391; and B. J. C. Claessens, W. Van Eerde, C. G. Rutte, and R. A. Roe, "Planning Behavior and Perceived Control of Time at Work," *Journal of Organizational Behavior* (December 2004), pp. 937–950.

95. See, for example, G. Lawrence-Ell, *The Invisible Clock: A Practical Revolution in Finding Time for Everyone and Everything* (Seaside Park, NJ: Kingsland Hall, 2002); and B. Tracy, *Time Power* (New York: AMACOM, 2004).

96. R. W. Renn, D. G. Allen, and T. M. Huning, "Empirical Examination of Individual-Level Personality-Based Theory of Self-Management Failure," *Journal of Organizational Behavior* 32, no. 1 (2011), pp. 25–43; and P. Gröpel and P. Steel, "A Mega-Trial Investigation of Goal Setting, Interest Enhancement, and Energy on Procrastination," *Personality and Individual Differences* 45, no. 5 (2008), pp. 406–411.

97. P. Salmon, "Effects of Physical Exercise on Anxiety, Depression, and Sensitivity to Stress: A Unifying Theory," *Clinical Psychology Review* 21, no. 1 (2001), pp. 33–61.

98. K. M. Richardson and H. R. Rothstein, "Effects of Occupational Stress Management Intervention Programs: A Meta-Analysis," *Journal of Occupational Health Psychology* 13, no. 1 (2008), pp. 69–93.

99. V. C. Hahn, C. Binnewies, S. Sonnentag, and E. J. Mojza, "Learning How to Recover From Job Stress: Effects of a Recovery Training Program on Recovery, Recovery-Related Self-Efficacy, and Well-Being," *Journal of Occupational Health Psychology* 16, no. 2 (2011), pp. 202–216; and C. Binnewies, S. Sonnentag, and E. J. Mojza, "Recovery During the Weekend and Fluctuations in Weekly Job Performance: A Week-Level Study Examining Intra-Individual Relationships," *Journal of Occupational and Organizational Psychology* 83, no. 2 (2010), pp. 419–441.

100. E. R. Greenglass and L. Fiksenbaum, "Proactive Coping, Positive Affect, and Well-Being: Testing for Mediation Using Path Analysis," *European Psychologist* 14, no. 1 (2009), pp. 29–39; and P. Miquelon and R. J. Vallerand, "Goal Motives, Well-Being, and Physical Health: Happiness and Self-Realization as Psychological Resources under Challenge," *Motivation and Emotion* 30, no. 4 (2006), pp. 259–272.

101. M. M. Butts, R. J. Vandenberg, D. M. DeJoy, B. S. Schaffer, and M. G. Wilson, "Individual Reactions to High Involvement Work Processes: Investigating the Role of Empowerment and Perceived Organizational Support," *Journal of Occupational Health Psychology* 14, no. 2 (2009), pp. 122–136.

102. "100 Best Companies to Work For," *Fortune* (August 17, 2011), http://money.cnn.com/magazines/fortune.

103. L. Blue, "Making Good Health Easy," *Time* (November 12, 2009), www.time.com; and M. Andrews, "Americas Best Health Plans," *US News and World Report* (November 5, 2007), pp. 54–60.

104. K. M. Richardson and H. R. Rothstein, "Effects of Occupational Stress Management Intervention Programs: A Meta-Analysis," *Journal of Occupational Health Psychology* 13, no. 1 (2008), pp. 69–93.

105. D. Brown, "Wellness Programs Bring Healthy Bottom Line," *Canadian HR Reporter* (December 17, 2001), pp. 1ff.

106. P. S. Goodman and L. B. Kurke, "Studies of Change in Organizations: A Status Report," in P. S. Goodman (ed.), *Change in Organizations* (San Francisco: Jossey-Bass, 1982), p. 1.

Appendix

Research in Organizational Behavior

> For every complex problem, there is a solution that is simple, neat, and wrong.
>
> —H. L. Mencken

A number of years ago, a friend of mine was excited because he had read about the findings from a research study that finally, once and for all, resolved the question of what it takes to make it to the top in a large corporation. I doubted there was any simple answer to this question but, not wanting to dampen his enthusiasm, I asked him to tell me of what he had read. The answer, according to my friend, was *participation in college athletics.* To say I was skeptical of his claim is a gross understatement, so I asked him to tell me more.

The study encompassed 1,700 successful senior executives at the 500 largest U.S. corporations. The researchers found that half of these executives had played varsity-level college sports.[1] My friend, who happens to be good with statistics, informed me that since fewer than 2 percent of all college students participate in intercollegiate athletics, the probability of this finding occurring by mere chance is less than 1 in 10 million! He concluded his analysis by telling me that, based on this research, I should encourage my management students to get into shape and to make one of the varsity teams.

My friend was somewhat perturbed when I suggested that his conclusions were likely to be flawed. These executives were all males who attended college in the 1940s and 1950s. Would his advice be meaningful to females in the twenty-first century? These executives also weren't your typical college students. For the most part, they had attended elite private colleges such as Princeton and Amherst, where a large proportion of the student body participates in intercollegiate sports. And these "jocks" hadn't necessarily played football or basketball; many had participated in golf, tennis, baseball, cross-country running, crew, rugby, and similar minor sports. Moreover, maybe the researchers had confused the direction of causality. That is, maybe individuals with the motivation and ability to make it to the top of a large corporation are drawn to competitive activities like college athletics.

My friend was guilty of misusing research data. Of course, he is not alone. We are all continually bombarded with reports of experiments that link certain substances to cancer in mice and surveys that show changing attitudes toward sex among college students, for example. Many of these studies are carefully designed, with great caution taken to note the implications and limitations of the findings. But some studies are poorly designed, making their conclusions at best suspect, and at worst meaningless.

Rather than attempting to make you a researcher, the purpose of this appendix is to increase your awareness as a consumer of behavioral research. A knowledge of research methods will allow you to appreciate more fully the care in data collection that underlies the information and conclusions presented in this text. Moreover, an understanding of research methods will make you a more skilled evaluator of the OB studies you will encounter in business and professional journals. So an appreciation of behavioral research is important because (1) it's the foundation on which the theories in this text are built, and (2) it will benefit you in future years when you read reports of research and attempt to assess their value.

Purposes of Research

Research is concerned with the systematic gathering of information. Its purpose is to help us in our search for the truth. Although we will never find ultimate truth—in our case, that would be to know precisely how any person or group would behave in any organizational context—ongoing research adds to our body of OB knowledge by supporting some theories, contradicting others, and suggesting new theories to replace those that fail to gain support.

Research Terminology

Researchers have their own vocabulary for communicating among themselves and with outsiders. The following briefly defines some of the more popular terms you're likely to encounter in behavioral science studies.[2]

Variable

A *variable* is any general characteristic that can be measured and that changes in amplitude, intensity, or both. Some examples of OB variables found in this textbook are job satisfaction, employee productivity, work stress, ability, personality, and group norms.

Hypothesis

A tentative explanation of the relationship between two or more variables is called a *hypothesis*. My friend's statement that participation in college athletics leads to a top executive position in a large corporation is an example of a hypothesis. Until confirmed by empirical research, a hypothesis remains only a tentative explanation.

Dependent Variable

A *dependent variable* is a response that is affected by an independent variable. In terms of the hypothesis, it is the variable that the researcher is interested in explaining. Referring back to our opening example, the dependent variable in my friend's hypothesis was executive succession. In organizational behavior research, the most popular dependent variables are productivity, absenteeism, turnover, job satisfaction, and organizational commitment.[3]

Independent Variable

An *independent variable* is the presumed cause of some change in the dependent variable. Participating in varsity athletics was the independent variable in my friend's hypothesis. Popular independent variables studied by OB researchers include intelligence, personality, job satisfaction, experience, motivation, reinforcement patterns, leadership style, reward allocations, selection methods, and organization design.

You may have noticed we said that job satisfaction is frequently used by OB researchers as both a dependent and an independent variable. This is not an error. It merely reflects that the label given to a variable depends on its place in the hypothesis. In the statement "Increases in job satisfaction lead to reduced turnover," job satisfaction is an independent variable. However, in the statement "Increases in money lead to higher job satisfaction," job satisfaction becomes a dependent variable.

Moderating Variable

A *moderating variable* abates the effect of the independent variable on the dependent variable. It might also be thought of as the contingency variable: If X (independent variable), then Y (dependent variable) will occur, but only under conditions Z (moderating variable). To translate this into a real-life example, we might say that if we increase the amount of direct supervision in the work area (X), then there will be a change in worker productivity (Y), but this effect will be moderated by the complexity of the tasks being performed (Z).

Causality

A hypothesis, by definition, implies a relationship. That is, it implies a presumed cause and effect. This direction of cause and effect is called *causality*. Changes in the independent variable are assumed to cause changes in the dependent variable. However, in behavioral research, it's possible to make an incorrect assumption of causality when relationships are found. For example, early behavioral scientists found a relationship between employee satisfaction and productivity. They concluded that a happy worker was a productive worker. Follow-up research has supported the relationship, but disconfirmed the direction of the arrow. The evidence more correctly suggests that high productivity leads to satisfaction rather than the other way around.

Correlation Coefficient

It's one thing to know that there is a relationship between two or more variables. It's another to know the *strength* of that relationship. The term *correlation coefficient* is used to indicate that strength, and is expressed as a number between −1.00 (a perfect negative relationship) and +1.00 (a perfect positive correlation).

When two variables vary directly with one another, the correlation will be expressed as a positive number. When they vary inversely—that is, one increases as the other decreases—the correlation will be expressed as a negative number. If the two variables vary independently of each other, we say that the correlation between them is zero.

For example, a researcher might survey a group of employees to determine the satisfaction of each with his or her job. Then, using company absenteeism reports, the researcher could correlate the job satisfaction scores against individual attendance records to determine whether employees who are more satisfied with their jobs have better attendance records than their counterparts who indicated lower job satisfaction. Let's suppose the researcher found a correlation coefficient of +0.50 between satisfaction and attendance. Would that be a strong association? There is, unfortunately, no precise numerical cutoff separating strong and weak relationships. A standard statistical test would need to be applied to determine whether the relationship was a significant one.

A final point needs to be made before we move on: A correlation coefficient measures only the strength of association between two variables. A high value does *not* imply causality. The length of women's skirts and stock market prices, for instance, have long been noted to be highly correlated, but one should be careful not to infer that a causal relationship between the two exists. In this instance, the high correlation is more happenstance than predictive.

Theory

The final term we introduce in this section is *theory*. Theory describes a set of systematically interrelated concepts or hypotheses that purports to explain and predict phenomena. In OB, theories are also frequently referred to as *models*. We use the two terms interchangeably.

There are no shortages of theories in OB. For instance, we have theories to describe what motivates people, the most effective leadership styles, the best way to resolve conflicts, and how people acquire power. In some cases, we have half a dozen or more separate theories that purport to explain and predict a given phenomenon. In such cases, is one right and the others wrong? No! They tend to reflect science at work—researchers testing previous theories, modifying them, and, when appropriate, proposing new models that may prove to have higher explanatory and predictive powers. Multiple theories attempting to explain common phenomena merely attest that OB is an active discipline, still growing and evolving.

Evaluating Research

As a potential consumer of behavioral research, you should follow the dictum of *caveat emptor*—let the buyer beware! In evaluating any research study, you need to ask three questions.[4]

Is it valid? Is the study actually measuring what it claims to be measuring? A number of psychological tests have been discarded by employers in recent years because they have not been found to be valid measures of the applicants' ability to do a given job successfully. But the validity issue is relevant to all research studies. So, if you find a study that links cohesive work teams with higher productivity, you want to know how each of these variables was measured and whether it is actually measuring what it is supposed to be measuring.

Is it reliable? Reliability refers to consistency of measurement. If you were to have your height measured every day with a wooden yardstick, you'd get highly reliable results. On the other hand, if you were measured each day by an elastic tape measure, there would probably be considerable disparity between your height measurements from one day to the next. Your height, of course, doesn't change from day to day. The variability is due to the unreliability of the measuring device. So if a company asked a group of its employees to complete a reliable job satisfaction questionnaire, and then repeat the questionnaire six

months later, we'd expect the results to be very similar—provided nothing changed in the interim that might significantly affect employee satisfaction.

Is it generalizable? Are the results of the research study generalizable to groups of individuals other than those who participated in the original study? Be aware, for example, of the limitations that might exist in research that uses college students as subjects. Are the findings in such studies generalizable to full-time employees in real jobs? Similarly, how generalizable to the overall work population are the results from a study that assesses job stress among 10 nuclear power plant engineers in the hamlet of Mahone Bay, Nova Scotia?

Research Design

Doing research is an exercise in trade-offs. Richness of information typically comes with reduced generalizability. The more a researcher seeks to control for confounding variables, the less realistic his or her results are likely to be. High precision, generalizability, and control almost always translate into higher costs. When researchers make choices about whom they'll study, where their research will be done, the methods they'll use to collect data, and so on, they must make some concessions. Good research designs are not perfect, but they do carefully reflect the questions being addressed. Keep these facts in mind as we review the strengths and weaknesses of five popular research designs: case studies, field surveys, laboratory experiments, field experiments, and aggregate quantitative reviews.

Case Study

You pick up a copy of Soichiro Honda's autobiography. In it he describes his impoverished childhood; his decisions to open a small garage, assemble motorcycles, and eventually build automobiles; and how this led to the creation of one of the largest and most successful corporations in the world. Or you're in a business class and the instructor distributes a 50-page handout covering two companies: Wal-Mart and Kmart. The handout details the two firms' histories; describes their corporate strategies, management philosophies, and merchandising plans; and includes copies of their recent balance sheets and income statements. The instructor asks the class members to read the handout, analyze the data, and determine why Wal-Mart has been so much more successful than Kmart in recent years.

Soichiro Honda's autobiography and the Wal-Mart and Kmart handouts are case studies. Drawn from real-life situations, case studies present an in-depth analysis of one setting. They are thorough descriptions, rich in details about an individual, a group, or an organization. The primary source of information in case studies is obtained through observation, occasionally backed up by interviews and a review of records and documents.

Case studies have their drawbacks. They're open to the perceptual bias and subjective interpretations of the observer. The reader of a case is captive to what the observer/case writer chooses to include and exclude. Cases also trade off generalizability for depth of information and richness of detail. Because it's always dangerous to generalize from a sample of one, case studies make it difficult to prove or reject a hypothesis. On the other hand, you can't ignore the in-depth analysis that cases often provide. They are an excellent device for initial exploratory research and for evaluating real-life problems in organizations.

Field Survey

A lengthy questionnaire was created to assess the use of ethics policies, formal ethics structures, formalized activities such as ethics training, and executive involvement in ethics programs among billion-dollar corporations. The public affairs or corporate communications office of all *Fortune* 500 industrial firms and 500 service corporations were contacted to get the name and address of the "officer most responsible for dealing with ethics and conduct issues" in each firm. The questionnaire, with a cover letter explaining the nature of the study, was mailed to these 1,000 officers. Of the total, 254 returned a completed questionnaire, for a response rate just above 25 percent. The results of the survey found, among other things, that 77 percent had formal codes of ethics and 54 percent had a single officer specifically assigned to deal with ethics and conduct issues.[5]

The preceding study illustrates a typical field survey. A sample of respondents (in this case, 1,000 corporate officers in the largest U.S. publicly held corporations) was selected to represent a larger group that was under examination (billion-dollar U.S. business firms). The respondents were then surveyed using a questionnaire or interviewed to collect data on particular characteristics (the content and structure of ethics programs and practices) of interest to the researchers. The standardization of response items allows for data to be easily quantified, analyzed, and summarized, and for the researchers to make inferences from the representative sample about the larger population.

The field survey provides economies for doing research. It's less costly to sample a population than to obtain data from every member of that population. (There are, for instance, more than 5,000 U.S. business firms with sales in excess of a billion dollars; and since some of these are privately held and don't release financial data to the public, they are excluded from the *Fortune* list). Moreover, as the ethics study illustrates, field surveys provide an efficient way to find out how people feel about issues or how they say they behave. These data can then be easily quantified.

But the field survey has a number of potential weaknesses. First, mailed questionnaires rarely obtain 100 percent returns. Low response rates call into question whether conclusions based on respondents' answers are generalizable to nonrespondents. Second, the format is better at tapping respondents' attitudes and perceptions than behaviors. Third, responses can suffer from social desirability; that is, people saying what they think the researcher wants to hear. Fourth, since field surveys are designed to focus on specific issues, they're a relatively poor means of acquiring depth of information. Finally, the quality of the generalizations is largely a factor of the population chosen. Responses from executives at *Fortune* 500 firms, for instance, tell us nothing about small- or medium-sized firms or not-for-profit organizations. In summary, even a well-designed field survey trades off depth of information for breadth, generalizability, and economic efficiencies.

Laboratory Experiment

The following study is a classic example of the laboratory experiment. A researcher, Stanley Milgram, wondered how far individuals would go in following commands. If subjects were placed in the role of a teacher in a learning experiment and told by an experimenter to administer a shock to a learner each time that learner made a mistake, would the subjects follow the commands of the experimenter? Would their willingness to comply decrease as the intensity of the shock was increased?

To test these hypotheses, Milgram hired a set of subjects. Each was led to believe that the experiment was to investigate the effect of punishment on memory. Their job was to act as teachers and administer punishment whenever the learner made a mistake on the learning test.

Punishment was administered by an electric shock. The subject sat in front of a shock generator with 30 levels of shock—beginning at zero and progressing in 15-volt increments to a high of 450 volts. The demarcations of these positions ranged from "Slight Shock" at 15 volts to "Danger: Severe Shock" at 450 volts. To increase the realism of the experiment, the subjects received a sample shock of 45 volts and saw the learner—a pleasant, mild-mannered man about 50 years old—strapped into an "electric chair" in an adjacent room. Of course, the learner was an actor, and the electric shocks were phony, but the subjects didn't know this.

Taking his seat in front of the shock generator, the subject was directed to begin at the lowest shock level and to increase the shock intensity to the next level each time the learner made a mistake or failed to respond.

When the test began, the shock intensity rose rapidly because the learner made many errors. The subject got verbal feedback from the learner: At 75 volts, the learner began to grunt and moan; at 150 volts, he demanded to be released from the experiment; at 180 volts, he cried out that he could no longer stand the pain; and at 300 volts, he insisted that he be let out, yelled about his heart condition, screamed, and then failed to respond to further questions.

Most subjects protested and, fearful they might kill the learner if the increased shocks were to bring on a heart attack, insisted they could not go on with their job. Hesitations or protests by the subject were met by the experimenter's statement, "You have no choice, you must go on! Your job is to punish the learner's mistakes." Of course, the subjects did have a choice. All they had to do was stand up and walk out.

The majority of the subjects dissented. But dissension isn't synonymous with disobedience. Sixty-two percent of the subjects increased the shock level to the maximum of 450 volts. The average level of shock administered by the remaining 38 percent was nearly 370 volts.[6]

In a laboratory experiment such as that conducted by Milgram, an artificial environment is created by the researcher. Then the researcher manipulates an independent variable under controlled conditions. Finally, since all other things are held equal, the researcher is able to conclude that any change in the dependent variable is due to the manipulation or change imposed on the independent variable. Note that, because of the controlled conditions, the researcher is able to imply causation between the independent and dependent variables.

The laboratory experiment trades off realism and generalizability for precision and control. It provides a high degree of control over variables and precise measurement of those variables. But findings from laboratory studies are often difficult to generalize to the real world of work. This is because the artificial laboratory rarely duplicates the intricacies and nuances of real organizations. In addition, many laboratory experiments deal with phenomena that cannot be reproduced or applied to real-life situations.

Field Experiment

The following is an example of a field experiment. The management of a large company is interested in determining the impact that a four-day workweek would have on employee absenteeism. To be more specific, management wants to know if employees working four 10-hour days have lower absence rates than similar employees working the traditional five-day week of 8 hours each day. Because the company is large, it has a number of manufacturing plants that employ essentially similar workforces. Two of these are chosen for the experiment, both located in the greater Cleveland area. Obviously, it would not be appropriate to compare two similar-sized plants if one is in rural Mississippi and the other is in urban Copenhagen because factors such as national culture, transportation, and weather might be more likely to explain any differences found than changes in the number of days worked per week.

In one plant, the experiment was put into place—workers began the four-day week. At the other plant, which became the control group, no changes were made in the employees' five-day week. Absence data were gathered from the company's records at both locations for a period of 18 months. This extended time period lessened the possibility that any results would be distorted by the mere novelty of changes being implemented in the experimental plant. After 18 months, management found that absenteeism had dropped by 40 percent at the experimental plant, and by only 6 percent in the control plant. Because of the design of this study, management believed that the larger drop in absences at the experimental plant was due to the introduction of the compressed workweek.

The field experiment is similar to the laboratory experiment, except it is conducted in a real organization. The natural setting is more realistic than the laboratory setting, and this enhances validity but hinders control. In addition, unless control groups are maintained, there can be a loss of control if extraneous forces intervene—for example, an employee strike, a major layoff, or a corporate restructuring. Maybe the greatest concern with field studies has to do with organizational selection bias. Not all organizations are going to allow outside researchers to come in and study their employees and operations. This is especially true of organizations that have serious problems. Therefore, since most published studies in OB are done by outside researchers, the selection bias might work toward the publication of studies conducted almost exclusively at successful and well-managed organizations.

Our general conclusion is that, of the four research designs we've discussed to this point, the field experiment typically provides the most valid and generalizable findings and, except for its high cost, trades off the least to get the most.[7]

Aggregate Quantitative Reviews

What's the overall effect of organizational behavior modification (OB Mod) on task performance? There have been a number of field experiments that have sought to throw light on this question. Unfortunately, the wide range of effects from these various studies makes it hard to generalize.

To try to reconcile these diverse findings, two researchers reviewed all the empirical studies they could find on the impact of OB Mod on task performance over a 20-year period.[8] After discarding reports that had inadequate information, had nonquantitative data, or didn't meet all conditions associated with principles of behavioral modification, the researchers narrowed their set to 19 studies that included data on 2,818 individuals. Using an aggregating technique called *meta-analysis*, the researchers were able to synthesize the studies quantitatively and to conclude that the average person's task performance will rise from the 50th percentile to the 67th percentile after an OB Mod intervention.

The OB Mod–task performance review done by these researchers illustrates the use of meta-analysis, a quantitative form of literature review that enables researchers to look at validity findings from a comprehensive set of individual studies, and then apply a formula to them to determine if they consistently produced similar results.[9] If results prove to be consistent, it allows researchers to conclude more confidently that validity is generalizable. Meta-analysis is a means for overcoming the potentially imprecise interpretations of qualitative reviews and to synthesize variations in quantitative studies. In addition, the technique enables researchers to identify potential moderating variables between an independent and a dependent variable.

In the past 25 years, there's been a surge in the popularity of this research method. Why? It appears to offer a more objective means for doing traditional literature reviews. Although the use of meta-analysis requires researchers to make a number of judgment calls, which can introduce a considerable amount of subjectivity into the process, there is no arguing that meta-analysis reviews have now become widespread in the OB literature.

Ethics in Research

Researchers are not always tactful or candid with subjects when they do their studies. For instance, questions in field surveys may be perceived as embarrassing by respondents or as an invasion of privacy. Also, researchers in laboratory studies have been known to deceive participants about the true purpose of their experiment "because they felt deception was necessary to get honest responses."[10]

The "learning experiments" conducted by Stanley Milgram, which were conducted more than 30 years ago, have been widely criticized by psychologists on ethical grounds. He lied to subjects, telling them his study was investigating learning, when, in fact, he was concerned with obedience. The shock machine he used was a fake. Even the "learner" was an accomplice of Milgram's who had been trained to act as if he were hurt and in pain. Yet ethical lapses continue. For instance, in 2001, a professor of organizational behavior at Columbia University sent out a common letter on university letterhead to 240 New York City restaurants in which he detailed how he had eaten at this restaurant with his wife in celebration of their wedding anniversary, how he had gotten food poisoning, and that he had spent the night in his bathroom throwing up.[11] The letter closed with: "Although it is not my intention to file any reports with the Better Business Bureau or the Department of Health, I want you to understand what I went through in anticipation that you will respond accordingly. I await your response." The fictitious letter was part of the professor's study to determine how restaurants responded to complaints. But it created culinary chaos among many of the restaurant owners, managers, and chefs as they reviewed menus and produce deliveries for possibly spoiled food, and questioned kitchen workers about possible lapses. A follow-up letter of apology from the university for "an egregious error in judgment by a junior faculty member" did little to offset the distress it created for those affected.

Professional associations like the American Psychological Association, the American Sociological Association, and the Academy of Management have published formal guidelines for the conduct of research. Yet the ethical debate continues. On one side are those who argue that strict ethical controls can damage the scientific validity of an experiment and cripple future research. Deception, for example, is often necessary to avoid contaminating results. Moreover, proponents of minimizing ethical controls note that few subjects have been appreciably harmed by deceptive experiments. Even in Milgram's highly manipulative experiment, only 1.3 percent of the subjects reported negative feelings about their experience. The other side of this debate focuses on the rights of participants. Those favoring strict ethical controls argue that no procedure should ever be emotionally or physically distressing to subjects, and that, as professionals, researchers are obliged to be completely honest with their subjects and to protect the subjects' privacy at all costs.

Summary

The subject of organizational behavior is composed of a large number of theories that are research based. Research studies, when cumulatively integrated, become theories, and theories are proposed and followed by research studies designed to validate them. The concepts that make up OB, therefore, are only as valid as the research that supports them.

The topics and issues in this book are for the most part research-derived. They represent the result of systematic information gathering rather than merely hunch, intuition, or opinion. This doesn't mean, of course, that we have all the answers to OB issues. Many require far more corroborating evidence. The generalizability of others is limited by the research methods used. But new information is being created and published at an accelerated rate. To keep up with the latest findings, we strongly encourage you to regularly review the latest research in organizational behavior. More academic work can be found in journals such as the *Academy of Management Journal, Academy of Management Review, Administrative Science Quarterly, Human Relations, Journal of Applied Psychology, Journal of Management, Journal of Organizational Behavior,* and *Leadership Quarterly.* For more practical interpretations of OB research findings, you may want to read the *Academy of Management Executive, California Management Review, Harvard Business Review, Organizational Dynamics,* and the *Sloan Management Review.*

Endnotes

1. J. A. Byrne, "Executive Sweat," *Forbes,* May 20, 1985, pp. 198–200.

2. See D. P. Schwab, *Research Methods for Organizational Behavior* (Mahwah, NJ: Lawrence Erlbaum Associates, 1999); and S. G. Rogelberg (ed.), *Blackwell Handbook of Research Methods in Industrial and Organizational Psychology* (Malden, MA: Blackwell, 2002).

3. B. M. Staw and G. R. Oldham, "Reconsidering Our Dependent Variables: A Critique and Empirical Study," *Academy of Management Journal,* December 1978, pp. 539–559; and B. M. Staw, "Organizational Behavior: A Review and Reformulation of the Field's Outcome Variables," in M. R. Rosenzweig and L. W. Porter (eds.), *Annual Review of Psychology,* vol. 35 (Palo Alto, CA: Annual Reviews, 1984), pp. 627–666.

4. R. S. Blackburn, "Experimental Design in Organizational Settings," in J. W. Lorsch (ed.), *Handbook of Organizational Behavior* (Upper Saddle River, NJ: Prentice Hall, 1987), pp. 127–128; and F. L. Schmidt, C. Viswesvaran, D. S. Ones, "Reliability Is Not Validity and Validity Is Not Reliability," *Personnel Psychology,* Winter 2000, pp. 901–912.

5. G. R. Weaver, L. K. Trevino, and P. L. Cochran, "Corporate Ethics Practices in the Mid-1990's: An Empirical Study of the Fortune 1000," *Journal of Business Ethics,* February 1999, pp. 283–294.

6. S. Milgram, *Obedience to Authority* (New York: Harper & Row, 1974). For a critique of this research, see T. Blass, "Understanding Behavior in the Milgram Obedience Experiment: The Role of Personality, Situations, and Their Interactions," *Journal of Personality and Social Psychology,* March 1991, pp. 398–413.

7. See, for example, W. N. Kaghan, A. L. Strauss, S. R. Barley, M. Y. Brannen, and R. J. Thomas, "The Practice and Uses of Field Research in the 21st Century Organization," *Journal of Management Inquiry,* March 1999, pp. 67–81.

8. A. D. Stajkovic and F. Luthans, "A Meta-Analysis of the Effects of Organizational Behavior Modification on Task Performance, 1975–1995," *Academy of Management Journal,* October 1997, pp. 1122–1149.

9. See, for example, K. Zakzanis, "The Reliability of Meta Analytic Review," *Psychological Reports,* August 1998, pp. 215–222; C. Ostroff and D. A. Harrison, "Meta-Analysis, Level of Analysis, and Best Estimates of Population Correlations: Cautions for Interpreting Meta-Analytic Results in Organizational Behavior," *Journal of Applied Psychology,* April 1999, pp. 260–270; R. Rosenthal and M. R. DiMatteo, "Meta-Analysis: Recent Developments in Quantitative Methods for Literature Reviews," in S. T. Fiske, D. L. Schacter, and C. Zahn-Wacher (eds.), *Annual Review of Psychology,* vol. 52 (Palo Alto, CA: Annual Reviews, 2001), pp. 59–82; and F. L. Schmidt and J. E. Hunter, "Meta-Analysis," in N. Anderson, D. S. Ones, H. K. Sinangil, and C. Viswesvaran (eds.), *Handbook of Industrial, Work & Organizational Psychology,* vol. 1 (Thousand Oaks, CA: Sage, 2001), pp. 51–70.

10. For more on ethical issues in research, see T. L. Beauchamp, R. R. Faden, R. J. Wallace, Jr., and L. Walters (eds.), *Ethical Issues in Social Science Research* (Baltimore, MD: Johns Hopkins University Press, 1982); and J. G. Adair, "Ethics of Psychological Research: New Policies, Continuing Issues, New Concerns," *Canadian Psychology,* February 2001, pp. 25–37.

11. J. Kifner, "Scholar Sets Off Gastronomic False Alarm," *New York Times,* September 8, 2001, p. A1.

Comprehensive Cases

Managing Motivation in a Difficult Economy

Learning Goals

In this case, you'll have an opportunity to assess a motivational program designed to reenergize a troubled company's workforce. Acting on behalf of the company's executive board, you'll evaluate the board's current strategy based on survey data. You'll also advise board members about improving the effectiveness of this program based on what you've learned about goal-setting and motivation in organizations.

Major Topic Areas

- Changing nature of work
- Diversity and age
- Goal-setting
- Organizational downsizing
- Organizational justice

The Scenario

Morgan-Moe's drug stores are in trouble. A major regional player in the retail industry, the company has hundreds of stores in the upper Midwest. Unfortunately, a sharp decline in the region's manufacturing economy has put management in a serious financial bind. Revenues have been consistently dwindling. Customers spend less, and the stores have had to switch their focus to very low-margin commodities, such as milk and generic drugs, rather than the high-margin impulse-buy items that used to be the company's bread and butter. The firm has had to close quite a few locations, reversing its expansion plans for the first time since it incorporated.

Being that this is uncharted territory for the company, Jim Claussen, vice president for human relations, had been struggling with how to address the issue with employees. As the company's fortunes worsened, he could see that employees were becoming more and more disaffected. Their insecurity about their jobs was taking a toll on attitudes. The company's downsizing was big news, and the employees didn't like what they were hearing.

Media reports of Morgan-Moe's store closings have focused on the lack of advance notice or communication from the company's corporate offices, as well as the lack of severance payments for departing employees. In the absence of official information, rumors and gossip have spread like wildfire among remaining employees. A few angry blogs developed by laid-off employees, like IHateMorganMoe.blogspot.com, have made the morale and public relations picture even worse.

Morgan-Moe is changing in other ways as well. The average age of its workforce is increasing rapidly. A couple of factors have contributed to this shift. First, fewer qualified young people are around because many families have moved south to find jobs. Second, stores have been actively encouraged to hire older workers, such as retirees looking for some supplemental income. Managers are very receptive to these older workers because they are more mature, miss fewer days of work, and do not have child care responsibilities. They are also often more qualified than younger workers because they have more experience, sometimes in the managerial or executive ranks.

These older workers have been a great asset to the company in troubled times, but they are especially likely to leave if things get bad. If these older workers start to leave the company, taking their hard-earned experience with them, it seems likely that Morgan-Moe will sink deeper toward bankruptcy.

The System

Claussen wasn't quite sure how to respond to employees' sense of hopelessness and fear until a friend gave him a book entitled *Man's Search for Meaning*. The book was written by a psychologist named Victor Frankl, who survived the concentration camps at Auschwitz. Frankl found that those who had a clear sense of purpose, a reason to live, were more likely to persevere in the face of nearly unspeakable suffering. Something about this book, and its advocacy of finding meaning and direction as a way to triumph over adversity, really stuck with Claussen. He thought he might be able to apply its lessons to his workforce. He proposed the idea of a new direction for management to the company's executive committee, and they reluctantly agreed to try his suggestions.

Over the last 6 months, stores throughout the company have used a performance management system that, as Claussen says, "gets people to buy into the idea of performing so that they can see some real results in their stores. It's all about seeing that your work serves a broader purpose. I read about how some companies have been sharing store performance information with employees to get them to understand what their jobs really mean and participate in making changes, and I thought that was something we'd be able to do."

The HR team came up with five options for the management system. Corporate allowed individual managers to choose the option they thought would work best with their employees so that managers wouldn't feel too much like a rapid change was being forced on them. Program I is opting out of the new idea, continuing to stay the course and providing employees with little to no information or opportunities for participation. Program II tracks employee absence and sick leave and shares that information with individual employees, giving them feedback about things they can control. Management takes no further action. Program III tracks sales and inventory replacement rates across shifts. As in Program II, information is shared with employees, but without providing employee feedback about absence and sick leave. Program IV, the most comprehensive, tracks the same information as Programs II and III. Managers communicate it in weekly brainstorming sessions, during which employees try to determine what they can do better in the future and make suggestions for improving store performance. Program V keeps the idea of brainstorming but doesn't provide employees with information about their behavior or company profits.

Since implementing the system, Claussen has spoken with several managers about what motivated them to choose the program they did. Artie Washington, who chose Program IV, said, "I want to have my employees' input on how to keep the store running smoothly. Everybody worries about their job security in this economy. Letting them know what's going on and giving them ways to change things keeps them involved."

Betty Alvarez couldn't disagree more. She selected Program I. "I would rather have my employees doing their jobs than going to meetings to talk about doing their jobs. That's what management is for." Michael

Ostremski, another proponent of Program I, added, "It's okay for the employees to feel a little uncertain—if they think we're in the clear, they'll slack off. If they think we're in trouble, they'll give up."

Cal Martins also questions the need to provide information to the whole team, but he chose Program II. "A person should know where he or she stands in the job, but they don't have to know about everyone else. It creates unnecessary tension."

This is somewhat similar to Cindy Ang's reason for picking Program V. "When we have our brainstorming meetings, I learn what they [the employees] think is most pressing, not what some spreadsheet says. It gives me a better feel for what's going on in my store. Numbers count, of course, but they don't tell you everything. I was also a little worried that employees would be upset if they saw that we aren't performing well."

Results to Date

Claussen is convinced the most elaborate procedure (Program IV) is the most effective, but not everyone in the executive committee is won over by his advocacy. Although they have supported the test implementation of the system because it appears to have relatively low costs, others on the committee want to see results. CEO Jean Masterson has asked for a complete breakdown of the performance of the various stores over the past 4 years. She's especially interested in seeing how sales figures and turnover rates have been affected by the new program.

The company has been collecting data in spreadsheets on sales and turnover rates, and it prepared the following report, which also estimates the dollar cost of staff time taken up in each method. These costs are based on the number of hours employees spend working on the program multiplied by their wage rate. Estimates of turnover, profit, and staff time are collected per store. Profit and turnover data include means and standard deviations across locations; profit is net of the monthly time cost. Turnover information refers to the percentage of employees who either quit or are terminated in a month.

To see if any patterns emerged in managers' selection of programs, the company calculated relationships between program selection and various attributes of the stores. Program I was selected most frequently by the oldest stores and those in the most economically distressed areas. Programs II and III were selected most frequently by stores in urban areas and in areas where the workforce was younger on average. Programs IV and V were selected most frequently in stores in rural areas, and especially where the workforce is older on average.

Program	Methods	Number of Stores	Average Turnover	Weekly Profit per Month	Monthly Staff Time Cost
Program I	Traditional management	83	Mean = 30% SD = 10%	Mean = $5,700 SD = $3,000	None
Program II	Share absence and sick leave	27	Mean = 23% SD = 14%	Mean = $7,000 SD = $5,800	$1,960
Program III	Share sales and inventory	35	Mean = 37% SD = 20%	Mean = $11,000 SD = $2,700	$2,440
Program IV	Share information and brainstorm	67	Mean = 17% SD = 20%	Mean = $13,000 SD = $3,400	$3,420
Program V	Brainstorm without sharing information	87	Mean = 21% SD = 12%	Mean = $14,000 SD = $2,400	$2,750

Your Assignment

Your task is to prepare a report for the company's executive committee on the effectiveness of these programs. Make certain it is in the form of a professional business document. Your audience won't necessarily know about the organizational principles you're describing, so make sure you provide detailed explanations that someone in a real business can understand.

When you write, make sure you touch on the following points:

1. Consider the five management systems as variables in an experiment. Identify the independent and dependent variables, and explain how they are related to one another.
2. Based on the discussion of independent and dependent variables in the textbook, is there anything else you'd like to measure as an outcome?
3. Look over the data and decide which method of management appears most effective in generating revenues and reducing turnover, and why. Which methods appear least effective, and why?
4. Are there any concerns you have about these data?
   a. Does a comparison of the number of stores using each method influence your conclusions at all?
   b. Does the fact that managers are selecting the specific program to use (including Program I,

which continues the status quo) affect the inferences you can draw about program success?
   c. What are the advantages of randomly assigning different conditions to the stores instead of using this self-selection process?
5. How does the changing nature of the workforce and the economy, described in your textbook and in the case, affect your conclusions about how to manage retail employees? Does the participation of a more experienced workforce help or hurt these programs? Why might these programs work differently in an economy that isn't doing so poorly?
6. Claussen essentially designed the program on his own, with very little research into goal-setting and motivation. Based on your textbook, how well has he done? Which parts of the program appear to fit well with research evidence on goal-setting? What parts would you change to get more substantial improvements in employee motivation?
7. Describe the feelings employees might have when these systems are implemented that could help or hinder the program's success. What advice would you give managers about how to implement the programs so they match the principles of organizational justice described in your textbook?

Repairing Jobs That Fail to Satisfy

Learning Goals

Companies often divide up work as a way to improve efficiency, but specialization can lead to negative consequences. DrainFlow is a company that has effectively used specialization to reduce costs relative to its competitors' costs for years, but rising customer complaints suggest the firm's strong position may be slipping. After reading the case, you will suggest some ways it can create more interesting work for employees. You'll also tackle the problem of finding people qualified and ready to perform the multiple responsibilities required in these jobs.

Major Topic Areas

- Job design
- Job satisfaction
- Personality
- Emotional labor

The Scenario

DrainFlow is a large residential and commercial plumbing maintenance firm that operates around the United States. It has been a major player in residential plumbing for decades, and its familiar rhyming motto, "When Your Drain Won't Go, Call DrainFlow," has been plastered on billboards since the 1960s.

Lee Reynaldo has been a regional manager at DrainFlow for about 2 years. She used to work for a newer competing chain, Lightning Plumber, that has been drawing more and more customers from DrainFlow. Although her job at DrainFlow pays more, Lee isn't happy with the way things are going. She's noticed the work environment just isn't as vital or energetic as the environment she saw at Lightning.

Lee thinks the problem is that employees aren't motivated to provide the type of customer service Lightning Plumber employees offer. She recently sent surveys to customers to collect information about performance, and the data confirmed her fears. Although 60 percent of respondents said they were satisfied with their experience and would use DrainFlow again, 40 percent felt their experience was not good, and 30 percent said

they would use a competitor the next time they had a plumbing problem.

Lee is wondering whether DrainFlow's job design might be contributing to its problems in retaining customers. DrainFlow has about 2,000 employees in four basic job categories: plumbers, plumber's assistants, order processors, and billing representatives. This structure is designed to keep costs as low as possible. Plumbers make very high wages, whereas plumber's assistants make about one-quarter of what a licensed plumber makes. Using plumber's assistants is therefore a very cost-effective strategy that has enabled DrainFlow to easily undercut the competition when it comes to price. Order processors make even less than assistants but about the same as billing processors. All work is very specialized, but employees are often dependent on another job category to perform at their most efficient level.

Like most plumbing companies, DrainFlow gets business mostly from the Yellow Pages and the Internet. Customers either call in to describe a plumbing problem or submit an online request for plumbing services, receiving a return call with information within 24 hours. In either case, DrainFlow's order processors listen to the customer's description of the problem to determine whether a plumber or a plumber's assistant should make the service call. The job is then assigned accordingly, and a service provider goes to the location. When the job has been completed, via cell phone a billing representative relays the fee to the service rep, who presents a bill to the customer for payment. Billing representatives can take customers' credit card payments by phone or e-mail an invoice for online payment.

The Problem

Although specialization does cut costs significantly, Lee is worried about customer dissatisfaction. According to her survey, about 25 percent of customer contacts ended in no service call because customers were confused by the diagnostic questions the order processors asked and because the order processors did not have sufficient knowledge or skill to explain the situation. That means fully one in four people who call DrainFlow to hire a plumber are worse than dissatisfied: they aren't customers at all! The remaining 75 percent of calls that did end in a customer service encounter resulted in other problems.

The most frequent complaints Lee found in the customer surveys were about response time and cost, especially when the wrong person was sent to a job. A plumber's assistant cannot complete a more technically complicated job. The appointment has to be rescheduled, and the customer's time and the staff's time have been wasted. The resulting delay often caused customers in these situations to decline further contact with DrainFlow—many of them decided to go with Lightning Plumber.

"When I arrive at a job I can't take care of," says plumber's assistant Jim Larson, "the customer gets ticked off. They thought they were getting a licensed plumber, since they were calling for a plumber. Telling them they have to have someone else come out doesn't go over well."

On the other hand, when a plumber responds to a job easily handled by a plumber's assistant, the customer is still charged at the plumber's higher pay rate. Licensed plumber Luis Berger also does not like being in the position of giving customers bad news. "If I get called out to do something like snake a drain, the customer isn't expecting a hefty bill. I'm caught between a rock and a hard place—I don't set the rates or make the appointments, but I'm the one who gets it from the customer." Plumbers also resent being sent to do such simple work.

Susie McCarty is one of DrainFlow's order processors. She's frustrated too when the wrong person is sent to a job but feels she and the other order processors are doing the best they can. "We have a survey we're supposed to follow with the calls to find out what the problem is and who needs to take the job," she explains. "The customers don't know that we have a standard form, so they think we can answer all their questions. Most of us don't know any more about plumbing than the caller. If they don't use the terms on the survey, we don't understand what they're talking about. A plumber would, but we're not plumbers; we just take the calls."

Customer service issues also involve the billing representatives. They are the ones who have to keep contacting customers about payment. "It's not my fault the wrong guy was sent," says Elizabeth Monty. "If two guys went out, that's two trips. If a plumber did the work, you pay plumber rates. Some of these customers don't get that I didn't take their first call, and so I get yelled at." The billing representatives also complain that they see only the tail end of the process, so they don't know what the original call entailed. The job is fairly impersonal, and much of the work is recording customer complaints. Remember—40 percent of customers aren't satisfied, and it's the billing representatives who take the brunt of their negative reactions on the phone.

As you can probably tell, all employees have to engage in emotional labor, as described in your textbook, and many lack the skills or personality traits to complete the customer interaction component of their jobs. They aren't trained to provide customer service, and they see their work mostly in technical, or mechanical, terms. Quite a few are actually anxious about speaking directly with customers. The office staff (order processors and billing representatives) realize customer service is part of their job, but they also find dealing with negative feedback from customers and co-workers taxing.

A couple of years ago a management consulting company was hired to survey DrainFlow worker attitudes. The results showed they were less satisfied than workers in other comparable jobs. The following table provides a breakdown of respondent satisfaction levels across a number of categories:

	DrainFlow Plumbers	DrainFlow Plumber Assistants	DrainFlow Office Workers	Average Plumber	Average Office Workers
I am satisfied with the work I am asked to do.	3.7	2.5	2.5	4.3	3.5
I am satisfied with my working conditions.	3.8	2.4	3.7	4.1	4.2
I am satisfied with my interactions with co-workers.	3.5	3.2	2.7	3.8	3.9
I am satisfied with my interactions with my supervisor.	2.5	2.3	2.2	3.5	3.4

The information about average plumbers and average office workers is taken from the management consulting company's records of other companies. They aren't exactly surprising, given some of the complaints DrainFlow employees have made. Top management is worried about these results, but they haven't been able to formulate a solution. The traditional DrainFlow culture has been focused on cost containment, and the "soft stuff" like employee satisfaction hasn't been a major issue.

The Proposed Solution

The company is in trouble, and as revenues shrink and the cost savings that were supposed to be achieved by dividing up work fail to materialize, a change seems to be in order.

Lee is proposing using cash rewards to improve performance among employees. She thinks if employees were paid based on work outcomes, they'd work harder to satisfy customers. Because it's not easy to measure how satisfied people are with the initial call-in, Lee would like to give the order processors a small reward for every 20 calls successfully completed. For the hands-on work, she'd like to have each billing representative collect information about customer satisfaction for each completed call. If no complaints are made and the job is handled promptly, a moderate cash reward would be given to the plumber or plumber's assistant. If the customer indicates real satisfaction with the service, a larger cash reward would be provided.

Lee also wants to find people who are a better fit with the company's new goals. Current hiring procedure relies on unstructured interviews with each location's general manager, and little consistency is found in the way these managers choose employees. Most lack training in customer service and organizational behavior. Lee thinks it would be better if hiring methods were standardized across all branches in her region to help managers identify recruits who can actually succeed in the job.

Your Assignment

Your task is to prepare a report for Lee on the potential effectiveness of her cash reward and structured-interview programs. Make certain it is in the form of a professional business document that you'd actually give to an experienced manager at this level of a fairly large corporation. Lee is very smart when it comes to managing finances and running a plumbing business, but she won't necessarily know about the organizational behavior principles you're describing. Because any new proposals must be passed through top management, you should also address their concerns about cost containment. You'll need to make a strong evidence-based financial case that changing the management style will benefit the company.

When you write, make sure you touch on the following points:

1. Although it's clear employees are not especially satisfied with their work, do you think this is a reason for concern? Does research suggest satisfied workers are actually better at their jobs? Are any other behavioral outcomes associated with job satisfaction?

2. Using job characteristics theory, explain why the present system of job design may be contributing to employee dissatisfaction. Describe some ways you could help employees feel more satisfied with their work by redesigning their jobs.

3. Lee has a somewhat vague idea about how to implement the cash rewards system. Describe some of the specific ways you would make the reward system work better, based on the case.

4. Explain the advantages and disadvantages of using financial incentives in a program of this nature. What, if any, potential problems might arise if people are given money for achieving customer satisfaction goals? What other types of incentives might be considered?

5. Create a specific plan to assess whether the reward system is working. What are the dependent variables that should change if the system works? How will you go about measuring success?

6. What types of hiring recommendations would you make to find people better suited for these jobs? Which Big Five personality traits would be useful for the customer service responsibilities and emotional labor?

Building a Coalition

Learning Goals

Many of the most important organizational behavior challenges require coordinating plans and goals among groups. This case describes a multiorganizational effort, but the same principles of accommodation and compromise also apply when trying to work with multiple divisions within a single organization. You'll create a blueprint for managing a complex development team's progress, steering team members away from negative conflicts and toward productive discussion. You'll also be asked to help create a new message for executives so they can lead effectively.

Major Topic Areas

- Group dynamics
- Maximizing team performance
- Organizational culture
- Integrative bargaining

The Scenario

The Woodson Foundation, a large nonprofit social service agency, is teaming up with the public school system in Washington, D.C., to improve student outcomes. There's ample room for improvement. The schools have problems with truancy, low student performance, and crime. New staff quickly burn out as their initial enthusiasm for helping students is blunted by the harsh realities they encounter in the classroom. Turnover among new teachers is very high, and many of the best and brightest are the most likely to leave for schools that aren't as troubled.

The plan is to create an experimental after-school program that will combine the Woodson Foundation's skill in raising private money and coordinating community leaders with the educational expertise of school staff. Ideally, the system will be financially self-sufficient, which is important because less money is available for schools than in the past. After several months of negotiation, the leaders of the Woodson Foundation and the school system have agreed that the best course is to develop a new agency that will draw on resources from both organizations. The Woodson foundation will provide logistical support and program development and

measurement staff; the school system will provide classrooms and teaching staff.

The first stage in bringing this new plan to fruition is the formation of an executive development team. This team will span multiple functional areas and establish the operating plan for improving school performance. Its cross-organizational nature means representatives from both the Woodson Foundation and the school district must participate. The National Coalition for Parental Involvement in Education (NCPIE) is also going to be a major partner in the program, acting as a representative for parents on behalf of the PTA.

Conflict and Agreement in the Development Team

While it would be perfect if all the groups could work together easily to improve student outcomes, there is little doubt some substantive conflicts will arise. Each group has its own interests, and in some cases these are directly opposed to one another.

School district representatives want to ensure the new jobs will be unionized and will operate in a way consistent with current school board policies. They are very concerned that if Woodson assumes too dominant a role, the school board won't be able to control the operations of the new system. The complexity of the school system has led to the development of a highly complex bureaucratic structure over time, and administrators want to make sure their policies and procedures will still hold for teachers in these programs even outside the regular school day. They also worry that jobs going into the new system will take funding from other school district jobs.

Woodson, founded by entrepreneur Theodore Woodson around 1910, still bears the hallmarks of its founder's way of doing business. Woodson emphasized efficiency and experimentation in everything he did. Many of the foundation's charities have won awards for minimizing costs while still providing excellent services. Their focus on using hard data to measure performance for all their initiatives is not consistent with the school district culture.

Finally, the NCPIE is driven by a mission to increase parental control. The organization believes that when communities are able to drive their own educational methods, students and parents are better able to achieve success together. The organization is strongly committed to celebrating diversity along racial, gender, ethnic, and disability status categories. Its members are most interested in the process by which changes are made, ensuring everyone has the ability to weigh in.

Some demographic diversity issues complicate the team's situation. Most of the students served by the Washington, D.C., school district are African American, along with large populations of Caucasians and Hispanics. The NCPIE makeup generally matches the demographic diversity of the areas served by the public schools. The Woodson foundation, based in northern Virginia, is predominantly staffed by Caucasian professionals. There is some concern with the idea that a new group that does not understand the demographic concerns of the community will be so involved in a major change in educational administration. The leadership of the new program will have to be able to present an effective message for generating enthusiasm for the program across diverse stakeholder groups.

Although the groups differ in important ways, it's also worth considering what they have in common. All are interested in meeting the needs of students. All would like to increase student learning. The school system does benefit from anything that increases student test scores. And the Woodson Foundation and NCPIE are united in their desire to see more parents engaged in the system.

Candidates for the Development Team

The development team will consist of three individuals— HR representatives from the Woodson Foundation, the schools, and the NCPIE—who have prepared the following list of potential candidates for consideration.

Victoria Adams is the superintendent of schools for Washington, D.C. She spearheaded the initial communication with the Woodson Foundation and has been building support among teachers and principals. She thinks the schools and the foundation need to have larger roles than the parents and communities. "Of course we want their involvement and support, but as the professionals, we should have more say when it comes to making decisions and implementing programs. We don't want to shut anyone out, but we have to be realistic about what the parents can do."

Duane Hardy has been a principal in the Washington area for more than 15 years. He also thinks the schools should have the most power. "We're the ones who work with these kids every day. I've watched class sizes get bigger, and scores and graduation rates go down. Yes, we need to fix this, but these outside groups can't understand the limitations we're dealing with. We have the community, the politicians, the taxpayers— everyone watching what we're doing, everyone thinking

they know what's best. The parents, at least, have more of a stake in this."

"The most important thing is the kids," says second-year teacher Ari Kaufman. He is well liked by his students but doesn't get along well with other faculty members. He's seen as a "squeaky wheel." "The schools need change so badly. And how did they get this way? From too little outside involvement."

Community organizer Mason Dupree doesn't like the level of bureaucracy either. He worries that the school's answer to its problems is to throw more money at them. "I know these kids. I grew up in these neighborhoods. My parents knew every single teacher I had. The schools wanted our involvement then. Now all they want is our money. And I wouldn't mind giving it to them if I thought it would be used responsibly, not spent on raises for people who haven't shown they can get the job done."

Meredith Watson, with the Woodson Foundation, agrees the schools have become less focused on the families. A former teacher, she left the field of education after being in the classroom for 6 years. "There is so much waste in the system," she complains. "Jobs are unnecessarily duplicated, change processes are needlessly convoluted. Unless you're an insider already, you can't get anything done. These parents want to be involved. They know their kids best."

Unlike her NCPIE colleagues, Candace Sharpe thinks the schools are doing the best they can. She is a county social worker, relatively new to the D.C. area. "Parents say they want to be involved but then don't follow through. *We* need to step it up, *we* need to lead the way. Lasting change doesn't come from the outside, it comes from the home."

Victor Martinez has been at the Woodson Foundation for 10 years, starting as an intern straight out of college. "It's sometimes hard to see a situation when you're in the thick of it," he explains. "Nobody likes to be told they're doing something wrong, but sometimes it has to be said. We all know there are flaws in the system. We can't keep the status quo. It just isn't cutting it."

Strategies for the Program Team

Once the basic membership and principles for the development team have been established, the program team would also like to develop a handbook for those who will be running the new program. Ideally, this set of principles can help train new leaders to create an inspirational message that will facilitate success. The actual content of the program and the nature of the message will be hammered out by the development team, but it is still possible to generate some overriding principles for the program team in advance of these decisions.

Your Assignment

The Woodson Foundation, the NCPIE, and the schools have asked you to provide some information about how to form teams effectively. They would like your response to explain what should be done at each step of the way, from the selection of appropriate team members to setting group priorities and goals, setting deadlines, and describing effective methods for resolving conflicts that arise. After this, they'd like you to prepare a brief set of principles for leaders of the newly established program. That means you will have two audiences: the development team, which will receive one report on how it can effectively design the program, and the program team, which will receive one report on how it can effectively lead the new program.

The following points should help you form a comprehensive message for the development team:

1. The development team will be more effective if members have some idea about how groups and teams typically operate. Review the dominant perspectives on team formation and performance from the chapters in the book for the committee so it can know what to expect.
2. Given the profiles of candidates for the development team, provide suggestions for who would likely be a good group member and who might be less effective in this situation. Be sure you are using

the research on groups and teams in the textbook to defend your choices.
3. Using principles from the chapters on groups and teams, describe how you will advise the team to manage conflict effectively.
4. Describe how integrative negotiation strategies might achieve joint goals for the development team.

The following points should help you form a message for the program team:

1. Leaders of the new combined organization should have a good idea of the culture of the school district, the NCPIE, and the Woodson Foundation because they will need to manage relationships with all three groups on an ongoing basis. How would you describe the culture of these various stakeholder organizations? Use concepts from the chapter on organizational culture to describe how they differ and how they are similar.
2. Consider how leaders of the new program can generate a transformational message and encourage employee and parent trust. Using material from the chapter on leadership, describe how you would advise leaders to accomplish these ends.
3. Given the potential for demographic fault lines in negotiating these changes, what would you advise as a strategy for managing diversity issues for program leaders?

Boundaryless Organizations

Learning Goals

The multinational organization is an increasingly common and important part of the economy. This case takes you into the world of a cutting-edge music software business seeking success across three very different national and organizational cultures. Its managers need to make important decisions about how to structure work processes so employees can be satisfied and productive doing very different tasks.

Major Topic Areas

- Organizational structure and boundaryless organizations

- Organizational culture
- Human resources
- Organizational socialization

The Scenario

Newskool Grooves is a transnational company developing music software. The software is used to compose music, play recordings in clubs, and produce albums. Founder and CEO Gerd Finger is, understandably, the company's biggest fan. "I started this company from nothing, from just me, my ideas, and my computer. I love music—love playing music, love writing programs for making music, love listening to music—and the money is nice, too." Gerd says he never wanted to work for someone else, to give away his ideas and let someone else profit from them. He wanted to keep control over them, and their image. "Newskool Grooves is always ahead of the pack. In this business, if you can't keep up, you're out. And we are the company everyone else must keep up with. Everyone knows when they get something from us, they're getting only the best and the newest."

The company headquarters are in Berlin, the nerve center for the organization, where new products are developed and the organizational strategy is established. Newskool outsources a great deal of its coding work to programmers in Kiev, Ukraine. Its marketing efforts are increasingly based in its Los Angeles offices. This division of labor is at least partially based on technical expertise and cost issues. The German team excels at design and production tasks. Because most of Newskool's customers are English speakers, the Los Angeles office has been the best group to write ads and market products. The Kiev offices are filled with outstanding programmers who don't require the very high rates of compensation you'd find in German or U.S. offices. The combination of high-tech software, rapid reorganization, and outsourcing makes Newskool the very definition of a boundaryless organization.

Gerd also makes the final decision on hiring every employee for the company and places a heavy emphasis on independent work styles. "Why would I want to put my company in the hands of people I can't count on?" he asks with a laugh. "They have to believe in what we're doing here, really understand our direction and be able to go with it. I'm not the babysitter, I'm not the school master handing out homework. School time is over. This is the real world."

The Work Culture

Employees want to work at this company because it's cutting edge. Newskool's software is used by a number of dance musicians and DJs, who have been the firm's core market, seeing it as a relatively expensive but very high-quality and innovative brand. Whenever the rest of the market for music software goes in one direction, it seems like Newskool heads in a completely different direction in an effort to keep itself separate from the pack. This strategy has tended to pay off. While competitors develop similar products and therefore need to continually lower their prices to compete with one another, Newskool has kept revenues high by creating completely new types of products that don't face this type of price competition.

Unfortunately, computer piracy has eroded Newskool's ability to make money with just software-based music tools, and it has had to move into the production of hardware, such as drum machines and amplifiers that incorporate its computer technology. Making this massive market change might be challenging for some companies, but for an organization that reinvents itself every 2 or 3 years like Newskool does, the bigger fight is a constant war against stagnation and rigidity.

The organization has a very decentralized culture. With only 115 employees, the original management philosophy of allowing all employees to participate in decision making and innovation is still the lifeblood of the company's culture. One developer notes, "At Newskool, they want you to be part of the process. If you are a person who wants to do what you're told at work, you're in trouble. Most times, they can't tell you what they want you to do next—they don't even know what comes next! That's why they hire employees who are creative, people who can try to make the next thing happen. It's challenging, but a lot of us think it's very much an exciting environment."

The Boundaryless Environment

Because so much of the work can be performed on computers, Gerd decided early to allow employees to work outside the office. The senior management in Berlin and Los Angeles are both quite happy with this arrangement. Because some marketing work does require face-to-face contact, the Los Angeles office has weekly in-person meetings. Employees who like Newskool are happiest when they can work through the night and sleep most of the day, firing up their computers to get work done at the drop of a hat. Project discussions often happen via social networking on the company's intranet.

The Kiev offices have been less eager to work with the boundaryless model. Managers say their computer programmers find working with so little structure rather uncomfortable. They are more used to the idea of a strong leadership structure and well-defined work processes.

"When I started," says one manager, "Gerd said getting in touch with him would be no problem, getting in touch with L.A. would be no problem. We're small, we're family, he said. Well, it is a problem. When I call L.A., they say to wait until their meeting day. I can't always wait until they decide to get together. I call Gerd—he says, 'Figure it out.' Then when I do, he says it isn't right and we have to start again. If he just told me in the first place, we would have done it."

Some recent events have also shaken up the company's usual way of doing business. Developers in the corporate offices had a major communications breakdown about their hardware DJ controller, which required many hours of discussion to resolve. It seems that people who seldom met face to face had all made progress—but had moved in opposite directions! To test and design the company's hardware products, employees apparently need to do more than send each other code; sometimes they need to collaborate face to face. Some spirited disagreements have been voiced within the organization about how to move forward in this new environment.

The offices are experiencing additional difficulties. Since the shift to newer products, Sandra Pelham in the Los Angeles office has been more critical of the company. "With the software, we were more limited in the kinds of advertising media we could access. So now, with the hardware—real instruments—we finally thought, 'All right, this is something we can work with!' We had a whole slate of musicians and DJs and producers to contact for endorsements, but Gerd said, 'No way.' He didn't want customers who only cared that a celebrity liked us. He scrapped the whole campaign. He says we're all about creativity and doing our own thing—until we don't want to do things his way."

Although the organization is not without problems, there is little question Newskool has been a standout success in the computer music software industry. While many are shuttering their operations, Newskool is using its market power to push forward the next generation of electronic music-making tools. As Gerd Finger puts it, "Once the rest of the industry has gotten together and figured out how they're all going to cope with change, they'll look around and see that we're already three miles ahead of them down the road to the future."

Your Assignment

Gerd has asked for your advice on how to keep his organization successful. He wants to have some sort of benchmark for how other boundaryless organizations in the tech sector stay competitive despite the challenges of so many workers heading in so many different directions. You will need to prepare a report for the company's executive committee. Your report should read like a proposal to a corporate executive who has a great deal of knowledge about the technical aspects of his company but might not have much knowledge of organizational behavior.

When you write, make sure you touch on the following points:

1. Identify some of the problems likely to occur in a boundaryless organization like Newskool Grooves. What are the advantages of boundaryless organizations?

2. Consider some of the cultural issues that will affect a company operating in such different parts of the world and whose employees may not be representative of the national cultures of each country. Are the conflicts you observe a function of the different types of work people have to perform?

3. Based on what you know about motivation and personality, what types of people are likely to be satisfied in each area of the company? Use concepts from job characteristics theory and the emerging social relationships perspective on work to describe what might need to change to increase employee satisfaction in all areas.

4. What types of human resources practices need to be implemented in this sort of organization? What principles of selection and hiring are likely to be effective? Which Big Five traits and abilities might Newskool supervisors want to use for selection?

5. What kind of performance measures might you want to see for each office?

6. How can the company establish a socialization program that will maximize employee creativity and independence? Do employees in all its locations need equal levels of creativity?

The Stress of Caring

Learning Goals

One of the most consistent changes in the structure of work over the past few decades has been a shift from a manufacturing economy to a service economy. More workers are now engaged in jobs that include providing care and assistance, especially in education and medicine. This work is satisfying for some people, but it can also be highly stressful. In the following scenario, consider how a company in the nursing care industry is responding to the challenges of the new environment.

Major Topic Areas

- Stress
- Organizational change
- Emotions
- Leadership

The Scenario

Parkway Nursing Care is an organization facing a massive change. The company was founded in 1972 with just two nursing homes in Phoenix, Arizona. The company was very successful, and throughout the 1980s it continued to turn a consistent profit while slowly acquiring or building 30 more units. This low-profile approach changed forever in 1993 when venture capitalist Robert Quine decided to make a major investment in expanding Parkway in return for a portion of its profits over the coming years. The number of nursing homes exploded, and Parkway was operating 180 homes by the year 2000.

The company now has 220 facilities in the southwestern United States, with an average of 115 beds per facility and a total of nearly 30,000 employees. In addition to health care facilities, it also provides skilled in-home nursing care. Parkway is seen as one of the best care facilities in the region, and it has won numerous awards for its achievements in the field.

As members of the Baby Boom generation become senior citizens, the need for skilled care will only increase. Parkway wants to make sure it is in a good position to meet this growing need. This means the company must continue expanding rapidly.

The pressure for growth is one significant challenge, but it's not the only one. The nursing home industry has come under increasing government scrutiny following investigations that turned up widespread patient abuse and billing fraud. Parkway has always had outstanding patient care, and no substantiated claim of abuse or neglect in any of its homes has ever been made, but the need for increased documentation will still affect the company. As the federal government tries to trim Medicare expenses, Parkway may face a reduction in funding.

The Problem

As growth has continued, Parkway has remained committed to providing dignity and health to all residents in its facilities. The board of directors wants to see renewed commitment to the firm's mission and core values, not a diffusion of its culture. Its members are worried there might be problems to address. Interviews with employees suggest there's plenty to worry about.

Shift leader Maxine Vernon has been with Parkway for 15 years. "Now that the government keeps a closer eye on our staffing levels, I've seen management do what it can to keep positions filled, and I don't always agree with who is hired. Some of the basic job skills can be taught, sure, but how to *care* for our patients—a lot of these new kids just don't pick up on that."

"The problem isn't with staff—it's with Parkway's focus on filling the beds," says nurse's aide Bobby Reed. "When I started here, Parkway's reputation was still about the service. Now it's about numbers. No one is intentionally negligent—there just are too many patients to see."

A recent college graduate with a B.A. in psychology, Dalton Manetti is more stressed than he expected he would be. "These aren't the sweet grannies you see in the movies. Our patients are demanding. They complain about everything, even about being called patients, probably because most of them think they shouldn't be here in the first place. A lot of times, their gripes amount to nothing, but we have to log them in anyway."

Carmen Frank has been with Parkway almost a year and is already considering finding a new job. "I knew there were going to be physical parts to this job, and I thought I'd be able to handle that. It's not like I was looking for a desk job, you know? I go home after every

Year	Patients	Injuries per Staff Member	Incidents per Patient	Certified Absences per Staff	Other Absence per Staff	Turnover Rate
2000	21,200	3.32	4.98	4.55	3.14	0.31
2001	22,300	3.97	5.37	5.09	3.31	0.29
2002	22,600	4.87	5.92	4.71	3.47	0.28
2003	23,100	4.10	6.36	5.11	3.61	0.35
2004	23,300	4.21	6.87	5.66	4.03	0.31
2005	23,450	5.03	7.36	5.33	3.45	0.28
2006	23,600	5.84	7.88	5.28	4.24	0.36
2007	24,500	5.62	8.35	5.86	4.06	0.33
2008	24,100	7.12	8.84	5.63	3.89	0.35
2009	25,300	6.95	9.34	6.11	4.28	0.35

shift with aches all over—my back, my arms, my legs. I've never had to take so much time off from a job because I hurt. And then when I come back, I feel like the rest of the staff thinks I'm weak."

"I started working here right out of high school because it was the best-paid of the jobs I could get," says Niecey Wilson. "I had no idea what I was getting myself into. Now I really like my job. Next year I'm going to start taking some night classes so I can move into another position. But some of the staff just think of this as any other job. They don't see the patients as people, more like inventory. If they want to work with inventory, they should get a job in retail."

Last month, the company's human resources department pulled the following information from its records at the request of the board of directors. The numbers provide some quantitative support for the concerns voiced by staff.

Injuries to staff occur mostly because of back strain from lifting patients. Patient incidents reflect injuries due to slips, falls, medication errors, or other accidents. Certified absences are days off from work due to medically verified illnesses or injuries. Other absences are days missed that are not due to injuries or illnesses; these are excused absences (unexcused absences are grounds for immediate firing).

Using Organizational Development to Combat Stress and Improve Performance

The company wants to use such organizational development methods as appreciative inquiry (AI) to create change and reenergize its sense of mission. As the

chapter on organizational change explains, AI procedures systematically collect employee input and then use this information to create a change message everyone can support. The human resources department conducted focus groups, asking employees to describe some of their concerns and suggestions for the future. The focus groups highlighted a number of suggestions, although they don't all suggest movement in the same direction.

Many suggestions concerned schedule flexibility. One representative comment was this: "Most of the stress on this job comes because we can't take time off when we need it. The LPNs [licensed practical nurses, who do much of the care] and orderlies can't take time off when they need to, but a lot of them are single parents or primary caregivers for their own children. When they have to leave for child care responsibilities, the work suffers and there's no contingency plan to help smooth things over. Then everyone who is left has to work extra hard. The person who takes time off feels guilty, and there can be fights over taking time off. If we had some way of covering these emergency absences, we'd all be a lot happier, and I think the care would be a lot better."

Other suggestions proposed a better method for communicating information across shifts. Most of the documentation for shift work is done in large spiral notebooks. When a new shift begins, staff members say they don't have much time to check on what happened in the previous shift. Some younger caregivers would like to have a method that lets them document patient outcomes electronically because they type faster than they can write. The older caregivers are more committed to the paper-based process, in part because they think switching systems would require a lot of work. (Government regulations on health care reporting require that any documentation be made in a form that cannot be altered after the fact, to prevent covering up abuse, so specialized software systems must be used for electronic documentation.)

Finally, the nursing care staff believes its perspectives on patient care are seldom given an appropriate hearing. "We're the ones who are with the patients most of the time, but when it comes to doing this the right way, our point of view gets lost. We really could save a lot of money by eliminating some of these unnecessary routines and programs, but it's something management always just says it will consider." Staff members seem to want some way to provide suggestions for improvement, but it isn't clear what method they would prefer.

Your Assignment

Parkway has taken some initial steps toward a new direction, but clearly it has a lot of work left to do. You've been brought in as a change management consultant to help the company change its culture and respond to the stress that employees experience. Remember to create your report as if for the leadership of a major corporation.

When you write your recommendations, make sure you touch on the following points:

1. What do the data on employee injuries, incidents, absences, and turnover suggest to you? Is there reason for concern about the company's direction?
2. The company is going to be making some significant changes based on the AI process, and most change efforts are associated with resistance. What are the most common forms of resistance, and which would you expect to see at Parkway?
3. Given the board of directors' desire to reenergize the workforce, what advice would you provide for creating a leadership strategy? What leader behaviors should nursing home directors and nurse supervisors demonstrate?
4. What are the major sources of job stress at Parkway? What does the research on employee stress suggest you should do to help minimize the experience of psychological strain for employees? Create a plan for how to reduce stress among employees.
5. Based on the information collected in the focus groups, design a survey to hand out to employees. What sort of data should the survey gather? What types of data analysis methods would you like to employ for these data?

Indexes

Name Index

References followed by b indicate boxes; e, exhibits; f, figure; n, notes

Organization Index

*References followed by b indicate boxes;
e, exhibits; f, figure; n, notes*

Index A Combined Glossary/Subject Index